Infancy

Infant, Family, and Society

FOURTH
EDITION

ALAN FOGEL

University of Utah

In collaboration with

MARK REESE

Reese Movement Institute

WADSWORTH

THOMSON LEARNING

Australia | Canada | Mexico | Singapore
Spain | United Kingdom | United States

WADSWORTH

THOMSON LEARNING

Psychology Publisher: Edith Beard Brady
Marketing Manager: Marc Linsenman
Marketing Assistant: Megan Hansen
Project Editor: Lisa Weber
Print Buyer: Robert King
Permissions Editor: Robert Kauser
Production Service: G&S Typesetters, Inc.
Text Designer: Rita Naughton
Art Editor: Gretchen Otto/G&S Typesetters

Photo Researcher: Terri Wright
Copy Editor: Barbara Norton
Illustrators: Rolin Graphics,
    Johnny Alvarez/G&S Typesetters
Cover Designer: Bill Stanton
Cover Image: Phil Babb/Tony Stone Images
Cover Printer:
Compositor: G&S Typesetters, Inc.
Printer:

Wadsworth/Thomson Learning
10 Davis Drive
Belmont, CA 94002-3098
USA

For more information about our products, contact us:

Thomson Learning Academic Resource Center
1-800-423-0563
http://www.wadsworth.com

International Headquarters
Thomson Learning
International Division
290 Harbor Drive, 2nd Floor
Stamford, CT 06902-7477
USA

UK/Europe/Middle East/South Africa
Thomson Learning
Berkshire House
168-173 High Holborn
London WC1V 7AA
United Kingdom

Asia
Thomson Learning
60 Albert Street, #15-01
Albert Complex
Singapore 189969

Canada
Nelson Thomson Learning
1120 Birchmount Road
Toronto, Ontario M1K 5G4
Canada

Library of Congress Cataloging-in-Publication Data

Fogel, Alan.
    Infancy : infant, family, and society / Alan Fogel ;
in collaboration with Mark Reese.—4th ed.
        p. cm.
    Includes bibliographical references and index.
    ISBN 0-534-36783-6 (alk. paper)
    1. Infants.   2. Infants—Family relationships.
3. Child development.   4. Parent and infant.
5. Family.   I. Title.

HQ774 .F63 2001
305.232—dc21   00-043593

For my father and mother, Walter and Sherry Fogel,
and my grandparents, Abraham and Julia van Kollem
and Daniel and Gussie Fogel

Alan Fogel is a professor of psychology at the University of Utah. Born in Miami, Florida, he earned his B.S. in physics at the University of Miami (1967, Coral Gables, Fla.) and his M.A. in physics at Columbia University (1968, New York, N.Y.) where he was a Faculty Fellow. During his three-year term with the United States Peace Corps in Bogotá, Colombia, Fogel taught physics and worked on developing physics curricula for high schools. Through this experience Fogel became interested in how people learn, which led to his completion of a Ph.D. in education, in 1976, with a focus on early childhood development, at the University of Chicago.

Dr. Fogel is active as a researcher and author. He has written a book on early social and communicative development, *Developing through Relationships* (University of Chicago Press). He has co-edited three books on research in child development: *Emotion and Early Interaction* (with Tiffany Field), *Origins of Nurturance: Biological, Cultural, and Developmental Perspectives in Caregiving* (with Gail F. Melson), and *Dynamics and Indeterminism in Social and Developmental Processes* (with Maria Lyra and Jaan Valsiner). He has also written an undergraduate text on child development, *Child Development: Individual, Family, and Society* (with Gail F. Melson). Fogel's scholarly papers on development in infancy, which include studies of emotional development, social and communicative development in relation to parents and to peers, and topics of infant development of concern to health care providers and early childhood educators, have been published in *Child Development, Developmental Psychology, Developmental Science, Early Development and Parenting, Infant Behavior and Development, International Journal of Behavioral Development,* and *Social Development.*

Fogel has been supported in his research through grants from the National Science Foundation, the National Institutes of Health, the National Institute of Mental Health, the National March of Dimes Foundation, and the United States Department of Agriculture. He has ongoing collaborative research projects with scholars in Brazil, Canada, France, Italy, Japan, the Netherlands, Norway, the United States, and the United Kingdom. He has lectured widely in the United States, Japan (where he spent the 1983–1984 academic year as a senior research scholar under a Fulbright fellowship), Brazil, and Europe (where he was a visiting professor at the Free University in Amsterdam in 1990 and again in 1995, at the University of Florence in Italy in 1996, and the University of Rome in 1999).

Brief Contents

Contents

Preface

Babies evoke mixed feelings in almost everyone. Common descriptions of babies range from wonderful, cute, delightful, cuddly, soft, and warm on the positive side to noisy, smelly, demanding, and frustrating on the negative side. The way we feel about babies usually depends on how much experience we have had with them, how old we are, what kind of mood we happen to be in, and what we have heard from others about babies.

Everyone has a relationship with infancy, if only because everyone has been a baby. All of us cried, wet our diapers, and felt tiny and dependent on those whom we trusted to provide everything we needed. Because all of us have a different experience as a baby and different experiences with babies, there cannot be a single truth about babies. Babies mean different things to different people.

This book is about what babies mean to me and the experiences I have had with them as a behavioral scientist, friend, and father. This book draws heavily on infancy research that has been conducted in the past 25 years and provides a scientifically based account of infant development. Science has a lot to offer our relationship with infants, but it is not the only source of evidence. The research results reported in this book, combined with your own experience with infants, should lead you closer to an understanding of what babies are for you.

This book is designed not only to report the facts about infants but also to convey the vitality of infants as developing human beings. One way this is accomplished is by taking a chronological approach to infant development. The goal in each chapter is to construct a multifaceted picture of babies in a particular age period. Similar topics are covered in each chapter, with an eye toward distinguishing the developmental uniqueness of babies at each age. In most chapters, these topics include motor and physical development, perceptual and cognitive development, and social and language development. I have also endeavored to include research that describes what infants actually do, think, and feel and on how they behave in everyday contexts.

The chronological approach is not perfect, however. Some topics seem to work better for me, as an author, if I treat them coherently rather than divide them up by age period. When this happens, I cover some topics completely in a single chapter, even if the topic applies across a number of stages. Examples of this are differences in parental treatment of firstborn and laterborn children (Chapter 5) and sex differences in treatment of infants and sex-role identity

(Chapters 11 and 12). These and other topics can be found with an active use of the table of contents and the index. Students can reread the same topics from an earlier chapter to help clarify how the infant has changed in a particular domain.

Instructors can encourage such integration by asking students in class, in study questions, on homework exercises, and on exams to explicitly differentiate, for example, the perceptual abilities of 3- and 7-month-old infants. For a shorter course, instructors can skip similar sections in each chapter. Instructors wishing to focus on the infant can skip the "Family and Society" and "Applications" sections. Those desiring a more applied course or a more socially oriented course could skip the "Motor Development" and "Perceptual Development" sections. Another way to shorten the course is to drop whole chapters. Chapter 4 (birth) and Chapter 12 (early experience and individual differences) could be dropped without serious discontinuity.

Students and teachers should be aware that Chapter 3 (prenatal development) is particularly long and difficult. This is inevitable due to the large number of technical terms related to conception and prenatal health and development. Instructors wishing to focus entirely on postnatal development could skip this chapter. If the chapter is used in the course, instructors may wish to treat it as two separate chapters, one on normal conception and prenatal development and another on developmental disorders.

Pedagogical Features

Another way in which infants are brought to life is in each chapter's "Family and Society" section. In it you will find such topics as the effects of infants on parent and caregiver development, father-mother differences, infant-sibling interactions, maternal employment, and social policies toward infants. Of particular importance is that in most chapters, this section contains a significant discussion of cultural differences in infancy and infant care. Students should be reminded that cultures are each unique and that there is no one best way of rearing infants. Each chapter also addresses a current issue in infant development under the heading "Applications." These issues include sudden infant death syndrome, day care, and child abuse.

Three additional methods are used to focus on infants' real lives. The first is that most chapters have a section entitled "Co-Regulating with Baby." This section contains concrete suggestions for infant care and social interaction with infants. Based on the research reviewed earlier in the chapter, it is written in an informal tone so that students can apply the information if and when they have an opportunity to spend time with babies.

A second method, new to the fourth edition, is the "Awareness through Movement"® section that appears in most chapters. These sections were written by Mark Reese, Ph.D., a certified Feldenkrais method practitioner and trainer. As explained in Chapter 2, the Feldenkrais method is one of several types of body awareness and movement education methods for older children and adults that are based on observations of how infants learn and experience the world. The "Awareness through Movement" sections contain brief and simple lessons that may help readers to approximate the infant's psychological experience by practicing infant-like movements. I am grateful to Mark Reese for writing these highly educational and easy-to-follow lessons. Instructions for doing the lessons are found in the "Awareness through Movement" section of Chapter 3, the first chapter in which these lessons appear. Use these instructions for all the chapters. It helps to have someone read the steps while you do the lessons. This can also be done in a classroom. The reader should take each step slowly, giving the student time to experience the movement. The more you practice each lesson, the more aware you can become. The lessons can also lead to a greater sense of relaxation and well-being. Suggestions for integrating the lessons into a self-study project are given in Chapter 2.

The third method is also new to this edition: a section at the end of each chapter entitled "The Author's View." In this section, I say more about what infants mean to me. Students are encouraged to contrast my ideas and opinions with their own, and teachers are invited to encourage debate and discussion. Remember that everyone is an expert on infancy by virtue of having lived in that condition for three years of his or her life.

This book contains a chapter covering the third year of life (Chapter 11). It provides an opportunity for students to imagine how infants become preschoolers. This transition, from prelanguage to language and from the concrete to the symbolic, is one of the more fascinating and difficult-to-understand developmental changes.

In addition to the chapters covering each stage of infant development, there are several topical chapters that cover broad issues. Chapter 1 provides a basic orientation to infancy in the 21st century, includes a historical review of infancy, and gives an overview of some of the basic research techniques used in infant studies.

Chapter 2 acquaints the student with the current theories of infant and early childhood development. This theoretical review has been completely rewritten and updated for this edition. It now better reflects theoretical perspectives that are actively used by infancy researchers and clinicians. After each theory is presented, it is critically evaluated. The chapter urges an eclectic approach to theorizing about infants, rather than a contest over which theory is best. Instructors who wish to teach a more theoretically based course should guide students in the theoretical interpretation of the research presented in each chapter.

Chapter 3 covers the area of prenatal development. First, the chapter places the prenatal period in a developmental context. The emphasis is on the continuities between prenatal and postnatal development. A second feature of this chapter is its strong emphasis on prenatal behavior, learning, and psychological experience. Attention is devoted to behavioral developments and to the effects of prenatal motor and sensory experiences on later development. Traditional topics of genetic, chromosomal, and teratogenic influences are treated in depth.

Finally, Chapter 12 addresses the effects of the infancy experience on the formation of individual differences. Such topics as intelligence, sociability, and temperament are covered in detail. Although individual differences are addressed in each chapter, the large problem of how individual differences are formed and maintained requires us to look back on the period of infancy in its entirety.

The appendix contains standard growth charts for boys and girls, as well as a list of potential careers in the field of infancy. This is included because changes in our society have led to a new focus on the early childhood years. Demand for quality day care providers and infant clinicians is increasing, and there is a growing professionalism to be found among persons whose careers involve working with infants. This benefits everyone. The parents of infants prefer to trust their babies to the care of professionals. Professionalism encourages higher pay and better working conditions for providers, as well as the establishment of standards of professional excellence.

This fourth edition retains the same basic structure as the third edition, so that instructors familiar with the earlier volume can easily adapt their course materials. The major changes in this edition, in Chapters 1 and 2, were made in order to integrate a new focus on infant experience and create a foundation for the Awareness through Movement exercises. In addition, "On the Web" sections at the end of each chapter provide a list of interesting, relevant web sites where students can explore chapter topics. Please note that the web site addresses may be subject to change.

Another improvement in this edition is a thorough updating of the research and theory in the field. In revising the book, I did an in-depth search of the current literature. If some topics are covered primarily with pre-1990 references, it means that no new work has been done in that area. Many pre-1990 references are retained even when new material is available because the older material continues to contribute to our understanding. This edition contains several new sections. Chapter 1, for example, has a section on the importance of studying infancy and on qualitative research methods. In Chapter 2 there is a new section on clinical theories that includes methods focused on psychotherapy and on body awareness. Among other new sections is one in Chapter 4 on birthrates and one in Chapter 10 on infant mental health.

I would like to thank the following consultants for their important and thoughtful contributions and suggestions: Marc Lewis (Ontario Institute for Studies in Education, University of Toronto), Janet Mann (Department of Psychology, Georgetown University), Elaine Marie (Watsu practitioner and teacher, Harbin, CA), Mark Reese (director, Reese Movement Institute, San Diego, CA), Jen Shurtliff (Rosen method practitioner, Salt Lake City, UT), Esther Thelen (Department of Psychology, Indiana University), Sandra Wooten (director, Rosen Method Southwest School, Santa Fe, NM).

The comments and suggestions from the following reviewers were invaluable: Nameera Akhtar (University of California, Santa Cruz), Julia Braungart-Riegler (University of Notre Dame), Joseph Campos (University of California, Berkeley), Susan Churchill (University of Nebraska-Lincoln), Esther Devall (New Mexico State University), Cynthia Frosch (Arizona State University), Phyllis Gilbert (Stephen F. Austin State University), Robin Harwood (University of Connecticut), Dorothy Jackson (Ohio State University), Peggy Jessee (University of Alabama-Tuscaloosa), Gary Levy (University of Wyoming), Carolyn Mebert (University of New Hampshire), Brenda Volling (University of Michigan), and Diane Wille (Indiana University, Southeast).

I had excellent research assistants and student readers, all from the Department of Psychology at the University of Utah, Salt Lake City: Kari Applegate, Heather Bittinger, Tim Fowles, J'lene George, Cassandra Holloway, Jessica Keys, Jill Pecchia-Beccum, Prabhath Shettigar, and Scott Vice. I am indebted to my editorial assistant, Emilie Wilkinson, who put in long hours making sure everything fit together, from tables and figures to references. Finally, thanks again to my family—Jacqueline, Dan, and Menasheh—for providing me the time, space, love, and support to accomplish the task.

Chapter

1

Basic Concepts of Infant Behavior and Development

CHAPTER OVERVIEW AND OUTLINE

The Importance of Infancy	*What can be gained from the study of infants? What can be learned by reading this book?*
A Brief History of Babies	*How have responses to and ideas about infants changed historically? What are the historical origins of our current ideas about infants?*
The Scientific Perspective on Infancy	*What is the current scientific conception of infants? How does it change our view of infancy?*
Research Methods in Developmental Science	*What are the main scientific approaches to the study of human development? Is science a viable source of information about infants?*
Experimental Research Methods	*What are the possibilities and limits of controlled experiments with infants? How can experimental research help us understand how infants think, perceive, or feel?*
Observational Research Methods	*What can be learned from the observation of naturally occurring infant behavior? How has video and computer technology contributed to the accuracy of observation?*
Qualitative Research Methods	*What is the infant's experience of the world? What does it mean when a baby cries or smiles? What are the advantages and sources of bias that occur when adults try to answer these questions from their own point of view?*
Applications: Advocacy and Public Policy for Infants and Their Families	*How can public policy be changed to benefit infants and their families? Do child advocates play a role in changing public policy?*

Have you ever wondered about the details of your own birth? Do you think it was painful or pleasurable? Did you cry a lot? Do you remember learning to crawl or to walk? What was the first word you ever said? If you know the answer to any of these questions, it is likely you have asked or were told about it by someone who was an adult when you were a baby. Infancy is mysterious to us. We appear to have no memory of our own infancy; we must rely on the memory of others who were there. And babies themselves cannot tell us what they feel, at least not in words. The mystery of the infant's mind has intrigued parents, philosophers, and theologians for thousands of years.

The twentieth century, however, has given us powerful new methods for understanding infancy. Scientific research has helped us understand the limits and possibilities of the infant's ability to sense, move, and feel. We now know some types of environments and forms of care that are conducive to the development of healthy and happy babies. Advanced technologies allow us to monitor the brain's development and to observe the stages of prenatal growth. Clinical methods have been discovered that can bring older children and adults into contact with their own experiences as a baby. Contact with our infant experience creates a sense of wholeness and promotes healing in mind and body. These methods have generated strong public interest in babies. Why are babies so interesting?

The Importance of Infancy

If you read the newspapers or watch television news programs, you will recognize some of these headlines and advertisement leads.

Discoveries allow for the prenatal detection of genetic disorders.

Sixty-year-old women can give birth to their own babies.

Mothers may transmit AIDS to their babies through breast milk.

Parents can recognize their newborn infants by touch alone.

Day care may have harmful effects on the mother-infant relationship.

You can teach your infant to read before the age of two.

Inadequate parenting of infants causes lasting psychological damage.

If these statements are correct, they have a profound impact on our lives and on society. A sixty-year-old mother may die before the child is an adolescent or become too frail to care for the child. If day care is harmful to infants, we will have to reassess the value of parental work. But are these statements correct? In fact, there is some truth to all of them—but only under certain special conditions. A sixty-year-old can give birth by having a fertilized ovum implanted into her uterus, but only if she is in good health and can tolerate taking supplemental hormones. Day care can be harmful in settings where teachers are poorly trained and facilities are inadequate; otherwise, it can have some beneficial effects, such as giving children advanced social skills with their peers. By the end of this book, you should have a much better idea about how to evaluate claims such as the ones listed above. You will read about these and other issues and learn ways to understand research so you can look up the answers for yourself.

The study of infancy is important for many reasons. A few will be listed here, and you may be able to add some of your own.

Parent and Caregiver Education

Infants require adult guidance, love, and support. For a young couple ready to provide this care, their first baby can be both rewarding and anxiety provoking. What is the best way to feed babies? How much sleep do they need? Can babies be spoiled with too much holding and affection? What does it mean if a baby cries for long periods? You will find some answers to these questions in this book. Aside from information about infants, each chapter reviews research on the experiences and development of parents. Generally speaking, the more parents know about infants and children, the less anxious they will be, and the better the outcomes will be for the child. Although they cannot substitute for direct experience with infants, books like this one can provide valuable information that enhances the parenting experience. Infant caregivers—such as day care providers, grandparents, and other relatives—can also profit from this book. Clinicians who work with infants, or who work with adult clients and want to know more about the role of infant experiences, will also find this book helpful.

Infancy Is a Unique Period in the Life Course

Infancy is a special time in one's life. This is not only because it is the earliest stage of life but because all of life's stages are unique. Each has its pleasures and problems. For the first few years of life, infants are totally dependent on their caregivers for all their needs. Most of what happens to them is not within their understanding or control. They cry easily and feel their pain deeply. They get frustrated with their own clumsiness and relative incompetence to achieve their goals. For reasons we do not fully understand, nature has required all humans to pass through this period and to experience its total reliance on others, its helpless emotional lows and its carefree emotional highs.

Babyhood has a number of high points. Infants can spend hours immersed in the pleasure of play and exploration. They are not plagued by self-doubt, worries, bills to pay, and the other things that can distract adults from living in the moment. Most healthy infants are keenly attuned to their environment. Their bodies are flexible and soft, they breathe fully and deeply, and they are completely open to being held and touched. As you study this book and do the exercises at the end of each chapter, allow yourself to appreciate and to reexperience what is really special about being a baby. It can feel like a breath of fresh air.

The Experience of the Body and Its Movements and Senses

The consciousness of young infants is almost entirely occupied with bodily sensations and sensory experiences. Once children acquire the ability to talk, think, and conceptualize, they acquire an intellectual power that distinguishes humans from other animals. On the other hand, the preverbal

experience of being a baby in a baby's body is also uniquely human. After infancy, many physical and mental disorders of children and adults can be traced to their having lost touch with their own body. Cultural values can often run contrary to the needs of the body, as when work or family stresses cause muscular tension (headaches or backaches, for example) or when cultural ideals of physical beauty lead a person to eat less than her or his own body uniquely requires. But for a baby, losing touch with the body would be nearly impossible. For a baby, after all, what else is there?

In this book, you will read about research on the sensorimotor world of the infant. Most of the chapters have lessons you can do to appreciate the actual experience of being a baby, or at least of your own body as you move it in a more babylike way. With practice, these lessons may allow you to step back from thinking, reasoning, judging, and evaluating, and simply be present to your senses and movements.

Reexperiencing Infancy Is Healing and Rejuvenating

Lessons like the ones in this book have been used by movement, body awareness, and dance educators to help children and adults develop an awareness of their body. These procedures have proved useful in expanding the range of movement for all individuals. Regular practice of the lessons in this book may promote relaxation and personal growth. Movement education works especially well with people who are afflicted with muscular disorders, such as cerebral palsy, and with those who have suffered accidents and injuries. It is also helpful for the relief of everyday tension and muscular pains.

There are other approaches to self-awareness about infancy. Some psychotherapeutic techniques recreate within the patient-therapist relationship the innocence and trust found in healthy parent-infant relationships. Some touch therapies use gentle, noninvasive contact to create the type of relaxation and self-awareness that babies experience in their mother's arms. Practitioners from all these therapeutic and educational methods assume that there will be a healing effect of recreating—in a safe and protected setting—some of the conditions of being a baby. Reexperiencing some of the traumas of one's own infancy, especially within the supportive contexts of these treatment approaches, can also be therapeutic. Such clinical methods will be discussed in more detail in Chapter 2.

Improving Health by Early Prevention

Many of the diseases of childhood and adulthood have their origins in the prenatal period and infancy (see Chapters 3, 4, and 12). During prenatal development, for example, the brain is highly vulnerable to disease, malnutrition, and toxic substances to which the mother may be exposed. Many disorders can be prevented by changing maternal behavior during pregnancy, such as eating properly, avoiding particular drugs and chemicals, and reducing stress. In addition, medical research has discovered remarkable new treatments for prenatal and infant disorders. In the most serious cases, parents may choose to terminate the pregnancy. In a growing number of cases, however, treatments given to fetuses directly can permanently eliminate the effects of such disorders (see Chapter 3). Due to advances in medical technology, premature infants are more likely to survive and live normal lives than ever before. In poor nations, simple treatments for combating infant death, caused primarily by diarrhea, are saving millions of lives (see Chapter 4).

If infants from a wealthy nation survive past birth, the chances that they will die from a serious disease are extremely small due to widespread immunizations and health care. Public health officials are beginning to make progress in reducing the largest cause of infant death in these countries: accidents. Parent education in infant health and safety, safer toys, better infant restraints for automobiles (more infants and children lose their lives in auto accidents in North America than from all other causes of death combined), and better enforcement of seat belt laws are all helping to reduce injury and mortality (see Chapter 8).

Informed Public Policy

Because of infants' vulnerability, many social and medical problems could be prevented by making sure that they receive proper care and that young parents receive all the support necessary to provide the best environment for their children. Society can take positive steps toward the achievement of such goals. Citizens who are knowledgeable about the possibilities and risks of prenatal and infant development can make better-informed decisions when asked to vote—as lawmakers or as part of the electorate—on legislation regarding infant, family, and child welfare. Should all families with infants be guaranteed the right to housing, proper nutrition, medical care, and parent education? Currently, these are not guaranteed rights in the United States. They are guaranteed, however, in northern European countries such as Sweden and the Netherlands. Because the quality of day care influences infant development and the parent-child relationship, should there be national standards for day care providers? The United States is one of the few industrialized countries without such standards. You can read more about public policy issues throughout this book, beginning with the "Applications" section of this chapter.

Origins of Individual Differences

Each human being is different. A lot of these differences come from experiences as a child and adult, such as one's school experience, the effects of family and friends, the world of work, and unplanned opportunities and losses that occur during one's life. But do any of the differences between people have their origins in early infancy? If so, which parts of one's uniqueness are most likely connected to what happened to one as a baby? This is an extremely difficult question to answer because early experiences are rarely preserved in some pure form but rather combine in complex ways with later experiences. Nonetheless, many differences between people during the prenatal and infancy periods do have a lasting impact. In Chapter 12 you will discover what is known and what is yet to be discovered about the infantile origins of differences between people.

The importance of studying about infants, as illustrated by each of the topics above, may seem self-evident. The importance of infancy, however, is not always appreciated. An infant born into today's world may experience poverty or wealth, love or abuse, health or disease. More must be done to educate parents and political leaders about the need for protecting infants, who cannot protect themselves.

Was it always this way in the life of infants—this mixture of good and bad? In general, yes. In all periods of the past for which there are archaeological or historical sources, we can find evidence of both kindness to and neglect of infants. Nevertheless, there is more money, time, and care devoted to infants today than at any other known period of history. How-to articles, products, and books on child rearing, pregnancy, and childbirth are squeezing other items off store shelves. Most large supermarkets in Europe, Asia, and North America devote an entire aisle to baby products: diapers, oils, powders, foods, furniture, toys, designer clothing, strollers, packs, books, and magazines. In wealthy countries, it is not unusual for infants to be dressed in expensive high-tech running shoes and athletic clothes before they can even walk! More seriously, many countries devote a portion of their tax revenues to fund scientific research on the medical and psychological aspects of infancy, research that has led to many of the findings reported in this book.

To give you some insight into why infancy has become so important, the next section reviews some of the historical trends in the role of the infant in society. Because of limitations of space, the focus will be on the history of Western cultures (European and American). The heightened importance of infancy in today's Western society began in the eighteenth century, with an increase in pediatric medical practice, advice for parents and parental devotion to the individuality of each child, children's books, and other infant care products and resources. Readers are encouraged to integrate what is known about their own cultural history into this story.

A Brief History of Babies

Early Civilizations

The history and literature of the ancient Greeks and Romans (200 B.C.–300 A.D.) indicates that they advocated a rather harsh upbringing for infants. Shows of affection were avoided, and infants were wrapped tightly in swaddling bands in order to mold the child's body into one worthy of a citizen. Cold water was used to bathe the child to prevent the child from becoming too soft. Babies hated their baths all the more because nurses would push on the child's skull to make it round as possible and pull and stretch other body parts in order to shape them.

Similar beliefs in shaping the physical body of the adult by binding and manipulating the infant can be seen in such non-Western ancient practices as the foot binding of girls in China (which made their feet small but deformed). Head binding among both the ancient Maya of Mexico and among eighteenth-century Europeans was used to give the head an oblong shape (Johnson, 1992).

While it may seem surprising to people today, Roman parents felt this treatment to be an expression of their love. They wanted their children to grow up strong, their bodies nicely proportioned and held in a proper posture. Roman literature, in fact, testifies to a strong devotion between parents and children, especially among the wealthy classes, and attests to the importance of hugging, kissing, and affection after infancy, as the child grew older and began to form his or her own character (Dupont, 1989; Gies & Gies, 1987). Historians of ancient Egypt (2,000–100 B.C.) and Greece (800–200 B.C.) have found evidence of toys and games for children and written documents describing the need to love and protect infants (Greenleaf, 1978).

The recognition of the role of the body in the development of the person is an important aspect of Westerners' Greco-Roman heritage. Both Greeks and Romans believed that exercises for the body led to the development of a strong moral character. Upper-class boys learned athletics and gymnastics, while girls learned music and dance.

Many early civilizations, such as ancient Rome, practiced **infanticide,** the deliberate killing of unwanted infants. It was the duty of the head of the family to decide if a newborn should live or die. This practice eliminated infants who were malformed, but many healthy babies too were left to die because the family was poor or the child unwanted (Dupont, 1989). Infanticide continued in Europe throughout the Middle Ages, and some societies today still practice it (see the "Applications" section on family planning in Chapter 3).

The Middle Ages and the Renaissance

A similar mix of concern for children coexisting with what people today would consider to be harshness and deprivation continued throughout recorded Western history. The early Middle Ages in Europe (300–1100 A.D.) began with the fall of the Roman empire and the gradual spread of Christianity throughout the continent. The largely rural population began to move in large numbers to cities and towns. At the same time, the political boundaries changed frequently as empires dissolved and local powers asserted themselves. These social changes contributed to an increasingly educated urban population, on the one hand, and to the growth of a class of urban poor who suffered from disease, malnutrition, pollution, and ignorance, on the other. The poor people in the cities lived in much more unhealthy conditions than did the poor in the countryside.

Because of inadequate sanitation and other sources of urban pollution (pollution is not a new problem), infants of the urban poor were more likely to die or to suffer birth defects than those from rural areas. Because cities drew people away from family roots and because disease claimed the lives not only of infants but of mothers in childbirth, many orphaned children walked the streets as beggars, thieves, and prostitutes. As you can see, childhood among the urban poor then was not too much different from what it is today. This does not mean that poverty inevitably causes problems for parents and children, but it does increase the risk that problems will occur.

The Christian church began to have an impact on the beliefs and practices of European child rearing after around 400 A.D. Christians, following ancient Jewish practices, advocated parental love and worked to protect children from infanticide, abortion, and maltreatment. Gravestones for infants began to appear at this time, as well as special penances if a parent had done some wrong to a child (Gies & Gies, 1987).

During the late Middle Ages (1100–1300 A.D.), a few written medical texts giving advice on childbirth and early infant care appeared. Trotola, a female physician in twelfth-century Italy, advised rubbing the newborn's palate with honey, protecting the infant from bright lights and loud noises, and stimulating the infant's senses with cloths of various colors and textures and with "songs and gentle voices" (Gies & Gies, 1987). In England during the same period, birth often occurred in a warm chamber with plenty of bathwater, accompanied by the scent of olives, herbs, and roses. It was attended by a female midwife and female friends wishing mother and baby good fortune and joy (Hanawalt, 1993).

Infanticide, however, was still practiced. Although parents had to suffer penances, it was not a crime equivalent to homicide, as it is today. By the thirteenth century, some cities in Europe had created church-run hospices to adopt orphaned children as an alternative to infanticide, since, according to church doctrine, a child who died unbaptized was barred from heaven for all eternity (Le Goff, 1987). In some countries today, because of urban stress and poverty, infants are left in woods, rivers, and trash bins. Some cities in the United States have begun programs that allow mothers to drop unwanted infants at local hospitals without fear of prosecution. Social workers then help to find foster homes for these children. Times may have changed, but some of the problems still remain.

Not until the European Renaissance (1450–1650) do we begin to see the emergence of written philosophies of child rearing in Western cultures. Writers, mostly from the church, condemned the ancient practice of giving children to wet nurses from the poorer classes (a wet nurse was a woman who was paid to nurse the child with her own milk to spare wealthy women the task of nursing the baby themselves) because the child could pick up the habits and diseases of the nurse. The famous Renaissance artist Michelangelo jokingly claimed that his skill in sculpture came from his wet nurse, who was the wife of a stonecutter (Gies & Gies, 1987).

During the early Middle Ages, religious paintings depicted Christ as an adult. By the late Middle Ages, interest in children was growing, and Christ

Scala/Art Resource, NY

Painting from the late Middle Ages depicting Christ as an infant, but in stylized clothing with adult-like features and gestures.

began to appear as an infant. However, the infant Christ in medieval art is typically shown in stylized clothing, with adult facial features and mannerisms. One painting depicts Christ as an infant making the Catholic gesture of benediction to a group of people kneeling before him. In Renaissance art, by contrast, infants and children began to look and behave differently from adults. Children were sometimes shown playing with toys (Koops, 1996). Not only does the infant Christ begin to look more like a real baby, but we also see the emergence of secular paintings of everyday family life and portraits of individual children.

The Enlightenment

By the eighteenth century, new ideas about the value of human life, dignity, and freedom had begun to emerge, a shift of consciousness called the Enlightenment. In France, for example, Jean-

Jacques Rousseau (1712–1778) argued that childhood was a time of special privilege, that children bring goodness, not original sin, into the world, and that education should be sensitive to the needs and inclinations of the infant and young child. The social movement Rousseau represented was called **romanticism.** Its followers included such great English romantic poets as William Wordsworth (1770–1850), who wrote of childhood in idealized terms.

Behold the Child among his new-born blisses,
A six years' darling of pygmy size!
See, where 'mid work of his own hand he lies,
Fretted by sallies of his mother's kisses,
With light upon him from his father's eyes!

(From "Imitations of Immortality from Recollections of Early Childhood," in Williams 1952, 263).

William Blake (1757–1827), another English poet, rejected these simple romantic notions of innocence. In a poem called "The Scoffers," Blake suggested that the scientific achievements of Sir Isaac Newton were far more lasting intellectual milestones than the mocking voice of Rousseau. Charles Dickens was another author who rejected romanticism. Instead of depicting childhood in nineteenth-century England as a time of happy contentment, in *Oliver Twist* and other famous stories he courageously exposed the effects of disease, poverty, child abuse, and child labor for all to see.

All of these writers revealed a new concern for the individual and for the value of children, but they disagreed about what was "natural" compared to what needed to be provided for the child's healthy development. The English philosopher John Locke (1632–1704) accepted the importance of early education for children but believed that children needed more structure than the romantics advocated. Locke is known for his rational approach to education, which was decidedly not a romantic one, because he thought children needed specific guidance and discipline. Beginning with the assumption that the infant's mind is a *tabula rasa*, a blank slate on which anything could be written, Locke argued that education should provide the skills to make rational choices. The philosophical movement to which he belonged is called **empiricism.**

Both Rousseau and Locke revived the ancient Greek ideals of the body's importance in healthy moral development. Locke wrote that "a sound mind in a sound body, is a short but full description of a happy state in this world." Rousseau suggested that children should "run, jump, and shout to their heart's content." Their ideas were carried into educational practice by nineteenth-century educational reformers in Europe and North America, who made sure that school curriculums offered art, music, and physical education (Friedrich-Cofer, 1986).

The romantic ideas of freedom and happiness combined with the empiricist ideas of reason and realism to create the philosophical foundations for the revolutions in France and the United States. This period also saw the rise in society of the value of the individual. It had been the custom in the past to give a newborn the same name as an older sibling, or the name of a sibling who had died. Such practices gave way in the eighteenth century to a newfound respect for the individuality of the child. Not only did advice books for parents proliferate, but by 1800 a wide range of inexpensive books was being published exclusively for young children. There was a corresponding recognition of the importance of the nuclear family and the maintenance of a private and sacred family home.

Domesticity became a value for the first time. During the American colonial period, the main value of the family was to raise children according to the family's particular beliefs and values. Many of these families came to the New World specifically in order to practice their own beliefs, away from the conservatism and religious persecution then pervasive in Europe (Clarke-Stewart, 1998). These values of individuality, autonomy, and self-determination had never before existed in the history of the world, and they changed how adults conceptualized the meaning and value of infancy and childhood.

These ideas also led in the nineteenth century to the growth of social responsibility toward infants and children and the rise of the idea of the child as an integral part of the definition of the family. The "discovery" of the child was due to urban forces in Europe and North America that segregated the family from the workplace, defined the mother's role as major supervisor of the domestic scene, and allowed love or sentiment (rather than family inheritance or economic well-being) to be the bond holding the family together (Hareven, 1985).

Educators in the nineteenth century continued to emphasize the importance of the young child's body in the development of the whole individual. Children who were obese, physically awkward, or handicapped could expect to get guidance from the school. The curriculum included free expression and creativity for the body, such as gymnastics and dance. Team sports and other exercise programs were meant to lay the foundation for the continuation of physical exercise through adulthood. Students were expected to understand the principles of health and hygiene. These programs grew out of the Greco-Roman and Enlightenment emphasis on the importance of the body as well as the mind (Friedrich-Cofer, 1986).

Not only did the child emerge as an individual during this period, but the role of full-time mother and housewife appeared on the historical stage for the very first time. It may be shocking for people in Western cultures in the twenty-first century to realize that the idea of a loving mother taking full-time care of an infant is a very recent cultural invention brought about by the rise of the nuclear family. For most of human history, infants were raised by many different caregivers, such as nurses, siblings, and other relatives.

It should be noted, however, that the development of this segregated nuclear family and its full-time mother was at first confined to the white middle class. Families from other classes and ethnic and racial groups preserved the preindustrial extended family, in which love, work, and education all took place within the home, and child care was shared by all family members. Women worked in the fields and in the home in the company of their babies, just as they had done for most of human history. Changes in the family have not occurred uniformly in all parts of American society, and these cultural patterns still account for many of the differences among families today (Hareven, 1982). Other cultural and economic forces have led most recently to the decline of the nuclear family, the reemergence of extended families and communal living, and the rise of single-parent families.

Social changes in the nineteenth century led to the growing awareness of the public's responsibility for the welfare and development of infants. Although the first English-language pediatric textbook appeared in 1545, welfare and medical institutions devoted exclusively to children did not open in Europe and the United States until the 1850s, around the same time as the rise of immunization and the pasteurization of milk. Maternal deaths during childbirth declined in this period due to the invention of anesthesia and procedures for sterilizing medical instruments (Greenleaf, 1978).

These medical advances further solidified the family by reducing infant mortality. As each child could be counted on to live a healthy life, families began to consciously reduce the number of children so as to invest more emotional energy in each child. By the middle of the nineteenth century, infancy and childhood had emerged in the public mind as a separate and valuable stage of life (Hareven, 1985). Manufactured baby dolls first appeared in Europe in 1825. In 1840, half of all three-year-olds in

Massachusetts were attending infant schools, a practice that later declined because experts began to doubt the wisdom of sending such young children to school (Clarke-Stewart, 1998). The first public playground was developed in Boston in 1885 (a few heaps of sand dumped in a vacant lot), but by 1915, there were well-planned public playgrounds in 430 U.S. cities (Blank & Klig, 1982; Greenleaf, 1978; Zeitz, 1969).

Imagine what it must have been like to raise a baby in North America or Europe before 1850. The pain of childbirth could be helped by home remedies and the advice of a midwife, but there was no protection from serious problems and severe pain. Women could not be sure if they would survive childbirth, and many husbands were left without a wife and mother to raise the new baby. Infants died frequently of unknown (at the time) causes. Daily life with the baby was also much harder than it is today. There were no disposable diapers, no manufactured toys, and no baby foods you could buy. Parents had to make the infant's clothing, diapers, toys, and food from scratch. A baby gets a lot of diapers dirty in a day, and there were no washers and driers. In fact, cotton fabric did not become widely available until the early nineteenth century (the textile mills of that period contributed to the exploitation of child labor, as depicted in the novels of Charles Dickens, among others). Most clothing before that time was made of wool and was hot and heavy. If you were among the few who were wealthy, you could hire a servant and a wet nurse to care for and feed the baby (although wet-nursing declined rapidly at the end of the nineteenth century because maternal love was deemed better for children). For most families, however, having a baby affected all aspects of their lives. There were no readily available forms of contraception, so most women gave birth regularly every three to five years.

Infants Enter the World of Science

The beginning of the twentieth century saw the rise of the scientific study of infant development. Earlier debates over romanticism versus empiricism were replaced by discussions about the contributions to development of **nature** (genes) versus **nurture** (environments). (See Chapter 2 for a discussion of the role of genes and environments in the emergence of individual differences between infants.) Arnold Lucius Gesell (1880–1961), working out of the romantic tradition, thought that the orderly changes seen in early development were specified by the genes. In this regard, Gesell also followed the ideas of Charles Darwin, whose theory of the evolution of species will be discussed in greater detail in Chapter 2. The genetic timetable for the patterning of development was called **maturation.** Gesell made a career out of the careful measurements of developmental changes in size, motor skill, and behavior in infants and young children. He was the first scientist to use a one-way mirror to observe infants unobtrusively and the first to use film to record their behavior.

Because Gesell believed in genetic maturation, he cared little about individual differences and focused instead on the "average" child. This created anxiety in parents who read his works and discovered that their own children walked or talked later than the average child. Even today, most parents want their babies to be above average. We now know that babies vary widely in the ages at which they attain developmental milestones and that most babies—whether slow or fast—develop normally. There is, in fact, no such thing as an "average child," since all children are unique, according to the perspective of the European Enlightenment. The normal and expected variability between infants will be discussed in later chapters.

In the empiricist tradition, and contrary to Gesell, John B. Watson (1878–1958) believed that children could be trained to do almost anything, given the right kind of "nurture." He demonstrated this by doing studies in which he taught small children to be afraid of cuddly animals by making loud noises whenever they touched the animals. This type of research would be considered unethical today. Nevertheless, Watson's work suggested that all our behavior, even the most basic and innocent, could possibly be controlled by outside forces. This kind of belief, in extreme form, still persists in some science fiction stories of a future in which an all-powerful government manipulates every aspect of learning and development to produce robotlike cit-izens who are slaves to the rulers. Recently developed dynamic systems theories (see Chapter 2), on the contrary, suggest that not all behavior can be controlled or predicted. Human life is full of surprises and unexpected twists and turns.

Watson nevertheless left a lasting imprint on North American society. The waves of immigrants who landed on the shores of the United States and Canada all believed that they could make a new life for themselves and their children. Watson's idea that anyone could succeed regardless of past history or genetic heritage sustained the hopes of many of the new arrivals. Watson placed responsibility for a child's outcome directly on the shoulders of the parents; if the child failed, it was the parents' fault. He encouraged parents to avoid kissing and holding their babies, in order to make them independent individuals. Today we recognize that a wide range of parenting styles is acceptable and appropriate for babies, and later chapters review individual and cultural differences in infant-care patterns. I will also discuss systems theories of development (Chapter 2) that propose that the family, parent, and infant all make important contributions to developmental outcomes; human development is not so simple that blame or credit can be assigned to a single individual.

Sigmund Freud (1856–1939) presented strong counterarguments to Watson and Gesell. Freud focused on psychological experience rather than on behavior. He recognized that all infants experienced emotional highs and lows and that even infants felt the need for love and possessed powerful desires. Freud's daughter, Anna, devoted most of her life to bringing her father's insights out of the adult psychoanalytic session and into the real lives of parents and children. Anna Freud taught parents to hold and cuddle babies and to be patient while babies discovered and tried to manage their own desires in appropriate ways (A. Freud, 1965). Nurture was important here too, but only to the extent that it encouraged the child's nature to blossom. Unfortunately, Anna Freud too faulted parents for their children's developmental problems—in this case, for giving them too little attention and affection and for "selfishly" not understanding the situation from the child's point of view. Even the most understanding parent sometimes has bad days, and

A North American family and their baby in 1913. Note the children's elegant clothing. Well-educated parents probably were aware of the competing ideas of Watson's behaviorism and Gesell's maturationism.

Bettman /CORBIS

there are many times when infants are in fact incomprehensible. I will discuss Sigmund Freud at much greater length in Chapter 2.

The scientific theories of infant care and infant development spread rapidly through Western culture in the nineteenth and twentieth centuries because of the rise of the mass media and electronic communication. Urbanization and the automobile created an increasingly mobile and nuclear family, separated from grandparents and dependent on the advice of child-care experts. Society thus created a demand for better-trained and better-supported behavioral scientists who could share their expertise with a public hungry for rational approaches to child rearing.

Let us return to the question raised earlier in the chapter. Why is infancy even more in the public

mind today than it was fifty years ago? Although there is no single answer, I think it is a reaction to the rapid growth of scientific approaches to psychology and human development since the 1960s. This growth was inspired in part by the Cold War, when Western leaders decided that the education and training of their citizens was the best way to combat the technological threats of advanced weapon systems.

The scientific revolution in behavioral research on infancy during these years was very much in the empiricist tradition, but unlike Locke's focus on the whole child's mind and body, the research of the 1970s emphasized infant learning and cognitive development. Cognitive and learning theories rose in importance. The publication in 1973 of Stone, Smith, and Murphy's *The Competent Infant* reflected a desire to discover ever-earlier signs of intelligence in infants. Parents strove to train their infants to achieve the maximum mental potential at the earliest possible age. This was based on the belief that education, rather than natural endowment, was the best guarantee of child success (Clarke-Stewart, 1998). Many parents placed their infants into tightly structured study programs to teach them reading, word learning, music, and mathematics before they reached the age of three years.

This new scientific focus on childhood, for all its benefits, came at a price for children. The research became more focused on using quantitative measures of children's growth and on reporting statistical averages. Much of the research on children in the nineteenth and early twentieth centuries had focused on individual children using qualitative case studies (see the "Research Methods" section in this chapter). The individual child became lost in the quest for scientific generalizability and validity.

Another consequence that affected the lives of children more directly is that the emphasis on intelligence and mental development led to a steady decline in a balanced view of the whole child as needing education not only for mind but for body. According to one historian, "as the individual child and adolescent with bodies faded from view, many of the humanistic ties which bound scientist, teacher, family, and child faded with them" (Friedrich-Cofer, 1986, p. 133). Children's progress began to be reported in the form of standardized test scores rather than individualized assessment of mental and physical health. Physical education, music, and art programs that had been created for all children declined or disappeared entirely from schools, replaced by competitive athletics and music programs designed for an elite group of talented students.

This focus on the early structuring of the infant's intellectual growth was followed in the 1980s by an interest in targeting infants who were at risk for developmental difficulties, such as those who were premature, handicapped, or victims of abuse. The focus on risk was associated with the idea that all humans could become perfect if given the right kind of child rearing. For healthy and wealthy infants, this meant a quest for developing a "super-baby" and giving children a "head start" (Clarke-Stewart, 1998). It also brought the ideal of a "supermom" who could be employed outside the home and at the same time be a great mother and a wonderful and loving wife. The 1980s also saw a rise in the amount of time fathers spent with their babies.

More recently, however, romantic ideas have returned to scientific studies in psychology and in infant development (Schneider, 1998). Perhaps in reaction to what was seen as an overemphasis on intellectual achievement, since the 1990s we have seen a rise in studies of parent-child relationships, emotional development and attachment, the role of the body and touch, and communication and language. Of course, the more rational approaches to infant development continue to grow in such fields as cognitive neuroscience and behavior genetics. On the other hand, some of the trends of the 1970s and 1980s, which focused on babies growing up and getting smart as quickly as possible, were replaced by ideas about slowing down and appreciating the beauty of each phase of a baby's life and the specialness of being a baby.

It may be enlightening to realize that the view of science as quantitative and the focus on the study of the mind to the exclusion of that of the body is a relatively recent cultural invention that temporarily replaced a long Western cultural history of belief and practice in the holistic integration of body and mind. In the next few sections, a conceptualization of infancy based on these scientific approaches will be discussed, followed by a review of some of the research methods that have been devised for the study of infant development.

The Scientific Perspective on Infancy

Conceptualizing Infancy

How you conceptualize infancy depends on what you want to know about infants. If you are a painter, a poet, or a filmmaker, infants may serve as metaphors for divinity or innocence. If you are a clinician, contacting one's infancy experience is a source of healing and new psychological and physical growth. Scientists strive to understand infants in their own right, detached from social and cultural conceptions about infancy. Many scientists admit that they, as products of their own society and culture, can never rid themselves completely of cultural bias. Later in this chapter, I will discuss different scientific methods that either ignore the cultural beliefs of the researcher or take them explicitly into account.

Topics in Infant Development

A large number of topics in infancy have been studied scientifically. Some of these topics are discussed in the next paragraphs.

Perceptual/sensorial skills. These involve the development of the infant's senses—vision, touch, hearing, smell, vestibular-proprioceptive movement and balance, and taste—and the way the infant uses these sensory modalities to acquire knowledge about the world. Perceptual skills are not fully developed at birth; in fact, the human infant has a relatively rudimentary perceptual system for the first months of life. Perception and sensation are central to the experience of being an infant. Unlike older children and adults, infants can spend several hours each day just watching, listening, and feeling. Their senses are alive and salient for them.

Sensorimotor/tool using. Movement is fundamental to all forms of developmental change. As infants make simple movements, such as turning their heads, the visual images on the retina change. These self-produced spontaneous movements allow the child to compare perceptual inputs and to begin constructing a clearer view of the solidity of objects and spatial patterns. The development of motor skills usually is correlated with changes in other areas. Crawling and walking allow infants to access new parts of their world and enhance the awareness of the self as an independent agent. Infants often move just for the pleasure of it, like dancers exploring different possibilities for their bodies. Infant motor skills progress from simple acts, such as turning over, to locomotor skills, to fine motor coordination of objects and tools, such as toys and crayons.

Conceptual/thinking. Cognitive developmental studies chart changes in the infant's capacity to make sense of the world. For example, a major cognitive change occurs at about the age of six months, when infants begin to form conceptual categories. Infants of this age have been shown to distinguish males from females and adults from children. By nine months, infants are beginning to develop an awareness of the fact that objects exist independently from the self. It is only in the latter part of the second year that infants behave as if they are actually thinking, reasoning, and planning actions mentally. Up until this time, the infant could execute a plan of action but had to act out all of the trial and error of the attempt; the infant lacked the mental ability to preselect appropriate courses of action and eliminate others.

Representational/symbolic. The crowning achievement of cognitive development in the first three years of life is the emergence of representational and symbolic thinking: the ability to grasp the idea that a sound or a picture (a spoken or a written word) can represent something entirely different. The written word for "dog" bears no visual similarity to a real canine, nor does the sound of the spoken word "dog." This achievement ushers in a rich new phase of the children's development: pretend play and shared meaning with others through language.

Communicative/linguistic. Learning a first language in the short space of three years is an educational accomplishment of such magnitude that it would be hard to duplicate it at any later point in life. There is more to language than just learning the meanings of words. It is also necessary to learn how words are used, when to speak and when to listen, and how to understand what others are saying. Language in this sense is really only one form of a broader intention to communicate, to share information, and to learn more about the world.

Language, if we look at how it is used in everyday situations, is just as much a social skill as a cognitive skill.

Social/interactive. Infants begin to learn social skills long before they ever acquire their first words. Some of the social skills that infants need to learn are so basic to human life as we know it that it is hard to believe that there was a time in our lives when we did not possess such capabilities. One of these very basic social skills is the ability to take turns in a conversation. Although infants seem to be born with naturally occurring bursts and pauses in their behavior, any semblance of taking turns is apparently created by the adult partner, who learns to insert smiles, coos, and words into the natural silences left by the infant. Although the infant does not initially intend to leave these spaces, the experience of having them filled by the adult eventually leads to the child's growing awareness that he or she is indeed a partner, one who can initiate, pause, speak, or act in concert with another. This ability usually does not appear before the age of five or six months.

Expressive/emotive. An important part of the infant's social skills is the ability to experience certain kinds of emotional states, as well as to express what is felt. Most of the research on infant emotional development seems to indicate that the kinds of emotions infants can feel change with age. It is generally agreed that infants do not know the feeling of fear before about eight months and that they cannot experience complex feelings, such as guilt, pride, or shame, until they are almost three years old. Even though most of the basic emotional expressions can be observed in newborns, infants develop the capacity to express mixed emotions and subtle shades of feeling as they mature. They also develop the ability to control the kinds of emotions they wish to express, but this usually does not happen until the second and third years of life.

Self-regulatory/coping. Most parents would probably be delighted to watch their babies develop each of the skills listed above. But the development of self-regulatory skills is greeted by parents with a sense of relief that goes beyond delight. The ability of an infant to cope with the stresses of everyday life removes a considerable burden from the parents' shoulders. The hallmarks of successful self-regulation are sleeping through the night, waiting patiently while a meal is being prepared, handling the fear and distress of separation from parents, and fighting assertively to retrieve a toy from a meddling sibling. All of these milestones, and many others that occur during the first three years of life, represent the growing autonomy of the child's functioning and therefore lead to a greater sense of freedom for the parents or caregivers. Common to all these events is the ability to continue to function in the face of high levels of arousal. We shall see in later chapters that not only do infants need to cope with high levels of negative arousal, but they must also learn to deal with high levels of positive arousal in situations where excitement and enjoyment threaten to become overwhelmingly intense.

Stages and Changes in Infant Development

The definition of infancy also includes how we mark the important developmental transition points during the infancy period. In reality, infancy is a slow and continuous process of **developmental change.** Not all changes that we observe in infants are developmental changes. A baby can change from being happy to being angry, but we would not call such changes developmental, since the child frequently changes back and forth between these two emotions. Developmental change is characterized by the following three features.

Developmental changes are not reversible. Developmental change is a reorganization of the entire person such that the earlier patterns of behavior, thought, and feeling cannot be easily recognized or recaptured.

Developmental changes are stable. Organized patterns that emerge in development persist over relatively long periods of weeks, months, or years.

Developmental changes occur in sequence. Development occurs in an orderly sequence that is similar across infants.

The progression of language development, for example—crying, cooing, babbling, one-word speech, and multiword speech—has all the required features of developmental change. These changes reflect a reorganization of the whole infant in relation to the social world. Once babies learn to talk, for example, they can express their needs more clearly and participate more fully as partners in relationships. They can acquire conceptual thinking and social understanding. The change is not reversible, since babies rarely go back to simply crying when they need something. The only evidence for reversibility in development would be in the case of neurological damage due to accident or disease. Even here, what is occurring is not, strictly speaking, reversibility, but rather a different reorganization of the whole person that takes account of the deficit.

The developmental progression from crying to speaking also shows stable and persistent patterns called **developmental stages** that last for long periods. The period during which infants cry to get their needs met lasts for three or four months at the beginning of the first year. One-word speech begins around ten months and lasts almost one year, for most babies. Even though development is a continuous process of change, people can recognize that there also appear to be persistent stages. Stages also have the characteristic of occurring in an ordered sequence. Few infants can speak in whole sentences without first passing through the period of one-word speech.

Each culture views the stage divisions of an infant's life differently. The Alor people of the Lesser Sundra Islands do not even count the infant's development in days or months, but rather in terms of a series of stages of development. The first stage lasts from birth to the first smile, the second from smiling to sitting up alone or crawling, and the third from this point to the onset of walking. The Chagga of Tanganyika apply different names to infants depending upon their stage of development. A newborn is called *mnangu*, or "incomplete." A *mkoku* is "one who fills the lap," and a *mwana* is an infant before the age of three years (Mead & Newton, 1967). These linguistic labels are comparable to the terms *newborn, infant,* and *toddler* in English.

Parents and other infant caregivers may use another type of division for the first three years. They may be more concerned about the ages at which infants become capable of independent play with other infants, the age of the beginning of toilet training and the onset of bowel control, or the age at which infants become more relaxed when separated from their parents.

Developmental scientists tend to divide stages according to milestones having to do with one of the areas mentioned in the last section, such as the progression in communication from crying to speech. Another example is the motor development sequence. In deciding how to divide this book into chapters, Jean Piaget's six sensorimotor substages (see Chapter 2, Table 2.1) were chosen as the organizing unit. Piaget's work has received wide acclaim and acceptance. Although some do not agree with Piaget's explanations of development and others say he ignored important aspects of development, his three books on infancy (Piaget, 1952, 1954, 1962) provide one of the most detailed descriptions available of infant skills. In addition, each of his substages was conceptualized as a stable reorganization of the whole infant in relation to the environment, and they emerged in the same order for each infant.

Using Piaget's stages as a way to organize the book does not mean that each chapter focuses only on Piaget's ideas. On the contrary, a wide variety of research, theory, and applications that pertain to infants and their families at each of the age periods will be presented in each chapter. Thus, Piaget's theory will be used to organize infant development into stages and to give a sense of coherence to our understanding of the baby at each age, but we will not be limited to viewing infancy only in these terms.

Research Methods in Developmental Science

What causes people to develop along different pathways and to acquire different ways of experiencing the world? Each culture has its own theory of the formation of individual differences. As explained earlier, for example, the ancient Greeks and Romans believed that exposing an infant to a variety of fearful and stressful events early in life would make the child less fearful and more emotionally balanced later. Nineteenth-century Europeans believed just the opposite—that protecting the child from fear-producing experiences was the best way to create an outgoing child (Kagan, Kearsley, & Zelazo, 1978). Which one of these "folk" theories is more correct? How could you decide?

The position taken in this book is that while folk theories are important parts of people's beliefs and structure the way that people behave, scientific theories are a viable alternative for conceptualizing the processes that create developmental change and individual differences. The reason is that the scientist relies on many sources of evidence (folk theories may be based only on experience within one's own family), tries to separate what is repeatable and stable from what is coincidental (folk theories tend to infer general patterns from a small number of instances), and attempts to rid observations of bias (folk theories often embody what the observer hopes to see or believes should occur, rather than what actually does happen).

This does not mean that scientists always succeed in reaching these ideals. As research in the behavioral sciences has returned to a more romantic approach, many scientists are beginning to question this ideal. No scientific study can be flawless, and all science is infused with the values and perspectives of individual scientists. Some scientists have attempted to put themselves into the scientific study using qualitative, as contrasted with quantitative, research methods.

Quantitative research methods represent complex behavioral processes using a numerical index called a variable. **Qualitative research,** on the other hand, attempts to capture the meaning or quality of the behavior. Qualitative researchers use verbal or pictorial descriptions of behavior rather than numbers, and they try to understand how their own perspectives influence the subjects and shape the findings and interpretations. They make explicit the idea that science is one type of human interpersonal relationship. These qualitative researchers are like folk theorists in that they do not divorce their own beliefs from the observations, but they maintain a scientific stance by taking multiple perspectives and entertaining alternative interpretations. In the fol-

lowing sections, traditional quantitative research methods will be discussed, including methods for experimental and observational research. This will be followed by a section that discusses qualitative research methods.

Jean Piaget (1896–1980), one of the founders of the field of developmental psychology (Chapter 2), began his career in research on children by making extensive written notes, often on a daily basis, about the behavior of his three infant children. Piaget not only observed natural behavior, but tried out little experiments to test alternate interpretations of what the children could do. At one point, Piaget tried to determine whether his eight-month-old daughter Jacqueline (J.) was capable of imitating mouth movements and sounds.

In the following example, Jacqueline seemed to imitate her father's biting movements. Or did she? Piaget was not sure whether Jacqueline only appeared to imitate him because he had started out by imitating movements she could already make.

J. was moving her lips as she bit on her jaws. I did the same thing, and she stopped and watched me attentively. . . . J. began to imitate me an hour later. . . . In order to understand this new development, two circumstances must be noted. Firstly, for some days she had not merely imitated sounds for their own sake but had watched the mouth of the model with great attention. Secondly, as she moved her lips, J. began by making a slight noise with her saliva . . . and I had imitated this sound at the outset. Her interest in the movements of the mouth was thus clearly due to interest in the production of sound. [Three days later] I resumed the experiment without making any sound and without J. herself having made the movement beforehand. She watched my lips moving and then distinctly imitated me three times, keeping her eyes fixed on my mouth. (Piaget, 1962, pp. 30–31)

Experimental Research Methods

In this example, Piaget combined observational research with an **experiment.** An experiment is a research study in which one aspect of the situation is manipulated while all other aspects are held constant or controlled. In this case, in order to discover Jacqueline's ability to imitate mouth movements on her own, Piaget waited for a time when Jacqueline had not made the movement spontaneously for some time, and he did not produce any sound when he made the movements himself. The prior condition (the child makes no similar spontaneous movement and the adult does not imitate the child) and the presentation of the adult model (absence of sound) were controlled. The experimental manipulation is the presence or absence of a movement-only adult model.

In modern versions of Piaget's famous imitation experiment, many other aspects of the situation are controlled: the position in which the child is sitting, the behavior of the adult model, the familiarity of the infant with the adult, and the observation procedures (see Chapter 5). The following are some standard experimental procedures.

Control groups that do not receive any manipulation are compared to a group of infants who receive the experimental manipulation. Alternatively, different groups can be compared if each receives a different type of manipulation. These are called **contrast groups.** In imitation research, for example, different contrast groups of infants are presented with a different model (e.g., tongue protrusion, mouth movement, or a facial expression). If imitation occurs, the frequency of tongue protrusion following the model should be highest in the group that has seen the tongue-protrusion model. This procedure controls for the fact that most babies produce tongue protrusion spontaneously, so that some tongue protrusion would be seen in all the groups.

Random assignment is used to determine which subjects belong to each experimental group. A flip of a coin or some other random process is used to assign subjects to groups. In some cases, it is unethical to use random assignment in a study. For example, suppose we want to compare the effects on language development of differences in mother's speech to infants. We obviously cannot randomly assign mothers to infants.

Experiments generally have two important measures, also called variables. The **independent variable** is that which is controlled or manipulated by the experimenter. In the case of imitation studies, the independent variable is the type of model given to the infant. The independent variable is the presumed cause of the phenomenon—that is, different types of models are presumed to cause the infant to imitate different movements. The **dependent variable** is the outcome behavior that is observed in response to the changes in the independent variable. In the case of the imitation study, the dependent variable is the frequency of different actions of the infant, such as the frequency of mouth movements or tongue protrusions. The dependent variable is presumed to be affected by the causal independent variable such that manipulations of the independent variable should lead to systematic changes in the dependent variable.

Infants are not as easily studied as older children or adults. Infants cannot describe their inner states, take standardized written tests, or respond to interview questions. Because of the difficulty of working with infants, special procedures have been devised to measure their behavior.

Standardized Experimental Procedures for Use with Infants

In **paired-preference procedures,** infants are shown two visual stimuli side by side, or they hear sounds presented to one or the other ear. Researchers then try to determine which of the two stimuli is preferred by the infants. During such procedures, infants are either held quietly by their mothers or sit in an infant seat in a darkened room to reduce competing sources of stimulation. Directly in front of the infant there is usually a blank screen on which is mounted a display of flashing lights. A small peephole in this screen, invisible to the infant, allows an observer to look directly at the infant's face and judge where the infant is looking and for how long (Fantz, 1961). In a more sophisticated variation of this procedure, an invisible infrared light is reflected off the infant's cornea, and the angle of reflection is detected by an electronic sensor. The angle of reflection can be translated electrically to determine the precise position of the infant's gaze (Haith,

Bergman, & Moore, 1977). The latter procedure has also been used to examine the developmental changes in the way infants scan visual objects (see Chapter 6).

At the beginning of an experimental trial (a presentation of one pair of stimuli), the light display flashes to attract the infant's attention to the center. When the infant is judged to be looking at the center, the flashing lights are turned off and the paired visual display is presented, usually by a rear-screen slide projector (for example, mother on left, stranger on right). The length of time the infant looks left or right is recorded before the visual displays go off. On the next trial, the flashing lights are again used. After the infant looks to the center, the mother appears on the right and the stranger on the left. The order of presentation of the stimuli is counterbalanced across trials to eliminate any bias due to an infant's preference for turning to one side or another. Preference is determined by the average across trials of the length of time the infant looks to its mother and to a stranger.

Paired-preference methods have been used in many research studies that will be reviewed in this book. Using this method, for example, infants in the first month of life have been found to prefer the sound of their mother's voice to that of another woman and the odor of their mother's breast milk to the milk smell of another woman (Chapter 5). Five-month-old infants prefer a video image of their own legs as they would appear normally to the infant compared to a manipulated video image in which the left and right legs have been reversed (Chapter 6).

A second procedure for the assessment of infant psychological experience uses repeated exposure to the same visual or auditory stimulus. Each time the stimulus is repeated is one trial. If a researcher repeatedly shows the same picture to a baby—say, a picture of a face with a sad expression—the baby spends less and less time looking at the picture with each new presentation, acting as though he was getting bored with the same old thing. The gradual decline in looking time over repeated trials of the same stimulus is known as **habituation,** which results from increasing familiarity with the stimulus.

Researchers select some minimum amount of looking time as the criterion to decide when the baby has become habituated to a stimulus. For ex-

ample, if the baby's initial looks at a facial expression last about thirty seconds, a reasonable habituation criterion for subsequent trials might be five seconds. Once the baby has reached the criterion looking time, researchers change the picture or sound—in our example, from the face with a sad expression to the same face with a happy expression. If the baby cannot tell the difference between the two expressions, he or she will go on looking at the happy expression for durations shorter than the habituation criterion. However, if the baby can detect a change, the infant will begin to look longer at the happy face than at the last presentation of the sad face. This abrupt increase in looking time after a change in the stimulus is called **recovery.** Field et al. (1982) used this technique with newborns to see if they could differentiate between happy, sad, and surprised facial expressions. Remarkably, they could.

A final standardized procedure we will review is called the **response-contingent procedure,** which is often used in studies of auditory and taste perception. In this technique, infants are trained to change their behavior if they can detect certain features of the sounds or tastes. Once taught, infants will alter their behavior in order to hear their favorite sound or to receive their preferred taste.

DeCasper and Fifer (1980) used this technique with an automatic suck recorder. The suck recorder is a pacifier that is connected to a pressure transducer (which converts varying degrees of pressure into electrical impulses), which in turn is connected to recording equipment. Each infant in the study was equipped with a set of headphones and a suck recorder. After a two-minute adjustment period, the infant's sucking was recorded for five minutes with no sounds coming through the headphones. During this period, the experimenter computed the median duration of the pauses between sucking bouts (see Chapter 5). If you make a list of the durations of all the pauses observed for the infant, the median is the duration at the midpoint of the list: half the durations are above the median and half below.

In the experimental period, infants sucked as usual, such that half of their pauses were below the median and half above. When the experimenters detected a pause that was longer than the median interval, they presented the infants with the recorded voice of either their mother (reading a segment of a Dr. Seuss story) or a stranger (reading the same segment). Five of the infants were randomly assigned to a group that could evoke their mother's voice by pausing their sucking for longer than the median pause length and evoke the stranger's voice by pausing for less than the median pause interval. The other five infants had the reverse conditions.

Because the presentation of the adult voices was made contingent upon the duration of the sucking pause, infants quickly learned that by speeding up or slowing down their sucking, they could produce one or the other voice. If the infants had a preference for one or the other voice, they could then systematically shift their pause length to "suck for" that voice. Eight of the ten infants showed a tendency to shift their pause length to produce their own mother's voice. Four of the infants were retested twenty-four hours later in a situation in which the criterion for obtaining the mother's voice was reversed from the previous day. All four continued to suck for their mother's voice.

Babies can tell us very little about themselves using ordinary means of communication. These remarkably creative research methods, therefore, are very useful for finding out more about what infants know. The main problem with all these techniques is that the failure of an infant to respond does not necessarily mean the infant *cannot* respond. The infant may recognize the difference and *choose* not to respond. Thus, it is necessary to test the same infants repeatedly. One could also use a relatively large sample of infants with the expectation that if a sizable number of infants at a particular age can detect a difference, then infants at that age are in general capable of detecting a difference.

Physiological Recording

Because infants cannot report on their internal states, physiological activity is one method of discovering more about what is going on inside the baby. Please note, however, that physiological recording can be used for both experimental and observational research. The level of arousal in the autonomic nervous system (ANS) can be measured with a variety of techniques. Heart rate recordings tell us about the level of the infant's physiological

arousal associated with particular types of observed behavior and in different situations. An example of the use of heart rate in research is in the measurement of whether infants can perceive depth. Gibson and Walk (1960; see Chapter 8) discovered that infants older than six months would not continue to crawl to their mothers if they suddenly saw a deep drop-off between themselves and the mother. The drop-off was created by a trough several feet deep that interrupted the surface on which the infant was crawling. To protect unwary infants from harm, the researchers covered the trough with plexiglass, creating the so-called visual cliff device.

The visual cliff could not be used to study depth perception in infants under six months because it required that the infants be able to crawl. When attached to heart rate monitors and placed next to the visual cliff, however, infants as young as two months showed some changes in their heart rate indicating moderate arousal (though not fear) and thus perception of the depth (Campos, Langer, & Krowitz, 1970). It was not until infants began to crawl that they showed heart rate changes similar to those measured during a fearful response. Thus, although two-month-olds perceive the depth, they must have the experience of crawling around in the real world to be able to appreciate the depth with an appropriate level of fear (Campos, 1976).

Behavior can be automatically recorded using a number of techniques. Gross motor activity has been recorded with a device called an actometer, which can be fixed to the infant's clothing or attached to a crib mattress. It records the number of position shifts made by the infant as a function of time. Infant sounds can be studied with a sound spectrograph that shows the duration, pitch, and frequency of vocalizations. Changes in sucking, respiration, and gaze direction can also be detected by electronic devices and recorded as a continuous function of time.

Hormonal activity can be recorded from blood tests, but some hormones can be detected more easily from saliva. Saliva contains the hormone cortisol, which has been shown to increase in response to environmental stresses, such as during medical treatments, and to decrease during periods of relaxation.

Central nervous system (CNS) activity has been measured with a variety of so-called brain wave

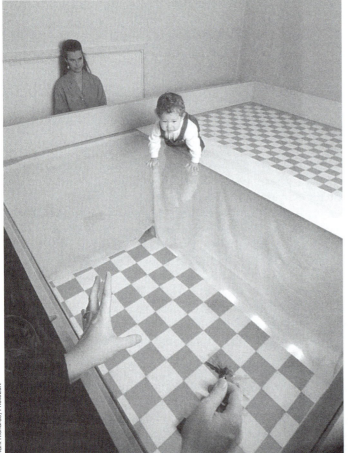

In this experimental laboratory, the age of onset of the fear of heights is tested using a "visual cliff" that is covered with glass.

Mark Richards/PhotoEdit

techniques. Electrodes are fastened to the infant's scalp with a small amount of petroleum jelly. The electrodes detect the minute changes in electrical activity inside the brain without hurting the infant. Because the currents generated in the brain are small, infants must be presented with a particular stimulus—a sound or a visual object—many times, and the electrical responses must be averaged by a computer in order to detect the existence of the "signal" of the response to the stimulus against the "noise" of normal spontaneous brain activity. The resulting averages are called averaged event-related potentials (ERPs). Although such techniques cannot be used to monitor an infant's ongoing mental state, they can tell us whether there is a general ability to detect a stimulus. ERP methods have also been used to diagnose brain disorders in the form of abnormal patterns of electrical activity or lack of predicted responses.

Although physiological recording devices allow us to detect information we could not otherwise observe, and although they reduce human error, they have important limitations. For one thing, we can never be sure of the precise meaning of a change in a physiological measure. Many events other than emotion or perception could trigger a change in heart rate or brain activity. Second, physiological activity is itself a response. Just because the heart rate changes when the infant is afraid does not mean the heart is the source of the emotion. All bodily systems are intimately linked together as a complex system such that small changes in one part can have major repercussions throughout the entire system. There is no way to say when and where a response originates or is encoded in the body.

Observational Research Methods

The inability to randomly assign subjects to groups is a major limitation in the application of the experimental method to infant studies. Many of the important questions in infancy research—such as the effects of prematurity and of variations in parental styles of child care—cannot be studied experimentally. We cannot randomly assign infants to be premature, and we cannot randomly assign particular types of parents to particular types of infants. We use instead the natural variations within the existing population of infants and mothers.

Methods that rely on natural variations rather than random assignment to create contrast groups are called **observational research** methods. The obvious advantage of observational research is that we can study many issues of grave importance to our understanding of early human development that would be unethical or impossible to study experimentally. The problem with observational studies is that the variable on which the groups are assigned (e.g., the style of parental child rearing) may also correlate with other factors (such as the mother's social skills and general expressiveness). If this occurs, it is impossible to say which factor—child rearing, social skills, or expressiveness—is the cause of differences in infant behavior.

In most cases involving human infancy, however, observational studies are all we can do. As discussed later in this book, researchers have developed ways to examine the mutual influences of many potential causes that enter into an observational study. Observational studies can be either longitudinal or cross-sectional. In a **longitudinal study,** researchers follow the same group of children as they get older. Longitudinal studies are important for determining how particular early experiences of individuals affect their later development and also for revealing patterns of change over time. Change is measured against the individual's own record of growth. The disadvantage is that the researcher must wait for the child to grow, although this takes less time for infants than for older children because infants grow at a faster rate; few researchers can find the research

funding to support such long-term efforts. Another problem is **attrition,** which occurs when subjects of a longitudinal study drop out of the study before they complete the entire period of observation. Not only does attrition lower the number of subjects in a study, but researchers worry whether the subjects who remain are different from those who drop out, making the study less representative of the larger population.

One of the methods most commonly used today to study developmental change is a **cross-sectional study,** in which the researcher selects children of different ages. Cross-sectional studies have the advantage of giving us a sense of age change in development without having to wait for the children to grow up. An additional advantage is that researchers who observe children from only two or three different age groups have more time to collect data from a large number of children and thus may find patterns of between-individual variation in behavioral characteristics and age of attainment of developmental milestones. Thus, while cross-sectional studies allow us to make generalizations about groups of infants, they cannot tell us how individual infants develop over time.

Observational research, like experimental research, can be quantitative. This means that observations are transformed in numerical indices called variables. The variable that is the presumed cause—such as child-rearing styles—is called the **predictor variable.** The presumed effect—child behavior—is called the **outcome variable.** There is an analogy between independent variables and predictor variables, and between dependent variables and outcome variables.

Reducing Bias in Research

Regardless of whether one does observational or experimental research, caution must be taken to assure that variables reflect accurate and unbiased measures of the phenomenon. **Reliability** and **validity** procedures are ways of attempting to reduce bias in quantitative research. Reliability is a measure of the consistency with which an assessment procedure is applied. If one is trying to measure an infant's preference for looking at her mother compared to an unfamiliar woman, observers may be asked to record the duration of time the infant spends looking at each adult. If two people, working independently, are asked to judge the duration of the same event, the measurement of duration is reliable to the extent that the two observers agree with each other.

Validity is the degree to which the procedure accurately measures what it is intended to measure. For example, one might ask if the duration of time the infant spends looking at the mother versus that spent looking at the stranger is a valid measure of the infant's preference for one or the other. A baby may look longer at an unfamiliar face because it is new and the baby is curious about it, not because the baby prefers to look at that face. In this case, the duration of time the infant looks at the stranger would not be a valid measure of preference for the stranger. To test whether the duration of the infant's looking is a valid measure of preference or of curiosity, one would have to compare this measure with other measures of preference and curiosity. An additional measure of preference might be the duration of time the infant smiles at and vocalizes to each adult. An additional measure of curiosity might be the duration of time the infant looks at pictures of novel compared to familiar objects.

To test the validity of the measure, a group of infants would have to be assessed on that measure and also on the other validating measures. The same infants, for example, would be tested to measure the duration of time they looked at the stranger compared to their mother. In addition, measures would be taken of the duration of time spent smiling at the stranger (a preference measure) and the duration of time spent looking at unfamiliar objects (a curiosity measure). If the babies who had high durations of time spent looking at the stranger also had high durations of time spent smiling at her, but low durations of time spent looking at unfamiliar objects (a curiosity measure), one could conclude that the duration measure of an infant's looking at a stranger is a valid measure of preference for the stranger. It could also turn out that high durations of time spent looking at the stranger are related to high durations of time spent looking at novel objects, suggesting that looking at the stranger is a valid measure of curiosity. Finally, it may be that there is no consistent relationship between the duration of time the infant looks at the stranger and the duration of the other two measures. If this happens, it means that looking at the stranger may sometimes reflect preference and sometimes curiosity. It cannot, therefore, be considered a valid measure of either one.

Another means of lowering research bias is to protect the outcomes of a study from the unintended influence of the subjects on the experimenters. This is usually accomplished by assuring that both the subjects and the experimenters are blind to the specific purpose of the research and to the group assignment of the subjects. **Blindness** in quantitative research refers to limiting the access of researchers and participants to knowledge that may bias the outcomes of the study. In a study on the relationship between infant language and mother's speech, for instance, experimenters who administer the tests of infant language should not be the same as those who observe the mother's speech, and they should not know anything about the mother's speech score. The mothers should not be aware of the precise measures and relationships being tested, although they might be told that they are participating in a study on infant language development.

Finally, bias in research can be reduced by assuring that the group of infants and parents who participate in a research study is representative of the larger population of infants (**representative research**). A study is representative if its conclusions can be applied to infants who were not direct participants in the study. Most infancy research is done with white, middle-class North American and European infants. It is important to ask whether these findings apply equally to infants from other ethnic groups, cultures, and socioeconomic groups. Research grants from the National Institutes of Health in the United States, which funds both medical and behavioral research on human subjects, cannot be obtained unless the subjects of the study represent both genders and a cross-section of ethnic groups.

Research Ethics and Informed Consent

Research ethics adopted by most institutions in North America require that human subjects give their **informed consent** to participate in research.

Informed consent is a voluntary agreement to participate in a research study. It must be based on accurate information about the purpose, procedures, risks, and benefits of the research study (Keith-Spiegel, 1983). Special provisions are required for research subjects who cannot give consent for themselves, specifically infants and small children. In these cases, one or both parents must sign the consent to participate. Parents are told about the possible risks and benefits of the research, both for themselves and for their infants.

In order to meet requirements of informed consent as well as the scientific requirement that subjects be blind to the purpose of the research, researchers usually tell subjects about the general purpose of the study but not about the specific measures to be used. Subjects must be told about all the procedures, but they need not be told about the specific purpose of the procedures. Most researchers will provide a debriefing session for subjects following the completion of their participation. During the debriefing, more details are provided, and all the subjects' questions should be answered frankly. In research using human subjects, researchers have the responsibility of designing studies of lasting value to society and respecting the rights and dignity of the individuals who volunteer their time to participate. Due to these controls over research ethics, some of the early studies of infant behavior and development—such as John Watson's research in which he made infants fear cuddly animals—would not be allowed today.

Researchers must pledge to keep the subjects' identity confidential and to limit access to their data only to those persons directly involved with the research. There are several situations, however, in which confidentiality cannot be assured. In the event that the researchers observe behavior constituting child abuse, they are required by law to report it to the appropriate community agency. Also, researchers cannot protect their data if they are subpoenaed in a child custody dispute. Parents need to be informed about these limits to confidentiality before they agree to participate. Fortunately, these situations rarely occur. In the past twenty-five years of doing infancy research with hundreds of families, I have never had to violate a subject's confidentiality for these or any other reasons.

Methods of Observational Research

A large portion of research on infants involves the observation of their behavior in relatively natural circumstances without experimental control. Observing the ongoing behavior of infants is difficult because many things are happening at the same time. Imagine trying to write down everything that happens during a social interaction between two partners in the exact sequence in which it occurs, including not only what they say to each other, but all of the nonverbal social behaviors, such as looking, facial expressions, gestures, and body movements. This research approach, focusing on minute changes in behavior, is called **microanalysis.**

Researchers have developed a number of techniques to simplify the task of microanalysis and to increase accuracy. First of all, it is important to be selective in what you want to observe. Since you cannot see everything, your choice should be guided by some conceptual framework. Suppose, for example, you wanted to observe how an infant interacted with her mother before and during the approach of an unfamiliar person. Based on the theory of infant attachment (Chapters 2 and 8), we expect that the presence of a stranger may be associated with behavior categories such as the child approaching the mother, following the mother, and staying near the mother's side. Older infants may also ask about the stranger or ask to be picked up and held.

After choosing a list of relevant behavioral categories, the observer is trained to recognize each category until an acceptable level of inter-rater reliability can be obtained. The process by which observers record the presence or absence of the predefined categories as they are watching an infant is known as **coding.**

One relatively easy coding strategy is pencil-and-paper recording of live observations. When any one of the categories is seen, it is checked off on a sheet of paper on which the categories have been listed. Audio and video recordings can improve the accuracy of observational data. Once behavior is recorded on tape, observers can replay the tape as often as necessary to code the entire observation period. Videotapes can be made with a digital clock image in the corner of the screen so that elapsed time between behavior onsets and offsets can be recorded.

In addition to increasing the accuracy of observational research, videotape has been revolutionary in showing us things babies do that are not apparent in traditional observation. One example is discussed in Chapter 6. Hand movements and facial expressions of two-month-old infants often give a picture of disorganized or chaotic movement. Looking at them in slow motion on a videotape, however, one can see recognizable patterns of smiling, brow raising, and finger pointing. Computers can be electronically interfaced with videotape players. A timing signal is recorded on the videotape. When the observer presses a key representing a particular behavior category, the computer automatically records and saves the category and the time of onset. The observer can ask the computer to fast-forward through the tape, stopping at all previously coded events in order to compare them or to do more detailed coding.

New methods have been devised for using the computer to automatically identify behavior from a videotape recording, without the need for an observer. The computer is programmed to recognize particular images, such as when an infant smiles, frowns, or moves his or her body in a particular way, and to record the onset and offset time as well as dynamic changes in intensity. This is similar to the voice recognition programs often used in automatic telephone answering systems. Scientists hope that by using these tools for microanalysis, they will be better able to understand the complexity and dynamic changes in human communication.

A final type of observational research, called **macroanalysis,** focuses on the overall or summary features of behavior rather than its details and sequences of occurrences. Macroanalysis is usually done with the use of a **rating scale.** Rating scales allow observers to use a number to differentiate the amount or quality of a particular type of observed behavior. In the example of a stranger approaching an infant, described earlier, the microanalytical coding categories were discrete behaviors: approaching, following, and staying near the mother when a stranger is present. The observer recorded each category separately whenever it occurred and noted the onset and offset times. A macroanalytical rating scale for the entire interaction could be devised that would eliminate the need for detailed behavior records. For example, after watching the entire observation session of the infant with mother and stranger, an observer might rate the child on a scale of 1 to 5, where 1 is comfort with the stranger (not approaching or following the mother), 3 is some discomfort (maintaining a moderate distance from the mother), and 5 is extreme anxiety (clinging to the mother and following her closely).

Macroanalytical ratings are effective when the measure of interest to the research need not be equated to specific behaviors—in this case, only the overall level of comfort versus anxiety. Ratings are easier to do, but they often require more coder training since they are open to subjective interpretation. Microanalytical behavior codes are often simpler to learn but require more coder time since they must be assessed continuously during an observation period. Microanalysis is necessary when one is interested in the dynamics of behavior—in how it unfolds over time.

Using macroanalysis, an infant's social play might be assessed according to Mildred Parten's (1932) scale of mutual involvement in play (see Table 1.1). One could observe children and rate the highest level of play. A rating of 3, for example, means that children have achieved associative but not cooperative play. Bakeman and Brownlee (1980) used Parten's coding categories but did a microanalysis. They observed three-year-old children in out-of-doors free play. Instead of rating, they recorded the presence or absence of each category of play during successive fifteen-second time intervals for about a hundred minutes.

Besides learning about the overall level of play in the children, Bakeman and Brownlee were interested in the sequence of play. For example, when did parallel play occur in relationship to group play? It could be that parallel play occurred during the first half of the observation, and then group play took over. However, the microanalysis revealed that parallel play was sandwiched between episodes of group play.

What does it mean for the children that parallel play occurs between episodes of group play? The microanalysis and macroanalysis are not sufficient

Table 1.1   Types of Play between Young Children

Type of Play	Description	Example
Solitary play	Child plays alone.	A child sits alone in a sandbox and fills a pail with sand.
Parallel play	Play in close proximity to other children but without interaction.	Two children sit next to each other in a sandbox, each filling a pail.
Associative play	Children respond to each other during play but maintain separate goals.	Two children talk to each other while playing with sand in a sandbox.
Cooperative play	Play is organized around joint activities.	Two children work together to build a sand castle.

Source: Adapted from M. B. Parten, Social participation among preschool children, 1932. *Journal of Abnormal and Social Psychology, 27,* 243–269.

to answer this question. In order to find out, it is necessary to observe what happens during these periods of parallel play. What happens when the children change to group play? The authors took their findings from the quantitative microanalysis and went back to the playground to observe the situation without focusing on a particular type of behavior. They discovered that for children of this age, parallel play was a "time out" from group play. During periods of parallel play, children could relax, work momentarily on their own, or observe each other's behavior before reentering the mainstream of group activity. This type of research, which focuses on the meaning of the behaviors for the participants, is called *qualitative research.*

Qualitative Research Methods

In the previous sections, I discussed quantitative research using experimental and observational methods. In quantitative studies, the phenomenon is measured—that is, it is codified into a number. The number could be an onset time, a duration, a frequency, or a score on a rating scale. Qualitative research, on the other hand, does not use quantity or number. It is characterized by one or both of the following features.

1. The observers focus on the meaning of the situation for the participants.

2. The role of the researcher in the situation is taken explicitly into account.

In order to infer the meaning of the situation and to take account of the observer as part of the situation, qualitative research needs to examine the situation in its broader context. The child is observed in relation to the setting, the actors, the sequences of behavior, the history of previous encounters in similar situations, and the presence of the observer. If the researcher is part of the observation situation, as a **participant observer,** he or she has a direct effect on the people being studied, and they have an effect on the researcher. If the observer is watching a videotape or some other already collected data, their interpretations play a role in deciding what the participants' behaviors mean.

One example of qualitative research is the final part of the study by Bakeman and Brownlee (1980). This part of the study fits the first characteristic of qualitative research: a focus on the meaning of the behavior for the participants. The study done by Piaget on Jacqueline's imitation was described earlier as an example of quantitative research in the sense that Piaget counted the number of times Jacqueline imitated him under different experimental conditions. It is also an example of qualitative research, because he used a verbal narrative of the whole situation to highlight the broader meaning to Jacqueline of the behavior. Piaget also was explicit about taking account of his own role in the outcome. Having recognized the possible effects of his own behavior on his daughter, he was better able to sort out the possible causes and effects, which led him to design a better experiment.

The earliest known systematic observation and recording of infant behavior was done by educated European and North American parents during the eighteenth and nineteenth centuries. Some of these parents kept a daily dairy about their baby's life, a **baby biography.** These diaries satisfied the first characteristic of qualitative research: they were narratives intended to understand the meaning of infant behavior rather than to measure it. The German philosopher Dietrich Tiedemann (1748–1803), for example, recorded the development of motor skills, language, thinking abilities, and social behavior in his infant son. Tiedemann described what we now call the Moro reflex (see Chapter 5) as follows:

> *If he was held in arms and then suddenly lowered from a considerable height, he strove to hold himself with his hands, to save himself from falling; and he did not like to be lifted very high. Since he could not possibly have any conception of falling, his fear was unquestionably a purely mechanical sensation, such as older persons feel at a steep and unaccustomed height, something akin to dizziness. (Tiedemann, 1927, p. 216)*

Notice that Tiedemann not only described his son's behavior in the manner of observational research but also interpreted the meaning of the behavior for the infant when he speculated that the infant's experience was "purely mechanical." Tiedemann may have been an accurate observer, but he would not be considered a good qualitative researcher by today's standards. Although we readers can see that his interpretations of the meaning of the child's behavior is based on his own point of view as an adult, Teidemann did not take explicit account of his role in the interpretive process. He was not, in other words, aware of his own biases.

Charles Darwin, whose theory of natural selection will be discussed in Chapter 2, was also a baby biographer. Darwin was very aware of his role in the interpretive process. When his son, William, was only a few months old, Darwin was a relatively objective observer. But as William became more active and expressive, Darwin added more references to himself and his affections for William. Because Darwin thought these references to himself were unscientific, however, they were deleted in the versions of his diary that he published (Conrad, 1998).

Qualitative researchers today do not think it is unscientific for observers to take account of their own reactions. They suggest that a deeper understanding of the meaning of behavior for the subjects can only come from a deeper self-awareness of the researchers about their own reactions and biases (Moustakas, 1994). Perhaps the only way to get to know another person meaningfully is to share a long-term relationship full of emotions, opinions, and attachments.

Researchers always have some kind of relationship with their subjects. In the quantitative approach, the relationship is one of keeping a distance and remaining objective as an observer. In qualitative research, observers allow themselves to experience some of the feelings of participation that might be present in any interpersonal relationship (Aureli, 1997). Their training and self-awareness, however, allow them to use their own feelings to enhance their understanding of the subject's perspective. On the other hand, quantitative researchers also have biases, which they quantify by means of reliability and validity measures. Each type of research has its advantages and disadvantages.

The assessment of a student's performance in school, for example, can occur through either a distant or a close teacher-student relationship. In large classes, a quantitative approach is most typically used. Instructors use primarily numerical and presumably objective indices of student performance, based on a limited number of exams and other graded assignments. In small classes, on the other hand, evaluations are based not only on grades but also on a more in-depth interpersonal relationship between teachers and students. In this situation, the teacher has an opportunity to get to know each student. Experienced teachers are able to develop meaningful interpersonal relationships with their students while maintaining the ability to judge the student's performance and guide her or his learning. Experienced clinicians, such as psychotherapists, also have this skill of being able to evaluate their client's progress while maintaining a strong interpersonal relationship.

Validity in quantitative research is based on comparing different types of numerical measurements with each other. It is an assessment of the quality of the measurement instrument, such as an automatic recording device or category of behavior. In qualitative research, *the researcher is the instrument of observation*. Researchers' **credibility** depends upon their skill, experience, and rigor (Denzin & Lincoln, 1994). Credibility in qualitative research is similar to validity in quantitative research. Credibility is enhanced if the researcher is highly trained, has spent many hours doing comparable observations, and has had a prolonged engagement with the particular subjects of the study. This is true for Piaget, since he was a trained scientist and he obviously had prolonged contact with his own children. In the example of teaching, more experienced teachers tend to be more credible.

Even if researchers are credible, however, they can still be biased, because the interpretation of meaning is always from their own point of view. Qualitative researchers feel there is a trade-off between the accuracy but limited scope of a quantitative measure compared to the flexibility, human insight, and awareness of broad meaning of a highly trained qualitative observer (Patton, 1990). In some qualitative research methods, the researcher allows the subjects to give feedback and to play a role in the interpretation of the data. This is impossible with infant subjects, but sometimes parents can participate as co-researchers.

In quantitative research, reliability is assessed by comparing the coding or rating of behavior between two independent observers. In qualitative research, on the other hand, the same observers go over the same data many times in order to check and revise their interpretation of the meaning of the behavior for the participants. Revisions are repeated until the observers feel confident that the interpretations are consistent throughout and new interpretations do not emerge during the process (Patton, 1990). This is called the **constant comparative method,** because researchers compare current interpretations with earlier ones (Strauss & Corbin, 1990).

Because prolonged engagement with data is important to assure the credibility of the observer, and also in order to use the constant comparative method, many qualitative researchers use case studies. In a **case study,** the same subjects are observed over a long period of time, as in the baby biographies and Piaget's studies of his own children. Case studies are often used as a means for emphasizing data on individuals in their real-life contexts. They are also used to study changes in individuals over time. Generally, case studies provide more detail about individuals than can be obtained using quantitative methods on large groups of individuals.

Generalizability is the characteristic of a research study the results of which can apply to people other than the ones who were observed. Research that is done on many individuals using representative samples of subjects is more likely to be generalizable. On the other hand, if there are a lot of subjects, the research can only obtain a limited amount of quantitative information about each individual. When researchers focus on a few cases, they can obtain a more detailed picture of the lives of those individuals and the meaning of their behavior. Once again, there is a trade-off between the kind of meaning and detail in a case study compared to the generalizability of a large sample quantitative study. The best approach is to use qualitative research on several different cases combined with quantitative research on a large sample.

The Author's View

The study of infancy is valuable for our society, increasing knowledge and enriching lives. I am proud to have been a small part of the history of infancy research during the past thirty years. The study of infants has helped me understand my own early development, guided me as a father, and given me a rewarding professional career.

There is no single best way to do research on infants. Many people believe research is not scientific unless one uses quantitative methods such as representative samples, control groups, random assignment, and reliable and valid measures. For me, on the contrary, a scientific approach is not defined by a particular type of method but rather by the flexible combination of different methods that best allow the scientist to appreciate the beauty and complexity of nature. A scientific stance allows me to

Applications Advocacy and Public Policy for Infants and Their Families

In this chapter, we learned that the twentieth century has been a period of increased public awareness about the development of infants. There is a strong perception that some proportion of tax revenues should be spent for the benefit of all infants. It was not always this way. The United States was founded on basic principles of self-reliance and upon the idea that parents had both the responsibility and the right to raise their children without undue intervention from the government. Legally, children are viewed as the possessions of their parents, and the government may only interfere with families in extreme circumstances of abuse and neglect. This legal concept, called *parens patriae,* was part of English common law originating in the 15th century.

The effects of parens patriae can be seen in the history of public welfare in the United States. The first nursery schools, day care centers, and public health programs in the United States were established in the 19th century. The state Boards of Charity, begun in 1863, were the first government welfare institutions. They provided protection from abuse for children living in orphanages and working in factories, but not for those living at home with parents. Two White House conferences on children, in 1909 and 1930, led to the creation of the Social Security Acts of the 1930s, which established a welfare system, aid to dependent children, and financial and rehabilitation services for needy children and their families.

Because of the ideals of self-reliance and parens patriae, the government confined its protective activities to the most needy segment of society, children whose parents could not provide support for them. Receiving welfare and public funds—even if the funds were used to protect infants from abuse and exploitation—was thought of as a social stigma.

Contrast these narrow ideas of the public interest in children with the infant- and child-related discussions going on in the halls of state legislatures today. At issue is proposed legislation to provide minimum standards for all day care centers and day care homes, whether attended by the rich or the poor. Surprisingly few states have such standards, and there is no national day care policy. Recently, national and state legislatures have passed laws to provide, as a basic right, liberal parental leave policies so that parents (men and women) with young infants may take unpaid time off from work after their baby is born without fear of losing their jobs.

Although few programs provide direct benefits to families with infants, tax money is used to benefit families in some indirect ways. Corporations receive income tax deductions for providing on-site day care centers. Parents can deduct the cost of child care from their incomes, thereby reducing their overall income tax burden. This, however, is not much of a help to families in which both parents have to work just to get by. They often cannot afford child care of good quality, and the lack of legal standards encourages the proliferation of poor-quality for-profit day care.

In many ways, the United States is unique among the developed countries of the world in its reluctance to support infant development as a national policy. Infant health care, proper nutrition, clean and well-managed child care that is affordable, and parental leave policies have all been publicly supported by law with tax funds for many years in such countries as France, Sweden, the former Soviet Union, China, and Japan.

In those countries, there is no argument that infants and children are in the national trust, that they are the most valuable resources a society has, and that all families with infants and children deserve encouragement and government support. In the United States, these issues are controversial because of the fear that government will impinge on the rights of individuals and families. In the United States, it seems that the damage done daily to the mental and physical health of millions of poor and homeless, and even some middle-income, infants and children is the price we are willing to pay for our frontier-days notions of personal freedom and self-reliance.

In the absence of a set of nationally recognized values in support of infants and children, advocacy groups that speak out for children's rights have formed at the local, state, and national level. Most of their members are volunteers, and they are supported entirely by private funds.

Child and family advocacy has become an important part of the social and political fabric of the United States. Professional advocates—whose salaries are paid by the organizations—work with volunteers, parents, child care professionals, and researchers to make phone calls, prepare position papers, and contact lawmakers. Not all these advocacy groups have similar positions. Some want more funds for day care centers, while others want tax breaks to allow parents to stay home and raise their own children.

In a complex society that contains many different cultures and many different value systems, advocacy will always be an essential part of democracy. It is important to realize that even though you believe in particular rights for infants, those rights may not currently be guaranteed by law and are not likely to become so without the combined efforts of many concerned individuals.

concentrate my attention on one tiny aspect of nature, to be open to letting that aspect be a "teacher" for me.

The playful communication between mothers and babies that I typically study is one of my teachers. One of the most important lessons I have learned is that mother-infant play can only be partially understood by quantitative research methods. Mothers and infants are people, and I am a person too. I can learn more if I get to know each mother-infant couple in depth. I use case studies to video-record the same mothers and babies playing, week after week, for up to two years. My students and I watch these videotapes many times, getting to know these people who have allowed us this opportunity to observe their private lives. I show my respect for their human complexity by sustaining my relationship with them long enough and deeply enough to get to know them.

Scientists are people who need special training and plenty of experience in order to have this kind of deep relationship while retaining a questioning stance. I train students to use a variety of research methods to focus their attention, to not get distracted, and to evaluate their beliefs and assumptions. It is only human to become attached to one's ideas and insights and to the subjects of the research study. I try to train scientists who can retain their attachment and love for nature but who are willing to give up their most precious ideas if nature reveals itself in a way that changes those ideas.

As a consumer of research information, you can train yourself to respect your human attachments and needs while at the same time remaining open to sources of data that may contradict your beliefs. It is important to remember that research on infants is above all a human enterprise, a relationship between scientist-persons and subject-persons. Every research study is, therefore, a particular point of view on nature, a point of view at the intersection of the scientist's focus of attention and what that scientist has allowed herself or himself to be taught by the subjects.

A single study on a topic is always limited in this way. More information can be gained by reading different studies that use a variety of different measures and research methods. A study on infants from one culture many not apply to another. Research on normal children may not apply to children who are at risk because of poverty, abuse, or prematurity. I hope that reading this book will give you at least some training in how to decide whether research results can be applied to your personal or professional situation.

SUMMARY

The Importance of Infancy

- Prenatal and infant development are frequent topics in the news, on television, and in the movies today.

- The more a parent knows about infants and children, the lower his or her anxiety will be, and the better the outcomes will be for the child.

- Infancy is a unique stage in the life course. This is not only because it is the earliest stage of life but because all life's stages are unique.

- The preverbal experience of the body is uniquely human. After infancy, many physical and mental disorders of children and adults can be traced to a person's losing touch with one's own body.

- Practitioners from different therapeutic and educational methods assume that a healing effect will ensue from recreating—in a safe and protected setting—some of the conditions of being a baby.

- Many disorders can be prevented by changing maternal behavior during pregnancy. Advances have been made in the treatment of prenatal disorders and in the care of premature and sick infants.

- Because of the vulnerability of infants, many social and medical problems could be prevented by making sure that infants receive proper care and that young parents receive all the support necessary to provide the best environment for their children.

- Many differences between people during the prenatal and infancy periods have a lasting impact on later individual differences.

A Brief History of Babies

- During all periods of recorded history, some infants and children have received love and care while others have been abused or neglected.

- Beginning in the Middle Ages, urbanization brought about changes in the family and in the health and safety of infants.

- In the eighteenth century, the ideas of romanticism and empiricism marked the beginning of philosophical and educational efforts directed toward infants.

- In the nineteenth century, the development of the nuclear family, along with advances in infant medical care, led to the discovery of infancy as an important period in the life course.

- In the nineteenth and twentieth centuries, infants became the subjects of scientific study sparked by the debate over whether nature or nurture has the most influence on behavioral development.

The Scientific Perspective on Infancy

- Infancy can be divided into topical areas, such as perceptual/sensorial, sensorimotor/tool using, conceptual/thinking, representational/symbolic, communicative/linguistic, social/interactive, expressive/emotive, and self-regulatory/coping.

- Developmental changes are nonreversible and permanent, and they occur in a sequence.

- The division of infancy into stages of development is somewhat arbitrary and depends on the purposes of the culture or group.

Research Methods in Developmental Science

- Individual differences between infants may or may not be stable over the course of infancy. Scientists are still trying to determine whether these differences are due to genetic or environmental factors.

- Scientists rely on many sources of evidence, try to separate what is repeatable and stable from what is coincidental, and attempt to rid observations of bias.

Experimental Research Methods

- An experiment is a research study in which one aspect of the situation is manipulated while all other aspects are held constant or controlled.

- The independent variable is that which is controlled or manipulated by the experimenter. The independent variable is the presumed cause of the phenomenon. The dependent variable is the outcome behavior that is observed in response to the changes in the independent variable.

- Automatic recording of behavior involves measurements of heart rate, respiration, brain activity, and aspects of behavior.

- Paired-preference tests, habituation procedures, and response-contingent procedures are techniques for testing perception and cognition in infants.

Observational Research Methods

- Methods that rely on natural variations rather than random assignment to create contrast groups are called observational research methods.

- Longitudinal studies follow the same children at different ages, while cross-sectional studies use different children at different ages.

- In observational studies, the variable that is the presumed cause is called the predictor variable. The presumed effect is called the outcome variable. There is an analogy between independent variables and predictor variables, and between dependent variables and outcome variables.

- Bias is reduced in research by attention to reliability, validity, observer bias, and representativeness.

- Since infants cannot provide informed consent to participate in research, their parents must do so. Researchers need to observe ethical guidelines when using human subjects in research.

- Research focusing on minute changes in behavior is called microanalysis.

- Macroanalysis focuses on the overall or summary features of behavior rather than its details and sequences of occurrences. Macroanalysis is usually done with the use of rating scales.

Qualitative Research Methods

- Qualitative research does not use quantity or number. It is characterized by one or both of the following features: (1) the observers focus on the meaning of the situation for the participants; and (2) the role of the researcher in the situation is taken explicitly into account.

- Qualitative researchers' credibility depends upon their skill, experience, and rigor.

- Using the constant comparative method in qualitative research, the same observers go over the same data many times in order to check and revise their interpretation of the meaning of the behavior for the participants.

- In a case study, the same subjects are observed over a long period of time.

Applications: Advocacy and Public Policy for Infants and Their Families

- In a society based on **parens patriae,** public funds are typically allocated for only the most needy cases.

- Societies differ in how much of their public funds go to the welfare of children and their families.

- All individuals in a democratic society must participate in the process of changing local, state, and federal policies regarding infant and family development.

ON THE WEB

www.ehsnrc.org The Early Head Start National Resource Center web page provides information on training and technical assistance regarding Head Start's new Early Head Start program. This program supports the healthy development of infants, toddlers, and their families, including pregnant women.

www.connectforkids.org The Connect for Kids web page is an excellent source of information for adults who are interested in making their communities better places for children. This site offers information on e-mail newsletters and radio, print, and television ads aimed at helping people become more active citizens, from volunteering to voting.

www.childadvocacy.org The National Association of Child Advocates (NACA) web page is directed at strengthening the capacity of state and local child advocacy organizations. NACA is a nationwide network of child advocacy organizations working at the increasingly critical level of America's state legislatures, county commissions, and city councils.

www.nccic.org The Child Care Bureau is a program designed to administer federal child care programs to states, tribes, and territories for low-income children and families. This site also provides helpful links to the Tribal Child Care Technical Assistance Center, Child Care Partnership Project, and Healthy Child Care America.

GLOSSARY

Attrition The loss of subjects over time in longitudinal research studies.

Baby biography A detailed written observation of the day-to-day changes in the behavior of a single infant; one of the first forms of scientific observations of infant behavior.

Blindness The provision of limited information about the goals and conditions of a research study in order to prevent bias from subjects or observers.

Case study The focus on a single individual, or a single interacting group such as a family or classroom, in order to follow changes in them over time.

Coding The process by which observers record the presence or absence of predefined behavioral categories as they are watching an individual or a group.

Constant comparative method The process of revising the researchers' interpretations of the data upon repeated reviews of it until there are no further changes in interpretation.

Contrast group A group used in experimental studies that receives a different manipulation or intervention from the experimental group.

Control group A group used in experimental studies that does not experience the intervention or manipulation received by the experimental groups; allows a test of the effects of the manipulation compared with no manipulation.

Credibility A form of validity in qualitative research based on the skill, experience, and rigor of the observer.

Cross-sectional study A research study in which age differences are studied using different infants at each age.

Dependent variable Measurable outcome behavior observed in response to changes in an independent variable; the presumed effect of a causal independent variable in an experimental study.

Developmental change Change that is non-reversible, not temporary, and not haphazard.

Developmental stage A stable and persistent pattern of behavior, thought, and feeling that continues over a long period of time (months or years).

Empiricism An eighteenth-century philosophical idea that knowledge is derived from direct observation and that human problems can be solved with logical reasoning.

Experiment A research strategy in which some factors are manipulated by the experimenter, while others are controlled or held constant across groups.

Generalizability The ability of the results of a study to be correct for people other than those who were part of the study sample.

Habituation The gradual decrease in looking or listening time across repeated presentations of the same visual or auditory stimulus.

Independent variable The variable controlled or manipulated by the experimenter; the presumed cause of the effects measured by the dependent variables in experimental research.

Infanticide The deliberate killing of newborn infants as a means to limit family size.

Informed consent The voluntary consent by human research subjects, based on a complete description of the procedures, risks, and benefits of the research; a fundamental ethical principle of human research.

Longitudinal study A research study that follows developmental changes in the same individual over time.

Macroanalysis The focus on overall patterns of behavior and summary variables rather than on events and sequences.

Maturation Developmental change that is controlled by hereditary timing mechanisms.

Microanalysis The focus on the occurrences and changes of specific events and event sequences.

Nature Refers to the belief that behavior and development are controlled primarily by hereditary influences.

Nurture Refers to the belief that behavior and development are controlled primarily by environmental influences.

Observational research A research strategy in which the experimenter does not manipulate the subjects but takes advantage of natural variations in the environment.

Outcome variable The presumed effect of a cause represented by a predictor variable in observational research; analogous to the dependent variable in experimental research.

Paired-preference procedure A research technique that relies on differences in infant looking time to assess perceptual preference.

Parens patriae The legal concept that children are possessions of their parents.

Participant observer A form of qualitative research in which the observer is explicitly part of the process of observation and takes account of his or her effect on the subjects.

Predictor variable The presumed cause of an effect measured by an outcome variable in observational research; analogous to the independent variable in experimental research.

Qualitative research Research that focuses on the meaning of behavior for the participants.

Quantitative research Research that focuses on representing behavior using numerical variables.

Random assignment A procedure in which subjects are placed into experimental and control groups by the flip of a coin or some other non-biased method.

Rating scale A summary judgment about behavior, expressed as a numerical value along an ordinal scale.

Recovery An increase in infant looking time in response to a change in the stimulus during a habituation procedure.

Reliability   The extent to which multiple observers agree about the coding of ongoing behavior.

Representative research   A study in which the results from the group of infants who are observed can be generalized to a wider range of infants from different cultures and socioeconomic groups.

Response-contingent procedure   A research technique in which different stimuli are made contingent upon different infant actions. Display of one or the other action by the infant usually means a preference for the contingently related stimulus.

Romanticism   An eighteenth-century philosophical idea that children are inherently good and have the ability to develop successfully with minimal guidance.

Validity   The extent to which an assessment procedure accurately measures the concept or goal of the experimenter.

2
Theories of Infant Development

CHAPTER OVERVIEW AND OUTLINE

Biological Approaches	*In what way has the evolutionary history of the human species contributed to infant behavior and development? Does genetic inheritance account for behavioral and psychological differences between infants?*
Learning Theories	*How do infants learn? What are the conditions most conducive to infant learning?*
Cognitive Theories	*What are the developmental origins of perceiving, remembering, thought, and language? Are infants intelligent before they can speak?*
Systems Theories	*How are infants connected to the world of people and objects around them? What is the role of the parent-infant relationship in early development?*
Clinical Theories	*What has therapy with adults and children revealed about how infancy contributes to psychological development? What are the therapeutic effects of re-experiencing normal infant behavior and development?*

People acquire a personal theory about infants in the course of working with infants or raising one of their own. A **scientific theory** differs from personal theories in several ways. In essence, it is a set of concepts that explains the observable world with structures, processes, or mechanisms that are presumed to exist but that cannot be observed directly.

1. A scientific theory helps to organize observations derived from systematic research, using accepted methods of observation and assessment.
2. A scientific theory is phrased in terms of general principles that can be applied to specific research findings and applications.
3. A scientific theory should accurately predict future observations in a majority of cases. A theory whose predictions are not confirmed should be changed or abandoned.

Scientific theories of human development focus on describing and predicting the ways in which children change over time and the origins of individual differences. Why does one child become adept at language skills from an early age, for example, while another is slow to pick up these abilities?

In this chapter, we shall examine a variety of theories of human development that have been applied to infancy: biological, learning, cognitive, systems, and clinical theories. The main principles and concepts of each theory are described, the historical trends within each are reviewed, and the contributions of the theory to contemporary research are outlined. Finally, the main limitations of the theory are discussed.

Biological Approaches

Biological approaches are based on the work of Charles Darwin, who discovered that species characteristics and between-individual differences are shaped by **natural selection.** Natural selection is the process by which some individuals reproduce while others do not. Those who can survive long enough to reproduce will pass some of their characteristics down to the next generation. Thus, the environment—as much as any characteristics of individuals—influences which types of characteristics will survive and evolve (Darwin, 1859).

Part of what gets passed down between generations is the genetic code. In sexually reproducing species, each parent passes half of his or her genetic code to the offspring (see Chapter 3). The genetic code is a set of chemical instructions for producing proteins in the nucleus of a living cell. This raw genetic code, made up of large molecules of deoxyribonucleic acid (DNA), is called the **genotype.** Through a complex set of chemical interactions between the genotype and the environment of the cell, particular types of proteins are produced. These interactions yield the neural, skeletal, muscular, and other tissues that underlie mental and behavioral abilities.

The other part of what gets passed down between generations is a particular type of environment, including the physical and social environment. Children inherit not only the parent's genes but also the parent's environment. Prenatal development, for example, could not occur outside of the special environment of the female reproductive system. The temperature, chemistry, biology, and physics of that environment are just as important for the development of the individual and the evolution of the species as the composition of the DNA. Individual differences in that environment are just as important as individual differences in the DNA in the formation of the next generation (see Chapter 3).

The outcomes of the genotype-environment interactions—the resultant products—are called **phenotypes** and include not only tissues but also behaviors, intelligence, and temperament. Thus, it is important to understand that the genotype does not directly determine the phenotype; rather, *the genotype determines the opportunities by which the environment may have an influence on the phenotype* (Gottlieb, 1991b). Natural selection, then, does not operate on the genetic code directly. Natural selection operates on the phenotypes, the characteristics of the individual in his or her environment. In this section, we will review two biological approaches: behavior ecology theory and behavior genetics.

Behavior Ecology Theory

Species-specific behavior. Behavior ecology theory is the study of behavior from an evolutionary perspective. Drawing upon Darwin's ideas, behavior ecology theory suggests that all animal species have **species-specific behaviors** that evolved through the process of natural selection. Species-specific behaviors are those that are seen in only one species, such as chimpanzee calls or human speech. Although these two behaviors are species specific, both are examples of a more general function of communication. The selection of a specific form of communication in a species is presumably related to the survival of its members over many generations and the maintenance of a particular environment in which that form of communication can flourish.

Another example of a cross-species behavior related to survival is the close relationship between mother and infant seen in most mammalian species. Each species has a different set of species-specific patterns of behavior that reflect the attachment bonds between mother and infant. Mother cats lick and nuzzle their infants, while mother monkeys groom and cuddle their babies and carry them around. All mammals nurse their young, but the styles of nursing differ between species. In dogs, the mother lies on her side while her puppies nurse. The mother does not look at her babies, but she may lick them and smell them.

Critical periods. Another aspect of behavior ecology theory is the prediction that species-specific behaviors are enhanced and modified in specific environments and at specific times during the life course. Typically, in many animal species, the young seem biologically more susceptible to the acquisition of new behavior than do older individuals. Often there is a limited period of time early in life during which environmental input can make a difference in later behavior. This period of maximum susceptibility is called a **critical period** and is a relatively short (compared to the individual's life span) and clearly demarcated period of time in which learning can occur and during which whatever the animal learns has a permanent and irreversible effect.

In some species of birds, for example, attachment of the infant to an adult occurs only during a period of about two hours, several days after hatching. If a gosling follows its mother around during the critical period, it will develop a preference for the mother over other adults and will stay close to her after the critical period ends and for a long time afterward. This learning of preferences is called **imprinting.**

Konrad Lorenz (1965) found that goslings could become imprinted on a number of different objects during this period. Lorenz made goslings imprint on flashlights, electric trains, and even himself. He would walk near the goslings during the critical period, squatting and honking like a mother goose. In his description of these early studies, he wrote, "In the interest of science, I submitted myself literally for hours on end to this ordeal" (Lorenz, 1952, p. 42). For this and other work, Lorenz won a Nobel Prize in 1973. He is one of only three behavioral scientists to have received this honor. The other two—Niko Tinbergen and Karl von Frisch—were also behavior ecologists.

A large number of studies—mostly with mallard ducklings—have been done on imprinting since Lorenz's classic work. One of the main findings is that imprinting occurs only after the ducklings leave the nest and only if they can follow a moving duck that is calling to them (Bateson, 1966; Hess, 1959). One study (Dyer, Lickliter, & Gottlieb, 1989) suggests that before imprinting, ducklings may be more sensitive to the visual images of their walking siblings than to the mother duck. Ducklings may initially leave the nest as they see other ducklings doing so. Once this happens, the ducklings will respond as a group to the mother duck's call, follow her as a group, and thus become imprinted. Other factors also affect the imprinting process. Ducklings need to hear their own call prior to hatching. In experiments in which duck embryos were unable to vocalize, they did not recognize the mother's call after hatching (Gottlieb, 1991a). If quail chicks are exposed to patterned light during the first days after birth, instead of seeing their mothers or siblings, they will not imprint even if they can hear the mother's call (Lickliter & Hellewell, 1992).

Courtesy of the University of Wisconsin Primate Laboratory

In research by the Harlows, infant monkeys preferred the substitute mother that was covered with a soft cloth, rather than the wire mother to which the food was attached. This study showed that attachment in monkeys is more related to contact comfort than to feeding. In humans, attachment is related to play and communication.

The picture of imprinting that emerges from these studies is that a series of related environmental events must be tied together. Imprinting involves age mates, locomotion, and auditory and visual perception and cannot be thought of as simple photographic images of the mother printed on the duckling's brain. Indeed, due to the complexity of many developmental processes, it is unlikely that a simple notion of critical periods can apply to human behavior (Gottlieb, 1991b).

Imprinting does not occur in humans and other primate species because the infants are too immature to follow their parents around. Parents, therefore, play a role in the mutual maintenance of proximity. The lasting emotional tie that promotes this proximity is called attachment (see Chapter 8). Attachment in humans, for example, does not seem to fit the idea of a critical period. Studies of infants reared with little adult interaction in orphanages in Eastern Europe and in the Middle East showed that these children developed severe symptoms of withdrawal. Infant monkeys reared without adults tend to show similar symptoms: rocking, head banging, extreme fear in the presence of strangers, and an inability to form relationships with other individuals (Harlow & Harlow, 1965; Spitz, 1965). This seems to be evidence for a critical period.

On the other hand, some of the early orphanage studies have been criticized for confusing the symptoms of malnutrition—common in those institutions—with those predicted for maternal deprivation. Since research that deliberately deprives infants of their mothers is ethically forbidden with humans, researchers have used nonhuman primates for this research. Follow-up studies on monkeys deprived of their mothers early in life showed that some social experiences—in particular, interactions between the deprived monkeys and monkeys younger than themselves—provided when the deprived monkeys were juveniles had the effect of partially reversing the social withdrawal (Suomi & Harlow, 1972).

Gorilla infants who are raised by human mother surrogates develop more aggressive and antisocial behaviors than do gorillas raised with their mothers. After spending time in a group of gorilla peers, however, human-reared juvenile gorillas will act more like those who were reared by their own mothers (Meder, 1989). These studies seem to suggest that critical periods may not exist for primate species, including humans.

Another potential example of a human critical period is the development of language in the first three years of life. Some confirmation of this view is found in the case of a girl named Genie, who was found in 1970 at the age of thirteen after having been isolated in a small room since infancy. Her father, apparently a psychotic who hated children, forced Genie to remain in a closet and refused to let anyone speak to her. Susan Curtiss, a developmentalist who spent many years trying to help Genie recover, reported that Genie learned some language (Curtiss, 1977) and after several years of practice could string up to three words together to make her intentions and thoughts known. But she never seemed to grasp the idea of grammar, and she never learned to ask questions.

The problem with this single case study is that we have no way of knowing whether Genie suffered from some form of brain damage or other impairment early in life. Such an organic deficit might be the real cause of Genie's language retardation. Ethically, we cannot do language deprivation experiments on groups of healthy children.

In summary, there is little concrete evidence that critical periods exist for humans. The clearest example of a critical period in human development is the first six months of prenatal development. Environmental influences—such as maternal nutrition and environmental toxins—can have severe effects on the health and behavior of the fetus that last for a lifetime. These processes will be reviewed in detail in Chapter 3.

Behavior Genetic Theory

Another biological approach to infant development is the search for genetic causes of individual differences between members of a species. We have known for a long time that individual differences in physical and health characteristics are partly determined by some combination of environmental and genetic differences between people. **Behavior genetics** is the study of possible environmental and genetic explanations for individual differences in behavior and personality characteristics.

In doing research in behavior genetics, it is essential to know how individuals are genetically related to each other and whether the environments in which they are raised are similar or different. A typical research strategy is to observe behavior, such as intelligence or temperament (a word researchers use to talk about infant personality; see Chapter 6), in identical compared to fraternal twins. Identical twins have the same set of genes, while fraternal twins share only a portion of their genes. Thus, if identical twins reared at home are more similar to each other than are fraternal twins reared at home, it is possible to conclude that at least some portion of the observed behavior is explained by a genetic contribution (since identical twins have more genes in common than fraternal twins, who are no more related to each other than any two siblings in a family).

Another research approach is to study identical twins who are adopted at birth and raised in different families. They will have the same genes but be reared in different environments. Twins reared together will be more similar than twins reared apart, showing that some of the similarity between identical twins is due to the fact that they are raised in the same **shared environment** rather than to their genetic similarity. The shared environment of identical twins can be observed because twins look alike and are the same sex, so they are more likely to be treated alike by parents than fraternal twins. Identical twins may be dressed alike and encouraged to spend time together, creating opportunities for mutual imitation and similar experiences. Even in the same home, however, each twin may have somewhat different experiences, called the *nonshared environment* (Loehlin, 1989; Plomin, 1994).

The study of similarities in characteristics between family members is another approach to behavior genetic research (Lemery & Goldsmith, 1999). This kind of study is useful if a particular trait, such as a suspected genetically caused disease, occurs disproportionately within particular families.

Identical twins share 100 percent of their genetic material, while other siblings from the same parents share 50 percent of their genetic material, the same amount shared by parents with their children. Uncle and nephews, aunts and nieces, grandparents and grandchildren, and half siblings share 25 percent of their genetic material. If genetics plays a role for a characteristic, there should be a decreased probability of the occurrence of that characteristic in family members who are more distantly related and an increased probability of occurrence among those who are more closely related.

The **heritability** of the observed behavior measures the extent to which individual differences in the behavior are due to genetic factors. Heritability is usually expressed in terms of a percentage, the percentage of variability between individuals that can be explained by genetic variability. It varies between 0 and 1.00. Research findings show modest heritability (about 30 percent, on average) for some measures of intelligence, temperamental inhibition, empathy, self-esteem, and the ways in which individuals select, modify, create, or avoid specific features of their environments (Plomin, 1994; Robinson et al., 1992; Scarr, 1993; Zahn-Waxler, Robinson, & Emde, 1992). This means that 30 percent of the differences between people in these characteristics can be explained by genetic variability.

Because heritability is expressed as a percentage, results from behavior genetic research are **probabilistic.** That is, if you possess a particular set of genes, you have a higher probability of developing a particular kind of behavioral characteristic than a person without those same genes. The action of the genes is not *deterministic,* since there are environments that might lessen the impact of those genes on the behavioral outcome (Scarr, 1993; Scarr & McCartney, 1983).

Some genetic predispositions, for example, may never appear in the phenotype because the genotype is never exposed to a "needed" environmental resource at a particular time in life. Thus, a gosling will never manifest its species-typical attachment behaviors if it is not exposed to an adult goose during the critical period for imprinting. This is an example of a genetic predisposition that is easily influenced by the environment. In this case, *environmental variability has a larger probability of predicting individual phenotypes than does genetic variability.* In fact, genetic variability usually accounts for only a small proportion of behavioral variability. Many genes, each with a small influence, rather than a single gene, are typically involved in influencing behavior (Plomin, 1990, 1994).

Other genotypes may be less susceptible to variations in the environment. If infants have a color blindness genotype, variability in the amount of exposure to visual stimuli will have little influence on the phenotype of color blindness. In this case, *genetic variability between individuals* (inheriting or not inheriting color blindness genes) *has a larger probability of predicting individual phenotypes than does environmental variability.*

No genes and no environments are 100 percent deterministic. Some genetic disorders can be eliminated in the phenotype through surgery, by drug treatments, or by avoiding certain environmental factors (e.g., controlling diabetes through diet). There is also hope that some will be "cured" by as yet undiscovered techniques (see Chapter 3).

In some cases, genetic variability may predict variability in phenotypes early in life but not later. A stable pattern of temperamental withdrawal tends to be correlated with eye color (withdrawn infants are more represented in the group of blue-eyed infants than would be expected by chance) during the first three years of life. During the preschool period and later, there is no correlation between eye color and temperament (Kagan, Reznick, & Snidman, 1987). These findings suggest that temperamental withdrawal may be genetically based, but after several years, the variability of that phenotype in the population is better predicted by environmental rather than genetic variability. The opposite could also be true: a genetically based skill in language might account for between-infant differences at age three, but not earlier in infancy (Fagard & Jacquet, 1989; Ramsay, 1980).

The relationship between genes and environments is made more complicated because they influence each other. People with a particular genetic predisposition—for temperamental withdrawal, for example—may prefer to be with one or two other people rather than in large groups. Their choice of environments then influences the kinds of skills they develop (Scarr & McCartney, 1983).

It is generally assumed that the environment of the home is independent of the child's genetic predispositions. Studies based on parents who are identical and fraternal twins, however, reveal that parental warmth and affection are partly heritable. If the child inherits similar genes from genetically more affectionate parents, the environment created by those parents is also to some extent genetically determined (Losoya et al., 1997). Behavior genetic research is still in its early stages, but it promises to provide important new ways of understanding the origins of differences between people.

What Are the Problems with Biological Approaches?

Behavior ecology theory assumes that all behavior evolved through natural selection. While this may seem clear for species-specific behaviors such as attachment and language, the evolutionary basis of the effects of television on infants or their preference for one storybook over another is a more difficult theoretical problem. Because televisions and books were not in the environment in which the current species-typical characteristics evolved, they are not easily understood from this perspective. It may be, however, that our ability as humans to invent tools and technologies underlies the more specific abilities. This allows us to do things that did not evolve by natural selection, things that are nevertheless adaptive and enhance our ability to pass these characteristics to the next generation (Buss & Goldsmith, 1998).

One criticism of behavior genetics is that in most human situations, it is extremely difficult to sort out the relative effects of genetic and environmental variability. It is difficult to find cases of identical twins reared apart. Even when this happens, the reasons for the twins' separation at birth may make them unrepresentative of the rest of the population. Also, adoptions tend to occur within similar racial, ethnic, and social-class groupings, increasing the degree of shared environment, which may account for the twins' similarity (Baumrind, 1993; Jackson, 1993).

Another problem with behavior genetic research is that while it gives some numerical estimate of genetic and environmental influences for groups of people, it does not tell us anything about a particular individual and his or her probability of inheriting the genetic potential or showing the characteristic in the phenotype (Gottlieb, 1995). Also, behavior genetic research tells us nothing at all about the ways in which the genes and environment act to produce a phenotype, so it gives no guidelines for intervention should a genetic problem be suspected, nor for how to enhance the development of a particular child (Baumrind, 1993). As the future brings more technological advances in the field of microbiology, it may be possible to find the particular genes associated with those characteristics that have been shown to have a higher heritability (Plomin, 1994; Plomin & Rutter, 1998). Until that time, however, behavior genetic research is not likely to have a strong impact on how we raise children.

Learning Theories

Traditionally, learning theories have been contrasted with evolutionary theories as being on opposite sides in the nature-versus-nurture debate. Learning theories suggest that the environment is the most potent influence, while evolutionary theories dwell on genetic influences. As we saw in the section on behavior ecology theory, this simple characterization is not accurate. There is no clear separation between nature (the views of Rousseau and Gesell) and nurture (the views of Locke and Watson).

Evolutionary theory researchers believe that *the genes regulate the kinds of learning possible in a species and the ages at which it can take place.* Often, their research methods are nearly identical to those of learning theorists: both are studying the conditions under which learning takes place. On the other hand, learning theorists are cognizant of species differences in learning, since the vast majority of work based on learning theory has been done with nonhuman species.

Learning theory researchers have contributed to our understanding of development in several ways. First, they have discovered simple yet powerful ways to enhance learning. Second, they have shown that with the proper kinds of environmental supports,

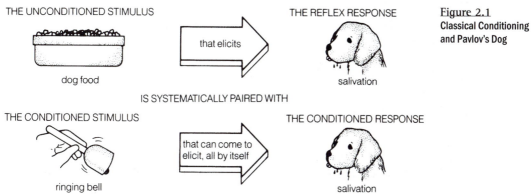

THE UNCONDITIONED STIMULUS

dog food

that elicits

THE REFLEX RESPONSE

salivation

IS SYSTEMATICALLY PAIRED WITH

THE CONDITIONED STIMULUS

ringing bell

that can come to elicit, all by itself

THE CONDITIONED RESPONSE

salivation

Figure 2.1
Classical Conditioning and Pavlov's Dog

Source: J. P. Dworetzky & N. J. Davis, *Human development: A life span approach*, 1989, p. 34. St. Paul, MN: West. Copyright © by West Publishing Company. Reprinted by permission. All rights reserved.

individuals and species can be trained to achieve considerably more than what might have been expected from evolutionary models of species-typical behavior. We might say that learning researchers work at the upper end of a species's range of abilities, as they search for more optimal strategies to enhance learning skills.

Classical Conditioning

The Russian physiologist Ivan Pavlov (1849–1936) published one of the first demonstrations of learning as a result of systematic environmental manipulation. Pavlov attempted to teach dogs to salivate on cue, not simply in the presence of food. He discovered that if a bell was rung every time a hungry dog was presented with food, the dog would later salivate at the sound of the bell without any food present. This process, called **classical conditioning,** or learning by **association,** is illustrated in Figure 2.1.

In classical conditioning, there must be an unconditioned stimulus that induces the unconditioned response. An example from human infancy is the fear (unconditioned response) induced by strangers in strange places (unconditioned stimulus). Learning occurs when the unconditioned stimulus occurs at the same time as some new conditioned stimulus. Following repeated exposure to this pairing of conditioned and unconditioned stimuli, the unconditioned response will occur in the presence of the conditioned stimulus. For example, if the infant's doctor wears a white coat, the fear of the strangeness of the doctor's office may be-

come associated with white coats. Thus, the infant may later cry at the sight of anyone—even a familiar person—wearing a white coat.

Operant Conditioning

In an experiment that led to a later development in learning theory, B. F. Skinner (1938) tried to condition birds. Since classical conditioning theory assumes that all unconditioned responses must be related to unconditioned stimuli, Skinner faced a problem. He could not discover the unconditioned stimuli for most of the animal's actions: it seemed to emit behavior spontaneously without any obvious external stimulation. Skinner referred to these spontaneously emitted actions as *operants.* Pigeons, for example, peck (the operant) even when not eating. Skinner was not interested in what caused the operants, and he accepted the fact that each different species will have different types of operants. His goal was to change the way in which the animal emitted the operants.

Skinner discovered that the rate of emitted behavior could be controlled by the consequences of the behavior, that is, by what happened in the environment immediately following the operant's occurrence. In one experiment, a pigeon was placed in a cage with no food tray. On the side of the cage was a colored disk. As the pigeon in the cage emitted the operant of pecking, it pecked at all the parts of the cage at random. When the bird happened to peck the colored disk, a small bit of food was dropped into the cage. Over time, the bird began to narrow down its pecking to the region of the cage containing the disk, and eventually it pecked exclusively at the disk: the animal discovered the contingency between its own operant, the disk, and the food. This is similar to our description of the response-contingent method of infant research (see Chapter 1). The process by which the frequency of an operant is controlled by its consequences is called **operant conditioning.**

Consequences that increase the frequency of the preceding operant are called **reinforcers.** A **positive reinforcer** is an action or reward that follows the operant and increases its frequency. In some cases, the frequency of an operant is increased following the removal of an aversive stimulus. Thus, the absence of a consequence that increases the frequency of the operant is called a **negative reinforcer.**

Suppose an infant performs some action that the parents would like to encourage, such as drinking all his or her milk. Parents can increase the frequency with which this happens by praising the child after he or she has finished the milk (a positive reinforcer). On the other hand, the child may increase the frequency with which he or she finishes the milk to avoid being scolded for not finishing it. The absence of scolding becomes a negative reinforcer. A negative reinforcer is not negative in the sense of being bad or unrewarding, but rather in the sense of being absent. Not getting scolded is a rewarding consequence for the child.

Unrewarding consequences have the effect of decreasing rather than increasing the frequency of a particular behavior. An unrewarding consequence that decreases the frequency of an operant is called a **punishment.** In the above example, the scolding may act as a punishment to decrease the probability of the child's *not* finishing the milk.

Another way to decrease the frequency of a behavior is by **extinction.** This is the process by which the frequency of an operant decreases when a reinforcing consequence is removed. In the first few months of life, it is important to respond promptly to an infant's crying. This response, however, may increase the frequency with which the infant cries (although the intensity and duration of the crying episodes may decline over time). When the infant is several months older and is better able to tolerate distress, parents may want the infant to calm down

on his or her own. Parents can extinguish crying by not responding to it as frequently or as promptly as before.

Both classical and operant conditioning are able to explain particular learning phenomena in infancy, especially in situations in which there are repeated opportunities for exposure to similar environmental consequences. There are, however, developmental differences in an infant's susceptibility to conditioning and to the types of environmental stimuli and conditions that are most likely to serve as reinforcers or punishers. Unfortunately, learning theory cannot explain how these individual differences and development changes are caused.

Social Learning Theory

Researchers began to notice that simple conditioning was not enough to explain patterns of behavior seen in infants and children. Several theoretical developments led to social learning theory. First of all, researchers discovered that as infants change their behavior to adjust to the contingencies between their behavior and the environment, the infants seek to change the environment to preserve or enhance the same pattern of contingencies. Thus, infants come to control not only their behavior but also the behavior of other people around them (Bijou & Baer, 1965).

Suppose, for example, a parent reinforces the child every time the child asks for help and ignores the child whenever the child whines or cries to get help. The child is likely to increase the frequency of verbal requests for help, but in addition, the child will come to *expect* help whenever it is asked for in the appropriate way. On the parent's side, when the child asks for help verbally and without whining, the parent is more likely to provide the assistance. Thus, the increase in the child's verbal requests will condition the parent to increase the frequency with which he or she gives help. As a result of this complex social process, the child's recognition of the contingency has ultimately changed that child's social environment.

A second theoretical development was the discovery that infants could change their behavior in ways that had nothing to do with conditioning. Entirely new behaviors could be acquired al-

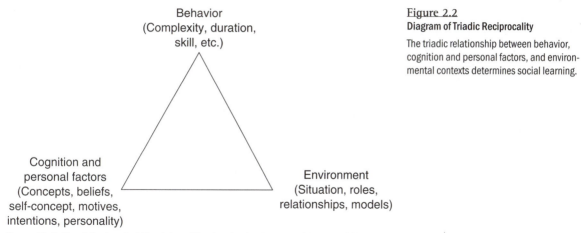

Behavior
(Complexity, duration,
skill, etc.)

Cognition and
personal factors
(Concepts, beliefs,
self-concept, motives,
intentions, personality)

Environment
(Situation, roles,
relationships, models)

Figure 2.2
Diagram of Triadic Reciprocality

The triadic relationship between behavior, cognition and personal factors, and environmental contexts determines social learning.

Source: Adapted from A. Bandura, *Social foundations of thought and action: A social cognitive theory,* 1996, p. 24. Englewood Cliffs, NJ: Prentice-Hall. Reprinted by permission.

most immediately through **observational learning** (Bandura, 1977). Just by watching an adult or peer model, an infant could imitate the behavior and incorporate that imitated act into the infant's own goals.

A final theoretical advance of social learning theory is the idea that infants are more likely to acquire new behaviors in some situations than in others. Both conditioning and observational learning are more likely to occur if infants are motivated to pay attention to the consequences of their action or to the model. Thus, an infant's goals help to organize the way in which he or she picks up information from the environment. In a word, social learning theory introduced the self (including cognitions and motivations) as an intelligent actor and organizer of information. As Figure 2.2 shows, learning is an interaction between the behavior to be learned (is it easy or difficult to master?), the environment in which it is learned (does the environment support or inhibit the learning?), and the factors the person brings to the situation (is the person motivated to learn?).

If someone gives the infant a task to learn and models a behavior that is too difficult for the infant, if the infant is not interested at that moment in learning, or if consistent and positive help from others is not provided, this affects not only learning but the infant's emotional experience as well. If the infant's experiences are contingent upon his or her actions, and if those actions subsequently change

the behavior of others in ways that accord with the infant's goals, a feeling of self-efficacy emerges (Bandura, 1989). If, on the other hand, the infant's goals are typically thwarted and the social environment behaves capriciously, feelings of helplessness and despair emerge (Seligman & Maier, 1967).

Social learning theory has been applied to a wide variety of issues in infant development. It suggests that environments can be structured in ways that are conducive to infant learning and to longer-term feelings of self-efficacy. The theory focuses on the immediate context of behavior and shows the importance of the environment's being responsive to the infant's current goals and needs and not merely a mechanical producer of reinforcers.

In the first few months, infants are largely dependent upon the pushes and pulls of their emotions. Later, they develop the ability to self-regulate their emotions through a process of social learning. Infants come to identify particular feelings with particular expressions and verbal labels. In this view, infants have feelings that they do not understand or recognize. Through a process of parental labeling of their feelings (e.g., saying things like "You must be angry" or "Why are you sad today?"), children learn to construct the social meaning of their emotions. Children also imitate adults' use of emotion expressions in particular situations. If adults are smiling, the infant will also smile. In the process, the infant comes to associate the inner feelings of enjoyment with the expression of smiling in others and with the typical situations in which such feelings tend to occur. In addition, strong emotions become less frequent with age and are expressed in more socially appropriate forms, by saying, "I'm really angry," as opposed to screaming and hitting (Izard & Malatesta, 1987; Lewis & Michalson, 1983).

What Are the Problems with Learning Theory?

Although learning theory has had remarkable success in predicting infant behavior during controlled laboratory experiments, real-life environments are never so simple or so contingent. Many processes, including genetic contributions, may influence the way behavior is acquired. Because learning theory focuses on the immediate conditions of learning, it appears to suggest that an infant can acquire any behavior at any age if the environmental and motivational conditions are right. Since this is clearly not the case, learning theory cannot explain the sequence and timing of developmental stages in infancy. Although learning theorists deny that stages exist, insisting instead that behavior is acquired gradually and cumulatively, the existence of universal developmental sequences cannot be denied. Learning theory also cannot explain the spontaneous emergence of new behaviors, such as stranger anxiety even when children have no prior experience with a stranger, or smiling in blind infants. Cognitive-constructivist theory, to be reviewed next, provides one explanation for the developmental stages of infancy.

Cognitive Theories

Cognitive developmental theories focus on the mental experience of the person. The goal is to understand intelligence: how people of different ages know about, perceive, plan, and remember their experiences. In cognitive theory, behavior is considered to be a form of intelligence because most of what people do is goal directed and depends upon

their knowing what to do under particular circumstances. In this book, I focus on cognitive theories that have been applied to the study of developmental change in infancy.

Constructivist Theory

One of the central theories of infant cognitive development is that of Jean Piaget (1896–1980), who was trained as an invertebrate biologist before he became interested in the study of human development. Biologists used evolutionary theory to study development from the point of view of each individual's **adaptation** to the environment. Adaptation is a change in an individual's functioning that makes the individual better suited to survive in a particular environment. Piaget's contribution to cognitive development was to conceptualize human intelligence as a form of adaptation to the environment. In his view, even small infants can act in intelligent ways, not by thinking but by acting physically on the environment in order to meet their own goals (Piaget, 1952).

For Piaget, an infant who is touching an object is developing an intelligent way of "knowing" that object. Knowledge is conceived of not as a static library of information but as an active process of **co-construction** between the knower and what is to be known. Co-construction means that what one knows depends upon how one acts on the environment and how the environment responds to those actions. Imagine what you would know about an object if all you could do were grasp it and bring it to your mouth, like a four-month-old (you would not have the skill to inspect it visually, to test its properties, or to feel its subtle details with your fingers). All complex forms of knowing develop out of simpler actions found in infants, such as sucking, chewing, touching, and crawling.

Piaget brought two principles of biological adaptation into his study of the development of intelligent action: **assimilation** and **accommodation.** Assimilation refers to the process by which individuals use their existing abilities in response to challenges from the environment. It is the application of what one already knows or does to the current situation. Accommodation is the alteration of existing abilities to better fit the requirements of the task

Jean Piaget is known for his theoretical contributions and also for his empathic sensitivity with young children. His many experiments with his own three infants take account of his effects on them and were embedded into the infants' daily activities.

or situation. Accommodation is more likely to occur if assimilation does not result in an effective adaptation to the environment.

Typically, most actions involve both assimilation and accommodation. Between the ages of six and twelve months, human infants must learn to eat solid foods. This is not an easy task, because the infant's tongue is not yet coordinated enough to keep food in the mouth. While sucking on a breast or a bottle, the baby's tongue moves in and out like a piston. When a baby is first given solid food on a spoon, the baby's response is to move the tongue as if he or she were sucking, which has the effect of expelling food from the mouth. Thus, the infant assimilates the tongue and mouth actions of sucking to the eating of solids. Since this simple assimilation leaves the infant hungry, the child must accommodate mouth and tongue movements so they are better adapted to the shape of the spoon and the consistency of the solid foods. The infant's knowledge about food, therefore, is a co-construction between assimilation and accommodation, as each process influences the other to create the resulting action.

Piaget's main goal was to apply his theory to the development of human intelligence, and he looked for the origins of intelligence in human infancy. He referred to the first two years of life as the **sensorimotor substage** because at that age infants were primarily involved in explorations involving their movements and senses. The primary feature of

Table 2.1 Piaget's Substages of Sensorimotor Development

Approximate Age (Months)	Stage	Description
0–2	Reflex schemes	Inborn reflexes such as sucking, looking, and crying establish the infant's first connection to the world.
2–5	Primary circular reactions	Repeated actions (circular) that involve connections within the infant's own body (primary) such as cooing and coordinating arm movements with the mouth to suck on the thumb. Initial occurrence of the behavior is discovered by chance.
6–9	Secondary circular reactions	Repeated actions (circular) that involve the connection between the infant and the environment (secondary) such as kicking the crib to make a mobile move or smiling to get another person to smile back. Initial occurrence is discovered by chance.
10–12	Coordination of secondary circular reactions	First sign of goal-directed behavior not motivated by chance occurrences. Combining different circular reactions to achieve goals, such as using one hand to hold an object while the other explores it, or using one object to retrieve or to act on another one.
12–18	Tertiary circular reactions	The use of familiar secondary circular reactions in order to make new things happen, such as when the child explores how different objects fall from his or her high-chair table, creates new relationships between different objects in play, or uses trial-and-error problem solving.
18–24	Invention of new means through mental combinations	The ability to think before acting by representing actions as mental pictures and symbols. The infant can solve problems without trial and error.

sensorimotor development is the growth of infants' understanding of their bodies and how their bodies relate to other things in the environment (Piaget & Inhelder, 1969). Piaget divided the sensorimotor stage into six substages. We will discuss substages 1–6 in Chapters 5–10, respectively. These are described in Table 2.1. Although they will not be discussed in this book, Piaget's discoveries of stages beyond the infancy period are summarized in Table 2.2.

The sensorimotor stage was thought to contain the seeds for the development of thought, language, social skills, and morality. According to Piaget, the earliest forms of thinking, seen around the age of eighteen months, are "interiorized actions," the actions of the sensorimotor period. Three basic principles about human infants characterize Piaget's theory:

Individuals play an active role in their own development. The major motivation for developmental change comes from the individual's failure to reach an adaptation to the environment. This experience of failure, when accommodation and assimilation fall short of adaptation, is called **disequilibrium.** Since disequilibrium is defined in relation to what each individual wants to accomplish, it cannot be imposed from the outside: babies seek knowledge about those things that motivate their curiosity.

Infants develop knowledge by means of their own actions on the environment. The accommodation process literally changes the infant's view of the world, since, by altering his or her own actions, the child comes to "know" new uses for the same objects. Through action, individuals create knowledge. Since knowledge is an active process of creation, this is often referred to as **constructivist theory,** according to which knowledge is built up by the child's own action rather than imposed on the child from the outside.

Infants will learn better from experiences if those experiences can be assimilated to their current developmental level. The currently available set of skills

Table 2.2   Piaget's Cognitive-Developmental Stages of Child Development

Approximate Age (Years)	Stage	Description
0–2	Sensorimotor	Infants learn through direct experience of the senses and by handling objects and moving them around. They do not understand that things exist outside their own actions.
3–7	Pre-operational	Ability to form mental representations, language, thinking as internalized action but centered on the self's perspective; inability to think logically.
7–11	Concrete operational	Thinking takes the perspective of others and is logical with respect to concrete actions and objects, such as the rules of a game; inability to think about abstract things.
12–adult	Formal operational	Thinking about non-concrete, abstract things; ability to solve word problems, form a coherent system of thought relating many ideas, and think about future possibility.

Source: A. Fogel & G. F. Melson, *Child development*, 1988, p. 39. St. Paul, MN: West. Copyright © by West Publishing Co. Reprinted by permission. All rights reserved.

and knowledge is known as the infant's **schemes.** Schemes can be sensorimotor, that is, involving physical actions, such as reaching and chewing. Schemes can also be conceptual, involving ideas, concepts, or thoughts. In order for accommodation to occur, the infant has to assimilate the existing set of schemes to the environment. For this to happen, the environment should present challenges that are moderate, not overly difficult or beyond the infant's grasp. Thus, the first solid foods have to be soft in consistency (the infant does not have teeth yet) and given on a spoon that is small enough to fit in the infant's mouth. Adults have to hold the spoon at just the right angle and move it in and out of the infant's mouth at the appropriate time.

Piaget's original work on infancy was based on observations of his own three children, Jacqueline, Laurent, and Lucienne, and he is known to have been empathically attuned to young children. His observations are unrivaled in their clarity, accuracy, detail, and theoretical import (see Chapter 1). Piaget's work is clearly distinguished from learning theories and from evolutionary theories. Piaget believed that development is not imposed on the infant from the outside, nor is it guided solely by maturational change. Adaptation suggests a more active, infant-centered perspective.

Piaget referred to emotional processes only very briefly, but he believed that emotional development was parallel to the developmental of intelligence and should therefore follow his sequence of sensorimotor substages. The emotions of shame and pride, for example, do not appear in children until they have the cognitive ability to separate self from other and to recognize the existence of standards of behavior. Shame is the feeling of being exposed, and that means exposed in front of some other person. To be able to feel shame, we must realize that other people can see us as we see them. Similarly, pride is a sense of meeting or achieving some standard in the eyes of another person (see Chapter 10).

What Are the Problems with Piaget's Theory?

One problem with Piaget's theory is related to how Piaget decided to divide development into stages. As we discussed in the previous chapter, there is a certain arbitrariness in choosing a particular behavioral milestone to mark the beginning or end of a stage of development. Once you pick an indicator of a stage transition, then you do not expect to see that behavior appearing earlier or later in development. Unfortunately for stage theories, this often happens.

Research has shown, for example, that certain behaviors may appear earlier than Piaget's stages suggest that they should. A good example is imitation. Piaget (1962) claimed that infants younger than nine months could not imitate movements, such as a facial expression, that they could not see themselves make. Yet current evidence indicates that such imitation may be possible at birth (see Chapter 5).

Perhaps a more critical problem for Piaget's theory is that he failed to take account of the effects of adults on infants. Although he is given credit for helping us understand that infants are active learners, he did not attend to the facilitating and supportive environment that parents often provide and in which infants may exercise their curiosity. The role of parents is more explicit in systems theories, discussed later in this chapter.

Information Processing Theories of Cognitive Development

Imagine a toddler, about two years old, playing with her peers in a day care center. The toddler playroom is enclosed by glass windows that separate it from the entrance foyer of the day care building. Out of the corner of her eye, the toddler sees her mother come into the foyer. Her mother stops to speak with someone. The little girl gets up, walks to the door that opens onto the hall, walks down the hall, turns left, enters the foyer, and runs up to Mommy with arms outstretched. The child has solved a difficult problem in communication.

Piaget's explanation of this behavior, assuming this is not the first time it happened, would be simply "assimilation." Piaget might also place our toddler in the fifth or sixth sensorimotor substage, since she was able to see her mother as a separate person, stop what she was doing, and walk around a barrier to reach her mother. A younger baby might recognize her mother but try to walk directly to her by going toward the glass wall.

Many developmentalists are dissatisfied with this kind of explanation because it leaves unspecified the mental processes that may be involved. Let us think about what they might be. First of all, the child must be able to focus her *attention* on the person who walks in. Next, the jumble of colors, lines, and moving images must be organized into a coherent picture that has a meaning for the child; this is known as the *perceptual process*. The particular perception is organized according to specific categories using the processes of *recognition* and *recall memory*. The child interprets this perception as one that she has seen before, and she remembers what this perception means to her (Mommy!). At this point she can invoke *thought processes* to make some decisions. Should I go to see Mommy? How can I get there? Should I go through the door or wave at her through the window?

Information processing theories attempt to specify the way in which the mind handles the information presented to it by the environment (see Figure 2.3). This type of cognitive theory does not run counter to Piagetian theory; it simply tries to provide a more specific picture of mental processes and their changes in the course of development. Research in information processing generally requires sophisticated technology to measure such things as visual fixation time, eye movement patterns, auditory sensitivities, and the like (see Chapter 1).

During the past twenty-five years, information processing research has become the primary tool for studying infant cognition. Most of the research on perception and cognition reported in this book is based on an information processing theory rather than on Piaget's theory of development. Piaget's work mapped the basic features of infant cognitive development. Information processing research is now filling in the details.

Information processing theory can be applied to the study of emotions. Changes in different components of the information processing system may change the way emotions are expressed and experienced during infancy. Emotions become more complicated as different ones are combined (e.g., joy and anger mixed will become mischief). Emotional expressions can be modulated by cognitive processes such as remembering, thinking, and planning. These lead to emotion regulation and coping (e.g., biting the lower lip to hold back crying). Finally, emotional states become detached from direct emotional experience and associated with cognitive beliefs and expectations (e.g., trying to smile in a social situation even though one is feeling sad). This latter achievement, however, does not begin until after the infancy period.

Figure 2.3
Components of Information Processing

One advantage of information processing theory is that it can be applied to problems in early education and in the treatment of handicapped infants. In Piaget's view, infants pass through major stages in which all of their capacities are integrated and centered around a single stage. Information processing views predict that infants may get off their cognitive developmental track if only one of their component processes is faulty. For example, an infant with poor perceptual skills may show signs of retardation even if everything else about the infant is intact and healthy. Without perception, however, nothing else can operate well. Simple interventions to improve hearing or eyesight, for example, may be all that is necessary to dramatically improve the developmental prognosis for some infants.

What Are the Problems with Information Processing Theory?

One problem with information processing theory is that it offers few clues about how each of the informational processing components develops. Each component—such as memory and perception—is presumed to change gradually, leading to overall improvements in cognition. Information processing is more a theory of how infants act and think than a theory of how action and thought develop.

Another problem is that there are many different approaches to information processing theory and research and many thousands of research studies. Making sense of these different approaches is sometimes difficult, especially since there is no broader theoretical framework to use in interpreting the findings. So please beware. One should not expect the current knowledge on infant cognition to come neatly wrapped in nicely understandable packages.

Systems Theories

Systems theories share the view that all facets of the child and the environment are important and that development is a complex process in which outcomes are determined through the active interaction of these facets. Rather than focusing on one element—emotion, cognition, or learning—systems theories attempt to understand developmental change in its entirety: the whole child in the whole environment.

A **system** is a set of interdependent components, each of which affects the others in reciprocal fashion. Systems theories recognize the mutual dependencies between the infant and the environment. The process by which systems components affect each other in a bidirectional and reciprocal way is known as **transaction.** In the parent-infant interaction system, for example, the behavior of a parent is likely to depend on the sociability of the infant. Infants who smile more and cry less are likely to have parents who are more relaxed and socially attentive to the infant. This parental social attentiveness in turn will affect the infant's continued sociability.

Consider this parent-infant system during a transactional process. The infant's sociability affects the parents, which makes the parents more relaxed and which then affects the infant in ways that promote sociability. **Feedback** is a process by which components of a system have an effect on their own behavior during their transactions with other components. The behavior of the infant is fed back to the infant in terms of how the infant's behavior affected the parent's.

Feedback transactions show how systems have the property of **self-organization:** the emergence of organized patterns due to the mutual influences of each component of the system on the others. Nothing from outside the system is required to maintain the transaction that enhances the infant's sociability; it is a product only of the system's transactions. The infant sociability transaction is an example of feedback that maintains the system over time. If the parent or infant has a bad day and is not so relaxed or socially attentive, it is likely that the sociability of one partner will help the other to calm down. Feedback that maintains a system's characteristics over time in spite of small deviations is called **deviation-correcting feedback** (or *negative feedback*).

In other cases, however, the deviation from the normal state of affairs is larger than the system can tolerate and still maintain itself. Suppose, for example, the infant becomes ill and fussy. Under normal conditions, the parent would remain cheerful and attentive. If the parent too is under stress, however, the infant's fussiness could lead to an increase in the parent's level of stress, which then leads to the infant's feeling even more distress and crying more, which leads to parental despair or anger. Feedback that drastically changes a system as a result of a small deviation is called **deviation-amplifying feedback** (or *positive feedback*).

Deviation-amplifying feedback generally works to change a system, while deviation-correcting feedback works to maintain it. Deviation amplification could also change a system for the better. The infant's sociability may, with the support of the parents' attentiveness, lead to the enhancement of the infant's social skills with peers and other partners and to the growth of a wider range of shared communication between parent and infant.

Another facet of systems is that they have multiple levels. A parent-child relationship system, for example, is embedded within a larger family system. In addition to the feedback between parent and child, a parent's relationship to the infant may also be affected by the parent's marital satisfaction, his or her relationship with other family members, the financial well-being of the family, his or her own job satisfaction, and even society's attitudes about the parenting role. Conversely, the successful functioning of society depends on the patterns of interaction and socialization within the family, where infants and children are initially prepared for their roles in that society.

Ecological Systems Theory

One of the first applications of systems theory to developmental psychology was the work of Urie Bronfenbrenner. He developed a conceptual framework for understanding the complex relationships between the infant, the family, and society. The **ecology of human development** is "the study of the progressive, mutual accommodation, throughout the life span, between a growing human organism and the changing immediate environments in which it lives, as the process is affected by relations obtaining within and between those immediate settings, as well as the larger social contexts . . . in

which the settings are embedded" (Bronfenbrenner, 1979). Bronfenbrenner defined four levels of system functioning between persons:

Microsystem. The **microsystem** is made up of all the relationships between the person and his or her environment in a particular setting. For example, all of the transactions that take place between the child and the physical and social environment of the family form a microsystem. Other settings in which children are typically found are schools, camps, hospitals, play groups, and churches or synagogues. Children are affected by many aspects of their immediate microsystem environment, including social interactions, housing, and nutrition (Melson, 1980). We shall deal with a number of these aspects in the course of this book.

Mesosystem. The **mesosystem** includes the relationships between the major settings in which children are found. An example would be the interaction between the family and the day care center. A child who is experiencing many difficulties in day care is likely to force the family to have more interactions with the center's teachers and administrators, and those family-school interactions should in turn have an effect on the child's functioning.

Exosystem. The **exosystem** extends the mesosystem to include other social systems that do not contain the developing child but have some effect on him or her. The world of work, neighborhood institutions, the media, the government, the economy, and transportation affect the functioning of the family, school, and other social settings in which children are found.

Macrosystem. The **macrosystem** contains all of the various subsystems that we have been discussing. It contains all of the general tenets, beliefs, and values of the culture or subculture and is made up of the written and unwritten principles that regulate everyone's behavior. These principles—whether legal, economic, political, religious, or educational—endow individual life with meaning and value and control the nature and scope of the interactions between the various levels of the total social system.

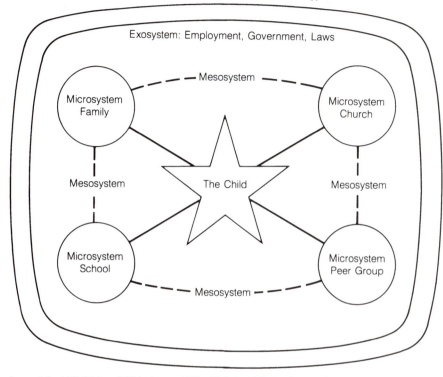

Macrosystem: Culture, Values, Ideology

Exosystem: Employment, Government, Laws

Mesosystem

Microsystem
Family

Microsystem
Church

Mesosystem

The Child

Mesosystem

Microsystem
School

Microsystem
Peer Group

Mesosystem

Figure 2.4
Ecological Systems Theory

The child is contained within a nested system of social relationships and institutions. Except in microsystems, children are not direct participants in any of the other social systems that may affect their lives.

Source: A. Fogel & G. F. Melson, *Child development,* 1988, p. 50. St. Paul, MN: West. Copyright © by West Publishing Company. Reprinted by permission. All rights reserved.

The idea of the macrosystem suggests that cultural values and practices have an effect on child-rearing practices and on the development of children. Throughout this book, we shall cite examples of cross-cultural studies showing how culture affects children's development. The relationships among these various subsystems are shown in Figure 2.4.

An example of ecological systems theory as applied to the family system suggests that infants may be influenced by and influence others either by **direct transactions** or by **mediated transactions.** A direct transaction occurs as part of a social relationship in which the child is an active participant: the infant-parent, infant-peer, or infant-sibling relationship. A mediated transaction occurs when the infant affects or is affected by people with whom the infant does not share an active relationship.

An example of a mediated transaction concerns the child's relationship with grandparents. Though children in North American society often spend little time with their grandparents, visiting perhaps only once or twice a year, they nevertheless seem to develop special relationships with them. This can be accounted for by parental mediation. Since the parent's relationship to his or her own parents is so important, this importance is transmitted to the child, who then comes to think of Grandma and Grandpa as special people (Lewis & Feiring, 1978).

One model of the family system that incorporates these ideas is depicted in Figure 2.5 (Belsky, 1981). With mediated effects, the acts of one individual affect another, who then affects a third person. This model includes the effects of one individual (for example, the infant) on the relationship between the parents and, conversely, the effects of the marital relationship on the infant directly and indirectly as it affects each spouse's ability to parent. One other notable aspect of this model is that it includes feedback transactions. For example, the marriage may affect a spouse's ability to parent, which may affect the infant, whose subsequent behavior may affect the marital relationship. Each component is capable of affecting every other component in a mutually influential manner.

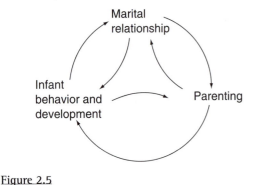

Figure 2.5
Model of Family System Functioning

Source: J. Belsky, Early human experience: A family perspective, 1981, p. 16.
Developmental Psychology, 17, 3–23. Copyright © by the American Psychological
Association. Adapted with permission.

Ecological systems theory has contributed to research and applied work with infants. Since this theory's conception, a growing number of studies have examined the infant in the context of the family or the school. In addition, we are becoming more aware of the effects of the larger social and cultural ecosystem on infants. Nuclear radiation and environmental toxins affect prenatal development and mother's milk. The effect of having two parents working outside the home—on both the infant and the parents—is a complex family and social issue. We are becoming aware that child abuse and neglect are social ills related to poverty, discrimination, drug use, and stress.

What Are the Problems with Ecological Systems Theory?

A problem with ecological systems theory is that it does not specify the processes by which these effects might occur. For example, a disturbed parent-infant interaction may depend in part on the mother's drug use or the father's absence from the family. The precise transactional process by which the parent-infant interaction mediates these ecological factors is not explained by the theory. In addition, the theory does not provide any guidance concerning which of the many ecological factors are most likely to affect a family and under what circumstances the family is or is not affected. In other words, the richness of the conceptualization of multiple interacting effects is not supported by enough detail to guide research or practice. For that reason, most research based on

ecological systems theory is descriptive of the processes that occur under a variety of social conditions.

Another problem with ecological systems theory is that it is not developmental. Although the theory points to factors that might affect infants of different ages, it is not a theory about how infants develop from one age to the next. Because adults are the primary mediators of ecological factors on infants, other versions of systems theory, which will be discussed next, focus on the infant-adult interaction in order to explain infant development. These theories deal with the process by which cultural skills, such as language, are transferred from parent to infant during social interaction.

Interactive Systems Theory

Up until the 1960s, the parent-infant relationship was viewed as a one-way process: parental behavior affects infant behavior. This was due to the general acceptance of learning theories, which view the parent as the primary socializer. In these theories, parents got all the credit for child-rearing success and all the blame for child-rearing failure. Cognitive theories had little to say about the role of the parent, assuming that cognitive development was the result of the individual's transactions with the physical environment.

In the early 1960s, an infant psychiatrist, Louis Sander, developed a theory of the early mother-infant relationship in which he explicitly recognized the reciprocal mutual transactions and feedback processes between mother and child (Sander, 1962). Sander's stages of development in the mother-infant interaction are given in Table 2.3. The importance of this theory is that it recognized that both parent and infant develop as a system in relationship to each other over time.

A large body of research since then has confirmed the transactional nature of the parent-infant interaction. The evidence is so persuasive that most developmentalists today accept the idea of transaction in the parent-infant system as fact. This change in theoretical orientation toward the parent-infant relationship contributed in part to a revival in the 1970s and 1980s of the nearly forgotten work of Lev Semanovich Vygotsky (1896–1934), a Soviet educator who worked with parents and founded a number of schools.

Table 2.3 Louis Sander's Stages of the Development of Mother-Infant Reciprocity

Approximate Age (Months)	Description
0–3	The parent is concerned with helping the infant cope with biological function and the establishment of regular patterns of sleeping, feeding, arousal, and quieting. The infant begins to show differential responsiveness to the caregiver.
4–6	The beginnings of mutual play and reciprocal interactions can be seen. The parent and infant learn to anticipate signals from each other to coordinate feeding, playing, and caretaking activities.
7–9	The infant begins to take the initiative in social exchanges and shows preferences for certain kinds of social activities over others. The infant experiences feelings of success or frustration in meeting goals.
10–13	The infant makes directed demands on the mother and tries to test her availability. The parent is used as a secure base for exploration.
14–20	Infants take their own initiatives in a wider variety of settings. Infants learn to achieve success and pleasure autonomously (apart from the mother).

Source: Adapted from L. W. Sander, Issues in early mother-child interaction, 1962. *Journal of the American Academy of Child Psychiatry, 1,* 141–166.

Vygotsky did most of his work in the early years after the Russian revolution. Following from the political theory of Marxism-Leninism, which viewed society as a complex system of mutual and cooperative influences, Vygotsky suggested that all individuals are defined by the social group and that their knowledge is an active social construction. Vygotsky suggested that adults do not directly socialize the child into the culture but rather follow the child's own motivations to learn. By careful observation of what the infant wants to understand, adults can introduce forms of guidance that allow the infant to realize his or her goals.

The timing of parental guidance is crucial. According to Vygotsky, parents should wait for times when the infant appears to be trying to learn some new skill but has not yet mastered it (see Figure 2.6). Vygotsky referred to this phase of skill development as the **zone of proximal development,** that is, the time during which the proximal (next) achievement in skill is about to occur but has not occurred yet (Wertsch & Tulviste, 1992). Adults who tailor their guidance to fit the child's needs for support and information in the zone of proximal development will have the most lasting impact on learning.

Suppose, for example, the child is trying to express his or her desire for an object using grunts. If the adult suggests more culturally appropriate ways of requesting (speech, pointing, etc.), the child will

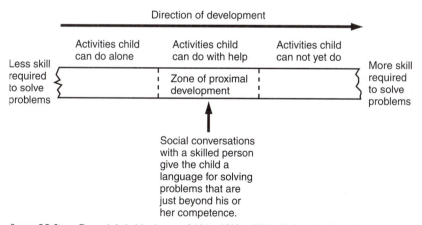

Figure 2.6
Vygotsky's Concept of the Zone of Proximal Development

Source: F. B. Steuer, *The psychological development of children,* 1994, p. 323. Pacific Grove, CA: Brooks/Cole. Used with permission.

pick up the cultural skills because those skills best serve the child's motivation at that particular moment. If the adult models appropriate forms of requesting when the child is not interested in requesting, the adult's model will not have an impact on the child.

The concept of the zone of proximal development, therefore, suggests that children will acquire culturally acceptable practices only if parents can adjust the timing and level of their actions to the ongoing motivational state of the children; mutual, cooperative transaction is at the heart of Vygotsky's theory, which is why it is sometimes called *sociocultural theory*. Because Vygotsky became ill and died at the young age of thirty-eight, he was not able to elaborate his theory. Developmentalists today are taking over where he left off.

One of the theories derived from Vygotsky's work is that of Jerome Bruner (1983). Bruner suggests that language development arises out of earlier social-communicative routines between parents and infants. These routines must be ones in which the infant is an active participant. Bruner focuses on simple parent-infant social games, such as peekaboo. The infant's participation in the game is part of his or her zone of proximal development because parents not only help to create the game's structure, they also make sure the game is a challenge for the infant that goes slightly beyond what the infant is capable of doing. Because the infant wants to play, he or she is more attuned to learning about the rules of the game and the behavior necessary to play. In Bruner's examples, the necessary behaviors are turn taking and language, which the child learns as part of play in the company of an adult.

In many interactions, adult and infant are working on something together, but each has a different purpose. The adult is perhaps intent on instructing the child in the culturally appropriate uses of words and objects. The child may be more motivated by being a direct participant in the social world. The concept of **guided participation,** which is also based on Vygotsky's theory, reflects the active role that children play while observing and participating in the organized activities of the family and society in the company of adults (Rogoff, 1990). Although, from the adult's perspective, the child is merely "playing games" or "playing at" cooking or taking care of a doll, from the child's perspective,

Table 2.4 **Components of Guided Participation between Adults and Young Children**

Child sets the agenda according to interest and skill level

Adult adjusts level of child's participation according to child's skill

Adult constrains child's participation for the safety and rights of others

Adult transfers responsibility to child according to ongoing assessment of child's abilities

Source: Adapted from B. Rogoff, *Apprenticeship in thinking: Cognitive development in social context,* 1990. New York: Oxford University Press.

the child is actually doing the task as an active participant.

Typically, in adult-child interactions, the children set the agenda for what they want to do and for how much they want to be involved. The more skilled partner collaborates in the child's goals by giving the child responsibility for certain actions that are part of the larger task but within the range of the zone of proximal development. The adult must also constrain the child's participation for the sake of the child's, or of others', safety or rights. Eventually, the adult transfers responsibility for larger segments of the task to the child, in relation to the growth of the child's competence as assessed by the adult (Bruner, 1983; Heckhausen, 1988; Kaye, 1982; Lock, 1980; Rogoff, 1990). These points are summarized in Table 2.4.

There are cultural differences in styles of guided participation. In one study (Rogoff et al., 1989), mothers from the United States were compared with Maya Indian mothers from Guatemala on how they helped their twenty-month-old children to use a set of nesting dolls. The U.S. mothers acted more like peers, wanting to take turns in combining dolls and commenting on the process. These mothers took their roles as teachers seriously. The Maya mothers retained more of an adult-child status difference. They assumed the children would eventually learn the task. They monitored the children's progress and gave verbal instructions, but they did not get very involved in the task.

One U.S. mother tried to play games with the dolls, then offered them to the child for "his turn." She gave instructions ("Put the lid on") and then cheered when the child did this ("Yeah! You're so smaaart!"). This mother tried to change the agenda when she judged that the baby's attention waned. She commented on all the child's actions and made requests for actions throughout the task.

A typical Maya mother demonstrated how the dolls come apart and go back together, using a few words to encourage the child to look. The baby wanted to handle the doll, but soon after, the mother took it back and again demonstrated how to do the task. She pointed out the features of the task verbally as she performed the action. After that, she let the infant try for some time on his own, while she watched but did not intervene. When he ran into trouble, the mother would say something to help ("Do this one first"). When the child made a successful move, the mother would simply say "Okay" or "I see" in a quiet tone. This study shows that the principles of guided participation work even in very different cultural situations and different styles of maternal teaching.

Interactive systems theories have had a major impact on research and on practice. Even during Vygotsky's era, these ideas influenced early childhood education. Teachers in day care centers and nursery schools have known for generations that education begins with the child's motivation and that it is the teacher's job to adapt to the skill level of the infants. Many parents do this intuitively, and most current child-rearing advice books encourage this behavior. Teaching young parents how to pay attention to the inclinations of their babies is a major component of parent-education classes for parents who are having difficulty with their babies, such as teenage parents, single parents living in poverty, parents with clinical depression, and parents who have a handicapped infant (see Chapter 9).

Simple, one-directional parent-to-child socialization theories would not be acceptable in developmental research journals today. Research based on interactive systems theories has given detailed descriptive accounts of the ways in which parents and infants play games, come to understand each other, and develop over time.

What Are the Problems with Interactive Systems Theory?

One problem with interactive systems theory is that it focuses primarily on short-term developmental changes such as acquiring a new skill during guided participation with an adult. It does not provide a framework for understanding how these short-term changes contribute to the changes that move infants from one developmental stage to the next.

Another criticism of interactive systems theory is that it focuses on parent-infant relationships, or small groups of co-participants, without taking account of the broader issues, such as those raised in ecological systems theories. Many interaction theorists study primarily the mother-infant interaction and fail to consider the family systems processes described earlier, including the roles of the father and siblings. Research inspired by Vygotsky's work, on the other hand, does take explicit account of cultural factors and cultural differences in the developmental process.

Dynamic Systems Theory

Some of the pioneers in the study of human development—Darwin, Vygotsky, and Piaget—were interested in the problem of how new forms arise during development. At different times in evolutionary history, for example, new species emerge that have never been seen before. Similarly, during the life span of a person, new abilities, emotions, and experiences arise as stages unfold in time. The story of all living systems, in fact, is about the generation of novelty, the creation of something new that was not there before.

Until recently, however, the emergence of novelty could not be explained. Many developmentalists turned their attention to other topics, such as the age at which children acquired particular skills and the environmental conditions that facilitated the infant's development. The introduction of dynamic systems theory into developmental research, however, has given scientists the conceptual and methodological tools to return to the fundamental question that motivated Darwin, Vygotsky, and Piaget: the emergence of novelty in development (van Geert, 1998).

Dynamic systems theory takes its current form from the work of the physicist Ilya Prigogine (Prigogine & Stengers, 1984). Most of the matter in the universe slowly expends its energy and then burns out. But Prigogine was interested in phenomena that make their own energy, preserve themselves across time, and become increasingly complex by generating novel forms. The ability of systems to maintain themselves and to develop new forms is called *self-organization*. The "self" in self-organization means that the maintenance and development of the system arises from the mutual transactions and feedback processes between the components of the system, rather than being imposed on the system by some preexisting plan.

Prigogine began his research by studying some nonliving physical systems that had the capacity to create their own energy and become more complex in form. One example is the weather, in which the forms—such as seasons—develop and maintain themselves over time. In spite of its dynamic complexity, the weather has patterns that repeat. Every year you can expect it to be cold in the winter and warm in the summer. Every winter is different from every previous winter in particular ways, however, and it is not possible to predict in advance what each new winter will be like.

Many dynamic systems display the following two properties.

1. They form predictable and stable patterns in their macroscopic behavior. The seasons in the weather system are one example; the stages of human development are another. All infants go through the same Piagetian substages in the same sequence, just as each year the earth goes through the same four seasons.
2. They are relatively unpredictable in their microscopic behavior. One may be able to predict the weather over the coming week or two within a range of possibilities depending upon the season, but the complexity of the weather system always leaves room for something novel to emerge. Similarly, we can describe what ten-month-old infants are likely to do, but their precise behavior on a given day and how they develop within the range of their possibilities cannot be predicted. Something novel happens every day that cannot be anticipated.

This microscopic unpredictability in the context of macroscopic stability is known as **chaos.** Chaos is a mathematical concept that expresses the property of complex systems to have some general structure that repeats over time but never in exactly the same way. The drawing in Figure 2.7 represents chaos. It is the trajectory of a mathematical equation that traces a path in three-dimensional space that is similar on each cycle but is never exactly the same as any previous cycle. Each person's life course is similar in the transitions between developmental stages, but no two lives are exactly the same. The concept of chaos suggests that dynamic systems are partially determinate and partially indeterminate.

The concepts of chaos and indeterminism suggest how the application of dynamic systems theory to human development is different from all other developmental theories. All scientists will admit that with something as complex as human development, there is no way to predict precisely how a person will turn out. Most scientists believe, however, that if we could somehow measure all the relevant variables in the system it would in fact be possible to predict a person's future. This idea of **determinism** suggests that all events have a cause and that that cause can be found with enough scientific work. In this view, we are unable to predict events in a person's life because we simply do not have sufficient data.

On the other hand, dynamic systems theory allows for the possibility of **indeterminism.** Indeterminism expresses the idea that not everything a person does, and not every turn in that person's development, can be predicted from known laws or principles. Indeterminism suggests that even if we could measure all the relevant variables in a system, we still could not completely predict its future behavior. This is because self-organization spontaneously creates novelty, something that did not exist prior to its creation and that could not have been predicted. Most living systems display a certain degree of indeterminism in their growth (Fogel, Lyra, & Valsiner, 1997; Prigogine & Stengers, 1984).

Scientists use the following example. Imagine a butterfly is flapping its wings somewhere in Asia. This movement is just enough to change the flow of a tiny bit of warm air. This tiny change in airflow may happen at just the right moment to trigger a much larger change in airflow because of deviation-amplifying feedback, which then causes a change in the temperature distribution at higher elevations. At some point and without a specific cause, the con-

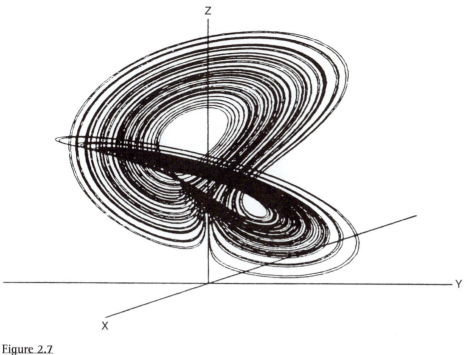

Z

Y

X

Figure 2.7
A Trajectory of Chaos

A mathematical equation generates a curve that repeats a similar shape in three-dimensional space. Each time the curve repeats the shape, however, it is in a slightly different place from where it has passed through before.

Source: F. Capra, *The web of life,* 1996, p. 135. New York: Anchor Books.

ditions are created for a thunderstorm to emerge in the United States. Because of complex feedback processes and emergent novelty, it is impossible to trace the cause of the thunderstorm back to a single source (even the flight of the butterfly is part of the existing weather system).

A **butterfly effect** occurs when a very small perturbation creates unpredictable novelty in a system, which then results in macroscopic developmental change in the system. Self-organization, chaos, and the butterfly effect have been used to explain why all snowflakes are similar but no two are exactly alike, the unpredictable heart rhythms during a heart attack, and the development of differences and similarities within the living cell (Capra, 1996; Hopkins & Butterworth, 1997).

Esther Thelen and I were among the first to apply dynamic systems theory to developmental psychology. We used it to explain infant locomotor development and infant socioemotional development (Fogel & Thelen, 1987; Thelen & Fogel, 1989).

We proposed that infant development is not fixed to a genetic or maturational timetable, nor is it entirely predictable from adult guidance or infant learning. While these factors provide the context for development, new abilities emerge through the dynamic indeterminacy of self-organization.

Infants have the locomotor skills for walking as early as six months, but they do not walk until ten or twelve months. By six months, infants can move their legs in a walking pattern, can support their own weight on their legs, and can take steps if held by an adult. They seem to have all the abilities but one—balancing themselves while upright. This balancing ability develops between six and ten months through a variety of experiences alone and with an adult. When the ability develops—and the exact age is unpredictable—infant walking self-organizes spontaneously. In just a few days from the first independent steps, the infant can walk across the room (Thelen, 1989; Thelen & Smith 1994). This spontaneous and sudden developmental transition is one of the behavioral markers of a self-organizing process (Prigogine & Stengers, 1984): something novel emerges that was not present earlier.

Dynamic systems theory has the advantage of trying to explain development from the perspective of multiple possible causes and connections. Unlike most theories, dynamic systems gives credit to indeterministic factors in development, suggesting that there is a creativity and spontaneity in human development that goes beyond the inputs to produce unique effects: the special qualities of particular infant personalities and infants' remarkably inventive actions. Human development has many examples of butterfly effects, small and unexpected events that can change the course of a life (Fogel, 1990a; Thelen, 1990).

I have applied dynamic systems theory to the parent-infant communication system (Fogel, 1993; Fogel & Lyra, 1997; Fogel & Branco, 1997). Many forms of interpersonal communication are transactional, that is, they work by means of feedback between the participants. I discovered that this transaction has two important features: the continuous mutual adjustment of action and creativity.

Unlike adults, whose conversations are in the form of speaking turns in which one person waits while the other talks, parents and infants communicate nonverbally in such a way that both participants are continuously active at all times. As a baby makes cooing vocalizations, for example, the parent is smiling at the infant, holding him, and moving him in rhythm with the vocal sounds. You can see this continuous mutual adjustment of actions in adult conversation if you take note of the facial expressions and body movements of the adults and not just their vocalizations. It also appears during dancing, group singing, and other forms of co-movement activity.

The other feature of communication is creativity. During conversation, for example, people form their sentences and stories in order to express something they have in mind. There is never a perfect match between what someone wants to express and the way in which it is actually said. People have to make up their sentences as they speak, and no two sentences are ever exactly alike. In addition, as we hear the responses of others to our words, that feedback sometimes makes us work to clarify our meaning or even to change it according to the other's perspective. In this sense, communication is

creatively self-organized because it emerges in the process of transaction. A participant's words and actions can have a butterfly effect, changing the direction of an interaction toward new topics and introducing a certain amount of indeterminism.

Communication that is continuously mutually adjusted and creative is co-regulated (Fogel, 1993). **Co-regulation** is a synonym for self-organization as applied to interpersonal communication. It accounts for why communication systems maintain repeating patterns of co-activity such as greetings, parent-infant games like peekaboo, or particular topics of conversation between a couple. Repeating patterns in a communication system, such as a topic of conversation, are called **frames.** Co-regulation also provides a way for novelty to enter into the system. Because communication in inherently creative, it contains the sources for its own change over time (Fogel, 1993).

Dynamic systems theory has been applied by an increasing number of infant researchers. The applications are in areas such as motor development (Goldfield, 1993; Clark, Truly, & Phillips, 1993; Thelen & Smith, 1994), cognitive development (van Geert, 1993; Thelen & Smith, 1994), perceptual development (Bertenthal & Pinto, 1993; Butterworth, 1993), personality and temperament (Lewis, 1995), emotions (Camras, 1993; Fogel et al., 1992; Wolff, 1993), and peer play (Eckerman, 1993).

Consider the development of infant emotions. Infant self-soothing, to take one example, emerges quite suddenly when infants develop the ability to put their hands in their mouths, usually around the age of five months. This achievement reduces the intensity of crying and allows infants immediate control over the direction of their attention and action. Hand-mouth coordination would not normally be considered part of emotional development. When we look at the whole system, however, we can see that each component of the system may be affecting the others. In addition, a simple butterfly effect of the change of one small component can have big effects on the self-organization of the whole system. In addition to self-calming, infant laughter and sustained engagement in social and object play also occur around five months of age (Fogel, 1985; Fogel, Nwokah, & Karns, 1993; see also Chapters 6 and 7).

At each developmental period, dynamic systems theory suggests an important role for creativity in everyday action. When babies begin to acquire language, for example, they can create novel sentences never spoken before. These experiments with playful creativity provide the opportunities for novelty to enter the system and enhance growth and development.

What Are the Problems with Dynamic Systems Theory?

Because dynamic systems theory is relatively new, its description of infant development is still rather general. Dynamic systems theory points to the inclusion of all the components of the system and the search for butterfly effects but does not have any specific guidelines for where to look for such things. It will take a great deal more research to fill in the blanks of the theory (as it took twenty-five years for information processing theory to fill in the blanks of Piaget's more general theory of cognitive development; research can be a slow process).

Because it came from physics, dynamic systems theory is based on complicated mathematical models. Applying such models directly to human development is difficult because it is not easily reduced to measurable quantities such as velocity and acceleration. The mathematics of the theory has been most successfully applied in the study of motor development, because moving limbs can be measured according to displacement, velocity, and acceleration. We do not know whether socioemotional development fits the same mathematical principles as the physical systems on which the theory was originally based or whether a very different mathematical approach will be needed to understand the more qualitative aspects of human experience. It is possible that there is a form of mathematics for the human psyche, but it has not been invented.

Clinical Theories

The infant's psychological experience of the world—what the infant knows, perceives, and feels—is not observable. Theories function to go beyond what is observed in order to explain what cannot be observed. Virtually all scientific theories of infant experience, such as Piaget's, are based upon direct observations of infants, creating a picture of infancy known as the **observed infant** (Stern, 1985).

An alternative source of evidence about infants' psychological experience comes from clinical work with older children and adults. During psychotherapy, for example, people sometimes appear to remember their experiences during childhood. Memories of particular incidents and events are called **conceptual memories.** Conceptual memories are composed of specific categories for type of event ("I was left alone"), time ("when I was five years old") and place ("at the preschool"). Conceptual memory is recall *about* an event that is communicated in the form of a verbal narrative or story.

Memories of early infancy, however, are very different from conceptual memories of particular incidents. Memories of infancy are **participatory memories.** Participatory memories are nonconceptual. They are not *about* a past experience; rather, they are felt as a *being with* or a *reliving of* past experiences. They are composed of emotions, desires, and a sense of familiarity, without any specific time or place (Bråten, 1998; Fogel, 1993; Heshusuis, 1994; Stern, 1985). A participatory memory, for example, is the re-creation of a feeling of what it was like to be cuddled and comforted rather than a specific situation of being cuddled. An adult's participatory memory of feeling cuddled may include the adult's body curling into a fetal posture and the feeling of being very tiny and held by a much bigger person.

The **clinical infant** is the participatory memory of infancy that emerges from therapeutic encounters with children and adults. The observed infant is constructed primarily from quantitative research methods. The clinical infant is based primarily on qualitative research methods. Clinicians are participant observers as they work with their adult clients, and they typically report their data—clients' reexperiencing their own infancy during therapy—in terms of narrative descriptions of case studies. The quantitative researcher relies primarily on conceptual analyses, describing and narrating *about* what has been observed. The qualitative researcher, on the other hand, uses a participatory method. The goal is *being with* the subject of the study, being a participant observer in the sense of *reliving* the subject's experiences rather than standing outside those experiences (Heshusius, 1994).

Theory and qualitative research based on the clinical infant are often not accepted within the scientific community because of the belief that they cannot be proven. In part, this is due to a negative bias attached to qualitative and case study research methods by people who favor quantitative research as the only true scientific method. Also, it is very difficult to ascertain, for example, if an adult's participatory memory of his or her infant experience during psychotherapy is the "truth."

It is important to realize, however, that even scientific theories based on the observed infant cannot be proven. No matter what research method is used, *infants' psychological experience will always be unobservable by adults.* Adult scientists cannot get inside the skin of the infants being observed; they must use theory to fill the gap between what can be observed and what cannot.

Scientific theories are not "truth" but reasonable conclusions based on a systematic application of the assumptions of the theory and the methods of research. There are many instances in the history of psychology in which theoretical conclusions about the infant's psychological experience have changed—witness the historical changes and controversies regarding ideas about infants during the twentieth century (Chapter 1) and the different views of infant experience that emerge from each of the scientific theories reviewed earlier in this chapter.

Scientists of human behavior can never prove that one theory is better than another. It is unethical to do the critical experiments required for this kind of proof. Each theory, then, is just one perspective on nature. No single theory can ever deal with the entire range of human developmental phenomena. Researchers, clinicians, parents, and educators can examine each of these theories and take what is most meaningful for any given application. These theories should be seen not as mutually exclusive but rather as complementary.

The purpose of this section on clinical theories is to describe several theories of infancy that are based on the clinical infant. In addition, I briefly explore the possible therapeutic effects on children and adults of the participatory remembering of infant experiences during clinical work.

Can Children and Adults Remember Their Infancy Experiences?

The clinical theories reviewed in this chapter assume that children and adults are shaped by their experiences during early infancy and the prenatal period. Is there any evidence that this is so? With regard to conceptual memory, people typically can recall only one or two specific incidents from early childhood, and not before the age of two or three years. Adults can have more detailed conceptual memories of events and situations beginning from when they were five or six years old. This is why it is commonly believed that we cannot remember our infancy, a phenomenon known as **infantile amnesia.**

As mentioned earlier, however, during therapeutic encounters, people have participatory memories of the prenatal and infancy periods that had been previously forgotten. Some therapeutic situations appear to allow people to recover the **unconscious,** that part of the self that is not remembered during ordinary waking states (Wade, 1996). Participatory memories are likely to be unconscious ones because they occurred at a time when we did not have words to describe them or because they were in some way traumatic. We know this from research on three-year-olds remembering traumatic injuries that occurred when they were one or two years old (Peterson, 1999; Peterson & Bell, 1996; Peterson & Rideout, 1998; see also Chapter 11).

While conceptual memories are primarily mental, participatory memories often involve the whole body. When particular patterns of movement, posture, and/or emotions occur repeatedly in particular situations, they are more likely to be remembered by the neuromotor system (Shore, 1994; Thelen & Smith, 1994). This is true, for example, in learning any skilled activity, such as music or athletics. Musicians may have conceptual memories of written music, but it is the participatory memory of moving their bodies that allows them to actually play or sing. Research on adults who experienced traumas as adults (such as assault, emotional trauma, or an automobile accident) also shows that their memories of the trauma are fragmentary (they do not have a particular time or place) and relived in the body. They may shake or break out in a cold sweat and experience a feeling of intense fear (Smyth & Pennebaker, 1999; Terr, 1994; see also Chapter 11).

If an infant's needs are repeatedly ignored, for example, the infant develops feelings of distress and hopelessness. As the infant grows older, as a child or adult, similar situations will evoke similar participatory memories. If that person feels ignored, it is likely to lead to the experience of hopelessness. If that experience occurs repeatedly in life, it can lead to depression. The depression, therefore, may have its origins in a participatory memory from early infancy. There are also many ordinary, nontraumatic participatory memories. Movement patterns learned in infancy, such as kicking, reaching, crawling, and rolling over, underlie all later complex movements of older children and adults (Thelen & Smith, 1994). Patterns of emotional responses in infancy form the basis for many later adult emotions (Stern, 1985).

Participatory memories are often transformed over time. The memory of being ignored in infancy, in the above example, is changed into feelings of depression in the adult. The adult has a long history following infancy, which may include other experiences of being ignored or of being recognized and loved. The early participatory memories, therefore, are filtered through this history of related experiences. These early memories may remain, or they may become lost.

Participatory memories are not verbal. For this reason, therapeutic methods that evoke these memories succeed by taking people away from their ordinary patterns of conceptual thinking and reasoning. The most common example of participatory memories in adults is dreams, which cannot be completely comprehended by verbal or logical means. Dreams are often used in therapeutic situations as a way to bring these participatory memories into conscious awareness.

Although the idea of participatory memories of infancy is theoretical, there is some evidence that they exist and can be reexperienced. This evidence comes from dreams and from experiences during therapeutic encounters. In the remainder of this section, we review two different types of approach to the clinical infant: psychotherapeutic and somatic awareness. **Somatic** refers to the individual's conscious awareness of the experiences of their bodies. Psychotherapeutic theories use talking between client and therapist as the principal tool for enhancing awareness of participatory memory and how it affects the adults' psyche. Somatic awareness approaches use some combination of talk, movement, touch, and somatic awareness in order to access participatory memory. It is not the purpose of this section to review all types of clinical methods. We focus only on a few that have explicitly recognized the role of infant and other developmental experiences in the therapeutic process.

Psychotherapeutic Approaches

Sigmund Freud was a physician who noticed that his patients often came to him with physical symptoms that had no apparent medical cause. Freud saw that in some cases, people exhibited behavior that was thematically related to their physical symptom. A person with constipation, for example, might tend to be overly concerned with behavioral cleanliness, order, and punctuality. The mode of retention in the body organ corresponded with retaining tight behavioral control over one's life.

Freud speculated that these patterns of behavior might have their origins early in a person's life, around the time when infants are being toilet trained and becoming aware of the process of holding onto and letting go of the contents of their bowels. This occurs in children in Western cultures around the age of two years. Freud wanted to explore whether such people had any memory of a trauma that might have occurred around that age. He experimented with an early form of hypnosis and then later discovered a method that he called **free association.** He asked his clients to lie down and encouraged them to relax by providing a comfortable couch and a safe environment in which they could say anything without fear of retribution or judgment. As they talked about whatever came to mind, Freud helped them become aware of the possible participatory memories that were behind the behavioral symptoms, memories of which the client's conscious mind was unaware. The use of free association along with interpretation in psychotherapy is called **psychoanalysis.**

During free association, people who are overcontrolled in their daily life may express participatory memories of fear, such as the fear of punishment or the fear of being controlled. This participatory memory is not of any specific toilet-training situation. These memories may be connected with unconscious desires to lose control, to be uninhibited in their behavior, to let go of what they are carrying, and to release their pent-up feelings of frustration. This type of uninhibited behavior is what Freud (1903) referred to as the **id.** The id can be thought of as all of the person's needs and desires, but especially those desires that are irrational, overwhelmingly compelling, and not tolerant of any delay.

According to Freud, infants are dominated by the id and gradually learn to control some of these impulses. Their crying becomes less insistent, for example, and they develop the capacity to wait for gratification and to regulate their own needs. The **ego** is the ability to tolerate discomfort and frustration and to moderate the pursuit of pleasure. The ego refers to the regulatory functions of the person.

As the infant grows older, the ego relies increasingly on thought processes, mental representation, problem solving, and rational approaches to the world. Freud realized that thinking and reasoning about oneself are important for self-control and appropriate social behavior. These tools of the ego, however, are not useful in accessing the unconscious id memories, because the ego was developed specifically in order to repress the id. This is why Freud turned to free association: in order to get people temporarily out of the rational conceptual way in which they regulated their everyday life.

Based on what his adult clients revealed during free association, Freud theorized that the development from id to ego recurs during the life course, as new sources of id experiences mature. Id experiences relate to pleasurable feelings of the body, and the pleasurable areas of the body change as the person grows older. He distinguished two major phases of id development during the first three years of life: the oral stage and the anal stage.

During the first year of life, the infant is particularly aware of sensations of pleasure and displeasure in the mouth region through activities such as sucking, chewing, biting, and swallowing. This period is called the **oral stage.** During this stage, according to Freud's theory, the infant views the world from the point of view of consuming it. Freud felt that infants at this stage of development believe that they can incorporate everything and everyone—that the world is centered upon their own gratification—and trust in the inevitability of satisfaction.

The **anal stage** begins sometime in the second year of life, when the primary sensitive zone becomes the anal region of the body. Freud recognized that children find pleasure in the distension of the bowel, the withholding of feces, and the elimination of feces. Gaining self-control over the bladder and bowel muscles is a major personal achievement, and the feelings associated with producing, owning, holding onto, and voluntarily giving up one's feces are thought to relate to the child's growing sense of self and personal autonomy.

The person with constipation, for example, may be holding onto things, according to Freud, because his anal id desires to let go and be messy either were not recognized or were punished by his family. He retains a participatory memory of his anal desires (to be messy), but that memory has become unconscious because the behavior was not tolerated when he was two years old.

These two stages and later developmental stages postulated by Freud are included in Table 2.5. A more detailed description of the later stages is beyond the scope of this book.

Erik Erikson (1950) accepted Freud's basic premise that changes in body sensitivity from oral to anal awareness form the core of the developing infant. He viewed each stage of development (eight stages in all across the entire life span) as a potential crisis of the personality leading to a sense of individual identity. An individual might continue his or her forward progress in development, or he or she might become sidetracked at any point. Erikson's developmental stages are also given in Table 2.5. Parents and parental behavior are a topic of this book as well, and parents are typically in Erikson's stage of generativity versus stagnation, the period of young adulthood and parental responsibility that follows the stage of

Table 2.5 Psychoanalytic Stages of Development

Approximate Age (Years)	According to Freud	According to Erickson
0–1½	*Oral:* Focus on experiences of the mouth such as sucking, eating, crying, biting	*Trust vs. mistrust:* Development of expectancy for either gratification or frustration
1½–3	*Anal:* Focus on experience in anal region such as elimination and retention	*Autonomy vs. shame/doubt:* Self-assertiveness and self-control or uncertainty and shame
3–6	*Phallic or oedipal:* Focus on genitals and desire to possess opposite sex parent	*Initiative vs. Guilt:* Independent activity is approached with either a sense of purpose (initiative) or questioning (guilt)
6–11	*Latency:* Interest in learning new skills but no overt sexual desires	*Industry vs. inferiority:* Interest in learning and skill development or a sense of inadequacy and loss of motivation
11–20	*Genital:* Adult sexual desires and the establishment of sexual relationships	*Identity vs. role confusion:* Perception of self as a unique individual; development of personal values or confusion about identity and role in life

Source: A. Fogel & G. F. Melson, *Child development,* 1988, p. 34. St. Paul, MN: West. Copyright © by West Publishing Co. Reprinted by permission. All rights reserved.

identity versus role confusion shown in Table 2.5. *Generativity* means to create and to nurture.

Instead of emphasizing participatory memory of the body, as Freud did, Erikson focused on the way in which the infant's body related to the family and to society. The first conflict of the life cycle was related to the development of a sense of basic trust in the environment. This trust developed if the parent was able to recognize and gratify the infant's id needs in such a way that the baby came to expect the environment to be friendly and supportive. Mistrust occurred when the parent did not allow the infant to experience id feelings (trust in self) or when the infant came to expect that needs would not be met adequately (trust in others). In an adult, participatory memories of this period may be related to feelings of being ignored or supported by others.

In the second stage, the infant could develop either a sense of purpose and autonomy or else a sense of shame and doubt. This again depended upon the parent's ability to support the infant's desire to feel his or her own experiences of control and letting go, and to reward and to share in the infant's personal achievements. If the parent chastises the infant for being assertive or fails to delight in the infant's accomplishments, the infant may feel ashamed and develop a sense of doubt about his or her ability to be independent. In adults, participatory memories of this period may be felt as a fear of failure or a lack of self-confidence.

Both Freud and Erikson relied on observations of the clinical infant, the infant as experienced by adults during free association. Somewhat later, psychoanalysts began to rely on data from the observed infant. The issue of the growth of personal autonomy, for example, was studied by Margaret Mahler (1975). Mahler was a practicing psychoanalyst who devoted her clinical work to helping young children and their families. She believed that many psychopathologies could be prevented by intervention with families in the early years of the child's life.

Mahler's work and that of others led to the refinement of the field of **infant psychiatry,** the application of clinical psychology work directly to infants and their families (see the section on infant mental health in Chapter 10). Because of the psychoanalytic emphasis on the parent-infant bond, most clinical interventions in infancy involve a large component of parent education and enrichment. When infants have severe feeding, toilet-training, emotional regulation, or autonomy problems, clinicians will most often work with the mother-infant dyad.

Daniel Stern (1985) followed Mahler's approach of using data from both clinical and observed infants. Stern's theoretical emphasis is on self-awareness, and his theory is one of the most detailed regarding the types of infant experiences that correspond to later participatory memories of adults. He theorized that even from birth, infants have a sense of self. The early senses of self during the first three years of life remain with the person even as new ways of knowing the self emerge in development.

Stern postulated that during the first two months, infants have a sense of an **emergent self** (see Chapter 5). They are aware of how the different movements, sensations, and feelings cohere into recognizable states. Between two and eight months, infants develop a sense of a **core self** (also called the *ecological self*; see Chapter 6). This is the experience of being an active agent that does things in the world, has feelings, and has a history of prior experiences. Between eight and fifteen months, infants discover that they have inner experiences that are different from others around them. This **subjective self** (see Chapter 8) can choose to share feelings and experiences with others and is aware of its dependence upon and attachment to others. After fifteen months, the **verbal self** (which this book divides into the *categorical self* [Chapter 10] and the *conceptual self* [Chapter 11]) comes to use language to talk about inner states and to construct a coherent identity in the company of other people. The verbal self is the beginning of the individual's conceptual memory.

According to Stern, the ability to fully experience each of these senses of the infant self is fostered when parents recognize and support the infant in his or her endeavors to explore the self, its possibilities and boundaries. These senses of self are very vulnerable to being overwhelmed when parental action is not attuned to the infant's process of self-discovery. If parents are too controlling, infants may lose their sense of an emergent, core, or subjective self. They cannot feel any of their own control over their feelings and actions. Although this happens regularly to all babies and is part of the process of growing up, in some cases infants are chronically deprived of any ability to sense themselves.

Stern's theory suggests that adults may have both positive and negative participatory memories of the emergent, core, and subjective selves. In adults, the participatory memory of the emergent self is the feeling that things are "coming together,"

or, in contrast, that the events in one's life are chaotic or confusing. In adults, the participatory memory of the core self is the sense of having a lasting identity and the person's willingness to fully feel one's emotions. Alternatively, core self memories may be experienced as identity confusion, avoidance of emotions, loss of direction, and helplessness. In adults, the participatory memory of the subjective self is the presence or lack of sharing, security, and trust with which we relate our inner feelings to other people.

The work of Mahler and Stern led to a developmental approach to the treatment of children and adults who have lost touch with their infant selves. A developmental approach allows people to reexperience the core self—in a therapeutic context, for example—and then to use those experiences to recreate a more optimal sequence of self-development than they had in their own families.

The treatment method is similar to Freud's. Work with clients, who may be suffering from a mistrust of others, occurs in a setting that is conducive to relaxation and total acceptance of their feelings. Relaxation and acceptance are universally part of all therapeutic efforts—both psychotherapeutic and somatic awareness approaches—to relive one's infancy and to recreate a better developmental process. These are the basic conditions under which people can be made aware of their participatory memories of infancy.

The therapist also helps the client to focus attention on the threads of their early experience in order to explore the consequences for the self. This allows the client the freedom to weave these threads into a coherent pattern that promotes renewed developmental change. The basic elements of developmental therapeutic processes are given in Table 2.6. Working with young children, these goals can be accomplished using play therapy (Ryan & Wilson, 1995).

Somatic Awareness Approaches

The other branch of developmental clinical theory and practice that will be discussed here is grouped under the heading of **somatic awareness approaches.** In psychotherapeutic methods, thera-

Table 2.6   Techniques of Developmental Therapies

Using these techniques, clinicians have found that clients are more likely to reexperience unconscious events from infancy and early childhood and to use that information to recreate a more optimal developmental process.

Technique	Description
Safety	The client is allowed to feel secure. This is done by creating a comfortable and stable physical setting and by the therapist's maintaining an open and accepting attitude.
Exploration	Clients and therapists are allowed to follow the leads of whatever comes up and to explore their consequences and meanings for the client. Clients should be allowed to feel their unconscious emotions and thoughts in this protected situation, which is more like pretend play than "for real." This defuses the power of the unconscious to control the clients' behavior.
Awareness	The therapist's role is to help the clients maintain their attention on the sources and consequences of the unconscious patterns. The therapists are not expected to heal the clients. Rather, the clients heal themselves as they develop a sense of competence and control over their own actions, which is a direct result of their expanded awareness of their previously unconscious processes.

pists usually talk with their clients while they are seated or lying down. Somatic awareness approaches may also use talk, but they typically use body movement and touch as a way to access the participatory memories of early childhood. Since infants experience their world via movement and touch, for many somatic awareness practitioners, this seems to be a more direct route to an adult's infant experience than merely talking.

Somatic awareness approaches also use the three aspects of developmental therapy shown in Table 2.6: safety, exploration, and awareness. Safety is created in part by the physical environment. Some methods use soft music and low lighting. Safety is also created by an attitude on the part of the practitioner that permits openness and allows people to relax. If touch is used, clients are reassured that it will be for therapeutic and strictly nonsexual purposes. Exploration is created by letting the client direct the flow of the session. Awareness is enhanced as the practitioner helps clients to pay attention not only to their words but to their body movements, emotions, and sensations. Because it is difficult for most adults to do this, access to participatory memory is aided by the creation of a deep state of relaxation that facilitates attention to the inner self.

One somatic awareness method that explicitly attempts to recreate an optimal infant experience is **Watsu.** In this technique, the practitioner floats the client in a pool of warm water. It was created by Harold Dull, who studied a Japanese massage method called zen shiatsu, in which the body is gently stretched in order to release tension. Dull found that the effects of zen shiatsu were enhanced in the water.

During a session, clients are moved freely in the water, stretched gently, and cradled in the practitioner's arms. In their parent's arms, fussy infants are comforted and touched, their tensions are eased, and they can return to focusing their relaxed attention on what they are doing and feeling. In this safe environment, they can really explore their bodies and continue to grow. A similar effect occurs in Watsu. "By being moved so freely through the water, by being stretched and repeatedly returned to a fetal position, the adult has the opportunity to heal in himself whatever pain or loss he may still carry from that time" (Dull, 1995, p. 65).

With the head and body in water, sound is muted, and clients can hear the rush of the water and the sound of their own heartbeat. They can also hear the practitioner's heartbeat and feel the contact of skin against skin. This is believed to evoke a preverbal experience, possibly even a prenatal experience, that provides a sense of wholeness.

In the **Rosen method,** clients lie on a padded table while the practitioner's open and relaxed hands make gentle contact with areas of the body that appear to hold muscular tension and restrict free breathing. By listening to the client's body with gentle touch and to the words they use to describe their experience, the practitioner can help the client to relax, relieve pain, and breathe easier. The Rosen method was developed by Marion Rosen, who began her studies of the body as a young woman in Germany in the 1930s. After working many years as a physical therapist, she began incorporating her own observations into her treatments. Following the client's natural breathing pattern with gentle touch resulted in deep relaxation. She listened as clients sometimes talked about how their injuries had occurred. Often the client would connect with the felt sense of an earlier experience that related to the injury. When this happened, the client's breath would deepen, relaxation would occur, and pain would often disappear.

Rosen began to understand that the body tells its own story, shaped by our early life experiences, many of them forgotten and unconscious. If we are born healthy, we come into the world breathing fully, with the full swing of our diaphragm moving every muscle in our body. We expect to have all our needs met and to be loved. But these expectations cannot be fully met even under the best of circumstances. As a result of either ordinary or traumatic events, we shape ourselves through muscular tension in whatever way that helps us to survive.

These situations are believed to be registered deeply in our bodies as participatory memories, which contribute to our characteristic patterns of muscular tensions, emotions, and postures. These emotions are unconsciously held in abeyance by muscular tension until we feel big enough, strong enough, and safe enough to finally allow ourselves a felt sense of the old experience. Through the gentle touch of the Rosen method, as we deeply relax and breathe more easily, we begin to remember the experiences that we had learned to unconsciously contain and through that knowledge we regain fuller movement, ease, and well-being (Wooten, 1995).

Moshe Feldenkrais (1904–1984), originally a physicist and judo instructor, invented a system of body movement education—the **Feldenkrais method**—that reawakens, develops, and organizes capacities for kinesthetic (sensorimotor) learning. Whereas children before the age of three learn movements by relying on their sensorimotor experience, older children and adults in technological cultures often behave according to social expectations, distancing themselves from their bodily feelings. Feldenkrais also observed that very young children use all their senses and every part of their bodies, a process he called **organic learning.** Adults appear to involve less of themselves, unless they are fully absorbed in what they are doing.

Feldenkrais believed that such alienation from the body contributes to habitual, usually unconscious, patterns of muscular tension and psychosomatic illnesses. Because the Feldenkrais method involves the emulation of how young children learn, its therapeutic value hinges on releasing capacities for learning that had been left behind in childhood (Reese, 1985).

In order to teach his methods, Feldenkrais invented thousands of Awareness through Movement lessons, many of which are based on the movements performed by babies as they first learn to roll, sit, crawl, walk, and explore their bodies in the environment. Students are asked to make small, slow movements, reduce their efforts, and sense how even simple movements are connected with every part of the body. This book contains a series of Awareness through Movement lessons to help you access your own participatory memories of infancy. Feldenkrais practitioners also use hands-on techniques called *functional integration*. In this work, students lie on a padded table as a practitioner gently touches and moves them, often in babylike ways, in order to promote deep relaxation, kinesthetic awareness, and openness to learning new ways to move.

Feldenkrais methods are used to increase physical coordination and integration and to bring greater enjoyment and satisfaction in life. They are also used for adults and children with minor muscular problems, cerebral palsy, Down's syndrome (see Chapter 3), and other developmental problems, and with adults who suffer from neurological or orthopedic problems.

Bodymind centering is a method of body and movement awareness in which adults perform exercises based on the normal stages of infant sensorimotor development (Hartley, 1995). Bodymind centering was created by a dance teacher and physical therapist, Bonnie Bainbridge Cohen, during the 1960s and 1970s. Cohen discovered that she could help many of her clients by taking them step by step through the sensorimotor stages of prenatal and infant development. This is done by giving verbal directions and using touch to guide movement when necessary. In this way, clients can reconnect with a sense of self and self-discovery that may have been lost as they grew up.

Clients are first guided through the prenatal experience of feeling the pull of gravity, the movement of their breathing, and their heartbeat. Then they do exercises focused on feeling the sensations around the mouth, just as a newborn baby explores with mouth and sucking movements. The infant's first movements are generated through the torso and spine, and these are explored before movements that entail pushing and pulling with the arms and legs. "First we simply *feel* the new sensations, perceptions, and mobility in a very direct and immediate way, as does an infant or child. Conscious recognition of change may occur in the adult only after the movement has been fully experienced" (Hartley, 1995, p. 99).

What Are the Problems with Clinical Theories?

Clinical theories have offered an alternative perspective for understanding infant development, the perspective of adults who are taught how to become aware of their participatory memories of being a baby. Although no theory can be proven, clinical theories have not been subjected to quantitative research tests of their predictions in the same way as the other theories reviewed in this chapter.

Clinical research is rooted in qualitative methods, which is a strength because they help us to understand how particular individuals have been shaped by their infant experience. On the other hand, more could be learned from clinical approaches by a systematic introduction of qualitative research and also by the complementary use of quantitative methods. Claims about increased relaxation and a renewed sense of well-being could be measured easily in treatment and no-treatment contrast groups.

It is difficult to substantiate whether the participatory memory of infancy revealed during a therapy session is the same as what that adult actually experienced as a baby. First of all, memories of early infancy are typically about feelings and body states,

not about particular incidents. Second, the adult clients' middle-aged or elderly parents would find it difficult to remember whether a particular event happened, and even if they did, their experience of it as a parent would not be the same as the infant's experience. It may be that the acceptance of particular body feelings as belonging to a person's past, regardless of how they actually occurred, is of such significant therapeutic value that an exact verification is unnecessary.

A problem with psychoanalytically oriented psychotherapeutic theories is that like learning theories, they tend to focus reward or blame for the child's behavior on the parents. Our earlier review of systems theories suggested, on the contrary, that children contribute to their own development by influencing parental behavior. It is easier to be sensitive and calm with a relaxed and happy baby than with one who cries much of the time.

All clinical approaches are limited in the effectiveness of their treatment. Most approaches work best for a particular range of adult concerns and problems. No one approach can treat all behavioral and psychological issues of adults. Clients should be informed about both the possibilities and the limitations of each approach.

The Author's View

My own research has been informed by each of the theoretical and clinical approaches reviewed in this chapter. I have studied the scientific theories and tried to apply all of them to my studies on the observed infant. I am particularly drawn to systems theories in general, and dynamic systems theory in particular, because I believe that life is a complex, dynamic, and partially indeterminate process.

As I mentioned in Chapter 1, my definition of science means to examine all sources of data from multiple methods and perspectives. For this reason, I have reviewed theories of the clinical infant in this chapter. As a client, I have personally experienced each of the psychotherapeutic and somatic awareness clinical approaches that were discussed. I have studied psychotherapy and am currently receiving training to become a practitioner in the Rosen method. I have found these methods to be personally enriching and growth producing for myself and others.

Because the infant's psychological experience is unobservable, one might conclude that understanding an infant is no different from understanding the psychological experience of a nonhuman animal. Adult humans, however, have all been human infants, and we have all had infant experiences. On scientific grounds, it would be pointless to ignore such a rich source of potential data on infancy as the clinical infant. Scientists, however, need not give up their healthy skepticism as they continue to weigh the validity of different sources of data on infancy.

My own experiences using the clinical approaches reviewed in this chapter have been informative for my understanding of the infant's psychological experience. Many of the later chapters in this book include movement awareness lessons written by Mark Reese, a certified Feldenkrais method practitioner and trainer. These exercises will allow you the opportunity to experience the clinical infant for yourself.

When I teach infant development courses at my university, I ask students to do a qualitative case study of their own reactions while doing the Awareness through Movement lessons. I typically begin the session with a bodymind centering exercise that helps students relax. Lying on their backs on a carpeted floor, I ask students to become aware of their breathing by noticing where their body moves when they breathe. Then I ask them to notice the pull of gravity by sensing the parts of their backs, arms, and legs that are touching the floor. Finally, they notice the sensations on their skin, the air, and their clothing. These simple forms of awareness are probably what the fetus and newborn experience.

Following the traditions of Feldenkrais practitioners, I read the lessons out loud during class time while students follow each step. It is important to do this in a quiet room where students can recline comfortably, to say only what is written in a clear and even voice, and to allow students time to do each of the steps. In addition, I ask students to practice the lessons at home and to include in their study any opportunities to interact with infants (see the "Co-Regulating with Baby" sections in most chapters for ideas about this). I invite you to do a similar qualitative research study. You can do the lessons on your own if you are not part of a group or class.

In order to transform your experiences into research, keep a journal of your reactions to each of these lessons and encounters with babies. It is best to write in your journal immediately following the lesson or exercise. As a participant observer, note your physical and emotional reactions. Note if you have any strong impressions of having an infantile participatory memory and what gives you this feeling. If you think the memory is from later in childhood, note this and say why.

Writing a narrative about your observations and experiences is an essential part of qualitative research. Why? For a study to count as qualitative research, the researcher has to interpret the meaning of the observations. This can only be done by talking or writing about them. Writing is preferred to talking because it is easier and more accurate to compare written observations (the constant comparative method; see Chapter 1) than spoken ones, which are easily forgotten. The other aspect of qualitative research is that the observer is an explicit part of the study. No problem here. You are a participant-observer.

Talk to your parents or guardians about what they remember about your infancy. Were you a healthy baby? Were you born prematurely? Did you experience traumas as an infant, or was your infancy reasonably happy? What was that time like for your mother and father? Was their relationship supportive or difficult, intact or separated? Did either of your parents have a physical or mental illness? Did either of them leave or die when you were a baby? Did one or both of them work, and was that work satisfying or stressful? Was your family rich or poor? Did you spend a significant amount of time with someone other than your parents? What was life like for those individuals?

Try to match your spontaneous experiences of participation in the lessons and exercises with what you can find out from others about you, the family, and the environment that you lived in as a fetus and as an infant. Review the principles of qualitative research from Chapter 1 as well as the research on the observed infant presented in this book and ask yourself: Is this is a useful way to study myself? Does this help me understand my own infancy? Did I have any participatory memories of my infancy? Does it help me understand infants in general? Is this a valid scientific approach to doing research on infant development?

In my class, I ask students to write a term paper in which they try to answer these questions and report the findings of their qualitative research study on themselves. Putting all their journal observations together into a coherent narrative in the term paper is where the constant comparative method is most useful. As you see differences and similarities between your journal entries, it helps you interpret the meaning of your experiences for yourself. Below are some of the things I learned from the students' term papers when I taught this class most recently.

Many students were honest about being hesitant at the start of the semester. This was partly because they felt self-conscious and foolish about doing the lessons in class in front of their peers and partly because they were genuinely skeptical. One student said, "Coming into this class, I thought these lessons were going to be silly. I told friends of mine about what we did and they would laugh." Another wrote, "I admit that I was very apprehensive when we began the lessons and I was not sure I wanted to stay in the class." Students who were initially hesitant changed their minds after actually doing the lessons for a while.

All of the students agreed that this was an important way to study themselves. They reported becoming more aware of their bodies both during the lessons and in everyday life. Some said they learned to notice the tension in their bodies when sitting or doing ordinary tasks. One student said, "I wonder how many times I've ignored the tension in my back, and what impact doing this has had on me?" Another said, "We are so preoccupied with responsibilities and obligations that we overlook how we feel and what is going on around us." Others remarked that because of the lessons, they paid more attention to what they ate and drank and to their health. This was particularly striking because none of the lessons are about health behaviors. It shows how even simple somatic lessons like the ones in this book can generate a more pervasive somatic awareness that promotes health.

Most said that they become more open to their feelings and to new experiences. Many students reported feeling a sense of relaxation, peace, calm, and enhanced well-being. One word the students used to describe these effects was "therapeutic." The therapeutic and healing effects, of course, are the reasons Feldenkrais and other practitioners developed lessons like these in the first place. Students compared doing these lessons to other kinds of movement and somatic awareness education in which they had participated, such as dance, yoga, massage, meditation, and athletics. One student who was not involved in these other activities said, "I never experienced movement for the sake of movement before, at least not as an adult."

Students also felt this was a great way to understand infants, because when they observed babies they could see some of the same joys and struggles they themselves had experienced while doing the lessons. They said things like, "Being an infant is not as easy as I used to think it was." Some reported a sense of certainty that having done this qualitative study would contribute to how they raised their own children. The students who had infants in their close families or infants of their own were made more aware of what the babies were trying to accomplish. They changed their approach from being an observer of the infants to being someone who, they felt, could really share the infant's feelings and experiences. This is a shift from a conceptual stance of *learning about* infants to a participatory stance of *being with* infants.

A big question for all the students was whether they had experienced participatory memories of their own infancy and whether their qualitative study was valid enough to convince others. I will say more about some of their conclusions in the "Author's View" section in Chapter 6, in which studies of the observed infant's memory are reported. In Chapter 12, I will describe the students' opinions about whether or not this kind of qualitative research on the self is scientifically valid.

I believe that if there is proof about the infantile origins of some participatory memories, it can only come from the experience of participation, from doing and feeling the lessons rather than from reading and thinking about them. I came to this conclusion after I took the opportunity to do a qualitative study on myself using Feldenkrais movement lessons like the ones in this book, added to my experiences with Rosen, Watsu, bodymind centering, and other forms of somatic education. That study is still ongoing. I agree with the way one student in my class described this kind of research. He wrote, "I now strongly believe that in order to understand human behavior it is imperative that you understand yourself."

SUMMARY

Biological Approaches

- Species and individual phenotypes evolve by natural selection.

- Behavior ecology theory is the study of a species's evolved behavior characteristics.

- Although certain survival functions are present across species, each species has a unique species-specific behavioral pattern.

- Critical periods are less useful for explaining development in humans than in other species of animals, although they do occur during human prenatal development.

- Behavior genetics studies the probabilities of predicting individual differences between phenotypes using differences between either environments, genotypes, or both.

Learning Theories

- Classical conditioning is learning by association that occurs when unconditioned and conditioned stimuli are paired during training.

- Operant conditioning occurs when the frequency of behavior is controlled by its consequences: reinforcement, punishment, and extinction.

- Social learning theory suggests that learning occurs when the individual is motivated to attend to the consequences. Infants can also learn by observation and imitation.

Cognitive Theories

- Piagetian constructivist approaches suggest that infants develop intelligence by means of their own explorations in the world. Infant intelligence is of a sensorimotor rather than a verbal-symbolic form.

- Information processing theories break cognition down into a series of component processes, each of which can function independently of the others. Breakdowns in the cognitive system may occur if any of the components are not properly functioning.

Systems Theories

- A *system* is a set of interdependent components, each of which affects the others in reciprocal fashion. The process by which systems components affect each other is known as *transaction*.

- Ecological systems theory suggests that infant development is related in direct and indirect ways to the family and to society, and vice versa.

- Interactive systems theory focuses on the process of communication between parents and infants and the ways in which that communication leads to developmental change in the infant.

- Dynamic systems theory introduces elements of self-organization and indeterminacy into the process of development. Individual differences are not always predictable as a direct result of particular causes, but rather emerge creatively as part of the complex dynamics of action.

Clinical Theories

- Clinical theories use evidence from children and adults during therapeutic transactions in order to construct a view of infant experience and its meaning in later development.

- Children and adults remember their infancy in unconscious ways, via forms of body movement, muscular tension, and emotions.

- Psychoanalysis uses talking in the form of free association to evoke unconscious memories. It uses these memories to help adults understand sources of tension and emotion that were acquired during the oral and anal stages.

- Somatic awareness approaches use a combination of talk, movement, and touch to evoke unconscious memories, allowing people to remember the spontaneous capacities for organic learning and the full use of the senses and emotions that they experienced as an infant.

ON THE WEB

www.psych.utah.edu/alan_fogels_infant_lab
The site for the author's research laboratory. Contains summaries of ongoing studies, descriptions of the personnel, contact information for people doing collaborative research with the author, and information for potential research assistants and research subjects. There are links to the author's web page in the Department of Psychology at the University of Utah. That page contains information about the author's publications and background.

www.idealist.com/children This child development web page offers a great deal of information on child development and ongoing research. The message forum index provides service for people with questions and answers regarding child development. The tutorial, a month-by-month look at development of children from one to thirty-six months of age, provides information based on the classic theories of child development of Freud, Erikson, and Mahler. A newsletter is also available.

www.cforums.com Contemporary Forums is a corporation dedicated to continuing education. This web site has access to many different conferences throughout the year. It provides a calendar of events regarding continuing education needs of physicians, nurses, and other health professionals.

www.zerotothree.org This web site from the National Center for Infants, Toddlers, and Families provides information on children from zero to three years of age. It offers an easy-to-understand parent's guide to understanding development assessment procedures, a glossary of terms used in assessments, and a resource list to help guide parents to local organizations for support. Zero to Three concentrates exclusively on the critical period when a child undergoes the greatest human growth and development. During this period, the parent or professional has the opportunity to make a great impact and positively influence a child's future. Zero to Three's mission is to help children best navigate their first three years of life in order to develop a solid intellectual, emotional, and social foundation.

www.rosenmethod.org This is the main site for the Rosen Institute. The site offers information about Rosen method bodywork and its goals and methods. There is also information about how to receive training in the Rosen method and where to find a practitioner in your area.

www.feldenkraisglobal.com This is the site of the Reese Movement Institute. Information is available about the Feldenkrais method and about the classes and training offered at the institute. Recorded tapes for the lessons in this book are also available from this site. There are links to the main site for the Feldenkrais method and suggestions for finding a practitioner in your area.

www.waba.edu This is the main site for the World Aquatic Bodywork Association. Information is available about Watsu and other water-based bodywork methods. One can find information about receiving training, taking classes, and finding a practitioner in your area.

www.careeratyourfingertips.com/bodywork .htm/ This site is a general source of career information with specific information about careers in bodywork. It provides links to the Rosen Institute, Feldenkrais, and Watsu organizations, as well as many other methods that may deal directly or indirectly with reexperiencing infant and fetal development as well as healing traumas associated with those developmental periods.

GLOSSARY

Accommodation A change in individual functioning and skill in order to meet new environmental demands.

Adaptation The process of becoming better suited to survive and succeed in a particular environment.

Anal stage A period that begins sometime in the second year of life when the primary sensitive zone becomes the anal region of the body.

Assimilation The adaptive utilization of those aspects of the environment that are within the limits of our skills and biological processing capacities.

Association The psychological linkage between a stimulus and a response that occur in the environment at about the same time.

Behavior genetics   The study of between-individual variability in phenotypes as a result of variability in environments or in genotypes.

Bodymind centering   A somatic awareness technique in which verbal directions and touch are used to guide people step by step through the reexperiencing of the sensorimotor stages of prenatal and infant development.

Butterfly effect   The idea that small effects can have major consequences as they are amplified in a dynamic system, with the implication that it is impossible to trace the system backward in time to isolate single causes for later changes in the system.

Chaos   A mathematical concept that expresses the property of complex systems of having some general structure that repeats over time but never in exactly the same way.

Classical conditioning   Learning by association; the linking together of a stimulus and a response occurring at the same time.

Clinical infant   The view of infant experience that emerges from therapeutic encounters with children and adults.

Co-construction   The process by which what one knows depends upon how one acts on the environment and how the environment responds to those actions.

Conceptual memories   Memories of specific categories for type of event ("I was left alone"), time ("when I was five years old"), and place ("at the preschool"); recall about an event that is communicated in the form of a verbal narrative or story.

Constructivist theory   A theory in which knowledge is built up by the child's own action rather than being imposed on the child from the outside.

Co-regulation   A form of self-organization as applied to interpersonal communication that involves continuous mutual adjustment and creativity.

Core self   The experience of being an active agent that does things in the world, has feelings, and has a history of prior experiences.

Critical period   A relatively short, well-defined period in the life cycle when the individual is particularly receptive to certain kinds of environmental stimulation; if that stimulation is not received, the individual is not likely to profit from later exposure to similar stimuli, and other normal developmental processes may be disrupted.

Determinism   The idea that all events have a cause and that that cause can be found with enough scientific work.

Deviation-amplifying feedback   Feedback that drastically changes a system as a result of a small deviation.

Deviation-correcting feedback   Feedback that maintains a system's characteristics over time in spite of small deviations.

Direct transaction   A transaction that occurs as part of a social relationship in which the child is an active participant: the infant-parent, infant-peer, or infant-sibling relationship.

Disequilibrium   The infant's experience during failures at adaptation; the motivational force that leads the infant to adapt by means of assimilation and accommodation.

Ecology of human development   The physical and social environments in which children develop.

Ego   The sum total of the person's regulatory functions, which includes coping, information processing, and emotions; the ego mediates between the person's needs and the demands of the environment.

Emergent self   The awareness of how different movements, sensations, and feelings cohere into recognizable psychological states.

Exosystem   Includes systems that do not contain the developing child but that do affect the child's well-being, such as the parent's work, the government, and the economy.

Extinction   The elimination of learned behavior by ceasing to reinforce the behavior.

Feedback   A process by which components of a system have an effect on their own behavior during their transactions with other components.

Feldenkrais method   A system of somatic awareness and movement education that reawakens, develops, and organizes capacities for kinesthetic (sensorimotor) learning.

Frames   Repeating patterns of co-activity such as greetings, parent-infant games like peekaboo, or particular topics of conversation between a couple.

Free association   A method of recovering unconscious memories by having clients lie down and encouraging them to relax in an environment safe enough to say anything without fear of retribution or judgment.

Genotype   The set of chemical messages within the DNA that direct the formation of protein within a cell nucleus; an individual's genetic inheritance.

Guided participation   Phases in the development of transmission of a cultural skill from the parent to the child.

Heritability   The proportion of individual variability in a group that can be explained as owing primarily to individual differences in genetic make-up.

Id   The uninhibited expression of the individual's basic needs; during infancy, these needs are centered primarily around the oral and anal zones.

Imprinting   A process in which the young of some animal species become attached to an object or person by means of a brief exposure to that object or person.

Indeterminism   The idea that not everything a person does, and not every turn in that person's development, can be predicted from known laws or principles.

Infant psychiatry   The application of clinical psychology to work with infants and their families.

Infantile amnesia   The lack of adult conceptual memory of one's life before the age of two years.

Macrosystem   The system of beliefs, values, and rules of the society and culture.

Mediated transaction   A transaction that occurs when the infant affects or is affected by people with whom the infant does not share an active relationship.

Mesosystem   The system of relationships between the settings in which children live, such as between the home and the school setting.

Microsystem   The system of interpersonal relationships between the child and other people.

Natural selection   The theory of the evolution of species, proposed by Charles Darwin, in which genetic changes are explained by different survival rates of offspring that have characteristics that are better or less well suited to the environment.

Negative feedback   Feedback that maintains a system's characteristics over time in spite of small deviations.

Negative reinforcer   The absence of a consequence of an action that increases the frequency of that action.

Observational learning   Learning without reinforcement or association by watching how others perform in certain situations.

Observed infant   A view of infant experience that derives from scientific observations on infant behavior.

Operant conditioning   An increase in the likelihood that a particular response will occur following a reinforcement of that response.

Oral stage   The period during the first eighteen months of life when the infant is particularly aware of sensations of pleasure and displeasure in the mouth region through activities such as sucking, chewing, biting, and swallowing.

Organic learning   The use of all one's senses and every part of the body in the process of learning new movements.

Participatory memories   Memories that are in the form of feeling or sensation rather than being conceptualized as a specific incident; composed of emotions, desires, and a sense of familiarity, but without any specific time or place.

Phenotype   The functioning organism; everything other than the DNA.

Positive feedback   Feedback that drastically alters a system as a result of a small deviation.

Positive reinforcer   A consequence of an action that increases the probability of that action in the future.

Probabilistic   Refers to the nondeterministic influence of the genotype over the phenotype. A particular genotype will not lead to a specific phenotype for all individuals.

Psychoanalysis   The use of free association in psychotherapy leading to the interpretation of unconscious and participatory memories from the perspective of early childhood experiences.

Punishment A consequence that decreases the frequency of the behavior that it follows.

Reinforcer An environmental stimulus that, when it appears following a specific individual response, increases the likelihood that the response will occur again.

Rosen method A somatic awareness approach that uses listening to the client's body with gentle touch and to the words they use to describe their experience, allowing the client to relax, relieve pain, and breathe more easily.

Schemes The currently available set of skills and knowledge that a person has.

Scientific theory A system of concepts that explains the observable world with structures, processes, or mechanisms that are presumed to exist but that cannot be observed directly.

Self-organization The emergence of organized patterns and processes in dynamic systems due to the mutual influences of each element of the system on the others.

Sensorimotor substage According to Piaget, the first two years of life, in which the child "understands" the world through action and sensation rather than through concepts and ideas.

Shared environment That part of the family environment that contributes in the same way to the development of more than one sibling.

Somatic Individuals' conscious awareness of the experiences of their bodies.

Somatic awareness approaches Clinical approaches that use talk, body movement, and touch as a way to access the participatory memories of early childhood.

Species-specific behavior Behavior patterns that occur only in one species and are the result of evolution by natural selection.

Subjective self A sense of self that involves an awareness of the feelings and experiences of others and of its dependence upon and attachment to others.

System A set of interrelated components that are governed by feedback processes and that exchange information and material between themselves and between the environment and themselves.

Transaction The process by which systems components affect each other.

Unconscious That part of the self that is not remembered during ordinary waking states.

Verbal self That part of the self that uses language to talk about inner states and to construct a coherent identity in the company of other people.

Watsu A somatic awareness technique in which the practitioner floats the client in a pool of warm water, using stretching and water resistance to create a state of relaxation.

Zone of proximal development Those infant skills that are in the process of developing and are the most uncertain.

Chapter 3

Before Birth:
Prenatal Behavior
and Development

CHAPTER OVERVIEW AND OUTLINE

Conception and Fertility

What is the process of fertilization? What causes infertility and how can it be treated? What are the most common methods of contraception?

Developmental Processes before Birth

What are the stages of prenatal development? What are the main behavioral, physical, and psychological characteristics of each stage?

Individual Differences in Prenatal Development

In what ways do fetuses differ? What are the major causes of individual differences? What types of problems can occur during prenatal development?

Family and Society

What are the physical and psychological aspects of the mother's adaptation to being pregnant? How do fathers and siblings adapt to the pregnancy?

Applications: Family Planning

How is the birth rate controlled in different countries? How do cultural differences affect choices of contraceptive methods?

Although many people think of birth as the beginning of life, it is now known that much of what takes place in the 9-month period of gestation has important effects on subsequent development. During prenatal development, all of the major organ systems of the body, including the brain, undergo rapid development. It is just at the point of the most accelerated development that an organ is most susceptible to environmental influences.

As we shall see in this chapter, the womb—uterus and placenta—is not an impenetrable shield of nurture and security. The placenta functions as a link between mother and fetus. In some cases, the placenta becomes a wonderfully adept censor, keeping potentially harmful substances from crossing into the immature fetal circulatory system. Often, however, it does not. The womb is an environment, albeit a very special and uniquely suitable environment, to which the developing person must adapt during this phase of their lives. Even variations of the prenatal environment within the normal range contribute to individual differences between fetuses, some of which have long-term effects on the form of body structures, movement patterns, and sensory awareness.

This chapter will cover the development of the fetus from conception until the last month of pregnancy. In the first section, we discuss conception and heredity. The next section covers the stages of prenatal development. This is followed by a section on individual differences between fetuses and prenatal risk, including such topics as genetic and chromosomal disorders, teratology, and genetic counseling. The last section of the chapter addresses physical and psychological changes in the mother and the response of the rest of the family to her pregnancy.

Conception and Fertility

Conception

Human development begins with **conception,** the union of a female **ovum** and a male **spermatozoon.**

Collectively, spermatozoa and ova are known as **gametes.** During sexual intercourse, many millions of sperm cells enter the vagina. These cells are propelled through the uterus and into the Fallopian tubes, partly via the pumping action of the vaginal and uterine muscles and partly by the swimming movements of the spermatozoa. Only a few hundred sperm cells will reach the Fallopian tubes, and even those will die if they do not encounter an ovum within 24 to 48 hours.

Ova are produced in the ovaries, usually one for each menstrual cycle. Adult females will have about 350 ovulations over approximately 30 years of fertility. The ovum is covered with small hairlike appendages that can be dissolved by an enzyme secreted by the spermatozoa, and it eventually decomposes if it does not encounter a sperm cell. For fertilization to take place, many spermatozoa must bind to the surface of the ovum, after which an opening is made at random for the entrance of a single sperm cell. Once that sperm cell enters the ovum, a chemical reaction occurs to prevent other sperm cells from entering. The fertilized ovum is called a **zygote.**

Fertility

The ability to contribute successfully to fertilization or conception is called **fertility.** Male fertility begins at puberty and, for most males, lasts their entire life. Female fertility begins at puberty and lasts until menopause, the cessation of menstrual cycling that occurs when the woman is about 50 years old.

All of a girl's ova are already formed in her ovary at birth, but they remain immature until the girl reaches puberty and begins to menstruate. Near the end of each menstrual period, the time during the menstrual cycle when vaginal bleeding occurs, the pituitary gland secretes a hormone that allows one of the immature ova to ripen. This event leads to the secretion of estrogen, which stimulates the development of a lining in the uterus that will nourish a possible fertilized ovum. About 14 days after the onset of the menstrual period, the ovum is ready to be fertilized as it makes its way from the ovary to the Fallopian tubes. The zygote will journey to the uterus, where it becomes implanted in the newly formed uterine lining. If fertilization does not occur, the uterine lining is discharged through the vagina during the next menstrual period.

In some cases, more than one ovum ripens. If two ova are fertilized, two different zygotes, called fraternal or **dizygotic (DZ) twins,** develop. Identical or **monozygotic (MZ) twins** develop when the fertilized zygote divides and splits into two separate zygotes. Twinning happens in about 1 in 80 pregnancies. About three-fourths of the twins are MZ twins, and the rest are DZ twins. Since they split from the same zygote, MZ twins share identical sets of genetic material, while DZ twins are no more related than any two siblings from the same mother and father. Triplets occur in 1 out of 6,400 births, while quadruplets happen in 1 out of 512,000 births. Triplets and quadruplets can be either MZ or DZ or some combination.

Boys are not born with spermatozoa. Instead, the onset of puberty in the male triggers the production of hormones that stimulate the manufacture of about 2 million sperm cells per day for the rest of his life. Male fertility, therefore, is not cyclic as female fertility is. During ejaculation, 2 to 4 million sperm cells are expelled through the penis in a liquid medium called seminal fluid or semen. The testes produce the sperm, and the prostate gland and seminal vesicles produce the semen.

Infertility

During a female's childbearing years, about one in six couples suffers from **infertility:** they are unable to conceive successfully for at least one year. Either the male or the female, or both, may be infertile. Female infertility is usually caused by a failure to ovulate (that is, the failure of the immature ova to ripen) or by some process that impedes the journey of the ripened ovum from the ovary to the Fallopian tubes. Failure to ovulate can be caused by a number of treatable factors, such as excessive exercise or weight loss, obesity, some sexually transmitted diseases, excessive alcohol use, exposure to toxic chemicals, and hormonal imbalances (Ford, MacCormac, & Hiller, 1994; Grodstein, Goldman, & Cramer, 1994). Changes in diet, exercise, and hormonal treatments, called fertility drugs, can be used. In cases of blockage, both drugs and surgery have been tried. Fertility drugs sometimes lead to

twinning and multiple births because they stimulate ovulation.

Causes of male infertility include using marijuana and cigarettes, wearing excessively tight underwear, taking hot baths or saunas, inability to maintain an erection, and premature ejaculation or failure to ejaculate (Howard, 1995). These can be treated with changes in behavior and sex therapies. Male infertility may also be caused by underdeveloped testes, prior injuries, and some childhood diseases. Some of these problems may not be treatable.

Enhancing Fertility

The chances of a successful conception can be improved by timing sexual intercourse to the period of the menstrual cycle when ovulation is taking place. Usually, this period lasts about 5 or 6 days before the day of ovulation (Wilcox, Weinberg, & Baird, 1995). Couples can monitor ovulation daily by recording the woman's body temperature, which rises about 1 degree Fahrenheit during ovulation. Ovulation can also be monitored by charting the changes in color, amount, and consistency of the cervical mucus. Kits are now sold in drugstores to monitor changes in hormone levels by testing urine samples.

Lovemaking and sexual intercourse should be a relaxed experience for the couple. Fertility is also enhanced if both partners are in good physical health, maintain appropriate body weight, eat nutritious diets, exercise regularly, and avoid excessive smoking and drinking. Males should avoid or reduce the use of hot tubs and saunas to prevent elevation of temperature around the testes.

If these natural methods fail and standard drug and surgical treatments for infertility are not successful, couples can choose several more expensive and higher-risk measures. The approach recommended by physicians is artificial insemination, in which sperm from the father or another male donor is transferred directly to the mother's fallopian tubes (Velde & Cohlen, 1999).

If artificial insemination fails, another approach is called **in vitro fertilization,** sometimes referred to as *assisted reproductive technology.* In cases where healthy ova ripen but cannot pass to the Fallopian tubes, one of the mother's ova is surgically removed and joined with spermatozoa from the father in a sterile biological medium. After fertilization has taken place and the zygote has made a few cell divisions (it is now called an *embryo;* see below), it is surgically implanted into the mother's uterus.

The failure rate for in vitro fertilization can be as high as 30%. Couples who choose these methods have a strong desire for children. One or more such failures can lead to depression and to doubt about themselves and their marriage. Because of the uncertainty of the procedure, many IVF couples delay their psychological preparation for parenthood (McMahon, Tennant, Ungerer, & Saunders, 1999; see the "Family and Society" section in this chapter). These couples require empathy and support (Osofsky, Rosenthal, & Butterbaugh, 1999). On the other hand, if the fertilization procedure is successful, long-term pregnancy outcomes for embryos fertilized in vitro are similar to those of natural conceptions, with the exception that there are more multiple births with in vitro fertilization (Winston & Handyside, 1993). After birth, babies conceived in vitro are no more likely to have medical problems than are normally conceived infants (Leslie, Gibson, McMahon, Tennant, & Saunders, 1998).

There are many variations of in vitro fertilization. In some cases, more than one ovum may be fertilized at a time. This procedure is reasonably common because the success rate for pregnancy is higher if more than one embryo is implanted. Also, it may take many menstrual cycles for success to be achieved. If a woman needs radiation treatments for cancer that might damage her ova, or if she is approaching the end of her reproductive years and has not yet conceived, she may wish to have some of her ova removed for fertilization. These excess embryos are frozen in a process called **embryo cryopreservation.** This method is still experimental because the data on long-term pregnancy outcomes are still insufficient (Winston & Handyside, 1993), although it can be useful when other approaches fail (Grover & Permezel, 1994). If sperm function too poorly to break down the lining of the ovum, they can be injected directly into the ovum using **sperm microinjection,** which has shown good success rates.

In other variations of in vitro fertilization, gametes from a donor may be substituted for those of the parent who cannot produce his or her own.

Donors can be family members, friends, or anonymous public donors (Winston & Handyside, 1993). An in vitro zygote from the mother and father can also be implanted into the uterus of another woman, called a **surrogate mother,** who carries the infant until birth and then gives the baby to the parents who contributed the zygote. This practice is more controversial, however, and is rarely used.

Generally, in vitro fertilization is very expensive, ranging from $60,000 up to almost $1 million, depending on the problems and the number of unsuccessful cycles (Neumann, Gharib, & Weinstein, 1994). About 14% of attempts lead to successful births; the success rate is higher if two zygotes are transferred to the mother's uterus (Winston & Handyside, 1993). Two seems to be the optimal number, since more than two zygotes does not increase the chances of conception but does increase the chance of multiple births (Templeton & Morris, 1998).

What are the social issues related to in vitro fertilization methods? Advances in technology to treat infertility have raised new social issues about the nature of conception, birth, and parenthood. If the genetic parents contribute the embryo but a surrogate mother carries the baby to birth, whose child is it?

Although some states in the United States have laws regulating contracts between the genetic parents and the surrogate, courts have struggled with lawsuits from surrogate mothers who wanted to retain custody of the child (Hansen, 1993). In 1993 Florida passed a statute, the Florida Assisted Reproductive Technology Act, that grants parental rights under two conditions: parents are those who contribute the child's genetic inheritance and those who hold the original written intent to be the child's parents (Maun, Williams, Graber, & Myers, 1994). This law also applies to frozen embryos, which may be used later by the genetic parents or by others.

The underlying premise of this law and others like it is that parenting is a matter of choice rather than destiny. In the freedom-granting politics of the United States, people have come to believe that choosing to have or not to have a child is a right, even if factors such as disease, age, or infertility conspire against it (R. Mead, 1999). As new methods for manipulating reproductive outcomes are invented, each individual and the society as a whole will have to struggle with the morality of such freedoms.

What if parents have fertilized zygotes frozen and then divorce? In one New York case, the mother wanted to use her eggs to get pregnant, but her ex-husband objected. New York courts ruled in the husband's favor, suggesting that parents who undergo this procedure should decide what happens to the zygotes in the event of a separation (Associated Press, May 8, 1998). In Los Angeles, a woman's husband, a 30-year-old man, died suddenly of an allergic reaction. Doctors extracted the sperm from his testicles after death, froze them, and used them to impregnate the wife 15 months later. She had a normal pregnancy and birth (Associated Press, March 28, 1999).

Some women cannot produce healthy ova. A lively business of egg donation has developed during the past few years. Donors are catalogued on the Internet or in private agencies in order to be matched to infertile couples. One recent newspaper ad read: "Egg donor needed. You must be at least 5′10″ and have a 1400+ SAT score." The couple was offering $50,000 for the donation. Such ads appeal to young women with financial needs, since most donors receive considerably less money. Donating eggs is a painful and risky procedure requiring the donor to be injected with large doses of hormones that substantially alter her body chemistry and functioning. The long-term effects on donors' health and fertility are currently unknown. In addition, egg and sperm donation raises the possibility that couples can introduce desired genetic traits into their family line, especially privileged, primarily Caucasian families, who can afford the high cost (R. Mead, 1999). On the other hand, behavior genetics research (see Chapter 2) shows that the effects of genes are probabilistic, meaning that the child may have not have the same phenotype (body form or intelligence, for example) as the donating parents.

We now have the technology to implant postmenopausal women with their own previously frozen embryos or the embryo of a donor couple. Medical evidence shows that women between the ages of 50 and 60 are just as capable of carrying a pregnancy to birth as younger women, although the risks of pregnancy to the mother are somewhat higher. In a survey conducted in Australia, only 38% of respondents from a representative sample approved of the donation of embryos to postmenopausal women (Bowman & Saunders, 1994). Society will have to ponder the question of what happens to children in middle childhood and adolescence when their parents are of an advanced age and perhaps less capable of the physical demands of parenting (Winston & Handyside, 1993). On the other hand, as older adult parents become more common, they may reveal forms of resilience in older adults that have never been observed.

Recall that during prenatal development, a lifetime supply of ova is formed inside the ovaries of female fetuses. Due to a shortage of donor ova for women needing transplants for in vitro fertilization, a fertility laboratory in Great Britain implanted ova from an aborted fetus into an infertile woman. On the one hand, this method could give new hope to infertile women and also in some ways replace the loss of the aborted fetus. On the other hand, it raises the possibility of "fetus farming," where women would conceive infants only to have an abortion and sell the fetus for profit.

Some of the social, legal and ethical problems of these technologies might be eliminated if human cloning was available. **Cloning** is a method of creating a zygote by removing the donor mother's DNA from the ova and implanting the DNA from any cell in the body of another person—for example, the intended mother or father. This bypasses the need to use a particular person's ova or sperm. The cloned zygote is genetically identical to the adult DNA donor. Currently, cloning has been successful in a few animal species but is against the law for humans. If the techniques are perfected, cloning may be used simply to grow tissues or organs needed to implant in an ailing adult donor from whom the genetic material was harvested. Or it could be used to create babies with the particular characteristics of the DNA donor. Cloning may solve some problems, but it raises others. Society is only beginning to grasp the ethical issues related to these new technologies (see also the later section on ethical issues in genetic counseling).

Controlling Fertility: Contraception

One of the simplest and least expensive methods of contraception is called **natural family planning.** The same methods used to chart ovulation for the purpose of enhancing fertility can also tell a couple when to avoid intercourse if they wish not to conceive. If used properly and with the guidance of a physician or family planning counselor, natural family planning can be very successful.

A limited number of other options for contraception are also available. Methods that work prior to fertilization include male or female sterilization, which prevents the production or transport of gametes (used by 15% of couples); birth control pills, which prevent ovulation (used by 39%); condoms and diaphragms, which block the passage of sperm to the vagina (used by 25%); and spermicides (foams, sponges, and suppositories), which kill sperm before they can fertilize and are often used in combination with other methods (Forrest & Fordyce, 1993b).

Several methods that work after fertilization are also available. The intrauterine device (IUD) prevents the zygote from implanting in the uterine wall. A drug known as RU-486, the so-called abortion pill, causes the uterine lining to be expelled, taking the embryo with it. The pill must be followed 2 days later by an additional drug that causes the uterus to contract and complete the expulsion process. Finally, there is the Preven Kit for emergency contraception, approved by the FDA in 1997. It is a series of birth control pills taken for up to 5 days within 72 hours after having unprotected sex. Each of these methods has advantages and disadvantages that depend upon one's religious beliefs, values, convenience, and medical conditions and risks. Couples should consult their doctors or family planning clinics for specific advice and information.

The World Health Organization reports that about one-quarter of pregnancies worldwide are unwanted, and about 50 million of these end in abortion each year. Although it is theoretically possible to develop new methods of contraception as advanced as those used for in vitro fertilization, relatively little research has been done on new contraceptive methods during the past 20 years.

If there is a need for more contraception research, why is it not being done? The reason seems to be that most of the research on fertility and infertility is done in wealthier countries, where drug companies can make considerably more profit from infertility treatments than from contraception (R. F. Service, 1994). Individuals in advanced countries are not satisfied with existing contraception methods, however, and would like to see more research on new methods (Rosenfeld, Zahorik, Saint, & Murphy, 1993). See the "Applications" section of this chapter for a longer discussion of family planning in different countries.

Developmental Processes before Birth

It is difficult to see how a fully developed human can emerge from its beginnings as a zygote. At the start of development, several processes are important in inducing developmental change. One process comes from inside the cells themselves, and another relates to the cells' interactions with the environment inside the mother's body. In this section, I review the stages of prenatal development that are common to all humans. In the next section, we discuss individual differences in prenatal development.

The Period of the Zygote

Within the cell nucleus, the genetic material is in the form of a spiral-shaped molecule called deoxyribonucleic acid **(DNA).** Inside this spiral are locations at which any one of a number of different types of smaller molecules called *bases* may be attached. The DNA is segmented into sections, each of which contains a different set of bases. Each segment is called a **gene.** The genes are arranged in long strings, much like beads on a necklace, into structures called **chromosomes.**

Chromosomes can be seen under a microscope, as shown in Figure 3.1. Most chromosomes look

(a)   (b)

Figure 3.1
Human Chromosome Pairs before and after Karyotyping

Humans have 23 pairs of chromosomes, and in the karyotype, the pairs have been matched. One member of each pair is from the mother and one is from the father. The X chromosome of the 23rd pair is shown in the middle of the bottom row.

Source: Courtesy of Dr. J. Aznar.

like the letter X. The X is made up of two strands that are joined near their middle. The genes can be seen in Figure 3.1 as alternating bands of light and dark. Chromosomes come in matched pairs, as shown in part *(b)* of Figure 3.1. This arrangement of chromosomes into pairs is achieved by cutting the photo in part *(a)* and placing the chromosomes in order. The rearranged photo is called a **karyotype.** Note that chromosomes come in different sizes and that a single Y-shaped chromosome on the 23rd pair contains the genetic code for a male.

Every cell in one's body, except for the gametes, contains 46 chromosomes, representing about 1 million bits of genetic information. Each of the body's cells contains the same set of genes and chromosomes. Each gamete normally contains only 23 chromosomes. The 46 chromosomes in most body cells represent 23 pairs.

Individual cells develop by dividing into two identical daughter cells. During **mitosis,** each chromosome within the cell nucleus makes a copy of itself before cell division occurs. The original set of chromosomes and their identical copies do not get mixed up: each set pushes away from the other until they occupy opposite sides of the nucleus. The cell will divide into two only after this physical sepa-

ration of the two identical sets of chromosomes occurs (McIntosh & Koonce, 1989).

Although every cell in an individual's body carries the same set of genes and chromosomes, every individual has a slightly different set. This genetic variability arises first during the creation of the gametes. In the special biological environment of the female ovaries and the male testicles, cells divide in the absence of the chromosome copying process that is characteristic of mitosis. In **meiosis,** each daughter cell contains only 23 chromosomes. When sperm and ovum unite during fertilization, the resulting zygote will have a unique combination of 46 chromosomes, half from the mother and half from the father. Since each individual gamete contains a slightly different set of chromosomes and genes and the particular pair that unite for fertilization is random, the number of genetically different individuals is enormous. This explains how siblings can be genetically different.

Every individual begins life as a zygote that progresses through the initial state of mitosis. As a result of mitosis, the number of cells in the developing organism grows rapidly, doubling every few hours. Because mitosis is an exact copying process, each of these cells has the same genetic material.

One of the great mysteries of early development is how, given identical genes in each cell, the different tissues and structures—muscles, blood, sensory receptors, and so on—can develop. The biologist Waddington expressed it thus:

a simple lump of jelly . . . eventually turns into a recognizable small plant or worm or insect or some other type of organism. Nothing else that one can see puts on a performance which is both so apparently simple and spontaneous and yet, when you think about it, so mysterious. (Waddington, 1966, p. v)

To find some solutions to this mystery, we have to go outside the cell and examine its environment.

Research on nonhuman prenatal development has shown that in almost all species of animals, the cells of the zygote form a spherelike cluster (Sameroff, 1984). Because some of the cells are on the surface and some on the interior of the sphere, these different regions are in contact with different environments. The interior cells are next to other cells like themselves, while the exterior cells will have a different cellular environment on each side.

Each of these environments exposes the cell to different molecules that may be transported into the cell from the neighboring cells. In addition, physical forces on the cell will cause it to produce specific molecules in the cell's body. When these molecules enter the cell nucleus, they activate some of the cell's genes and inhibit the action of others. When the genes are activated, they begin to send chemical messages back out to the main cell body, changing the cell's structural characteristics. This is the beginning of the process of differentiation of the properties of the interior cells from those of the exterior cells.

As cell division proceeds, cells form groups in which distinct molecular processes occur. Boundaries form between the different groups that prevent the processes of one group from leaking into another (Trevarthen, 1973). Thus, the development of the phenotype—the cell's specific characteristic as neuron or muscle—is the result of a constant and dynamic interaction between the genotype and the intra- and extracellular environment (Antonelli, 1985).

The effect of the cell's environment has been shown in a series of experiments on nonhuman em-

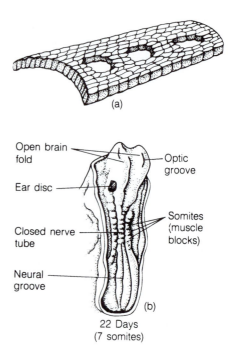

Figure 3.2
Creation of a Structure

(a) During the process of cell differentiation, some cells begin to create structures. The early formation of a tube with holes is shown. The cells become less elastic on one side and more elastic on the other, causing the sheet of cells to bend. Differential rigidity around the region of the holes can create spaces between cells. **(b)** In the 22-day-old embryo, such a tube structure will eventually become the spinal cord and spine.

Source: C. Trevarthen, Neurological development and the growth of psychological functions, 1980. In J. Sants, *Developmental psychology and society*, 46–95. New York: St. Martin's Press. Copyright © by J. Sants. Reprinted by permission of St. Martin's Press, Inc.

bryos. Early in the process of the formation of different regions, cells can be removed from one region and placed in an entirely different one. After a few cell divisions, the transplanted cells resemble the region in which they were placed, not the region that they came from (Spemann, 1938; Ebert & Sussex, 1970).

As cells begin to differentiate into distinct regions, physical structures begin to form. The most common type of embryonic structure is the formation of a tube. Figure 3.2 shows how this occurs. In *(a)*, cells on the top of the sheet have been genetically activated to reproduce cells with the ability to stretch. Cells on the bottom of the sheet have been genetically activated to produce contraction. As cells divide and increased differential stretching and contracting occur, the sheet eventually curls into a tube. Tubes can also be formed when a ball of cells contracts in the center, eventually making a kind of doughnut shape. In vertebrate animals, one of the early-forming tubular structures is the spinal cord and spine (see Figure 3.2(b)).

It is usually assumed that development is a continuous series of acquisitions along the road to maturity. Prenatal development does show a number of aspects that are continuous, but there are also instances in which certain structures form only to disappear at a later point. The types of prenatal changes are as follows (Meredith, 1975).

Changes in kind. One of the most noticeable prenatal changes is the gradual differentiation of multiple kinds of tissue from the relatively uniform zygote. Certain structures also emerge and disappear. For example, the pronephros, the precursor of the kidney, is only there for 2 weeks, gill arches are present for three weeks, an external tail appears and disappears between the second and fourth months, and finger pads are seen between the third and fifth months.

Changes in number. Depending upon the particular structure or organ, cell numbers increase and decrease over time. Obviously, the overall number of cells continues to increase.

Changes in position. The relative orientation and position of the organs in the fetus change. When the heart is formed, for example, it lies near what will become the face. Over time it moves lower, more toward the back, and rotates and tilts. Other organs and limbs undertake their own particular paths of migration.

Changes in size. Changes in size vary with the time and location of the organ. During the second month, the head and neck regions grow faster (**cephalocaudal development**), there is more growth near the spine than in the front (**dorsoventral development**), and the growth rate is

higher near the shoulders and hips than near the extremities (**proximodistal development**). As development proceeds, these trends reverse.

Changes in shape. Immediately after fertilization, the organism has an oval shape. Several weeks later, its shape is elongated and is mostly head. There are also changes in the shape of cells and organs.

What Are the Major Phases of Prenatal Development?

The prenatal period is usually divided into three parts: the zygote, the embryo, and the fetus. The period of the zygote begins at the time the ovum is fertilized and lasts about 2 weeks, or until the ovum is implanted in the uterine wall. The period of the **embryo** begins about 2 weeks after fertilization and extends until the end of the second month, at which time the embryo is designated a **fetus.** This designation is applied when the organism begins to resemble a human in its external features and the bones begin to harden into a more rigid skeletal structure. In this book, the fetal period will be divided into three phases (7–16 weeks, 17–22 weeks, and 23–36 weeks). These divisions correspond to changes in structure and behavior that will be explained later. The period of human gestation lasts about 38 weeks, but this can vary from between 36 and 40 weeks for a full-term infant.

In the first half week, the zygote divides to about 20 cells, and at the end of the week, some differentiation can be noted. At the end of the second week, there is a clearly defined **embryonic disk** that lies between the **amniotic sac** and the **yolk sac,** which themselves have differentiated out of the original zygote. This organism is now called the **blastocyst,** and it implants itself in the lining of the uterus sometime during the third week. The blastocyst, still only $\frac{1}{125}$ of an inch long, triggers the secretion of hormones that inhibit menstruation. As the concentration of these hormones, known as **human chorionic gonadotropin (HCG),** increases, they can be detected in the urine; they are used in laboratory pregnancy tests (see Figure 3.3).

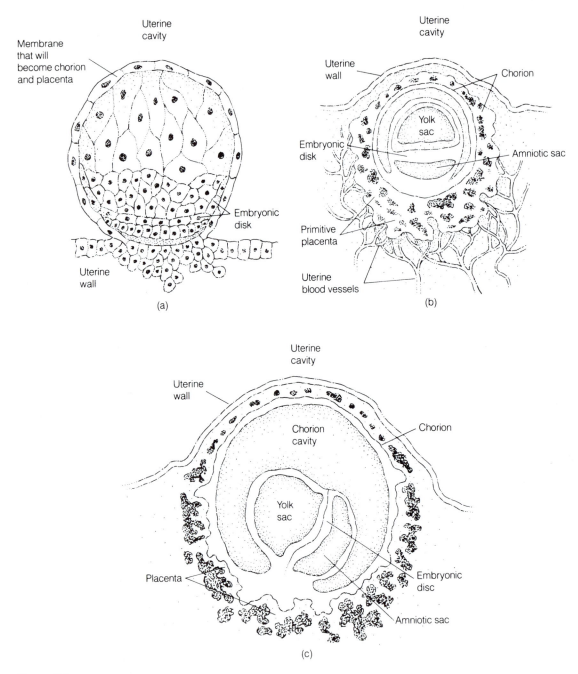

Figure 3.3
Early Stages of Prenatal Development

(a) Blastocyst stage: The fertilized egg (zygote) has made its way down the fallopian tube and has undergone repeated cell division and multiplication on the way. It attaches to the uterine lining and begins to grow into the uterine wall in search of nutrients. **(b), (c)** Cell division and differentiation continue at a rapid pace, and specific structures begin to take shape. The developing organism is now a bulge on the uterine wall. **(d), (e)** Embryo stage: Gradually, the form of the embryo takes shape. By the end of the 1st month, the head and the arm and leg buds are visible, a primitive heart has started to pump, and other organs are beginning to develop. At this stage, the human embryo closely resembles the embryos of most other animals.

Source: M. J. Gander & H. W. Gardiner, *Child and adolescent development,* 1981, p. 63. Boston: Little, Brown. Copyright © by M. J. Gander & H. W. Gardiner. Reprinted by permission of the publisher.

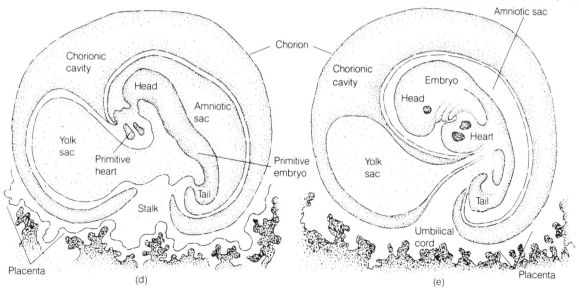

(d)   (e)

The Period of the Embryo

The blastocyst structure—the embryonic disk, the yolk sac, and the amniotic sac—will differentiate further. The embryonic disk differentiates into three layers. The **endoderm** eventually becomes part of the digestive, urinary, and respiratory systems. The **mesoderm** will become the muscles, bone, circulatory system, and reproductive system. The **ectoderm** will become the central nervous system and brain, the sense organs, and the skin, hair, nails, and teeth.

The yolk sac produces blood cells and becomes part of the liver, spleen, and bone marrow, all of which later produce blood cells. By the end of the embryonic period, the yolk sac has disappeared. The amniotic sac persists throughout gestation. It grows to cover the embryo and contains the amniotic fluid, which provides a cushion for the fetus against sudden movements of the mother's body.

Surrounding all of these developments is a membrane called the **chorion.** The placenta, which forms from the outer surface of the chorion, functions as a link between the bloodstreams of mother and embryo, which are not directly connected. The placenta passes nutrients and oxygen from the mother's blood to the fetus's through the umbilical cord and serves to eliminate the fetal wastes via the mother's bloodstream. The fetus is in the upright position throughout most of the pregnancy, so there is no danger of the cord choking the fetus because of its location, the effect of gravity, and the relative inflexibility of the cord from the pressure of the blood circulating in it (like a hose with the water turned on). The risk of choking increases at birth because the fetus has changed positions— head down for delivery—and the head may now come in contact with the cord.

By the third week, one can distinguish the head and primitive circulatory and skeletal systems. By the end of the first month, the heart is beating, and there are cavities for the ears, nose, and mouth (see Figure 3.4). The head is large relative to the rest of the body and has gill arches, and the body has upper limb buds and a small tail. At this point the embryo may be between 3 and 5 millimeters (⅙ inch) long.

Now development is occurring very rapidly. In the next 2 weeks, the beginnings of the eyes, nose, lungs, and liver grow, and bones begin to form. The gill structures are transformed into bones of the inner ear, the neck, and cartilage of the larynx, as well as the eustachian tubes, thyroid and thymus glands, and the trachea. By 6 weeks, the limbs are beginning to differentiate rapidly, and fingers and toes will appear shortly. The tail is still present and

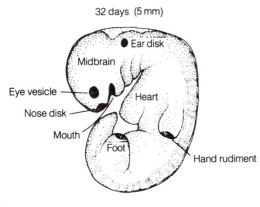

32 days (5 mm)

Ear disk
Midbrain
Eye vesicle
Nose disk
Mouth
Foot
Heart
Hand rudiment

Figure 3.4
Sensory Surfaces of a Human Embryo at Four Weeks
Source: Adapted from C. Trevarthen, *Behavioral embryology.* In E. C. Carterette
& M. P. Friedman, eds., *Handbook of Perception* (Vol. 3), 1973, p. 93. New York:
Academic Press. Adapted by permission of the publisher and author.

may comprise 15% of the embryo's total length of 12 millimeters (½ inch). The total weight is about 2 grams (¹⁄₁₄ ounce). About half of the weight of an 8-week-old embryo is in its head. It has all of the major organs except genital organs. It has a skeleton, eyebrows, knees, fingers, toes, and buds for teeth. Its rapid growth during this period makes the embryo more vulnerable to environmental risks (see the "Individual Differences in Prenatal Development" section below).

The first evidence of prenatal behavior is seen during the embryonic period in the movements of the muscles of the heart. The movements are jerky and spontaneous at first but gradually become more rhythmic as they pump blood cells between the heart, yolk sac, and chorion. The origin of these rhythmic movements is unknown, since they occur before the embryo has developed its nervous system (Hofer, 1981).

By the 32nd day of life (4½ weeks), the human embryo has a rudimentary sensory system (see Figure 3.4), but these sense organs are not yet connected to any nerve fibers. The first nerve cells form between 4 and 5 weeks, and the first spontaneous movements of the body occur a week later. By 7 weeks, the embryo is responsive to touch in the mouth region and will turn its head to the side (Trevarthen, 1973).

The Period of the Fetus: Seven to Sixteen Weeks

During the early part of the fetal period, a large number of spontaneous behaviors emerge, including mouth and limb movements. The fetus can be stimulated to act by a number of occurrences. These include maternal muscle contractions, sounds, and changes in maternal glucose and oxygen levels. The whole body may shudder or jerk when a sensitive area like the mouth is touched. As the fetus develops during this period, movement responses become more localized to the stimulated area, and specific reflexes emerge. Areas of reflex activity spread out to the peripheries of the body, including hands and feet.

The behavior developments during this fetal period are listed in Table 3.1. Fetal behavior can be observed using several different methods. **Ultrasound** is a method in which high-frequency sound waves are be bounced off the fetus's body to reveal the outline of the soft tissues (T. R. B. Johnson, Besinger, & Thomas, 1989). Ultrasound does not produce clear images of details, but it can record gross body movements and structures.

The purpose of these early fetal movements is not entirely clear. One experimental technique used with nonhuman embryos involves studying development after a fetal movement has been prevented from occurring, either through severing the nerve connections or by introducing a local anesthetic. Chick embryos that have been prevented from moving in this way were unable to move later. The muscles and nerves of these chicks developed normally, but their joints had become frozen into bone (Drachman & Coulombre, 1962). In another study with mice, inability to move the tongue embryonically resulted in deformation of the soft palate (Walker & Quarles, 1976). The relatively high incidence of cleft palate in infants of alcoholic mothers may be due to the anesthetic effects of alcohol on fetal mouth movements (Hofer, 1981). Other experiments have shown that movement in the fetus helps to induce the development of nerve endings in the sensory receptors.

Fetal movements may also serve to help the fetus survive as an organism trying to adapt to its environment. As the mother moves about during her

Table 3.1   Chronology of Fetal Behavior (First Period)

Age (Weeks)	Behavior
8	Stroking the mouth region produces flexion of upper torso and neck and extension of arms at the shoulder.
9	Some spontaneous movements. More of the whole body responds when the mouth is stroked. Startle reflex.
10½	Stroking the palms of the hands leads to partial closing of the fingers. Hiccups. Cyclic movements begin.
11	Other parts of face and arms become sensitive. Head rotation.
11½	Sensitive area spreads to upper chest. Hand-face contact.
12½	Specific reflexes appear: lip closure, swallowing, Babinski (see Chapter 5), squinting, sucking.
14	Entire body is sensitive, with more specific reflexes, such as rooting, grasping, finger closing. Body stretching.
15	Can maintain closure of the fingers (grasp) with muscle tightening, muscle strengthening. Yawning.
16	Frowning, grimacing.

Sources: D. Hooker, *The prenatal origin of behavior,* 1952. Lawrence: University of Kansas Press; T. R. B. Johnson, R. E. Besinger, & R. L. Thomas, The latest clues to fetal behavior and well-being, 1989. *Contemporary Pediatrics,* 66–84; C. D. Laughlin, Pre- and perinatal brain development and enculturation: A biogenetic structural approach, 1991. *Human Nature, 2,* 171–213; S. S. Robertson, Temporal organization in fetal and newborn movement, 1990. In H. Bloch & B. I. Bertenthal (Eds.), *Sensory-motor organizations and development in infancy and early childhood.* Netherlands: Kluwer Academic; C. Trevarthen, Behavioral embryology, 1973. In E. C. Carterette & M. P. Friedman (Eds.), *Handbook of perception: Vol. 3. Biology of perceptual systems.* New York: Academic Press.

The 6-week-old embryo is less than an inch long. It has a heartbeat, eye patches, a rudimentary brain, and a stomach and liver. At this age there are no connections between the brain and the rest of the body.

Just after three months, the fetus is about 2½ inches long and weighs ½ ounce. Most of the internal organs are formed, and fingers and toes can be seen. At this age, the fetus is capable of reflexive movements such as sucking, swallowing, grasping, and stretching.

Lennart Nilsson. Photo originally appeared in *Behold Man*, by Lennart Nilsson (Boston: Little, Brown, and Company)

normal routine, her movements can shift the position of the fetus, and her activity may change the chemistry and composition of the amniotic fluid and blood supply. Fetal movements may have the effect of reorienting the fetus to the most comfortable position for itself and maximizing its chances of being protected and well nourished (Gandelman, 1992). This is an example of a developmental systems transaction.

As tissues and structures form, spontaneous movements are produced. The movements induce further development in those same tissues and structures, which by feedback strengthens the movement pattern, making it more responsive and predictable.

Aside from behavioral development, physical development is also occurring. By about 16 weeks, the

fetus has become about 3 inches long and weighs about ½ ounce. During the period from 12 to 16 weeks, the external genitals form as a result of the interaction of the fetus's genes with the environment of the cells.

The genetic determination of sex occurs at conception. Females have two X-shaped chromosomes in the 23rd pair, while males have one X- and one Y-shaped chromosome. All of the ova a woman produces have only X chromosomes. About half of the spermatozoa produced by men contain an X and the other half a Y chromosome in the 23rd place. The genetic sex of the zygote will thus depend on which of the father's spermatozoa actually fertilizes the ovum. For reasons not fully understood, more males are conceived than females, in the ratio of 105 to 100. Over the course of the life span, an increasing number of females survive at every age, so that by age 60, the ratio of males to females is 70 to 100.

Up until the third month after conception, genetic males and genetic females have similar external structures in the genital area. During the second month, the hormone testosterone is secreted in male fetuses; it activates particular genes that induce the development of the internal ducts that will later connect to male genitals. The continued action of testosterone causes the development of the external male genitals at around three months. Female genitals do not require any specific hormone to develop at this stage (Lamb & Bornstein, 1987).

The Period of the Fetus: Seventeen to Twenty-Two Weeks

Up until the 16th week, the list of newly acquired spontaneous and stimulated fetal behavior continues to grow. Between 17 and 22 weeks, however, the fetus becomes strangely quieter, after which activity begins again and lasts until birth. The reduction of movement is due to the rapid development of the brain during this period (Hofer, 1981).

You might think that the development of the brain would induce more movement, rather than less. Up until this time, the brain stimulated large movements that involved the whole body, including arms and legs. These uninhibited movements originated in the brain stem regions. During the period between 17 and 22 weeks, the brain is beginning to develop subcortical and cortical cells and pathways to inhibit such uncontrolled, spasmlike movements. The result is that after 22 weeks, the movements of the fetus will be more specialized and controlled (see Table 3.2). After this point, for example, specific facial expressions and coordinated hand movements begin to emerge.

This period of prenatal development, therefore, is characterized by rapid brain development. As shown in Figure 3.5, the brain's weight and volume increase by a factor of four during this period. Throughout fetal development, the major process of brain growth is cell division and intercell connections in the nervous system. After 22 weeks, new brain cells continue to be formed, but at a much slower rate. Following birth, the major processes of brain development are an increase in intercell connections and in cell specialization. Thus, during the early fetal period, when the brain is growing the most rapidly, it is the most susceptible to influences from the environment.

Table 3.2 Chronology of Fetal Behavior (Second and Third Periods)

Age (Weeks)	Behavior
19	Gag reflex. Early coordinated body movements in response to noxious stimulation (these are different from whole-body spasms of the early part of the first fetal period).
21	Audible crying.
22	As sensitive to touch as a 1-year-old. Beginnings of prenatal learning ability.
24	Hearing structures developed, listens to mother's heartbeat, can blink eyes. Sleep-wake pattern first appears.
25	Moves in rhythm to drumbeats.
26	Lungs can breathe on their own, can regulate body temperature, remembers sounds heard previously, reacts to differences in maternal emotions, can open eyelids, can survive if born prematurely.
32	Brain wave patterns show all primary brain areas functioning. REM sleep and mature sleep-wake pattern. Fetuses sleep about 75% of the time. First signs of visual attention.
34	Can habituate, active visual attention.
35	Evidence of visual recognition memory.

Sources: J. A. DiPietro, D. M. Hodgson, K. A. Costigan, & T. R. B. Johnson, Fetal neurobehavioral development, 1996. *Child Development, 67*(5); R. Gandelman, *The psychobiology of behavioral development,* 1992. New York: Oxford University Press; C. D. Laughlin, Pre- and perinatal brain development and enculturation: A biogenetic structural approach, 1991. *Human Nature, 2.*

Figure 3.5
Development of the Human Brain

Upper set: Human brains at the same scale of magnification. Lower set: Development of the corpus callosum linking the hemispheres and of the cerebellum.

5 Months

4 Months

8 Months

6 Months

Term

Adult

16 Weeks

1 cm

40 Weeks (term)

10 cm

Adult

10 cm

Corpus callosum

Cerebellum

Source: C. Trevarthen, Neurological development and the growth of psychological functions, 1980. In J. Sants, *Developmental psychology and society,* 46 – 95. New York: St. Martin's Press. Copyright © by J. Sants. Reprinted by permission of St. Martin's Press, Inc.

During this period of development, the fetus is changing its physical characteristics. In the fourth month, a fine, long hair, **lanugo,** grows over most of the body. Coarser hair appears on the head in the fifth month, and eyebrows and eyelashes grow in the sixth month. During this period, the skin glands secrete a waxy substance, the **vernix caseosa,** that serves to protect the delicate skin. This period is also marked by the formation of fingernails, toenails, and the adult tooth buds.

The inhibition of movement by the brain makes sense from the point of view of physical development. The rapid increase in fetal size means that the fetus has less space in which to move around. At 6 months, the fetus weighs about 900 grams (2 pounds). Most babies born at this age do not survive, and if a baby is less than 600 grams or less than 24 weeks, the chances of survival are exceedingly slim.

The Period of the Fetus: Twenty-Three to Thirty-Six Weeks

During this period, fetuses are active about 20% to 30% of the time. They move less often than during the first fetal period but with more vigor (DiPietro, Hodgson, Costigan, & Johnson, 1996). The beginning of this period is the time when mothers can first feel the fetus moving. By now, a doctor can detect the fetal heartbeat with a stethoscope. Data from infants born prematurely and also from ultrasound recordings of the fetus inside the womb provide evidence for a large number of new patterns of movement that begin during this period.

The fetus has been observed to cry, grunt, and yawn. By the 8th month, the fetus can suck its thumb and open its eyes. Grasping and postural adjustment movements have also been observed. By this time, the fetus can see, hear, feel, and smell. Thus, by about the seventh month, most fetuses could survive if born, given appropriate intensive care (see Chapter 4). The Awareness through Movement lessons at the end of this chapter will give you a more participatory feeling for what it may feel like to be a late-term fetus.

One of the most remarkable achievements of the late fetal period is the development of clear-cut states of arousal (Hofer, 1981; T. R. B. Johnson et al., 1989). A **state of arousal** is an organized pattern of infant physical and physiological response that is related to the internal level of arousal or activation. States are alternating periods of activation and quiescence. During the fourth and fifth months, periods of activation and quiet in the fetus are irregular, and transitions from quiet to active are sudden and jerky. By the sixth month, a clear and regular alternation between activity and rest occurs about once every 40 minutes, based on data taken from sensors placed on the abdomens of sleeping women (Sterman & Hoppenbrouwers, 1971). This basic rhythm continues unchanged until after birth (S. S. Robertson, 1987).

These earlier periods of activity and rest become waking and sleeping states during this period. Fully developed sleep states appear in the fetus as early as 24 weeks (DiPietro et al., 1996). From its first appearance, sleep is divided into a period of quiet sleep and a period of active or REM sleep. **REM (rapid eye movement) sleep** is characterized by short, jerky, vertical eye movements, spontaneous body movements, and irregular respiration. The 32-week-old fetus spends about three-quarters of its time in REM sleep.

The purpose of REM sleep is not fully understood. One hypothesis (Ruffwarg, Muzio, & Dement, 1966; Vertes, 1986) is that it is a form of self-stimulation similar to earlier body movements. The last month of gestation is a period during which the fetus gains a considerable amount of weight. From 900 grams at 24 weeks, the fetus typically grows to about 3,500 grams at 36 weeks (about 7 pounds); most of this weight is subcutaneous fat tissues that will provide the newborn with insulation against the cold. Because of this weight gain, the fetus becomes too cramped to move its body. REM sleep may provide a less physically demanding source of

movement stimulation to assist the development of the fetal brain and sensory organs.

Another remarkable achievement of the last few months of prenatal development is the emergence of the ability to learn. A number of people have speculated that fetuses may become imprinted to the heartbeat sounds of their mothers so that after birth, the sound of heartbeats is comforting to the infants. Indeed, it has been found that a majority of adults hold infants on the left side of the adult's body, closer to the heart (Salk, 1973).

Using a response-contingent procedure (see Chapter 2), DeCasper and Sigafoos (1983) found that newborn infants will change their rate of sucking to imitate the sound of a heartbeat. Although these studies do not prove that newborns recognize the specific heartbeat of their mothers, they seem to suggest that a general preference for heartbeat sounds may have been learned. Holding the infant on the left side has another advantage, however: it frees up the right hand to do other things.

In another study (Panneton & DeCasper, 1986), researchers asked pregnant women to sing "Mary Had a Little Lamb" frequently during the period 2 weeks prior to their due dates. After birth, the newborns' preference for "Mary Had a Little Lamb" over the song "Love Somebody" was tested using the conditioned sucking procedure (see Chapter 1). The newborns could clearly perceive the difference between the two songs, and in addition, they preferred to listen to the song that they had heard prenatally. DeCasper and Spence (1986) found postnatal preferences for stories read prenatally. Along these same lines, infants preferred hearing their mother's voice, compared to that of a stranger, when the voices were filtered for only the low-frequency components that the fetus might have heard through the insulating uterine wall. When higher-frequency whispered voices were used, newborns showed no preference (Spence & Freeman, 1996).

Newborns also prefer familiar smells. They orient more to the odor of their mother's amniotic fluid than to formula milk or to amniotic fluid taken from another woman (Marlier, Schaal, & Soussignan, 1998a; Marlier, Schaal, & Soussignan, 1998b).

The studies reviewed so far have tested newborns for preferences related to their experiences before birth. Several studies have tested fetuses before birth and found an ability to learn in utero. One study examined whether fetuses 36 to 39 weeks old could distinguish between a male and a female voice (Lecanuet, Granier-Deferre, Jacquet, Capponi, & Ledru, 1993). One voice was presented until the fetal heart rate became habituated, and then the voice was changed. The criterion for fetal recognition of a change from one voice to the other was the dishabituation of the heart rate. Heart rate changes were significantly different when the voice was changed from male to female, or vice versa, and were significantly different from a control group for whom the voice was not changed. Fetal heart rate was also found to habituate to a vibro-acoustic sound presented at intervals near the fetal head (Sandman, Wadhwa, Hetrick, Porto, & Peeke, 1997).

Prenatal learning has been convincingly demonstrated in other animals. Rat pups that had been exposed prenatally to a mint smell after birth preferred to suck on mother's teats to which the same smell had been applied (Smotherman & Robinson, 1987). Other work with animal fetuses shows conditioning effects from stimulation due to sound, light, and chemicals (Gandelman, 1992).

What is the purpose of this learning ability in the fetus? It may be that it has no particular purpose for the fetus and that its importance is for the development of learning ability that will be required after birth. On the other hand, this research demonstrates that prenatally learned associations become postnatal preferences. Fetuses exposed to prenatal maternal sounds and chemicals are more likely to recognize and prefer those same sounds and sensations after birth, and they are more likely to avoid sounds and smells that they found aversive prenatally. Thus, prenatal learning ability may serve as an early mechanism for mother-infant attachment and for the orientation of infants to the smells, tastes, and sounds of the environment into which they are born (Gandelman, 1992). It may also be that prenatal learning experiences, like prenatal movements, play a role in the development of connections between sensory, motor, and information processing areas of the brain before birth (Laughlin, 1991).

So far, we have traced the early development of behavior, brain, and body in the prenatal period.

The processes discussed apply generally to prenatal development. We now turn to a consideration of individual differences in fetal development, their causes, and their consequences.

Individual Differences in Prenatal Development

Fetuses are not just genetically different. Each fetus is exposed to an environment different from that of every other fetus. The experiments on fetal learning, for example, show that newborns can remember some of their sensory experiences as fetuses: the particular sounds, tastes, and smells of their fetal home. We also know that the form of bodily structures and sensitivities of children and adults is the result of their exposure to the physics, chemistry, and nutrition of the uterine environment. This section is divided into genetic, chromosomal, and environmental influences.

Genetic and Chromosomal Influences on Development

In Chapter 2, we discussed how behavior geneticists view the origins of individual differences in the phenotype as being the result of individual differences in genotypes and/or environments. Individual variations in phenotypic characteristics that are closely correlated with individual characteristics in genotypes are less susceptible to variations in the environment. Physical characteristics, such as hair and eye color, baldness, and height fall into this category, although all of these phenotypes can be influenced by the environment to some extent. Let us examine some of these processes in more detail.

Genes rarely act alone in determining a phenotype. Most phenotypes are derived from **polygenic**

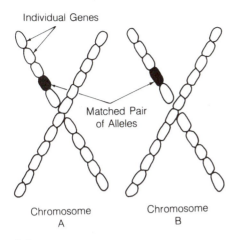

Individual Genes

Matched Pair
of Alleles

Chromosome
A

Chromosome
B

<u>Figure 3.6</u>
The Relative Position of Two Alleles in a Chromosome Pair

Source: A. Fogel & G. F. Melson, *Child development,* 1988, p. 89. St. Paul, MN: West.

inheritance; that is, they arise from the action of a combination of genes interacting with the environment. In most cases, at least two genes enter into the phenotype: one from the mother and one from the father. With a polygenic characteristic such as skin color, a number of genes from the mother combine with an equal number from the father, and the offspring's skin color is likely to be somewhere between the skin colors of the parents. Children in the same family may exhibit a range of skin colors.

Because chromosome pairs in an individual are made up of singles from each parent, genes that typically interact with each other to produce a phenotype are located at similar sites along the chromosome of each member of the pair. This is illustrated in Figure 3.6. Genes that act together to express a particular phenotype are called **alleles.**

In the past, it was believed that some phenotypic characteristics were inherited by a simple two-allele combination called **dominant-recessive inheritance.** Eye color is one example. The dominant allele (the one related to brown eyes) will always be expressed, even in the presence of a recessive mate (the allele for blue eyes). Thus, a person with brown eyes might actually carry a recessive allele for blue eyes, and two brown-eyed parents could produce a blue-eyed child if the zygote happens to contain two blue recessive alleles and no brown dominant allele. It takes two recessive genes for a trait to ap-

pear in the phenotype. The dominant trait appears in the phenotype, however, if only one dominant gene is present, either from the mother or from the father, or if both genes are dominant. Therefore, the dominant characteristic will appear in the phenotype 75% of the time.

It is rare for only one or two genes to determine a phenotype, however. Even characteristics that are strongly influenced by a pattern of dominant-recessive inheritance act along with other genes to produce the phenotype. Therefore, eye color, like skin color, comes in many different shades and variations—the typical signature of polygenic inheritance.

Another pattern of inheritance relates to those characteristics that are displayed differentially between the sexes. **Sex-linked inheritance** relates to phenotypes that are tied to genes that appear on the 23rd chromosome. Recall that genetic males have an X and a Y chromosome as their 23rd pair. Not only is the Y chromosome missing one of its arms compared to the X chromosome, but the Y is also considerably smaller than the X. For this reason, one might think that women would have more sex-linked characteristics than men, but this is not the case. For females, the alleles on the X chromosome will express themselves in interaction with their matched alleles on the other X chromosome of the 23rd pair. For males, alleles on the X chromosome of the 23rd pair will express themselves in the absence of an interaction with a matched allele.

Sex-linked inheritance produces primary (genitals) and secondary (facial hair, body shape, etc.) sexual characteristics in males and females. Other sex-linked characteristics are baldness, color blindness, and a disorder of blood clotting processes called hemophilia, all of which occur primarily in males.

In most cases, these latter sex-linked characteristics are caused by a recessive allele on the X chromosome. If the recessive allele is paired with a dominant allele on another X chromosome, that dominant allele will override the influence of the recessive gene. Recall that it takes two recessive genes to produce the characteristic in the phenotype. Females are thus less likely to display the phenotype for baldness because they can inherit both the dominant and recessive allele. A male who inherits a re-

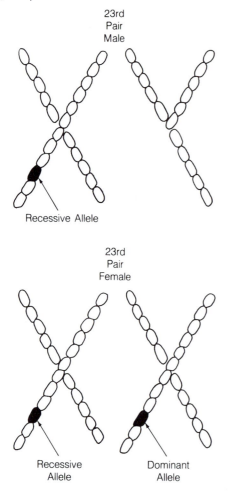

23rd
Pair
Male

Recessive Allele

23rd
Pair
Female

Recessive
Allele

Dominant
Allele

Figure 3.7
Sex-Linked Inheritance

The male Y chromosome is missing dominant alleles that are found on the lower left-hand branch of the female's X chromosome.

Source: A. Fogel & G. F. Melson, *Child development,* 1988, p. 89. St. Paul, MN: West. Copyright © by West Publishing Co. Reprinted by permission. All rights reserved.

In some cases, however, a woman will inherit two recessive alleles for a characteristic such as baldness. Some of these women will bald, while others will not. In addition, while most men who inherit a recessive baldness gene actually bald, some of these men retain their hair. How can this happen?

Much like the formation of the external genitals in the third month of prenatal development, baldness is a characteristic that is expressed in the phenotype only when the gene for baldness interacts with the hormone testosterone. Because men typically have higher levels of circulating testosterone than females, their baldness gene will almost always be expressed. Men who do not bald are either not genetically predisposed to baldness or are predisposed but have low levels of circulating testosterone. Similarly, females who bald carry two recessive genes and have higher-than-average testosterone levels. Female baldness can be treated with estrogen (a female hormone) supplements, but these have undesirable side effects, such as the prolongation of menstruation and the disruption of normal menopausal processes.

In addition to genetically based differences in physical appearance, there may be genetically based differences in prenatal behavior. During the third fetal period, male fetuses are more active than females (DiPietro Hodgson, Costigan, & Johnson, 1996). Male fetuses also appear to develop organized states of arousal earlier than females (DiPietro et al., 1996). The findings on activity level suggest that boys are born with more motor experience. Since boys are more active postnatally, this suggests that early gender differences are not due entirely to postnatal environmental and parental influences (see Chapter 12).

cessive allele for baldness on his X chromosome will not have the corresponding dominant allele on his Y chromosome: there is no site for it to occupy (see Figure 3.7).

Because the X chromosome in the male's 23rd pair always comes from his mother (Y chromosomes are only produced by males), women are the carriers of these sex-linked characteristics. A male is more likely to have a hairline like his maternal grandfather's than like his own father's (McClearn, 1970).

Genetically Based Disorders

Occasionally, problems more serious than baldness can be carried by the genes from one generation to the next. These genetically based disorders are not deterministic of a particular phenotype. Rather, if an individual carries a particular gene, the probability of acquiring its related disorder is increased.

In some cases, genetic disorders are so severe that the fetus will die and be expelled from the mother's body. This is called spontaneous abortion. It has been estimated that two out of every three conceptions are spontaneously aborted in the early months of pregnancy. In a large majority of these cases, the embryo has genetic or chromosomal abnormalities. In addition, over 80% of newborn deaths can be accounted for by neural tube defects (15%) and chromosomal and genetic abnormalities (67%) (C. Roberts & Lowe, 1975; Strobino & Pantel-Silverman, 1987; Tharapel, Bannerman, & Tharapel, 1985; I. D. Young, Clarke, & Rickett, 1986). Thus, spontaneous abortion and mortality of malformed fetuses seem to be natural biological functions to eliminate malformations. In other cases, infants stricken with a genetic disorder can live for several years or even longer, depending on available treatments.

Most of the evidence for genetic disorders is derived from genealogical studies in which the path of a disorder can be traced through a family tree. For example, manic-depressive disease occurs in a high incidence in the Old Order Amish community in Lancaster, Pennsylvania. Because the entire population of this Amish community is descended from fewer than 100 people who settled there before 1750, and because the community kept excellent genealogical, disease, and death records, researchers were able to study the chromosomes of hundreds of afflicted individuals. When this is done, the specific gene that causes the disorder can be detected because it is the only one that is identical in all cases. However, other characteristics also occur along with this gene, making it difficult to say what the gene actually causes. Some forms of manic-depressive disorder (also called bipolar disorder) may be related to multiple genes, while other forms may not be genetically related.

When a specific gene can be isolated, it gives hope for the early detection and possibly the treatment of the disorder. Treatment takes many forms, but one of the most effective is to prevent exposure of the individual to the types of environments in which the phenotype is most likely to emerge, or conversely, to provide environments that are conducive to health. Environmental treatments have been effective for physical disorders, such as PKU (see below). They may also be useful as behavior genetic researchers discover the genetic basis for

behavioral disorders such as particular types of psychopathologies (Plomin & Rutter, 1998).

Of the 3,000 known genetic disorders, researchers have isolated the genes for only about 30 of them. This kind of work is extremely difficult to do. First, one needs good family genealogies, and second, it takes years to find the single gene or genes out of the many thousands of genes carried by humans.

Consistent sex differences are also used as clues to the genetic origins of certain disorders. Sex-linked inheritance accounts for color blindness and hemophilia in males. Hemophilia is known as the "disease of royalty," because the female descendants of England's Queen Victoria were carriers of the disease, and many of the males in the family inherited it. Hemophilia can be treated today with various medications that aid in blood clotting. Other sex-linked disorders are color blindness and some forms of muscular dystrophy.

Fragile X syndrome, another sex-linked disorder, is caused by an abnormal gene on the bottom end of the X chromosome. It is the most common inherited cause of mental retardation. Males affected with the disorder have autistic-like symptoms (see Chapter 10 on autism) such as hand flapping, biting, poor eye contact, shyness, repetitive behaviors, and mild to moderate mental retardation. They may also have deficits in attention and information processing. Girls who are carriers show only mild cognitive deficits. These children tend to have long faces and prominent ears (Burack et al., 1999; Hagerman, 1996).

In some cases, a single recessive gene can have multiple effects. Marfan's syndrome is one example. This disorder is associated with a weakened heart, mild bone structure deformities, long fingers, and eye lens problems. It is believed that Abraham Lincoln suffered from this disease. **Phenylketonuria (PKU)** is a recessive disorder in which the person cannot properly metabolize phenylalanine, an essential amino acid found in most forms of protein. If detected early, the level of phenylalanine-containing foods in the child's diet can be lowered, thus reducing the chances that mental and nervous deficits will develop. Even with appropriate treatment, however, preschool children with PKU showed less ability for planning and search behaviors, although their memory skills were similar, compared to matched control children who did not have PKU (Welsh, Pennington, Ozonoff, Rouse, & McCabe, 1990). These effects are related to the concentration of phenylalanine in the child's blood, suggesting that additional dietary and drug treatment may provide hope for treatment (Diamond, Prevor, Callender, & Druin, 1997). PKU occurs in 1 in 25,000 births. It can be tested for at birth, and parents can be counseled about their baby's diet (H. L. Levy, Karolkewicz, Houghton, & MacCready, 1970).

Another recessive disorder is **cystic fibrosis,** which affects 1 in 2,500 births. It is the most common genetic disorder among people with a northern European ancestry. The disorder is characterized by the clogging of the lungs with mucus, which leads to infection and death in young adulthood. It can be detected prenatally, and many countries routinely screen newborns for the disease.

Some disorders afflict particular racial or ethnic groups whose members are likely to intermarry, increasing the chances of having a child inherit two recessive genes. Jewish couples in which both members can trace their origins to European ancestry (Ashkenazic Jews) have a 1 in 3,600 chance of producing a baby with **Tay-Sachs disease,** an enzyme deficiency that brings about a steady deterioration of mental and physical abilities. Infants may become blind or deaf, have paralysis, and lose the ability to swallow. Few live past the age of 5 (Silver, 1985).

Black infants have a 1 in 400 chance of inheriting **sickle-cell anemia,** a disorder of the red blood cells in which they tend to clot and block off blood vessels. People afflicted with sickle-cell anemia may become mildly retarded or have heart and kidney problems. Unlike Tay-Sachs disease, sickle-cell anemia can be partially treated, and its victims can live normal lives. The sickle-cell gene is also associated with a positive side effect: those who have the disease as well as those who are merely carriers of the gene are partially immunized against the deadly disease of malaria. People with sickle-cell genes are not good hosts for the malarial parasite, which spends part of its life cycle in the blood. Malarial protection is probably the reason why the sickle-cell gene was maintained in the population.

Huntington's disease is a particularly poignant genetic disorder. It is caused by a dominant gene, so half of the children of a parent with the disease will also acquire it. The problem is that the symptoms do not appear until the age of 35 or 40, well after those children have begun to have children of their own. The symptoms include depression, loss of memory and motor control, and other problems caused by the death of brain cells. It occurs in 1 out of 18,000 births, and there is no treatment. A recently developed test can determine whether an individual carries the gene for Huntington's disease. While such a test may be useful for counseling these individuals about whether or not to have children, it also tells them whether they will acquire the disease themselves. Because many people do not want to learn that they might have an incurable disease, relatively few individuals at risk for this disease come to a clinic for genetic screening (S. D. Taylor, 1994). Another dominant disorder is **familial Alzheimer's disease,** which is also associated with brain deterioration and loss of social and cognitive control.

Other genetic disorders are polygenic. Because these disorders require a combination of factors in order to occur, their incidence is less than that of the single-gene sex-linked and recessive disorders. Polygenic disorders include cleft lip and cleft palate, spina bifida (exposed spinal cord), some forms of diabetes, and some forms of heart defects. Genetic causes may also be implicated in some forms of schizophrenia, alcoholism, and homosexuality, although less is known about these conditions. Considerably more research is required to investigate these and other genetic causes.

Chromosomal Disorders

During the process of meiosis, errors sometimes occur as chromosomes split and recombine. One gamete may wind up with too many chromosomes, another with too few. A **monosomy** is an abnormality of the 23rd pair, the sex chromosomes. Monosomies occur when one member of the pair is missing. In **Turner's syndrome,** a female has only one X chromosome. This is associated with a lack of complete sex determination, other physical deformities, and mental retardation.

A **trisomy** is a chromosome pair that has an extra chromosome accidentally attached to it. Trisomies can occur on the sex chromosomes, resulting, for example, in **Kleinfelter's syndrome**

Table 3.3   Risk of Down's Syndrome as
            a Function of Maternal Age

Age of Mother	Proportion of Births
30	1/885
35	1/365
40	1/109
45	1/32
49	1/12

Source: P. A. Baird & A. D. Sadovnick, Life expectancy in Down syndrome, 1987, p. 852. *Journal of Pediatrics, 110,* pp. 849–854.

(XXY) in which the male has female behavioral characteristics and may be mentally retarded, although normal in appearance. The best-known of the trisomies is trisomy 21, in which an extra chromosome is attached to the 21st pair. The resulting disorder, which in the past was sometimes called "mongolism" but is now known as **Down's syndrome,** is characterized by short stature, flabbiness, cardiac and glandular abnormalities, small mouth, mental retardation, and folds of skin over the eyes.

It is known that Down's syndrome is more prevalent in infants born to mothers nearing the end of their fertility (see Table 3.3). For this reason, most women over the age of 35 are counseled to have amniocentesis (see below) to test for the presence of chromosomal abnormalities during pregnancy. It has recently been hypothesized that estrogen levels in the mother may explain Down's syndrome. Since estrogen production is highest between the ages of 20 and 35, women older than this may be more likely to have a Down's baby than are women between those ages. Estrogen may enhance the process of meiotic cell division, and its lack may cause incomplete cell division (Crowley, Gulati, Hayden, Lopez, & Dyer, 1979).

Furthermore, the risk of Down's syndrome increases when fathers are younger than 20 and older than 55 years; errors in the genetic material of sperm cells may account for as much as one-fourth of all Down's cases (Arehart-Treichel, 1979). Since older mothers typically have older male partners, there is no way to determine whether the risk of Down's syndrome is caused by maternal or paternal factors.

Aside from the risk of Down's syndrome, older couples face no more significant risks to either parents or the fetus than do younger couples. In several studies of first-time mothers over 35 years of age, the rate of complications of pregnancy and birth was no different than for younger first-time mothers (P. F. Hughes & Morrison, 1994; Melchor et al., 1994; Prysak, Lorenz, & Kisly, 1995). Nevertheless, due to the social and psychological issues surrounding childbearing for older women (see the earlier section on infertility), they can be helped by prenatal counseling and genetic screening of their fetus for Down's syndrome (O'Reilly-Green & Cohen, 1993).

Environmental Influence on Prenatal Development

In this section, I will examine environmental influences on the development of individual differences. Little is known about how variations in the prenatal environment are related to normal individual differences that develop postnatally. We are, however, learning a great deal about more serious variations in the prenatal environment, those that lead to birth defects and complications of pregnancy. As mentioned at the opening of this chapter, many kinds of hazardous substances can penetrate the otherwise peaceful world of the fetus. For a pregnant woman and her family, therefore, this section is perhaps the most important in this chapter. It is reasonably easy to avoid many of the things that may cause harm to an unborn baby if you are aware of them. The purpose of this section is not only to report the current research findings on this topic, but also to keep you informed about the ways to achieve a healthy pregnancy.

The study of birth defects is known as **teratology,** from the Greek word *tera,* meaning monster—hardly a pleasant association. Teratology, however, is an extremely valuable area of investigation because it attempts to find the causes of birth defects so that they may be avoided in the future. Up until this century, birth defects were mysterious. They were often attributed to magical, spiritual, or supernatural causes, or else they were read as omens or signs. The ancient Babylonians considered birth defects to be omens because that is how they viewed any "unnatural" occurrence. Many primitive societies today have some theories of the causes of birth defects, but these are mostly superstitious beliefs, such as the admonition that eating twisted

98 | Chapter 3

or deformed plants may lead to birth deformities (M. Mead & Newton, 1967).

If the birth defect arises because of some environmental cause rather than a chromosomal or genetic abnormality, then the agent responsible for the defect is known as a **teratogen.** Teratogens come in many different forms, from viruses to chemicals to nuclear radiation, and their existence testifies to the importance of environmental-infant interactions even before birth.

The general public was made aware of the devastating effects of toxic agents on fetal development through two drugs that were once widely prescribed for pregnant women: thalidomide and DES. Thalidomide was a mild tranquilizer that was available in Europe in the 1950s. Pregnant women took it in the early months of pregnancy to help control nausea and insomnia. It was discovered to be teratogenic after a number of physicians traced the presence of heart defects and deformed or missing limbs to the mother's use of the drug during pregnancy. It was found that the time in pregnancy at which the mother had taken the drug determined the particular deformity. If she took it just at the time when the arms were forming, for example, then the arms suffered the most deformity.

Another way in which teratogenic agents may operate is illustrated by the case of the drug diethylstilbestrol (DES), a hormone given to pregnant women between 1948 and 1969 to help prevent miscarriage and to enhance reproductive health. Between 500,000 and 2 million women are believed to have taken this drug. In this case, however, the effects did not show up at birth, but rather when the offspring of these women had reached adolescence. A rise in the number of cases of vaginal cancer in teenage girls and of sterility and other genital abnormalities in teenage boys was eventually traced back to DES.

As a general rule, the effects of toxic agents on the fetus will depend upon a number of factors. Among them is the point in pregnancy at which the exposure occurs. Since two-thirds of all birth defects occur in the first trimester, the first 3 months of pregnancy (Heinonen, Sloane, & Shapiro, 1976), the earlier in pregnancy one is exposed to a toxic agent, the greater the risk (see Figure 3.8). In reality, the first few days and weeks of fetal life allow for a minimum of susceptibility. The effect of the teratogenic agents increases and peaks during the pe-

riod of the rapid differentiation of the organs and limbs and then declines again. If the exposure occurs during the time when organs are growing at a rapid rate, the result will likely be a structural defect. If it occurs after organ growth is mostly completed, the result will more likely be growth retardation or a behavioral abnormality (Kopp & Parmelee, 1979). Other factors include the size of the dosage and the length of exposure, with longer, larger doses creating the greatest risk. A **dose-response relationship** occurs when levels of the drug consumed are directly correlated with the strength of the outcome effect (Bookstein, Sampson, Streissguth, & Barr, 1996; Vorhees & Mollnow, 1987).

As more research has been done, the list of teratogenic agents has increased. Some of these are given in Table 3.4. For some of these agents, the effects are well established in both animal and human studies. Effects that are listed as suspected may have been confirmed in animals but not in humans. One problem with isolating the effects of particular agents is that more than one factor may occur at the same time. For example, it is difficult to determine the effect of an antinausea drug apart from the condition that caused the severe nausea in the first place (Vorhees & Mollnow, 1987).

Perhaps the area of teratology that has attracted the most research is the effects of maternal alcohol consumption. **Fetal alcohol syndrome (FAS),** which was discovered in 1973, is associated with some forms of mental retardation, facial abnormalities such as small narrow heads with widely spaced eyes and an underdeveloped jaw, hyperactivity, growth retardation, more premature births and miscarriages, lower birthweight, and heart defects. FAS occurs at an incidence of 1 to 3 per 1,000 births in the United States (Fifth Special Report to the U.S. Congress on Alcohol and Health 1984). The heaviest drinkers, those who consume more than five drinks per day on the average, have a 30% higher risk of having an FAS child (Landesman-Dwyer, 1981; Rosett, 1980).

Infants born to moderate drinkers, those who consume one or two drinks per day, are not likely to have physical deformities. Follow-up studies show that by age 4, however, these children have mild to severe learning disabilities and slightly retarded physical growth. This pattern of outcomes has been called *fetal alcohol effects (FAE)* (Abel, Randall, &

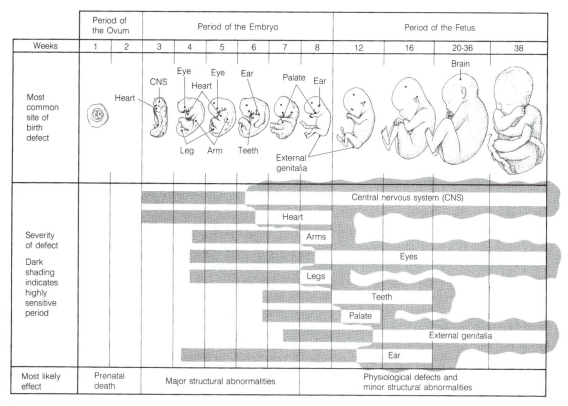

Figure 3.8 chart: Stages of Prenatal Development and Birth Defects

	Period of the Ovum		Period of the Embryo						Period of the Fetus			
Weeks	1	2	3	4	5	6	7	8	12	16	20-36	38

Most common site of birth defect: Heart, CNS, Eye, Heart, Eye, Ear, Palate, Ear, Leg, Arm, Teeth, External genitalia, Brain

Severity of defect — Dark shading indicates highly sensitive period:
Central nervous system (CNS), Heart, Arms, Eyes, Legs, Teeth, Palate, External genitalia, Ear

Most likely effect: Prenatal death | Major structural abnormalities | Physiological defects and minor structural abnormalities

Figure 3.8
Stages of Prenatal Development and Birth Defects

Source: A. Fogel & G. F. Melson, *Child development,* 1988, p. 106. St. Paul, MN: West. Copyright © by West Publishing Co. Reprinted by permission. All rights reserved.

These 5-month-old fraternal twin girls have some of the characteristic symptoms of fetal alcohol syndrome: narrow heads, widely spaced eyes, underdeveloped jaws, and growth retardation.

Table 3.4   Common Teratogenic Agents and Their Effects

Agent	Known or Suspected Effects
Drugs	
Alcohol	Growth retardation, heart problems, mental retardation.
Amphetamines (stimulant)	Intrauterine growth retardation (suspected).
Analgesics (for pain)	Respiratory problems at birth.
Antibiotics	Streptomycin can cause hearing loss; tetracycline can stain teeth and inhibit bone growth.
Arsenic (in water)	Suspected growth retardation and malformation.
Aspirin	In large amounts, suspected respiratory problems and bleeding at birth for mother and infant.
Barbiturates (sedatives)	No known long-term effects, but newborns may experience withdrawal and respiratory problems.
Caffeine	No known long-term effects for moderate use, but increased activity, heart rate, and arousal in fetus during periods of maternal consumption; also, caffeine may enhance the negative effect of other drugs such as tobacco and alcohol.
Cocaine	See text.
Diethystilbestrol (DES)	Genetic abnormalities; genital cancer in female infants.
Heroin, morphine	Respiratory problems, growth retardation, increased risk for mortality, sleep disturbances; newborns experience withdrawal.
Hydantoins, dilantin, valproic acid (anticonvulsants)	Can cause heart defects, cleft lip and palate, limb reduction, and mental retardation, but some of the effects may be caused by maternal epilepsy.
Lithium (for depression)	Cardiovascular disorders (suspected).
Marijuana	Few long-term effects; sleep disturbance by age 3; newborns may experience withdrawal.
Prozac (and related antidepressants)	No known effects.
Sex hormones (for birth control, fertility, & prevention of miscarriage)	Suspected cardiovascular disorders; no known effects in humans.
Thalidomide	Limb deformities, hearing loss, higher risk of mortality.
Tobacco	Higher risk for newborn mortality, low birthweight, neurological changes, post-natal growth retardation, cleft lip and palate, sudden infant death.
Tranquilizers	No known long-term effects, but newborns may experience withdrawal.
Vitamins	Large doses of vitamin A (used to treat acne) cause defects in heart, head, neck, and brain, and other deformities; large doses of other vitamins are suspected of causing defects.
Diseases (sexually transmitted)	
AIDS	See text.
Chlamydia	Eye infection and risk of pneumonia in newborn.
Gonorrhea	Prematurity and eye infection in newborns, higher risk of newborn mortality.
Hepatitis B	Prematurity, low birthweight, higher risk of newborn mortality.
Herpes simplex	Mental retardation, eye damage, higher risk of newborn mortality (can be prevented by cesarean section).
Syphilis	Mental retardation, blindness, deafness, higher risk of mortality.
Diseases (others)	
Anemia (iron deficiency)	Higher risk of stillbirth, newborn mortality, brain damage.

Table 3.4 *(continued)*

Agent	Known or Suspected Effects
Diabetes	Can cause malformations and higher risk of mortality.
Hypertension	Higher risk of mortality and miscarriage.
Influenza	Cardiovascular and central nervous system defects, spontaneous abortion.
Mumps	Higher risk of spontaneous abortion and stillbirth.
Rh incompatibility	Higher risk of stillbirth, miscarriage, heart defects, and mental retardation.
Rubella	Deafness, cataracts, heart disease, mental retardation, higher risk of spontaneous abortion and stillbirth.
Other viruses	In particular, cytomegalovirus and chicken pox increase the risk of skin and muscle defects, deafness, blindness, mental retardation, and infant mortality.
Environmental hazards	
Lead	Anemia, hemorrhage, increased risk of miscarriage.
Radiation	Small head size, growth retardation, leukemia, cataracts, higher risk of miscarriage and stillbirth.
Methylmercury (in contaminated fish)	Cerebral palsy, neurological disorders.
Pesticides, PCB	Higher risk of stillbirth, low birthweight, mental delays.
Cleaning agents, solvents	Possible effects of low birthweight and some defects (suspected).
Maternal conditions	
Stress	Pregnancy complications, increased risk of Down's syndrome, attentional and motor deficits.
Malnutrition	Prematurity, low birthweight, growth retardation, mental retardation.
Age	Older women have higher rates of Down's syndrome in their fetuses.
Depression	Depressed behavior and higher stress hormones (cortisol) at birth.

Sources: B. A. Buehler, V. Rao, & R. H. Finnell, Biochemical and molecular teratology of fetal hydantoin syndrome, 1994. *Neurological Clinics, 12;* D. Bukatko & M. W. Daehler, *Child development* (2d ed.), 1995. Boston: Houghton Mifflin; R. E. Dahl, M. S. Scher, D. E. Williamson, N. Robles, & N. Day, A longitudinal study of prenatal marijuana use: Effects of sleep and arousal at age 3 years, 1995. *Archives of Pediatric and Adolescent Medicine, 149,* 145–150; R. Gandelman, *The psychobiology of behavioral development,* 1992. New York: Oxford University Press; M. S. Golub, M. S. Macintosh, & N. Baumrind, Developmental and reproductive toxicity of inorganic arsenic: Animal studies and human concerns, 1998. *Journal of Toxicology and Environmental Health, 1*(3), 199–241; E. M. Hetherington & R. D. Parke, *Child psychology: A contemporary viewpoint* (4th ed.), 1992. New York: McGraw-Hill; S. W. Jacobson, G. G. Fein, J. L. Jacobson, P. M. Schwartz, & J. K. Dowler, The effect of intrauterine PCB exposure on visual recognition memory, 1985. *Child Development, 56,* 853–860; D. Kennedy & G. Koren, Valproic acid use in psychiatry: Issues in treating women of reproductive age, 1998. *Journal of Psychiatry and Neuroscience, 23*(4), 223–228; C. B. Kopp & A. Parmelee, Prenatal and perinatal influences on infant behavior, 1979. In J. Osofsky (Ed.), *Handbook of infant development.* New York: Wiley; N. A. Kulin, A. Pastuszk, S. R. Sage, B. Schick-Boschetto, G. Spivey, M. Feldkamp, K. Ormond, D. Matsui, A. K. Stein-Schechman, L. Cook, J. Brochu, M. Rieder, & G. Koren, Pregnancy outcome following maternal use of the new selective serotonin reuptake inhibitors, 1998. *Journal of the American Medical Association, 279,* 609–610; B. M. Lester & M. Dreher, Effects of marijuana use during pregnancy on newborn cry, 1998. *Child Development, 60,* 765–771; B. L. Lundy, N. A. Jones, T. Field, G. Nearing, M. Davalos, P. A. Pietro, S. Schanberg, & C. Kuhn, Prenatal depression effects on neonates, 1999. *Infant Behavior and Development, 22*(1), 119–129; M. L. Martinez-Frias, E. Rodriguez-Pinilla, E. Bermejo, & L. Prieto, Prenatal exposure to sex hormones: A case-control study, 1998. *Teratology, 57*(1), 8–12; A. Nehlig & G. Debry, Potential teratogenic and neurodevelopmental consequences of coffee and caffeine exposure: A review of human and animal data, 1994. *Neurotoxicology and Teratology, 16,* 531–543; T. A. Rizzo, B. E. Metzger, S. L. Dooley, & N. H. Cho, Early malnutrition and child neurobehavioral development: Insights from the study of children of diabetic mothers, 1997. *Child Development, 68*(1), 26–38; T. S. Roy, J. E. Andrews, F. J. Seidler, & T. A. Slotkin, Nicotine evokes cell death in embryonic rat brain during neurulation, 1998. *Journal of Pharmacology and Experimental Therapy, 287*(3), 1136–1144; D. H. Rubin, B. Krasilnikoff, J. M. Leventhal, B. Weile, & A. Berget, Effect of passive smoking on birth-weight, 1986. *Lancet, 2,* 415–417; M. L. Schneider, E. C. Roughton, A. J. Koehler, & G. R. Lubach, Growth and development following prenatal stress exposure in primates: An examination of ontogenetic vulnerability, 1999. *Child Development, 70*(2), 263–274; P. Schuetze & P. S. Zeskind, Relation between reported maternal caffeine consumption during pregnancy and neonatal state and heart rate, 1997. *Infant Behavior and Development, 20*(4), 559–562; R. Taylor, Cracking cocaine's legacy in babies of drug abusers, 1989. *Journal of NIH Research, 1,* 29–32; C. V. Vorhees & E. Mollnow, Behavioral teratogenesis: Long-term influences on behavior from early exposure to environmental agents, 1987. In J. D. Osofsky (Ed.), *Handbook of infant development.* New York: Wiley.

Riley, 1983). Long-term follow-up studies have shown continuing effects in children in a dose-response relationship as late as 14 years of age, including problems with attention, speed of information processing, and learning problems (Streissguth et al., 1984; Streissguth, Barr, Sampson, & Bookstein, 1994). The effects are relatively small for children whose mothers had one drink per day but increase rapidly with higher rates of consumption.

The evidence is not strong that low levels of alcohol consumption during pregnancy will have an effect, but there may be unmeasured consequences. Pregnant women are best advised to eliminate all alcohol consumption until after their babies have been born. On the other hand, if you are currently pregnant and have been a light or occasional drinker since conception, the chances of this having an effect on your baby are relatively small. Nevertheless, you should terminate further alcohol consumption until after the birth of the baby.

Smoking both tobacco and marijuana has been shown to cause respiratory problems, birth complications, and learning disabilities in early childhood (Lester & Dreher, 1989; Moss, Colombo, Mitchell, & Horowitz, 1988; G. A. Richardson, Day, & Taylor, 1989). Remarkably, the effect of cigarette smoking on reducing the birthweight of the fetus is the same whether it is the mother or the father who smokes, and if both smoke, the effect is doubled. As in related studies of older children and adults, passive smoking has effects just as severe as those of direct smoking and causes respiratory problems in those exposed (D. H. Rubin, Krasilnikoff, Leventhal, Weile, & Berget, 1986). Both parents should refrain from smoking during the mother's pregnancy.

With cocaine and intravenous drug use on the rise, there is an increasing incidence of cocaine-addicted pregnant women, as well as women infected with the AIDS virus. Cocaine use by mothers reduces birthweight and creates circulatory, respiratory, and urinary problems. It also increases the risk of Sudden Infant Death Syndrome (see Chapter 6), attentional difficulties, and lags in motor development. Although cocaine-exposed infants often fall within the normal range, they have slight deficits in attention and emotional responding compared to nonexposed infants. Also, as with other teratogenic effects related to drug and alcohol abuse,

mothers who abuse substances may have other health risks such as poor diet and poor prenatal care, and these other risks, rather than the drug itself, may be the cause of problems in the newborn. The long-term effects of cocaine on the infant may also be confounded with behavioral factors associated with drug abuse, such as poverty, maternal depression, family disruption, child abuse, and neglect (Alessandri, Sullivan, Imaizumi, & Lewis, 1993; Arendt, Singer, Angelopoulos, Bass-Busdiecker, & Mascia, 1998; Bendersky & Lewis, 1998; Bingol, Fuchs, Diaz, Stone, & Gromisch, 1987; Espy, Riese, & Francis, 1997; T. L. Hawley & Disney, 1992; Mayes, Granger, Bornstein, & Zuckerman, 1992; Mayes, Granger, Frank, Schottenfeld, & Bornstein, 1993; Mayes et al., 1997; Mitra, Ganesh, & Apuzzio, 1994; T. R. Moore, Sorg, Miller, Key, & Resnik, 1986; L. T. Singer et al., 1999; R. Taylor, 1989; Woods, Eyler, Behnke, & Conlon, 1993).

One of the problems that occurs with infants born to substance-abusing mothers is that professionals who come in contact with the infant, such as nursing staff, may inadvertently provide less adequate care. This is due to the popular belief by professionals that cocaine and other recreational and illegal drugs have strong and lasting effects on the infant, even though the research evidence suggests that there is considerable controversy about whether such effects actually occur. The lower quality of care by professionals may also be due to stereotypes that stigmatize drug abusers. It is recommended that professionals maintain a neutral and unbiased demeanor toward such infants, who certainly have had no choice in their own fates and may be just as healthy at birth as nonexposed infants (Mayes, Granger, Bornstein, & Zuckerman, 1992; Meyers & Kaltenbach, 1992).

It is also important to treat both the mother and the infant for the effects of drug withdrawal and to help the family recover from drug abuse. Extra support services are needed to help the family become economically and emotionally stabilized. Comforting an infant who is experiencing withdrawal symptoms is also difficult. It is recommended that the infant be kept quiet in a room with dim lights and low noise levels. Play soft music, hold and rock the baby gently and frequently, speak softly and calmly, and give gentle massages (Pawl, 1992; White, 1992).

Another area of recent research work is the transmission of acquired immune deficiency syndrome (AIDS) from the pregnant woman to the fetus. AIDS has become a global epidemic, affecting more than 6 million people worldwide. More than 20 million are infected with HIV-1, the virus that causes AIDS. In the United States, AIDS is the leading cause of death among younger men and the fourth leading cause of death among younger women (T. C. Quinn, 1995). The proportion of infants who contract AIDS prenatally varies across studies, but reported percentages range from 15% (Europe and North America) to 30% (Africa).

AIDS may contribute to low birthweight, although it is difficult to separate its effects from the effects of other risk factors like drug abuse (drug abusers may have contracted the AIDS virus from unclean needles). The biggest risk comes after birth, when infants begin to show signs of the disease. These infants are susceptible to infections that may lead to mental or motor deficits. It is not entirely clear how infants become infected with the AIDS virus. Some may get it prenatally. As with other sexually transmitted diseases (see Table 3.4), the may be a risk of infection by the virus as the infant comes into contact with the mother's body fluids during its passage through the birth canal. In some, but not all, cases, the risk may be reduced by as much as half by cesarean birth (A. Blank, Mofenson, Willoughby, & Yaffe, 1994; Paiva, Hutto, Antunes, & Scott, 1994; Spinillo et al., 1994; Touraine, Sanhadji, & Firouzi, 1994; Towers, Deveikis, Asrat, Nageotte, & Freeman, 1993). A third possible route of transmission is through breast milk after birth (see Chapter 4).

One problem with understanding teratology is that so much of our modern environment is made up of potentially harmful chemicals, pollutants, and radiation. Some are harmful to people of all ages, causing cancer and other diseases. In some cases, the fetus may be more susceptible than older children and adults. Another problem in establishing the effects of a teratogenic agent is that these effects are not always seen immediately. Some effects may take 20 or 30 years to develop, if, for example, they affect the functioning of the adult (Karcew, 1994). Teratogens may not always operate through the mother, although there is relatively little evidence at the current time that the father's exposure to drugs and other agents causes birth defects either through the sperm or by contact with the mother during pregnancy (Little & Vainio, 1994).

Experts advise that pregnant women should take no drugs unless explicitly advised by a physician. Even a seemingly harmless drug like aspirin, especially when taken late in pregnancy, can cause problems with labor and delivery. With all prescription drugs, it is wise for the mother to question the physician about the availability of research on the drug's teratogenic effects. Women are counseled to avoid alcohol, cigarettes, X rays, microwaves, food containing preservatives, colorings and other artificial additives, and contact with people who have viral diseases and other infections. Consult with a physician before taking vitamins or using caffeine (note that many cola drinks contain caffeine). Use sodium bicarbonate (baking soda) as an antacid and natural fiber foods as a laxative. Literature on making pregnancy safe for the baby and mother is available from the March of Dimes Birth Defects Foundation, 1275 Mamaroneck Avenue, White Plains, New York 10605.

Can Birth Defects Be Prevented?

The prevention of all forms of birth defects involves two aspects: diagnosis and treatment. If parents suspect that they may be at risk for having children with genetic, chromosomal, or teratogenic disorders, they should consult with their physician. Usually, parents are referred for **genetic counseling,** a service that can help investigate family histories and prescribe certain kinds of diagnostic approaches.

Most chromosomal abnormalities and many genetic disorders can be detected in fetuses as young as 16 weeks by **amniocentesis.** During this procedure, a small amount of amniotic fluid is withdrawn from the mother's uterus through a long hollow needle inserted into the mother's abdomen. The fetal cells present in the fluid can be tested for the presence of more than 100 genetic or chromosomal abnormalities. The sex of the fetus can also be determined.

Usually, amniocentesis is done only in circumstances where some problem is suspected—for example, if the mother is over the age of 35 or if there is a history of genetic disorders in the family—

because some risk is associated with the procedure. One or 2 out of every 200 women will have a spontaneous abortion after the procedure, and 4 to 6 fetuses may receive minor injuries due to puncture wounds. In addition, the cost of the procedure increases depending upon the number of laboratory tests that are needed to analyze the amniotic fluid. On the positive side, a long-term follow-up study of children aged 7 to 18 whose mothers had amniocentesis, compared to a group of children whose mothers did not undergo the procedure, found no significant differences in the two groups on learning skills and motor and physical development (Baird, Yee, & Sadovnick, 1994).

Another procedure for diagnosing genetic abnormalities is ultrasound. Ultrasound carries less risk than amniocentesis, but it is less able to detect genetic and chromosomal problems: only gross abnormalities of the body can be seen and detected using this procedure. Ultrasound has also been used during amniocentesis to help locate the position of the fetus's body before the needle is inserted. Ultrasound can detect the presence of multiple fetuses and the placement of the fetus (Barss, Benacerraf, & Frigoletto, 1985).

One problem with these methods is that they cannot be done until relatively late in the pregnancy, usually at the beginning of the second trimester. By that time, the parents' anxiety levels are likely to be high, and the decision to abort a malformed fetus is more difficult because of the mother's growing emotional attachment to it and because an abortion will require more complex surgical techniques.

In **chorionic villus sampling (CVS),** a recently developed test, a bit of the chorion is sampled. CVS has the advantage of diagnosing a wider range of disorders, and it can be done during the first trimester. It does not require that the physician puncture the amnion, and it is relatively painless since the uterus is entered through the vagina rather than through the abdomen. Ultrasound may be used to guide the sampling procedure. CVS causes only minor discomfort to the mother and has a 100% diagnostic success rate. The data on the safety of CVS for the fetus are mixed. Some research reports no increased risk from the use of the procedure (J. E. Green et al., 1988; Smidt-Jensen & Hahnemann, 1988; Von Hemel, Majoor-Krakauer, Jahoda, & Sachs, 1986). On the other hand, several studies have found that CVS produces a higher percentage of both spontaneous abortion and limb defects. The incidence of limb deformities may depend on the timing of the test, so more research is needed (Hsieh et al., 1995; Palo, Piiroinen, Honkonen, Lakkala, & Aula, 1994). On the other hand, the actual percentage of problems resulting from these procedures is very low—from 0.5 to 2.0% of all the tested pregnancies. Families need to weigh the benefits and risks of the procedure against their reasons for seeking genetic counseling (Boss, 1994; Cutillo et al., 1994).

Unfortunately, many types of disorders cannot be detected with any of these diagnostic procedures. In addition, each disorder requires a specific test, and each test can be quite costly. Thus, genetic counseling must be selective and done only with a thorough knowledge of the family history.

In actuality, very few of the causes of birth defects and prenatal disorders are clearly understood, and when defects or disorders are discovered, parents are often upset and confused. Research shows that it is better for parents to consult professional genetic counselors rather than their primary care physicians. Many physicians do not know the field of genetic research and may not understand the options available for parents when a prenatal disorder is detected (Geller et al., 1993; Wright, 1994).

A number of new procedures for prenatal diagnosis have been developed. Several disorders, including spina bifida (exposed spine) and anencephaly (exposed brain), can be detected by testing the mother's blood between the 15th and 18th weeks of pregnancy. The test is for **maternal serum alpha-fetoprotein (MSAFP),** and it is safe for both mother and fetus. Researchers are developing experimental methods for testing the fertilized zygote before it is implanted. Called **preimplantation genetic diagnosis (PGD),** the test may provide significant information without spontaneous abortion of an already implanted embryo, which may be an unacceptable risk for some families who would otherwise choose CVS (Verlinsky & Kuliev, 1994). PGD requires procedures similar to those used during in vitro fertilization: the zygote would be removed from the mother for testing and then implanted if it proves healthy.

After such tests are made and a prenatal disorder is discovered, what can be done to treat the problem? Currently, three avenues of treatment are available: the fetus can be treated medically while inside the uterus, the doctor and family can make concrete plans for treatment following the birth, or the family can choose to abort the fetus.

Fetal medicine is one of the fastest-growing fields of medicine. Doctors have had success treating certain disorders by giving vitamins to the mother. In other cases, tubes have been inserted into the fetus to draw blood or to drain harmful buildups of fluids from the head or the bladder. Some malformations, such as intestinal openings or blockages and respiratory and neural disorders, can be repaired surgically. Ultrasound can be used to monitor the progress of the disease, the intervention, and the treatment. Fetal medicine can pose risks to both mother and fetus, however, and these need to be carefully evaluated by future research. Among the problems of doing surgery on a fetus are how to move it into the desired position for the intervention, how to make the fetus relax during the procedure, and how to administer anesthetics, all without undue risk to the mother (Collins, 1994; Forestier, Kaplan, & Cox, 1988; Frigoletto, Greene, Benacerraf, Barss, & Saltzman, 1986). A growing number of advanced post-childbirth surgical and drug treatments are becoming available for such disorders as heart defects, facial deformities (cleft palate, for instance), and PKU. Information on genetic counseling is also available from the March of Dimes Birth Defects Foundation.

What Are Some Ethical Issues Raised by Genetic Counseling?

Like in vitro fertilization, genetic counseling and screening for prenatal disorders raise significant ethical questions. If a serious disorder is discovered, few treatments are available, and abortion is often the only option for a family that does not want to bring a child into the world who is likely to be severely handicapped (see the next section). Another side of the picture is the use of prenatal screening to enable parents to choose to carry or abort a child who does not meet their specifications but is otherwise healthy. Already parents can use CVS to determine the embryo's sex and choose to carry to term only a boy or a girl, depending upon their preference.

It is possible that these procedures may produce a higher percentage of wanted compared to unwanted infants. Research in Sweden shows that better parent-child relationships, even over a long-term follow-up lasting 25 years, result from raising children who fit the parents' prenatal sex preference (Stattin & Klackenberg-Larsson, 1991). However, this does not mean that selecting one sex and aborting another will automatically lead to better parent-child relationships.

Consider the following futuristic possibility. Using in vitro fertilization methods, one cell is removed from the developing embryo. In the relatively near future, we will be able to analyze the entire genetic code of this embryo, and we may have full knowledge of how the entire genotype transforms into the phenotype of the whole individual. According to one scientist,

> All of this information could be transferred to a super-computer, together with information about the environment—including likely nutrition, environmental toxins, sunlight, and so forth. The output will be a color movie in which the embryo develops into a fetus, is born, and then grows into an adult, explicitly depicting body size and shape and hair, skin, and eye color . . . speech and musical ability; the mother will be able to hear the embryo—as an adult—speak or sing. (Lodish, 1995, p. 1609)

Could medical technology make this happen? That depends upon your theoretical point of view (see Chapter 2)—in particular, on whether you believe that the development of the individual is completely determined by the genes, the environment, or their links. One theory, called *dynamic systems,* suggests that we will never be able to predict the outcome of human development, even if we know everything about the genetic code. Development involves a certain amount of indeterminism—butterfly effects—that could easily change the course of a person's development and for which no direct causes could be found.

Perhaps future computers will be so sophisticated that they will be able to introduce a few butterfly effects, such as a kind word said by a teacher or a chance meeting that leads to a career choice, and thus generate a lot of possible future adults from a single embryo. Would parents then be permitted to abort an embryo if they did not like any of these simulated adults? Or could parents, with this knowledge, know when and how to expose their children to particular butterfly events, thereby controlling the children's entire lives so as to sculpt them into the kind of persons the parents imagine? Would children become mere puppets in the hands of such godlike parents and scientists? Are these ideas any more than fantasy and science fiction? Only the future will tell us.

Elective Abortion

There are many reasons why parents might make the choice to end the pregnancy by means of induced or elective abortion: to prevent birth defects, to protect the life or health of the mother, in cases of rape or incest, because of poverty, and as a means of birth control. The last two reasons—low income and birth control—account for most abortions.

On an international level, the worldwide trend is toward the liberalization of abortion laws (Henshaw, 1994). Abortion is legal in the United States. The Constitution of the United States includes the right to privacy, and that right pertains especially to personal decisions made in the context of the home and the family. In their 1973 decision in *Roe v. Wade,* the justices of the U.S. Supreme Court concluded that the decision to terminate a pregnancy is part of a woman's right to privacy guaranteed by the Constitution. The Court's decision further divided pregnancy into three equal periods. In the first period (conception to 12 weeks), the decision to abort was up to the mother and her physician. In the second period (13 to 24 weeks), because abortion is more complicated, the health and safety of the mother was the main deciding factor. No limitations were placed on the reasons for abortion during these two periods. After 25 weeks, abortions were not permitted, except when the mother's life or health was in extreme danger. In 1992, in *Planned Parenthood v. Casey,* the Court made clear that states may not criminalize abortion prior to 24 weeks nor prevent any woman from exercising her choice to terminate her pregnancy (Kolbert & Miller, 1994).

A central issue in *Roe v. Wade* was the question of fetal viability. **Viability** refers to the ability of the fetus to survive on its own, without dependence on the mother. Medically speaking, a fetus is viable if after birth it can be sustained on life-support systems in a neonatal intensive care unit (see Chapter 4). Viability begins between 24 and 30 weeks (Grobstein, 1988). These medical findings are consistent with the *Roe* decision.

An entirely different issue is, "When does human life begin?" According to Lewis Thomas of the Memorial Sloan-Kettering Cancer Center in New York City, the question of when human life begins can be resolved "only in the domain of metaphysics. It can be argued by philosophers and theologians, but it lies beyond the reach of science." Taking the opposite view, Charles A. Gardner states:

> *There will always be arguments based on spiritual or ethical beliefs to convince an individual of the rightness or wrongness of abortion, but each person should first understand the biology to which those beliefs refer.* (Gardner, 1989, pp. 557–559)

With regard to biological development, it is often argued that the zygote at conception is human because it contains all of the necessary genetic instructions to make an individual human being. As we saw earlier in the chapter, however, the zygote can develop only by a complex process of interaction with the environment. The location and biochemical environment of a cell, not just its genetic code, are what determines the phenotype. There is no preformed person residing in the zygote or even in the embryo; the person is a complex gene-environment interaction that takes a long time and the proper nutrients to grow.

Abortion foes suggest that one way to decrease the number of abortions due to family planning is simply to encourage more contraception. This idea has both merits and drawbacks (see the "Applications" section on family planning in this chapter). Another alternative to abortion is carrying the infant to term and placing the infant for adoption. However, because most abortions are performed on young women living in poverty who may suffer from drug and alcohol abuse and poor prenatal care, removing abortion rights from these women increases the chances of teratogenic effects ranging from preterm birth at one extreme and retardation and deformity on the other. The costs to society (who will take care of these children, and who will pay for their care?) and the ultimate quality of life of the children (related to their particular ailments and to the fact that handicapped children in foster care have a high probability of being subjected to child abuse) must be taken into account in formulating public policies on adoption versus abortion.

Another argument in favor of the human individuality of the embryo and fetus is that the fetus feels pain. Given the chronology of fetal behavior and development established by research (see Tables 3.1 and 3.2), we can see that reflexes begin to appear at twelve weeks. Compare this development, however, to the development of the brain and nervous system (Figure 3.4). The 12-week-old fetus has an extremely rudimentary nervous system. Anything even closely resembling a human brain does not form until the twentieth week, and brain electrical activity (EEG) resembling that of adults does not begin until between 26 and 30 weeks. This age corresponds with other measures of viability, suggesting that a brain that is capable of feeling pain and behaving intentionally develops only late in fetal life (Grobstein, 1988).

Should these scientifically based observations take precedence over moral and ethical considerations? Certainly not. The decision to seek an abortion is a personal one based on social, scientific, medical, and moral considerations and made in consultation with genetic counselors, physicians, family members, or religious leaders.

Abortion rates can be reduced by providing individuals with more education and access to family planning methods (see the "Applications" section on family planning). In the Netherlands, abortion rates have declined steadily due to a reduction in unwanted pregnancies. The Dutch have achieved this decline through their success in preventing teenage pregnancies (by means of sex education, open discussion of sexuality in the mass media, educational campaigns, and family planning services that are available to everyone) and also through the growing acceptance of sterilization as a contraceptive practice (Ketting & Visser, 1994).

Prenatal Mortality

Prenatal mortality, or pregnancy loss, is rather common. *Spontaneous abortion* (the rejection of the zygote or embryo by the mother's body) is believed to occur in 40 to 60% of pregnancies (Little, 1988). In many cases, women may not even be aware that they were pregnant. Many spontaneous abortions occur due to genetic and chromosomal abnormalities of the embryo. *Miscarriage* is another term for spontaneous abortion. The term "spontaneous abortion" typically applies to an embryo, while "miscarriage" is used with respect to a fetus. Miscarriage during the fetal period is caused by genetic and chromosomal abnormalities and also by some teratogens, and by diseases of the maternal reproductive system. Finally, *stillbirth* is the loss of a full-term infant who dies just before or during delivery. Stillbirth may be caused by some of the same factors as miscarriage and also by poor prenatal care and poverty (Kapoor, Amand, & Kumar, 1994; Katz & Kuller, 1994).

Following miscarriage and stillbirth, both mothers and fathers (Puddifoot & Johnson, 1999) suffer from grief due to the loss. Often they feel self-blame and anger (Madden, 1994; Wheeler, 1994). It helps parents to enter a support program that empathizes with their situation and helps them work through their strong emotions (A. F. Hartmann, Radin, & McConnell, 1992; Speraw, 1994). Non-Western and ancient cultures have developed a variety of healing rituals to help parents resolve their grief and even to attempt to prevent the loss. These practices include ritual purification, special prayers, and herbal medicines. The rituals emphasize the depth of feeling both men and women have for the loss of their child (Kuller & Katz, 1994). In the next section, we examine the effects of pregnancy on the family.

Family and Society

Although new parenthood can be thought of as a crisis, it is perhaps more appropriate to call it a major phase of adult development. It is a phase, not unlike infancy or adolescence, that requires a good deal of adaptation. Like most other important developmental phases, parenthood has its own pleasures and sorrows, rewards and misgivings, and memories both fond and painful. For most people, the first step in becoming a parent is pregnancy.

The first issue that new parents must deal with is the physical changes that a woman's body undergoes during that 9-month period.

What Are the Physical Changes Associated with Pregnancy?

As can be seen from our discussion of risk factors during pregnancy, maternal and fetal health is extremely important in maintaining fetal development on a normal course. In this section, I will review some of the factors and behaviors that promote health during pregnancy. These include checkups, diet, and exercise.

What are the first signs of pregnancy? The failure to menstruate is usually considered to be the most reliable indicator, but it is not foolproof. A woman may menstruate for 2 or three months after she has conceived, and failure to menstruate may occur for other reasons, such as age, illness, or emotional upset. Breast changes may also be symptomatic of pregnancy. These may occur in the form of fullness, tingling, or hypersensitivity. About half of all women experience some nausea, usually in the morning, but this typically passes after 8 weeks. Some believe "morning sickness" is related to biochemical changes, while others think it is an adaptive mechanism that functions to provide a reason for the mother to get more sleep and rest or to enhance the development of the placenta and embryo. Morning sickness may be controlled naturally by changes in diet and rest patterns. In extreme cases, some physician-prescribed antihistamines are effective and have no known teratogenic effects (Seto, Einarson, & Koren, 1997).

Other symptoms of pregnancy are fatigue and frequency of urination. Conclusive diagnosis can only be obtained through laboratory tests, however. Pregnancy test kits are currently available for use at home, but they are not reliable in all cases.

During pregnancy, the uterus grows from about 2 ounces to 2 pounds, and the abdominal muscle fibers grow to about 10 times their original length. Maternal uterine muscles are extremely important for a number of reasons. They will open the cervix at birth to provide a passage for the baby, contract to push the infant out, and continue to contract after birth to restrict the continued flow of blood to the uterus. The latter function is essential to avoid a major blood loss. The vaginal muscles also change during pregnancy. The vagina increases in length and capacity, and more blood is supplied to the area. In addition, vaginal secretions increase in quantity and in bacteriological action.

Because of these secretions, sexual intercourse during pregnancy may be more satisfying to some women than it was before. In general, sexual intercourse during pregnancy is not harmful. Consultation with one's physician is suggested since each woman is different, and intercourse during late pregnancy may not be advisable.

Physicians who care for the health of the mother and fetus during pregnancy and who deliver babies are called **obstetrician/gynecologists.** Midwives (see Chapter 4) also provide prenatal care and support. Those who care for the baby immediately after birth and during childhood are called **pediatricians.** Women should be encouraged to discuss all aspects of their pregnancy and delivery with their obstetricians. Obstetricians differ in their willingness to answer questions and to allow a mother to make decisions about the course of her labor and delivery. To the extent possible, women should select an obstetrician whose beliefs and practices accord with their own. Most midwives and obstetrician/gynecologists recommend regular prenatal checkups. The frequency of these checkups and what is done depend upon the mother's health status and risk factors.

Proper health care during pregnancy has been shown to prevent many environmentally caused birth defects, reduce the rate of premature births, and reduce prenatal mortality and health risks for both mother and fetus. Due to poverty, fear, or unwanted or teen pregnancy, as many as 20% of women in the United States do not receive prenatal care during the first trimester of pregnancy. Government and health care officials are working to reduce this percentage (Fischer & Rozenberg, 1999; Klerman & Goldenberg, 1999).

As pregnancy proceeds, the placenta forms within the uterus and secretes hormones that nurture the fetus and also prepare the mother's body for birth. The placenta is constructed to enhance the ex-

Artery to mother's system

Vein to mother's system

Mother's blood

Umbilical arteries

Umbilical vein

Placenta (cross section)

Figure 3.9
Changes in Maternal Circulatory System during Pregnancy

A detailed cross section of the placenta is shown here. Note that the placenta has two portions—the embryo's portion and the mother's—and that they are interwoven. Those parts of the drawing that belong to the embryo are shown in light gray; those of the mother are in a darker gray. The gray umbilical vein and arteries carry the embryo's blood, exchanging nutrients, wastes, and the like, with the mother's blood, but the two blood supplies do not come in direct contact.

Source: A. Fogel & G. F. Melson, *Child development*, 1988, p. 108. St. Paul, MN: West. Copyright © by West Publishing Co. Reprinted by permission. All rights reserved.

change of nutrients and other substances between the mother's and the fetus's blood supply (see Figure 3.9). As we saw earlier, the placenta filters some things and allows others to pass through.

In reality, because the fetus has genes from the father as well as the mother, it exists within her as a foreign body. Under most circumstances, such foreign cells would be attacked by a person's immune system. Why does this not happen to the fetus? Apparently, the cells in the uterus near the placenta are responsible for blocking the local production of the immune response system. Studies of how the uterus does this may have applications in cancer research (because cancerous tumors may block the immune system) and in organ transplants, where doctors would like to stop the normal process of rejection (Silberner, 1986).

The placental hormones also induce changes in the breasts as they become ready for lactation. They increase in size as fat is replaced by mammary gland tissue and more blood supply. A clear, yellowish liquid called **colostrum,** high in protein and antibodies, may be secreted by the fourth month of pregnancy. Colostrum is the first food of the breast-fed infant. It is gradually replaced by milk during the first few days after birth.

In general, the mother's body adapts itself to work harder. The mother's digestive and eliminative systems (kidneys, intestines, and sweat glands) must begin to take on the requirements of the developing fetus. These extra requirements are often accompanied by discomfort. Typical complaints of pregnant women include leg cramps, varicose veins, temporary changes in skin pigmentation, stretch marks on the abdomen, shortness of breath, lethargy, indigestion, constipation, and moodiness. The quality of sleep also changes. Women wake up more frequently during the night and sleep less deeply (Brunner et al,. 1994). The severity of these symptoms depends upon the woman's body structure, nutritional status, fatigue, and psychological sense of well-being.

All of these facts show how the mother and fetus comprise a unique biological system in which feedback between them accounts for their mutual development. As the fetus changes, the mother's body changes in response, and continued changes in her body and its functioning provide the nourishment and biological support necessary for fetal growth and development. Both mother and fetus act as a system in their exchange of materials with the outside environment. One of the most important aspects of this interchange is the intake of food by the mother.

The main purpose of good prenatal nutrition is to avoid depletion of maternal stores of nutrients and to allow the mother to produce sufficient milk for breast-feeding (Guthrie, 1979). Malnutrition during pregnancy does more than simply deplete the mother's nutritional supplies; brain development can be severely hampered in an infant born to a malnourished mother. Because the number of neuronal brain cells does not substantially increase after 20 weeks' gestational age, the early months of pregnancy are a critical period for brain development, and the nutrition that the fetus receives from the mother will determine how many cells are produced.

The average weight gain for women in pregnancy is about 24 pounds, although it can be as high as 50 pounds or more depending upon the size of the infant and the mother's constitution. Severe restriction of calories during pregnancy is not recommended and may even be harmful. Too little weight gain is associated with low-birthweight infants, while excessive weight gain is associated with overly high birthweights (Cogswell, Serdula, Hungerford, & Yip, 1995). Adolescent girls require even more nutritional enrichment than adults because their bodies are still growing. Mothers are advised to eat a diet of balanced foods rather than taking vitamin and mineral supplements, since some vitamins may harm the fetus if taken in large quantities.

Mothers may continue to exercise during pregnancy and will derive benefits of cardiovascular fitness similar to those they experience when they are not pregnant. Maternal exercise during pregnancy is not associated with any known harmful effect on the fetus or newborn, and it contributes to the mother's sense of well-being. Mothers should check with their physicians to determine the right level of exercise in relation to the condition of their pregnancy (Technical bulletin no. 189, 1994).

Aside from nutrients, the mother receives information from the social environment, and the feedback processes that govern this exchange may ultimately affect the health and development of the baby. One of the most important sources of interchange for the mother is her relationship with her family and her own psychological adjustment to the state of becoming a parent. Although the effect is most apparent in first-time parents, each new baby brings with it a continuing psychological adaptation within the mother and within each of the other family members.

How Do Mothers Adapt Psychologically to Pregnancy?

In writing about this phase of adult development, Alice Rossi (1968) coined the term "transition to parenthood" as a way of capturing the developmental aspects of the change but avoiding any connotation of its being a major crisis. According to Rossi, parenthood, and not marriage, is the major transition into adult life. Erik Erikson referred to parenting as generativity, the giving of one's time and energy to the next generation (see Chapter 2). The birth of an infant is both a physical and a psychological point of no return. Unlike marriage, birth and parenthood are irreversible processes.

One of the reasons that pregnancy and childbirth are psychologically important is that to some extent they constitute a break from one's own childhood. Once people have a child of their own, they lose the "innocence" of being only a child of their parents. Ironically, pregnancy and childbirth often move women closer to their own mothers at the same time that the women are moving apart from them. The new mother moves away from her previous sense of dependency on her own mother and toward a greater sense of identification with her mother. Meanwhile, the new mother's parents may be encouraged to renew or readjust their feelings about their daughter by attempting to reestablish bonds that were strained or broken during adolescence or young adulthood. In later chapters, I will discuss the next phases of the transition to parenthood after the baby is born. In this chapter, I cover the parents' adaptation to pregnancy.

Pregnancy is not entirely free of difficulties. The stress of carrying the child and adapting to the physiological changes of one's body, and the psychological conflicts attached to the awareness of inevitable, impending parenthood, help contribute to the difficulty of the adaptation (Grimm, 1967). In general, adaptation to pregnancy involves coping with these unexpected emotions and with the physical changes of one's body.

During the later stages of pregnancy, many women in North America become preoccupied with their weight gain. In this culture, a high value is placed on a slender and attractive female body. Even though some women enjoy the sense of being pregnant, most worry about their appearance in some way. Many women feel as though they are losing control over their own bodies; they feel conspicuous or embarrassed at times. In the last months, women begin to feel awkward and sexually less attractive, and some worry about losing their husbands to more attractive women. Mothers who were ambivalent about their pregnancies and who were concerned about their appearance and behavior eventually adapted to the parenting role (M. Leifer, 1980).

Although some women report a decline in cognitive abilities during pregnancy, research shows that this is not the case. Pregnant women outperform other women on recognition and recall of pregnancy-related words (Christensen, Poyser, Pollitt, & Cubis, 1999). In the later months of pregnancy, however, women report an increase in daily hassles and a decrease in events that are uplifting (L. M. Thompson, Murphy, O'Hara, & Wallymahmed, 1997). Research shows that knowledge of pregnancy and childbirth helps a woman adapt successfully to the changes she experiences during pregnancy. Thus, prenatal education programs are particularly helpful for mothers (Rautava, Koski, Sillanpaa, & Tuominen, 1992).

Other factors that are related to women's successful adaptation to pregnancy include the presence of the father, marital satisfaction, low levels of family stress, social support from family and friends, ability to remain active, and emotional well-being (Dragonas, Petrogiannis, & Adam, 1997; Klinnert, Gavin, Wamboldt, & Mrazek, 1992; H. Taylor, Baker, & ALSPAC and the Study Team, 1997; K. J. Thorpe, Dragonas, & Golding, 1992). Regarding the protective factor of remaining active, some studies have reported that women adapt better if they continue to work at their jobs during pregnancy, while others have not found this effect. It may be that working is helpful if the mother wants to work and has low family stress (H. Taylor et al. 1997). Mothers who are more conscientious in their prenatal health care appear to be more psychologically involved with their fetus (Fares & Adler, 1998).

One study found that women who worried the least about the pregnancies were the most committed to becoming a parent and had the most involved husbands (M. Leifer, 1980). On average, there appears to be a slight decline in reports of marital satisfaction during the first few years of parenthood. Parents who were more likely to report that their marriages were satisfying, however, were less likely to experience a decline in feelings of tenderness and less likely to quarrel. Their infants were more securely attached at 12 months (Gloger-Tippelt & Huerkamp, 1998).

What Is the Father's Adaptation to Pregnancy Like?

The first-born child is a major source of excitement for the entire family. Aside from the mother, the father is the most closely involved with this process, and the evidence suggests that he, too, undergoes some important developmental changes as well as some specific changes in mood and behavior during this period.

For the male, pregnancy may be seen as a sign of his masculine potency, but it may also be interpreted as a sign of bondage—an end to his fantasy of a life of adventure and freedom. Pregnancy can seem, at least initially, either welcoming or threatening.

Many expectant fathers do not see themselves in merely a supportive role. They have a sense that they, like their mates, are experiencing an important development in their lives. Some cultures have traditions, called **couvade,** that encourage expectant fathers to identify with their mates and to act out the female role in a culturally approved manner. Cross-cultural studies have shown that couvade occurs primarily in societies where females are salient and valued in their roles (B. Whiting, 1974). It may be that the increased involvement of fathers in the childbirth process in our own culture reflects our increasing recognition of the importance of women's contributions to the family and to society. For a father to take time off from work, spend that time going to prenatal classes, discuss feelings openly, attend the delivery, and actively share in the "woman's" world of childbearing is an open expression of the value and worth of that world.

How is couvade expressed in other societies? Fathers in the Ifugao tribe of the Philippines are not permitted to cut wood during their wives' pregnancy, as a form of identification with the changes in lifestyle associated with being pregnant. In the Easter Islands of the Pacific, the wife leans against the husband during labor and delivery. Among the Lepcha, both parents undergo a ceremonial

Table 3.5 Maternal and Paternal Responses
of Feelings about the Unborn Baby

Response	Percentage of Women	Percentage of Men
Worry, anxiety, concern	8	4
Pleased, hopeful, positive	14	11
Talks to, loves, attached	18	8
Ambivalent, negative	13	12
Anticipating birth, curious	48	66

Source: R. T. Mercer et al., Further exploration of maternal and paternal fetal attachment, 1988, p. 92. *Research in Nursing and Health, 11,* 83–95.

cleansing in the fifth month of pregnancy (M. Mead & Newton, 1967).

Many men do not share these feelings; they see the work of childbearing as less important or too threatening. The temptation to engage in extramarital sex increases during pregnancy, and some men report feeling emotionally distant from their wives during pregnancy and childbirth (Gelles, 1978; K. J. Thorpe et al., 1992). Unfortunately, physical abuse by men of their pregnant partners is not uncommon, affecting about one in six adult women in the United States (Parker, McFarlane, & Soeken, 1994). Risk for abuse increases with factors such as teenage pregnancy, low social support, low income, unmarried status, unplanned pregnancy, drug and alcohol abuse, and poor prenatal care (Gielen et al. 1994; Parker et al. 1994; D. E. Stewart & Cecutti, 1993; Webster, Sweett, & Stolz 1994). Abuse during pregnancy is a significant predictor of continued abuse after the child is born (Geilen, O'Campo, Faden, Kass, & Xue, 1994; D. E. Stewart 1994).

At the same time, it is clear that most fathers develop a psychological attachment to the fetus. Mothers' and fathers' attachment to the fetus was assessed in a sample of 218 women and 147 of their mates. The sample was randomly distributed among income, ethnic, and racial groups, and the pregnancies were developing normally. The parents rated their attachment to the fetus and other feelings, as shown in Table 3.5. Both mothers and fathers were similar in their ratings, although fathers were more likely than mothers to be anticipating the birth, while mothers were somewhat more likely to express overt feelings of love for the fetus (Mercer et al. 1988).

Some of the same factors predict a smooth adaptation to pregnancy for both fathers and mothers; they include knowledge of pregnancy and childbirth, social support, marital satisfaction, low levels of family stress, and emotional well-being. Research shows that no single factor is more important than any other, that a successful transition to fatherhood depends on many different processes, and that men may differ with respect to what helps them the most (Hyssala et al. 1993; Klinnert et al. 1992). Many hospitals offer a variety of prenatal education and childbirth preparation classes. These can be very beneficial for maximizing the chances for a healthy and happy pregnancy and childbirth experience.

How Do Siblings Adapt to the Pregnancy?

Advice books for parents tend to recommend that the first child be prepared for the arrival of the baby, although there are differences of opinion about how much to say. An early study (Sewall 1930) found that differences in preparation of the first child during pregnancy did not relate to the severity of the jealousy reactions of the child following the birth of the baby. Other studies (J. Dunn & Kendrick 1982; Trause et al. 1978) have also found no relationship between prenatal preparation and the later quality of the sibling relationship.

It seems that the first child, typically only three or 4 years old, is unlikely to understand the meaning of the mother's attempts at preparation. Even if the child does understand, he or she is unlikely to anticipate the emotional experience that occurs when the new baby arrives. In families in which there is a high level of confrontation between the mother and the first child and in which the mother used prohibition and restraint, the first child was more likely to behave in an interfering or irritating manner toward the new baby (J. Dunn & Kendrick 1982).

Teenage Pregnancies: The Problem That Will Not Go Away?

The majority of infants with birth defects in the United States are born to teenage mothers. The rate of teenage births increased until the late 1980s in the United States and then gradually declined through 1997 for all racial and ethnic groups. The largest decline was for African American teenagers and for second births for teens who already have one child (Ventura, Mathews, & Curtin 1998). In 1997, the birthrate for teens aged 15 through 19 was 36 in 1,000 for whites, 90 in 1,000 for African Americans, and 99 in 1,000 for Hispanic Americans. Thus, in spite of the declines, many teens are still giving birth, and the rate of teen pregnancy is almost twice as high for African Americans and Hispanic Americans as that of Caucasian Americans (Guyer et al. 1998). Teen pregnancy is still a major social problem because teenage mothers require great expenses from society in order to cover their health care and financial support.

Teenage mothers tend to be at risk for all kinds of birth complications. The death rate for infants of teenage mothers is twice that for infants of older mothers, and the incidence of low-birthweight infants is much higher among infants born to teenagers. Are these problems associated solely with the age of the mother? The evidence suggests that there is nothing inherent in the age of the mother alone that would account for these problems. But teenage mothers seem to be at risk for childbearing because such a large proportion of teenage mothers come from poor socioeconomic conditions, with their attendant problems of poor nutrition, high stress, poor medical care, and poor family relationships (Coley & Chase-Lansdale 1998; Gunter & LaBarbera 1980; Phipps-Yonas 1980; Scaramella et al. 1998). Teenage mothers are seven times as likely to be poor before pregnancy as older mothers (Alan Guttmacher Institute 1994).

Marriage and parenting also place increased stress on teenagers. The demands of child and spouse often conflict with the teen's own needs for development, education, and health, and of mature romantic and marital relationships (Coley & Chase-Lansdale 1998). Teenage marriages often end in divorce, leaving many teenage mothers with the additional stress of being a single parent. In general, teenage mothers are less likely to be responsive to their young infants than older mothers are, and teenage mother-infant pairs experience less mutual affection and enjoyment compared to infants with older mothers (Barratt & Roach 1995). Males and females between 30 and 55 years old, both African

American and Caucasian American, who married as adolescents earned less income, completed fewer years of school, and held lower-paying jobs than those who married later (Hardy et al. 1998; Teti and Lamb 1989; Teti, Lamb, & Elster 1987).

Thus, the risks of adolescent pregnancy can best be understood from the perspective of social systems. These studies show how society has a direct impact on the developing infant and on the family. A family that is already stressed by economic factors is likely to view the pregnancy with apathy and resentment, leading to insufficient care during the prenatal months and after the infant is born.

The treatments for the teenage pregnancy problems are complex. They should involve the entire community and culture (Coley & Chase-Lansdale 1998). In general, teenagers are caught in a web of conflicting cultural standards (Marecek 1987). At home, they may receive the message that sex out of wedlock is prohibited. In school, there is peer pressure to engage in sexual behavior, and in the movies and on television, sexuality and sexual activity are glorified. Many movies and shows present macho and sexist themes in which men repress women (S. Gordon 1982; Sprafkin & Silverman 1982). Girls from impoverished homes or those who have suffered physical and sexual abuse may see pregnancy as a way to leave home or establish their own identity.

Other the other hand, better pregnancy outcomes are associated with reduction of psychosocial stress, social support, prenatal care, and a sense that these factors would continue through time (Boyce, Schaefer, & Uitti 1985). In addition, parent education programs tailored to teen mothers have been shown to enhance parental involvement (Zaslow & Eldred 1997).

Teenage fathers are similar to teenage mothers. They are more likely to be poor and to have come from troubled families. They work and earn more than non-parent peers, but because they obtain less education, their lifetime earning ability is considerably reduced. Because of high rates of divorce among teenage parents, only about 50% of teen fathers live with the mother and child sometime after the birth. Cohabitation rates are highest for whites compared to African Americans and Hispanic Americans. By the time the child is of school age, fewer than 25% of teen fathers are still in contact with

Due to national differences in family planning, large families—like the one to which these children from Mexico belong—are common in many places. Often the older children are expected to care for the younger ones.

John Neubauer/PhotoEdit

their children. This low rate of father involvement is related primarily to unstable or hostile relationships between mothers and fathers (Coley & Chase-Lansdale 1998).

Recent research in the United States shows that the majority of teenagers do not have basic knowledge of sexuality, conception, and contraception (Ammerman et al. 1992). For this reason, sex education programs in high school can significantly reduce the risk of teenage pregnancy and increase the incidence of sexual abstinence among adolescents. The most successful programs tend to encourage abstinence, include information about sexuality and contraception, and also provide students with concrete skills for avoiding situations that could lead to unprotected sex (Barth et al. 1992; Glazer 1993a; Weed & Jensen 1993). Sex education programs can also help teens who do become parents by providing important information about prenatal health and nutrition and postnatal child-rearing methods, factors that teen parents often neglect. Another program that has been successful with teenage parents has been to provide them with contact with older parents who can serve as mentors, people to whom they can turn for advice regarding child rearing, staying in school, and other concerns (Rhodes 1993).

The Author's View

The prenatal period is a crucial period (see Chapter 2) of the life course for mental and physical health. Thousands of research studies have documented the importance of regular prenatal care, proper nutrition, and the avoidance of stress and environmental toxins during pregnancy. Genetic and chromosomal factors interact with the intra-uterine environment in ways that regulate the growth of the body and brain. In some cases, the effects of prenatal development can be altered—either enhanced or alleviated. In other cases, deformations in the body and brain cannot be changed. Once a limb or organ is damaged during its critical period for development during the first 6 months of prenatal life, it may never become normal.

A more controversial question is whether prenatal development is a critical period for behavioral and psychological factors. In cases of mental retardation, for example, it is clear that prenatal brain growth has profound psychological consequences. We also know that genetic and chromosomal factors account for at least some differences in people's intelligence and temperament in later life. The research on fetal behavior and the ability of late-term (eight- and nine-month) fetuses to learn, however, raises the possibility that people can retain participatory memories of their prenatal life (see Chapter 2).

In order to have a participatory memory, late-term fetuses must have psychological experiences of sensation and emotion. Is this the case? In my opinion, the data suggest that late-term fetuses can feel their body movements, hear their mother's voices, heartbeats and other sounds, and have rudimentary emotionlike experiences connected with distress and arousal. Their psychological world is probably similar to that of the newborn (see Chapter 5) but not as richly textured with the opportunities for learning that occur after birth. As you do the Awareness through Movement lessons of this chapter, try to follow your own awareness into different sensory, motor, and emotional experiences.

The fetus in this period is probably aware of the sensations generated by the different reflexes. There may also be an awareness of the quality of reflexive movement. Reflexes have a build-up and sudden release. They also have a feeling of inevitability, because once they are set into motion, they will continue until they finish. This would be like feeling a sneeze coming on, building up, and releasing. To be a fetus at this age would be like having each part of your body sneezing in its own way. There would not be any sense of control or any awareness of something beyond these spasmodic experiences and the rest periods between them. Although we cannot be certain, as neural developments allow for more motor control, fetal awareness may begin to emerge. The vestibular system begins to develop after 22 weeks, probably providing an awareness of the orientation of the body with respect to gravity and an awareness of the movement of the whole body as the mother moves and as the fetus turns inside the mother. In adults, this would be like the sensation of being a passenger in a moving vehicle as it turns, stops, and starts. Of course, the fetus has no concept of moving and turning. The fetus is just aware of the feeling of being moved.

The onset of REM sleep may also be a developmental continuation of an increasing awareness of internal processes. It is likely that the fetus becomes aware of rhythmical and cyclical movements during the late fetal period. Fetuses can probably sense the feelings of waking up and falling asleep. They may also be aware of the rhythms of their mother's heartbeat and breathing and of the sound of her voice.

The fetus's awareness and the possibility that infants retain some participatory memories of this period suggest another question. Does enriched or impoverished experience during the last few months of pregnancy lead to positive or negative developmental pathways? We know that healthy prenatal environments lead to positive development for all periods of prenatal development. Perhaps a better question is whether specifically enriching the prenatal environment—playing classical music or massaging the fetus, for example—has any lasting effect.

Just because newborns can recognize sounds heard prenatally does not necessarily make them smarter or more talented for having heard them. Fetuses will move their bodies to loud or percussive music, but this does not mean they like it or that it will help them grow. Many books and Internet sites make strong cases for providing this kind of enrichment to the fetus. Beware when reading these materials, and examine the research they present very carefully to be sure about the limitations of their findings. In many cases, the goal is to get you to buy the book, tape, or equipment that is supposed to enhance fetal development.

Having said all that, singing to, talking to, and massaging the fetus can be a healthy and rewarding thing to do for both mother and fetus. These methods give the fetus a sense of familiarity after he or she is born. They are also natural and enjoyable for mother and father and their attachment to the fetus develops. Singing has all the important features of the human voice and language. Lullabies and other songs convey feelings of love and attachment that are essential for the mother to express and certainly cannot hurt the fetus. These things are free of charge, spontaneous, and can be done anytime of the day or night, and they make parents feel good.

Does the intrauterine environment earlier in pregnancy affect how older fetuses learn and therefore contribute to later development? The earlier development of the brain and sensory organs obviously prepares the fetus to learn. Fetal activity and

Applications Family Planning

At the turn of the millennium, January 1, 2000, the world had an estimated population of 6 billion people. This is double the number of people living in 1960 and triple the number who inhabited the planet in 1927. Although the rate of population growth is slowing, there are likely to be twice as many people alive in 2030 as there are today. Experts do not know how many people the earth can support, but all are concerned about the quality of life that will result. Although some of the growth is due to the fact that people are healthier and living longer than in the past, much of it is due to high birthrates.

Family planning is the voluntary alteration of normal reproductive patterns. The type of family planning used, if it is used at all, depends on a complex network of social and cultural factors interacting with moral and interpersonal factors within the family. In wealthy countries, family planning is a matter of personal choice for middle- and upper-income families. Family planning becomes a critical issue when the population of a country exceeds the ability of the environment to provide for the health and welfare of all the people. The same is true for low-income families in the United States.

Countries can be divided into two groups based on whether they have low or high population growth rates. In countries with low growth rates, the population increases by about 1% each year. The United States falls into this group. In high-growth countries, the population may increase as much as 3% per year, doubling every 25 years or so. This high rate of growth increases the chances of pregnancy and birth complications, prematurity, maternal and infant mortality, and a continuation of the cycle of poverty.

India, for example, has one-third the area of the United States but three times the population. A significant proportion of the people are illiterate and live below the poverty level. They have inadequate food, shelter, and clothing. There is active resistance to family planning, since these families depend for their livelihood on large numbers of children. In the 1970s, India passed a law requiring sterilization for all parents with two or more children who wanted to continue receiving welfare. Although the law was repealed in 1977, sterilization remains the most common form of birth control. The voluntary use of contraception has increased but not sufficiently to halt the population growth (Kumar, 1994).

China has been more successful in reducing its high birthrate. China has about the same area as the United States, but it has five times as many people. In the past 20 years, however, the Chinese have reduced their birthrate to 1% per year by allowing only one child per family (Feeney, 1994). The one-child policy is implemented by granting those who comply more vacation time and more welfare benefits. Elderly women in each village, called "granny police," are charged with counseling and disciplining women who wish to have a second child (Galvin, 1989; Associated Press, 1985). One problem that has arisen in China is that rural families have a strong desire to have a male child who can help with the farmwork. This preference has resulted in increased loss of female infants, partly through surgical abortion once the infant's sex is determined by genetic counseling or

self-stimulation appear to have an effect on fetal development in animals. The early fetal period is likely to affect the later period, but we have no longitudinal studies in humans showing specific effects for individuals.

Do people have memories of their prenatal life, and if so, how would these be experienced by an older child or adult? My interpretation of current research (see also Chapter 2) is that there is no verifiable evidence for people having specific conceptual event memories for anything in their lives before the age of 2 or three years, after language is acquired.

On the other hand, participatory memories of the prenatal period may exist in the form of preferential orientations for certain kinds of movement, posture, sound, taste, and touch. The evidence, however, comes entirely from clinical case studies. If you have chosen to do a qualitative case study on your own experiences doing the Awareness through Movement lessons, you may be able to decide for yourself whether such memories exist and whether you think this is a scientifically valid way of verifying their existence.

Here are some suggestions about what you might observe in yourself. We know, for example, that lying in a fetal posture on a comfortable surface can be relaxing and soothing for children and adults. Infants and young children often curl into fetal postures and suck their thumbs, a behavior commonly found in later-term fetuses. Heartbeat-like sounds, such as drumming and other deep rhythms, can be either soothing or arousing in pleasurable ways. In addition to these experiences, by selective infanticide of female newborns. A recent change in government policy allows families who give birth to a female child first to have the opportunity for a second child (Coale & Banister, 1994).

Other Asian countries such as Taiwan, Japan, and Korea have also reduced their birthrates to 1% per year. In these countries, the change was due not to government policy but rather to trends toward increased modernization over the past 30 years. With modernization, more people move to the cities, where they become better educated and have access to better health care. As a result, the infant mortality rate declines, and more children in the family survive and require financial support. Families therefore voluntarily limit the number of children they choose to have through various contraceptive procedures, including sterilization (Feeney, 1994; Thike, Wai, Oo, & Yi, 1993).

In many African countries, such as the Ivory Coast, where the population is growing at 4% per year, women have as many as seven children apiece, and as the infant mortality rate has declined, the population has increased drastically (Remez, 1996). Women use birth control to space births rather than to reduce the number of children. In some African countries, oral contraceptives are believed to be harmful, and in others, religious taboos against touching one's own genitals prevent the use of condoms and diaphragms. Some new birth control devices are proving highly effective, however. One device is a skin implant similar to birth control pills that prevents conception for 5 years and has been well accepted in cultures that use skin scarification as a beauty practice. Injections of birth control hormones work in areas where people have come to associate injections with good health. The use of female, but not male, sterilization is also becoming more accepted (C. Holden, 1988; Jack & Chao, 1992; Were & Karanja, 1994).

On the whole, it seems that culturally adapted interventions work the best and that education of the people is a necessary ingredient in a successful family planning program. The problem of finding the most appropriate method of family planning is particularly acute among the poor of all nations who lack education. For these women, abortion will continue to be the preferred method of family planning unless policy is changed considerably to provide birth control education and birth control devices on a regular basis.

In the United States, this kind of policy change might mean making birth control education and devices readily available to sexually active teenagers. One bar to such a change is that antiabortion religious values frequently go hand in hand with a prohibition on premarital sex, so that, paradoxically, young people feel they cannot seek alternate methods of contraception. Teenagers, aware of such attitudes among adults, are often reluctant even to broach the subject of their sexuality with parents or counselors. The fact is, however, that a significant proportion of this population is engaging in sexual activity, and society needs to respond to this reality in ways that respect and protect these youths, their families, and their children within the bounds of constitutional protections of rights and privacies.

which are common for many people and may reflect memories, are there individual participatory memories for fetal preferences? Do we like (or dislike) the kind of food that our mothers ate while they were pregnancy with us? Are we more prone to depression or joyfulness because of our mothers' experiences and the possible physiological effects on our fetally developed neurotransmitters?

These questions are likely to be difficult to answer. This is because emotional and behavioral development continues after birth, a period during which the mother's mental health continues to have an impact on the child. In addition, few memories from early life are exact replicas of the early experience. They have been transformed and changed through later experience and interpreted in terms of the remembering person's self-understanding at that time. The impact of the prenatal period on behavioral and psychological development, therefore, is a complex systemic process that has yet to be fully understood.

AWARENESS THROUGH MOVEMENT

Introduction

The prenatal environment is alien compared to life outside the womb. We are surrounded by liquid and largely free from the effects of gravity. Even though capable of many movements, we are restricted by our tight encapsulation in the womb. Also, while our other senses are beginning to function, our mother's body blocks any visual stimulation. Perhaps we can get a glimmer of what prenatal experience might be like by changing our relation to gravity, relearning some fetallike movements, and altering how we use our senses. Here are some experiments you can try.

How to Do the Movements

1. In order to fully experience each movement, read the instructions into a tape recorder and then follow the taped lesson.

2. Lie on a padded floor or firm bed.

3. Move very slowly and make very small movements.

4. Try to reduce your efforts even further, with every movement you make. Do not stretch or strain, and avoid movements that are uncomfortable. Pay particular attention to relaxing your mouth, face, hands, and feet.

5. Notice reactions throughout your body with each movement you perform, and search for ways to coordinate all parts of yourself to make the movement more efficient.

6. After completing a movement, pause fully before repeating the movement or going onto the next step.

7. At the end of a lesson, lie on your back and observe differences in sensation between your left and right sides. After completing the movements on one side, you will probably notice that that side lies on the floor differently from the other. You may experience body-image changes in the apparent sizes and proportions of your two sides, together with changes in the impression of different parts of your body.

The Primacy of Hearing and Touch

Blindfold yourself for a period of at least 1 hour, preferably up to 24 hours. Do this at home so that you are in a familiar environment. Try to go about your various activities to the extent that the blindfold allows. The longer you stay blindfolded, the more you will grow accustomed to relying on your hearing and sense of touch. For sighted people,

the majority of information from the environment comes from vision. The longer we interrupt our use of vision, the more we will depend on our other senses, and those senses will therefore become more acute. In the womb, our hearing and sense of touch developed before our visual sense. Despite the vast array of visual information we receive, the other senses may remain, in some way, more fundamental. What can we learn from reacquainting ourselves with such a different relationship to the world?

Sucking

Position: Lie on your right side in a fetal position. In other words, curl into a ball with your knees and arms bent, and place your hands not far from your mouth.

1. With your mouth slightly open, gently protrude your lips and tongue and then relax them. As you protrude your lips, allow them to turn slightly inside out. Keep your lips full, soft, and moist. Experiment with slower and faster rhythms. Try protruding your mouth sometimes a little to the left, sometimes to the right (rooting movements), and feel the difference in ease between the two directions due to the pull of gravity.

2. With your lips and tongue slightly protruded, begin to make soft sucking movements with your jaw and mouth. Note that this is very different from the ways we squeeze our lips when we suck through a straw. Try to sense how your head, neck, and the rest of your body become involved in the sucking movement. Rest often, and continue sucking. You will probably find that the longer you suck, the more you will feel how the movement involves your entire body. There is a tendency for the head to move a little forward and tilt slightly back, as if to help the movement of opening the mouth and reaching with it. This gentle movement of the mouth, jaw, and head tends to produce a soothing, wavelike movement down the entire spine, all the way to the pelvis and legs. Rest.

3. In order to help relax your mouth, use your fingers to gently pull your lower lip forward,

softly coaxing it to turn inside out. Relax your mouth in order to make your lip more elastic. Rest and notice the differences in sensation between your upper and lower lips.

4. Repeat the same movements with your upper lip.

5. Return to the sucking movements performed in step 2 and feel the difference. Is it easier? Is your mouth softer and more elastic? Begin to experiment with the lengths of the sucking bouts, making fewer or greater rhythmical sucking movements before pausing. Rest.

6. If you want to continue the experiment, repeat movements 1–5 while lying on your left side, and also on your back. Feel how the subtle effects of gravity are different in each position. After birth, the infant must suck differently due to the new needs to coordinate breathing and swallow milk. This is more complex than it might sound. Notice the timing of when you swallow in relation to sucking and how you move your mouth while you swallow. How does sucking influence your breathing just before and just after the swallowing takes place?

Comments

Sucking is one of many movements that we learn to do while still a fetus. Throughout our lifetimes, and especially during our fetal development, our movements help shape the forms of our bodies. Just as later in infancy, weight bearing will alter the curvature of our legs and spine, sucking helps to form our palate. Babies who do not suck normally do not form the high palate that other children have. Also, how infants suck affects the development of their teeth and future patterns of swallowing and speech.

Sucking is the first mouth movement that we master. Later we build on our infant sucking ability as we learn to control thousands of other movements of our mouth and face, including chewing, expressing our emotions, speaking, and singing. Many people experience a deep relaxation of the facial muscles after doing the sucking movements in this lesson. What was your experience?

SUMMARY

Conception and Fertility

- Fertilization takes place when one spermatozoon enters the ovum, creating a zygote.

- Female ova are present but immature at birth. Males do not begin to produce spermatozoa until adolescence.

- Male infertility is caused by different factors than female infertility. Fertility can often be enhanced by natural methods.

- When natural methods fail, surgery and/or in vitro fertilization may be required. In vitro fertilization is usually safe and effective.

- In vitro fertilization raises social and ethical issues that both parents and society need to consider carefully.

- Contraceptive practices vary between individuals. Most people can find a contraceptive method that suits their needs; however, more research needs to be done to find newer methods.

Developmental Processes before Birth

- All cells in the body except the gametes have the same set of genes and chromosomes.

- Development of a cell depends as much on its location and chemical environment as on its genetic composition.

- The period of the embryo begins when the zygote implants in the uterine wall.

- Embryos display rudimentary behavior patterns, such as heartbeats, respiration, and whole-body jerky movements.

- The period of the embryo ends when most of the major internal organs are formed.

- During the period of the fetus, the major developments occur in the brain and nervous system. Later in fetal development, we see the beginnings of controlled movements, such as facial expressions and grasping. After 28 weeks, fetuses have states of arousal and REM sleep, and they can learn.

- Fetal behavior has two purposes: to prepare the child for establishing initial preferences after birth, and to stimulate growth and development of bones, muscles, and the central nervous system.

Individual Differences in Prenatal Development

- Genetic influences can occur through polygenic inheritance, dominant-recessive inheritance, or sex-linked inheritance.

- The action of the genes, as well as the occurrence of genetic disorders, depends on the interaction of the genes with their environments.

- Chromosomal disorders involve additions and deletions of chromosomes.

- Teratogenic effects occur when the maternal environment transmits harmful substances to the fetus. Alcohol, drugs, and diseases are among the common teratogens that produce birth defects of varying severity.

- The higher incidence of birth defects and premature births among teenage mothers can be attributed to the effects of poverty and poor prenatal care, rather than to the age of the mother alone.

- Many birth defects can be diagnosed prenatally through genetic counseling. Treatments include fetal medicine, postnatal intensive care, and abortion.

- Abortion is a controversial issue in the United States, especially if it is done because of low income or for family planning. The rights of a woman to privacy conflict with the possible rights of the fetus in most legal decisions. It is difficult to establish when human life begins, but scientific research can add important information to the debate.

Family and Society

- Mothers must learn to cope psychologically with the physical changes in their bodies that occur during pregnancy.

- Fathers often identify with their mates' changes and act in supportive roles, depending upon their personality and cultural expectations.

- Preparing a first child for the birth of the second child does not seem to affect the amount of later sibling rivalry.

Applications: Family Planning

- The choice of family planning methods depends on personal and cultural values. Family planning is most needed in societies where the size of the population outstrips the ability of the economy and resources to provide for everyone's welfare.

 ON THE WEB

www.kencrest.org "Ken-Crest provides opportunities for people with disabilities to test the limits of their human potential." This web site provides information about Ken-Crest and the services that it provides for children and adults. This web site is routinely updated and provides feedback and other links.

www.waisman.wisc.edu/earlyint/pathways "The Pathways: Service Coordination Project collaborates with key stakeholders in participating states to provide training and technical assistance in early intervention service coordination." This site also provides information on parent-professional partnership, participant-centered training, and collaboration.

www.babycenter.com BabyCenter provides access to thousands of articles on pregnancy and babies in a colorful, user-friendly format. It has a large community of parents and a baby store, along with expert advice and guidance for parents on how to prepare for and take the best possible care for their newborn. The site includes links to information on preconception, pregnancy, fetal development, and the new baby, as well as weekly information on the development of your fetus.

www.childsecure.com This site provides "big health for little kids." It is a pediatric health destination and provides links to expert advice, support groups, breaking news, and more.

www.birthpsychology.com This site provides information on the latest studies and findings regarding the prenatal emotional development of infants. "In these pages you'll be able to explore the many mental and emotional dimensions of pregnancy and birth in everything from scholarly articles to personal stories and late-breaking headlines."

GLOSSARY

Allele A gene whose action depends upon at least one other gene, its allelic counterpart, to produce the phenotype. Usually, alleles are at the same location on each chromosome of a pair.

Amniocentesis Sampling a small amount of amniotic fluid for the purpose of determining the genetic and chromosomal make-up of the fetus.

Amniotic sac A membrane that encloses the embryo and fetus and contains amniotic fluid in which the fetus floats, providing a natural cushion.

Blastocyst A fertilized ovum during the first 2 weeks of prenatal development, before implantation in the uterus.

Cephalocaudal development Growth that proceeds from the top of the body to the bottom.

Chorion The inner lining of the placenta separating it from the amniotic sac.

Chorionic villus sampling (CVS) A test for birth defects in which a small amount of the chorion is sampled. It can be done earlier in pregnancy than amniocentesis.

Chromosome An arrangement of about 20,000 genes, aligned in a long string. Each cell in the body contains 46 chromosomes, except for the gametes, which contain 23 chromosomes.

Cloning A method of creating a zygote by removing the donor mother's DNA from the ova and implanting the DNA from any cell in the body of another person.

Colostrum A clear, yellowish, high-protein liquid secreted by the breasts beginning in the fourth month of pregnancy and continuing until several days after birth.

Conception The fertilization of an ovum.

Couvade A father's attempt to experience the mother's feelings during pregnancy and delivery, seen in the form of culturally accepted rituals.

Cystic fibrosis A genetic disorder that causes clogging of the lungs with mucus.

Dizygotic twins Twins formed when two ova are fertilized at the same time.

DNA (Deoxyribonucleic acid) A molecule that contains a biochemical code for the production of body tissues. Genes are sections of DNA that control the development of specific characteristics and functions of the individual.

Dominant-recessive inheritance A two-gene inheritance pattern in which the recessive gene appears in the phenotype only if no dominant gene is present.

Dorsoventral development Growth that begins at the spine and moves toward the front of the body.

Dose-response relationship A relationship between a drug's dosage and its effects in which increasing dosages lead to stronger effects.

Down's syndrome A chromosomal disorder that causes short stature, cardiac abnormalities, flabbiness, small mouth, and mental retardation.

Ectoderm One of the cell layers in the embryonic disk that will become the central nervous system, brain, sense organs, skin, hair, nails, and teeth (see also endoderm and mesoderm).

Embryo The period of prenatal development beginning in the second week after conception and extending until the third month of pregnancy.

Embryo cryopreservation Freezing fertilized embryos for later implantation into the uterus.

Embryonic disk A layer of cells in the blastocyst that will eventually become the embryo's body.

Endoderm A layer of cells in the embryonic disk that will become the digestive, respiratory, and urinary systems (see also ectoderm and mesoderm).

Familial Alzheimer's disease A genetic disorder that causes deterioration of the central nervous system, leading to lack of mental and motor control.

Fertility The ability to achieve fertilization and become pregnant.

Fetal alcohol syndrome (FAS) A teratogenic disorder caused by excessive alcohol consumption by a pregnant mother. Effects include physical malformations and attentional disorders.

Fetus The period from the third month of prenatal life until delivery of the newborn.

Fragile X syndrome A sex-linked genetic disorder that is the most common inherited cause of mental retardation.

Gametes Spermatozoa or ova: reproductive cells having 23 chromosomes each.

Gene   A section of the DNA molecule that comprises the smallest unit of the codes for inherited characteristics.

Genetic counseling   Assessing the parents' likelihood of producing a child with genetic or chromosomal abnormalities.

Gynecologist   A physician who specializes in women's reproductive health (see also obstetrician).

HCG (human chorionic gonadotropin)   A hormone whose presence signals the onset of pregnancy.

Huntington's disease   A genetic disorder that causes progressive brain damage and death.

Infertility   Failure to achieve fertilization.

In vitro fertilization   Fertilization achieved in a laboratory, outside the mother's body, by surgically removing ova and uniting them with spermatozoa.

Karyotype   An arrangement of chromosome pairs for easy examination; made by photographing a micrograph of a set of chromosomes and then cutting the photograph and placing the chromosome pairs in order.

Kleinfelter's syndrome   A chromosomal disorder that causes female-like males and mental retardation.

Lanugo   Fine hair that grows over most of the fetus's body, beginning in the fourth month.

Maternal serum alpha-fetoprotein (MSAFP)   A prenatal test for spina bifida (exposed spine) and anencephaly (exposed brain) using the mother's blood, performed between the 15th and 18th week of pregnancy.

Meiosis   The process of cell division that produces gametes, resulting in only half the usual number of chromosomes.

Mesoderm   A layer of cells in the embryonic disk that leads to the development of muscles, bones, and the circulatory and reproductive systems (see also ectoderm and endoderm).

Mitosis   The cell-division process by which each chromosome makes a copy of itself before cell division takes place.

Monosomy   An abnormality of the 23rd chromosome in which one member of the pair is missing.

Monozygotic twins   Twins formed by the splitting of the same zygote.

Natural family planning   Limiting or enhancing the possibility of conception by using a method for determining the days of ovulation.

Obstetrician   A physician who specializes in prenatal care, delivery, and reproductive health (see also gynecologist).

Ovum   Female gamete; pl. *ova*.

Pediatrician   A physician who specializes in the care of infants and children.

Phenylketonuria (PKU)   A genetic disorder that causes central nervous system damage if not treated by dietary control.

Polygenic inheritance   When multiple genes are responsible for a single phenotypic characteristic.

Preimplantation genetic diagnosis (PGD)   A method of testing cells from the zygote for genetic and chromosomal disorders before it becomes implanted in the uterus.

Proximodistal development   Parts of the body closer to the trunk develop faster than the extremities.

Rapid eye movement (REM) sleep   Sleep in which rapid vertical eye movements are accompanied by irregular body and respiration movements.

Sex-linked inheritance   Refers to those characteristics that are carried in the genes of the sex chromosomes.

Sickle-cell anemia   A genetic disorder that causes blood clots to form.

Spermatozoon   Male gamete; pl. *spermatazoa*.

Sperm microinjection   Injection of sperm directly into a ripe ovum.

State of arousal   An organized system of physical and physiological responding that is related to the internal level of arousal, from sleep to waking.

Surrogate mother   A woman who carries the fertilized embryo of another woman and brings the embryo through pregnancy to birth.

Tay-Sachs disease   A genetic disorder that causes mental retardation, physical disabilities, and early death.

Teratogen   An agent that causes birth defects.

Teratology   The study of birth defects.

Trisomy A chromosome pair with an extra chromosome attached to it.

Turner's syndrome A chromosomal disorder that causes incomplete sexual determination and mental retardation.

Ultrasound Obtaining an outline of the fetus by means of high-frequency sound wave reflections.

Vernix caseosa A white, cheesy coating that protects the fetal skin.

Viability The ability of the fetus to maintain its own life outside the uterus.

Yolk sac A region of cells in the blastocyst that will eventually become the embryonic blood supply and internal organs.

Zygote A fertilized ovum.

4

Childbirth and
Newborn Health

CHAPTER OVERVIEW AND OUTLINE

The Childbirth Experience	*What is the process of labor and delivery? What are the common methods of childbirth?*
The Baby at Birth: Health and Risk	*What are the physical features of the newborn? What are the typical complications of birth? What is premature birth, what are its effects, and what are the most effective interventions to help premature infants?*
Perinatal Mortality	*How many babies and mothers die during the perinatal period? How do families respond to infant death?*
Family and Society	*What are the mother's psychological reactions to childbirth? What are some cultural differences in childbirth practices? Is it better to breast-feed or to bottle-feed babies?*
Applications: The Case of Baby Doe	*What is euthanasia? Under what conditions is euthanasia applied to newborns?*

This chapter deals with the infant's transition from prenatal to postnatal life. Family members have been anticipating the moment of birth with both hope and concern, while the fetus is making movements that prepare for the next phase of its life. In normal circumstances, the pregnancy period ends with parents already being attached to their infants. The baby is born not only into a world of light and air, but also into a world of love.

After reviewing some data on birthrates, I shall discuss the process of birth and some of the birth complications that may affect the infant's development. I will review the physical features of the newborn infant and cover aspects of newborn health. I examine the causes and cures for infant mortality in the United States and in different parts of the world. Finally, I discuss the parents' psychological adaptation to the birth process, breast- versus bottle-feeding, and some cross-cultural differences in the management of birthing. In the next chapter, I discuss newborn behavior, perception, and learning abilities.

The Childbirth Experience

Birthrates

How many babies are born each year? The **birthrate** is the average number of infants born for every 1,000 women of childbearing age. Birthrate data is usually kept by government agencies as part of a country's vital statistics. **Vital statistics** are numerical estimates in a population of events related to birth, death, and the incidence of illnesses and accidents. The birthrate for women in the United States between 1950 and 1996 is given in Table 4.1. The 1996 birthrate is between 60 and 70 for all racial and ethnic groups in the United States with the exception of Hispanic Americans, whose birthrate is 105 (Guyer, MacDorman, Martin, Peters, & Strobino, 1998).

The birthrate has been cut in half in the United States since 1950. Another way to look at birthrates is to examine the number of births for each

Table 4.1 Vital Statistics for Births

Year	1950	1980	1996
Birthrate per 1,000 women (USA)	106.2	68.4	65.3
Multiple-birthrate per 1,000 women (USA)	—	18.9	25.9
Average number of births per woman:			
USA	3.0	1.8	2.0
UK	2.1	1.8	1.6
France	2.8	2.0	1.6
Japan	3.5	1.6	1.3
Italy	2.5	1.6	1.3

Source: B. Guyer, M. F. MacDorman, J. A. Martin, K. D. Peters, & D. M. Strobino, Annual summary of vital statistics: 1997, 1998, p. 780. *Pediatrics, 102*(6), 751–792; Associated Press, Aug. 2, 1998.

woman of childbearing age. In 1950, women in the United States had an average of three children. This dropped to two children in 1980 and remains the same today. Table 4.1 also shows the number of children per family in other industrialized countries. Some countries, such as Italy and Japan, have an average of only one child per family today. This birthrate is not enough to maintain the present population of those countries, so their work force is increasingly being filled by immigrants. The effect of this is that the racial and cultural balance of these two countries, which traditionally have had a relatively homogenous population, changes.

Another notable vital statistic is the rate of multiple births (twins, triplets, etc.). As shown in Table 4.1, the multiple birthrate has almost doubled since 1980. This is believed to be due to the use of treatments to enhance fertility, discussed in Chapter 3, which have the effect of increasing the chance of multiple births. The effect of reproductive technologies on society is, therefore, more than theoretical. The multiple birthrate of 25.9 in 1996 translates into 107,000 multiple births, signaling a small but significant change in family composition.

The Stages of Labor

The birth process itself begins during the last several weeks of pregnancy. The muscles in the uterus begin to contract and expand at irregular intervals, sometimes days or weeks apart. These gentle muscle contractions, called **Braxton-Hicks contractions** or false labor, have two important effects. First, they

Left occipital   Prolapse of cord   Frank breech   Shoulder presentation   Incomplete breech

Figure 4.1
Various Deviations from the Most Optimal Vertex Presentation
The first drawing on the left shows a minor deviation, in which the head is first but is turned to the side. The next shows a prolapsed cord. The more extreme presentations are shown in the three drawings on the right.

Source: J. F. Rosenblith & J. E. Sims-Knight, *In the beginning: Development in the first two years,* 1985, p. 158. Belmont, CA: Brooks/Cole.

help to widen (dilate) the cervix to a width of 1 to 2 centimeters. The **cervix** is the membrane at the opening between the uterus and the vagina. Normally closed during pregnancy, the cervix must dilate to a width of about 10 centimeters (5 inches) to enable the fetus to pass from the uterus into the vagina.

Second, the Braxton-Hicks contractions may help to move the fetus closer to the cervix in preparation for birth. In almost all cases, the fetus's head is oriented downward. About 4% of all births are **breech presentations** (with the buttocks first), and a small fraction are **transverse presentations** (the fetus is oriented on its side). These presentations are shown in Figure 4.1. Cesarean deliveries are usually recommended when there is a breech or transverse presentation, since the fetus cannot be turned once it has descended into its prebirth position.

Labor begins when contractions start to appear at regular intervals spaced about 10 to 20 minutes apart. Labor is usually divided into three stages (see Figure 4.2). The first stage lasts until the cervix is fully dilated to 10 centimeters and effaced (made thin). Contractions in this stage help to efface and open the cervix. This is the longest stage of labor and may vary in duration from a few minutes to a few days (Guttmacher, 1973). The mean duration of the first stage is about 8 to 14 hours for **primiparous** mothers (mothers giving birth for the first time) and about 6 hours for **multiparous** mothers (Danforth, 1977; Parfitt, 1977).

During the first stage of labor, the pain of the contractions increases over time. During the early part of the first stage, contractions are regular and moderately intense. Women may be able to walk around, do household chores, watch television, nap, or take a bath. During the late part of the first stage is the time to go to the hospital or birthing center. Contractions last 40 to 60 seconds and are spaced at intervals of 3 to 4 minutes. The pain is especially intense in the final phase of the first stage, when the cervix must dilate between 8 and 10 centimeters. This is the time to begin the use of pain control methods (see next section). Mothers can move around, change positions, or take a warm bath or shower.

In the second stage of labor, the infant passes through the cervix and vagina. For women who choose natural childbirth, the pain of this phase of labor may be accompanied by panic, anger, and confusion (Lesko & Leski, 1984). Some mothers begin to shake or feel nausea. Contractions last 60 to 90 seconds and come once every 2 or 3 minutes. Fortunately, this stage is not as long as the previous stage. As the infant begins to descend into the vagina, contractions serve to push the baby out. In natural childbirth, mothers will feel an urge to push. If a local anesthetic is used, mothers feel pressure and will need coaching to determine when to push. The intensity of the pain and feelings of nausea or disorientation are balanced by the sense of relief that the end is near. Some women may begin to feel euphoria.

The final stage of labor is the birth of the placenta, often called the afterbirth. This stage takes

Figure 4.2
Birth Process: Stage 1
and Part of Stage 2

(a) End of the first stage of labor. The baby's head is moving through the cervix. **(b)** Transition. The baby's head is moving through the birth canal, the vagina. **(c–e)** The second stage of labor. The baby's head is moving through the opening of the vagina **(c)**, it emerges completely **(d)**, and the head is then turned so that the rest of the body slides out **(e)**.

Source: A. Fogel & G. F. Melson, *Child development*, 1988, pp. 116–117. St. Paul, MN: West. Copyright © by West Publishing Co. Reprinted by permission. All rights reserved.

less than 1 hour in most cases. By that time, the mother's attention and emotion is occupied with the newborn and most women do not pay much attention to what is happening in the vaginal area. Contractions continue for several hours as the placenta is expelled and the uterus closes up to prevent bleeding. These contractions are not as intense as during the previous stages, but the woman may continue to experience some pain.

If you ever wondered where the name labor comes from, it is because difficult muscular work is involved. Although some fortunate women go through all three stages in a matter of several hours, other mothers may be in labor for 20 or 30 hours,

during which time they have little chance to sleep or rest.

Babies are expected to be born 280 days from the first day of the mother's last menstrual period, but only about 4% of all births occur on their exact due date. Births occurring within 2 weeks before or after the due date are generally considered to be in the normal range.

The timing of birth is controlled by a protein called corticotropin-releasing hormone (CRH). Women with the highest levels of CRH in their blood during the fourth month of pregnancy were more likely to deliver their infants prematurely. Tests for the concentration of CRH are currently

Sam Sweezy/Stock, Boston

Childbirth can be an exceptionally moving experience for all members of the family. In many hospitals, fathers are encouraged to attend the childbirth, providing support for their mates and enhancing their own feelings of participation.

being developed. Given the risks of premature birth (see the section on prematurity in this chapter), it may be possible in the future to delay birth by regulating the production of CRH during pregnancy (R. Smith, 1999).

Technologies for Labor and Delivery

Advances in medical technology have led to the development of a variety of tools to assist childbirth. These include fetal monitoring, mechanical aids to speed delivery (forceps and vacuum extraction), cesarean section (a surgical rather than vaginal delivery), and drugs to reduce pain and speed labor. Following this section, I will discuss the human side of childbirth: the different options available for technologically assisted or natural childbirth, and the pros and cons of each.

Fetal monitoring is the use of electronic devices to detect and display the fetal signs (heart rate, respiration, blood gases, pH balance) during the delivery and birth process. In invasive fetal monitoring, electrodes are inserted through the vagina and cervix and attached to the fetus. This procedure deprives the mother of opportunity for movement. In a less

invasive form, the mother may wear a belt around her abdomen. Invasive fetal monitoring is controversial because it restricts the mother, often requires additional drugs for pain control, and carries a risk of infection for both mother and baby. Experts suggest that fetal monitoring should only be used in high-risk deliveries (Freeman, 1990; Shy et al., 1990). The American College of Obstetrics and Gynecology does not consider fetal monitoring part of standard care for childbirth. Furthermore, research shows that fetal monitoring does not produce healthier infants with fewer complications (Birth, 1988). Ultrasound can also be used to determine the position and behavior of the fetus prior to birth.

Forceps are instruments, usually made of metal or plastic, that are shaped to fit around the newborn's head and used to pull the infant through the birth canal. The use of forceps is declining in favor of cesarean section and spontaneous vaginal delivery because they may cause brain and spinal cord injuries if used during early phases of labor (high forceps). The effect of forceps used at the very end of delivery (low forceps) has not been studied. It seems generally safe, although bruises may be left on the head in some cases. With **vacuum extraction,** a cup connected to a suction device is placed on the baby's head. Research shows that the risks of vacuum extraction are lower than with cesarean section or high forceps (Meyer et al., 1987; Nagan et al., 1990). These mechanical methods are used more frequently in the United States than in Europe (Korte & Scaer, 1990).

Vaginal deliveries occur in about 77% of all births in the United States; the remainder are done by cesarean section (Placek, 1986). In a **cesarean section,** an incision is made in the mother's abdomen and uterus while she is under a local or general anesthetic. Then the baby and placenta are both removed. Cesarean sections, also called C-sections, are used in the case of breech or transverse presentations. C-sections are also recommended in multiple births (twins, triplets, etc.), when the baby's head is too large for the mother's pelvis, when the fetus becomes dangerously entangled in the umbilical cord, and in the case of fetal distress. Some diseases that infect the mother's vagina, such as syphilis, herpes simplex, and AIDS, can be transmitted to the infant during delivery, and a C-section birth helps to prevent the transmission of this infection to the infant. A new drug, nevirapine, can reduce the risk of transmitting AIDS to the newborn. It is inexpensive and can be used in African countries where AIDS has reached epidemic levels.

Fetal distress is a sudden loss of oxygen or a change in the heart rate or respiration of the fetus, usually determined by fetal monitoring. Severe fetal distress can cause serious complications. For example, too much pressure on the fetal head during delivery can cause excess blood pressure and possibly bleeding inside the scalp, called *intraventricular hemorrhage*. Loss of oxygen, which sometimes occurs in long and difficult labors, can lead to fetal brain damage. Using a fetal monitor, a physician can decide if the risk to the infant requires an emergency C-section.

C-sections have saved the lives and health of many mothers and infants. They are not without risk to the mother, however. Because a C-section is a surgical procedure, the mother is at greater risk of infection and postoperative stress. In the past, it was thought that once a woman had a C-section, she could not have vaginal deliveries in the future. This belief is changing as an increasing number of C-section mothers are having vaginal deliveries of later-born children.

The number of C-sections performed in the United States has increased over the past 20 years, which is hard to account for since the proportion of breech and difficult labors has not changed. Some people have complained that obstetricians are too quick to perform C-sections in an attempt to avoid lawsuits against them if the baby or mother suffers during a vaginal delivery or in an effort to make more money by doing surgery compared to a routine delivery. It is difficult to prove these claims, however. Other explanations for the increase in C-sections are better nutrition and therefore larger babies and more accurate fetal monitoring that allows a more sensitive and early detection of fetal distress.

There is little evidence that a C-section has any lasting negative side effects on mothers or on infants, even in long-term follow-up studies (Entwisle & Alexander, 1987; Field & Widmayer, 1980; Hollenbeck, Gewirtz, Seloris, & Scanlon, 1984). Fathers may be more involved with C-section infants because the mother receives more medication and takes longer to recover than with a vaginal delivery. In sum, although C-sections carry some increased risk for the mother due to complications of surgery, if the mother or infant is at risk, the health benefits justify the procedure.

Drugs and delivery. In either a vaginal or a cesarean delivery, many mothers are given some type of medication to control pain and/or to regulate the course of labor. According to Judeo-Christian tradition, women are supposed to suffer during childbirth as punishment for Eve's sins: "In sorrow thou shall bring forth children" (Genesis 3:16). This belief persisted until 1847, when a Scottish obstetrician, James Young Simpson, gave ether to a delivering mother to ease her pain. In his fight to use pain relievers during childbirth, Simpson had to combat both medical practice and religious values. He argued that the Hebrew word previously translated as "sorrow" should have been translated as "work" or "labor." Furthermore, he cited the "deep sleep" that God imposed on Adam when Eve was "delivered" from one of his ribs. Painless childbirth rapidly became popular and was encouraged by the use of chloroform during two of Queen Victoria's childbirths (Brackbill, 1979).

Today, the science of drug use during labor and delivery is complex. Perhaps because obstetricians who delivered babies were less concerned with the infant than with the mother, the development of **anesthesia** (loss of sensation) and **analgesia** (pain relief) proceeded without much concern for the welfare of the infant, although this has recently been changing.

In most industrialized nations, the method most used for pain control is drugs. Although drugs are medically controlled and have been proved safe for the mother, it is now well established that most general anesthetics administered to the mother cross the placenta during labor and delivery. Unfortunately for the neonate, those organ systems that are the most susceptible to chemical insult (primarily the central nervous system) and those that would be the most effective for drug clearance (the liver and kidneys) are the least well developed. Other organs of the newborn, such as the heart and lungs, are better developed, but these systems have little or nothing to do with helping the system get rid of the drugs.

How long the drugs remain in the newborn's system depends on the type of drug, the time during labor at which it was given, and the dosage given to the mother (Golub, 1996). Low to moderate dosages of drugs do not have measurable effects, and when effects are found, they are small in magnitude and do not last beyond the newborn period.

One should not conclude from this review that most drugs are without impact. Even though no effects can be shown overall, some infants and mothers may show extreme but short-term reactions. Some drugs may impair a mother's ability to participate in her delivery by paralyzing muscles normally used to push the baby out, while others may make her drowsy. Many women seem to suffer from gaps in their memories of the childbirth experience. In one study (Affonso, 1977), 86% of the women interviewed could not remember some of the events of their childbirth and wanted to know more. They would ask the doctor and nurses; they had bad dreams and felt somewhat frustrated. Some mothers asked the same questions over and over. This problem seems to occur when labor is either extremely long or extremely short, in high-risk conditions, or when the level of medication is high.

Epidurals are a local anesthetic administered in the lower (lumbar) spine that block pain sensation in the pelvic area but allow the mother to remain awake and aware. Epidurals have been shown to cause fevers during childbirth in about 15% of women. Although there is no measurable effect on the newborn, some doctors may react to the maternal fever by preventive treatment of the newborn for infection (Lieberman et al., 1997). Epidurals also increase the risk for postpartum depression (see the "Family and Society" section in this chapter). Before electing them, women should discuss the use of epidurals with their doctors or midwives.

On the other hand, for some mothers anxiety and pain increase dramatically prior to and during labor and delivery (Westbrook, 1978). Drugs serve to calm these mothers and reduce their discomfort, making them better able to enjoy the birth of their infant (Field & Widmayer, 1980; Shnider, 1981). Prenatal preparation for childbirth is important in order for the doctor and the parents to understand all the different options available for pain control and to choose the one that is best for mother and infant. In the next section, we turn to different types of childbirth practices, including methods for the behavioral and psychological control of pain.

The Management of Childbirth

Most childbirths in North America today take place in hospital settings. From a medical perspective, the hospital environment allows a large staff to assist in labor, delivery, and the care of the newborn. Hospitals also provide access to emergency medical care in the event of fetal distress or complications with labor.

At the beginning of the 20th century, most childbirths took place in the home. Once it became accepted practice to give birth in the hospital, however, the experience of childbirth for women and their families changed. In the home, the mother could be surrounded by familiar sights and sounds and have the support of other family members. In the early days of hospital births, mothers were left in sparsely furnished rooms for labor, and birth took place in a sterile operating chamber. Family members were prohibited from accompanying the mother. The babies were separated from the mothers for several days, bottle feeding was encouraged, and hospitals stays could last up to a week for normal deliveries.

Today, childbirth in hospitals has become more humane. There is a growing recognition of the need to treat childbirth less like a disease and more like a normal event. Labor and birthing rooms are comfortably furnished and can accommodate other family members. Because of a new awareness about the psychological benefits of early mother-infant and father-infant contact (see the section on parent-infant bonding in Chapter 5), babies are separated from parents only in the case of a medical complication. Otherwise, early and frequent contact is desirable.

Every hospital has different practices, however. Parents who desire the presence of fathers during delivery, rooming in (allowing the newborn to sleep in the mother's room rather than in the hospital nursery), or natural childbirth need to consult their health care providers and inquire about hospital practices. It helps if the parents make their desires known and act assertively to get their personal needs met. Hospitals, like all large institutions, have rules of standard practice, but sometimes these can be tailored to fit the individual and family, if their needs are made known to the hospital staff.

Early discharge. In the case of normal deliveries, hospital stays can last from 1 to 3 days. Some hospitals allow discharge within 3 hours after the birth if the mother receives no analgesia or anesthesia and the infant is in good health. Under these conditions, there is no increased risk associated with early discharge (Mehl, Peterson, Sokolsky, & Whitt, 1976). More recently, early discharge has been allowed on demand in consultation with the physician.

Women who elect early discharge feel that the home is a better and more supportive environment for comfort, recovery, and early adaptation to their babies. Early-discharge mothers report more social support in the home (availability of relatives and friends) and are more confident in their ability to manage on their own (Lemmer, 1987). On the other hand, early discharge limits the ability of the hospital staff to provide parent education and to detect feeding problems and other abnormalities (Kiely, Drum, & Kessel, 1998). It may also deprive

women of some needed rest to recover from the delivery. Women should try to evaluate their preferences and discuss them with staff.

Behavioral pain control and childbirth preparation. While drugs offer the advantages that they can be administered in controlled doses and are effective, a number of behavioral and psychological alternatives to speed labor and relieve pain are available. Many diverse kinds of pain-relieving methods have been used throughout human history. One common practice, used by the Laotians, the Navaho, and the Cuna of Panama, among others, is the use of music during labor. Among the Comanche and Tewa Indian tribes, heat is applied to the abdomen (M. Mead & Newton, 1967).

Some groups believe that pain and ease of delivery are functions of the mother's body position during labor and delivery. Many cultures encourage women to give birth in a sitting position, usually held from behind by another woman. The Taureg of the Sahara insist that the laboring mother walk up and down small hills to allow the infant to become properly placed to facilitate delivery. Taureg women usually deliver from a kneeling position. In fact, most obstetrics textbooks in the United States at the turn of the century advocated an upright position during labor (M. Mead & Newton, 1967).

For some peoples, prevention is the best cure. The Ainu of Japan believe that maternal exercise will make the fetus small and encourage a shorter labor. (The Japanese value smaller newborns and are not pleased with multiple births, which they consider too animal-like.) In a number of other cultures, including the Hopi of the American Southwest, women are encouraged to exercise during pregnancy (M. Mead & Newton, 1967).

Nonchemical pain control during labor in developed Western countries today is sometimes achieved using the **Lamaze method.** Working in France, Frederick Lamaze developed a system of exercise, breathing, and massage that was based on a theory of pain during labor developed by Grantly Dick-Read in Great Britain (Dick-Read, 1933/1972). According to Dick-Read, women become afraid during childbirth due to the pain that develops when muscles are contracted. He suggested that if women were to employ some commonly known methods of relaxation, their experience of pain would be lessened. Female animals naturally fall into panting and breathing patterns. Using these observations and the work of Dick-Read, Lamaze based his method on the use of rhythmic breathing as a mental distraction from pain and on relaxation methods to prevent it (Karmel, 1959).

Pain has also been associated with negative attitudes toward pregnancy and childbirth (Nettlebladt, Fagerstrom, & Udderberg, 1976) and with a lack of support from the husband. Women whose husbands were present during the labor and delivery, as well as those whose husbands stayed with them for longer periods, perceived childbirth as less painful (Davenport-Slack & Boylan, 1974; Nettlebladt et al., 1976). It could be, however, that women who were more likely to view childbirth as less painful were those who requested their husbands' presence for longer periods during the delivery. In addition, people who choose such approaches are a self-selected group whose positive attitudes about labor and delivery might help them, even under adverse conditions.

There is some debate, though little concrete data, on how childbirth preparation affects women (Wideman & Singer, 1984). Some suggest that the effect is due to education and the ability to anticipate fearful events. Some think it is due to the relaxation techniques and/or the social support provided by the Lamaze approach, while others think the effect is related to positive images about the childbirth experience (Nichols & Humenick, 1988). Here are some examples of imagery techniques that have been used (C. Jones, 1987):

Imagine that you and your baby are breathing in harmony. Now imagine that you are inside the womb, face-to-face with your unborn child, who is comfortable and secure in a private sea of crystal-clear water. (p. 87)

Imagine yourself opening. Envision the baby's head against the cervix and the cervix widening to let it pass. At that time, mentally say yes to the contractions as they come and fade away. (p. 145)

Some research has shown, however, that relaxation techniques may be superior to this approach since these images tend to be transitory, whereas breathing and massage can be sustained for longer periods (Markman & Kadushin, 1986). Lamaze-

trained mothers, especially if they are accompanied by the father and receive professional support during the delivery, require less pain medication and fewer episiotomies (surgical cutting of the labia to prevent tearing during delivery) (Copstick, Taylor, Hayes, & Morris, 1986; Hodnett & Osborn, 1989).

The enhancement of relaxation to control pain is also at the heart of the somatic awareness methods reviewed under the clinical theories in Chapter 2. The Rosen method, the Feldenkrais method, Watsu, and bodymind centering all rely on helping clients to relax and easing chronic tension and stress. Although these methods are probably not useful during childbirth, they may be helpful in childbirth preparation and recovery. Acupuncture and acupressure, massage, hypnosis, relaxation techniques, yoga, warm baths, walking, and music have also been shown to help ease labor pain. Somatic education helps a mother to be more in touch with her body. This reduces anxiety and pain and gives mothers greater confidence in their decisions to use or not to use drugs during delivery.

Upright postures. During traditional hospital labors and deliveries, women have been confined almost the entire time to a supine position. There is a growing recognition that upright postures may be beneficial to both mother and infant. Anatomically, when a mother is upright, her pelvis widens, access to the birth canal is easier for the fetus, and pushing is more effective because of the assistance of gravity. Upright postures also seem to improve the blood circulation to the mother's abdominal muscles and increase the oxygen supply to the fetus (Cottrell & Shannahan, 1987).

Research is somewhat inconclusive about the benefits of upright postures. Some studies find beneficial effects such as fewer birth complications, shortening of labor, less backache pain, and easier pushing, while others find none. In general, it can be concluded that upright postures do not have negative effects and that, in some cases, they may relieve discomfort (Gardosi, Hutson, & Lynch, 1989; Holland & Smith, 1989; Lupe & Gross, 1986).

Upright postures can be achieved in a number of ways. During labor, some women find it helpful

Figure 4.3
Birthing Chair

A modern birthing chair can be adjusted for both vertical and horizontal delivery positions according to the comfort of the mother.

Source: Adapted from J. F. Rosenblith & J. E. Sims-Knight, *In the beginning: Development in the first two years,* 1985, p. 180. Belmont, CA: Brooks/Cole. Copyright © by Wadsworth, Inc. Reprinted by permission.

to get up and walk around, stand, or squat. Just changing positions sometimes relieves discomfort. During the actual delivery, some hospitals use a birthing chair (see Figure 4.3), although some evidence suggests that a squatting cushion (Figure 4.4) is more effective and more practical (Gardosi et al., 1989). In other places a birthing bar is used. The bar is suspended about two feet above the bed. It allows the mother to pull herself upright anytime during labor.

Midwives and doulas. A **midwife** is a practitioner who has been trained to assist women who are giving birth. Lay midwives receive informal and formal training, while nurse midwives are registered nurses who receive their training as part of their nursing education. Midwives often work alongside doctors and assist the mother as long as the labor is without complications. They are trained to recognize which complications require the attention of a physician. Midwives are usually less costly to parents than physicians, and they also provide both prenatal and postnatal care for the family. Midwives help families understand the various birthing options and the risks and benefits of drugs and surgical procedures, and they work with the family to enhance the healthy development of parents and baby. Midwives assist in the delivery of 80% of births worldwide.

Doula is an ancient Greek word meaning "an experienced woman who guides and assists a new mother in her infant-care tasks." A doula works alongside doctors or midwives to provide emotional support during labor and delivery. Doulas are trained to recognize birth as a key life experience that the mother will remember all her life. Doulas serve as advocates and supporters of the parents in preparing for and carrying out their plans for the birth. Doulas attend the birth, provide emotional support and physical comfort measures, and help the mother and her partner communicate with the hospital staff. Randomized clinical trials using low-income first-time mothers found that doula-assisted delivery shortened the labor, reduced the number of oxytocin, forceps, and cesarian deliveries, and increased satisfaction with the childbirth experience. Doula-assisted mothers also were more likely to initiate and maintain breast-feeding (Glink, 1998).

Doulas can be used by any woman who would like support and advocacy at an important and sensitive time in her life. If women have a close relationship to their physician or midwife, and if they believe they can obtain the kind of delivery they desire, a doula may not be necessary. On the other hand, even in the best of circumstances, physicians and midwives will have relatively little time to spend with each individual patient. Doulas take the perspective of the mother and serve as her support and

Figure 4.4
Supported Squatting on the Birth Cushion

Source: J. Gardosi, N. Hutson, & C. Lynch, Randomized, controlled trial of squatting in the second stage of labor, 1989, p. 75. *Lancet, 2,* 74–77. Copyright © The Lancet Ltd. Used with permission.

advocate. When the clinician is too busy with assisting the actual delivery, the doula remains by the mother's side, explains what is happening, ands helps her to make decisions if she becomes confused or disoriented. Finding the right doula can alleviate a lot of anxiety for the mother and father, who can then concentrate their energies on preparing themselves physically and emotionally for the birth.

Birthing centers. Birthing centers are alternatives to standard hospital deliveries. They are based on the idea that most births are natural and nonmedical and should take place in a comfortable, homelike environment. Birthing centers are typically located in hospitals, but they keep medical technology to a minimum and provide comfortable furnishings, quiet, and privacy. Thus, they combine the relative comfort and privacy of a home birth with the availability of medical assistance if it is required. Most birthing center childbirths are assisted by midwives rather than physicians (Rooks et al., 1989). Birth-

ing centers encourage mothers to be prepared through Lamaze and other similar methods. As in the case of home births (see the next section), birthing centers screen their clients and accept only low-risk pregnancies.

Parents find birthing centers very rewarding and enriching for their childbirth experience (Eakins, 1986; Waldenström, 1999); such centers are a safe and effective alternative to hospital deliveries for low-risk pregnancies (Rooks et al., 1989). They have some of the same advantages of using midwives and doulas. Birthing centers are especially effective for low-income mothers who benefit from the additional social support and long-term care (Lubic, 1999). Low-income mothers who used a birthing center in New York City tell about the effectiveness of the birthing center in their own words:

If you have given birth, you have given life, and if you have given life then you can do anything—you can get a job and you can go to school and you can do anything you want as long as you put your mind to it.

That's the best thing about the birth center concept. It empowers women, and in turn, they empower their families, and families empower the community and it just grows and grows. (Lubic, 1999, p. 21)

Home births. An alternative to hospital delivery is the modern practice of birth at home. Home births are standard practice in some countries, such as the Netherlands and most of Scandinavia. These births are assisted by professional midwives, and the incidence of infant mortality is lower in these countries than in the United States. On closer examination, though, this effect is due not to home birth itself but to other factors. These countries have a relatively high level of education and a low incidence of poverty. In addition, women who are at risk are not allowed to have home births. These women include very young or very old mothers, unmarried women, low-income women, and those with medical risks (Rosenblith & Sims-Knight, 1985). With a trained professional in attendance, screening for risk, and a nearby hospital in case of emergency, home births in the United States are no more risky than hospital births (R. Cohen, 1981; Hazell, 1975; Howe, 1988).

The Leboyer method: Birth without violence. Before leaving this section, I will discuss alternatives for the infant. Frederick Leboyer (1975) suggests that some hospital routines are traumatic for the infant: holding the infant upside down in the cold air, placing the baby on a cold metal scale, putting silver nitrate in his or her eyes, separating the infant from the mother, putting the baby under bright lights, exposing him or her to loud sounds, and prematurely cutting the umbilical cord. With the **Leboyer method,** the delivery room is quiet and dimly lit, and the infant is placed on the mother's warm abdomen right after birth until the umbilical cord stops pulsing. After the cord is cut, the infant is placed in a warm-water bath. Leboyer reports that infants so treated tend to be more relaxed and alert than other infants. This method has many similarities to Watsu (see Chapter 2).

Leboyer's claims that such procedures increase the newborn's alertness have not been verified scientifically. Most studies reporting positive effects were biased by the observer's preference for the method and the lack of a control group (e.g., Rappoport, 1976). One well-controlled study (Nelson et al., 1980) found no difference in alertness between Leboyer and non-Leboyer babies, nor were there any differences in developmental test scores between the two groups at 8 months. Furthermore, half of the Leboyer babies reacted to the warm-water bath following birth with irritated crying. As with upright postures and childbirth preparation classes, it is difficult to establish a conclusive effect for these practices. On the positive side, most of the practices discussed here cannot be shown to have any harmful side effects, and they may be effective for many of the people who use them.

Regardless of whether a mother chooses a physician, midwife, or doula, it is a good idea to make a birth plan in which the mother, her partner, and her care provider discuss what they would like to happen during labor and delivery. Several Internet sites are also available to help mothers understand their options and to construct a birth plan that suits their needs.

In the next section, I look more closely at the infant following birth. First, I examine the physical characteristics of the normal newborn infant, and later I discuss newborns who are at risk.

The Baby at Birth: Health and Risk

The transition from an essentially aquatic existence to a world of air, light, and gravity is one of the most abrupt and remarkable developmental shifts in the human life span. Much of what we can observe in the human newborn is the result of making this adaptation to extrauterine life. Some of the souvenirs of their prior home will stay with the infants as they make this change.

As you might imagine, the newborn's lungs are filled with mucus and amniotic fluid, making its initial attempts at breathing difficult. As the mucus gradually drains over the first few weeks of life, the infant's breathing becomes more regular and quieter. Just about any kind of stimulation can induce respiration, even the mere exposure to air. Breathing can also be stimulated by a sneeze, cough, yawn, or cry. Some alternative birthing methods use massage or dip the infant into warm water as a stimulus to start breathing. Slapping the baby is not necessary.

Another major adaptation of the newborn to extrauterine existence is the loss of the umbilical connection to the mother. Immediately after birth, the abdominal muscles surrounding the umbilical vessels contract to inhibit the circulation of blood in the cord. Once the cord has been cut, the navel opening usually heals within a week, and the dried remains of the cord fall off in another few days. The umbilical cord contains cells that assist in the manufacture of new blood cells, much as the cells in bone marrow do. For this reason, physicians have begun to collect umbilical cords for use in the treatment of blood and immune disorders, such as leukemia and AIDS, in children (C. Thompson, 1995).

Once the umbilical cord has been severed and respiration has begun, it takes about 30 hours for the oxygen level of the blood to reach nearly normal levels. The blood pH balance needs about 1 week to become established, and blood pressure takes about 10 days to reach normal levels.

Just after birth, infants are wet with amniotic fluid, and their skin may still be coated with the

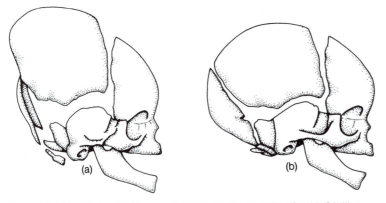

Figure 4.5
Skull of a Newborn

(a) Molding of the bones of the baby's head during passage through the birth canal.
(b) By the 3rd day of life, the bones return to their normal position.

white, cheesy vernix caseosa. The color of the skin may be pale to pink, or it may be slightly yellowish due to **normal physiological jaundice.** Jaundice is caused by unbalanced liver function. It can be treated by placing the baby under special lamps.

Almost all babies are born with smoky blue eyes, which do not develop their true color until later in the first year. Even neonates from parents of color may have light skin and blue eyes for the first few days of life, since eye and skin pigments depend on white light for further development.

At birth, the newborn retains some of the physical characteristics of the fetus. The newborn's head is about one-fourth its total length, the legs about one-third. A newborn has virtually no voluntary control over his or her head, although if the head is cradled, the infant can turn it from side to side. The newborn has somewhat bowed legs, with the feet bent inward at the ankles so that the soles of the feet are almost parallel. The typical "baby face" includes a very short neck, no chin, and a flattened nose. Newborns' heads are often temporarily misshapen from the pressures of the birth process. This gradually disappears by the end of the second week of life. Some fetal hair may remain on the infant's head, eyebrows, and back (the lanugo). This hair usually is replaced by more permanent hair within the first few months.

Newborns have six soft spots on the top of their heads, called **fontanels.** These openings provide some room for the various bones of the skull to move during the birth process, called molding. The fontanels also allow for the growth of the brain during the first years of life. They do not fully close un-til about 18 months. The initial shifting of the fontanels after birth is shown in Figure 4.5. The time of fontanel closure is unrelated to infant sex, race, birth measurements, or later growth measurements; slowly closing fontanels are not a sign of abnormal development (Kataria, Frutiger, Lanford, & Swanson, 1988).

At birth, virtually all the nerve cells in the brain are present, but they have not developed very far. During the first year, the brain doubles in size (from 350 to 750 cubic centimeters), and it doubles again by the sixth year. Most of the postnatal brain growth is accounted for by the increase in **myelination,** the development of a protective sheath around the nerve pathways, as well as by an increase in the volume and density of dendritic connections between the cells. **Dendrites** are the branchlike filaments that connect the nerve cells and transmit nerve impulses between the cells.

While these processes of brain development are occurring, the cells that receive fewer inputs and connections will eventually die. Thus, postnatal experience tends to actively select certain areas and cells in the brain for further development. Those areas and cells that are not used will eventually be lost (Greenough, Black, & Wallace, 1987). I will return to the topic of brain development in Chapter 7.

Other important changes are occurring in other parts of the newborn's body. At birth, the newborn's genitals appear large and prominent. Both sexes may have slightly enlarged breasts that may excrete a white, milklike substance, and females may have a brief "menstrual flow." These phenomena are caused by the massive infusion of maternal hormones during the birth process, and the effects disappear quickly. Newborns may also look withered because they have very little body fat except in the cheeks, where it is needed for sucking. This withered look is even worse for premature infants, since the fat pads in their cheeks are underdeveloped.

Each baby's body has a characteristic muscle tone and response to tactile stimulation. Some babies are cuddly: they will mold into the arms of the caregiver and curl up when held. Others are tense and tight; some squirm and some sprawl. An adult can almost hold the entire infant in one hand.

Taking in food through the mouth is not an entirely new experience to a newborn, since babies suck in the uterus. Nevertheless, one of the major prenatal-to-postnatal transitions involves the handling of nutrients. Before birth, nutrient intake and waste matter both pass through the umbilical cord. After birth, the newborn's digestive system must take over those functions. The intestines of the newborn are filled with a greenish-black substance called **meconium,** which consists of digested bits of mucus, amniotic fluid, shed skin, and hair that was ingested prenatally. Due to the excretion of meconium and also because the mother's milk does not develop before the first few days, the infant typically experiences weight loss during the first week, but the weight is rapidly regained. The fluid that is excreted by the mother's breasts in the first few days is called the **colostrum** (see the section on feeding in this chapter).

The process of keeping physiological signs at a steady level is known as **homeostasis.** At birth, temperature homeostasis is not fully functioning, and infants can easily become chilled if not wrapped. Infants can also become easily overheated if they are too heavily clothed. Infants should not be overdressed; as a general rule, they should wear the same number of layers of clothing as the adults in the same room. Infants need to be exposed to cold as well as warmth to help them develop the capacity to regulate their body temperature. This capability will not fully develop until after 1 month of age, when the sweat glands become more fully functional.

In the next section, I discuss methods of assessing the health status and behavioral abilities of the newborn infant. Following that, I consider risks to the newborn.

Assessing the Infant's Status at Birth

Once a baby is born, a series of assessments may be done to determine whether there are any complications or whether the infant is in need of special attention. Assessments are divided into three basic groups. **Screening assessments** give an indication of the newborn's ability to survive and whether there are any immediate medical needs. **Neurological assessments** test for problems in the newborn's central and peripheral nervous system, such as major brain, spinal cord, or sensory damage. **Behavioral assessments** are used to rate the presence and strength of behavioral responses to stimulation and spontaneous activity. Some of the more common newborn-assessment procedures are listed in Table 4.2.

Table 4.2 Newborn Assessment Tests

Type of Test	Name of Test	Description of Test
Screening	Apgar	Heart rate, respiration, and other vital signs.
Neurological	Dubowitz assessment of gestational age	Differentiation of small-for-date infants from infants with appropriate weight for gestational age.
	Neurological examining of Prechtl and Beintema	Test of reflexes, posture, and motor development.
Behavioral	Graham-Rosenblith tests	Responses to physical objects, strength of grasp, and response to covering the nose and mouth.
	Brazelton neonatal assessment	Reflexes, responses to social and physical stimuli, response to covering nose and mouth, time spent in different states, and number of changes between states.

Table 4.3 The Apgar Rating Scale

Area	Score 0	Score 1	Score 2
Heart rate	Absent	Slow (<100)	Rapid (>100)
Respiration	Absent	Irregular	Good, infant crying
Muscle tone	Flaccid	Weak	Strong, well flexed
Color	Blue, pale	Body pink, extremities blue	All pink
Reflex irritability:			
Nasal tickle	No response	Grimace	Cough, sneeze
Heel prick	No response	Mild response	Foot withdrawal, cry

Source: V. Apgar, A proposal for a new method of evaluation in the newborn infant, 1953, p. 260. *Current Research in Anesthesia and Analgesia, 32,* 260.

One of the most common newborn screening tests was developed by Virginia Apgar (1953) and is known as the **Apgar score.** The test is relatively easy to do and takes only a few seconds. The rating usually is made at 1 minute and again at 5 minutes after birth. Table 4.3 shows the categories of the Apgar rating and the possible score an infant may receive in each of five areas: respiration, heart rate, muscle tone, color, and reflex irritability. The infant's total score is summed over each of the five areas. A total score of 7 or greater usually indicates that the infant is in no immediate danger, whereas a rating of less than 7 indicates some kind of severe risk to life. If the rating is less than 4, the infant is in critical condition.

The reason for making two ratings is to encourage hospital staff to continue to monitor the newborn over several minutes. Often staff members are distracted by other events and may miss the possible deterioration of the infant's condition. In addition to the Apgar, the infant can be screened on the basis of its physical appearance, color, and the presence of any obvious deformities (Judd, 1985; Olds, London, & Ladewig, 1984; Sardana, 1985).

Apgar scores have been found to relate to a variety of prenatal and birth complications. The scores are less likely to predict later outcomes of the infant, however, probably because low scores indicate the need for immediate treatment that may alleviate the problem (Francis, Self, & Horowitz, 1987). On the other hand, low Apgar scores are strongly correlated with infant mortality, especially if the scores decrease between the two testings.

Although the Apgar score is useful for determining the infant's viability, it is a relatively crude assessment scale. It tells us little about the actual complications the infant may have. Accordingly, pediatricians and developmentalists require an assessment procedure that aids early identification of childhood behavioral and functional disorders. If such problems can be detected in the newborn, medicine and psychology could more effectively concentrate their efforts on prevention, rather than simply treating problems after they appear. A number of neurological and behavioral examinations of the newborn infant can be used for specific diagnoses (see Table 4.2). Each of these examinations has its specific limitations and range of usefulness (Self & Horowitz, 1979).

Among the neurological tests, the Dubowitz scale tests for the gestational age of the infant at birth. The **gestational age** is the number of weeks since conception. (Gestation is another word for pregnancy.) To check the gestational age, raters use the infant's muscular control, physical size measurements, skin texture and color, amount of lanugo, and the size and development of the ears, breasts, and genitals. The Dubowitz can predict the gestational age within a few days (Dubowitz, Dubowitz, & Goldberg, 1970; Jaroszewicz & Boyd, 1973). The neurological test of Prechtl and Beintema examines all of the newborn's basic reflexes. It is related to the short-term status of the newborn, but like the Apgar, it is less clearly related to long-term outcomes (Francis et al., 1987).

The Graham-Rosenblith test and the Brazelton behavioral assessments use similar types of procedures. For example, the infant's head is placed face down on a mattress. Most normal infants will turn their heads to one side to free the nasal passages. In a similar test, a cloth is placed gently over the face. In another test, the infant is pulled by the arms into a sitting position to check for head control and muscle tone. A flashlight and a bell are moved from side to side to see if the infant can localize the stimulus by turning his or her head. Faces and voices are also used in the Brazelton test. In addition, observations are made about the infant's ability to control distress and maintain an awake state.

Because the Brazelton test involves a larger range of newborn behavior, it is the most frequently used. The Brazelton test has been studied extensively. It relates well to other newborn tests, such as the Prechtl and Beintema test. The test finds reliable individual differences between normal infants and can also be used to diagnose the behavioral difficulties of high-risk infants (Brazelton, Nugent, & Lester, 1987; Francis et al., 1987).

Another use of the Brazelton test is as an intervention. Research has found that mothers and fathers increased their knowledge of and responsivity to the baby if they observed their baby while it was undergoing the Brazelton test, especially if the examiner explained the test and responded to the parents' questions (Liptak, Keller, Feldman, & Chamberlain, 1983; Myers, 1982; Worobey & Belsky, 1982).

The field of newborn assessment is rapidly improving as researchers determine the most reliable indicators of long-term problems. Improved scoring procedures and statistics and a large number of longitudinal follow-up studies have also contributed to the development of better assessments. The hope of predicting many childhood disorders from newborn assessments, however, has not been realized. In the last chapter of this book, I will discuss the findings on the possible long-term persistence into childhood and adulthood of individual differences between infants.

Birth Complications

For the purpose of discussion, the infant's early history is usually divided into three main phases: the prenatal, the **perinatal** (the period from 1 month before birth to about 1 month after), and the **neo-**natal (the newborn until the age of 4 to 6 weeks). Although the leading cause of severe impairment stems from prenatal problems (Kopp & Parmelee, 1979), most of these problems do not show up until the perinatal period. In addition, a number of complications of the perinatal period are due to the birth process itself. Between 3 and 5 children in 1,000 show severe developmental problems before entering school, and about 85% of these problems can be attributed to prenatal and perinatal causes. Compared with the effect of prenatal and perinatal causes on later development, the contribution of neonatal problems—illness, disease, and accidents—is relatively small (Kopp & Parmelee, 1979).

Perinatal problems usually derive from disorders of delivery, perinatal infections, asphyxia, hypoglycemia (low blood sugar levels), prematurity, and cardiac and respiratory difficulties. Several of these problems appear to be caused by prenatal factors, many of which we discussed in the last chapter. There is considerable evidence that a number of the complications of the perinatal period can be overcome if the infant is exposed to a supportive social and physical environment. Infants who are raised in inadequate social and economic conditions are more likely to develop permanent deficits as a result of a perinatal complication (Kopp & Parmelee, 1979; Sameroff & Chandler, 1975). We will discuss the developmental outcomes of early deficits in the last chapter.

One birth complication, prematurity, has received a good deal of attention recently from psychologists, parents, and physicians. Much of this interest has to do with modern improvements in neonatal intensive care that have permitted more low-birthweight infants to survive.

What Is Prematurity?

Some confusion surrounds the labeling of various classes of premature infants. In general, a number of factors can vary in the determination of an infant's status. These are the birthweight, the gestational age, and the relationship between the two. Table 4.4 lists some of these classifications.

In the previous chapter, we looked at a variety of genetic, chromosomal, and teratogenic agents that may lead to premature birth. Although they are

Table 4.4 Forms of Prematurity

Classification Factor	Premature Category
Birthweight:	
Less than 1,000 grams	Extremely low birthweight (ELBW)
Between 1,000 and 1,500 grams	Very low birthweight (VLBW)
Between 1,500 and 2,500 grams	Low birthweight (LBW)
More than 2,500 grams	Normal birthweight
Gestational age:	
Less than 37 weeks	Premature birth
More than 37 weeks	Full-term birth
Weight less than expected for gestational age	Intrauterine growth retardation
Weight appropriate for gestational age	See weight and term classifications above

not the only causes, lower birthweight often results from such factors as smoking and alcohol use and poor maternal health or nutrition. Indeed, cigarette smoking during pregnancy is the largest single preventable cause of low birthweight, accounting for 20 to 30% of low-birthweight cases (Ogunyemi, Hullett, Leeper, & Risk, 1998). Exceptional stress and persistent family discord during the pregnancy period have also been associated with low birthweight (Chomitz, Cheung, & Lieberman, 1995; Ramsey, Abell, & Baker, 1986; Reeb, Graham, Zyzanski, & Kitson, 1987; A. Stein, Campbell, Day, McPherson, & Cooper, 1987). Infertility treatments that produce multiple births and low maternal weight gain also contribute to the incidence of low birthweight (Ogunyemi et al., 1998). A small percentage of infants are low birthweight even if the pregnancy had no risk factors.

The incidence of low birthweight and infant mortality varies by ethnicity (see Table 4.6). There is also a strong correlation between low birthweight and mortality. Note, however, that the mortality rates are only one-tenth as high as the rates of low birthweight. Typically, low birthweight and mortality increase as the availability of good prenatal health care and nutrition declines. It is therefore curious that the rates of mortality and low birthweight for African Americans exceed those of all other groups in industrialized countries. On the average, African American mothers have less education, are less likely to be married, are more likely to give birth during their teenage years, and have more general health problems than do other ethnic groups in the United States. These differences, however, are

not enough to account for the fact that rates of low birthweight and mortality in African Americans are nearly double those in other ethnic groups, so more research is needed (Chomitz et al., 1995). One thing is clear: poor, young, African American women are at special risk for birth complications and should be the focus of national efforts to prevent low birthweight (see below).

Problems and Prospects for Premature and Low-Birthweight Babies and Their Families

In 1975, about 40% of premature infants developed serious intellectual and neurological deficits. Due to improvements in medical technology and knowledge about the premature infant, the percentage of later deficits continues to decrease. Infants who would have been severely handicapped a generation ago, had they even survived, have a better prognosis for developing normally.

The youngest and smallest babies still run the most risk of complications and death. Babies under 1,000 grams (extremely low birthweight, or ELBW) or of less than 32 weeks' gestational age are currently considered to be at the most risk. Although more of these babies are saved each year, it increases the chances that babies with handicaps will survive from this group (Hack, Klein, & Taylor, 1995). Infants under 1,000 grams (ELBW) show the least improvements in outcomes.

Recent research shows that a large proportion of infants born prematurely, regardless of weight, may

Premature infants often spend weeks in intensive care units. With appropriately gentle medical intervention and sensitive handling, most of these infants will develop normally into adulthood.

Elizabeth Crews

have more health, motor, and intellectual problems than full-term infants, both in the short term and in the long term. In this section I will discuss the short- and long-term consequences of premature birth. Following that, I review some of the research on improvements in neonatal intensive care.

Short-term effects. Because of their early birth and/or low birthweight, prematures are often at a disadvantage in getting a good start on adaptation to the real world. They suffer more from a lack of oxygen during the birth process (respiratory distress), they are more likely to have jaundice and to suffer physical and mental impairments as a result of the birth process, and about one-fourth to one-third of them will die, depending upon the severity of their complications (Kitchen & Murton, 1985).

Generalizing about the abilities of premature infants is difficult because they vary widely in weight and gestational age, because prematurity has many different causes, and because the quality of neonatal care is highly variable. Researchers today categorize infants into experimental groups on the basis of weight, gestational age, and whether they have medical complications in addition to the prematurity. In follow-up studies of the effects of prematurity, researchers compare normal infants with premature infants of the same gestational age, rather than comparing infants of the same natal age. For example, a 3-month-old normal infant might be compared with a 4-month-old premature infant, both of whom were conceived about the same time.

Using gestational age rather than birth age is based on the ideas of Gesell (see Chapter 1), who charted the ages at which the average infant reached developmental milestones. In many cases, gestational age is the best indicator of developmental status. Many premature infants cannot suck from a bottle successfully until they have reached a gestational age of 35 weeks, about the age of a full-term newborn (Brake, Fifer, Alfasi, & Fleischman, 1988). Typical patterns of sleep and waking displayed by full-term babies do not begin until 34 weeks' gestational age; until then, premature infants spend considerably more time sleeping than waking (Korner et al., 1988). Thirty-four weeks appears to be the age at which premature infants show a marked increase in their ability to respond appropriately to external stimulation. Before that age, it takes a considerable effort on the part of an adult to keep the baby still and alert in the presence of a new tactile, auditory, or visual stimulus (Als, Duffy, & McAnulty, 1988). The problem with using gestational age is that it is based on averages and thus may not fit the developmental abilities of any particular infant.

Long-term effects. The long-term effects of any particular event or risk factor in early infancy are particularly difficult to assess. In Chapter 12, I will return to the general problem of how to determine the effects of early experiences. For now, you should keep in mind that the effects of prematurity independent of other factors cannot be determined. This is because many premature infants have other complications, and we cannot assign infants randomly to experimental groups based on prematurity and health status. In addition, many premature and sick infants receive a variety of short-term and long-term interventions—including special attention from their families—that may alleviate their conditions. It would be unethical to withhold intervention or family support just so we can observe how a baby would develop without these resources.

Individuals who were born prematurely are shorter and smaller on average than people who were full term at birth. The difference is greatest during the first 2 years of life, during which babies who are small at birth often show some catch-up growth if they receive appropriate care and nutrition (Peña, Teburg, & Hoppenbrouwers, 1987). **Catch-up growth** refers to a more rapid growth rate than for normal infants early in life and a more normal growth rate once the infant reaches a weight that is appropriate for his or her gestational age. For most prematures, catch-up growth is the most rapid during the first year of life (Peña et al., 1987). Catch-up growth may occur at any point in childhood if the individual suffers a deprivation, accident, or illness and is later restored to normal functioning (Barrett, Radke-Yarrow, & Klein, 1982; Tanner, 1970). Catch-up growth does not mean that the individual will eventually enter the normal range, but rather that they will grow faster than normal following the trauma.

The effects of prematurity on intelligence, motor skills, perceptual skills, and emotion are often compounded by heath factors. In one study, a group of premature infants was classified according to health status at birth: high-, moderate-, and low-risk groups were formed according to respiratory problems in the hospital. At 12 and 18 months of age, the high-risk premature infants had considerably more difficulty coping with stressful situations, and once they became distressed, they were more difficult to soothe (Stiefel, Plunket, & Meisels, 1987). This study shows that health risk, when added to prematurity, has a significantly greater impact on emotional regulation than prematurity alone.

In another study, infants who experienced intraventricular hemorrhage (IVH) were assessed on motor and behavioral measures at 1 and 2 years (Sostek, Smith, Katz, & Grant, 1987). The infants were grouped according to severity of IVH and birthweight. Birthweight and IVH had a minor correlation with outcome at 1 year and no relationship at age 2. More recent research, on the other hand, finds that IVH is one of the most important predictors of long-term motor and health deficits (Messinger, Dolcourt, King, Bodnar, & Beck, 1996). Many but not all infants who have IVH will suffer from deficits. Some children are able to recover although it may take several years. This pattern of recovery is called **self-righting** and is comparable to catch-up growth.

For factors related to the parent-infant relationship, we find in some cases no differences between full-term and very-low-birthweight infants (less than 1,500 grams) in mother- and father-infant attachment at 1 year when the comparison is made at equivalent gestational ages (Easterbrooks, 1989). Other research shows that parents of premature infants are more active and stimulating than parents of full-term babies, at least during the first year. Premature infants receive more holding, vocalizing, and care taking during the first year, even though these infants are less attentive and less likely to play and vocalize than full-term babies. As the more healthy prematures catch up with the full terms, their parents also show more normal levels of behavior toward them (Barratt, Roach, & Leavitt, 1996; Branchfeld, Goldberg, & Sloman, 1980; Crawford, 1982). It may be that these additional parental actions are used to compensate for a less active infant, and they may actually help the infant to recover.

For some parents, however, dealing with a premature infant can have short-term effects and may lead to lasting difficulties in the relationship. Parents experience additional stress and emotional trauma just by the fact of having their baby in a hospital for a long period of time (Conner & Nelson, 1999; Cronin, Shapiro, Casiro, & Cheang, 1995; Hughes, McCollum, Sheftel, & Sanchez, 1994; L. T. Singer, Salvator, Guo, Collin, Lilien, & Baley, 1999). In early infancy, prematures become easily overwhelmed with stimulation, smiling less and fussing more, and parents may experience them as unrewarding (Eckerman, Hsu, Molitor, Leung, & Goldstein, 1999). Some parents experience burnout in their role (Barnard, Bee, & Hammond, 1984), and there is a higher than expected percentage of premature infants among children who are later abused or neglected (R. S. Hunter, Kilstrom, Kraybill, & Loda, 1978). In general, the quality of the home and school environments can have an effect on alleviating long-term effects of prematurity (Dittrichová et al., 1996; Kalmar, 1996; Sansavini, Rizzardi, Alessandroni, & Giovanelli, 1996).

Many prematures, especially those who were very low birthweight (VLBW), have deficits that last until middle childhood and adolescence and perhaps even longer. These deficits are in such areas as attention, behavior problems and emotional maturity, language skill, intelligence and educational performance, perceptual and motor function, serious illnesses, and mental retardation (Blackman, Lindgren, Hein, & Harper, 1987; Botting, Powls, Cooke, & Marlow, 1998; Grigoroiu-Serbanescu, 1981; Hack et al., 1995; Lefebvre, Bard, Veilleux, & Martel, 1988; Rieck, Arad, & Netzer, 1996; Robson & Cline, 1998; Skeoch, Rosenberg, Turner, Skeoch, & McIlwaine, 1987). In general, researchers have discovered long-term effects of perinatal risk only for the most extreme cases of illness or very low birthweight. This may be because such effects are more easily detectable. More subtle and as yet unmeasured effects of prematurity may last a lifetime.

Remember also that even when there are few differences between premature and full-term infants in later life, it does not mean that life has been normal or easy for the prematures and their families. Their improved status in later life may have been the result of persistent, difficult, and costly interventions on the part of parents and professionals (Lewit, Baker, Corman, & Shiono, 1995). In the next section, I will discuss some of these early intervention procedures.

Interventions for Premature Infants

Improvements in neonatal intensive care have saved many lives and improved the health of many premature babies (Battin, Ling, Whitfield, MacKinnon, & Effer, 1998; Richardson et al., 1998). Better ways have been found to manage the hospital care for these infants, and new methods have been developed to help parents once the infants have come home. Only about 5% of newborns require intensive care; most of these are due to low birthweight. Most infants in intensive care will require between 15 and 50 days (Hack et al., 1995).

Medical procedures in the hospital. In a modern neonatal intensive care unit (NICU), an increasing number of procedures are adapted to the special needs of premature infants. The smallest infants need high levels of oxygen, warm temperatures, bedding that does not bruise their thin and delicate skin, and nutrients. In the past, providing these needs produced more complications for the infants, who were exposed to dangerously high levels of noise and light inside incubator boxes, bruised from touch, and scarred from needle pricks. Blindness resulted from too much oxygen and deafness from too much noise.

Research has demonstrated that late-term fetuses, premature infants, and full-term newborns feel pain. Repeated experience of untreated pain has the effect of making infants hypervigilant during social interaction and causing them to exhibit increased tension in response to tactile stimulation. In addition, preemies may suffer from the stress of separation from their mothers and long-term isolation due to hospitalization (Karns, 2000).

Today, premature infants are on open beds in a nursery that has higher concentrations of oxygen in the air. They are warmed with low-intensity lights, and their bedding is extremely soft. Some hospitals use sheepskins or water beds. The babies are touched gently and as little as possible, sound and light are kept at moderate levels, and the oxygen content of the blood is monitored continuously by a probe attached to the skin surface, reducing the need for blood sampling. Pain control is managed by drugs, pacifier sucking, giving sucrose, and providing soothing sounds (Furdon, Pfeil, & Snow, 1998; Kawakami, Takai-Kawakami, Kurihara, Shimizu, & Yanaihara, 1996; Korner, 1987; Sell, Hill-Mangan, & Holberg, 1992; Stevens et al., 1999).

Behavioral procedures in the hospital. A variety of approaches have been used either to compensate for missing intrauterine experiences or to try to enhance catch-up growth. One important form of stimulation that a premature lacks is whole-body movement, called **vestibular-proprioceptive stimulation.** Premature infants have received rocking stimulation from adults, in hammocks, from a breathing teddy bear, and from oscillating waterbeds. This rhythmic stimulation has been designed to be similar to the kinds of movements and breathing rhythms that a full-term infant would feel inside the mother during the last weeks of pregnancy. If these natural rhythms are attuned to the needs of individual infants so as not to overstimulate them, the infants increase weight gain, improve sleeping and other physiological indicators, and can be discharged earlier from the hospital (Gatts, Wallace, Glasscock, McKee, & Cohen, 1994; Ingersoll & Thoman, 1994; Korner, 1987; E. B. Thoman, 1993).

Although prematures, especially the smallest ones, cannot ingest fluids, they can suck readily on a pacifier; this is called **nonnutritive sucking** (NNS). Fetuses of the same gestational age inside the uterus also suck regularly. In several studies, premature infants who were provided with pacifiers on a regular basis required fewer tube feedings, started bottle feeding earlier, slept better, gained more weight, and were discharged earlier from the hospital (G. C. Anderson, Burroughs, & Measel, 1983; T. Field et al., 1982; Woodson, Drinkwin, & Hamilton, 1985). NNS reduces the infant's average heart rate, thus allowing the infant the opportunity to use its energy resources for growth instead of life maintenance (Woodson & Hamilton, 1988).

Another form of behavioral intervention is stroking and handling. It appears that for very-low-birthweight infants (less than 1,500 grams), stroking can actually be detrimental due to the extreme sensitivity of the infant's skin. In studies of this group of infants, talking helped to bring the infants into an attentive state, while talking plus touching caused the infant to withdraw (Eckerman, Oehler, Medvin, & Hannan, 1994; Oehler & Eckerman, 1988).

For babies between 1,500 and 2,500 grams, stroking in the form of back massage, neck rubbing, and movement of arms and legs had remarkable effects. In a 12-day test period, the prematures who received the stroking had a 50% increase in weight compared to prematures who did not receive stroking. The stimulated infants had larger heads and fewer complications (Field & Sostek, 1983). Studies of animal infants have shown that touch stimulates hormones that regulate the action and development of the brain (Schanberg, Bartolome, & Kuhn, 1987). These studies clearly show that the overall amount of stimulation is not important. Rather, some specific forms of stimulation work better than others, and the most effective stimulation will depend on the infant's gestational age and weight. Music in the form of male and female singing voices, for example, leads to earlier discharge, improved respiration, and more weight gain (Cassidy & Standley, 1995; Coleman et al., 1997).

Another approach that emphasizes touch and handling is known as kangaroo care. In **kangaroo care,** the infant, wearing only a diaper, is placed on the parent's chest. The infant's head is turned to the side so the baby's ear is against the parent's heart. Any tubes or wires are taped to the parent's clothing. Kangaroo care originated in Bogotá, Colombia, in 1983 because electrical power often failed and expensive equipment did not often work. Infant mortality was reduced significantly. Since then, many studies have been conducted showing positive effects on preterm infants and their families. Preterms who get kangaroo care cry less, sleep for longer periods, gain more weight, have more coordinated breathing and heartbeat patterns, and need less supplemental oxygen. Parents also feel closer to their babies, and it increases their confidence that they can take care of the babies at home (G. C. Anderson, 1999; Ludington-Hoe, Ferreira, & Goldsten, 1998; Ludington-Hoe & Swinth, 1996; Messmer et al., 1999). Kangaroo care's close skin-to-skin contact is probably a good way to handle all babies. Because babies live in a world of touch and warmth, they respond best when these ingredients are provided. A behavior ecology theorist would not be surprised to hear about kangaroo care; it has been around for millions of years.

Finally, interventions can be made with the parents to educate them about the special needs of the premature infant. Parental visitation to the NICU gives the infant more opportunities for stimulation and aids in the parents' positive perceptions of their infant. Both mothers and fathers benefit from frequent visitations (Levy-Shiff, Sharir, & Mogilner, 1989), and infants who are visited more frequently by parents are released sooner from the hospital (Zeskind & Iacino, 1984). Since many mothers of prematures are low-income teenagers, educational interventions directed at making mothers more aware of their responsibilities and setting more realistic goals are effective in improving the outcomes for their babies (Field, Widmayer, Stringer, & Ignatoff, 1980; Pridham, 1998; Zeskind & Iacino, 1987).

Parents may have difficulty communicating with a premature infant because they fear that the child may be vulnerable, and indeed premature infants are more passive and slower to respond to adult social contacts. Premature infants often show a pattern of having either rigid or floppy body posture, and their facial expressions and crying may be different from those of normal babies. Parents need to understand that these differences are normal and will eventually disappear with sensitive handling (van Beek & Samson, 1994).

Even though low-birthweight and premature infants make up only 9% of births, they account for 35% of the medical costs devoted to infants. In 1988 dollars, a normal birth costs about $2,000–$3,000 depending upon the length of hospital stay. Low-birthweight infants as a group average about $6,000 per birth, while the cost for a very-low-birthweight infant is $26,000. Neonatal intensive care is very expensive, at least $100,000 per infant depending on the length of the hospital stay (Rogowski, 1998, 1999). Low-birthweight infants require additional medical treatment during childhood, amounting to an extra $1,200 per year more than normal children. Because many of the families who have low-birthweight children are poor, these costs are borne by government assistance programs such as Medicaid and by increased health insur-

ance premiums for everyone. In addition, prematurity may lead to other long-term costs such as the prosecution and incarceration of persons who exhibit criminal and delinquent behavior that may result from early brain damage and later deprivation. Thus, it is essential that governments devote funding to study the causes and preventions of prematurity (Lewit et al., 1995).

Prevention costs considerably less. Good prenatal care for low-income women could reduce prematurity and complications radically and cost less than $1,000 per child. Simple hospital interventions such as those described here also have long-term benefits to society. Unfortunately, low-income women find it difficult to obtain good prenatal care, Medicaid places limits on the number of allowable prenatal visits, and it takes a long time to process claims. Ultimately, the prevention of birth defects will require radical changes in our society, including the elimination of poverty and prejudice (Alexander & Korenbrot, 1995).

What Can We Learn about Fetal Psychology from Premature Infants?

Infants born prematurely are the same age as late-term fetuses and have the same behavioral, sensory, and neurological abilities. Because preemies have experienced the birth process, and because they had to adapt to life outside the uterus, they may have acquired abilities that the fetus does not possess. On the other hand, the NICU behavioral interventions that are most successful seem to offer clues to the characteristics of the prenatal environment that are most conducive to fetal psychological development.

In Chapter 3, we learned that in the third fetal period, the fetus was responsive to movement, touch, and sound, and that it could suck. Because of the success of interventions involving these modalities with preemies, it is reasonable to conclude that fetuses *require* vestibular-proprioceptive, tactile, and auditory stimulation, as well as opportunities for sucking. The prenatal environment is uniquely suited to provide these requirements for growth. Vestibular-proprioceptive stimulation comes from maternal movements. Tactile stimulation is provided in terms of the soft feeling, warm temperature, and constant flow of the amniotic fluid. Auditory stimulation is provided by the mother's heartbeat and voice.

These forms of stimulation are apparently necessary to sustain normal fetal development. They probably are related to feelings of pleasure, comfort, and security. It is also possible that the fetus has a sense of an emergent self (See Chapters 2 and 5), as these various sensory modalities are experienced in an integrated way that provides a sense of completeness.

Perinatal Mortality

Like prematurity and health risk, infant mortality is greatest in groups who have low incomes and inadequate health care. Most of the causes of perinatal death can be found in poor prenatal care, ill health, or malnutrition of the mother during pregnancy. Statistics for infant mortality are shown in Tables 4.5 and 4.6. Although infants are more likely to die than mothers, those countries and ethnicities that have high infant mortality also have high maternal mortality (United Nations Department of Economic and Social Affairs, 1986). The causes of maternal mortality are very different from the causes of infant mortality, however. The leading causes of maternal death in the United States are pregnancy-induced high blood pressure, hemorrhage (excessive bleeding following childbirth), and respiratory failure (Grimes, 1994).

Apparently, the trend over time toward decreasing mortality has been going on since records began to be kept in 1750. Balog (1976) traced the changes in mortality over the last 200 years in the United States and found no obvious dips in the rate after major medical advances, such as drugs and sterilization procedures. He concluded that changes in mortality rates reflect trends in general economic growth, a higher standard of living, and better education—in short, social and economic factors.

The one place in the world where maternal mortality has been increasing over the past 20 years is sub-Saharan Africa. The maternal mortality rate between 1983 and 1988 in West Africa was 760 maternal deaths per 100,000 births. During the same

Table 4.5 Rates of Infant Mortality by Country per 1,000 Live Births (1996)

Country	Rate
Japan	3.8
Norway	4.0
Sweden	4.0
France	4.9
Denmark	5.7
Australia	5.8
England	6.1
Italy	6.0
USA	7.3

Source: B. Guyer, M. F. MacDorman, J. A. Martin, K. D. Peters, & D. M. Strobino, Annual summary of vital statistics: 1997, 1998, p. 782. *Pediatrics, 102*(6), 751–792.

period, the rate in Mexico was 90 deaths per 100,000 and in the United States 8 deaths per 100,000. There are several explanations for this extraordinarily high incidence of maternal deaths in Africa. The deteriorating economic, political, and social conditions that lead to starvation and deprivation for all people are a factor. Another is the high rate of sexism and violence against women. Women are expected to have as many children as possible even in the worst of circumstances. Many of these countries also practice female genital mutilation, a widespread procedure in which a young girl's clitoris is removed to prevent her from experiencing sexual pleasure. Thus, the African situation is complicated by cultural factors over and above the usual social and economic factors that cause maternal death (WIN News, 1992).

In the United States, even though mortality has fallen for ethnic groups, African American infants are still twice as likely to die as Caucasian Americans (Table 4.6). A closer look at the causes of death shows that African American infants succumb to conditions that are indicative of poor prenatal care. Homicides, birth injuries, and congenital abnormalities are nearly the same among whites and non-whites. These categories have little to do with the quality of prenatal care, health, or nutrition. The most common causes of neonatal mortality among the poor in the United States and in developing nations are respiratory problems and diarrhea. They derive from the immature system's inability to cope with normal bacterial infections and physical insults

Table 4.6   Percentage of Low-Birthweight Babies and Infant Mortality by Ethnicity in the United States (1997)

Group	Very-Low-Birthweight Babies (<1,500 Grams)	Low-Birthweight Babies (<2,500 Grams)	Mortality (Under 1 Year)
Caucasian American	1.1	6.5	0.6
African American	3.0	13.0	1.4

Source: B. Guyer, M. F. MacDorman, J. A. Martin, K. D. Peters, & D. M. Strobino, Annual summary of vital statistics: 1997, 1998, p. 781. Pediatrics, 102(6), 751–792.

and stem largely from deficits acquired prenatally. Studies have shown, for example, that adequate nutritional supplementation during pregnancy can cut the infant death rate by as much as half (Werner, 1979). In the United States, only a very small percentage of infant or maternal deaths can be attributed to ineffective hospital care during and after birth (Escobar et al., 1998).

Apparently, malnutrition, poverty, and ill health act as a system: one condition feeds upon another to worsen or maintain high death and disease rates. In many countries, people who cannot make a living on farms move into the cities to join the growing poor population in the inner city. Forced to live in slums with poor sanitation, they have little food and no money. Urban employment places special burdens on mothers who must travel away from home, and there are seldom adequate child care facilities. Lack of energy from malnutrition contributes to the inability to cope with these enormous problems.

The prevention and elimination of these problems depend on intervention in the cycle of poverty and ill health. Community-based clinics providing medical care during pregnancy, simple disease-screening procedures, immunizations, nutrition education, fertility advice, upgrading of parental competence, improved sanitation, and the effective management of diarrhea already are being implemented in many less developed countries (Puffer & Serrano, 1973; WIN News, 1992; World Health Organization, 1976).

Supplemental nutrition given to mothers has a greater effect on infant mortality than on infant birthweight. In a study done in Bogotá, Colombia, supplemental food for malnourished mothers increased birthweight by only 77 grams but decreased the neonatal death rate from 42 to 23 per 1,000

births. Food availability for pregnant mothers in developing countries can be increased by larger contributions from rich nations. This assistance will reduce pressures to use land for cash crops (such as coffee and cocoa) and allow local farmers to grow their own food. Supporting local health care and breast-feeding will also help to reduce infant mortality (Falkner, 1985).

The United Nations has developed and tested a successful health education program called GOBI, which stands for Growth charts, Oral rehydration, Breast-feeding, and Immunization (Werner, 1986). By comparing their own infant's development to standard growth charts, parents can detect growth retardation and conditions such as failure-to-thrive. **Failure-to-thrive** is a condition in which infants fail to respond to the environment and continue to deteriorate even when intervention is available and even when parents do everything possible. Failure-to-thrive has unknown causes, but intervention can help in some cases even though failure-to-thrive children may permanently lag behind others in language, intelligence, and emotional maturity.

Oral rehydration—providing fluids—is the primary treatment for infantile diarrhea. Breast-feeding provides adequate and sanitary nourishment as well as natural immunization (see the section on breast-feeding in this chapter). Immunization protects children from many infectious diseases.

An alternative explanation for the reduction in infant mortality is that it may be associated with the decrease in the number of pregnancies a woman will have. In the 1700s, a woman might expect to carry 10 to 15 conceptions to term, which would mean an increased probability of mortality for each infant. The age of the mother, the spacing between pregnancies, and the number of pregnancies all account for a portion of the risk of infant death.

Age and sex are also important factors in determining the probability of infant death. The highest probability of death is when an infant is less than 24 hours old. In fact, if a baby survives beyond the first day, the odds of mortality are extremely low, about 1 per 1,000 or less. With regard to sex, males tend to have a higher death rate all through their life spans. More males are conceived, but more are miscarried or spontaneously aborted.

These raw statistics are sobering, but they do little to make us aware that each time an infant dies, the family feels a major loss. The next section will try to give you insight into the human element behind the mortality tables.

How Does the Family Respond to the Death of an Infant?

The loss parents feel when a newborn dies may not be the same feeling as when an older child or some other close relative dies, but neonatal death can deeply affect parents (Helmrath & Steinitz, 1978). If parents are not encouraged to mourn the loss and deal successfully with the painful feelings and memories, the incomplete bereavement may lead to disturbed perceptions and inappropriate behavior with later children (Drotar & Irvin, 1979; Hesse & van Ijzendoorn, 1998).

The normal sequence of emotions parents experience after neonatal death is similar to other kinds of grief reactions. Upon hearing the news that their baby has died or will soon die, parents experience shock and denial. They think a mistake has been made and wonder if it can be corrected. The next phase is feelings of sadness and loss mixed with anger. This anger may be directed at others, such as the obstetrician, or it may be directed at themselves in the form of self-blame. Gradually, parents come to accept the death and readjust the reality to their lives. This can often take several years. Having healthy children later on helps this process, but parents continue to fear that something will go wrong with the next child and wonder what their lost child might have been like.

A number of practitioners have argued that the loss of the newborn should be treated like any other death in the family. Some hospitals simply dispose of the body without allowing the parents any option to view it. Parents often are concerned about the actual disposition of the infant's body. They may have painful and frightening fantasies: perhaps the infant did not die naturally but was used for some strange experiment; perhaps the child's body is on display in a jar for medical students to look at; was the infant cremated or just thrown away? As unlikely as these fantasies are, they are quite common among such parents (L. Cohen, Zilkha, Middleton, & O'Donnohue, 1978).

In one program (L. Cohen et al., 1978), parents are offered the option of viewing the body. If they elect to do this, a nurse brings the infant wrapped in a blanket. The blanket is tucked to hide any abnormalities. At the sight of the deceased infant, mothers are less afraid than expected. In all cases in this program, infants are given appropriate religious services and burials.

Between life and death, there are some gray areas. Infants may be born viable but suffer from gross deformities or other conditions that would impair later functioning. The issues faced by parents and doctors in these situations are not unlike those faced by the families of persons in comas or with terminal and painful diseases or by those close to the elderly and infirm. **Euthanasia** is the act of causing a painless death or of letting someone die naturally without trying to prolong life with "heroic" medical procedures. As you can imagine, the idea of euthanasia involves some serious and difficult religious, ethical, legal, medical, and personal issues that are not easily resolved. With the advent of sophisticated neonatal intensive care, parents and pediatricians are facing these issues more and more (see the "Applications" section in this chapter).

Some hospitals take photographs of sick infants at birth. Because parents are distressed to hear that their infant is ill and may die, the hospital photo may be the only one that is taken. Many states now have support groups for parents following perinatal death. Similar grief reactions are seen in cases of miscarriage, especially in instances of repeated miscarriage, and in sudden infant death syndrome, in which death occurs unexpectedly between 1 and 6 months of age (see Chapter 6). In all cases, factual and frank discussions with medical personnel, the availability of the autopsy report, and a funeral service help the parents cope (Dyregrov & Matthiesen, 1987; Kotch & Cohen, 1986).

Family and Society

What Are the Attitudes and Emotions of Women following Childbirth?

As with every other major event in life, we would expect childbirth to have a lasting impact on the individual and to be the source of a good deal of psychological adjustment in the days and weeks that follow. Westbrook (1978) asked women to remember their feelings during pregnancy, labor, and the hospital stay and upon returning home. Of the 200 women interviewed in Sydney, Australia, most reported high levels of positive feelings all the way through. In discussing their anxieties and worries, however, they noted changes depending on the stage the woman was at in the process. For example, women experienced the highest levels of total anxiety, fears of death, and fears of mutilation during pregnancy and labor. Most of these severe anxieties declined right after the birth.

One emotional change that can occur after birth is *postpartum blues,* which seem to occur in some form in about two-thirds of all women after childbirth (O'Hara, Schlechte, Lewis, & Varner, 1991; Yalom, 1968). These "blues" usually take the form of brief episodes of crying, mood swings, confusion, or mild depression that seems to begin and end suddenly and without warning. Postpartum blues lasts only a few hours or a few days.

Postpartum blues should be distinguished from the more serious occurrence of clinical postpartum depression. **Postpartum depression** is characterized by dysphoric mood, disturbances of sleep or appetite, fatigue, feelings of guilt, and suicidal thoughts. It occurs in between 8% and 15% of women following childbirth (O'Hara, 1997). One mother reported:

Although I've got a routine with the kids, I've lost my own routine. . . . It's a terrible thing to admit but

I went for two days without even washing. I sat down and had a good cry and I said to Mark "This just isn't on because I'm really going to go down if I'm not careful." And you think at the back of your mind "Oh God, am I suffering from depression?" (S. E. Lewis & Nicolson, 1998, p. 189)

Postpartum depression has been linked with prenatal factors such as life stresses, a perceived lack of social support, poor marital adjustment, depressed mood, and a history of psychiatric illness (Berthiaume, David, Saucier, & Borgeat, 1998; J. M. Green, 1998; O'Hara et al., 1991; Whiffen, 1988). Following childbirth, women with postpartum depression report having the need for greater emotional support from their partners and lower levels of marital satisfaction compared to nondepressed women (Mauthner, 1998; O'Brian, Asay, & McCluskey-Fawcett, 1999; Stuchbery, Matthey, & Barnett, 1998). A small percentage of men also show symptoms of postpartum depression, especially if they are stepfathers or if their wives are depressed (Areias, Kumar, Barros, & Figueiredo, 1996).

Some mothers may experience childbirth as traumatic and suffer from **post-traumatic stress disorder** (PTSD), characterized by intrusive thoughts, fears, nightmares, and heightened arousal. The causes of PTSD are different from those of postpartum depression. They include feelings of loss of control, fear of harm to self or infant during labor and delivery, having an induced labor, and having epidural anesthesia (S. Allen, 1998; Lyons, 1998). Other research has shown, however, that these effects are similar to those of any traumatic surgical event and are not specific to childbirth (Mandy, Gard, Ross, & Valentine, 1998). In most cases, women recover from these feelings after several weeks.

In general, the moods of women after childbirth are relatively stable and positive (Murai, Murai, & Takahashi, 1978; O'Hara, 1998). In a sample of 129 women in Australia, only 16 were severely depressed, and only 15 showed no mood changes following childbirth. The rest of the sample experienced one or more brief episodes of crying (Meares, Grimwalde, & Wood, 1976). How childbirth is experienced, however, is dictated in large measure by the cultural beliefs of the society.

What Are Some Cultural Differences in Childbirth and Infant Care Practices?

Not all societies greet the event of birth in the same way. Some peoples consider it an illness or an abnormality, whereas others view it as part of the fabric of everyday affairs. The Cuna of Panama consider birth to be a secret event. In the United States, birth is considered a private affair, with only medical personnel and a few family members in attendance. Some cultures on the extreme end of the privacy dimension consider birth to be defiling and insist that women give birth in a separate area, which often is reserved for such things as childbirth, menstruation, and excrement (M. Mead & Newton, 1967).

At the other extreme, the Jahara of South America give birth under a shelter in full view of everyone in the village—even small children. A number of Pacific Island communities also regard the birth of a child as an event of interest to the entire community.

To illustrate the cultural influences on childbirth and child care practices in the newborn period, a portrait of three cultures from widely different parts of the globe will be presented: Zinancantecan Indians from Mexico, originally of Mayan descent; villagers from the south of Italy; and the Japanese.

No drugs are used during labor among the Zinancantecans. The mother is supported and encouraged by an ever-present midwife. After birth, the newborn is placed naked before a fire. The midwife, who is still in attendance, begins to say prayers asking the gods to look kindly upon this child. A long skirt made of heavy fabric is brought out and put on the infant. Extending beyond the feet, the skirt is worn by both males and females throughout the first year of life. For fear of losing parts of the soul, the newborn is wrapped snugly in several layers of blankets; even the face is covered, except during feedings. This practice is believed to ward off evil spirits and illnesses during the first few months of life (Brazelton, 1977).

On the other side of the Atlantic, birth in a small village in southern Italy usually takes place in a hospital, attended by a midwife. Just after the birth, as in Mexico, the newborn is dressed in clothing and ceremonial linens the family has provided. When the infant is dressed and usually within about

Owen Franken / Stock, Boston

Each culture has different rituals for childbirth and newborn care. In most places, newborns are immediately integrated into family life. This family is from Morocco.

10 minutes of the birth, the midwife goes into the hall, where the mother's entire immediate and extended family has been waiting. They all accompany the midwife back to the mother's room, where everyone takes a turn congratulating, kissing, and fondling both the mother and the baby.

The family then provides a party of pastries and liqueurs to share with one another and with those who attended the birth. During the labor, the mother was never left alone, and she will continue to be supported by rituals like this one. The mother will be visited by many of her friends and relatives for some time after the birth. These visits have the effect of recognizing the contribution the mother has made to the community. This social support system is embodied in the role of the mother-in-law; from a few days before until about 1 month after the birth, she feeds the mother ritual foods of broth, marsala, and fresh cheeses. All mothers breast-feed their infants, and the infant usually sleeps in the same bed as the mother or in a nearby cradle (Schreiber, 1977).

Finally, in traditional Japanese society, interdependent relationships between people are viewed as extremely important. Children are valued and loved, and their development is celebrated by a number of community rituals. These rituals start during the fifth month of pregnancy, when the woman begins to wear a special belt (called an *iwata-obi*) around her abdomen under the kimono. This ritual is believed to establish the child's first tie to the community. After birth, the umbilical cord is dried and saved in an ornamental box, reminding the mother and child of their once-close physical bond. From birth until late childhood, children sleep with their parents, since it is believed that sleeping alone breaks the family psychological bonds.

On the day of the birth and on the third and seventh day of the infant's life, elaborate feasts are celebrated among all the relatives. Since these early days are thought to be critical to the infant's survival, the feasts ensure health for the baby. A special naming ceremony is performed on the seventh day, and at 1 month, the baby is taken to the Shinto shrine for blessing. At the age of 100 days, the infant is given a grain of rice as its first token solid food (Kojima, 1986). Although some of these traditional practices are changing due to the urbanization of Japan, the basic commitment to the infant's value remains.

Newborn Feeding Practices

In the United States, breast-feeding was the general practice until the beginning of the 20th century. In 1900, only 38% of mothers breast-fed, and this percentage declined until only 18% were breast-feeding in 1966. The number of women breast-feeding took a major turn upward in the 1970s, so that by 1976, about half of all mothers were breast-feeding at the time of discharge from the hospital. The incidence of breast-feeding in the United States varies with class and education. The rate of breast-feeding in the United States is highest among higher-income, college-educated women who are more than 30 years old and live in the Mountain and Pacific regions of the country. In 1995, about 60% of mothers were breast-feeding their newborns, though only 21% were still nursing at 6 months (American Academy of Pediatrics, 1997).

The major factor for predicting success in breast-feeding is the desire of the mother to do so. The evidence suggests that mothers automatically produce milk after birth. Milk will be produced even under conditions of maternal malnutrition. In such cases, the milk will be made in less quantity, but it will have the same nutrient quality as that of well-nourished mothers (Guthrie, 1979). This quality is usually maintained at the expense of the mother's reserve stores of nutrients.

Because breast-feeding is being encouraged as a way to prevent infant death in developing countries, the reduced quantity of milk from malnourished mothers presents a dilemma for the mother who is undernourished. The World Health Organization recommends teaching mothers when and how to supplement the diets of breast-fed babies with foods prepared from locally available products (World Health Organization, 1985).

Some women can even breast-feed without having given birth, as reports from around the world show. In one study of mothers who nursed adopted babies, the sample consisted of 18 women who had never been pregnant, 7 who had been pregnant but had never lactated, and 40 who had previously lactated. All were able to nurse their adopted infants. Their success seemed to depend on factors such as the support of the husband and family, preparation by either hand-pumping the breast or nursing another infant at least 1 month in advance, having an

Felicia Martinez/PhotoEdit

Breast-feeding can be a great source of pleasure for the mother and infant, especially in quiet family times. For some mothers, breast-feeding is inconvenient and difficult. Although breast-feeding is recommended, each family should choose the feeding option that best suits their lifestyle.

infant as young as possible, and nursing a great deal at first. Apparently, sucking stimulation is more effective than hormone treatments in inducing lactation (Hormann, 1977).

Sucking stimulation can maintain the supply of breast milk even if the infant is feeding only once a day. This kind of minimal breast-feeding is often used by mothers who work outside the home, who are weaning a baby from the breast, or who are using breast-feeding for "comfort" nursing for older infants. It is not necessary to mechanically express milk to maintain the supply during periods of minimal breast-feeding (Michaelson et al., 1988).

The nutritive demands of the lactating mother are far in excess of the demands made during prenatal life because of the accelerated weight gain of the infant just after birth. The milk secreted in just 1 month represents more calories than the net energy cost of pregnancy (Guthrie, 1979). The mother can meet this increased nutrient need by eating the equivalent of an additional meal of 500 kilocalories each day.

The composition of human milk not only differs from cow's milk, but changes over the first few weeks of life (see Table 4.7). **Colostrum,** the clear, yellowish liquid that is present in the first few days, is relatively high in protein. It also has enzymes that

Table 4.7 Composition of Breast Milk Compared with Leading Formulas (per 100 Milliliters of Milk)

	Colostrum (1 to 5 Days)	Transitional (6 to 10 Days)	Mature	Enfamil	Similac
Energy (kilocalories)	58.0	74.0	71.0	67	68
Fat (grams)	2.9	3.6	4.5	3.7	3.6
Protein (g)	2.3	1.6	1.2	1.5	1.6
Calcium (milligrams)	31.0	34.0	33.0	55	58
Carbohydrate (g)			6.8	7	7.1
Sodium (mg)			16	28	25
Cholesterol (mg)			7–47	1.4	1.6
Iron (mg)			0.05	1.2	1.2

Source: H. A. Guthrie, *Introduction to nutrition*, 1979, p. 286. St. Louis: Mosby.

inhibit the growth of bacteria, microorganisms (*Lactobacillus bifidus*) that depress the growth of pathogens, and large "eating" cells (microphages) that enhance the immune system against bacteria and some viruses (American Academy of Pediatrics, 1997; Bocci et al., 1993; Guthrie, 1979).

To make cow's milk used for most commercial infant formulas more similar in composition to human milk, it is usually modified. The protein content is lowered, and the milk is treated to make it more easily digested (the whey protein of human milk is easier to digest than that of cow's milk). Vitamins A, D, and C, and sometimes iron, are added to fortify the formula (C. H. Robinson, 1978). Formulas can also be tailored to infants with special needs, such as soy formulas for infants with allergies. Today, formula and breast milk have similar nutrient values, but human milk is more nutritionally matched to infants and contains other important substances that promote immunization.

Human milk has a sweet taste. It also takes on some of the flavors found in the maternal diet. Amniotic fluid is also flavored with the mother's foods, suggesting that there is an acculturation toward local foods that begins prenatally (Mennella, 1997). Human milk is also low in sodium, and breast-fed infants have less of a preference for salt than bottle-fed infants (Karns, 2000).

The Effects of Breast- and Bottle-Feeding on Mother and Infant

Breast-feeding has important health benefits for both the mother and the infant. One advantage of breast-feeding is that it serves as a natural way to help mothers recover from childbirth. The sucking stimulation from the infant triggers the release of several maternal hormones, in particular oxytocin and prolactin. Oxytocin, as you may recall, is used as a drug to speed up contractions during labor. It is essential following the third stage of labor, since continued uterine contractions are necessary to shrink the uterus to normal size and prevent uterine hemorrhage. The oxytocin released by sucking does this naturally. If mothers do not breast-feed, they must be given oxytocin. Oxytocin also stimulates the breast to deliver milk only when sucking occurs and not otherwise. Prolactin stimulates the mammary glands to produce more milk.

There is some evidence that breast-feeding has a long-term effect on mothers, in particular, the partial prevention of ovarian and breast cancer. Women who breast-fed their firstborn infants longer than 1 month had a significantly lower risk of developing breast cancer, at least during the period before the onset of menopause (American Academy of Pediatrics, 1997; Byers, Grahm, & Rzepka, 1985; Siskind, Schofield, Rice, & Bain, 1989). Breast-feeding also lowers the risk of hip fractures in the postmenopausal period and helps women retain minerals in their bones.

There are also health benefits to the infant. Mother's milk contains immunizing agents that protect against a variety of infections such as respiratory infection, ear infection, bacterial meningitis, and urinary tract infection. Breast-feeding may also reduce the risk of sudden infant death syndrome (SIDS; see Chapter 6), diabetes, allergic diseases, and digestive diseases. Finally, there is some evidence that breast-feeding may enhance cognitive development and reduce the risk of obesity (American Academy of Pediatrics, 1997; Jelliffe & Jelliffe, 1988).

Breast-feeding for more than 6 months significantly reduces their risk of developing childhood cancer, especially lymphomas. Non-breast-fed children are five times more likely to get lymphoma, a form of cancer that is higher in children with immune deficiencies (American Academy of Pediatrics, 1997; Smigel, 1988).

The immunologic effect of human milk derives from the protein called *secretory IgA,* or SIgA. This protein coats the inner lining of the baby's intestines, acting to trap and kill harmful bacteria. SIgA also enters the lungs and breathing passages whenever the infant gurgles and blows milk bubbles and thus may protect against respiratory diseases. If a mother has a bacterial infection, her milk contains higher levels of SIgA, which helps to further protect the infant from catching the mother's infection (Pollitt, Garza, & Leib, 1984).

If breast milk protects the infant against disorders of the immune system, what happens if the mother has an immune system disorder such as AIDS? There is some controversy about whether infants can acquire AIDS from their mothers by breast-feeding. If a mother is infected with AIDS, HIV is typically present in her breast milk. The chance of an infant's acquiring AIDS from its mother is about 15%, but part of this transmission may occur either prenatally or during the birth process (see Chapter 3). It is difficult to determine which of these routes is most likely to infect the infant.

Medical agencies have come up with conflicting recommendations about whether an AIDS-infected mother should breast-feed. It is thought that SIgA may neutralize the AIDS virus and that the risk of an infant acquiring other diseases because of a lack of breast milk SIgA may be just as high as the risk of getting AIDS from breast milk, especially in poor countries where the incidence of AIDS and other diseases is high. Others believe that the chance of acquiring AIDS from breast milk is not worth the risk of spreading the disease and therefore recommend against breast-feeding. Infected women should consult their physician before making the choice to breast-feed (American Academy of Pedi-

atrics, 1997; D. T. Dunn, Newell, Ades, & Peckham, 1992; Goldfarb, 1993; Kennedy et al., 1990; Peckham, 1993; Porcher, 1992; Van de Perre et al., 1993). Breast-feeding is also not recommended if the mother uses illegal drugs or is receiving chemotherapy for cancer.

Behavioral differences between breast- and bottle-fed infants have been found. A study of 100 healthy, full-term, vaginally delivered newborns found that breast-fed infants are more irritably fussy than bottle-fed infants (DiPietro, Larson, & Porges, 1987). This irritability, however, was associated with a more optimal physiological functioning, such as a slower heart rate, compared to bottle-fed infants. The physiological functioning of breast-fed infants is more energy-efficient, as judged by differences in the patterns of heart rate, breathing, and sleeping of bottle- and breast-fed infants (Zeskind, Marshall, & Goff, 1992). The higher irritability of breast-fed infants is not due to a less optimal mother-infant interaction. Some research has shown, on the contrary, that breast-fed infants get talked to, smiled at, touched, looked at, and rocked more by their mothers (J. Dunn, 1975; Lavelli & Poli, 1998) during feeding, although no long-term behavioral differences have been found. Nor is the effect due to the fact that breast-fed babies get hungrier than bottle-fed infants (DiPietro et al., 1987).

Rather, DiPietro and associates (1987) propose that "the irritability of breast-fed neonates be regarded as the norm of neonatal behavior. Formula may have a depressant effect on behavior" (p. 472). This may be due to the differences in the specific types of proteins and sugars that constitute the two types of milk. If more irritability is the norm, these authors argue that it serves two purposes. First, it enhances physiological functioning by giving the infant experience with varying degrees of arousal. Second, crying may serve to stimulate more mother-infant interaction and provide more opportunities for feeding (Hunziker & Barr, 1986).

Taken together, the benefits of breast-feeding appear to be immunological, physiological, behavioral, and psychological.

Because of the growing number of research studies supporting the superiority of breast milk and breast-feeding for both mother and infant, the American Academy of Pediatrics (AAP), the Canadian Paediatric Society, and the American Dietetic Association all strongly encourage breast-feeding (Karns, 2000). The AAP recommends:

Exclusive breast-feeding is ideal nutrition and sufficient to support optimal growth and development for approximately the first 6 months after birth. Infants weaned before 12 months of age should not receive cow's milk feedings but should receive iron-fortified infant formula. Gradual introduction of iron-enriched solid foods in the second half of the first year should complement the breast milk diet. It is recommended that breast feeding continue for at least 12 months, and thereafter for as long as mutually desired. (American Academy of Pediatrics, 1997, p. 4)

Although breast-feeding is recommended, personal preferences, illness, family and social support, and cultural norms may influence the choice of feeding method. An effort is being made in the United States to encourage health care professionals to promote breast-feeding. Mothers can also receive information and support from local hospitals, clinics, and breast-feeding advocacy groups. These supports are necessary to counteract the effects of cultural beliefs against breast-feeding, embarrassment, lack of self-confidence, and family attitudes (Karns, 2000). The wishes of other family members may play a role in the choice. Some fathers have feelings of jealousy, uselessness, and sexual frustration associated with their mates' breast-feeding. Some men may also experience feelings of ambivalence about the breast: who does it "belong" to? Who and what is it for? Research shows that these feelings can be alleviated somewhat by enhancing the father's participation in the birth experience and by improving father-mother communication on such issues as infant care and sexual fulfillment (Karns, 2000; Waletzky, 1979).

The Author's View

The perinatal period is unique in the life course. It is a major developmental transition for the family as the pregnancy ends and a new person is born. Parents, especially first-time parents, must learn new roles and take on important new demands and pleasures. Perhaps the transition is not as crucial for the infant. Although the baby must learn to breathe and live in an atmospheric as opposed to an aquatic environment, the ability to breathe, feel, suck, hear, and move had already been established in the last months of gestation.

Childbirth itself is an event full of powerful human emotions. Parents are filled with excitement and fear when the baby first appears. These emotions can turn suddenly into overwhelming joy with a normal baby or crushing despair and sadness if the baby has birth defects or suffers from a perinatal trauma or prematurity. With the exception of parents whose own poor health, malnutrition, drug addiction, or mental illness keeps them from appreciating the full impact of childbirth, the emotions of childbirth can be life-changing events that fix the experience indelibly within the person. I speak not only from my knowledge of the field but also from experience. I was fortunate to be present at the births of my own two sons in the early 1970s, one in a traditional hospital environment and the other using natural childbirth at home.

In previous editions of this book, I have taken a neutral stance on the topic of breast- versus bottle-feeding. In spite of my own personal advocacy of breast-feeding, I felt this was necessary because the research was not sufficiently strong to warrant a strong choice. I am pleased that the American Academy of Pediatrics has finally taken a strong position in support of breast-feeding and that there is finally a significant body of research to support it. I was bottle-fed in the 1940s at a time when breast-feeding was strongly discouraged by the medical community. My sons were breast-fed in the 1970s when breast-feeding was on the rise for college-educated people. The AAP and the federal government want to achieve the goal of 75% of babies being breast-fed by the first years of the 21st century. It can be achieved if there is enough cultural, medical, and family support.

Given what we are also learning about the importance of holding, touch, and a sense of security

Applications   The Case of Baby Doe

On April 9, 1982, a baby was born in Bloomington, Indiana, who was given little chance to survive. The baby had Down's syndrome and multiple complications, including a blocked esophagus and an enlarged heart. In this case, the physicians agreed that surgery would not be worthwhile because it had a limited chance of success and would only prolong the infant's life for a few weeks, increasing the suffering of both the infant and family.

The medical decision, to which the parents agreed, was to withhold treatment for the infant. Because of the infant's state of health, this decision was an act of euthanasia: keeping the infant comfortable and well fed while waiting for an inevitable death.

This baby continued to live longer than the doctors expected, and the case caught the attention of the county prosecutor, who charged the parents and physicians with criminal neglect. Two county judges agreed with the parents' decision, but the prosecutor eventually asked the Indiana Supreme Court to issue an order to provide treatment for the infant, who later became known as Baby Doe.

The issues in the Baby Doe case are similar to the issues in the abortion debate. On the one side are those who feel that newborns should have a constitutional right to treatment even without the consent of their parents, and on the other side are those who argue for the newborn's right to die peacefully in cases where the low quality of life is considered to outweigh the need to preserve life.

Because of Baby Doe and other similar cases, in 1984 the U.S. Senate amended

the 1974 Child Abuse and Prevention Act. The amendment states that "withholding of medically indicated treatment from disabled infants with life-threatening conditions" could be considered a form of child abuse and neglect. However, the amendment lists three exceptions to this rule, which specify when euthanasia is permitted:

1. The infant is chronically ill and irreversibly comatose.
2. The provision of such treatment would merely prolong dying and would not be effective in ameliorating or correcting the infant's life-threatening condition.
3. The provision of such treatment would be virtually futile in terms of the survival of the infant, and the treatment under such circumstances would be inhumane.

While many accepted this legislation, the American Medical Association did not endorse it because the amendment does not mention issues related to the quality of life. Suppose, for example, that the infant would survive with an appropriate medical intervention. The law clearly states that such an intervention must be provided. But what if the infants who survive are so deformed, sick, or handicapped that their lives would involve constant pain, discomfort, and severe restriction of movement? It is this quality-of-life issue that doctors would like to have the freedom to consider in making recommendations to parents.

The Baby Doe case raises important questions about how society is to decide what is in the best interests of children. Is life worth preserving at any cost? Is the best intervention in some cases not to inter-

vene? How should quality of life and stress—emotional and financial—on the family be weighed in decisions about the rights of children? As our technology advances, we can do extraordinary things, such as save the life of an extremely fragile or extremely low birthweight newborn. Unfortunately, individuals and governments are not able to cope with the complex ethical and legal issues that this technology raises.

Some examples illustrate the strong emotions and conflicting values involved in such cases. In 1994, Gregory Messenger of Michigan removed his extremely low birthweight (ELBW) son from life support and was later charged with manslaughter. In 1989, Rudy Linares of Illinois unhooked a respirator from his 15-month-old son while holding a gun on the hospital staff. The child had been comatose for 9 months after swallowing a balloon. Linares was not charged with a crime. A mother in Virginia, on the other hand, fought a hospital's decision to end life support for her 2-year-old, who was born without most of her brain. Meanwhile, the number of parents—often poor, on drugs, or mentally ill—who abandon their infants in the hospital is increasing. There were 22,000 such infants in 1991. Who should take care of these babies, and what is to be done if they are at risk for major disorders? To help resolve these difficult problems, professionals in the field of medical ethics are beginning to create a philosophical standard to guide doctors, nurses, parents, lawyers, and hospital administrators. Many hospitals today employ medical ethicists as consultants.

in early infancy (Chapters 2, 5, and 6), breast-feeding and methods such as kangaroo care seem to be the most natural way to achieve these goals. If mothers cannot breast-feed, it is important to provide extra physical contact, preferably skin-to-skin

with plenty of touching, to make up for the increased physical distance and lowered feeding frequency that comes with bottle-feeding. You and your baby will not regret having these special experiences.

SUMMARY

The Childbirth Experience

- The overall birthrate in first-world nations has been declining, but the rate of multiple births has been increasing.

- Labor occurs in three stages: the opening of the cervix, the passage of the infant through the vagina, and the birth of the placenta.

- Both risks and benefits are associated with medical technologies such as fetal monitoring, forceps, and vacuum extraction.

- About 16% of births are done by cesarean section. There seem to be no ill effects of C-sections compared to vaginal deliveries.

- Drugs are used to speed labor and ease pain. Drugs can be safe if used sparingly. Short-term effects are common, but few long-term effects can be demonstrated.

- Conventional hospital childbirth was compared with a number of alternatives, including early discharge, Lamaze childbirth, upright postures, midwives, birthing centers, home births, and the Leboyer technique. If implemented properly, these practices are all effective and safe for those who choose to use them.

The Baby at Birth: Health and Risk

- The newborn has unique physical characteristics, most of which disappear after a few weeks of life. These characteristics are the remnants of prenatal life and the effects of the birth process.

- The art of newborn assessment is rapidly improving. Reliable and valid tests exist for determining the newborn's risk in terms of survival, neurological problems, gestational age, and behavioral status.

- Perinatal problems account for a large proportion of later deficits.

- Prematurity is the largest single category of birth complication and seems to be caused by a variety of prenatal factors.

- Premature infants are likely to be smaller and sicker and to lag behaviorally, compared to full-term infants.

- The most severe long-term deficits occur primarily for very-low-birthweight infants, under 1,500 grams. Most infants between 1,500 and 2,500 grams tend to recover eventually and lead normal lives, but many will show mild to severe effects of prematurity.

- The type of intervention that improves the long-term outcome for premature infants depends on the infant's gestational age and health. Medical interventions are improving and becoming less invasive. Behavioral procedures are extremely effective in improving health and weight gain at low cost. Parent education is also an effective strategy.

- The research on preterm infants suggests that late-term fetuses require movement, touch, sound, and sucking in order to continue their development, all forms of stimulation uniquely found in the prenatal environment.

Perinatal Mortality

- Poverty and disease are the biggest causes of infant mortality worldwide.

- Supplemental maternal and infant nutrition, breast-feeding, growth monitoring, rehydration, and immunization can prevent many perinatal deaths.

- Parents who lose an infant can be expected to grieve in the usual manner and thus should be helped through this process by medical personnel and family.

- Euthanasia for newborns is a controversial topic that involves social, psychological, legal, and moral issues.

Family and Society

- Most women adjust to the birth of their children rapidly and without long-term psychological effects. A small percentage of women suffer from postpartum depression.

- Each society has its own unique way of welcoming newborns into the world. This involves a variety of rituals that ensure the health of the newborn and mother and carry a blessing for a happy life.

- Breast milk is superior to other forms of infant feeding. Infants should be breast-fed until twelve months and for as long after as mutually convenient for mother, infant, and family. Solid foods should be supplemented after 6 months.

Applications: The Case of Baby Doe

- Euthanasia for newborns is practiced under conditions in which the infant is likely to die or in which the treatment would unnecessarily prolong suffering.

- Parents and physicians need to consider a number of ethical issues in making decisions about euthanasia for newborns, including quality of life in the future for the child and family.

ON THE WEB

www.dona.com This is the home page of Doulas of North America (DONA). It gives information about doulas and what it is that they do. It also helps you find a doula near you and provides links to certification information, membership, and bookstores, as well as other birth-related links.

www.lalecheleague.org La Leche League International is dedicated to providing education, information, support, and encouragement to women who want to breast-feed. Through this web page you can contact a La Leche League member in your area to answer any questions you may have regarding breast-feeding.

www.chss.iup.edu/postpartum Postpartum Support International's web page provides detailed information for parents, students, and researchers. It includes an APA style paper on the topic, a searchable research database, prevention helps, information on increasing social support both before and after childbirth, a list of sites and support groups including sites specific to fathers, mothers, and professionals, self-assessments, information on reducing anxiety and stress, and more.

www.sbpep.org This web site for Postpartum Education for Parents includes a self-assessment questionnaire, a suggested reading list, advice for fathers, families, and friends, and support contacts by region as well as information on symptoms and general information.

GLOSSARY

Analgesia Pain-relieving drugs.

Anesthesia Drugs used to mask the sensation of pain.

Apgar score A screening test used to rate the infant's current health status and likelihood of crisis, rated at 1 and 5 minutes after birth.

Behavioral assessments Tests used to measure the newborn's behavioral status, including reflexes, orientation to external stimuli, and state control.

Birthrate The average number of infants born for every 1,000 women of childbearing age.

Braxton-Hicks contractions Contractions that serve to move the fetus into its prebirth position; also called false labor.

Breech presentation A presentation in which the fetus is aligned buttocks first against the cervix.

Catch-up growth The higher rate of physical development seen in some cases of early deprivation or birth complications, compared to the normal growth rate.

Cervix The opening between the uterus and the vagina.

Cesarean section Delivery of the fetus through an incision in the mother's abdomen and uterus.

Colostrum A clear yellowish liquid that is secreted by the mother's breasts for several days after birth and before the onset of milk production.

Dendrites Fibers that extend outward from nerve cells and enhance the connections to neighboring cells.

Euthanasia Letting an individual die naturally without medical intervention, except to relieve pain.

Failure-to-thrive The slow deterioration of an infant's condition and lack of responsiveness to intervention; seen in cases of malnutrition and disease.

Fetal distress A sudden loss of oxygen to the fetal brain caused by respiratory or heart problems or a restriction of the blood supply through the umbilical cord.

Fetal monitoring The use of electronic equipment to detect fetal heart rate, breathing, and other physiological signs during the birth process.

Fontanels   Spaces between the bones of the newborn's skull, which can be felt as soft spots on the scalp.

Forceps   An instrument that clamps around the infant's head to pull it through the birth canal.

Gestational age   The age of the infant starting from the date of conception.

Homeostasis   The maintenance of biological functions within normal levels, for example, the regulation of body temperature.

Kangaroo care   A method of communication with premature infants in which the infant, wearing only a diaper, is placed on the parent's chest. The infant's head is turned to the side so that the baby's ear is against the parent's heart.

Labor   Muscle contractions leading to the birth of the fetus and placenta.

Lamaze method   Pain relief during labor that uses breathing and relaxation techniques.

Leboyer method   An approach to delivery in which the newborn is kept warm in a water bath and subjected to low levels of sound and light.

Meconium   The contents of the newborn's intestines; a greenish-black substance containing digested amniotic fluid and particles of hair and skin.

Midwife   A professional trained to assist women during childbirth.

Multiparous   A mother who has given birth more than once.

Myelination   The development of a protective coating over nerve conduction pathways that improves transmission of information.

Neonatal   The period immediately following birth.

Neurological assessment   Testing of newborn reflexes and postures to determine the intactness of the brain and nervous system.

Nonnutritive sucking (NNS)   Sucking in the absence of fluids, including spontaneous sucking and sucking on a pacifier.

Normal physiological jaundice   A slight yellowing of the skin caused by immature functioning of the liver.

Perinatal   The period from about 1 month before to about 1 month after birth.

Postpartum depression   Sudden, transitory episodes of sadness or emotional lows; not related to pathological depression.

Post-traumatic stress disorder (PTSD)   A response to traumatic childbirth characterized by intrusive thoughts, fears, nightmares, and heightened arousal.

Primiparous   A woman who is giving birth for the first time.

Screening assessment   Tests of newborn functioning used to predict the need for medical interventions.

Self-righting   The rapid behavioral and psychological development often seen in infants who are recovering from birth complications.

Transverse presentations   A presentation in which the fetus is oriented on its side.

Vacuum extraction   The use of a suction device attached to the head to extract the infant from the birth canal.

Vestibular-proprioceptive stimulation   The movement of the infant's body, usually accomplished by carrying and rocking.

Vital statistics   Numerical estimates of events in a population related to birth, death, and the incidence of illnesses and accidents.

Chapter

5

The First Two Months

CHAPTER OVERVIEW AND OUTLINE

Physical and Motor Development

How is the newborn's behavior organized? How does the brain develop?

Perceptual Development

What can newborns see, hear, taste, feel, and smell?

Cognitive Development

Can newborns learn? Can they imitate?

Emotional Development

What can newborns feel?

Family and Society

How do newborns and adults coordinate their behavior? Are firstborns different from laterborns?

Applications: Parent-Infant Bonding

How important is early contact between parent and infant for the establishment of lasting emotional ties?

At birth, the baby must adapt to the physical changes needed to breathe air, to obtain nutrients orally, and to self-regulate body temperature. Birth also introduces a vast array of lights, sounds, touches, tastes, and smells that challenge the newborn's senses. What must the first taste of milk be like, or the first look at a human face? Do these things have any meaning for the newborn infant?

From another perspective, birth is not a major developmental change for the infant. As we saw in Chapters 3 and 4, studies of preterm infants and ultrasound studies of fetuses show that many of the motor and perceptual systems of the newborn are already developed by 36 weeks' gestational age. By this age or before, for instance, the fetus can suck. Furthermore, the amniotic fluid has tastes similar to the mother's milk, since both are flavored by what the mother eats. The mother's voice is already familiar to the infant. And even an infant who is raised by someone other than the mother is already familiar with movements like breathing and crying, has developed receptors and neural pathways for all the sensory systems, and has a distinct pattern of sleeping and waking states.

The abilities of the newborn infant have been the subject of a great many speculations and investigations by scholars. For thousands of years, philosophers have built theories of the human mind based on what they presumed was acquired by experience and what already endowed at birth. In the last 150 years, the sciences have taken up the investigation of the newborn's abilities, as psychologists, biologists, physicians, and nurses have tried to answer questions related to their own areas of interest.

The amount of information collected on the newborn in just the past 30 years alone could fill a small library. Studies have been done on such diverse topics as treating newborn diseases, finding the best way to soothe a crying baby, understanding the development of sleeping and waking states, and the ability of the newborn to recognize his or her mother.

In the last chapter, I covered the physical features of the newborn and his or her initial adaptations to postnatal life. In this chapter, I examine some of the sensorimotor and psychological abilities of the newborn and how they change over the next 6 or 8 weeks. I will look at some of the perceptual and cognitive aspects of newborn behavior and at the newborn's initial social interactions with adults. The issue of the role of early contact in the formation of attachment bonds will be covered in the "Applications" section. This chapter contains the first "Co-Regulating with Baby" section, a regular feature of this and the following chapters. This section describes some ways to enjoy the company of newborns and to provide them with developmentally appropriate stimulation. There is also an "Awareness through Movement" section.

Physical and Motor Development

States of Rest and Activity

During the fetal period, distinct periods of rest and activity begin to emerge at about 26 to 28 weeks' gestational age. These primitive patterns of activity and quiescence change cyclically about once every 40 minutes. By 32 weeks, both rest and activity are more complex and are divided into distinct states. As defined in Chapter 3, a **state** is an organized pattern of physical and physiological responding that is related to the infant's level of activation or arousal. Once infants enter a particular state (see Table 5.1), they are likely to remain in that state for as little as 15 minutes or as long as several hours. It is not easy to soothe newborns who are crying, to induce sleep, or to arouse them once they are sleeping. This suggests that states are relatively stable behavioral processes that form the base from which all other actions of the newborn must be understood (Wolff, 1993; Zeskind & Marshall, 1991).

At least two sleep states are present at 32 weeks' gestational age: rapid eye movement sleep (called REM sleep or active sleep) and non-REM sleep (called NREM sleep or quiet sleep). By 38 weeks, or full-term gestational age, several other sleep states are present, including periodic sleep (a combination of REM and NREM sleep) and drowsiness (a transitional state between sleep and waking). These states are described in Table 5.1, along with the

Table 5.1   Newborn States of Arousal

State Name	Description
Quiet sleep (NREM)	Respiration is regular, eyes are closed and not moving, and the baby is relatively motionless.
Active sleep (REM)	Muscles are more tense than in quiet sleep, the eyes may be still or display REMs, breathing is irregular, and spontaneous startles, sucks, and body movements occur in rhythmic bursts.
Drowsiness	Opening and closing of the eyes, increased activity, more rapid and regular breathing, and occasional smiling.
Quiet alert	Eyes are open and the environment is being scanned; the body is still, and respiration is more rapid than in sleep.
Active alert	Awake with body and limb movements, although infants are less likely to attend to external stimulation and focus their eyes less often than in the quiet alert state.
Crying	Elevated activity and respiration rate, cry vocalization, and facial expression of distress.

waking states of the normal full-term newborn infant. Researchers disagree about the number and type of infant states. Table 5.1 shows 6 levels of state, but some researchers have used as many as 11 different state distinctions (Zeskind & Marshall, 1991).

Sleep States

How much time a newborn spends sleeping and when during the day or night the baby sleeps are issues of great concern to parents. Newborns sleep an average of 16 to 17 hours per day, although this can vary between 11 and 21 hours (Parmelee, Schultz, & Disbrow, 1961). By 2 weeks, the average sleep time is decreased to about 14 to 15 hours, again with large differences between infants (St. James-Roberts & Plewis, 1996). Unlike adult sleep, infant sleep does not occur as one continuous period. Sleep periods range from 2 to ten hours. For the first few weeks after birth, these periods can occur almost anytime during the 24-hour day, to the dismay of sleepless parents. By 3 or 4 months of age, infants regularly sleep more at night than during the day, but night wakings are common throughout infancy and early childhood (Anders, Goodlin-Jones, & Zelenko, 1998; Kleitman, 1963).

Some babies show a preference for night sleeping, while others are more likely to wake at night. Individual infants appear to be highly consistent. Their preference for sleeping through the night or for waking at night remain stable over many years.

There is recent evidence that these preferences may appear during the late fetal period, affected in unknown ways by maternal patterns of activity during the day/night cycle and by daily fluctuations of maternal and infant hormones. The propensity to sleep through the night, then, may be partially acquired prenatally (Cofer et al., 1999; Colombo, Moss, & Horowitz, 1989; Zeskind & Marshall, 1991).

These individual differences affect the person's later interactions with others. Infants who are awake more at night are perceived as more difficult. During childhood, children who prefer being awake during the evening hours have a harder time getting up for school and do less well in school. It helps if parents are aware of whether their child is a morning person (goes to bed early and gets up early) or an evening person and adjust their expectations accordingly (Cofer et al., 1999).

Whether the child goes to bed early or late, some research shows that infants can be trained to sleep through the night during the first month of life. The procedure is based on reducing stimulation in the late afternoon, when infants naturally tend to become more fussy, and creating the habit of an early bedtime (Godfrey & Kilgore, 1998). The procedure is given in Table 5.2. After using this procedure for 3 to 4 weeks, parents report that their infant is more likely to sleep through the night and to avoid fussing during night wakings. If the time between night feedings is gradually increased, even breast-fed infants can learn to tolerate not getting a night feeding. If the infant does not get fussy until

Three newborn states: Sleeping, alert inactivity, and crying.

Table 5.2

For families who value independent sleeping, this method can be used to teach young infants to sleep through the night.

1st Month	Place the baby on back or side on a firm mattress.
	Do not let the baby sleep with breast, bottle, or pacifier in mouth, or while being held.
2nd Month	Reduce the amount of handling and stimulation after 4 P.M., or when evening fussiness begins. Bathe the baby in early evening, 6–7 P.M., followed by a gentle rubdown or massage, and dress the baby for the night. Feed the baby and then put the baby to bed around 7 P.M. Some fussing may persist for 3–5 days. If the baby cries loudly, enter the room every 5–10 minutes and then leave without turning on an overhead light. If feeding is necessary, keep it brief, do not turn on the light, and reduce the amount of stimulation.
	If this routine is interrupted due to travel or sickness, retraining is necessary.

later in the evening, then parents can adjust the times accordingly.

While this procedure may work for some families, training babies to sleep on their own is not necessarily desirable. In some families and some cultures, co-sleeping with parents is the norm. While no research exists, co-sleeping advocates estimate that worldwide, 80% to 90% of parents co-sleep with their infants for as long as 1 to 4 years. In North America, co-sleeping goes against the white middle-class cultural norm of raising an independent child and is not recommended by many of the best-known infant care advice books. On the other hand, a large number of North American parents from diverse ethnic and cultural backgrounds report co-sleeping with their babies at least occasionally, and many report long-term co-sleeping arrangements.

There is no research that addresses the short-term or long-term effects of independent sleeping versus co-sleeping. This is unfortunate, since young parents ask more questions to pediatricians and nurses about sleeping than any other topic. It seems to be a choice that is mediated by parental family and cultural values and mutual convenience. Co-sleeping tends to be favored by breast-feeding mothers, who prefer to bring the baby to bed during night wakings and feedings rather than sit in the child's room. It is also preferred by parents who feel uncomfortable leaving their child alone at night. Independent sleeping is favored when there is a strong family and cultural value for independence. Some parents become concerned about a reduction in sexual activity if the baby sleeps in the same bed. In either case, parents can expect to experience

some sleep deprivation during the first few months, until the family finds a mutually beneficial way of sleeping.

If the average newborn sleeps 17 hours a day, what happens during the rest of the time? On the average, about 3 hours are spent in quiet alert, 2 hours in active alert, and 2 to 3 hours in crying. Of course, some babies are awake more than 3 hours and some less. Some babies cry for as much as ten hours per day and others as little as one hour.

Waking States

Waking states are important for the processing of stimulation from the environment—processing that will lead to perceptual and cognitive development. Newborn infants have two basic modes of response to stimulation: orienting and defense. The **orienting response** is a heightened alertness on the part of the individual that includes behavioral localization toward the source of the stimulation (a head turn to the source of a sound). A **defensive response** is a behavioral action that involves withdrawal from the source of stimulation.

Stimulation that is moderate in intensity will elicit orienting responses: soft talking, moderate light levels, and holding and rocking can enhance alertness in the newborn. Stimulation that is intense and sharp produces defensive reactions. A sudden change in light level, a loud noise, or a sudden change in body position will produce a blink or a startle response. If the intense stimulus continues, newborns will turn away, grimace, or cry. Low-intensity stimulation, such as gentle rocking or whispering, may not produce any reaction in the new-born. When newborns orient to a source of stimulation, they are relatively slow to respond compared with a 2-month-old, whose latency to respond is similar in speed to an adult's (Berg & Berg, 1987; Graham, Anthony, & Zeigler, 1984; Karrer, Monti, & Ackles, 1989).

As infants develop, they become able to orient to a wider range of both low- and high-intensity stimulation (Field, 1981b; Krafchuk, Tronick, & Clifton, 1983). It is as though the newborn were looking at the world through a very small window centered on the moderate range of stimulation. Developmental changes expand the size of the window to include both lower and higher intensities of stimulation so that the older infant is more sensitive to subtle cues and less sensitive to intensity (Berg, 1975).

Developmental Change in State Is Related to Brain Development

During the first few months of life, infants become more tolerant of a wider range of stimulus intensity and complexity, and they are less likely to withdraw from potentially interesting sources of information. How does this developmental change occur? Experience with moderately intense and moderately complex stimuli can have a profound effect on the development of the brain, which in turn allows for more sustained attention and less withdrawal.

To understand how this process works, it is necessary to take a look at the structure of the neuron. **Neurons** are the information storage and transfer cells of the central nervous system. The anatomy of the neuron is shown in Figure 5.1. Neurons code

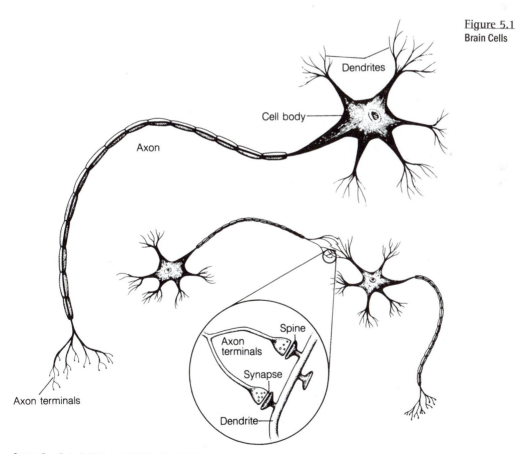

Figure 5.1
Brain Cells

Dendrites

Cell body

Axon

Axon terminals

Spine

Axon terminals

Synapse

Dendrite

Source: From Teyler & Chiaia, in *A child's brain* (ed. M. Frank). New York: Haworth Press, 1984. In A. Fogel & G. F. Melson, *Child development*, 1988, p. 222. St. Paul, MN: West. Copyright © by West Publishing Co. Reprinted by permission. All rights reserved.

and transmit information in the form of electro-chemical currents, called *action potentials,* that travel from the cell body along the axons to the axon terminals. Information is transmitted to the next cell at a junction called the synapse by chemicals called neurotransmitters. The **synapse** connects the axon terminals of the transmitting cell to the dendrites of the receiving cell, as shown in the figure.

The brain develops by four basic processes:

1. New cells are created via mitosis. This process occurs almost entirely during the prenatal period of development.

2. The axons lengthen and the cells migrate to form distinctly different regions of the brain that are connected to different sensory systems. Brain development occurs from the inside out, as cells destined to become part of the visual cortex, for example, send out axons and connections that eventually meet the visual receptors in the optic nerve (Greenough, Black, & Wallace, 1987). Neuronal growth and migration are guided by the glial cells, which are the structural cells in the brain that hold the neurons in their place. This process is usually completed by the 7th prenatal month.

In addition to lengthening, the axons also become more efficient conductors by developing a kind of insulation called **myelin.** Myelination improves the speed of information flow along the axon by a factor of about three. Myelination occurs most rapidly during the end of gestation and the first few postnatal months. One-month-olds process information about three times faster than newborns.

3. The cells become more complex, growing more dendrites and axon terminals and making an increasing number of synaptic connections. This process is called *synaptogenesis.* By 1 year, the child's brain has 150% of the number of synapses in the adult's; this number begins to decline in the second year (M. H. Johnson, 2000). By the age of 2 years, a single neuron may have as many as 10,000 different connections to other cells (Adinolfi, 1971). These new connections are thought to be related to the rapid behavioral and cognitive developments that take place during the infancy period. The rapid rate of synaptogenesis in different areas of the brain is shown in Figure 5.2.

4. A final process of brain development is the specialization of cells and regions of cells. At the end of the prenatal period, the human brain appears to have connections that allow newborns to perform their basic survival and adaptive functions: sucking, crying, states, reflexes, and orienting and defensive reactions.

Neuromotor pathways that prepare the infant for survival are called **experience expectant** because the brain appears to be ready and waiting for a specific type of environmental input (such as pain) for which a particular behavioral skill (such as crying) is best adapted. Many areas of the brain, on the other hand, do not have a specialized function at birth. Some cells and synapses have developed prenatally whose only purpose is to become ready to learn about a particular individual's experiences. These cells and connections are called **experience dependent.** As particular sensory and motor patterns are repeated in early development, specific experience-dependent synapses and cells are used more than others. The synapses that are used the most become strengthened, while those that are used the least eventually die (Greenough et al., 1987; Thelen & Smith, 1994).

In reality, all neurons and neural connections are experience dependent in the sense that they develop at some point in time with respect to the kind of environment to which the infant is exposed (M. H. Johnson, 2000). Cells and pathways that at birth are experience expectant were, at some time during prenatal development, made up of more general cells that were experience dependent. Recall that sucking, which is a well-established experience-expectant pathway at birth, develops out of the tactile and motor experiences of the fetus and requires stimulation and repetition during the fetal period in order for the neural pathways to become strengthened into an experience-expectant behavior at birth. All during development, as we acquire new actions, the neural pathways become more expectant of skill-specific information, which increases the skillfulness of the action.

The developmental changes in numbers of synapses follow a similar course in each of the major areas of the cortex, the most advanced part of the brain that controls voluntary actions, including motor skills, perception, and emotion regulation. The

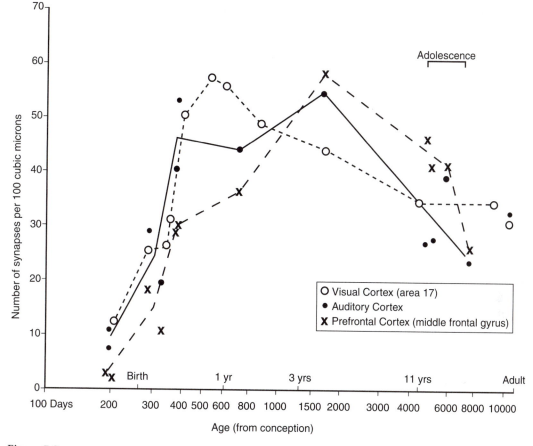

Figure 5.2
Developmental changes in synaptic density of the human brain.

Adapted from P. Huttenlocher & A. Dabholkar, Regional differences in synaptogenesis in human cerebral cortex, 1997, p. 387. *Journal of Comparative Neurology* (4).

number of synapses increases rapidly until birth and then decreases gradually, stabilizing at about the age of 3 years (Goldman-Rakic, 1987).

In summary, these changes in cell and synapse development show that the brain's development is highly dependent on the individual's experiences. The brain's construction tailors its development to the experiences of its owner. These neural developmental processes help us to understand how birth defects occur. Alcohol that the mother ingests during pregnancy limits the production of new axons and dendrites (Dow & Reoppelli, 1985), while lead exposure destroys myelin (Lampert & Schochet, 1968). These conditions limit the number of experience-dependent connections and cause informa-

tion processing to be slower, making for a less adaptive, less intelligent individual.

These results, and others like them, demonstrate the dynamic system linkages between brain, experience, and behavior. And during the first few months, infants experience stimuli of increasing intensity and complexity, and connections favoring those types of stimuli will be strengthened. Via feedback from brain to behavior, the window of sustained attention will widen. As sustained attention allows the infant to inspect and explore specific stimuli, feedback to the brain will correspondingly create connections that make those specific events more easily recognized on subsequent occasions (K. W. Fischer, 1987; Goldman-Rakic, 1987; Hebb, 1949; Thelen

& Smith, 1994). Developmental changes in the brain affect not only waking states but sleeping and crying as well. In the next section, I turn to an examination of crying and its development.

Crying State

Infants have different kinds of cries that seem to be associated with different kinds of distress. Cries have four phases: expiratory (exhaling; the actual creation of the crying sound), a rest period, an inspiratory period (inhaling), and another rest period. As Table 5.3 shows, the different types of infant cries can be distinguished on the basis of the length of these phases.

One feature of the neonatal pain cry, for example, is an exceptionally long rest phase, which gives the listener the feeling that the baby has stopped breathing. This long silence no doubt accounts for the salience of this cry to an adult. The pain cry also has a long expiration phase, much like the cry evoked when the infant is teased by having a pacifier pulled out of his or her mouth repeatedly. The expiration of the teased cry, however, is not followed by a long rest. These cry patterns repeat themselves over and over to form a crying bout.

Crying also involves a pattern of body movement including facial expressions of distress, movement of the arms and legs, changes in muscle tone and skin color, and alterations in breathing patterns. The intensity of pain or distress changes not only the acoustic features of the cry but also the body expressions (J. A. Green, Gustafson, Irwin, Kalinowski, & Wood, 1995; Lock, 2000).

Neonatal crying is symptomatic of a range of "normal" internal states, but it may also reflect a number of abnormal conditions. A series of studies has examined variations in neonatal cry patterns under various conditions of mild to severe abnormalities. Cries were elicited by snapping a rubber band against the sole of the infant's foot. The cry sounds were recorded on a sound spectrograph. In general, infants with more complications required higher levels of stimulation to initiate the cry, took a longer time before they started to cry, had a shorter first cry expiration, cried for a shorter total time, and had cries of a higher pitch than infants with few or no complications. Higher infant arousal also changes the pattern of cry acoustics (Boom & Gravenhorst, 1995; J. A. Green, Gustafson, & McGhie, 1998; Lester, 1976; Lester & Zeskind, 1978; Zeskind & Lester, 1978, 1981).

These studies have several implications. Parents and caregivers can use crying to "read" an infant's internal state, and health professionals can use it to diagnose potential abnormalities. An abnormal cry, however, is not always associated with a serious or permanent underlying abnormality. Such a cry may merely indicate that the infant was born under conditions of stress. Many birth complications have no lasting effects, and the infants' cries eventually return to normal. Crying, then, just as your grandmother could have told you, is a fairly reliable indicator of a newborn's degree of discomfort, pain, or stress.

Differences between Infants: Quiet and Colic

Among normally developing newborns with no health complications, there is an increase in the frequency of crying between birth and 2 months of age, particularly during the later afternoon and early evening hours (Anders et al., 1998). After that time, the amount of crying begins a decrease that continues over the first year of life. This developmental phenomenon is similar for infants in many different cultures having different patterns of infant care and response to crying (Barr, 1990). Nevertheless, during this 2-month period of the most intense crying, infants differ with respect to how long they cry during the day. And although there are striking differences within cultures, there are even bigger ones between cultures.

Table 5.3 Properties of Neonatal Cries*

Cry Phase	Basic Cry	Angry Cry	Pain Cry	Being-Teased Cry
Expiratory	0.62	0.69	3.83	2.67
Rest	0.08	0.20	3.99	0.07
Inspiratory	0.04	0.05	0.18	0.13
Rest	0.20	0.11	0.16	0.13

*All values are time in seconds.
Source: P. H. Wolff, The causes, controls, and organization of behavior in the neonate, 1966. *Psychological Issues 5*, 202–204.

Hunter-gatherer societies are composed of small bands of humans who sustain themselves by hunting game and gathering wild roots and plants to eat. Although hunter-gatherer societies are believed to have been the only form of human society before the invention of agriculture some 10,000 years ago, relatively few such societies survive today. Research on their child-care practices provides an important comparison for understanding child development in non-Western societies.

In hunter-gatherer societies in Africa, for example, infants cry as frequently as in Western countries. The hunter-gatherer infants, however, sustain their cries for only brief periods, while Western babies cry for much longer. This difference seems to be due to the fact that in hunter-gatherer societies the infant is in almost constant contact with a caregiver, who carries the infant in a sling or pouch at all times. The infant is never left alone, and the caregiver responds immediately to any fussiness (Barr, 1990).

Western infants are not tended so closely. They are typically carried only for brief periods and are kept physically separate from the caregiver. Even when parents sensitively respond to the infant cry, the physical separation requires a longer response time than in hunter-gatherer societies. Infants have more time to build the pitch and volume of their cries and they cry for longer periods until they are tended. In some cases their crying continues even after they are picked up.

Of particular concern is a group of infants who cry excessively. **Colic** is crying in which (1) the infant cries at least 3 hours per day, on at least 3 days per week, and for at least 3 successive weeks; (2) the parents judge the crying to be very intense; (3) the infant is otherwise normal; and (4) the infant is relatively unresponsive to soothing and feeding (Barr, Rotman, Yaremko, Leduc, & Francoeur, 1992).

Research has shown that infants with colic, compared to noncolicky infants, are more likely to cry following feeding, to have more distress-related facial expressions, to have more turbulence in the cry sound, and to be rated as more difficult and negative by their parents. No differences have been found between colicky and noncolicky infants in the amount of stomach swelling after feeding, vomiting, hiccuping, or bowel movements (Barr et al., 1992; Lester, Boukydis, Garcia-Coll, Hole, &

Peucker, 1992; Zeskind & Barr, 1997). Furthermore, the parents' negative feelings about the infants ended after 3 months when the infants' crying decreased. Thus, both the colic and the parents' response to it are short-lived (Bohlin, Hagekull, & Lindberg, 1994).

What causes colic? Research suggests that it is not digestive problems, as is commonly believed. In hunter-gatherer and other societies in which there is almost continual close physical contact with infants, colic and excessive crying do not exist (Barr, 1990). Given the opportunity to cry because parents do not respond immediately, otherwise normal babies will indeed differ in the amount that they cry. Research in Germany has shown that when parents are generally slower to respond to infants, the infants cry more. This suggests that colic is a symptom of the Western infant-care practice of physical separation of parent and infant during all or part of the day. The research on colic also shows that crying has an important function in the newborn period, to keep the caregiver near the infant and to encourage a close physical connection between them (H. Keller et al., 1996; M. Papousek & von Hofacker, 1995).

If we consider the parent-infant relationship as a dynamic system, small factors in early infancy may lead to excessive crying by means of deviation-amplifying feedback. If the infant is neurologically immature, if the parents are under stress or uncertain about themselves (as in the case of first-borns), or if the culture inhibits parental responsiveness, it may take only a short time for infant crying to increase to levels that are difficult to regulate (Cuisinier, Janssen, de Graauw, & Hoogduin, 1998; M. Papousek & von Hofacker, 1995). For some infants who cry a great deal during the newborn period, crying and fussiness will continue to be characteristic of their behavior during the first year of life and perhaps later (St. James-Roberts, Conroy, & Wilsher, 1998; St. James-Roberts & Plewis, 1998).

The only prevention for colic would be constant contact with and immediate response to the infant when he or she is fussy. Clearly, this type of infant care is not feasible in Western cultures, where parents would experience that level of contact as too demanding. Unless we change the structure of our society, which is not likely, we are certain to hear a lot of infant crying. Fortunately, the research also suggests that such crying has little or no known lasting effect on parents or infants, although more research is needed on this topic. In the short term, however, infants and adults may find it extremely frustrating and distressing.

The Effects of Crying on Adults

Even when infants do not have colic, their crying affects adults in important ways. Adult women can perceive differences between basic cries and pain cries, whether they are mothers or not (Gustafson & Harris, 1990). These same women, however, when observed with an infant mannequin that emitted either a pain or a basic cry, showed no differences in their responses to each type of cry. Regardless of the type of cry, the women rocked, talked to, touched, held, distracted, and checked the diaper of the mannequin when asked to pretend to take care of it. They first tried actions to soothe the infant (such as holding and rocking) and later attempted to relieve the source of distress (by diapering or feeding). Crying, therefore, is heard as a general index of infant distress, and adults then try to figure out the source of that distress.

Particular aspects of the cry are more likely to affect how adults perceive the cry. Adults rate cries of high pitch and of long duration as urgent and irritable while cries of variable pitch are rated as signs of infant sickness (Gustafson & Green, 1989; Zeskind, Klein, & Marshall, 1992; Zeskind & Marshall, 1988). Experimental modifications of infant cry sounds show that adults perceive cries with extremely short pauses as more arousing, aversive, and rough (Zeskind, Wilhite, & Marshall, 1993).

Nonparents appear to be about as responsive to crying as parents (Zeskind, 1980), and generally equal levels of physiological arousal and responsiveness to crying have been found for men and women (Frodi, Lamb, Leavitt, & Donovan, 1978). On the other hand, child abusers have greater physiological arousal and express more annoyance at cries than nonabusers (Frodi & Lamb, 1980).

You might think, therefore, that infants who cry a great deal or who have especially irritating cries are more at risk for insensitive or abusive parental treatment. This seems to be the case only when irritable crying is also associated with abnormal behavioral tendencies typical of infants with mental and motor perinatal defects and prematurity (Field, Widmayer, Stringer, & Ignatoff, 1980) or when mothers have a preexisting negative attitude toward their infants that in part contributes to the high levels of infant distress (Crockenberg & Acredolo, 1983; Crockenberg & Smith, 1982). For normally developing infants, crying brings adults closer to them. More-irritable infants are held more in the newborn period, and parents spend more time in social play with them at 2 months (Lowinger, 1999).

Infants who are rated by their parents as having a **difficult temperament** in early infancy, based on their irritability and responsiveness to adults, can remain difficult for periods up to several years, although the majority of infants rated as difficult early in life do not remain difficult for more than a few months (Boom & Hoeksma, 1994; C. Lee & Bates, 1985; Swets-Gronert, 1984). Difficultness has few consistent effects on normal parent-infant relationships and is not related to measures of maternal warmth or responsiveness (J. E. Bates, Olson, Pettit, & Bayles, 1982; Daniels, Plomin, & Greenhalgh, 1984; Olson, Bates, & Bayles, 1984; Wachs & Gandour, 1983). Some studies have actually found increased maternal attention directed to infants rated as difficult (J. E. Bates et al., 1982; Pettit & Bates, 1984).

In summary, most adults find crying to be arousing, and they reliably can perceive differences between types of crying. Adults also respond to crying infants in an attempt to soothe the cry and relieve the source of the discomfort. Since most adults use similar means of trying to relieve infant distress, it is important to examine what research has shown about the effectiveness of these soothing techniques.

What Are the Best Ways to Soothe a Crying Baby?

Many calming techniques have been used historically: sucking, swaddling, rocking, and singing. Do they really work? Under what conditions does one technique work and not another?

Sucking on a pacifier. Whether sucking pacifiers is harmful or beneficial is a question of practical concern to parents. Sucking on a pacifier, or nonnutritive sucking (NNS), occurs in many forms throughout the infancy period. If we count any incidence of NNS—on pacifiers, toys, fingers, thumbs, and adults' fingers—about 60 to 90% of all infants will do it. NNS usually stops at the end of the first year of life. It may continue to occur, however, when a child is hungry, tired, or unhappy, until the child reaches 4 to 7 years of age. A small proportion of children suck their thumbs until adolescence. In infants, thumb sucking after the age of 4 months appears primarily during sleep (Kessen, Haith, & Salapatek, 1970).

It would appear from these statistics that NNS is not an unusual occurrence in infancy and early childhood. It may even serve some important functions for the infant. We will deal with thumb sucking and the issue of self-calming and pacification in a later chapter. Here we will merely note that a number of hypotheses have been advanced about why newborn infants suck nonnutritively.

Pacification is one reason infants suck. Sucking is an activity that immediately induces a state of calm in the infant, whether it is associated with nutritive intake or not. You may have felt a similar sense of calm while doing the sucking in the Awareness through Movement lesson in Chapter 3. Another reason for NNS is that it feels good. This could come about because sucking is genetically associated with pleasure or because the infant develops a conditioned association between the sucking response and the pleasurable intake of nutrient. Sucking could also have an inhibitory effect on other states or behavior.

Regardless of the particular reason, NNS appears to be a spontaneous behavior that has some important benefits to the newborn and the older infant. One study (R. G. Campos, 1989) examined the effects of pacifiers on calming infants at 2 weeks and 2 months of age during routine medical exams. At 2 weeks, the infants received a heel prick to draw blood, and at 2 months, they received an injection. Pacifiers were immediately effective in reducing crying and heart rate acceleration in response to the pain at both ages.

Swaddling. Swaddling, or wrapping the infant in a blanket, tends to reduce motor movement and spontaneous startles. Swaddling is less effective than the pacifier in reducing pain-elicited distress in 2-week-olds, although it lowers their heart rate (R. G. Campos, 1989). When a pacifier falls out of an infant's mouth, they will begin to cry again. Once swaddled, on the other hand, infants remain calm for long periods.

Swaddling is practiced among many traditional cultures such as the Quechua Indians living at high altitude in the Peruvian Andean Mountains. The Quechua swaddle infants in a pouch. The temperature inside the pouch is higher and more stable than in the outside atmosphere, and the humidity is higher. The pouch protects the infant against environmental stress due to cold temperatures and dryness. On the other hand, in the closed environment of the pouch, the infant gets less oxygen and less stimulation that it would without the pouch. Since the Quechua live in unheated surroundings and spend a great deal of time out of doors, the benefits of the pouch seem to outweigh the potential risks (E. Z. Tronick, Thomas, & Daltabuit, 1994).

Massage. Massage is a technique related to swaddling in that the whole body is stimulated and the infant's movements are controlled. Massage has been shown to increase weight gain and responsiveness in preterm infants (see Chapter 3). In normal full-term infants, regular massage for 15 minutes each day has been shown to enhance alertness when awake, deepen sleep, reduce stress, modulate emotions, and lower the amount of crying (Field, 1998). Massage may also have calming effects on adults. Grandparents were assigned either to receive massages for 1 month or to give massages to their grandchildren. Giving massages had more positive effects than receiving them. Those who gave massages had lower depression scores, increased their self-esteem, and enhanced their health behaviors (Field, 1998). Parents who take relaxation and massage baths with their babies have higher levels of marital satisfaction and self-esteem and lower levels of postpartum depression (Stack, 2000).

Massage is used regularly in a variety of cultures, for example in India and Guatemala. Touching and massage are known to reduce stress in animals, adults, and infants. Touch stimulation reduces hormones related to stress and increases hormones related to growth (Stack, 2000). Gentle massage has no negative effects, and it can be a rewarding and relaxing experience for both infant and adult, even if not used directly in response to crying. A book on infant massage techniques for caregivers and parents is available (McClure, 1989).

Rocking. The effects of rocking were studied in a group of 36 crying infants who were offered either vertical (on the adult's shoulder) or horizontal (supine) rocking to calm them. In general, rocking in any form helped calm the infants. The best form of rocking to calm a distressed infant turned out to be rocking intermittently (rather than continuously) in the vertical plane. The best form of rocking for putting the infant to sleep was continuous rocking in the horizontal plane (Bryne & Horowitz, 1979).

Sound. Sound, too, has a calming effect on the baby, but apparently not all types of sound work. Intermittent sound increases infant arousal, whereas continuous sound is calming. The calming effect of continuous sound is enhanced when the sound is moderately loud and in the low frequencies of the vocal range (Brackbill, 1971; Friedman & Jacobs, 1981; Hazelwood, 1977). Humming and singing lullabies have these features. Singing has been shown to lower stress among pre-term infants (Coleman, Pratt, Stoddard, Gerstmann, & Abel, 1997). High-pitched vocal sounds can be used to alert infants or attract their attention.

The soothing effects of continuous stimulation are not limited to sound: any stimulus that is continuous can work. Sucking, rocking, swaddling, and humming are all forms of continuous stimulation. Using more than one method has a cumulative effect. Individual infants also show a wide range of differences. Some infants are better soothed by one method than another, and some infants appear to be more easily consoled than others, regardless of the particular method used.

Developmental changes also affect what best soothes the baby. While any kind of continuous auditory stimulation soothes in the infant's first 2 months, the mother's voice is more effective by 3 months (Kopp, 1982). Visual stimulation becomes increasingly effective by 3 months, as does stimulation from objects to touch and hold (Kopp, 1982; Wolff, 1966).

In summary, state is important for the newborn infant for a number of reasons. First, the body needs periods of tranquility and rest in order to consolidate its resources for growth. Second, the infant's attention to the environment is dependent upon maintaining a stress-free state of quiet alertness. Finally, state regulates the types of interactions newborns have with their adult caregivers. Babies who are fussier require different resources from their parents compared to calmer babies.

Motor Coordinations of the Newborn: Reflexes

The basic rest-activity cycle that is characteristic of states is believed to originate in primitive areas of the brain that are responsible for autonomic activities, such as respiration, heart rate, body temperature, and sucking. This area of the brain is at the lower back of the head and is referred to variously as the brain stem, medulla, or hindbrain. At the next higher level, called the midbrain, which is located more or less in the very center of the head, such processes as attention, sleeping, waking, and elimination are regulated. These two areas are the most functional at birth. Although all the cells of the external surface of the brain, the cortex, have developed, their connections with other cortical and subcortical (hindbrain and midbrain) regions have only begun to develop.

Aside from state and temperature regulation, newborns possess a variety of semiautomatic patterns of behavior—such as grasping, head turning, and sucking—that actually began to function prenatally, during the last trimester. This kind of semiautomatic behavior is called a **reflex.** Reflexes are triggered only by specific elicitors, such as the presence of fluid in the mouth or an object in the palm, and they look about the same every time they are triggered. Once triggered, a reflex must run its course without stopping.

The actual brain location that controls the reflexes is not known. They are presumed to originate in subcortical areas since they do not show evidence of any voluntary control. Voluntary control is shown when behavior can be adjusted, modified, or stopped to suit the demands of the environment. Voluntary control over behavior has its source in

Table 5.4 Newborn Reflexes

Body Part	Name of Reflex	Description	Baby's Age at Reflex's Disappearance (Months)
Head and Face	Head turning	Place baby face down on a mattress. Baby will turn head to side to free breathing passages.	4
	Rooting	Stroke baby's cheek gently near the mouth. Baby will turn head to the side that is being stroked.	5
	Sucking	Place a nipple-sized object in baby's mouth. Baby will start sucking movements.	6
	Defensive reaction	Cover the baby's nose and mouth with a cloth. Baby will turn head and move arms in an attempt to free breathing passages.	4
Arms	Asymmetrical tonic neck reflex	Turn the baby's head to one side or the other. The baby's arm will extend in the direction in which the head is turned and the other arm will flex upward. This is also called the fencer's reflex.	4
	Moro	Drop the baby's head slightly but abruptly. The baby's arms and legs will spread open and make an embracing movement, as if to grasp hold of something. This is a kind of startle reaction.	6
Hands	Palmer	Lightly touch the baby's palm. The fingers will clamp into a fist.	4
Torso	Swimmer's reflex	While baby is lying on its stomach, gently tap the back along the side and above the waist. The baby will twist its lower extremities toward the side that was touched.	3
	Crawling	Push against the soles of the baby's feet while the baby baby is lying on the stomach and rudimentary crawling movements will result.	4
Legs	Standing	Hold the baby gently under the arms while the feet touch a table. As you release support slowly, the baby will begin to show some resistance to the weight by stretching the muscles of the legs.	3
	Stepping	Hold the baby under the arms with the baby's feet touching a table and move the baby forward, keeping contact between table and feet. The baby will take "steps."	3
Feet	Plantar	Similar to the Palmer reflex. The toes will curl inward when the instep is lightly touched.	9
	Babinski	Gently stroke the outer side of the bottom of the baby's foot. The toes will curl outward like a fan.	12

the cortex. The cortex also contains most of the sources of sensation, perception, language, and cognition and is considerably larger in humans than in other animals.

Reflexes associated with different parts of the body are listed in Table 5.4. Some of these reflexes reflect primitive forms of orienting behavior, including rooting, sucking, and grasping. Other reflexes are primitive defensive reactions, including the Moro reflex and the reaction to a cloth on the face or the head placed face down. Other reflexes seem to contain the elementary coordinations needed for later adaptive and voluntary movements. These include the stepping, standing, crawling, and swimmer's reflexes. Other reflexes do not seem to have a clear function, such as the Babinski reflex;

however, the lack of a Babinski response may indicate neurological disorder.

In spite of the semiautomatic structure of reflexes, there is a wide variability in their display. In the same infant tested on different occasions, a reflex might be present at one time and not later. Some reflexes become more prominent in the days following birth, having been absent immediately after birth due to birth recovery processes. Some reflexes are easier to elicit in sleep states and others in waking states. The strength and clarity of response also differ between infants. After their cheeks are stroked to elicit rooting, one baby may barely turn his or her head to that side, while another may make a strong head turn, open the mouth, and begin to suck. Other factors that affect the strength and quality of a reflex response are age, time since last feeding, and the number of repeated attempts to evoke the reflex (Kessen et al., 1970; Prechtl, 1977).

These observations suggest that reflexes may be partly controlled by the cortex because they are more variable than the midbrain and hindbrain autonomic responses, such as breathing and heart rate. Another explanation is that reflexes are only partly specified by neural circuitry. It is not only the brain that is developing, but the body as well. A reflex, or any behavior for that matter, could not happen without the particular muscles, bones, joints, and body proportions that are part of the baby's physical development. It may be that slowness to respond to stimulation is the result of poor motor coordination rather than slow brain processing.

Each reflex has its own developmental course starting at different gestational ages. Some reflexes persist throughout life—such as startle and blinking—while others disappear in early infancy. Since the reflexes that disappear do so between 3 and 6 months of age, traditional explanations have assumed that the disappearance is the result of the development of the motor cortex, whose ability to regulate voluntary movement suppresses the semiautomatic signals from the hindbrain (Fiorentino, 1981; Illingworth, 1966; Molnar, 1978; Peiper, 1963). When adults receive damage to the motor cortex, some of these primitive reflexes reappear (Paulson & Gottlieb, 1968).

If motor and physical factors might account for the variability of expression of reflexes, could they also account for the developmental disappearance of reflexes? Stepping is elicited in a newborn when the infant is held upright with the foot gently touching a flat surface. When the foot touches the surface, the newborn will pick up the foot by bending the leg at the knee in a kind of march-step movement. Remarkably, newborns do not pick up both legs at the same time: they alternate steps in the manner of later walking.

Stepping disappears earlier in infants who have the most rapid weight gain. Researchers studied 4-week-olds who could still step reflexively. To experimentally simulate weight gain, they added weights to the babies' legs in amounts predicted to reflect the possible weight gain of the legs in the next few weeks. These weights practically eliminated stepping. In another experiment, 4-week-olds were tested for stepping while their legs were submerged under water and then again on dry land. The step rate was much higher underwater, again suggesting that weight and gravity, rather than brain development alone, contribute to the disappearance of stepping (Thelen, Bradshaw, & Ward, 1981). The researchers also found that stepping movements could be seen in the form of kicking in any age infant when the infant was lying on his or her back.

In this experiment, the decline in stepping was not due to the effect of weight gain alone. Rather, stepping declines because after birth, fat grows faster than muscle. This means that babies' legs simply became too heavy for them to lift on their own! In another study, stepping did not disappear in babies who were given stepping exercises every day. The workout program may have built their tiny muscles to be capable of lifting more than those of the average baby of a particular age. Similar practice also helps babies to sit earlier (P. R. Zelazo, 1976; N. A. Zelazo, Zelazo, Cohen, & Zelazo, 1993).

In summary, newborn reflexes are extremely important for orienting the infant to the environment and for protecting the infant from harm. Although we do not know the purpose of all the reflexes, many of them—such as the defensive reaction—have obvious functions. The data also suggest that reflexes are not simply discharges in the brain, but require active muscle effort and control. Thus, like prenatal spontaneous movements, reflexes play a role in the active development of the muscles, leading to increased strength and coordination.

You can simulate the newborn's experience of the reflexes by practicing the Awareness through Movement lessons at the end of this chapter. Although adults no longer have reflexive response to being touched on the palm, our hands still open and close in the same way as newborns' hands. Our bodies seem to prefer the configuration of the Asymmetrical Tonic Neck Reflex. Through practicing different kinds of body awareness exercises or experiencing some of the forms of body awareness therapies mentioned in Chapter 2, it is possible to rediscover some of the ways in which our bodies have retained some characteristics from our newborn period.

Asynchronous Growth

The finding the newborn stepping reflex disappears when the infant's legs become too heavy is not meant to suggest that 1-month-olds should go on diets, exercise their legs, and do weight training. First of all, giving babies stepping exercises does not make the babies walk any sooner than if they receive no such training (P. R. Zelazo, 1976). Second, there is a good reason why babies of this age need to increase fat rapidly: to keep warm and protect their muscles against shocks. Fat is kept at a minimum prenatally to make birth easier and because most of the fetal energy resources go into brain

development. Muscles get stronger later in the first year.

These findings show that infants do not grow "all at once." Different body regions grow faster at different times; this is called **asynchronous growth** and is shown in Figure 5.3. Because physical growth depends on the body's ability to metabolize nutrients to create energy to support the growth, the body invests its growth resources in at most a few domains at a time.

What makes some areas turn on their growth spurt and others turn off? This is difficult to determine, but it may be in part genetically controlled and in part related to opportunities in the environment. Fetal resources are used primarily to develop the brain and perceptual systems. This is due partly to the fact that movement opportunities are limited for a fetus, and muscles do not develop without exercise. Because newborns rely on the care of adults, they do not need strong and able muscles early in life. Chimpanzees, on the contrary, have to be strong enough to cling to their moving and swinging mothers from the day of birth. Their survival depends more on physical strength and speed compared to human newborns.

A comparison of chimpanzee and human newborns' scores on selected items of the Brazelton newborn assessment test confirms this. Chimpanzees score about the same as human newborns on state control, alertness, and attention to social and nonsocial stimuli. Chimpanzees score higher on

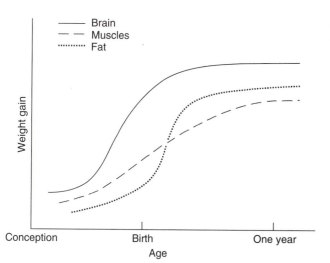

Figure 5.3
Asynchronous Growth

motor skills in the pull-to-sit task and on irritability (Bard, Platzman, Lester, & Suomi, 1992; Hallock, Worobey, & Self, 1989).

Sucking

One reflex that is clearly part of the lower brain system is sucking, perhaps because of its crucial importance to survival. Sucking is an example of a reflex that begins prenatally and does not disappear. This statement is a bit misleading, however, since sucking becomes more voluntary and changes form and mode of expression in later infancy. Sucking is accomplished through the combined action of three sets of sucking pads: the lips, the gums, and the fat pads inside the cheeks. It is the gums—not the lips—that form a closed pressure seal around the nipple, while the cheek pads prevent the oral cavity from collapsing from the negative pressure created (Kessen et al., 1970).

As you may have noticed when practicing the Awareness through Movement lesson in Chapter 3, sucking is a two-phase process. In the first phase, the lower jaw drops to create **negative pressure** in the mouth. This method works because the gums form a closed seal around the nipple, but it differs from that used by an adult, who creates negative pressure by breathing in. In the second phase of sucking, called **milk expression,** the newborn's tongue presses the nipple against the hard palate while moving from the front to the back of the mouth. Finally, the presence of fluid in the mouth triggers the swallowing reflex. Apparently, the newborn sucks and swallows in a single-action pattern

in which the tongue moves in and out while the baby swallows. Did you discover this for yourself when you practiced the Awareness through Movement sucking lesson?

The action of the tongue in sucking explains why young infants have trouble eating solids and drinking from a cup: the pushing action of their tongues tends to expel more material from their mouths than they are able to successfully ingest. The ability to separate the expressing and swallowing movements does not occur until late in the first year.

Sucking, like crying, tends to occur in a rhythmic pattern. While the infant is actually sucking, there are usually about two sucks per second. Typically, infants suck in a **burst-pause pattern:** bursts of successive sucks separated by pauses. The bursts usually last from between 5 and 24 sucks. Like the other reflexes, the sucking rate depends primarily on the state of arousal rather than on factors related to hunger. The number of pauses is primarily determined by the milk flow. If the flow is too fast, pauses disappear, reappearing only when the flow is reduced (see Figure 5.4). Pauses do not appear to be associated with fatigue, since infants can suck without pausing for long periods under high milk-flow conditions (Kessen et al., 1970).

I discussed earlier in the chapter how nonnutritive sucking provides a source of pacification for the newborn infant. It would seem natural that infants under 2 months, who cry more than older infants, would use their own hands and fingers as sources of sucking stimulation. In fact, hand-to-mouth behavior is a relatively rare occurrence at this age, but it does happen under some conditions. For example,

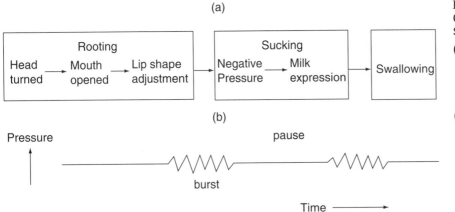

(a)

(b)

Figure 5.4
Organization of Sucking Behavior

(a) Sequence of acts comprising sucking behavior, from initial orientation to the nipple until swallowing has occurred.

(b) Changes in sucking pressure with time, showing the characteristic burst-pause pattern.

Figure 5.5
Hand-to-Mouth Contact during Distress at Two Months
The hand is "found by accident" when the baby turns its head to the side. The hand cannot be pulled to the midline for sucking.

Source: E. Thelen & A. Fogel, Toward an action-based theory of infant development, 1989, p. 51. In J. Lockman & N. Hazen (Eds.), *Action in a social context: Perspectives on early development*, 23 – 63. New York: Plenum Press.

it occurs in newborns when the arms are flexed and the hands come near the mouth when the baby begins to cry (Hopkins, Janssen, Kardaun, & van der Schoot, 1988), if the infant is given sweetened water when upset (Blass, Fillion, Rochat, Hoffmeyer, & Metzger, 1989; Rochat, Blass, & Hoffmeyer, 1988), or if the infant's hand is held near the mouth by an adult (Fogel, 1985), as shown in Figure 5.5. Apparently, infants do not do this intentionally until about 4 months of age. Before then, the meeting of the hand and the mouth is a happy accident from which the infant can take temporary comfort (Fogel, 1985; Hopkins et al., 1988). Giving the infant a mildly sweet solution to suck not only increases the frequency of hand-to-mouth contact, but has the additional effect of calming infants who are crying (Barr, Quek, Cousineau, Oberlander, Brian, & Young, 1994; Blass & Ciaramitaro, 1994; Buka & Lipsitt, 1991).

On the other hand, newborns will actively search for a nipple with their mouths. If they feel a nipple with their cheek, they will move their head backward, open their mouth, and move their mouth toward the nipple in one smooth movement (Koepke & Bigelow, 1997). This pattern of action is called *rooting.* Although it is considered one of the basic reflexes, rooting varies according to the size, shape, and location of the nipple.

Newborn Hand and Arm Movements

The newborn's arms and hands are among the least controlled part of the body. By contrast, actions of the face—such as sucking and crying—are highly developed and can be used by the infant to meet specific needs. Nevertheless, newborn hand and arm activity is more controlled under certain conditions. In the previous section, for example, we saw that if infants are given a mild sucrose solution to suck, it increases the probability that they will bring their hand to the region of the mouth. Similarly, hand-to-mouth contact is more likely to occur just before feeding and is often accompanied by anticipatory mouth opening as the hand approaches the region of the mouth (Lew & Butterworth, 1995).

Newborn hand and arm movements may appear random in real time, but patterns are revealed when these movements are observed carefully in slow motion. In one study on hand and arm movements, newborns were presented with three conditions: a person facing them, a ball moving slowly in front of them, and a control condition with neither a person nor a ball. Results showed a higher frequency of finger movements and flexion of the hand in the social condition compared to the other two conditions. In the object condition, infants were more likely to extend the fingers of their hand (as if to anticipate a grasp), to move the thumb and index finger (as if to grasp), and to extend their arms forward (as if to reach) (Ronnqvist & Hofsten, 1994). In a related study, newborns resisted attempts at manipulation of their arms and were able to visually follow the movements of their arms if they could see them (Meer, Weel, & Lee, 1995). Finally, studies have found that newborns presented with an object in different locations direct more arm and hand movements in the direction of the object (Bloch, 1990).

These studies show that even though newborns cannot actually reach or grasp, they already have motor patterns that are adapted to particular kinds of social and object situations. This research also reveals a surprising amount of coordination in newborn activity that has never before been suspected. It is likely, however, that you could not observe these newborn responses with the naked eye. As explained in the section on research methods (Chapter 1), we can only detect some of these sophisticated infant abilities through the use of controlled experiments and detailed videorecording.

Summary of Physical and Motor Development

In many ways, the newborn infant is a highly organized individual. In a sense, we are more tightly organized and predictable as newborns than at any later time in life. These babies cycle regularly through states of rest and activity. Although parents cannot predict exactly when a baby will wake up or fall asleep, they have a pretty good idea of how much their baby sleeps and how alert he or she can be and under what conditions.

Behavior ecology theories suggest that the regularities of the newborn's behavior—states, state changes, and reflexes—can be explained by genetic programming in which the sources of these behaviors lie in precise locations in the brain. The argument is that the newborn needs to suck, cry, calm, sleep, and self-stimulate in order to survive and develop.

Dynamic systems theory, on the other hand, suggests that all behavior is the result of a complex interaction among a large number of related factors. We saw in Chapter 3 that not even prenatal development is under the direct control of the genotype: a series of events in the environment of the cell and in the uterine environment of the mother must be present in order for a gene to express its message in the phenotype.

Postnatally, we observe even more complexity in developmental pathways. Whether we observe a strong or a weak reflex or no reflex at all, for example, is explained by a combination of factors, including whatever genetic codes exist for giving the newborn's body its particular structure, whether the baby has had time to unstretch its prenatally flexed arms, the rate of development of fat versus muscle, and whether or not the baby has something in its mouth at the moment. In addition, even reflexive movements are not rigidly programmed. They vary according to the infant's past experience and the contextual conditions under which they are elicited. As we will see in the next sections, perceptual and cognitive development show similar patterns of adaptability to current conditions and individual experiences.

Perceptual Development

The sensory systems of the body—sight, sound, taste, smell, and touch—provide the basic fabric of our psychological experiences. The senses form the basic ways in which we are connected to the environment. A baby "knows" the mother because she has a characteristic visual shape, auditory pattern in her voice, and quality of touch. She is permeated with fragrance from her body and clothing. Her milk tastes sweet and is flavored by the food she eats. These sensations fill up the baby's psychological experience of other persons and things. There is no overlay of thought or judgment, so common in adults. The baby's connection to the world is direct.

This kind of experience that relies on direct perception through the senses is called **ecological perception** (J. J. Gibson, 1966). Ecological perception is available to people of all ages, but its purest form exists during early infancy. The infant is totally attuned to the play of light and color, the melodies of sound, and the pleasure of being touched. This kind of experience remains intense during childhood but gradually fades into the background as we devote more of our time to thinking, doing, achieving, and working, and less to simply being fully present to our sensory experience and how that experience connects us directly to the rhythms of the earth and to its inhabitants. One of the goals of the body awareness clinical methods reviewed in Chapter 2 is to help children and adults reconnect with their senses. Practicing the Awareness through Movement lessons in this book is also a means to reawaken one's ecological perception.

The sensory world of the newborn infant is not as sharply focused or as discriminating as that of the adult. Nevertheless, newborns have the ability to see, hear, taste, smell, and feel. There has been a great deal of research on the topic of the newborn's perceptual abilities, especially in the areas of vision and audition.

The Visual World of the Newborn

Vision is one of the most powerful of the senses because it is so diverse. One sees shape, color, distance, texture, and the relative locations of objects in space. Compared to touch, which only takes in information that can be physically contacted by the hand or mouth, vision takes in the entire environment.

The visual world of the newborn, however, is focused primarily on the near environment. When people ask whether newborns can see, they usually are wondering about visual **acuity.** Visual acuity is a measure of the lens's ability to focus images on the retina, as well as the retina's ability to decode the light. A common measure of acuity is the Snellen

chart, with the large letter E on the top and successively smaller letters below. An acuity rating of 20/20 is given to a person who can see a particular line on the chart clearly at 20 feet. A person with 20/50 vision is able to see at 20 feet with the same clarity as a person with 20/20 vision can see at 50 feet.

Newborns' visual acuity is tested by their ability to see stripes of decreasing thinness in comparison to an all-gray stimulus, using a pattern preference test (see Chapter 1). Although the estimates vary between studies, a newborn's visual acuity is between 20/300 and 20/800, with an average of about 20/500 (Aslin, 1987). This low level of visual acuity in newborns is not related to an inability of the lens to focus. Rather, it seems to be the result of the immaturity of the dendrites and axons of the neurons in the retina and optic nerve and the relative lack of myelination (L. B. Cohen, DeLoache, & Strauss, 1979; Salapatek & Banks, 1978). By 6 months, visual acuity improves to nearly 20/20 in most infants.

This means that the visual world of the newborn is rather blurry, like an out-of-focus photo or film. On the other hand, newborns can see colors (Aslin, 1987). Thus, their visual world is probably filled with fuzzy regions of one color adjoining regions of other colors, each with different levels of brightness, forming an abstract mosaic of light. If you are, like me, sufficiently nearsighted, you will have no trouble replicating the newborn's visual world by simply removing your glasses or contacts. If not, try looking around when your eyes are bleary, when you are very sleepy or just after waking up.

The eyes do a lot more than just focus their lenses. **Oculomotor skills** are the movements that the eye must make to bring objects into focus, follow moving objects, and adjust for objects at different distances. Newborns' tracking of moving objects is a bit jerky, and they are able to follow only relatively slowly moving objects. More adultlike following begins between 6 and 8 weeks (Aslin, 1981; Kremenitzer, Vaughan, Kurtzberg, & Dowling, 1979).

Scanning occurs as the eye traces a path across a visual stimulus. Since the eye cannot see an entire image all at once, it must make small, rapid movements to move from one point of fixation to the next. One-month-olds tend to scan small, localized

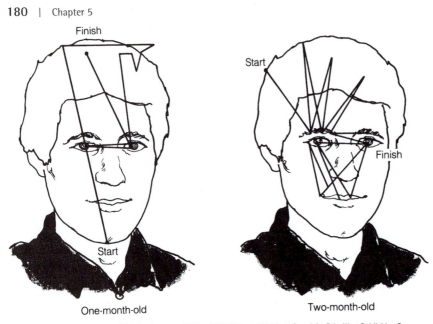

Finish

Start

Finish

Start

One-month-old

Two-month-old

Figure 5.6
Facial Scanning Patterns

The superimposed lines show where a baby will look at a face. One-month-olds look mostly around the outside, while older babies look at the inner details, especially at the eyes.

Source: A. Fogel & G. F. Melson, *Child development,* 1988, p. 158. St. Paul, MN: West. Copyright © by West Publishing Co.

regions of a figure, usually around its edges, while by the age of 3 months, infants spend more time scanning finer details of a figure (see Figure 5.6). Adults scan like newborns when they look at large objects from a distance, like a city skyline or a mountain range.

Oculomotor control adjusts the eyes to see objects at different distances. The ability to judge the relative distances between two objects and determine whether objects are close or far is called *depth perception.* We have the sensation of depth because each of our eyes sees a slightly different view of the same object. To see for yourself, try looking at an object nearby with one eye and then the other. The ability to compare the two retinal images, and therefore to see distance, emerges slowly between 3 and 6 months. Thus, until about 2 to 3 months of age, infants have functional but limited oculomotor skills. However, in spite of these limitations, infants can use their vision in a variety of ways and may even be able to recognize visual patterns after repeated exposure.

Can newborns see patterns within the complex jumble of lines, depths, and colors that they can see? We know from a number of studies that newborns can detect differences between visual images and seem to prefer some images more than others.

Newborns prefer to look at objects with clearly marked edges and outlines. They also prefer circular patterns to straight lines (Fantz, Fagan, & Miranda, 1975). Newborns like to look at the external contours of a figure, especially if the edges are sharp; their gaze tends to follow these lines, and once on a line, they rarely break out to scan other regions of a figure (Haith, 1980; Maurer & Salapatek, 1976; Milewski, 1976).

These pattern preferences in newborns seem to match their relatively poor visual acuity, while allowing them to actively explore objects with their eyes. As we saw in the fetus, active sensory and motor exploration seems to be a form of self-stimulation that is necessary to maintain continued development of the CNS and the associated motor skills. In this view, the patterns the newborn prefers are not necessarily meaningful: they merely serve to help the visual system develop by the age of 3 months to a point at which the infant can see the world more clearly and pick out enough details to make meaningful distinctions, such as between a familiar and an unfamiliar person.

This perspective suggests that infants need experience with the perceptual world before they can make sense out of it. Starting with some simple preferences for physical features of a stimulus, the infant later comes to attach particular features with other sources of information. Thus, the sounds, smells, and touches that an infant has come to understand as "mother" will only match up with the visual recognition of her at 3 months. This view is similar to that of Piaget, who held that infants gradually build up representations of the world by means of repeated encounters, each of which is compared with the others via assimilation and accommodation. The infant constructs perceptions by active engagement and experience.

Although infants have to build up a concept such as "mother" through repeated experiences over many months, they also have preferences at birth that guide them in their search for meaning. Newborns have visual preferences that seem to be attuned to social stimulation, orienting them to the most important figures in their environment—adults—who will help them survive. These early perceptual preferences are predicted by behavior ecology theory (J. J. Gibson, 1966). Newborns have inherited perceptual preferences that are most likely to bring them into contact with things that enhance their survival.

Infants are attracted to facelike stimuli and prefer faces over other objects (M. H. Johnson, Dziurawiee, Ellis, & Morton, 1991). Even more remarkable is that infants only 1 day old will change their sucking response to see a picture of their mother's face rather than the face of an unfamiliar female. When the mother is shown wearing a scarf, however, the newborn does not distinguish the mother from a stranger. These findings show that the outline of the face, including the hairline, is an important recognition cue for infants at this age (Pascalis, de Schonen, Morton, Deruelle, & Fabre-Grenet, 1995; Walton, Bower, & Bower, 1992). Perhaps more remarkable is the finding that newborns prefer to look at faces judged by adults to be more attractive. The preference is found regardless of the age, gender, or race of the face (Slater et al., 1998).

In summary, research has shown that infants as young as 1 month respond to their mother's face in a meaningful way and prefer attractive faces, supporting behavior ecology theory. Nevertheless, in accord with constructivist (Piagetian) theory, additional meanings will be built through active experience. Due to their relatively poor visual acuity and the slowness of their visual response, newborns' vi-

sual relationship to the world is relatively limited; the onset of more mature visual perception does not begin until at least 3 months of age (see Chapter 6). On the other hand, it is not so bad to begin one's life bathed in the intense sensation of colors and pleasing shapes. In order to draw or to paint, visual artists must relearn this infantlike way of seeing the world in terms of color and shape, rather than in terms of objects. The infant has other senses in addition, and these are considerably more acute at birth than vision.

Auditory Perception

Auditory perception does not require the same motor components as vision. Thus, developments in the sensitivity of the ears are likely to depend on the maturation of the auditory nerve and the components of the ear's anatomy. These structures are more mature at birth than those associated with vision. The auditory nerve is almost completely myelinated, and the bones of the middle ear are almost adult size at birth. After birth, most development occurs in the expansion of the auditory canal and the eardrum and the articulation of the auditory cortex in the brain. These processes reach adult levels by about 1 year, which is the same time that speech begins (Eilers & Gavin, 1981).

Auditory sensitivity. Sensitivity to sounds involves two basic aspects: loudness and pitch. Loudness is usually measured in decibels (dB). Loud thunder is about 120 dB, 70 dB is a noisy street corner, 60 dB is a normal conversation, and 40 dB is a whisper. Pitch is the frequency of the sound wave and is usually measured in hertz (Hz). One Hz is one cycle per second. A high C on a piano is 3951.07 Hz, and the low C is 65.41 Hz. This range of notes also corresponds to the frequency range of the human voice.

How loud does a sound have to be before a baby can hear it? Sensitivity to sounds is measured by observing a change in heart rate, a blink response, or a head turn; by recording brain waves; or by using a conditioned head turning or conditioned sucking procedure (see Chapter 1). The softest sounds a newborn baby can hear are in the range of 40 dB to 60 dB (Berg & Berg, 1979), although sounds from 50 dB to 70 dB are necessary to awaken a sleeping infant (Wedenberg, 1956).

In general, the research shows that while most adults can hear sounds as low as 0 dB to 5 dB, the most sensitive newborn cannot hear below about 20 dB (Schulman-Galambos & Galambos, 1979), although this ability improves over the first year. Babies are more sensitive to sounds in the middle range of the piano's notes, although they tend to prefer higher to lower pitched sounds (Kessen et al., 1970). Finally, babies prefer sounds made up of more than one note, of a wide band of frequencies (Eisenberg, 1976).

If we put together all the characteristics of sounds that are most easily heard, and in fact preferred, by newborns, the most common source of such sounds is an adult female voice either talking or singing. Newborns, in fact, prefer to listen to an adult singing infant-directed songs rather than adult-directed songs (Masataka, 1999). Although newborns are sensitive to a wide range of sounds and will orient to men who raise the pitch of their voice, researchers have speculated that prenatal experience with the sound of the mother's voice may have attuned infants to sounds of that level of loudness and mixture of pitches.

Recognition of mother's voice. We saw in Chapter 3 that newborns preferred to listen to a song or story that their mothers had sung or read aloud 2 weeks prior to birth compared to a song they had not heard, and that newborns seem to prefer heartbeat sounds similar to those they must have heard prenatally. Other research seems to support the view that infants can distinguish the voice of their own mother from the voices of other women. Thus, in addition to recognizing his or her mother visually, as we learned in the last section, a newborn can recognize her voice; as we shall see in the next section, newborns can also recognize their mother's smell. Prenatal and postnatal exposure to the mother thus set the infant on the path to developing a special tie to that particular person. The strong attachments to a particular person that develop later in the first year, therefore, are built upon early perceptual orienting preferences that begin in the last month of prenatal life.

Recognition of speech sounds. How, though, do newborns recognize their mother's voice and distinguish between different songs and stories that they have heard prenatally? They may detect overall patterns of rhythm and pitch that differentiate one person from another (Nazzi, Floccia, & Bertoncini, 1998; Sansavini, 1997; Sansavini, Bertoncini, & Giovanelli, 1997). In addition, infants may be able to hear differences among syllables that give them cues about a speaker's uniqueness.

One-month-olds can distinguish between two very closely related speech sounds: "p" having the sound "puh," and "b" having the sound "buh" (Eimas, Siqueland, Jusczyk, & Vigorito, 1971). By 2 months, babies can recognize not only consonant differences but also vowel differences in sounds (Kuhl, 1981; Swoboda, Kass, Morse, & Leavitt, 1978). Newborns can remember sounds to which they were exposed the day before, and they will change their sucking in order to hear recordings made in their native language rather than those in a foreign language (Bijeljac-Babic, Bertoncini, & Mehler, 1993; Moon, Cooper, & Fifer, 1993; Swain, Zelazo, & Clifton, 1993).

It seems that newborns can not only recognize the broad category of speech compared to nonspeech and mother compared to nonmother, but they can also distinguish between some of the finer aspects of speech sounds. As discussed earlier with respect to vision, behavior ecology theory suggests that this match may be necessary to ensure the survival of the human newborn, who is totally dependent on adults. On the other hand, learning theory suggests that newborns construct a preference for human voices and a recognition of their native language and their mother's voice as a result of hearing these voices prenatally. This early exposure to sound enhances the development of the auditory components of the CNS and predisposes the infant to similar sounds in the future.

Taste, Smell, and Touch

Newborns appear to be able to distinguish the four basic tastes: sweet, salty, sour, and bitter. We saw earlier how a sweet solution helped to calm a crying baby. Infants will consume more of a sweeter solution than a less sweet one, although they will stop sucking if the solution gets too sweet (Crook, 1978; Desor, Miller, & Turner, 1973). Sweet fluids seem to relax infants, as shown by the sequence of facial actions in Figure 5.7. At first, babies show

Figure 5.7
Facial Expressions Elicited by the Sweet Solution
Initial negative facial actions are followed by relaxation and sucking.

201343

201501

201060

Source: D. Rosenstein & H. Oster, Differential facial responses to four basic tastes in newborns, 1988, p. 1561. *Child Development, 59,* 1555–1568. Copyright © The Society for Research in Child Development, Inc. Used with permission of the author and publisher.

a negative expression, followed by relaxation and sucking (Blass, 1997; Rosenstein & Oster, 1988; Steiner, 1973).

In response to sour and bitter tastes, newborns show more consistently negative expressions, especially upper lip raising (as in disgust) and nose wrinkling. They also become more restless and stop sucking (Rosenstein & Oster, 1988; Steiner, 1973). Newborns do not like salty solutions (Crook, 1978).

Some of the same facial expressions as those described above for tastes have been seen in response to smells (Steiner, 1977). Newborns can differentiate between such odors as vinegar, licorice, and alcohol. In response to unpleasant odors, newborns will make faces of disgust. They will turn away from unpleasant odors and turn toward pleasant ones (Lipsitt, Engen, & Kaye, 1963).

Odors may be another way, besides sounds, that infants recognize their mothers. Infants older than 6 days tend to turn their heads more often to a pad containing their own mother's breast milk than to a pad containing the milk of another woman (Mac-Farlane, 1975). In a study using similar methodology, breast-fed infants were able to recognize pads containing their own mother's underarm odor compared to pads worn by unfamiliar women, although bottle-fed babies showed no evidence of recognition (Cernoch & Porter, 1985). Breast-fed infants can also distinguish their own mother's perfume from other perfume smells, and they show a clear olfactory preference for breast milk from any woman over other types of smells (Porter, Makin, Davis, & Christensen, 1992; Schleidt & Genzel, 1990). These differences between breast- and bottle-fed infants are probably due to the fact that breast-fed babies spend a longer time in direct contact with their mother's bare skin than bottle-fed babies do.

Interestingly, new mothers—whether their deliveries were vaginal or cesarean—were able to recognize their own infant's odors (Porter, Cernoch, & Perry, 1983; Russell, Mendelson, & Peeke, 1983). There seems to be a mutual olfactory (odor) sensitivity between infants and mothers. Thus, infants and mothers have a number of alternative and complementary channels of communication that ensure the beginnings of an emotional bond.

Olfactory and taste responses are probably not mediated by the cortex at this age. Both normal infants and deformed infants born without a cortex were able to detect odors and tastes (Steiner, 1977). This suggests that these perceptions are linked to the midbrain and hindbrain survival functions related to sucking and feeding.

Finally, newborn infants seem highly sensitive to tactile stimulation. The presence of the newborn reflexes bears witness to this fact. In addition, researchers have found changes in behavior and heart rate when infants are stimulated with touch or with an air puff on various regions of the body (Bell & Costello, 1964; Rose, Schmidt, & Bridget, 1976). Infants' mouths and hands are especially sensitive, and even in the first few weeks of life, they make different kinds of hand and mouth movements when soft or hard objects are placed in their hands or mouths (Rochat, 1987). Newborns are also able to change their hand movements depending upon whether a surface is smooth or textured (Molina & Jouen, 1998). Although it is possible that infants use touch to recognize their mothers, no studies have been done on this topic.

Newborns also feel pain. In response to normal medical procedures, such as injections and circumcision, infants show increased distress and may exhibit disturbances of sleep for the next few days (Emde, Gaensbauer, & Harmon, 1976; Karns, 2000). Newborns during vaginal delivery show more pain-related facial expressions than those born by cesarian section (Delevati & Bergamasco, 1999). Although medical procedures have traditionally been done without anesthetics, recent findings on pain sensitivity in newborns are leading to the increased use of local anesthetics.

In summary, infants are able to perceive with all their senses, and their sensitivity improves rapidly over the first few weeks and months of life. Certainly, this improvement is due in part to changes in the brain. On the other hand, the changes in the brain depend closely on the kinds of experiences the infant has during this period. There is also evidence that newborns recognize many forms of perception as meaningful: they recognize their mothers, and they cry in response to pain. It is also true that many forms of stimulation have no particular meaning for the infant: a face may be perceived simply as a series of lines, a melody as a sequence of sounds. The process of making sense of sensation is one of the major developmental tasks of infancy and we should not expect infants to come into the world with an understanding of more than a few simple things. Those simple things, however, are ecological in the sense that the infant has a direct connection with the thing perceived. In the next section, I take up the issue of the newborn's ability to understand, learn, and feel.

Cognitive Development

The ability to think conceptually, using words or symbols, does not begin until the middle of the second year of life. Newborns and young infants, however, possess a number of ways to process information that are collectively referred to as *cognition*. These processes include learning and memory, orienting and habituation, and imitation.

Can Newborns Learn?

The answer to this question is yes. We have already reported that in late pregnancy, the fetus is capable of learning certain sound patterns, such as songs, and can recognize their mother's voice. This means that fetuses not only learn to distinguish the sounds, but also remember the differences when they hear the sounds weeks later, after they are born, implying that they also have a memory of what they learn. Newborns have important limitations on their learning ability, however. Perhaps a better way to ask the question of whether newborns can learn is to ask under what conditions they are most likely to learn.

Newborns can learn by classical conditioning (see Chapter 2), at least under the specific circumstances of a certain type of research study. Researchers used the unconditioned response of rooting and sucking to the unconditioned stimulus (UCS) of a sweet fluid in the mouth. The presentation of the sweet fluid was paired during training with a light stroking of the infant's head (the conditioned stimulus, or CS). After training, the infants rooted and sucked to the stroking stimulus in the absence of the sweet fluid. In addition, when the sweet fluid was re-

moved entirely, the babies rooted and sucked to the stroking, but they also cried, showing that they had learned a connection between the stroking (CS) and the sweet taste (UCS) (Blass, Ganchrow, & Steiner, 1984). Classical conditioning may be possible when the UCS evokes a powerfully rewarding natural response, such as a sweet taste. This may explain the common observation that after a few days of feeding experience, newborns will root and suck at the sight of a nipple, even before they begin to taste the milk. If no milk comes out, they will cry or fuss.

Operant conditioning is much easier to demonstrate in the newborn. Recall that the conditioned sucking procedure (Chapter 1) involves the operant conditioning of infants to alter their sucking rate in the presence of particular sounds or pictures (DeCasper & Fifer, 1980) or syllables (Jusczyk, 1985). Head turning can also be conditioned successfully (H. Papousek, 1967). Once the infants learn the connection between their behavior and the reinforcement, they can signal their preferences with the "correct" sucking rate or head turn direction.

These studies of operant conditioning show that newborns can remember the link between their behavior and its consequence long enough to complete the experiment on that day. Suppose, however, that you trained a week-old infant to suck for the sound of her mother's voice by increasing her sucking rate. Now, if you bring the same baby back to the laboratory on the following day and put her in the experimental setting with no further training, will she remember the training and begin to suck at a faster rate?

This kind of procedure is the basis for most studies searching for infant memories. Do babies under 2 months of age remember what they learned 24 hours ago? It is very likely that they may remember under certain conditions, although not enough research has been done on this age group. Babies of this age seem to remember the sound of their mother's voice and some of her characteristic odors. When a group of mothers was asked to repeat the same word 60 times a day each day to their babies who were between 2 and 4 weeks of age, the infants recognized the word after delays of between 15 and 42 hours (Ungerer, Brody, & Zelazo, 1978). Perhaps the key to establishing a long-term memory in the newborn is a great deal of repetition, rather than a single exposure. In the next chapter, I will review research showing that by 3 months of age, infants can remember things, even from brief exposures, up to 2 weeks later.

Newborn memory is also demonstrated by the fact that newborns are more attracted to familiarity rather than novelty. Unlike older infants who seem to prefer novelty, newborns prefer the sound of their mother's voice, the smell of their mother's milk, and the sight of their mother's faces (Lock, 2000). They will also choose a familiar face from a set of faces and a familiar sound from a set of sounds (Barrile, Armstrong, & Bower, 1999).

Can Newborns Habituate?

Another form of infant learning and short-term memory is habituation. Like conditioned sucking, habituation is a reliable response that is used as the basis of a number of infant testing procedures (see Chapter 1). Recall that habituation is the gradual decline in the strength of a response following repeated presentations of the same stimulus. For example, if you live on a noisy street, you eventually habituate to the noise; that is, you no longer notice it on a regular basis. If some new element is added to the noise, for example, a siren or the screech of brakes, this is enough to renew your interest in the street noise. This renewal of interest is called *dishabituation* or *recovery*.

Researchers have found evidence of habituation in newborns' motor and heart rate responses to auditory stimuli (P. R. Zelazo, Brody, & Chaikan, 1984), visual stimuli (Slater, Morison, & Rose, 1984), and tactile stimuli (Kisilevsky & Muir, 1984). In addition, habituation can be shown in premature newborns (Field, Dempsey, Hatch, Ting, & Clifton, 1979). In one study, infants born without a brain cortex (anencephalic) did not habituate to noise (Brackbill, 1971), while other studies have found heart rate response habituation to an auditory stimulus in such infants (Graham, Anthony, & Ziegler, 1978).

In summary, studies of learning and habituation in newborns show that some simple forms of learning take place between the late fetal period until about 2 months of age. These rudimentary learning abilities may be mediated by the cortex, but they

also could be built into the lower structures of the brain as basic survival mechanisms. These simple learning and memory processes are fundamental to the survival of newborns. The recognition of maternal sounds and smells orients the newborns to their primary resource for survival. Learning how to orient themselves to and approach sources of food (sweet fluids and milk) and how to avoid noxious smells and tastes on future exposures seems so fundamental to survival that a brain stem mediation of such responses is quite plausible. More sophisticated forms of learning and cognition—complex associations, long-term memory, categorization, and inference—must await the further development of the brain's cortical connections and the enhanced acuity of the senses.

Can Newborns Imitate?

A final area of newborn cognition that we will discuss is imitation. Piaget believed that newborns lacked the cognitive skills to imitate. He thought this ability began only at 8 or 9 months of age. More recent studies have shown that infants can indeed imitate under certain conditions. Researchers studied 12- to 21-day-old infants' abilities to match tongue protrusion, lip protrusion, mouth opening, hand opening, and hand closing (A. Meltzoff & Moore, 1977). In this study, each infant was shown a series of gestures made by the same adult. If the infant could reliably produce the same gesture following the adult's display of that gesture, compared with following the adult's display of another gesture, imitation could be inferred. The researchers found that infants were much more likely to demonstrate a particular gesture following the modeling of that gesture than at any other time (see Figure 5.8).

A number of replications of this study have been successful in producing correct matching of gestures in very young infants. Another study found correct matching of tongue protrusion and hand-opening models, but it also found that other stimuli could evoke the same responses in the newborns. Moving a ballpoint pen toward and away from the infant's face in the same manner as a tongue might move in and out was also successful in eliciting tongue protrusion in infants. A dangling ring elicited hand

Figure 5.8
Imitation of Facial Expressions in Newborns

Sample photographs from video-tape recordings of 2-to-3-week-old infants imitating **(a)** tongue protrusion, **(b)** mouth opening, and **(c)** lip protrusion demonstrated by an adult experimenter.

Source: A. Meltzoff & W. Moore, Imitation of facial and manual gestures by human neonates, 1977, p. 77. *Science, 198,* 75–78. Copyright © by the American Association for the Advancement of Science. Reprinted by permission of the publisher and the author.

opening and closing. It was concluded that the infants were not imitating a particular gesture as much as they were imitating a movement pattern or responding with some oral exploratory behavior (S. W. Jacobson, 1979; S. S. Jones, 1996).

Other work shows that infants do match expressions. During the demonstration of the surprise face, newborns showed more wide eyes and wide mouth opening. During the demonstration of the sad face, they had tight mouths, protruded lips, and furrowed brows; during the happy-face demonstration, infants had more wide-lip expressions. Matching was more likely to occur during the middle trials, suggesting that it is not due to the immediate arousal of the visual display nor is it a reflexive response. These possibilities could be true only if the infants imitated on the first few trials (Field, Woodson, Greenberg, & Cohen, 1982).

Other replications of this work have reported imitation of head movement (A. Meltzoff & Moore, 1989), lip widening and lip pursing with a sample of Nepalese newborns (Reissland, 1988),

and tongue protrusion and mouth opening. Infants who imitated more at birth gazed away from their mothers less during social interaction at 3 months, suggesting that early imitation reflects a possible social receptivity (Heimann, 1989).

On the other hand, some teams of researchers have failed to replicate the findings (Koepke, Hamm, Legerstee, & Russell, 1983; B. McKenzie & Over, 1983). Others have argued that although there is a slightly elevated probability of the baby displaying the modeled gesture, in fact all babies display a wide variety of gestures following the model; furthermore, there are wide individual differences between babies (Anisfeld, 1979).

Thus, although the evidence is in favor of some form of newborn imitation, the response is fleeting and hard to detect. Its occurrence in any form reflects a rather remarkable capacity of the immature human brain and perceptual system to process information and reflect it back to the outside world. Like learning and habituation, even occasional imitative responses are likely to orient the caregiver in a positive way toward the infant and enhance the probability of an early parent-infant attachment.

For newborns, imitation may be a way of relating to people by establishing a connection of similarity between the baby and another person. Even as adults we are drawn to people that we perceive as being like us in some way. Imitation is a nonverbal way of establishing this social connection. Six-week-old infants were exposed to an adult who modeled mouth opening and tongue protrusion, which the infants imitated. Then after a delay of 24 hours, the infants saw the same adult once again. Without the adult doing anything, the infants spontaneously produced the imitative response they had learned the day before (A. N. Meltzoff & Moore, 1994). Copying another person as a way of knowing and connecting with them can be seen in later behaviors such as taking another person's point of view, following another person's lead, and letting oneself be influenced by a role model (A. N. Meltzoff & Moore, 1997). It is remarkable that newborns have the rudimentary ability to connect with other people in this way.

Do Newborns Have a Sense of Self?

When a newborn imitates mouth opening or tongue protrusion, it is necessary for them to match a facial expression of their own with that of the adult. This is surprising because newborns have never seen their own face in a mirror, yet somehow, out of all the possible facial expressions, they can pick one of their own that fits with the one they see. This may mean that newborns can distinguish the movements of their own bodies from the movements of others, an early form of a sense of self (A. N. Meltzoff & Moore, 1997).

Some research suggests that newborns can tell the difference between being touched on their cheeks by another person and touching themselves on the cheek. They are more likely to root when being touched by another person than when touching themselves (Rochat & Hespos, 1997). Newborns also cry more and suck less when they hear the cries of another infant played on a tape recorder compared to when they hear their own cries played on the tape recorder (Dondi, Simion, & Caltran, 1999).

It is possible that these studies merely show that newborns can tell the difference between familiarity and unfamiliarity. On the other hand, the familiarity comes from their own bodies. It may be that a rudimentary sense of self emerges from the repeated familiarity of living in the same body and experiencing the same sounds and feelings many times. This sense of sameness and familiarity is also enhanced by the parents, who tend to respond to the infant's repeating actions in similar ways each time they occur. Thus, the infant's growing awareness of self-familiarity is enhanced by the parent's consistent form of responding (Kaye, 1982).

This early sense of self that appears during the first 2 months of life has been called the **emergent self,** the perception of sameness over time in behavior, feelings, and states of arousal (Stern, 1985; see Chapter 2). The emergent self is the sense of familiar experience of the body and of the familiarity in the way others respond to those experiences.

In summary, although newborn cognition is limited to some simple forms of learning, memory, habituation, imitation, and a sense of self, the research reveals that they are capable of adapting to their environment in order to promote their growth and development. Not only can newborns distinguish familiarity from unfamiliarity, they seem to prefer familiar sights, sounds, tastes, and feelings, including themselves. For the first 2 months of life, the infant finds satisfaction in the comforts of home. Newborns do not like to be stressed or challenged, and they do not show much initiative to go out and conquer the world (see the "Co-Regulating with Baby" section in this chapter). These abilities begin to appear in the 3rd month (Chapter 6).

Emotional Development

Do newborns have the ability to experience emotions? If they can see, hear, taste, smell, learn, and remember, it makes sense to conclude that they also have feelings. In the past, however, many hospital staff assumed that newborns could not feel pain, and medical procedures were administered without anesthetic. Fortunately, this practice is changing, along with the belief that newborns cannot feel.

One of the more interesting demonstrations of the existence of newborn feelings was the result of an accidental discovery. A group of researchers at Brown University were studying the newborn's ability to learn and also exploring the range of newborn sensitivity to taste and smell (see the earlier sections of this chapter). While investigating newborn preferences for sweet fluids, Lipsitt (1979b) and Crook (1978) found that the babies sucked in longer bursts, with shorter pauses between bursts. Within a sucking burst, the interval between sucks is higher for sweetened water than for plain water, and the newborn's heart rate increases while he or she is sucking the sweet water. Thus, the babies were sucking for longer periods and holding the sweet liquid longer in their mouths before swallowing. The researchers concluded that the babies were "savoring" the pleasurable sensation of the sweet taste. In addition, when plain water was given following the sweet water, the babies showed aversive reactions.

All researchers today agree that newborns can feel. The current debate is about the range and depth of the newborn's emotional experience. Newborns, for example, do not feel many of the emotions that are experienced by older infants and children. They show no signs of fear (which begins about 9 months), anger (which begins about 6 months), or shame (which begins about 18 months).

From the perspective of discrete emotion theory (see Chapter 2), there are a small number of basic human emotions and these emotions are associated with specific facial expressions. Some studies (Oster, 1978; Rosenstein & Oster, 1988) find that newborns have the expressions for most of the adult discrete emotions. Some of these expressions, such as disgust responses to tastes and smells (see Figure 5.7), are appropriate to the stimulation in the sense that an adult would respond in a similar way to the same stimulus. Crying occurs in situations in which the child should feel some distress or pain. In addition to facial expressions, newborns can convey emotion with other parts of their bodies. During distress, for example, there may be reddening of the entire body, kicking and thrashing, contorted arm movements, and stiffening of the body.

In addition to disgust and distress, newborns appear to experience the emotions of interest and surprise (Dondi, 1999; Lavelli, 1999). These expressions occur during waking states and are keyed to the infant's attention to faces, social interaction, and moving objects. Newborn attention may shift between states of simple attention (simply observing), concentrated attention (when there appears to be an effort made to recognize or to take in the object of attention) and excited attention (when the infant seemed momentarily startled but still attentive). These expressions are shown in Figure 6.8 (Chapter 6).

On the other hand, some expressions do not occur with any clear link to the situation. Newborns smile during sleep and drowsy states rather then when awake. Newborn smiling may be related to some kind of simple contentment or relaxation rather than to the feeling of joy that we begin to see more clearly around 3 months of age. In addition, newborns have a wide variety of facial movements that do not fall neatly into one of the discrete emotion categories: odd-seeming twists and turns of facial muscles. Only after 2 months of age do these movements begin to coalesce into organized and recognizable patterns of facial expression that are clearly linked to discrete emotions.

Emotions—like perceptions and cognitions—are not given at birth. They develop over time. The process of emotional development depends in part on how these incomplete forms of expression are interpreted by adults. Even when adults do not know what the infant wants, feels, or needs, they are quick to attribute meaning to the infant's behavior and respond according to this attribution. In these cases, the adult responds "as if" the baby had a fully developed emotion (Adamson, 1995; Kaye, 1982). Adults observe a contraction of the infant's lip corners, assume the baby is happy, and make happy expressions and sounds to the baby. Or, an infant may cry in such a way as to make the adult think the baby is hungry or tired or angry.

After many repetitions of adult interpretive responses to incomplete infant expressions, those expressions begin to consolidate into recognizable patterns. According to a dynamic systems perspective, discrete emotions emerge from the interaction of the infant's relatively unformed facial displays and the social environment in which particular patterns of facial display are interpreted by adults as being communicative (Dondi, 1999; Fogel, Nwokah, et al., 1992; Fogel, Dickson, et al., 1997). This transaction process consolidates the diffuse expressions and experiences of the child into socially recognizable emotional expressions and feeling states. The resulting infant emotion is not made up by or shaped by the adult. Rather, emotions emerge in their relationship as a process of development. I will return to this point in the next chapter.

It seems wise for us as caregivers to make the assumption that infants of all ages have feelings, since it helps us to understand their needs. The interventions we make that are consonant with our interpretations of infant emotions often seem to have the intended effect. We pick up a crying baby to soothe what we believe to be the child's pain or discomfort as much as to stop the crying, and the subsequent relaxation of the infant confirms our belief about his or her feelings. I now turn to a discussion of infant-caregiver interactions.

Family and Society

Early Adult–Infant Interaction: The Beginnings of Emotional Ties

As we saw in the last chapter and earlier in this one, adults and infants have sensitivities and responses that make a good mutual fit. Newborn sucking responses are perfectly suited to obtain milk from the breast; the newborn's appearance, sound, and smell are powerful attractors of adult attention and care; and the newborn is primed to recognize the primary caregiver by smell, sound, and possibly touch.

According to behavior ecology theory, especially that of John Bowlby (1969), in the early weeks and months of life, we share a common heritage with most other mammals who nurse and show a good deal of solicitude toward their young. Not every order of animals behaves this way. Reptiles give birth to eggs and usually leave the young to fend for

themselves after hatching. Bird species do not nurse their young, nor do they give birth to live infants; however, they do show parental caregiving behavior.

After the domestic cat gives birth, the mother lies on her side to expose her nipples. She licks the kittens, which are blind at birth, and the licking helps them orient to her body, nuzzle into her fur, and begin to search for the nipple. After only a few days, each kitten has a preferred nipple, and there is rapid improvement in the speed with which a kitten can find its nipple (Rosenblatt, 1972).

The example of the domestic cat illustrates the idea that a complex series of co-actions occurs between mother and infant by which each learns to adjust to the other. Over time, the initial trial-and-error response is reduced, and nursing and other forms of interpersonal interaction become more efficient. In this case the mother, no less than the infant, is subject to the tug of powerful evolutionary forces that ensure the survival of the young. In one study, human mothers of newborns were blindfolded and then guided to touch the hand and cheek of three newborns, their own and two other infants. Two-thirds of the mothers were able to identify their own infant from touching the infant's hands, while half identified their infant from touching the face (Kaitz, Meirov, & Landman, 1993). This study shows that mothers have a nonverbal and nonvisual sensitivity toward their own babies that matches the infant's recognition of their own mothers by auditory, taste, visual and tactile cues.

These mutual emotional ties that bring mother and infant together are the first manifestations of attachment (Bowlby, 1969). **Attachment** is the maintenance of mutual proximity between two individuals over time. At first, during the newborn period, attachment for the infant involves simple interactions and perceptual recognition cues. By the end of the first year (see Chapter 8), infants become so attached to their caregivers that they begin to show signs of distress at separation.

From the very start, the human adult-infant relationship involves more than just a streamlining of the behaviors necessary for feeding and caretaking. There is also a social-psychological component that may form the basis of later interpersonal communication and attachment between adult and infant. Mothers and infants were observed on the day after birth and again at 2 weeks of age during breast- or bottle-feeding while the mother jiggled the infant (Kaye, 1977; Kaye & Wells, 1980). Jiggles were anything the mother did to stimulate sucking, such as shaking the infant or gently moving the nipple in and out of the mouth. Jiggles rarely occurred, but when they did, they tended to occur during pauses in sucking, and mothers claimed they were using the jiggling to get the infant to start sucking again. To test whether the jiggling was effective, the duration of the pauses without jiggles was measured in relation to the duration of the pauses containing a jiggle. When the mother jiggled during a pause, the jiggling actually lengthened the pause. The mother's intervention tended to delay the onset of the next burst of sucks by about 2 seconds. This pattern held true so long as the mother continued to jiggle the infant.

If, however, the mother jiggled momentarily and then stopped, the infant was more likely to begin a burst of sucks than in either the no-jiggle or the continuous-jiggle condition. The pattern that developed—suck-pause, jiggle-stop, suck-pause, jiggle-stop, and so on—is the precursor to later forms of social discourse. The pattern looks very much like a dialogue in which there is an exchange of turns: baby, mother, baby, mother.

This turn-taking situation is still rather one-sided. Although the infant can adjust the timing of the onset of the burst of sucking within a limited range, he or she cannot change the pattern altogether. The mother, on the other hand, is quite capable of changing her behavior to fit the situation. She is able to choose what to do and when to do it. It is almost as if the pauses in sucking serve as "slots" or "spaces" into which the mother can insert her interventions. Although the whole thing has the appearance of turn taking, that seems to be an illusion created mostly by the mother's ability to adapt to the infant.

As we saw in the section on emotion, newborns require an adult to make them complete, to fill in the missing pieces of their ability, and to give their world psychological coherence. This takes a lot of patience, because newborn expressions and movements are subtle and sometimes confusing.

Bringing coherence to the newborn's awake states is difficult for these reasons and also because the newborn is awake and alert relatively infre-

quently, and alertness is a rather fragile and easily disrupted state. On the other hand, just as jiggling prolongs sucking pauses, animated adult faces and brightly colored objects prolong periods of alertness (Sander, Stechler, Burns, & Lee, 1979; Wolff, 1987). As a result of repeated attempts to engage, taking advantage of initially brief periods of alertness, the duration of parent-infant face-to-face play and infant attention gradually increases over the first 2 months of life (Lavelli, 1999; Thoman, Acebo, Dreyer, Becker, & Freese, 1979). This increase is clearly a product of the dynamically changing parent-infant system.

Most of the studies of early parent-infant interaction have been done with the infants' mothers; only recently have investigators begun to look at the father-newborn interaction. Some of these findings are summarized in the next section.

What Is the Father's Role with Newborns?

Are fathers important to their newborns? Some studies have found that fathers spend very little time interacting with their newborns; others have found that fathers would like to spend more time with their babies; and still others have shown that when fathers actually do spend time with newborns, they can be just as competent as mothers in administering care and affection. In reality, these studies are not contradictory; they merely represent different aspects of the fathering role. Although we will discuss the father's role and behavior in more detail later, in this chapter we will confine our discussion to studies of fathers and newborns.

Studies of large-scale national samples of parents and infants show that fathers spend between 20 and 35% as much time as mothers in direct participation in infant care. Mothers appear to take the primary responsibility, while fathers take the role of helpers and baby-sitters (Lamb, Pleck, Charnov, & Levine, 1987; Pleck, 1983). Fathers have a strong desire to share in the experience of parenting but need a good deal of support to do so. Men's ability to participate in parenting tasks depends on the amount of social support they receive (Fein, 1976).

Father-infant and mother-infant interaction can be enhanced by specific interventions to orient fathers to their newborns. In one program, fathers

Michael Newman/PhotoEdit

Both fathers and mothers can become attached to their newborns.

were given instruction in baby massage and bathing methods when the infants were 4 weeks old. When the infants were 12 weeks old, the fathers who had received the instruction reported more marital satisfaction and less depression, compared to a control group of fathers who were not trained. In addition, 12-week-old infants in the massage and bathing group were more likely to maintain eye contact, smile, and vocalize with their fathers, and the fathers were more likely to be involved with their infants (Samuels, Scholz, & Edmundson, 1992; Scholz & Samuels, 1992). Parents who were given information about newborn responsiveness and behavior when the infant was 2 days old were more likely to interact synchronously with their infants (Wendland-Carro, Piccinini, & Millar, 1999).

Men who adjust better to parenthood have more knowledge about children and better relationships with their wives than men who have trouble adjusting to being fathers. This is in contrast to the factors predicting parental adjustment in women, which include self-esteem, identification with the mothering role, and adaptation to the pregnancy experience (Entwisle & Doering, 1981; Feldman & Nash, 1986; Wente & Crockenberg, 1976).

In a series of studies (Parke & Sawin, 1980; Parke & Tinsley, 1981; Sawin & Parke, 1979), infants were observed with mothers and fathers in a maternity ward of a hospital. During feeding and other caretaking tasks, fathers were at least as active as mothers and showed similar levels of sensitivity and affection. New fathers' heart rates and blood pressures were elevated while holding their newborns compared to when they were not holding the babies, suggesting heightened arousal (L. C. Jones & Thomas, 1989). On the whole, however, mothers spend more time caretaking during this period than the fathers.

On the other hand, the involvement of the father in caregiving affects the mother-infant relationship. Working mothers who left their newborn infants with fathers compared to other infant-care providers reported less anger, depression, and anxiety (Vandell, Hyde, Plant, & Essex, 1997). From the perspective of family systems theory, families in which the fathers are more involved have wives who show more interest and affection toward the neonate (Sawin and Parke, 1979). Of course, this result could be explained the other way around: interested, affectionate mothers may be more adept at encouraging fathers to take part in the care of the infant. Fathers do play an important role, even in the newborn period. They may not do as much as mothers overall, but with some encouragement and training, they are able to become competent caregivers.

Do Firstborns Have Different Interactions with Their Mothers than Laterborns?

Another factor influencing the family system at this period of time is whether the parents have had prior experience with an infant. As a general rule, newborns who are firstborn receive more caregiving interaction (Kilbride, Johnson, & Streissguth, 1977). Perhaps because of the novelty of the experience, parents devote more time and energy to the care of the firstborn than to infants born later. One study examined family photo albums and found considerably more photographs of firstborn children than of children born later (Titus, 1976).

One of the possible reasons for the differences in parental behavior toward first- versus laterborn children is that primiparous mothers (women who have given birth for the first time) receive more obstetrical medication than multiparous mothers (mothers who have given birth more than once),

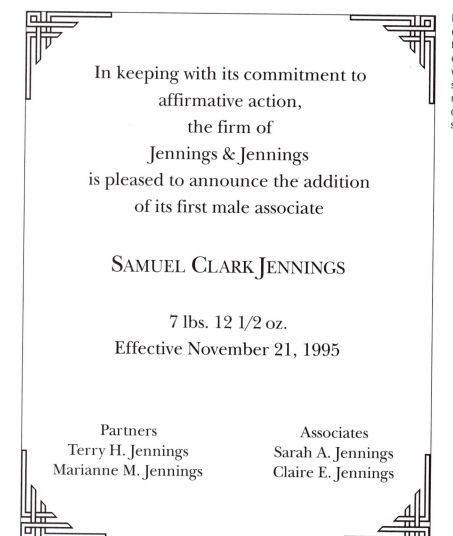

In keeping with its commitment to
affirmative action,
the firm of
Jennings & Jennings
is pleased to announce the addition
of its first male associate

SAMUEL CLARK JENNINGS

7 lbs. 12 1/2 oz.
Effective November 21, 1995

Partners	Associates
Terry H. Jennings	Sarah A. Jennings
Marianne M. Jennings	Claire E. Jennings

Many new parents are proud of their babies regardless of gender or birth order. Birth announcement cards or notices printed in the newspaper are ways that parents communicate this special event to others. Unfortunately, not all parents have the financial ability or family stability to give newborns such special attention.

which may result in an infant who is somewhat slower to respond to stimulation. Not only do mothers spend more time with their firstborns, but firstborns are more passive and nonresponsive than babies born later. Could it be that mothers have to spend more time simply to get the infant sufficiently aroused to feed (Brown et al., 1975)?

Another explanation of the difference is that the mothers of firstborns are less skilled as caregivers. Do they spend more time because they are less efficient at getting the normal caregiving tasks accomplished? Primiparous mothers spend more time in nonfeeding activity during a feeding session. They are more likely to change activity frequently, such as shifting the infant's posture, providing more stimulation, and talking more to the newborn. Their infants spend less time on the nipple and do less sucking when attached than infants born later. These mothers could be spending more time because they are more uncertain about how to handle their infant or because they are more excited by the infant and wish to touch, explore, and talk to the infant. The number of changes of activity decreased over the first 3 days for primiparous mothers, suggesting that it does not take them very long to get down to the business of feeding during the feeding period (E. Thoman, Barnett, & Leiderman, 1971; E. Thoman, Leiderman, & Olson, 1972).

Another explanation is that first-time mothers are simply more anxious than other mothers. An anxious mood is likely to be caused by lack of security in the child-rearing role, and it may be enhanced by such factors as separation from the infant due to prematurity and illness. Anxiety in first-time mothers at birth is correlated with anxiety at 1 month but not at later follow-up observations (Fleming & Orpen, 1986; Fleming, Ruble, Flett, & Van Wagner, 1990), suggesting that most early insecurities that might influence behavior are reduced after a few months' experience.

In summary, adults and infants seem ready to interact with each other and have feelings and behaviors that mutually complement. Under the right conditions, any adult can interact successfully with a newborn and with enough exposure to the baby can develop a lasting attachment. The emotional tie between adults and infants does not seem to depend on a particular experience or a particular starting time (see the "Applications" section below).

Rather, emotional bonds develop slowly and in a variety of ways. Many senses and behaviors can be involved, and if one pathway is absent (the parents do not have the opportunity for early contact, for example), other pathways are available to enhance the adult-infant communication process.

The Author's View

The first two months of life is a period of dramatic change. In many ways, the newborn is not very different from the late-term fetus. On the other hand, the environment of the fetus is radically different from that of the newborn. The fetus is kept warm, nourished, submerged, and tightly held. It is bathed in soft sounds in cozy darkness. No postnatal environment can replicate the womb. As a result, even well-wrapped, breast-fed, and constantly held newborns will need to change in order to adapt to the relative inconstancy of the postnatal world. New senses are challenged, like sight and smell, and the body is freer to move. Sucking has to accommodate to a nipple and to milk. Emotions such as pain, disgust, and interest may not have been experienced before.

It takes 2 months for the newborn to get settled and secure. After that age, crying decreases, waking increases, perception improves, and a wide range of emotional experience becomes available. During that 2 months, the newborn becomes aware of an occasional sense of self-sameness that emerges through the cloud of change. Imagine being very busy, on the move, unsettled, or seriously ill. People in these situations are so preoccupied that they have little time for themselves. Their sleep and waking patterns may change day to day, and they find it difficult to know when or if they are hungry. Some things, however, emerge as islands of permanence and security: the feeling of falling asleep, a warm shower, a familiar voice, or a predictable routine.

Part of what creates the sense of consistency and familiarity is the pattern of relating to the environment. The parent and infant, both of whom are changing and adapting to the newness, find moments together that are quiet, comforting, predictable, and mutually satisfying. As they get to know each other and develop routines for being together, starting from initial attractions that are part of the species's ecology, they get to know themselves at the same time. It is as if the newborn's goal in life is to create and seek familiar routines as a way of bringing some sense of comfort and order to the sea of change.

The infant is never isolated. Infants move from a fetus-womb system into a newborn-parent system. The constancy that is at the heart of the infant's experience of self is a constancy created by the system, in the establishment of routines for mutually co-regulating. Dynamic systems have the characteristic of creating stability in the midst of change. One of the remarkable abilities of the newborn is to be able to detect that stability, within the flow of change, as a sense of and a preference for familiarity. It seems, therefore, that the human mind from its earliest beginnings is matched to the complex dynamics of the natural ecology, extracting just enough stability to insure survival without losing an awareness of the distressing and unpredictable feeling of change.

AWARENESS THROUGH MOVEMENT

Instructions for doing these lessons are found in the preface and in Chapter 3. These lessons will not be very effective unless you give them your complete attention. It helps to set aside a special time for doing the lessons that is not interrupted by other demands. It is important to go through each step slowly, allowing yourself the opportunity to experience multiple dimensions of somatic and self-awareness.

Head Turning/Tonic Neck & Primitive Crawling/Swimmer Movements

1. Lie on your stomach with your face to the right. Bring one arm up so that your elbow is bent and your hand rests near your head, palm facing the floor. Extend your other arm down alongside your body. Your elbows should rest on the floor. There are two possible arm positions. Is your face turned toward the arm that is bent or the one that is straight? Slowly reverse the position of your arms by sliding your hands on the floor in circular arcs, if possible without lifting your elbows. Your long arm will bend, and you will bring up one hand near to your face, while the other arm lengthens down along your side. Reverse the position of your arms a few more times and notice which position is more comfortable for your shoulders and neck. Continue to alternate which arm is bent and which straight by slowly making a half-circle with each hand. Both arms move at the same time in opposite directions, so that midway through the arc your arms will be extended straight out to the sides at shoulder height. Lie on your back and rest.

2. Return to lie on your stomach with your face in the middle, both elbows bent, and with both of your hands lying under your face, palms down. Begin to roll your pelvis from side to side and notice how your entire body responds passively to this wobbling of your pelvis. Find the most effortless rhythm in order to create an oscillatory movement that spreads through your whole body.

3. Now slow this movement down and gradually increase the amount you roll your pelvis side to side. As your pelvis rolls to the side, one knee begins to bend by itself. Gradually increase how far you roll your pelvis until your knee is light enough for you to easily draw it upward toward your abdomen. The leg straightens as your pelvis returns to the middle, and as your pelvis rolls to the other side, draw up the other knee. Alternate rolling your pelvis back and forth, drawing up one knee and then the other. Lie on your back and rest.

4. Lie again on your stomach and resume rolling your pelvis and drawing up your knees. Now, at the same time you move your pelvis and legs, synchronize turning your face from side to side, while reversing your arm positions back and forth, as you did in step 1. In the middle of the movement, both of your legs are straight, your arms are out to the sides, and your face is in the middle. Lie on your back and rest.

5. Observe that there are eight possible configurations for your face, arms, and knees: Your face

Applications   Parent-Infant Bonding

What is bonding?

People use the word **bonding** to signify the relationship of attachment between infant and parent, speaking of a relationship as either "bonded" or "not bonded." Bonding also has been used to refer to the events that take place during the first few hours after birth, when mother and infant are placed alone together and in skin-to-skin contact. Finally, some individuals presume or try to prove that skin-to-skin contact in the first hours after birth will predispose the mother-infant pair to a closer, more affectionate attachment relationship later.

How has bonding been studied?

The concept of bonding grew out of the pioneering work of Marshall Klaus and John Kennell of Case Western Reserve University. Their first reports detailed an apparently universal pattern of behavior seen in mothers presented with their naked newborns immediately after birth. The mothers in their study first began to touch the neonates' fingers and toes. This phase usually lasted between 4 and 8 minutes. After this, the mothers began to move inward, touching the infants' limbs, and ended their exploration by an encompassing palm contact with the infant's abdomen, accompanied by massaging movements (Klaus, Kennell, Plumb, & Zeuhlke, 1970). The same study found that mothers of premature infants progressed through the same phases but spent more time in each one.

Since then, the pattern of maternal behavior at first contact with the neonate has been replicated on many occasions and in a wide variety of settings. It has been shown that fathers, when given the same opportunity to lie next to their newborn children, progress through the same sequence of phases (D. McDonald, 1978; Rodholm & Larsson, 1979). Remarkably, this same pattern of exploration of the newborn has been observed in chimpanzee mothers with their newborn infants (Bard, 1994). The adult response to the first contact with the newborn is similar to adult responses to the cry, the smile, and the facial configuration of the neonate, a part of the species survival characteristics considered by behavior ecology theory.

What are the long-term effects of early contact?

Although few doubt the validity of the first-contact behavior pattern, controversy arises over the relative importance of this behavior, or the lack of it, for the infant's later development. Not long after the first-contact phenomenon had been reported, Klaus and colleagues published a study showing that mothers who had early contact with their infants in the newborn period were more likely to spend more time holding their infants in a face-to-face position. The study involved 28 primiparous mothers of low-income families who did not plan to breastfeed. The experimental group had 1 hour of extra contact at birth and another 5 hours of extra contact each afternoon while in the hospital. The observers at 1 month were not aware of the group identity of the mothers (Klaus et al., 1972). Since that report appeared, many other studies have been done, and the results have been inconsistent. The goal of this review is not to present all the studies that have been done on the effects of early contact but to provide a representative sampling of the types of findings that have appeared.

One study used a sample of middle-class white infants from Canada who had had normal deliveries. The experimental group had 1 hour of extra contact beginning at 45 minutes after birth. In follow-up observations at 1 and 3 months, the mothers who had extra contact did more smiling, singing, holding of the babies in the face-to-face position, and playing without the use of a toy than the mothers in the control group. The amount of touching behavior did not differ between the groups. This study was somewhat flawed, however, because only one of the two observers at the 1- and 2-month sessions was unaware of the mothers' group identity. We have no way of knowing how the informed observer might have influenced the naive observer (Kontos, 1978). Another study that used a sample and schedule of observations similar to that in the Kontos study (Curry, 1979) but employed blind observers failed to find any differences at 36 hours and at 3 months in the amounts of holding; encompassing, affectionate close contact; face-to-face holding; smiling; or kissing of the infant.

In a well-controlled study done in Sweden, Schaller, Carlsson, and Larsson (1979) found evidence of higher levels of proximal contact in the extended-contact mothers

---

can be turned to the right or left. Your hands can be near your face or down along your sides. Your knees can be drawn up or straight. Slowly and playfully, try all the combinations, taking frequent rests on your back between variations. Some of the patterns will feel awkward and others will be more comfortable.

Which patterns do you prefer? Which positions would you expect to see in a 1-month-old infant? Lie on your back and rest.

6. When you get up, turn from side and side, looking to the right and left. Notice if your neck is freer than usual.

(rubs, pats, kisses, and touches) at 2 and 4 days, but they found no differences at 42 days. A replication study by the same group of investigators (Carlsson et al., 1979) yielded similar findings: differences in the first few days but no differences 1 month later. DeChateau (1980, 1987) reported some differences between extended and control groups at 36 hours, but only in the position in which the mothers sat to hold their infants while feeding them. A 3-year follow-up, also from Sweden, reported no differences.

A number of other studies have also failed to support the claims of the importance of early contact (Goldberg, 1983; Lamb, 1982; Myers, 1987). Furthermore, similar research on the effects of early contact on fathers has failed to turn up any lasting effects (Palkovitz, 1985). The important factor in paternal involvement with newborns is an ongoing interactive relationship, whether it starts at birth or several days or weeks later.

Although it is impossible to prove that early contact has no long-term effects, these studies, done in different countries and under many different conditions, seem to suggest that any differences due to extended or early contact are at best transitory, lasting no more than a few days or months. It is also extremely important to note that all the studies, without exception, have focused on maternal attachment or changes in maternal behavior following the experience of early contact. There is absolutely no evidence that any of these manipulations have any effect on the baby's future attachment to the mother.

There is some evidence that early contact has effects on mothers from low-income groups or on mothers at high risk for attachment problems. In these cases, the additional contact seems to be an important boost to get the mother-infant system started. Ordinarily, however, the mother-infant relationship has a number of alternative feedback systems that enable it to maintain its course without the benefit of early contact.

What are the implications of these findings?

The implication of this research is that mothers who do not have the opportunity for early contact need not worry about the well-being of their infants. Indeed, early contact is impossible in many situations, such as with premature infants, sick infants, sick mothers, or adopted infants. In these cases, it is especially important for the parents not to worry about what may have been lost and to concentrate on developing their relationship with their babies.

I will discuss some of these issues again in the final chapter, where I consider the effects of early experience. To set the stage for that chapter, consider that the human species would be severely limited in its adaptive flexibility if the future well-being of its individual members depended on a few short minutes following birth. These studies also teach us something about how systems function. A complex system usually has multiple possible pathways to the same end point; the more alternative pathways in the

system, the more adaptive the system can become.

None of this is meant to deny the fact that it may be extremely satisfying for parents to have the opportunity for early contact with their babies, rather than being artificially isolated from them by hospital rules and regulations. We have already described how early discharge and immediate contact during home births have demonstrated that such alternatives as rooming in have no ill effects. A much more solid argument for early and extended contact would be based on the immediate satisfaction of the parents or on ensuring that each parent gets the fullest possible enjoyment from the childbirth experience, rather than on any lasting impact of that early contact on the infant.

The search for the effects of early contact perhaps reflects our society's more general need to justify everything in terms of its ultimate usefulness or its payoff down the road. This social value has made the path to changing childbirth practices a rocky one, and because of this prevailing attitude, the failure to replicate the effects of early contact may disappoint many well-intentioned individuals. On the other hand, the research initiated by Klaus, Kennell, and colleagues led the way for more humane treatment of newborns and mothers, making the hospital experience more emotionally meaningful for both parents and infants.

Comments: It is common for adults to experience neck tension. Part of the problem is that because of our sitting culture, we often move our heads and eyes without moving the rest of our bodies. When babies turn their heads from side to side, they also involve their arms, shoulders, spine, pelvis, and legs. We can regain flexibility and coordination by experimenting with our earliest movement patterns.

There are observable patterns in most infants' positions and movements. These patterns reflect many factors, including the structure of the skeleton, muscles, and nervous system, and the physical and social environment. When we as adults perform

Co-Regulating with Baby

Co-regulation (see Chapter 2 and Fogel, 1993) refers to periods of communication when people are continuously adjusting their actions to each other, and when both participants have the feeling that something new and creative is occurring. Co-regulation is more than just being responsive and sensitive. It is about being open to the emerging possibilities in your relationship with another person and being sufficiently spontaneous to allow for improvisation and innovation. A co-regulated conversation between adults is one in which ideas and feelings are mutually accepted, in which there is a continuous flow of ideas and feelings, and in which participants have a sense of discovering something new about themselves and each other.

In the Awareness through Movement lessons, it is important to focus your awareness on your body's movements and sensations. Co-regulating with baby is a type of awareness through social communication. As you interact with the baby (or with any person), it is important to pay attention to your own experiences. Usually, if you are feeling unhappy or uncomfortable when communicating, the other person is feeling that also. So, as in qualitative research, you can use your own experiences as a guide to help you relate to the baby.

Co-regulating with a newborn infant is not easy because they have limited social skills and the time in which they are awake and alert is relatively brief. With patience, however, co-regulating with a newborn can be a wonderful and surprising experience.

A baby's first attempts to gaze at people and objects may be brief. If infants are shown an object while they are alert, they may learn to look for longer periods. For newborns, objects should be brightly colored with simple shapes, such as a striped ball, a mirror, a shiny bracelet, or a white paper plate with a face painted in thick black lines.

Hold objects about 8 to 10 inches from the baby's face. The infant can best focus his or her vision at this distance. Hold the object steady or move it slowly from side to side. Some newborns show a clear preference for looking at certain objects. Watch to see which ones the baby seems to prefer. Try to vary the distance and speed of the object and see what happens.

An infant may enjoy looking at objects from different points of view and from different positions, such as while being cradled in mother's arms, lying on his or her back, or sitting in an infant seat. A baby's attention may be attracted by objects that make noise or music.

---

these same movements, we exhibit far more variability in how we tend to position our head, arms, and legs. This is because, over the course of time, we have formed muscular habits that predispose us to particular patterns. Perhaps infants move in very efficient ways that we can learn from.

Hands and Feet: Palmer/Plantar Reflex

Position: Lie on your back with your legs long. Bend your elbows so that your forearms are perpendicular to the floor and your hands directed toward the ceiling. (The instructions are designed for right-handed people. If you are left handed, do all the movements on your left side.)

1. Slowly begin to close and open your right hand. Make very small movements so that you avoid fully opening or fully closing your hand.

Keep reducing your effort in order to make the lightest possible movement. Repeat this movement many times, resting before you get tired. It may take as long as 5 or 10 minutes to produce significant changes in the muscular tonus of your hand and arm. Rest with your arm down at your side.

2. What would be an analogous movement for you to do with your foot? Begin to flex your right foot slowly and gently, curling your toes toward the sole of your foot, and then slowly allow your toes to extend. Repeat this movement many times, reducing your effort with each repetition. Rest.

3. Put your right arm in the same position as in step 1 and do the movements of your hand and foot at exactly the same time, so that you curl

Baby's attention is especially attracted to the high-pitched voices of caregivers.

If the infant becomes overstimulated when watching objects, try showing just one at a time and moving the object more slowly in the baby's visual field. If the baby still appears to be overstimulated (turning away, crying, sucking a fist, etc.), the game should be put aside until a later time. Use your own feelings as a guide to tell when the infant wants more or has had enough. It is very satisfying when a baby actually engages with you. If you are experiencing feelings of rejection or frustration, it probably is a good indication that you need to change your play or wait until a later time.

Although true eye contact does not begin until about 6 weeks, infants will look in the direction of your eyes and face. You can encourage this by talking gently while holding the baby up near your face. Cutting down on outside sources of stimulation will also help encourage the baby to focus on the caregiver. If a baby will not look at your face, cut back on the level of stimulation and give the baby a chance to look at you. Remember that some babies are slow to focus and cannot sustain their attention for long periods. It is important to not take this personally. The baby is not capable of rejecting anyone at this age. Your patience and understanding of the difficult time babies have in attending will eventually be rewarded.

You can follow the baby's direction of gaze with your face until the baby is looking at you, and then give the baby a big smile while saying "Hi!" Newborns like to hear soft whispers and humming sounds. After the baby is looking at you, smiles can sometimes be elicited by quiet, high-pitched voices, gentle tummy strokes, and smiling faces. You will probably be so delighted to be looked at in this way that these responses will seem very natural.

Aside from these activities, babies of this age like to listen to music, to be held and touched, and to be bathed and massaged. In all these activities, try to create simple routines that the baby can recognize. Observe for signs of overstimulation and give the baby a chance to rest and relax. Co-regulation may take some trial and error to figure out what is best for you and the infant. When you really connect, it is worth all the effort. Even though newborns have only a limited capacity for attention and interaction, with some gentleness and patience, the caregiver can be rewarded with periods of mutually co-regulated attention and enjoyment.

and uncurl both your fingers and toes. Repeat this many times in a very relaxed way. You may begin to feel subtle changes in the muscles all along your right side. Rest.

4. Alternate curling and uncurling your right hand and foot, so that now one is opening at the same time that the other is closing. Vary the rhythm. Which pattern feels more "natural"? Do you prefer closing and opening the hand and foot at the same time or moving them in alternation? Rest. Experiment with these two variations in different rhythms. As you move, and during your rests, notice if you feel subtle reactions throughout the right side of your body while you do the hand and foot movements. Rest and feel the differences in sensation between your right and left sides.

Comment: Primitive movements of the hands and feet like the ones in this lesson are known to begin during fetal development. Such movements occur spontaneously throughout infancy. In fact, such primitive movements of the hands and feet occur throughout our lifetimes, although we might not recognize them as originating in infancy. Consider how we make the movement of grasping. Sometimes we overuse the grasping muscles, such as when gripping a steering wheel or holding a pen. Also as a result of stress, there may be an increase in the muscular tension in our hands. Notice whether your hands feel more relaxed and open after doing this lesson. When we perform these primitive hand and feet movements with relaxation and attention, they can be a powerful technique for reducing muscular tension and stress.

SUMMARY

Physical and Motor Development

- The fetal states of rest and activity develop into sleeping and waking states.

- Newborns sleep about 17 hours per day.

- Responsiveness to the environment is related to orienting and defensive responses. Newborns will orient to stimuli of moderate intensity and complexity.

- Brain development depends on experience with the environment. Part of the brain is experience expectant, while other parts are experience dependent. Brain growth involves cell loss as well as increases in connections.

- Crying is an organized rhythmic activity that has reliable effects on adults. Infants who cry a great deal are not necessarily at risk for problems in parent-infant attachment.

- Colic is a pattern of excessive crying with no known cause. It does not seem to have lasting effects on parents or infants.

- Each method of soothing infants has advantages and disadvantages.

- Reflexes are highly variable within and between infants. Many disappear by about 6 months, while others remain with us for life. Both brain and motor factors may contribute to the disappearance of reflexes.

- The infant does not grow all at once; different parts of the body grow at different rates and at different times.

- Sucking is a complex activity that can be adapted to the environment.

- Newborn arm and hand movements are directed to objects in different locations and differ between social and physical objects, although detailed videotape analysis is required to observe these patterns.

Perceptual Development

- Newborn visual acuity and visual processing are poor but improve rapidly during the first 3 months.

- Infants can perceive some meaningful visual patterns, but in most cases, they do not attach meanings to their perceptions.

- Hearing, smell, and taste are more acute at birth than vision, perhaps due to prenatal experiences. Infants can recognize their mothers by sound and by smell.

Cognitive Development

- Newborns are susceptible to both operant conditioning and classical conditioning.

- Habituation and conditioning reflect rudimentary memory processes as infants need to compare current with past experiences. Most newborn memories seem to last no more than a few hours, unless the stimulus is repeated often.

- Newborns appear to be able to imitate simple gestures they themselves can make. Imitation is irregular and not especially salient to a casual observer.

- Newborns appear to have a rudimentary sense of self, experienced as a feeling of the familiarity of their own bodies, feelings, and behaviors.

Emotional Development

- Newborns have a large repertoire of facial expressions and body movements, some of which are related to emotion expression.

- Newborns can feel distress, contentment, disgust, interest, and surprise.

Family and Society

- Adults and infants seem to have mutually complementary communications that get their interaction started and set the stage for later emotional ties.

- There are many alternate pathways for adult-infant communication and recognition, suggesting that early physical contact is not crucial for the formation of attachments.

- First-time parents are somewhat more hesitant with their babies than other parents, but this difference disappears after several months.

Applications: Parent-Infant Bonding

- Early physical contact between parents and newborns is satisfying and important to all participants, when it is possible and available.

- There are no known long-term effects of a lack of physical contact between parents and newborns, since the parent-infant relationship has many subsequent opportunities to create affectionate ties.

 ## ON THE WEB

www.nncc.org   The National Network for Child Care web page provides child-care information from America's leading colleges and universities. It is an excellent site offering a database of over 1,000 publications and resources, a national and international discussion group, and national newsletters for family child care, center-based care, and school-aged care. Maps, catalogs, and newsletters, along with information on conferences and other resources, are also available.

childdevelopmentinfo.com/development   The child development section of this site provides parents with information on physical, mental, and emotional growth and development in children and teenagers. The information on the pages in this section helps parents know what to expect from their children as they mature. It provides information from the Child Development Institute on physical, social, intellectual, and language development of children and adolescents.

www.babyonline.com   Baby Online.Com offers comprehensive information to both parents and childcare professionals, addressing pregnancy, prenatal/postnatal, baby, and parenting issues. It also features excerpts from best-selling books on pregnancy, childbirth, and parenting and live, prescheduled chat forums, hosted by experts. It also gives information on toy safety and provides links to the Family Research Council and Pregnancy Web Ring. The site is updated monthly.

GLOSSARY

Acuity   The ability of a perceptual system to resolve incoming information into sharp focus.

Asynchronous growth   Refers to the fact that growth occurs in different regions of the body at different times and different rates.

Attachment   The maintenance of close proximity between infant and adult as part of an enduring relationship.

Bonding   The feelings of attachment the caregiver derives from close contact with the baby.

Burst-pause pattern   The pattern of sucking behavior in which the baby sucks for a few minutes, stops, and resumes sucking.

Colic   A complaint of excessive crying (at least 3 hours per day, for a least 3 days per week, for at least 3 weeks) in an otherwise normal infant.

Defensive response   Avoidance or aversive response to noxious or potentially threatening stimuli.

Difficult temperament   A parental judgment regarding the relative nonresponsiveness of the infant to parental interventions.

Ecological perception   The kind of experience that relies on direct perception through the senses, not mediated by thought or judgment.

Emergent self   The perception of sameness over time in behavior, feelings, and states of arousal; the sense of familiarity of the body that persists even when objects and people come and go.

Experience dependent   Brain regions and pathways that are not fully formed and must await environmental input for their development.

Experience expectant   Brain regions and pathways that are more or less fully developed at birth, allowing the infant to adapt to particular types of environmental stimuli related to basic survival.

Milk expression   The second phase of sucking, in which the infant presses the nipple against the roof of the mouth with the tongue to force milk out.

Myelin   A protective coating over nerve cells that aids in the conduction of action potentials.

Negative pressure   The first phase of sucking, in which the gums create a seal around the nipple and the jaw drops to create suction inside the mouth.

Neuron   A conductive cell in the central nervous system.

Oculomotor skills   The movements of the eye, including lens focusing, convergence and divergence, scanning, and tracking.

Orienting response   The direction of attention and action toward an attractive stimulus.

Reflex   A semiautomatic response to a specific stimulus that, once elicited, must run its course.

Stereopsis   The ability to compare the different images coming from each eye.

State   An organized pattern of physical and physiological responding that is related to the infant's level of activation and arousal.

Synapse   The connection between axons and dendrites by which action potentials are transmitted between neurons.

6

Two to Five Months

CHAPTER OVERVIEW AND OUTLINE

Physical and Motor Development	*What are the features of physical growth during this period? What types of motor skills do infants have?*
Perceptual Development	*What perceptual abilities develop during this period? Can infants perceive their own actions?*
Cognitive Development	*What types of things do infants remember? What type of intelligence do infants have at this age?*
Emotional Development	*What types of emotions can infants at this age feel? What are their capacities for emotion regulation?*
Social Development	*How do adults typically behave with babies of this age? What are some cultural differences in adult-infant interaction? What are the effects of adult behavior on infants? What is the infant's sense of self at this age?*
Family and Society	*What are the developmental tasks of adults in the transition to parenthood? Are there differences in parenting between men and women?*
Applications: Unexpected Death in Infancy	*What is SIDS? How is it caused? Can it be prevented?*

During the first few months, babies seem to be in a world of their own. They sleep a great deal, they have few means of communication other than crying, and their movements seem self-contained and repetitive. These newborn behavior patterns are organized and highly adaptive for the initial tasks of postnatal survival.

Around the age of 2 months, most babies experience their first major developmental transition since birth. Their motor movements become more purposeful and deliberate, a change from the earlier cyclical and reflexive movements. Their perceptual systems, especially vision, become more acute. Waking time and attention span increase rapidly. Adults first notice these changes at 6 to 8 weeks, when infants become able to establish and maintain eye contact. Around this time, demanding crying wanes and is replaced by other forms of emotional communication, especially smiling in response to other people. These changes lead to more prolonged and satisfying adult-infant social interactions and the beginnings of social play.

As the quality of their attention becomes more focused, infants begin to have memories of past experiences. These memories form the basis of infants' feelings of enjoyment in the company of familiar people and in the ability to anticipate recurring routines, such as meals and baths. This period is truly an exciting time for parents as their baby seems to come alive and to engage with them.

Physical and Motor Development

Physical Development

In infancy and early childhood, physical development occurs as a natural accompaniment to psychological development. Physical development is usually measured in terms of height and weight. Additional indices include the circumference of the head, the fat-to-muscle ratio, the emergence of baby teeth, and bone growth. Standard charts for height and weight for boys and girls from birth to 36 months are given in the Appendix.

At birth, most infants are 19 to 21 inches in length and weigh between 7 and 8 pounds. Boys are slightly longer and heavier than girls and remain so, on the average, throughout life. The most rapid growth in both height and weight occurs in the first 6 months of life. By this age, height increases by a factor of 1.5, while weight increases by a factor of 2. This is a lot of growth in a short period. Imagine a teenager (the teenage years are the other period of life when rapid growth occurs) whose height increased by half again in 6 months—say, from 5 feet to 7½ feet! Teens grow fast, but not that fast.

Individual differences in birth height and weight are relatively small, since they are limited by the need for the infant's body to fit through the mother's pelvis and vagina during birth. Individual differences become larger with age (the range of heights and weights is wider among 2-year-olds than among 1-year-olds). In addition, as the infants get older, their height becomes a better predictor of their adult height. Infant weight is not a very good predictor of adult weight, since weight is more variable than height and more dependent upon environmental factors. As we saw in Chapter 3, weight gain in premature infants can be influenced not only by diet but also by age-appropriate stimulation. In Chapter 7, I will return to the topic of infant nutrition and its effects on growth.

Also, keep in mind that growth is asynchronous (see Chapter 5). Different parts of the body grow at different rates, and growth spurts occur at different times in each body region. Before birth, the head grows faster than the rest of the body, while after birth, the body begins to grow faster. The process in which head growth precedes body growth is called **cephalocaudal development.** Growth also proceeds outward, first centered on the body and later on the developing limbs in a process called **proximodistal development.** Because their limbs develop more slowly than the central part of the body, it takes almost a year for babies to begin standing and walking. These growth processes are illustrated in Figure 6.1.

Infant sleep also changes during this period. By 3 months infants are still sleeping about the same amount as newborns, but they can sleep for longer periods before waking up and are more likely to

Figure 6.1
Developmental Changes in Body Proportion

The very different proportions of body length accounted for by the head, trunk, and legs at different ages or stages of development. The disproportion is greatest in fetal life. The head decreases from 50% of total body length at 2 months postconception to only 25% at birth and 12% in adulthood.

| 2 month (fetal) | 5 month (fetal) | Newborn | 2 yr | 6 yr | 12 yr | 25 yr |

Source: J. F. Rosenblith & J. E. Sims-Knight, *In the beginning: Development in the first two years,* 1985, p. 296. Belmont, CA: Brooks/Cole. Copyright © by Wadsworth, Inc. Reprinted by permission.

Table 6.1   Commonly Used Infant Development Tests

Name of Test	Areas of Competency Assessed
Gesell Scales (Gesell, 1925)	Motor behavior, language behavior, adaptive behavior, and personal-social behavior.
Bayley Scales of Infant Development (Bayley, 1969)	Motor area (gross body coordination) and mental area (adaptability, learning, sensory acuity, and fine motor coordination).
Denver Developmental Screening Test (Frankenburg et al., 1975)	Personal-social behavior, fine motor-adaptive behavior, language behavior, and gross motor coordination.
Einstein Scales of Sensorimotor Development (Escalona & Corman, 1968)	Prehension, object permanence, and space (detour behavior and perspective taking).
Infant Psychological Development Scales (Uzgiris & Hunt, 1975)	Object permanence, development of means, development of imitation, development of causality, development of objects in space, and development of schemes for relating to objects.

Source: A. Fogel & G. F. Melson, *Child development,* 1988, p. 150. St. Paul, MN: West. Copyright © by West Publishing Co. Reprinted by permission. All rights reserved.

sleep through the night. About half of their sleep time is in REM sleep. This percentage decreases gradually so that in adults, only 20% of sleep is REM sleep. I will discuss sleep more fully in the "Applications" section of this chapter, since most SIDS (Sudden Infant Death Syndrome) deaths occur during sleep.

Motor Development

At the same time that their body is growing physically, the infant is also becoming more skilled at a variety of motor movements. In the realm of motor development, I will consider control over pos-ture, locomotion, and the movements of the hands and arms.

Motor development was studied extensively in the early part of the twentieth century (Gesell, 1928; McGraw, 1935; Shirley, 1931). Because of this research, the infant's level of motor development can be assessed today using a variety of standardized testing situations. Some of the commonly used motor developmental assessment tests are listed in Table 6.1. Based on results from using these tests with many infants, both the average age of achievement of a skill and the range of ages seen in normal infants is usually reported. The age norms for the achievement of body postures and hand and arm

Table 6.2   Norms for the Development of Motor Behavior Patterns in North America

Test Item	Average Age	Normal Age Range
A. Head and body control		
Holds head erect when upright	7 weeks	3 weeks–4 months
Holds head steady when upright	2.5 months	1 month–5 months
Elevates chest and head in prone position	2.2 months	3 weeks–5 months
Thrusts arms and legs in supine position	1 month	1 week–2 months
Turns from side to back	2 months	3 weeks–5 months
Turns from back to side	2.5 months	2 months–7 months
Sits with support	2.2 months	1 month–5 months
Sits with slight support	3.7 months	2 months–6 months
Sits alone momentarily	5.2 months	4 months–8 months
Pulls self to sitting position	5.7 months	4 months–8 months
B. Hand and arm control		
Holds onto large ring in supine position	1 month	3 weeks–4 months
Grasps 1-inch cube with palm	3.7 months	2 months–7 months
Grasps cube with partial use of thumb	5 months	4 months–8 months
Reaches with one hand	5.5 months	4 months–8 months

Source: Bayley Infant Development Tests, as reported in and adapted from J. F. Rosenblith & J. E. Sims-Knight, *In the beginning: Development in the first two years,* 1985, Tables 8.2 and 8.5. Reprinted by permission of Sage Publications.

control between 2 and 5 months of age are given in Table 6.2 using the standard scores from the Bayley test. Between 2 and 5 months of age, boy and girl infants do not differ in motor skills or amount of motor activity (Cossette, Malcuit, & Pomerleau, 1991).

These assessment procedures are useful for diagnosing retardation and motor deficits in infants, but they only work well under specific conditions. First, the test norms apply only to infants in a particular cultural and economic group. Second, the test is applicable only if it is administered in precisely the same manner for each infant. The ability to grasp a cube is supposed to be assessed when the infant is supported in a sitting position. What if, instead, you presented the cube while the baby was lying supine? How might such a postural change affect the infant's hand motor skills?

Physical exercise and environmental support for motor skills can enhance the infant's ability to achieve motor coordination. As a simple case, consider how an infant seat, a high chair, and an infant walker provide postural support so that the baby can execute manual and locomotor movements that they would not be able to do while lying on their backs. Similarly, the positions in which adults hold infants also influence the range of motor skills that

the infants can display. In general, the ability of a baby to perform a motor skill depends in part on two factors: the difficulty of the task and the supports and resources present in the environment in which the task is carried out.

Task difficulty.   We saw in the last chapter that the stepping reflex disappears after 2 months. When the infant is held upright with the feet placed on a surface, they cannot execute stepping movements. When the same infant's legs are underwater or when the infant is lying supine, on the other hand, stepping becomes easier. In conditions where the stepping task is less difficult, in other words, infants can do it (Thelen, Skala, & Kelso, 1987).

Similar effects of task difficulty have been shown for fine motor skills, such as manipulating objects. Between the ages of 2 and 5 months, infants have more difficulty handling objects like balls and cubes than objects that have graspable appendages, such as a cube with holes into which the baby can insert his or her fingers or a ring (which is simply a ball with a hole in the middle).

At 3 months, grasping movements are relatively primitive. Babies will grasp an object and move it directly to their mouths without even looking at it. Beginning at about 4 months, however, babies will alternate putting the object in their mouths and looking at it, and they can hold the object in one hand while looking at it and finger the object with the other hand (Rochat, 1989). The older baby uses more motor actions and more perceptual systems in exploring the environment (Bushnell, 1982; Ruff, Saltarelli, Capozzoli, & Dubiner, 1992).

At 2 months, however, one can observe more sophisticated object-directed hand movements when the task is less difficult, as when infants do not actually make hand contact with objects. When an object can be seen but not grasped, 2-month-olds can move their hands and fingers to make grasping and fingering movements. Their fingers can move in graceful and rhythmic patterns, and they can point and make pincher grasp movements (Trevarthen, 1977). The ability to make sophisticated movements toward objects also differs according to the baby's emotional state (Fogel, 1981; Hannan,

1987; H. Papousek & Papousek, 1977; Trevarthen, 1977). Figure 6.2 shows some of these state-related arm and hand movements. Infants 2 and 3 months of age were more likely to point if they were in an alert and attentive state. Typically, the pointing movements are not directed to the object of the infant's attention: pointing is more like an expression of interest than a direct communication about the object at this age (Fogel & Hannan, 1985; Thelen & Fogel, 1989) (see Figure 6.3).

In general, therefore, infants will perform better on easier motor skill tasks. This, of course, is no different at any age. Children can ride a bike with training wheels before they can ride without them. Adults can help infants by making appropriate adjustments when tasks are too difficult. As you will see in the Awareness through Movement lessons in this chapter, you can make simple tasks easier on yourself if you pay attention to each part of the movement and how it affects your body.

Figure 6.2
State-Dependent Hand and Arm Expressions

The position of hands in different behavioral states of infants: **(a)** alert waking state; **(b)** closed fists in uncomfortable or distressing situations; **(c)** passive waking state; **(d)** transitional states to sleep; **(e)** sleep.

Source: H. Papousek, Mothering and the cognitive head start: Psychobiological considerations, 1977, p. 71. In H. R. Schaffer (Ed.), *Studies in mother-infant interaction,* 63 – 85. Copyright © by Academic Press, Inc.

Source: E. Thelen & A. Fogel, Toward an action-based theory of infant development, 1989, p. 53. In J. Lockman & N. Hazen (Eds.), *Action in a social context: Perspectives on early development,* 23 – 63. New York: Plenum Press.

Figure 6.3
Development of Pointing

(a) Point at 2 months during face-to-face interaction with mother. Index finger extends while arms are flexed and does not indicate direction of gaze. **(b)** Point at 9 months during free play with mother. Both arm and finger are extended in the direction of the object of interest.

Supports and resources. As infants develop, they can perform tasks that were once too difficult for them. How do these changes come about? What is the cause of motor development? As explained in the previous chapter, brain development is not enough to explain changes in motor skill. In fact, the infant has to practice making movements with easy tasks in order for the brain to develop. Since human infants have such a limited ability to move around in the environment or to think about how to make tasks easier, they need social partners to help them. Usually, the infant's caregiver creates supports and resources by which object manipulation and motor movements are made easier.

During simple social play with objects, adults help infants to practice their budding motor skills (Lyra & Ferreira, 1987; Lyra & Rossetti-Ferreira, 1995). At first, when infants are unable to reach, adults will show an object to the baby and demonstrate the object's properties (shaking a rattle or squeezing a soft toy). During this period, adults may also place the object into the infant's hands, allowing the infant to grasp and hold the object or bring the object to the mouth. After infants acquire the ability to reach for objects, mothers stop showing and placing and begin to hold the objects steady and within reach of the babies, apparently to give the babies the opportunity to practice reaching. Once reaching is mastered, mothers begin to challenge the babies with more complex objects and with two objects at one time (Fogel, 1990b; Reimers & Fogel, 1992; West & Fogel, 1990).

Another way in which adults provide supports and resources for motor skills is by holding the infants in postures that are most conducive to the execution of those skills. For example, when infants first are learning to sit, they need to balance their bodies with one hand. This detracts from their ability to reach for things with two hands (Rochat, 1989). When adults hold babies upright, it frees both of the infant's hands. We have found that upright babies are more attentive to the physical environment, while supine babies are more likely to look at their mothers (Fogel, Dedo, & McEwen, 1992; Fogel, Nwokah, Hsu, Dedo, & Walker, 1993). Similarly, infants in upright rather than supine positions are more likely to reach for objects that are presented within their reach (Savelsbergh & Kamp, 1993).

The effect of adult support for motor development is also seen in some African cultures. One study done in Mali (Bril & Sabatier, 1986) found that mothers put babies through some active workout routines. From birth, the babies were given postural control exercises, including training in sitting and standing. Mothers also stretched the babies' muscles and suspended the babies by their arms and legs (see Figure 6.4). Similar patterns have

STRETCHING

(1) 1 month   (2) 1 month   (3) 1 month

SUSPENSION

(4) 1 month   (5) 1 month   (6) 1 month

(7) 2 months   (8) 1 month   (9) 2 months   (10) 5.5 months

Figure 6.4
Postural Manipulations by Adults

Source: B. Bril & C. Sabatier, The cultural context of motor development: Postural manipulations in the daily life of Bambara babies (Mali), 1986, p. 445. *International Journal of Behavior Development, 9,* 439 – 453.

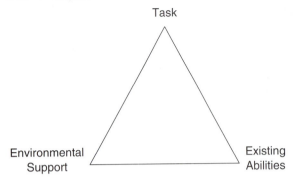

Figure 6.5
Systems Model of Task Difficulty
A task will be easy or difficult for an infant depending upon what the infant is being asked to do (the task), the help and resources the infant received from others (environmental support), and the skills that the infant brings to the task (existing abilities).

been found for West African families living in Paris (Rabain-Jamin & Wornham, 1993).

As a result of this practice, many African babies have advanced motor coordination compared to Caucasian babies. In addition, because the babies' limbs are exercised frequently, certain reflexes such as stepping do not disappear after 2 months, as was found in North American infants (Super, 1976). On the opposite end of the spectrum are Navaho infants, who spend many hours strapped tightly onto cradle boards. Their motor development is slower than that of the other groups (Chisholm, 1983).

In summary, differences in task difficulty and in supports and resources for motor development seem to influence the age at which the motor skill is first acquired. Eventually, however, all babies achieve the important motor milestones. These findings show that motor and physical development in the first half year is the result of a systems interaction between infants, adults, and the environment. Generally speaking, the ability of a person to perform a coordinated task is based on three systemic factors: task, environmental supports, and existing abilities. This is shown in Figure 6.5.

Whether a baby can reach for objects, for example, can be explained according to Figure 6.5 as follows. The task is to reach for an object. The environmental supports are whether the object is within reach or out of reach, whether it is held by an adult or not, and the size and shape of the ob-

ject. The abilities are whether the infant has learned to reach (after 4 months, usually) and whether the infant can turn, sit upright, or move toward the object. Reaching will be coordinated and successful depending upon how these factors come together.

Perceptual Development

As we saw in the last chapter, perceptual development is also influenced by the kinds of experiences the child encounters. Lack of exposure to sensory information can impede the articulation of brain pathways for sensory acuity and information processing. The period from 2 to 5 months includes a major shift in perceptual development. During the first 2 months, infants can see, hear, smell, taste, and feel. Infants have clear preferences for certain types of perceptual experiences, such as looking at sharp and bold outlines of figures or listening to high-pitched voices. In some cases, infants under 2 months can recognize particular patterns that seem to have a meaning to them—looming objects, their mothers' voices and smells—but pattern detection is the exception rather than the rule. Between 2 and 4 months, infants recognize and prefer meaningful patterned stimuli (a smiling face, for example) regardless of its level of intensity, complexity, or sharpness.

Visual Pattern Perception

The visual world comes to us in the form of line, shape, brightness and color. Adults do not perceive these simple features, however; they perceive whole objects. Newborn infants perceive the lines and colors but do not detect the patterns. Adults perceive like a newborn when they are trying to draw or paint an object and they need to break it down into its basic elements. Consider the following figure: 毌. Does this mean anything to you? To a Chinese

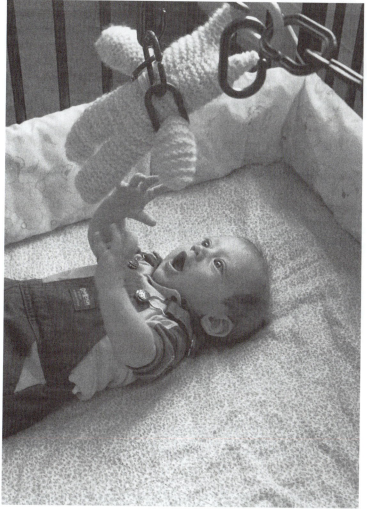

Visual perception develops by seeing the same object from a number of different perspectives. Colorful mobiles with varied shapes are particularly interesting. Research using mobiles has found that babies of this age can tell the difference between a familiar mobile and the same one with only a single piece removed.

or Japanese speaker, this figure means "mother." To the rest of the world, it is just an interesting shape made by intersecting lines. Before 2 months, many of the things babies see may seem as if they are looking at Chinese without knowing the language.

The ability to perceive whole patterns, rather than lines and shapes, first appears at about 3 months. To discover this, researchers show infants a picture of a figure—usually two-dimensional—during a familiarization period. Then, using habituation procedures, the familiar figure is replaced with either an unfamiliar one or the same figure rotated into different orientations or seen from different angles. Generally, by 3 months, infants will dishabituate when a totally novel figure is introduced but not when a different view of the familiar figure is shown (Bornstein, Krinsky, & Benasich, 1986; Caron, Caron, & Carlson, 1979; Fagan, 1979; Gibson, Owsley, Walker, & Megaw-Nyce, 1979; McKenzie, Tootell, & Day, 1980). This means they see the different images as if they were different views of the same figure. If they were just seeing lines, the different orientations of the same figure would appear to the babies to be different figures.

Another procedure is to observe scanning movements made by infants looking at pictures of simple figures, such as circles and squares, drawn with dashed or dotted lines. Infants older than 3 months will scan these figures as if they were drawn with a solid line. If one of the dashed-line elements is

(a) (b)

(c) (d)

Figure 6.6
Stimuli Used in Face Preference Studies

Source: J. L. Dannemiller & B. R. Stephens, A critical test of infant pattern preference models, 1988, p. 212. *Child Development, 59,* 210 –216. Copyright © by The Society for Research in Child Development, Inc.

drawn at an orientation that does not follow the outline of the figure, infants will scan this element more than the other elements that appear to them to be part of a pattern (Van Giffen & Haith, 1984). This means they expect visual patterns to form into a meaningful whole.

By 3 months, infants are able to visually differentiate familiar from unfamiliar faces from a variety of live and photographed faces of mothers compared to unfamiliar women (Barrera & Mauer, 1981; Kurzweil, 1988). Infants of this age prefer looking at faces over nonface stimuli that have been carefully constructed to have exactly the same complexity, brightness, and black-and-white contrasts (Dannemiller & Stephens, 1988) (see Figure 6.6). Remarkably, both 3-month-olds and 6-month-olds prefer to look longer at faces that adults have judged as attractive than at faces adults judged as less attractive (Langlois et al., 1987).

Why should infants prefer faces over other types of visual stimuli? Faces do have clear outlines and moderate complexity. They are composed of closed circular shapes that babies like to look at. Babies seem to prefer shapes that are symmetrical (shapes in which one side is the mirror image of the other). Faces have vertical symmetry, and 3-month-olds prefer vertical symmetry to horizontal symmetry (Bornstein & Krinsky, 1985; Fisher, Ferdinandsen, & Bornstein, 1981).

Is it a fortunate coincidence that faces happen to have just those elements that make them attractive to babies? Or is the visual system designed in such a way that its first preferences direct it toward social objects? It could be that both things are true. We share similar visual systems with other vertebrate species, and most vertebrates have symmetrical faces. Perhaps both faces and visual systems evolved together in relation to each other.

Preference for the face continues to develop throughout the first year of life (Maurer, 1985). Three-month-olds can perceive some facial expressions. They are best at recognizing a smile, particularly if it is a wide, open-mouth smile and if their mothers encourage attention to faces (Kuchuk, Vibbert, & Bornstein, 1986). Not until 6 months, however, do infants become competent at recognizing a variety of specific facial expressions and emotions.

Perception of Moving Objects

One problem with the research presented so far is that most of the test stimuli are drawings or photographs—in other words, static two-dimensional representations. You might think that babies would be more familiar with moving three-dimensional objects and faces and thus might recognize differences between moving objects better than stationary ones.

This seems to be true. Infants at this age look longer at dynamic faces and moving patterns than at static ones (Kaufmann & Kaufmann, 1980; C. A. Samuels, 1985). By 3 or 4 months, infants perceive moving objects as whole units. By 5 months, infants will reach for small moving objects that appear to be in front of larger stationary objects, but do not

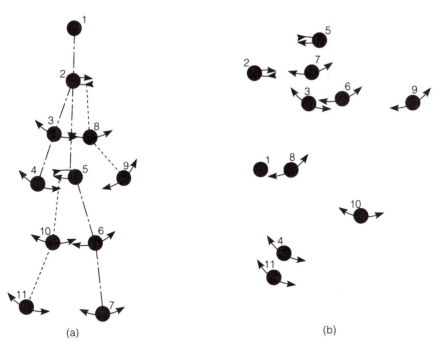

(a)   (b)

Figure 6.7
Motion Perception Stimuli

Panel **(a)** shows a display of eleven point-lights moving as if attached to the head and major joints of a person walking. The arrows drawn through the points represent the perceived motions of the display. Panel **(b)** depicts the scrambled walker display, which is identical to **(a)** except that the relative locations of the point-lights are scrambled. Correspondingly numbered points in the two displays undergo identical motions.

Source: B. I. Bertenthal, D. R. Proffitt, & J. E. Cutting, Infant sensitivity to figural coherence in biomechanical motions, 1984, p. 217. *Journal of Experimental Child Psychology, 37*, 213–230.

reach for small moving objects that are behind the larger object (Van de Walle & Spelke, 1996; Von Hofsten & Spelke, 1985).

By using movement cues, 4-month-old infants are also aware that objects are solid and that they take up their own space. In one study, a platform resembling a drawbridge was rotated back until it hit the top of an object projected on a screen; then the platform stopped. In another condition, the platform kept rotating as if it were passing directly through the solid object. Babies looked longer at the second event, suggesting that they were puzzled by this spatial impossibility (Baillargeon, 1987).

Finally, infants appear to detect complex patterns of motion. Using a "point-light display" technique (Figure 6.7), the movements of a human body walking can be represented by a series of moving lights on the joints. A computer can then invert this light display or move the lights to create displays that would not be biologically possible (joints in incorrect locations and body parts moving in opposite ways). Between 3 and 5 months, infants prefer to look at normal walkers or runners over inverted or biologically impossible ones (Bertenthal,

Proffitt, & Cutting, 1984; Bertenthal, Proffitt, Kramer, & Spetner, 1987; Fox & McDaniels, 1982).

As with the infant's preference for faces, it appears that the perceptual system early in life is disposed to detect real-world information. Infants are able to see whole objects and not just patterns. They are better at detecting relevant information (such as whether the object can be reached and grasped or whether the object is familiar) if they are able to see the object from multiple perspectives and in motion.

Some have suggested that the perception "this is a whole object" is derived from detecting the object's invariant properties as seen from different perspectives (Ruff, 1978; 1985). **Invariance** refers to those aspects of an object that remain the same regardless of how the object is viewed. For example, a ball always has a round shape no matter how you look at it. A cube has sides of equal length and three sides that meet in right-angle corners regardless of which side of the object you are looking at or from what direction. Adults immediately detect the invariances of most simple objects without much thought. It is not clear whether babies do the same or have to puzzle over whether two views of something are indeed the same thing. We also do not know how infants detect invariance (do they compare angles, distances, overall shapes, or what?); but there is no doubt that infants like to seek out invariant properties of objects at a very early age. In other words, the infant is *able* to perceive meaningful wholes because human infants are *predisposed* to finding the similarities and differences between things; no one has to tell a baby to do this.

Auditory Perception

We saw in the last chapter that infant auditory perception is rather good during the first 2 months of life. Infants recognize and prefer their mothers' voices at birth, for example. By 4 months, infants prefer human speech to nonspeech sounds (Fernald, 1985). Four-month-olds also prefer to listen to a speech style that is typically used with young infants, called **infant-directed (ID) speech** (also called **motherese;** see the "Social Development" section in this chapter). Infant-directed speech has a higher pitch and more exaggerated contrasts between high- and low-pitched sounds and is more melodic than speech directed toward adults. These characteristics seem to fit the kinds of listening preferences of infants after the age of 4 months (Colombo, Frick, Ryther, Coldren, & Mitchell, 1995; Cooper, Abraham, Berman, & Staska, 1997; Cooper & Aslin, 1989; 1994; M. Papousek, Bornstein, Nuzzo, Papousek, & Symmes, 1990).

Infants appear to be able to detect different emotions expressed in the voice earlier than they can see differences between facial expressions. Five-month-old infants listen longer to positive compared to negative vocalizations, and they smile more to voices expressing approval and frown more to voices expressing disapproval (Fernald, 1993). Since the babies cannot understand the content of the speech, they must detect the emotional information from the auditory cues alone: pitch, timing, and intensity. The ability to detect emotion from speech improves if the infant can also see the adult's face making an expression that is related to the positivity or negativity of the sounds (Walker-Andrews & Lennon, 1991).

Infants at 4 months like music. When exposed to consonant (as opposed to dissonant) music, they look more in the direction of the sound and become less motorically active, apparently because they are listening more intently (Zentner & Kagan, 1998). Infants like play songs ("Eensy Weensy Spider") and lullabies ("Rock-a-Bye, Baby") better if they are sung directly to them in a loving tone of voice, compared to prerecorded songs (Trainor, 1996; Trainor, Clark, Huntley, & Adams, 1997), suggesting that the song is less important to the infants than the way it is sung to them. Infants also direct more attention to their own bodies when being sung lullabies and more attention to the singer when being sung play songs (Rock, Trainor, & Addison, 1999). Perhaps these traditional melodies were developed over many centuries simply by watching how infants respond to the sounds.

Speed of auditory processing also improves. At birth, infants can recognize sounds and locate sound sources, but only if the sound is repeated many times or is heard for at least 20 seconds. By 3 to 4 months, sounds can be recognized after shorter exposures, and infants can localize the source of briefly heard sound at wider angles from the midline of the body than they could at birth (Aslin, 1987; Jusczyk, Kennedy, & Jusczyk, 1995; Morrongiello, Fenwick, & Chance, 1990). This means that infants at this age appear to process sounds at about the same speed as adults.

Cross-Modal Perception

Infants of this age have **cross-modal perception,** the ability to integrate information coming from at least two sensory modalities. After about 4 months, infants expect sights and sounds to "go together." Infants prefer, for example, to hear a film soundtrack where the visual object's movements and the sound are synchronized, rather than a soundtrack that has been altered (Bahrick, 1988) and they prefer to look at moving faces in which the lips are moving in synchrony with the vocalizations (Patterson & Werker, 1999). Babies prefer to look at visual objects that make a noise compared to silent objects (Lawson & Ruff, 1984). Sound localization is improved by 3 months if the infant has visual cues about the sound source, compared to a sound heard in the dark or made from behind a screen (Morrongiello & Rocca, 1987). Cross-modal perception between vision and touch occurs at about 4 to 6 months, a bit later than between vision and sound, probably because infants do not have exposure to handling objects much before this age (Rose & Ruff, 1987; Streri & Spelke, 1989).

These studies show that by the time infants reach the age of 3 or 4 months, their world is not disjointed. Objects are perceived as coherent wholes. Infants expect the different properties of the same objects to go together, and they will respond by looking away more if things are presented to them in a disjointed form. As we will see later in this chapter, this ability extends beyond object perception to include social communication. When communication patterns are experimentally altered, infants of this age notice the difference and may even become upset.

Cognitive Development

Cognition involves the processing of perceived information. Cognition includes learning and memory and the ability to mentally compare different situations in order to evaluate their similarities and differences. In actuality, since perception involves memory (the comparison of past and present in the detection of the familiar and of invariant properties of objects and sounds) it is often difficult to separate one from the other.

In Chapter 5, cognition was discussed in terms of different information processing steps: perceiving, habituating, learning, and remembering. A number of important developmental changes take place in these areas between the ages of 2 to 5 months. Another way to think about cognition is not as separate information processing steps but as a unified approach to understanding and acting in the environment. This approach is more typical of Piaget's theory of cognitive development in infants (see Chapter 2). In this section, I will first discuss the

developments in habituation and memory as examples of information processing and then describe Piaget's views on infants of this age.

Habituation

From the ages of 2 to 5 months, infants improve in their speed of information processing, due in part to rapid changes in myelination and the formation of synapses and in part to an increasing ability to focus attention on familiar types of tasks. While a newborn could take as long as 5 or ten minutes to habituate to a repeating stimulus, by 3 months of age, infants typically habituate within 1½ to 2 minutes. By 6 months, this time drops to half a minute (Bornstein, 1985). Like all cognitive and perceptual tasks, the speed of information processing also depends on the complexity and difficulty of the stimulus and on the infant's alertness at the time of testing.

There are individual differences in the speed of habituation. Infants who are fast habituators at 3 months are more likely to be fast habituators at 6 months (Colombo, Mitchell, O'Brien, & Horowitz, 1987; Mayes & Kessen, 1989). Infants who are faster habituators tend to have parents who stimulate their ability to focus visual attention (Bornstein & Benasich, 1986). Slower habituators are more likely to have perinatal risk factors, illness, malnutrition, and poor state control (Bornstein, 1985; Moss, Colombo, Mitchell, & Horowitz, 1988), and faster habituators are more efficient in their information processing (Colombo, Mitchell, Coldren, & Freeseman, 1991; Frick, Colombo & Saxon, 1999). Thus, speed of habituation may be used as an early index of cognitive differences. Although these individual differences seem to be fairly good predictors over a period of 4 or 5 months, they are not likely to predict long-term differences in cognitive development.

Long-Term Memory

We saw in the last chapter that infants have short-term memories lasting several hours or days right from birth. By 3 months, infants can remember situations for up to 2 weeks, as was shown using a contingent learning procedure (Sullivan, Rovee-Collier, & Tynes, 1979). Babies were placed supine in cribs with brightly colored mobiles suspended overhead. Experimenters decided beforehand that they would move the mobile if the baby kicked with either the right or the left foot (but not with both feet). The mobile was moved more the harder the infant kicked, thus increasing the speed of conditioning. On the initial training day, the babies were given about 15 to 20 minutes of training. Then the babies were brought back to the same laboratory a few days later and placed in cribs without any further training.

Infants who were tested less than 2 weeks after training managed to repeat the same leg movements they learned during training, although the longer the delay between training and testing, the longer it took the infants to remember to kick in a particular way. After a delay of longer than 2 weeks, infants behaved as if they had never seen the mobile.

If infants are retrained at intervals shorter than 2 weeks, the memory can be reactivated for an indefinite period (Rovee-Collier, Enright, Lucas, Fagan, & Gekoski, 1981). In another study, infants were given a reminder by showing them a mobile 24 hours before 2 weeks had elapsed since their original training. If the mobile was moving, the infants remembered their earlier training when tested the next day, but if the mobile was stationary, the infants could not remember their initial training (Hayne & Rovee-Collier, 1995; Rovee-Collier, Evancio, & Earley, 1995). On the other hand, giving the infants a reminder by showing them a cloth of the same color that had draped the crib during training was just as effective as the moving mobile in helping them to remember the earlier procedure as much as 4 weeks after training (Hayne & Findlay, 1995). These studies suggest that infants can remember for an indefinite period, so long as they continue to receive non-verbal reminders of the early situation (Rovee-Collier & Barr, 2000).

Infant memory, however, is very specific to the situation in which the initial learning occurs. When babies are retested in different cribs, in the same cribs with different colored bumpers, or with different mobiles, they are less likely to remember the event (Butler & Rovee-Collier, 1989). When infants are retested with different odors in the room

or with different music playing, they are also more likely to forget the training (J. Fagen et al., 1997; G. B. Rubin, Fagen, & Carroll, 1998). These findings suggest that familiar, routine environments may be important for infant memory at this age, as they begin to develop a sense of permanence and stability of the world and what to expect from it. The findings also show that infants pick up visual, auditory, and odor cues that become part of the memory for them.

On the other hand, lack of stability in the environment may have negative consequences for cognitive development. Crying and the negative emotion associated with it seem to create a kind of amnesia for experiences associated with the crying (J. W. Fagen, Ohr, Singer, & Klein, 1989). Using a similar mobile-kicking contingent procedure, during training the experimenters substituted a mobile with only 2 components for one with 10 components. Some of the infants cried as a result of this change; others did not. The infants who cried were not able to reactivate the kicking technique to the 10-component mobile even 1 week later. The infants who did not cry when the mobile was changed could easily reactivate the kicking.

Apparently, the emotion associated with a learning situation becomes part of the memory, as do the specific sights, sounds, and smells of the surrounding environment in which the training takes place. This suggests that infants remember whole situations, rather than specific events. Supporting this perspective, one study exposed infants to a mobile in which the pieces had an S symbol and then 24 hours later to a mobile showing a vertical line, I. After 24 hours, the infants recognized a mobile with a dollar sign, $, as well as mobiles with the S and I. This suggests that infants blend their different experiences into a unified memory for the situation (Adler, 1997), which helps them to understand both similarities and differences between situations (Hespos & Rochat, 1997; Needham & Baillargeon, 1998).

These studies suggest that learning and development occur in an integrated way that involves the whole infant, as well as the whole situation in which the learning occurs. These memories can last indefinitely with periodic reminders, but over time, novel aspects of a repeating situation may become integrated into the memory. These findings suggest that infants of this age have a sense of **self-history,** the experience that the past can be connected to the present by means of recreating one's own actions in similar situations.

These findings call for a reevaluation of the common observation that people do not remember their experiences as infants, a phenomenon known as **infantile amnesia.** To remember specific infantile experiences, one would have to be in almost exactly the same situation and the same emotional state as during the original experience. Since older children and adults are unlikely to ever be in exactly the same kinds of situations as when they were infants (primarily because their perceptual, cognitive, emotional, and physical abilities have all changed), they are unlikely to be able to retrieve early memories *for specific events* (Hayne & Rovee-Collier, 1995).

On the other hand, people may in fact have memories of early infancy, but because it is difficult to replicate the exact context, they may be unable to locate the memories in a specific time and place (Rovee-Collier & Barr, 2000). In one study, children who were 2½ years old were retested in a procedure that had required them to reach for objects in the dark when they were 6 months of age. Compared to infants who did not have the experience at 6 months of reaching in the dark, the children who had the experience were better at the task at 2½ years, even though it is unlikely that these children remembered the actual experience of doing this when they were 6 months old (Perris, Myers, & Clifton, 1990).

These studies of infant memory provide support for the idea of *participatory memories* (see Chapter 2) of early infancy, reported by people during somatic awareness and psychotherapeutic encounters. It may be possible to reexperience a feeling, an odor, a body posture, or a pattern of movement without remembering a specific time or place when it first occurred. Even though the specific time and place cannot be remembered, these memories seem to come from a very early period in one's life. When older individuals have memories in which a sense of familiarity is coupled with an amnesia for how, when, and where the memory was acquired, such memories may "feel" babylike. In the "Author's View" section in this chapter, I will discuss my students' reports of such infantile participatory memories that occurred while they were doing the Awareness through Movement lessons.

Piagetian Perspectives on Cognitive Development

The findings on the holistic and integrative way in which infants remember support the theories of Jean Piaget (refer to Chapter 2). Piaget viewed infant actions as adaptations to the environment that involve the whole infant; motor, cognitive, and emotional aspects are interconnected. During the newborn period, which Piaget called sensorimotor Stage I, the majority of the infant's actions are in the form of mostly automatic reflexes. The infant uses reflexes (such as rooting, sucking, and grasping) to adapt to the environment, but reflexes are not rigid and mechanical. We saw in the last chapter that even reflexes can be accommodated to a particular situation, as in sucking on different-shaped nipples or displaying stepping movements only when lying supine.

During the period from about 1 to about 5 months, called sensorimotor Stage II, infants begin to act more purposefully. They are able to recognize the connections between their behavior and events in the environment, as we saw in the research related to making mobiles move when kicking. We know from some studies that even newborns can recognize the connections between their behavior and the environment. For example, infants can be trained using conditioned sucking techniques to suck in a particular way to hear their own mother's voice. However, it takes a long time to train newborns to do this, and the training is not always successful.

By 2 to 3 months, the ability to recognize simple connections between behavior and its effect is very well established and can be seen in almost everything the baby does. Piaget noticed this in each of his own children—Laurent, Lucienne, and Jacqueline. As they discovered the relationship between their behavior and its effects, they would repeat the same behavior many times and often with great delight. Observations 6.1 and 6.2, taken directly from Piaget's observation notes, describe how Laurent at

---

OBSERVATIONS

Stage II Behavior (Piaget, 1952, pp. 70, 79)

Observation 6.1

At 0;2(21), in the morning, Laurent spontaneously bends his head backward and surveys the end of the bassinet from this position. Then he smiles, returns to his normal position and then begins again. . . .

Observation 6.2

In certain special cases the tendency to repeat, by circular reactions, sounds discovered by pure chance, may be observed. Thus at 0;2(12) Lucienne, after coughing, recommences several times for fun and smiles. Laurent puffs out his breath, producing an indefinite sound. At 0;2(26) he reproduces the peals of his voice which ordinarily accompany his laughter, but without laughing and out of pure phonetic interest. At 0;2(15) Lucienne uses her voice in similar circumstances.

---

2 months and 21 days of age repeatedly bends his head back to look at his crib. At about the same age, Lucienne repeatedly coughs for the "fun" of it.

Piaget called these repetitive movements *circular reactions.* During sensorimotor Stage II, the circular reactions described in the box are called **primary circular reactions.** Primary circular reactions are repetitive movements in which the infant focuses on his or her own actions. In some cases, the actions involve other objects (like kicking to get a mobile to move), and in other cases, they involve the infant's own body. The infants at this stage do not appear to be interested in the object for its own sake.

According to Piaget, *the meaning of a particular object or person to the infant is the action and experience the child brings to it.* For example, a rattle means "graspable, seeable, suckable." During this stage of sensorimotor development, the rattle is not yet "an *object* to be grasped, seen, or sucked," for that kind of conceptualization of the rattle as object would require that the infant understand the object as if observing it from outside the self, which does not begin until 8 months of age. In Stage II, the "object" is "known" simply by the actions that can be performed on it. Infant actions are not intended to explore the object's properties but rather to experience their own behavior and its effects. This suggests that infants during this period are developing a sense of **self-agency,** the feeling that they are a causal agent that can successfully affect their own bodies and the environment.

Later in Stage II, infants begin to combine different primary circular reaction schemes into more unified behavior patterns. An example of this is the development of visually guided reaching at about 4 months. Piaget viewed this as the integration of vision, arm, and hand actions: the baby somehow makes the connection between seen objects and his or her own actions. These observations are consistent with the finding that babies of this age have the ability for cross-modal perception and that their memories are integrated wholes of sights, sounds, smells, and movements. This suggests that infants have a sense of **self-coherence,** the feeling that they and the objects around them are integrated wholes that have distinct boundaries.

One aspect of self-agency and self-coherence at this age is the experience of contingency (see Chapter 5). Two-month-olds are capable of discovering contingencies, and one study has shown that the babies enjoy it. In a study done by Watson (1973), the movements of a mobile were linked to infants' head presses on an automatic pillow. If the infants discovered that the mobile would move with respect to their head presses, they usually smiled and cooed. In contrast, if the pillow was "capricious" and inconsistently rewarded head presses, infants became frustrated and distressed. Other research shows that infants are more likely to display these emotions when people behave contingently than when objects behave contingently (Legerstee, 1997).

Once a contingency is discovered, infants come to expect or anticipate a similar pattern in the future. Infants of this age prefer to interact with strangers who have been trained to respond with the same kinds of contingencies as the infant's mother (A. E. Bigelow, 1998). Related research has shown that if infants are exposed to a visual series of repeating events, they can anticipate the likely next event in the sequence (Canfield & Haith, 1991; S. W. Jacobson et al., 1992; Wentworth & Haith, 1992).

These findings have implications for the kinds of experiences adults should provide for infants during Piaget's Stage II. If babies realize that their environment is controllable—that their own actions will produce predictable responses in the people and objects around them—they will show increasing positive involvement with the world. If the environment is capricious, infants will become distressed, angry, and withdrawn or simply uninterested (Watson, 1973). It is important, therefore, for adults to adapt their behavior to be responsive to infants so the infants will gain a sense of efficacy that will lead to further exploration. In early infancy, exploration, cognition, and motor behavior are all part of the same underlying developmental process.

The primary circular reactions create powerful motivations for babies to become engaged in the environment. They especially enjoy when adults create highly ritualized and repetitive situations as in feeding, playing, bathing, and diapering. A limitation of babies of this age is that they do not enjoy deviations from the routines, which makes it difficult for them to adapt quickly to new caregivers. Even though Piaget integrated motor, perceptual, cognitive, and emotional aspects of the infant, he failed to recognize the role of adults in supporting infant development. Even before infants can reach for and manipulate objects, adults bring objects into view, manipulate the objects in appropriate ways (like shaking a rattle and turning a ball around), and place them into the babies' hands (see the earlier discussion of supports and resources for motor development in this chapter). I will return to these interactive systems processes in the section on social development.

Emotional Development

The studies of contingency learning clearly show that the infant's emotions are affected by changes in the contingency of the environment. In this section, I take a closer look at emotional development in terms of three related topics: emotion expression, emotion experience, and emotion regulation. The development of emotional expression involves the study of the behavioral manifestations of emotional experience, the inner world of feelings. Self-control over emotions is called **emotion regulation.**

These three areas of emotional development—expression, experience, and self-regulation—will concern us throughout this book. Many other areas of interest also fall under the general heading of emotional development. These include people's verbal expression of their emotions, their ability to conceptualize their emotions, and their ability to perceive another person's emotions (Fogel, 1982c). These abilities mostly apply to the older infant and young child, and the later chapters of this book will touch on them.

Emotional Expression and Experience

Distress, anger, and wariness. Infants were once thought to have all the basic emotional expressions at birth (Peiper, 1963), but these are reflexive movements that disappear after several weeks. A 1-month-old infant has only a relatively small number of functional expressions, and these are primarily related to the emotion of distress. The expression involves frowning (knitted brows with the mouth turned down at the corners). It usually is accompanied by crying, generally with the eyes closed. Younger infants often exhibit a trembling of the lips during crying, as well as a reddening of the face if the cry is intense enough. Chapter 5 described the different auditory characteristics of the types of crying seen in young infants. Adults have a difficult time categorizing the distress expressions of infants under 4 months into recognizable adult emotions, which suggests that infants do not have a fully differentiated set of adultlike facial expressions (Matias & Cohn, 1993; Oster, Hegley, & Nagel, 1992).

The duration of distress significantly decreases during the first 3 months. In spite of this, adults rate the cries of 6-month-olds as more intense than the cries of younger infants, primarily because the older infants' cries, while shorter in duration, are louder and more energetic (Leger, Thompson, Merritt, & Benz, 1996). After 3 months, infants develop a brief negative-sounding vocalization, usually called *fussing* as distinguished from crying, that accompanies a distress facial expression. Fussing babies usually vocalize for a brief period, then become silent or coo for a while, and then return to fussing (Hopkins & von Wulfften Palthe, 1987). Even though crying lessens in almost all infants over the course of the first year, infants who cried more during the first 3 months, such as those with colic, are likely to cry more on average for the rest of the first year of life (McGlaughlin & Grayson, 1999).

By 4 months, infants may still exhibit intense distress cries, but now they often cry with their eyes open, an expression interpreted as anger. In fact, the longer infants look, the longer they cry, suggesting that the attention may play a feedback role to increase or lessen the anger (Axia, Bonichini, & Benini, 1999; M. D. Lewis, Lamey, & Douglas, 1999). Crying may also be accompanied by directed actions such as kicking, pulling, or pushing, and it may involve few or no tears.

Fear, another expression related to distress, does not appear until later in the first year, but infants at 4 months can show "wary" or hesitant expressions. Infants of this age are capable of turning their heads or looking away from an unpleasant or confusing situation. Their wary or ambivalent expressions consist of an increased rate of gazing away from and looking back at the situation, combined with a reduction of expressions of positive affect (Bronson, 1972; Sroufe, 1979).

Attention and enjoyment. During waking states, infants of 1 month may exhibit a range of expression between alertness and drowsiness. When infants are alert, their eyes are wide and bright, and their brows and mouth may alternate between movement and stillness. During "obligatory attention" episodes, infants may stare motionless for long periods. Infants of this age often fade into brief periods of "dulling." Their eyes, although open and fixed, take on a glazed or dull quality. Smiles usually are not seen during alert states until about 6 weeks of age.

Around the age of 2 months, a significant change can be seen in infants' facial expressions. They are more complex and animated and better coordinated with events in the environment around them (Sroufe, 1995). Attention and enjoyment become differentiated experiences for infants of this age. When smiling, infants look for longer periods and

learn cognitive tasks more slowly than when showing an attentive expression. This shows that positive expressions correspond to a less analytical emotional experience and also that attention is one kind of emotion (Rose, Futterweit, & Jankowski, 1999).

The expressions of attention and enjoyment develop primarily during face-to-face communication with adults. Between 1 and 3 months, one can observe a developmental sequence of facial expressions shown in Figure 6.8. In the first months during face-to-face interaction, infants show primarily simple and concentrated attention. After 2 months, more complex attention expressions, as well as smiling and cooing expressions, appear (Lavelli, 1999; Lavelli & Fogel, 1998). These developments in the expression of attention suggest that the infant is also developing attention-related emotional experiences such as concentration, excitement, and astonishment.

Smiling during face-to-face interaction also develops between 2 and 5 months. Beginning at 3 months, smiling occurs in clusters during social interactions. Infants smile four or five times in rapid succession, followed by a relative pause of 20 or 30 seconds, after which a new bout of smiles begins (Fogel, 1982a). By this age, infants show multiple types of smiles that communicate different types of positive emotional experience. A smile involving the raising of the cheeks and some wrinkling around the eyes (called a Duchenne smile) is observed in the context of mother-infant face-to-face play when the infant is held upright and is able to see the mother smiling and talking (see Figure 6.9). A smile that involves an extremely wide-open mouth and dropping of the jaw (play smile) is observed when infants are held closer to the mother, kissed, or tickled (Messinger, Fogel, & Dickson, 1998). Duchenne smiles appear to be related to visually and cognitively pleasurable events, while play smiles are related more to tactile and physically arousing events. In the period between 2 and 5 months, all types of smiles may occur interchangeably during social play, suggesting that the infant is beginning to experience a complex range of positive feelings (Messinger, Fogel, & Dickson, 1998).

After 2 months of age, infants also begin to express positive emotions through vocalizations. During the first 2 months of life, infants' vocalizations are of three sorts: cry, discomfort, and "vegetative" (Stark, Rose, & McLagen, 1975). The cry is used to

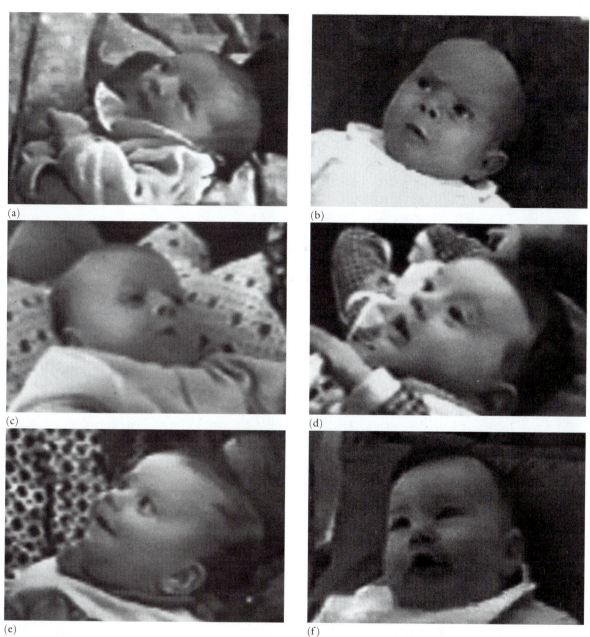

Figure 6.8
Interest and Enjoyment Expressions

(a) Simple attention: Visual fixation in a quiet alert state.
(b) Concentrated attention: Visual fixation with effortful movements of brow and mouth.
(c) Excited attention: Visual fixation with active motor movement of arms, legs, and /or mouth.
(d) Astonished attention: Fascinated and motionless visual fixation.
(e) Smile: Relaxed visual fixation with smiling.
(f) Cooing: Visual fixation, with mouth making the shape of a vocalization, either with or without actual vocalizing.

Source: Manuela Lavelli / University of Verona, Italy

Figure 6.9
Duchenne and Non-Duchenne Smiles

An infant's non-Duchenne smile (on the left) followed approximately 2 seconds later by a Duchenne smile (on the right), in which the cheeks are raised more prominently.

express acute distress, whereas discomfort sounds are associated with distress that is not as severe; they are more like fussing or complaining than crying. The infant's vegetative repertoire includes a series of biological noises, such as the cough, burp, sneeze, hiccup, suck, snort, grunt, and sigh. These sounds are all so basic to the biological necessities of the infant organism that there is very little individual variation across infants, nor do they change much in sound characteristics over time.

Somewhere between 5 and 8 weeks, most infants begin to "coo." As distinguished from the other sounds already in the infant's repertoire, cooing is primarily an expression of comfort. If all the infant's sounds are analyzed with sophisticated sound recording and frequency amplitude–resolving equipment, all the auditory properties of cooing can be found in the more primitive forms of sound making. According to Stark (1978), these findings suggest that infants are beginning to take the sounds they made reflexively and recombine them in the form of exploratory vocal activity. Recalling Lucienne's coughing for fun, we see that infants begin to use their voicing in repetitive ways reminiscent of other circular reactions.

Two kinds of infant non-distress vocalizations appear after 2 months: speechlike and non-speechlike. Speechlike sounds are produced in the front of the mouth and have a more resonant quality. Non-speechlike sounds are produced in the back of the mouth, lack projection, and have a more nasal qual-

ity. Speechlike sounds increase between 2 and 5 months, while non-speechlike sounds decline (Hsu, Fogel, & Cooper, 2000).

According to a dynamic systems theory of emotion (see Chapter 2), emotion is closely related to the social communication system. So, different communicative tasks—different types of play (social-visual versus social-tactile), for example—will require different forms of facial communication and will be accompanied by different types of internal feelings (J. J. Campos, Campos, & Barrett, 1989; Fogel et al., 1992). Just as the infant's cognition is integrated across different perceptual modalities, infants have organized patterns of expressive movements that are integrated across the face, vocalization and body movement that occur in specific types of communicative situations (Lavelli & Fogel, 1998; Weinberg & Tronick, 1994; Yale, Messinger, Cobo-Lewis, Oller, & Eilers, 1999).

Examples of organized patterns of emotion are positive engagement (positive facial expressions and vocalizations, looking at adult or objects, mouthing parts of own body); attentive engagement (facial expressions of attention, looking at adult or objects, mouthing objects); passive withdrawal (facial expressions of sadness, fussy vocalizations); and active protest (facial expressions of anger, fussy and cry vocalizations, pickup requests, and escape movements). These organized patterns are flexible, dynamic, and tied into the communication system. These patterns also show that infants have some control over the type of social and emotional processes in which they participate; that is, they are developing emotion regulation skills.

Development of Emotion Regulation

Emotion regulation, the ability to control one's internal state and outward expression, gradually emerges over the first years of life. During the first 4 months, increases in emotion regulation are shown by several transitions: a decrease in the overall amount of crying, a reduction in the force of obligatory attention, and the mastery of continuous and repeated bouts of smiling.

If emotion regulation works well, it allows the individual to control the negative or overwhelming aspects of a situation without losing touch with it. Although looking away is a total break with something, it is only a momentary one, allowing the baby time to regroup his or her emotional forces for a new assault on the environment. Emotion regulation is shown not merely by looking away but by the overall pattern of looking away and then back in a repeated fashion.

A second important emotion regulation skill that develops in the infant's third month is the smile itself. Studies on the relationship between heart rate changes and the occurrence of smiling have shown that smiles occur neither when the heart rate is increasing nor when it is at its peak but rather when the heart rate is on the decline (Sroufe & Waters, 1976). Smiling is a relaxation response, and it seems to be a way of reducing arousal without turning away from the situation. On the other hand, after particularly intense smiles, 5-month-olds may need to look away from the situation, an indication that with intense positive emotion, multiple emotion regulation strategies may be required (Stifter & Moyer, 1991).

While infants are developing new ways to maintain attention during periods of emotional arousal, they also are widening the range of arousal levels they can tolerate. At the upper end of arousal, the 1-month-old is able to tolerate stimulation only if it is gentle and slowly changing, whereas the 3-month-old can handle a wider variety of stimulation with

Figure 6.10
Hand-to-Mouth Activity

Source: E. Thelen & A. Fogel, Toward an action-based theory of infant development, 1989, p. 51. In J. Lockman & N. Hazen (Eds.), *Action in a social context: Perspectives on early development*, 23 – 63. New York: Plenum Press. Reprinted by permission.

more abrupt changes, such as a highly animated, talking adult.

A final contribution to emotion regulation is the baby's developing sensorimotor skills. During this period, the ability of infants to regulate their own distress improves as they can reach for objects and hold them without dropping them (Kopp, 1989). In relation to hand-to-mouth activity, discussed in the last chapter, infants can calm themselves down after 4 months, when they can reliably get the hand to the mouth and keep it there while engaged in other activities, as shown in Figure 6.10 (Thelen & Fogel, 1989; Toda & Fogel, 1989). During experimental perturbations of the mothers' behavior (see the "Experimental Disturbances of Interactions" section below), 6-month-olds, but not 3-month-olds, were able to retain their composure by putting their hands in their mouths or focusing their visual attention on what their hands were doing (usually exploring their clothing or the infant seat) (Toda & Fogel, 1993).

Researchers are gradually beginning to recognize that young infants use their whole bodies in emotion expressions and emotion regulations. Emotion regulation derives from the use of some nonemotional action pattern (like reaching for objects) to help the baby calm down when upset (J. J. Campos, Campos, & Barrett, 1989; Kopp, 1989). On the other hand, reaching for objects and other sensorimotor skills bring the infant into contact with situations never before encountered. The ability to reach generates new pleasures and also new sources of frustration. In this sense, emotion and emotion regulation are not mere responses to the situation but also represent the baby's goals in the situation (J. J. Campos, Campos, & Barrett, 1989).

Thus, by about 4 or 5 months, emotions and their regulation are future oriented and depend in part on motivations, memories, and cognitive expectancies. The role of the adults should not be forgotten. Often caregivers can provide just the right support that, when combined with the infant's own abilities, results in a spontaneous relaxation. Adults can also introduce new objects or challenge the baby to learn new social routines and games. These then become part of the baby's future orientation. We can better understand, in this case, why a baby is happy when a familiar game is repeated many times and why a baby gets upset if adults fail to play by the rules. From a dynamic systems view, when we take account not only of facial expression but also of other infant actions and cognitions as well as the actions of adults, we may see more clearly the conditions conducive to emotion regulation (Fogel & Thelen, 1987). We can also see that emotional expressions are never simply a response, but are part of a dynamic flow of action and feeling that moves the baby from the present situation into a desired future one.

Social Development

Infants of this age show the widest range of emotion expressions primarily in the company of adults. By the age of 2 months, infants make distinctly different actions toward adults compared to other animate stimuli. For example, infants are more likely to smile, vocalize, and make relaxed arm movements with responsive adults than with peers (Fogel, 1979), inanimate faces (Field, 1979a), or animate or inanimate toys (Ellsworth, Muir, & Hains, 1993; Legerstee, 1991, 1992; Legerstee, Pomerleau, Malcuit, & Feider, 1987).

First, I will examine the effects of infants on adult behavior and some cultural differences in adult behavior. Next, I will discuss how adult behavior affects infants.

The Effect of Infants on Adult Behavior

Exaggeration. With young infants, adults tend to exaggerate particular aspects of their speech and body movement. Facial expressions are made larger than usual, as in mock surprise and mock sadness. Adults shake and nod their heads in deliberate movements. When speaking, adults raise the pitch of their voices and have wider variations in pitch than when speaking to other adults. This has been found in a large number of different cultures (Fernald & Kuhl, 1987; Fernald & Simon, 1984; J. L. Jacobson, Boersma, Fields, & Olson, 1983; M. Papousek, Papousek, & Bornstein, 1985; Stern, Spieker, Barnett, & MacKain, 1983). Even in languages in which the pitch of a syllable conveys linguistic meaning—tonal languages such as Mandarin Chinese—researchers have found overall increases of pitch when adults talk to babies compared to other adults (Grieser & Kuhl, 1988).

Slowing down and simplification. A second aspect of adult behavior with young infants is the tendency to slow down and simplify behavior. Each action, such as a head nod or a facial expression, is held for a longer period with an infant than with another adult. In addition, when talking to infants, adults leave longer pauses between their individual actions (Fernald & Simon, 1984; M. Papouseket al., 1985; C. E. Snow, 1977; Stern, 1977). Adults prolong particular syllables and speak more slowly overall, giving their speech a melodic or singsong quality (M. Papousek & Papousek, 1981). Similarly, adults reduce the complexity of their behavior and their speech when talking to infants, using single words instead of sentences or simple actions, such as a single head nod and a wide smile.

Rhythm and repetition. Adults also use highly repetitive and rhythmic activities. They may say the same word or phrase many times with minor variations or make a series of exaggerated head nods punctuated with a clap or a vocalization. Different rhythms are used depending upon the purpose of the behavior (soothing versus attention getting) and the baby's responsiveness to the adult (Fogel, 1977; H. Papousek & Papousek, 1987).

Parental speech to infants contains characteristic melodies that are related to ordinary tasks of parent-infant communication. For example, adults use different melodic contours to prohibit, elicit attention, encourage infant participation, encourage imitation, approve, and soothe. Furthermore, these melodies are similar in many different languages, including tonal languages such as Chinese (M. Papousek, 1994; M. Papousek, Papousek, & Symmes, 1991).

When applied to speech, exaggeration, slowing down, rhythm, and melody make up a package that investigators have called **infant-directed (ID) speech** or more commonly, *motherese*. Not only does it appear to occur in many different languages, but babies actually prefer to listen to motherese compared to normal adult speech (Fernald, 1985). The features of motherese even appear in deaf mothers using signed languages. One study found that a mother's signs to an infant, compared to signing to another adult, are significantly slower in tempo, are repeated more frequently, and use exaggerated movements related to each sign (Masataka, 1992). Mothers of deaf infants exaggerate their nonverbal and facial behaviors when with their infants, although they also exaggerate their directiveness and control over the infants (Koester, 1994). Similar patterns of motherese appear in lullabies. When lullaby melodies from different areas of the world were played without words to adults who were unfamiliar with those particular lullabies, the adults could differentiate them from songs not meant to be sung to infants (Trehub, Unyk, & Trainor, 1993). There are only a few cultures, such as the Quiche Maya in Guatemala, where motherese has not been observed in adult speech (Pye, 1986).

Matching and attunement. A large share of adult behavior is aimed at matching or imitating the infant's behavior. Although infants can imitate adults, adults imitate babies much more. This imitation may involve matching infant vocal sounds, pitches, rhythms, facial expressions, body movements, and so on (Malatesta & Haviland, 1982; Moran, Krupka, Tutton, & Symons, 1987; H. Papousek & Papousek, 1987). A concept related to matching is **attunement** (Stern, 1985), in which the adult's behavior is similar to the infant's but not an exact copy. For example, the infant may shake his or her arm up and down in a rhythmical motion. The parent may respond in a different modality, such as vocalizing "yea-yea-yea-yea" in exactly the same rhythm as the baby's arm movements.

Turn taking. Adults also engage in turn-taking behavior with babies. In the early months, infants do not yet have a concept of turn taking. Adults fill in the natural pauses of the infant's actions with their own actions, creating the appearance of turn taking (Brazelton, Koslowski, & Main, 1974; J. Cohn & Tronick, 1988; Fogel, 1977; Trevarthen, 1977). This adult-controlled pattern of turn taking has been called **protoconversation** (M. C. Bateson, 1975; Trevarthen, 1977). During this early period, adults often overlap their vocalizations and actions with those of the infant, creating a sense of shared emotion, as when adults vocalize at the same time the baby is cooing (G. P. Ginsburg & Kilbourne, 1988; Stern, Jaffe, Beebe, & Bennett, 1975).

Between 4 and 6 months, infants begin to shift to a more interactive mode of behavior: they learn to wait until the adult pauses before beginning their own actions. Infants appear to take the initiative more often by looking in the mother's direction and waiting until she responds before smiling or vocalizing (J. Cohn & Tronick, 1988; Kaye & Fogel, 1980). By about 5 months, then, infants are beginning to become true social partners rather than merely appreciative audiences for the display of motherese.

These developmental changes in infants coupled with the special features of infant-directed adult behavior create regularly recurring communication routines called **frames** (Fogel, 1993). Some of the frames that emerge during this period are social games like face-to-face play, tickle and other tactile games, peekaboo, and frames for playing with toy objects. There are also frames for caregiving such as bedtime, bathing, and feeding routines. Frames are the natural result of everyday communication (see the "Co-Regulating with Baby" section for more details). While some frames are similar between families (see the section on cultural differences below), parents and infants often develop frames that are unique to their relationship and give it a special meaning and sense of familiarity for the participants.

The effects of individual differences between infants on adults. Just as infants prefer to listen to adults making infant-directed speech, adults prefer infant vocalizations that are relaxed and resonant and have greater pitch contours. These types of sounds are considered more speechlike (K. Bloom, D'Odorico, & Beaumont, 1993; K. Bloom & Lo, 1990). With Eva Nwokah, I studied when and why mothers laugh at their infants (Nwokah & Fogel, 1993). Table 6.3 summarizes reasons for maternal laughter with infants between the ages of 2 and 12 months. Unlike other vocalizations, maternal laughter occurs at times when mothers are particularly enjoying their babies and thus may reflect a deep sense of appreciation for specific aspects of infant behavior. As Table 6.3 shows, mothers especially enjoy it when the infant discovers something new or masters a skill, smiles or laughs, or plays a game with her, or when the mother perceives her own behavior as funny or enjoyable.

Adults are drawn to facial features that have baby-like characteristics, such as large eyes, a round face, thin eyebrows, and a small nose bridge (Zebrowitz & Montepare, 1992). Individual differences in infant facial attractiveness affect maternal behavior. In a study of newborns and 3-month-olds, mothers were more affectionate and playful if their infants were judged by adult raters to be attractive. Mothers with less attractive infants were more attentive to other people besides the infant and were more likely to spend time in caretaking routines rather than affectionate behavior. These differences were not as strong at 3 months as they were at birth. In a related study, mothers of 6-month-olds expected less attractive infants to be more developmentally advanced (Langlois, Ritter, Casey, & Sawin, 1995; Ritter, Casey, & Langlois, 1991). Mothers of infants

Table 6.3   Summarized Descriptions of Probable Causes of Maternal Laughter

1. *Onset of infant behavior or facial expression.* Child produces a change in bodily posture, movement, or facial expression, e.g., smiling, banging a toy, or tilting the head.

2. *Onset of infant vocalization.* Child produces a sound, string of sounds, words, or phrase, excluding those related to bodily functions such as a sneeze or cough.

3. *Onset of infant laughter.* Child laughs aloud with a long or short laugh and accompanying active smile facial expression.

4. *Premastery.* Child strives to achieve a goal such as standing up, holding a large object, or holding two objects at a time, but does not succeed.

5. *Social games.* A game is a playful social interaction in which a behavior is repeated more than twice. Games are characterized by repetition, nonliterality, mutual involvement, and usually turn alternation. At an early age, mutual involvement may be only attentiveness, and turn alternation may be minimal. There is almost always a lack of negative affect.

6. *Maternal interaction.* The mother engages in any playful social activity, such as shaking a toy near the infant or tickling him or her, that is not repeated more than twice.

7. *Other.* Includes mastery achievement such as walking for the first time, no apparent cause, reaction to a continued infant state such as sleeping, and mother laughing at her own joke or comment.

Source: E. Nwokah & A. Fogel, 1993.

with cleft lip and cleft palate are less sensitive and more directive with their infants compared to mothers of normal infants (Koomen & Hoeksma, 1992).

Gender differences between infants also affect adult behavior, at least in middle-class white North American and northern European families. When talking to girls, both mothers and fathers are more likely to comment on the present situation and the infant's current state. Comments about absent or future events are more common when parents talk with boys. Parents use first names more when talking to boys compared to girls (Pecheux, Labrell, & Pistorio, 1993). Mothers of male infants stimulate them more in general, while mothers of girls are more likely to stroke and caress their infants (Grant, 1994). Apparently gender-typical socialization can begin very early in life.

Even at birth, babies differ from each other in emotional responsivity and social behavior. Some babies have highly expressive facial and body movements, and others are relatively poker-faced or inexpressive (Field, Greenberg, Woodson, Cohen, & Garcia, 1984; N. A. Fox, 1985; Lipsitt, 1981). Such differences can be found throughout the first year of life (Stifter, Fox, & Porges, 1989). I will discuss these differences in infant temperament in more detail in Chapter 7.

Some research has shown that the infants who are less expressive are actually more aroused by stimulation than the more expressive infants. The low-expressive infants tend to have higher overall heart rates, higher cortisol (a hormone related to arousal), and higher muscle tension (Field, 1987; N. A. Fox & Davidson, 1988; Kagan, Reznick, & Snidman, 1987). These children have been referred to as *inhibited*, because they are physiologically predisposed to be highly responsive to stimulation but tend to withdraw from stimulation rather than express signs of engagement or enjoyment. Very similar patterns of individual differences have been observed in infant monkeys (Suomi, 1987).

It is clear that babies make some contribution to how others respond to them. A baby who is easily aroused is likely to withdraw from social interaction rather quickly. Adults often overreact to this withdrawal by trying even more aggressively to get the baby's attention, which in turn causes the baby to withdraw even more (Field, 1987; Gianino & Tronick, 1988). Under most circumstances, adults are highly attuned to the baby's responses. Most adults, regardless of age or parenting experience, are able to correctly identify an infant's state just by hearing the sounds the baby makes in each state (M. Papousek, 1989). On the other hand, if infants are persistently difficult to handle, mothers rate their own self-efficacy as parents lower than mothers whose infants are not so difficult (Teti & Gelfand, 1991). When communicating with infants, it is important for adults to be aware of their own emotions and the effects of those emotions on their behavior, as described in the "Co-regulating with Baby" section of this chapter.

In summary, adult behavior is consistently different toward boys and girls, toward attractive and unattractive infants regardless of gender, and toward infants differing in expressiveness. These findings are not surprising if one thinks about Western culture, which encourages independence, values different attributes in boys and girls, and promotes an abstract ideal of beauty in its products and practices (just look at the infants in any advertisement for baby products or, for that matter, at any adult models used in commercial advertisements). Perhaps the surprising point is that these cultural ideals begin to be instilled as early as the first months of life. In the next section, I turn to the topic of cultural differences.

Cultural Differences in Adult Behavior toward Infants

We have already mentioned that some aspects of motherese may be universally seen in all cultures. In general, because babies are similar around the world, we can expect them to elicit similar sorts of behavior from adults. On the other hand, there are some interesting cultural differences in adult-infant communication.

We have already seen how some African mothers interact with their babies using a large variety of postural manipulations and motor exercise. In a study of infant development in Nigeria, Elauma infants were compared to a group of infants in Oxford, England (Whiten & Milner, 1986). The Elauma are hunter-gatherers. At 3 months of age, Elauma infants spend almost all their time, whether awake or asleep, in physical contact with an adult or within three feet of the adult. When the Elauma infants cry, they are responded to more often and more quickly than are the English babies, and the response from the adult is more likely to be physical than verbal. The Elauma infant is more a part of the mother's everyday life. She carries the baby around with her, and babies often ride on the mothers' backs or sit in their laps while the mothers go about their daily chores. The babies sleep next to their mothers.

The pattern of close physical contact and rapid response to crying is common among hunting and gathering cultures worldwide (Konner, 1977). Hunter-gatherer groups move camps several times per year. They are egalitarian with respect to age

Table 6.4 Examples of Baby Talk Used by Japanese Mothers

English Equivalent	Adult Speech	Baby Talk	Explanation
Are you hungry?	Onaka suita?	Onaka shuita	Phonological change
Let's play	Asobimashoo	Achobimachoo	Phonological change
Please	Doozo	Doojo	Phonological change
Eye	Me	Meme	Duplication
It hurts	Itai	Itai-tai	Duplication
Get up	Okiru	Okki	Shortening
Hiccup	Shakkuri	Hikku hikku	Mimic sound of action
Lamp	Denki	Denki-san	Use of honorific
Dirty	Katanai	Batchii	Entirely new word

Source: S. Toda, A. Fogel, & M. Kawai, Maternal speech to three-month-old infants in the United States and Japan, 1990, p. 287. *Journal of Child Language, 17,* 279–294.

and gender differences and have little political hierarchy. In one study, a hunter-gatherer group (the Aka) was compared with a neighboring agricultural group (the Ngandu) in Central Africa. The Ngandu are sedentary farmers with strong chiefs and clear inequalities in age and gender roles. In the Aka, men and women contribute equally to infant care and other tasks. Roles are divided along traditional lines in the Ngandu. The Ngandu have more infant care devices, the infants wear more clothing, and are more likely to be physically separate from their mothers compared to the Aka. The Ngandu mothers are more likely to let their infants fuss or cry. Like mothers in the urban cultures, they tend to use more distal play and object play with their babies (Hewlett, Lamb, Shannon, Leyendecker, & Schölmerich, 1998). This study shows that differences in infant care are not due simply to urban versus rural factors, or Western versus non-Western, but rather to differences in lifestyle. The more egalitarian society, used to equality and sharing of resources, seems to promote closer and more lasting contact with the infant.

Japanese mothers also react in different ways to their babies than North American mothers. Japanese mothers spend less time in physical contact with their babies than American mothers when the babies are awake, although Japanese babies sleep with their mothers at night. American mothers hold, rock, bounce, touch, and kiss their babies considerably more than Japanese mothers, and when interacting with babies, American mothers hold their faces closer to the babies (Caudill & Weinstein,

1969; Fogel, Toda, & Kawai, 1988; Otaki, Durrett, Richards, Nyquist, & Pennebaker, 1986; Shand & Kosawa, 1985).

When they verbalize to babies, Japanese and American mothers are quite different. Over the course of an entire day, Japanese mothers tend to use more negative vocalizations, such as prohibitions and expressions of negative feelings. When actually engaged in a playful interaction with their babies, Japanese mothers use more nonsense sounds and more baby talk, as shown in Table 6.4, while American mothers use more complete sentences and more recognizable adult words. When an American mother might use vocalizations to get her baby's attention, a Japanese mother either uses vocal noises or makes noise with her hands, like clapping and finger snapping (Bornstein, Tal, et al., 1992; Fogel, Toda, & Kawai, 1988; Toda, Fogel, & Kawai, 1990). American mothers are more likely to label objects, while Japanese mothers are more likely to talk about how to incorporate objects into social play (Fernald & Morikawa, 1993).

Navajo mothers rarely talk to infants, although they are responsive to babies' cries and touch the babies a great deal. Traditional Navajo keep babies more physically distant from their mothers with the use of cradle boards (Callaghan, 1981; J. S. Chisholm, 1983). Similar patterns of behavior have been observed among the Maya Indians of Mexico (Brazelton, 1977).

In the Japanese and Native American cultures, adults believe, as did the 17th-century European romantics, that infants are precious and innocent

Table 6.5 Hindu Beliefs about the Stages of Infancy and Childhood

Stage	Mode of Relationship	Ritual Performed at the End of the Stage
Garbha (fetus)	Symbolic	Jatakama: Birthing ritual
Ksheerda (infancy)	Dyadic intimacy (0–1 month)	Namakarana: Naming ceremony; the child meets the father and siblings for the first time
	Dyad in family (1–4 months)	Nishakarmana: First outing, first look at the sun and moon
	Dyad in world (4–8 months)	Annaprasana: Introduction to solid foods, weaning from the breast
Ksheerannada	Dyad dissolution (8 months–3 years)	Chudakarana: First ritual cutting of (early childhood) the hair

Source: P. Sharan, One view of the cultural context for the study of childrearing in India, 1988, p. 8. *Newsletter of the International Society for the Study of Behavioral Development, 13*, 1–8.

beings who are close to God, and that they should generally be kept quiet and not influenced by adults until they begin to make some of their own initiatives, around the age of 6 months. This "hands-off" respect for the infant's autonomy and individuality is not found in the West. Influenced by John Locke's 17th-century idea of empiricism, we try to affect sleeping, feeding, and interactive social behavior from an early age. We want our babies to be scheduled, to smile at us, and not to cry (Fogel, Stevenson, & Messinger, 1992). American and European adults especially like to encourage independence through didactic (teaching) behaviors leading to infant socialization (Bornstein, Tamis-LeMonda, et al., 1992).

The East Asian (Indian) philosophy of child rearing is summed up in the elaborate rituals performed for infants in Hindu culture in India (see Table 6.5). Indian families tend to keep the babies quiet and introduce them very gradually to the world. This introduction does not begin in earnest until 6 to 9 months, when early childhood is considered to begin. Indian mothers talk to and touch their babies more than the Japanese. Infant massage is commonly practiced in India, and even the mothers receive regular massage from their female relatives.

Some of the recent interest in somatic awareness and touch therapies in North America and Europe has been adapted from ancient Indian somatic practices such as Yoga, Buddhist meditation, and massage. Chinese and Japanese somatic awareness methods such as tai chi, judo, kendo, and zen also have their origins in ancient Indian culture.

The Effects of Adult Behaviors on Infants

We do not know to what extent the parent's use of motherese and related verbal and nonverbal baby-directed communication actually contributes to infant social and emotional development. A large number of studies have documented correlations between mother behavior during social interaction and infant behavior at the same age and also at later ages. Unfortunately, it is impossible to determine whether these correlations result from the effects of the parents on the infants or from differences between infants that may affect the way the parents behave.

Some research, however, asks mothers to modify their normal behavior with their infants so that the effect of such changes on the infants can be assessed. These studies reveal that beginning at 2 months of age, babies seem highly sensitive to how others interact with them.

The effect of adult contingent responsiveness. Contingency refers to the responsiveness of the adult to the infant's behaviors. A contingent response is an appropriate one that immediately follows some infant action, like a maternal smile following an infant's smile. When responses are contingent, infants tend to smile, coo, and look more at the adults. When responses are noncontingent, infants fuss, cry, or look away (P. J. Dunham, Dunham, Hurshman, & Alexander, 1989; Legerstee, 1997; Symons & Moran, 1987). Infants also look and smile more when adults are producing the kinds of exaggerated behavior described earlier, such as motherese (Cooper, Abram, Berman, & Staska, 1997).

Experimental disturbances of play frames. The infant's reaction to contingent responsiveness can also be assessed by experimentally perturbing inter-action sequences during normal play frames. In one type of study, infants and mothers play face-to-face games with each other, but instead of actually being face-to-face, they are each viewing a videotaped im-age of the other. Under these conditions, the in-fants respond normally. The researchers then show the infant a videotape of the mother playing with the infant that was made on an earlier occasion. In this condition, the mother's behavior is more or less the same, but she is no longer responding contin-gently to the infant. When this occurs, infants de-crease the amount of smiling and gazing at the television monitor compared to when they were interacting "live" (Hains & Muir, 1996; L. Murray & Trevarthen, 1985; Nadel, Carchon, Kervella, Marcelli, & Plantey-Reserbat, 1999).

In another type of study, peekaboo games are played with infants, some in the normal way and other times in a disorganized way, such as by saying "peekaboo" before covering the face. Once again, infants smile and gaze more when the frame is or-ganized in the expected way compared to the dis-organized play (Rochat, Querido, & Striano, 1999).

In another type of study procedure used with ba-bies between 2 and 5 months, the mother is asked to play with and talk to her baby as she might do at home. After several minutes of positively toned play, the experimenter asks the mother to perturb her behavior by ceasing to talk and holding her face in a neutral, nonexpressive pose. This is called the **still-face** procedure. In other studies, mothers are asked to simulate depression during the perturba-tion period.

What do babies do when confronted with this unexpectedly unresponsive mother? Some babies continue to smile and look at the mother for a few seconds; then they stop smiling and look away from the mother for increasingly longer periods of time. If the distorted mother behavior goes on for more than a few minutes, the baby becomes increasingly distressed and withdrawn. When mothers are asked to resume their normal interactions, most of the in-fants begin to cry if they have not cried already, per-haps with the intent to communicate the prior dis-tress (J. F. Cohn & Elmore, 1988; J. F. Cohn & Tronick, 1983; Toda & Fogel, 1989; Tronick, Als, Adamson, Weise, & Brazelton, 1978). The same effects are observed in different cultures (Kisilevsky et al., 1998) and with both mothers and fathers (Braungart-Rieker, Garwood, Powers, & Notaro, 1998; Kisilevsky et al., 1998).

At the age of 3 to 4 months, infants are more dis-tressed at the still face than at separation from the mother (Field, Vega-Lahr, Scafidi, & Goldstein, 1986). Babies get equally upset if the still face is posed by the live mother or an image of the mother over closed-circuit television, but there is no change in the infants' behavior if the television mother con-tinues to be expressive while the sound is turned off (Gusella, Muir, & Tronick, 1988). Apparently, it is the sight of the unresponsive mother, rather than the absence of the mother, that is upsetting to the babies.

In another variant of the procedure, mothers are allowed to touch their infants while maintaining the still face. In this case, the effect of the still face on the infant is significantly less noticeable. When be-ing touched during the still face, infants continue to smile and gaze, at both the mothers' hands and face (Stack & Arnold, 1998; Stack & LePage, 1996; Stack & Muir, 1992). Therefore, touching can compensate for the sight of an unresponsive mother. If both of the infant's parents are present and the parent with whom the infant is interacting is asked to perform a still-face, the infant turns to the other parent and begins to interact normally (Fivaz-Depeursinge & Corboz-Warnery, 1999). Fi-nally, if mothers are more contingently responsive during the normal play episodes, infants recover more quickly following the still-face episode (Kogan & Carter, 1996).

These studies reveal that infants are certainly sen-sitive to changes in contingency and breaks in com-munication frames. In addition, infants also seem to be able to recover from such breaks via simple in-terventions such as having access to touch or to an-other adult. More serious effects on the infants are seen when parental unresponsiveness goes on for a long period of time and there is no one else to whom the infant can turn.

The effects of maternal depression on infants.
Some of the effects of lasting maternal nonresponsiveness on infants are seen with maternal depression. Compared to normal psychological states and to other psychological problems, depression has the strongest effect on infants since its main symptom is a lack of emotionality. Depressed people are not merely sad; rather, they are characterized by a flat emotional tone and preoccupation with themselves. These factors make depressed mothers less responsive as parents, which can be a major problem, since severe depression occurs in 10 to 12% of women following childbirth (Field, 1987).

Depressed mothers with infants under 6 months of age do not use the exaggerated and positive actions typical of normal mothers (Bettes, 1988; Campbell, Cohn, & Meyers, 1995; Kaplan, Bachorowski, & Zarlengo-Strouse, 1999); they are less affectionate and show more negative forms of touch such as poking and pulling (Fleming, Ruble, Flett, & Shaul, 1988; Malphurs, Raag, Field, Pickens, & Pelaez-Nogueras, 1996); they are not often contingently responsive to their babies (Bettes, 1988; Donovan, Leavitt, & Walsh, 1998; Field et al., 1985; Zlochower & Cohn, 1996); they rate their infant's behavior more negatively than nondepressed mothers (Field, Morrow, & Adelstein, 1993; Field, Grizzle, Scafidi, & Schanberg, 1996; C. R. Fox & Gelfand, 1994); or they alternate between disengagement and intrusiveness (J. F. Cohn, Matias, Tronick, Lyons-Ruth, & Connell, 1986).

Depressed mothers have trouble tracking the activities of their infants and may fail to protect them from potential dangers by letting the babies fall off their laps, for example, or letting them get into electrical equipment. Compared to nondepressed mothers, depressed mothers report having more parenting stress, more daily hassles, less marital satisfaction, and less social support (C. R. Fox & Gelfand, 1994; Gelfand & Teti, 1990; Gelfand, Teti, & Fox, 1992; Simons, Lorenz, Wu, & Conger, 1993).

Infants of depressed mothers are more likely to be fussy, to show more negative facial expressions, to have low levels of physical activity, and to be withdrawn. They orient less to their mothers and gaze less at them compared to infants of nondepressed mothers. Infants of depressed mothers also have higher levels of circulating stress hormones as well as asymmetries in brain activity indicative of a withdrawn mood state. These patterns can be seen even when these infants interact with nondepressed adults (J. F. Cohn et al., 1986; J. F. Cohn, Campbell, Matias, & Hopkins, 1990; Dawson et al., 1999; Field et al., 1985; Field et al., 1988; Field, Healy, & LeBlanc, 1989; S. Hart, Field, Letourneau, & Del Valle, 1998; N. A. Jones et al., 1997; Pickens & Field, 1995).

There is some controversy, however, about the consequences of maternal mental illness for the infant. Most of the studies showing infant depression when interacting with nondepressed adults have used adults who are unfamiliar to the infant, which could account for the less than positive behavior of the infants. When infants of depressed mothers are observed interacting with their nondepressed fathers or with familiar nursery school teachers, these infants do not show signs of depression (Hossain et al., 1994; Pelaez-Nogueras, Field, Cigales, Gonzalez, & Clasky, 1994). A large-scale demographic study of 262 families found no significant effects of maternal mental illness on infant behavior at 4 and 12 months (Seifer, Sameroff, Anagnostopolou, & Elias, 1992). Effects on infants are more likely to show up if their mothers remain depressed over many years and if the infants have few opportunities to interact regularly with nondepressed adults.

Unfortunately, the causes of depression are not well understood, and treatments are slow and not always successful. Clinical depression, on the other hand, has no higher rate of occurrence for postpartum women than for non-childbearing women. Depression can occur for a variety of reasons, most of which are poorly understood. Since infants and children of depressed mothers are at increased risk, these mothers should be under some form of psychological or psychiatric treatment.

A number of intervention programs have become available to help mothers who are depressed. We have already seen that nondepressed family members can make a significant difference in the positive development of infants. One type of program teaches depressed mothers to focus on child-care tasks, to pay attention to the needs of their infants, and to use touch in addition to facial and vocal behavior (Field et al., 1985; Gelfand & Teti, 1990; Leitch, 1999; Pelaez-Nogueras, Field, Hossain, & Pickens, 1996). Another type of intervention program focuses on increasing positive moods in the mothers and infants. This can be accomplished either by giving infants and/or their mothers daily massages or by using music therapy (Field, 1998; Field, Grizzle, Scafidi, F., & Schanberg, 1996). Sensitive touch, apparently, can partially alleviate the effects of negative mood for mothers and for infants during periods of maternal unavailability.

In summary, during play frames, parents modify their behavior in a way that infants can most readily appreciate and infants' smiling and gazing encourage the parents to continue. During everyday communication, the mutual influence is co-regulated and dynamic. The effects of one partner on the other can only be determined by looking at individual differences between infants (such as infants who are difficult) or between parents (such as maternal depression) or during experimental perturbations of adult behavior. During the process of interacting with people and objects, infants are beginning to develop a new sense of themselves called the ecological self.

Putting It All Together: The Sense of an Ecological Self

We know that infants of this age perceive objects and people as coherent wholes. They perceive familiar patterns of interaction—frames—as coherent wholes, and they get upset when those patterns are altered. We also learned that infants of this age practice a form of self-exploration, the primary circular reactions by which they feel themselves move and act. Given these abilities, can young infants perceive themselves as a coherent entity?

The traditional test of self-recognition is done by secretly putting a spot of red makeup (rouge) on the infant's forehead and placing the infant in front of a mirror. Touching the red spot while looking in the mirror is taken as evidence that the infant recognizes his or her own image in the mirror. Infants do not pass this rouge test of mirror self-recognition until 18 months (see Chapter 10).

Many infancy researchers now believe that infants between 2 and 5 months can also recognize themselves as separate and whole individuals, but not by their image in a mirror. How is this possible? Infants under 6 months of age have what is called

an **ecological self.** This conclusion is based on some of the research I have already reviewed on infant perception, cognition, emotion, and social behavior. The ecological self has four basic features (Kaye, 1982; Neisser, 1991; Stern, 1985).

1. *Self-agency* is the sense that one is capable of generating one's own actions and expecting that these self-generated actions will have consequences, such as the sense that it gets dark when the eyes are closed or the arm moves when one wants it to move.

2. *Self-coherence* is the sense of being a whole physical entity with boundaries and limitations, such as sensing the difference between touching someone or something and being touched by someone.

3. *Self-affectivity* is the sense of having inner emotional feelings that routinely go together with specific experiences, such as feeling happy when one's mother approaches and sad when she leaves.

4. *Self-history* is the sense of enduring, of having a past, of going on even through changes, as when one acts and feels in similar ways with familiar people or in familiar situations.

Each of these four aspects of the ecological self is experienced *in relation to* something else. One senses self-coherence, for example, by feeling where one's own body ends and where the environment begins. According to ecological systems theory, an ecology is a system of relationships, as in the ecosystem of plants and animals. Plants and animals cannot live without each other. They exchange oxygen and carbon dioxide. Animals eat plants and plants depend upon animals (worms and insects) to decompose their remains to create soils in which the plants can grow. So, while plants and animals are mutually interdependent, they each have their boundaries and can be identified one from the other.

Infants (and adults) can see some part of their own bodies—their nose, at a minimum—at all times in their field of vision. You can check this by closing one eye and looking straight ahead: you will see your nose in your peripheral vision. This means that at the same time you are seeing things in the environment, you are also seeing part of yourself. Thus, your perception of the environment is also a

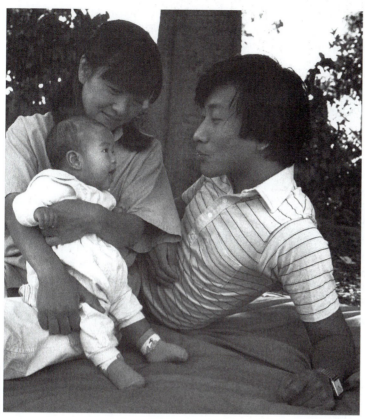

Family times together can have a special meaning for a couple with a new baby. It is important for families to take time out from work and chores to play and relax together.

Elizabeth Crews

perception of yourself in relation to the environment (Fogel, 1993; J. J. Gibson, 1966). This is why this early sense of self is called the ecological self, the self sensed as being situated in relation to the environment. **Self-agency** is the sense of the relationship of one's action and its effect on the environment. **Self-affectivity** is the sense of one's emotions as experienced in the company of another feeling person. **Self-history** is a sense of the relationship with one's past (Fogel, 2000).

Cross-modal perception, the relationship between the different senses, is one source of the ecological self. By 3½ months, infants begin to watch their hands moving in front of them. Because they can also feel their arms and hands making these movements, it is likely that this cross-modal experience gives the infants a sense of self-recognition through self-coherence. Babies recognize their hands as their own because the hands are the same ones the babies have been feeling for months (Neisser, 1991; Stern, 1995). In a similar way, in-

fants can recognize their own sounds because their different forms of vocalization (contented or distressed) will be cross-modally associated with different internal feelings (Gustafson, Green, & Kalinowski, 1995).

Young infants also explore their own bodies, feeling the relationship between the touching hand and the part of their bodies that is being touched. In the first few hours of life, newborns touch their own head in an ordered sequence beginning with the mouth, then moving to the face, head, ear, nose, and eyes. This process occurs only when the infant is awake (Kravitz et al., 1978, as reported in Butterworth, 1990). As described in Chapter 5, just prior to hand-to-mouth contact, newborns will open their mouth in anticipation. Once infants can reach, around the fourth month, they self-explore by touching different parts of the body beginning with the fingers and ending months later with the toes (Kravitz et al., 1978, as reported in Butterworth, 1990).

In one experiment, 3-to-5-month-old infants were shown videotaped images of their own legs. The video cameras were suspended above the infants to photograph the legs. The infants could see the video image of their legs, but they could not see their own legs directly. The infants were wearing striped leg-length socks to make their legs visually salient. Using this method, the researchers could manipulate the video image to show the infant's legs either as the infant would see them normally or in mirror image, with the right leg on the left side and vice versa. Infants gazed longer and kicked more to the reversed mirror image of their legs, suggesting that they could recognize the normal configuration of their own bodies and were curious about the unusual-looking reversed legs. The increased kicking also suggests that the infants were trying to figure out if the video legs were indeed their own (Rochat & Morgan, 1995). Similar experiments have been done using infant arm movements (Schmuckler, 1996).

Another unique experiment was done with Siamese twins who were born connected at their lower abdomens, facing each other. A week before they were surgically separated at 4 months, researchers noticed that the twins sometimes sucked on their own hands and sometimes on their sister's hands.

When twin A (Alice) was sucking on her own fingers, one of us placed one hand on her head and the other hand on the arm that she was sucking. We gently pulled the sucking arm away from her mouth and registered (in our own hands) whether her arm put up resistance

to being moved from her mouth and/or whether her head strained forward to go after the retreating hand. In this situation, Alice's arm registered the interruption of sucking, but she did not give evidence of straining forward with her head. The same procedure was followed when Alice was sucking on her sister Betty's fingers rather than her own. When Betty's hand was gently pulled from Alice's mouth, Alice's arms showed no resistance, but Alice's head did strain forward. Alice seemed, in this case, to have no confusion as to whose fingers belonged to whom and which motor plan would best reestablish sucking (Stern, 1985, pp. 78–79).

This suggests that the ecological self is experienced in relation not only to the physical environment but also to the social environment. As one interacts with another person, it is possible to feel the part of the interaction that comes from the self in comparison to that part contributed by the other. This is illustrated in Figure 6.11. Even during a continuous movement, such as when the mother takes the infant's arms and pulls the infant into a sitting position, there is a co-regulated dialogue in which the effort of the mother and baby changes but remains in balance. Sometimes the baby pulls a bit harder than the mother, feeling himself or herself as an agent in the co-regulation. Sometimes the baby does not have the strength to pull so the mother pulls harder, allowing the infant to feel the mother's side of the co-regulated dialogue. The baby can feel his or her effort as less than, more than, or the same as the mother's. As with the example of seeing the nose in the visual field, the experience of the ecological self is always an experi-

Figure 6.11
Self and Other Experiences during Co-Regulation

The diagram shows the amount of effort exerted by mother and infant when the infant is pulled by the mother from a supine to a sitting position. The dashed curve shows the infant's effort, while the solid curve shows how the mother exerts more or less force depending upon the co-regulated dialogue. Infants feel themselves when they are exerting more force than the mother, and they feel their mothers when the mother's force is more dominant.

Source: A. Fogel, *Developing through relationships,* 1993, p. 18. Chicago: University of Chicago Press. Reprinted with permission from the University of Chicago Press.

ence of a self in relation to the environment (Fogel, 1993). This kind of participatory co-regulated relationship with another person also gives the infant information about the other person in relation to the self, a sense of **intersubjectivity** (Bråten, 1998; Trevarthen, 1998).

In summary, the ecological self is a sense of one's body in the environment and the ability to recognize one's own movements. This sense of self comes from the infant's experiences relating to other people, the environment, and their own bodies. You can better appreciate the infant's and your own ecological self by doing the Awareness through Movement lessons at the end of each chapter. Participating in active communication with an infant, as suggested by the "Co-Regulating with Baby" section, is a way to sense your own compared to the infant's contribution to the dialogue. Infants of this age do not have a cognitive concept of themselves or of their mothers as whole people with different feelings, ideas, and motivations. The emergence of self-concepts begins during the third year of life (see Chapter 11). Thus, when doing the movement lessons, try to focus your attention on the movements and sensations of your body. To the extent that you can do this in a *participatory* way—without thought, judgment, evaluation, or conceptualization—you will be connecting with your ecological self, that part of yourself that began when you were between 2 and 5 months old. In the next section, I turn to a discussion of the factors affecting the infant's parents.

Family and Society

In Chapter 2 I reviewed some of the current theories about the nature of family interaction. Family systems theory suggests that each member of the family is part of a feedback system with every other family member. In addition, when families have three or more members, the relationship between two of them can affect the third and vice versa (Belsky, 1981). From this perspective, we might predict that the birth of a baby would bring major changes for a family. If it is a first birth, the married couple must adjust to becoming a three-person system. In a three-person family, a new baby creates disequilibrium and necessitates an adjustment by each of the other family members. In addition, developmental changes occur in all members of a family, including the adults and older siblings. In this section, we consider how adults develop through the transition to parenthood that occurs after the birth of the baby.

Developmental Tasks of Early Parenthood

After a child is born, parents must learn to cope with a variety of new conditions, including a total alteration of lifestyle, lack of sleep, and the adjustment of the marital relationship to include new family members. In general, new parents must address four types of problems (Sollie & Miller, 1980).

First, there are the energy demands associated with infant care, such as loss of sleep and extra work resulting in fatigue. Mothers, if they are the primary caregivers, must continue with the ordinary household tasks while trying to keep up with the baby. Fathers in the United States spend about half the time that mothers do in caregiving, and there are no differences across Caucasian, Hispanic, and African-American groups (Hossain, Field, Pickens, Malphurs, & Del Valle, 1997). This suggests that there are few ethnic differences in the amount of father involvement, contrary to cultural stereotypes.

Women who are employed before the birth of the child must decide whether or not to continue working after the child is born. Theoretically, men should make the same decision, but in the vast majority of cases, it is the woman who decides whether or not to return to work. In general, women who are most concerned about the potential conflicts between family and work are the most likely to remain home with the infant. The type of work done by the mother outside the home does not predict whether she will stay home or go back to work (Symons & McLeod, 1994). On the other hand, if the mother chooses to work, some work environments are more consistent with the maintenance of positive parenting. In particular, parenting is enhanced if the mother works in an environment that is challenging, includes a complex variety of different people, and is stimulating (Greenberger, O'Neil, & Nagel, 1994; see Chapter 7 for a complete discussion of maternal employment).

Second, new parenthood places stress on the marital relationship. Problems may include less time spent together and perhaps jealousy of the baby for taking time away from the marriage. It may take many months for sexual relationships to become mutually gratifying and still more time before the couple is free to go out alone. Parents generally perceive a decline in marital satisfaction over the first year of the infant's life (Gloger-Tippelt & Huerkamp, 1998). Interpersonal conflicts increase over the first year, and parents report less marital cohesion, less partner support, and less ability to cope. In general, couples with more conflicts felt less mutual support and found it more difficult to cope. These findings suggest that, while not a crisis that ends marriages, the first year of parenthood may be a difficult adjustment period for some couples (Frosch, Mangelsdorf, & McHale, 1998; Levy-Shiff, Dimitrovsky, Shulman, & Har-Even, 1998; Wicki, 1999).

Third, parents begin to feel the responsibility of caring for and rearing a child. No matter how psychologically prepared one is before the birth, the reality of the child's presence makes clear the lifelong commitment of parenthood. Parents may have doubts about whether they can manage this responsibility and be good parents for their child.

Finally, parents must cope with the additional costs of raising a child, in the form of food, clothing, and education. Just going to see a movie may cost double what it did before the child was born, after the cost of a baby-sitter is included. Whatever income a working mother might earn will be lessened by the cost of the child's daytime care. In addition, parents worry about day-to-day problems, such as infant health and sickness, crying, nutrition, and how to resolve conflicts (McKim, 1987; Wilkie & Ames, 1986).

Predictors of Success in the Transition to Parenthood

In general, the degree to which parents will adopt the parenting role depends on both developmental factors in the life of the adult and concurrent factors inside and outside the family system. Developmental factors include the adults' relationships with their own parents, their prior experience with child care, their self-esteem and belief in their own self-efficacy as a parent, and their readiness to have children. Concurrent factors include the marital relationship, other family members, the amount of social support available to the parents, and nonfamily factors, such as income and job satisfaction.

One of the key issues in the transition to parenthood is the effect of the infant on the marriage. Having a baby does not seem to alter existing marital relationships. Couples who have the most conflicts prenatally also have the most postnatally (Cowan & Cowan, 1981). The equality versus inequality of role relationships before childbirth tends to predict the amount of marital satisfaction after birth. In general, couples who are more likely to share responsibilities report higher marital satisfaction after childbirth than more traditional couples (Cowan & Cowan, 1981; Wicki, 1999). Other factors found to increase marital satisfaction following childbirth are a positive and warm relationship with one's own parents (Belsky & Isabella, 1985) and a postbirth experience that is not more difficult than anticipated (Belsky, Ward, & Rovine, 1986). The latter difficulty affects women more than men, since women, even in nontraditional marriages, are more likely to have most of the burden of care in addition to the fatigue following childbirth.

Marital quality itself is strongly associated with both men's and women's involvement in the parenting role. For mothers, a high level of marital satisfaction is related to warmth and sensitivity toward infants, and the amount of father involvement in the marriage plays a major role in the long-term ability of mothers to cope with child rearing. For fathers, marital satisfaction is associated with more positive attitudes toward the parenting role and with more time spent with the infant (Cox, Owen, Lewis, & Henderson, 1989; S. S. Feldman & Nash, 1986; Heinicke, 1984; Vandell, Hyde, Plant, & Essex, 1997).

Personality factors also affect adaptation to parenthood. Men who have had a good relationship with their own fathers and who have some personality traits traditionally associated with femininity (affiliation, warmth, nurturance) make better parents. Fathers who are more invested in their careers and who are in midlife are less likely to show warmth toward infants, although they are more involved in the practical and financial aspects of child care, since they make more money than younger fathers (S. S. Feldman & Nash, 1986; Levy-Shiff, 1994; R. D. Parke & Tinsley, 1987).

Interestingly, a very different set of personality factors is associated with parenting for women. Women who have higher self-esteem and a less ego-centric orientation, that is, away from their own needs and toward the needs of others, show more nurturance toward their children. Unlike men, women who have children later in life show higher caregiving responsibility and more satisfaction with parenthood. Older primiparous mothers are more confident of their skills and may interact more successfully with their babies than younger primiparous mothers (S. S. Feldman & Nash, 1986; Heinicke & Guthrie, 1992; R. D. Parke & Tinsley, 1987; Ragozin, Bashan, Crnic, Greenberg, & Robinson, 1982).

While men's involvement in infant care depends primarily on social factors, such as marriage, job, and the social acceptability of parenting, women are more likely to be involved parents without such social supports. On the other hand, women's parenting suffers most when their self-esteem is low or when they experience depressed moods (Belsky, 1984; S. S. Feldman & Nash, 1986; Fleming et al., 1988). In an earlier section, we discussed the serious nature of maternal depression for infants.

The Author's View

During this age period, infants blossom into attentive, feeling people who can connect with other people in meaningful ways. Recent research sheds light upon what it may feel like to be an infant during this age period. Infants appear to be developing a sense of their own bodies: they are getting to know the movements, feelings, and sensations that belong to them. This occurs as they explore their bodies and as they co-regulate with other people's bodies and the environment. The communication frames created by parents and infants serve to create a sense of history and an opportunity to compare the self with others. All of this experience of self, however, is participatory rather than conceptual. Infant memories are strictly nonverbal, and the infant has to be in more or less the same situation and doing the same kinds of things to remember.

This research on the observed infant's cognition and emotion tells us something about the kinds of adult experiences that may be closely related to an infant's experience. Recall that the clinical infant, as opposed to the observed infant, is the participatory memory of infancy that emerges from therapeutic encounters and somatic awareness experiences with children and adults. In Chapter 2, I raised the question about the scientific validity of using clinical infant experiences as a companion to the scientific research on the observed infant. At a minimum, the experiences of adults doing Feldenkrais Awareness through Movement lessons or receiving a Watsu session are participatory and nonconceptual and lead to a feeling of relaxation. These somatic awareness methods are valuable for this reason alone, even if these particular experiences are not related to memories of the adults' own infancy.

On the other hand, the theory behind these somatic awareness methods and some psychotherapeutic techniques is that adults can, in fact, recapture and remember some of their infant experiences. This type of therapeutic participatory remembering is believed to have particularly beneficial healing effects for adults, a kind of rejuvenation by means of reexperiencing one's early infancy.

The research reported in this chapter tells us that it is possible for children and adults to remember their experiences from early infancy. It is not merely theoretical. Participatory memories of infancy are adult nonverbal experiences that feel familiar and infantile, such as the experience of being comforted or rejected, of feeling contented or helpless, or of discovering some way of moving or feeling as if for the very first time. There is, however, an amnesia for the specifics of the early experience. This research suggests, therefore, that while it is possible to recapture infant-like moods and states, it is impossible to recall the specific times and places in which those states occurred. These participatory memories may come from infancy, or they may be some combination of both infantile and childhood experiences of being comforted.

These research findings are consistent with the reports of my students doing Awareness through Movement lessons (see the "Author's View" section of Chapter 2 for a description of a qualitative research study and the term project that my students did in conjunction with some of the lessons in this book). Virtually all the students in the class reported having some kind of participatory memory while doing the sucking lesson (Chapter 3). Most of the students felt overcome with calm, comfort, relaxation, and a sense of trust. They said things like, "From my recent observations of infants, I have noticed a wave of calmness and quietness while sucking, identical to the response I had to the exercise." Many reported being initially uncomfortable or self-conscious, but these feelings gave way to others. "I thought that I would feel silly sucking, but it felt comforting and left me with a warm feeling inside."

On the other hand, several of the students continued to feel discomfort during the lesson. One wrote, "When starting the sucking process I felt tension crawl up my neck and my muscles tighten." This student thought the tension might have been just a reflection of her feeling on that day, but she tried the lesson at home several times and felt the same thing. Another student said, "I felt anxiety and I was nervous, and I thought that was really strange."

These were clearly participatory memories because of their nonverbal and nonconceptual nature. But were these reports of *infant* participatory memories? Almost all the students were convinced that their feelings were unusual and out of the ordinary. Here are some typical statements, each from a different student. "When I finished the lesson, I could not believe how real it felt." "I was surprised to find that the lesson felt both natural and comforting. Before this, I would never have thought my body could remember something from that long ago. After comparing my body's reactions to the lesson and my daily life actions, I am more convinced than ever that my body remembers things that my brain doesn't." "The movement was so familiar to me and felt so natural that I have little doubt that I experienced this movement before, though I have no conscious memory of doing so. I can describe this occurrence as nothing other than memory of some-

thing from my infancy." "I can't explain why I felt like that, but I know that I was experiencing what a baby experiences." "There seemed to be a memory encoded in my mouth and body that I never realized before."

Many students, obviously surprised by what they had experienced, asked their parents about what happened to them as a baby, in this case with respect to sucking and feeding. One student who felt calm and comfort during the lesson learned that she had been breast-fed for about 1 year, during which period her family was having a major crisis. "It was sort of a sanctuary for me as a child to be alone with my mother away from all the chaos in our lives. It was a time of peace, serenity, and quiet." Students who had normal infancies connected that to their sense of peace and calm while sucking.

Without exception, all the students who had reported continuing anxiety during the sucking lesson learned from their parents that as babies, they had some type of sucking or feeding problem. One student's mother told her she did not suck well as a baby. Her mother "explained that I would eat only when I was starving and I was losing weight. The physician finally had to feed me through a tube." Although this student did not consciously remember her infant feeding problems, she was very aware of her teenage and adult eating disorder. As a result of doing this lesson, she developed a new understanding of herself and her eating disorder that was of therapeutic significance. Another student's mother told her that as a baby, she hated having nipples in her mouth, either bottles or pacifiers.

These discoveries that the students made almost always came as a great surprise to them. It was a surprise that their bodies remembered things unconsciously, and it was a surprise that their parents' recollections of them as infants were consistent with these participatory memories. One student's case is particularly telling. Before beginning each lesson, I ask students to just lie down in the silent and partially darkened classroom, relax, and bring their awareness into their bodies. During one of these periods, a male student reported feeling a "remarkable and overwhelming sense of loneliness. I imagined myself as an infant lying down helplessly in my yellow crib, all alone in a dark quiet room at night. I felt a longing to be held, to be with someone and to be comforted and secure. It was hard to say if this was an actual memory or something I was imagining, but at age 23 and being 6′3″ and 200 pounds, I do not usually feel a longing to be held and comforted at night." Another student put his experience of participatory remembering this way: "It is a way of knowing without knowing how one knows."

About half the students were convinced that these participatory memories had their origins in their own infancy. This was especially true for those whose parents' stories seemed to confirm their experiences. The other half admitted some doubt and skepticism. It is clear to me—from my own experience and from those reported by the students— that adults have participatory memories and that these memories are experienced as real and full of feeling. These memories are like dreams because they are reenactments rather than conceptual thought about something. They typically come as a surprise. They are convincing as experiences but difficult to understand or to explain. It is most likely that participatory memories of infancy are not simple reenactments of a single occurrence but feelings that happened frequently. This means that each time the feeling recurred, it was transformed in some way. Not all early feeding problems lead to later eating disorders, but this one student's case is an example of how events during infancy combined with later events to create a participatory experience of anxiety about sucking.

Doing the Awareness through Movement lessons and other forms of somatic awareness is not necessarily a direct route to infancy. Rather, it can be a way to contact the unconscious processes by which some experiences originating during infancy have survived by combining with later experiences along complex developmental pathways. The "inner child" probably does not exist, but there may be an "inner person," who has developed from infancy through adulthood, whose experiences can only be remembered in participatory rather than conceptual ways, via somatic rather than mental activity.

The issue of whether our infant experience leaves us with participatory memories is related to the more general issue of the long-term effects of infancy on later childhood and adulthood. This is the topic of Chapter 12, and in "Author's View" section of that chapter, I'll report some of the students' conclu-sions about whether qualitative research using somatic awareness methods, such as the Awareness through Movement lessons, is a valid way of studying the effect of infancy on our adult lives.

AWARENESS THROUGH MOVEMENT

Rolling from Side to Back

Position: Lie on your right side in a fetal position. Lean your head on the floor or, if necessary for comfort, place a pillow under your head. Bend both of your legs. Have your legs lying one on top of the other, and draw your legs up near your abdomen. Place your arms in a position similar to that of your legs. Both elbows should be bent, with one arm placed on top of the other. Have your forearms and hands in contact with each other and your hands resting on the floor, not far from your mouth. Make sure you are in a position where you could lie very comfortably, without any sense of effort, stretching, or straining.

1. While lying on your side, begin to rock yourself side to side, moving only an inch or two, while breathing in a very relaxed way. Keep this movement small, light, soothing, and rhythmical. The movement is similar to the feeling of being rocked in a cradle. Your trunk, left shoulder, and hip will oscillate forward and back, and your head will wobble a little on the floor. Try moving a little quicker or slower, until you find a rhythm that suits you. Find the rhythm that allows you to rock with the least amount of effort, so that you could even imagine falling asleep while rocking—as some babies (and adults) actually do. Rest on your side.

2. While lying on your side, move your eyes slowly to the left in the direction of the ceiling, as if interested in something behind you, and then move your eyes to gaze in front of you again. Repeat this movement slowly many times. Notice how the movement of your eyes creates a tendency for your head to turn also. Rest on your side.

What are some causes
of unexpected death in infancy?

In Chapter 4 I discussed some of the causes of infant death during the newborn period. We saw then that the vast majority of infant deaths occur during the first few days of life. After the first month, the primary causes of infant death may be labeled "unexpected," since in most industrial societies, fatal infant diseases have all but been eliminated through the use of vaccines and preventive care.

Accidents are one of the major causes of unexpected death in the first year of life. These may be traffic accidents or home accidents, such as suffocation, burns, poisoning, and drowning. Another major cause

of unexpected death is homicide, including maltreatment, infanticide, sexual offenses, kidnapping, and killing accompanied by parental suicide (Hartmann & Molz, 1979).

The most frequent cause of unexpected death in the first year of life is sudden infant death syndrome **(SIDS),** also called *crib death.* Figure 6.12 shows the incidence of SIDS compared with all other causes of infant death in the United States. SIDS claims the life of 1 infant in every 1,000 (Karns, 2000).

What causes SIDS?

One of the problems in diagnosing and preventing SIDS is that no single disorder accounts for all the cases. The only thing they have in common is the manner of death. The SIDS diagnosis is applied if parents discover

that their baby has died, perhaps at night or during a nap, and there is no apparent cause of death. Sometimes an investigation will reveal a non-SIDS cause of death. Some other causes of death appear to be SIDS related but are not; they include accidental asphyxiation, overheating, and infant abuse (Bass, Kravath, & Glass, 1986).

In the past, a case of SIDS might have brought the parents under suspicion of murder by suffocation. The threat of this insinuation, plus the shock, grief, and guilt brought on by the loss of the baby, placed an unusually heavy burden on the parents, many of whom wondered if they indeed had been the cause of death.

The fact that many SIDS cases seemed to be associated with colds or some mild

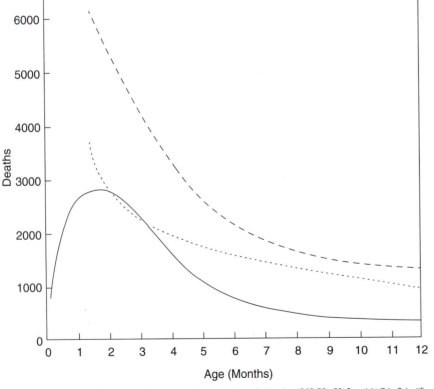

Figure 6.12
Infant Deaths in the United States

The solid curve shows infant deaths from SIDS. All other causes of infant deaths are charted by the dotted curve. The dashed curve indicates the total number of deaths between the ages of 10 weeks and 12 months. SIDS is the most frequent cause of death between the ages of 1 month and 1 year, and it exceeds all other causes.

Source: R. Naeye, Sudden infant death syndrome, 1980 (April), p. 59. *Scientific American, 242,* 56 – 62. Copyright © by Scientific American, Inc. All rights reserved.

respiratory problem led some researchers to study the relationship between respiration and SIDS. Very young infants often cease breathing for brief periods, a condition known as **apnea.** These pauses in breathing, or apneic pauses, almost always occur during sleep. Since most crib deaths occur during sleep, researchers have attempted to establish some connection between apnea and SIDS.

The problem with the SIDS infant may not be the apnea, since all infants have apneic episodes, but may be related to some sensorimotor deficit that prevents the infant from making the correct movements and heart rate changes that will assist in recovery from the apnea (Lipsitt, 1979a; Lipsitt, Sturges, & Burke, 1979). Some of the sensorimotor deficits that may prevent recovery from apnea during the first year may have been caused by loss of oxygen during the perinatal period, by other inadequacies in the perinatal environment, or by genetic factors associated with low motor control over breathing. There is some evidence that all three factors may cause respiratory weakness (Black, Steinschneider, & Sheehe, 1979; Lipsitt, 1979a; Naeye, 1980; Schiffman, Westlake, Santiago, & Edelman, 1980). Slower brain development related to the control of breathing has also been found in SIDS infants (Cruz-Sanchez et al., 1997).

Around the age of 2 to 3 months, infants are beginning to exert voluntary control over respiration both to produce vocal sounds, such as cooing, and to inhibit crying. Because this developmental change coincides with the onset of SIDS, it also suggests a sensorimotor or neuromotor deficit in this voluntary motor control (McKenna, 1988).

What are some other possible causes of SIDS?

A number of other possible causes have been associated with SIDS. Heat is one suspected cause of SIDS, and SIDS victims have symptoms similar to those of heat stroke. Some victims of SIDS were found to be ex-cessively covered or dressed at the time of death (Stanton, Scott, & Downhan, 1980).

The inability to cope with relatively mild stresses, such as heat, apnea, or even mild toxicity, may result from some other systemic weakness. Oxygen deprivation in the perinatal period may be one cause. Another may be vitamin deficiency. Some researchers have suggested that at least some SIDS victims are deficient in biotin, a B vitamin.

Respiratory infection has been studied as a possible cause of SIDS. In some cases, the infection may be acquired prenatally, but it is more likely to have environmental causes. Higher rates of SIDS have been found during outbreaks of influenza (Moreno, Ardanaz, Olivera, Castilla, & de Pedro, 1994). A more consistent link has been found for cigarette smoking in the home, which accounts for 28% of SIDS cases (Blackwell et al., 1994; Hilder, 1994; Lindsay, Johnson, Wallace, & Soos, 1994; Peduto, Musu, Gatto, & Ghilli, 1994).

Although no one symptom can predict SIDS in all cases, SIDS infants have some of the following: difficulty in waking, shrill crying, few movements during sleep, poor oxygenation of the blood, pneumonia, and repeated hospitalization (Einspieler, Widder, Holzer, & Kenner, 1988; Golding & Peters, 1985).

Can SIDS be prevented?

There is currently no foolproof method of preventing SIDS. Some infants may be identified at birth as being at risk. Infants who are from deprived socioeconomic settings, who have suffered oxygen deprivation, who have a high apnea rate, who have biotin or hormonal imbalances, or who have siblings who died or nearly died of SIDS are all at risk for SIDS.

Since the causes of SIDS are related to respiratory, feeding, and state control problems, some simple procedures are recommended for use with all infants (see Table 6.6). Of these recommendations, perhaps the most important is to avoid a prone sleep-ing position. A supine position makes it easier for the infant to breathe. Controlled studies have shown a significant reduction—up to 50%—in the SIDS death rate when parents are told to place their infants in the supine position (Goldman, 1994; Helweg-Larsen, Lundemose, & Bille, 1994; Wigfield, Gilbert, & Fleming, 1994).

Table 6.6   How to Prevent SIDS

Do:

Place the baby on back (supine) or side when sleeping.

Use a firm mattress and bedding materials.

Breast-feed if possible.

Obtain adequate prenatal care.

Don't:

Overheat the baby with excessive clothing or bedding.

Smoke near the baby.

Place the baby on stomach (prone) to sleep.

A parent can also use a home apnea monitor, which emits an alarm if the infant stops breathing during sleep. This system has both advantages and disadvantages for use in the home. Monitor use can cause extreme anxiety for the first month and lead to a restricted social life for the parents. Once they get over their initial anxiety, however, parents feel that home monitoring is beneficial; it causes few marital problems, and few parents resent the extra burden involved. Also, new research shows that monitoring for only 24 hours can determine if the infant is at risk for SIDS (Cain, Kelly, & Shannon, 1980; l'Hoir et al., 1994; Rebuffat, Groswasser, Kelmanson, Sottiaux, & Kahn, 1994).

If SIDS is caused by a basic impairment in sensorimotor development, it may be possible to train infants to exert more effective control over breathing failures. One possibility is to encourage parents to let their babies sleep with them until the risk period for SIDS

(continues)

Applications (continued)

is past. If a baby is likely to make errors in respiratory control, exposure to parental breathing can have a significant effect on the regularity of the infant's breathing by creating a rhythmic cue to which the infant can become entrained. It is extremely unlikely that parents would suffocate an infant by rolling over on the infant while sleeping, since they are mutually attuned to one another's position even when sleeping (McKenna, 1987; McKenna & Mosko, 1994; McKenna et al., 1994).

How can the SIDS victim's parents and family be helped?

Bereavement over SIDS victims shows a similar pattern over time as that for neonatal death: negativism, anger, shock, disbelief, and guilt (see Chapter 4 and Mandell, McAnulty, & Reece, 1980; Smialek, 1978). Following the death of the infant, wives may become more dependent on their husbands for support. This, combined with the possibility that a husband may secretly resent or blame his wife for the death, may cause mar-

ital discord (Gruen, 1987). Siblings in the family may also be affected, both because of a sense of loss and because parental preoccupation may detract from the parents' relationship with the older children. Siblings may also suffer from grief reactions similar to those of the parents (McConkie-Rosell & Iafolla, 1993; M. Powell, 1991). In some cases, even professionals, such as nursing staff, who come in contact with the family may also be affected by the death (McCalin & Mandell, 1994).

The more knowledgeable the parents' community, friends, relatives, and physicians are, the easier it will be for the parents to cope with the loss. Perhaps the best source of possible comfort and assistance is the family's pediatrician. Often, however, the pediatrician is either unwilling or, because of ignorance, unable to help. In such cases, parents may contact one of several national groups that have been organized by parents of SIDS victims, such as the National Foundation for Sudden Infant Death, Inc. (1501 Broadway, New York, NY 10036), or the In-

ternational Council for Infant Survival (1515 Reisterstown Road, Baltimore, MD 21208). These groups are dedicated to medical research, providing support for survivors and public education and informing the parents of their right to an autopsy. Autopsy is considered an essential element in relieving parents' guilt (Terjesen & Wilkins, 1979), although there are often delays and difficulties in dealing with local coroners and medical committees (Bluglass & Hassall, 1979).

For these reasons, parents of SIDS victims would benefit from contact with such groups and other knowledgeable individuals in the community, particularly other families of SIDS victims. Legal, social, and psychological assistance is part of a complete intervention package to help parents fully recover. Parents should also treat the death as meaningful and rely on the same religious and spiritual rituals that would help them in the event of death for any family member (Fabrena & Nutini, 1994).

3. While lying on your side, very, very slowly roll back *only a few inches,* as if in the direction of lying on your back, and then very, very slowly roll forward those same few inches until you lie on your side again. You are no longer rocking, although the direction of the movement is similar to the rocking movement in step 1. As you repeat this movement, notice how your limbs are carried back and forth by the movement of the center of your body. Notice how your shoulder and hip tend to move apart as your eyes move to the left and your trunk moves in such a way that you tend toward lying on your back. Notice how your shoulder and hip tend to move closer together as you slowly move your eyes to the right, and your trunk moves so that you tend toward lying on your side. Rest on your side.

4. Gradually begin to roll more and more toward lying on your back. Each time, return to lie fully on your side and rest before starting to roll back again. Slowly increase the size of your movement in very small increments, so that it might take ten to fifteen movements to complete the movement of rolling onto your back. As you very slowly roll back, allow your left arm and left leg to extend. As you return to your side, allow your left knee and elbow to bend. Synchronize the movements of your limbs and trunk. This means that it should take the same time for you to arrive completely on your back as it takes for your left arm and left leg to elongate fully. Similarly, flex yourself into the fetal position simultaneously with the movement of rolling to your side. Try to keep your head, feet, and hands in contact with the

Co-Regulating with Baby

Between 2 and 5 months, infants are only beginning to become aware of themselves. They do this primarily by engaging in primary circular reactions, repeated explorations of their own bodies and the effects of their bodies on the environment. As part of that environment, you can help babies to discover themselves by encouraging circular reactions and playing co-regulated games involving repetition with variations. In the first month or two, you can gently talk to the baby each time you feed, diaper, or bathe him or her. The infant will come to recognize a particular voice in a particular place; this will contribute to a sense of familiarity and encourage positive feelings associated with recognition.

Gently move the baby's arms and legs up, down, in, and out, playing an "exercise" game. Gently touch the baby's cheeks and other skin surfaces, or blow softly and repeatedly on the arms and abdomen. Remember that at this age, the baby has a limited range of arousal tolerance and cannot handle too much stimulation. You have to be sensitive to cues for termination: head turning, avoidance reactions, crying, and spitting up are common responses to overstimulation. Do not be discouraged if this happens; use what you learned from this experience to adjust your behavior the next time you play. When you feel the play is going right, it is probably because it is also going right for the baby too.

I have already mentioned appropriate kinds of face-to-face play as the baby approaches 2 to 3 months. Remember to imitate, to exaggerate your expressions, to use themes and variations, and to make your responses contingent upon the baby's. You also can buy or design toys that are contingent: mobiles and other objects that dangle and can be swiped at. You can place a rattle in the infant's hand so the child can have the experience of "making" noise, or let the baby bang a pot with a spoon. Do not try to force the infant into a play situation; just be available to support the infant when he or she wants to get involved.

In general, your job is to encourage the baby to move, see, feel, and hear in a way that is safe and that leads to growing discovery of the self-other relationship. This happens best in mutually satisfying, co-regulated communication frames that are appropriate for this age. Toys are less important now than they will be later, because it is very hard to construct a toy that can co-regulate with the baby.

Do not forget that all babies are different. Whereas one infant seems to be able to take as much play as you care to offer, another may be slow to warm up and require a much more relaxed and gentle pace. Being aware of your own feelings in relation to the baby is the key to success. You may become impatient, for example, with a baby who is slower to respond to you. Try to examine the source of that impatience in your own life and self-history. Perhaps the impatience is a participatory memory from your own early life, or perhaps it is due to a current stressful situation. You may not be able to rid yourself of impatient feelings, but you can make an effort not to let those feelings interfere with entering into a creative co-regulation with this particular baby. If you can allow yourself to do that, the mutual enjoyment will certainly play a role in helping you to relax, which will be beneficial for both yourself and the baby.

floor during the entire movement. If this is not possible, then lift any of them the very minimum amount that is necessary.

5. Lie on your back and rest, and feel the differences between your right and left sides. Walk around and feel the difference between the two sides.

Note: Normally people have to practice many movements in order to learn how to do this. If you lengthen your left side too soon and your body is totally straight before your back is on the floor, you will tend to fall jerkily or make unnecessary efforts, like pushing with your left foot into the ground in order to stabilize yourself. If you can synchronize the rolling together with the flexing and straightening, your movement will become incredibly smooth and efficient, and you will never feel as if you are pushing against the floor. Similarly, avoid any tendency to lift parts of your body away from the floor. One of the chief differences between the way adults and babies shift from side to back, and back to side again, is that while adults needlessly push against, or lift away from, the floor or bed, babies do not make these efforts. They roll more like a cylinder or ball, similar to the movement of a cat.

Further Explorations: Experiment with making the movement faster or slower and notice the changes in your breathing, coordination, effort, and the pressure put on the floor by various parts of your body. How slowly can you do it? How fast? Instead of initiating the movement with your eyes as if looking at something that captures your interest, initiate the movement with your mouth as if reaching for a nipple or bottle. Notice how the movement changes when you change your intention. Repeat the lesson starting on your left side, and feel how the left side of your body is affected. After experiencing rolling to the right and left sides independently, alternate between rolling to one side and the other.

Smiling and Cooing

Position: Lie on your back with your knees bent and your feet standing on the floor about shoulder width apart. Lie with your arms down at your sides. Please feel free to lie in a more fetal-like way on your back or side if you can find a comfortable way to do so.

1. With your mouth slightly open, gently protrude your lips and tongue and then relax them. As you protrude your lips, allow them to turn slightly inside out. Repeat this many times, as if reaching for a nipple or bottle. Experiment with slower and faster rhythms. Rest.

2. Continue to protrude your lips many times, as in step 1. Each time you relax your lips, notice how the corners of your mouth widen. Imagine the corners of your mouth widening as if you were beginning to smile. Rest.

3. Widen your lips as if to smile, and notice how your lips come forward as they relax. Begin to alternate between protruding your lips and smiling as you relax the muscles of your face and neck. Rest.

4. With each exhalation, make an "ooo" sound as you softly bring your lips forward. Imagine you are expressing a deep sense of satisfaction. Repeat this many times. Pause and then smile a few times. Notice the increased softness of your face. Now alternate between smiling and making the "ooo" sounds while protruding your lips.

Comments: An infant's facial expressions and sounds directly reflect his or her feelings and actions. In later childhood and adulthood, we learn to assume a "mask," which may conceal as much as it reveals about our inner state. Our masks often become so habitual that we are no longer aware of our expressions and facial tensions. These masks can perform useful social functions; but if we wish to make choices, we need to be able to observe in ourselves the difference between spontaneous expressions and ones that are consciously controlled. After this lesson, your face will probably be relieved of some of its habitual tensions, and you will become more aware of how you use your face in every day life.

SUMMARY

Physical and Motor Development

■ The most rapid period of physical growth in human life occurs between birth and 6 months.

■ Some developmental disorders may be detected from standardized tests of infant motor skill.

■ Motor performance depends on the level of brain development, on the complexity of the task, and on the types of supports and resources available in the environment, especially from adults.

Perceptual Development

■ Acuity and speed of information processing improve in all perceptual modalities between 2 and 5 months.

■ Infants can detect color differences and a wide variety of visual patterns. They can perceive the solidity of objects and can recognize them from different points of view and using different sense modalities.

- Infants have a strong preference for looking at faces and at moving objects and are better able to perceive differences between objects if the objects are moving.

- Infants show a preference for infant-directed speech and songs.

- Cross-modal perception is the ability to perceive that different sense modalities give complementary information on the same object.

Cognitive Development

- The time taken for habituation decreases, and the infant's attention span increases.

- Infants have participatory memories for up to 2 weeks, but reminders make the memories longer. Memory is dependent upon emotional and contextual cues present at the time of the learning.

- Infantile amnesia may be due to the fact that infant memory is so closely related to the situation in which the infant was first exposed to the stimulus. Since the exact situation rarely recurs later, people seem to forget what happened to them as infants. People do, however, have participatory memories of feelings and sensations from infancy, even though they cannot locate the exact time, place, or situation.

- The main form of adaptation is primary circular reactions, in which the infants are exploring the effects of their own body movements and vocalizations.

Emotional Development

- A distinction can be made between emotion expression, emotion experience, and emotional regulation.

- The infant's emotional expression becomes more complex and varied. Infants can use their whole bodies for emotional expression.

- Negative emotions decrease over time, while positive emotions increase.

- Improvements in emotional regulation occur, but new challenges create new sources of frustration for babies.

Social Development

- Adults display characteristic patterns of behavior with infants that include motherese-type vocalizations and actions.

- Some aspects of motherese are universal, but cultures differ in the amount and type of verbal versus nonverbal behavior that is directed toward infants.

- Research shows that adults are affected by their infants' behavior, and infants are affected by adult behavior, making the origins of individual differences hard to determine in most cases.

- Infants are at risk when mothers have emotional disorders, such as depression.

- Infants can perceive an ecological self, the sense that they have agency, coherence, location in the environment, and feelings that belong to them.

Family and Society

- Parents must adapt to a number of new challenges during the transition to parenthood.

- Different factors predict the success of adaptation to parenthood for men and women.

Applications: Unexpected Death in Infancy

- SIDS does not have a known cause but is believed to be linked to sensorimotor difficulties of respiration.

- Several preventive steps can be taken with infants at risk for SIDS, but none is foolproof.

- Parents who lose a baby to SIDS need special counseling and understanding from relatives and their community.

 ON THE WEB

www.nmchc.org The National Maternal and Child Health Clearinghouse Home Page produces and disseminates educational material on SIDS. Links take you to the National Maternal and Child Health Clearinghouse 1998 Publications Catalog, Full-Text Publications, Publications from Other Sources, Maternal and Child Health State Resource

Sheets, National SIDS Resource Center Materials, and Forums.

www.cjsids.com "The CJ Foundation for Sudden Infant Death Syndrome is a nationwide voluntary health organization dedicated to recognizing the special needs of the SIDS community through funding SIDS research and support services. The Foundation hopes to increase public awareness of SIDS and to contribute to a future in which no parent is faced with the tragedy of losing a loved one to SIDS."

sids-network.org SIDS Network provides a world of information and support. The web site offers up-to-date information and support for those who have felt and know the tragedy of SIDS and other infant deaths. There are over 1,000 files containing over 3,000 pages of information on this site.

GLOSSARY

Apnea Short cessation of respiratory movements.

Attunement Cross-modal matching of infant behavior by an adult or vice versa.

Cephalocaudal development Growth that proceeds from the top of the body to the bottom.

Cross-modal perception Integration of information across more than one perceptual modality.

Ecological self The ability to recognize the body and its senses, feelings, and movements.

Emotion regulation The ability to control the form and timing of one's emotional expression and feeling state.

Frames Regularly recurring communication routines such as social games, play with toy objects, and bedtime, bathing, and feeding routines.

Infant-directed (ID) speech A style of speech that includes exaggerated pitch, loudness, marked rhythms, and clear melodies (see also *motherese*).

Infantile amnesia The lack of memory of older children and adults for the infancy period.

Intersubjectivity The experience of another person in relation to the actions of the self.

During participatory co-regulated dialogue, the infant can feel how their agency affects the other person and how the other's agency affects the infant's own.

Invariance Detection of what is similar about an object in spite of variations in the conditions under which it is perceived; the basis of recognizing the same object from different perspectives.

Motherese Changes in speech patterns involving exaggeration of pitch, higher pitch, use of rhythm and melody, slowing down, and simplification.

Primary circular reactions Repetitive movements of the infant's body that are discovered by chance and repeated for fun.

Protoconversation An initial form of turn taking in adult-infant interaction in which the parent fills in the natural pauses in the infant's behavior, but the infant does not take any social initiatives.

Proximodistal development Refers to the fact that the parts of the body closer to the trunk develop faster than the extremities.

Self-affectivity People's sense of having inner emotional feelings that routinely go together with specific experiences.

Self-agency People's feeling that they are causal agents that can successfully affect their own bodies and the environment.

Self-coherence People's feeling that they and the objects around them are integrated wholes that have distinct boundaries.

Self-history People's feeling that the past can be connected to the present by means of recreating one's own actions in similar situations, a sense of self-similarity.

SIDS Sudden infant death syndrome; a cause of death of unknown origins believed to be associated with errors in respiratory regulation, especially during sleep.

Still-face An experimental manipulation in which mothers are asked to hold their faces in a neutral pose and cease talking to or otherwise interacting with their infants.

7

Six to Nine Months

CHAPTER OVERVIEW AND OUTLINE

Physical and Motor Development	*What are the infant's motor skills at this age? Do infants have a preferred hand? How do motor skills develop?*
Perceptual Development	*Can infants perceive object properties at this age? Can they appreciate pictures in books and on television?*
Cognitive Development	*What kinds of concepts do infants of this age have? Do they know that objects exist when out of sight?*
Emotional Development	*What are the negative emotions at this age? What are the positive emotions? Can infants recognize the facial expressions of other people? Do infants have lasting temperamental characteristics?*
Social and Language Development	*What are the typical frames of parent-infant communication at this age? In what ways is infant babbling related to speech? Can infants recognize speech sounds? What are some cultural differences in communication? What is the infant's sense of self at this age?*
Family and Society	*What are the effects of maternal employment on infants and families? Are males and females equally responsive toward infants?*
Applications: Infant Nutrition	*What are the nutritional requirements of infants? How should solid foods be introduced? When can infants be expected to feed themselves?*

Between the ages of 6 and 9 months, infants grow more adventurous. This development is physical in that babies can creep or crawl, at least for short distances, on their own. It is also psychological in that infants begin to take initiatives and to call attention to themselves. Infants of this age develop a serious interest in the object world, and they come to understand that objects are whole entities with an existence separate from their own.

Physical and Motor Development

By the age of 5 months, infants can sit supported, and they can reach and grasp objects. Between 6 and 9 months, improvements in posture lead to independent sitting and to supported standing. Muscle strength improvements allow babies to turn over and to move their bodies by creeping or by crawling. By 9 months, infants can take a few steps while holding on to furniture or an adult hand. Their grasp becomes more precise so that by 9 months, infants can pick up small objects such as peas or carrot slices using just the tips of the thumb and index finger. These developments are listed in Table 7.1. In this section, I will review the topic of handedness in infants. Following that is a discussion of the process by which these different motor skills develop.

Do Infants Have a Preferred Hand?

One of the distinguishing features of the human brain is that the left and right hemispheres serve different functions. Although researchers disagree about the precise allocation of functions to each side of the brain, the right hemisphere is believed to control spatial patterns and nonlinguistic information processing, while the left hemisphere is more sensitive to sequential processing of the sort used in understanding language. These left-right brain differences are found in right-handed people; in left-handed people the hemisphere functions are reversed.

Because brain hemisphere specialization is linked to **handedness,** or the preference for the use of one

Table 7.1 Norms for the Development of Motor Behavior Patterns in North America

Test Item	Average Age	Normal Age Range
A. Body control		
Sits alone steadily	6.5 months	5–9 months
Pulls self to sitting	8.2 months	6–11 months
Pulls self to standing	8.5 months	6–12 months
B. Locomotion		
Stepping movements while standing	8.7 months	6–12 months
Walks with help	9.5 months	7–12 months
Sits down	9.5 months	7–14 months
C. Hand and arm control		
Can scoop small pellet	5.5 months	4–8 months
Finger-to-thumb grasp of cube	7 months	5–9 months
Finger-to-thumb grasp of pellet	9 months	7–10 months
Rotates wrist while holding cube	5.7 months	4–8 months
Combines objects at midline	8.5 months	6–10 months
Pat-a-cake at midline	9.7 months	7–15 months

Source: Bayley Infant Development Tests, as reported in and adapted from J. F. Rosenblith & J. E. Sims-Knight, *In the beginning: Development in the first two years,* 1985, Tables 8.3, 8.4, and 8.5. Belmont, CA: Brooks/Cole. Copyright © by Wadsworth, Inc. Reprinted by permission of Sage Publications.

hand over another, the emergence in infancy of a preferred hand is thought to be related to milestones in the development of the brain. If there is a hand-use preference in early infancy, it might suggest that the left and the right cortices of the infant's brain are already functioning differently.

At first glance, there seems to be good evidence for left-right differences. Infants begin to exhibit a hand preference at about 2 months of age, around the time when visually guided reaching begins. Like adults, more infants preferentially reach with their right than with their left hands. Furthermore, this hand preference is relatively stable in babies over the first year of life (McDonnell, Anderson, & Abraham, 1983; Young, Segalowitz, Misek, Alp, & Boulet, 1983).

These left-right differences are not the same as those found in adults, however. About 90% of adults in all cultures are right handed. However, only about 30 to 50% of infants under 1 year show a preference for the right hand in reaching, while 10 to 30% have a left-hand preference. The remaining infants show no hand preference. In adults, hand preference is correlated with the hand preference of one's parents, but this is not true for infants (McCormick & Maurer, 1988). Thus, it seems that infants do have a right-side bias, but it is not nearly as strong nor as stable as adults'. In other words, the majority of infants show a hand preference at any age, but the preferred hand may change as the infant gets older.

If infant hand-use preference is not linked to heredity, as is the case for most adults, what does determines it? According to one perspective, hand preference may develop out of earlier postural preferences. Most newborns, for example, prefer to turn their heads to the right side. It could be that the right-hand preference develops because that is the hand infants can see the best if their heads are turned to the side (Michel & Harkins, 1986). Adults may also have an effect on which hand is used by presenting objects preferentially to the infant's right or left side (Fogel, Karns, & Kawai, 1990; Harkins & Michel, 1988). More-permanent hand preferences in infants do not emerge until the second year of life, perhaps as an interaction between heredity and environmental influences.

Effects of Hand Preference on Infant Motor Development

Why should we prefer to use one hand more than the other? Because the sides of our brains are specialized, perhaps handedness is merely a reflection of the brain structure. Actually, handedness does not mean that we use one hand and not the other; it means that each of our hands may be doing different things. When a baby explores an object, the hand that is doing the grasping and manipulating is no less important than the hand that is holding the object steady. Perhaps handedness evolved in order to allow each hand to perform a different but complementary function (Fagard & Jacquet, 1989).

When infants first begin to reach for objects, they use two hands and reach symmetrically toward the midline of the body. More mature reaching, beginning at around 6 months, involves reaching with a single hand for the object. What happens to the nonreaching hand at this time? The babies, who by 6 months are just learning to sit without support, extend the nonreaching hand backward to balance their upper bodies as the reaching hand moves forward (Rochat & Senders, 1990). Single-handed reaches would be impossible for babies without the postural counterbalance provided by the other hand and arm.

Being able to extend one arm independently of the other is also believed to be important for the development of crawling. Observations of infants reveal that there are different types of crawling (see Table 7.2). As long as babies are still reaching with two hands at the same time (showing no hand preference), they either creep or rock. They begin to crawl as soon as they can reach with one hand, probably because crawling requires the extension of one hand and leg and then the other (Goldfield, 1989). The Awareness through Movement lessons in this chapter may help you to understand how this works.

Not all infants go through the sequence of types of crawling shown in Table 7.2. Some infants creep before they crawl, while others skip the creeping phase and go directly to crawling. Infants who creep before they crawl, however, are better at crawling than those who do not creep. When they crawl, the

Table 7.2   **Operational Definitions of Locomotor Stages**

Pivot	Arms alternatively flex and extend, one after the other, causing the trunk to pivot on the abdomen. Symmetrical leg extension is followed by forward flexion of one knee, in adduction. Head lifts.
Low creep	Both arms are flexed symmetrically or extended symmetrically, or one is flexed while the other is extended. Legs flex, one at a time. Face is lifted, but chest and abdomen contact supporting surface.
High creep	Both arms are extended, and both legs are flexed symmetrically. Knees are forward under trunk in adduction, lifting abdomen and chest from supporting surface. Head is well up from floor, and eyes look ahead.
Rocking	Arms extend symmetrically, and both legs are flexed symmetrically. Knees are forward under trunk, lifting abdomen and chest from supporting surface. Infant rocks back and forth, remaining in one location.
Crawling	Both arms extend downward from shoulder, then extend forward, alternately. Legs flex forward alternately. Arm and leg on opposite sides of the body move simultaneously.

Note: These definitions were modified from Gesell and Ames (1940).

Source: E. C. Goldfield, Transition from rocking to crawling: Postural constraints on infant movement, 1989, p. 916. *Developmental Psychology, 25,* 913–919. Reprinted by permission.

creepers move faster and their movements are larger and more efficient, although the non-creepers become proficient crawlers after a couple of weeks (Adolph, Vereijken, & Denny, 1998). There is no evidence, therefore, of any permanent effects of the delay in crawling proficiency for the non-creepers. On the contrary, infants are creative in combining all of the types of movements related to crawling, each in their own unique way. Apparently, infants use whatever means are available to achieve their goals, rather than staying with the most advanced form of movement all the time (Goldfield, 1993).

How Motor Skills Develop

The research on crawling shows that even though infants can get up on their hands and knees in a crawling posture, they still cannot crawl because they lack one of crawling's necessary skill components: alternate extension of the arms and legs. When doing the Awareness through Movement lessons in this chapter, you can see how difficult it is to achieve this skill. This is similar to the younger infants, discussed in the last chapter, who could not step because their leg muscles lacked the strength to lift the legs. Dynamic systems theory predicts that new motor skills develop by adding additional components to existing skills.

A similar analysis could be applied to the development of walking. In the age period covered in this chapter, 6 to 9 months, infants can stand and take a few steps, but they cannot yet walk. Why not? Nine-month-old infants seem to possess the prerequisites of walking. They can pull themselves into a standing position, take steps while holding onto something, and alternate their leg movements. What they lack, however, is the ability to control balance. This was discovered in research using a "moving-room" technique (see Figure 7.1). A baby stands in a miniature room, the floor of which is stationary but whose walls and ceiling are moved either toward or away from the baby. Infants under 1 year will fall in the direction in which the wall appears to be moving. Infants older than 1 year may sway but are less likely to lose their balance (Bertenthal & Bai, 1989). The moving room recreates the visual experience of moving without asking the baby to take steps at the same time. It is this visual experience of the room seeming to flow past the eyes that appears to cause babies to lose their balance.

This research suggests that perception of one's own movement in space is a key ingredient in controlling the posture necessary for locomotor development. A similar effect of balance and posture also influences other motor developmental processes. The difference between a creep and a crawl (Table 7.2 and the "Awareness through Movement" section of this chapter), for example, is the ability to balance on the hands and knees while moving forward. Once balance is acquired in the crawl, infants' movements become more efficient

Figure 7.1
Schematic Drawing of Moving-Room Apparatus

Depicted inside the room is a child falling backward as a function of the room moving toward the child. This compensatory response would occur if the child perceived the optical flow produced by the room movement as specifying a forward sway rather than a movement of the walls.

Source: B. I. Bertenthal & D. L. Bai, Infant's sensitivity to optical flow for controlling posture, 1989, p. 39. *Developmental Psychology, 25,* 936–945. Copyright © by the American Psychological Association. Reprinted with permission.

and uniform (Adolph, Vereijken, Denny, Gill, & Lucero, 1995). Infants who had experience with creeping or crawling were observed in the moving room apparatus and compared with infants who had not yet begun to locomote themselves. Those infants who had already begun self-produced locomotion were better able to make postural adjustments to the moving room, showing that the balance needed for walking may come from earlier experiences of balance while trying to crawl (Higgins, Campos, & Kermoian, 1996).

Postural control while sitting is important for the development of skilled reaching. Before infants can sit upright steadily, they reach for objects with two hands at the same time. After they can sit steadily, they are able to reach with a single hand, allowing them to use their other hand for something else. Infants of this age also seem to know how far they can reach for an object based on how stable they are in a sitting posture. They reach out farther when they feel more stable and do not reach when they feel unstable (Pieraut-Lebonniec, 1990; Rochat, 1992; Rochat & Goubet, 1995; Rochat, Goubet, & Senders, 1999). Thus, not only is motor development a complex systems interaction of the different parts of the motor system (legs, trunk, and arms), but it also includes the perceptual system and the type of environment in which the child is moving.

Infants can execute walking movements, for example, if they are supported in their posture—by an infant walker or an adult—and allowed to move their legs cyclically (Thelen & Ulrich, 1991). The onset of walking is later in infants with fewer opportunities to exercise these movements. Infants in northern climates who are born in summer and fall will walk on their own an average of 3 weeks later than infants born in winter and spring. The reason for this is that the babies born in winter and spring are more likely to be practicing walking skills in the summer or fall, and the warmer temperatures give them more opportunity for movement without the constriction of a lot of clothing (Benson, 1993).

In the next section, I discuss perceptual developments. Just as motor development involves a complex interplay of perception and environmental processes, perceptual development involves the motor system and its development. At this age, therefore, it is not really possible to divide the infant's development into distinct categories like motor skill, perception, and cognition. They are all part of a dynamic developing system.

Perceptual Development

New Developments in the Recognition of Objects and Depth

In the last chapter, we saw that by 4 months, infants are able to recognize objects even though they may look different when seen from different orientations. By 4 months, infants perceive objects as being solid and will become puzzled if one solid object appears to pass through another. Infants of this age can also perceive differences in distances between objects and will reach preferentially to objects they perceive as nearer to them. For infants under 6 months, however, object recognition and depth perception are easier if the objects are moving and if real objects, rather than pictures of objects, are presented.

After 6 months, however, infants can infer object properties and depth merely from visual cues alone (Craton, 1996; Wilcox & Baillargeon, 1998). Another way to say this is that by 6 months, infants can "see" three dimensions when they are shown objects in two dimensions, as in a drawing or a photograph. Suppose two pictures of different sizes but of the same object, such as a car, are placed next to each other. Adults looking at the pictures with one eye (monocular vision) would assume that the smaller car is farther away. Looking with two eyes, adults can easily see that two cars are at the same distance but of different sizes. These perceptual conclusions must be based only on the relative sizes of the pictures and not on the movements of one car away from the other or the movements of the perceiver in a three-dimensional space.

By about 7 months of age, infants with a patch over one eye will reach toward the larger of two identical pictures of a face, apparently perceiving it as closer (Yonas, Pettersen, & Granrud, 1982). If a small and a large checkerboard are used, the infants do not reach more frequently for the larger one, since checkerboards have no standard size. If the infants are allowed to reach while looking with both eyes, they do not show a preference for the larger

object, either the car or the checkerboard. Thus, by 7 months, infants use visual cues, such as size, to judge depth.

Also by 7 months, infants can use other visual cues to judge depth. If one object partially blocks the view of another, the blocked object is perceived as farther away (Granrud & Yonas, 1984), and relative shading in a drawing depicting a bump or a depression causes 7-month-olds, but not 5-month-olds, to reach for the object shaded like a bump (Granrud, Yonas, & Opland, 1985). Both 5- and 7-month-olds reach for actual bumps. Finally, by 7 months, when objects are presented in a perspective drawing, infants use the perspective information to reach for the object that is apparently nearer to them (Arterberry, Yonas, & Bensen, 1989). Infants' ability to recognize objects in two dimensions leads to increased interest in picture books and television at this age.

During this period, infants learn to perceive object properties through touch as well as through vision. Perception of the properties of an object using touch is called **haptic perception.** Through haptic perception, infants soon after birth can distinguish different properties of objects primarily by using their mouths. In the early months, the mouth is perhaps the most sensitive haptic organ. Between 4 and 6 months, infants begin examining objects by active exploration combining hand, mouth, and vision (Morange-Majoux, Cougnot, & Bloch, 1997; Oakes & Tellinghuisen, 1994; Ruff, 1986). After 6 months, infants develop specialized hand movements to detect information about specific object properties (Bushnell & Boudreau, 1993). To perceive an object's relative size, for example, infants will enclose their hands around the outside of the object. Other perception-action correspondences are shown in Table 7.3. Through both haptics and vision, therefore, infants become increasingly sophisticated in their knowledge of object properties.

Other Perceptual Developments

Besides recognizing pictures in books, infants in this age period can recognize differences between simple melodies. Six-month-olds can discriminate between six-note melodies differing by only one note (Trehub, Bull, & Thorpe, 1984), and they can

Table 7.3 Haptic Perception-Action Correspondences for Infants

Object Property	Haptic Action
Size, volume	Enclosing external contours
Hardness	Applying pressure
Exact shape	Following the contour with fingers
Temperature	Static palm or finger contact
Texture	Side-to-side movements of palms or fingers
Weight	Holding in palm without enclosing, lowering and raising

discriminate between melodies in which the pauses between notes are varied (Thorpe & Trehub, 1989). By this age, therefore, babies can recognize some nursery rhymes and simple melodies heard in songs.

Also by this age, babies show continuing evidence of cross-modal perception. Thus, infants are sensitive to distortions in the sound track of a film showing a rattle shaking at a particular rhythm. If the sound is faster or slower than the rattle's movements, the babies notice the difference (Bahrick, 1987). As the visual and auditory display becomes more complicated, however, infants preferentially process the sound but not the vision, reflecting the fact that even at 6 months, auditory perception is more advanced than visual perception (Lewkowicz, 1988, 1996). This auditory dominance is also true for adults, as when light displays flashed to accompany music seem to move at the same beat as the music. If the visual displays are flashed in a regular manner that makes their rhythm salient, however, infants and adults will pay more attention to the visual compared to the auditory display (Lewkowicz, 1994). These findings are important because they show that cross-modal perception is becoming more controlled for infants: under certain conditions, they can distinguish between the separate attributes of each modality.

Infants older than 6 months can also use cross-modal perception to infer information about object properties. Infants of this age who are familiarized with an object only by touch can recognize the object by sight alone (Ruff & Kohler, 1978) and infants will alternatively look at and touch objects and put them into their mouths while exploring them (Ruff, 1984). Furthermore, if babies hear a sound in the dark, they will reach for an object in the direction of the sound. Infants can also distinguish whether the object is within or out of their reach based on hearing its sound in the dark (Clifton, Perris, & Bullinger, 1991; Perris & Clifton, 1988). Finally, infants were given sweet and tart foods in cups of different colors. On subsequent color-choice trials, the infants consistently picked the color that had been paired with the sweet food (Reardon & Bushnell, 1988).

In summary, these studies of perception show that by the middle of the first year of life, infants can use subtle cues to infer regularities in their perceptual world. They can now learn from pictures in books and on television. They can pick up relationships between different senses in order to pay attention to aspects of their environment that most interest them, such as the color of the baby food jar that contains their favorite flavor. These perceptual abilities lead to clear preferences, as we will see later in the chapter. Babies begin to take the initiative in expressing their desires for particular pictures, objects, and tastes. As we saw in the last chapter in relation to the topic of the ecological self, as infants learn to perceive the world, they also learn about themselves.

Cognitive Development

Memory

During the period from 6 to 9 months, the infant's brain continues to develop. Studies using kicking to make mobiles move have shown that infant memory during this period is similar to memory at 3 months. However, while 3-month-olds can remember how to produce mobile movements for up to 14 days, 7-month-olds can remember for as long as 21 days without a reminder (Hill, Borovsky, & Rovee-Collier, 1988). In the previous chapter, we saw how 3-month-olds required the exact duplication of the original learning situation in order to remember something. By 7 months, their memories are somewhat less context dependent, meaning that infants can remember a salient event that has been learned in several different but related situations. Infants of this age have more control over reactivating their own memories and do not have to rely entirely on contextual cues (Amabile & Rovee-Collier, 1991; Bhatt, Rovee-Collier, & Weiner, 1994).

Although the memory of infants of this age is improving, it is still limited and localized to the situation, at least compared to that of a preschool child or an adult. Nevertheless, one can begin to see the seeds of more lasting participatory memories. The fact that infants can remind themselves means that they are beginning to take a role in creating their own self-history that transcends particular situations. By 6 months, therefore, infants take a more active role in the processing of information.

Increasing Use of Concepts to Organize and Process Information

This increasingly active information processing means that infants are able to group different stimuli into higher-order conceptual categories. Using a habituation procedure, researchers showed babies a series of pictures of the same face in different poses. During the test trial, the infants dishabituated to an unfamiliar face but not to the same face in a different pose. This shows that the babies had organized all the different poses they saw into a higher-order concept of a particular face. Seven-month-olds, but not 5-month-olds, were able to do this (L. B. Cohen & Strauss, 1979). In a similar type of study, 7-month-old infants were habituated to different faces having the same facial expression (a smile). They dishabituated to a different face with a non-smile expression but not to a different face with a smile expression (R. F. Caron, Caron, & Myers, 1982).

In an interesting variant of this procedure, infants were familiarized with somewhat distorted versions of a prototype figure (Younger & Gotlieb, 1988; see Figure 7.2). A **prototype** figure is one that is the clearest example of the form being represented. If infants are actively organizing the images of the distorted figures into a category, then they should prefer to look at a related prototype, compared to an unrelated prototype in a test trial in which both are available to look at. Infants who were familiarized with the "plus sign" distortions preferred the "plus sign" prototype at ages 3, 5, and 7 months. Only 7-months-olds could recognize the prototype from the distorted versions of the odd-shaped figure shown in the lower part of Figure 7.2.

Because of their ability to perceive objects as whole entities, infants of this age are beginning to relate objects together into higher-order classifications. Seven-month-olds, for example, can distinguish horses from some other four-legged mammals such as cats, zebras, and giraffes (Eimas & Quinn, 1994). Infants develop motor categorizations for objects, grouping them into things shakable, drinkable, squeezable, and so on (Baldwin, Markman, & Melartin, 1993; Bushnell & Boudreau, 1993; Catherwood, 1993). By 9 months, infants can distinguish these object properties visually as well as haptically (Coldren & Colombo, 1994).

Infants of this age are able to judge whether objects are too big to fit into containers, when shown objects and containers of various sizes (Aguiar & Baillargeon, 1998). They understand that moving objects should follow along their prior path of movement and that larger objects can support smaller objects (Baillargeon & De Vos, 1991; Baillargeon, Needham, & De Vos, 1992; Sitskoorn & Smitsman, 1995). Infants will respond differentially when the same object is placed above as opposed to below another object, showing that they have a category for these kinds of spatial relationships (Quinn, Cummins, Kase, Martin, & Weissman, 1996).

Infants of this age may even have a concept of number or quantity of objects. Infants were habituated to a puppet jumping in the air either two or three times. They dishabituated when the number of jumps changed, from two to three or from three to two (Wynn, 1998). Piaget discovered that his children had a sense of quantity at 11 months of age when he tried to get them to imitate sounds (Piaget, 1952, p. 241). If Piaget said "papa," Laurent replied with "papa." If Piaget said "pa," so did Laurent. By adding more "pa" syllables, Piaget discovered that Laurent had trouble with more than three. Saying "papapapapapa" only got a "papapapa" in return. Other research found that 10- to 12-month-olds could easily discriminate visual ar-

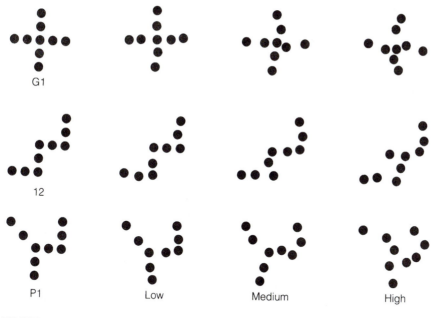

Figure 7.2
Prototypes and Variations

Prototypical patterns shown with examples of corresponding low-, medium-, and high-level distortions.

G1

12

P1   Low   Medium   High

PROTOTYPE   **LEVEL OF DISTORTION**

Source: B. Younger & S. Gotlieb, Development of categorization skills: Changes in the nature or structure of infant form categories, 1988, p. 614. *Developmental Psychology, 24,* 611–619. Copyright © by the American Psychological Association. Reprinted with permission.

rays that differed only in number, particularly for one versus two objects, one versus three objects, and two versus three objects. They had a harder time with four versus three objects, and no luck at all discriminating four from five objects (M. Strauss & Curtis, 1981). Studies like these show that infants of this age have a concept of quantity—more versus less—but they do not prove that infants of this age know numbers and can do math problems. That ability begins in the third year (Mix, Levine, & Huttenlocher, 1997). All of the infant's rudimentary categorical abilities will develop rapidly after 9 months (see Chapter 8).

Piaget's Third Sensorimotor Stage: Secondary Circular Reactions

The infant's growing abilities to perceive and conceptualize the properties of objects were also noticed by Piaget. Beginning at about 4 months and continuing until about 8 or 9 months, infants pass

through Piaget's third stage of sensorimotor development: the stage of **secondary circular reactions.** This stage is a natural extension of the preceding one. Instead of only repeating actions that they discover by chance on their own bodies (the primary circular reaction), infants soon begin to repeat actions that, by chance, produce some effect on the objects and people in the environment. The idea of *chance*—the fortuitous discovery of some interesting result—is what distinguishes this stage from the ones that follow. Once the chance discovery is made, however, infants make deliberate, intentional attempts to repeat that action.

In a primary circular reaction, babies repeat a movement of their own bodies but do not make the connection between that movement and its effect. The movement creates a good feeling (a sound or a sight), but the babies seem focused on the efforts of their own bodies. In secondary circular reactions, babies are focused more on the objects in the environment. They not only repeat actions that produce effects on objects, they also vary the actions in order to explore changes in the effect. Piaget

---

OBSERVATIONS

Stage III Behavior (Piaget, 1952, pp. 187, 195)

Observation 7.1

Laurent: at 0;4(21) has an object in his hands when, in order to distract him, I shake the hanging rattles which he is in the habit of striking. He then looks at the rattles without relinquishing his toy and outlines with his right hand the movement of "striking."

Observation 7.2

At 0;7(10): Laurent cries in the morning as soon as he hears his mother's bed creak. Until then, although awake, he did not show his hunger. But, at the slightest creak, he moans and thus demands his bottle.

(1952) suggested that infants are trying to "make interesting sights last."

Babies between 6 and 9 months will drop objects off the edge of their high chairs, perhaps listening for different sounds or looking at different movements when the objects hit the floor. They shake objects in different ways to notice the effect or repeatedly dump things (such as their food) out of containers.

Infants in this period tend to apply the movements they use for particular objects as a way of representing or referring to the object. When Piaget shakes his son's rattles, Laurent at 4½ months is too busily engaged in playing with the toy he is holding to actually strike his rattle. He seems to indicate the potential action by making a striking movement in the air. Instead of saying verbally, "Those are my rattles," Laurent expresses himself through a motor movement that has the exact form of his previous interactions with that object (see Observation 7.1).

At the same time, repeated occurrences in the environment take on meaning for the baby. By 7 months, Laurent knew that he would be fed shortly after he heard his mother's bed creak. Earlier in his life, he would cry with hunger as soon as he woke up. Now he cries in relation to certain environmental events that have come to have a meaning for him. Like the act of "pretend" striking, the cry is a motor way of saying, "That's the sound of my food!" (see Observation 7.2).

These observations suggest that infants are becoming more intentional and goal directed, and also that they can perceive the intentional behavior of other people. Nine-month-old infants were shown an actor grasping first one toy and then another. They were also shown an actor touching one toy with the back of her hand and then touching another toy the same way. The infants looked longer when the grasping hand contacted the second toy than they did when the actor touched the second toy with the back of her hand (Woodward, 1999). This suggests that infants are more interested in actions of other people that seem to have a clear goal.

Out of Sight, Out of Mind?

Another aspect of conceptualizing objects is whether infants believe that objects have a permanent existence. **Object permanence** is the ability to remain aware of an object even after it has gone out of sight. Piaget (1952) showed that infants will not actively search for an object that has been hidden until after the age of 9 months, during Stage IV. Can infants at a younger age keep track of a visually hidden object in a setting that does not require the use of the motor skills that Stage III infants do not have?

Given what we know about the memory of infants under 9 months, it seems quite likely that they should be able to remember objects when they can no longer see them. In one study, infants aged 7 to 8 months saw an object sitting on one of two red placemats that were 8.5 inches (21.5 centimeters) apart. Next, two purple screens big enough to hide the object were slid in front of the placemats (see Figure 7.3). A hand then reached behind the screen and reappeared holding the object in either a possible situation or an impossible situation (Figure 7.3). Infants looked longer at the hand following the impossible situation compared to the possible one, showing that they remembered the object's location and were surprised when the object appeared from behind the screen opposite that behind which they had seen it placed (Baillargeon & Graber, 1988).

Possible event   Impossible event

Figure 7.3
Sequence of Events Used in an Object Permanence Task

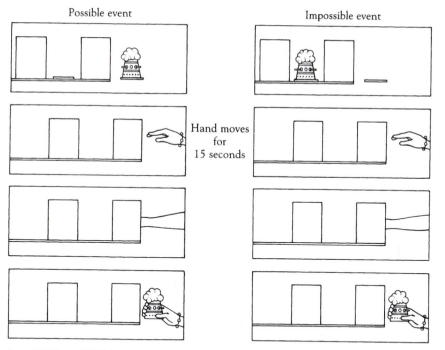

Hand moves for 15 seconds

Source: R. Baillargeon & M. Graber, Evidence of location memory in 8-month-old infants in a nonsearch AB task, 1988, p. 505. *Developmental Psychology, 24,* 502–511. Copyright © by the American Psychological Association. Reprinted with permission.

This type of research has been repeated for different kinds of visual events in which objects appear and disappear in possible and impossible ways. Infants between 3 and 7 months come to understand that objects seen in the light will still be in the same place when the lights are turned off (Clifton et al., 1991; Clifton et al., 1994). In one study, infants were shown an object falling and making a noise on impact, after which they were allowed to reach for the fallen object. Next, the lights were turned off. When the infants heard the sound of the impact they reached for the object in the dark at the same location (Goubet & Clifton, 1998; McCall & Clifton, 1999).

In summary, infants of this age are becoming aware of objects and people and whole entities. They can appreciate that objects have features and boundaries, that they occupy unique locations in space, and that they do not disappear when out of sight. The same is also true for infant's conceptions of people. People, however, are understood by infants as having intentions. The ability to perceive another's intentions corresponds with the infant's awareness of their own intentions, their ability to

have an effect on the environment. I will return to this topic when I discuss the sense of self at this age. Another characteristic of people is that they experience and display emotions, a topic to which I shall turn next.

Emotional Development

The Development of Negative Emotions

Until the beginning of Piaget's Stage III (around 5 months), babies have basically one response to a negative experience: they cry. With the onset of secondary circular reactions, infants become more "aware" that they can cause things to happen in the environment. This sense of themselves as a causal agent—part of the ecological self—accounts in part for the reduction in the amount of crying that occurs between 3 and 5 months. When infants cannot succeed at being an effective causal agent—when they cannot get a toy they want, for example—a new source of negative experience enters their lives: *anger*.

Anger in infants is a direct result of their having their motives disrupted. Although both anger and distress are accompanied by crying, the facial expression during anger is different from that of distress, as is the baby's underlying feeling (Izard, 1981; Sroufe, 1979). In one study, infants' reactions to inoculations were observed at 2, 4, and 7 months. At 2 and 4 months, infants reacted with physical distress, a direct response to pain. Distress is expressed by crying with tightly shut eyes. By 7 months, the babies responded with more angry expressions, crying with open, vigilant eyes (Izard, 1981; Izard, Hembree, & Huebner, 1987).

It is almost as if the quality of the gaze signals that the infant is angry at the person being watched. If you have an opportunity to experience this with a baby (see the "Co-Regulating with Baby" section of this chapter), you can feel what it is like when an upset baby looks at you in this particular way. Anger can be expressed in many different ways as infants get older, such as by kicking, biting, sulking, yelling, pouting, or temper tantrums (Barrett, 1993; Barrett & Campos, 1987; Campos & Barrett, 1984).

Separation from the mother is another situation that causes negative emotions. Before the age of 6 months, infants cry with distress, particularly if their mothers leave, act depressed, or perform a still face in the middle of a feeding or play session. The distress arises from the cessation of the pleasurable interaction. After 6 months, infants respond to parental separation with some anger, especially if the parent happens to be a part of the infant's activity—such as during play or feeding—when he or she leaves (Izard, 1981). Expressions of anger are also seen in 7-month-olds when a teething biscuit is removed from their mouths or when their arms are restrained (Stenberg, Campos, & Emde, 1983).

Another negatively toned emotion seen at this age is **wariness.** Infants may become quiet and stare at a stranger or a strange situation, knit their brows,

become momentarily sober, and look away (Bronson, 1972). Because wariness allows the infant to observe what is happening, it is a considerably more adaptive reaction to strange situations than is the withdrawal of infantile fussing and crying of previous ages (Emde, Gaensbauer, & Harmon, 1976; Malatesta et al., 1986).

Aside from these general trends, there are also individual differences. Infants of this age were taught to pull a string attached to their wrist in order to activate a slide projection of an infant's face accompanied by the *Sesame Street* theme song. After they learned this procedure, the experimenters stopped turning on the slide projector and music when the infant pulled the string. Most of the infants reacted to this contingency failure with anger, although some showed expressions of sadness. When the contingency was renewed, the infants who expressed anger immediately became interested again in the task, while those who showed sadness reacted to the renewal of the contingency with less enjoyment (Lewis et al., 1992). This shows that anger is an adaptive and useful response for some babies, who perceive the renewal of the contingency as under their control. The babies who were saddened, however, may perceive themselves as helpless to change the course of events.

At this age, then, the helpless fussing of earlier ages gives way to demanding crying, anger, and wariness. Each of these forms of negative emotional expression is considerably more adaptive from the infant's point of view and these developments reflect some significant advances in the infant's ability to cope with negative situations. Wariness, for example, allows for even more prolonged inspection of the potentially worrisome stimulus rather than a simple rejection of it. We might say that the end result of this increasing sophistication in the realm of negative responding is to bring the infant back into a positive engagement with the environment.

The Development of Positive Emotions

The positive emotions also become more complex during this age period. In one study, mothers and infants were observed playing peekaboo and tickle games. Different types of smiles had different emotional meanings depending upon whether the infant was attending to the mother or not (Fogel, Nelson-Goens, Hsu, & Shapiro, in press). Simple smiling (lip corner retraction without cheek raising; see Chapter 6) accompanied by gazing at the mother during peekaboo represents an *enjoyment of recognition* or perhaps an *enjoyment of readiness to engage in play.* The feeling may be similar to an adult's experience of being delighted to be with a familiar person and to engage in enjoyable things together. Simple smiles occurring without gazing at mother after a previous tickle are often accompanied by gasping for air and sighing. The feeling associated with these smiles may be an *enjoyment of relief* or perhaps an *enjoyment of relaxation,* similar to pauses between laughter episodes in playful conversations of children and adults.

Duchenne smiles (lip corner retraction with cheek raising) occur with gazing at the mother primarily when she uncovers her face during peekaboo. These smiles may reflect an *enjoyment of agency,* sensing oneself as an active rather than passive participant in the game (Holt, Fogel, & Wood, 1998; Stern, 1985). This may mean that the pleasure of peekaboo is in the experience of active visual searching for when and how the mother will reappear after hiding. Duchenne smiles without gazing at the mother occur most frequently during a tickle, often as infants turn their whole bodies away as if trying to hide or to protect themselves. These Duchenne smiles may reflect an *enjoyment of hiding* or perhaps an *enjoyment of escape,* as during hiding and chasing games in older infants and children.

These findings reveal that infants of this age are showing the beginnings of adultlike emotional experiences. When co-regulating with an infant of this age, one gets the impression that babies are aware of their feelings and of some of the effects of those feelings on others. These results also show that infant emotional experiences are co-regulated with adults during social interaction (see the "Co-Regulating with Baby" section in this chapter).

The first laughs could be seen in the previous stage, primarily as a result of tickling and other vigorous stimulation. By the age of 6 months, babies will laugh at your jokes. They will laugh when you play tug with them, when they see you suck on their pacifiers or bottles, and when they try to pull the bottles out of your mouth (Fogel, Nwokah, & Karns, 1993; Nwokah et al., 1993; Sroufe, 1979).

Babies also laugh at very abrupt and highly arousing stimuli. They may laugh at things that once made them cry, such as a loud noise or a loss of balance. The laugh will sometimes follow a very serious or wary expression, almost as if the babies were trying to make up their minds about whether to get upset or enjoy the situation. In one study, 8-month-old babies watched while someone wearing a scary mask approached them. When the mask was worn by a stranger, the babies cried. When it was worn by their mothers, the babies laughed (Sroufe & Wunsch, 1977).

Emotion Regulation

This experiment suggests that by this age, the infant is beginning to use cognition to *decide what to feel,* a process known as **appraisal.** This means that there is a growing relationship between infant emotion and attention to the events and processes related to that emotion. Seven-month-old infants were familiarized with a computerized drawing of a face and asked to choose between the familiar face and an unfamiliar one using a paired preference procedure. If infants studied the familiar faces with a neutral facial expression, they looked at the pair of faces for a shorter time and were better able to distinguish the familiar from the unfamiliar faces. If the infants were smiling, they looked longer at the familiar faces and were less efficient in their discrimination during the paired preference test. This means that positive emotions are related to a less analytical style of attending (Rose, Futterweit, & Jankowski, 1999).

Because of the connection between infant emotion regulation and adult-infant communication, you might expect that different patterns of communication between mothers and their male and female infants would be related to gender differences in emotion regulation. Six-month-old boys and girls were observed during face-to-face play, followed by maternal still face (see Chapter 6). During the still-face condition, boys were more likely than girls to show expressions of anger, to fuss, to gesture to be picked up, or to try to get out of the infant seat.

Boys also were more likely to try to get the mother's attention by smiling and vocalizing to her. Girls, on the other hand, spent more time gazing at objects and showing expressions of interest. The boys also had a more positive interaction with the mother during the normal face-to-face period (Weinberg, Tronick, Cohn, & Olson, 1999).

You might think these findings are counterintuitive. Under the assumption that girls may be more social, should not girls be more positive with their mothers and more upset during the still face because of an apparent break in the mother-infant communication? This study, however, does not reveal that boys are more social than girls but, rather, that boys are less able to regulate their emotions under stressful conditions. The girls were able to manage their emotions during the still face by becoming more observant of the objects in the environment. The more positive interaction between mothers and sons during the normal condition may reflect a necessity to achieve co-regulated communication because boys are more upset when there are breakdowns in communication (Weinberg et al., 1999).

In summary, the findings on emotion regulation show that infants of both genders are highly tuned into their emotional communication with others. They are able to experience subtle differences of emotion as a function of how their attention is directed and whether the communication is co-regulated or disrupted. In older children and adults, emotions are related to changes in interpersonal communication. People's ability to regulate their emotions depends strongly on whether things go well or badly with their friends and romantic partners. This research shows that infants are beginning to feel these same types of social and emotional connections.

Recognition of Emotional Expressions

Research shows that infants' ability to recognize and discriminate among different emotional expressions increases between 6 and 9 months. Babies seem more capable of recognizing smiles than other expressions. Infants were familiarized with pictures of faces with smiles of different inensities. Later, they dishabituated to nonsmile expressions but not to smiles differing in intensity (Ludemann, 1991; Ludemann & Nelson, 1988). Their ability at this age to distinguish between other expressions, such as fear and anger, is relatively poor (Nelson, 1987). On the other hand, as we saw in the last chapter, infants recognize emotion in the voice earlier than emotion in the face. When facial expressions of emotions are combined with voices expressing those emotions, 7-month-olds improve considerably in their ability to distinguish between emotions (Caron, Caron, & McLean, 1988; Phillips et al., 1990; Soken & Pick, 1992). When faces are presented dynamically, that is, via videorecordings rather than still pictures, 7-month-old infants' ability to distinguish different types of expression also improves (Soken & Pick, 1999).

Except for a happy expression, to which infants will respond with a smile, there is little evidence that infants of this age view facial expressions alone as meaningful emotion signals (Nelson, 1987). The ability to extract meaning from viewing another person's face is extremely slow to develop, but we will see the beginnings of this skill in the next stage (see Chapter 8). It is not clear why infants have a concept for smiles earlier than they do concepts for other facial expressions. It makes sense, however, that the infant would be particularly attuned to facial expressions related to happiness, which probably increase the infant's sense of connection to the other person.

Infants of this age prefer to look at faces judged by adults to be attractive, regardless of the race or gender of the faces they are looking at (Langlois et al., 1991). Apparently, attractiveness, like recognition of particular people, can be inferred from more global features of the face that do not involve specific expressions (Rubenstein, Kalakanis, & Langlois, 1999). Infants can also distinguish between the faces of children and adults (Bahrick, Netto, & Hernandez-Reif, 1998). In summary, infants of this age have a rudimentary ability to perceive information from the face, and this ability will continue to improve in the coming months.

Infant Temperament

Another question related to infant emotional development is whether there are lasting patterns of emotional responding in infants. We know that

Table 7.4 Temperamental Characteristics Crucial in Classifying Children as Easy or Difficult*

Temperamental Quality	Two Months	Two Years
Activity level	Does not move when being dressed or during sleep. *Moves often in sleep. Wriggles when diaper is changed.*	Enjoys quiet play with puzzles. Can listen to records for hours. *Climbs furniture. Explores. Gets in and out of bed while being put to sleep.*
Rhythmicity	Has been on 4-hour feeding schedule since birth. Regular bowel movement. *Awakes at different time each morning. Size of feedings varies.*	Eats a big lunch each day. Always has a snack before bedtime. *Nap time changes from day to day. Toilet training is difficult because bowel movement is unpredictable.*
Approach/Withdrawal	Smiles and licks washcloth. Has always liked bottle. *Rejected cereal the first time. Cries when strangers appear.*	Slept well the first time he stayed overnight at grandparents' house. *Avoids strange children in the playground. Whimpers first time at beach. Will not go into water.*
Adaptability	Was passive during first bath, now enjoys bathing. Smiles at nurse. *Still startled by sudden, sharp noises. Resists diapering.*	Obeys quickly. Stayed contentedly with grandparents for a week. *Cries and screams each time hair is cut. Disobeys persistently.*
Intensity of reaction	Does not cry when diapers are wet. Whimpers instead of crying when hungry. *Cries when diapers are wet. Rejects food vigorously when satisfied.*	When another child hit her, she looked surprised, did not hit back. *Yells if he feels excitement or delight. Cries loudly if a toy is taken away.*
Quality of mood	Smacks lips when first tasting new food. Smiles at parents. *Fusses after nursing. Cries when carriage is rocked.*	Plays with sister; laughs and giggles. Smiles when he succeeds in putting shoes on. *Cries and squirms when given a haircut. Cries when mother leaves.*

*Temperamental ratings and behaviors for difficult children are in italic type; those for easy children are in regular type.
Source: From Thomas, Chess, & Birch, 1970. In A. Fogel & G. F. Melson, *Child development*, 1988, p. 209. St. Paul, MN: West. Copyright © by West Publishing Co. Reprinted by permission. All rights reserved.

at any age infants exhibit different amounts of difficulty, fussiness, or happiness. The question is whether these differences persist over time. Is the same infant who is difficult at 3 months also difficult at 6 or 12 months? **Temperament** is a persistent pattern of emotion and emotion regulation in the infant's relationship to people and things in the environment.

Researchers have identified a number of expressive and responsive dimensions along which infants vary. One list of temperamental dimensions is given in Table 7.4. On each dimension, some children are especially high or especially low, and such extreme cases have been referred to as "easy" or as "difficult" (see Table 7.4; Thomas & Chess, 1977). Considerably shorter lists of temperamental dimensions have been developed by other groups of researchers and are shown in Tables 7.5 and 7.6.

In addition to proposing different definitions of temperament, each research team has a slightly different view of the origins of stable temperaments. According to Thomas and Chess, temperament is a style of approach to the environment and may be affected by the situation. For Plomin (Buss & Plomin, 1984; Plomin & Saudino, 1994), temperament is stable because it is an inherited personality trait that appears early in life. While some traits are acquired, the three dimensions shown in Table 7.5 are believed to have some inherited basis (Goldsmith et al., 1987; Goldsmith, Buss, & Lemery, 1997; Goldsmith et al., 1999).

Research done using twin studies and behavior genetics methods (see the section on behavior ecology theory in Chapter 2) has found that some aspects of temperament are partly inherited. Inhibition to the unfamiliar (see Table 7.6), as observed

Table 7.5   Dimensions of Infant Temperament According to Buss and Plomin (1984)

Temperamental Quality	Description
Emotionality	Emotional infants have strong fear, anger, or distress responses, as shown by high ANS activity. Emotional infants may also respond more to minimal aversive events and may be less easy to calm or to appease. Emotional infants tend to "specialize" in one emotion, showing, for example, strong anger but not strong fear or distress.
Activity	Active infants tend to be busy and energetic. They move around a lot and prefer more active forms of play.
Sociability	Sociable infants tend to spend more time in the company of others. This concept refers more to frequent initiation of contact with a wide range of individuals than to intimate contact with attachment figures. Sociable infants prefer being with people rather than alone and seem genuinely pleased by social contact.

Source: Information from A. H. Buss & R. Plomin, *Temperament: Early developing personality traits,* 1984. Hillsdale, NJ: Erlbaum. Used with permission.

Table 7.6   Temperamental Dimensions of Reactivity (Rothbart & Derryberry, 1981) and Inhibition (Kagan, 1987)

Reactivity	Includes brain activation, ANS processes, and hormonal processes. High reactivity includes both a rapid response and a high-intensity response, and it may also include a slow recovery from the response.
Inhibition	Inhibited children are restrained, watchful, and gentle. They tend to experience uncertainty about how to respond or how to think about a situation. Inhibition can also be characterized by particular brain, ANS, and hormonal processes.

in the laboratory, and infant negative emotions, as rated by parents, both have some genetic influence (Emde et al., 1992). Negativity and inhibition both appear early in life and are persistent characteristics in 5 to 10% of all infants up until the ages of 5 to 7 years. In addition, similar proportions of persistently inhibited children are found in different countries and even in infant monkeys, which further suggests some genetic contribution (Garcia-Coll, Kagan, & Reznick, 1984; Kagan, 1997; Kagan & Reznick, 1984; Kagan et al., 1988; Kagan et al., 1994; Lewis, 1993; Mullen, Snidman, & Kagan, 1993; Reznick et al., 1986; Shwalb, Shwalb, & Shoji, 1994; Worobey & Lewis, 1989).

According to both Rothbart (Rothbart & Derryberry, 1981; Rothbart, Derryberry, & Posner, 1994) and Kagan (1987), temperament is rooted in biological processes but not necessarily inherited. For these researchers, behavioral characteristics called temperamental must be associated with specific central nervous system (CNS) and autonomic nervous system (ANS) activity (S. D. Calkins, Fox, & Marshall, 1996; Kagan, Reznick & Snidman,

1987; Rothbart, 1986). In this view, temperament is a somatic pattern, involving both mind and body. A number of other researchers have found such physiological correlates for children rated as highly reactive, emotional, or inhibited.

For example, inhibition (see Table 7.6) is related to brain wave and heart rate patterns as well as to stress responses to frustration. Physiological stress responses to frustration, such as heart rate acceleration, are present at an early age for some inhibited infants and may persist for periods of up to 1 year (S. Calkins & Fox, 1994; N. A. Fox, 1989; M. Gunnar, 1994; M. Gunnar, Mangelsdorf, Larson, & Hertsgaard, 1989; Healy, 1989; Huffman et al., 1998; M. Lewis & Ramsay, 1995; C. A. Nelson, 1994).

For some researchers, environmental influences on temperament are more salient than somatic physiological or genetic influences. Some research has shown that infant temperament is correlated with parental personality. Infants who are more inhibited, for example, are more likely to have parents who are introverted, shy, and anxious (Rickman & Davidson, 1994). Also, persistent infant inhibition and high levels of negativity are related to lower scores on maternal adaptation to pregnancy, maternal sensitivity to the infant after birth, and maternal self-esteem (Fish, Stifter, & Belsky, 1991; Martin, Noyes, Wisenbaker, & Huttunen, 1999). Mothers who rate infant cries as more aversive are more likely to rate their infants as difficult (Pedersen & Moran, 1996). These findings, while they suggest that parents play a role in the development of infant temperament, do not necessarily rule out a partial genetic explanation for inhibition, since parents and infants could both share similar genetic make-ups.

Another finding that may call the genetic explanation into question is that children do not necessarily exhibit continuity of temperament. Inhibited children may, with appropriately sensitive child rearing, eventually lose their extreme sensitivity. Normal children may become more inhibited in extremely stressful environments. While extreme fussiness at birth predicts later emotionality in full-term infants (Worobey & Blajda, 1989), fussiness at birth is not related to later behavior in premature infants (Riese, 1987). The stress of premature birth may have made it impossible to assess the infant's temperament at the time of birth. If there is a biological predisposition toward inhibition or other temperamental factors, such as emotionality, it does not operate in the absence of environmental influences (Kagan, 1987; Wachs, 1988).

Temperamental characteristics in infancy do not seem to predict long-term personality characteristics or behavior disorders. Temperament may have short-term influences on cognitive information processing, as when an inhibited infant is unlikely to approach a novel stimulus, but there is less evidence that temperament contributes to longer-term cognitive deficit or enhancement (J. E. Bates, 1987; Kagan, 1987; M. D. Lewis, 1993). One reason may be that parents adjust their short-term behavior to the child's reactivity. If parents respond cautiously to inhibited children or work to desensitize them, and if they reduce the intensity of stimulation for highly active children, the parental behavior may attenuate the long-term effects of the early temperamental characteristic (Gandour, 1989; Kagan, 1987; Kagan, Snidman, & Arcus, 1998; S. Park, Belsky, Putnam, & Crnic, 1997).

Aside from parental factors, factors in the infant may contribute to the stability of temperament. Inhibited children who showed more positive emotion were less likely to be inhibited at age 3 than inhibited children who tended to be more negative (S. Park et al., 1997). It seems that both parental and child factors can interact to influence the stability of temperament over time.

On the other hand, temperament assessed at the end of the infancy period, between 2 and 4 years of age, does tend to show long-term stability (Lemery, Goldsmith, Klinnert, & Mrazek, 1999). Two-year-olds who were rated as more difficult had more attention problems and aggressive behavior at 12 years (Guerin, Gottfried, & Thomas, 1997). Three-year-olds who were rated low on self-control had more adjustment problems and interpersonal conflicts as adults (Newman, Caspi, Moffitt, & Silva, 1997).

In summary, temperamental characteristics such as inhibition and negativity clearly exist in infants and may persist over many years. Less clear is the origin of these temperamental characteristics. The evidence suggests that they have multiple and complex causes related to inheritance, physiology, environment, and parent-child relationships. Temperament is apparently best explained by some type of systems theory. In the next section, I turn to the problem of how temperament is measured.

The Measurement of Temperament

One of the problems in studying temperament is that it must be observed over a long period of time. Temperament is *by definition* characterized by developmental continuity; that is, temperamental dimensions are those aspects of infants that are consistent over time. A child who is sociable on a particular day is not necessarily temperamentally sociable unless there is a consistent pattern of such behavior over a long period. For this reason, the study of temperament is more difficult than other areas of research because the investigator has to identify what stays the same when other things are changing. Because infants change in so many ways, it is difficult to capture their essence (J. E. Bates, 1987; J. E. Bates, Wachs, & Emde, 1994; Kagan, 1987; Wachs & Bates, 2000).

Another problem is that of language. Even though we might have some strong intuition about the consistent temperament of a baby we know, it is hard to describe that consistency in words. Once a word such as "inhibited" is chosen, it cannot describe exactly what the temperamental quality is, and the word itself often distorts what is unique about the baby (Kagan, 1987). To call a baby "inhibited" does not do justice to the fact that the child may play, walk, and talk like most other children. Under certain circumstances, however, such as in the presence of an unfamiliar person, this child may be especially shy.

Given the difficulties in identifying a commonsense concept of temperament, it should come as no surprise that researchers have found temperament to be a difficult construct to measure in a reliable and valid manner. Some have attempted to observe children's responses to particular situations over a long period, such as their reactions to distress and separation, or to examine their overall activity level. More typically, parents are asked to rate their children's temperaments under the assumption that the parents have the most complete, long-term experiences with the children and can better assess any stable characteristics (J. E. Bates, 1987).

On the other hand, what is probably the best source of information about the child's temperament is not always reliable. When mothers and fathers are asked to rate the same child, their reports agree only about half the time (J. E. Bates & Bayles, 1984; H. H. Goldsmith & Gottesman, 1981; Hubert, Wachs, Peters-Martin, & Gandour, 1982). Similarly, there is only a moderate amount of agreement between mothers and outside observers (J. E. Bates, 1980), although there is more overall agreement about the difficulty of an infant than about any other dimension of temperament.

Some evidence also suggests that temperament is related to other measures of the infant's behavior. Infants rated as "distractable" by their parents at 2 weeks, for example, had lower scores on the Brazelton Neonatal Assessment Scale at 1 week and lower scores on the Bayley infant assessment test at 10 weeks (Sostek & Anders, 1977). Infants who were rated as "difficult" had cries that were independently rated as more irritating and had longer pauses between cry sounds, as revealed by sound

spectrograph analysis (see Chapter 5), giving their cries a greater sense of urgency (Huffman et al., 1994; Lounsbury & Bates, 1982). Mothers' ratings of infant temperamental fussiness correlated with direct observations of crying behavior at 3 months (Crockenberg & Acredolo, 1983). Infant fear and pleasure responses as measured in a laboratory setting correlated with similar dimensions of parent-rated infant temperament (H. H. Goldsmith & Campos, 1990). The correlation between parental reports and actual behavior is improved if infants are selected only from the extreme ends of the behavioral scale. Infants who were either extremely inhibited or extremely uninhibited in a laboratory situation had parents who also rated them in this manner (Garcia-Coll et al., 1984). These findings suggest that although there is some correspondence between parental reports and actual behavior, in many cases, correspondence is lacking.

It could be that each parent and each observer have different experiences with the child and thus have different databases from which to draw conclusions. Also, the child may actually behave differently across situations and in the company of different observers. It could also be that the questions asked on rating forms (ranging from general questions about the overall difficulty of the child to specific questions about the child's reaction to strangers) are not sufficiently sensitive to capture the individuality of the child.

Another possibility is that the parental reports reflect the parents' personalities more than the child's (Matheny, Wilson, & Thoben, 1987; Miebert, 1991; Vaughn, Bradley, Joffe, Seifer, & Barglow, 1987) or reveal something about the current psychological state of the parents. Mothers who were multiparous and extroverted were more likely to rate their infants as easy than other mothers (J. E. Bates, Freeland, & Lounsbury, 1979). Other studies found that mothers from low-income groups who were African American, had a history of mental illness, or scored high on tests of anxiety rated their infants' temperament as more difficult than mothers who did not fall into any of these groups (Sameroff, Seifer, & Elias, 1982; Vaughn, Taraldson, Crichton, & Egeland, 1981).

Another way to test the validity of temperament measures is to study their consistency over repeated testings. On the whole, parental reports and observational measures are only moderately stable over the infancy period. In other words, children who are rated as "fearful," "inhibited," or "sociable" at 1 year are not necessarily rated the same way at 3 years (J. E. Bates, 1987; Seifer, Sameroff, Barrett, & Krafchuk, 1994).

In summary, parents' ratings of infant temperament have some usefulness, but they must be interpreted with caution. Some ratings reflect the parents' own personalities or current levels of stress and may be inconsistent over time. It is not surprising that parents' interpretations of their infant's temperament are colored by their own experiences. No less is true of adults' interpretations of the behavior and personality of other adults. The best research strategy is to use a combination of parental reports and direct observations made at repeated intervals in the child's life.

Social and Language Development

Social-Object Frames

Because of the newly developed motor, perceptual, and cognitive abilities for acting upon objects, a good deal of parent-infant communication at this age is focused on objects. In the previous developmental period, much of the parent-infant communication involved mutual gazing and frames for face-to-face play in the absence of objects. While infants smiled and cooed, their parents made exaggerated facial expressions and vocalizations. These types of frames are very satisfying to both participants. The research on disruptions of play, such as during the still-face situation or when mothers are depressed, reveals how rapidly positive emotions can change into negative emotion and avoidance. As infants become increasingly interested in objects, between 4 and 6 months of age, and the earlier face-to-face frames give way to social-object frames, parents sometimes feel a sense of disappointment. For the infant's part, the developmental task is to integrate interest in objects with the desire to remain socially and emotionally connected to the parents.

In the first part of this developmental period, infants are primarily focused on the objects themselves. It is up to the parents to provide frames for mutual communication about objects. Typically, this is done by holding objects within the infant's reach, making objects attractive to infants, helping the infants steady the object in order to explore it, and sometimes just sitting nearby and commenting while the infant manipulates or sucks on a toy. The types of actions performed by parents at this age are shown in Table 7.7.

When using the actions shown in Table 7.7, parents employ strategies with toys similar to those they used earlier with their own faces, taking advantage of simple changes in rhythm, timing, and exaggeration to help infants to attend to particular objects or to particular properties of objects. Parents will

Table 7.7   Attention-Directing Strategies of Parents

Act-ons	Moving the infant through some activity, such as pulling the infant up and saying "up."
Shows	Moving an object across the infant's line of sight, or moving the object toward and away from the infant.
Demonstrations	A particular action on an object is shown, such as how to comb a doll's hair or how to shake a rattle.
Points	Using a gesture to direct the infant's attention to a particular feature of an object or to a specific location in space, such as *over there.*

Source: Adapted from P. Zukow-Goldring, A social ecological realist approach to the emergence of the lexicon: Educating attention to amodal invariants in gesture and speech, 1997. In C. Dent-Read & P. Zukow-Goldring (Eds.), *Evolving explanations of development: Ecological approaches to organism-environment systems* (pp. 199–250). Washington, DC: American Psychological Association.

animate a toy dog, for example, by making it jump and matching the intensity of the jumping to the changes in the infant's delight (Stern, 1985). When trying to get the infant's attention to a jar of vitamins, a mother shook it rhythmically, saying, "shakey, SHA . . . KEY, SHA . . . KEY!," increasing the volume and changing the timing of pauses between syllables (Zukow-Goldring, 1997).

The infant's ability to coordinate his or her attention to people and to objects is enhanced if parents regularly create frames in which these kinds of object-directed actions occur. The more attentive and animated the parents are with respect to the infant's attention to objects, the more likely it is that the infant will learn to co-regulate attention with others (Brighi, 1997). This is important, because infants who are more attentive to what adults do and say are more likely to learn language and share the mental perspectives of other people (Moore, Angelopoulos, & Bennett, 1997; Morales, Mundy, & Rojas, 1998; Striano & Rochat, 1999).

By the end of this developmental period, infants begin to be more aware of the adult and of the connection between the object, the self, and the adult. As discussed earlier, by around 8 months, infants become aware that other people have intentions, that they are agents. This change is also seen in the infant's growing ability to appreciate and to make "jokes" with adults.

By 8 or 9 months, infants can appreciate frames involving clowning. Prior to 8 months, the infant might bang a ball on the table. If the parent discourages the activity, the infant may stop momentarily and begin again or else ignore the parent. By about 8 months, the infant may bang the ball on the table, look at the parent, and grin mischievously (Lock, 2000; Reddy, 2000).

At 6 months, infants appear to be in a receptive mode, ready to participate in the frames created by the parents. By 8 months, infants are beginning to take initiatives in social frames. In one experiment, mothers were asked to see if infants would take the initiative in asking for help. During ordinary play with objects, mothers were asked either to hold a toy out of the infant's reach, stop demonstrating a toy, or delay giving help even if the child seemed to need immediate assistance. One-third of the 6-month-olds and two-thirds of the 9-month-olds showed evidence of asking the mother for help by

gazing at her, making a demanding vocalization, or making a gesture (such as pulling on her arm) that indicated a help request (Mosier & Rogoff, 1994). By 8 months, infants "ask" to be picked up by making sad facial expressions or raising their hands above their heads, especially if adults indicate a willingness to pick them up (Service, Lock, & Chandler, 1989). Finally, the frequency with which infants make demands of mothers increases markedly once the infants begin to walk (Biringen, Emde, Campos, & Appelbaum, 1995).

Another aspect of initiative taking is that infants during this period are becoming more selective with respect to adults than during the previous period. By 8 or 9 months, infants will smile and laugh more toward familiar and trusted adults than toward unfamiliar ones. They may show some wariness in response to unfamiliar persons, but this has not yet blossomed into the more severe fearful reactions to strangers seen in some infants after the age of 10 months.

Babbling: A Prerequisite for Later Vocal Communication

When infants are somewhere between 4 and 6 months of age, their vocal tracts begin to undergo major anatomical changes, bringing them closer to the vocal apparatus of the adult. At birth, the infant's tongue fills most of the oral cavity and can only execute some primitive thrusting movements designed to help in sucking and swallowing (see Chapter 5).

Figure 7.4 shows how the vocal tract of the adult differs from that of the very young infant. Besides the differences between infant and adult tongues, note that the infant's epiglottis is in contact with the palate. This configuration covers the air tube from the lungs (the larynx) and helps prevent choking and inhaling of food particles. Beginning at 4 months, the oral cavity and vocal tract widen and lengthen and the epiglottis begins to move away from the palate. The net effect is to allow air to be taken in and pushed out through the infant's mouth more readily (Kent, 1981).

Before the age of 4 months, infants cannot breathe well through their mouths. This is why it is important to keep the very young baby's nasal passages clear of mucus. After 4 months, oral breath-

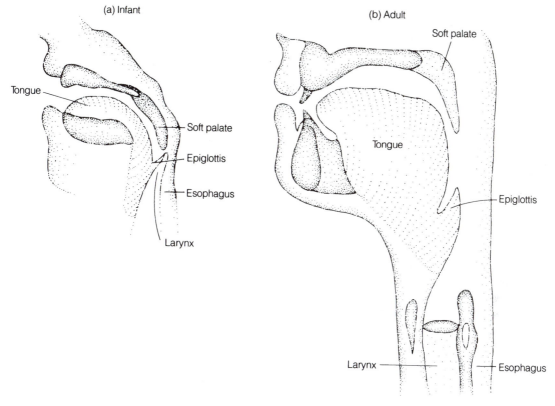

(a) Infant
Tongue
Soft palate
Epiglottis
Esophagus
Larynx

(b) Adult
Soft palate
Tongue
Epiglottis
Larynx
Esophagus

Figure 7.4
Comparison of Infant and Adult Vocal Tracts

Source: R. D. Kent, Articulatory-acoustic perspectives on speech development, 1981, p. 109. In R. Stark (Ed.), *Language development in infancy and early childhood,*
105–126. New York: Elsevier. Copyright © by Elsevier Science Publishing Co., Inc. Reprinted by permission of the publisher.

ing allows the infant a much greater latitude for making new types of sounds.

After 6 months, infants begin to explore sound production by using their ability to vary the direction of air flow, the pitch of the sound, and its loudness by abruptly stopping the air flow with the epiglottis (Zlatin, 1973). We can compare the oral and laryngeal manipulation of airflow to the manual manipulation of objects. The "goo"s and "gah"s that result, or **babbling,** sound almost as though the babies are talking to themselves as they roll off a string of related vowel and consonant sounds to accompany their eating or playing.

Many parents report that babbling sounds like speech. Although infants of this age are not imitating the words of speech, there is evidence that babbling imitates the intonation contours (the rising and falling pitches) of sentences (Nakazima, 1972). Indeed, in a study done in French-, Chinese-, and

Arabic-speaking homes, the intonation contours of babbling match quite well the contours of the speech spoken in the infant's home (DeBoysson-Bardies, Sagant, & Durand, 1984).

The relationship of babbling to speech is supported by research showing that right-handed reaching and rhythmical banging with the hands increases in frequency at the same age infants begin to babble (Locke, 1993). The right hand is controlled by the left brain, and the left brain is known to be the primary location of speech processing. This means that the infant's vocalizations at this age come increasingly under the control of the left brain, setting the stage for linking vocalization to later speech.

Early observations suggested that even deaf babies babble in ways similar to hearing babies up until about 9 months of age (Lenneberg, 1969). More recent research suggests that this is not the case, as shown in a careful descriptive analysis of babbling in deaf infants (Oller & Eilers, 1988). First of all, the onset of babbling in deaf infants is substantially delayed, in some cases occurring between 6 and 18 months later than in hearing infants. Second, the deaf infants produce considerably fewer well-formed consonant-vowel syllables. Although this study does not show that hearing infants copy the speech sounds of adults at this age, it does show that the ability to hear oneself vocalize contributes to the development of vocalization.

Speech Perception

Indeed, the development of auditory perception seems to parallel the development of sound production in hearing infants. Before the age of 6 months, infants are universal language perceivers. They can distinguish important sound contrasts from many different languages. Infants between 6 and 9 months are beginning to organize sounds, especially speech sounds, into conceptual categories. Recall that in research on visual perception, after being familiarized with a set of somewhat distorted figures, infants preferred to look at the prototype figure that best fit the series of distorted figures seen before. A similar study done with distorted versions of speech syllable prototypes yielded very similar results (Grieser & Kuhl, 1989). The auditory stimuli were syllables in which the vowel sound was subtly altered in pitch using a computer simulation.

This means that infants of this age hear the variations of the sound as the "same" as the prototype sound. Since the prototype sounds for most babies are those most commonly heard in their linguistic environment, it means that infants will be less likely to hear a wide diversity of sounds and more likely to hear sounds that "sound like" those occurring in the native language (Kuhl, 1998).

A developmental study (Werker & Tees, 1984) looked at infants between 4 and 6 months and between 10 and 12 months from three different language groups: English, Salish (a Native Canadian language), and Hindi. Babies from each group were tested with syllable contrasts from each language. Syllables were chosen in such a way that a native speaker could hear the differences between them, but a nonnative speaker could not. An example of

this is the contrast in English between /ra/ and /la/. Japanese speakers cannot distinguish perceptually between these two syllables and often get them mixed up when they speak English. English speakers have a similarly difficult time distinguishing between the Japanese syllables /ki/ and /kii/, as in *kite* (come) and *kiite* (listen). In the second syllable, the /ii/ sound (pronounced like the "e" in "be") is held just slightly longer than the /i/ sound in the first syllable; otherwise, the two sounds are identical.

The results of the study showed that the younger infants could distinguish the syllable contrasts from all the languages, but the older infants could only distinguish between the contrasts of the language heard in the home. A later study replicated these findings using computer-simulated sound contrasts similar to those found in English and in Hindi (Werker & Lalonde, 1988). Thus, between the ages of 6 and 9 months, infants lose a perceptual sensitivity that they had at an earlier age.

The loss of perceptual sensitivity may be related to the selective processes of brain development discussed in Chapter 5. At first, synapses are overproduced, and later some (those that are responsive to the sounds heard in the environment) are selected and strengthened, while synapses for sounds that are not heard disappear. In the auditory cortex, the overproduction occurs during the first 6 months; by 10 months, the number of synapses has started to drop (Goldman-Rakic, 1987).

Infants of this age can distinguish between a wide variety of speech sounds in their native language but are less sensitive than adults (Aslin, 1987). Their ability to distinguish between sounds improves when the test sounds are embedded in a series of familiar speech sounds (Karzon, 1985) or in sentences in which adults are speaking motherese (Fernald, 1985).

Infants can apparently distinguish between the intonation patterns of different languages. Some infants from monolingual English-speaking homes and some from bilingual English- and Spanish-speaking homes were familiarized with a video display of a woman reciting a passage in either English or Spanish. In the test condition, infants dishabituated to the woman reciting a passage in the language they had not heard during familiarization but not to a different passage read in the language with which they had been familiarized (Bahrick & Pickens, 1988). In American English, the majority of two-syllable words are stressed on the initial syllable (strong-weak pattern of stress). By 9 months, American infants preferred to listen to words having a strong-weak stress pattern, compared to a weak-strong stress pattern. Six-month-olds showed no such preference (Jusczyk, Cutler, & Redanz, 1993).

Overall, these results show that by the second half of the first year of life, even though infants would not be considered to be speaking or understanding language, they are beginning to recognize and produce some of the characteristics of language as a system of sounds. Babbling infants may sound to adults as if they are trying to talk but it is more appropriate to view them as exploring how to make familiar sounds, those heard in the home environment, rather than as trying to communicate with sounds. Nevertheless, this is a remarkable ability. The intonation patterns of language are complex and rich. It seems as if babies first learn the music and later they learn the words. This music is learned in the context of parent-infant frames, including social games.

Parent-Infant Games

By 8 months, the infant is much more likely to take the initiative in play situations rather than simply respond to the caregiver (Gustafson, Green, & West, 1979; Kaye & Fogel, 1980). Social play is more frequent and more spirited, with laughter and squealing in the sound track.

A large variety of new social frames emerge in the parent-infant relationship at this age. Table 7.8 describes the typical playful frames found in parent-infant play during the second half-year of life. Figure 7.5 shows the relative frequency of each game

Fathers and mothers play different types of games with their babies. Both paternal and maternal styles of play are important to infant development.

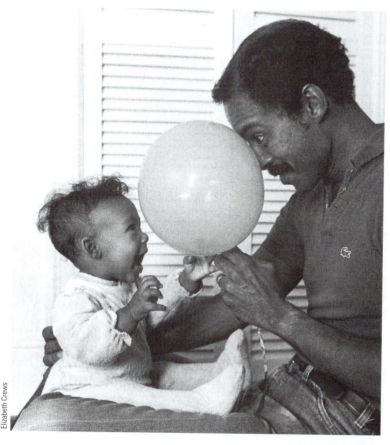

Elizabeth Crews

Table 7.8 Descriptions of Conventional Games

- *Gonna get you:* Mother repeatedly tickles, grabs, jostles, or provides other tactual/kinesthetic stimulation to the infant. Often includes a repeated vocalization such as "I'm gonna get you" or "Ahhhhhh-boom!" that terminates just as physical contact is made. (Active participation by an infant could include fleeing when approached or attempting to "get" the mother.)

- *Pat-a-cake:* Primary components are the mother's saying "pat-a-cake" and clapping or banging performed by either the mother or the infant. (Active participation by the infant would include beginning to clap only after the mother said "pat-a-cake" or patting the mother's hands.)

- *Horsie:* Primary component is the mother's bouncing the infant, who is sitting on her knees or foot. The mother's verbalizations include "Want to play horsie?" or "Ride the horsie." (Active participation by the infant involves initiating the game or tying to prolong it by continuing to bounce after the mother has stopped.)

- *Peekaboo:* One member of the dyad is hidden and reappears. Hiding is typically accompanied by the mother's calling to the child (if the mother is hidden) or by her asking "Where's [child's name]?" (if the child is hidden). Reappearance is typically accompanied by verbalizations such as "Peekaboo," "Peepeye," or "There he/she is!" (Mother may control all the hiding and uncovering, or the infant may actively perform some of these activities.)

- *Ball:* Involves the infant's repeatedly receiving and losing the ball. (Mother may hold up both ends of the game by tossing the ball to the infant and then taking it away, or the infant may actively participate by presenting or returning the ball to the mother.)

- *Vocal game:* Minimal requirement is that the mother be attempting to elicit a word or vocalization from the infant. In expanded form, these interactions are verbal or vocal-verbal "conversations."

- *Build tower–knock down:* One member of the dyad builds a tower of blocks, and the other knocks the tower over. The sequence may be repeated many times. (Active participation by the infant is typically limited to knocking the tower down.)

- *Give and take:* Involves repeated giving and receiving of objects. Receiving by the mother is often accompanied by a carefully articulated "Thank you." Typically, the infant gives and the mother receives, although mother often returns the object to the infant.

- *Point and name:* One member of the dyad (usually the infant) repeatedly points to objects, each time waiting for a vocalization by the other (usually the mother, in the form of naming the object), before pointing to the next object. Pointing is sometimes accompanied by a questioning vocalization or by the query, "What's this?"

- *Miscellaneous:* Any traditional infant game that occurs very infrequently at a particular age. Included are the game "Overboard," in which the mother repeatedly turns the infant upside down and says "Little girl overboard," and the game "So Big," in which the mother says, "How big are you?" and the infant stretches his or her arms out while the mother says, "So big." Also included are sequences with a toy telephone in which the receiver is put to the infant's ear and the mother says "Hello," and interactions in which one or both members of the pair wave or say, "Bye-bye."

Source: G. E. Gustafson, J. A. Green, & M. J. West, The infant's changing role in mother-infant games: The growth of social skills, 1979, p. 304. *Infant Behavior and Development, 2,* 301–308. Reprinted by permission of Ablex Publishing Co.

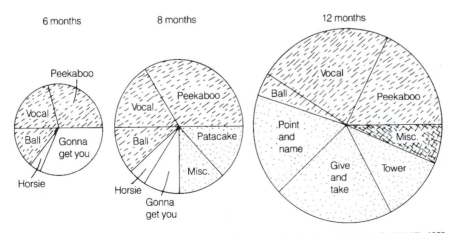

Figure 7.5
Relative Frequency of Parent-Infant Games

Dotted areas represent games in which the infant's role is explicitly active; blank areas represent games in which the infant's role is typically passive. Hatched areas represent games played at all ages. Cross-hatched areas represent both active and passive games.

Source: G. E. Gustafson, J. A. Green, & M. J. West, The infant's changing role in mother-infant games: The growth of social skills, 1979, p. 304. *Infant Behavior and Development, 2,* 301–308. Reprinted by permission of Ablex Publishing Co.

at 6, 8, and 12 months of age. As infants get older, they learn to play an increasing number of new social games, such as "point and name" and "give and take" at 12 months. In playing those games that are played at every age—such as "ball," vocal games, and peekaboo—infants take an increasingly active role as they get older. Games like "gonna get you" and "horsie," in which the 6-month-old played a relatively passive role, occur only rarely at 12 months (Gustafson et al., 1979; Rome-Flanders et al., 1995).

Note that these games are typical of white middle-class North American populations and do not necessarily represent what parents and infants do in other cultures. Furthermore, even in this particular population, games were observed in only about 10% of all social interaction episodes. The rest of the time is taken up with frames for caregiving (such as feeding, calming, bathing and bedtime rituals) and for infant solitary play with objects, which increases at this age.

Cultural Differences in Parent-Infant Interaction

As infants get older, their mothers tend to spend less time with them. When mothers do spend time with babies, the proportion of time devoted to games and play over simple caretaking increases with the baby's age. One cross-cultural study found that the infant's rate of receiving social stimulation does not change appreciably with age, but the proportion of time that the infant's primary social partner is the mother declines. Evidently, infants receive an increasing amount of stimulation from other sources, such as relatives and peers (Landau, 1976).

There are wide differences between cultures in the amount of time mothers spend with babies, as well as in the types of activities they perform when with the babies. Climate is one factor that accounts for cultural differences in child-rearing patterns. In warm countries, infants tend to be carried by their caregivers, to remain in close physical contact throughout most of the day and night, and to be breast-fed longer than infants reared in cold climates. Infants in cold climates are more likely to be separated from their mothers at an earlier age. They sleep in cradles, are carried in strollers and buggies, and are kept at a distance from the parents through the use of infant seats and playpens (Agiobu-Kemmer, 1986; Whiten & Milner, 1986; J. Whiting, 1981).

These differences are believed to be due to the need to wrap babies in cold climates against the cold (see Figure 7.6). Since both the adult and infant must wear many layers of protective clothing, parent-infant skin contact is very difficult. Over many centuries, child-rearing practices have evolved to adapt to this fundamental ecological constraint (J. Whiting, 1981).

There are very few studies in this age period on differences in parent-infant interaction in different subcultures within the United States. Franco, Fogel, Messinger, & Frazier (1996) did a study of mother-infant physical contact during play between 26 Hispanic American and 26 Anglo-American mothers and their 9-month-old infants. Although the overall amount of touching and physical contact did not differ between groups, Hispanic mothers touched, kissed, hugged, and held their infants physically closer than Anglo mothers. On questionnaires, the Hispanic mothers reported placing a higher value on touch and affection than Anglo mothers. These cultural differences were the same in all income levels in our sample.

As a general rule, the cultures of southern Europe and Central and South America have close patterns of touching, physical contact, kissing, and hugging even between adults. Puerto Rican mothers, for example, are more likely than Anglo mothers to physically direct the child's body and behavior during play and feeding situations. The Anglo mothers are more likely to use praise and suggestions, focusing on verbal means of communication (Harwood, Schölmerich, Schulze, & Gonzalez, 1999).

Hispanic Americans, as the minority culture, often feel self-conscious about their cultural styles of raising infants. They report feeling self-conscious in the company of their Anglo-American neighbors and think of themselves as "too affectionate" with their infants (Franco et al., 1996). These patterns of cultural tension reveal how difficult it is for some parents to maintain the traditional values and practices of their minority culture. Each of these cultural styles of physical contact is, however, valuable in its own right. One is not better than the other.

The type of play that occurs between infants and adults also differs between cultures. In more

Figure 7.6
Infant-Carrying Practices

In warm climates, infants spend more time in skin-to-skin contact with adults. Infants in cold climates must wear protective clothing, making them more difficult to carry for long periods.

(a) North America

(c) Africa

(b) North America

(d) Africa

technical and industrial societies, mother-infant play is embedded in a matrix of communication and warmth. In these societies—including, for example, Japan, Europe, and North America, and urban families everywhere—the parent will begin to *interpret the infant's intentions.* Assuming that the parent has made a correct interpretation, the next step is usually to *help the infant carry out the intended act.* In addition, parents often *create new intentions* that were not there in the first place. Instead of simply helping infants get objects they see, parents may hold out an object to get the baby interested or make sounds or movements to try to get the baby to imitate them (Adamson, 1995; Kaye, 1982; Lock, 1980; Rogoff, 1990).

The parent creates, interprets, and completes intentions even though the infant may not be fully aware of these intentions. The situation is much like the study of music or language, for example, in which teachers require that their pupils learn simple exercises. The student has little notion of the purpose of learning scales, arpeggios, the parts of speech, or conjugations. Nevertheless, the instructor understands the relationship of the exercises to the final skilled performance. Some examples of these kinds of instructional interactions involving a 7-month-old baby are given in Observations 7.3 and 7.4.

By contrast, in nontechnical agricultural and hunter-gatherer communities, adults are more directive and ritualistic in their interactions with infants (Whiten & Milner, 1986). Among the Gusii, an agricultural community in Kenya, when mothers taught children to do a task, they used a lot of repetition, provided direct demonstration of the whole task (they did not break it into simpler components), and pulled on the infants' hands to encourage participation. The mothers used very little vocalization and little praise or reinforcement (Dixon, LeVine, Richman, & Brazelton, 1984). Chomorro

OBSERVATIONS

Early Communicative Interactions Rely on Adult Interpretations (Lock, 1980)

Observation 7.3

Mary: age 7(10): A spoonful of food has just been placed in Mary's mouth when the telephone rings. Mother takes Mary's left hand and wraps it round the spoon handle, which is sticking from Mary's mouth.

Mother: "You take it while Mummy answers the phone."

Mary: pulls the spoon from her mouth and while eating waves it about. While still holding the spoon, she pushes her hand around in her dinner and then starts licking her hand. While she is doing this mother returns.

Mother: "There's a clever girl, are you feeding yourself? Here, let's wipe you, you're ever so mucky."

She takes the spoon from Mary to wipe her. Mary cries and struggles, then reaches out toward the spoon.

Mother: "All right, here you are. Let me show you."

She gives Mary the spoon and then guiding her hand, places it into the dish and then to Mary's mouth.

Mother: "Oh, aren't we clever! Aren't we clever!"

Observation 7.4

Mary: age 7(27): Mary is in her chair, having finished her afternoon meal.

Mother comes through the door with a packet of biscuits in her hand. The door is behind Mary and out of her view. As mother comes in, Mary coos and smiles, turning around to see her mother.

Mother: "Yes, you heard me coming, didn't you?"

She enters Mary's field of view, and Mary reaches out towards her mother's hand; her whole body straining in the chair.

Mother: "Yes, they're your favourites, aren't they?"

---

mothers, from a fishing community on the Pacific island of Guam, were highly directive when interacting with infants; they talked quickly, dominated the interactions, were highly repetitive, and abruptly shifted activities in a manner more suited to their own pace than to the infants' (Carlile & Holstrum, 1989).

Once again, it is not necessarily the case that one style of play and teaching is better than another. Each style has evolved to fit the needs of the particular culture. Problems may arise, however, when cultures are forced to interact. Cultural-minority families from traditional backgrounds are often at a disadvantage when they enter urban environments. Their styles of interaction are not well suited to the urban lifestyle and the demands of school-based learning. According to ecological systems theory, this is a conflict between the microsystem of the family and the macrosystem of the culture, especially when the family values are different from those of the dominant culture. The research reviewed in this section shows that cultural differences become important in early development, well before the child enters school.

The Sense of Self

In the previous stage, infants developed a sense of an ecological self. Between 3 and 5 months, infants can perceive a sense of their own agency in relation to others, their own emotions, a sense of coherence across sensory systems, and a sense of their own history. This sense of self comes from self-exploration via primary circular reactions, repeated actions of the infant's own body. However, it is rather rudimentary. Infants between 3 and 5 months old may feel as if there is a coherence between moving their hand to touch their own face and the sensation felt in the face. They know that this feels different from other kinds of contact with their face, say, from their blanket or another person's touch.

Infants of that age, however, do not know that there is a self and another person who are different centers of subjective experience. All they know is that some touches feel different than others and that there is a special significance to touches that are accompanied by a sense of their own movements (that is, self-touches). Babies between 3 and 5 months cannot put labels on these different kinds of touches. They have a sense of agency, but only for these simple actions on their own body. They do not know they can affect the world beyond their body. They experience the world receptively and unquestioningly.

A 3-month-old baby is aware of the environment in the same way that a fish is aware of water. A fish "knows" that to propel its body it must exert a certain force and that the force is different at different times (we as outside observers would call these different times changes in the speed and direction of the water currents). The fish, however, does not know water as a separate entity, different from itself. The fish has an ecological self. It knows what to do and how to move, has a memory of past experiences, and can adapt to changes, but it cannot separate itself from the ecology. It is unified with the ecology.

Between 6 and 9 months, we see the first evidence that babies are becoming aware of a world "out there." They are still part of the ecology of relationships with things and people (indeed, so are all of us), but now they are starting to see that the ecology has local regions, each of which has different properties and each of which has an existence independent of the self. As they begin to differentiate objects as whole entities having an existence even when out of sight, they also begin to see themselves as being different from those objects.

Infants of this age call attention to themselves in a number of ways that did not exist in the previous stage. These features make up a sense of a **differentiated ecological self.**

1. *Asking for help.* If their needs are not met, infants are beginning to find ways to let others know.
2. *Taking the initiative.* Infants will start games, like covering their face as if to ask to play peekaboo. It is as if they are "waking up" to the fact that the world does not always act for their benefit and that they can actually do something to change it.
3. *Clowning and showing off.* Infants begin to do things to get an emotional reaction from others. They act clever or silly, violate rules to get a laugh from others, make odd facial expressions, put their pajamas on their head, and blow "raspberries" (Reddy, 2000).
4. *Demanding.* The quality of crying changes as infants become angry at others and persist until something changes.
5. *Hiding and escaping.* Infants like to play peekaboo, tickle, and chase games that involve a temporary separation from the other followed by a reunion.

Another indication of a differentiated ecological self is the emergence of gender and temperamental differences at this age. Infants begin to seem as if they have their own personalities. Their emotions

are becoming more complex, and they are beginning to take events into their own hands. Infants of this age, however, do not yet have a sense of subjectivity. They have feelings—getting angry or happy—but cannot yet stand apart from those feelings. They do not have a sense of an "I" that feels, and, consequently, they do not have a sense that other people are separate subjects with their own feelings. The sense of a subjective self begins after the age of 10 months (see Chapter 8).

Family and Society

In the section on social development, I looked at styles of mother-infant interaction in different cultures. We saw how ecological systems theory helps to explain that microsystem cultural factors external to the family may influence the style of mother- or father-infant interaction. In this section, I will take a look at maternal employment as one ecological factor that affects the family. According to ecological systems theory, the world of work is in the exosystem. Even though infants may never enter the workplace, work will have a mediated effect on them through their parents. Also in this section, I will also examine the roles of fathers and siblings.

Maternal Employment and Its Effects on Infants

Since 1950, the number of working mothers in the United States has increased by 70%. In 1984, 46% of mothers with children under 1 year of age, 53% with children under 2 years, and 58% with children under 3 years were working full time. This group of mothers is the fastest-growing segment of the workforce (Yale Bush Center Infant Care Leave Project, 1985). Among other things, this increase in the number of working mothers raises the problem of how to provide adequate care for their infants. I will return to this problem in the next chapter.

In this chapter, I discuss the impact the maternal work role has had on the American family and especially how it has affected both parents and infants. It should be noted that our discussion focuses on paid work, either inside or outside the home. Mothers do a substantial amount of unpaid work—child care, cooking, cleaning, gardening, and chauffeuring—which is estimated to be worth about $27,000 per woman per year. Much of this work goes unrecognized (Eyer, 1996).

First of all, how does maternal employment affect the mother's relationship with her infant and the infant's development? In general, infant-mother attachment is not seriously altered by maternal employment (Easterbrooks & Goldberg, 1985; Vaughn, Grove, & Egeland, 1980; Youngblut, Loveland-Cherry, & Horan, 1993). On the other hand, if attachment is going to be affected, it is most likely to decline between employed mothers and their infant sons rather than their daughters (Chase-Lansdale & Owen, 1987).

Why are boys more affected? It may be that boys are perceived as more independent and as requiring less parental nurture and attention than girls, who are seen as more vulnerable (Parke & Sawin, 1980). Thus, when mothers are under extra stress and time pressures from their jobs, they may spend less time with their sons than with their daughters. Other research suggests that there is a correlation between a son's insecure attachment and a mother's perceived level of stress. Mothers who felt more stressed by their jobs and the demands of family life had less securely attached sons (Benn, 1986). The effects of stress are compounded for low-income mothers, for whom not just employment but also the stresses of living in poverty may affect attachment in both sons and daughters (Barglow, 1987a).

These results suggest that the impact of maternal work on infant-mother attachment is mediated by the mother's adjustment to the work role. Better psychological adjustment will lead to more-sensitive infant care. Thus, researchers have asked what factors promote maternal adjustment to employment. A number of studies find that the important variable is the mother's desire to work, not the mere fact of working. Mothers who are doing what they prefer—either working or staying at home with their children—tend to be well adjusted. On the other hand, there are adverse affects on adjustment if the mother does not want to work but has

to for economic reasons, or if the mother would like to return to work but feels she should stay home with her children (Alvarez, 1985; DeMeis, Hock, & McBride, 1986; Pistrang, 1984; Stifter, Coulehan, & Fish, 1993).

On the other hand, staying home with the baby is also stressful for some mothers. Research has shown that problems with coping, dissatisfaction with life, depression, and loneliness are significantly higher in young mothers who do not work outside the home than in those who do, and that there are higher levels of functioning in families in which the mothers are employed (Sogaard, Kritz-Silverstein, & Wingard, 1994; Vandell & Ramanan, 1992). The type of work done by the mother also has an impact. In Chapter 6, I reported that if work was more challenging, complex, and stimulating, it enhanced the mother's parenting role.

Whether mothers work by choice or because of necessity, they typically end the day fatigued because of a phenomenon called **role overload.** Role overload occurs when the demands of a role are more than an individual can easily cope with or when the same person is required to perform too many roles. After a full day at work, many women come home to traditional conceptions of the roles of both wife and mother. Women often continue to do most of the infant care and most of the housework, compared to men, even if they are working as many hours outside the home as the men (L. C. Jones & Hermann, 1992; Scarr, 1984). Role overload is inevitable for single parents. Even though fathers with working wives do more infant care and housework than husbands of women who are not employed outside the home, men with working wives increase their contribution to family work by only an average of 15 minutes per day (Crouter, Perry-Jenkins, Huston, & McHale, 1987; Pleck & Rustad, 1980).

Lest you think this is entirely the fault of men, research shows that men do proportionately more work at home if their wives have a less traditional attitude toward the male role. Thus, it may be the mother's own perception of her central family role and her failure to strongly encourage the husband's participation in the family that leads to low levels of father involvement. Women may be trying too hard to be "supermoms" (R. C. Barnett & Baruch,

A working mother must learn to balance multiple demands of work and family, even if she does not take her baby to work with her.

Andy Cox /Stone

1987; Palkovitz, 1984; Scarr, 1984) and in the process may be contributing inadvertently to role overload.

When women work, however, there are more pressures on fathers, and they too can experience a form of role overload. When women remain at home, fathers can choose when and how to become involved with their infants. These fathers show more positive emotion toward their infants and are more attuned to the infants' needs. In contrast, fathers whose wives work experience more tension and frustration with being called upon to take more child care responsibility. During the first year, such fathers show more negative behavior with their infants. After the first year, however, they are just as sensitive to their infants as the husbands of mothers who do not work outside the home (Grych & Clark, 1999). These are general patterns, however, so each family may be different in the balance of mother and father roles.

Parental Leave Policies

Unfortunately, the amount of work a person does outside the home is only partially defined by the individual. Much has to do with cultural and economic demands placed on workers by society and by employers. Most work situations in the United States take little account of a person's obligations to family. An inflexible daily work schedule leaves little time or opportunity for parents to be involved in the day-to-day life of the family. Corporations often have a policy of moving their employees from city to city as part of a training and advancement program.

This is especially the case for women. Even when mothers are paid, they earn only 71 cents for every dollar earned by a man in the same position. They are often relegated to low-paying jobs such as secretary (98% are women), child care providers (98%), nurses (93%), and bank tellers (91%). Even highly educated women face job and salary discrimination, especially if they get pregnant or are raising a child (Eyer, 1996). These sources of discrimination in the ecological system make working especially burdensome for women and increase their level of guilt.

Some alternatives exist, but they are not widespread. More flexible work schedules (**flextime**) began to be instituted in Europe in the early 1960s. Workers can have time off to take a child to the doctor, watch their child participate in sports, or do whatever they desire. After a child is born, Swedish workers, for example, are legally entitled to maternity and paternity leaves. Some Swedish employers allow husbands and wives to share the same jobs. That way both can work *and* spend time at home. Swedish women earn about 90% the wages men do for similar jobs, and 86% of women with young children are in the workforce (Eyer, 1996).

The opportunity to take infant care leave of some type, without suffering loss of income or profession, is mandated by law in at least 75 nations, including all the industrial societies in the world. In 1993, the U.S. Congress enacted the Family and Medical Leave Act of 1993 (FMLA, Public Law 103-3), which established a family leave policy. This law provides unpaid leave from employment for up to 12 weeks without loss of rank or position in the workplace in businesses with more than 50 employees. The leave applies to both mothers and fathers as well as to non-pregnancy-related illnesses. Unfortunately, 95% of businesses are exempt from the FMLA because they have fewer than 50 employees. In addition, most parents cannot afford to take unpaid leaves (Eyer, 1996).

Although mothers are more likely to take a parental leave, research done in the United States in 1993 found that almost all fathers took at least a few days of leave. The average length of leave for fathers was 5 days, with 71% of fathers taking 5 or fewer days (Hyde, Essex, & Horton, 1993). Research shows that mothers who take shorter leaves are more likely to feel stress, show negative emotions toward their infants, and experience depressive symptoms (R. Clark, Hyde, Essex, & Klein, 1997). This means that even with the FMLA, too few parents are able to take advantage of parental leave, with negative consequences for themselves and their children.

Better pay and benefits for part-time work could also be helpful for young parents. Many employers provide medical insurance, unemployment compensation, and other benefits only to full-time employees. A parent who would like to spend more time at home is caught between the demands of the family and the very real needs to be covered by those benefits. Employer-sponsored day care, a topic to which I will return in the next chapter, is also helping working parents.

Age and Sex Differences in Nurturance toward Infants

As the results of research on maternal employment suggest, infant care is thought to be part of women's work. Implicit in this belief is that nurturance is part of the female biological heritage and that women should be able to do this under any circumstances and without support. In actuality, these beliefs are simply not true. Research has shown that the interest and ability to care for babies is present in both males and females early in life and will continue in both genders if fostered by the social environment. In the following sections, I review age and sex differences in responses to infants.

Preschool Age

One study that used a single female infant placed in a playpen in a nursery school found that girls approached the baby more than did boys. Once the children were near the baby, however, both boys and girls spoke to, reached out for, and touched the baby equally (Berman, Monda, & Merscough, 1977). Another study used both male and female infants in a waiting-room situation. Preschool children were asked to wait in a laboratory room with a baby and mother for 10 minutes. In this rather unusual situation, many children did not approach the baby. When they did, boys and girls approached in equal numbers, and there were no differences in the types of interaction attempted by male and female children. They usually sat down on the floor, handed the baby toys, or showed the baby his image in a mirror (Melson & Fogel, 1982).

These children almost never talked to the baby. If they wanted to find something out or make a comment, they would talk to the baby's mother about the baby. In addition, there was a same-sex effect for these unfamiliar infant-preschooler pairs similar to that found for sibling pairs (Dunn & Kendrick, 1982). At the ages of 2 and 3 years, boys were more likely to approach male babies, and girls were more likely to approach female babies (Melson & Fogel, 1982).

One interesting twist in this study was that by the time children were 4 to 5 years old, there were still no overall sex differences in the amount of time males and females interacted with the baby. However, both the males and the females preferred to interact with female babies. Perhaps the older boys no longer identify with the babies. By the time the boys were 5 years old, being a boy and being a baby were no longer compatible.

In later work, Melson and I found that if adults encouraged children to become involved with unfamiliar infants, both boys and girls increased their amount of interaction with the babies and both boys and girls asked the adults many questions about the babies (Fogel, Melson, Toda, & Mistry, 1987). When we interviewed children in kindergarten and second grade about babies, we found both equal interest and equal knowledge about infant care on the part of boys and girls (Melson, Fogel, & Toda, 1986). In general, the research suggests that few sex differences are found among children in their attitudes, knowledge about, and behavior toward infants if they are exposed to infants with adult guidance (Melson & Fogel, 1988). For most children, this exposure occurs in the context of the family, with baby brothers or sisters.

Siblings

Similar types of sex differences have been observed among siblings; that is, same-sex dyads tend to be more positive in their interactions than mixed-sex dyads (Dunn & Kendrick, 1982; Lamb, 1978b). On the other hand, when preschool-age children talk to their infant brothers and sisters, both boys and girls modify their speech to make it sound more like motherese (Dunn & Kendrick, 1982; Sachs & Devin, 1976; Shatz & Gelman, 1973).

The children's speech includes simple utterances, repetition, and high pitch as in the following example taken from a 4-year-old talking to her younger brother: "Harry! Harry! Have my camera! Have my camera! Naughty boy. You . . . aah! Aah! No!" (Dunn & Kendrick, 1982, p. 124). In some cases, the preschoolers used repetition twice as often as their mothers when talking to babies. About 25% of the preschool-age children were observed to use endearing terms toward the baby and to ask soliciting questions (Are you hungry? Are you getting frustrated?). On the other hand, the majority of the preschoolers rarely asked questions of the baby, whereas question asking is a major form of adult speech to infants (Dunn & Kendrick, 1982).

Later Childhood

Among children aged 8 to 14 years, girls interact more with babies and ignore them less than do boys. Interestingly, however, there are no sex differences in blood pressure, skin conductance, and heart rate: both boys and girls are equally aroused or unaroused by the sight of an infant. Girls, it would seem, make the choice to interact, whereas boys do not (Frodi & Lamb, 1978). A similar study of African American children also found that girls are more likely to look at the babies than boys (Berman, Goodman, Sloan, & Fernandez, 1978).

These differences in male versus female interest in babies continue through high school (Feldman & Nash, 1979a) but they seem to vanish for college students and for young adults (Feldman and Nash, 1978, 1979a; Frodi, Lamb, Leavitt, & Donovan, 1978). Some studies with adults have compared the responses of parents to babies with those of nonparents. The most responsive group is usually new mothers. Men's child-rearing status does not affect their responsiveness to babies (Feldman & Nash, 1978; Sagi, 1981). Mothers tend to be more accurate in their identification of the type of cry (pain, distress, and so on) than fathers but both mothers and fathers can distinguish their own infant's cry from cries of unfamiliar infants (Wiesenfeld, Malatesta, & DeLoach, 1981).

Parenthood: Mothers versus Fathers

In most comparisons of fathers' and mothers' styles of interaction with infants, fathers are found to be more physical and active with infants than mothers. Fathers are reported to be less contingently responsive with infants and have a style of play and interaction that is more directive and characterized by abrupt changes of activity. By contrast, mothers' games are quieter and more likely to depend on the pace set by the infant. Mothers also engage in proportionately more caregiving than fathers (Lamb et al., 1982; Parke & Sawin, 1980; Pedersen, Suwalsky, Cain, & Zaslow, 1987; Ricks, 1985; Sagi, 1981). These differences are considered important for infants. While contingent responsiveness fosters infants' understanding of the connections between their own actions and those of others, the more directive and unexpected style of father-infant play may lead infants to develop adaptive responses to challenges as they strive to keep up with the father's expectations.

We observed mother-infant and father-infant play in 60 middle-class families (K. L. Dickson, Walker, & Fogel, 1997). Unlike previous studies done as much as 15 or 20 years earlier, our observations of North American, primarily Caucasian fathers in the 1990s found virtually no differences in play style or contingent responsiveness with their 1-year-old infants. It is quite likely that cultural changes in the past 15 years have made middle-class fathers more involved and sensitive parents. In another study, mothers and fathers in England were videotaped interacting with their infants with an observer present and later without the observer present. There were fewer mother-father differences when the observer was absent. This suggests that fathers may be somewhat more self-conscious when observed and therefore may appear to be less sensitive (C. Lewis et al., 1996).

On the other hand, there are large cultural differences in the amount of father involvement. In most Asian countries, mothers are expected to play a more traditional role and devote most of their time to the infant while the father works outside the home. In one study done in Taiwan, for example, mothers held, smiled, talked to, and played with infants more than fathers, but both parents displayed similar amounts of soothing and affection toward their infants (Sun & Roopnarine, 1996).

Anthropologists studied primate species that differed in the amount of father involvement. Orangutans and chimps are species in which mothers do virtually all the infant care. Siamangs and gorillas have about as much father care as humans. Owl monkeys and titi monkeys are species in which the fathers do more of the care than mothers. There was a direct correspondence between the amount of infant care and the average life span. Generally speaking, doing more child care is correlated with living longer. Females outlive males in those species where there is more female care, and vice versa (Allman, Rosin, Kumar, & Hasenstaub, 1998). Although this study does not prove that individuals who do more child care will live longer, it certainly suggests that there may be important health benefits, for both men and women, to being involved in child care.

Grandparents

Finally, investigators studied the responsiveness to babies of 30 parents of adolescents, 28 parents whose grown children had left home, and 26 grandparents of infants. As you might have guessed, grandparents were more responsive to babies than the other two groups. Grandmothers were more responsive than grandfathers, but grandfathers were more responsive than men at other ages, who tended to be less responsive to babies than their wives (Feldman & Nash, 1979b).

It seems that differences in male versus female responsiveness to infants appear in middle childhood and adolescence. Preschool boys, men of child-rearing age, and grandfathers are about equally responsive to babies as their female counterparts. These studies suggest that sex differences in interest in babies may be related to society's expectations of how males and females should behave rather than to some underlying biological predisposition favoring females. Males' interest in babies corresponds to the times in the life cycle when men are exposed to babies and are expected to take an interest in

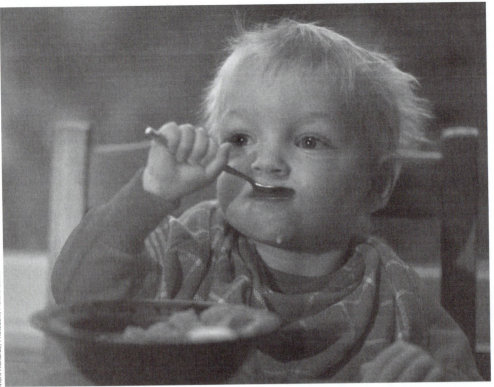

Mark Richards/PhotoEdit/Picture Quest

Self-feeding requires more coordination than most infants can manage. Parents need to give infants foods that are easily handled.

them. Women are more likely to be expected to be interested in babies all through their lives.

The Author's View

At this age, infants are in a transition between directly experiencing their relationship with their social and physical ecology and having the sense of a self that experiences the ecology, a sense of subjectivity. I used the analogy of a fish in water for the infant's earlier sense of self. Perhaps it should be written as "fish-in-water." The infant is aware of one thing, the ecosystem, rather than two separate things. The later sense of self is that the fish becomes aware of the water and how the water's currents and temperatures affect the fish's movements and feelings. This, as far as we know, never occurs for a fish,

but it does occur for babies around 10 months. At this age, infants begin to point at objects in the company of others, as if to say they have a sense of having a perspective on the world that differs from that of others. This means that by 10 months, infants begin to have a sense of being a subject, an "I" who can perceive or feel and who can share those feelings with other people.

What makes the period between 6 and 9 months transitional? In the simplest sense, this age period is developmentally situated between the ecological self and the subjective self. This period is also transitional in a more meaningful sense. The infant's interest in objects in the company of adults creates a triadic (three-way) relationship where before there was primarily a dyadic (two-way) relationship. In the earlier period there was primarily the dyadic ecology and in the next period there is the triad, in which, to use the example of pointing, the infant seems to be aware that there are three different things—self, other, and object—and that one needs an explicit gesture to acknowledge this. Between 6 and 9 months, the infant participates in triadic relationships but does not yet see all the connections. It appears that an interest in objects outside the dyad is a bridge from immersion in the ecology to being a subject in the ecology.

Another sense in which this age period is a transition is with respect to emotions. In the next period, the subjective self seems to have an understanding that other people can feel similar types of emotions as the self. Between 6 and 9 months, the infant's positive and negative emotions become more complex, and each has some interpersonal significance. Anger is typically directed toward another person. It highlights the concerns of the self that may have been violated. The enjoyment of escape during tickle and chase games is a feeling of trying to get away from someone else. It is as if emotions become triadic too, so that instead of just feeling distress or happiness, the infant begins to feel happiness with respect to a particular interpersonal situation, such as getting out of tickle range. Clowning is also triadic, a way of playing that involves another person. So, while infants of this age are not yet aware of others as separate subjects, they are beginning to experience others as a meaningful part of their own emotional life. These interpersonal emotions also bridge the immersion in the ecology with the soon-to-arrive sense of subjectivity.

As you are doing the Awareness through Movement lessons and/or the Co-Regulating with Baby exercises, try to see if you can experience this differentiated ecological self. After a lot of practice in the crawling lessons, for example, you are asked to look around the environment. As you do this, what do you experience about yourself in relation to the environment? Is it ecological, transitional (differentiated ecological), or subjective? How do you know?

AWARENESS THROUGH MOVEMENT

Low Creep

Position: Lie on your stomach with both elbows bent, your hands resting palms down on the floor near your head.

1. Begin to slowly roll your pelvis back and forth from right to left, keeping your legs as limp as possible. Reduce your efforts to the minimum necessary for the movement. Is it easier to roll your pelvis in one direction? Now turn your face to the opposite side and continue to roll your pelvis. Does changing the direction you are facing influence which direction it is easier for you to roll your pelvis? Rest.

2. Turn your face to the right and again roll your pelvis right and left. Begin gently to increase the range of the movement of rolling your pelvis to the left, until your right knee starts to bend by itself. Your right foot should remain on the floor and turn so that the inside edge of the foot eventually makes contact with the floor. Rest.

3. This time, turn your face to the left and increase the movement of rolling your pelvis to the right, until your left knee starts to bend by itself. Rest.

4. Now, with your face to the right, roll your pelvis to the left until your right leg becomes light, and draw up your right knee. Then, turn your head to the left, roll your pelvis to the right, and draw up your left knee. Alternate back and forth very slowly, until you can create a smooth movement of turning your head, rolling your pelvis and drawing up your knees. Your feet should always be in contact with the floor, without pushing against the floor. The legs should do very little active work, because they are carried by the movement of your pelvis.

5. Begin to lift your head and look around. Is there something you are interested in reaching, something you want to see, touch, or put in your mouth? Begin to move toward that object of interest, pulling yourself with your elbows and alternating bending your legs a little more and then allowing your legs to straighten a bit as you pull yourself forward. Rest on your back and feel the changes in your contact with the floor.

Beginning to Crawl

Position and Suggestions: Stand on your hands and knees. You may want to use extra padding

Applications   Infant Nutrition

Coincidences are common in human development. For example, the depletion of fetal supplies of iron coincides with the beginning of the teething period, the ability to make fine motor movements with the hands to grasp and pick up objects, and the decline of the extrusion reflex of the tongue, in which most things placed in the mouth are pushed out.

Just at the time when the infant's body is beginning to need a supplementation of nutrients (mother's milk has little iron), in other words, the baby begins to develop the ability to handle food, chew it, and swallow it. Is this more than a chance coincidence? We will probably never really know, but it all works out nicely for the baby, who develops the skill to consume solid foods at just the time when he or she needs them.

The American Academy of Pediatrics maintains that infants do not need supplementary foods besides milk until 4 to 6 months (American Academy of Pediatrics, Committee on Nutrition, 1981; A. S. Anderson, Purvis, & Chopra, 1979; Barness, 1981). By 6 months, the baby has certain abilities that will help in processing solid foods. These include enzymes to digest carbohydrates, chewing and swallowing skills, and the ability to express satiety by head shaking (R. A. Stewart, 1981). Data indicate no relationship between the early introduction of solid foods or the amount of food the baby eats and whether the baby will sleep through the night. Thus, no clear benefits can be gained from the early introduction of solid foods (Chubet, 1988; Grunwaldt, Bates, & Guthrie, 1960).

Can the early introduction of solid foods do any harm?

Some hazards are associated with the early introduction of solid foods. The best source of nutrition for infants under 6 months is milk—preferably human. Any solid food is inferior nutritionally, so proportionately more is required to satisfy nutritional needs. This will lead to less consumption of milk and to a tendency to distend or overtax the stomach, resulting in the short term in gastrointestinal upset and in the long term in possible obesity. Early feeding of solids also has been associated with the development of food allergies, kidney malfunction, and an increased likelihood of developing strong food dislikes (Guthrie, 1979; Pipes, 1985; C. H. Robinson, 1978; Weir & Feldman, 1975).

How should solids be introduced?

By the age of 5 months, the digestive systems of most babies develop the enzymes to digest most proteins, and saliva production increases to lubricate swallowing. Drooling begins about this time, because the production of saliva exceeds the baby's ability to keep it under control. Furthermore, chewing, swallowing, and teeth pushing up under the gums all make it easier to handle the demands of eating solids (Guthrie, 1979; Pipes, 1985; Sheppard & Mysak, 1984).

The first teeth typically do not erupt through the gums until about 8 months, although individual infants may vary from the average dates of tooth eruption by as much as 6 months before or after (Lunt & Law, 1974; R. McDonald & Avery, 1983). In response to teething, some babies become fussy, while others do not seem to notice, although most babies like to bite semisoft objects as their teeth are coming in. Infants under a year may be given biscuits to chew on, and babies older than 1 year may be given large carrot sticks.

Weaning is the process by which children become accustomed to the foods eaten by adults. General guidelines on how to introduce solid foods are available from a number of sources. Because of the possibility of food allergies, most experts recommend introducing one food at a time—for at least a week or two—before trying another. New foods should be offered in small amounts at first, and caregivers should never force infants to take a food they do not like. Food should be seasoned lightly or not at all. Salts and sugars are not harmful in small quantities, but there is no need for them. They seem to be more important for the feeder than for the baby (Guthrie, 1979; C. H. Robinson, 1978). Some commercially available baby foods contain added sugars and salts.

Solid foods are usually introduced to babies in the following order: cereals (one at a time), strained fruit or juice (except orange), vegetables, proteins (meat and cheese), egg

---

under your knees if the pressure on the floor is too uncomfortable. Rest a while on your back after each variation before going on to the next one.

1. In slow motion begin to lift your right knee a millimeter (one-eighth inch) or two away from the floor and return it to the floor. Do not lift your foot, only the knee. Notice how your pelvis shifts over the left leg and then

returns to the middle when your right knee returns to the floor. Each time you lift your knee, notice how the weight distribution changes on the two hands. Now, gently lift and lower your left knee just a small amount and return it to the floor. Notice how you shift your weight onto your right knee, and alter the weight on your hands in order to yolk (not until 8 months), and egg white (not until 10 to 12 months) (Guthrie 1979; C. H. Robinson, 1978). This order is related to a number of developmental factors, such as production of digestive enzymes, the consistency of the food and the ability to chew, and the possibility of an allergic reaction (egg whites are one of the biggest troublemakers in this regard). Since cow's milk should not be used for the first year, dry cereals should be mixed with breast milk or formula. Rice cereals are the most easily tolerated in the first year, and rice milk formulas can also be found (Karns, 2000).

Infants can eat a vegetarian diet with certain precautions (Karns, 2000). Vegetarian diets are high in bulk, and infants need denser foods such as nuts, olives, dates, and avocados. Macrobiotic diets present the greatest risk, but infants who eat milk and /or eggs have normal growth patterns. Infants need to ingest dietary fat for a number of reasons: it is a source of energy; it is a carrier of fat-soluble vitamins such as A, D, E, and K; and infants need certain essential fatty acids.

Up until 1 year, food should be mashed or chopped until it is fine enough not to cause choking. Foods most likely to cause choking are hot dogs, grapes, raw vegetables, popcorn, nuts, and hard candy (Karns, 2000). Finger foods are good for 6-month-olds, and by 9 to 12 months, infants can begin to feed themselves with a spoon. Until about 18 months, spilling and messing food is quite common. Why should babies not explore food just as they do everything else? A good recommendation is for the feeder to come armed with a towel, a sponge, and a sense of humor.

If infants persist in spilling food as part of a game or to get the caregiver's attention, caregivers can remove the food temporarily, while firmly stating that food is for eating. It is usually not necessary to coax infants to eat: they will eventually eat to satisfy their hunger. Thus, intake in any one meal is not so important. Caregivers may wish to insist on proper mealtime behavior (considering the limits of the infant's motor abilities and allowing for a little bit of fun), but insisting that the infant eat particular foods and particular amounts of foods is generally not recommended. Babies may avoid food because of its taste or because they are not hungry.

At the end of the first year, babies who are teething like to chew on carrots or dry toast but tend to mangle these foods more than consume them. Babies often go on food jags, refusing to eat more than one or two different kinds of foods. They can be erratic in their appetites and seem to have strong ideas about when and what to eat (Pipes, 1985).

How to eat is also a big concern for most babies. They may eat something only if it is presented in a ritualized way—cut or arranged a certain way or served on a certain dish. There is not too much the caregiver can do except live with these idiosyncrasies, accepting them with good humor and the recognition that preferences are part of being human. Some people like their hamburgers with catsup and others like mustard; some people like grits with their breakfast and others eat bagels.

For a baby, a meal is more than food intake: it is an occasion for play, learning, and socializing. Mealtimes are an important part of the infant's social, cognitive, and emotional development, not just a refueling for physical growth. Parents should try not to rush meals and should cut down on stimulation, such as the television, that might compete with the social aspects of feeding the baby.

As shown in the examples in the observation box related to communication, mealtimes contain complex sequences of co-regulated social interaction. Issues of control arise often. The baby wants to hold the spoon, for example, but is doing more banging than eating. The mother takes the spoon and begins to feed the baby, who starts to protest and refuses to eat. Mother eventually returns the spoon to the baby. The best solution is to allow the baby as much time as needed to complete the meal. When this is not possible, caregivers do need to model more appropriate eating habits, but without undue domination. In eating as in other aspects of development, infants will never learn independent behavior unless they are allowed to develop their own sense of control and achievement in this realm. Patience and praise are the best teaching tools.

---

lift your knee. Do everything in slow motion and pause between movements so you can discover the nuances. Alternate lifting one knee and then the other. Which knee is easier to lift? Rest on your back.

2. Bring your knees and feet together to touch each other. Again, lift one knee and then the other just a small amount. Notice how easy it is to lift the knees when the legs are together. Your base of support is now more narrow, so that you are less stable but more movable. Rest on your back.

3. Move your knees very far apart. Again alternate lifting one knee and then the other, and notice how much more difficult it is. Your base of support is now wider, so that you are

Co-Regulating with Baby

At the beginning of this stage, babies are just beginning to reach out and grasp things with some success. Over these 4 to 5 months, babies get better at grasping and holding onto objects, and they get better at locomotion. Any kind of play in which objects are handed to or taken from the baby is most appealing in this stage. As the baby gets good at moving around, you can play a kind of "catch and fetch" game by rolling a ball across the floor and letting the baby retrieve it. Babies have their own version of this game. They love to push toys off tables or throw them down, and they expect the caregiver to rush to pick them up, put them back, and wait for the next round of pushing and throwing. You can guess who gets tired of this game first. Play these games, but be aware of your own limits of patience. Change the game and the setting before you get upset with the baby.

You can create inviting places into which infants can crawl, like cardboard boxes and "houses" of couch pillows. Place objects on the floor away from the infant in order to encourage crawling to them. You will need to prepare the house, because now the baby can get into cupboards and closets. Make sure dangerous substances are in locked cabinets. It helps to provide one lower-level cabinet the baby can get into, filled with things that the baby can empty out and put back. The more comfortable you feel about the house being safe for the baby, the more likely you will be to let the baby explore.

Toward the end of this period, babies really get the idea of listening to words. Their favorite words are often names—their own names, of course, and names like "Mommy" and "Daddy." Try to punctuate all your games with words. Babies quickly learn to associate tonal patterns with behavioral sequences. When the infant responds with delight, you will know that you have gotten the rhythm right. Give yourself an opportunity to make mistakes, and forgive yourself when you do.

This is the stage in which the baby perfects the art of anticipation. Games that have a set pattern and a "punch line" the baby can look forward to are perfect. A good example is singing "Pop Goes the Weasel." Chase games, like "I'm gonna get you," tickle games, and the classic peekaboo, are just right for babies of this age group. Watch for different types of smiles (with cheek raises and/or wide open mouth) and see if you can tell what each of them means for the baby.

Although the baby does not understand the words of the sentences you say, he or she can use differences in tonal patterns as a way of sensing the significance of your words. Games that ask questions of the baby begin to work in this stage. Questions have a pattern of rising intonation near the end of the sentence that a baby can recognize as being different from other kinds of statements. This rising pitch creates a sense of anticipation. Of course, you have to answer the questions yourself, but your answer gives the baby a sense of completeness and therefore delight. Examples are "How big is the baby?" and "Where is the baby?" (a variant on peekaboo).

Babies of this age know when things are about to happen. They watch out the window as their parents leave for work, and they look for them when they hear the door opening or footsteps ringing in the hall. Babies also learn the sounds and sights of siblings and friends and usually get excited when they see or hear them approach. These behaviors give the baby's family members the clear sense that the baby recognizes and appreciates them. Notice how your feelings change when the infant seems to learn these routines.

It is important to exercise babies' bodies as well as their minds. Helping babies stand, holding their arms to let them "walk," and picking them up are good ways to do this. Babies of this age like vigorous games, such as being tickled or tossed up in the air and swung around. Gentleness and care are important, since babies' bodies are somewhat weak, and it is easy to dislocate an arm if you are not careful. Seek a level of excitement at which both you and the baby are having fun.

Babies of this age develop their own motor games. They will rock themselves, bounce on their legs, bang on things, and crawl and climb around the house to the extent of their ability. In general, these motor games and rhythmical movements are essential for normal motor and mental development. However, the caregiver must be on the alert for potentially dangerous situations. Make sure the things babies like to hold onto to pull themselves up are secure, as well as that there are no dangerous objects—too heavy, too sharp, or too small—in their normal path of movement. The baby's delight at finding their way around will more than compensate you for these efforts.

more stable, but it is harder to move. Rest on your back.

4. Now experiment with different distances between your knees in order to find the optimum position. Where is the best balance between stability and instability? Rest on your back.

5. Repeat movements 1–4 with your hands. Discover how you need to shift your weight and determine the best distance for your hands to be apart. Rest on your back.

6. Now lift your right hand and foot just a small amount, and at the same time see if you can lift and lower them simultaneously. Discover how you need to balance and shift your weight. Always pause after each movement. Now lift and lower your left hand and left foot. Alternate between lifting the right hand and foot and then the left hand and foot. Which side is easier to lift? Rest on your back.

7. Lift and lower your right hand together with your left knee. How do you need to shift your weight? Now do the other diagonal, lifting and lowering your left hand together with your right knee. Try to lift the knee and hand at exactly the same time. Which diagonal is easier to lift? Which is easier, lifting diagonals or lifting the hand and foot on the same side? Rest on your back.

8. Lift both hands off the floor and move in the direction of sitting on your heels. As you shift your weight back, begin to lift one hand before the other and see which hand you lift first. Rest on your back.

9. Rock back and forward on your hands and knees. Find a comfortable rhythm. Can you find a rhythm that feels connected to the movement of crawling? Do you feel like you are preparing yourself to advance forward? Look around. Does anything in the environment draw your attention?

10. Now begin to crawl forward several steps and then back. Notice the order you use in lifting the hands and knees. If you move the hand and knee on the same side, this is called *homolateral crawling*. If you move your hand on one side as you move your knee on the other side, this is called the *contralateral crawling*.

As you crawl, experiment with both homolateral and contralateral crawling. Does it change from one to the other when you change direction to crawl either backward or forward? Is it easier to go backward or forward? Many babies go backward first. Can you feel why this is so? If you are confused, maybe you are not yet ready to crawl.

11. Return to the movements in step 1. Is it easier than it was at the beginning? After resting on your back, get up on your feet and walk. Has revisiting crawling improved the fluency of your walking?

SUMMARY

Physical and Motor Development

■ During this period, infants learn to locomote by crawling; they can sit alone and pull themselves up to standing. Grasping and reaching are well coordinated.

■ Infants have a preferred hand, but their hand preference may change during the first year of life. Hand preference leads to the development of different uses for each hand that are necessary for the acquisition of unimanual reaching and crawling.

■ Walking develops after infants gain postural control.

Perceptual Development

■ Infants can now perceive objects from visual cues alone, allowing them to process information in pictures and on television.

■ Haptic perception is also used to perceive object properties through action.

■ Infants can recognize melodies and relate sound patterns to visual patterns.

Cognitive Development

■ Infant memory improves in duration, and infants can process information faster than in the previous stage.

■ Infants now try to form concepts out of their perceptual experiences. Concept formation appears to be organized around prototypes.

- Using secondary circular reactions, infants discover relationships between their actions and the environment, and they will vary their actions to observe the effects.

- Infants of this age can remember object locations, so long as they do not have to act on the objects.

Emotional Development

- Anger and wariness are two new negative emotions seen during this period.

- Laughter emerges as a new positive emotion, and other positive emotions develop at this age.

- Infants can recognize positive facial expression better than negative expression; however, they do not seem to attribute meaning to those expressions.

- Infants have stable temperamental characteristics, although the origins of these patterns are not understood.

- Measuring temperament is difficult because it requires understanding how the infant changes or remains the same over long periods of time.

Social and Language Development

- Infants can communicate nonverbally through action; however, they do not fully understand the meaning of their own behavior. Adults are required to interpret the infant's meaning, which ultimately contributes to the infant's understanding of communication.

- Infant social play becomes oriented toward objects, and parents can play a role in directing the infant's attention to objects and their properties.

- Parent-infant games are elaborated during this period. There are cultural differences in the amount of play versus caregiving that are related in part to ecological factors.

- The infant develops a differentiated ecological self. They do things to call attention to themselves and thus make the first distinctions between self and other.

- Babbling mimics the intonation patterns of speech and develops in conjunction with auditory perception of speech sounds. However, infants are not using babbling to express themselves in a meaningful, linguistic manner.

- In specializing in their perception of the language spoken in the home, infants lose their sensitivity to sound contrasts that are not made in that language.

Family and Society

- Typically, maternal employment does not affect the attachment between mothers and infants. The important factor is whether the mother desires to return to work, in which case her adjustment is more successful.

- Parental leave policy helps the family's initial adjustment to a new baby, but few parents can take advantage of it.

- At all ages, boys and girls are equally responsive to and knowledgeable about babies. Differences arise in social situations in which individuals are encouraged toward or away from nurturing roles.

- Preschool-age siblings are capable of adapting their speech and behavior to the needs of the baby.

- Fathers often have a more directing and challenging style than mothers, but in most cases, their behavior with infants is similar.

Applications: Infant Nutrition

- The age at which solid foods are started coincides with changes in the infant's physical and motor development that make eating solids possible.

- Foods should be introduced one at a time to allow babies to express possible allergies.

- Younger babies need food that is ground or mashed.

- Eating is a social experience, and parents should allow plenty of time for meals.

 ON THE WEB

www.nnfr.org   This site for the National Network for Family Resiliency has access to many subjects regarding family. These links refer to adolescent sexuality, evaluation of family programs, family economics, public policy, general family resiliency, intergenerational connections, Money 2000, parenting education, the program and curriculum, research, surviving childhood cancer, and violence prevention. You can also learn about many conferences that are taking place.

www.nara-licensing.org The Child Development and Education pages of the National Association for Regulatory Administration web site provide information and activities concerning children and their health and safety, educational resources, special Internet directories, search engines, provider resources, policy and advocacy groups, and much more. Also available in the General Subjects pages is information on aging, disabilities, child welfare, psychology, brain development, health and safety, government agencies, law, licensing sites, food, news, maps, weather, policy interest groups, general and writing reference tools, management, and so forth, as well as directories and search engines.

GLOSSARY

Appraisal The process by which an individual uses cognitive judgments to regulate emotional experiences.

Babbling Vocal behavior that includes reduplication (repetition) of consonant-vowel syllables.

Differentiated ecological self The awareness that the ecology has localized entities, such as self and other or self and object, shown by the different ways in which infants call attention to themselves such as asking for help, taking the initiative, clowning and showing off, demanding, and hiding and escaping.

Flextime A policy allowing flexible work schedules for working parents.

Handedness The preferential use of one hand over the other; also refers to the use of each hand to do different things.

Haptic perception The perception of the properties of an object using touch.

Object permanence The ability to remember the location of objects that are out of sight.

Prototype The clearest example of a particular form or sound. Prototypes also represent the average of all exemplars across all relevant dimensions.

Role overload Refers to one person trying to fill too many roles or facing excessive demands from a single role.

Secondary circular reaction Deliberate repetition of an association between an action and its effect. In this case, each repetition is a slight variation of the one before in which the infant is exploring different ways to create effects.

Temperament A persistent pattern of emotion and emotion regulation in the infant's relationship to people and things in the environment.

Wariness A quieting or sobering of an infant, usually in response to a novel situation. Wariness is believed to be a precursor to fear.

8

Ten to Twelve Months

CHAPTER OVERVIEW AND OUTLINE

Physical and Motor Development	*How do infants learn to walk? What are the developments of the infant's ability to explore?*
Perceptual and Cognitive Development	*What kinds of concepts do infants have at this age? Are infants aware of objects when the objects are out of sight?*
Emotional Development	*What new emotions can infants feel at this age? How do infants use adults to regulate their emotions?*
Social and Language Development	*What words and gestures do infants use at this age? How do attachments develop and what are some individual differences in attachment? What is the sense of self at this age?*
Family and Society	*Can infants form attachments to people other than the mother? Can infants become attached to adoptive parents?*
Applications: Infant Health and Safety	*What are the main threats to health and safety? What kinds of immunizations are recommended for infants?*

The period from 10 to 12 months brings several of the most important developmental achievements of the infancy period. First of all, infants develop strong and permanent attachments to their primary caregivers, typically the members of the immediate family. They prefer to stay close to these people, they do not like separations, and they may become afraid of strangers under certain circumstances. The infant's sense of security or insecurity in those attachment ties has lasting implications for mental health and the success of interpersonal relationships. Second, infants develop a subjective sense of self. They learn ways to communicate their perceptions and feelings to others and at the same time learn that others have a view of the world different from their own. It takes a lifetime, of course, to learn how to communicate our ideas to others and to appreciate how other people feel and think. At this stage, however, infants have begun this journey into intersubjectivity.

Physical and Motor Development

By the age of 1 year, infant growth rates have leveled off (see the growth charts in the appendix). Most year-old boys are between 28¼ inches (71.75 cm) and 32 inches (81.25 cm) in length, and girls are between 27½ inches (69.85 cm) and 31¼ inches (79.38 cm). Both boys and girls will continue to grow at a rate of about 4 to 5 inches (10 to 13 cm) per year for the next several years. At 1 year, boys weigh between 18½ and 26½ pounds (8.4 to 12.0 kg), while girls weigh between 17¼ and 24¾ pounds (7.8 to 11.2 kg). By the 12th month, most babies are eating a variety of solid foods, including table foods that are cut up for them. Most infants are holding their own spoons and can drink from a cup with both hands. By this time, almost all infants will have experienced teething pains and will have several teeth to help them chew their food.

With respect to motor developments, 11 months is the average age at which infants can stand alone (the range is 9 to 16 months), and at 11¾ months, the average baby can walk alone (the range is 9 to 17 months). By 1 year, most infants can sit down from a standing position, and most can climb up and down stairs by crawling.

Infants between 3 and 15 months were observed every 3 weeks in a laboratory going up and down a moderate slope (Adolph, 1997). The methods used to go up and down depended upon whether the infant was a belly crawler (also called a creeper; see Chapter 7), a hands-and-knees crawler, or a walker (see Figure 8.1). Most of the infants adapted their locomotion to the slope on-line, that is, by checking out the slope in relation to their abilities. The more experience they had with the slope, the more conservative they became in their method and the less need there was to rescue the infant from a possible fall. With experience, infants began to make "smart" locomotor decisions that required less adult guidance, and parents reported a similar progression at home.

Infants used four different strategies, depending upon their ability. There was the quick glance followed by a plunge, typically when infants felt the surface was safe enough to proceed. If the glance suggested some difficulty, the infants took a long look while swaying their bodies, then proceeded with their typical method of locomotion. If that did not work, infants took more time to look, and they also touched the slope to check the slant. This was sometimes followed by their typical means of locomotion and sometimes by an alternative means. If these techniques did not work, as a last resort, infants would hold onto the landing and try out different means of locomotion before proceeding. At this point, if they perceived the slope as too risky they would await a rescue from the adult. If not, they typically chose a sliding method.

The first months of independent walking initiate what some refer to as the toddler period of infant development. The label "toddler" seems to derive from the characteristic gait of the child who has not fully mastered the skill of walking. The earliest forms of childhood bipedalism have a distinct resemblance to a duck out for a jog—a sight that never fails to produce humorous delight in most caregivers.

What accounts for this precarious-looking form of locomotion? When adults walk, both legs are moving at the same time: while one is moving forward, the other moves backward relative to the

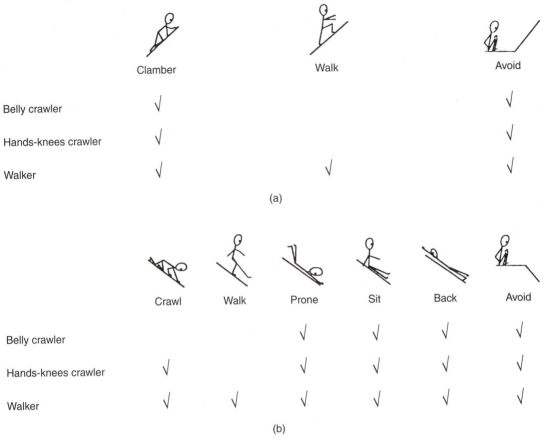

Figure 8.1
Possible locomotor methods for going up and down hills for belly crawlers, hands-and-knees crawlers, and walkers.

(**a**) = uphill, (**b**) = downhill

Source: K. E. Adolph, Learning in the development of infant locomotion, 1997, p. 51. *Monographs of the Society for Research in Child Development, 62*(3).

body. This kind of movement is called symmetrical gait. In the gait of toddlers, many steps are symmetrical, but many are also unsymmetrical. This happens because the toddlers often plant one foot and then seem to fall forward onto the other foot in a robot-like walk. Toddlers still have trouble balancing and they need to walk this way to keep from falling. Doing the Awareness through Movement lessons in this chapter will help you to understand the difficulty of keeping one's balance.

Thus, while adult walkers are smoothly making every step symmetrical, toddlers have much more variable steps. Smoothness of gait reaches nearly adult levels about 6 months after the infant begins walking, regardless of the age at which the infant started taking steps (J. E. Clark, Truly, & Phillips, 1993; J. E. Clark, Whitall, & Phillips, 1988). If in-

fants are given support by an adult, their variability lessens, and they seem to be better-coordinated walkers. This suggests that balance, not the timing of the limb movements, is the limiting factor (Bril & Breniere, 1993; Clark, Whitall, & Phillips, 1988).

Locomotion has benefits other than the ability to move from place to place. After beginning to walk, 10-month-old infants increase their frequency and duration of social contacts. This occurs whether the walking is supported or unsupported. It appears that an upright infant is more likely to be able to look, vocalize, and smile at adults (Gustafson, 1984).

Even more surprising is that locomotor experience enhances cognitive development. As we will see in the next section, one of the tests typically used to assess cognitive knowledge is the ability to

The infant's delight at mastering walking is not hard to decipher. Coordinated walking develops about 6 months after the infant's first independent steps. Coordination is better if an adult helps the infant to walk.

Elizabeth Crews

search for hidden objects. Infants with more loco-motor experience, who are apparently more accustomed to moving around in the environment, are the most likely to persist in searches for hidden objects. The locomotor experience could be either crawling or assisted walking (Bai & Bertenthal, 1992; Bertenthal, Campos, & Barrett, 1984; Kermoian & Campos, 1988). The development of walking also facilitates the search for hidden objects by blind infants, even though blind infants walk later than sighted infants (Bigelow, 1992). Being able to move oneself through the environment is essential for understanding spatial arrangements and the locations of things in that space.

The motor skill of reaching continues to improve during this period. Between 6 and 8 months, in-fants discover that they can lean forward to get objects just outside their reach. By 10 months, infants understand the limits of how far they can reach both by leaning forward and by extending their arms. By 12 months, infants are able to use mechanical and social aids to get things out of their reach, such as using a long object to get another or asking an adult for help (McKenzie, Skouteris, Day, Hartman, & Yonas, 1993).

Fine motor development also is intimately linked to cognitive and perceptual development. In one research study (Ruff, 1984), infants at 6, 9, and 12 months were observed while playing with objects that differed in weight, shape, or texture. Infants were handed one object to explore and then given another differing only in one property (for example, two cubes of the same size and weight, one with a bumpy texture and the other with a smooth texture). Between 6 and 12 months, mouthing the objects decreased, while fingering increased. The 12-month-olds also used more actions that were specific to the properties of the object. If only the object's texture was changed, babies increased the amount of time they looked at and fingered the object. If only the shape was changed, looking at and fingering the object increased, but so did rotating the object and transferring it between both hands. Weight changes did not evoke a differential response.

Related research has shown that by 12 months, infants use touching, listening, watching, and mouthing as alternative sources of information gathering. This involves more than intersensory coordination; it is the coordination of different types of motor skills in the service of directed exploration of objects (Bushnell, 1982; Gottfried, Rose, & Bridger, 1977).

This research shows that by 12 months, infants are using specific actions that are adapted to the type of object they are holding. Motor skill improvements and improvements in the ability to relate information cross-modally (such as between vision and touch) are essential in fostering cognitive development because they put infants into direct contact with more aspects of their world.

Perceptual and Cognitive Development

Conceptualizing Relationships between Objects and Events

By the age of 7 months, infants are just beginning to understand that objects exist as whole entities and they are starting to categorize objects on the basis of their similarity to a prototype. By 10 months, infants are beginning to discover the relationships be-

tween objects, between people and objects, and between people. This can be seen, for example, in the development of **relational play.** Relational play is action that demonstrates a knowledge of the relationships between two objects, for example, putting lids on pots, cups on saucers, or spoons in cups (Fenson, Kagan, Kearsley, & Zelazo, 1976). The more perceptually distinct the two objects, the more likely it is that babies will combine them correctly (Bates, Carlson-Luden, & Bretherton, 1980). For example, if a box and its lid are different colors, infants will be more likely to see how they go together. Also, if the adult places the lid of the box on a table positioned near the top of the box, rather than near the bottom, babies are more likely to put the lid on the box in an appropriate manner. Year-old infants can tell the difference between a visual display of a block that enters an opening of a box and one that rests precariously on the rim of the opening (Sitskoorn & Smitsman, 1997). These studies suggest that infants understand how different objects may be related to each other. A block is supposed to go inside the opening rather than rest on the rim.

Infants of this age are also able to perceive the relationship between a tool and its use. Infants first saw a toy sitting on the far end of a long piece of cloth. The near end of the cloth was pulled by an experimenter, moving the toy closer to the experimenter. Next they saw the toy sitting next to the cloth. In one instance the cloth was pulled and the toy did not move closer (as expected) and in another instance the cloth was pulled and the toy moved closer (an impossible event). The infants were surprised when seeing the impossible event, suggesting that they understood the relationship between the cloth tool and the object being retrieved (Schlesinger & Langer, 1999).

Forming relationships between objects can also be seen in studies in which infants were placed in front of a tray containing different groups of identical objects, for example, four identical human figures, four balls of the same color, and four identical toy cars. Six-month-olds pick up the objects in random sequence, even though they can visually distinguish the different types of objects in a standard habituation procedure. By 12 months, infants will pick up three or four identical objects in a row before going on to pick up other objects. About 40%

of 12-month olds will take those identical objects and place them in a new pile by themselves (Starkey, 1981). By 10 months, infants are able to classify pictures of animals (dogs versus cats), male versus female faces, African American versus Caucasian American female faces, and plants versus kitchen utensils (G. Levy, in press; G. Levy & Haaf, 1994; Mandler & McDonough, 1998; B. A. Younger & Fearing, 1999). The ability of infants of this age to categorize objects is related to their familiarity with those objects rather than to some abstract ability to categorize objects (McDonough & Mandler, 1998; Oakes, Coppage, & Dingel, 1997).

Infants of this age are also able to perceive the relationship between a prior event and a subsequent event, that is, between a cause and an effect. Infants can understand that when one toy car hits another toy car, the second one should move as a result of the collision (L. B. Cohen & Oakes, 1993). They also understand the relationships between faces and voices, that a male voice belongs with a male face and a female voice belongs with a female face (Poulin-Dubois, Serbin, Kenyon, & Derbyshire, 1994).

The Emergence of Intentional Action

In these studies, infants are acting as if their object play has particular goals, such as combining objects in a meaningful way. This deliberate combination of different actions into a unified pattern of behavior suggests that infants are intending to act in this way. This is different from what occurred in earlier periods, when infants first discovered actions by chance and then repeated those actions as primary or secondary circular reactions. This intentional and deliberate form of action is what Piaget (1952) called the *coordination of secondary circular reactions*. In

Observations 8.1 and 8.2, Jacqueline's pushing away of her parent's hand shows how the infant can combine different actions with each hand to achieve a goal.

Notice that to perform these deliberate actions, the infant must relate two simpler secondary circular reactions, such as holding the toy in one hand and pushing the adult away with the other. Infants are also relating two actions when they search for hidden objects. In order to find an object that they see being hidden behind a barrier or a cover, infants have to move the barrier with one hand and grasp the uncovered object with the other hand. We saw in the last chapter that younger infants remember the hidden object's location, although they do not reach for the object once it is out of sight. Piaget found that by 10 months, infants will readily search for the hidden object and seem delighted to find it under the cover.

Now suppose you have two identical handkerchief-sized pieces of colored cloth on a table at which you are sitting opposite the infant. You engage the infant with an attractive toy, such as a set of colored keys, and then you hide the keys under one of the pieces of cloth. Infants 10 months and older, but not younger, will lift the cloth to retrieve the keys. Now suppose you take the keys back from the baby and hide them under the other piece of cloth. Infants younger than about 15 months typically will look under the first piece of cloth and will not persist in looking under the second piece of cloth to find the object even though it was hidden in their plain view! This is easy to demonstrate with a year-old infant, if you want to convince yourself that babies could actually make such an obvious error.

This mistaken search for the missing object is called the **A-not-B error** by infancy researchers. The infants who find the object at location A, the first location, cannot find the object at location B,

---

OBSERVATIONS

Stage IV Behavior (Piaget, 1954, p. 219)

Observation 8.1

At 0;8(8) Jacqueline tries to grasp her celluloid duck but I also grasp it at the same time she does. Then she firmly holds the toy in her right hand and pushes my hand away with her left.

Observation 8.2

At 0;8(17) after taking a first spoonful of medicine, she pushes away her mother's hand which extends to her a second one.

When an object is hidden, young infants often act as if it does not exist anymore.

Bob Daemmrich/PhotoEdit

the second location. This error has aroused the curiosity of many infant researchers. Why does it happen?

According to Piaget, the infants act as if part of their definition of the object includes its location. In other words, infants do not yet conceive of a whole independent object as you and I might. Rather, infants define the object as the "keys-under-the-cloth," or the "ball-under-the-chair." This sort of thing also happens to adults. Most of us have had the experience of meeting someone briefly, say, at a party, and then failing to recognize the same person in another location, such as the grocery store. If we encountered that person at another party at the same place, we would have no trouble recognizing the individual.

Following Piaget's elegant first experiments and his contextual explanation, there have been a number of seemingly contradictory results. First of all, it should be noted that by 9 months, infants are almost 100% correct in reaching for hidden objects at the A location (Wellman, Cross, & Bartsch, 1986). Second, if objects are displaced at several different locations without being hidden or if objects are hidden under transparent covers, so long as the infants are first familiarized with the covers and objects, they are almost 100% correct in reaching for the object in either location, A or B (Butterworth, 1977;

Yates & Bremner, 1988). The only case in which this is not true is if the object or the infant is moved along complex paths with many twists and turns (B. Landau & Spelke, 1988). This suggests that following the path of a moving object in space is not limiting the infant's search when the objects are hidden.

Memory of the hidden object cannot be a problem for 9-month-olds, as shown by the studies of Baillargeon (discussed in Chapter 7), in which 8-month-old infants remembered an object's location so long as they did not have to act on it. It appears, then, that infants of this age already have a concept of objects as existing when out of sight, and they do not appear to associate objects with particular locations, since they will directly search for the object in multiple locations so long as they can see the object.

The A-not-B error is made most frequently when the object is out of sight, but even then, infants succeed under certain conditions:

1. If there is no delay between the hiding and the opportunity to search for the object, they can find it. Errors are increased if infants are restrained for at least 3 seconds after the object is hidden at location B (Diamond, 1988; Diamond & Doar, 1989).

2. If the infants are shown the object being hidden in the A location multiple times, they are more likely to search in the B location (Marcovitch & Zelazo, 1999).

3. If the infants are allowed to lean their bodies in the direction of the hidden object, they can sometimes find it even after a delay by following the direction of their lean (Diamond & Doar, 1989).

4. If the objects are hidden under covers that are perceptually very different, it is easier for the infants than if the objects are hidden under identical covers (Bremner, 1978).

5. It also helps if the infants are familiar with the objects or if the objects are interesting to them (Munakata, 1997). They will search more readily for their hidden mothers than for an unfamiliar person or a large object (Bigelow, MacDonald, & MacDonald, 1995).

The A-not-B error is not a serious deficit for infants, and they overcome it within a few months or if the objects are presented in ways that facilitate their search, as described above. The importance of the A-not-B error lies in questions it raises for understanding human development. Development offers many examples in which the emergence of a new skill (like searching for hidden objects) is accompanied by a curious but not serious deficit (like being unable to search in more than one hiding place). When we discuss language development in Chapter 9, we will encounter another example, called *overgeneralization,* which occurs when children begin to make grammatical errors after they have seemingly acquired the correct rule. Developmental researchers would like to better understand why these patterns occur.

Imitation

Imitation is another skill that requires making a conceptual relationship between two actions, in this case, between another person's actions and one's own. The imitations of newborns occur only for acts that they can already do. Observing an adult doing the same types of acts increases the probability of the newborn's selecting a similar act. However, newborn imitation is slow and does not happen for all infants. Six-month-olds can imitate actions

that they have not done before, but only if you give them many demonstrations and allow them plenty of time to process the information (Kaye & Marcus, 1978). Between 10 and 12 months, infants become more proficient at imitating actions that they see for the first time or have not done before.

Typically, babies are better at imitating actions that are close to what they can already do. Nine-month-old infants can imitate simple actions on objects such as opening a box, shaking a toy rattle, and pushing a button. In addition, when the same babies were shown the objects 24 hours later, they reproduced the actions that had been modeled previously (A. Meltzoff, 1988). Imitation that occurs following a delay from the time the action is observed is called **deferred imitation.** Deferred imitation also shows that infants can remember the relationships they learn, at least for a short time.

Individual Differences in Cognition and Attention

The basic trends in cognitive development discussed in this chapter have been found to occur at about the same ages in different cultures around the world (Agiobu-Kemmer, 1986). On the other hand, within any group there are individual differences in the age of attainment of cognitive milestones and in the quality of cognitive abilities.

One important component of cognition is the ability to attend to objects for a long enough time to remember their locations, watch their paths of movement, or learn about their properties during exploratory play. Individual differences in the duration of sustained attention to objects have been found at the age of 1 year (Power, Chapieski, & McGrath, 1985). Infants who can sustain attention for longer periods engage in higher levels of exploratory play (Caruso, 1993; L. Fenson, Sapper, & Minner, 1974) and score higher on developmental tests of mental and motor abilities (Kopp & Vaughn, 1982; Ruff, Lawson, Parrinello, & Weissberg, 1990).

What factors account for individual differences in attention? To some extent, these differences may be related to differential development of the brain and may be partly constitutional (Rothbart & Posner, 1985). I will return to evaluate this explanation in the last chapter. On the other hand, differences in the caregiving environment have been shown to influence the quality of infant attention.

When mothers are trained to enhance their object-related behaviors during social play with infants—by demonstrating object properties, pointing to and naming objects, and questioning—the complexity of the infants' exploratory play is enhanced (Belsky, Goode, & Most, 1980; Tamis-LeMonda, Bornstein, Cyphers, Toda, & Ogino, 1992; Tomasello, 1995). Actually, this effect works best for infants who have short attention spans. Their duration of attention increases following an intervention in which adults work to point out object properties and refocus the infants after a loss of attention, while the duration of attention for high-attending infants does not change following the intervention (Lawson, Parrinello, & Ruff, 1992; Parrinello & Ruff, 1988).

Another approach to the study of individual differences in cognitive ability is to assess the infant's **mastery motivation.** Mastery motivation is an inherent motivation to be competent in a particular situation, and its measurement involves persistence in solving problems. At 12 months of age, persistent goal-directed actions on objects are typically followed by the expression of smiling or laughter by infants (McTurk, McCarthy, Vietze, & Yarrow, 1987), suggesting that persistence is in fact motivated by a goal and that the achievement of the goal results in positive feelings of efficacy.

Like adults' effects on infant attention, adult object-related behavior increased the level of mastery motivation only for 12-month-olds who were rated as being temperamentally low in activity. For infants who were highly active, parental intervention had no effect or an interfering effect on the infants' mastery (Wachs, 1987). Thus, more active infants are less in need of adult encouragement and intervention in their play than less active infants.

These studies suggest that adults can play important roles in the cognitive development of infants, particularly if their actions are designed to enhance the infants' attention to objects and their properties. The adults need not so much teach or reinforce as support the infants' own initiatives and help the infants to regulate their limited attention spans. These results also suggest that adult behavior needs to be adapted to the individual infant. Babies who are less active and poor attenders may need a more involved adult to help organize their play. Babies who are more active and attentive may have different needs for adults, perhaps needing them to be an appreciative audience to whom the infants can show off their self-directed achievements.

In summary, infants of this age are making the discovery that objects and events are related to each other. They can combine objects according to their function (lids on pots), their category (toy cars), or how they need to be combined to achieve a goal (using a fork to get food). As we shall see, this ability to form mental relationships between things is related to important developments in emotion, communication, and the sense of self.

Emotional Development

As the sections on cognitive and motor development suggest, the infant's life is becoming increasingly integrated into patterns of relationships. Motor skills create the tools with which the infant can operate on the environment to achieve goals, and goals increasingly structure the way in which the infant behaves. During the previous age period, infants became upset when someone caused them pain or when some expected event did not happen. Between the ages of 10 and 12 months, infants become upset when their goals are blocked and are pleased when they achieve an intended goal. Infant emotions, therefore, are intimately connected to the infant's goals.

The Development of Anger

Anger is the emotion most frequently elicited in infants when their goals have been disrupted. An angry expression has distinct characteristics. The mouth is open with a squarish shape that is angled downward toward the back of the mouth. The brows are lowered, and the eyes are opened and intense (see Figure 8.2). In the expression of distress, the mouth is similar, but the eyes are usually closed or partially closed (Figure 8.2). Anger typically involves a bracing of the jaw. In the Awareness through Movement lessons, you can explore how it feels to move your jaw in different ways and the importance of jaw movements in facial expressions.

When the infant is crying and making the anger expression at the same time, the state of emotion is more intense. When anger expressions were observed without crying, EEG recordings from the infants' scalps showed heightened activity in the left frontal region. When the infants were angry and crying, there was more activity in the right frontal region. The right frontal area is believed to be associated with more-intense states of negative emotions. These results suggest that low levels of anger, without crying, are probably adaptive and maintain the infant's orientation toward the environment (N. A. Fox & Davidson, 1988).

The emotion of anger began in the previous stage as a more vigilant and intense form of distress. Between 10 and 12 months, anger becomes more purposeful and directed. Infants do such things as stomp their feet, hit away objects or interfering hands, or slap and kick (Sroufe, 1979). These expressions have the quality of outbursts, and they coincide with the development of goal-directed behavior seen in other realms of infant functioning during this period.

The Development of Wariness and Fear

Around the age of 6 months, infants develop a wary look, which may involve a raised brow furrowing above the nose and a relatively relaxed mouth. Wariness is related to the emotion of fear, since both involve an inhibition of action and may reflect a tendency for the individual to withdraw from the situation. The expression of fear includes the raised and furrowed brow of wariness while the mouth corners are retracted straight back (Figure 8.2).

True fear expressions are rare in infancy, but they first appear around the age of 10 months (Demos, 1982). Fear expressions may appear briefly and then change to anger or sadness (see Figure 8.2). Fear may also be shown by behavioral inhibition in the absence of a facial expression. Infants may stop their movements or actively avoid approaching the source of the fear. Infants feel fear when unexpected or threatening events occur. Below are some of the situations that may arouse fear in year-old infants.

Heights. Fear of heights has been assessed using the **visual cliff** situation. A piece of hard, clear plastic is extended over a box with a shallow side and a deep side. Beginning at 9 months of age, infants show fear in approaching the deep side of the cliff (see Chapter 1, p. 20; E. J. Gibson & Walk, 1960; A. Schwartz, Campos, & Baisel, 1973).

Unpredictable objects and movements. Infants will show fear responses to any objects—either people or inanimate moving objects—that loom unexpectedly in front of them (Bronson, 1972; Cicchetti & Mans, 1976). Surprising events, like a jack-in-the-box popping up, may also cause fear (Ricciuti & Poresky, 1972). Unpredictable, noisy mechanical toys can cause fear. However, in one study, infants were given control over the movements of such toys. When the infants were in control, the toys were significantly less fearsome (Gunnar, Leighton, & Peleaux, 1984).

Acquired fears. Infants may become fearful of an otherwise benign situation because it reminds them of something they found stressful, fearful, or painful in the past. These fears can be said to arise from a conditioned association. They are different from fears of such things as heights or looming objects, which may be universal. Acquired fears are learned. Examples are fear of particular people, of doctor's offices, or of certain kinds of sounds, such as a dog's bark (Bronson, 1972; see Observation 8.3).

Strangers. Fear of strangers takes two forms. One is a response to particular people or people wearing a particular kind of clothing or hairstyle. This is an acquired fear, or a **categorical stranger reaction** (Bronson, 1972). The other is a general wariness of the unfamiliar that appears in most infants in every culture beginning about 8 months of age.

(a) Enjoyment

(b) Sadness

(c) Distress

(d) Anger

(e) Fear

Figure 8.2
Infant Expressions

Source: C. Izard, The maximally discriminative facial movement coding system, 1983 (January), p. 97. Instructional Resources Center, University of Delaware, Newark, Delaware, pp. 93, 95 – 98.

OBSERVATION

Stage IV Behavior (Piaget, 1952, p. 249)

Observation 8.3

At 1;1(10) she [Jacqueline] has a slight scratch which is disinfected with alcohol. She cries, chiefly from fear. Subse-quently, as soon as she again sees the bottle of alcohol she recommences to cry, knowing what is in store for her. Two days later, same reaction, as soon as she sees the bottle and even before it is opened.

Infants of this age are naturally wary of new situations. They find great comfort in the company of familiar caregivers.

Robert Brenner/PhotoEdit

Although infants' reactions to strangers are usually different from their responses to their mothers, infants are not always afraid of strangers. Recent research indicates that infants fear strangers the most when the strangers' presence contains any of the elements of the unconditioned fear responses mentioned above. Factors such as the height of the stranger, the familiarity of the setting, and whether the stranger looms in rapidly all play a part in the baby's appraisal of the situation.

Infants show more positive reactions if the stranger approaches them slowly and keeps an appropriate distance (Kaltenbach, Weinraub, & Fullard, 1980; Ricard & Decarie, 1993; Trause, 1977); if their mothers are present when the stranger approaches (Eckerman & Whatley, 1975; Ricciuti,

1974; Trause, 1977); if they are with familiar caregivers, such as baby-sitters or child-care providers (N. A. Fox, 1977; Ricciuti, 1974); if the stranger is a little person or a child (Bigelow, MacLean, Wood, & Smith, 1990; Brooks & Lewis, 1976); if the stranger does not tower over them (Weinraub & Putney, 1978); if the stranger is sensitive to the infants' signals and allows the approach to be regulated by the infants (Mangelsdorf, 1992); and if the infants are in an unfamiliar setting, such as a laboratory, compared to a home (Brookhart & Hock, 1976; Skarin, 1977).

You might expect a baby to be less fearful at home than in a strange place, but this is not the case. In strange places, infants seem to expect to see unusual or unfamiliar things. When the stranger intrudes on the familiar and predictable setting of the home, however, the infant gets disturbed. In fact, mothers take their babies many places, such as doctors' offices and grocery stores, and the babies are rarely upset by the many unfamiliar people they meet in those situations.

Surprisingly, infants are less fearful of attractive than of unattractive strangers (Langlois, Roggman, & Rieser-Danner, 1990). An adult stranger wore a mask showing either an attractive or an unattractive face to a baby. The adult stranger was an attractive female. A professional mask maker made a cast of the woman's face and then created two lifelike masks. One was essentially a replica of the woman's face and the other had been altered according to previous research on attractiveness. To make the mask unattractive, the eyes were narrowed and moved closer together, the eyebrows were lowered, and the nose was lengthened. These changes did not make the mask look abnormal or deformed. The experimenters placed a mask over the woman's face and asked her to interact with infants. She was not told which mask she was wearing and was asked to behave as much as possible the same way every time she interacted with an infant.

When the stranger wore the attractive mask, infants showed more positive expressions and less withdrawal and got more involved in play with the stranger, compared to when she wore the unattractive mask. The results can only be explained by the infants' preference for attractiveness, since the stranger was unaware of which mask she was wearing. The same experimenters gave infants attractive and unattractive dolls to play with. The infants played longer with the attractive doll. There is currently no accepted explanation for this effect. It is important to point out that these behavioral differences showing a preference for attractiveness are short term. Infants are unafraid of familiar people, regardless of how attractive those people are.

A number of studies have shown that babies can engage in positive and rewarding social interaction soon after meeting a new person. If the stranger proves acceptable to the baby, the baby often will spend more time playing with this interesting visitor than with his or her own mother (Klein & Durfee, 1976; Ross & Goldman, 1977b).

In contrast, if the stranger approaches too quickly, looms toward or towers over the baby, or otherwise violates the infant's personal space, fearful reactions can easily be evoked. But would an adult react any differently? In one study (Kaltenbach, Weinraub, & Fullard, 1980), mothers and their 8-month-old infants sat side by side as unfamiliar female adults approached them quickly. The mothers showed more quizzical looks, frowns, and gaze aversions as the stranger got closer than did their infants. This suggests that "stranger fear" is not a stage of development that all babies go through. It may represent a growing awareness of situations that all humans fear—a step toward becoming more adult. Hesitancy toward strangers—especially intrusive ones—is something that stays with people throughout their lives.

If you want to make friends with a baby of this age, the rules are much the same as with anyone else: go slowly, be sensitive to signs of withdrawal or wariness, let the baby get to know you on his or her own terms, and make sure the baby is properly chaperoned by his or her mother or caregiver before you make any serious proposals. Finally, do not forget that year-old babies develop acquired fears. If the baby screams in terror at the mere sight of you, it could be that you remind the baby of a negative encounter. Even though it is hard to keep from feeling downright insulted, it is probably not your fault. It may take some extra sensitivity on your part to help the baby learn to like you for yourself.

The Development of Sadness

The emotion of sadness has a different expression than anger and fear. During sadness, the brows are raised at the center and drop at the sides, and the mouth corners are drawn back and down (see Figure 8.2). As we reported for anger, sadness without crying is less intense, showing left-frontal brain activity. With crying, sadness is accompanied by right-brain activation. In the earlier months, sadness accompanies disappointment when an expected event fails to happen, for example, when the baby expects to receive a treat or a hug and does not get it. By 9 or 10 months, sadness accompanies a feeling of loss. Because infants can now connect their memory of absent objects with some concrete action on the objects, the infants may become sad if an object disappears and they cannot find it after a search.

In some cases, but not all, sadness accompanies separation from caregivers. This emotion is sometimes called *separation distress*. Research has shown, however, that if mothers leave their babies behind in the company of the regular caregiver (the grandmother, baby-sitter, father, and so on), there is little or no separation distress (Ricciuti, 1974; Stayton, Ainsworth, & Main, 1973; Suwalsky & Klein, 1980). One study of children admitted to residential care found that if they were admitted with a sibling, they showed less separation distress than if admitted by themselves, even when the sibling was not old enough to take care of the infant (Heinicke & Westheimer, 1966). Another study found that infants left with a total stranger cope significantly better with separation than infants left completely alone (Ricciuti, 1974).

Infants respond more positively to separation from their mothers if they are left with any other person, particularly a familiar one; if they are left with toys of any kind; if they can see or hear their mothers in an adjoining room (Corter, 1977); and if they are left with their own pacifiers (Halonen & Passman, 1978; Hong & Townes, 1976). The mothers's saying "bye-bye" or making some other parting gestures before they left had no effect on 1-year-olds (Corter, 1977). These parting gestures do seem to help older infants, however. In general, the longer parents take to say good-bye, the harder it is for the babies to initially adjust to the new situation (Field, Gewirtz, et al., 1984; Weinraub & Lewis, 1977). Babies who go to a new preschool or day care center or who must be hospitalized show less distress if accompanied by peer friends or by siblings (Field, Vega-Lahr, & Jagadish, 1984; J. Robertson & Robertson, 1971).

These findings suggest that the infant's response to separation is not entirely up to the infant but depends in part on the relationship between the infant and the people involved. One might expect cultural differences in response to separation, as shown by a study of brief (30-second) mother-infant separations in Japan (Hoshi & Chen, 1998). About half of the Japanese infants showed distress, even at this brief separation, perhaps because of the close contact between Japanese mothers and their infants and because separation is relatively rare. In addition, about one-third of the mothers apologized to the infant during the reunion. Their apologies were done in an intonation pattern that matched the infant's crying, such as saying *Hai, hai, gomen nei, gomen nei, oh, oh* (yes, yes, oh, I'm so sorry, so sorry, well, well). The mothers seemed to endorse the infant's feelings as if to join in their misery and seek their forgiveness, a pattern of emotional sharing commonly seen in Japanese adults. Whether Western mothers do the same is unknown but such behavior has never been reported in the thousands of studies on separation in Western countries.

If infants are separated from parents for long periods and are not provided with adequate substitute caregivers, more serious depression and withdrawal can result, including both behavior and physiological changes (Reite, Kaemingk, & Boccia, 1989; Tizard & Tizard, 1971). These effects can be ameliorated once the infants are restored to stable adult care, either with their biological parents or with adoptive parents (Reite et al., 1989; Suomi & Harlow, 1972; Tizard & Tizard, 1971). The effect on infants of substitute care by nonparental caregivers is an important topic to which I will return in the next chapter.

The Development of Enjoyment and Affection

In the earlier months, infants showed positive responses to their caregivers. The smile of recognition appears at 2 months, and laughter of enjoyment during social play appears at 5 months. At 10 months, the infant has a deeper and more lasting type of positive feeling that has been called affection (Sroufe, 1979). Affection has a characteristic expression that is similar to a simple smile in the mouth region accompanied by a widening of the eyes (see Figure 8.2). Such smiles occur at the approach of familiar caregivers and are accompanied by right-brain activation. Infants' smiles at strangers usually lack the wide-eye component; such smiles activate the left side of the brain (N. A. Fox & Davidson, 1988).

After a brief separation, infants often feel genuinely happy to see the caregiver. This is a positive emotion that goes beyond the particular situation and expresses a lasting bond. Infants express these feelings not only to caregivers but also to favorite toys and to siblings. Infants of this age smile more in the presence of people, especially familiar people, and their favorite objects (S. S. Jones, Collins, & Hong, 1991). As we saw in the last chapter, smiling is related partly to emotion and partly to communication with others. Smiling is a reflection of a socially shared emotion.

Differential responsiveness to people on reunion is probably one of the earliest and most reliable ways of telling who the most important people in a baby's life are (Stayton, Ainsworth, & Main, 1973). In a stressful situation, if both the mother and another caregiver are present, infants will approach the mother (Klein & Durfee, 1976). Even when infants spend more hours of the day in the company of caregivers, as on an Israeli kibbutz, they show more positive responses when reunited with their mothers after a brief separation than when reunited with their **metapelets,** or caregivers (N. A. Fox, 1977). These findings suggest that babies have a growing awareness of the specialness of certain

people and respond to them in ways that communicate the depth of their feelings.

The Development of Mixed Emotions

Before leaving the topic of emotions, it is necessary to touch on the subject of mixed emotional expressions. In one study, a stranger presented dolls and teddy bears to infants of this age. The babies alternatively reached out toward the objects and pulled their arms back (Ricciuti & Poresky, 1972). Lest we think this sort of ambivalence was merely an artifact of testing infants in an unfamiliar laboratory setting, we should note that another study found evidence for mixed emotions by naturalistic observation in the infants' homes. This study found that pure expressions of joy, anger, distress, excitement, or fear occur only about half the time. The other half of

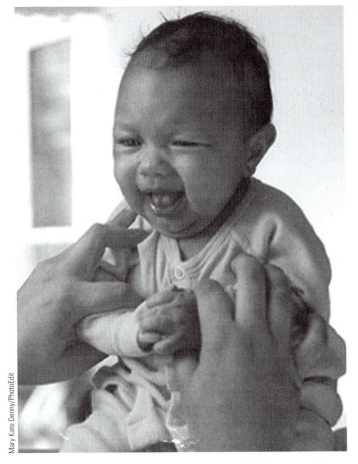

This baby is experiencing a mixed emotion. If you cover the eyes and look only at the mouth, what would you say the baby feels? Now cover the mouth, looking only at the eyes, and guess the baby's feelings. Putting the two parts together gives a mixed emotion.

Mary Kate Denny/PhotoEdit

OBSERVATIONS

Teasing Games (Nakano, 1995; Reddy, 1991)

Observation 8.4

Rebecca (8.5 months) "accidentally" discovers her impact on others of going in front of the television in her walker while someone is watching. After that, each time the television is turned on, Rebecca scoots, stands in front of it and giggles. Mother makes getting Rebecca away from the television into a game by playing "I'm gonna get you," while grabbing her away.

Observation 8.5

Stephanie (7 months) developed a shrill shriek that she used when she was not getting enough attention. In the supermarket, her mother heard the shriek, turned toward Stephanie quickly and with alarm, to find Stephanie sitting in her stroller grinning at her mother.

Observation 8.6

Mother claps her hands rhythmically to get her 10-month-old's attention. When the infant looks at her hands, the mother says, "my hands are stuck together and I can't pull them apart." She shrieks with an exasperated tone and asks the baby for help getting her hands apart. At the moment when the baby reaches out to help, the mother startles the baby by pulling her hands apart, saying "Bang!" at the same time. The mother answers the baby's surprised look with a smile and laugh and then the baby smiles joyfully.

the time the infant's face expresses more than one emotion (Demos, 1982).

Enjoyment, for example, often is expressed with elements of excitement or surprise, as when a smile is combined with a "jaw-drop," producing a wide-open, smiling mouth. This is called a *play smile* (see Chapter 7). In my research, play smiles in 12-month-olds occur during games involving some physical activity or touch combined with an element of excitement. These are games like tickle, chase, and tossing the baby in the air. Play smiles are more likely to occur in physical games and thus appear more during father-infant play than in mother-infant play (L. Dickson, Fogel, & Messinger, 1997). Smiles have also been observed to occur with nose wrinkles, blinks, blows, and waves; each combination reflects a slight variation in the meaning of the enjoyment. Try each one out and see if you can figure out what it might mean.

In the next stage, distress will be combined with biting or stiffening the lip, showing that the baby is trying to control the crying. One-year-old babies do not do this, but they often alternate between distress and enjoyment, showing that they are able to maintain interest in a toy or in social interaction even though they may be tired or frustrated. One-year-olds will sometimes look directly at the caregiver when crying, or they may pull at the caregiver, gesture to be picked up, or point to the offending object or event (Gustafson & Green, 1991). The caregiver can provide encouragement for the infant's efforts to gain control over frustration, teaching the baby the capacity to persist. The baby can learn that feeling distressed and frustrated does not

necessarily mean the end of the game—that these "negative" affects are both tolerable and manageable (Demos, 1982).

Another example of a mixed emotion appearing at this age is jealousy. Year-old infants were observed while their mothers and a strange adult female played with a picture book or a child-sized doll. Infants showed more protest and negative vocalization and their play was more inhibited primarily in the mother-with-doll condition (Hart, Field, Letourneau, & Del Valle, 1998). These responses were interpreted as jealousy because the infant was not upset about the mother with a book, nor about the stranger's behavior. Jealousy is an example of wanting to approach the mother but avoiding her at the same time.

Because of the emergence of mixed emotions, new forms of parent-child play develop as a way to help infants understand and cope with emotional changes. Teasing games are especially important in this regard. A tease takes something that has a serious emotional tone and alters it into a more positive tone. Between 9 and 12 months, infants learn the art of teasing and also become able to appreciate the teases of others (see Observations 8.4, 8.5, and 8.6). The contradictory messages in these games provide important opportunities for infants to learn how to regulate their emotions, how to affect other people, and also how to have fun (Nakano, 1995; Reddy, 1991; Reddy, 2000). Teasing is relatively more frequent in father-infant than in mother-infant play (Labrell, 1994).

In summary, these findings show that infants are becoming emotionally complex. Not only are they aware of the relationships between objects and between events, they are also aware of the relationships between their different feelings. They may not always be able to resolve these relationships. but at a minimum, their emotional life is becoming more diverse. In the "Social Development" section in this chapter, we shall see that infants are also becoming more aware of interpersonal relationships. Indeed, findings show that jealousy and teasing are clearly emotions that take account of different kinds of interpersonal relationships.

Individual Differences in Emotion Regulation

One of the more important aspects of emotional development is the ability to regulate one's emotions: to maintain some self-control in the face of highly arousing (either exciting or distressing) situations. At this age, infants show differences in how they use people or objects to regulate emotions.

Heart-rate measures have shown that even when infants do not cry during maternal separation, they do get aroused. We may observe an extended glance at the door, perhaps a sad expression, and then a concerted effort to become involved with the toys. It is almost as if the babies were using the toys to prevent feeling sad and lonely. Conversely, other infants who may ignore their mother when she returns from a separation also show elevated heart rates. These babies are coping with their ambivalent feelings about their mother in relation to the feeling of loss they must have experienced when she was out of the room. The manner in which the infants cope with these feelings is not necessarily adaptive, since it effectively removes them from the only source of comfort they might receive: their mothers (Sroufe, 1979).

Some infants are temperamentally more fearful and withdrawn, and they are more likely to become fearful or sad in stressful situations, such as during separations and in the presence of strangers or unusual situations (Blackford & Walden, 1998; Bohlin & Hagekull, 1993; K. A. Buss & Goldsmith, 1998; J. J. Campos, Emde, Gaensbauer, & Henderson, 1975; Connell, 1985; Kagan, 1989; R. A. Thompson, Connell, & Bridges, 1988). These differences

in emotionality are associated with individual differences in brain asymmetry. That is, infants who become easily distressed to the point of crying by a maternal separation have more marked differences between left- and right-brain activity in the frontal area (N. A. Fox & Davidson, 1987). These findings show that the infant's ability to remain attentive to the situation, rather than to withdraw, may be in part responsible for higher levels of regulation of fear (Kochanska, Coy, Tjebkes, & Husarek, 1998; M. D. Lewis, Koroshegyi, Douglas, & Kampe, 1997).

This suggests that there is a relationship between measures of cognition (attention) and measures of emotion regulation. Findings reported earlier in this chapter, that sustained attention to tasks is related to exploratory play, are also relevant here. Some infants are more focused, attentive, and not easily upset, while others seem more emotional and require more support from adults in challenging situations. We do not know about the long-term consequences of these differences. Most likely, they are simply normal temperamental differences that need to be taken into account when co-regulating with a baby.

Developments in the Infant's Ability to Use Emotional Information Expressed by Other People

In the last chapter, I reported research showing that by 6 or 7 months, infants are capable of perceiving a few simple facial expressions. By 9 or 10 months, however, infants can distinguish more expressions, and they are beginning to use the emotional information displayed by others in a meaningful manner. These developments in the perception of emotions in other people are one of the ways in which the infant is becoming increasingly aware of relationships between people. Even more important, infants at this age are beginning to get the idea that other people have emotions that differ from their own. This is shown by some of the following processes.

Affective sharing occurs when infants wish to communicate their feelings to another person or to confirm their feelings with another person. An example would be when a baby discovers an interesting relationship (such as how a lid goes onto a pot), smiles, and then looks to the caregiver. In this case, the infant is expecting a smile in return, as a way of confirming their own feeling of accomplishment.

Social referencing occurs when infants face an uncertain situation. In this case, they look to another person's emotional expressions to help them decide what to do in this situation. When infants are presented with a noisy, unpredictable toy, they may look around to see how adults are responding to the toy. Positive responses from the adults may encourage the infants to approach the toy.

Underlying both affective sharing and social referencing is the development of the ability to delay an immediate emotional reaction to a situation and to evaluate how one is going to feel about the situation. **Appraisal** is the ability to use cognitive comparisons of alternate interpretations to regulate one's emotions. In affective sharing, the infant has a spontaneous reaction (such as a smile) and looks at others to appraise that reaction. A confirmation leads to continued smiling. In social referencing, the infant may be unable to appraise a situation and uses information from others to decide whether the uncertain event (a strange toy) should be greeted with delight or wariness.

The appraisal at this age, however, differs from the appraisal seen during the period between 6 and 9 months. In that earlier period, infants are often observed to show a slight delay in their emotional reactions, as if deciding what to feel in a particular situation. After 10 months, however, the infant looks to *another person* to decide what to feel.

Between 9 and 12 months of age, affective sharing is the most common response in social situations, and it tends almost always to involve positive emotions (Hornick & Gunnar, 1988; Klinnert, 1984; Walden & Ogan, 1988). When infants in this age range are given novel toys or shown a rabbit in a cage, for example, they tend to focus mostly on the objects and look at the caregiver for confirmation, primarily the display of a positive expression by the caregiver (Hagekull, Stenberg, & Bohlin, 1993).

Between 10 and 12 months, infants begin to use social referencing systematically, although social referencing does not occur as frequently as affective sharing in naturalistic situations (Hornick & Gunnar, 1988; C. A. Nelson, 1985). Social referencing

occurs when infants look at adults in an uncertain situation, when infants look as much at negative as positive adult expressions, and when infants change their behavior (or at least pause before acting) as a result of the emotional information in the adults' faces.

Thus, by 10 months, if mothers display a negative expression, some infants will avoid crossing a visual cliff, avoid playing with toys or avoid approaching a rabbit in a cage, and they will show more aversive responses to strangers to whom the mothers show negative expressions. Opposite patterns of behavior can be seen if the mothers display positive expressions in these situations, although negative expressions seem to have a more powerful effect on regulating infant behavior at this age (Feiring, Lewis, & Starr, 1984; M. R. Gunnar & Stone, 1984; Hornick, Risenhoover, & Gunnar, 1987; Sorce, Emde, Campos, & Klinnert, 1985; Zarbatany & Lamb, 1985). Infants will reference almost any available adult and show equal responsiveness to mothers, fathers, and strangers (Dickstein & Parke, 1988; Klinnert, Emde, Butterfield, & Campos, 1986).

Female infants are more likely to regulate their distance from fearful objects as a result of maternal referencing than are males (Blackford & Walden, 1998; W. D. Rosen, Adamson, & Bakeman, 1992). These findings are consistent with the gender differences reported in the previous chapter, in which females were observed to be more effective at regulating their emotions at still-face condition than males. By 10 months, when emotional regulation becomes more social for both boys and girls, girls begin to use other people more effectively to regulate themselves than boys. A study of 9-month-olds in Sweden found that mother-daughter dyads spent more time in close proximity than did mother-son dyads, once again suggesting that girls begin to use their mothers as emotional guides more than boys at this age (Lindahl & Heimann, 1997).

In addition to this directed referencing in uncertain situations, infants are influenced by adults' emotions and attention. During a play period, mothers were instructed to use facial and vocal expressions of either joy or sadness. In the joy condition, infants expressed more joy and looked more at their mothers while engaging in higher-level play behavior.

In the sadness condition, infants expressed more negative emotions, looked less at their mothers, and played less (Stenberg & Hagekull, 1997; Termine & Izard, 1988). Infants of this age regulate their behavior to vocal information in the absence of visual information, but only when the voice expresses fear rather than enjoyment (Mumme, Fernald, & Herrera, 1996). Infants preferentially reference adults who are looking at the infants over adults who are looking away from the infants, suggesting further that infants are aware of the adult as another person who has the intention to communicate with the infants or not to communicate (Striano & Rochat, 2000).

In summary, these studies show that by the second half of the first year of life, emotion is no longer a private experience. Perhaps without intending to do so, infants nevertheless begin to alter their own emotions according to what others are expressing. It would not be correct to infer that infants understand the feelings of others at this age or even that infants can differentiate their own feelings from those of others. These developments begin almost a year later. They are simply aware that feelings can be shared and that they "have" feelings. Coupled with new perceptual and cognitive skills, infants probably discover that particular types of facial expression are related to actions that either enhance or interrupt their own activities. Thus, by the end of the first year, those facial expressions of adults have become part of the means by which infants regulate their own actions. From the adult's perspective, the infants are becoming more socially responsive and are entering into more meaningful social communications.

Social and Language Development

In this section, I cover new developments in the infant's communication with adults, including the beginnings of spoken language. Following that, we discuss caregiver-infant attachment. Finally, I will look at the beginnings of infant-peer relationships.

Developments in Parent-Infant Communication

The development in emotional communication, affective sharing, and social referencing at this age is tied in to a new pattern in parent-infant communication. During this period infants seem to become less obsessive in their attention to objects and more likely to share their interest in objects with adults. It is as if the infant realizes, for the first time, that others have different intentions and that the infant must act in a way that helps to coordinate intentions between self and other (Lock, 2000). This ability is called **intersubjectivity** (Trevarthen & Hubley, 1978) or **coordinated joint attention** (Adamson, 1995).

In addition to looking at the adult in order to share information about objects on which they are acting, infants of this age begin to follow the adult's line of gaze or pointing in order to detect something about what the adult is looking at. This ability to follow another person's line of regard is called **joint visual attention** (Butterworth, 2000; Corkum & Moore, 1995). Infants are especially likely to follow the gaze of people, or of objects that behave in some intentional way like a person (S. Johnson, Slaughter, & Carey, 1998). This means that gaze following is genuinely a way to communicate with another mind, not simply a mechanical act of following a moving object.

Developmentally, infants first become involved in frames for coordinated joint attention between 9 and 10 months. Next, they begin to produce simple gestures, like pointing and requesting at around 10 months. Finally, at 11 months, infants begin to follow the direction of the adult's gaze or pointing gesture. These developments are followed during the next few months (see Chapter 9) by increasing gesture and word use. In fact, the more coordinated joint attention shared by mother and infant during this age period, the more rapidly infants will develop skills for linguistic and gestural communication in the second year (Carpenter, Nagell, & Tomasello, 1998).

The Emergence of Intentional Gestures

At this age, infants are becoming more intentional in their use of gestures in communication. At 3 to

Figure 8.3
Infant Pointing Pattern

At 1–2 months
Spontaneous pointing.

At 6 months
Pointing used to
explore objects.

At 9 months
Pointing intentionally
used as a gesture.

Source: A. Fogel & G. F. Melson, *Child development,* 1988, p. 175. St. Paul, MN: West. Copyright © by West Publishing Co.
Reprinted by permission. All rights reserved.

5 months, pointing is a spontaneous display of attention or interest (Fogel & Hannan, 1985); after 5 months, pointing is used instrumentally to touch or tap objects while exploring (Bates, O'Connell, & Shore, 1987; Fogel & Thelen, 1987), but it is not until about 10 months that infants use pointing in intentionally communicative ways (see Figure 8.3). We can say that infants use pointing and other gestures to intentionally communicate if they look between the adult and the object alternately and if they keep trying to communicate when the initial

attempt does not succeed (Bates et al., 1987; Lock, 1980; see Figure 8.4).

During this age period, infants begin to use gestures such as pointing, showing, offering, giving, and requesting. These gestures are different from the actions the child might perform on an object (see Figure 8.3). Their form is designed to direct another person's attention to an object rather than to act alone on it (Camaioni, 2000).

In research done in my laboratory (D. S. Messinger & Fogel, 1998; Reinecke & Fogel, 1994),

(1)   (2)

(3)   (4)

Figure 8.4
Gestural Communication
at One Year

Source: A. Lock, *The guided reinvention of language,* 1980, p. 98. London: Academic Press.

we examined the development of infant offering of objects. Before 10 months, infants hand objects to their mothers in the course of exploratory play with the objects. When this happens, the infants never take their eyes off the object. They look at the object as their mothers take it and then hand it back. If mothers playfully keep the object, the infants become frustrated. Beginning at 10 months, infants alternate their gaze between mother and object during the offering, especially if the infant initiates the object exchange. When the mother requests an object, the infant does not look at her during the offer. Finally, and importantly, when infants initiate offers and alternate gaze, they are likely to smile or laugh when the offer is completed. Although communicative offering continues to be part of the infant's repertoire, the smile and laugh during offering lasts only a few weeks. It suggests

that infants are pleased with the discovery of a new communicative ability and that positive emotion may help to consolidate the developmental achievement.

Parents can use the infant's ability for joint visual attention to direct his or her attention to an object ("Look, there's a doggie"), a person ("Where's Daddy?"), a picture in a book, or even a particular feature of an object ("Where's Mommy's nose?"), thus creating a host of new opportunities for learning and communication (Zukow-Goldring, 1997). The infant's attention to the adult's gestures means that the infant wants to be included in what the adult is doing. If the adult turns away to talk to another person, the infant may try to engage also with the other person (Nadel & Tremblay-Leveau, 1999), or they may shows signs of jealousy, as discussed earlier.

Adults typically respond to infant gestures by interpreting what the infant wants. This includes coordinating their activities using objects with those of the infant, such as playing an object manipulation game by building with blocks or feeding a baby doll. In addition, caregivers are using words more deliberately as part of their actions on objects. An example would be describing in words what the baby is doing, requesting objects, offering objects, and saying, "Here's the baby's bottle" (Bakeman & Adamson, 1984; Hodapp, Goldfield, & Boyatzis, 1984; F. T. Hunter, McCarthy, MacTurk, & Vietze, 1987). In the next sections, I will discuss the infant's use of words and the infant's understanding of the parent's words.

Speech Production by Infants: First Words

Between 9 and 12 months, in the context of frames for coordinated joint attention, infants begin to make a variety of sounds that attentive caregivers recognize as words or wordlike utterances (Camaioni, Aureli, Bellagamba, & Fogel, 1999). As in the development of babbling, these new sounds are made possible by further anatomical developments of the vocal tract. The sounds are used repeatedly in similar situations and not in other situations. Table 8.1 lists the first seven "words" in a child's vocabulary, recorded in one of the early studies of language development. Some research suggests that the child's first words of this sort have sound patterns similar to the favorite sounds the child makes when babbling. Since the babbling sounds are also similar to those heard in the linguistic environment of the home (see Chapter 7), these early words will begin to sound intelligible to adults (DeBoysson-Bardies, 1990).

Researchers disagree over whether these sounds are true words or true names for things, since they are arbitrary and idiosyncratic, rather than conventional. Instead, they seem like accompaniments to action, like saying "brrroom" when moving a toy car or grunting when exerting physical effort (Bates et al., 1987; McCune, 1989).

The meaning of such sounds, as well as of many of the infant's gestures, still depends on the interpretive activity of the caregiver who recognizes a relationship between the sound or gesture and the situation in which the child uses it (Adamson, Bakeman, Smith, & Walters, 1987; Lock, 1980). Observations 8.7, 8.8, and 8.9 provide some examples of caregiver interpretations of infant acts, both verbal and nonverbal, at this age.

This combination of communication and emotion that we saw with gestures has also been

Table 8.1 The First Seven "Words" in One Child's Vocabulary

Utterance	Age (Months)	Meaning
eh	8	Said to people, distant objects, and toys.
Dididi	9	Disapproval (loud) or comfort (soft).
Mama	10	Refers to food; also means tastes good, and hungry.
Nenene	10	Scolding.
tt!	10	Used to call squirrels.
Piti	10	Always used with a gesture and always whispered; means that's interesting.
Duh	10	Used with same gesture as for piti; seems to be a comment on ongoing action.

Source: From W. Leopold, *Speech development of a bilingual child,* 1949. Chicago: Northwestern University Press, 1949. Copyright © by Northwestern University Press. Also in A. Fogel & G. F. Melson, *Child development,* 1988, p. 177. St. Paul, MN: West. Copyright © by West Publishing Co. Reprinted by permission. All rights reserved.

OBSERVATIONS

Coordinated Joint Engagement

Observation 8.7 (Trevarthen & Hubley, 1978, p. 200)

At 40 weeks, Tracey's mother become an acknowledged participant in actions. Tracey repeatedly looked up at her mother's face when receiving an object, pausing as if to acknowledge receipt. She also looked up to her mother at breaks in her play, giving an indication of willingness to share experiences as she had never done before.

OBSERVATIONS

Communicative Behavior (Lock, 1980)

Observation 8.8

Mary; age 12(20): (1) Mary turns around in her chair and tries to pick up an apple from behind her. (2) She fails and turns back to her mother, who has been watching her, and cries. (3) Mother: "What do you want?" (4) Mary gesturally reaches toward the apple. Mother then gives it to her.

Observation 8.9

Mary; age 11(5): Mary is sitting in her high chair with mother next to her. She has finished eating. Some of her toys are on the table in front of her. Mother picks up a squeaky duck and shows it to Mary. Mother: "Who's this?" (squeak, squeak) "Who is it? Is it the duck? What does the duck say?"

Mary: "ugh."

Mother: "He doesn't say 'ugh.' He says 'quack, quack, quack, quack' . . . 'quack, quack, quack, quack.' Ooh, and who's this? It's the doggie isn't it? And what does the doggie say? What does the doggie say? Mary? Oh he doesn't yawn? What does the doggie say? 'Woof, woof, woof, woof, woof,' 'Woof, woof, woof, woof, woof.' Don't you want the doggie? Oh, you say it, 'woof, woof, woof, woof, woof.' Mary say it, 'Woof, woof, woof, woof, woof.' And who's this? Who's this? It's Teddy, isn't it? and Teddy says 'aah.' It's Teddy, isn't it? Aah, love Teddy. Ah, is it Teddy? Aah."

Mary picks up the dog.

Mother: "Oh, is that your doggie? What does the doggie say? What does the doggie say? What does the doggie say? 'Woof, woof, woof, woof, woof.' 'Woof, woof, woof, woof, woof.' Doesn't he?"

---

discovered in relation to the use of first words. When infants actually utter a word, they tend to have a neutral facial expression. Immediately following the word, their expression changes, typically to a positive expression (Bloom & Beckwith, 1989). Once the infants begin to use the words more regularly, they no longer smile after saying them. The smiling is related to the infant's achievement of making their very first words.

Developments in Infant Perception of Adult Speech

Before the age of about 10 months, infants are capable of perceiving differences in intonation patterns, which allows them to recognize differences between melodies and passages of speech. We also described how babbling seems to reflect the intonation patterns of speech but not its meaning.

In speaking to year-old children, adults continue to raise the overall pitch and to exaggerate the intonation contours of sentences. In one study, adults were recorded while talking to 1-year-olds and to other adults about attention getting, approval, prohibition, comfort, and play. Then the tapes were synthetically modified to remove all speech content while preserving the intonation. These modified tapes were played to other adults who were asked to judge the content of the speech. The judges were significantly likely to be more correct about the

original content of the speech (e.g., whether the speech was about approval or prohibition) when they heard the modified speech to babies rather than the modified speech to adults (Fernald, 1989). This means that there are more cues to speech content in intonation patterns alone when adults are speaking to babies than in speech to other adults.

Thus, the exaggerated speech to year-old infants seems to emphasize the meaningful aspects of the intonation patterns of speech, making it easier to recognize meaning from intonation alone. In related work, speech to year-old infants was sampled in France, Italy, Germany, Japan, Britain, and the United States. In all cases, the speech had similar exaggerated intonation contours, although the American mothers did the most exaggeration (Fernald et al., 1989). There is no doubt that infants at this age, as well as adults, can differentiate between these different speech intonation patterns (Ferland & Mendelson, 1989; Trehub, Thorpe, & Morrongiello, 1987). Thus, the capacity to recognize meaningfully different speech intonation patterns is well established by the age of 1 year. In addition, these patterns appear to hold up in the majority of languages that have been studied systematically.

There is some evidence that adults actually make their speech more exaggerated and simpler for year-old infants than they did earlier in the first year. When the baby was 3 months old, the parents mostly were content to comment on the baby's condition or state or make some general inferences about their relationship to the baby (see Chapter 6). By the time the baby is 8 months old, parents tend to use more commanding and directive language in relation to specific aspects of their baby's behavior. Compared with parents' speech to 4-month-olds, their speech to 8-month-olds is more related to what the child is doing; it is somewhat simpler in structure, almost as if the parents are simplifying their sentences because they think the infant is capable of understanding now (Davis, 1978; Sherrod et al., 1977; Sherrod et al., 1978).

The parents begin to make specific verbal responses in commenting about infant activity, such as saying, "Put the toy over here," which enhances the infant's ability to make connections between action and speech. Parents also provide the infant with some very detailed utterances. Not only do they name objects, but they name small details of the objects, such as color, texture, response properties, and the infant's familiarity with the object. They also make the object more real, such as making a toy cow moo or a stuffed dog bark.

In some cultures, infants are treated to pop quizzes: "What does the cow say?" The mother corrects the baby's pronunciations and gives little compliments when things are done correctly. She instructs the child on how to play with a toy or how to behave, and she uses polite expressions, such as "please" and "thank you" (West & Rheingold, 1978).

Parents often do not correct infants, and they seem to enjoy the verbal mistakes infants make. The Marquesas Islanders enjoy their infants' incomplete development. They try to get the babies to perform their incomplete movements or to make verbal mistakes. These are humorous and enjoyable moments for the family (Martini & Kirkpatrick, 1981).

In addition to becoming perceptually attuned to the speech spoken in the home, infants are beginning to grasp the meanings of some words and gestures. For example, around 9 months, infants will make the appropriate action when parents say things like "play pat-a-cake" or "wave bye-bye to Daddy." Soon parents begin spelling out words like "bottle" or "candy" when speaking to each other in the baby's presence, so as not to get the baby interested at that moment (Bates, O'Connell, & Shore, 1987).

The Development of Attachment

It is not a coincidence that the developments in cognition, emotion, and communication occur in the same age period as we begin to see the emergence of clear and lasting attachments to parents and other significant figures in the child's life. These abilities set the stage for the child to see others as intentional beings who are important for the continued development of the child's goals, for the resolution of emotionally difficult situations, and for the expression and receipt of affection.

Attachment refers to a lasting emotional tie between people such that the individual strives to maintain closeness to the object of attachment and acts to ensure that the relationship continues. The process by which infants develop lasting, affectionate emotional ties to adults over the first few years of life has been the subject of a great deal of scientific research. Before reviewing the findings of these studies, let us first look at some of the theoretical perspectives on how attachment develops.

Psychoanalytic theory suggests that attachment is the normal resolution of the oral stage of development (see Chapter 2). If the id's oral urges are gratified regularly during the first few months of life, the baby will develop the expectation that needs can be met and that distress will not continue for long without some relief.

After the baby is 2 or 3 months old, parents begin to notice that the baby's cry is a little less urgent when the baby is hungry or tired. At this time, psychoanalytic theory prescribes that the parents should wait a short time before responding to the baby. If the baby calms down, the parents have allowed the baby to meet this small crisis with his or her own resources. Not only do these minor frustrations lead the baby toward self-control, but they also make the baby aware of the person who is responsible for satisfying the oral needs. This awareness gradually expands into a dependency on that particular person and later into affection, attachment, and trust.

Learning theory has focused not on the feelings or concepts of the infant, but on the behaviors observed when caregivers and infants are together. Caregivers seek positive reinforcements from their infants. For example, when parents pick up a baby, they expect the baby to become calm or to smile. When parents feed the baby, they expect the baby to coo and gurgle. When these positive reinforcements occur, the frequency of the same parental actions is increased on future occasions, which in turn reinforces the calming down, smiling, cooing, and gurgling of the baby. Learning theory, therefore, predicts that attachment behaviors develop by a complex process of mutual reinforcements (Cairns, 1979; Gewirtz, 1972).

Behavior ecology theory suggests that adults have inherited some kinds of caregiving responses that are triggered in the presence of infants and young children and that infants are innately drawn to particular aspects of the caregiver. In a classic study of the maternal-infant feedback system in infant monkeys (Harlow & Harlow, 1965), the babies were provided one "mother" made of wire mesh with a milk bottle attached and another "mother" of the same size made of wire covered with a soft cloth. The monkeys took food from the wire mother but spent almost all of the rest of the time with the softer mother substitute. In fearful situations, the monkeys clung to the soft mother and, when they got older, were even seen to carry the cloth mother around as a security object.

For monkeys, contrary to the predictions of psychoanalytic theory, physical contact with the mother is more important than food in the formation of attachments. Contrary to the predictions of learning theory, infant monkeys became attached to the soft object (an innate preference) and not to the object that gave positive reinforcement—the food-giving wire mother.

Studies of human infants (Schaffer & Emerson, 1964) have shown that they are most attached to the people who play and interact with them. Some babies who live in extended families with many siblings and who have mothers who concentrated primarily on caretaking tasks such as feeding and diapering are less attached to the mother than to any aunt, uncle, or older sibling who spend the most time playing with the baby. This suggests that attachment in humans is based more on social interaction and communication than on feeding or physical contact as predicted by psychoanalytic theory.

Dissatisfaction with the psychoanalytic and learning theory accounts of attachment led John Bowlby (1969) to develop a behavior ecology theory of attachment in humans. Bowlby suggested that mutual responsiveness and attraction between adults and infants resulted not because of mutual reinforcements but because the physical appearance and behavior of both the adult and the infant innately attract the other. Table 8.2 shows the stages in the development of attachment as proposed by Bowlby.

The newborn and small infant's physical appearance, called *babyishness*, elicits protective responses from adults. Babies also have a host of behaviors, such as crying, sucking, smiling, looking at the caregiver preferentially, following the adult around, and becoming distressed when the adult leaves, that have the net effect of orienting the caregiver to the infant and increasing the time that the infant spends in proximity to the caregiver. Because of the universality of this mutual attraction and its importance for survival, attachment can be thought of neurologically as experience expectant (see Chapter 5) because neurological processes exist at birth that require the presence of an adult (Barnett, Butler, & Vondra, 1999).

Bowlby suggests that as the infant develops cognitively, attachment shifts from relying on innate responses to any adult to identifying and recognizing a particular adult and seeking that adult in an intentional, goal-oriented manner. This facet of attachment is neurologically experience dependent (Chapter 5), because the child's developmental history plays a role in the nature of his or her attachment to the parent (Barnett et al., 1999). The baby establishes a goal of maintaining proximity to the parent and uses information about the parent's present and past movements as well as the his or her own locomotor skills and current needs to keep the parent within view or to seek contact when needed.

By 8 or 9 months of age, because of the developments in goal-oriented action reviewed earlier in this chapter, infants begin to develop some of the same kinds of emotional feelings of closeness to the parents that the parents had felt for the infant since before the birth. We know this because infants of this age begin to display affectionate responses to the parents. During reunions after brief separations, 1-year-olds feel genuinely happy to see the parent and may approach briefly for a hug or kiss (Sroufe, 1979). Infants will follow the parent and may be distressed at separation.

Table 8.2   Stages in the Development of Attachment (Bowlby, 1969)

Approximate Age (Months)	Stage	Description
0–2 and over	Orientation to signals without discrimination of a figure	The infant shows orientation to social stimuli—grasping, reaching, smiling, and babbling. The baby will cease to cry when picked up or when he or she sees a face. These behaviors increase when the baby is in proximity to a companion, although the baby cannot distinguish one person from another.
1–6 and over	Orientation to signals directed toward one or more discriminated figures	Orientation behaviors similar to those in Stage I appear, but they are markedly directed toward the primary caregiver. Evidence of discrimination begins at 1 month for auditory and at 2½ months for visual stimuli.
6–30 and over	Maintenance of proximity to a discriminated figure by means of locomotion as well as signals	The repertoire of responses to people increases to include following a departed mother, greeting her on return, and using her as a base for exploration. Strangers are treated with caution and may evoke alarm and withdrawal; others may be selected as additional attachment figures (e.g., fathers).
24–48 and over	Formation of a goal-corrected partnership	The child begins to acquire insight into the mother's feelings and goals, which leads to cooperative interaction and partnership.

Source: Adapted from J. Bowlby, *Attachment and loss: Vol. 1. Attachment,* 1969. New York: Basic Books.

Bowlby's theory has been refined and expanded by others. Mary Ainsworth, who studied attachment in Uganda and North America (Ainsworth, 1979), suggests that there is a distinction between the **attachment system** (the network of feelings and cognitions related to the object of attachment) and **attachment behavior** (the overt signals such as crying and following that bring the parent and child into close proximity). She points out that each child's attachment system would be expressed through behavior in a unique way. For example, if a baby does not get upset when his or her mother leaves, it does not indicate a lack of attachment. Rather, it may indicate the infant's relative feelings of security to carry on temporarily without the mother present.

Ainsworth believes that virtually all infants are attached to their parents but differ in the sense of security they feel in relation to the adult. The ease with which a distressed infant feels comforted by a caregiver is called the *quality of attachment* and has four basic patterns: securely attached, insecurely attached–resistant, insecurely attached–avoidant, and disorganized-disoriented (Ainsworth, Bell, & Stayton, 1971, Ainsworth et al., 1978; Main & Solomon, 1986).

Attachment quality is assessed in the Ainsworth Strange Situation Test, in which infants are observed with their caregivers in an unfamiliar playroom (Ainsworth & Bell, 1970). The test consists of eight episodes:

1. Parent and infant are brought to the observation room by the observer.
2. Parent and infant play together for several minutes.
3. Parent and infant play with an unfamiliar adult.
4. The mother leaves the baby with the stranger for 3 minutes.
5. The stranger leaves, and the mother returns.
6. The mother leaves the baby alone.
7. The stranger returns without the mother.
8. The stranger leaves, and the mother is reunited with her baby.

An infant who demonstrates *secure attachment* will seek comfort from the caregiver during the reunion (episode 8) and, once comforted, will return to independent play. Securely attached infants show interest in objects and in the stranger and will get acquainted with the unfamiliar setting by making brief forays, always returning to the adult's side, and using the caregiver as a *secure base* from which to explore. Such infants will feel comfortable and secure in most situations.

There are three types of insecure attachments. Infants who demonstrate *insecure-resistant attachment* have a more difficult time feeling comfortable in a strange situation. They will vacillate between mother and an interesting object, but once near the object, they will not explore as freely as will the securely attached infants. The resistant infant is more wary of strangers and tends to get more upset when the mother leaves the room. During the reunion, such infants show ambivalent responses to the mother, first approaching her and then pushing her away. Insecure-resistant infants (also called insecure-ambivalent) tend to be temperamentally vulnerable to stress, have limited coping skills, have mothers who are inconsistently available, and have limited skills at independent exploratory behavior (Cassidy, 1994; Cassidy & Berlin, 1994).

Infants who display **insecure-avoidant attachment** tend not to be upset when left with an unfamiliar person or in a strange setting. During the reunion episode, they may avoid approaching caregivers for comfort and may actively resist any attempts to be comforted by turning away and squirming to get down if picked up. Insecurely attached–avoidant infants seem neutral in their emotions regarding the mother. However, this apparent calm may be superficial. These infants show a pattern of physiological arousal indicative of masked anger (Cassidy, 1994; Spangler & Grossman, 1993).

Infants who exhibit **disorganized-disoriented attachment** display contradictory behavior during the Strange Situation Test. The infant may give a broad smile and then abruptly turn away from the mother. Or, the infant may approach the mother by crawling backward toward her with gaze averted from her. Other infants may have frozen postures during reunion, sitting and staring at a wall or sucking their thumbs. Although this pattern of attachment occurs less often than the first three, it is very disturbing to watch these infants. Almost all infants who show this type of attachment come from families with a history of child abuse, maltreatment, infant malnutrition, and/or alcoholism. Some infants with disorganized attachment may also suffer from neurological deficits (Carlson et al., 1989; Main & Solomon, 1985; O'Conner, Sigman, & Brill, 1987;

Pipp-Siegel, Seigel, & Dean, 1999; Valenzuela, 1990). These infants tend to show hostile, aggressive, and other maladaptive behaviors when they enter preschool (van Ijzendoorn et al., 1992; Lyons-Ruth, Alpern, & Repacholi, 1993). Most of the discussion that follows will be about the first three types of attachment, all of which fall more within the normal range of individual differences in infants.

The Ainsworth Strange Situation Test and the four types of attachment quality by which infants can be classified have been shown to be highly reliable and valid. Test-retest reliability has been found in middle-class North American samples (Waters, 1983). This means that a baby who is classified as securely attached at one age will typically remain so at later ages—but not always. Those babies whose security classification changes over time come from homes with a high level of social and economic stress, such as divorce, job changes, and poverty (Vaughn et al., 1979).

Stability of security classification does not mean that the children display the same kinds of behavior in the strange situation at different ages (Sroufe, 1979). For example, infants were observed in the Strange Situation test at 12 and 18 months. A baby may have been classified as avoidant at 12 months because he turned his head away from his mother when she picked him up, while at 18 months the same baby's avoidance might be expressed by arching his back and pushing away from the mother (Waters, 1983).

Antecedents of Attachment

What are the possible causes of secure and insecure attachments at 1 year of age? There are three possible explanations: variations in the parent's ability to create a warm and sensitive relationship with her baby during the first year, temperamental factors in the child that no parental response can change, and issues that arise in the relationship between parent and infant that cannot be attributed directly to either one of them.

Because Bowlby's theory focuses on the mother-infant relationship as the source of attachment, Ainsworth and others have predicted that sensitive maternal behavior toward the infant will be one of the main causes of secure attachment. Many studies have shown that the more responsive the mother is to the infant's needs at 3 months, such as during face-to-face play or in responding relatively soon to the infant's cries, the more likely the baby is to be securely attached at 1 year (Ainsworth, Bell, & Stayton, 1971; Belsky, Rovine, & Taylor, 1984; Blehar, Lieberman, & Ainsworth, 1977; Carmen et al., 1993; De Wolff & van Ijzendoorn, 1997; Grossman et al., 1985; Pedersen & Moran, 1996). Related research has revealed similar maternal factors during the first year that are associated with attachment at 12 months. For example, there is a relationship between secure attachment and maternal tender style, including a moderate tempo of speech, expressions of quiet pleasure, few directives, no impatience, even attentiveness, prompt soothing, and general responsiveness to all types of infant behavior; reciprocal and mutually rewarding social interactions are also associated with secure attachment. Infants and mothers who show coordinated joint attention are more likely to be securely attached (Grossman et al., 1985; Isabella, 1993; 1998; Isabella & Belsky, 1989; Isabella & Belsky, 1991; Schölmerich et al., 1995; Schölmerich et al., 1997; Vereijken, Riksen-Walraven, & Kondo-Ikemura, 1997).

Behavior ecology theory does not expect all mothers to be equally sensitive. According to this theory, the parent's investment in time and effort toward the child must be balanced by an investment in the parent's own survival. In cases where the mother is under stress, living in poverty, or depressed, or has limited physical or emotional resources, behavior ecology theory predicts that the infant will adapt by displaying more demanding and dependent behavior. The insecure patterns of attachment, therefore, are just as adaptive from the perspective of survival as the secure attachment pattern (Thompson, 1995). This means that the "causes" of security or insecurity are not "in" the mother's handling of the infant but rather "in" the relationship between the mother and her ecological context: her family of origin, her relationship with her husband, economic status, job, neighborhood, and other mesosystem, exosytem, and macrosystem factors (Belsky, 1995; Hrdy, 1999; Thompson, 1995). This perspective takes the blame away from the mother and leads one to examine the larger systems in which the mother lives.

This systems perspective is supported by a number of findings. First of all, factors in the mother's family affect attachment. There is a relationship between rejecting or intrusive mothering and later insecure attachment, and mothers who perceive themselves as having little control over their children's behavior and who suffer from depressed moods are more likely to have insecurely attached infants (Donovan & Leavitt, 1989; Isabella, 1998; Izard et al., 1991; Smith & Pederson, 1988; Teti et al., 1995). Many of these maternal behaviors are the result of family history factors.

Mothers of infants who are rated as having disorganized attachment are especially likely to show disturbed communication patterns with their infants. These mothers give contradictory messages, such as verbally inviting the infant to approach them and then withdrawing. They often fail to respond to the infant's clear communications, such as not comforting a distressed infant. Some of these mothers seemed frightened or confused by the infant, some sought reassurance from the infant (a kind of role reversal), and others intrusively teased or mocked the infant. The severity of these maternal behaviors often can be explained by trauma, harsh punishment, and/or sexual abuse in the mother's early history (Lyons-Ruth, Bronfman, & Parsons, 1999).

In such cases, one can clearly see a pattern of intergenerational transmission of psychopathology. The parent's attachment to their own parents can be assessed using the Adult Attachment Interview. The parent's rating of security or insecurity with regard to his or her own parents is moderately associated with their child's attachment to them as assessed in the ASST at 12 months (Steele, Steele, & Fonagy, 1996).

Second, in studies that measure other factors besides maternal sensitivity, attachment can be partially explained by some combination of maternal behavior and other factors (Goldsmith & Alansky, 1987; Isabella, 1993; Lamb et al., 1984; Rosen & Rothbaum, 1993). One such factor is infant temperament, which may mediate the mother's responsiveness. It is possible that a mother who has a fussy baby might respond to the baby less often simply because she has learned that her interventions are not always effective. Lack of security of attachment may therefore reflect primarily an inborn inability on the part of the baby to regulate distress and a heightened feeling of anxiety or wariness and only secondarily an effect of the mother's behavior.

Some studies suggest that infant temperament is a direct predictor of attachment (Seifer et al., 1996). For example, temperamental fearfulness is related to resistant behavior in the strange situation (Thompson, Connell, & Bridges, 1988). Children who at 3 months were less sociable and preferred playing with toys to playing with people were more likely to be scored as avoidant at 12 months (Lewis & Feiring, 1989). Infant negative emotionality is also associated with insecure attachment (Vaughn et al., 1992). Some scholars have suggested that whether the child is secure or insecure is related primarily to maternal sensitivity, while different types of insecurity may be more related to the infant's temperament (Susman-Stillman et al., 1996). On the other hand, infants rated as secure are more likely to show affective sharing and to enjoy being touched, and less likely to be difficult (Pedersen & Moran, 1996).

It is unlikely, however, that either the mother or the infant is the sole determiner of attachment quality. In other cases, for example, 3-month-olds cry more because their mothers are not responsive to their needs (Belsky, Rovine, & Taylor, 1984), thus setting up a negative cycle of infant fussiness countered by maternal insensitivity that leads to a lack of security of attachment at 1 year. In an even more complex pattern of findings, highly active and intense young infants became securely attached so long as their mothers did not try to pick them up and cuddle them often. On the other hand, active and intense infants became avoidant in the strange situation if they had mothers who insisted on a great deal of physical contact (Bohlin et al., 1989).

A third set of findings supporting the systems theory perspective on attachment is that concurrent social support for the family is a predictor of the infant's attachment. Support can alleviate situations in which the infant or the parent is at risk. Take the example of difficult infant temperament. Insecure attachments at 12 months were predicted by newborn fussiness, but only for those mothers who were not responsive to the infant's cries at 3 months and who had few opportunities for social support outside the home (Crockenberg, 1981). In addi-

tion, parents who are at risk for failures of attachment—teenage mothers, adoptive mothers, or single parents—can often inspire babies toward secure attachments. It is only when these parental risk factors are compounded by a lack of support networks, poverty, or a history of psychiatric disorders that insecure attachments develop (Allen et al., 1984; Belsky, 1995; Brooks-Gunn & Furstenberg, 1986; Jacobson & Frye, 1991; Sameroff & Seifer, 1983; Singer et al., 1985).

These findings suggest that neither parent nor infant is solely responsible for the attachment outcome. Bowlby's concept of attachment suggests that it does not evolve from one or another person's sole influence, but rather has more to do with the way the parent and infant have developed their relationship to maintain proximity in times of stress (Sroufe, 1995). This idea is supported by evidence showing that infants can form different types of attachments in different relationships. Mothers and fathers form unique attachments to infants and make unique contributions to their development (see below), and infants also can form independent attachment relationships with professional caregivers (Cox et al., 1992; Easterbrooks & Goldberg, 1984; Goossens & van Ijzendoorn, 1990; Oppenheim, Sagi, & Lamb, 1988; Schaffer & Emerson, 1964; Volling & Belsky, 1992).

Each relationship has a unique character and develops through its own life history, in much the same way that each person has a unique temperament and developmental course (Fogel, 1993). The types of attachment security represent ways parents and infants have developed to communicate about their feelings and needs in a stressful situation. As in any interpersonal relationship (think of your own relationships with friends, for example), some couples can easily communicate their feelings and support each other in times of stress. Other couples tend to become anxious and hesitant under stress (insecure resistant/ambivalent), while still others resolve the problem by avoiding difficult topics of discussion (insecure avoidant).

Support for the connection between attachment and relationships is also found in intervention research. During the first year of the infant's life, mothers who were at risk for attachment problems (due to low income, poor social support, and anxiety or depression) were allowed to participate in a program that provided social support, education for infant care, and psychotherapy. Compared to control families of the same group who did not receive the intervention, there was a higher percentage of securely attached infants in the intervention groups (Boom, 1994; Lieberman, Weston, & Pawl, 1991). These results suggest that attachment quality is not the direct result of mother's or infant's behavior. Rather, attachment is related to the communication system of the mother-infant relationship and to the larger family and social systems in which the dyad is embedded. Another point, to which we will return in the "Family and Society" section, is that infants may become attached to more than one person, and each of those attachments similarly depends upon social and ecological factors.

Cultural Differences in Attachment

According to the systems theory of attachment, cultural differences in the macrosystem should also contribute to differences in attachment, independent of maternal and infant behavior. Cross-cultural research has generally found this to be the case. While all cultures that have been studied have about the same percentage of secure infants (Posada et al., 1995), they differ according to the types of insecurity found. In general, avoidant classifications are more frequent in North America and northern Europe, while resistant classifications are more frequent in Japan, Indonesia, and Israel (Grossman et al., 1985; Miyake, Chen, & Campos, 1985; Sagi et al., 1985; Thompson, 1995; Van Ijzendoorn & Kroonenberg, 1988; Zevalkink, Riksen-Walraven, & van Lieshout, 1999).

A number of explanations have been offered for these differences. The Strange Situation Test may be too stressful for Japanese infants, who are rarely separated from their mothers or exposed to strangers during their first years of life (Takahashi, 1986). The higher percentage of resistant infants in the Japanese sample may be the result of the infants' becoming overly stressed during the testing situation and thus resisting attempts by the mother at comforting. We saw earlier that Japanese infants be-

came rather upset at even a 30-second separation, and the separation period in the ASST is longer and repeated frequently. A similar pattern of closeness and rapid response to infant distress may be observed in Indonesia (Zevalkink et al., 1999).

The resistant attachments in Israeli infants come primarily from infants who are reared in a communal setting called a kibbutz. These infants spend most of their time with peers and caregivers and see their parents relatively infrequently (Sagi et al., 1994). These infants may prefer to be comforted by people other than their parents, especially in the context of the ASST. In partial confirmation of this hypothesis, the parent's security on the Adult Attachment Interview was less strongly related to the infant's security of attachment in Israeli kibbutz samples in which the infant slept at home with the parents than in kibbutz samples in which infants co-slept communally with other infants. The home sleeping samples were more similar to those found in North America and northern Europe (Aveizer et al., 1999; Sagi et al., 1997).

On the other hand, it is thought that the higher percentages of avoidant infants in North America and northern Europe may be due to higher demands for infant independence in those countries. As infants are encouraged to play independently and to occupy themselves at a distance from the mothers, they may be less likely to approach the mother for comfort.

A related issue concerns the security of attachment of infants who from an early age spend a good deal of time in day care. Although the results are mixed, with many studies finding no differences in attachment between day care and home care infants, some studies find that day care infants are more avoidant than home care infants (see Chapter 9 for a fuller discussion). This is consistent with the pattern of more avoidant infants in countries that encourage independence at an early age.

Researchers disagree about how to interpret these findings on cultural differences. On the one hand, they are clearly consistent with the ecological systems theory. Certain factors in the cultural norms and expectations may make mothers more or less protective or more or less encouraging of independence. These factors, in turn, unwittingly affect the mother's relationship with the infant.

On the other hand, these findings may also reflect a potential limitation of the ASST. It may be too stressful for Japanese infants, for example, who are not used to such separations from their mothers. On the contrary, infants who are used to daily separations from mother may not be disturbed by the series of separations and strangers in the ASST, and they may appear avoidant when their mothers return. At a minimum, the findings on cross-cultural differences reflect the need to interpret the results of the ASST with some sensitivity to the cultural and contextual factors of the infant and family.

Does Attachment Security in Infancy Predict Later Behavior?

One of the successes of the ASST is its ability to predict child behavior many years into the future. Securely attached children at 1 year, for example, were found during later infancy and early childhood to be more sociable with peers (Arend, Gove, & Sroufe, 1979; Fagot, 1997; Park & Waters, 1989; Slade, 1987b) and unfamiliar adults (Main & Weston, 1981; Thompson & Lamb, 1982), to be more aware of their emotions (Steele et al., 1999), and to be more securely attached to their mothers at 6 years of age (Main & Cassidy, 1988; Teti et al., 1991). Securely attached infants are also more likely to be better problem solvers in preschool and kindergarten, to be more persistent and enthusiastic, to be more socially competent and less lonely, and to have fewer behavioral problems (Bates, Maslin, & Frankel, 1985; Berlin, Cassidy, & Belsky, 1995; Block & Block, 1980; Erickson, Sroufe, & Egeland, 1985; Meins, 1998; Sroufe, 1983; Wartner et al., 1994).

Children who were maltreated in infancy and were scored as having a disorganized attachment at 1 year continue to be disorganized during early childhood (Barnett, Ganiban, & Cicchetti, 1999). Disorganized children are more likely to display evidence of child behavior problems (disobedience, fighting, withdrawal) and adolescent psychopathology, in particular dissociation (confusion, unpredictable behavior, accident proneness, and self-harm or suicide proneness) (Carlson, 1998; Lyons-Ruth, Easterbrooks, & Cibelli, 1997). Clearly, disorga-

nized attachment in infancy is a serious developmental problem and should be cause for concern and possible intervention at an early age.

In most of the studies reported here, the investigators who measured the child's behavior in preschool were unaware of the child's classification rating on the Ainsworth Strange Situation Test. Thus results cannot be accounted for by observer bias. On the other hand, these patterns of findings are correlational; therefore, they only show a pattern of association rather than cause and effect.

We are still left with the question of how these early ratings are maintained over time and are translated into a variety of behavioral competencies. Bowlby (1969; 1980) proposed that attachment has long-term effects because of an **internal working model**. An internal working model is a sense of self and of other people that allows one to anticipate future behavior, react to new situations in a competent manner, and appraise the likelihood of success for action. For example, based on past experiences with the mother, the infant constructs a model of her as the person from whom particular types of support are likely to be received. As the infant's internal working model becomes solidified through experiences with the mother, actual behavioral monitoring of the mother becomes less necessary, and the infant is able to tolerate separations and react favorably to reunions.

Thus, the internal working model is relatively stable and is updated gradually. The model is determined in part by interactive experiences but eventually comes to affect interactions. Thus, a baby who has been disappointed by the mother many times in the past is not likely to accept changes in the mother's behavior if at a later time she desires more closeness to the baby (Bretherton, 1985). The notion of an internal working model is related to a number of cognitive and emotional theories that postulate the existence of a generalized representation of the individual's history of interpersonal experiences between self and other (Bretherton, 1987; Stern, 1985).

These ideas may have potential for explaining some of the long-term correlations of child behavior with earlier attachment classification, especially if we consider that caregivers also have internal working models of themselves and their infants.

The long-term stability of interaction patterns between mothers and infants may be maintained by stable internal working models in both mother and infant, which may enhance or inhibit interpersonal closeness over a long period of time (Main, Kaplan, & Cassidy, 1985).

Of interest in this regard is a study on adolescents who were evaluated in the Strange Situation Test with their mothers when they were 12 months old. No relationship was found between their 1-year attachment classification and their behavior and emotional adjustment during adolescence. On the other hand, their behavior was related to their views on the supportiveness and emotional availability of their parents, information obtained from the Adult Attachment Interview when the adolescents were 10 years old. This research suggests that relationships between parents and children can change over time and that the most recent pattern of emotional communication between them—the most updated internal working model—best predicts child behavior. As we have seen, some parents may not be able to be emotionally available to their infants. This research shows that parent-child relationships can improve—or worsen—leading to corresponding changes in the child's well-being (Sameroff & Emde, 1989; Sroufe, 1989; Zimmermann et al., 1995).

In summary, parent-child attachment has been the subject of a great deal of research. Although there are different theoretical interpretations of the findings, one thing is clear. The early development of the parent-infant relationship is crucial for the continuing social and emotional development of the infant. On the other hand, attachment can change as relationships improve or worsen, and infants can derive benefits from a secure attachment to any person. The results speak not only to the negative effects of inconsistent, unavailable, and abusive parents, but also to the resiliency of relationships and their ability to change for the better under optimal conditions of social and cultural support.

Infant-Peer Relationships

At the beginning of the first year of life, infants make different responses to peers than to their parents. At 3 months of age, infants are more likely to look at a peer for long periods and to make abrupt, jerky movements of the body while watching the peer. Their behavior toward their mothers is much smoother, with more smiling and vocalizing (Fogel, 1979).

At 6 months, infants are more likely to look at and vocalize to a peer but more likely to touch their mothers. As they get older, touching mothers increases and touching peers decreases, although by the end of the first year, infants are taking initiatives that will bring them into proximity with the peer (Vandell, 1980).

From 6 to 12 months, peer play is more likely in the absence of objects (Eckerman & Whatley, 1977; J. L. Jacobson, 1981; Vandell, Wilson, & Buchanan, 1980). When babies get together, they explore each other with mutual touches, smile and gesture at each other, and imitate each other. By the age of 1 year, peer play in the absence of objects begins to take on the quality of a dialogue, with mutual exchanges of tickling, touching, and laughing at each other (Ross & Goldman, 1977a). However, by 12 months, toys are becoming more important to the maintenance of the social interaction (J. L. Jacobson, 1981; Vandell et al., 1980). Games with toys have the same reciprocal quality as purely social games. There is mutual giving and taking of objects, offering and receiving, rolling and throwing balls back and forth, and so on. By this age, taking turns is such an essential part of peer play that interactions usually are disrupted if one child fails to take his or her turn (Ross & Goldman, 1977a). In comparison, infants at 12 months express a wider range of emotions in their interactions with their mothers and take more turns with them, perhaps due to the mothers' attempts to create dialogues through active structuring of the interaction (Adamson & Bakeman, 1985; Vandell & Wilson, 1987).

The Sense of a Subjective Self

During this age period, a new sense of self emerges in infants. Our review of affective sharing and social referencing, for example, shows that infants have a sense of themselves, as people who can feel and whose feelings can be appraised not only by others but also by the self. The fact that infants begin to gesture and use words suggests that they make a deliberate attempt to share what is on their mind with others. Behaviors like clowning and showing off also reveal that there is an "I" that wants to be recognized.

This sense of "I" is the *subjective self* (Stern, 1985). The subjective self is a participatory (see Chapter 2), rather than a conceptual, sense of "I." When infants of this age show off, they act as if they are saying, "Look at me." The infants are not, however, actually saying "look at me." Babies of this age do not use the word I, nor do they have a language to describe themselves or a concept of "self." These will take almost another year to develop. This is the crucial difference between the subjective self and the conceptual self, which emerges around the child's second birthday. On the other hand, intentional communicative actions like showing off, pointing and requesting, and social referencing are also fundamentally different from the fish-in-water sense of the ecological self.

How can an infant have a sense of "I" but no word or concept for it? Imagine looking into someone's eyes in a way that says "I love you" or "I'm afraid of you." You do not need any words to express this. It is clear, however, that there is an "I" that feels love or fear, and also that this "I" comes into awareness in the act of trying to communicate nonverbally, in a participatory way, with another person. Teenagers will sometimes show off and act silly when around members of the opposite sex. Perhaps all people do this when they are falling in love! These behaviors call attention to the self in a way that says "look at me" without actually saying it. In many cases, the person who is doing the showing off is not even conceptually aware of it. Their behavior is a participatory way of highlighting the self in communication.

The development of attachment during this age period is another way in which infants reveal the sense of a subjective self. They begin to look at other people in a participatory way that says "I love you" or "I'm afraid." The infant's showing off at this age means "look at me," and also "I know you will look at me because we love each other." They communicate their sense of affection, fear, or loneliness by making deliberate attempts at approaching or avoiding, by signaling their desire to be with particular people, and by asking for comfort and assis-

tance. Because the subjective self is participatory, babies do not think about whether or not to do these things, they just engage in the actions and experience the consequences.

Family and Society

Since this chapter introduces attachment and its development, in this section I will discuss attachments to other family members besides the traditional attachment figure—the infant's mother. I discuss differences and similarities of infant attachment to mothers versus fathers and then discuss the role of grandparents in infants' lives.

Are Infants More Attached to Mothers or to Fathers?

On the whole, there are few differences between attachment to mother and to father (Bridges & Connell, 1991; N. A. Fox, Kimmerly, & Schafer, 1991). This does not mean that infants have the same kind of relationship with each, but only that they can be adequately comforted in a stressful situation by either parent. Some research has shown that if their mother and father are both present in a stressful situation, infants will choose the mother (Bridges, Connell, & Belsky, 1988; L. J. Cohen & Campos, 1974). Other work shows that infants would much rather be with one of their parents than with a stranger (Lamb, 1977).

Other research has shown that there are differences among families. Most infants develop roughly equal attachments for their mothers and fathers. In a sample of 41 maritally intact families in the United States, 78% of the infants had the same type of attachment security with both parents (Rosen & Burke, 1999). The remaining 22% of the sample was more attached to one than the other (not necessarily the mothers). In general, the more time the father spends with the infant, the more extroverted the father, and the greater the father's marital and work satisfaction, the more likely it is the father and infant will share a secure attachment and mutual communication (Belsky, 1996; Cox, Owen, Henderson, & Margand, 1992; Pedersen, Suwalsky,

Cain, & Zaslow, 1987; Volling & Belsky, 1992). Failure to become securely attached to one person does not preclude becoming attached to another. In a small percentage of families, however, infants will be insecurely attached to both parents (Lamb, 1978b; Main & Weston, 1981). If an infant becomes securely attached to either the mother or the father, the baby will be significantly less wary of strangers than an infant who is not securely attached to either parent (Main and Weston, 1981).

Grandparents and Their Infant Grandchildren

There are very few empirical studies of grandparents and grandchildren and only a handful on grandparent-infant relationships. With the decline of the extended family living under one roof, developmentalists have not taken much interest in grandparents as a source of influence on infants. In many cases, grandparents do not live near their children, and the once-a-year contact with the family is hardly enough to make much of an impression on an infant.

The degree to which grandparents become involved in infant care varies considerably. In some families, grandparents have daily contact with the infants and participate in caregiving as well as play. In others, there may be little or no contact. One reason for this difference may be that adults can become grandparents as young as 30 years of age or as old as 90. Younger grandparents are still employed and have little time for infant care (Cohler & Grunebaum, 1981; Kornhaber & Woodward, 1981; Tinsley & Parke, 1984).

A few studies have been done on grandmother-infant attachment at 1 year. The subjects were white, primarily middle-class families in which the grandmother lived nearby and had relatively frequent

In all cultures, grandparents and infants share a special relationship.

contact with the infant. This research shows that mothers and grandmothers are nearly interchangeable as attachment figures: infants approach both in times of stress. The more time a grandmother spends with the baby, the more secure the attachment relationship (Myers, Jarvis, & Creasey, 1987; Schaffer & Emerson, 1964).

Spending time with the infant also means spending time with their own daughters or daughters-in-law. This allows for more communication about differences of opinion and belief about child rearing, which improves the mother-grandmother relationship and also the grandmother-infant attachment. In the 1990s, mothers and grandmothers were generally in agreement over beliefs. Mothers, however, were more accepting on the whole than grandmothers of table messiness and nudity indoors, more relaxed about when to begin toilet training, and less rigid in differentiating sex roles in child play. This sample did not, however, differ in their basic beliefs about moral domains; the disagreements were more about personal and social behaviors (Honig & Deters, 1996).

Some studies have shown that grandmothers in African American families are considerably more involved with their infant grandchildren than in Caucasian families. The grandparents tend to live close by their grown children and devote much of their free time to their children's infants (Cherlin & Furstenberg, 1986; Pearson, Hunter, Ensminger, & Kellam, 1990; Wilson, 1986). Compared to Caucasian parents, African American parents of infants have more frequent contact with kin—including grandmothers—and respect the advice of relatives, showing concern for what the relative thinks is important (Wilson, 1986).

This strong network of ties between relatives was carried to the Americas from traditional African societies. Research has shown that the extended family system is important in the reduction of family stress, especially for low-income, teenage, and single mothers. Typically, the grandmothers are warmer and more patient with the infants than are the infants' teenage mothers. In addition to providing a buffer against the effects of mothers who have too many of their own problems to cope with their babies, the grandmothers serve as valuable sources of advice and instruction about parenthood for their own daughters. With the support of their mothers,

many of these adolescent and at-risk parents are able to continue in their education and eventually become economically self-supporting and caring parents (Colletta & Lee, 1983; Furstenberg, Brooks-Gunn, & Morgan, 1987; Spieker & Bensley, 1994; Stevens, 1984; Wakschlag, Chase-Landale, & Brooks-Gunn, 1996).

These studies suggest that involvement between infants and grandmothers is dependent on ecological systems factors, including ethnicity, culture, and patterns of residence. These factors also determine the amount of mutual reliance and mutual trust between family members, both of which affect the quality of the social network of kinship in which the child develops. I will discuss social support networks more thoroughly in Chapter 10.

Adoptive Parents and Their Infants

The transition to parenthood for adoptive parents is rather different than for biological parents. Adoptive parents are already in a special category because typically many of them cannot have children of their own. They may have a history of infertility and may have made many attempts to treat it (see Chapter 3). They are also people with a very great desire to have children. If adoptive parents are not infertile, then they probably have a strong desire to rear children who would otherwise be disadvantaged. Thus, it is not surprising that adoptive parents enter parenthood with much higher expectations for success than biological parents. Adoptive parents also experience more stress, at least initially. The "delivery" of their infants is often sudden and may follow a period of several years of waiting. They are thrust into the parenting role without the prior stage of pregnancy during which most new parents adjust to that role. Also, they may worry about how their own parents will feel about having a grandchild who is not their kin. Adoptive couples want to be seen as "real" parents by family, friends, and the workplace (Levy-Shiff, Goldschmidt, & Har-Even, 1991; Shahmoon-Shanok, 1999).

Research on the outcomes of parent-child attachment and marital relationships during the infancy period shows that there are few differences between adoptive and nonadoptive families in spite of the differences in the transition to parenthood (Humphrey

& Kirkwood, 1982; Levy-Shiff et al., 1991; Singer et al., 1985). Even when adoptive infants come from at-risk groups, attachment can be facilitated with simple interventions that prepare the parents for the task at hand (Juffer, Rosenboom, Hoksbergen, Riksen-Walraven, & Kohnstamm, 1997). There is about the same percentage of secure infants (about 70%) in nonadoptive samples as in domestic adoptions within the same racial group, transracial adoptions, and adoptions of infants from other countries (Juffer & Rosenboom, 1997; Marcovitch, Goldberg, Gold, & Washington, 1997). This pattern also holds for infants adopted from Romanian orphanages, in which infants are known to have suffered deprivations of care, although the longer time spent in the orphanage has a negative effect on adoptive parent-infant attachment (K. Chisholm, 1998; Marcovitch et al., 1997)

One reason for this may be that adoptive parents are older and take a more mature approach to the adjustments required to help the infant adapt. Adoptive parents are more likely to name their children after family members (parents and other relatives) than are nonadoptive parents, perhaps as a way to integrate the child into the family (J. L. Johnson, McAndrew, & Harris, 1991). These findings may also reflect the resilience of infants and their ability to respond to loving care when it is provided.

On the other hand, research on adults who were adoptees shows that they are more likely to rate their parents as more critical and less fair minded than nonadoptees (Silverman, Dickens, Eals, & Fine, 1993). There is an apparent contradiction between the studies of adoptees as infants and adoptees as adults. One explanation for the differences is that the adopted adults come from an older generation when treatment of and attitudes about adopted children may have been less tolerant than today. When these adults were infants, there were no treatments for infertility and no such thing as surrogate parents. Another explanation is that differences between adopted and nonadopted children may not emerge until later childhood and adulthood. A final explanation is that the findings on adults are from their own report of their adoptive parents. These reports may be influenced by a feeling of loss about not being raised by their birth parents rather than by the quality of the adoptive parent-child relationship. We are unlikely ever to know which of these explanations is correct. The results suggest that adoption is a viable alternative for infertile parents and can provide a nurturing environment for infants who have been given up by their own parents. On the other hand, adoptive parent-child relationships are always going to be different from those in nonadoptive families. This difference need not be considered a deficit. Rather, adoption is a reflection of the human capacity for multiple and unique forms of love that transcend biological ties.

The Author's View

The emergence of the subjective self is a major developmental achievement. Now for the first time, the infant is aware of a self who feels and experiences the world. The importance of this achievement should not be underestimated. It is the beginning of a uniquely human consciousness, a consciousness that is aware of itself thinking, feeling, and doing.

What is this new sense of "I"? Why is it a developmental achievement to acquire an "I"? Imagine the experience of an intense emotion, such as losing one's temper at someone. During the experience there is no sense of "I" or "you." There is just the anger, as if one is primarily an ecological self. Later, however, a person can say, "I completely lost myself," or "I didn't know what I was doing." At the time such statements are made, one is subjectively aware of oneself as *having had an experience of anger*. One is also conceptually aware of the differences between self and other, so that, hopefully, apologies and restitutions can be made.

Now imagine teenagers or adults who are strong enough to really inflict harm on others or the self but who do not have a sense of a subjective or conceptual self. These people would be a danger to themselves and to other people, and a number of psychopathological conditions stem from this problem. Some of these disturbances of the mature sense of self have their origins during this early period of infancy (see the section on clinical theories, Chapter 2).

According to psychoanalytic theories, for example, when the infant's intentional communicative

During this stage of development, the baby begins to crawl and toddle around the house, which can lead to potentially dangerous situations. Beginning at this age and continuing into early childhood, infants need to be protected from some of the obvious dangers their environments present.

What are the main threats to infant safety?

Each year, about 3,500 children under the age of 4 years die in the United States from unintentional injuries. This accounts for about 35% of all deaths in this age group, making injuries the leading cause of death (Karns, 2000). Many more injuries occur that do not result in death. For every death, there are 1,120 emergency room visits and an unknown number of untreated injuries or injuries treated at home. Infant mortality due to unintentional injuries can be categorized as follows: motor vehicle collisions (32%), fire (19%), drowning (18%), choking (7%), falls (3%), poisoning (2%), and other causes (19%) (Lewit & Baker, 1995). In this section, I will discuss each of these different causes of injury.

Collisions and falls: Automobile accidents are the leading cause of injury and death among infants. In the United States, about 1,100 children under 4 years of age die every year in such accidents, and 7,000 infants per year suffer injuries. The tragedy is that most of these could be prevented by the use of well-designed car seats and seat belts, since most injuries occur when infants are riding in the front seat of a car on someone's lap. Even though every state has a safety restraint law for infants, less than half of all infants are safely strapped in. Safety restraints are highly effective, and the number of deaths per year has been dropping under the new safety belt laws (D. Davis, 1985; National Safety Council, 1987).

Buy an infant car seat that is easy to install correctly. The seat should be in the center of the back seat. Be firm with the baby and do not let him or her out of the seat even if the child fusses. Do not let the child eat lollipops or hold sharp or pointed objects while the car

is moving, and do not put loose items like groceries in the back seat (Chubet, 1988).

At home, falls and collisions can be prevented by taking simple precautions. Never leave a baby unattended on a table or a bed, block off access to stairs, and keep the baby's high chair away from a table or wall that could be used as leverage to push the chair over. Even though babies at this age have developed a wariness of the deep side of a visual cliff (see the "Emotional Development" section earlier in this chapter), most infants do not have sufficient control over their locomotor skills at this age to prevent a fall. All infants suffer minor tumbles and shocks as they try to expand their motor skills. These are generally not serious unless there is some suspicion of a broken bone or a severe head injury. A number of excellent books are available for parents and other caregivers on the diagnosis of medical problems in infants and children. Be sure to read about the signs of concussion and know what to do if you see one.

Infants can also fall from cribs, high chairs, walkers, windows, and grocery carts. Cribs should be checked for sturdiness and should have a mattress that can be lowered as the baby grows. The posts or slats should be no more than $2\frac{3}{8}$ inches apart to prevent infants from getting their heads stuck. Be sure that mobiles are securely fastened and will not fall if the baby grabs them. Do not use plastic bags to cover the mattress, and do not allow any strings within reach of the baby. Do not tie pacifiers to strings, as the baby can easily become entangled or choke (Chubet, 1988).

High chairs should not have sharp edges, springs that can catch the baby's skin, or straps in which the baby can become entangled. The seat should not be so slippery that it causes the baby to slide down. It should be extremely easy to remove the tray without hurting the baby. Walkers are safe if the wheelbase is wider than the seat and grip area and if they are not used near stairs or near furniture with sharp edges. Always strap infants into grocery carts, and never allow

children to stand in a cart. For high chairs, walkers, jumpers, grocery carts, and changing tables, the most important rule is that *under no circumstances are you to leave the baby unattended.* If the phone rings, either ignore it or take the baby with you to answer it.

Finally, if you live in a building with more than one story, do not trust screens to keep an active toddler from falling out a window. Windows can be blocked so that they can open only enough for ventilation but not wide enough for a baby to fit through. Safety gates are recommended near stairs or to block off rooms that hold dangers for the baby. Buy gates that will not pinch a baby and that are easy for adults to open and close (otherwise they will stay open).

Poisoning: Modern households are filled with lethal poisons, and most of them are kept within easy reach of an inquisitive infant. The cabinets under the kitchen and bathroom sinks are the most likely repositories of poisonous substances in the house: soaps, detergents, cleaning fluids, cosmetics, insecticides, and other toxic substances. It is wise to keep all such substances completely out of the infant's reach, since parental discipline is often not effective at this age in totally keeping the infant away from these dangers. Cabinets should be locked or childproofed or the toxic substances moved well out of the infant's reach. Even if most things have childproof caps, the caps and outer surfaces of the containers may contain enough toxin to make the infants ill if they should put them in their mouths. Child-care providers and parents should learn some of the common poisons and their antidotes. A poison antidote chart is available from most hospitals and pediatricians and should be posted in the kitchen or bathroom, where it can be readily consulted in an emergency.

Other potential sources of poisonous material include the leaves and flowers of houseplants and lead and lead-based paints. Never allow babies to be in rooms where there are paint flakes and plaster dust. Like plaster dust, baby powders can be toxic and are so fine that they can easily clog immature lung passages. Breathing can also be obstructed by plastic bags, and uninflated or broken balloon pieces are especially dangerous (although inflated balloons are not). Finally, infants—like fetuses—are affected by passive smoking; for infants, the danger lies in inhaling the smoke from burning cigarettes or the exhalations of smokers.

Swallowing small objects: If a small object becomes lodged in an infant's throat, it can disrupt breathing or cause choking. As with poisons, any object that can easily fit into an infant's mouth should be removed from the child's reach. The most common cause of suffocation at this age is latex balloons. Mylar and paper balloons are better, but all balloons can explode, which may cause pieces to become lodged in the baby's throat. Beads, coins, uncooked grains, paper clips, and so on are candidates for chokers. Be sure the button eyes of stuffed toys are sewn on securely and that rattles (with beads inside) are not cracked. As the infant learns to stand while holding onto furniture, small objects on the tops of tables and desks are vulnerable to the infant's reach. Make sure they are on high shelves or in childproofed drawers. Foods that are cut too small can also be dangerous for babies who cannot yet chew effectively. Hot dogs, peanuts, and other hard foods are not recommended. Parents may want to be trained in the Heimlich maneuver and other methods for helping a choking infant.

Burns and drowning: Infants suffer more from home fires and smoke inhalation than do older children and adults. They are less mature and have more sensitive skin and lungs. They are also less able to escape on their own. Many burns also occur from overly hot bathwater, stove tops, splashing grease, and radiators. Be sure the child knows the meaning of the word "hot." Keep the infant away from sources of heat, and always test the bathwater before putting the baby in.

Baths also present the danger of the child's slipping and/or drowning. Be sure to use nonslip pads in the bottom of the sink or tub. You can also buy a molded sponge in which the baby can sit. Keep infants away from pools, and keep toilet seats down. Never leave a baby unattended near or in water. Parental attention is imperative at all times when a baby is near water; bathtub seats and molded sponges are no substitute for an adult's vigilance.

Other dangers: Sharp and pointed objects are another common source of danger. Pencils, pens, and screwdrivers should never be given to infants of this age. If they want to scribble, let them use a nontoxic crayon (not a felt-tipped marker). Heavy objects, especially those infants can pull down on top of themselves, are also potential dangers. Keep the baby away from ropes or cords (such as venetian blind pulls), and avoid clothing that ties around the neck. The best way to prevent many dangers is to crawl around and look at the house from the point of view of someone who is 2 feet tall, curious, and clumsy.

Finally, toys are potentially dangerous. They should have no small parts, such as buttons, that are detachable, and small objects, such as marbles should not be used. Toys should have no sharp edges, small holes, or openings that can cut, trap, or pinch fingers or tongues. Toys should be sturdy. Plastic is always better than glass, which can break or shatter. Toys should not contain any strings, elastic bands, or ropes longer than 10 or 12 inches. Stuffed toys should not be so soft that the baby can suffocate, and they should be easy to wash.

Emergency procedures

Even with the best attempts at prevention, infants will sometimes face life-threatening accidents or injuries. It is recommended that parents and caregivers be familiar with the basics of first aid and cardiopulmonary resuscitation (CPR). A number of excellent infant health books are available, and first aid classes can be found through local health organizations. CPR is useful in cases of shock or drowning to help the infant resume breathing and provide heart massage. Simple but specific techniques should be learned to control bleeding, treat burns, stop choking, stop electrical shock, and treat poisoning (Chubet, 1988).

What are some important health considerations?

Most of the serious diseases of infancy and early childhood have been eliminated due to immunization procedures. Babies should be given a series of inoculations during the first 2 years of life. These are shown in Table 8.3.

Table 8.3   Immunization Schedule for Infants

Age (Months)	Immunization
2	Diphtheria, pertussis, tetanus (DPT); polio; meningitis (HibCV); hepatitis B (birth to 2 months)
4	DPT; polio; hepatitis B
6	DPT; polio
12	Tuberculosis test
12–15	Measles, mumps, rubella (MMR); hepatitis B; HibCV
18	DPT; polio
4–6 years	DPT; polio; MMR

Sources: R. A. Beck, S. Kambiss, & J. W. Bass, The retreat of Hemophilus influenzae type B invasive disease: Analysis of an immunization program and implications for OTO-HNS, 1993, p. 718. *Otolaryngol Head Neck Surg., 109,* 712–721; Centers for Disease Control, Recommended childhood immunization schedule—United States, 1995, p. 6. *Morbidity and Mortality Weekly Report, 44,* no. RR-5, 1–8; R. K. Zimmerman & G. S. Grebink, Childhood immunizations: A practical approach for clinicians, 1992, p. 1768. *American Family Physician, 45,* 1759–1772.

(*continues*)

Applications (continued)

It is generally recommended that children not receive immunizations later than scheduled so as to avoid unnecessary exposure.

Most of the common diseases of infancy involve gastrointestinal or respiratory problems. Symptoms of the former include vomiting, stomach pains, diarrhea, and constipation. Signs of the latter are a runny nose, sore throat, coughing or wheezing, and trouble breathing. A fever is also a sign of illness. Consult medical care manuals. They generally give advice about which conditions can be treated at home and which require a doctor's attention.

Although some illnesses are caused by viral or bacterial infections, repeated occurrences of particular symptoms should be taken as warning signs. The infant may be exposed to infectious or unsanitary conditions, or the illness may be a symptom of an allergic reaction. In the latter case, the physician should work with the family to isolate the possible source of the allergy.

---

actions are not recognized by the family system to help the infant appreciate what acts lead to what consequences, then the inner experience will not be felt as the infant's own (Sander, 1962). Indeed, this may be the case for infants with disorganized attachments. The capricious and confusing messages given by their parents may fail to create a sense of "I" for the infant. If these conditions persist until they become teenagers, these children suffer from *dissociation,* or the inability to connect themselves with their experiences. They hurt themselves and others as if there were no self to feel the hurt.

People can also lose their sense of "I" when they become depressed or alienated. In these conditions, one feels helpless to change circumstances, as if the "I" is not an effective, intentional being. Infants who experience their world as excessively controlling or intrusive develop a similar loss of subjectivity. So, the sense of a subjective self is crucial to mental health. We need to know who we are, what we need, and how to communicate about those things with other people.

At this age, babies begin to develop some of the human frailties that plague us all: vulnerability to loss and separation from loved ones, irrational fears, and insatiable curiosity. There are some limits to this. Babies of this age do not suffer from self-doubt or pride. These peculiarly human vulnerabilities need at least another year before they begin to flower.

The wonderful news is that the vast majority of infants at this age develop a healthy sense of a subjective self with at least one person and that this sense of self arises naturally and spontaneously dur-

ing frames for coordinated joint attention. Infants simply need to be able to express themselves though gestures, to have someone respond appropriately, and to take pleasure in creating playful and satisfying communicative routines. It is not necessary to teach babies about themselves. You only have to be aware of the signs of their budding self-awareness and to be available when infants need your assistance, when they look to you for guidance, and when they want you to share in their discoveries.

AWARENESS THROUGH MOVEMENT

Balancing

As adults we can easily take for granted the enormous achievement we made as children when we learned to balance in an upright posture. Balancing is accomplished in a variety of ways: we use our eyes and ears to know where we are in space; we receive feedback about our verticality from the vestibular system in our inner ears; we have awareness of changing contact with the ground through our feet; and we feel our muscles stretching and working as we stray from balance. All of these elements are explored in the following simple movements.

1. Stand still with your feet shoulder width apart. You may feel like you are standing still, but we know from fine measurements that our bodies are always wobbling slightly in what is called

Co-Regulating with Baby

The year-old infant is awake and aware. There is not too much you can do that the baby will not notice. This will give you the sense that the baby has become more of an equal participant in play and love. The year-old infant is cocky and assured, generally quite happy, and easily delighted by small surprises, like finding a hidden object or the mother's face behind a blanket. The ability to do things for themselves—things they have done with help in the past or that have been done for them—is a great source of amusement for babies. Letting babies hide things, such as their own face or their mother's during peekaboo games, is one example. Self-feeding is another, as is letting babies get their own diapers, hold the pins (if they are closed), or wash themselves in the bath. Needless to say, all these baby-ish attempts at self-care are as much a delight to the caregivers as to the infants.

Do not let the first birthday pass without an appropriate celebration. Babies can really join in the festive spirit, although they have no idea what it is all about and have no conception of themselves as objects of all the attention. At age 1, babies are just going along with everyone else's fun. They will imitate when their parents try to blow out the candles, they will clap along with everyone else, and they will have a great time pulling off the wrapping paper. Do not be too surprised if the wrapping gets more attention than the gift. For the baby, each is just an interesting object to explore. The ideas of gifts, giving, gratitude, and politeness are still a long way down the developmental path.

There are a number of games you can play with the baby. Hiding is a popular one; be sure to try all the variations of hiding objects and people, as well as letting the baby do some of the hiding. Babies of this age like to be picked up, thrown, and swung around (carefully and gently, of course). They like to have cross-modal experiences. Make a book with different colors, shapes and textures; let them smell and touch flowers or soaps of different colors. Sounds and sights can be combined with nursery rhymes acted out with the hands and face (for example, "Eensy Weensy Spider"). Add some bouncing on the knee or tickling to complete the experience. Dancing with the baby to music combines all these experiences with physical closeness. This closeness can also be achieved by taking the baby into the bath with you if you have the opportunity.

Babies like to play with their own images in mirrors, although they do not yet recognize the images as themselves. Do not leave a baby alone with a breakable mirror. Read books with the baby and name pictures in them. Ask the baby if he or she can recognize the pictures from the words you say.

There are many other things to do with babies of this age: consult child care books and your own imagination. The main thing to keep in mind is that play is a form of learning—one that affects the whole child. A knee-bouncing nursery rhyme has cognitive, perceptual, linguistic, motor, and social elements. It is also important to encourage the baby's efforts by showing your enthusiasm for accomplishments, as well as by encouraging the effort involved in the attempts. Most important of all, plan to give the baby at least some "quality" time during the day. This is a time when you are not distracted by other chores or worries and can devote your full attention to the baby; it may be during play, bathing, or feeding. The baby needs to bask in the warm light of total attention, love, and approval for at least some part of the day in order to develop a healthy sense of a subjective self that is connected in meaningful ways to other people. The baby also needs to learn how to control his or her needs, how to wait when you are busy, how to defer gratification, and other socialization tasks. You will find these easier to teach the baby if you provide enough pure and simple indulgence at other times. I will have more to say about socialization and discipline in later chapters. At age 1, the main message is, Enjoy!

postural sway. Ideally our skeletons carry most of our weight, leaving our muscles relaxed and free for generating movement. We tend, however, to carry areas of muscular tension in ways that force our muscles and not our skeletons to keep us upright. Can you sense areas of muscular tension in such typical areas as your neck and shoulders, lower back, or calves? Where is your weight placed on your feet? On the heels? On the toes? Toward the inside or outside of the feet?

2. Stand in this position with eyes open, and keep your feet glued to the floor. Begin to sway very slowly forward and backward, as if you wanted to move like a stick. Most of the movement will take place in your ankles. How far can you go forward and backward without lifting your heels or toes while keeping your breathing and your muscles relaxed? Do a few movements with your eyes closed and feel the difference. Some will find the movement smoother when the eyes are closed, and some will not.

3. Now do the same movement swaying from side to side, first with your eyes open, then with your eyes closed.

4. Now begin to make circles, as if your head were moving a pencil that drew circles on the ceiling. Do it first in one direction, then in the other. Try moving with your eyes open, then closed, and feel the difference.

5. Place your feet together so that the insides of your feet touch. Now your base of support is much smaller, and it is harder to balance. This is one reason why toddlers stand with their feet wide apart. Now repeat the movements you did in steps 1–4. Make your movements small and slow enough so that you can feel how you are moving, and keep your heels and toes on the floor. In some directions it will be more difficult to move in a straight line or in circles, and you will need to move other parts of your body to avoid falling.

6. Now repeat steps 1–4 with your feet shoulder width apart again. Are your movements more symmetrical? Are you moving with less effort? Is your balance better? Do you feel your feet making better contact with the floor?

Upright balancing for humans ideally involves all the joints of the body doing their share of adjusting to shifts over our base of support. Our ankles and hips are the most important areas where balancing movements take place. As we get older, some people's ankle movements diminish, and this may contribute to a more precarious upright posture. Movements like the one in this lesson can help us to improve how we use our feet and the other parts of our bodies.

Movements of the Mouth and Jaw

Think of all the activities we do that involve our mouth and jaw. The act of eating includes tasting, chewing, swallowing, and using our tongues to clean our teeth. Speech involves many complex movements of the mouth and jaw, as do our emotional expressions. Even breathing requires coordination of the mouth and jaw, and you probably have not forgotten kissing. Imagine the kind of coordination needed to speak, express emotions, and eat, all at the same time!

1. Lie on your back on a firm bed or padded floor, with your knees bent and feet flat on the floor. Can you sense any tension in your facial muscles? Notice the feelings in your forehead, eyebrows, eyes, cheeks, lips, and jaw. Begin to slowly open and close your mouth. How far can you open your mouth without any stretching or strain? Notice the points at which the movement is smooth and where it is not. Rest.

2. Put your thumb inside your mouth and very slowly glide your lower teeth against your thumbnail as you slowly move your lower jaw forward a small amount, and then bring it back. Pause and fully relax your jaw, then move it forward again. Repeat this movement very gently many times. Rest.

3. Place your thumb inside your mouth again. Bring your jaw a little forward and stay there, with your lower teeth resting against your thumbnail. Now slowly move your lower jaw a little to the right and then back to the middle again. Bring your lower jaw back to its normal position, pause and relax a few moments, and then repeat the movement. Move your jaw for-

ward and, while keeping it forward, move it to the right and then back to the middle.

4. Do the movements in step 3 on the left side.

5. Now repeat step 2 and notice whether your jaw moves forward more easily.

6. Repeat step 1 and notice the differences you feel in how you open and close your mouth. Close your eyes and notice the feeling in your face. Are you more relaxed? Does your face have a different expression? Are your mouth and jaw are in a different position, a different shape?

Placing your thumb inside your mouth helps you to sense more clearly the movement of your jaw and is another way to recreate some early behaviors. Many emotional expressions involve either retracting (bringing back) or protracting (bringing forward) the jaw. For example, our jaws tend to jut forward when we are angry and retract when we are afraid. Virtually all of our expressive facial movements involve some degree of movement in the jaw. Our jaws remain in a fixed position when we are in a fixed emotional state, and when we are relaxed and comfortable our jaw stays mobile and in a more neutral position.

S U M M A R Y

Physical and Motor Development

- During this period, infants begin to walk. Balance is the limiting factor in the stability and regularity of their steps.
- The onset of independent locomotion enhances both cognitive and social development.
- Infants' exploratory actions are more coordinated and adapted to the properties of objects.

Perceptual and Cognitive Development

- Infants can perceive and act on relationships between objects, such as between cups and saucers, between causes and effects, between objects and their hiding places, and between the actions of others and their own actions.
- Infants act in deliberate and intentional ways, persisting until a goal is achieved.

- Although infants can find hidden objects in some circumstances, they are still puzzled by complicated paths of movement and multiple hiding places.
- Infants can now imitate actions that they have never performed before and can reproduce acts even after a 24-hour delay.
- Individual differences in cognition result from an interaction between infant temperament and attentional skills and adult intervention.

Emotional Development

- New forms of expression of anger, fear, sadness, and joy all develop at this age.
- Infants can now express mixed emotions and ambivalence.
- Affective sharing and social referencing both enhance infants' ability to use information about other people's emotional expressions, although infants do not yet understand that others have emotions.
- Teasing games are opportunities for infants to experience mixed emotions and develop their skills at emotion regulation.

Social and Language Development

- Infants and parents develop frames for coordinated joint attention and joint visual attention.
- Infants become more selective in their perception of speech, losing their ability to recognize sound contrasts in languages other than the one heard in the home.
- Intentional communication begins at this age, more with gestures than with words. Most gestures are related to infants' interactions with objects.
- Specific attachments develop. The quality of attachment can be assessed using the Ainsworth Strange Situation Test (ASST).
- The ASST has both advantages and disadvantages. The results for a particular infant may reflect the infant as much as the infant-caregiver relationship and the ecological system.
- At this age, genuine turn-taking exchanges with peers begin. Infant-peer relationships evolve

around different themes from those that define infant-adult relationships.

Family and Society

- Infants are able to form attachments equally with mothers and fathers, although the type of attachment with each parent varies across families and depends on time spent and quality of interaction.

- Grandmothers and infants also form attachments. Grandmothers are more likely to be involved with their infant grandchildren in African American families than in Caucasian families.

- Adoptive infants and their parents can form close and lasting attachments.

Applications: Infant Health and Safety

- Caregivers need to be aware of the common sources of danger and accidents for infants.

- Caregivers should learn emergency treatment techniques to handle a variety of potential hazards.

- Health care and immunization is essential for normal development.

 ON THE WEB

www.kidsource.com/NICHCY/speech.html
This site gives general information on speech and language disorders. Other links are www.angelfire .com/nj/speechlanguage/ and www.larynxlink .com/welcome.html.

www.managedcareinfo.com "Managed Care– INFO [a division of the National Healthcare Benefit Corporation (NHBC)] was developed to be a managed care reference library, resource and information center" for the public. Its provides information on aspects of managed care.

www.cfc-efc.ca Child & Family Canada is a Canadian education web site. This site provides creditable resources on children and family. It also has a virtual library, with subjects ranging from adolescents to special-needs children.

GLOSSARY

Affective sharing   Occurs when the child seeks confirmation from others for his or her own felt emotion.

A-not-B error   An error in finding hidden objects that occurs when an object is hidden first in one place (A) and then in another place (B). The child finds the object at A but not at B.

Appraisal   The ability to evaluate a situation and its circumstances before making an emotional response.

Attachment   The maintenance of close proximity between infant and caregiver as part of an enduring relationship.

Attachment behavior   The overt set of signals, such as smiling, crying, and following, that bring parent and infant into close proximity.

Attachment system   The network of feelings and cognitions related to the object of attachment.

Categorical stranger reaction   An acquired fear of a particular type of stranger.

Coordinated joint attention   The process by which the infant co-regulates intentions with other people (also called *intersubjectivity*).

Deferred imitation   Imitation that occurs following a delay from the time the action is seen modeled.

Disorganized-disoriented attachment   The infant shows confused behavior in the Strange Situation Test, such as approaching the mother and then suddenly withdrawing.

Insecure-avoidant attachment   The infant does not approach the mother during the reunion episode of the Strange Situation Test and makes active efforts to get away if the mother tries to comfort the infant.

Insecure-resistant attachment   An ambivalent pattern of responding in the Strange Situation Test such that the infant cannot feel comfortable with either the mother or the toys. Not as extreme or as abrupt as the disorganized-disoriented pattern.

Internal working model   A set of mental representations and expectations one has about attachment figures.

Intersubjectivity   See *coordinated joint attention*.

Joint visual attention   The ability of partners to follow the direction of the other's gaze or pointing gesture.

Mastery motivation   The desire to become competent at a particular goal.

Metapelet   A substitute caregiver on an Israeli kibbutz.

Relational play   The ability to combine two or more objects appropriately according to their function.

Secure attachment   The infant returns to independent play following comfort seeking from the mother during the Strange Situation Test.

Social referencing   A form of appraisal in which infants use the emotional expressions of others in order to regulate their own emotional reactions.

Visual cliff   An experimental apparatus used to determine the nature of an infant's fear of heights.

9

Twelve to Eighteen Months

CHAPTER OVERVIEW AND OUTLINE

Physical and Motor Development	*What kinds of motor skills can infants perform at this age?*
Cognitive Development	*What are the developments in conceptualization and categorization?*
Emotional Development	*How does the infant use speech and gesture to express emotions?*
Social and Language Development	*What are the properties of early language production and comprehension? How does the infant relate to peers and parents at this age?*
Family and Society	*What are some ways of helping infants with special needs? How do infants with special needs affect the family and society? What is the effect of day care on infants and their families?*
Applications: Social Policy and Day Care	*How does public policy affect the types of day care available to infants and their families?*

Babies of this age are full of energy. They start getting into everything, or so it seems. With their almost constant activity and newfound mobility leading them into forbidden or dangerous areas, babies of this age require much more supervision than was necessary in earlier stages. This chapter will trace the beginnings of spoken language. Language acquisition began at earlier ages in the form of nonverbal social exchanges between the infant and the parent or caregiver. Between the ages of 9 and 12 months, some infants develop a rudimentary vocabulary. In this chapter, we will see how these prelinguistic interactions lead naturally into linguistic communication. This chapter will also cover the concurrent emotional and social developments in the first half of the second year of life. In addition, I will be taking a close look at infants with special needs and at the family and social issues surrounding the topic of day care.

Physical and Motor Development

Walking over Different Types of Surfaces

As we saw in the last chapter, balance is the limiting factor in the emergence of stable walking. A complete sense of balance takes a long time to develop. Walking tends to smooth out and have less of an unstable toddler look about 6 months after the infant begins to walk (J. E. Clark, Whitall, & Phillips, 1988). Around this time, infants begin to show the ability to stand on one foot with help and to walk up and down stairs with help. These skills emerge at about 16 months for the average baby (a range of 12 to 23 months) (Rosenblith & Sims-Knight, 1985). Babies still need to use crawling for going up and down stairs (see the "Awareness through Movement" section of this chapter).

Infants of this age period begin to adjust their behavior to the type of surface on which they walk. When jogging, for example, people run more slowly

and step more carefully on a rocky surface than on a smooth one. They do not wait until they step onto the rocks to slow down. Instead, they use perceptual information about the surface to adjust their steps before they get to the rocks. Do walking infants have the same kind of link between their perception and action?

Several studies suggest that infants can perceive how different types of surface affect their locomotor actions. Infants prefer to walk on matte rather than shiny surfaces. If the matte surface looks like it is moving in waves (the researchers used a water bed), infants shift to crawling (Gibson et al., 1987). We saw in the last chapter how infants adjusted their locomotor behavior when encountering a sloping surface. Fourteen-month-old infants are able to regulate their locomotor behavior depending upon the steepness of the slope. If they perceived the slope as too steep for walking down, they sat and slid down (Adolph, Gibson, & Eppler, 1990). These studies show that an awareness of the surface on which one is acting is an essential ingredient of advanced motor skills. As at earlier ages, these skills develop as a complex system between perception, action, and the difficulty of the task.

Coordinated Actions with the Hands

The same holds true for fine motor skills. During explorations of different types of toys, year-old infants were placed at either a foam or a hard table. At the foam table, infants did more mouthing and held the object with both hands. At the hard table, infants used each hand differently (one for support and the other for object manipulation, or each hand held a different object), and they used the table to explore the objects by scooting and banging (Palmer, 1989). Babies of this age are beginning to discover what properties of the environment are best suited to support their motor actions. This matching of motor action with the type of surface is essential for operating safely and successfully.

As infants progress in their ability to adapt their skills to the properties of objects and surfaces, they are more able to use objects as means toward goals rather than as goals in themselves. Thus, at the beginning of the first year, we see the emergence of

Clenched transverse digital
grip (ulnar)

Transverse digital grip
(ulnar)

Clenched transverse digital
grip (radial)

Digital palmar grip

Transverse palmar grip
(radial)

Transverse digital grip
(radial)

Adult grip

Inter-digital grip

Transverse palmar grip
(ulnar)

Adult clenched grip

Ventral clenched grip

Figure 9.1
Grip Patterns

Source: K. Connolly & M. Dalgleish, The emergence of a tool-using skill in infancy, 1989, p. 898. *Developmental Psychology, 25,* 894 – 912.

deliberate tool usage in infants (see the "Awareness through Movement" section of this chapter for a lesson in fine motor skills). A practical tool infants in many cultures need to use is the spoon. One research team has charted the development of spoon use in the second year of life in detail (Connolly & Dalgleish, 1989). Their work has produced a fascinating story about the developmental unfolding of a skill. They classified different types of spoon grips (Figure 9.1), different heights at which the spoon

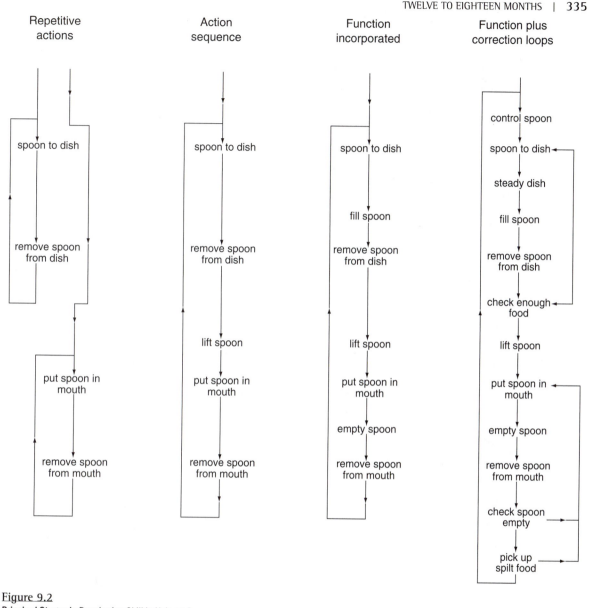

Figure 9.2
Principal Stages in Developing Skill in Using a Spoon

Source: K. Connolly & M. Dalgleish, The emergence of a tool-using skill in infancy, 1989, p. 910. *Developmental Psychology, 25,* 894–912.

was lifted between bowl and mouth, different paths the spoon takes between the bowl and the mouth, and different uses of the opposite hand. Their findings are summarized in the diagrams shown in Figure 9.2.

In the first stage, infants take the spoon in and out of their mouths or in and out of their dishes, but these two repetitive cycles are not connected. No food actually makes it from the dish to the mouth. In the second stage, we have the outlines of the complete action sequence but babies are not paying attention to how much food gets onto the spoon. Often the only taste the babies get is the food that manages to cling to the convex surface of the spoon. The movements from the dish to the mouth are jerky, and the spoon is not held in a grip that permits it to contain the food. During these two stages, caregivers need to help feed infants.

By the third stage, the action sequence of moving the spoon from the dish to the mouth now incorporates the function of moving the food. Although still not very efficient, at least the babies are getting somewhere. In this stage, not only is the action sequence functional, but it is correcting itself for errors. Thus, the babies will keep dipping the spoon into the dish until they are satisfied that it is holding enough food. They will also hold the dish steady. Similarly, at the mouth, the infants will continue to put the spoon into their mouths until it is clean. Infants at this stage can also alternate which hand holds the spoon and the type of grip (McCarty, Clifton, & Collard, 1999).

This study shows that spoon use can be a complicated motor challenge for a baby. The developments shown in Figure 9.2 take 6 to 8 months from the onset of spoon use. Successful tool use involves not only making all the right moves at the right time but also the ability to adjust the movement to correct errors that occur in the process. In mature eating, few errors are made, and if they occur, they are adjusted very quickly.

Cognitive Development

The period between 12 and 18 months encompasses Piaget's Stage V of sensorimotor development. As Observations 9.1 and 9.2 show, infants in Piaget's Stage V are not merely using familiar means to achieve their goals: they are creatively inventing new ways of doing things. This is the stage of what Piaget called the **tertiary circular reactions,** the beginnings of active experimentation and the search for novelty. In the previous stages, infants were most comfortable in familiar settings and were most likely to use the means they had discovered—largely by chance—to handle situations that arose. In Stage V, children become able to adapt to brand-new situations, both by using tried and true methods and by seeking out and discovering new methods of acting upon the environment. Stage V sometimes is called the stage of trial-and-error behavior, since infants attempt new combinations of action schemes until they find the one that will solve the problem.

A characteristic behavior of infants at this age is experimenting to discover new ways of doing things. It is almost as if they are aware of themselves as a persistent part of the series of actions in the experiment, a manifestation of their growing subjective self. Infants discover that a distant object can be retrieved by pulling the blanket on which the object sits, or they find new ways to open containers. They try to figure out which objects best fit into particular containers. Unlike the previous stage, in which infants tried out new means to reach a single goal, babies in this stage seem to have multiple goals, and they examine the techniques available to determine which are best suited to the particular goal they have in mind at the moment and which are better suited to other goals.

In the previous stage, the infant was able to find a hidden object if the adult showed the baby where the object was being hidden. The baby often was fooled, however, if the adult moved the object in plain view to a new location. The Stage V infant is no longer so easily tricked. So long as the object can

---

O B S E R V A T I O N S

Stage V Behavior (Piaget, 1952, pp. 269 and 285)

Observation 9.1

At 0;10(11) Laurent grasps in succession a celluloid swan, a box, etc., stretches out his arm and lets them fall. He distinctly varies the position of the fall. Sometimes he stretches out his arm vertically, sometimes he holds it obliquely, in front of or behind his eyes, etc. When the object falls in a new position (for example on his pillow), he lets it fall two or three more times in the same place, as though to study the spatial relation; then he modifies the situation.

Observation 9.2

At 0;10(27) seated on her bed Lucienne tried to 'grasp a distant toy when, having by chance moved the folded sheet she saw the object sway slightly. She at once grasped the sheet, noticed the object shake again and pulled the whole thing toward her.

be seen moving from one place to another, the baby can follow the path of the object and find its hiding place, even after a long series of moves. This accomplishment implies that the infant has an increased awareness of space and an increased cognitive ability to comprehend longer periods of time.

In the area of imitation, the infant is able to model acts that are completely different from those seen before. This flexibility allows the toddler to become a very good copycat. The baby will try to imitate complicated actions done by an older sibling or a peer without having much understanding of the reason for those actions. These are the origins of role play and dramatic play, both of which will take on increased significance after 18 months, when the infant will begin to understand what it means to play a role and get vicarious experience by so doing. Babies between 12 and 18 months are simply having fun copying. Often babies will copy to get a laugh out of the person being copied rather than to try on a role for size (see the later discussion of this behavior).

Imitation has been used as a way to study infants' understanding of the world and their memory skills. As we saw in the last chapter, before the age of 1 year, infants are beginning to understand that other people have intentions. In one study, 14-to-18-month-olds watched adults operate simple tools, such as one in which a party favor appears after pressing a lever. Sometimes the adult said "There!" (intentional action) after pressing the level and other times "Whoops!" (accidental action). Infants were twice as likely to imitate if the action was intentional, showing that they use intention to make sense of adult behavior. They are not, in other words, simply reproducing a mechanical action but acting for a purpose, the same purpose observed in the adults (Bellagamba & Tomasello, 1999; Carpenter, Ahktar, & Tomasello, 1998). In another study, 12-month-olds were more interested in a toy the experimenter reached for inside of a transparent box than in the box, also showing that the infants seemed to understand the purpose of the adult's reaching (Woodward & Sommerville, 2000).

Imitation has also been used to demonstrate how infants of this age remember. During the first year, memory is nonverbal and participatory (see Chapters 2 and 6). Infants under 1 year can re-member how to kick to make a mobile move, remembering the task in action. Can infants older than a year remember a task they observed but did not actually perform? Researchers have found that infants as young as 13 months can do this, but the infants' "descriptions" of what they saw are given by means of imitation.

An infant of this age period is shown a teddy bear, a blanket, and a book, and the experimenter enacts a scene of putting the teddy bear to bed. A week later, given the same materials, the child will reenact the sequence of pretend events (Bauer, 1996; Chen, Sanchez, & Campbell, 1997; Hanna & Meltzoff, 1993; A. Meltzoff, 1988). Infants will remember for longer if they are given multiple demonstrations and if they can imitate the demonstration immediately. In addition, children of this age will spontaneously use words as they are reenacting the original event, commenting on their own actions in a way that suggests that verbal memories are beginning to form around the nonverbal participatory memories (Bauer, 1996).

These memory studies once again reveal that under the appropriate conditions, we do not observe infantile amnesia. When infants are tested using familiar objects and events, when they are allowed multiple exposures, when they can enact the sequence in action rather than in words, and when there are reminders, they can recall events for long periods of time. This age period is also a transitional period for infant memory. In the next period, infants begin to have verbal-conceptual memories. It is difficult for the older infant and child, however, to translate the earlier participatory memories into conceptual memories. Thus it may seem that most people "forget" their infant experiences (see Chapter 6).

Finally, infants develop more advanced categorization skills during this period. Recall that in the first year, infants could understand the relationships of particular examples to a simple category, such as faces, birds, or geometric figures of a certain prototypical shape. A simple categorization task is to recognize different sizes and shapes of birds as belonging to the category "bird." A higher-order task is to be able to group birds, fish, lions, cats, and dogs into an "animal" category. Experiments have shown that by 15 months, infants can correctly form higher-order categories for familiar objects. They can classify animals together, but they will not include cars with the animals (Oakes, Plumert, Lansink, & Merryman, 1996; Roberts & Cuff, 1989).

These two sections on motor and cognitive development are briefer than in previous chapters. This is not because 12-to-18-month-olds are less interesting. Rather, it is because very little research has been done on the motor and cognitive aspects of infants this age, perhaps because the more salient developmental change at this age is the rapid growth of language, a topic to which I will return after a review of emotional developments during this period.

Emotional Development

In this stage, the infant gains a new sense of self-awareness and control over emotional expressions. In the previous stage, infants were able to use the adults around them to regulate their own level of arousal. Social referencing enabled the infant to determine the appropriate way to react to a situation simply by watching a nearby adult. Infants also approached an adult caregiver when they needed comfort, and they used the caregiver as a secure base from which to explore the environment. After 12 months infants still seek help from adults in regulating their emotions, but now we can see the beginnings of an attempt to control their own positive and negative emotions.

Positive Emotion

In the previous stages, infants might smile at their caregivers or laugh at a "joke," but these emotions were direct responses to the environmental events that provoked the emotion. Now infants can remain happy over a long period without the continuation of the stimulating event. This prolonged feeling of enjoyment has been called *elation* (Sroufe, 1979).

Infants also play an active role in creating situations in which happiness is produced and maintained. During the last age period, babies would show off to provoke repeated laughs from the caregiver. During the period between 12 and 18 months, babies will self-consciously exaggerate facial expressions, making funny faces or sticking out their tongues for an especially receptive audience (Demos, 1982). This exaggeration of actual routines in play can also be seen during co-regulated communication frames. By 18 or 20 months, babies and mothers play emotion games in which the children slap their mothers lightly, for example, the mothers pretend to cry, and then the children comfort them (Bretherton, Fritz, Zahn-Waxler, & Ridgeway, 1986).

Finally, infants show delight in their own achievements (Sroufe, 1979). Because they are becoming aware of their own abilities to act on the environment, to create new means, and to experiment, they appreciate the sense of accomplishment that mastery over a new task brings. It is another indication of an expanding sense of a subjective self, a person who persists and achieves. The babies' obvious delight when they take their first steps or find a toy they have been searching for is an example of this new sense of self-appreciation.

Babies continue to show their affection for the special people in their lives. These expressions may change from physical contact to expressions from a distance, such as a smile and a wave. In one study of infants' behavior upon reunion with their mothers after a brief separation, 11-month-olds approached their mothers and sought physical contact immediately. Fourteen-month-olds, in contrast, were less likely to approach the mothers upon their return and more likely to use some form of signaling from a distance: crying, whining, or raising their arms as if to ask to be picked up. By 19 months, the babies rarely even used this form of signaling. When their mothers returned, the babies were content merely to look at them before resuming their play (Serifica, 1978).

Negative Emotion

In the previous stages, situations of stress tended to evoke fear or distress from the infant almost immediately. During an episode of separation from the mother, for example, infants were likely to cry or approach another friendly adult for comfort. After 12 months, infants visibly fight back tears and use other self-comforting behaviors such as stroking and hugging themselves and redirecting their attention to a toy (Bridges, Grolnick, & Connell, 1997; Parritz, 1996; Sroufe, 1979). Since these babies are not overwhelmed with the distress, they search more for their mothers (Serifica, 1978). When their mothers are out of the room, infants often alternate between pouting and frowning (Sroufe, 1979) or biting their lower lips to control distress (Demos, 1982). As previously mentioned, the baby who so successfully fought back the tears during separation almost certainly will burst into tears upon the mother's return. Studies done in the United States and in the Gusii agricultural society in Kenya have shown a relative reduction of attachment behavior during the period between 12 and 18 months, that is, fewer approaches to the mother and fewer bids for attention and support (Reed & Leiderman, 1981).

As infants get older, parents are more willing to expose them to potentially stressful events. Parents are less likely to intervene when the infant has an everyday problem—such as an argument with a sibling, waking up at night, a nonserious fall, or needing attention. Parents are also more likely to leave the infant with a babysitter or in day care, and they are more likely to take trips without the infant. This is partly because infants are beginning to cope with these events (Hildebrandt, Lake, & Parry, 1994). There are individual differences in the infant's ability to cope. Infants who are temperamentally inhibited and who have insecure attachments are more likely to show distress at even minor stresses (Nachmias, Gunnar, Mangelsdorf, Parritz, & Buss, 1996).

When the mother takes a short (2- or 3-day) trip, leaving the infant in the company of the father or another caregiver, infants of this age experience relatively few sleep or behavior problems and can maintain their typical level of positive smiling and verbal interaction with adults. For longer separations, such as when the mother is in the hospital for a prolonged period, infants are likely to show more severe disturbances in their routines and less positive engagement, both while the mother is away and for some weeks after she returns. Infants with more difficult and withdrawn temperaments take these separations harder than others (Field, 1994). These findings suggest that infants of this age can cope with a wide range of stresses, but they need adult support and encouragement. After the parents return, they should also expect to spend extra time reestablishing the infant's routines and providing emotional reassurance.

Social and Language Development

Since this stage is important in the development of language and since I already have hinted at the importance of spoken language for human behavior and development, this section will introduce some of the basic concepts of language development used in the next three chapters.

What Are the Basic Properties of Languages?

Hundreds of languages, as well as countless dialects, are spoken around the world today. Some other languages, such as American Sign Language, are not spoken at all. All human languages—no matter where or how they are used (spoken, signed, or written)—share important properties that distinguish them from other kinds of communication systems, such as those found among other animals or those used for specific purposes, such as computer languages.

Roger Brown (1973) has defined three properties of human language. The first, **semanticity,** is the capacity of a language to carry meaning for both speaker and listener. Human adults are geared to find meaning in words and in all forms of social behavior. It is not unusual for an adult to try to interpret a gesture or a phrase made by someone else, whether that person intended it as meaningful or not. I have already discussed how adults try to find meaning in the more or less automatic behavioral expressions of very young infants. Not until the last quarter of the first year do infants begin to use words and gestures in meaningful ways, however.

Productivity, Brown's second property, refers to the ability of a speaker to express many different meanings with a relatively small number of words simply by rearranging them into novel combinations following the rules of grammar. Infants during the one-word stage of this age period cannot be productive in their language use, but when they begin to combine words into sentences, after 18 months, language becomes productive.

Displacement is the property of language that enables speakers to describe distant or absent objects and communicate abstract notions such as peace and justice, and it allows speakers to discuss the past, present, and future. Displacement is based on the fact that words bear an arbitrary relationship to the things they represent. The English word "cat" does not look or sound like a cat, but English speakers can understand what it means. Arbitrary words must be used when describing abstract concepts, since there is no concrete physical image to which a concept like justice corresponds. Infants of this age do not understand abstract concepts but they are beginning to use words that have an arbitrary relationship to the objects they represent.

Aside from these three properties, language has a characteristic structure and function that set it apart from other systems of communication. The structure of language, called grammar or **syntax,** refers to the fact that out of all possible combinations of word order, only a small number are meaningful to the native speaker. The function of language everywhere is to communicate. The study of a language's social and communicative function is called **pragmatics.** Pragmatics is more concerned with why people say something than with how they say it.

What Are the Theories of Language Acquisition?

Learning theory. Developmental psychologists and developmental psycholinguists of this century first viewed language development in behavioral terms. Like any other behavior, speech can be con-ditioned and imitated. Although children must use imitation to acquire the speech patterns of their own linguistic community, developmentalists differ over the extent to which these processes can account for how children acquire a language's syntax and how they come to use language productively. Learning theorists explain these accomplishments with concepts like "delayed imitation" and "generalization" of learned responses (Bandura, 1977; Bijou & Baer, 1965; Whitehurst & Vasta, 1975).

Nevertheless, learning theory cannot fully account for the fact that sentences have a very similar structure all over the world (subject, verb, and object—though not necessarily in that order). Imitation and reinforcement may help explain the learning of specific words and phrases but not the presence of linguistic universals of syntax. Another problem with the learning theory perspective is that it cannot explain why language is acquired at the particular time in the infant's life that it is. Why does it happen right at the end of the first year and coincident with Piaget's Stages IV and V? If learning were the only mechanism available, we might expect to see a much wider range of ages for language acquisition than we now see.

Behavior ecology theory. Theories based more on biological factors arose to try to explain these two problems with learning theory. As for the observation that all language has essentially the same structure, Noam Chomsky (1975) reasoned that each infant is born with a rudimentary notion of syntactic structure—an innate universal grammar. According to Chomsky, this is the only way to explain how infants, especially after 18 months, can take sounds and organize them into meaningful sentences. Careful scrutiny of children's one-word productions and the incipient word order found in early two- and three-word utterances led to an attempt to write down grammatical rules for infant speech (McNeill, 1970).

The problem is that infant speech could not be easily fitted into these simple rules: there were too many exceptions. Martin Braine (1976) has concluded that rather than expressing some underlying universal grammar, the child's "first productive structures are formulae of limited scope for realizing specific kinds of meanings" (p. 4). Language acquisition, according to Braine, is better understood from the point of view of pragmatics—what the child is trying to say and why—than from a syntactic, or structural, perspective.

Functional theory. As a response to the deficiencies in both learning and biological theories, functional theories of language acquisition have attempted to study language development in its natural context: the parent-infant interaction. The functional theory of language acquisition is one type of *interactive systems theory* (see Chapter 2). In contrast to purely psychological, or individual-oriented, theories, the functional approach attempts to study language development in relation to the social system in which it naturally occurs. As we will see, the key milestones of the functional theory of language acquisition are not individual achievements (such as babbling, single-word utterances, and multiword sentences) but achievements of the parent-infant dyad, such as taking turns, paying **joint attention** to an external object (i.e., both parent and infant direct their attention to the same thing), and sharing meaning of particular gestures, words, and phrases (Camaioni, 2000).

Coordinated Joint Attention as a Frame for Language Development

In the previous chapter, we saw how parents and infants create frames for coordinated joint attention. From a functionalist perspective, these frames are essential prerequisities for the emergence of language. Once a joint focus of attention is created, it is relatively easy for infants to begin to associate objects and events with words. Studies in which words are introduced when the infant is looking at an object, compared to when the infant is looking elsewhere, show that infants are more likely to acquire the correct object word if they are looking at the object being named (P. J. Dunham, Dunham, & Curwin, 1993; Woodward & Hoyne, 1999). In addition, infants who are more skilled in establishing joint attention to an object acquire language at an earlier age than children who are less able to jointly attend (Mundy & Gomes, 1998).

During frames for coordinated joint attention, the adult's level of language use, the specific instruction regarding objects and their uses and names, has

a great impact on the child's language development (Broerse & Elias, 1994; McCune, 1995; Tamis-LeMonda & Bornstein, 1990; Tamis-LeMonda, Bornstein, Baumwell, and Damast, 1996). Play with peers involves much less language and gesture than play with adult caregivers. With mother, compared to with peers or being alone, infants use significantly more words and gestures, and their play is more symbolic and relational (Turkheimer, Bakeman, & Adamson, 1989; Zukow, 1986). A similar finding has been reported comparing parent-infant and older sibling-infant interactions (Teti, Bond, & Gibbs, 1988). During experimental manipulations when mothers are asked to temporarily cease being responsive during play, infants increase their requests for assistance from the mothers (Ross & Lollis, 1987).

Once the infant's attention is on the object, adults can use combinations of pointing, showing, and words to highlight specific features of the object. The more mothers do this, the more advanced the child's language skills (Baldwin, 1995; Zukow, 1990; Zukow-Goldring, 1996). Some mothers are more likely to emphasize single words in their speech. They do this either by saying only one word in an utterance ("dog"), by repeating the same word in a subsequent utterance ("That's a dog; look at the dog"), or by changing a word in a repeating sentence frame ("That's a cat; that's a dog"). Mothers who were more likely to do this had children who, as their language skills improved, were more likely to speak clearly and not run their words together (Pine, Lieven, & Rowland, 1997). Finally, the child's participation in frames for shared book reading at 14 months predicted language skills 4 months later (Laakso, Poikkeus, & Lyytinen, 1999). These studies all show that participation in frames for coordinated joint attention significantly enhances language acquisition, providing support for the functionalist theory.

The adult's role in creating frames for coordinated joint attention is also matched by the infant's ability to participate in these frames and pay attention to objects and words. Earlier than 12 months, when adults point at an object, infants are more likely to look at the adult's hand than at the object. Around 15 months this changes, and infants are more likely to pay attention to an object or a feature of an object when adults point (Desrochers,

Morissette, & Ricard, 1995). At the beginning of the second year, infants begin to take the initiative in creating joint frames of references. They develop the ability to follow their mothers' line of vision (Butterworth & Cochran, 1980; Collis & Schaffer, 1975; Scaife & Bruner, 1975); they begin to use pointing to direct their mothers' interest to something they want (Leung & Rheingold, 1981; Murphy, 1978); and they begin to imitate their parent's words more consistently (Masur & Rodemaker, 1999).

The ability to search for new means to reach goals imparts this persistence to the infant's communicative attempts. If infants do not get what they want by pointing or reaching for it, they are likely to look at their mothers, pull on them, point or reach for something, and look back at their mothers until they get what is needed (Blake, McConnell, Horton, & Benson, 1992; Harding & Golinkoff, 1979; Lock, 1980; Mayes, Carter, & Stubbe, 1993). If the mother is asked not to respond to the infant's requests or pretends not to understand the infant, the infant will repeat the request using more exaggerated movements, like leaning or whining, or will change the form of the request such as by replacing a gesture with a word or vice versa (Marcos & Chanu, 1992). These studies suggest that a good deal of language acquisition is infant-initiated. The infant has something to say or wants to know a word and approaches the adult for assistance (L. Bloom, Margulis, Tinker, & Fujita, 1996). These observations are consistent with Piaget's descriptions of an active and persistent infant during this stage.

In the last chapter, we saw the emergence of simple intentional gestures, such as pointing and offering. The child persists until a desired result is obtained but tends to repeat the same gesture. After 12 months, infants begin to use gestures in combinations to communicate more complex meanings (Lock, 1980), as shown in Observation 9.3. In this example, the child first cries intentionally, and then, after the mother arrives, the child points.

Intersubjectivity, the ability to act cooperatively and to incorporate others as meaningful agents in one's actions, also expands at this age. During the previous age period, infants became aware of how their communicative actions affected others. Between 12 and 18 months, infants become more aware of the relationship between self and other. **Metacommunicative events** are communicative acts that refer to the communication in the relationship itself, in contrast to ordinary communicative events, which refer to the world outside the relationship, such as gesturing toward or talking about objects and other people. When infants persist in trying to get an adult's attention or assistance, they are using metacommunication by referring—implicitly or explicitly—to a failure of communication within the relationship.

We have studied metacommunication in infants during this age period during mother-infant play with a pair of toy telephones (Fogel & Branco, 1997; Reinecke & Fogel, 1994). When infants are less than 1 year old, they treat the telephone as a physical object, something to push and bang. When mothers try to get the infants to pretend that the

---

OBSERVATIONS

Communicative Behavior (Lock, 1980)

Observation 9.3

Paul; age 13 months (27 days): Paul is playing with his football, which becomes stuck among chair legs. He tries to free it but is unable to. He starts crying while on his hands and knees, then moves to a sitting position and continues wailing. Mother comes in.

Mother: "What's the matter? What's the matter?"

Paul continues crying but also points in the direction of the chair.

Mother: "Oh, have you got it stuck again? I think you do it on purpose some times," and she gives him the ball.

Paul continues crying but less and less vigorously, until he stops.

Observation 9.4

Peter; age 13 months (13 days): (a) Mother is putting Peter's slippers on.

Peter reaches upwards, laughs and shrieks "Lieee."

Mother: "Yes, it's the light."

Peter: "Dieee."

Mother: "That's right, light, light."

(b) I am talking to Mother. Peter comes up to me and touches my wrist.

Peter: "Dik do."

Andy: "Yes, it's a tick tock."

I continue talking to mother, the above occurring without intruding into our conversation.

toy phone is a real phone, that is, to pretend to talk to someone, the infants resist. The infants' metacommunication consists of pushing the phone away if the mother tries to hold it to their ear, making disgusted facial expressions, shaking their heads, and grabbing the phone away from the mother.

Metacommunication changes as the relationship changes. One infant who could pretend play with a toy phone put it to her ear and said, "Dada?" The mother, talking on the other phone, said, "No, it's Grandma." The infant responded with "Dada," and this exchange continued for five rounds, with mutual smiling. In the last round, however, the baby's tone of voice became more serious. The mother interpreted this as a metacommunication and said, "Should we put the phone away?" The baby held the phone and without looking at the mother said (in a robotlike tone), "Da-da-da-da-da." The mother took the phone away saying, "OK," showing that she understood the infant's metacommunication meant not wanting to pretend talk to grandma. After the phone was taken away, the baby continued, "Da-da, da-da, da-da," almost squealing the sounds and smiling at the mother. This type of behavior is different from clowning, seen during the previous age period, because the infant seems to be commenting on the mother-infant relationship rather than simply being a participant.

The Emergence of Conventional Gestures and Words

During the previous age period, infants used a variety of gestures and words. Their gestures were simple acts of directing another person's attention, such as pointing and requesting. Prior to 1 year, infant words are most likely to mimic sounds that accompany an action, like saying "vrooom" when playing with a toy car. After 1 year, gestures and words become conventional. **Conventional actions** are those that represent an action or object using some type of ritualized manner of expression (Acredolo & Goodwyn, 1985; Camaioni, 2000; McCune-Nicolich, 1981). For example, a child who wants her hair combed will hold a comb and pretend to comb her hair. Pretending to drink from a cup might signal the need for a drink. Waving "bye-bye" is another conventional gesture. Such gestures

may refer to the past or the future and to objects that are out of sight. Thus, they have the character of words that are used to name objects and events. There is some evidence, however, that gestures may be easier to learn for infants than words (Goodwyn & Acredolo, 1993).

Sometime between 10 and 16 months, most infants begin to use words to communicate some intention. One manifestation of this developmental change is the onset of *naming*. Naming is the intentional use of a gesture or a word to refer to a specific object or event. Carlotta, one of the infants whose speech development has been reported in the literature (E. Bates, Camaioni, & Volterra, 1975; E. Bates, O'Connell, & Shore, 1987), used the sound "bam" when knocking over a tower of blocks. Several weeks later, Carlotta was sitting silently among her toys. She stopped, looked up, and said "bam," and then she turned and started to bang on her toy piano. What has changed here? The word "bam" has been removed from its original context as an accompaniment to action and is now being said in advance of the action to stand symbolically for the action that is about to occur. Another example of naming is given in Observation 9.4 above.

Around the same time, Carlotta began to do other naming procedures. When asked during the reading of a book, "How does the doggie go?" Carlotta consistently replied, "Woowoo." She also said "woowoo" when she saw a dog in real life or heard a dog barking. At the same age, she was rapidly developing names for toys, foods, and clothing.

Children first acquire words for objects (*car, shoes, teddy, cup*), for social interaction (*hello, no, yes, bye-bye*), and for some simple concepts (*gone, more, there*). Infants of this age acquire only about one to three words per month (Adamson, 1995; Camaioni, 2000). Once they begin to use words, infants seem to prefer objects and events for which they already have a word or name (Schafer, Plunkett, & Harris, 1999). During picture-book reading, for example, infants will spend more time on pictures for which they already know a name.

These early words tend to be used like conventional gestures in the sense that they are like the conventionally used adult word and that they are used consistently in similar situations. These words lack an important property that is discovered by infants only after 18 months: words are symbols.

Symbols, as we will see in the next chapter, stand for or represent something else. A word is not the real thing, it is an arbitrary pattern of sound that represents that thing. Between 12 and 18 months, infants seem to use the words and gestures as if they are part of the real thing, and they use those words only when the real thing is present or nearby. To use Brown's terminology, infants of this age are aware of semanticity but not of displacement.

When children first acquire a word or first make one up, a considerable period of time passes before they use that word in the same way adults use it. Infants make many errors in the application of words. In one type of error, called **overextension,** the child uses the word for instances not included in the adult's definition. For example, a child might use the word "car" for a wide range of vehicles, including motorcycles, bicycles, trucks, and planes. Does this mean the child does not really understand the true meaning of the word "car"? Or does it mean that the child has a faulty concept of cars and believes that all vehicles are cars?

Children's overextending while naming an object reflects their active attempt to try to categorize objects. By naming all vehicles "cars," children "elaborate for themselves the similarities among things" (K. Nelson, Rescorla, Gruendel, & Benedict, 1978, p. 964). Bowerman (1978) reported that her daughter Eva first used the word "moon" to describe the real thing and then extended the word's use to such things as grapefruit sections, lemon slices, and steer horns—anything she saw with a crescent shape. In such cases, the child does not appear to be saying that "a car is a plane" or "a lemon slice is a moon." Instead, the child may be saying that "a car is like a plane" or "a lemon slice is like a moon," much as an older child might say, "It looks like a car," or "Look, it's crescent shaped."

Generally, adults have three choices when infants overextend their word use. They can accept the child's own version of the word; they can say that the child is not correct; or they can provide the correct label for the object (Gruendel, 1977). However, even when the adult says something like "That's not a cookie" in response to the child's overextension of the word "cookie" to refer to a hamburger, the child may not understand or hear the negation. Failure to understand the word "not" may lead the child to interpret the adult's response

to mean "It's okay to call that a cookie. Mommy said it, too" (Gruendel, 1977). As soon as the adult stops referring to the object with the child's overextension and uses only the adult word for it, the child soon picks up the correct name.

Relationship of Production to Comprehension

The same child who used the word "car" to describe many different vehicles was able to readily point out the correct vehicle when asked a question like "Where's the truck?" In another case, a child could correctly point out strawberries when asked but insisted on calling them "apple." Research has shown that 13-month-olds can understand about 50 words, but they cannot speak 50 words until they are about 19 months of age. Thus, infants can comprehend a word considerably earlier than they can produce it.

The earliest instances of word comprehension have been found at the age of 10 months for objects that are both salient and very familiar. At that age, however, it takes great effort to teach infants to understand a word, and they may rely more on the adult's pattern of intonation and gesture in identifying the correct object. By 17 months, however, infants can acquire word meanings easily—sometimes after a single exposure (Masur, 1993; Oviatt, 1978; Woodward, Markman, & Fitzsimmons, 1994).

Not all children have such noticeable lags between comprehension and production; in fact, some children can understand far more than they produce, while for others production is much more closely related to comprehension. How can this be? Some children who produce little but understand a great deal may suffer from a speech or hearing disorder, but this accounts for only a small percentage. Some children may be overly cautious about speaking out until they are certain that they understand how to use the word, which may be related to a temperamental propensity to shyness (E. Bates, Thal, Whitesell, Fenson, & Oakes, 1989). Lags in production may also be related to the amount of explicit naming done by caregivers (Vibbert & Bornstein, 1989). Currently, there is no complete explanation of what accounts for these individual differences.

On the other hand, those children who have high linguistic comprehension show high levels of gestural production. Thus, even though they hesitate to communicate with words, they have articulated a rich array of symbolic gestures (E. Bates et al., 1987). This can be seen clearly in deaf children, who develop a large number of gestural signs that signify objects and actions at ages similar to when hearing children develop linguistic names (Petitto, 1985; Reilly, McIntire, & Bellugi, 1985). Thus, virtually all children at this age try to make themselves understood in one way or another.

The lag between comprehension and production suggests that children in the second year know more than their verbal behavior would indicate and that their efforts to speak are not crude groupings reflecting incomplete understanding but active efforts to make sense out of a complex world of objects and people. The young child's speech may be an important part of the process of concept formation, rather than a mere comment on a concept the child already has attained. At least one study has shown that after adults label novel objects for infants, the infants pay closer attention to those objects (Baldwin & Markman, 1989). Thus, in complex ways, the acquisition of language may place the infant on a fast track toward conceptual and cognitive development.

How Do Infants Communicate with Peers at This Age?

Peer relationships are one way to observe the growing link between language and social development. Peers increasingly attempt to show contingent responses to one another (Mueller & Lucas, 1975), for example, in sharing behavior, which begins in this stage (Rheingold, Hay, & West, 1976). In response to a verbal request or a visual regard on the part of one infant, a peer will show or give an object to the infant who requests it. Although this does not happen all the time, peers tend increasingly to focus their attention jointly on the same object of interest (Eckerman, Whatley, & Kutz, 1975). In general, however, joint attention occurs much less at this age during peer play, compared to adult play (Turkheimer, 1989). At this age, about 77% of peer play is parallel play (see Table 1.1, Chapter 1); that is, peers play alongside each other but independently (Howes & Matheson, 1992).

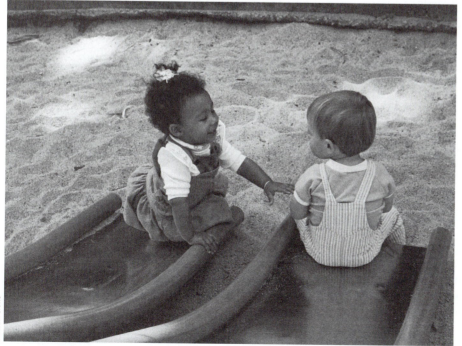

Toddler friendships are genuine and important. Sharing and contingent responses are just beginning at this age.

Elizabeth Crews

Between peers, toys have a different role from the one they have between adults and infants. With adults, toys can be objects of a request or an offer, or the subject of naming and labeling routines. Toys are just part of a more complex interaction involving many levels of meaning. On the other hand, with peers, toys become the major focus of attention and serve as vehicles for the initiation and maintenance of social interactions. If someone else in the room is touching or manipulating a toy, the infant is likely to approach that person and make contact with the toy. Intentional communication—unlike a single-minded interest in the toy itself—requires that the infant not only touch the toy but also look at the other person and verbalize to that person about the object. Babies 11 to 13 months of age were likely to smile, vocalize, and gesture to an adult just before and just after making contact with the toy the adult was touching, but this happens less often between peers (Eckerman, Whatley, & McGehee, 1979; Turkheimer et al., 1989). In one study of infants during this age period, a novel toy was introduced into play between adults and infants and between infant peers (Marcos & Verba, 1990). In the infant-adult interaction, the infant pointed to the toy and looked at the mother, requesting the toy's name and wanting to use it. When the same toy was introduced between two peers, they just looked at each other and laughed.

Does the Mother's Presence Affect the Way an Infant Plays with Peers?

Because of the infant's newfound awareness of persons as potential communicators, we might expect the parent's presence to affect peer interaction. Infants still approach peers for different reasons than they approach parents. In general, given the simultaneous presence of both mother and peer, a child is more likely to initiate play with a peer (Vandell, 1979). With their mothers, children are more likely to seek physical contact and show negative emotions like distress and anger.

To answer the question posed at the beginning of this section, however, we need to compare the infant's behavior toward peers when the mother is present with that when she is absent. In a familiar setting—a parent co-op nursery school—10- and 14-month-olds were found to be more social and less negative to peers when their mothers were out of the room (Field, 1979). The main difference between the mothers' presence and their absence was that more conflict, toy snatching, and crying occurred when the mothers were present, even when the infants were playing with peers. These behaviors may serve as signals to the mother of the infant's relative discontent about something.

What Other Situational Constraints Affect Peer Relationships?

The mother's presence during a peer interaction is referred to as a **situational constraint**—an aspect of the environment that affects the nature of the peer relationship. We saw in Chapter 2 how factors outside a social system can affect the functioning of that system. The presence of a third person is one such constraint. Others include the infant's familiarity with the peer and each infant's level of peer experience.

Familiarity has been shown to affect how 1-year-olds play together. When children are asked to identify which other children are their friends, friends are more likely to interact together than nonfriends, even under controlled laboratory situations in which friend and nonfriend pairs are formed artificially and allowed to play by themselves for a short period of time (Becker, 1977; Young & Lewis, 1979). Friends are more likely than nonfriends to touch and lean on each other, more likely to initiate interactions with each other, and more likely to show positive affect with each other (M. Lewis, Young, Brooks, & Michalson, 1975).

Apparently, then, friendship can be shown to exist as early as 12 months of age. Although it is not clear from these studies whether infants at this age have the same kind of attachment to their friends as older children and adults do, infants are more comfortable and expressive in the company of familiars.

The amount of experience an infant has had with peers is not as strong a situational constraint as peer familiarity. Some evidence suggests that experienced toddlers are more active in peer encounters than relatively inexperienced toddlers and that the experienced toddlers are more likely to show more complex social behaviors such as mutual imitation and cooperative play (Mueller & Brenner, 1977; Vandell, 1979). Nevertheless, infants seem to need little prior exposure to other infants to act competently in their company, and infants seem to understand the ins and outs of peer play very quickly.

The Sense of an Elaborated Subjective Self

During the period from 9 to 12 months, the subjective self emerged. At this age, the infant has a sense of being a subject who can feel and experience and who is different from other subjects. The subjective self is shown by such behaviors as showing off, intentional communication, and social referencing. These same behaviors continue during the period between 12 and 18 months, and other similar behaviors are added. In the realm of showing off, for example, infants at this age will exaggerate their facial expressions and other social actions as if they are exploring their own subjectivity in relation to another person. In the realm of intentional communication, 12-to-18-month-olds will not only gesture or use a word, they will persist when their attempts are not understood. They lean toward the adult, whine, use additional gestures, or pull on the adult's arm.

In the realm of social referencing, infants of this age still rely on adults, but they also discover that they have some emotion regulation skills of their own. They attempt to control their own distress by biting their lip or hugging themselves. When with another person, babies will look toward that person for confirmation of an achievement, but they will also smile, jump, or wave their arms to recognize the achievement for themselves. Finally, infants of this age will metacommunicate, showing that they have a concept of themselves as a participant in a relationship that persists over time.

One gets the sense that the subjective self in this age period is becoming more elaborated, that the infant is filling in the blanks of self-experience and trying out the possibilities and limitations of it. It is

interesting that all of this self-exploration and self-knowing goes on for at least 9 months before the infant acquires the word "I," which begins during the next developmental period. During the period between 12 and 18 months, it appears that subjectivity becomes more active. Infants not only become more persistent in expressing themselves, they begin to imitate complex sequences of adult action. It is also notable that infants imitate not just any adult action, but intentional adult action. This means that the infants are understanding the action subjectively, that is, as actions done by a person for a purpose. By copying these actions, the infants are coming to feel themselves as purposeful, feeling subjects.

Family and Society

In this section, I discuss two important topics. First, I look at how infants with special needs affect families and their functioning, a topic that does not fit neatly into a single age period. Second, because many mothers are returning to work by the time their infants are 1 year old, I discuss how infant development is affected by nonparental caregivers. In relation to this, the "Applications" section of this chapter examines the role of society in providing day care for all families who need it.

When an infant has a long-term or permanent challenge—a disability, deformity, or special need—a systems approach predicts that this infant will affect the entire family and that the family's response to the infant will affect the infant's own development. This section will explore these possibilities. You might want to go back and read the section in Chapter 3 on teratology, as well as the sections in Chapter 4 dealing with euthanasia for neonates with birth defects and with birth complications. Because the infant will affect every member of the family for a long time, the issues discussed in this section should be a part of any decision regarding life, death, or institutionalization for these infants at the time of birth.

Infants with Special Needs

How does an infant with special needs affect the family? Infants with special needs constitute an important population of babies. Such infants may have suffered from a birth defect that affects the brain or body, or they may have acquired a disability following birth. This population of infants is referred to in many ways: special needs, developmentally challenged, developmentally disabled, handicapped, or developmentally delayed. One problem with some of these terms is that they have a negative connotation. Although the babies to whom the terms refer have some deficit with respect to the population of typically developing infants, a great deal can be done to improve their developmental outcomes. To help parents and professionals realize the enormous potential for growth in these babies, we refer to them as **infants with special needs.** Infants with special needs create some degree of emotional trauma for most families.

Effects on individuals. Parents, siblings, and other relatives go through a series of difficult feelings. They almost always experience a chronic sorrow or depression—a feeling that the child will never fit into their lives or dreams. Individuals around the infant with special needs may feel an emotional rejection of the infant that may result, in part, from a lack of knowledge about the infant's condition. Family members also experience difficulty adapting—even to everyday demands—and they find most of their interpersonal relationships strained (Blake, Stewart, & Turcan, 1975; Brooks-Gunn & Lewis, 1982; Preisler, 1997; Rapoport, Rapoport, & Strelitz, 1977).

Parents may be in a state of high emotional arousal much of the time. The shame and guilt they feel at being the "cause" of the problem are coupled with the extra difficulties of caring for the child. These may include extra visits to doctors and hospitals, special difficulties (such as soiling and wetting), special housing or equipment needs, financial difficulties, special care arrangements, special clothing, and special transportation (Rapoport, Rapoport, & Strelitz, 1977). In the course of all this, a parent may swing between the extreme attitudes of either wanting to abandon the child or trying to overprotect the child.

Siblings have unique individual responses to the situation. They may have trouble with peer relationships, become restless and disobedient, display temper tantrums, or live in a state of emotional misery. Part of the difficulty for siblings is that the added stress on the parents reduces the amount of parental time and emotional energy available to give them.

Infants with special needs even affect their grandparents. In one study (D. Davis, 1967), maternal grandmothers were less supportive of their daughters if the daughters had infants with special needs rather than typically developing infants. The feedback a mother receives from her own mother may make her feel less supported and therefore affect her ability to care for the baby. If the grandmother senses that her daughter is not doing her job, the grandmother may withdraw even further. These mutual feedback effects show how the family system can work against the benefit of the infant. However, mutually supportive feedback can lead to a strengthening of the family to the ultimate benefit of the infant.

Effect on the marital relationship. Most of the research on the effect of a child with special needs on marital discord has shown that there is little or no effect. Couples who separated or divorced after having a child with special needs did so because of some problem in the marriage that existed before the child was born (Howard, 1978). Marital discord that could be directly traced to the child amounted to only 4% of the cases studied in a sample of 243 children with a rubella-related birth defect (Korn, Chess, & Fernandez, 1978). Indeed, in some cases, having a child with special needs brings the couple closer together because the parents collaborate more on child-rearing issues than do parents in families without an infant with special needs (Becker, Houser, Engelhardt, & Steinmann, 1993).

Effects on the family. In contrast, the child with special needs has a definite impact on family interaction patterns. Effects may include changes in family routines, lack of vacations and other out-of-home visits, a limited social life, and parents' neglect of other children. These problems only occurred in about one-fourth of a sample of 243 children with a rubella-related defect (Korn et al., 1978), but some of these families had experienced similar disruptions even before the infants' births.

In general, most families who are provided with adequate social, economic, and psychological support come to an effective resolution of these issues, although it may take a long time. A resolution usually means a realistic assessment of the child's abilities and limitations, continued feelings of sadness—but about the child rather than about the effect on the parents—and a recovery of the parents' self-esteem (Mintzer, Als, Tronick, & Brazelton, 1985; Shonkoff, Hauser-Cram, Krauss, & Upshur, 1992).

How do disabilities affect the parent-infant interaction? Most evidence suggests that interactions are adversely affected by a child's disabilities. The amount of disruption of the parent-infant interaction depends on the severity of the disability (Landry, Chapieski, & Schmidt, 1986). Perhaps the mildest effects are seen in premature infants, many of whom would not be classified as disabled. Mothers of these infants are often overindulgent and overstimulating during the first year (Field, 1981a). Disturbances in the mother-infant communication depend upon the severity of the deficits due to prematurity, some of which may last for many years. Premature infants who were delayed in smiling, for example, were smiled at less by their mothers (Field, 1982; Malatesta, Grigoryev, Lamb, Albin, & Culver, 1986).

Many but not all of these differences tend to disappear after the first year, perhaps because the preterm infants gradually catch up with full-term infants (Branchfeld, Goldberg, & Sloman, 1980; Crawford, 1982). Even though preterm infants showed less vocalization, play, and attentive behavior than full-term infants in interaction with their mothers at 6, 8, and 10 months, most of these differences were no longer significant at 12 months. In addition, the extra holding and caretaking that preterm infants received during the first year, compared with full-term infants, was no longer apparent at 12 months (Crawford, 1982). Even though the differences between preterm and full-term groups were lessened by 1 year for these behavioral indicators, other studies have shown that more subtle effects of prematurity may persist until early and middle childhood in such areas as emotional

Deborah Gilbert / The Image Bank

Many infants with special needs are capable of social relationships. Some require regular medical interventions. All such infants demand special care and attention from their families.

maturity, language skills, and perceptual-motor functioning (Grigoroiu-Serbanescu, 1981; Taub, Goldstein, & Caputo, 1977).

In general, however, by the time the children reach the age of 3 years, differences between preterm and full-term groups are typically absent. In preterm groups, as for full terms, individual differences are best predicted by security of attachment at 1 year (Plunkett, Klein, & Meisels, 1988), by the severity of birth complications independent of prematurity (Landry et al., 1986), and by the infant's history of illness during the first years of life (Jarvis, Myers, & Creasey, 1989). Thus, the factors that complicate preterm birth have a longer-lasting impact than the prematurity itself.

Another example of a less severe developmental disability is infants with an unattractive craniofacial deformity. Here we see a pattern similar to that observed for premature infants. Mothers of these infants appear to be less nurturant than parents of typically developing children during the early part of the first year (Barden, Ford, Jensen, Rogers-Salyer, & Salyer, 1989). By the end of the first year, however, there are no differences in attachment security between these infants and typically developing infants (Speltz, Endriga, Fisher, & Mason, 1997).

Lasting interactive deficits are seen in more serious disorders (Hauser-Cram, 1996). One study of 110 infants with special needs (with Down's syndrome, cerebral palsy, and developmental delay) found that the infants with special needs smiled and vocalized less than the matched sample of typically developing infants (Brooks-Gunn & Lewis, 1982). In fact, one-third of the infants with special needs never smiled in the first two years of life, although by age 3, 80% had smiled. These babies cried more at older ages than the controls. Children with cerebral palsy are likely to receive less maternal warmth if they are not walking by 3 years of age than if they walk earlier (Korn et al., 1978). In the second year, parents of infants with any kind of physical disability are both more reinforcing of what the child actually can do and more likely to ignore the larger number of difficulties the child experiences than are parents of typically developing infants (Wasserman, Allen, & Solomon, 1985).

Down's syndrome babies tend to be slower to develop than typical infants. Parents tend to interrupt their Down's syndrome infants' vocalizations more than their typically developing infants', even though the Down's infants vocalize less (Berger & Cunningham, 1983). Although most 4-month-old infants, when presented with a maternal "still face" during social interaction (see Chapter 6), will cease smiling and gaze away, Down's infants actually gaze longer and may even smile (Legerstee & Bowman, 1989). This suggests that Down's babies may be overstimulated by social interaction and find it easier to express themselves when mothers are relatively quiet. Other research has shown that maternal attention-directing strategies during object play are usually less successful with Down's babies, and coordinated joint attention episodes are less frequent (Cielinski, Vaughn, Seifer, & Contreras, 1995; Landry & Chapieski, 1989; Legerstee & Weintraub, 1997). In response to these actions, mothers of

Down's babies are likely to respond less and to attempt new interactions less than mothers of typically developing infants (Brooks-Gunn & Lewis, 1982; O. Jones, 1977). Down's syndrome infants are also less likely to be securely attached than are typically developing infants, although this may be due in part to their cognitive deficits and inability to understand the strange situation (Atkinson et al., 1999). The prognosis for Down's syndrome infants is better when there is high family cohesion and a sensitive mother-infant relationship (Hauser-Cram et al., 1999).

Blind and deaf infants are a special case because they have sensory but not cognitive or motor deficits. Parents of blind infants feel less attached and are likely to interact less with their infants (Fraiberg, 1974). Blind children, for example, are delayed by up to 1 year in the communicative skills discussed in this and the previous chapter. During the second year, they do not use gestures like pointing, showing, or giving, they do not seem to be oriented to external objects, they show few intentional behaviors, and they do not, of course, look at the parent for social referencing. Blind infants do not engage in pretend play or use spoken language until their third year or later. They also do not imitate adults (Preisler, 1997).

These deficits make it very difficult for parents to establish frames for coordinated joint attention, a cornerstone of development of the self and of communication. This means that parents must work hard to observe subtle signs of attention in the infant. They tend to overcompensate, which further delays the emergence of initiative taking in the child. Once language begins to be acquired in the third year, blind children become more socially oriented. Even so, they require an environment in which others remain visually attentive to them and can pick up their sometimes subtle cues (Preisler, 1997; Recchia, 1997).

Deaf children in general fare better developmentally than blind children. Most of the forms of establishing coordinated joint attention are visual, and the deaf child can observe parents, imitate, gesture, and produce typical facial expressions. Even with gesture and sign language, deaf children may be somewhat delayed compared to hearing children (Bornstein, Haynes, Pascual, Painter, & Galperin,

1999). Interestingly, deaf mothers of deaf infants and hearing mothers of hearing infants are both rated as more sensitive than unmatched dyads in which either mother or infant is deaf. The matched dyads also spend more time in episodes of coordinated joint attention. These findings suggest that the more attuned the mother is to the infant's communicative actions, the more the dyad is coregulated (Meadow-Orlans & Spencer, 1996).

Some research has shown that the developmental prognosis is better for infants with special needs whose social interactions with their mothers are more like those of typically developing infants. The frequency of social interaction in the early part of the first year of life predicted a child's competence at age 2 on the Gesell Developmental Schedule, the Bayley Scales of Infant Development, and a language development scale (S. E. Cohen & Beckwith, 1979). This suggests that the more parents treat their infants as if they were typically developing children with special problems rather than as abnormal or problem children, the better off the children are in the long run. Several studies have shown that if maternal question asking, which is found at high frequency for typically developing infants, is maintained at a high level for special needs and language-disordered infants, it can have a marked effect on their social and communicative development (J. S. Leifer & Lewis, 1983; Yoder, 1989).

One problem is that often parents may not understand the nature of their child's disorder. Another is that parents have trouble being happy and playing with a baby that is less responsive. Even when the baby makes an occasional response, the parent often is unprepared and is not able to anticipate an appropriate answer (Fogel, 1982b; Koester, 1994).

What can be done to help parents help their children with special needs? Intervention programs designed to educate parents about their children's disabilities, to provide emotional support and the supportive network of a system of peers (other parents with similar problems), and to teach parents how to respond to and anticipate the needs of their individual children have a significant success rate. Mothers in such intervention programs enjoy and respond more to their infants (Bromwich & Parma-

lee, 1979; Calhoun, Rose, Hanft, & Sturkey, 1991; Field, 1981a; Fraiberg, 1974). Parents who are more positive about improving the family communication are more likely to participate in such programs (Gavidia-Payne & Stoneman, 1997).

In addition, local and state governments provide support services for children with special needs through day care and school systems, as well as through hospital programs. Federal funds are available through such programs as Developmental Disabilities, Early Periodic Screening Diagnosis and Treatment, Head Start, Education of the Handicapped (PL 94-142), Title XX Social Services, and the National Institute for Mental Health. Most of these programs make funds available through community and state education and welfare agencies (McPherson, 1983).

Another federal law (PL 99-457) provides for family-centered, rather than child-centered, services. This law encourages the states to implement comprehensive, multidisciplinary, and interagency services for early intervention with families and children who have special needs. The program focuses on identifying family strengths, goals, and needs while developing an intervention plan to meet those needs (Rounds, 1991).

John D. McKee, who was born in 1919 with cerebral palsy, writes articles and books about what it is like to grow up as a special needs individual. In his autobiography, he writes eloquently about his life and family (McKee, 1974). His works express ideas that modern scientific research is only beginning to discover: that knowledge burns brighter than ignorance, that all children need love and a chance to make it on their own, and that a sense of humor is one of the best shields against depression and guilt. McKee wrote:

At home with my family, I was perfectly relaxed. If I spilled something at the table, it was only as if one of my brothers spilled his milk or dropped his bread butterside-down on the floor. Once in a while, if I was having a particularly tough time and was spreading my food around the dining room with a lavish hand, Mother would say, "Why don't you sit on the floor, Jack? Anything that falls up, we'll hand down to you." In the laugh that followed, the tension was broken, and I could usually finish my meal with a minimum of spilling. (McKee, 1974, p. 201)

In the next section, I turn to the topic of the effects of alternate and multiple caregivers on infant development.

The Effects of Nonparental Care on Infants and Parents

In the first edition of this book, published in 1984, I reviewed research on the effects of out-of-home care for infants. There were relatively few studies, and most showed no harmful effects, so long as the infants were left in high-quality care. Since 1984, there has been an explosion of new research, new findings, and, especially, new public interest in the question of child care.

One of the most significant contributions to this important research issue has been the National Institute of Child Health and Human Development (NICHD) study of early child care. Child care in this case means care given by any person other than the child's mother. A total of 1,364 children took part in the study, which began in 1991. The composition of this nationwide sample was 76% Caucasian Americans, 13% African Americans, 6% Hispanic Americans, and the remainder were other minorities. The study sample came from a wide range of income and education levels, using a wide variety of types of child care, including center day care, day care homes, and in-home care from relatives or nannies. The researchers assessed multiple variables, including the child's experience in child care, quality of child care, family income, parental psychological adjustment, quality of the mother-child interaction, and the home environment.

The statistics from this representative sample show the importance of child care for infants and their families in the United States. The children in this sample received an average of 33 hours of non-maternal care per week. Hispanic infants used non-maternal care the least, while black infants used it the most. Most of the infants were placed into some type of care prior to 4 months of age. When they first entered care, half of the infants were with the father or grandparent, 20% were in child care homes, and only 8% were in a child care center. I will report the findings from this and other child care research in the remainder of this section. Mothers with higher incomes and those who had

Table 9.1 Primary Child Care Arrangements Used by Working Mothers with Children under the Age of Five Years (1987)

Licensed Day Care Centers	25.6%
Day Care in Another Home	
Relatives	13.2%
Nonrelatives	22.4%
Care in Child's Home	
Mother working at home	8.9%
Father	15.3%
Other relatives	8.4%
Nonrelatives	6.2%

Source: U.S. Bureau of the Census, *Current Population Reports,* Series P-70, No. 20 (1988).

an economic need to work were most likely to place their children in child care. After the first year, there are an increasing number of children in center care (see Table 9.1)

After 15 years of research, we can now conclude with more certainty that the effects of child care on children still depend on the quality of that care. We know that high-quality child care is correlated with successful outcomes for children. Children in high-quality care receive better caregiving, are more securely attached to their caregivers, and are more competent with their peers and with adults than are children in low-quality care. Children in high-quality care score better on school readiness and on cognitive and linguistic abilities, have fewer behavior problems, and are more securely attached to both their mothers and their care providers (Burchinal, Bryant, Lee, & Ramey, 1996; Howes, 1997; Howes, Galinsky, & Kontos, 1998; Howes, Phillips, & Whitebook, 1992; NICHD Early Child Care Research Network, 1997a; 1998a) We also know what is necessary to create high-quality care (NICHD Early Child Care Research Network, 1996; see Table 9.2). These studies not only show that children do better in high-quality child care; they also reveal that children receive positive benefits such as cognitive, linguistic, and social skills from attending high-quality child care.

In addition to the quality of child care, research also shows that the quality of the family environment is one of the most important predictors of child outcomes for children who attend child care. In one large-scale study in Sweden, children who

Table 9.2   Accepted Standards of High-Quality Child Care*

Factor	Needed to Maintain Effective Development
Group size	Caregiver-child ratio between 1:4 and 1:10 over 3 years of age; between 1:4 and 1:8, over 2 and under 3 years; between 1:3 and 1:6, over 1 and under 2 years; and 1:3 under 1 year.
Caregivers	Trained in specialized, formal teacher training programs that emphasize early childhood education and experienced in working in child care settings. Caregivers should be nurturant, supportive, and responsive to children's cues; they should talk to, hug, and smile at children and enjoy their company. Also, they should be willing to firmly and appropriately enforce guidelines for behaviors that affect the rights and safety of others, as well as have respect for parents' points of view and concerns.
Staffing	Low staff turnover, staff support, and low burnout; only one or two caregivers should be responsible for the same child.
Curriculum	Planned in advance, emphasis on development. Age-appropriate and safe toys, flexible program with special events and outside trips. Curriculum adapted to needs of the individual child. Opportunities for diverse activities and movement.
Parents	Should be informed daily about child's day and any special problems or special achievements; should be encouraged to visit at any time and to participate if desired.
Facility	Clean, bright, safe, lots of room for toddlers to move about. Nap times and quiet areas, access to a fenced outside play area. Emergency essentials available. Food safe and nutritious.

*Applicable to day care centers and family day care.

Source: K. Magid & C. A. McKelvey, *High risk: Children without a conscience,* 1987, p. 170. New York: Bantam; S. Provence, Infant day care: Relationships between theory and practice, 1982, p. 34. In E. F. Zigler & E. W. Gordon (Eds.), *Day care: Scientific and social policy issues,* 33–35. Boston: Auburn House; S. Scarr, *Mother care/other care,* 1984, p. 212. New York: Basic Books; K. S. Weintraub & L. N. Furman, Child care: Quality, regulation, and research, 1987, p. 333. *Social Policy Report: Society for Research in Child Development, 2,* 317–342.

were in high-quality day care under the age of 1 year performed better in school at 8 and 13 years of age than other children (Andersson, 1992). Part of this result may be accounted for by the fact that children who entered day care early in this study had two professional parents. It is well known that parents with higher levels of education and income have children who achieve better in school. A similar study in Israel found that the social competence and communicative skill of children in preschool were more related to parental positive interaction with the children than to early day care experience (N. K. Rosenthal, 1991).

The NICHD study confirmed these findings. If mothers were depressed and/or not contingently responsive to the children, their children in child care had lower scores on social and cognitive tests, and had more behavior and attachment problems (NICHD Early Child Care Research Network, 1998a,b). These studies show that the quality of day care and the social and economic abilities of parents can buffer children against any adverse effects of early child care. Put another way, for children who come from supportive and loving families, placement in high-quality child care does not adversely affect development and may even enhance it.

Most researchers agree that child care after the age of 12 months is not harmful and might even be beneficial to the child. Compared to home-reared infants, day care infants are more cognitively and socially advanced and are more likely to show independence in compliance to rules (Caldwell, 1986; Clarke-Stewart, 1984; Schuetze, Lewis, & DiMartino, 1999; Siegal & Storey, 1985; Volling & Feagans, 1995). Infants older than 12 months are able to adjust to repeated separations from their mothers during ordinary day care attendance. The separation reactions of infants on their first day of day care are considerably greater than after 1 or 2 weeks (Field, 1991). Infants, even those who are insecurely attached to their mothers, are able to use caregivers and teachers as attachment figures and secure bases (Howes & Smith, 1995).

In contrast to these findings, a number of research studies have reported that the proportion of infants with insecure attachments increases if the infants have been in child care for at least 4 months beginning before the first birthday and for more than 20 hours per week (that is, children whose mothers are employed more than half time) (Barglow, 1987a; Belsky & Rovine, 1988; P. Schwartz, 1983; Vaughn, Grove, & Egeland, 1980). In

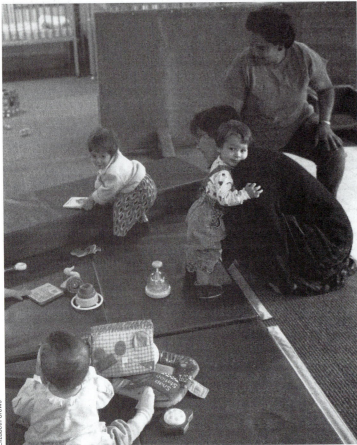

Elizabeth Crews

The effects of nonparental day care on infants depend on the conditions of the day care setting, the infant's age, and the parent-infant relationship. Only a small percentage of infants in the United States are able to attend a high-quality day care facility.

samples of infants in the United States whose mothers do not work outside the home, the proportion of secure attachments is about 65 to 75%. In these samples of early child care infants, the proportion of secure attachments, across all studies, is 57% (Belsky & Rovine, 1988). The difference in security between early child care and home care infants is small but statistically significant. In these studies, the dependent measure is attachment security as assessed by the Ainsworth Strange Situation Test.

What accounts for those infants who develop insecure attachments? The infants most at risk for insecure attachments tend to be boys who are rated as difficult and/or fussy, who are insecure-avoidant, and who have mothers who have strong career orientations, work full time, and express less anxiety about being separated from their infants. Generally speaking, the quality of the mother-infant relationship is a stronger predictor of insecure attachments

than the child care situation is. Insensitive mothering coupled with low-quality child care accounts for most of the reported insecurity of attachment (Barglow, 1987a; Belsky & Braungart, 1991; Belsky & Rovine, 1988; Chase-Lansdale & Owen, 1987; NICHD Early Child Care Research Network, 1997b). If the quality of care is high and mothers are sensitive, there appear to be no adverse effects of early day care experience on infant-mother attachment, either at 1 year or later (Burchinal, Bryant, Lee, & Ramey, 1992; Lamb, Sternberg, & Prodromidis, 1992; NICHD Early Child Care Research Network, 1997b; Roggman, Langlois, Hubbs-Tait, & Rieser-Danner, 1994).

In cases where the mother is insensitive, a high-quality child care experience can be beneficial. Research shows that the security of the early child care infant's attachment to mother does not predict social and emotional competence in preschool; rather, the security of attachment to the substitute care-giver and/or the quality of the early care setting is the best predictor of social and emotional competence in preschool (Howes, 1988; Howes & Stewart, 1987; Oppenheim, Sagi, & Lamb, 1988; Phillips, McCartney, & Scarr, 1987; Schindler, Moely, & Frank, 1987; Vaughn, Deane, & Waters, 1985). These relationships were found for infants in the United States in day care centers or family day care homes and on Israeli kibbutzim in which the child's primary attachment is with the metapelet. As we saw in the last chapter, for infants primarily reared at home, it is the child's attachment to mother that is the best predictor of preschool social behavior (Egeland & Hiester, 1995).

The data suggest that substitute care for infants under the age of 1 year is indeed a different experience for the infants than if they are placed in such care after the age of 1 year. Under the age of 1 year, infants appear to be more sensitive to the effects of child care quality and to the availability of non-parental attachment figures within the child care setting. These factors are less important for infants older than 1 year, who have already formed a strong attachment to one or both parents.

Does this mean that one should not place children under the age of 1 year in child care for more than a few hours a week and that mothers or fathers should plan to stay home with infants for at least 1 year? Some observers make a strong case for this position on the following grounds. First, this early experience outside the home somewhat reduces the importance of the parental role. Second, and more importantly, it may not be possible in the United States today to guarantee high-quality child care for more than a handful of children (see the "Applications" section of this chapter). If this is true, one may be justified in supporting home care for infants under a year (Barglow, 1987b; Belsky & Rovine, 1988; Magid & McKelvey, 1987). In addition, some mothers want to stay at home with their children if they can afford it financially.

On the other hand, some parents may not be disturbed by a change in their parental role. The findings do not mean that parents are unimportant, only that they have a different type of relationship and provide different sorts of needs for their children than parents who choose to stay at home. In many countries, such as Israel, China, and the for-mer Soviet Union, extensive out-of-home child care is an accepted part of the culture. Advocates of child care in the United States argue that if child care were made more of a national priority, we could guarantee high-quality care for all infants. In the meantime, these advocates provide guidelines for parents to use in evaluating the quality of care in order to assure a good setting for their infants (Howes, 1988; Phillips, McCartney, & Scarr, 1987; Scarr, 1984). I take up these issues at the interface between research, practice, and policy making in the "Applications" section.

The Author's View

The period between 12 and 18 months is one of consolidation and growth. Infants of this age acquire new words and gestures. They become more proficient at motor skills, refining their previous skills, like crawling, and manipulating and applying them to new tasks (see the "Awareness through Movement" section of this chapter). Infants experience more of themselves subjectively. These are all incremental advances that lead the way for the next major developmental transition at around 18 months. In the period between 12 and 18 months, the infant is still a participatory subjective self, a lived self rather than a conceived self.

Infants of this age period imitate extended sequences of intentional activity, almost as if trying the activity on for size. They may, for example, pick up a toy telephone and try to talk "like Mommy," imitating the mother's actual telephone conversation. Or they may want to type on the computer or stir the pot. Without any understanding of what the computer is used for, and without an "I" that wants to take control, what could these actions possibly mean for the baby?

This kind of behavior happens in older children and adults. Imagine listening to a song on the radio. You do not understand all the words, you do not want to be a rock star, you just like the way the song sounds and want to try singing it yourself. Maybe you can reproduce some of the words of the song. If not, you either hum or make up some of

Applications Social Policy and Day Care

Item: In 1968 the U.S. Department of Health, Education, and Welfare published minimum requirements for day care, referred to as the Federal Interagency Day Care Requirements (FIDCR). However, they were never implemented because of political controversies within the federal government over which agency would best administer them, whether they could be enforced at all, and whether the government could afford to maintain its own standards.

Item: The FIDCR were revised in 1972 by a noted Yale psychologist, Edward Zigler. He included in-home care in the regulations, specified meal requirements and minimum wages, and set child-to-adult ratios: zero to 18 months, 3:1; and 19 to 38 months, 4:1. The 1968 regulations did not set ratios for children under 3 years of age. Very few facilities could comply with the low child-to-staff ratios and the minimum wages so the revised regulations could not be enforced.

Item: Two years later, Congress put day care in the hands of the states under the Title XX amendment to the Social Security Act. In 1975, the Department of Health, Education, and Welfare published new child-to-staff ratios as follows: zero to 6 weeks, 1:1; 6 weeks to 18 months, 3:1; 18 to 36 months, 4:1. Congresspersons, state administrators, and caregivers launched a tide of protest. The requirements were never enforced.

Item: In 1987, Congress began to draft new federal child care legislation in collaboration with a number of child advocacy groups, including the Children's Defense Fund, the Society for Research in Child Development, the American Psychological Association, the American Academy of Pediatrics, and the American Federation of Teachers. Called the ABC bill (Act for Better Child-care), it was designed to provide child care for low-to moderate-income families and to provide incentives for states to improve the quality of care in centers and in family day care. The ABC bill was finally enacted in late 1990.

Item: Although we are one of the world's wealthiest nations, we are subsidizing child care for less than 10% of our children under 6 years, compared to 100% in Sweden, 90% in France, and 50% in Israel and Hungary.

Item: More than half of young children in the United States are in second-rate child care situations, with substandard facilities, poor staff training, and high staff turnover, in spite of the overwhelming evidence in showing the importance of high quality child care.

Item: Three million children in the United States under the age of 14 years are in programs guided by no national standards that reflect current knowledge obtained by research in child development. Licensed day care facilities currently account for only 25% of out-of-home care for children. The rest of the children are in nonlicensed, family-run day care homes.

Item: Although more employers are providing child care at work, these employers still represent less than .1% of the nation's employers. Only 2% of the 1.2 million companies with more than 10 employees have child care on site (Sancier & Mapp, 1992). The private sector is not stepping in and picking up the responsibility.

The generally poor care available to many children and the even worse care available to children from low-income and minority groups (B. P. Klein, 1985; Magid & McKelvey, 1987; Kontos, Howes, Shinn, & Galinsky, 1997; J. R. Nelson, 1982; Ruopp &

---

the words. It is all playful and enjoyable. You do not think about it as "I am singing this song," but you nevertheless feel yourself singing it and it feels good, or silly, or funny, or whatever. You are aware that there is an "I" singing; it is not the performer on the radio singing, for sure. If you liked doing it, maybe you will try another song.

People do this type of participatory, subjective imitation most frequently when developing new skills such as taking lessons in music, dance, or athletics, or taking a math or science class. When you first study physics, for example, you use the formulas, but you do not necessarily understand what they mean. This step of participatory involvement is a prelude to the emergence of a self who possesses a particular skill. When you can say, "I'm a dancer," "I studied algebra," or "I like to play tennis," you have moved on to a different kind of experience of self with respect to that skilled activity. When you do the Awareness through Movement lessons of this chapter, be sure to pay attention to what type of sense of self you are experiencing.

These examples reveal why infants of this age seem to be having so much fun. It is as if they are always experimenting with new things and feeling themselves doing it. On the other hand, they have not yet gotten to the point where they have formed a sense of self that has possessions, goals, or plans. So, while they are full of energy and love to feel themselves, they are not burdened by expectations for success or failure, they are not troubled by meeting a particular schedule, and they do not feel ashamed of themselves if they make a mistake. They do not even have a concept of a mistake. If we

Travers, 1982; Slaughter, 1980; Weintraub & Furman, 1987) testify to the large gap between children's needs and the willingness of our leaders to provide adequately for them. Slaughter (1980) gives several reasons for the lack of effective child care policies. The first is the myth that the modern family can be independent and self-sufficient. In spite of growing evidence to the contrary, people tend to think they are the masters of their own destiny. Hence, there is a strong resistance to the idea of social policy and social legislation (Bennett, 1987). Studies on the ecology of child development (Bronfenbrenner, 1979; Belsky, 1981) have shown that what happens to the child and the family depends, to a large measure, on the exosystem, mesosystem, and macrosystem of the surrounding society (see Chapter 2). Although a parent may believe that day care services should be found close to or in the home, the reality is that many parents leave their children in situations that are often inadequate and unregulated by state and federal laws.

A second reason given by Slaughter is the fragmentation of social services that exist for families, especially for high-risk families with low incomes. Support services are scattered among many different agencies, making it difficult for parents to obtain necessary services and nearly impossible for the government to exert reasonably efficient regulatory controls. Efforts to unify and streamline these services typically meet with strong political opposition, since many of them fall under the authority of different branches and departments of government (Weintraub & Furman, 1987). Contrast the fragmentation of child-care services with the unification of services to children with special needs under PL 99-457 (see the section on special needs above).

Cultural differences in child care have received relatively little attention. In some societies, nonmaternal care is the norm rather than the exception. In these cultures, the mother is not believed to be the sole contributor to the child's development. This is the case, for example, in African American culture. For most of the research on child care reported earlier in this chapter, outcome measures reflected the child's independent competence and ability, such as social and intellectual competence. In other societies, children are not expected to become autonomous but rather to focus on group sharing and cooperation. In such cultures, outcome measures should relate to group orientations rather than to individuals. The cultural diversity of child care philosophies, both for type of care and desired outcomes, have not been sufficiently studied (Friedman, Randolph, & Kochanoff, 2000; Leach, 1997; M. K. Rosenthal, 1999).

In summary, while a great deal of research and practice has been done with respect to child care, we have a long way to go in the United States. The recent federally funded research on the NICHD child care study is an important step in creating a database that encompasses a wider range of children from diverse settings. More work needs to be done to study how to improve child care quality, how to address cultural differences, and how to implement these findings into workable public policies.

---

adults could reserve part of each week for this kind of carefree joyfulness, we would probably be a lot happier with ourselves, both with our successes and our failures.

AWARENESS THROUGH MOVEMENT

Fine Movements of the Hand

Position: Lie on your back on a padded surface or firm bed. Lengthen both of your arms down along your sides. Bend or straighten your knees according to your comfort. Bend your right elbow at 90 degrees so your forearm is perpendicular to floor. (If you are left handed, do all the movements on your left side.) Your hand is directed toward the ceiling, but let your fingers be soft. Your palm faces your feet. If you relax your hand in this position, your fingers will be slightly flexed so that your hand is half closed.

1. Keeping your fingers relaxed, slowly and softly bend your wrist and observe how your fingers extend passively in the direction of your feet as your wrist flexes. Straighten your wrist and observe how your fingers partially close by themselves. Repeat these movements several times slowly and gently, while paying attention to the movements of each individual finger, one at a time.

Co-Regulating with Baby

In some ways, babies of this age seem quite fearless—walking into the street, putting screwdrivers into electrical outlets, sticking fingers into their eyes, and perching precariously at the top of a flight of stairs. Caregivers need to limit the child's access to certain dangerous or precarious areas or objects. This is best accomplished by establishing physical barriers, such as a baby fence across the entrance to basement stairs, or by offering the baby some alternatives for exploration. Although babies of this age understand the meaning of "no" and even come to use it on their own, overuse of negative language by parents ultimately may dilute its effectiveness. Of course, parents do not have to walk around saying "no" all the time. Other common and important prohibitive words include "yucky," "hot," or "that's Mommy's."

The major attractions of the baby's world at this age are adults and containers. Babies want to try out everything the adult does. This may mean trying to talk on the telephone, eat from Dad's plate, sit in Mom's chair at the table instead of the usual high chair, "smoke" Dad's pipe, or "read" the newspaper. While this behavior may seem cute at first, it often gets in the way of household routines and stretches the limits of health and safety. Adults can offer alternatives like toy telephones, feeding the baby first before the adults eat, or just spending time with the baby and allowing the child to play at being grown up.

At this age, babies love to pull things out of and put things into containers. Unfortunately, this could mean kitchen cabinets, fishbowls, detergent boxes, ears, mouths, and eyes. Some parents try to arrange the house so the baby has his or her own drawer, stocked with an array of harmless kitchen gadgets and plastic cups and dishes. The situation is not as easy to handle when the baby decides to tear the pages out of an older brother's favorite book. Toddlers' natural urges to test the limits of their environment are not intentionally negative or malicious in any way. Nevertheless, babies must come to understand the effects their actions have on people around them. The older sibling's angry responses and the adult's prohibitions are part of that process. So are the tears and tantrums that often result.

Babies do not restrict their exploratory activities to inanimate objects. Parts of others' bodies are also fair game. Babies will recklessly pull off your glasses, twist your nose, pull your hair, pull on your necklace, pat you, and even hit you. Toward the end of this developmental period, at 15 to 18 months, babies will do some of these things just to get your attention. Showing off, which I have already discussed, and putting on performances for admiring audiences are also part of trying to attract the attention and laughter of others.

To some extent, babies need to know that you recognize and appreciate them and that you are willing and able to share a laugh with them. It is also important to impose and enforce reasonable limits on what you consider to be overexuberance. This may be particularly true when attention getting begins to look downright mischievous, as in hitting, throwing food, or pulling and tugging.

Social games are still important to the baby, such as peekaboo or "give and take." Babies of this age like to sit on an adult's lap and identify mutual body parts, like touching their own nose and then the adult's. Looking at pictures and books, talking on the telephone with the baby, playing with puppets, and action rhymes like "Pop Goes the Weasel" and "This Little Piggy" are all favorites. Babies love it when you act as a tour guide to the world of the adult. This could involve holding their hands and walking places where they could not go on their own, like up and down stairs or outside. You can pick them up and let them see things that are not visually accessible from their normal viewing height, let them be a "helper" and carry a pot or utensil, or let them listen to your watch ticking (or sounding its alarm, if you have an electronic watch).

Although babies are starting to test the limits of their world, they have not yet fully discovered their own unique individuality, something that occurs in the next stage of development. For these reasons, many parents think that 12 to 18 months is the "best" age for a baby. The next stage, however, brings with it the mastery of the symbol, a genuine turning point in the child's development: the transition from action to thought.

2. Without stretching or straining, slowly bend your wrist backward and notice how your fingers close even more. Return to the neutral position and repeat this several times while paying attention to the movements of each individual finger, one at a time.

3. Alternate between bending your wrist forward and bending it backward, pausing each time you return to the middle or neutral position. Now alternate between dropping your hand forward and slowly bringing it back to the middle and then dropping it backward and slowly bringing it back to the middle. Let your fingers be passive.

4. Lower your arm, rest, and examine the differences you feel between your two hands and arms.

5. Bend your right elbow again so that your forearm is perpendicular to the floor. Slowly rotate your forearm to the right as you bend your wrist backward, and then slowly rotate your forearm to left as you bend your wrist forward. Allow your fingers to move passively.

6. Now do the opposite. Rotate your forearm to the right as you bend your wrist forward and rotate your arm to the left as you bend your wrist backward.

7. Lightly touch and rub your thumb against each of your fingers, one at a time as your wrist remains in the neutral position. Repeat this movement with your wrist bent forward.

8. Lower your arm, rest, and examine the differences you feel between your right and left sides in your hands, arms, and throughout the rest of your body.

Comment: In this lesson we examined how our hands move in connection with our forearms. We also saw how the position of our wrists causes our fingers to flex and extend passively, due to the arrangement of the finger tendons. We performed this lesson with our dominant hands, because it is easiest to pay attention to the hand that we use so often. It is not uncommon for there to be chronic tensions in the hand due to the strains of using tools, driving, writing, typing, and many other activities. Some of you probably noticed such tensions, and were able to relax them. Our hands are capable of extraordinary sensitivity and versatility, and their control depends upon the function of large areas of the brain. Many of you will notice relaxation throughout the entire side of the body of the hand that you worked with.

When infants close and open their hands, their movements resemble making a fist with all the fingers together. In order to grasp most objects, however, our fingers and hands must adjust themselves to fit the shapes of objects, and this requires controlling the individual fingers. Other manipulative actions require even further differentiation, or separate control, of individual fingers, without which we could not type or play the piano. In childhood we also learn how to oppose our thumbs to each of the other fingers. What activities require our being able to oppose the fingers to the thumb? Such activities would probably be impossible for an ape or a younger infant to perform.

Sitting Back from Hands and Knees

Position: Stand on your hands and knees on a padded floor. Be sure your hands are placed under your shoulders and your knees are placed under your hips, shoulder width apart, with right angles at your hip joints.

1. Keeping your right knee on the floor, slide your right foot to the right, that is, to the outside, and then return it to your starting position. Repeat the movement several times very slowly and gently, and without stretching or straining. Let your head hang toward the floor, relax your neck, and allow your hips to shift and your spine and chest to bend along with the movement of your leg. Now, while keeping your right knee on the floor, slide your right foot to the left, that is, to the inside, and then back to the middle. Repeat as before.

2. Rest on your back and sense the differences between the right and left sides of your body.

3. Repeat the movements in step 1, alternating between sliding your right foot to the left and sliding it to the right. Turn your head as if to look over your right shoulder at your foot as your right foot moves to the right. Then turn your head as to look over your left shoulder as you move your right foot to the left. Alternate

moving your foot right and left as you turn your head to look at the foot as it moves to the right and left.

4. Rest on your back and sense the differences between the right and left sides of your body.

5. Repeat step 3, but now turn your head to look over your right shoulder at your right foot when it moves to the left, and turn your head to look over your left shoulder as your foot moves to the right.

6. Rest on your back and sense the differences between the right and left sides of your body.

7. Repeat steps 1–6, doing all the movements with the left leg.

8. Rest on your back and sense the differences between the right and left sides of your body.

9. Stand on your hands and knees and alternate looking up toward the ceiling, and then down toward the floor. Do this slowly and gently, without straining or stretching. When you look down toward the floor, curve your entire spine like a cat, lifting the middle of your back toward the ceiling. When you lift your eyes and head, arch your entire spine so that your chest and abdomen hang like a hammock toward the floor. Continue, flexing and extending your toes at the same time. You will bend your feet to stand on the toes when you look up, and you will straighten your feet backward, so that your toenails touch the floor, when you look downward.

10. Rest on your back and sense the differences between the right and left sides of your body.

11. Stand on your hands and knees with your knees a little father apart. Bring your right foot to the left and then back to the middle. Gradually bring your foot enough to the inside so that can rest on the floor next to your left knee, and then return it to the middle. Leave your right foot on the floor near to your left knee. While keeping your right foot in that position, move back as if to sit behind your right lower leg, and then come forward again. Lower your head each time you sit back, and lift your head each time you come forward. In order to sit back you will need to lift one of your hands off the floor. Which one?

12. Rest on your back and sense the differences between the right and left sides of your body.

13. Repeat step 11 and sit back behind your left leg.

14. Now alternate sitting back behind one leg and the other, and alternate the hand you lift. Look up when you go back to sit and look down when you come forward onto your hands and knees. Gradually learn to sit fully behind each leg, without resting either hand on the floor, and always come forward to stand on your hands and knees before sitting back behind the opposite leg.

15. Rest on your back and sense the differences in how your body contacts the floor, and notice if your breathing is different. When you stand up, notice how your posture and walking are different. Are your movements easier and more supple?

Comment: During those months when babies are active crawlers, they are capable of great agility and maneuverability when standing on their hands and knees. They can sit up easily from this position, as you learned to do in this lesson. They can also use the movement of crawling and sitting back to manage the difficult task of going down stairs. Many people have extolled the benefits of crawling movements for adults for its effects on your muscles, joints, and brains. This lesson demonstrates some other aspects of the hands-and-knees position that give both the baby and the adult new possibilities of action.

SUMMARY

Physical and Motor Development

- At this age, infants can adjust their locomotor movements to the characteristics of the surface. They will not cross a wavy surface or downward-sloping surface while standing. They perform different actions on objects when the table is hard than when it is soft.

- Spoon use becomes more efficient during this period, including corrections for the amount of food on the spoon and entering the mouth.

Cognitive Development

- Infants are experimenting to find new ways to cause similar effects, such as trying alternate strategies to reach goals through trial-and-error exploration.

- Infants can now conceive of higher-order categories, such as "animals" and "vehicles."

Emotional Development

- Infants are getting better at making good feelings last and controlling negative feelings.

- Infants know how to tease adults by varying the patterns of normal routines or stopping just short of misbehavior and laughing.

Social and Language Development

- Languages have properties that distinguish them from other forms of communication.

- Functional theories of language are discussed at length, and most of the recent research is on how infants use language to communicate.

- At this age, infants develop both linguistic and gestural referential communication, naming, gestural combinations, and the ability to coordinate their communications with those of the adult.

- Infants typically comprehend more than they can produce, although the gap between comprehension and production is much larger for some infants than for others.

- Particular forms of adult response seem more conducive to infant language development than others.

- Infants are able to metacommunicate, that is, to communicate about their relationships with others and change the way in which the communication occurs.

- Linguistic communication is more likely in certain situations, and gestural communication is more likely in others.

- Peer interaction is more focused on direct actions on objects, while adult-infant interaction has more referential communication about objects.

- Peers are more likely to get along better when one of the parents is not around.

Family and Society

- Family members face a difficult period of adapting to an infant with special needs.

- The effect of a disability on the parent-infant interaction depends on the severity of the disability and how long it persists. In general, parents tend to adapt their behavior to suit the needs of the infant with special needs.

- Families are encouraged to seek support services to help with coping and education.

- Day care has different effects on infants and families, depending on the age of the child upon entering day care, the parent's feelings about day care and returning to work, and the quality of care.

Applications: Social Policy and Day Care

- There is a growing gap between the need for day care in the United States and public support for it.

- The role of the researcher in forming public policy has been limited by the belief that families should be self-sufficient and by the fact that child care services are fragmented.

- Cultural differences have not been adequately considered in research on and planning social policy for child care.

 ON THE WEB

www.nichcy.org This web site of the National Information Center for Children and Youth with Disabilities (NICHY) offers information on practically everything relating to children with disabilities: specific disabilities, early intervention, family issues, disability organizations, and so on. It includes news updates, downloadable publications, answers to frequently asked questions, and many other resources in a user-friendly format. Personal replies and publications in Spanish are also available.

www.dssc.org This web site of the Disabilities Studies and Services Center (DSSC) offers links to a variety of sites on different programs such as NICHY, the Federal Resource Center for Special

Education, and others. It also has four search engines for bibliographic, organization, model program, and conference databases.

www.babyhood.com "This site is dedicated to providing information about babies. Unlike many parenting resources on the Web, at Babyhood™ we limit our focus to infants (birth to about 24 months) in order to provide the best possible coverage of the information new and prospective parents need."

www.babycenter.com The BabyCenter web site provides information on pregnancy, parenting, child development, and nutrition. This site is updated weekly with new information and articles to help you raise your child.

GLOSSARY

Conventional actions Actions that represent another action or an object using some type of ritualized manner of expression, such as waving or saying "bye-bye."

Displacement The property of language to express concrete and abstract ideas and describe objects that are not physically in the speaker's presence.

Infants with special needs Infants who suffer from prenatal and postnatal deficits, deformities, and developmental delays that create additional challenges for them and their families.

Intersubjectivity Acting cooperatively and deliberately involving others as meaningful agents in one's actions.

Joint attention When communicating partners direct their attention to the same object or topic.

Metacommunicative events Communicative acts that refer to the relationship between partners rather than to the world outside the relationship.

Overextension Applying a single word to refer to more objects and situations than it normally refers to in adult speech.

Pragmatics The study of the functional uses of language, as opposed to the structural (grammatical) properties of language.

Productivity The ability of language to express multiple meanings using a small number of words simply by rearranging the word order in novel ways.

Semanticity The ability of language to carry meaning for both speaker and listener.

Situational constraints Elements of the context of a stimulus or event that determine a child's response to that event. In interactions with other children, for example, the peer's age, sex, and familiarity to the infant; the infant's experience interacting with other children; and the caregiver's location are all situational constraints that may determine the quality of the peer-infant interaction.

Syntax The structure or grammar of a language; the rules that determine word order.

Tertiary circular reactions Refers to the fact that new means are invented to achieve goals by trial-and-error experimentation.

10

Eighteen to Twenty-Four Months

CHAPTER OVERVIEW AND OUTLINE

Motor and Cognitive Development

Can babies of this age use a toilet and sleep through the night? What do symbolic thought and pretend play contribute to the child's thinking? What are the advances in the conception of self at this age? What is early childhood autism, and how does it affect the self at this age?

Emotional Development

How do symbolic thought and the sense of self affect the infant's emotions? How do children of this age cope with stress? How do they deal with separations from parents?

Social and Language Development

What are the patterns of parent-infant communication at this age? What is the best way to discipline infants? How do children begin to combine words? What are some individual differences in language development? How can adults facilitate language development? How do infants interact with peers?

Family and Society

What kinds of support and intervention programs are available for families with infants? What is the impact of these programs?

Applications: Poverty and Risk

How does poverty affect infant development? What are the causes and preventions of poverty?

This age period sees a change in the realm of cognition. Babies are now beginning to think; they are able to plan things out before acting, thus eliminating much of the trial-and-error quality seen in the last stage. The ability to think without having to act is at the root of our capacity to plan, dream, and solve complex problems. Infants of this age are beginning to establish a sense of themselves as individuals with intentions, rights, and possessions, an "I." With this sense of an "I" come the emotions of defiance and negativism, which bring the 2-year-old into direct conflict with caregivers, siblings, and peers. Self-awareness often can bring self-doubt and feelings of shame as well as feelings of pride. Infants need to discover how to handle the new experience of personal autonomy and yet still maintain close and affectionate ties with the people around them.

We will see how language develops rapidly during this period, as infants begin to express more-complex ideas in sentences rather than single words and peer relationships become more complex and more verbal. Finally, we will discuss issues related to the family in society, including the effects of social supports and intervention programs on parenting and the effects of poverty on family and infant development.

Motor and Cognitive Development

Motor Advances

Infants' locomotion is so stable that they now prefer to be independent walkers and may resist holding an adult's hand. They easily make the transition from walking to running, so by this age, most infants can run reasonably well (Forrester, Phillips, & Clark, 1993). It is not until the third year that infants living in cultures where there are homes with stairs can negotiate them on their own, however. Most 18-month-olds can feed themselves, and most prefer to manage their own food. Self-dressing is

well under way by 18 months, and many infants will be able to put on their own coats, shoes, and socks by the time they are 2 years old.

One of the big advances, from a parent's perspective, that is likely to occur at this age is toilet learning. Based on findings from some African countries in which toilet learning begins in the first month of life (see Chapter 6), it is likely that infants have the potential to regulate their bowels and bladders well before they are trained in most Western countries. So why should we wait so long? The reason is that in these African societies, there is almost constant physical contact between the mother and infant, enabling mothers to detect the signs of impending elimination. In societies where physical contact is at a minimum, infants must signal their intentions across a distance. Typically, this means using words. So the trick in Western societies is to help the child associate the need to eliminate with a verbal communication about being taken to the toilet. Toilet learning in industrialized cultures is most likely to begin between 18 months and 3 years, although it may take up to a year to complete.

Another aspect of physical development that concerns parents is the child's sleep patterns. Most infants of this age are still napping during the afternoon, and they can sleep through most of the night. It is not uncommon, however, for infants between the age of 1 and 3 years to wake occasionally at night (Richards, 1977). Out of 77 babies in one study, 29 were waking during the night at 1 year. The style in which parents handled the situation, such as how much the baby was encouraged to "cry it out," did not affect whether the baby woke at night. Families had tried different techniques to handle the problem: verbal battles with the babies; sleep deprivation by keeping the baby awake during the day; and, as a last resort, the modification of parental lifestyles so the parents could spend several hours awake with the baby at 3 A.M.

Since none of these parental methods seemed to change the babies, what accounts for night waking? Babies who woke at night at 1 year had been born after longer labors and were more wakeful—but more fussy—during the first 10 days of life. At 3 years, these same children slept through the night, but it was still difficult to get them to sleep (Blurton-Jones, N., Ferreira, C., Brown, M., & MacDonald, 1978; Richards, 1977). The findings suggest that night waking may result from a bio-logical predisposition. Some infants are night owls, probably from birth or even prenatally, and this pattern tends to persist for many years (Cofer et al., 1999; see also the discussion of sleeping in Chapter 5). Although no documented method exists for changing sleep patterns, some methods are available (see Chapter 5) to train children to sleep independently from parents. These methods, however, do not guarantee that the child will remain asleep throughout the night. It may help parents to know that they do not have the only baby who cannot sleep through the night and that they are probably not the cause of the problem.

Cognitive Development: Symbolic Play

Piaget has referred to the sixth and final stage of sensorimotor development as the *invention of new means through mental combinations.* In the previous stage, the infant could experiment with new ways of making things happen. However, all this trial and error happened in the sphere of real action. The child had to actually do all the alternatives to get to the goal. This is one reason why, in the last chapter, I remarked on the sheer energy of the toddler in Stage V.

All this changes in Stage VI, because children no longer have to physically carry out the actions: they can think about the possible paths to a goal, eliminate the most improbable ones, and only then act. According to Piaget (1952), the child's first thoughts are internalized action sequences. Babies now can find objects after any number of visible or invisible displacements; they can go around a detour to get at something.

At the heart of thinking is the **symbol,** a representation of a thing or event that is conventionally shared among the members of a community. A road sign is a symbol of what lies ahead, such as a curve or a steep hill or an intersection. A word is a symbol for the object it represents. A plastic bowl can be used for eating, or it can be used symbolically when a child pretends that the bowl is a hat or a boat.

David Young-Wolff/PhotoEdit

Exploring objects that are challenging to understand leads to a sense of mastery and personal competence. Exploratory play also contributes to cognitive development. At this age, play becomes more symbolic and includes pretending.

OBSERVATIONS

Stage VI Behavior (Piaget, 1962, pp. 121 and 124)

Observation 10.1

At 1;6(30) Jacqueline said cry, cry to her dog and herself imitated the sound of crying. On the following days she made her bear, a duck, etc., cry. At 1;7(1) she made her hat cry.

Observation 10.2

At 1;8(30) Jacqueline stroked her mother's hair, saying pussy, pussy. At 1;9(0) she saw a shell and said cup. The next day, seeing the same shell she said glass, then cup, then hat and finally boat in the water.

Symbols appear only gradually in children's repertoires. At first, children represent objects by performing some action related to the objects and physically similar to the represented objects, like moving one's open hand through the air to represent an airplane or a bird (Ungerer, Zelazo, Kearsley, & O'Leary, 1981). Later, symbols become arbitrary in the sense that the form of the symbol bears no physical resemblance to the thing it represents. The word "airplane," for example, neither looks nor sounds like an airplane. Words as verbal symbols are arbitrary in this sense, but they are also a form of **conventional communication:** how and when they are used in communication is not arbitrary but bound by the rules of meaning and grammar of the linguistic community. See the observations of verbal symbol usage that Piaget made on his own children in Observations 10.1 and 10.2.

In Stage VI, the symbol becomes detached from its original context of meaning and becomes something that, like objects, can be manipulated and explored. Several researchers have developed systems for classifying different levels of symbolic play (see Tables 10.1 and 10.2). Although there is no clearcut age at which infants begin to display a particular level of play, at 18 months, most babies are entering some of the early stages of pretend play. By the age of 2 years, most children can execute complex sequences of play requiring multiple symbols and advance planning, such as pretending to cook a whole meal using blocks and pegs to substitute for food and utensils (Belsky & Most, 1981; Nicolich, 1977; Ungerer et al., 1981).

One of the favorite forms of play of children this age involves containers. Children love to put things into containers, and they also enjoy nesting-cup toys, in which smaller cups are placed inside successively larger cups. By the age of 18 months, infants understand the concept of containment, as shown by the following experiment. Infants were shown videotapes of sand being poured into cups and tubes. In some cases, the sand poured right through the container and came out the other side (violation condition). In other cases, the sand did not go through the container but filled it up to the rim (nonviolation condition). Only infants older than 18 months looked longer at the violation condition, suggesting that they found it unusual (A. J. Caron, Caron, & Antell, 1988).

On the other hand, when actually presented with a set of nesting cups, children of this age period had trouble stacking them without errors. The infants might combine one or two cups correctly. Then they take a small cup and place it at the large end of their stack. Typically, infants under 24 months of age try to force the cup to fit, perhaps because they see that it might fit if the bottom cup were not in the way. At this point, most infants of this age will actually take the cups apart and start all over again or else just give up; they do not attempt alternative solutions, such as simply moving the cup to the other end of the stack (DeLoache, Sugarman, & Brown, 1985).

Table 10.1   Level of Symbolic Play

1. Presymbolic acts, such as combing one's own hair
2. Self-symbolic acts, such as pretending to be sleeping
3. Object-centered symbolic games, such as feeding a doll
4. Object-combination symbolic games, such as taking a baby doll and a teddy bear for a walk
5. Planned symbolic games, such as saying, "Let's cook dinner," before actually doing it

Source: L. M. Nicolich, Beyond sensorimotor intelligence: Assessment of symbolic maturity through analysis of pretend play, 1977. *Merrill-Palmer Quarterly, 23,* 89–100.

Table 10.2 Levels of Exploratory and Pretend Play

1. Mouthing: Indiscriminate mouthing of materials

2. Simple manipulation: Visually guided manipulation (excluding indiscriminate banging and shaking) at least 5 seconds in duration that cannot be coded in any other category (e.g., turn over an object, touch and look at an object)

3. Functional: Visually guided manipulation that is particularly appropriate for a certain object and involves the intentional extraction of some unique piece of information (e.g., turn dial on toy phone, squeeze piece of foam rubber, flip antenna of Buzy Bee toy, spin wheels on cart, roll cart on wheels).

4. Relational: Bringing together and integrating two or more materials in an inappropriate manner, that is, in a manner not initially intended by the manufacturer (e.g., set cradle on phone, touch spoon to stick)

5. Functional-relational: Bringing together and integrating two objects in an appropriate manner, that is, in a manner intended by the manufacturer (e.g., set cup on saucer, place peg in hole of pegboard, mount spool on shaft of cart).

6. Enactive naming: Approximate pretense activity but without confirming evidence of actual pretense behavior (e.g., touch cup to lip without making drinking sounds, tilting head back, or tipping cup; raise phone receiver in proximity of ear without making talking sounds; touch brush to doll's hair without making combing motions).

7. Pretend self: Pretense behavior directed toward self in which pretense is apparent (e.g., raise cup to lip; tip cup, make drinking sounds, or tilt head; stroke own hair with miniature brush; raise phone receiver to ear and vocalize).

8. Pretend other: Pretense behavior directed away from child toward other (e.g., feed doll with spoon, bottle, or cup; brush doll's hair; push car on floor and make car noise).

9. Substitution: Using a "meaningless" object in a creative or imaginative manner (e.g., drink from seashell; feed baby with stick as "bottle") or using an object in a pretense act in a way that differs from how it has previously been used by the child (e.g., use hairbrush to brush teeth after already using it as a hairbrush on self or other).

10. Sequence pretend: Repetition of a single pretense act with minor variation (e.g., drink from bottle, give doll drink; pour into cup, pour into plate) or linking together different pretense schemes (e.g., stir in cup, then drink; put doll in cradle, then kiss good night).

11. Sequence pretend substitution: Same as sequence pretend except using an object substitution within sequence (e.g., put doll in cradle, cover with green felt piece as "blanket"; feed self with spoon, then with stick).

12. Double substitution: Pretense play in which two materials are transformed, within a single act, into something they are not in reality (e.g., treat peg as doll and a piece of green felt as a blanket and cover peg with felt and say "night-night"; treat stick as person and seashell as cup and give stick a drink).

Source: J. Belsky & R. K. Most, From exploration to play: A cross-sectional study of infant free play behavior, 1981, p. 635. *Developmental Psychology, 17,* 630–639. Copyright © 1981 by the American Psychological Association. Reprinted with permission.

These studies show that even though infants recognize what is necessary for containment, they have trouble organizing their actions when a series of containers is present. This is similar to the A-not-B error in Stage IV, in which infants understand that objects exist when out of sight but persist in searching for them where they were last seen. If they fail, they give up the search. It is not until about 2½ years that infants are able to understand that two objects could have multiple relationships with each other: a cup that will not fit when placed on top of another might fit when placed under it. When younger infants place one cup on top of another, they fail to realize that the order of placement of the same two cups could be reversed.

Is It Appropriate for Infants to Watch Television?

During the previous age period, infants could imitate live adults doing complex sequences of action. During the period between 18 and 24 months, infants begin to be more interested in television and can imitate television sequences as easily as live sequences (Barr & Hayne, 1999). At this age children become fond of programs like *Teletubbies.* Four brightly colored characters—Tinky Winky, Dipsy, Laa-Laa, and Po—live in Tubbyland. They resemble chubby children in blanket sleepers with television screens on their stomachs and television antennae on their heads. Tubbyland has green hills with artificial flowers and a sun in the sky with a baby face in the center. The tubbies' homes have slides, a living vacuum named Noo Noo, and a machine for making "tubby custard." There is a lot of repetition of simple actions. The tubbies speak motherese in a high-pitched voice using mispronounced words. Sometimes there are video clips on the tummy television screens, like a child washing a car, watching rabbits, or packing for a trip.

Many parents and child advocates are strongly against the show. They claim television is not an appropriate stimulation for infants, who would be better off actively exploring their world. The critics think it will create television addicts and sedentary children. In North America, excessive television watching by children takes up time that could be used for other activities and for social interaction. Web sites accuse the show of everything from communism to devil worship. Those who market the show insist that it can be effective in language acquisition and making children comfortable with technology. They think the show creates a happy fantasy that can be a respite from the frustration of being a toddler. PBS, which airs the show in the United States, recommends that children watch it with an adult.

Because there is no published research on the effects of television on infants of this age, I asked one of the assistants who helped me do the research on this book to do a brief qualitative study. She unobtrusively observed three middle-class Caucasian American children, her 21-month-old nephew and her two nieces, 25 and 30 months, while watching the show. The children seemed to identify with the face in the sun (not with the tubbies!). They pointed and said "baby" and laughed. All three children wandered around during the program, but they paid attention at least some of the time. When watching with an adult, the children were more likely to name objects and to laugh appropriately than when watching alone.

Although this is not a representative sample, it suggests that these children are neither inactive nor couch potatoes. And, as PBS recommends, they did better when watching with an adult. Children of this age should not be left alone in front of the television. If parents choose to let their child watch and use it interactively, it may be an enjoy-able learning experience. And, like all television, the user and the user's parents have a choice of whether to turn it on or to leave it off. Most child development experts advocate that parents should carefully monitor children's television viewing and limit the amount of time children are allowed to watch.

Development of the Ability to Categorize Objects

Even during the first year of life, infants begin to organize the information they see and hear into meaningful groups of items or events. At first, this is done at the level of simple categories: faces, birds, cars, and the like. Next, infants group items into higher-level categories, such as animals and vehicles. By 18 months, another important principle of categorization emerges: categorization by sequential order, or by cause and effect. Infants at this age remember items and events better if they are organized into a sequence. For example, in a bath sequence with a teddy bear, the bear's shirt is removed, the bear is put into the tub, the bear is washed, and then it is dried. Infants can remember exact sequences up to 2 weeks later whether they are familiar sequences, such as the bath, or unfamiliar, such as events related to a train ride. Some evidence suggests that even when events are not related naturally, infants will remember them by the sequence in which the events were observed (Bauer & Dow, 1994).

When concepts and memories are organized in terms of how the events are related to each other in time, this kind of conceptual organization is called a **script** (K. Nelson, 1978). Scripts become increasingly important as ways of representing complex aspects of reality, such as remembering to get dressed, eat, get in the car, get out of the car, walk inside the day care center, take off one's coat, and go to one's assigned area. All of the separate events required to get from bed to the day care center would be difficult to remember if they were not organized into expectable sequences of events. Thus, although 2-year-olds cannot memorize long lists of new words or concepts, they can execute complex sequences of related actions.

The Sense of an Existential Self

From early in the first year, infants can differentiate their own feelings and movements from those of others, and they can distinguish their own acts relative to the environment. This is called the **ecological self** (see Chapter 6). Beginning at 9 months, infants have a sense of their own subjectivity, but they do not yet have a concept of "I."

With the advent of script-based conceptual memory, infants are now able to categorize and remember sequences of events that are most familiar to them. Among such sequences are the actions performed and the feelings experienced by the children themselves. Because of script-based memory, the infant at 18 months is beginning to put all of these self-experiences together into a whole picture of himself or herself as someone who can be recognized and distinguished, as a whole person, from other people. This ability for self-recognition is called the **existential self.** Beginning at 18 months, the infants can say things like "I cry" or "I tired," indicating that not only does the child have the subjective sense of one who gets tired, but he or she can also combine that with a pronoun indicating a person who has or possesses that feeling. Children's earliest linguistic references to the self are with the word *I* rather than words like *me, mine,* or *my.* When using *I,* children express their intended actions ("I do it," "I hold it"), make requests or proposals ("I wanna play with that one"), or state a proposition ("I have the crayon"). They rarely use the word *you* (Imbens-Bailey & Pan, 1998).

One method that has been developed to study the emergence of the existential self is to observe infants' reactions to their own mirror images (M. Lewis & Brooks-Gunn, 1979). Initially, infants are put in front of the mirror for a few minutes. Even young infants will show interest in the mirror image, touching the mirror or parts of themselves, smiling and showing other emotions. After this period of free play with the mirror, the experimenter removes the infants and pretends to wipe their faces with a cloth. In actuality, the experimenter dabs a bit of red rouge on the infants' noses without the babies realizing it. Then, the babies are returned to the mirror. If the infants recognize that the mirror image is of themselves, they will touch their own noses, but not the mirror image nose. By 24 months, the majority of children will touch their own noses after seeing the red spot. Table 10.3 describes the steps in the infant's development of self-recognition.

Recall that babies during the first year are able to form simple mental categories: they can recognize male versus female faces and infants compared to older children and adults. In the next chapter, I will discuss the development of the **categorical self,** or self-concept, which emerges when children can identify their own membership in one or more conceptual categories, such as "I am a boy," "I am a brother," and "I am not a baby" (Harter, 1983). Curiously, it takes until the third year for this conceptual skill to be applied to the self. One research study on the application of such concepts to self and to mother gives some insight into why it takes babies so long to discover themselves.

Elizabeth Crews

By 18 months, most babies can recognize their own image in a mirror.

Table 10.3   Stages in the Development of the Existential Self, the Ability to Recognize the Physical Features of the Self

Behaviors	Approximate Age in Months	Interpretation
Emergence of Self as Subject, as Active, Independent, Causal Agent		
I. Interest in mirror image; regards, approaches, touches, smiles, vocalizes. Does not differentially respond to self vs. other in mirror, videotape, or pictorial representation.	5–8	No evidence that self is perceived as a causal agent, independent of others. No featural differentiation between self and other.
II. Understands nature of reflective surface: contingency play, imitation, rhythmic movements, bouncing, waving; can locate objects in space, attached to body. Differentiates between contingent and noncontingent videotape representations of self.	9–12	Active agent in space emerges, awareness of cause-effect relationship between own body movements and moving visual image.
III. Uses mirror to locate people/objects in space. Reaches toward person, not image, and reaches toward object not attached to body. Distinguishes between self-movement and movement of others on videotape.	12–15	Self-other differentiation with regard to agency. Appreciates self as an active, independent, agent separate from others, who can also cause his or her own movements in space.
Emergence of Self as an Object of One's Knowledge		
IV. In mirror and videotape, demonstrates mark-directed behavior, sees image and touches rouge on nose. Points to self. Distinguishes between self and other in pictorial representation and videotape.	15–18	Featural recognition of self; internal schema for own face that can be compared to external visual image.
V. Verbal labeling: infant can state name, attach appropriate personal pronoun to own image in mirror. Can distinguish self from same-gender infant in pictures and can label self.	18–24	Appreciation that one has unique featural attributes that can be verbally labeled as the self.

Source: S. Harter, Developmental perspectives on the self-system, 1983, p. 283. In E. M. Hetherington (Ed.), *Handbook of child psychology: Socialization, personality, and social development* (Vol. 4), pp. 265–290. New York: Wiley. Reprinted by permission of John Wiley & Sons, Inc.

In this study (Pipp, Fischer, & Jennings, 1987), infants were given the standard rouge test on themselves and also on their mothers. A number of different self- and other recognition tasks were given to the children as well (see Table 10.4). (As an aside, these tasks are great fun to do with babies of this age and would work as exercises for co-regulating with baby.) In addition to these recognition tasks, infants were asked to perform actions either on a doll, on themselves, or on their mothers. An example would be pretend feeding the doll or self or pretend feeding the mother.

The results show that before 18 months, infants are able to correctly recognize their mothers and respond correctly to questions about mother at earlier ages than those at which they can recognize and respond to questions about themselves. This is consistent with studies of concept development done in the first year: infants are able to recognize the common features of objects and group them into categories. Before 18 months, on the other hand, infants are more successful at performing actions on themselves or the doll than on the mother. After 18 months, infants were equally adept at describing self and mother.

In the previous age period, infants preferred to imitate intentional rather than mechanical actions of adults. After 18 months, infants are also beginning to reason about other people's desires. In one study, 14- and 18-month-old infants watched while

Table 10.4   Self- and Other Physical Feature Recognition Tasks

Infant Version	Mother Version
Infant touches own nose with rouge after seeing self in mirror.	Infant touches mother's nose with rouge after seeing mother in mirror.
"Where's [child's name]?"	"Where's Mommy?"
"Who's that?" (said while pointing to child).	"Who's that?" (said while pointing to mother).
"Whose shoe is that?" (said while pointing to child's shoe).	"Whose shoe is that? "(said while pointing to mother's shoe).
"Are you a boy or a girl?"	"Is Mommy a boy or a girl?"

Source: S. Pipp, K. W. Fischer, & S. Jennings, Acquisition of self- and mother knowledge in infancy, 1986, p. 90. *Developmental Psychology, 23,* 86–96.

adults ate either crackers or broccoli. For some babies at each age, the adult said "Mmm," making a happy expression, when eating the crackers, and "Eeew," making a disgusted expression, when eating the broccoli. For other infants, the adult acted as if she liked the broccoli but not the crackers. The adult then asked the infants to offer her one or the other type of food. Fourteen-month-olds offered the adult only crackers, assuming that the adult would like what the child liked, regardless of the adult's expressed preferences. The 18-month-olds, on the other hand, offered whichever food the adult seemed to prefer. This means the older infants were beginning to be aware of the psychological desires of the adult and respond appropriately (Repacholi & Gopnik, 1997). These older babies realized that their own preferences were not necessarily the same as the adult's, a major advance in distinguishing between the internal experiences of self and other.

Infants differ in their level of self- and other understanding, however. Some infants are better at the task of self- and other recognition. These infants notice more details and can respond with more complex answers to the questions in Table 10.4. These more self- and other-aware infants are more securely attached to their mothers and fathers, show more concern for other's distress, they can coordinate mirror image imitation, and are more competent in peer play (Asendorpf & Baudonniere, 1993; Asendorph, Warkentin, & Baudonniere, 1996; Pipp, Easterbrooks, & Brown, 1993; Pipp, Easterbrooks, & Harmon, 1992; Zahn-Waxler, Radke-Yarrow, Wagner, & Chapman, 1992). These studies suggest that positive social relationships are likely to enhance one's understanding of oneself

and one's relationships to others. Other research shows that children who reacted with greater distress to inoculations during the first year of life were more likely to be able to recognize themselves in the mirror at 18 months than infants with who reacted with less distress during the first year. This finding suggests that infants who are more sensitive to their internal experiences are more aware of themselves at this age (M. Lewis & Ramsey, 1997).

In summary, cognitive advances at this age set the stage for a major transformation in the infant's sense of self. The experience of the past 6 or 8 months, of feeling one's own subjectivity as a participant, was a necessary precursor to the ability to recognize the self in the mirror and to distinguish self from other. There is now an "I" in the infant's vocabulary and also in the infant's conscious awareness. Infants who have had more opportunity to focus on their own internal experience and to appreciate the experiences of others will acquire an existential self earlier.

Infantile Autism: A Disturbance of Self and Relationships

Some children are slower to develop an existential self than others, but they still fall into the range of typical development. A small group of children, however, fail to develop an existential self: children who are diagnosed with **autism**. Autism is a developmental psychopathology with symptoms that include impaired ability to interact socially, speech and language deficits, and unusual movements of the body. About two to four times as many males as females are diagnosed with autism, which is believed to occur in about 1 in 1,000 individuals (Ozonoff and South, 2000). Autism is discussed here because it may be reliably diagnosed during this age period, although some research to be reviewed below suggests that it may be possible to diagnose autism even earlier.

Autistic children have a difficult time establishing coordinated joint attention with others, and therefore they are not able to enter into early forms of intersubjectivity by which typically developing infants acquire an understanding about relationships, self, and others. Autistic infants do not use social referencing or affective sharing, do not respond appropriately to the desires or distress of others, are less distressed at separation from mothers, are less likely to imitate others, do not pretend, and are unlikely to initiate social interaction. When they talk, it is typically in monologues, and they have a difficult time letting others contribute to the conversation. By the time typically developing infants are 18 months old, they have established a sense of an existential self and existential other. It is quite likely that many autistic children never develop this ability (Charman et al., 1997; Hobson, 1990; 1993; Ozonoff & South, 2000; Sigman & Kasari, 1995; Sigman & Ruskin, 1999; Tanguay, 1990; Trevarthen, Aitken, Papoudi, & Robarts, 1998).

On the other hand, autistic children can develop secure attachments with their mothers (Ozonoff & South, 2000). They can use pointing and requesting gestures to ask for what they want, even though they may have a difficult time in establishing coordinated joint attention (Camaioni, Perucchini, Muratori, & Milone, 1997). They can also be more advanced in some perceptual and object-related skills. They can imitate object-related tasks better than typically developing children but have a difficult time imitating facial expressions, vocalizations, and social movements.

Research has shown that autistic children differ from both typically developing children and children with other developmental disorders. Compared to children who are either hearing impaired, language impaired, or mentally retarded, or who have no disorders, 3-to-6-year-old autistic children are less likely to be able to perform motor imitation—such as imitating stirring a cup with a spoon, talking on a toy telephone, giving a drink to a toy animal, touching one's nose, or raising an arm. Autistic children's play is less likely to be symbolic and more likely to be aggressive or self-stimulatory and they are less likely to approach peers to initiate social play. Finally, autistic children are more likely to use toys in ways different from their appropriate functions, such as banging a toy telephone rather than pretending to talk (Heimann, Ullstadius, Dahlgren, & Gillberg, 1992; Sigman & Ruskin, 1999; W. L. Stone, Lemanek, Fishel, Fernandez, & Altemeier, 1990). On the other hand, they can acquire pretend play when adults use guided participation strategies (see the "Social Development" section in this chapter).

One of the more unusual features of a small number of autistic children is that they may be exceptional in one specific area. Some autistic children can solve remarkably complicated mathematical calculations in their heads much faster than any computer can do it. Some are gifted artists but draw only one subject, such as public buildings and monuments. Some have specialized knowledge in an odd area such as plumbing fixtures or animal classifications. The popular 1988 movie *Rain Man* starred Dustin Hoffman as an autistic adult who had exceptional abilities in arithmetic and baseball statistics but was unable to relate in ordinary ways to other people. It is important to remember, however, that autism covers a wide spectrum of symptoms and only a few autistic individuals will behave like *Rain Man*.

Autism is very difficult to treat. In the most severe cases, individuals may remain institutionalized all their life (as in *Rain Man*). Others, known as high-functioning autistics, have been able to hold jobs and create a life for themselves. One autistic adult, Temple Grandin, has become a well-known agricultural engineer and has written her autobiography (Grandin & Scariano, 1986). Another autistic adult, Donna Williams, has also written a series of books about her life (Williams, 1999), which was marked with abuse and neglect in addition to autism. The prognosis for most autistic children, however, is that they will change little and acquire only minimal social skills (limited receptiveness to others, socialization to rules) and self-care (Harty, 1990; Lelorde, Barthelemy, Martineau, & Bruneau, 1991). Since treatments for autism occur in later childhood, they are beyond the scope of this book.

A wide variety of treatments are available, however, with wide differences in their claims for success. Some people think autism can be cured while others believe that treatment can only improve the quality of life for autistic individuals and help their families to understand the unique characteristics and contributions of people with autism (Trevarthen et al., 1998).

Autism is believed to have its origins in early infancy and possibly prenatal development. It is known to be associated with some genetic and chromosomal abnormalities and may result from brain and other physiological problems that emerge during early development. These include abnormalities in the limbic system, the auditory region of the brain stem, and myelin pathologies (Herault, Martineau, Petit, & Perrot, 1994; Kemper & Bauman, 1993; Singh, Warren, Odell, Warren, & Cole, 1993; Trevarthen et al., 1998; Wong & Wong, 1991).

Even though autism originates in early infancy, it typically is not diagnosed until children are between 4 and 5 years of age. One reason for this is the low incidence of the disorder (5 per 10,000 children). In addition, the symptoms change with age and may overlap with other problems such as hearing and speech disorders. If autism could be diagnosed earlier, preventive and more successful treatments might be possible. Recently, some breakthroughs in the early diagnosis of autism have occurred.

The methodology used by the researchers involves comparing autistic children, diagnosed at age 4 or 5 years, with nonautistic children. The researchers search for records of these children's development before the age at which they were diagnosed. Past medical records, parent interviews and reports, home videos of children's first-year birthday parties, and various other records have all been searched for data. Although these data sources are not always reliable, a consistent pattern of findings is beginning to emerge.

By the age of 18 months, there are clear signs of difference between typically developing and autistic children. One study discovered four behaviors that, if they occurred together in the same 1-year-old child, led to a correct classification of these children as later diagnosed with autism. These behaviors were a lack of pointing, of showing objects, of looking at others, and of orienting to their name. Another

study found that children with two or more of the following symptoms at 18 months were most likely to be diagnosed as autistic at 30 months: a lack of pretend play, a lack of pointing, a lack of interest in social relationships, an absence of social play, and an inability to establish joint attention with the caregiver. Specialists recommend that an 18-month-old who shows this combination of symptoms should be referred to a specialist in autistic assessment for possible diagnosis and treatment (Adrien et al., 1993; Baron-Cohen, Allen, & Gillberg, 1992; Osterling & Dawson, 1994; Rogers & DiLalla, 1990).

Many of these signs of early autism are based on small sample research and anecdotal evidence. An alternative method is to sample a large randomly chosen population of infants at 18 months, assess them on a few chosen criteria, and then determine whether they later develop autism. A study of 16,000 children was done in England. At 18 months, all the children were assessed for ability to point, to engage in social communication, and to pretend play. Twelve out of the 16,000 children failed all three of these tests, and of these, ten were diagnosed as autistic at 3½ years of age. Of the children who failed one or two of the items, none was later diagnosed as autistic. In spite of the small numbers of autistic children that appeared in the sample, the three factors were highly predictive of autistic symptoms in early childhood (Baron-Cohen, Cox, Baird, Sweettenham, & Nightingale, 1996).

This large population study illustrates the difficulty of doing research on the early screening of autism. Autistic children make up a small percentage of the population, so many thousands of children have to be tested. This is extremely costly and time consuming. However, large population research and small sample studies together are yielding a converging pattern of social and symbolic deficits that characterize autism as a developmental disorder.

One of the implications of all this research is that autism is a disorder of the brain and of cognition that makes it difficult for these children to comprehend the features of social interaction and to process emotions that will lead to the development of a sense of self and other. Another possibility is that autism is related to a deficit in sensory and motor patterns that, from an early age, prevents these infants from engaging with the environment in such a way that their brains and minds can understand what is needed.

One recent research study has discovered abnormal movement patterns between 4 and 6 months of age that are presumed to distinguish autistic from typically developing infants (Teitelbaum, Teitelbaum, Nye, Fryman, & Maurer, 1998). The authors studied the home videos of 17 infants who had been diagnosed with autism when they were 3 years old and compared them with home videos of typically developing 4-to-6-month-old infants. When rolling over, for example, typically developing infants turn their pelvis to one side, followed by the trunk, and then the head. Later they lead with the head, followed by the trunk and pelvis. (You may recall this from doing the Awareness through Movement lessons in Chapter 6.) Three of the babies later diagnosed with autism turned over by lying on their sides and, while lifting their heads and legs at the same time, flopped their body in a single movement either onto their backs or to the stomachs. Some of the autistic infants fell from sitting positions easily, showing no compensatory actions, so that they appeared to topple like a cut tree. When learning to crawl, some of the autistic infants had a hard time adjusting their base of support (see the Awareness through Movement lessons in Chapter 7), leaned on their elbows instead of their hands, and had a difficult time distributing their weight evenly because of asymmetries between right and left sides.

Although this study provides some possible new directions for the study of the causes of autism, it must be read with caution. First of all, the authors were not consistent in reporting the numbers of children with such deficits. They typically discussed only one or two infants or used words like "some infants [showed the deficit]." Thus, we do not know if any of the autistic children were more typical, or if any of the typically developing children had some of these similar deficits. Finally, the coders of the infant's movement patterns were not blind to whether the child was autistic or typically developing.

It is well known that autistic children and adults have motor asymmetries and sometimes walk unsteadily. They often have an aversion to touch, eye contact, and other forms of sensory overstimulation. Autistic children's difficulty in imitating another person is believed to be due to neuromotor deficits, the failure to clearly link perception and action (Ozonoff & South, 2000). Both Donna Williams and Temple Grandin describe the difficulties they have with being touched, for example, and the lengthy process by which they discovered means to safely touch and be touched. It is plausible, therefore, that movement and sensory deficits may play some role in autism. If an infant has to struggle with something simple like turning over, their participatory experiences of everyday life may be extremely difficult, creating disturbances in the sense of an ecological self. In later development, one can imagine that these early disturbances of the ecological self may become transformed, though social and cognitive development, into later pathologies of the existential self.

In summary, diagnosis of autism in the second year involves deficits in the very behaviors and skills that are acquired by typically developing 18-month-old infants: social intersubjectivity, a sense of an existential self, and, as we shall see in the next section, a wide repertoire of self-conscious emotions. Diagnosis in the first year points to sensorimotor deficits. Most treatment approaches for young autistic children focus on improving the child's ability to engage with another person and to develop coordinated joint attention. The studies of sensorimotor deficits may lead to new ways of treating infants for movement and sensory disorders that might possibly affect the development of the brain and improve the chances for later cognitive and emotional development. There is always the hope that treatments begun early enough may have a more lasting effect than treatments begun after 4 or 5 years of age.

Infant Mental Health

Autism is one of several recognized mental health disorders that have been defined for infants in the official diagnostic handbook of the American Psychiatric Association, *Diagnostic and Statistical Manual of Mental Disorders, 4th edition,* 1994 (generally referred to DSM-IV). In addition to autism, infants may be classified as having pervasive developmental disorder, reactive attachment disorder, or separation anxiety disorder (Gelfand, 2000).

Pervasive developmental disorder is diagnosed when infants persistently fall behind on multiple assessments of developmental progress. The category does not apply to a typically developing infant who is slow to walk or to talk, but rather to a severe and prolonged delay in multiple areas of functioning. These children typically have mild to severe mental retardation and some kind of chromosomal or neurological abnormalities. Some children show deficits from birth, while others only show the symptom after 1 or 2 years of otherwise typical development.

Reactive attachment disorder is typically associated with a pattern of disorganized attachment (see Chapter 8 for a more detailed discussion and references). It is marked by disturbed behavior in the company of other individuals, not necessarily only with the parent. The child may display inhibition and watchfulness or else be indiscriminately sociable. This disorder is always associated with disturbances in parental care, such as failures to meet the child's physical or emotional needs, abuse and neglect, and changes in caregivers so that no stable attachment can form.

Separation anxiety disorder is much more severe than the typical separation anxiety felt by most infants. A child diagnosed with this disorder refuses to be separated from the parent, even to go to bed, and has excessive distress when not at home with parents. The behavior must be intense, last at least 1 month, and be inappropriate for the child's age. It is more prevalent in children who can voice their concerns verbally. This disorder in more likely if the child is temperamentally inhibited or if one parent or close relative has panic disorder or other forms of severe anxiety.

It is difficult to make mental health diagnoses for children under the age of 3 years because many disorders are slow to reveal themselves. Parents may suspect a problem, but mental health practitioners are often hesitant to make a firm diagnosis because many behavioral abnormalities of infants are transitory (see Chapters 4 and 12). Infants have a remarkable ability for self-righting when in supportive and loving environments. Also, little is known about how to treat some of these disorders. A diagnosis may stigmatize the infant or parent and do more harm than good. This may be frustrating for some parents who believe that something is seriously wrong with their infants but cannot find a professional who takes them seriously. On the other hand, to the extent that some of these disorders reflect mental health problems of the parents, practitioners may advise treatment for them rather than for the infant. Sometimes, problem behavior in infants is due to the social conditions of child rearing or to ignorance. In these cases, infants can best be served by enrolling them with their parents into a variety of support and intervention programs (see the "Family and Society" section in this chapter).

Emotional Development

The more complex event memories and concepts, the ability to think symbolically, and the emergence of the existential self, account for some of the changes in emotional development during this period of infancy. The infants' emotional expressions continue to become more complex and more closely related to communicative situations. During the second year, the infants' predominant emotional expressions are smiling and laughter (Malatesta, Culver, Tesman, & Shepard, 1989).

Prior to this period, smiles occur when infants accomplish a task such as the successful completion of an offering or a request gesture (Messinger & Fogel, 1997). After 18 months, infants are more likely to smile when both they and their mothers establish joint activity and attention and when they experience periods of affective sharing, rather than just at their own achievements (S. S. Jones, Raag, & Collins, 1990; Mundy, Kasari, & Sigman, 1992). Infants of this age are also increasingly likely to initiate positive emotions in their communications with the parent, acting like a more emotionally autonomous individual (Grolnick, Cosgrove, & Bridges, 1996).

Our studies on infant laughter have revealed significant changes between the first and second year of life (Nwokah, Hsu, Dobrowolska, & Fogel, 1994). During the first year, most infant laughter occurs while the mother is smiling or laughing. In the second year, infant laughter takes on a specific meaning within the mother-infant communication system. A solitary infant laugh might mean "this is fun," an infant laugh following the mother's laugh might mean "if you think this is funny, so do I," and infant laughter while the mother is not displaying positive emotion, especially during teasing situations, might mean "I enjoy it when you look shocked so long as you are not really angry." Laughter also serves as an attention-getting device. A laugh can reestablish visual attention or direct the mother's attention back to the infant who may laugh at his or her own antics.

We also found that mother-infant dyads developed their own styles of laughing together. For example, a mother would frame an opportunity for infant laughter by providing all the facial features of a laugh, such as a wide open mouth, and waiting until the infant provided the actual laugh before she laughed in unison. In another couple, mother and infant would stare silently smiling at each other and then burst out laughing almost simultaneously.

How Does Symbolic Thought Affect the Child's Emotional Experiences?

The ability to form mental images and create symbols increases the range of the infant's emotional experiences. In the previous stage, fear, for example, could be triggered by a concrete event that might remind the infant of a related and unpleasant past event. Seeing someone in a white coat might remind the infant of a doctor and cause the infant to become frightened and cry.

After 18 months, fear can be evoked by a symbolic mental image such as a monster or the thought of being sucked down the drain of a sink. Starting at this age, children develop fears of the dark and of things that might lurk behind doors, refrigerators, and other unseen places (Sroufe, 1979). Dreams, which at this age begin to take on representational forms that can be remembered and talked about, also can be a source of fears, although nightmares do not appear until after the second birthday (Piaget, 1962; also see Chapter 11 of this book). Piaget reported observing instances of dreaming in one child as young as 21 months; she called out the names of several of her friends in the middle of the night and on one occasion said, "Pussy's hiding."

Symbolic skills also increase the probability that infants will talk about their emotions. Indeed, by 20 months, about one-third of all children will talk about one or more of the following states: sleep/fatigue ("tired"), pain ("ouch"), distress ("sad"), disgust ("yuck"), affection ("love Mommy"), and value ("good," "bad") (Bretherton, Fritz, Zahn-Waxler, & Ridgeway, 1986; Ridgeway, Waters, & Kuczaj, 1985). By the age of 24 months, infants engage in conversations about their feelings, talk about the causes of their feelings, and play games with siblings in which they pretend to have certain kinds of feelings (J. Dunn, Bretherton, & Munn, 1987). These types of conversations are illustrated in Observations 10.3 and 10.4. Aside from the connection between emotions and symbols, this kind of talk also shows that the child is becoming in-

---

OBSERVATIONS

Communicative Behavior between Siblings (J. Dunn, Bretherton, & Munn, 1987)

Observation 10.3

Family M., child 24 months: Baby sibling is crying after child knocked him (accidentally). Mother comes into room.
Child: Poor Thomas.
Mother: What?
Child: I banged his head.
Mother: You banged it?
Child: Yes.
Mother: Are you going to kiss it?
Child: Yes.
Mother: Kiss his head.

Observation 10.4

Family Th., child 24 months: Older sibling has been showing child a book with pictures of monsters. Child leaves sibling and goes to Mother.
Child: Mummy, Mummy. (whines)
Mother: What's wrong?
Child: Frighten.
Mother: The book?
Child: Yes.
Mother: It's not frightening you!
Child: Yes!
Mother: It did, did it?
Child: Yes.

creasing aware of internal experience. The verbal expression of that internal experience is one of the major characteristics of the existential self compared to the subjective self of earlier ages.

How Does the Concept of the Self Affect Emotional Experience?

What kind of emotion might you expect infants to display at the moment they first recognize themselves in the mirror and touch the spot of rouge on their own noses? The primary emotion experienced is embarrassment. In one study, infants' reactions to the mirror were compared with infants' reactions to an unfamiliar adult. To the adult, the predominant expression was wariness, defined as an attentive look, a sober facial expression, and a cessation of ongoing action or vocalization, followed by a gaze aversion. To the mirror, infants were embarrassed, as shown by a turning to the nearest adult with a smiling facial expression, followed by a gaze aversion and movement to touch the hair, hands, or face in a self-conscious manner (M. Lewis, Sullivan, Stanger, and Weiss, 1989).

Embarrassment, or *shame,* is fundamentally different from the other emotions that infants had experienced up to this point in their lives. Shame is a **self-conscious emotion,** that is, it requires an awareness of an existential self in relation to an existential other. Self-conscious emotions begin to emerge around the child's second birthday. Shame

is always felt in the eyes of someone else. In order to feel shame, one has to realize that others are different from the self and that the self is exposed, separate, and likely to be evaluated by others (M. Lewis, 1995). Other self-conscious emotions are guilt, jealousy, and pride (K. C. Barrett & Nelson-Goens, 1997).

Pride occurs when infants see themselves as effective and competent individuals in the eyes of another person, able to achieve and to have an impact on others. In previous stages, children expressed enjoyment at being a cause, at being contingent, and at having an effect on others. In this stage, the feeling of pride is the result of meeting their own standards, as well as the awareness of having accomplished a personal goal.

Children observed an experimenter rolling a ball to knock down a bowling pin, and later the children were asked to do it themselves. Children smiled when the pin fell in both conditions but they only looked at the experimenter when they had done the task themselves. This look seems to be one indication of a sense of pride. Similarly, children of this age period are more likely to show pride reactions when achieving goals they determine for themselves rather than those set for them by their mothers (Stipek, 1995). Some behavioral characteristics of pride and shame are shown in Table 10.5.

Both pride and shame are developed in the context of communicating about success or failure in meeting socially accepted standards, rules, and achievements (K. C. Barrett & Nelson-Goens,

Table 10.5   Characteristics of Pride and Shame

	Pride	Shame
Situation	Success at achieving standard	Failure to achieve standard
Behavior	Approach others, show/tell, stand erect, smile broadly	Increase distance from others, reduce exposure, hide face
Social	Self as dominant, achiever	Self as submissive, small
Self	Maintenance of good feelings about self	Maintenance of other's respect
Other	"Everyone thinks I am good."	"Everyone is looking at me."
Vocalization	Wide, full voice	Narrow, thin voice
Physiology	High heart rate, flushed face	Low heart rate, blushing

Sources: K. C. Barrett, A functionalist approach to shame and guilt, 1995, p. 42. In J. P. Tangney & K. W. Fischer (Eds.), *Self conscious emotions: The psychology of shame, guilt, embarrassment, and pride,* 25–63. New York: Guilford Press; M. Lewis, S. M. Alessandri, & M. W. Sullivan, Differences in shame and pride as a function of children's gender and task difficulty, 1992, p. 633. *Child Development, 63,* 630–638; M. F. Mascolo & K. W. Fischer, Developmental transformations in appraisals for pride, shame, and guilt, 1995, p. 100. In J. P. Tangney & K. W. Fischer (Eds.), *Self-conscious emotions: The psychology of shame, guilt, embarrassment, and pride,* 64–113. New York: Guilford Press.

Defiance is one way infants come to know themselves in relation to other people.

Michael Newman/PhotoEdit

1997). Children at this age become aware of standards, such as completing an entire puzzle or finishing one's food. Rules include cleaning up after playing with toys or not touching electrical outlets. Achievements occur when the child reaches a level of new mastery after putting in some effort, such as putting on one's own shirt.

The parent's responses to these everyday events play a role in the development of the toddler's emotions. Children whose parents respond most positively to the child's achievements and to when the child follows everyday social rules are more likely to show guilt reactions when a doll they are playing with during an experimental situation breaks. The doll had been designed by the experimenter to come apart easily. When it appears they have broken the doll, these children are more likely to point out the problem to the experimenter and try to repair the doll. Children whose parents were more negative in response to children's failure during everyday social situations were more likely to pretend that the doll did not break and to avoid mentioning the problem to the experimenter. Children whose parents respond positively when they are successful at something are more likely to react nega-

tively when they are unsuccessful (K. C. Barrett & Nelson-Goens, 1997).

It is possible that the parents of these children react more positively because they can see the child is very sensitive to failure. It is also possible that when parents are highly supportive and positive, children develop high standards for themselves. Most likely, there is a co-regulation between parents and children such that their styles of emotional communication become more similar over time, with each influencing the other (K. C. Barrett & Nelson-Goens, 1997; Dunsmore & Halberstadt, 1997).

In the realm of *anger,* a growing sense of independence and a feeling that the self is separate from others leads to feelings of *defiance, negativism,* and *aggression* (Sroufe, 1979). These feelings, which arise out of earlier feelings of anger provoked by frustration or the immediate situation, are due more to the *mental idea* that the self is and should be independent. Defiance of parents is one way infants experience themselves—one way they make a declaration of self-sufficiency and explore the boundaries of the existential self.

Thus, in Stage VI, anger is no longer a private response to an unyielding situation; it becomes a communication tool used willfully to affect other people. It is, therefore, one of the first signs of the child's sense of personal autonomy and signals the first break in the cycle of initial dependency. These patterns of emotion as related to the development of the self have been nicely described by Erikson's theory of development (see Chapter 2). He referred to autonomy (pride, defiance) and shame (doubt, disappointment) as two emotional poles of this developmental phase. I will discuss more about the emotion of defiance in a later section on discipline and compliance.

How Do Infants of This Age Cope with Stress?

At this age, children come to rely on their teddy bears and favorite blankets to comfort themselves in stressful situations and when their parents are not around. Children can become attached to these objects in the sense that they desire contant proximity with the objects and show signs of anxiety and distress when separated from the objects. Studies compared the behavior of children who were attached to a blanket with others who were not (Passman, 1977; Passman & Weisberg, 1975). The children, who ranged in age from 20 to 40 months, were observed individually in a novel play situation with either their mother, their blanket, a favorite toy, or no available objects. There were no differences in exploratory behavior or in the amount of distress between children with their mothers present and blanket-attached children with their blankets. Children in these two situations performed considerably better (had more exploratory play and less distress) than either non-blanket-attached children with their blankets, all children with only a favorite toy, or children without any objects.

It seems that a 2-year-old may attach himself or herself to a blanket as an effective substitute for the mother, at least for brief periods. There are a number of reasons why this might be true. Blankets are soft and cuddly, and they carry plenty of familiar smells that may remind the child of the comforts of home and impart an increased sense of security.

Children's reliance on blankets as sources of comfort comes at a time when they are becoming aware of their physical and psychological separateness from the caregiver. Although this sense of self as an independent individual does not fully take hold until the third year of life, when the conceptual self emerges (see Chapter 11), the development of the existential self at the end of the second year can be thought of as an important transitional phase in the growth of independence. The blanket and other such attachment objects therefore have been called **transitional objects** (Mahler, Pine, & Bergman, 1975; Winnicott, 1971), because they seem to serve as an intermediate bridge between a child's total reliance and dependence on the mother and the development of individuation.

Not all children develop blanket attachments. In countries where there is relatively more physical contact between infants and caregivers, a blanket attachment is less likely to develop (Super, 1981). In a study of Italian children, only 4.9% of rural children had transitional object attachments, whereas 31.1% of urban children in Rome had them (Gaddini, 1970). Korean infants used transitional objects less than a matched sample of U.S. infants, and there is less sucking on fingers and pacifiers among the relatively more indulged (compared with North American) Japanese infants (Caudill & Weinstein, 1969; Hong & Townes, 1976). It seems that in societies where children have continued access to physical contact with other people, there is little need for transitional objects. On the other hand, in cultures where there is less close physical contact, transitional objects can be effective and adaptive for some children.

There are individual differences in infants' reactions to stressful or frustrating situations. In one study, infants were exposed to a variety of frustrating situations—for instance, a desirable object was placed in a Plexiglas container so the child could not get it or food was placed nearby but the child could not eat it or and the child was asked to sit for 5 minutes in a high chair. Some children screamed loudly when frustrated, while others showed little or no distress. Those who were more distressed were more likely to act out by hitting, kicking, or banging. These more distressed children were less able to use self-comforting strategies such as finding something to distract themselves, seeking the mother, or making a constructive attempt to get the toy or the food (S. D. Calkins & Johnson, 1998; Raver, 1996).

The mothers of the more distressed children were also more likely to do things to help the children rather than letting the children solve the problem themselves. This may be because the mothers know the children will have negative reactions and want to avoid the distress. Or it may be because the mothers never let the children do things on their own, so the children never acquire their own coping skills (S. D. Calkins, Smith, Gill, & Johnson, 1998; S. D. Calkins & Johnson, 1998). This may be another example in which it is impossible to sort out cause and effect. Rather, the parent and child co-regulate, each changing the other, leading to a relationship style that is either distress-prone and tense or calmer and adaptive (Fogel, 1993).

Generally speaking, children of this age adopt the emotional regulation styles found in their families (Dunsmore & Halberstadt, 1997). In one study of 2-year-olds in a preschool setting, children tended to seek comfort and assistance from caregivers who reported a family history similar to that of the children's mothers. If the mothers had a positive relationship with their own parents in the past and present, their children sought out caregivers who also had a positive relationship with their own parents. Similarly, if the children's parents were conflicted or ambivalent about their own parents, so were the caregivers that the children approached (Shulman, Becker, & Sroufe, 1999).

This finding is rather surprising. One might expect that children whose mothers were more conflicted would turn to more secure adults when given the opportunity. On the other hand, adults typically choose partners who have similar family histories and attachment styles, even when their partners show negative behaviors toward them similar to those that their parents displayed (P. A. Frazier, A. L. Byer, A. R. Fischer, D. M. Wright, & K. A. DeBord, 1996). This work supports that idea that children develop internal working models with expectations for particular kinds of attachment styles and continue to replicate those styles even when it is not in their best interests. Breaking out of the cycle of difficult interpersonal relationships often requires individual, couple, or family psychotherapy.

These findings show the importance of the parent-infant relationship and the active role of adults in emotion regulation at this age. A transitional object is useful but cannot replace an adult. Children of this age are better able to cope on their own with distress and frustration when an adult is nearby. They typically have limited ability to do this, such as finding alternative objects to play with when the one they want cannot be obtained, as shown in the study just reviewed and in other related research (Grolnick, Bridges, & Connell, 1996). Children of this age do not have the ability to comfort themselves verbally, which appears during the next age period. Even at this age, when children are beginning to acquire language, most of their emotion regulation is accomplished nonverbally. The participatory memories of these adult-child regulatory processes may help explain why they have a lasting effect on the formation of later interpersonal relationships.

What Happens to Children during Separations from Their Primary Caregivers?

We already know that when even very young infants are left in the company of familiar substitute caregivers, few problems are seen. Infants quickly adapt to the new situation, and they are able to use the familiar substitute as a secure base for exploration, as well as a source of support and comfort. This is true even though infants almost always prefer their mothers when given the choice (see Chapter 9).

By the end of the second year, because of cognitive advances related to understanding scripts and sequences, infants can understand that their parents will return after a separation, so they begin to take their own initiatives in separating from the parents. Infants of this age observed with their parents in a public park were not afraid to wander some distance from the parents. Although males left the parents' side more often than females, there were no significant sex differences in how far the children went or how much total time they spent at a distance (Ley & Koepke, 1982).

The situation is different, however, when the parents initiate a separation. This could happen for many reasons. The parents may want to go out in the evening, or they may need to travel away from the child for several days. This is often the age when mothers go into the hospital to have a second child. Other separation occasions include a parent's business trips and even brief hospitalizations for a child who is ill or needs an operation.

Research suggests that separation episodes are more tolerable to the infant if the parent prepares the child for them beforehand. In one study (Weinraub & Lewis, 1977), children were least upset during the separation if the mother explained that she would be leaving and gave the child instructions on what to do in her absence. This was especially true for children who were more developmentally advanced and could better understand the mother's instructions. It also seemed to help the child during the separation if the mother spent more time at a distance, and less time in close physical contact with the infant, in the 3 minutes just prior to the departure.

A somewhat contradictory finding was reported in another study. The longer a mother spent in preparing a child for separation (70 seconds versus 10 seconds), the less content the child remained during the separation (Adams and Passman, 1981). It could be, however, that mothers in this study who were assigned to the 70-second preparation condition also spent more time in close contact with the infant before departure.

In a related study (Lollis, 1990), mothers were instructed to be extremely brief in separating from their infants. They were told to say only, "I'm going to leave for a little while. You stay here and play until I come back." These departures took only about 20 seconds. Another group of mothers was asked to take leave of the infants quickly, but no instructions were given about what the mothers should say. These uninstructed mothers took a bit longer but prepared the infants for the separation more thoroughly. The infants who were prepared more thoroughly fared better during the separation. This suggests that it is not the duration of leavetaking but rather how well the infant is prepared by the parent during this time that is the important factor.

Several other related findings are of interest here. Infants are more predisposed to separate from parents if they are dropped off at a familiar day care setting or preschool, due primarily to the presence of peers already in the setting (Gunnar, Senior, & Hartup, 1984). This suggests that the environment in which the child is left is an important factor in regulating separation protest. Other research has found that infants left at the preschool or day care setting show more protest when dropped off by their mothers than by their fathers. The mothers took longer to leave the children than did the fathers (Field, Gewirtz, et al., 1984).

The best way for parents to prepare their 2-year-olds for a brief separation is to avoid close contact just before they leave, give the children some concrete suggestions about what they might do while the parents are gone, and try to tailor speech to the comprehension level of the infants. Even given this advice, and knowing that children of this age do quite well in brief separations, parents still find it difficult to leave their babies alone in a strange place with a new baby-sitter or to go out on their own for the first time. No matter how hard parents try to prepare themselves and their children, the children almost inevitably get upset as soon as they understand that their parents are *actually* leaving. Little in the annals of parenthood is more emotionally wrenching than the painful wails of a child being left behind. This phenomenon is called **parental separation anxiety.** Parental separation anxiety afflicts many working mothers and mothers who leave their children behind in day care (Hock & DeMeis, 1990; Jarvis & Creasey, 1991). Both mothers and fathers can experience parental separation anxiety.

One additional finding should provide at least a small measure of comfort to parents or prospective parents. Researchers discovered that the infant's immediate response to the parent's departure was not correlated with anything the parent said or did. Only after this initial response, when the infant finally calmed down, did the baby's behavior begin to reflect the efforts of the parent's work at preparation (Weinraub & Lewis, 1977). Indeed, it seems common for babies of this age to protest loudly during the actual departure of the parent. As soon as it is clear that these protests are ineffective, the 2-year-old generally is capable of quieting down and even enjoying the substitute caregiver.

Perhaps the most striking demonstration of this was offered in a study of children left by their parents in a British residential nursery for several days. The children were provided with a warm and affectionate substitute caregiver. Some of the younger children showed almost no signs of distress or despair, and they gradually became attached to the substitute. Some of the older children in their study—the 4-year-olds—started off their stay with some sadness and a lowered tolerance for frustration, but they were able to use the foster parent to sustain their feelings, and their intimacy with her increased over time. All the children in the study greeted their parents warmly upon their return. It was not the separation per se that caused the problems but the psychosocial environment of the situation in which the child was left. Similar findings have been reported for infants institutionalized over the long term and infants in foster-care situations. The lack of social interaction in the institution was the most important factor accounting for the delayed or disturbed development of some institutionalized infants (Robertson & Robertson, 1971; B. Tizard & Rees, 1974; J. Tizard & Tizard, 1971).

Social and Language Development

The period between 18 and 24 months is marked by a number of important changes in language, due in part to the child's more conceptual and symbolic forms of cognition. First of all, there is a dramatic increase in the size of children's vocabulary, and second, children begin to use multiword sentences.

The Vocabulary Spurt

Between 12 and 18 months, new words are acquired slowly, a few per week. Sometime around 18 months, there is typically a rapid increase in vocabulary in which children begin to acquire five or more words per week. This growth of vocabulary consists primarily of object names. It is as if children discover that objects have names and become ob-

sessed with naming things and asking for the names of things, in what has been called the *naming insight* (McShane, 1980). They may repeatedly ask "What-da?" to request object names and point to many different objects, wanting to hear the name (Camaioni, 2000).

By 18 months, children have an active vocabulary of about 90 words but by 24 months this has expanded to 320 words. A typical 6-year-old knows 14,000 words, and a high school graduate knows about 60,000. People learn nine or ten words per day between the ages of 2 and 18 years (Adamson, 1995). This means that most language is actually acquired after the infancy period.

Although nouns predominate, children in this age period also acquire some verbs (*play, kiss*), adjectives (*hot, yucky*), and adverbs (*up, more*). They can use words to make comments on objects (*gone, dirty*) and on their own actions and feelings (*uh-oh, tired*) (E. Bates, O'Connell, & Shore, 1987). When children use a verb or an adjective, it suggests that they are referring not simply to the word itself but to several words or things. Saying "gone," for example, implies that some object is no longer present; "hot" refers to an object that is at a high temperature.

When children under 18 months say "shoe," they may be referring to shoe in the form of simply naming. After 18 months, they may point to the shoe and say "dirty" or "Mommy." This type of behavior could be interpreted as "the shoe is dirty" or "this is Mommy's shoe." It seems, therefore, that just before the acquisition of multiword speech, infants begin to use single words in more complex ways that suggest a subject and a predicate (E. Bates et al., 1987; Greenfield & Smith, 1976; Lock, 1980). Nevertheless, their language is still limited in what can be expressed. The additional discovery of combining words increases what a child of this age can say, but it is not until the third year that children become able to speak in fluent sentences (Adamson, 1995).

Multiword Speech

The main advance in language is the emergence of the sentence. Correlational studies show that sentences emerge at about the same age (on the average, about 20 months) when children begin to

Table 10.6   Development of Conventionalized Semantics and Syntax

Age	Semantics	Syntax
9–12 months	Sensorimotor gestures	
12–18 months	Idiosyncratic words (symbols)	
19–24 months	Conventional words (signs)	Idiosyncratic word order
Over 24 months		Conventional word order

pursue objects after multiple hidings, use tools in deliberate ways, and engage in symbolic play. This is also the age at which they can combine symbolic objects and gestures in novel ways, classify objects by sorting, and solve complex problems mentally without trial-and-error behavior (E. Bates et al., 1987; McCune-Nicolich, 1981; Piaget, 1962; Shore, 1986; Sugarman, 1982; Zachry, 1978).

The onset of sentences with a series of words parallels the emergence of the use of a series of related gestures, or a combination of words and gestures, to communicate meaning (Acredolo & Goodwyn, 1988; Lock, 1980; Mayer & Musatti, 1992; McCune-Nicolich, 1981). An example would be pulling on the mother's skirt, lifting one's arms up, looking distressed, and perhaps saying, "Mommy up." The pragmatic view of language development, discussed in the previous chapter, suggests that language serves one main purpose for young children: to communicate their intentions. As children develop cognitively, they discover better ways to get their point across to others. During the previous stage, children relied on the context or situation, intonation patterns, and interpreting adults to communicate their meanings with single words.

In this phase, children discover they can create new meanings simply by changing *the order in which several words are spoken together*. When gestures and words first are used in intentional communication, they are a direct extension of some sensorimotor act of the child. These **idiosyncratic communication** gestures only gradually develop into **conventional communication** signs. We see a parallel development in the realm of grammar or syntax: the first two-word combinations are idiosyncratic usages that only later become conventionalized in the form of adult syntax (see Table 10.6).

The child's first multiword utterances are not as sophisticated as adult grammar. Apparently, children first use word order to express meanings with

a fairly limited set of speech patterns. These speech patterns are better thought of as **formulas** than as sentences: children seem to use a particular kind of word sequencing in which they can "fill in the blanks" to vary the meaning of the phrase. Table 10.7 gives these early formulas, along with their meanings and some examples.

Formulas similar to those found in Table 10.7 have been reported for children from six different

Table 10.7   Early Two-Word Combinations

Function	Formula	Example
Drawing attention to something	see + X here + X	see car here milk
Object's properties	big/little + X hot + X old + X	big house hot pipe old cookie
Possession	X + Y	doggy hold pig tail Kendall birthday
Plurality	number + X	two book
Recurrence	more + X other + X	more raisins other hand
Disappearance	all gone + X all done + X	all gone airplane all done juice
Negation	no + X not + X	no water not eat
Actor-action relations		sits doll sleeps baby Kendall break Mommy hit Kendall
Location	X + preposition	rock outside milk in there milk in cup
Request	want + X	want dessert want get down

Source: M. D. S. Braine, Children's first word combinations, 1976, p. 57. *Monographs of the Society for Research in Child Development,* 164, 56–57.

language groups. For example, "more milk" is found in Germany as "mehr Milch," in Russia as "yesche moloka," and in Finland as "lisaa kakkua" (Slobin, 1970). Similar patterns can be seen in the first word combinations of deaf children acquiring sign language. One study found hand signs that could be interpreted as "Daddy work" (Daddy is at work) and "Barry train" (referring to a brother's train) in a language-learning deaf child (Dale, 1976).

The speech examples in Table 10.7 are called **telegraphic speech,** because they tend to leave out small words such as prepositions and word endings such as *-ing, -s* sounds, and *-ed,* which add additional refinements to the meaning of words and sentences. Usually, simpler endings such as *-ing,* the plural *-s,* and the possessive *-'s* are acquired first, followed by the more difficult use of the verb "to be" with all its tenses, auxiliaries, and contractions (deVilliers & deVilliers, 1973).

Individual Differences: Two Types of Speech Style

While these syntactic refinements are taking place, children continue to develop a vocabulary. This entails increasing the number of conventional words they know how to use and refining the meanings of the words that have been overextended or used incorrectly in the past. Young children show two distinct styles of vocabulary acquisition: **referential speech** and **expressive speech.** Differences between referential and expressive word use are summed up in Table 10.8.

Some examples of expressive language are "I don't want it," "Don't do it," "I'll get it," and "I don't know where it is." These phrases have the characteristics of being spoken as a single word, since the individual words are poorly articulated. There is no evidence that the use of either of these styles of language acquisition relates to later behavior in any way. Indeed, most children use them both in different contexts, for example, in referential versus interpersonal situations (Camaioni, 2000; K. Nelson, 1981). Some studies have shown that as children get older, they tend to favor one style over another—a more social-oriented versus object-oriented approach—although the evidence is based almost entirely on a few case studies.

Children's use of one or the other style may reflect the speech spoken to them. If a caregiver responds to questions by clearly labeling objects, the child may focus more on individual words. If the caregiver uses social control language like "D'ya wanna go out" or "I dunno where it is," the child is likely to hear these as whole phrases rather than as a series of single words.

Relationship between Language Development and the Social Environment

It is extremely rare for adults to correct children's language errors directly. What do adults actually say and do that might be conducive to the development of speech? One major trend is an increasing reliance on verbal suggestions and commands, as

Table 10.8 Two Styles of Word Use in Infancy

Attribute	Referential Speech	Expressive Speech
Word Type	Object names	Social routines
Part of Speech	Nouns	Pronouns
Syntax	Single words	Phrases
Size of Vocabulary	Large	Small
Content	Substantive	Relational
Production	Original	Imitative
Articulation	Clear	Mumbled
Situational	Referential	Interpersonal
Context	As in reading books	As in free social play

Source: K. Nelson, Individual differences in language development: Implications for development and language, 1981, p. 182. *Developmental Psychology, 17,* 170–187. Adapted with permission of Katherine Nelson.

SW Productions/PhotoDisc

Picture-book reading is a particularly good setting for guided participation in language development.

compared to nonverbal gestures, in the last half of the second year. When this happens, mothers tend to emphasize two basic verbal forms: requests and comments. Requests may include asking for information through "what" and "where" questions ("What's this?" "Where's the doggie?"). Mothers also request that the children speak about something ("Talk to Daddy on the telephone"; "Tell me what you saw in the park"). Comments are responses to the children's utterances or attempts to initiate a conversation ("Yes, that's an apple"; "The duck is swimming"; "This is the same car we saw the other day") (Stella-Prorok, 1983).

Similar patterns were found in a study of picture book reading (Ninio, 1983). Mothers referred to pictures using simple labeling, "what" questions ("What's that?" "What does the doggie say?"), and "where" questions ("Where's the kitty?") that elicited pointing by the children. Mothers also imitated their infants' utterances. Imitation was most likely to occur when the child made an error of pronunciation. Rather than correct the child's speech, the mother simply repeated the correct pronunciation (Bohannon & Stanowicz, 1988).

Research that measures the total amount of maternal speech provides only indirect evidence that these methods actually promote speech development, although generally mothers who talk more to their infants have infants who are more advanced linguistically (Sigman et al., 1988; Tomasello, Mannle, & Kruger, 1986). More to the point, if mothers time their verbal inputs to instances when the infants are looking at them or at an object, the infants develop higher language production scores compared to situations in which the mothers first attract the children's attention to an object and then comment on it (M. Harris, Jones, & Grant, 1985; F. F. Schachter, 1979; Tomasello & Farrar, 1986; Whitehurst et al., 1988).

In general, the child develops greater linguistic competence when the adult uses speech that is more responsive to the child's focus of interest and uses the child's interest to achieve a joint focus of attention before talking (Aureli, 1994; Baldwin, 1993; Hoff-Ginsberg, 1986; Hoff-Ginsberg & Shatz, 1982; Olson, Bates, & Bayles, 1984; M. Papousek, Papousek, & Bornstein, 1985; Snow, 1984). To the extent that maternal speech around the world shares some of the characteristics mentioned above, then it is likely to be the particular style of speaking to the child, rather than simply the amount of child-directed speech, that is the important factor.

The use of requests and comments as the primary mode of maternal speech may also be understood from the results of a study on infant imitation of adult actions during the period from 18 to 24 months (Hay, Murray, Cecire, & Nash, 1985). Infants were shown how to use a party hat as a horn or a shoe and how to use a string of beads as a telephone or a comb. The infants showed a much greater tendency to imitate adults' novel actions using these objects if the adults explained in words what they were doing ("I think you need a new shoe. Here's a pretty new shoe!"). Thus, verbal requests for action, when embedded in an action sequence, are more likely to be acted on by the child, providing more opportunities for language to be coupled with action. Children are also more likely to learn words if the adult is actually pointing to the object or looking at the object when saying the word (Baldwin et al., 1996). These studies show that children play a role in what words they choose to try out, opting for words that appear to be connected to intentional adult action. They also suggest that adults adapt their speech style to that of the children.

Guided Participation between Infants and Adults

These studies on linguistic interaction reflect some more general patterns of adult-infant communication that emerge around this age. In most interactions, adult and infant are working on something together, but each has a different purpose. The adult may be intent on instructing the child in the culturally appropriate uses of words and of objects. The child may be more motivated by being a direct participant in the social world. The concept of **guided participation** reflects the active role that children take in observing and participating in the organized activities of the family and society in the company of adults (Rogoff, 1990). Although from the adult's perspective, the child is merely "playing games" or "playing at" cooking or taking care of a doll, from the child's perspective, the child is actually doing the task as an active participant.

Table 10.9   Components of Guided Participation between Adults and Young Children

Child sets the agenda according to interest and skill level.

Adult adjusts level of child's participation according to child's skill.

Adult constrains child's participation for the safety and rights of the child and others.

Adult transfers responsibility to child according to ongoing assessment of child's abilities.

Source: B. Rogoff, Apprenticeship in thinking: Cognitive development in social context, 1990. New York: Oxford University Press.

Typically, in adult-child interactions, the children set the agenda for what they want to do and how much they want to be involved. The more skilled partner collaborates in the child's goals by giving the child responsibility for certain actions that are part of the larger task but within the range of the child's competence. In this first phase, the task is to establish coordinated joint attention beginning from the child's initiatives.

The adult must also constrain the child's participation for the sake of the child's, or others', safety or rights. Eventually, the adult transfers responsibility for larger segments of the task to the child, in relation to the growth of the child's competence as assessed by the adult (Bodle, Zhou, Shore, & Dixon, 1996; Bruner, 1983; Heckhausen, 1988; Kaye, 1982; Lock, 1980; Raver, 1996; Rogoff, 1990). These points are summarized in Table 10.9.

There are cultural differences in styles of guided participation. In one study (Rogoff, Mosier, Mistry, & Goncu, 1989; Rogoff, Mistry, Goncu, & Mosier, 1993), mothers from the United States were compared with Maya Indian mothers from Guatemala on how they helped their 20-month-old children use a set of nesting dolls. The U.S. mothers acted more like peers, wanting to take turns in combining dolls and commenting on the process. These mothers took seriously their role as teacher. The Maya mothers retained more of an adult-child status differential. They assumed the children would eventually acquire the ability to do the task. They monitored the children's progress and gave verbal instructions, but they did not get very involved in the task.

One U.S. mother tried to play games with the dolls, then offered them to the child for "his turn."

She gave instructions ("Put the lid on") and then cheered when the child did this ("Yeah! You're so smaaart!"). This mother tried to change the agenda when she judged that the baby's attention waned. She commented on all the child's actions and made requests for actions throughout the task.

A typical Maya mother demonstrated how the dolls come apart and go back together, using a few words to encourage the child to look. The baby wanted to handle the doll, but soon after, the mother took it back and again demonstrated how to do it. She pointed out the features of the task verbally as she performed the action. After that, she let the infant try for some time on his own, while she watched but did not intervene. When he ran into trouble, the mother would say something to help ("Do this one first"). When the child made a successful move, the mother would simply say "Okay" or "I see" in a quiet tone.

Both of these cases illustrate the general principles of guided participation listed in Table 10.9, but they differ markedly from each other. Similar differences in levels of involvement have been observed between American and North African mothers with infants of this age (Guillain, Foxonet, Petersen, & Ramos, 1998). American mothers were more actively involved than those in North Africa, but both practiced guided participation.

It is generally true that when adults become collaborators or participants in what children spontaneously seem interested in doing, children can achieve higher levels of language play and cognitive development compared to when adults do not become involved. (O'Connell & Bretherton, 1984; Slade, 1987a; Zukow, 1980). Particular types of adult involvement, however, are more effective in promoting higher cognitive levels in the development of symbolic play. The establishment of coordinated joint attention with children of this age is less likely to occur if mothers are depressed or have a low sense of self-efficacy (D. F. Goldsmith & Rogoff, 1997; Teti, O'Connell, & Reiner, 1996). Parents who understand the relationship between play and development and who engage the child in higher levels of symbolic play are more likely to encourage the child's participation at a higher level of performance (Bornstein, Haynes, Pascual, Painter, & Galperin, 1999; Damast, Tamis-LeMonda, & Bornstein, 1996). Children develop higher levels

of symbolic play when their mothers give more options that stimulate the child's creativity. If a child tries to put a doll into a toy cup, an options-limiting maternal response might be, "No, dolls don't go like that. We play with dolls in the dollhouse." An options-promoting reply might be, "Is the doll going swimming in the cup? Maybe she would like to have some lemonade in the dollhouse when she's done?"

Remarkably, the same process of guided participation that helps human infants acquire language also occurs when baby chimpanzees and baby bonobos are taught to use signs in the company of human adults. Chimpanzees and bonobos, along with gorillas, are great apes and our closest primate relatives. Compared to animals who are raised by their own mothers, chimpanzees and bonobos who are raised with human adults acquire signs in way similar to that in which human infants acquire verbal language, at least up until the age of 2 years (Savage-Rumbaugh et al., 1993; Tomasello, Savage-Rumbaugh, & Kruger, 1993). There is no evidence that nonhumans can acquire grammar, outside of a few simple formulas.

In addition to attesting to the power of guided participation in the development of language, these studies also tell us about the evolution of language. That chimpanzees and bonobos can acquire some linguistic signs when taught by humans clearly shows that they have the cognitive ability for forming symbols to represent objects and events. This means that symbolic ability probably evolved before the evolution of speech. The likely evolutionary scenario is that as humans evolved upright, bipedal locomotion, the vocal organs in the throat were reoriented, permitting the closure of the soft palate. Recall that when this closure happens developmentally in infants at around 5 months (Chapter 6), it allows the infants to create consonant sounds and produce syllable-like utterances that sound like words. In this way, humans evolved the ability to create meaningful speech using that part of the cognitive system that is common to both apes and humans (Savage-Rumbaugh et al., 1993).

Aside from cultural differences in guided participation and development, there are also individual differences. More-explicit instructions (compared to sharing and mutuality) are given to children who are temperamentally difficult or who show attachment problems; such instructions are also more likely to be used by fathers than by mothers (Fagot & Kavanagh, 1993; Marcos, 1995). Sharing and mutuality also vary depending upon the task or situation.

In particular, instances of parent-infant pretend play evoke relatively more sharing than instances in which the child is trying to or is expected to learn something. Pretending can be used just for fun as parent and child together create pretend scenarios, such as going for a ride in the car (using the couch as the car), playing house (using a cardboard box as the house), or reversing roles (the mother becomes the child and vice versa). Pretending can also be used to meta-communicate about more serious conflicts or disagreements. Mothers may engage in pretend play to give the child something to do, to redirect an otherwise undesirable activity, or to make light of a negative emotion (Farver & Howes, 1993; Haight, Masiello, Dickson, Huckeby, & Black, 1994; Haight & Miller, 1992). Pretend play is more likely to be used for guidance, such as teaching proper conduct, in Taiwanese than in North American families. The North American families were more likely to use pretend play for fun and fantasy games (Haight, Wang, Fung, Williams, & Mintz, 1999).

The Development of Discipline and Compliance

As it turns out, these basic principles of guided participation and collaboration in infants' activities are the foundation for effective discipline of children at this age. These principles include adjusting one's actions to the child's agenda and providing clear guides to adult standards (T. Gordon, 1988; Rocissano, Slade, & Lynch, 1987). The Awareness through Movement lesson of this chapter may also provide some insights into why particular forms of discipline are more likely than others to foster compliance.

Research suggests that in western cultures the most effective forms of parental discipline combine empathy and firmness (Baumrind, 1973). Caregivers should be sensitive to the reasons for the child's behavior and to the natural negative reactions children are likely to have when restrictions are imposed. The most successful discipliners in Baumrind's studies made firm demands and were appropriately expressive of their own angry or distressed reactions to the child's behavior. These parents did not use power as a means of controlling the child. These kinds of parents, whose style Baumrind called **authoritative parenting,** have children who show purposive, independent behavior, are cooperative with adults, show friendliness to peers, and are more likely to imitate their mothers; they are also more likely to become upset when they have violated standards of conduct (Kochanska, Forman, & Coy, 1999; also see the "Emotional Development" section in this chapter). The key, therefore, seems to be a combination of love and control.

Some parents, however, use more coercive and controlling disciplinary techniques. One research study examined 69 families with their firstborn sons when they were 15 and 21 months old. Some of the families at each age were identified as "troubled." These families used control as the primary disciplinary method and were unlikely to use guided participation; the children in these families showed the most defiance and the most negative emotion. More troubled families included men who showed more negative attitudes and were less social and less friendly than men in nontroubled families. Both mothers and fathers in these families, however, were more likely to use control techniques in place of guidance and authoritative approaches (Belsky, Woodworth, & Crnic, 1996). Teenage mothers are more coercive and tend to infer more anger and defiance in emotion expressions of infants (Strassberg & Treboux, 2000).

Boys at this age tend to be more aggressive and defiant than girls (K. H. Rubin, Hastings, Chen, Stewart, & McNichol, 1998). By this age, it appears that the father begins to play a substantial role in family processes. Fathers who are rated as more sensitive and involved with their children have children who are more socially competent and less defiant in both Caucasian American and African American families with toddlers (M. M. Black & Krishnakumar, 1998; Kelley, Smith, Green, Berndt, & Rogers, 1998).

In order to get more specific details about ways to obtain compliance, mothers were asked to try to get their babies to play with all the toys that were set out in a laboratory free-play situation (Schaffer & Crook, 1979, 1980). Researchers distinguished three types of compliance. Orientation compliance refers to getting infants to look where the adult wants them to. Mothers succeeded in this about 50% of the time on the first try. It helped if they used a nonverbal gesture. Almost all the mothers succeeded in getting orientation compliance if they persisted long enough.

Contact compliance refers to getting children to touch a designated toy. First-time success rates ran at 33%. In this case, success was more likely if the children were already looking at the toy, either because of their own interest or as a result of orientation compliance. Task compliance is shown when an infant manipulates a toy in an appropriate manner. It occurred only one-fourth of the time, and as you might expect, the likelihood of task compliance was higher if the infant was already looking at and touching the toy.

What conclusions can we draw about compliance from this research? First, it is important to get the child's attention; second, it helps if the child already is starting to do what is wanted. In other words, the mothers made their children look more compliant than they actually were by timing their requests for compliance to coincide with a behavior of the child that was most likely to lead to the desired response.

If a baby is playing, for example, and you want to do something else, such as go out, give her a bath, or feed her dinner, one approach is to sit down on the floor next to the baby and start playing with her! The parent should become part of the baby's play for only a few minutes to maneuver the game to a logical conclusion. For example, the parent might pick up the ball the baby is playing with, roll it back and forth with the baby a few times, tap it playfully on the baby's stomach and nose, and then pick up the baby with a tickle and carry the baby to the dinner table or bathtub. In this way a parent can skillfully change the baby's goals without causing a confrontation (Spock, 1957).

The importance of these recommendations was confirmed in a study by G. W. Holden (1983). Unobtrusive observations were made of 24 middle-class mothers and their 2-year-old infants in the supermarket. What were mothers' strategies in dealing with undesired behavior, such as asking for food, reaching for things, standing in the cart, and ignoring the mothers' requests? One group of mothers used "contingent" responses; that is, they scolded or reprimanded the infant after the transgression had occurred. The other group of mothers used "preventive" responses, such as talking to the child while shopping and giving the child something to eat. The children of the mothers who used preventive measures showed fewer instances of undesired behavior. When it comes to discipline and compliance in the second year, prevention is the best cure.

Preventive measures fall under the heading of **parental proactive behavior,** including any action that has the goal of a positive outcome for the child. Table 10.10 lists some examples of proactive

Table 10.10 Examples of Parental Proactive Behavior

Type	Short Term	Long Term
Direct	Occupy with activities. Divert attention. Engage child in game. Prepare verbally for upcoming situations. Set limits in advance. Monitor child's action when danger is present.	Take child on an outing. Train child to be wary of dangers. Organize peer groups. Select a day care center.
Indirect	Place child in car seat. Dress child appropriately for weather. Use night light. Serve appropriate foods.	Buy a home in a neighborhood conducive to child's development. Build a fence to keep child from danger. Keep poisons locked up. Purchase safe toys and furniture.

Source: G. W. Holden, How parents create a social environment via proactive behavior, 1985, p. 130. In T. Garling & J. Valsiner (Eds.), *Children within environments: Towards a psychology of accident prevention,* 116–142. New York: Plenum Press.

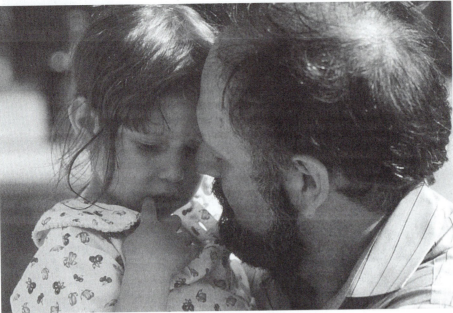

Effective discipline requires a balance of firmness and affection.

behavior used by adults. This approach to discipline suggests that one may avoid potential problems by proactively controlling or regulating access to the environment. In a healthy, safe, and developmentally appropriate environment, infants have fewer opportunities to get into danger or out of control.

Finally, it is worth noting that even though infants of this age want to try things out for themselves and often resist parental requests that directly interfere with their own actions, the infants also have a strong desire to be part of the social group and to join in with whatever adults might be doing. Infants are attracted to objects that adults are handling and want to do the same, and they seem to think that most household tasks the adult is doing are fun and want to join in (Hay, Murray, Cecire, & Nash, 1985; Rheingold, 1982; Rheingold, Cook, & Kolowitz, 1987). Rather than ignoring or complaining about the children being nuisances for interfering, adults can encourage the children's collaboration by giving them small tasks. This requires the adults to slow down and think about how to best include the children's efforts (Rogoff, 1990).

It is clear, however, that infants of this age are capable of developing self-control. In one study, an experimenter while talking with a child placed an attractive toy on the table. The experimenter then told the child that she (the experimenter) had to go out of the room to get something and asked the child to please wait and not to touch the toy. By age 2 years, children could wait on average for a full minute before being tempted to touch the toy, a long time for a 2-year-old (Vaughn, Kopp, & Krakow, 1984).

Compliance is more easily assured if it is clear to the infants that the expected behavior affects how they relate to others and if they are shown how their behavior affects others. For this to happen, verbal skills are necessary, and indeed, compliance with requests is correlated with verbal development (Kaler & Kopp, 1990; McLaughlin, 1983; Schneider-Rosen & Wenz-Gross, 1990; Vaughn, Kopp, & Krakow, 1984).

Peer Interactions

The last aspect of social development that I will discuss in this chapter is the change in the child's relationship to peers at this age. When given a choice of whom to play with, infants almost always choose a peer—familiar or unfamiliar—over their mothers.

They spend more time with the peer and make fewer bids for their mother's attention when a peer is present (Rubenstein, Howes, & Pedersen, 1982). A similar pattern can be seen in a day care setting: 2-year-olds spend more time with one another than with teachers (Finkelstein, Dent, Gallacher, & Ramey, 1978).

When the tables are turned and the adult is with an adult peer while the child is not, the child increases the number of bids for attention and close contact. In fact, the child is more demanding of the mother's attention when she is with a friend than when the mother and child are home alone (Rubenstein et al., 1982). This finding should come as no surprise to any parent who has tried to carry on a conversation with a friend while the baby is around. It is probably best not to ignore the child's need for attention and wish to be included. At the same time, children have to understand that they cannot necessarily be a part of everything that the parent does. Some balance between the parent's and the child's needs should be struck.

We saw in previous chapters that toddler-peer play is different in quality from toddler-parent play. Studies of 19-month-olds show that this trend continues with age. Toddlers are more likely to play with, imitate, offer toys to, and talk to peers than to their mothers, although they touch peers and mothers about the same amount of time (Rubenstein & Howes, 1976). When they play with their mothers, toddlers are more likely to have longer periods of sustained attention to single objects (N. L. Cohen & Tomlinson-Keasey, 1980).

Sometime between 18 and 24 months, peer play begins to take on a more gamelike quality. Children take simple turns involving complementary roles such as offering and accepting, throwing and catching, or simple verbal exchange ("You're a sissy"; "No, I'm not"). Words are used in such games, but not at the same level of elaboration as in adult-infant games. At this age also, there are few instances of actual collaboration on a task, as may be found during adult-infant interaction. Under 24 months, peer play seems to rest on the assumption that each child can influence the other, rather than on genuine cooperation (Brownell, 1986; Eckerman, Davis, & Didow, 1989; Howes & Matheson, 1992). Cooperation and complex verbal exchanges and

pretend play with peers will be discussed in the next chapter.

Children of this age are just beginning to form lasting relationships with peers. A **relationship** is a continuing pattern of communication between two or more people in which past encounters provide a historical background for future encounters. In the parent-infant relationship, for example, a relational perspective (Fogel, 1993) suggests that the history of their communication patterns during the first year leads to differences between dyads in their security of attachment at 1 year. It is not until the end of the second year of life that children can form lasting relationships with other children.

Children preferentially direct positive or negative behavior to particular others. Some children (compatible friends) direct mostly positive behaviors toward each other and refrain from conflicts. Other children (enemies, or fighting friends) tend to engage in conflicts most of the time they get together. Other children tend not to interact with each other (ignoring), either positively or negatively. It could be said that even these ignoring pairs have a relationship, since the same children tend to ignore each other day after day (Ross, Conant, Cheyne, & Alevizos, 1992).

Finally, the types of toys used in peer play influence the types of interactions between the children. Eighteen-month-old infants were observed playing in pairs in four different play settings: a typical play setting, one with no play materials, one with only small portable toys, and one with only large nonportable play equipment (DeStefano & Mueller, 1982).

The researchers found more sophisticated social interaction and a greater expression of positive emotion in the setting with the large play equipment (ladders, slides, and boxes). With the small portable toys, more conflict and more negative emotion was expressed. This is understandable, since children tend to fight over the possession of small toys. With only large toys, children tend to treat the environment as a space to be shared and enjoyed together.

Surprisingly, the children were most creative in the no-toy situation: they actually invented their own toys! The radiator became a "base," they took off articles of clothing to be used as play objects, and they even used each other as if they were toys.

By this age, children can cooperate in a common activity and develop sophisticated social pretend games.

Elizabeth Crews

When playing with infants, adults tend to introduce toys and other play materials to keep the pace of play up or keep the toddlers out of their way. Perhaps peer interaction provides time for the child to be more inventive and develop independent initiatives.

When conflicts over small toys do arise, children of this age are more likely to share than children older than 2 years. This may be because the older children have a more consolidated sense of self that includes possessions (see Chapter 11), and also because the younger child would prefer to avoid serious conflicts (Caplan, Vespo, Pedersen, & Hay, 1991; Hay, Caplan, Castle, & Stimson, 1991). Although it is relatively rare at this age, a third child may come over to intervene in the toy conflict between two other children (Ross et al., 1992).

Family and Society

I devote the "Family and Society" section of this chapter to some of the ways families with infants interface with their communities. Even well-

functioning, middle-income families require support and intervention from their families and communities. In cases of poverty and other risks to parenting, community support is essential and makes a difference in the outcomes for both parents and children. I will discuss both informal and formal supports for families with infants.

Informal Support Systems

Informal support systems are social networks that include friends, relatives, neighbors, co-workers, and other acquaintances, as well as community organizations that are not run by government agencies, such as churches, YWCAs, and community centers (Parke & Tinsley, 1987). One of the primary informal support systems is the marriage and extended family.

Research has shown that in two-parent families, the spouse is the most used and effective member of the social network. Spouses can provide relief from child care and consultation about child-rearing issues and can mediate when stresses on the partner predispose the partner toward impatience and harshness toward the children. Spouses can also provide needed encouragement and emotional support to each other (Levitt, Weber, & Clark, 1986; Parke & Tinsley, 1987; Weinraub & Wolf, 1983).

Typically, the infant's maternal grandmother is the next most frequent source of support; this is true for both two-parent and single-parent families. As discussed in Chapter 8, grandparents who live nearby and spend time with the infants share secure attachments with the infants and provide similar types of support for the parents as a spouse does. The special value of spouses and grandparents is that they are embedded in the family and are willing to intervene directly in the parent-child relationship. This may take the form of explaining child-rearing principles and mediating between the parent and the infant (Levitt, Weber, & Clark, 1986; McLoyd, 1990; J. H. Stevens, 1988). Teenage single mothers, both African American and Caucasian, are less punitive to their infants if the grandmother is involved (see the section on adolescent mothers in Chapter 3). The teens say things like "I would hit him more if it weren't for my parents" and "My parents won't let me spank him as often as I think he should be spanked" (McLoyd, 1990, p. 335).

As a general rule, emotional support is correlated with better parenting outcomes, regardless of where the support comes from. Parents, particularly mothers, who receive more support are less likely to be punitive in their child rearing (Colletta, 1981), more likely to play and be affectionate with their infants (Cotterell, 1986), respond more quickly to the babies' cries, have more secure attachments (Crockenberg, 1987; Crockenberg & McCluskey, 1986), are more nurturant, have more positive attitudes about child rearing (Weinraub & Wolf, 1983), and abuse their infants less (Garbarino, 1976). Having a larger and more complex support network is related to better-quality support and to parental competence in child rearing (Ball & Pianta, 1993; Melson, Hsu, & Ladd, 1993).

Factors Mediating the Impact of Informal Support Systems

Social attitudes. Unfortunately, however, not all families benefit from social support systems. In some cases, this is due to social attitudes associated with certain types of families and children. For example, studies comparing social support for families with

preterm and special-needs infants with families of typically developing infants find that the latter receive more social support. Well-functioning, middle-class families with preterm infants report receiving fewer offers of support and gifts, such as clothing and furniture, than similar families with full-term infants (Feiring, Fox, Jaskir, & Lewis, 1987).

Even when friends and family provide support to parents of preterm infants, the quality of that support may be diminished. With a preterm birth, network members may not know how to respond appropriately, and their attempts to help result in ambiguous or stressful communications, leading to a lessening of the impact of their support on the family (Zarling, Hirsch, & Landry, 1988). In general, social networks are more supportive when the psychological stress of the parents is relatively low, when the family is experiencing an expected or understandable life transition (such as a temporary job loss or a death in the family), and when the source of stress is a single event rather than a long-term problem (Crnic & Greenberg, 1987; Crockenberg, 1987; Dressler, 1985).

Parental personality. A number of studies have shown that abusive parents have small social networks and an overall poorer quality of support. This may be due in part to the fact that the personality of the abusive parent keeps the child and the social network at a distance. These parents may actively discourage those who seek to help (Crittenden, 1985; Trickett & Susman, 1988). Some parents may have poor interpersonal skills that lead to an inability to seek help and maintain supportive social ties (Parke & Tinsley, 1987). On the other hand, seeking help from family and friends entails some cost in the form of obligations for friendly behavior and doing favors in return. Some parents may prefer isolation to the burden of these obligations (McLoyd, 1990).

Cultural attitudes about seeking help. Finally, the effects of informal support networks may be lessened if parents distrust the sources of support. African American and Caucasian mothers find different types of supports most useful. For example, African American mothers tend to rely more on the extended family for support. They view professionals as unsympathetic and cannot reconcile professional advice with family norms and values. Caucasian mothers are more likely to rely on professional sources of support (Colletta, 1981; Crockenberg, 1987; J. H. Stevens, 1988). These differences may be explained by the fact that most professionals are Caucasian and may not appreciate the differences in values between their culture and the minority family culture.

Formal support systems. Formal support systems are structured programs designed to meet the special needs of parents and infants. These support systems include health care, education, counseling services, social services, housing, welfare, and recreational facilities (Parke & Tinsley, 1987). They offer services ranging from childbirth education (see Chapter 3) to well-baby care to parent training programs to early childhood education for disadvantaged toddlers. The variety of services available and their effects will not be discussed here for reasons of space; see Berlin, O'Neal, & Brooks-Gunn (1998); Greenspan & Wieder (1997); Parke & Tinsley (1987); and D. R. Powell (2000) for a more complete review.

Generally, educational interventions for parents, even in small doses, can be enormously effective, especially when combined with health care and income support (see the "Applications" section in this chapter). Short classes, films, and books can enrich the parenting experiences in well-functioning families and give parents needed confidence. For families at risk, a more comprehensive effort is most effective. Some of the more successful programs combine preschool education for the infants, a nurse–home visitor for home-based parent education, and an effort to link parents up with other formal and informal community supports (education, job training and placement, recreational facilities, etc.).

One example of a family support intervention program included a home visitor who served as a counselor and liaison with other agencies, pediatric care, day care, and developmental testing that the parents were able to observe. The families who participated were from a low-income inner-city area, the infants had no birth complications and were firstborns, and the mothers had no history of serious psychological illness. A follow-up study of the children 10 years after their participation in the pro-

gram compared the children who were in the program to a matched sample of children who did not attend. The children in the intervention program had better school attendance and required less welfare and special education programming. The mothers were more likely to be economically independent, had completed more years of school, and had fewer children than the control mothers (Field, Widmayer, Stringer, & Ignatoff; Provence & Naylor, 1983; Seitz, Rosenbaum, & Apfel, 1985).

Other multisite, multimethod intervention programs have been shown to decrease reliance on welfare, reduce parental substance abuse, and lower the incidence of criminal acts when the infants become adolescents (A. J. Reynolds, 1998). Generally speaking, the most successful programs are those that provide high-quality educational child care for the infant coupled with home- and center-based support services for the parents and families. Neither parent education alone nor child care alone is as effective as the two are in combination (M. M. Black & Krishnakumar, 1998; D. R. Powell, 2000; C. T. Ramey & Ramey, 1998; Yoshikawa, 1999).

Head Start is a federally funded national preschool (3 to 6 years) education program with goals similar to the projects mentioned above. Since it was started by President Lyndon Johnson in 1965, Head Start has enjoyed bipartisan support in Congress, but it has received funding for only 40% of all eligible children. In the 30 years between 1965 and 1995, Head Start served more than 14 million poor (83% had family incomes below $12,000) preschool children: one-third are Caucasian, one-third are African American, and the rest are Hispanic and Native American. In 1994, 740,493 children were enrolled at a annual cost of $4,343 per child.

Recent long-term follow-up research comparing Head Start children with those who attended other day care or had no support show that Head Start children were more advanced educationally and cognitively; however, the differences between the Head Start and the other groups diminished with increasing age (V. E. Lee, Brooks-Gunn, & Schnur, 1988; V. E. Lee, Brooks-Gunn, Schnur, & Liaw, 1990). Although the cognitive gains are not impressive, other research shows that 15 years after Head Start the participating children had fewer teen pregnancies and a higher high school graduation rate, and they were more likely to be employed and less likely to have been arrested (Schweinhart & Weikart, 1979; Berrueta-Clement, Schweinhart, Barnett, Epstein, & Weikart, 1984). Other research shows gains for Head Start similar to those found for the family intervention program described above (Lazar & Darlington, 1982). The problem is that these gains may obtain only for the highest quality Head Start programs in which the research is done. On the other hand, everyone agrees that Head Start children have a more enriched early childhood experience and do better in preschool and elementary school than controls. This, it can be argued, is sufficient reason to continue the program (S. L. Ramey, 1999).

Head Start continues to add new experimental programs. Currently, it is undertaking an initiative to include children under the age of 3 years. Other experimental programs include family service centers (to provide job training and education for parents), transition to elementary school programs (to provide training for elementary school teachers who will teach the Head Start graduates), comprehensive child developmental centers (to provide training in prenatal nutrition and parent skills), and family child-care projects (to allow single parents to work full time while supporting the child and family). These efforts combine services for the developing child with attempts to lift the family from poverty (D. L. Cohen, 1993; Glazer, 1993b).

The Author's View

This age period brings revolutionary changes in infant development. Symbolic thought, for example, is considered to be one of the major attributes of a human being. Although infants have already shown the seeds of symbolic thought, beginning with their first intentional gestures at 9 months, it takes another year or more for true symbols to emerge. For the first time, we can say that infants think in a way that is similar to adult thinking: with symbols that are words.

Symbols are conventionally shared among the members of a linguistic community. When children use the word "dog," they not only represent dogs

symbolically, they partake of a socially shared way of representing dogs. At the end of the first year, the child's first words were an example of **idiosyncratic communication:** they represented things but not in a way that could be shared by more than the people who were closest to the child. When the children use the word "dog," they are referring to that particular animal and they are accepting the rights and responsibilities of being a member of a community of people who have agreed to use that word. To be a member of a community is to comply by its rules (the animal we know as a dog is to be called by the word "dog") and also to be consciously aware of abiding by the rules.

The awareness that *communication* takes place in a *community* is the foundation of the existential self, which begins to develop after the age of 18 months. Babies of this age become aware that they are being watched. This must be a rather startling discovery for a baby, as the following example may illustrate. Think of some ways that you express yourself privately, ways you have not shown to anyone or even talked about with anyone, like singing in the shower, writing poetry, or drawing pictures. You are probably perfectly happy doing these things alone and you can feel yourself, your mind and body, as you do them. This is your subjective self coming out. Now imagine that someone overhears you, or finds your poems and reads them, or sees your drawings. Your privacy has been invaded and you would most likely be embarrassed. This is the voice of your existential self waking up to the fact that you can be exposed when you least expect it. Depending on your style of emotional regulation and on the person who discovered you and their way of behaving with you about this discovery, you might be defiantly angry and feel violated, or you might be relieved and proud that someone likes your work.

Whatever way you feel about it, your world has been changed. You cannot operate in total isolation anymore. You have to do something about your new awareness that you are living in a household community. One thing you might do is negotiate the boundaries of your privacy with the other person, coming to an agreement about what is yours alone and what you are willing to share. Alternatively, you could slam the door to your room and scream at the other person. Or, you could welcome the other person into your world and open that world to shared experiences. No one of these strategies is better than another. Each depends upon you and the situation

What they have in common, however, is that you are being compelled to recognize your membership in a community. The more of yourself that you open up to that community, the more of an opportunity you have to share, but the more you must comply with the standards and rules of the community. The dynamics of compliance is the topic of the Awareness through Movement lesson of this chapter. If you are willing to comply, it may lead to increased skills and self-awareness, such as when one takes singing, writing, or drawing lessons, for example. These activities provide access to community standards and practices and the symbols with which members of those communities communicate about their work.

The developmental challenge for infants of this age, then, is to open up to the pleasures (pride, mastery, sharing) and pains (shame, defiance, having to comply) of being an active member of a community. This is not easy to do, and in fact, as the Awareness through Movement lesson reveals, it is a lifelong issue that only *begins* at 18 months. How much of your willingness to comply in particular situations is related to an unconscious participatory memory of your style of compliance as a toddler? Perhaps you can ask the people who knew you as a baby about your style of compliance back then and compare it to your style of compliance today.

The other major developmental lesson of this age period is opening up to new dimensions of psychological experience. Up to this point in their development, children's awareness has been participatory. Now they can put symbolic labels on their experiences and attach those labels to a subject (e.g., "I," "you"). When a child says "I'm tired," they can identify their experience with a word and at the same time bring it into the community for guidance and assistance. "I'm tired" is a way of saying "pick me up" or "put me to bed."

Imagine feeling as though you are low in energy but not knowing why. You have a conversation with a friend, and somehow you realize that this feeling is because you have been working really hard or faced some new or difficult challenges. Because you were so caught up in what you had to do (subjective self), you did not have an opportunity to find a

name for your feeling and recognize that it was part of you (existential self). After the conversation you can say, "Oh, yes, I'm really tired," which may give you permission to take it easy or to treat yourself nicely for a while. You deserve it!

The clinical theories reviewed in Chapter 2, both the psychotherapeutic and somatic approaches, suggest that developmental change comes from the coupling of psychological and body awareness with words or gestures shared with another person in the context of a therapeutic relationship. Research and clinical practice have shown that simply communicating—verbally or nonverbally—with another person in a therapeutic situation about those areas of your mind and body that were hurting, confused, or in the darkness of anxiety is often sufficient to change them for the better (Feldenkrais, 1981; C. Ginsburg, 1999; Hartley, 1995; Hunt, 1995; Smyth & Pennebaker, 1999; Varela, Thompson, & Rosch, 1995; Wooten, 1995).

Co-regulation with another person in a safe and secure relationship, within the boundaries of a shared communication frame, is both the source and the container of developmental change (Fogel, 1993; also see Chapter 2). Co-regulation is inherently creative when people can be spontaneous with each other. Frames provide a sense of safety, a secure base from which people can venture into new areas of developmental challenges and can return for support and sustenance. At 18 months, infants are just beginning to appreciate the existence of community, themselves as members of it, and its mysterious power to expose them on the one hand and to shelter them on the other. We spend the rest of our lives on the boundary of these alternative possibilities, changing self and community in the process of co-regulation.

AWARENESS THROUGH MOVEMENT

Compliance and Related Issues

Do the following exercise with a partner. Both partners sit in chairs facing each other, with their chairs at least six feet apart. One partner should read the instructions to the other. The exercise relates to movement, but its primary purpose is to discover more about issues relating to compliance and how we respond to requests. Carefully observe both your mental and physical processes while doing the steps below.

1. Slowly and comfortably bend forward without any strain, and move in such a way as if you wanted to put your elbows on the floor in front of you. Come back to slowly sitting upright in your chair, pause a few moments, and then repeat the movement. Do not do anything to force yourself to do it. Slowly repeat the movement many times, and observe what you feel in your body while doing it and how you feel about listening and complying with the instructions.

   a. Do you comply, or try to comply, with the request immediately, or is there a time delay? What happens during the time delay?
   b. Are you trying to understand the request? How did you link the words in the request to the parts of your body, to the environment, and to the task?
   c. Do you feel any conflict about whether to comply with the request or not?
   d. Is the movement possible?
   e. Did you feel personally capable of doing the movement?
   f. If you feel a sense of difficulty, do you feel uncomfortable with yourself about it, or uncomfortable with the person giving you the instructions, or both?
   g. How do you feel about the possibility of complying or not complying? How does that make you feel about yourself and your relationship to the one making the request?
   h. Do you feel that you are successful in satisfying the request or not? How would you gauge your success?
   i. Do you attempt different ways of doing the movement, or stay with one strategy? If you try different strategies, do you wonder whether you are complying with the request or not?

2. Now continue to the same thing, except experiment and see if there is another way to bring your elbows to the floor that is not so difficult. Do not be too serious. Fool around. Is it pos-sible to bring your elbows to the floor? How many ways can you think of doing it?

Comments: Most people stay seated in their chairs and attempt to place their elbows on the floor by stretching. It is impossible to touch the elbows to the floor in this manner. However, it is easy to touch your elbows to the floor if you bend forward, get out of your chair, and go onto your hands and knees. You can also probably think of other ways of doing it. Small children react to such an exercise in very different ways than adults do. Although this particular movement is not appropriate for a baby, the exercise highlights issues that pertain to issues of compliance for the baby's, and our own, relationships. It is much more likely for young children than adults to arrive at a solution to bringing their elbows to the floor. What is different in the process of the child compared with that of the adult? Perhaps the child is less likely to assume that he or she must remain seated on the chair and focuses on the task rather than the position. Perhaps the child is more creative. Perhaps the child is less willing to put himself or herself through uncomfortable movements.

Small children are also more likely than adults not to comply with the request at all, and simply do nothing, or something completely unrelated to the request. Why is this? Is it because the child does not understand the instructions? Or does not feel like doing what is asked? Or does not want to accept the effort he or she believes will be required? This simple situation is very complicated because it entails understanding verbal instructions, and interpreting the parameters of the task and the purpose of the request. At the same time, one is assessing one's competency to perform the task, gauging one's comfort, and evaluating whether the task is worth the effort. Implicit in this situation is also an assessment of the significance of the person making the request and their feelings regarding it, as well as an assessment of our trust in the one who is making the request. In the course of performing the movements, as we become aware of different reactions in ourselves and the other, all the other feelings are in a dynamic process of change.

Although you were requested to move in comfort and not to strain or force the movement,

In 1960, one-quarter of all children under 5 years old in the United States were living in poverty. By 1980, this figure had fallen to 17%, but by 1994, it had risen again to 25% of all children. An increasing proportion of these poor children live in female-headed single families, which today constitute the fastest growing poverty group in the United States. These figures are shocking. When we compare them to statistics for other wealthy nations, they become a matter of national shame. When our childhood poverty rate was the lowest, in 1980 at 17%, the childhood poverty rate was 10% in Canada, 8% in West Germany, 5% in Sweden, and 11% in the United Kingdom. Child poverty rates have continued to decline in these other countries (Bane & Ellwood, 1989; Hernandez, 1997; Huston, 1994; McLoyd, 1998; Smeeding & Torrey, 1988).

What are some of the causes of these poverty rates and national differences?

Single parenthood: In all countries, as you might expect, single-parent families are poorer than two-parent families because of the reduced earning power of a single adult. In addition, due to the structure of most welfare systems, it is not advantageous for many single mothers to work outside the home because of the added costs and risks of child care.

For example, an unemployed single mother with two children in the United States in 1986 could collect $6,284 in welfare and food stamps. If she worked full-time in a minimum wage job, she would earn a salary of $6,700 and could still collect $2,744 in welfare. By the time she paid for child care (about $3,000) and taxes ($373), her resulting income would be $6,817, only $533 more than if she were unemployed

and stayed home with her children (Bane & Ellwood, 1989).

Diverse populations: In the United States, poverty level varies considerably as a function of race and ethnicity. The percentage of African American children living in poverty (the number of poor African American children divided by the total number of African American children) is three times as high as for Caucasian children, and the rate for Hispanic children is twice as high as for Caucasian children. Even so, the poverty rate of Caucasian children alone (11%) is higher than in most other wealthy nations. Obviously, not all poverty occurs in minority groups.

Lack of public support for families: In the United States, welfare and other public benefits are given to individuals, not to families. One of the problems is that children do not have their own rights to such benefits. While the poverty rate among the elderly has dropped in recent years due to increased medical and Social Security benefits to individuals, the poverty rate for children has increased. At least 25% of families with children living below the poverty level in the United States receive no welfare or other forms of support. In contrast, almost 100% of poor families receive benefits in Canada, Germany, Sweden, and the United Kingdom (Smeeding & Torrey, 1988). Contrary to popular belief, one or both parents work in over three-quarters of the poor families with children in the United States. Of the remaining 25% of families, 15% have parents who do not work because of illness or disability or because they are past retirement age (Bane & Ellwood, 1989). Thus, the welfare system cannot be blamed for keeping families in poverty. Most parents work if they are able to.

The economic system: Since none of the above factors by itself — single parenthood, race and ethnicity, and welfare — can explain why so many families are poor, what does? The best explanation seems to be the economy as a whole. If the economy slows down, middle- and upper-income families fare better than those at the bottom. Lower-income families suffer more from the lack of an annual raise or the loss of a job, since they have no other resources on which to depend. In addition, the number of blue-collar jobs is steadily declining in favor of jobs requiring more technical training, such as working with computers.

Analysts suggest some alternatives to welfare that might help these poor families. These alternatives include better tax credits for lower-income families (in the United States, higher-income families receive the most tax credits), a higher minimum wage, better child care alternatives that are not based on how much money you can afford to pay, and better medical care to alleviate the chronic health problems associated with poverty. Nonwelfare options may also contribute to a better life for such families. These include enforcing child support payments from absent fathers, parent education and job training, and community support and intervention services (Bane & Ellwood, 1989; Huston, 1994).

How are children affected by living in poor families?

Poverty breeds mental and health risks due to an increased and continuous stream of stressful life events, including job loss, worry about bills, eviction, illness, alcoholism and drug dependency, marital discord, assault, arrest, and imprisonment. In addition, poor children receive lower-quality prenatal care, lower-quality day care, and lower access to informal and formal support systems (McLoyd, 1998; NICHD Early Child Care Research Network, 1997). These factors feed off each other, leading to increasingly dismal cycles of loss, stress, and despair. When these factors are then compounded with racial and social-class prejudice, the risk to mental health is enormous (McLoyd, 1990; McLoyd, 1998).

Due to these stresses, poor parents have been shown to be less emotionally available for their children, less affectionate, harsher in their disciplinary styles, and more likely to respond punitively to relatively minor forms of child misbehavior. Fathers seem particularly affected; they grow more harsh, and many leave the family entirely. On the positive side, however, some families report greater parent-child closeness following job loss, as well as more family solidarity. Evidence from a variety of sources — including the effects of the Great Depression, the experience of inner-city families, and the results of job losses due to farm foreclosures and plant closings in middle-class America — reveals a surprising pattern of individual variation in family response to poverty, ranging from renewed parent-child closeness to child abuse and neglect (Coles, 1971; Elder, Nguyen, & Caspi, 1985; McLoyd, 1990; 1997; Perrucci & Targ, 1988; G. Peterson & Peters, 1985; Portes, Dunham, & Williams, 1986). Some research even suggests that harsher parental discipline may better prepare children for the hardships they will face growing up in poverty (Sameroff & Seifer, 1983). In general, however, poverty has more negative than positive effects on parent-child relationships.

Children from poor families suffer more from depression, poor peer relations, social withdrawal, low self-esteem, deviant behavior patterns, aggressiveness (particularly in boys), and lowered aspirations (especially for girls). In addition, these children often contract more infectious diseases, are less skilled verbally and interpersonally, and do less well in school and on other indices of cognitive development (Bronfenbrenner, 1986; McLoyd, 1990; McLoyd & Wilson, 1991; Patterson, Kupersmidt, & Vaden, 1990; Ramey & Campbell, 1991).

Conclusions

I have written in this section about children in general, but children under the age of 3 years are disproportionately represented in poverty rates. Because of their relative helplessness and vulnerability, infants may suffer more from the effects of poverty than older children (Bronfenbrenner, 1986).

Consider the following chain of events. A teenage girl or young woman has grown up in an inner-city culture of poverty. She has suffered from parental neglect and malnutrition. Even if she is lucky enough to have escaped physical or sexual abuse, she has been hardened against her own feelings and those of others. She gets sick often, takes alcohol and drugs to excess, eats mostly junk food, and gets no exercise or fresh air.

She is likely to become pregnant before her 20th birthday and is likely to bear and keep the child. She may not detect that she is pregnant until the second or third month, may not see a doctor until near the end of her pregnancy, and is unlikely to change any of her risky health behaviors. What would you predict is likely to happen to her child, based on what you know about the needs of a typically developing fetus?

It is statistically likely (see Chapter 3) that her baby will be born prematurely and in addition may suffer from a variety of prenatal and perinatal disorders, many of which will have lasting effects on the future development of the brain and body. The long-term follow-up data suggest that high-risk newborns who are raised in high-risk families are likely to develop mental and physical health problems, behavior disorders, and intellectual deficits (see Chapter 12). When this child becomes a teenager, will she fare better than her mother? The conditions of poverty, acting through generational developmental cycles, perpetuate the suffering and widen the gap between rich and poor.

Earlier discussions in this text about child development and public policy suggest that it will be a long time before the U.S. government places the welfare of families and children high on the national agenda. The attitude of the government seems to be that the community will take care of itself and that private business, if given enough tax credits, will share the burden. This has not happened. Indeed, corporations and businesses spend millions of dollars to lobby against federal legislation for day care, parental leave, and a higher minimum wage. Businesses that support the family, in the community and for their own employees, make up a very small minority of all businesses.

Even small amounts of community support can have lasting positive effects on families and children living in poverty (see the "Family and Society" section in this chapter). On the other hand, without intervention, some of the effects of early malnutrition, disease, abuse, and neglect may be irreversible. What kind of a future will deprived American children and their families face?

Co-Regulating with Baby

The most striking and remarkable aspect of this stage of development is the emergence of the child's sense of an existential self. For the first time, the baby no longer seems so much like a baby: the child begins to behave in more adult-like ways. Whole new realms of interpersonal communication are possible for those interested in taking advantage of them.

One of the most notable signs of the child's new grasp on personhood is the increasing use of negation. At first, this happens with an insistent "no!" Later, with improved language, it becomes something like, "I won't do it," or "I don't want to." Babies often say *no* just for the purpose of exploring its effect on others; at other times, they do so because they have a legitimate complaint or disagreement that needs attention.

This behavior signals a new recognition of personal boundaries and limitations. The difficulty during the "no" stage comes when caregivers and children are at odds on an issue or when the children insist on making up their own minds and then cannot handle the responsibility they seem to want to have for themselves.

It helps to give the children experience in making choices they can handle, for example, deciding what kind of juice they would like or what color socks they would like to wear. If the children know they can make responsible decisions about some things, it may be easier to discourage them from insisting on making other decisions that the caregiver knows they should not make. This is the essence of proactive parenting.

As in other aspects of dealing with children, a sense of humor is a good ally. You can sometimes make "no" into a game by repeating it back in an obviously playful tone of voice as well as by suggesting obviously silly alternatives to the child's unreasonable request or to the caregiver's snubbed demand. In this way, the toddler may discover that refusing to do something does not always have to end up in a fight with Mom or Dad.

It is not always possible to be so flexible, as when a child refuses to hold your hand when crossing the street. However, even this can be made into a kind of game ritual. Once you establish a pattern of doing things like crossing streets, changing diapers, putting the child to bed, or reading a story, a child likes to stick to the initial routines faithfully. At this age, some of these frames have a ritualistic quality because the child likes to do them the same way each time. Although rituals can become downright boring and tedious for a caregiver, it is important to realize that they are necessary ways of maintaining order, safety, and health in a generally peaceful manner. You may not understand why a sandwich cut in quarters tastes better than one cut in half, but if that is what it takes to get a meal down, then why not cut it that way? Good-natured co-regulation in areas like this is an effective way to build trust so the child will understand you when you need to insist on compliance in more serious situations.

One area in which children show self-assertion is getting dressed. It is very difficult to know how much

many people will nonetheless try to force the movement anyway. Where does this effort come from? Some people will feel satisfied with making gentle movements toward the floor, even though they do not reach the floor with their elbows. Others will feel conflicted about the relationship between themselves and the one giving the requests. Some people will treat the request as a problem-solving exercise, rather than a physical exercise, and that will result in more experimentation and play. As adults, our feelings about compliance affect our development and our relationships in many ways.

SUMMARY

Motor and Cognitive Development

- Motor advances include self-feeding, toilet training, and stable sleep patterns.

- The ability to think about actions without actually performing them develops. Infants can solve some problems mentally, without trial and error.

- Symbolic play develops by the combination of different types of symbols into complex event children need or want you to do for them and how much they can or want to do for themselves. Although babies of this age are just about able to put on their socks and shoes, for example, they still have some trouble getting socks over that inconvenient bend at the ankle or trying to figure out which shoe goes on which foot. Your effort to co-regulate can be courteous as well as respectful by helping get things started and then letting the child finish. Some examples are putting on a sock partway, giving the child an oversized sock to put on, or handing the child the proper shoe. Other situations include providing a step stool to reach the sink, turning on the faucet partway, pulling out the child's chair just enough for the child to climb up to the table on his or her own, and pushing the chair in once the child is settled.

Language helps all these problems immensely. Children are less likely to have a tantrum or cry when they are able to express their problems with words. Caregivers can help this along by modeling words related to inner feelings, such as *mad, tired, scared, happy, sad*, or *hurt*.

Language also leads to new and interesting games and conversations with the child. Naming is a compelling game at this age. Reading books becomes more fun. Also at this age, children discover the fun of playing outdoors, where there are many new things to name and explore. Car rides are usually a big treat, because children gradually come to recognize general categories of objects ("the cow like the cow in the book").

They also recognize specific things like the kind of gasoline station where their mother always stops. Every time they pass that type of gasoline station, children can recognize it, and they will happily search until they see another one. These kinds of discoveries almost always are accompanied by feelings of great pride on the children's part, and they want everyone else to appreciate the accomplishment.

As already mentioned, pretending and tool using are important at this age. In the realm of object exploration, children are discovering how to make towers and trains, as well as how to destroy them in a flash. The following are traditional pastimes guaranteed to delight any child of 1½ years: riding a tricycle or scooter; playing catch by rolling the ball; pushing and pulling large objects such as wagons or chairs; climbing on the sofa, chairs, and playground equipment; and playing a real game of hide-and-seek.

The second birthday is rather different from the first. Because of the ability to form mental representations, babies about to be 2 years old are able to look forward to their second birthdays, think about presents, get excited about the occasion, and ask whether they will have cake. Although they still do not fully understand the concept of a birthday, they are aware that they are part of a special event that is somehow centered upon them. In the next chapter, I will follow the development of that important sense of self-awareness as it unfolds in the third year of life.

sequences. Infants still do not understand all the connections between their own actions on objects.

- Script-based memories allow for categorization of events according to the sequences in which they typically occur.

- Children of this age become interested in simple television programs, but it helps if adults watch along with them.

- An existential sense of self emerges when children can recognize themselves in the mirror and when they begin to use the word "I."

- Infantile autism, a pathology of self and relationships, can be diagnosed as early as 18 months, which may lead to the development of new treatments.

- Aside from autism, there are three other diagnostic catgorgies used by infant mental health practitioners: pervasive developmental disorder, reactive attachment syndrome, and separation anxiety disorder.

Emotional Development

- Fears originate in mental and symbolic images, and some dreaming begins. Infants develop new emotions, such as defiance, embarrassment, and pride.

- Transitional objects serve to comfort infants when adults are unavailable.

- Smiling and laughter develop as important forms of communication about positive emotion.

- Pride and shame develop as emotions related to the existential self.

- Separations are easier for children if parents explain what will happen and when they will return, if the environment is one in which the infants feel comfortable, and if the infants have experience with separations.

Social and Language Development

- There is a vocabulary spurt that begins at this age, corresponding with the insight that things have names.

- Symbolic play and tool use correlate with the onset of multiword speech and the vocabulary spurt at around 20 months.

- Infants combine words in flexible formulas that allow different meanings to be constructed but are not as rigid as grammar.

- Individual differences in style and amount of speech emerge at this age.

- A linguistic environment conducive to infant language development is one in which adults are responsive to the infant's speech initiative by commenting and asking questions.

- Apes appear to have language abilities similar to those of human infants, and with human adult guidance, they can acquire signed languages.

- Guided participation is a general principle that applies to language, play, and discipline interactions.

- Discipline can be achieved by guided participation and by proactively regulating the environment.

- Peers begin to play more reciprocal games. They also begin to form lasting relationships.

Family and Society

- All families rely on both formal and informal sources of support during infancy.

- Factors mediating the effectiveness of support include social attitudes about different types of infants, parental personality and its effect on support sources, and cultural attitudes about seeking help.

- Early childhood intervention for disadvantaged families shows gains for infants in some areas but not in others.

Applications: Poverty and Risk

- The poverty rate for children in the United States is one of the highest among the wealthy countries.

- There is a higher percentage of poverty among racial and ethnic minorities, but there are also many poor Caucasian children.

- Poverty affects the psychological health of adults, which in turn affects how they interact with their children.

- A variety of welfare and nonwelfare solutions to alleviate the effects of poverty on children have been proposed.

ON THE WEB

www.autism.org/overview.html   This site is an online version of "Overview of Autism," by Stephen M. Edelson, Center for the Study of Autism, Salem, Oregon. According to the abstract, "It has been over 50 years since Dr. Leo Kanner, a psychiatrist at Johns Hopkins University, wrote the first paper applying the term 'autism' to a group of children who were self-absorbed and who had severe social, communication, and behavioral problems. This paper provides a general overview of the complexity of this developmental disability by summarizing many of the major topics in autism."

www.menninger.edu   This is the home page of Menninger, a psychiatric hospital in Topeka, Kansas, that provides services for adults, children, and adolescents. It also has programs such as the Child & Family Center, the Center for Learning Disabilities, training programs for mental health professionals, the Institute for Psychoanalysis, continuing education, and the Center for Clinical Research. The site provides links to news releases, the library, the *Bulletin of the Menninger Clinic,* the Menninger Bookstore, articles, the telephone directory, and contact information.

www.ehsnrc.org The Early Head Start National Resource Center offers complete documents, bibliographies, and annotated references for Early Head Start topic areas: early childhood development and health, family and community partnerships, and program design and management.

www.acf.dhhs.gov The web page of the Administration for Children and Families, part of the Department of Health and Human Services, provides many resources on ACF programs and services such as the Administration for Native Americans, the Administration on Developmental Disabilities, the Children's Bureau, Child Support Enforcement, the Family and Youth Services Bureau, the Head Start Bureau, the Office of Family Assistance, and more.

www.utmem.edu/bcdd/boling.html "The Boling Center for Developmental Disabilities (BCDD) is part of the University of Tennessee Health Science Center's College of Medicine [in Memphis]. Located near 17 hospitals and rehabilitation programs, the BCDD is an interdisciplinary program whose mission is to improve the lives of individuals with developmental disabilities and their families through research, training, service, technical assistance, and prevention activities."

GLOSSARY

Authoritative parenting A style of parenting that combines warmth and firmness.

Autism A developmental disorder whose symptoms include an impaired ability to interact socially, speech and language deficits, and unusual movements of the body.

Categorical self A concept of the self as belonging to one or more categories, such as that of baby or female.

Conventional communication A communicative act, such as a word, that is used by all members of the same speaking community.

Ecological self The ability to experience the body and its senses, feelings, and movements in relation to the environment.

Existential self The ability to recognize one's own features as different from someone else's. It involves an awareness of the self as someone who can be recognized and can be distinguished as a whole person from other people.

Expressive speech Speech that is socially oriented and uses more, but less well articulated, words per utterance.

Formal support systems Community programs that are specifically designed to serve the needs of parents and infants; usually funded by the government.

Formulas Flexible word orders that make up the first sentences of infants; not the same as mature grammar.

Guided participation Collaboration of a responsive adult on a task the infant is already doing, allowing the infant to take small, culturally appropriate roles.

Head Start A federally funded program for enriched early childhood education and parent education for disadvantaged families.

Idiosyncratic communication A form of communication that the individual makes up. It requires a familiar adult to interpret its meaning.

Informal support system A family's social network of relatives, friends, and community resources.

Parental proactive behavior An approach to discipline in which the adult controls the child's environment by anticipating future problems.

Parental separation anxiety A parent's feelings of loss or distress when he or she is separated from the child.

Referential speech Speech that is object oriented and contains a few, but clearly articulated, words per utterance.

Relationship A lasting pattern of communication between two or more people in which past encounters provide a historical background for future encounters.

Script A form of conceptual organization in which events are remembered according to the sequences in which they usually occur.

Self-conscious emotion An emotion that requires an awareness of an existential self in relation to an existential other; examples are shame, embarrassment, guilt, and pride.

Symbol   A representation of a thing or event that is conventionally shared among the members of a community.

Telegraphic speech   Speech having two or more words per utterance but with endings and connecting words left out.

Transitional object   An object to which the infant develops an attachment; it may be used for comfort in the absence of the caregiver.

11

Twenty-Four to Thirty-Six Months

CHAPTER OVERVIEW AND OUTLINE

Motor and Cognitive Development

How does the child's thinking affect action? What are some uses of and individual differences in pretend play?

Emotional Development

What are the different forms of positive emotion at this age? How do children talk about their emotions? Can children at this age understand the emotions of other people?

Social and Language Development

In what way are verbs acquired? How does grammar develop? What are the conversational skills at this age? What changes occur in parent and peer relationships? What are children's gender-role concepts and how are they formed?

Family and Society

What happens between children of this age and their siblings? Are there inter-family differences in sibling interaction?

Applications: Infant and Child Maltreatment

What are the causes and effects of child abuse? What are the limitations of research on child abuse?

This chapter is intended as a bridge between infancy and the preschool years. Although there is no clear demarcation between these two periods, a number of factors suggest that the infancy period is not completely over until late in the third year of life. At this time, infants can genuinely engage in linguistic and cooperative interactions with their peers, siblings, and parents. The 3-year-old has a command of family relationships that the 2-year-old does not. By the age of 3 years, the child can nurture a younger sibling and take independent stands against older siblings. Productive grammatical speech does not emerge until the end of the third year, although even this speech is still fairly simple in structure. Children of this age also develop an awareness of themselves as boys or girls. This chapter describes these important transitions in the third year. The "Applications" section of this chapter covers the topic of child maltreatment as it affects infants.

Motor and Cognitive Development

Motor Development

From a motor perspective, the third year is an exciting developmental period. Table 11.1 lists some of the motor achievements that occur in the third year. Age norms are not available for all these items, so I list them according to whether they develop early or late in the third year. It is important to remember that there are wide individual differences in the age these skills are acquired, so some children will not be doing all of these things by the end of the third year. The Awareness through Movement lesson of this chapter explores one of these motor achievements: jumping.

Most infants have developed their adult hand preference by the age of 3 years, although for some infants a stable preference does not finally emerge until the age of 5 years (Hardyck & Petrinovich, 1977; Ramsay, 1980). There is no evidence that left-handed children (about 12% of the population) have cognitive and motor deficits, and it is unjustified on

typical developmental grounds to try to encourage children to switch their hand preference (Tan, 1985).

Whether right or left handed, by age 3, children are drawing squiggles and making simple shapes on paper. Research shows that these early drawings are not usually mirrors of the child's emotional life but reflect the motor limitations of the arm and the hand (Freeman, 1980; Golomb, 1974). Once children begin to draw shapes, they prefer simple ones, such as circles and rectangles. Eventually, these shapes are combined into more complex pictures (Goodnow, 1977). The development of one child's ability to copy a square is shown in Figure 11.1. Note that even in the first drawings using spiral forms, there is a crude representation of a square. During the period when Matthew was using the spiral forms shown here, he was also representing human figures with spirals. After he was able to draw the square at 2 years, 9 months, and 13 days, his drawings of human figures began to look more realistic and include facial details. This research shows that children in the third year develop the ability to draw simple visual units (like circles and squares) from which they construct more complex images (Stiles, 1995). Children of this age, then, can make approximate drawings of physical objects. It takes at least another year for children to draw symbolic objects such as letters, words, and graphic symbols like smiley faces (T. C. Callaghan, 1999).

The drawings shown in Figure 11.1 were done when the child was asked to copy a particular figure. Not all the drawings that children produce during this period are meant to represent something in the world and it is not always appropriate for adults to interpret the drawings as being real or representational. Rather, the child may be using the materials to explore the medium: to discover what kinds of shapes, lines, and colors can be made with this brush or that crayon.

Another aspect of motor development is physical play. During the first 2 years, physical play consists primarily of explorations of the body's abilities, primary and secondary circular reactions, and the child's efforts to acquire new motor skills such as sitting, standing, and walking. These types of physical play are similar to doing Awareness through Movement lessons. During the second and third years, children develop what is called **exercise play.** Exercise play is playful locomotor movement that

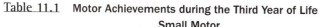

Table 11.1   Motor Achievements during the Third Year of Life

	Small Motor	Large Motor
First half of third year	Uses large crayons and pencils. Uses hand gestures and sign language.	Rides large-wheel toys. Walks up and down stairs with both feet on each step. Jumps with two-foot takeoff. Throws a ball 4 to 5 feet. Walks sideways and backward. Runs. Engages in free-ranging movement out of doors.
Second half of third year	Uses building toys with many possible shapes (blocks, Legos, etc.). Uses paints and clay. Hammers.	Walks up and down stairs by alternating each foot. Walks a line, heel-to-toe. Hops 2 or 3 times. Walks a short balance beam. Throws a ball 10 feet. Engages in rough-and-tumble play. Finds route in unfamiliar places.

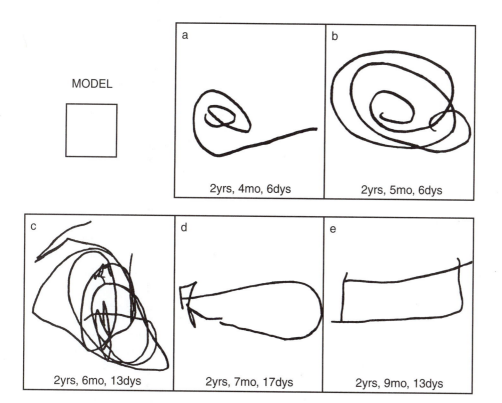

Figure 11.1

Squares Produced by Matthew When Asked to Copy the Square Model

Source: J. Stiles, The early use and development of graphic formulas: Two case study reports of graphic formula production by 2-to-3-year-old children, 1995, p. 132. *International Journal of Behavioral Development, 18*(1), 127–149. Reprinted by permission of the International Society for the Study of Behavioral Development.

is physically vigorous, such as running, chasing, and climbing; it may or may not be social. It accounts for about 7–14% of behavior in day care settings for 3-year-old children (Pellegrini & Smith, 1998). Boys tend to engage in exercise play more than girls, and boys of this age have a higher overall activity level than girls (Campbell & Eaton, 1999; Pellegrini & Smith, 1998).

Exercise play appears to have the same sorts of benefits for young children as for adults. It increases fitness, endurance, strength, and skill. There is some evidence that physical play in young children reduces fat and increases the ability of the body to regulate temperature. Some have suggested that exercise play enhances cognitive ability, but research has not been able to clearly distinguish the effects of exercise play from the effects of just having playground breaks during the more demanding cognitive tasks in day care and preschool. In any case, it is clear that both boys and girls need exercise play for the healthy development of both body and mind (Pellegrini & Smith, 1998).

Can Two-Year-Olds Remember Their Own Infancy?

As we saw in the previous chapter, by age 2, infants are beginning to organize their memories according to sequences of events. They can often remember complex sequences, and in some cases, they can remember sequences that happened some time ago so long as there is some kind of nonverbal reminder and the child is allowed to demonstrate the memory nonverbally via imitation.

The ability to remember experiences verbally is called **autobiographical memory.** Autobiographical memory serves to create a sense of one's life history. It is constructed in conversations with others beginning during the third year of life. Children whose autobiographical memory is more detailed have mothers who are more likely to elaborate on children's recall by filling in the details of the past event and asking questions of children to clarify their stories about themselves (Fivush, 1994; Harley & Reese, 1999).

By the beginning of the third year of life, children are beginning to show verbal autobiographical memories. Their ability to verbally narrate a past situation depends, however, on whether or not they had verbal skills at the time of the event they are trying to remember. Researchers in Canada studied children who had a traumatic injury that brought them to the hospital emergency room some time during their first two years of life (C. Peterson, 1999; C. Peterson & Bell, 1996; C. Peterson & Rideout, 1998). If the injury occurred around the age of 2 years, children could recall the situation verbally up to two years later. One such child had burned his hand on a lawnmower exhaust when he was just under 2 years old. A year and a half later, he could state that he burned his hand, who was there, why it happened, and that he saw a doctor.

Children who were injured before 18 months are interesting from the perspective of the transition from participatory to verbal memories. At 16 months, a child fell and cut his forehead. His emergency room visit was traumatic for him, since he had to be tightly wrapped in a blanket to keep him from moving during the stitching. For the next few months, he showed sleep disturbances and fear of strangers, did not want to leave the house, and became hysterical when blankets were put on him. He was interviewed by the researchers when he was 22 months old. At that time he still did not have verbal skills sufficient to describe the situation, but when he heard the word "hospital," he pointed to the place on his forehead where he had received the stitches. He was shown several pictures, one of which was of his doctor. He picked up the doctor's picture and showed it to his father, saying, "Doc, doc." When interviewed 18 months after the accident (at 34 months of age), he still had no verbal memory of it, but his parents said he still refused to be wrapped in a smock when getting his hair cut.

These studies clearly show that if an incident, especially a traumatic one, occurs earlier than age 2, participatory memories remain but are largely unconscious in the sense that they are expressed nonverbally (not wanting to be covered with a smock) but not verbally. As we saw in earlier chapters, individuals may have participatory memories of their early infancy that persist for long periods in the form of nonverbal patterns of action. Infantile amnesia is primarily a verbal amnesia.

People with adult amnesia due to brain injury are more likely to have participatory memories than verbal memories. They may look and act like "themselves" using their somatic participatory memories even though they do not remember autobiographically who they are when asked questions about themselves (Baddeley, 1994; Hirst, 1994). In addition, as we saw in Chapter 2, adult trauma victims are more likely to have participatory memories than verbal memories of their trauma. They may have recurring dreams or behavior patterns, or they may have fragmentary flashbacks in which they relive some part of the trauma, such as being suddenly intensely afraid and breaking into a cold sweat for no apparent reason (Smyth & Pennebaker, 1999; Terr, 1994).

The study of children's recall of emergency room visits also suggests that traumatic memories from infancy may be particularly likely to persist in the form of nonverbal, unconscious participatory memories. The child may not "know" why he is afraid of being wrapped up in a blanket because he is unable to verbally articulate and understand why, but the memory persists somatically and becomes part of the unconscious. Participatory somatic memories will continue to persist longer if the conditions that created the memories persist and continue to be reenacted (Hudson & Sheffield, 1998).

This research is consistent with other studies of infant nonverbal memory that I have reviewed in the previous chapters. These findings support the testimony of clinicians, especially those who work with somatic therapies such as the Rosen method and bodymind centering, who report that infantile participatory memories and traumatic memories are often experienced during therapeutic encounters (see Chapter 2). Therapeutic interventions that allow traumas to be relived safely and then transformed into verbal memories by writing or talking, diffuse the trauma and lead to increases in mental and physical health (Smyth & Pennebaker, 1999).

More research is needed, however, to better understand why some participatory memories remain and others do not. We also need to better understand the circumstances in which these memories can best be revealed. Are children and adults more likely to retain participatory memories of traumatic events that occurred before the age of 2 years than of everyday events that occurred during infancy? Or are infantile traumatic experiences less likely to be transformed into verbal memories in the absence of the emotional safety of a therapeutic situation? I will return to this topic when I discuss the traumatic effects of child maltreatment during the infancy period in the "Applications" section of this chapter.

What Is the Relationship between Action and Thought?

During the third year, children increase their ability to perform complicated sequences of action, as demonstrated by the following investigation (Bullock & Lutkenhaus, 1988). Researchers gave children three tasks. The first was to build a house from blocks in a particular fashion modeled by the experimenter. The next was to clean a blackboard, and the last was to dress a doll so that it would not be cold. After age 2, but not before, the children were able to perform all the actions in the sequence given by the experimenter (the constructed house, the clean blackboard, and the dressed doll).

When the younger children made an error in putting the blocks together to build the house, they simply stopped or went on to another activity. The older children were able to correct the error and persist until the task was completed to a reasonable approximation of the standard. This ability to combine a series of actions together in a flexible way and to persist until a standard or conventional goal is reached is a major cognitive achievement. This achievement is reflected in a variety of areas, including object play, pretend play, social play, peer play, self-control, and language (Bauer, Schwade, Wewerka, & Delaney, 1999; Brownell, 1988; Messer, Rachford, McCarthy, & Yarrow, 1987). Self-control is seen in the ability to wait as requested by an adult (Vaughn, Kopp, Krakow, Johnson, & Schwartz, 1986). In the realm of language, for example, children at this age are beginning to use grammatical syntax in which a number of words are combined according to conventional usage into a flexible sequence.

What causes these changes to occur? Since attention span also increases around the same age, you might think that an increase in some kind of cognitive capacity allows the infant to process a longer series of actions. Some researchers believe, on the contrary, that longer attention is the result of more skilled action sequences that require the child to spend more time following through with the details of completing a task (Ruff & Lawson, 1990).

In related studies, it has been found that the more children comprehend of television programs, such as *Sesame Street*, the longer they will watch, and that television watching increases markedly at 30 months, about the same time these other changes are happening (Anderson & Levin, 1976; Anderson & Lorch, 1983). This kind of more focused attention to television is different from what was observed during the previous age period, when children got distracted while watching *Teletubbies* and needed the assistance of an adult to sustain attention.

Self-produced action does appear to affect cognition. In one study, 3-year-olds were taken into a children's area in a natural history museum (Hazen, 1982). Some of the children were allowed to explore the area on their own, while others were led through it by an adult. Those who went on their own had a more accurate spatial cognition of the layout of the area than those who were led. This study shows that self-produced action involves active cognitive processing and that by their action, children are increasing their knowledge of the environment.

What Is the Relationship between Action and Language?

If attention increases as a result of more articulated action, that still leaves open the question of what causes action to develop. According to Piaget (1952, 1962), development of both action and language is caused by developmental increases in cognitive abilities such as logical thinking. Piaget also concluded that errors committed by children older than 2 years were errors of logical thinking: he assumed the primacy of cognition over action after age 2 years. He gave children problems, such as the following: "Bill is older than Tom. Tom is older than Steve. Who is older, Bill or Steve?" A typical 3-year-old, according to Piaget, will not be able to answer because of an inability to understand the logical chain of comparisons.

An alternative to the logical error hypothesis is that children have a difficult time comprehending the language used in such problems. Children often have difficulty understanding differences between similar words with different endings, such as the difference between *old* and *older*. Some research has shown that what children actually comprehend is

something like this: "Bill is old; Tom is not old. Tom is old; Steve is not old." This seems like contradictory information. How can Tom be old and not old at the same time? Thus, the error may be due to a linguistic problem, rather than to a deficit in cognitive ability (Bryant & Trabasso, 1971; Riley & Trabasso, 1974).

Let us return to the original question, that is, what accounts for the development of complex action sequences? In the last chapter, I reviewed research showing that younger infants appear more skilled in pretend play when in the company of adults. They are also more advanced linguistically with adults than with peers. The adult guidance and the adult language seem to regulate the infant's actions, providing a kind of external support system that the infant cannot maintain alone or with a peer. After 30 months, it seems, infants have begun to internalize this social-linguistic regulatory system as thought, carrying it over into their activities in the absence of adults.

How do we know this? Beginning at 30 months, children begin to use language to regulate their behavior. For example, in one study, children were given a peg-and-hammer toy and told to hammer the pegs into the board in a particular order according to the color of the peg. If the children were allowed to say out loud the given order while hammering, they were more accurate than if told not to speak (Balamore & Wozniak, 1984).

At around 30 months, children begin, literally, to talk to themselves. **Private speech** is the use of language to regulate one's own behavior without the intention of a social communication. Private speech is different from the child's speech play seen in the first year (such as saying "mmmmm" while eating) because private speech uses both conventional words and conventional syntax. Private speech reflects the transition from social regulation to individual self-regulation.

Research has shown that private speech occurs in the following situations: the child talks about an intended action ("I put that there"), describes ongoing action ("Banging it"), makes a statement to an inanimate object ("Get out of my way, chair!"), or asks a question and then answers it ("Why are you crying, dolly? Because I'm sad"). In all cases, these words are said without looking at anyone else or seeking social confirmation (Berk, 1986; Furrow, 1984).

In summary, according to Piaget's theory, the development of more complex action sequences is the result of developments in the cognitive realm: the ability to hold more events in mind and link them logically. The alternative perspective, derived from the work of Vygotsky (1978; see Chapter 2), sees language and social experience as the primary cause of the development of action sequences. Since private speech is an internalized version of what earlier occurred socially during the regulation of the infant's action by means of caregiver speech, the development of complex action sequences has its origins in earlier social interaction. In a sense, babies turn social dialogue into private monologue and language into thought, and the result is the self-regulation of action (Vygotsky, 1978).

The World of Make-Believe

Because they say out loud (private speech) most of what they are thinking, children of this age are delightful to watch. Pretend play, discussed in the last chapter, is a kind of private speech that allows chil-dren to construct their own version of reality. At the beginning of the third year, children develop more complex forms of pretending. The child begins to reconstruct whole scenes and experiences in play:

At 2;1(9) Jacqueline put her doll's head through the balcony railing with its face turned toward the street and began to tell it what she saw: "You see the lake and the trees. You see a carriage, a horse," etc. The same day she seated her doll on the sofa and told it what she herself had seen in the garden. (Piaget, 1962, p. 127)

In the previous example, the child tried to faithfully reproduce reality. In the following example, the child makes some attempt to change or correct reality to make it more to her own liking. These games are the beginning of **imaginative pretend play,** in which the child is able to invent whole new situations in make-believe:

At 2;4(8) Jacqueline, not being allowed to play with the water being used for washing, took an empty cup, went and stood by the forbidden tub and went through the actions, saying: "I'm pouring out the water." (Piaget, 1962, p. 131)

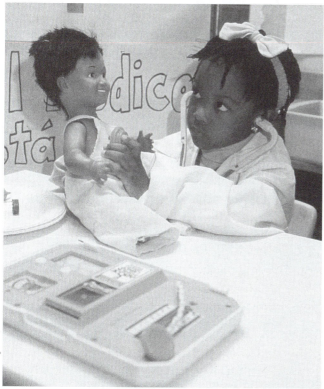

Pretend play is a common activity in the third year of life. Children pretend with adults, with other children, and often by themselves.

David Young-Wolff/PhotoEdit

The final type of pretend play that occurs during the third year of life is what Piaget called **liquidating pretend play.** This usually happens after the child experiences something unpleasant or threatening. Later, the child will try to relive the difficult situation in play as a way of coping with it. By removing it from its original unpleasantness, the child is better able to understand and assimilate what went on:

At 2;7(2) Jacqueline had fallen down and cut her lip. She consoled herself by projecting it all on to "Cousin Andree," who took the form of a doll: "Oh! It's Cousin Andree. They're washing her because she fell down and hurt her lip. She made a little hole in it. She cried."

At 2;7(15) a friend of her mother went for a walk with them. Jacqueline, who did not care for the presence of the third person, expressed frankly what she felt: "She's naughty . . . she can't talk . . . I don't like people to laugh." Then, as soon as the walk was over, Jacqueline accepted her, put her beside her in the bath, then in her bed, talked to her, and went for the walk again with her (all in imagination). (Piaget, 1962, p. 133)

These kinds of games allow the self to emerge victorious in the face of failure or to save face in the case of embarrassment. Children of this age also develop **pretend role play,** in which they act out the roles of mother, father, or other important figures in their lives, typically in the company of adults or peers.

During this same period in which children are developing their pretending skills, they can also understand when adults refer to pretend situations. In one study, adults pretended that a cup contained tea. The adults also did things like "pouring" or "spilling" the tea. After 28 months (2 years, 4 months), children can participate in these pretend episodes. They will "drink" from the cup and help "clean up" the "spilled" tea. The children also use language that makes clear they understand the situation is make-believe and not real (P. L. Harris & Kavanaugh, 1993).

Pretending is also manifested as dreaming, which children of this age can talk about for the first time. Dreams often concern experiences the child has had, physical changes such as toileting, and strong emotions.

At 2;2(23) X. woke up crying: "Poupette has come back." Poupette was a little girl she had met the day before and who had obviously worried her by unceremoniously taking possession of all her toys. At 2;8(11)

X. woke with a loud scream: "It was all dark, and I saw a lady over there (pointing to her bed). That's why I screamed." Then she explained that it was a horrid lady who stood with her legs apart and played with her feces. (Piaget, 1962, p. 177)

These dreams are examples of some of the things reported by 2-year-old children upon awakening. These dreams are classic nightmares, or dreams about fears that are still so frightening that the dream is unable to resolve them or make them better. In one case the child fears her toys will be stolen, and in another she fears her own feces. The latter is a common problem in 2- and 3-year-old children who are becoming aware that their own bodies can manufacture these products. Children of this age are both fascinated by their feces and repelled and confused by them at the same time (see the discussion of psychoanalytic theory in Chapter 2 and Erikson, 1950). Some children feel possessive about these products and may refuse toilet learning for fear of losing part of themselves. Other children may show more curiosity and playfulness about their stools and urine than most parents are able to tolerate, and still others do not seem to be at all concerned with these matters.

Another common dream in very young children is the "transposition of an organic stimulus" (Piaget, 1962). A good example is when children dream about a watering can at just the moment when they feel like (or are in the process of) urinating. Dreams other than nightmares may fulfill a wish, or they may take a painful event and finish it off with a happy ending. According to Freud (1900/1953), dreams are the "guardians" of sleep. Without dreams to transform and soothe our minds, we might keep waking up with painful or troublesome thoughts.

Are There Individual Differences in Children's Styles of Pretend Play?

The last chapter showed that there are two different styles of language acquisition. Referential approaches emphasize single words, clear articulation, and the use of nouns. Expressive approaches use phrases, mumbled speech, and pronouns; they tend to refer to social situations (K. Nelson, 1981).

Similar styles have been found for symbolic play in the third year. These patterns of individual

(a) Patterner's solution

Figure 11.2
Patterner's and Dramatist's
Solutions to the Classification
Task

(b) Dramatist's solution

Source: D. Wolf & H. Gardner, Style and sequence in early symbolic play, 1979, p. 80. In N. Smith & M. Franklin (Eds.), *Symbolic function in childhood,* pp. 64 – 92. Hillsdale, NJ: Erlbaum. Reprinted by permission of the publisher and the author.

difference cut across play, language, motor development, and problem-solving behavior. **Patterners** are concerned with properties of objects, shape, and form. **Dramatists** are more involved with storytelling, imagination, and social interaction. Children at age 2 were offered a set of 16 items (four people, four animals, four small blocks, and four large blocks). They were asked to put the items that were alike together. The patterners grouped objects according to their external forms, shapes, and colors. The dramatists grouped the objects by making a story out of them, such as a person in a house made of blocks (see Figure 11.2).

Emotional Development

The most important emotional developments during the third year are the ability to label and talk about emotions and the ability to understand the causes of emotional states in self and other. These are inherently linguistic, social, and cognitive achievements.

Changes in Emotional Communication: Laughter

During the third year of life, toddlers become more active and childlike when participating in social relationships with others. One way this occurs is by an increasingly sophisticated repertory of emotional forms of communication. The research I have been doing with my colleagues shows this pattern with respect to the development of laughter in the third year (Nwokah et al., 1993). Recall that infants can produce different types of smiles (Duchenne, or cheek-raise, smiles, and play, or jaw-drop, smiles). We found that these different types of smiles are associated with specific types of social communicative situations during the first year of life. Duchenne smiles are more likely with peekaboo games, for example, and play smiles with tickling games. A similar pattern occurs with laughter. Three-year-old children have different types of laughs—called comment, chuckle, rhythmical, and squeal—and

each laugh is associated with a specific type of communicative situation (Nwokah, Davies, Islam, Hsu, & Fogel, 1993).

A comment laugh is brief and sounds like an exclamation; typically, it follows a funny action on the part of the mother. Here is an example of a communicative situation for a comment laugh:

Mother and Betsy are playing with a toy picnic set. Betsy starts to open a bag of plastic potato chips. Mother makes a pretend, sad face and says quietly and wistfully, "Are you gonna share the chips with me?" Betsy replies, "Yeah." Mother opens her mouth, smiles, and says, "Okay," as she throws her head back and laughs. Betsy watches, smiles, and gives a short comment laugh while turning to peek into the chip bag.

A chuckle laugh is soft with a low tone and reflects mild amusement. Chuckles occur in situations involving more excitement than the situations that evoke comment laughs. The following is an example from our data:

Betsy is standing and puts a toy doll's feeding bottle into her own mouth. Mother says, "Yukk!" and attempts to grab the bottle from Betsy's mouth. Betsy quickly pulls backward and sits down so mother misses. As Betsy sits down she emits a chuckle laugh with a wide grin, but keeps the bottle in her mouth, continuing to look at mother.

A rhythmical laugh is the longest type of laughter; it consists of a series of regularly spaced syllables (ha-ha-ha). Rhythmical laughs occur in a wide variety of highly arousing situations, usually when both partners are laughing:

Mother has a Daffy Duck puppet on her hand. Betsy is lying on her back on the floor and mother makes the puppet talk. Betsy says, "Shut up, Daffy Duck!" Mother then tickles Betsy's leg with the puppet. Betsy makes a rhythmical laugh as she tries to roll away, her eyes half closed and her mouth wide open.

Finally, a squeal laugh is a long, high, shrill sound. The following example illustrates its occurrence:

Betsy is holding a puppet while lying on her stomach. Mother, while smiling, moves her hand slowly to the puppet to get hold of it. Betsy gives a squeal laugh as mother touches the puppet. Betsy's head is raised with a wide open mouth smile.

As this research shows, children use laughter and other facial expressions and body movements, along with words, to express their feelings. These findings also show an increasing awareness of the emotions of self and other.

What Is the Relationship between Emotion and Self-Understanding?

Because they now have the ability to take language out of its immediate social context and use it to talk to the self using private speech and talk to others about the self, children can be said to have a **categorical self,** or a self-concept, during this period. The categorical self is the ability of people to identify their own membership in one or more conceptual categories, such as "I am a boy," "I am a brother," and "I am not a baby"; it begins around the child's third birthday. Given a set of pictures of people of different sexes and ages, children of this age are quite accurate in labeling both age and sex differences in other people (Edwards, 1984; Keller, Ford, & Meacham, 1978). Thus, by the end of the second year, you might hear a child say, "I'm not a baby anymore!" I will discuss several aspects of the categorical self that emerge at this age: the sense of being a boy or a girl, talking about emotions, and understanding the emotions of other people.

Gender identity and gender roles. Children of this age develop **gender labeling,** when the child can identify self or other verbally as male or female. This begins at about 18 months (G. Levy, 2000; Poulin-Dubois, Serbin, & Derbyshire, 1998). Up until the age of 3 years, however, children do not understand that these labels reflect enduring characteristics of people. Two-year-olds will say correctly that they are a boy or a girl and will even engage in gender-stereotyped toy play, but they do not understand that a boy will always grow up to be a man. Children believe that gender might be changed by changing one's appearance or dress, which might explain why they are fairly rigid in their adoption of gender-role stereotypes ("Ladies can't wear pants"; "Boys don't play with dolls"). Children may actively discourage each other from playing with opposite gender–typed toys or even with members of the opposite sex (Gelman, Collman, & Maccoby, 1986; Slaby & Frey, 1975).

Interestingly, 2-to-3-year-old children who are more advanced in gender labeling (those who give the correct gender response to the question, "Who are you?") and who score higher on verbal intelligence tests are also more explicit about gender-role behaviors. That is, they will classify tasks and tools as male (car repair, shovels) or as female (cooking, irons). These children will also more readily adopt same-sex playmates in peer groups. Additionally, a number of studies have found that boys begin gender labeling and gender stereotyping somewhat earlier than girls. Girls, for example, are more likely to play with opposite-sex toys than are boys (Bauer, 1993; Fagot & Leinbach, 1989; Fagot, Leinbach, & Hagan, 1990; McGuire, 1988; O'Brien & Huston, 1985; Weinraub et al., 1984).

These studies of gender understanding suggest that cognitive and linguistic factors play some role, because children who are more linguistically and cognitively advanced are also more stereotypic in their gender-role concepts. However, it may be that children who are more articulate about gender roles have parents who talk more about such issues, so we cannot rule out a possible social influence in such factors.

One area that has been studied a great deal is parental influence over the child's choice of toys—specifically, parental reactions to traditional masculine toys (trucks, hammers, guns) and feminine toys (dolls, kitchen utensils) for their boys and girls. This is a difficult area in which to do research because reactions to a child's behavior regarding gender roles are highly culture specific. Interpreting this research is complicated because different studies use different measures (observations, questionnaires, parental reports) and because most of the research is done in middle-class Caucasian American families. However, with these qualifications, the following conclusions can be reached.

Few parents explicitly instruct their children in the gender-appropriate choice or use of toys. Gender-role stereotypes are communicated to children by the parents' emotional reactions to the children's choice of toys. First of all, when children are between 18 and 24 months, parents have more emotional reactions, both positive and negative and not necessarily gender stereotyped, to any kind of gender-related toy. At this age, parents react less to toy choices that are not gender related (such as blocks and nesting cups). Children who begin gender labeling early have parents who evince more emotional reactions to gender-typed toys during this early period (Fagot & Leinbach, 1989).

During the second year, as the children's toy choices become more gender typed, some parents begin to discourage gender-appropriate toys and encourage gender-inappropriate toys, again through emotional reactions rather than instruction (Caldera, Huston, & O'Brien, 1989; Fagot & Leinbach, 1989; Weinraub et al., 1984). Parents also contribute to gender-role identity by discouraging aggression and encouraging prosocial behavior in girls and by encouraging responsibility in boys. In addition, most parents dress and cut their children's hair in gender-appropriate ways in order to avoid other peoples' incorrect identification of the children's gender (McGuire, 1988; Power & Parke, 1986).

Sex differences in emotional communication occur outside the context of which toys are used. Girls talk more spontaneously and earlier in development about their emotions compared to boys (Cervantes & Callanan, 1998; Farver & Wimbarti, 1995). Research suggests that this may also be due partly to differences in parent-child emotional communication. Parents are more likely to respond to their daughters with a similar emotion, creating a shared emotional state (Robinson, Little, & Biringen, 1993). In talking about emotions with daughters, parents are more likely to provide a way to resolve their emotions with another person. With sons, parents more typically encourage the child to resolve the situation on their own. With anger, for example, parents encourage daughters to make up with their friend who took a toy by approaching or playing with the friend. Parents are more likely to encourage sons to retaliate. A daughter's expressed desire to retaliate is discouraged, while a son's desires to retaliate are typically encouraged (Fivush, 1994). Girls are being socialized to resolve their emotions within the boundaries of their ongoing relationships. Boys, on the other hand, are expected to be autonomous and to stand up for themselves.

Few studies have found differences between mothers and fathers in the encouragement of gender-appropriate behavior. Mothers and fathers typically agree on the kinds of gender roles they want for their children (Fagot & Hagan, 1991; Fagot & Leinbach, 1989). In one study, the types of speech, length of utterances, and number of questions and directives were the same for mothers and fathers when each interacted individually with the infant (Golinkoff and Ames, 1979). A study of verbal and nonverbal behavior of mothers and fathers found no parental sex differences in responsiveness to the infant, use of stimulation, affection, or effectiveness (A. Clarke-Stewart, 1978).

Even though mothers and fathers are using similar behavior toward the children, the early onset of gender labeling and the frequency of gender-typed toy play in children are predicted by personality characteristics of the father rather than of the mother. Early labelers, both boys and girls, have fathers who have more traditional gender-role orientations and who engage in more traditionally masculine tasks (car washing, lawn mowing, carpentry) than feminine tasks (laundry, cooking, dishwashing) at home. Additionally, in homes where mothers work outside the home or where fathers are absent (single-parent mother-headed homes), children have less traditional gender-role stereotypes (Fagot & Leinbach, 1989; Fagot, Leinbach, & O'Boyle, 1992; McGuire, 1988; Stevenson & Black, 1988; Weinraub et al., 1984).

This research is difficult to sort out. Why should gender-role development of children be correlated with the father's personality or absence, even though the mother and father in the same family encourage gender-role behavior in a similar way? Could it be that fathers are influencing the mothers' actions? Or could it be that these women married men who had similar beliefs? Finally, it could be that both parents are being affected by the child's behavior. Although a parent-to-child socialization effect is the most plausible explanation, it is difficult to get unambiguous evidence in support of this position.

There is really too little evidence and too much variability between studies and between families to draw firm conclusions about parent-infant sex differences and their effects on development. More evidence exists for older children whose gender-role behavior is more obvious and salient. The most we can say about gender-role development in the third year is that it is a topic of interest for both parents and children and that children are using information available in the environment, as well as their own thinking about self-concept, to form ideas about gender roles.

Talking about emotions. Another aspect of the categorical self is that children of this age can talk about their feelings and label emotional and physiological states accurately (Denham, 1986; M. Lewis & Michalson, 1983), they can talk about future and past emotions, and they can discuss the causes and consequences of emotions (Bretherton, Fritz, Zahn-Waxler, & Ridgeway, 1986; Reissland & Harris, 1991). By 28 months, most children have extensive emotion vocabularies for positive emotions (*happy, fun, good time, funny, like, love, feel better, proud*) and negative ones (*sad, scared, mad, yucky, messy, feel bad*). Children from different cultural groups also acquire emotion words around this age (Tardif & Wellman, 2000). Also common across different cultural groups is that children talk about their own and other people's emotions first, and then, about 6 months to 1 year later, begin to talk about their own and others' thoughts (*know, think*) (Tardif & Wellman, 2000).

Understanding other people and their emotions. As we saw in the previous chapter, the development of self-understanding develops in parallel with the development of understanding others. Children of this age are developing categories for other people, describing other's emotions, and understanding that other people have emotions and states of mind. These findings raise the question of whether infants of this age have a **theory of mind,** an understanding that other people have psychological states and that those states may be different from their own.

In addition to labeling their own emotions, 2-year-olds can talk about the emotions of other people (Bretherton et al., 1986; Hoffman, 1975; Radke-Yarrow & Zahn-Waxler, 1984). Emotion talk about self and others is shown in Table 11.2.

Children of this age appear to have a sense of empathy toward others. Two-year-olds are visibly affected by the emotions of others. In an experimental situation, children observed an experimenter having either an angry or a pleasant conversation

Table 11.2 Statements of Emotion Made by Two-Year-Olds

Positive	I give a hug. Baby be happy. I laugh at funny man. I not cry now. I happy. Mommy exercise. Mommy having a good time.
Negative	Me fall down. Me cry. It's dark. I'm scared. No cry, Mama. It will be all right. I feel bad. My tummy hurts. Mommy, you went away. I was sad. He's sad. He'll be happy when his daddy comes home. I'm mad at you, Daddy. I'm going away, good-bye. If you go on vacation again, I'll cry.

Sources: I. Bretherton, J. Fritz, C. Zahn-Waxler, & D. Ridgeway, Learning to talk about emotions: A functionalist perspective, 1986. *Child Development, 57,* 529–548.

with their mother. In the angry situation, the children expressed concern for their mother, sought her reassurance, and tried to comfort her (Cummings, Pellegrini, Notarius, & Cummings, 1989). Children of this age also show "concerned attention" toward others who are in distress, combined with helpful initiatives toward the other person and attempts to elicit help from bystanders (R. A. Thompson, 1998).

In general, girls show more caring and concern for the distress of others than boys do. In play sessions with peers, boys show slightly more anger than girls, but the differences are not strong (Malatesta-Magai et al., 1994). Children of mothers with severe depression show more caring behavior than children of nondepressed mothers, perhaps because the children have had to prematurely attend to the emotional states of others in order to get attention in return (Radke-Yarrow, Zahn-Waxler, Richardson, Susman, & Martinez, 1994).

In one experiment, children of this age were given a doll that would break as soon as they began to play with it. Most of the children reacted to the planned mishap with frustration, shame, anger, or sadness, and they attempted to correct the problem by putting the doll back together. On the other hand, children of depressed mothers were more likely to suppress their frustrations by showing more solicitude toward their depressed parent. It seems that children of depressed mothers may become disconnected from their own feelings in an attempt to protect their parent from undue emotional arousal (Cole, Barrett, & Zahn-Waxler, 1992). It also suggests that in some children, empathy may be coupled with feelings of guilt and responsibility for the adult's emotional well-being (R. A. Thompson, 1998).

On the other hand, children who score high on tests of understanding others' emotions are more likely to come from families in which there is frequent talk about feelings and the causes of feelings, in which children have a opportunity to observe parents talking with siblings about their feelings and behavior, and in which children are encouraged to cooperate with their siblings during coordinated play (J. Dunn, 1998). It seems that emotional understanding of others not related to guilt is facilitated in families in which emotional discourse occurs between all the members.

Some research suggests that children who are temperamentally inhibited are less likely to show understanding of others' feelings (S. K. Young, Fox, & Zahn-Waxler, 1999), but it is not clear how much of this inhibition can be explained by the family processes mentioned above. Children who are either inhibited or overly active may be less susceptible to observing the nuances of family emotional dialogues. They may require a more directive style of parental teaching in order to understand others' emotions (Zahn-Waxler & Robinson, 1995).

These findings suggest that children's concept of self and emotional states of self are associated with their relationships to other people. Children of this age are aware of multiple forms of self-other relationships (P. J. Miller, Mintz, Hoogstra, Fung, & Potts, 1992). They can talk about sharing activity with others ("We went down by the pool"), distinguish themselves as part of a relationship ("No one was holding my hand"; "You were far away"), and metacommunicate about their interpersonal relationships with others ("I hate Leslie"; "He wanted to play with me"). This suggests that the categorical self forms as part of a network of interpersonal relationships such that individuality is always defined in terms of one's connections, relations, similarities, and differences (Fogel, 1993).

Other findings also support this view that children can understand some aspects of others' mental states. Three-year-olds—both boys and girls—can modify their speech in the form of motherese when talking to a baby (J. Dunn & Kendrick, 1981; Shatz & Gelman, 1973). Children as young as 3 years are able to describe the kinds of things you might do to take care of a baby (Melson, Fogel, & Toda, 1986). When asked to show a picture to another person, 3-year-olds turned the picture around to face that person (Lempers, Flavell, & Flavell, 1977). Children of this age were more likely to gesture toward a "lost" object when they knew that the parent was unaware of the object's location than when the parent was aware of the location (O'Neill, 1996; Tomasello, Call, & Gluckman, 1997), suggesting that children of this age not only recognize but understand the intentions of other people.

These studies show that children have an understanding of some of the needs of other people that go beyond other's emotions and may include their mental state or level but they do not demonstrate conclusively that 3-year-olds have a theory of mind. A child can copy the parent's speech to a baby brother or sister or just describe what others do for a baby. Attempts to comfort a hurt adult have to be looked at with respect not only to what the child says (Table 11.2) but also to what the child actually does. Two-year-olds often try to comfort adults with blankets, bottles, and pacifiers, suggesting that the children may be trying to calm their own upset by stopping the crying of the adult (Hoffman, 1975). The use of emotion language could perhaps refer to facial expressions and actions of other people that the children have come to label in a particular way without realizing that others have feelings like themselves.

You do not have to presume that the child understands that other people have minds or feelings, and some scholars suggest that genuine empathy for others does not begin to develop until 4 or 5 years of age (Hoffman, 1975; Selman, 1980). Adults, for example, can operate computers just by following instructions without having any notion at all of what makes computers work. Similarly, 2-year-olds who are exposed to robot toys that respond to them and talk to them will enter into conversations with the robots, apparently without thinking about how the robots work or what the robots might be feeling (P. J. Dunham, Dunham, Tran, & Akhtar, 1991).

On the other hand, evidence in favor of a rudimentary theory of mind comes from studies of the development of the ability to deceive others. Three-year-old children were left alone in a room with what they were told was a surprise toy. They were asked not to peek while the experimenter left the room. Observed from behind a one-way mirror, almost all of the children peeked, but when the experimenter returned and asked, "Did you peek?" only 38% of those who peeked admitted that they had done so. The ones who confessed showed little change in facial expression. The ones who actually peeked but said they had not peeked showed an increase in smiling, while those who peeked but refused to answer the question showed an increase in nervous self-touching (Lewis, Stanger, & Sullivan, 1989).

Do these differences in facial expression suggest that children may be aware of what adults are thinking, that is, do the children assume that the adult believes they peeked and therefore try to change the adult's beliefs? In a related study (Chandler, Fritz, & Hala, 1989; Hala, Chandler, & Fritz, 1991), children were asked to hide a treasure from an experimenter. They could do this in a number of ways: by covering up the trail to the treasure, by creating false leads about where the treasure was hidden if the experimenter asked for help, and by lying. Children as young as 2½ years used all three strategies, suggesting that they were acting to create a false belief in the adult. To create a false belief, you have to have a theory of mind; that is, you have to assume that others are capable of holding some beliefs. According to the authors, the children "not only slyly lied and disingenuously misled, but they did so with what often amounted to disarming delight in leading others astray" (Chandler et al., 1989, p. 1275).

The child's cognitive sophistication is revealed by the way emotion and action go together in these examples. Nevertheless, even though a case can be made that children of this age have a theory of mind, it is likely to be a rather simple theory, something like: "Adults will believe what I want them to

believe, and they can't really tell that I'm trying to deceive them." In other words, children of this age probably believe that adults are in some ways extensions of themselves and entirely in tune with their wishes.

According to P. L. Harris (1989), children need the following abilities in order to have a genuine theory of mind: self-awareness, the capacity for pretending, and the ability to distinguish reality from pretending. We know that by the beginning of the third year, most children have both self-awareness and the ability to pretend. These factors are necessary because, as Harris suggests, a theory of mind requires one to imagine that others have feelings like one's own. Because we have no direct confirmation of another's feelings, we have to imagine what someone might feel under certain circumstances.

What 3-year-olds lack, however, is the ability to separate pretend from reality (R. P. Hobson, 1991). Until children can do this, they will see others as mere extensions of their own desires. How do we know children of this age cannot always separate reality from fantasy? One study found that when adults entered into a child's pretend game, the child became confused about the difference. A mother pretended to hold up an umbrella and suggested to her 30-month-old son that he hold out his hand to feel the rain. He did this and then very soberly looked at the palms of his hands to see if they were wet (DeLoache & Plaetzer, 1985). Another child while playing at cooking turned to a peer and said, "This is pretend, right?" (Slade, 1986). Another was pretending to be a monster by making growling noises. She became afraid of the noises she herself made and began to cry (DiLalla & Watson, 1988).

Of course, children in the third year can sometimes make the fantasy-reality distinction, but it would be more accurate to say that they are never really sure which is which. A greater feeling of certainty does not emerge until the age of 4 years, and therefore, it is not until this age that children solidify a theory of mind, an appreciation of the feelings and desires of others as independent from their own (P. L. Harris, 1989, 1998). In language, children before the fourth year do not produce words representing conditional or temporary states, such as *could* and *would* as opposed to *can* and *will* (Kuczaj & Maratsos, 1983). By the age of 4 years, a child might say to a younger sibling, "You don't get it. It's just pretend. I could have fooled you!" On the other hand, at the beginning of the third year, it is fair to say that children begin to catch glimmers of the differences between self and other as part of their ongoing social interactions.

As you can see from this discussion of emotional development, separating it from its origins in the social relationship and the sense of self is impossible. Emotion becomes increasingly social as it is subject to labeling and explicit regulation by others. The ways adults respond to happy expressions versus temper tantrums ultimately affect the child's own emotional understanding. In general, research suggests that adults should accept children's emotions as genuine expressions of feeling while working toward changing the manner in which the emotion is expressed or talked about ("I can see that you're angry, but I don't permit throwing things in the house"). The general principles for dealing with emotions are the same as those discussed in the previous chapter for guided participation: accept the child's initiative (even if this is negative) and then find ways to encourage the child into culturally and socially acceptable forms of expression (Demos, 1982; Lewis & Michalson, 1983; Rogoff, 1990). As children understand more about their own and other's emotions, it enhances the development of the categorical self.

Social and Language Development

Near the end of the second year, a vocabulary spurt occurs, as discussed in the last chapter. Sometime during the third year, or later for some children, there is a spurt in the **mean length of utterance (MLU).** The MLU is the average number of morphemes in each utterance spoken by the child. A morpheme is a meaningful unit of language; it is usually a word, but it can also be a word ending, such as *-ed, -s,* or *-ing.* The word "walking," for example, has two morphemes: *walk + ing.* Increases in MLU for three children are shown in Figure 11.3. Notice the wide range of individual variation. Eve has reached a peak in MLU development before Adam and Sarah have even begun to use more than one or two morphemes in an utterance (R. Brown, 1973).

These utterances are becoming less formulaic (see Chapter 10) and more like a flexible and productive standard grammar for the language spoken in the home (Bates, O'Connell, & Shore, 1987). Speaking in a sentence requires at least two basic components: a subject and a verb. In a grammatical sentence, the components must agree with one another in number (and gender in gender-based languages, such as Spanish and French). Sentences do not truly emerge until children begin to use verbs in a systematic manner—near the end of the second year of life.

In most cases, children acquire verbs more slowly than nouns. The time between when the first noun is acquired (about 10 months) and the first verb is acquired (about 20 months of age) is about the same as the time between birth and the first nouns acquired. While English is a noun-based language, other languages such as Korean and Mandarin Chinese are more likely to organize their sentences around verbs. In these languages, verbs occur at the ends of sentences and can occur alone. Verbs, therefore, are more salient to both children and adults using these languages. Children acquiring these languages have more verbs in their early vocabularies than those speaking English, but in all languages, nouns predominate over verbs during the second and third years (Tardif, 1996; Tardif, Gelman, & Xu, 1999).

Nouns and verbs are fundamentally different. Nouns represent the descriptions of things or objects; they serve a referential function. Nouns refer to concrete things the child can see, touch, or feel. Verbs, in contrast, tell us about the relationship between things—between the subject and the object, for example. Verbs are relational rather than referential. The ability to understand relationships between things and to express these in words begins during the second year (Gentner, 1978; S. S. Jones, Smith, & Landau, 1991; Waxman & Senghas, 1992).

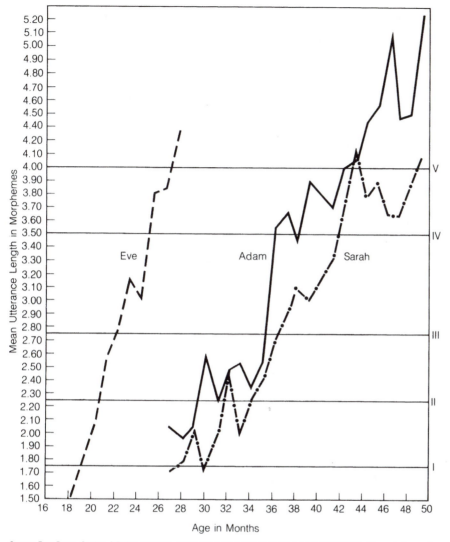

Figure 11.3
Average Length of Utterance in Morphemes at Different Ages for Three Children

Source: From Brown, Cazden, & Bellugi-Klima, The child's grammar from I to III, 1969, p. 29. In J. P. Hill (Ed.), *Minnesota Symposium on Child Psychology* (Vol. 2). Copyright © by the University of Minnesota Press. Reprinted by permission. Also in A. Fogel & G. F. Melson, *Child development,* 1988, p. 286. St. Paul, MN: West. Copyright © by West Publishing Co. Reprinted by permission. All rights reserved.

Because verbs are relational, they can express nontangible things. When you say "The ball rolls across the floor," the verb represents a transient action—one that relates the ball and the floor. The words *ball* and *floor,* in contrast, make fewer intellectual demands on the listener; these objects are there for all to see whenever they wish to. Verbs can also represent abstract properties that are difficult for a young child to appreciate, for example, *to think* and *to feel.*

When children first start to express action words, they often combine the action and its result in the same word. The word *up* can be used for a variety of situations, such as being lifted, being put down, asking to be picked up or to climb on someone's lap, climbing up or down stairs, or even requesting out-of-reach objects (Clark, 1978). *Off, on, out,* and *open* can be used in similarly extended ways.

The next step in the development of action expression is the use of simple verbs, such as *do* and

Table 11.3 Uses of *Do, Go,* and *Make* in the Third Year*

Verb	Utterance	Context
Do	I do it again.	Said as knocks over blocks.
	You . . . do . . . doing that.	Said as watches O build blocks into a tower.
	You do do it, OK?	Asking O to unroll some computer tape, after trying unsuccessfully to do it himself.
	You do that!	Indicating which toy O should take out of a box.
	Uh oh. I did.	Said as he turned off the tape recorder by pushing a knob.
	The clown do!	Asking O to make the toy clown do what clowns do.
Make	Make name!	Telling O to write his name.
	I make a little doggie.	Said as cut a dog shape out of Play-Doh.
	Make a dog.	Telling O what to draw next.
	Make it go in there.	Asking O to get a crayon back into its box.
	Make that.	Said as pointed to the hand moving on a clock; seemed to be request for O to move the hand on.
Go	It go there.	Talking about a block lying on the floor.
	Red went Boom.	Talking about a red block that fell on the floor.
	They go in the car.	Talking about two storybook characters.
	'N turn go up.	Said as turned a puzzle piece the right way up.
	'N go like that.	Said as dropped puzzle pieces on the floor.

*Examples cited come from the first month of recordings from S, a child taped at weekly intervals for 1 year from age 2–0. The utterances cited occurred without any immediately preceding use of the particular general purpose verb by either the observer (O) or the child's parents.
Source: From E. Clark, Strategies for communicating, 1978, p. 957. *Child Development, 49,* 953–959. Copyright by the Society for Research in Child Development. Reprinted by permission of the publisher and the author.

make. The initial meaning of these words is not always clear to the listener, because the child uses them in many different ways. Thus, it is important to see the child speaking in the context of the ongoing activity (Table 11.3).

A final way children express actions is by using an object word to talk about the action (E. V. Clark, 1978). Some examples include "The man is keying the door" (opening the door with a key); "I'm souping" (eating soup); or "Pillow me!" (throw a pillow at me).

Children of this age also make errors in the use of verbs similar to the overextension of nouns. Some examples are given in Table 11.4. Such errors usually happen after the children understand the similarity in meaning between verbs that they accidentally substitute for each other (Bowerman, 1978). *Put* and *give,* for example, are both words that a person uses to make an object move from one place to another. The substitution "errors" shown in Table 11.4 require that the child understand the basic relationship between *put* and *give,* since children rarely substitute words that have no semantic relationship to each other.

If you think about the order of events in an action sequence (rolling a ball from me back to you), some words represent the source of the action (*from, out, off, away*), some represent the path of the action (*back, up, down, across, through*), and some represent the goal or end point of the action (*to, in, at, there*). Children acquire these words in the same order: source-path-goal (Stockman & Vaughn-Cooke, 1992). Source words are acquired at the end of the first year ("Get this *out* her mouth [said taking a thermometer out of a doll's mouth]"; "Go *away* [telling a cat to leave the play area]"). Path words are acquired in the middle of the second year ("He climb *up* a tree [looking at a picture of a boy in a tree]"; "Make the man go *around* [placing a toy figure on a merry-go-round]"). Finally, goal words are acquired at the end of the second year ("All of 'em go *to* here [putting items in a purse]"; "I blow *at* Coty [aiming soap bubbles at Coty]").

These results show that language development is influenced by the temporal relations between elements in a sequence (Naigles & Kako, 1993; Stockman & Vaughn-Cooke, 1992). Children are better able to acquire new nouns when they occur in sentences with a familiar verb. If there are a number of foods on the table and the adult says, "rutabaga," the child may have difficulty picking out the right object and may not pay attention to the word. If

Table 11.4   Verb Substitution Errors*

A. Put *substituted for* give

E (2–2):	I go *put* it to Christy. (Starting off with a rubber band, then *gives* it to C.)
E (2–4):	Can I go *put* it to her? (Then takes juice and gives it to C.)
E (2–4):	M: It's all gone. (Re: C's juice.) E: Then *put* her some more.
E (2–4):	How come you're *putting* me that kind of juice? (As M prepares to give unfamiliar juice to E.)
E (2–4):	We're *putting* our things to you. (To D, after M has told children that it's time to *give* him their Father's Day presents.

B. Give *substituted for* put

E (2–7):	*Give* some ice in here, Mommy. *Put* some ice in here, Mommy. (Pointing to ice crusher.)
E (2–9):	*Give* those crayons right here. (Indicating to M spot on table near where she is sitting.)
E (2–10):	I'm gonna *give* your glasses right here. (M: Huh?) I'm gonna *put* your glasses right here.
E (2–10):	Don't *give* those next to me. (As C dumps things on couch near E's seat.)

*C = Christy, E = Eva, M = Mother, D = Daddy

Source: M. Bowerman, Systematizing semantic knowledge: Changes over time in the child's organization of word meaning, 1978, p. 984–985. *Child Development, 49,* 977–987. Copyright by the Society for Research in Child Development. Reprinted by permission of the publisher and the author.

the adult says, "Daddy is *eating* the rutabaga," it gives the child a clue about the object to which the word *rutabaga* refers (Goodman, McDonough, & Brown, 1998). This may help explain the vocabulary spurt that began during the previous age period. As children begin to acquire verbs it also helps them to understand more nouns.

Adding the Proper Endings

Children still have more to know about verbs in the preschool years, in particular about verb meaning and tense. One interesting phenomenon is that just after children acquire the past tense of regular verbs (such as *looked* for *look* or *helped* for *help*), they apply the *-ed* rule to all verbs, including irregular verbs. So, instead of saying *went*, the child says *goed*. Instead of saying *made*, the child says *maked*. This pattern of grammatical error is called **overregularization.** Overregularization errors are relatively rare, happening only 2.5% of the time the child intends to use an irregular past tense. They occur from the age of 2 years up through the elementary school years. These errors probably reflect minor memory slips and are not symptomatic of poor language development (Kuczaj, 1978; Marcus, Pinker, Ullman, & Hollander, 1992). In fact, they actually reflect progress in learning the underlying grammatical rules.

Similar processes occur in acquiring the plural forms of nouns. The way children acquire plurals is very similar to the way they acquire verb tenses. Children first acquire some irregular forms such as *men* and *children* almost without realizing that they are plurals of *man* and *child*. Once they acquire the general rule of adding an *s*, they apply that rule to anything, even the words they previously had acquired in the irregular plural forms: *mans* and *childs* (Berko, 1958).

Another type of meaningful word ending is negation. Although younger infants express negation by saying *no* or *not*, children of this age use contractions, such as *can't* and *don't* (H. H. Clark & Clark, 1977). Although the ability to put the proper endings on words is slow to be acquired, apparently by the age of 2 years children can understand the difference between words with different endings (Gerken, Landau, & Remez, 1990).

When Do Children Begin to Ask Questions?

After children master the subject-verb-object composition of sentences, they usually move quickly beyond simple declarative sentences to form questions. Questions usually begin with *wh-* words, and a definite developmental sequence in the order of acquisition of these words has been found (see Table 11.5). The ages listed in Table 11.5 are approximations, and we can expect individual differences in the age of acquisition.

Table 11.5   Order of Acquisition of wh- Questions

Age (Months)	Question
26	Where and What
28	Who
33	How
35	Why
36	Which, Whose, and When (occurred rarely at this age)

Source: L. Bloom, S. Merkin, & J. Wootten, Wh-questions: Linguistic factors that contribute to the sequence of acquisition, 1982, p. 1089. *Child Development, 53,* 1084–1092.

The reason for this developmental sequence is that the *wh* questions differ in their complexity. *What, where,* and *who* all ask for single-word responses that usually are simply extracted from a situation: "What did Bobby make?" "A tower." *Why, how,* and *when* require a more extended response giving a reason, process, or time.

The initial use of questions by 2-year-olds also reflects a rudimentary ability to use the questions in a fully expressive manner. Most of the questions addressed by children of this age are not dependent upon the previous topic of discussion. Thus, children use questions to start a conversation rather than to continue one. The only exceptions to this rule are *why* questions (L. Bloom, Rocissano, & Hood, 1976; L. Bloom, Merkin, & Wootten, 1982). Although some parents get annoyed with the constant "why"s of their young children, the ability to ask *why* reflects a growing linguistic sophistication that presages a more complex use of verbs and other *wh-* questions over the next few years.

Children's asking questions tells us that they have become aware of the importance of language for communication. When children ask *why* questions, they are not only requesting information but making a kind of statement as well. They are saying, "I know you know the answer," "I know I can use language to get a response or an explanation from you," and possibly even "I have the right, duty, and privilege to ask you this question." These unstated forms of linguistic awareness, or awareness about the function of language and of the implicit relationship between speakers, are known as **metalinguistic knowledge** (Kaye, 1982; P. J. Dunham

& Dunham, 1996; Y. Levy, 1999). Metalinguistic means "above" or "outside of" language itself.

In What Ways Is the Two-Year-Old's Language Limited?

In spite of the major accomplishments in the linguistic realm taking place during the third year of life, children still have a great deal more to learn about language. They still make errors in pronunciation, fail to comprehend certain words and sentences, and have only rudimentary conversational skills.

Young children acquiring English have an endearing tendency to confuse *r* and *l* and to make them both sound like *w*. Sound spectrographs (see Chapter 5) of children who said *gwass* for both *glass* and *grass* could detect differences between the child's pronunciation of the two words, however, even though the human ear could not (Kornfeld, 1971).

Another study examined a similar group of children who confused *r* with *w*. They all said *wake* to refer to the garden tool used to gather leaves. About two-thirds of the group, however, were able to tell the difference between an adult's pronunciation of *wake* and *rake*. Children become annoyed when adults try to mimic their mispronunciations (Locke, 1979; W. R. Miller, 1964).

The evidence suggests that comprehension continues to be ahead of production. Even though children can hear the difference, and even though they apparently are attempting to pronounce the words correctly, they are still unable to do this perfectly. This error tends to persist in the speech of some children until school age, whereas other children never have problems with the *r-l* distinction. All children, however, need a good deal of time to get the correct pronunciations of most of the words they routinely use.

Some researchers have collected tape-recorded samples of children's private speech with a microphone hidden in their cribs. During these monologues, children have been heard to practice their pronunciation. One child practiced the *r* in *story* as follows: "Stoly/Stoly here/want a stoly/Dave, stoly/story, story/story's de hat/story's de big hat/store's a hat" (R. H. Weir, 1966).

Finally, children of this age have trouble comprehending unusual grammatical sequences. If you were told that the robin is being kissed by the bluejay, how would you answer the questions "Who did the kissing?" and "Who was the kisser?" You are probably wishing all your test questions were this easy. However, 2-year-olds could not get the right answer. Half the time they said the robin was the kisser, and half the time they said the bluejay (Bever, 1970).

They all got the right answer when they were told "The bluejay kisses the robin" or "It's the robin that the bluejay kisses." The first sentence—the one that confused the children—is a passive construction. Evidently, whenever the children hear a noun followed by a verb, they assume the noun represents the actor. Not until children are in elementary school can they understand sentences such as "Donald Duck was liked by Goofy" (Maratsos, Kuczaj, Fox, & Chalkley, 1979).

How Well Can a Two-Year-Old Carry On a Conversation?

The mother and child in Table 11.6 were reading a Richard Scarry picture-book together. In the same study from which this conversation was taken, mothers and children also played with a set of toy teacups and plates, as well as with a Fischer-Price play family with a table, chairs, a dog, and a car, among other things (Kaye, 1982). The children were videotaped at 26 months and again at 30 months doing these things with their mothers (28 children in all).

Table 11.6 A Conversation

Mother	Child (30 Months)
1. (Points to a picture) What is that one?	2. Kitty cat.
3. Well what is it?	4. Kitty cat.
5. Well, I know there's a kitty in it; what's he in?	6. Huh?
7. What's he riding in?	8. Airplane.
9. Right.	10. (turns page)

Source: K. Kaye, The mental and social life of babies, 1982, p. 100. Chicago: University of Chicago Press. Copyright © The Society for Research in Child Development, Inc. Reprinted by permission of the publisher and the author.

What is the difference between this conversation and one you might hear between two adults? When adults talk to each other, the conversation is likely to continue because both partners are used to taking initiatives and starting new thoughts. In Table 11.6, the parent was more likely to get a response from the child if she asked the child a question or created a situation that required a response from the child. Thus, the parent needs to keep prompting the child to continue the conversation. At this age, the child does not have a mature ability to carry on dialogue, even though the child may have mastered the words and phrases of the language. As an apprentice conversationalist, the child can respond to the adult, who makes the child look more capable than he or she really is (Kaye, 1982; Shatz, 1978; C. E. Snow, 1977).

Aside from using prompts and questions in conversations, adults have other skills designed to make the infant a more active participant. Adults use a greater number of hand gestures and gestures of a more complex variety with their preschoolers than they do with their toddlers (Gutman & Turnure, 1979). These gestures are of three major types. From the beginning of the second year, parents use such gestures as pointing or otherwise specifying the location of something. As children acquire meanings and become symbol users, parents employ gestures that copy or imitate the attributes of an object or situation (as in "Eensy Weensy Spider"). Finally, parents use gestures that add emphasis to speech, much as they would when talking to another adult.

No doubt these gestures help the child understand more-complex sentences, much as gestures helped the prelinguistic child to interpret the parent's meaning. Gestures function the same as the mother's speech in Table 11.6, in that they help children maintain an active participation in a conversation that might otherwise be beyond their comprehension and production capacities.

Research has shown that by age 2, social class differences in linguistically based parent-child communication emerge. One study in the United States found that middle-income dyads spend twice as much time in mutual play as lower-income dyads. Mothers in lower-income groups spend more time reading to themselves, and their children are observed more often in independent play (Farran & Haskins, 1980). Even within middle-income groups, there seem to be individual differences. Parents with professional backgrounds—especially teachers—are more likely to read to and interact with their children than parents with blue- or white-collar jobs (Feiring & Lewis, 1981).

Lower- versus middle-income comparisons in Israel showed similar differences. Lower-income mothers thought infants were slower to acquire cognitive skills than did middle-income mothers. The tendency to see the infant as precocious, and therefore to create the "pseudodialogues" previously described, was found for middle-income parents only (Ninio, 1979). In observations of parents reading picture-books to their children, Ninio (1980) found that middle-income Israeli mothers asked more questions, talked more during the reading session, and modeled more new words than the low-income mothers. The final chapter will discuss whether these differences in parental behavior have any lasting impact on the child's social and intellectual development.

Discipline and Compliance in Parent-Child Relationships

During the third year of life, children widen the scope of their activities and language, not all of which fits into their parents' ideas about appropriate behavior. The parents need to provide continued discipline to orient the child toward acceptable and competent patterns of action. Parents introduce a wide variety of controls over toddler behavior. Children are told when to do things ("Tie your shoe") and when not to do things ("Don't yell"), and they are asked to control their future actions ("Be good while I'm gone"). Parents ask children to perform actions requiring a high level of competence ("Take care of your brother"; "Put the crayons away"; "Say thank you"; "Don't write on the wall"; "Go play in the other room"). Children can either comply or resist. Resistance can be passive or it can involve direct defiance, with the child exploring all the different ways of using the word *no* (Kuczynski & Kochanska, 1995).

The findings on parental discipline and child compliance at this age are similar to those reported in the previous chapter. Research shows that authoritative patterns of parental discipline (combining firmness, respect for the child, and warmth; see Chapter 10) are associated with cooperative and compliant children. On the other hand, oppositional children have parents who control their social behavior. Oppositional children receive fewer demands for performing competent behavior and fewer requests to control their future actions.

It is not clear whether this style of parenting causes oppositional children, or whether the parents adapt their style to a less compliant child by making fewer demands on the child. Most likely, this is a relational pattern that emerges during the history of their prior communications. In any case, the parent and child enter into a cycle in which the parents avoid confronting the child and the child is deprived of opportunities to become more competent. In other cases, a cycle of mutual conflict and parental nagging results (Achermann, Dinneen, & Stevenson-Hinde, 1991; Kuczynski & Kochanska, 1995; Leonard, 1993).

It is difficult to break these cycles, and they may persist for a year or more (Aber, Belsky, Slade, & Crnic, 1999). Intervention from a third party, another adult family member or a family therapist, may be needed if they persist and lead to breakdowns in parent-child communication. Intervention is helpful since these negative cycles often lead to behavior problems of the child with peers and in child care settings.

The good news is that during the third year, the frequency of defiance and refusals to cooperative gradually diminishes. It is replaced by children's use of negotiation strategies. Instead of simply saying "no" or "I don't want to," when asked to clean up their toys for example, by 30 months or so children may begin to say things like "Let me play a little longer and then I'll clean up," "You clean some and I'll clean some," or "Don't leave and I'll clean up" (Klimes-Dougan & Kopp, 1999).

Peer Interactions

By the third year of life, children are capable of engaging in social interaction and of adapting to the messages and demands of the listener (Wellman & Lempers, 1977). Between 22 and 30 months, infants increase their rates of verbalizations to peers, watch each other more, and increase their overall rates of social interaction (Mueller, Bleier, Krakow, Hegedus, & Cournoyer, 1977). Children also show

Table 11.7 Development of Emerging Skills in Achieving Coordinated Action

Age Period	Behavioral Skill	Characteristic Interaction
Younger than 16 months	Assume and maintain complementary role in familiar, ritualized games.	Sustained ritualized games, but little coordinated action in other contexts.
16–28 months	Imitation of nonverbal acts as general strategy for coordinated action in nonritualized contexts; repeated imitation across turns of action.	Widespread imitation of other's acts, resulting in imitation games and games with both imitative and complementary roles.
28–32 months	Verbalizations coordinated to another's actions begin to occur with appreciable frequency; increasingly accompany nonverbal forms of coordinated action with verbal regulations, descriptions, and imitations. Increasingly respond to another's overtures with alternative overtures composed of words and nonverbal actions or words alone.	Words coordinated to partner's actions increasingly occur in context of games structured largely by nonverbal imitation; words begin to serve as turns in games. Games intermixed with periods of negotiation of topic for interactions.
Older than 32 months	Use of overtures thematically related to ongoing activities to vary or elaborate on the ongoing coordinated action.	Games less repetitive across turns; coordinated action sustained for longer periods of time, with changes in topic occurring during the bout.

Source: C. O. Eckerman & S. M. Didow, Toddler's social coordinations: Changing responses to another's invitation to play, 1989, p. 803. *Developmental Psychology, 25,* 794–804.

a greater tendency to engage in mutual social play, and a decreasing amount of parallel play is seen near the end of the third year (Bakeman & Brownlee, 1980).

The kinds of interactions taking place, as well as the content of the interactions, are also undergoing important changes. Children gradually incorporate their symbolic play into peer interactions. No longer content to construct elaborate pretend sequences on their own, preschool children work together to elaborate a pretend game. At first, children simply copy or echo their partners in their peer exchanges. Later they provide complementary responses, and finally they elaborate and embellish the other's responses (Camaioni, Baumgartner, & Perucchini, 1991; Garvey, 1974; Gunnar, Senior, & Hartup, 1984).

Table 11.7 shows some of the social processes that account for this development in the ability of peers to achieve and maintain coordinated action (Eckerman & Didow, 1989). One important change is that peers begin to imitate each other, first nonverbally and later verbally. Based on both naturalistic observations and observations in which adults acted like peers and imitated children, research shows that the experience of being imitated is a powerful motivator of social behavior. Being imitated by someone gives one immediate and recognizable feedback of one's effect on the other person and inspires one to imitate him or her in return (Eckerman, 1993; Eckerman, Davis, & Didow, 1989; Eckerman & Stein, 1990). Some examples of imitation that are specific to peer relationships in the third year are given in Table 11.8.

A second component of increasing peer coordination, also shown in Table 11.8, is the emergence of complementary roles and alternative responses. In this case, the child makes a different but appropriate response to the partner's overture. This might even occur as a slight variation in the context of imitation: one child might throw a ball and the other a beanbag. A third developmental change is the growing use of language as part of a coordinated interaction. Instead of overt actions, the child begins to use words as directives, requests, or comments and responses.

Imitation, therefore, seems to serve as a social bridge between the simple kinds of uncoordinated peer play seen in the second year and the complex coordinated interactions seen later in the third year.

Table 11.8 Types of Imitative and Complementary Actions Seen in Peer Interactions during the Third Year

Type of Act	Example
Imitative	Exchanging an object; playing catch, peekaboo; hitting each other; both running, copying sounds, laughing, screaming; faking laugh or cry; clapping; sticking out tongues; singing; jumping
Complementary	Finding a hidden peer; playing leader and follower; giving/following directives ("Go jump"; "Come here"); answering a question

Source: C. O. Eckerman, C. C. Davis, & S. M. Didow, Toddlers' emerging ways of achieving social coordinations with a peer, 1989, p. 448. *Child Development, 60,* 440–453; L. Kuczynski, C. Zahn-Waxler, & M. Radke-Yarrow, Development and content of imitation in the second and third years of life: A socialization perspective, 1987, p. 280. *Developmental Psychology, 23,* 276–282.

One of the social functions of imitation is that it increases a feeling of closeness between two people (Nadel & Fontaine, 1989; Uzgiris, 1983). Thus, we might expect similar feelings of interpersonal closeness to emerge between 2-year-old peers.

Peers use both language and nonverbal action for metacommunication about their relationship. Children can engage in pretend fighting by metacommunicating (such as smiling or saying "This is pretend"). Or, a child can deflect a real attack by making it into a game with a teasing expression. Often children play in a very intense way and pretend to scream as if in pain. If one child accidentally gets hurt, a change in that child's intonation or posture can metacommunicate to the other children the more serious nature of the scream (Fogel & Branco, 1997).

Do Two-Year-Olds Behave the Same No Matter Whom They Are With?

The answer to this question is no. Children of this age can adapt their behavior to the characteristics of the other child and the type of relationship they have with that child. One dimension of relationship difference is friendship. Apparently, 2-year-olds can make friends. Research shows that there is a difference in social interaction between children who call themselves friends and those who do not (Ross & Lossis, 1987). In one study, children were left in an unfamiliar room either with a familiar peer, with an unfamiliar peer, or by themselves. The children with the familiar peer were the most comfortable, and the children left alone were the most upset (Ispa, 1981).

In another study, children were asked to rank all their nursery school playmates according to how much they liked being with each person. The children were paired off and taken to an unfamiliar place, where they played together. Half the pairs were made up of children who rated each other as preferred playmates, and half were made up of children who did not rate each other as preferred. At the end of 10 minutes of play in the new setting, an experimenter took one of the children off to play a special game, leaving the other in the room alone. Children whose friends left them behind were more likely to be disturbed during the separation than children left behind by nonfriends. Thus, there is some indication that peer friendships show an attachment-like quality—that children are fond of their friends and like to be with them (Melson & Cohen, 1981).

Another dimension of relationship difference is dominance. Beginning at this age, children's play groups form dominance hierarchies. A **dominance hierarchy** is a pattern of social relationships in which the members of a group are ranked according to their relative power or lack of power over others. A child who is with a more dominant peer will do more observing and take a less assertive and active role in exploring the environment. The same child with a subordinate peer will take more of a leadership role and have more initiative in the play (P. H. Hawley & Little, 1999).

Do Family Factors Affect Peer Relationships?

Family factors do affect peer relationships. One study found that children without siblings were more sociable with unfamiliar peers than were firstborns with siblings, and firstborns were more sociable than children born later. Children without siblings were the most outgoing of all. This could be because the children born later had the most nonpeers to play with or because they expected from peers the same kinds of aggressive rivalry they received from their siblings, making them more wary of peers (M. E. Snow, Jacklin, & Maccoby, 1981). The child's relationship to the parents also matters. Children who are more securely attached to their mothers and who demonstrate better self-control in frustrating situations also are more likely to show competence in peer encounters (Calkins, Gill, Johnson, & Smith, 1999; Leiberman, 1977; Matas, Arend, & Sroufe, 1978).

Do Sociocultural Factors Affect Peer Relationships?

Sociocultural factors also affect peer relationships. For example, Israeli children who were brought up in kibbutzim (farm cooperatives) showed more cooperative play with one another than Israeli children reared in an urban environment (Shapira & Madsen, 1969). The more a society is family oriented rather than peer-group oriented, the less the children will be encouraged to play in peer groups. This has been found in Mexico (Madsen & Shapira, 1970) and Switzerland (Boehm, 1977).

In smaller, agrarian societies, such as some African tribal societies, children have relatively few age-mates living in the same village. Children in these settings tend to play in mixed-age groups rather than peer groups (Konner, 1975). Mixed-age groupings are rare in modern, urbanized settings. They typically occur between siblings in the same family. Even preschools tend to be age segregated in Western countries. Although there is little research on the topic, we might suspect that some of the same benefits that exist in sibling relationships—such as the ability to lead and follow, to imitate and serve as a role model, to learn and teach—would exist in mixed-age groupings of children outside the family. For example, when socially isolated preschool children were asked to interact with children younger than themselves, the older child became more sociable over time (Furman, Rahe, and Hartup, 1979).

Societies differ in the amount adults supervise peer groups. In urban settings, young children are always under the watchful eyes of a caregiver, for obvious ecological reasons. In rural societies and smaller societies, children are relatively less supervised, even at a young age. The Foré people of New Guinea allow infants total freedom of movement as soon as they can walk (Sorenson, 1979). In the Marquesas Islands, starting at 2 years of age, children spend most of the day in unsupervised peer groups ranging in size from three to six children.

Societies differ in how much structure they provide for peer relationships. In Japan, young children wear uniforms, and their activities are coordinated by an adult.

Alan Oddie/PhotoEdit

They are allowed to play near the sea, in boat-houses, on bridges, and near streams (Martini & Kirkpatrick, 1981). Neither Sorensen nor Martini and Kirkpatrick ever observed children becoming lost or injured, but how the children avoided accidents is not clear. These examples suggest that 2-year-olds are indeed autonomous individuals, as well as that the social and physical ecology of the setting determines the manner in which that autonomy is expressed.

Family and Society

In earlier chapters, I discussed the infant's relationship with an older sibling. In this chapter, the infant will be discussed from the perspective of being both the older and the younger sibling. Sibling relationships in the family will be my main topic. I will cover types of interactions between siblings and interfamily differences in sibling interactions.

Types of Sibling Interactions

All sibling pairs share both positive and negative interactions. Furthermore, no matter what the interaction is, the children get something specific from their siblings that they do not receive in other relationships.

If the 2-year-old is a younger sibling, he or she will spend a lot of time paying attention to the older sibling and following him or her around. Younger siblings have been observed to imitate older siblings more often than they are imitated by older siblings; younger siblings are more likely to follow older

siblings' directions and suggestions, and they are more compliant in taking designated roles in games (Abramovitch, Corter, Pepler, & Stanhope, 1986; Brody, Stoneman, & MacKinnon, 1982; Lamb, 1978b; Stoneman, Brody, & MacKinnon, 1984).

In one study, 23-month-old children were observed both with and without their older siblings (H. R. Samuels, 1980). When they were with the siblings, the toddlers went farther from their mothers, left their mothers sooner, stayed away longer, and showed more independent exploratory behavior than did toddlers whose siblings were not present. The increased boldness seems to be due almost entirely to their following the older siblings around and imitating their behavior. In this way, younger children have the advantage of an older guide as they begin to explore the environment. This study does not suggest that the older sibling intentionally chooses to lead the way and teach the younger one, only that the younger one will follow what the older one does. Parents often remark that the laterborns seems to do things at a younger age than the firstborn; such imitative behavior may partially explain this observation.

On the other hand, older siblings are more likely to give directives, to orient the attention of the younger children, to command and prohibit, to support, and to tease. Older siblings address infants in a form of motherese, except they rarely ask questions of the babies (J. Dunn & Kendrick, 1982; Ellis & Rogoff, 1982; C. P. Jones & Adamson, 1987; R. A. Stewart, 1983). Observations 11.1 and 11.2 show representative directives of 2-to-3-year-old siblings to their baby sisters.

The evidence suggests that after the birth of a new baby, older children become somewhat more dependent compared with firstborns of the same

---

OBSERVATIONS

Speech to Younger Siblings by Three-Year-Olds

Observation 11.1 (England)

The younger sister, Robin, has just picked up a piece of candy from the floor and is licking it. The older brother, Duncan, tells Robin that the dog, Scottie, will eat it. When Robin doesn't listen, Duncan pushes her gently through the door.

Duncan: "No, don't you eat it. Scottie will eat it. Scottie will eat it. No, not you. Scottie will eat it. Not you. Scottie.

Not you. Shall we go in door? Right, come on. Come on. In door, Robin. In door" (J. Dunn & Kendrick, 1982, p. 126).

Observation 11.2 (Mexico)

Older sister Victoria and younger sister Lucha play in their courtyard with a small rabbit. Lucha is having some trouble keeping the rabbit in one place and is trying to do so by holding its ears.

Victoria: "Mira tu no sabes!" (Look, you don't know how!) Victoria then demonstrates how to hold the rabbit correctly (Zukow, 1990, p. 30).

Older children can be important as models and teachers for their younger siblings. The younger child seems to enjoy the company of the older, even if the younger one does not always understand what is going on.

Elizabeth Crews

age without siblings. They tend to seek help more, seek proximity to their mothers more, and cry more. Research shows that the older child has good reason for behaving this way. The mother's behavior to the older child changes somewhat when the new baby is around: confrontation increases and positive involvement with the firstborn decreases. Even when the mother is not occupied with the baby, she tends to spend less time with the older child (Kendrick & Dunn, 1980; R. A. Stewart, Mobley, Van Tuyl, & Salvador, 1987). The increase in confrontations between mother and firstborn is due primarily to an increase in "deliberate naughtiness" on the part of the older child. It seems that the older child's feelings of being displaced are met by the mother's increased workload as she cares for two young children instead of only one (Kendrick & Dunn, 1980).

On the other hand, 2-year-olds are becoming more sensitive to the dynamics of the family environment. They are really very skilled at knowing just how to annoy the younger sibling (teasing, making disparaging remarks, showing a toy spider to a sibling who does not like spiders), on the one hand, and enlisting the support of the mother during sibling conflicts (J. Dunn & Munn, 1985), on the other. Tattling occurs between siblings of this age in the majority of families. Sometimes children tattle to get the mother on their side during a conflict. Other times, tattling is used just to inform the parent about the sibling's misbehavior. Children do not tattle about just anything. They tattle primarily about physical aggression and about property damage and disputes (den Bak & Ross, 1996).

The older siblings also become adept at making eloquent justifications to the mother for their disputes with the sibling. For example, after taking a toy away from a younger brother, the older child might say to mother, "He took it first!" or "But I needed that" (J. Dunn & Munn, 1987). They also become able to steer the direction of a mother-baby interaction toward their own needs or concerns (J. Dunn & Shatz, 1989).

Although older siblings do not shy away from causing conflict with the younger ones, when the conflict is between the mother and the younger sibling, the 2-year-old sibling might be the first to come to the rescue of the baby. Some of the strategies used by the older child to diffuse the conflict between mother and younger sibling include repeating the sibling's action that the mother did not like (drawing the mother's attention away from the younger one), giving the younger child a similar object to the one the mother had just taken away, prohibiting or scolding the mother for her punishment of the sibling, and comforting the sibling.

Although some conflict is inevitable in family relationships, sibling relationships have many positive aspects. In conversations between siblings when the mother is present, for example, infants are able to join in the talk between mother and older sibling at a much higher level than when they are with the mother alone. This is because the older child does not always have the ability to reply as a full conversational partner (see Table 11.6), which leaves room for the young sibling to enter into the conversation (Barton & Tomasello, 1991).

There is also evidence that siblings have a special relationship that is different from the parent-child relationship. In particular, siblings like to talk more about their emotions with each other than with parents. Older siblings verbally label the younger sibling's emotional reactions ("You don't like that, do you? I don't want it!"). Siblings like to share jokes about "yucky" bugs or gender categories ("You like Barbie dolls!"). They also express feelings of liking and disliking ("I'm really proud of you [accompanied by kissing]!" "Ginny, you drive me mad!") (J. R. Brown & Dunn, 1992; N. Howe, 1991). There is also evidence that siblings form attachments to each other and would rather be together than with an unfamiliar peer (Kier & Lewis, 1993).

In some societies, it is common for older siblings, even those as young as 3 years, to have some responsibilities for taking care of babies (with adult supervision). Sibling caretakers for infants typically are found in societies that are relatively less complex and more traditional (Whiting & Whiting, 1975). If the division of labor in the family is such that the mother cannot stay at home to take care of the infant, siblings are likely to take over this function. In nontechnological societies, all family members are called upon to do extra work. The children have more chores around the house than children in technological societies, and infant care is one of these tasks.

In Taira, a village in Okinawa, preschool girls patted, bounced, and talked to infants to calm them. If this did not work, the girls returned them to mothers or grandmothers. Girls in Taira never bathed or fed infants, nor did they put them to bed. In Tarong, on the island of Luzon in the Philippines, child "nurses" were trained at age 3 to entertain, rock, and hold the baby, but adults continued to supervise them.

Among the Gusii living in Nyansongo, Kenya, child nurses were somewhat older (5 to 8 years), and they were given more responsibility. They were assigned the total care of an infant beginning when the infant was around 2 months of age. They fed, bathed, and cared for the infants while the mothers worked in nearby fields (Whiting & Whiting, 1975). In the Marquesas Islands, 2-year-olds are important as companions, instructors, and comforters of their infant siblings. The adults hold these children in high esteem and often ask them to show off the baby. Children are relied upon to calm an infant if an adult fails (Martini & Kirkpatrick, 1981).

In summary, these studies reveal that siblings are important to each other's development. Younger siblings benefit from the guidance and protection of a role model, and they also acquire self-protective social skills and learn how to resolve conflicts. Older siblings benefit from being tutors and caregivers by focusing their attention on the needs of others. When they are scolded for annoying the younger child, the older children understand the nature of codes of conduct and some complex social and emotional regulatory skills.

Interfamily Differences in the Types of Sibling Interactions

Why do some siblings fight more than others? What should parents do to help their children get along better with each other? A number of family and child factors have been associated with a higher incidence of both mother–older child and older child–younger child confrontations. I discuss the evidence for some of the factors in this section.

Each sibling's relationship with mother. Research shows that each sibling's attachment to the mother affects the quality of the sibling relationship. When the mother is present with the children, securely attached 2-year-old younger siblings are less likely to be aggressive to the mother or to the older sibling when the mother plays exclusively with the older sibling. Older siblings who are securely attached are more likely to respond to the needs and distress of the younger sibling in the mother's absence; older siblings who are not securely attached are less likely to do so (Teti & Ablard, 1989). A similar result has been found for twins (Vandell, Owen, Wilson, & Henderson, 1988). It is typical for both children in the same family to have similar attachment classifications (Ward, Vaughn, & Robb, 1988).

The older sibling's prior relationships outside the family. Research shows that higher-quality sibling relationships are associated with the older sibling's relationships with peers outside the family. Children who are more positive with their siblings show more positive peer play, fewer peer conflicts, more extended pretend play with peers, and more lasting peer friendships (Kramer & Gottman, 1992). Children with more knowledge of emotion and role-taking skills are more positive with their younger siblings (Garner, Jones, & Palmer, 1994).

Both sibling interaction and social competence with peers are related to the child's security of attachment, so you might think that the relationship between positive peer play and positive sibling interaction is simply the result of a more secure attachment to the mother. The research shows that while the parent-child relationship is important for developing the child's ability to care for the younger sibling, the child's experience with peers makes its own independent contribution (Kramer & Gottman, 1992). With peers, children are exposed to some basic rules of respect and responsibility for others that carry over into relationships at home, especially if the child's socially responsive behavior is supported by the parents.

Sex and age differences between the siblings. Another factor that may play a role in the incidence of positive versus negative sibling relationships is the sex composition of the sibling pair. Although there is a great deal of variability across families, same-sex pairs tend to have fewer instances of aggression than mixed-sex pairs, and parents are more likely to treat children in same-sex pairs equally than children in mixed-sex pairs (Corter, Abramovitch, & Pepler, 1983; R. A. Stewart et al., 1987). Firstborn females are somewhat more prosocial,

whereas firstborn males are somewhat more aggressive; however, these differences do not appear across all studies. Finally, the number of years between siblings does not seem to have any measurable effect on the amount of prosocial or aggressive behavior exchanged between them (Abramovitch, Corter, & Landau, 1979; Lamb, 1978c).

Temperamental differences between the siblings. Because the findings on age and sex differences between the siblings do not strongly predict the level of conflict between the siblings, some researchers have suggested that temperamental factors might be more important. Indeed, research shows that temperament is a better predictor. If one of the siblings is rated as having a generally negative mood and as being temperamentally nonadaptable, the siblings are less likely to engage in joint play. A mismatch in the temperament of the siblings is related to higher levels of conflict (Munn & Dunn, 1989).

One interpretation of these results is that the temperamental characteristics of the children affect the way that they relate to each other. Another interpretation is possible, however. One of the issues related to the measurement of infant temperament is that a parental rating of infant temperament is generally used (see Chapter 6). This introduces a possible bias in the parent's perception of the child, independent of the child's actual behavior.

The alternative interpretation related to differences in temperament between siblings is that these differences are created in part by the parents, who attempt to differentiate between siblings by viewing them as different individuals in a process called **sibling de-identification.** In this regard, research has shown that parents tend to rate the first two children in the family as having different temperaments, while temperaments for laterborn children are rated more alike (F. S. Schachter & Stone, 1985). In a longitudinal study in which observers studied mother-infant interaction for the first two children in the family when each was 24 months old, the researchers found that mothers expressed similar levels of affection and verbal responsiveness to both children but the amount of parental control of the children differed. Control was measured by the amount of direct interventions in the child's actions in the form of commands, rejections, and disciplinary actions (J. Dunn, Plomin, & Daniels, 1986).

In summary, many factors are likely to play a role in how well siblings get along with each other. From a family systems perspective, it is difficult to say with certainty that a single factor taken in isolation is the cause of sibling aggression. Temperament, although strongly related to sibling conflict, could be multiply determined by parent-child and child-child interactions over the course of the first years of life. Is the child really difficult, or has the child come to be labeled as difficult? Or is difficult temperament a stance one takes in the face of a sibling who is constantly rejecting or ignoring? It may be some time before we can sort out the answers to these questions.

Parent intervention in sibling disputes. Parents can choose whether or not to intervene in sibling disputes. The effects of their actions depend upon the age of the siblings. When the older child is under 3, parental noninvolvement in sibling disputes tends to predispose the siblings to continued conflict. Parents of children of this age tend to intervene primarily in the most serious fights. Before the intervention, children are most likely to use aggression and coercion in disputes. Immediately following the intervention, children are more likely to use negotiation strategies to resolve their conflicts, suggesting that parents can indeed play a role in helping children to negotiate. On the other hand, noninvolvement is a more effective strategy for older siblings who are less close and less involved with each other if the parent intervenes in their disputes in any way. This means that over time, siblings develop new ways to negotiate their disputes on their own. Self-interested justifications decrease and cooperative discourse increases (J. Dunn, Kreps, & Brown, 1996; Kramer, Perozynski, & Chung, 1999; Perlman & Ross, 1997).

At least in middle-class Caucasian North American families, when parents intervene, it is typically as third-party mediators. Parents tend to favor younger siblings in such disputes and to discipline the older sibling. When fathers in particular disciplined the older sibling primarily and mothers disciplined both siblings equally, these families were rated as more harmonious, both in the marital relationship and in the sibling relationships. If both parents pick on the older sibling, that child is more likely to show behavior problems in preschool (Volling & Elins, 1998). Better developmental outcomes are likely, therefore, when parents expect the older sibling to be the more responsible person and when the younger sibling is sometime disciplined by at least one parent. This not only helps the older sibling become more responsible but also helps prevent his or her feeling that the parents favor the younger sibling.

When parents intervene, they are not likely to get involved in children's claims of ownership ("It's mine") or possession ("I had it first"). Parents in general are more interested in getting children to share their activities rather than fight over who owns something, and they act to prevent property damage. Parents want children to resolve their differences, to play together harmoniously, and to end the dispute as quickly as possible (Ross, 1996).

In summary, parental involvement in sibling disputes decreases over age as children develop, primarily from their parents, new ways to negotiate peaceful settlements. There are, however, between-family differences in these patterns.

The Author's View

One of the major achievements of this age period is the emergence of verbal autobiographical memory and the use of verbal narrative—in stories, imaginative play, and conversation—as a tool to understand self and others. This achievement marks the end of infancy and the beginning of early childhood, although the distinction is arbitrary (see the discussion of developmental stages in Chapter 1). The infant lives in a participatory world of immediate and direct experience. The onset of imagination and the beginnings of a theory of mind at 30 months open up a psychological world that is bigger than life, filled with possibilities.

Children no longer have to be content with what actually happens. They can make up a better outcome as they play with dolls, siblings, and peers. We all do this when we imagine becoming famous, getting out of our difficulties and achieving success, or taking revenge on someone who has wronged us. The only problem for 3-year-olds is that they are never sure about the limits of this newfound ability to make up a more congenial world. If they could make things up so easily, why is everything not just pretend? Children may think they can make their parents disappear by wishing it. A boy might believe that he will change into a girl if he talks in a high voice for a long time. If the real can be imaginary then the imaginary could be real. Children fear their own imaginary monsters, get shaken awake by nightmares, and worry that they will lose themselves when their feces get sucked down the toilet drain. These fears are very real for children of this age and they often do not have a sufficient command of language to fully express themselves.

Do adults have such experiences? Recall a period after which you first entered into a completely different social and cultural situation. This might be going to a new school or college for the first time, going to a foreign country for the first time, moving to a new city or neighborhood where you do not know anyone, or signing up for a class about which you know nothing at all.

During the first few days or weeks of being in a completely new situation, you may have the feeling that there is something unreal about it. This may seem like a pretend world in which the language and customs are totally arbitrary. From the newcomer's perspective, this world seems to have been suddenly made up, so it could suddenly go away. On the other hand, there is often a fear of not being in control, of there being things out there that could sneak up on you and hurt you. Your conversations are limited to a few words, usually when people are asking you questions or when you need help. You do not always understand what people are saying to you.

These feelings usually pass after a while, when you can see that the people in this strange world are similar to the ones you knew before. They just dress and speak differently. As you begin to develop a theory of mind for those people, you can see their world is not just made up but has its own meaning and value. As you get acculturated, your fears of the unknown lessen and you begin to interact in a more adult way.

The third year of life, therefore, is transitional. New feelings of power and self-control are mixed with uncertainties and fears. Verbal narratives bring children into the world of emotional self and other understanding. They grow in their capacity to share feelings with others. On the other hand, they are still limited in their ability to express and understand themselves and may feel left out of conversations they do not understand. They often get confused by what people say. Children who are maltreated, or children whose parents talk little about their own emotions, are less able to participate in these verbal dialogues and are less likely to develop coherent autobiographical memories. Some of these children may continue to feel like the adult in a new situation. They may fail to develop a consistent sense of themselves, their conversations can remain limited, and they may be less likely to develop a theory of mind, conditions that may predispose a person to psychopathology.

The most effective way to help all children through this period of transition is to be open to their feelings, both positive and negative. Children will develop to the extent that they have opportunities to bring their private speech and participatory memory into a co-regulated verbal dialogue with another person. Children who have been severely maltreated will take a much longer time to trust even the most sensitive child clinical psychologist. Nonverbal methods, such as play therapy, can be a very effective way to break down their barriers of fear and anger.

Parents, teachers, and therapists will be rewarded by recognizing both the new verbal potentials as well as the special limitations and vulnerabilities of children at this age. This is best done by becoming aware of those parts of yourself that are most similar to the experiences of the child, by finding ways to activate your participatory memory for this age period.

AWARENESS THROUGH MOVEMENT

Jumping

1. Stand as you normally would, with your legs approximately shoulder width apart. Imagine there is a line drawn on the floor just in front

Applications Infant and Child Maltreatment

Child abuse and neglect are two forms of child maltreatment that should concern anyone who cares about the welfare of children. These problems can take a number of forms that vary in relative severity. *Abuse* typically refers to cases in which a child sustains a nonaccidental injury from a parent or other caregiver. *Neglect* is a pattern of ignoring the basic needs of the child for physical and psychological support and nourishment. Estimates of the incidence of child abuse and neglect are not very accurate due to deficiencies in reporting procedures. As many as several hundred thousand cases of abuse may occur in the United States every year.

What are the causes and effects of child maltreatment?

No one knows for sure what causes child maltreatment, although certain factors have been implicated. The four most important are (1) child characteristics, (2) parental personality, (3) the history of the parent-child interaction, and (4) the relative level of social stress on the family (Belsky, 1980; Lamb, 1978b).

Some infants and children, by virtue of being endowed with undesirable characteristics, are more likely to be maltreated. Infants who are handicapped, slow to develop, or relatively unresponsive, or who are judged to have a difficult temperament, place demands upon their caregivers that typically developing infants do not. Research suggests that premature infants and infants with special needs, Down's syndrome, and other illnesses are overrepresented in the maltreated population (Burgess, 1979; Sherrod, O'Conner, Vietze, & Altemeier, 1984). These babies are often expensive to care for and thus contribute to family stress. They require more effort and are more fussy and demanding than other infants. In addition, they show less positive emotion and therefore provide fewer reinforcements for the caregiver (see the "Family and Society" section in Chapter 9).

Parental factors play an important role in child abuse. Abusive parents show fewer positive emotions, interact with their babies less, are more likely to use control strategies and physical punishment with their infants, and talk less to their babies than are nonabusive parents (Boddy & Skuse, 1994; Burgess and Conger, 1978; Straus, 1994). Abusive parents are less adept at verbal skills in general, score lower in abstract reasoning, and show a reduced capacity for planning and control over impulses. Abusing fathers, in particular, are lower in parental warmth and interpersonal relationships, and they are more introverted than nonabusive fathers (Hyman & Mitchell, 1977). Child abusers have been found to be hypersensitive to their infants. Instead of adaptively tuning out a loud or piercing cry, the abusers are likely to become annoyed and aroused by the crying (Frodi & Lamb, 1980).

Abusers are less able to correctly identify emotion signals, and in some cases, they interpret negative emotion as positive (Kropp & Haynes, 1987). Compared to nonabusing parents, child abusers view child rearing as less satisfactory and more difficult, and they and their children tend to live more isolated lives (Hutcheson, Black, & Starr, 1993; Trickett & Susman, 1988). Some evidence suggests that parents who abuse their children were themselves abused as children (R. Parke & Collmer, 1975; Weston, Coolton, Halsey, & Covington, 1993).

Parents who neglect their children but do not abuse them seem to be somewhat different. The overall picture of the abusing parent is of a hypersensitive and nonempathic person. The neglectful parent, in contrast, seems to be more apathetic and depressed (Polansky, 1976). Fortunately, none of these factors conclusively predicts that parents actually are going to abuse or neglect their children. Many parents who suffer from these problems in their personality or personal histories never show signs of maltreating a child.

Another important factor in child maltreatment is family stress. Higher rates of child maltreatment have been recorded in lower social classes (Burgess, 1979; Garbarino, 1976; Garbarino & Crouter, 1978; Gil, 1970). The stress in lower-income families may be caused by a number of factors. Low income is one factor, but economic stress alone is not a major factor (Garbarino, 1976). More important ones seem to be the availability of social support systems and the stability and continuity of day-to-day existence. Families whose size, composition, and location are constantly changing are more at risk for maltreatment than others.

Maltreated children do not fare as well as children who have not been maltreated. At 2 years, maltreated children show more anger, frustration, and opposition, as well as a relative slowdown in developmental progress over the first year (Egeland & Sroufe, 1981). They are less likely to show pride in succeeding on a task and also less likely to show shame when they fail than are typically developing children, suggesting that they have deficits in their sense of an existential self (Alessandri & Lewis, 1996). In a day care setting, maltreated children are less likely to seek comfort from the adult caregivers, more likely to avoid contact with caregivers and peers, and more likely to be aggressive (George & Main, 1979).

Several studies have found that the attachment patterns of maltreated children do not fit into the three typical categories used in the Ainsworth Strange Situation Test. Resistant infants alternate between clinging and pulling away, while avoidant infants tend to ignore the presence of the mother and reject her advances. Maltreated infants' response to the Strange Situation has been described as disorganized/disoriented, comprised of a strong proximity seeking of the mother on reunion followed immediately by a strong avoidance of her or gaze aversion while approaching her (Carlson, Cicchetti,

Barnett, & Braunwald, 1989; Lamb, Gaensbauer, Malkin, & Schultz, 1985; Main & Solomon, 1986). This pattern may be the result of a fear of the mother mixed with normal attachment motivations, creating a conflict between approach and withdrawal (see Chapter 8).

Other negative effects of maltreatment on infants include a lack of concern for the distress of peers and an often inappropriate response to distress, such as physical aggression (Main & George, 1985). Compared to nonmaltreated ones, maltreated infants have shorter MLU (mean length of utterance), less speech related to their own emotional states, and less speech that is relevant to the ongoing topic of conversation (Coster, Gersten, Beeghly, & Cicchetti, 1989).

Since the children in these studies are under the age of 3 years, the conclusions are very disturbing. They suggest that abusing parents can disrupt the usual developmental process by which infants come to seek help, comfort, and information from people around them. In other words, maltreated children as young as 2 years old show behavior that is nonadaptive to the extent of avoiding those who might offer and extend support and encouragement.

These findings also suggest that maltreated children have already developed serious distortions in their sense of self. They do not seem to take an interest in their own achievements, do not share an appreciation of community standards, and do not have a well-developed theory of mind. If maltreatment occurs under the age of 3 years, children may retain participatory memories of the maltreatment that never become translated into verbal forms of knowing (see the "Motor and Cognitive Development" section in this chapter). This means that their autobiographical memories lack a means of understanding their nonverbal behavior. Therapeutic interventions—both psychotherapies and somatic therapies (see Chapter 2)—

that address the participatory memories are likely to be most helpful.

What are the limitations of the research on child maltreatment?

All the factors previously mentioned are probably interrelated in their impact on child maltreatment. For example, mothers of a lower social class have higher rates of special needs and premature infants. However, it is possible that the reporting rates are higher for lower-class children than for middle-class children. A more difficult problem is that the causes of child maltreatment are likely to be specific to the situation: some factors are more likely to operate with certain people than with others (Garbarino, 1982). Research designs that do not take into account the complex interactions among different types of people, circumstances, and infant characteristics will find few systematic effects.

Another problem with research on child maltreatment is that studies almost always begin with a sample of maltreated infants and maltreating parents. The search for causes of child maltreatment then is limited to only those people who actually demonstrate the symptom. Usually, researchers try to trace the maltreating adult's or the maltreated infant's history back in time. Findings such as "child maltreaters were maltreated as children" and "special-needs infants are more likely to be maltreated" are typical conclusions from this kind of research.

When a target sample's history is traced backward through time, the study is known as a *retrospective study.* While it may be the case that most abusing parents have been maltreated as children, it is not true that a person who was maltreated as a child will become an abusive parent. If we looked at the data prospectively, we would have to sample all children in a generation, follow them until they became parents themselves, and then see which of them maltreats their

children. Obviously, such a *prospective study* cannot be done. If it were, however, we would probably find that only a very small percentage of adults who were maltreated as children actually end up maltreating their own children.

What can be concluded from this evidence? A history of maltreatment in the family of origin is one factor that may contribute to a person's becoming a maltreating parent, but other factors must operate on maltreated children to make them into maltreating parents. We do not know what these factors are at present because of the difficulty of doing this kind of research. Social and cultural influences are major factors likely to affect the outcomes of parents with a history of maltreatment. We live in a society in which violence is accepted. It occurs in the streets, and we are inundated with mass media violence. Physical punishment is widespread, occurring in at least 35% of infants, and is often considered to be an accepted cultural practice in many communities (Garbarino, 1993; Gil, 1970; Holden, Thompson, Zambarano, & Marshall, 1997; Straus, 1994; Straus & Stewart, 1999).

Do these factors cause child maltreatment? It is hard to say, and still harder to do research that might establish a conclusive link between social values, physical punishment, and the incidence of abuse and neglect. We might think of doing a cross-cultural study in which we would select different cultural groups that place different amounts of value on violence and physical punishment and then look to see if this dimension correlates with child abuse or neglect. The problem is that these cultures are likely to differ on factors other than the value of violence, and we could not say whether violence alone, violence in combination with other factors, or those other factors alone were most responsible for the observed amount of child abuse.

(continues)

Applications (continued)

It would not be totally unwarranted at this time, however, to say that abuse and neglect are social and family problems—not merely the result of individual factors in the parent. If this is true, it suggests that we can act to prevent child maltreatment by strengthening community and neighborhood support systems for parents, providing human services for families as a whole rather than for single individuals, and taking preventive measures to strengthen community support systems when the child is born. Since the incidence of physical punishment for infants is much higher than even advocates for this disciplinary strategy would endorse, a stronger stand against its use and education about more authoritative parenting styles would also be helpful. The birth of a child invariably brings parents into contact with community institutions. Action at this time is essential, since some parents may not contact other community institutions until the child is in school, and by then it may be too late (Garbarino, 1982; Hamilton, 1989; Strauss & Stewart, 1999; Wiehe, 1989).

of your feet. In extreme slow motion, get ready to make a small jump over that line with both of your feet. Slowly return to your normal standing position, pause a few moments, and again slowly prepare yourself to jump. Repeat this process many times. Now and then make a little jump at normal speed so you can make sure that your small, slow movements accurately resemble a normal jump.

The object is to understand the body organization you need for jumping, in order to understand better what was required for us to jump as young children. Since jumping usually takes only a second, it is very difficult to notice the details involved. We could capture the details with the aid of slow-motion video analysis. Here, however, your own nervous system is the only equipment you have available. In order to become more aware of your movement, it is necessary to slow down your movements, and to repeat initiating the movement many times.

Try to give yourself at least 10 seconds to create gradually and smoothly the posture from which you are ready to jump, and take several seconds to return to your typical way of standing. People usually first notice that in order to jump they lean forward over the balls of their feet and then return to standing with more weight on the heels. If you examine yourself carefully, however, you will probably find that you must change your entire body alignment, including how you carry your chest over your pelvis, and your pelvis over your legs. In inefficient jumping, some body segments are pushed backward or down, which dampens the forces generated by the legs. In efficient jumping, on the other hand, the power of the legs lifts the entire body into the air and forward, without any buckling in the middle. Stand normally and rest awhile.

2. Now you will do a series a movements in order to improve the body alignment necessary for efficient jumping. Stand normally with your feet shoulder width apart. Begin to oscillate slowly backward and forward, shifting your weight on your feet, and try to bring more and more of your weight onto your heels. Lift your toes in order to go further back, but do not go so far that you strain or even stretch any muscles.

Continue to oscillate slowly forward and backward, and now focus on bringing your knees farther and farther back as you lift your toes.

Continue to oscillate slowly forward and backward, and now focus on bringing your coccyx, that is, the tip of your tailbone, back as you lift your toes. Each time you go back, you will stick your rear end out behind you.

Continue to oscillate slowly forward and backward, and now focus on bringing your hip joints farther and farther back as you lift your toes.

Continue to oscillate slowly forward and backward, and now focus on bringing the top of your pelvis farther and farther back as you lift your toes. The top of your pelvis is more or less where your belt would normally be. In order to do this, you will tuck your tailbone under slightly as you go back.

In the second year of life, children discover the power of assertiveness over their parents. In the third year, they can become more verbally and physically aggressive, although this begins to be replaced by more verbal negotiation strategies by the end of the third year. Aggressive behaviors are natural developments of the child's growing self-awareness and the child's exploration of the limits of the self's power and ability. It helps to remain calm in such situations, to ensure that the wronged child is properly attended, and not to overreact. Biting, however, needs to be dealt with firmly because of the risks to the health of the bitten child.

Parents may worry when they see their children manually exploring their genitals for the first time. A parent may want to distract the child by offering a toy, but reprimanding is not recommended. Self-exploration is a natural part of development, as is a child's curiosity about the sex organs of others, the origins of babies, and so on. It helps to keep your answers to sex-related questions simple, direct, and honest. The child does not treat these questions with any more prurient interest than questions about the moon, the grass, or the picture-book, so why should you?

Children need to be introduced to a wide range of experiences and places, but only gradually and at a pace that seems most comfortable to them. As children are developing self-help skills, it is easy to let them take greater responsibility for some of these tasks. Examples are picking out and putting on clothes, wiping themselves, washing and drying their own hands, and so on.

One of the most striking contradictions of this age is that the children's growing appreciation of reality and their own place in it is mixed with a growing fantasy life and a whole new crop of very unrealistic (at least to the adult) fears that come up in dreams and while awake. Remember that such fears are very real to children. The fears may arise because the children begin to notice things they never noticed before and realize there are things they do not understand.

Because a child's fears seem silly and inconsequential to an adult, there is a tendency to laugh at them or to tease the child about them. This does not help the child, who probably needs reassurance more than anything else. Two-year-olds are beginning to have worries just like anyone else. They may have nightmares, bite their nails, stutter, or show other signs of behavior disruption. Parents are justified in feeling concerned, but it is important to try to understand the source of children's worries and help them to solve the problems.

Children are also becoming more active participants in the adult world. They may want to help out around the house, preschool, or day care center. Even though this may mean getting work done more slowly with some extra mess, it pays to encourage these budding signs of helpfulness, at least once in a while. It is a good idea to talk about the next thing that is going to happen while you are engaged in a task. This helps the child understand that one thing leads to another. Telling the child about expectable future events may also help alleviate some fears. Talking about a visit to the doctor, a new baby-sitter, or some other potentially disturbing situation can be a very effective means of avoiding trouble before it begins. Teaching good habits such as staying clean, picking up toys, and putting away clothing can be started at this time, and the child's own initiatives are not to be ignored. You will have to play the role of a negotiator, reminder, and coach for many years to come, so do not be discouraged if the child does not understand how to do these things right away.

In the realm of play, 2-year-old children enjoy such activities as working with clay and finger painting. These activities are wonderful ways to let children creatively express their newfound fine motor skills. Children of this age also like sand and water, which go best with pails and shovels. Cars and pegboards are also of great interest. Be sure the toys you get are safe—nontoxic, not sharp or jagged, and with no parts that can be swallowed.

At this age, children get involved in many exciting things, and they want to have their own say about most things. The problem is that they have trouble striking a balance between alternatives and extremes. It is typical for 2-year-olds to play too long and get overtired. It is hard for children to relax at bedtime; they may need a story, a talk with parents, or just some time to themselves before they can settle down. It is common to see movement from one extreme to another at this age; for example, staying dry all day and then suddenly wetting, or screaming for dinner and then turning it down when it finally appears. These swings can be frustrating for parents, but they are necessary steps on the path to autonomous self-regulation.

Continue to oscillate slowly forward and backward, and now focus on bringing your lower ribs farther and farther back as you lift your toes. This is the area of your diaphragm. You will need to lengthen your lumbar spine as you do this. Allow your breath to relax into the area of your lower back.

Continue to oscillate slowly forward and backward, and now focus on bringing the area between your shoulder blades farther and farther back as you lift your toes. Do not pull your shoulders back. Let your shoulders relax and focus on bringing back the area of your spine between your shoulder blades.

Continue to oscillate slowly forward and backward, but now focus on bringing the back of your head farther and farther back as you lift your toes. Do not tilt your head back so that your chin comes up, but instead lengthen the back of your neck and keep your eyes at the level of the horizon. Be sure not to stretch or strain the muscles of your neck.

3. Now return to the process of jumping at normal speeds and in slow motion, as in step 1. Can you detect an increase in the efficiency of your jumping? Are you more aware of the role of balance and of the changes in alignment that are required?

Note: When most people think about jumping, they assume that the major requirement is power from the leg muscles. While it is true that muscular power is needed, this is only one element among many. Think of a growing baby. Early kicking movements are similar to jumping, and young babies can jump when supported in an upright posture. Jumping requires good balance so that we do not fall over when we lean forward on the toes, in order to use our calf muscles, and also for landing. Also, jumping requires precise skeletal alignment and proper timing, so that the forces generated from all the muscles are synchronized for greatest efficiency. It is certainly easier to jump when you already know how!

An additional benefit of this lesson is that getting ready to jump teaches many elements of good posture. If you maintain the alignment of the leaning-forward jumping posture and then bring your

weight back over your heels, straightening your knees and hips, you will produce an efficient standing posture.

Good posture entails a vertical alignment of the skeleton in order to minimize the downward force of gravity. Jumping improves posture because it also requires a vertical alignment of the skeleton, but for the purpose of organizing upwardly directed forces from the legs. If our standing posture is upright and efficient, it is possible to initiate jumping with minimal preparatory movements. More than likely, at the end of this lesson, you needed to do less realignment of your normal posture in order to jump. This means that your skeletal segments are better balanced, one on top of the other.

SUMMARY

Motor and Cognitive Development

■ Motor skills become more complex and adaptive during the third year, including running, jumping, constructing with blocks, and making art.

■ Motor skills become integrated with language and cognition, as language regulates the execution of a motor skill and self-produced movement enhances cognition.

■ Children are now able to execute complex sequences of action, work toward an adult standard, and correct their own errors. This leads to increases in attention span.

■ Language becomes internalized as private speech, such that prior forms of social regulation now become self-regulatory.

■ Make-believe and pretend become complex and creative.

Emotional Development

■ A sense of categorical self emerges, including age and gender self-labeling.

■ Descriptions of emotional states of the self and others become elaborate.

■ Three-year-olds can act by taking the behavior of others into account, but they do not yet behave as if they have a clear theory of the other's mind.

- Children of this age lack the ability to differentiate reality from make-believe in most cases.

Social and Language Development

- Grammar emerges with the use of verbs and the ability to add the appropriate endings to words for tense and number.

- Complex question asking emerges.

- Limitations of language include pronunciation problems, inability to appreciate complex grammar, and lack of skill in maintaining conversations.

- Toddlers who are more compliant have parents with more authoritative child-rearing styles.

- Peer interaction shows evidence of coordinated actions, imitative and complementary turn taking, and the emergence of friendships.

- The acquisition of gender-role stereotypes is a complex developmental process involving cognitive understanding of gender and family role relationships.

Family and Society

- Older and younger siblings derive different benefits from their mutual interactions. Younger siblings benefit from the guidance and protection of the older sibling and develop self-protection skills. Older siblings pay attention to the needs of others and develop skills in a leadership role.

- Interfamily differences in sibling conflict may depend on the children's prior relationships and attachments to parents and to their peers, on the sex similarity of the pair, on the temperament of the children, and on sibling de-identification by the parents.

Applications: Infant and Child Maltreatment

- Factors contributing to child maltreatment include child, parent, and societal influences. Child maltreatment is multicausal, and treatment approaches should recognize this.

- Research on child maltreatment is problematic because of the way the data are gathered and interpreted.

 ## ON THE WEB

www.childabuse.org   This web site has information regarding child abuse issues such as child abuse facts, organization facts, ways to help, tips for parents, press releases, state chapters, 1998 opinion polls, publications, links and resources, contacts, and employment opportunities.

www.apsac.org   The American Professional Society on the Abuse of Children is an organization that provides a professional response to everyone affected by child maltreatment. Its mission is to "provide professional education which promotes effective, culturally sensitive, and interdisciplinary approaches to the identification, intervention, treatment, and prevention of child abuse and neglect; by promoting research and guidelines to inform professional practice; by educating the public about child abuse and neglect; and by ensuring that America's public policy concerning child maltreatment is well-informed and constructive."

www.awlp.org   The web page of the Alliance of Work/Life Professionals, an organization for business, academic, and public-sector professionals who work to promote a good balance between work life and personal life. The site provides information about AWLP, its members, and its mission and goals; it also has links to the alliance newsletter and press releases.

GLOSSARY

Autobiographical memory   The ability to remember experiences verbally.

Categorical self   The ability of people to identify their own membership in one or more conceptual categories, such as "I am a boy," "I am a brother," and "I am not a baby."

Dominance hierachy   A pattern of social relationships in which the members of a group are ranked according to their relative power or lack of power over others.

Dramatists   Children who classify objects based on a script or story in which the objects are embedded.

Exercise play   Playful locomotor movement that is physically vigorous, such as running, chasing, and climbing.

Gender labeling   The ability to identify self or other verbally as male or female.

Imaginative pretend play   Play in which the child invents make-believe situations.

Liquidating pretend play   Play in which the child's make-believe situation alters reality to better suit the child's desires.

Mean length of utterance (MLU)   The average number of morphemes across all the utterances of a child.

Metalinguistic knowledge   An understanding of the uses and functions of language, independent of knowledge of semantics and syntax.

Overregularization   The extension of regular verb endings for the past tense to irregular verbs.

Patterners   Children who classify objects based on similarities in their forms or functions.

Pretend role play   A form of pretend play in which children act out the roles of their mother, their father, or other important figures in their lives.

Private speech   An internalized dialogue with the self in which children describe their thoughts and actions out loud.

Prospective study   A longitudinal research study in which data are gathered from subjects at periodic intervals, so that the subjects' current behavior and ideas are being observed.

Retrospective study   A research study in which the subject recollects his or her past or the experimenter traces the subject's records backward in time.

Sibling de-identification   The process by which parents differentiate between siblings.

Theory of mind   The awareness that other people have independent beliefs and feelings.

Chapter

12

The Effects of the Infancy Period on the Formation of Individual Differences

CHAPTER OVERVIEW AND OUTLINE

Development as a Complex Dynamic Process

What is the importance of infancy? How does one's experience as an infant affect one's life?

Research on Continuity between Early and Later Development

What are the ways in which experiences during infancy can be related to later outcomes?

Perinatal Factors

What are the long-term consequences of premature birth and of prenatal and genetic influences?

Motor Development

Do advances or lags in motor development affect later motor skills?

Parental Contributions

What are the effects of having a working mother or being in child care? Do parents make a difference in children's later behavior and development?

Risk and Disadvantage

What are the conditions under which infants can recover from early risk factors?

Culture

How do cultural differences affect developmental outcomes?

Gender

Does infant experience affect boys and girls differently?

Intellectual Development

Is intelligence predicted by the amount or type of stimulation an infant receives?

Temperament

Do temperamental characteristics persist for long periods?

Developmental Systems of Multiple Interacting Factors

Can any single event, trauma, or factor that occurs during infancy have lasting consequences in a person's life? Can the effects of early trauma be alleviated?

Is what happens to a person during their infancy important or critical for later development? Do traumatic experiences in infancy, such as extreme poverty or maternal depression, affect later cognitive or social functioning? Can we predict whether a child will be bright, average, or dull from scores on assessment tests done in early infancy? Can later developmental dysfunctions be diagnosed from early infant testing? What is the importance of infancy in the human life cycle?

These questions have been reserved for the last chapter of this book for several reasons. First, answering them requires an examination of individual continuity and change across the entire age span of infancy and from infancy to later childhood and adulthood. This type of long-term approach is difficult to discuss in chapters focused on particular age periods. Second, answering these questions requires an examination of the concepts and methods used in longitudinal research. Although I have discussed findings of longitudinal studies—such as the relationships between attachment at 12 months and peer competence in the preschool—I have not addressed the potentials and problems unique to the interpretation of such studies.

The questions raised in the first paragraph do not have simple answers. For some questions, we have no answers at all, aside from theoretical speculation. An appreciation of the research difficulties requires some familiarity with the way in which research in this area is carried out and the implicit and explicit theories that guide the work.

Development as a Complex Dynamic Process

Before getting into research and theory, it might help to put the questions raised in the first paragraph in a broader perspective. What do the answers to those questions mean to the children, their families, and society? How, for example, should we interpret strong evidence predicting later outcomes

from something that occurred during infancy? We might be pleased to find an early marker for some later disorder or an early sign of intelligence or social adjustment. If one is able to predict with certainty how a person will turn out based on some early factor, on the other hand, does that mean there is little hope for people who suffer some kind of deficit or trauma during infancy? Does it mean that people are marked for life by things that happened to them before they could walk or talk?

Perhaps, on the other hand, what people hope is that evidence of strong prediction will lead us to discover ways to break down the grip of early experiences on negative outcomes by discovering new treatments or interventions. Advocates for early intervention and early enrichment programs look to evidence of strong prediction to make a case for their work. This logic, however, is somewhat contradictory, since strong prediction implies *a lack of change*. Does it make sense that the justification for a program intended to induce change is research showing that people do not change? Medical research operates on this principle. Once a link between a gene or a virus and some disease is found, researchers can then seek out treatments that deal with the root cause of the disease.

Now, consider the opposite: research that shows a lack of ability to predict later from early factors. Should we take this research as saying that infancy has no value, in the sense that early experiences or predispositions are unimportant for later outcomes? People who are against investing money on early childhood education and intervention programs, who would prefer to see public and private funds invested in helping older children succeed at school or preventing crime, take this kind of research as an argument for their position (Bruer, 1999).

Development Is a Complex Process Involving Many Factors

The research on long-term outcomes, reviewed in this chapter, does not fit either of these extreme possibilities. No single early factor—such as the prenatal environment, parental sensitivity, or infant temperament—predicts later outcomes 100% of the time. Most of the factors that we have studied in this book turn out to be both necessary and influential for later outcomes, but only some of the time, and only for some people and not others. The answers to the questions raised in the first paragraph, therefore, are not simple. Early development is a complex process, and we need to take the time to understand that complexity if we are to do justice to the important issues facing infants, families, and society.

The phases of an individual's life are never completely unconnected; there is always some influence of the earlier phases on later ones. Perhaps the most salient example of apparent developmental disconnection is the life cycle of moths and butterflies. Here we have stages of development that are so radically different—larva, cocoon, and adult—that it seems almost certain that the experiences of the larva, for example, could not impact on the adult. And yet there are such influences. The olfactory (smell) experiences of the larva have been shown to influence the food choices of the adult (Klopfer, 1988).

In humans, developmental processes of the infant are embedded in social dyadic and family systems and families are embedded in the multiple and interconnecting systems of the larger society and culture. Several features of such complex systems are worth mentioning again here (see Chapter 2) in the context of this discussion of the effects of infancy on later development.

First, in complex systems, changes in one factor are likely to affect other factors in such a way that the system as a whole adapts to the change in any single part. We have seen countless examples of this kind of system effect in this book, as infants and parents, siblings and peers, and families and cultures affect each other in a variety of ways. Developmental outcomes are typically the result of a large number of factors acting in combination.

In the first paragraph of this chapter, I asked whether early factors have an impact on later outcomes. Perhaps a more systems-oriented way to ask the question is, *Under what circumstances, in what combinations, and for which types of individual do early factors impact later outcomes?* What are those combinations, and do they lead to positive or negative outcomes? Another way to say this is, *What is the developmental process by which desirable and undesirable outcomes are formed?* If a child exhibits a desirable tendency early in life, we would like to find ways to preserve it, and if he or she suffers an unfortunate circumstance early, we would wish to bring the individual back to a closer approximation of typical development and behavior.

Second, when systems are perturbed by some risk factor, the response of the whole system is not necessarily a change. Often, in fact, the system achieves a kind of dynamic balancing act in which it returns to a stable mode of functioning (Fogel, 1993; Fogel & Thelen, 1987; Thelen & Smith, 1994). A good example is the development of some premature infants. Due to the compensatory actions of the parents to provide extra support and stimulation for their infant at risk, the developmental course of the infant may approach that of full-term infants, and the family system may return to a stable mode of functioning following an earlier period of stress and uncertainty. Alternatively, system dynamics may progressively move a child and family off the typical developmental course. An example of a continuing spiral of negative effects that amplify each other is the cycle of persistent poverty, ill health, infant disadvantage, and maladaptive parental behavior.

An explanation for why some family systems achieve stable states of positive functioning, becoming self-righting after a trauma, and others become unstable must lie in the dynamic interactions between family members and between the family and society. The overwhelming body of research on the development of all species of animals suggests that the more complex the system and the more alternatives available (formal and informal supports, economic resources), the more likely it is that these multiple facets of the system will eventually absorb the initial trauma.

The more the continued trauma depletes the system of resources, the more likely that the child will develop some type of developmental difficulty (Brauth, Hall, & Dooling, 1991; Klopfer, 1988). Lack of resources constrains development and forces individuals into the limitations of their heredity and their early experiences. Availability of resources (home, family, nutrition, support, etc.) opens development up to a wider range of possibilities. In the research reviewed in this chapter, we will see examples in which early predispositions and risk factors were essentially eliminated as causal factors for later development and in which later outcomes are a product of a complex set of events that are unique to each individual.

No Two Individuals Respond in the Same Way to the Same Situation

Individuals vary in how they are affected by any single factor in infancy that contributes to later developmental outcome (Wachs, 2000). In the previous chapter, for example, we found that suffering abuse as an infant does not guarantee that individuals will go on to abuse their own infant. Only a small proportion of abused children become child abusers. The IQ range of children who were prenatally exposed to alcohol can range from retarded to having intelligence within a more typical range. There is a range of severe to mild retardation even in the case of major genetic disorders, such as fragile X syndrome (Chapter 3). There is a wide range of outcomes, therefore, even when individuals have some things in common at an earlier point in time.

A number of theories of development suggest that such variability and complexity of outcome is the rule rather than the exception. Behavior ecology theory, for example, suggests that species evolve because each individual is different. If everyone were the same, there would be no opportunity for natural selection to guarantee survival. Species evolve because those individuals who are best able to survive live long enough to reproduce.

Dynamic systems theories suggest that very small perturbations—butterfly effects—may have unpredictable consequences for the growth of the system. Suppose you were able to chart the developmental histories of many individual infants, recording all the relevant family and environmental factors that may affect their development. This cannot be done, of course, because of the complexity of human individuals and their social systems. But if it could be done, do you think you could find, ultimately, a reasonable explanation for everything that individual does and for how the individual develops over time? Many developmental researchers would say that yes, given all the important data, they could predict in all cases the developmental outcomes of the person. As one such scientist puts it:

"All scientists are determinists. It is difficult to imagine what not being a determinist could mean . . . There is no magical force . . . that shapes development, apart from genetic/biological systems that propel and guide development and environments that are necessary and provide opportunities for its expression." (Scarr, 1993, pp. 1342–1343)

Determinism is the view that all natural phenomena are the result of some specifiable cause or a series of interlocking causes (see Chapter 2). An alternative scientific perspective—based on dynamic systems theory—suggests that there is indeterminism in development:

"Webs and chains of historical events are so intricate, so imbued with random and chaotic elements, so unrepeatable in encompassing such a multitude of unique (and uniquely interacting) objects, that standard models of simple prediction and replication do not apply." (Gould, 1994, p. 85)

Indeterminism is the idea that not all natural phenomena can be predicted from known laws or principles. In Chapter 2, I talked about the weather as a complex system in which chaotic or indeterministic factors play a role. Another example of an indeterministic process is the history of society. Many natural processes are **historical processes** in the sense that they are not simple accumulations of past events. Rather, they are uniquely emergent creations that can never be exactly repeated. Indeterminism, "magic," and butterfly effects are just as much a part of human development as determinism and logic (see Chapter 2; Fogel, Lyra, & Valsiner, 1997; Prigogine & Stengers, 1984).

Although some aspects of developmental change are determined by specifiable sequences of events, many outcomes are indeterminate (Fogel, 1993; Fogel & Thelen, 1987). Individuals are continually open to opportunities that they do not plan and cannot predict. A baby may discover an important contingency between his or her own behavior and something in the environment merely by chance, because the baby happened to turn his or her head to see something and was ready to follow up the opportunity without fully understanding where this direction might ultimately lead. Sometimes the infant is able to make sense of this foray into the un-

What makes children different from each other? The formation of individual differences is a complicated field of study about which we understand relatively little. These children are all supposed to be doing the same thing, but each has interpreted it differently.

David Young-Wolff/PhotoEdit

known and sometimes not. Sometimes the meaning of the infant's attempt is clarified by an adult, who "explains" to the child what he or she just did.

One could argue that this "discovery" by the child is nothing more than a potentially knowable combination of genes and environments that predispose the child to make such a discovery. But is the fact that the child makes the discovery there and then, at that particular moment in his or her life, explainable? The child decides, in the emotion of the moment, to take the risk of jumping into something new and unknown or to stay within the safety of what is already understood. Is this decision determined in any logical way? And could the flowering into the social world of a previously shy or withdrawn child have been predicted even by the people most intimately connected with the child? Or could they have predicted that such a change would occur quite suddenly at a particular point in the child's developmental history?

In summary, there are two basic principles for developmental change. One is that *development is a complex multifactor process*. The other is that *no two individuals respond in the same way to the same factor—variability and the opportunity to capitalize on chance outcomes is inherent to the developmental process* (Fogel, 1993; Thelen & Smith, 1994; Wachs,

2000). In the next section of this chapter, I will review some of the findings on the relationship between early infancy factors and later developmental outcomes.

Research on Continuity between Early and Later Development

Developmentalists generally talk about lasting individual differences in terms of the concept of developmental continuity. **Continuity** is the extent to which aspects of the individual are preserved from one age to another. The existence of developmental continuity means that a particular sensitivity or ability acquired in infancy is likely to affect the functioning of the individual in some way at later ages. There are many forms of continuity, some of which are listed in Table 12.1.

Table 12.1 Forms of Developmental Continuity

Type of Continuity	Example
Absolute consistency	A lack of change during development. Once an ability is acquired, such as the ability to form attachments or to think symbolically, it is never lost or altered.
Consistent pattern of change	A particular ability has a predictable and invariant developmental course. For example, cooing, babbling, and single words precede the onset of language.
Consistent pattern of behavior	A predominant mode of behaving in spite of minor fluctuations. An infant who generally is withdrawn may show some instances of openness, but more usually, a pattern of withdrawal can be inferred across a variety of circumstances.
Consistent relation to the group	Even though developmental change occurs, individuals maintain their relative ranking within a group. For example, an infant grows taller but may always be short compared to other infants of the same age.
Consistency in process	Behavior is not consistent, but the underlying process may not be different across time. For example, a sensitive and warm social partner may be necessary at all ages, but the type of relationship will not be the same at each age (infant-mother, infant-teacher, infant-peer).
Consistency between early and later factors	Events and experiences early in infancy have an impact on some later outcome. For example, the security of early attachments predicts other social and cognitive abilities during the preschool years.

Source: M. Rutter, Continuities and discontinuities from infancy, 1987, p. 82. In J. D. Osofsky (Ed.), *Handbook of infant development* (2nd ed.), 67–86. New York: Wiley.

Continuity has been investigated in many different areas, and I cannot cover them all in this chapter. In this text, I have already reviewed a considerable amount of research related to continuity, although I have not labeled it as continuity research. I begin with a brief review of these topics, including perinatal factors; motor development; parental contributions; risk and disadvantage; culture; gender; intellectual development; and temperament. The student is encouraged to reread the relevant sections from earlier in the text from the perspective of continuity.

Perinatal Factors

The long-term effects of heredity on later behavior were discussed in Chapters 2 and 3. The data suggest that the effects of one's heredity are nondeterministic. That is, not everyone with the same types of genes or chromosomes will inherit the phenotypic characteristic typically associated with those genes or chromosomes. Even among those who show the phenotypic features, there will be a great deal of variation between individuals (Wachs, 2000). Some genetic structures have a higher probability of being expressed in the phenotype, and these structures are typically associated with severe disorders. The genetic contributions to behavior, cognition, emotion, and personality have a much lower probability of being expressed in the phenotype because many genes are involved and because they require a specific set of environmental contingencies in order to be expressed.

Hereditary influence is an example of continuity in which there is a consistency between early and later factors (Table 12.1); that is, an early factor (the genes) is consistently related to a later outcome (for example, PKU or temperament). Our earlier discussion of heredity shows that a strict continuity is observed only in some cases. It is more typical for environmental mediating factors to influence the way those genes are expressed or not expressed in the individual.

As we saw in Chapter 2, however, some researchers differ with this view. One behavior geneticist has claimed that the influence of the genes in explaining individual differences in outcomes is so strong that family influences "make few differences in children's personality and intellectual development" (Scarr, 1992, p. 3) unless the family is abusive or outside the typical range. More than 60 years ago, one of the pioneers of infant behavior research, Mary Shirley, reached a similar conclusion. She wrote that "although the personalities of the babies are undoubtedly influenced by training and treatment, strong characteristics are not ironed out by training" (Shirley, 1933, p. 207). The most recent research evidence suggests, on the contrary, that these statements are true for only a very small percentage of individuals. Most people are susceptible to a wide variety of influences—from family and society—that can limit or expand their genetic potentials (Plomin & Rutter, 1998; Wachs, 2000).

Another topic I have already discussed is premature birth and other perinatal factors (see Chapters 4 and 9). Newborns are susceptible to a wide range of perinatal problems ranging from oxygen deprivation to low birthweight. For all infants, the period immediately following birth is a time of adjustment from intrauterine to extrauterine life. An infant who suffers from one or more risk factors in the perinatal period may be unable to cope with the typical stresses of the first months of life and therefore may fall behind in developmental progress.

In general, research has found that many perinatal problems can be at least partially alleviated by a supportive environment. In a multiracial, multiclass sample of 670 infants born on the Hawaiian island of Kauai, all groups of children—regardless of race, social class, or age of mother—had about the same proportion of perinatal complications. In this sample, 13% suffered moderate complications, and 3% had severe complications. However, group membership predicted how well the infant recovered from the complication. Children born into lower-income families were less likely to recover fully by age 2. By age 10, the effects of perinatal problems had all but disappeared for all the groups, but children from lower-income groups had lower scores on intelligence tests and were doing worse in school than children from middle-income groups (Werner,

Bierman, & French, 1971). This research shows that between-individual variability is multidetermined in part by perinatal factors and in part by later environmental factors.

Other research in this area has supported these conclusions. In general, the more stressful the environment and the fewer economic and social support systems the parents have, the more likely it is that infants will not recover quickly from perinatal risk factors. The continuity with negative outcomes tends to be related to the total number of risk factors and/or traumas, which have an additive effect (Baker & Mednick, 1984; Bradley et al., 1994; Breitmayer & Ramey, 1986; Crockenberg, 1981; H. Johnson, Glassman, Fiks, Rosen, 1987; Rutter, 1987; Sameroff & Chandler, 1975; Sigman, Cohen, Beckwith, & Parmelee, 1981; Waters, Vaughn, & Egeland, 1980). In addition, even the same traumatic situation, if it continues over a long period of time, can also have cumulative effects. Short periods of harsh discipline, malnutrition, stress, or family instability have far less serious developmental outcomes than if those factors persist over many years (Wachs, 2000).

However, if there are adequate economic resources, if the parents are not under psychosocial stress, and if the perinatal complications are not too severe, the effects are usually not continuous over the long term. Continuity arises because of consistency in the environments to which the infant is exposed—environments that either alleviate or exacerbate the early risk factor.

In some cases, preterm infants may even be at some advantage with respect to full-term babies. At equivalent gestational ages (the time since conception), preterms have had more experience outside the uterus than full terms. Preterms begin to babble at earlier ages than full terms, presumably because they have had more exposure to auditory stimulation at the same gestational age (Eilers et al., 1993).

Another general proposition to emerge from this research is that the more severe the perinatal disorder, the more likely that long-term effects will be continuous. Infants who have very low birthweight (VLBW, less than 1,500 grams), for example, are doing less well in sensorimotor development during the first half year than other preterms (Gerner, 1999). Healthy preterms weighing more than 3,000 grams, on the other hand, are doing as well on sensorimotor tests as full terms (Bonin, Pomerleau, & Malcuit, 1998). By the gestational age of 2 years, when most preterms have caught up with full terms, VLBW infants are more passive, less attentive, and less securely attached to their mothers than the full terms of the same gestational age. Some VLBW infants have continuing social, cognitive, and attentional deficits at preschool and school age (Barrera, Rosenbaum, & Cunningham, 1987; Kanazawa, Shimizu, Kamada, Tanabe, & Itoigawa, 1997; Landry, 1995; Langkamp & Harris, 1992; Mangelsdorf et al., 1996; Tessier, Nadeau, Boivin, & Tremblay, 1997; Vohr & Coll, 1985).

Other extreme factors, such as auditory neurological deficits measured at birth that relate later to impaired auditory sensitivity (A. D. Murray, 1988) and other forms of severe brain damage at birth, have also been found to be related to later cognitive and sensory impairment (A. Stewart, 1983). Early visual impairment is associated with slower development in all domains during the preschool period (Hatton, Bailey, Burchinal, & Ferrell, 1997). Finally, particular types of early-onset teratogens, especially those that occur during the periods of rapid growth of the limbs, organs, and brain, are generally continuous with later disorders, such as fetal alcohol syndrome (Metosky & Vondra, 1995). Some recent research suggests that there is a continuity between exposure to particular types of teratogens, such as excessive maternal cigarette smoking, and violence in adulthood, especially for males (Brennan, Grekin, & Mednick, 1999; Karr-Morse & Wiley, 1997).

Nevertheless, it is important to remember that even in the worst cases of risk, there is variability in outcome between individuals (Wachs, 2000). Down's syndrome infants, for example, are better at daily living skills and communication if they come from cohesive families with sensitive parents (Hauser-Cram et al., 1999). On the other hand, findings from continuity studies suggest important ways to reduce the risk of serious disorders by means of simple interventions in the prenatal and perinatal periods.

These findings represent many of the types of continuity shown in Table 12.1. For example, the deformation of a limb or a disorder of auditory neurology reflects absolute consistencies in which the affected organ reaches a final state during early life and does not change later. The effects of very low birthweight could be part of an absolute consistency associated with brain damage, or they could reflect a general retardation of developmental progress and thus be an example of consistency in relation to the group (that is, these babies continue to score lower than full terms even after many years).

If infants are not at risk, their behavior in the perinatal period seems not to predict any later aspects of infant functioning. One study (Bell, Weller, and Waldrop, 1971) found virtually no perinatal behavior that predicted the behavior of children in the preschool years. The success (or lack of success) with which the mother and infant adjusted to each other during early feedings does not predict later mother-infant interaction patterns (J. Dunn, 1975).

These studies on both typically developing and at-risk infants speak to the newborn's **buffering** against difficulties of early adjustment. Infants have a **self-righting ability;** given an appropriately responsive environment, perinatal complications do not create any lasting organismic deficits (Sameroff & Chandler, 1975). Perhaps if mothers are not under stress and are predisposed to providing competent care, the infant at risk evokes more maternal attention and solicitude than typically developing infants (Bakeman & Brown, 1980; Beckwith & Cohen, 1978; Beckwith, Rodning, & Cohen, 1992; Crawford, 1982; Eizirik, Bohlin, & Hagekull, 1994; Landry et al., 1996; Liaw & Brooks-Gunn, 1993; Wijnroks, 1998). This increased solicitude may be a factor in alleviating the early deficits over the first year or two of life, even for infants who are have severe deficits such as VLBW infants (Landry, Smith, Miller-Loncar, & Swank, 1997; Landry, Smith, Miller-Loncar, & Swank, 1998). Thus, in certain circumstances, the environment can provide **compensation** for individual variation in perinatal factors.

Motor Development

Environmental influence on typical motor development was discussed in Chapters 6 and 7. As a general rule, environmental stimulation of particular motor systems does advance the infant receiving that stimulation in the short term, compared to other infants. I reviewed in particular the case of infant motor development in Africa, where infants are given a rigorous program of exercises and stretches, leading to an earlier onset of sitting, standing, and walking than in Europe and North America. I also discussed the research on attempts to give babies practice in standing and walking.

In general, however, these differences in environmental stimulation do not lead to long-term differences. Even though the exercised babies may sometimes achieve a motor milestone earlier, it does not mean that as preschoolers they will be superior in motor development to babies who achieved their milestone at a later date. However, in infants at risk, physical and motor stimulation can have an important remedial effect leading to catch-up growth.

At least as far as the evidence gleaned from typical variations of infant development shows, there does not seem to be any continuity between early motor practice, physical stature and weight, and later developmental outcomes (Gorman & Pollitt, 1993; Largo, 1993). As mentioned earlier, however, relatively little research has been done in the area of motor development, so drawing any general conclusions at this time would be unwarranted. In the preschool and later years, practice with a motor skill does have a definite effect on later ability, as when children are taught sports and music.

Some children may have a particular facility and desire for one area of endeavor or another, but this has not been shown to be related to hearing Mozart in the womb or being given aerobic workouts during the first few years of life (see Chapter 3). With appropriate guidance during the preschool and school years, children with talents that manifest themselves early may indeed achieve high levels of skill (Sternberg & Davidson, 1985; Wallach, 1985). If the child does not exhibit early desire and facility, however, early intensive skill testing and training are not advisable for the majority of children under the age of 3 years. A preschool education program that is responsive to the needs of the individual child and has the resources to challenge each child at his or her level of interest seems to be the most useful approach (Johnson, 1983).

Parental Contributions

Maternal Employment and Child Care

I discussed the effects of maternal employment in Chapter 7 and the effects of child care in Chapter 9. There does not appear to be a continuity between maternal employment or child care and later child developmental outcomes. Instead, the long-term effects are mediated by other factors (Chin-Quee & Scarr, 1994). One of the major risks related to maternal employment is for the mother herself, especially if she has an economic need to work but would prefer to stay at home, or if she is highly career motivated and suffers from role overload (Stifter, Coulehan, & Fish, 1993). In some, but not all cases, these mothers may have some difficulty establishing a secure relationship with their infants. We know little, however, about the long-term effects of maternal employment during infancy on later child development.

The risks in child care lie primarily in the quality of care available. The risks are highest for infants who do not have supportive family environments and who are in poor-quality care. These children may fare worse than their peers in preschool and kindergarten. The research, however, is difficult to interpret because of methodological problems and differences across studies. It is important to remember, once again, that the severity and duration of these effects vary greatly across infants. Some infants who are reared in low-quality child care show no deficits, while others do.

Attachment

Research on attachment has found consistency between early and later factors (Table 12.1), for example, in the relationship between parental sensitivity in the first year and later security of attachment, and between security of attachment at age 1 year and later social and intellectual competence in preschool. Consistency of process is shown by similarity of attachment security between the ages of 1 year and 6 years, even though the specific types of attachment behavior differ at each age (see Chapter 8).

Disorganized attachment in infancy shows the most consistency between early and later factors. Children with disorganized attachments are more likely to show behavior problems at all later school ages and more likely to develop psychopathologies in childhood and adolescence (separation anxiety disorder, oppositional disorder, depression, phobias, and dissociation). Even here, however, there is variability in the severity of the outcomes across individuals (Carlson, 1998).

The current explanation for these types of continuity is the concept of the internal working model of attachment, which suggests that individuals acquire particular expectations from their early social relationships that carry over into other relationships. Because internal working models are relatively stable and are changed only very slowly, they may account for the long-term consistencies in attachment across time. On the other hand, there is variability across families. While most attachments remain stable, some infants will change their attachment security, becoming either more or less secure over time (see Chapter 8).

Caregiving and Disciplinary Styles

In Chapter 10, I discussed guided participation in parent-infant interaction. Guided participation is based on following up the child's spontaneous interests and actions, structuring those actions in ways that enhance the child's competence and sense of participation, and then allowing the child to take increasing responsibility. Parents who use more guided participation with their children are more likely to have children with more-advanced language and cognitive skills.

Guided participation is also related to authoritative parenting styles that combine respect for the child's interests and points of view with parental firmness in the enforcement of rules. Such child outcomes as independence, cooperativeness, and social competence have been associated with authoritative parenting. I also noted that parental proactive behavior—preparing the environment or the child for anticipated positive outcomes—is part of guidance and authoritative disciplinary styles. Infant compliance is more readily assured if parents use proactive planning and guidance strategies, rather than confrontational approaches.

Social competence, intelligence and attentional control, emotion regulation, and language ability during early childhood are correlated with maternal vocalization, contingent responsiveness, mother-infant synchrony, and parenting involvement during the first two years and in the third year with parental proactive behavior, such as providing opportunities to interact with other people and to explore the environment (Bradley & Caldwell, 1995; Carew, 1980; Feiring & Lewis, 1981; Feldman, Greenbaum, & Yurmiya, 1999; Olson, Bates, & Kaskie, 1992; Vyt, 1993; Wachs, 1993; Wachs & Gruen, 1982). Lack of maternal responsiveness during infancy also predicts disruptive behavior problems (aggression, defiance, antisocial behavior) during middle childhood (Wakschlag & Hans, 1999). Teens who score as "dismissive" on the Adult Attachment Interview (denying and devaluing attachments) are more likely to have less sensitive mothers during infancy than teens who rated their adult attachments as more secure, but the effects of infant experiences were mediated by other life events during childhood, such as parental divorce (Beckwith, Cohen, & Hamilton, 1999). Maternal depression during early infancy predicts infant cognitive development at 18 months and preschool language, cooperation with peers, and behavior problems (Leadbeater, Bishop, & Raver, 1996; Murray, Fiori-Cowley, Hooper, & Cooper, 1996; NICHD Early Child Care Research Network, 1999).

The research in this area is not entirely conclusive. Global measures of parenting often are not sensitive to variations in disciplinary style that depend on the nature of the infraction and the responsiveness of the child to adult interventions. Furthermore, there are cross-family and cross-cultural differences in caregiving that are difficult to compare on any absolute scale of parental effectiveness or sensitivity. Finally, all of the findings in this area are based on correlations, which has two implications. First, the parent's style could be shaped by the child's behavior, at least in part. Second, the correlations are typically positive but small, meaning that while a general association exists between caregiving and child behavior, there is a wide variability between families. Simply put, children who experience maternal insensitivity during infancy will not all have behavior problems or attachment difficulties.

The important question is not whether sensitive parenting matters. It does matter. Parental figures are a necessary and irreplaceable part of infant development. Rather, we need to know whether the continuity between caregiving and positive outcome for the child is sustained by factors inherent in the child over time, by the consistency of adult care over time, or by an ongoing transaction between the adult and the child in which the interaction promotes consistent behaviors in both participants. Consistency, or a lack thereof, could also derive from the influence of mediating factors on the parent-infant dyad, such as the effect of social supports (Chapter 10) and economic advantage and disadvantage (Chapter 10).

Risk and Disadvantage

As we saw in Chapter 10, poverty is a clear case where consistency of negative outcomes can be maintained over long periods in the absence of other mediating factors. Children from poor families suffer more from depression, poor peer relationships, social withdrawal, low self-esteem, aggressiveness, and deviant behavior. They are more likely to have physical ailments, school problems, and language and cognitive deficits. In the "Applications" section of Chapter 10, I explored some of the cyclical processes that tend to maintain these negative outcomes over time. Stress, nutrition, health, and behavior interact to create increasingly negative patterns.

Another major risk factor in early development is severe stress on the infant and the family. Stress may be due to economic deprivation; disease; hospital-izations and other extended separations; parental psychopathology; family changes due to relocation or parental or sibling death; extreme conditions of social unrest, such as those created by war, persecution, or famine; and migration or flight as refugees. The research is complicated, detailed in some areas and not in others, and often dependent on personal recollections. Nevertheless, after extensive review of this literature, it can be concluded that a single stressful incident in early infancy has negligible long-term effects. However, multiple stresses create cyclical patterns of increasing risk and deprivation and are more likely to be associated with long-term emotional or behavioral disorders in later childhood (Rutter, 1979; Wachs, 2000).

Even with multiple stresses, however, some children show remarkable resilience and adaptability (Wachs, 2000). In some cases, an early stressor can prepare an individual to adapt to a similar stressor later in development, as when children who are repeatedly separated from parents in child care become less susceptible to the effects of routine separation from parents. On the other hand, some stressors can make people hypersensitive to repeated exposures, as in the example of the 3-year-old boy who did not like to be wrapped up in a cloth when getting a haircut because doctors had wrapped him in a blanket while stitching up an injury he had received when he was a baby (see Chapter 11). There is a great deal of variability in how a stressor will affect someone and how long the effect will be felt. Once again, there are no simple answers.

In Chapter 10, I also looked at the effects of early intervention programs, such as Head Start and other parent-infant programs. Although research on the long-term effectiveness of these programs is difficult to do, there is some evidence that such interventions do make a difference, especially for children from lower income groups or from dysfunctional families, and especially when the intervention contains some parent-educational component either in the home or at the program center (Burchinal, Lee, & Ramey, 1989; Caughy, DiPietro, & Strobino, 1994; Lyons-Ruth, Connell, Grunebaum, & Botein, 1990; Scarr & Eisenberg, 1993; Spitz, 1992; Wasik, Ramey, Bryant, & Sparling, 1990). High-quality educational child care, when combined with responsive care at home, can boost cognitive performance for poor African American children during the preschool period (Burchinal, Campbell, Bryant, Wasik, & Ramey, 1997).

Malnutrition can have severe short- and long-term effects on reducing infant energy, emotional responsiveness, attention, and play (Lozoff et al., 1998; M. A. McDonald, Sigman, Espinosa, & Neumann, 1994; Pollitt et al., 1996; Wachs, 2000). Interventions involving nutritional supplementation are generally successful if they are accompanied by parent-child behavior interventions to enhance maternal sensitivity (See Chapters 4 and 7; Cravioto & Arrieta, 1983; Pollitt et al., 1996; Z. Stein & Susser, 1985; Valenzuela, 1997; Winick, Knarig, & Harris, 1975). In a study done in Colombia, malnutrition was treated in one group with only food supplementation for the entire family and in another group with food supplementation plus parent education during home visits. The children in the group that received supplementation plus parent education were taller and heavier at the age of 6 years, and there were fewer cases of mental retardation than in the food-only group (Super, Herrera, & Mora, 1990).

Interventions designed for premature infants have also shown signs of success. The most successful interventions combine long-term pediatric care with parent education and family support. These programs enhance children's cognitive and behavioral development and also increase the competence and enthusiasm of the parents (Achenbach, Phares, Howell, Rauh, & Nurcombe, 1990; Brooks-Gunn, Klebanov, Liaw, & Spiker, 1993; Rauh, Achenbach, Nurcombe, Howell, & Teti, 1988; Spiker, Ferguson, & Brooks-Gunn, 1993).

One problem with intervention research is that the populations of children served vary enormously between locations. In addition, even clearly outlined interventions will vary in their application according to location, staff training and interpretation, and the reactions of the children and their families. The Mother-Child Home Program, which has been found to work well with disadvantaged children in the United States, for example, was relatively ineffective in a broader-based population of children in Bermuda (Scarr & McCartney, 1988).

Thus, the best statement that can be made at the current time is that some programs work some of the time for some groups and that, overall, intervention programs provide an important source of enrichment and encouragement for parents who are under social and economic stress. In this perspective, short-term relief from stress may be as valuable as any long-term developmental benefit. It could be that the long-term effects are present but that researchers have not been able to develop measures to assess them. Virtually all researchers and practitioners agree that early intervention is important and should continue for many years into the future.

Culture

I have reviewed many examples of the effects of culture in this book. In particular, we have seen many cultural differences in child-rearing styles. Cultures differ, broadly speaking, according to whether they focus on individual development and achievement or on the family and the group. We saw, for example, that in some cultures older children are expected to provide child care for their younger siblings. In these collectivistic cultures, children are socialized from an early age to respect authority, to give their time to support the family, and to avoid standing apart from the group. Many Asian, African, Latin/Hispanic, Native American, and other indigenous cultures are collectivistic.

These cultural influences can have a great deal of impact on social and emotional processes such as sharing, empathy, and self-disclosure. They can also affect gender-specific behavior, depending upon cultural attitudes toward traditional or nontraditional sex-role orientations.

Even though culture has a major impact on later outcomes, there is also a great deal of variability within cultures (Killen & Wainryb, 2000). Not all people raised in the North American culture of individuality are self-seeking and achievement oriented. Similarly, many people from collectivistic cultures are focused on getting ahead at the expense of others. In addition, culture interacts with all the other factors mentioned in this chapter. The cultural interpretation of poverty in North America may not be the same in South America, where a greater proportion of people are poor. Poverty may affect development differently in these two hemispheres.

Gender

We saw in Chapter 11 that by 3 years of age, children are beginning to express a gender identity and to adopt gender role–appropriate behavior. What has been difficult to establish is the extent to which individual differences in the gender-role orientations (from traditional to egalitarian) of children are consistent with any factors in their prior history. So far, research has not yielded any strong conclusions. Individual differences in gender-role orientations exist from a young age, but these differences do not possess a high degree of any form of continuity over time. The continuity of gender-role orientation may not emerge until later childhood or young adulthood. For example, the gender-role socialization behavior of the parents (selecting gender role–appropriate toys for children), especially that of the father, is strongly related to the father's prior history and beliefs about gender roles.

Sex differences during infancy have been related to factors other than gender-role socialization. For example, males seem to be more vulnerable to the effects of environmental stress. When they grow up in homes that are overcrowded, noisy, or confusing, males show deficits in their cognitive development, while females growing up in similar environments do not. Environmental opportunities to explore large areas in the home are more beneficial for the long-term cognitive development of males than females. Females, but not males, who are provided with a great deal of stimulus variety (different colors, shapes, and textures in the home) show higher levels of cognitive development (Rutter, 1979; Wachs & Gruen, 1982). Finally, higher levels of androgens (hormones associated with masculinity) at birth are correlated with lower scores on spatial

ability for girls at 6 years, but variations in androgen level have no effect on variability of spatial ability in boys (Jacklin, Wilcox, & Maccoby, 1988).

Although the reasons for these long-term continuities are not entirely clear, it may be that boys and girls process information differently or that they require different types of environmental inputs in order to maintain their levels of cognitive growth. This has been called the environmental specificity of long-term effects (Wachs, 1982). **Environmental specificity** occurs when certain aspects of the environment are more effective in promoting specific types of competencies than others, or when certain aspects of the environment are effective in promoting development in some children but not in others.

Intellectual Development

Environmental specificity effects have been found in long-term continuity studies of factors in early infancy that promote cognitive and intellectual development. For example, early exposure in the first year to an enriched home environment with a variety of inanimate objects and to contingently responsive inanimate objects leads to greater skill in problem solving and exploratory play in the second year (Molfese, DiLalla, & Bunce, 1997; Yarrow, Rubenstein, & Pedersen, 1975). The provision of age-appropriate play materials during the first two years strongly predicts a child's Stanford-Binet IQ score at 4½ years (Bradley & Caldwell, 1976), as well as elementary school achievement test scores between 5 and 9 years of age (VanDoorninck, Caldwell, Wright, & Frankenburg, 1981).

The development of spatial relations and perspective taking can best be predicted by avoidance of noise, confusion, and environmental overcrowding during the first two years. In contrast, exploratory play skills in the second and third year are best enhanced by caregivers' providing objects that respond when the child moves them—such as mobiles and rattles—and a variety of objects in the first year. These factors, plus a well-organized environment and the use of age-appropriate play materials, are the best predictors of a child's ability to invent new means and plan effective strategies (Wachs, 1982; Wachs & Gruen, 1982; Widmayer et al., 1990).

The variability of the efficiency of their information processing in the first six months predicts cognitive developmental outcomes. In a habituation task, for example, some infants habituate rather quickly and require less looking time overall to process the visual stimulus. These efficient information-processing strategies in early infancy are correlated with higher childhood standardized cognitive and language development test scores. Infants who at 4 months continued to fixate on an unchanging stimulus had lower intelligence test scores in middle childhood (Bornstein & Sigman, 1986; Dougherty & Haith, 1997; Rose & Feldman, 1997; Rose, Feldman, & Wallace, 1988; Rose, Feldman, Wallace, & McCarton, 1989; Sigman et al., 1986; Tamis-LeMonda & Bornstein, 1989). The efficient information processing, especially when combined with a maternal style focusing on directing the infant's attention to tasks, leads to more advanced cognitive and language outcomes (Lewis, Alessandri, & Sullivan, 1992; McCall & Carriger, 1993; Rose et al., 1989; Tamis-LeMonda & Bornstein, 1989, 1993; Thompson, Fagan, & Fulker, 1991).

More-specific measures of language behavior and its antecedents have also revealed strong predictive patterns. Verbal interaction with the child in the early years of life, not surprisingly, is one of the strongest and most distinctive predictors of later language competence in toddlers and preschoolers (Hart & Risley, 1992; Huttenlocher, Haight, Bryk, Seltzer, & Lyons, 1991; Sokolov, 1993; Wachs et al., 1993). Interventions for children at risk for poor language acquisition have been successful by training parents to talk with and read to infants. Children who stutter are helped when parents talk more slowly, giving the children time to take their turn in the conversation at their own pace (Ramig, 1993; Swan, 1993; Valdez-Menchaca & Whitehurst, 1992; Winslow & Guitar, 1994). These effects compound over time, so that children who talk early and competently also read earlier and are

more advanced conceptually; thus, they have a head start on the literacy skills required for schooling (Crain-Thoreson & Dale, 1992; P. J. Dunham & Dunham, 1995).

In play tasks, some 1-year-old infants are more focused on the particular toy and persist in exploring many of the toy's properties, while others show more-variable attention spans. They will move rapidly from one toy to the next without spending much time investigating the individual properties of each. These babies seem to move restlessly between things without fully appreciating the properties of any one item. Babies who are inattentive at 1 year also tend to be inattentive at age 3 and later score lower on intelligence tests (Heinicke, Diskin, Ramsey-Klee, & Oates, 1986; Heinicke & Lampl, 1988; Ruff, Lawson, Parrinello, & Weissberg, 1990; Wenckstern, Weizmann, & Leenaars, 1984).

In summary, the child's environment and information processing abilities during infancy play some role in the prediction of later intelligence. These factors interact, however, and no one factor can account for all the variability. In addition, as I have mentioned earlier, children who suffer from poor information processing during the first six months will vary in their outcomes, some scoring low and some scoring higher on IQ tests during later childhood. It is possible to enhance cognitive development for some children by talking with and reading to them. There is no evidence, however, that extra cognitive stimulation during infancy can create a genius.

Temperament

My review of **temperament** in Chapter 7 showed that there is limited evidence for continuity in infant temperament. Most of the research in this domain focuses on continuity with respect to group ranking, which is also called **stability.** Only when children fall into extreme groups on irritability, emotionality, reactivity, or inhibition can long-term stability be observed. We also found that stability in infant temperamental characteristics is more likely to be seen in the short term—six months to a year—rather than over several years. At older ages, stability can be seen for several years or more, but transformation and change are the rule just as often as stability (Caspi & Silva, 1995; Pedlow, Sanson, Prior, & Oberklaid, 1993).

Many of the factors that account for short-term continuity of temperament are likely to change over the long run. For example, infant irritability is one important temperamental dimension. Irritability is associated with a number of prenatal and perinatal risk factors, such as prematurity. As the effects of prematurity attenuate over time (see the earlier section on risk in this chapter), the early forms of irritability that may persist over the first year disappear or change in the second year (Coll, Halpern, Vohr, Seifer, & Oh, 1992). New factors, such as developmental challenges of autonomy and parent-child attachment, begin to account for individual differences in irritability and other temperamental factors in the second year. For a few children, first-year irritability persists into the second year, but most lose their infantile irritability. Some children transform it into more age-appropriate patterns of negativity such as anger and defiance.

While lack of continuity is the rule in temperament studies, the fact that development is marked by variability in outcome means that some children, under certain conditions, will show long-term continuity of temperament. This can occur when the parents have a temperamental pattern similar to that of the infant, and especially when both parent and infant show temperamental inhibition and shyness, which suggests that when parent and child share an attribute, their mutual interaction enhances the possibility that their genetically based inhibition will continue to be manifested in the phenotype (P. Cohen, Kasen, Brook, & Hartmark, 1998; Schmitz et al., 1999).

In summary, as we have seen in other sections of this chapter, research that shows statistical significance in long-term continuity does not mean that all children remain the same over time. We are still a long way from understanding the genetic, environmental, age, and context-specific conditions that promote continuity and change in temperament. Like intelligence and gender effects, temperament is continuous for some children under some conditions. In other cases, temperament may have some short-term continuity, but after several years, the child does not persist with the same characteristics. The study of temperament is confounded by inconsistencies in the definition of temperament and by the difficulty of obtaining reliable and valid measures (see Chapter 7). In the next section, I discuss the complexity of the findings reviewed in this chapter.

Developmental Systems of Multiple Interacting Factors

The research reviewed in this chapter shows that many factors in early infancy have significant effects on outcomes in childhood and adulthood. The prenatal and perinatal environment, genetics, parental sensitivity, culture, gender, and temperament, among many other things, play a role in creating the individual person. Throughout this chapter, two major principles have been discussed: that no one of these factors can work in isolation (development is multifactorial and complex), and that no two individuals are affected in the same way by any one factor or any set of factors acting in combination (there is an inherent between-individual variability in developmental process and outcome).

These two principles are not independent from each other. This can be illustrated by the results of a study in which infants were tested on the Bayley Mental Scale at 4, 8, 12, and 18 months and their performance later assessed on the Reynell Developmental Language Scales at 2, 3, and 4 years. The quality of the infants' home environments were also studied in this longitudinal study involving 148 infants (L. S. Siegal, 1981).

If we look at the Bayley scores as predictive of the language scores at 2 years, there was no relationship. Infants who scored low on the Bayley test could be developing typically at 2 years in the areas of language, or they could be slower than average.

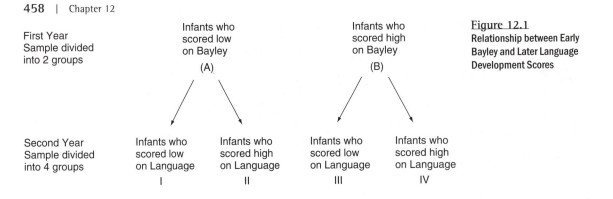

First Year
Sample divided
into 2 groups

Infants who
scored low
on Bayley
(A)

Infants who
scored high
on Bayley
(B)

Figure 12.1
**Relationship between Early
Bayley and Later Language
Development Scores**

Second Year
Sample divided
into 4 groups

Infants who
scored low
on Language
I

Infants who
scored high
on Language
II

Infants who
scored low
on Language
III

Infants who
scored high
on Language
IV

The same two outcomes were possible for children who had more typical scores on the Bayley test in the first year (see Figure 12.1). Of the four groups of 2-year-olds shown in Figure 12.1, two of them fit a single factor pattern. In group I, low Bayley scores led to low language scores; in group IV, more-typical Bayley scores led to high language scores. Groups II and III do not fit the single factor pattern. In each of these cases, another factor—the home environment—played a significant role (L. S. Siegal, 1981).

Infants in group II, who had low Bayley scores in the first year but scored high on language at age 2, had home environments that were significantly more enriched and stimulating than the home environments of group I babies. Infants in group III, who had low language scores even though they were developing typically in the first year, had a less enriched environment than infants in group IV (L. S. Siegal, 1981; Ungerer & Sigman, 1984).

Notice how the two different factors interact in complex ways. The home environment is more important for some infants (those in groups II and III), and the early psychomotor abilities, as measured by the Bayley score, are more important for the others. Another aspect of these findings, not shown in Figure 12.1, is that there is variability in outcome *within* each of the groups. In group I, for example, some infants with low Bayley scores had higher language scores than others within the group, even though the whole group was in the low range.

Multifactor processes with between-individual variability have been found for virtually every research study in which more than one factor is measured on the same group of infants (Wachs, 2000). Consider some of the following results from research.

Maternal smoking during pregnancy has known effects on neurological development of the fetus, with long-lasting effects on the child. Pregnant women who smoke, however, are more likely both to be depressed and to be poor (Leftwich & Collins, 1994). Depression and poverty affect the mother's behavior during pregnancy, which creates neurological deficits and an infant who is then more likely to succumb to the combined effects of maternal depression and poverty after birth. Children who are malnourished are more likely to be living in a home with low stimulation value and low parental responsiveness (Lozoff, 1998). The parental negligence is probably affected by poverty and stress, which compounds the effects on an already weak child. In these examples, one factor amplifies the effects of other factors. If fewer risk factors are present, such as maternal depression in the absence of prenatal smoking and poverty, the effects will be different and specific to the particular combination of factors.

The age of exposure to a particular factor is also an important interacting factor in determining outcome (Bronfenbrenner & Evans, 2000; Wachs, 2000). We have seen this in prenatal development, when teratogens have a much more serious effect if the exposure occurs at critical periods in the formation of an organ system. Child care may have different effects on younger and older infants. Another aspect of the multifactor process is that children may be affected in one domain of functioning and not in another. Maternal alcohol consumption during pregnancy, for example, affects neurological development but not physical development. At-

David Burnett/Contact Press Images/Picture Quest

Many complex factors must combine to ensure healthy development during the infancy period. Adults have an important responsibility to provide the best possible environments and care that bring out the highest potential of each child.

tachment disorganization affects psychosocial functioning but not intelligence.

In summary, one should distrust any claims that a single factor from early infancy has lasting outcomes for all infants exposed to it. Traumas are serious, but they do not always have lasting effects. On the other hand, products and interventions that promise to make a child into a genius by exposing the infant to Mozart prenatally or providing extra cognitive stimulation during the first year of life also do not have consistent outcomes. Some children may benefit, but many will not. Development is a complex dynamic system that resists simple explanations. Each baby's life is as rich and complex as an adult's in the sense that there are no easy answers, only more questions.

To return to the questions posed at the beginning of this chapter: does this mean that infancy is not important? Does it mean that we should not provide the best parental care, nutrition, enriched environments, health practices, and love to infants? The answer to these questions is clearly *no*. Babies—indeed, people of all ages—should be afforded healthy, safe, enriched, and loving opportunities. These factors promote development without question. We do not need research to convince us that every human being is entitled to good prenatal care, a warm and loving home, quality education, and economic security. It is just the right thing to do. On the other hand, research clearly shows that people are more likely to become healthy, happy, productive, and intelligent if they have these things.

Parents, educators, practitioners, and policy makers need to understand, however, that while infants benefit from having these opportunities, we cannot predict with certainty that a particular event or program will have particular outcomes. We can only say that, in general, intelligence, social skills, and emotional control are promoted in healthy, safe, and loving environments. We can only say that, in general, these abilities are more likely to be deficient in impoverished and insensitive rearing conditions. We *can* say with certainty that *infancy is important* and that each person will get something different from their early years, both potentials and limitations.

The Author's View

In this chapter, I have stressed two important developmental principles: that development is multifactorial, and that each person will respond differently to the same circumstances. The latter principle focuses on individuals and their unique pathways through time. One of the problems with research on long-term developmental outcomes is that the factors presumed to have an influence—such as genes, environments, parents, attachments, and the like—are conceptualized in terms of reliable and valid measurements. The very process of measurement, as a tool for quantitative research, requires that the measures be relatively insensitive to the daily life of the individual child. What good is a measurement of attachment security, for example, if the results change between morning and afternoon, or if the test is done on a day when the mother and baby are feeling good about each other instead of a day of frustration and anger?

There is an inherent opposition between the demands for standardized measurement in quantitative research and the basic principles of development showing that each person is special, unique, and individual. Suppose you participated in a quantitative study of the academic development of college students. In the study, you were interviewed as a freshman and your course grades that year were recorded. A similar interview was conducted when you were a senior, and your senior-year grades were noted. Perhaps the grade point averages of all the students in the study did not change much. While you were a solid B student as a freshman and also as a senior, another classmate was consistently an A student (which demonstrates consistency of ranking). The researcher concludes that you did not change much. This study does not give credit to the wealth of experiences you had in college and tells us almost nothing about the processes in your life.

Unfortunately, this is the type of continuity study that is most frequently done on infants. Few studies observe the process of development within individuals to determine how they solved daily problems and did or did not maintain their equilibrium to stay on course. Research that looks at developmental processes rather than just the outcomes would be based on case study qualitative methods (Chapter 1). Until there are more such studies, our conclusions about how to foster desirable development and how to remedy early risk factors are going to be oversimplified. We know that multiple factors are involved, of course, but we do not know how they might operate for a particular person. This type of research is difficult to do, and relatively few researchers are doing it. The problem is how to get sufficient detail about an individual's life and still have the time to study many individuals in order to make more general conclusions.

Development is a continuously unfolding process of change. Every day in one's life presents new opportunities and new challenges. Infants, like people of all ages, are remarkably adaptable and uniquely individual. Little by little, many influences, actions, feelings, and thoughts transform us as we live from day to day. Day-to-day change is subtle, sometimes regressing rather than going forward, like babies who first crawl backward when they are really trying to move ahead. At some point we look back in time and realize that we have changed, that we are not the same anymore. No single factor caused this, no single day—nothing we can define clearly.

One advantage of qualitative research is that it has the potential to better capture indeterministic factors in development, those chance occurrences and serendipitous events that, without planning or premeditation, change our lives. These are things we cannot explain, that do not seem logical. In my opinion, human development and relationships, without a bit of magic, are dry and inhospitable. Creativity, surprise, and the excitement of the unknown keep pulling us forward as much as our genes and environments push us from behind. An individual whose developmental fate is determined by a predictable set of causes and effects could not also be open to the opportunity for discovery, exploration, risk taking, and personal growth in the absence of predictable guarantees.

Aside from this, infancy is a particularly magical time because much of what the infant does is not logical, deliberate, or scientific. Infants are grounded in their own ecological experiences. They accept what is. It is not until late in the second year that infants begin to seek control over external events, defy or try to change their world, and reason according to a set of community standards. I hope that you had an opportunity to relive the ecological and participatory experience of infancy while you were doing the Awareness through Movement lessons and/or the Co-Regulating with Baby exercises. These experiences can bring those feelings back into your adult life if you have temporarily lost touch with them.

Recall the qualitative research study that my students did on themselves as participant observers for their term projects in one of the infancy courses I teach (see the "Author's View" sections of Chapters 3 and 6). I asked students to evaluate this type of qualitative study on the clinical infant (see Chapter 2). What can this research reveal that is scientifically valid about the students themselves and about infant development in general?

All the students agreed that this qualitative research method was a useful way to study themselves. They discovered many things about themselves doing the Awareness through Movement lessons, which led to their discovering some of their unconscious and participatory ways of moving and feeling and to an expanded sense of themselves. According to one student, "These lessons have given me a renewed understanding of the importance of knowing one's own body. The sensations that one feels should not be taken for granted or overlooked. Allowing yourself to experience and understand these sensations will help you grow and maintain good physical and mental health." Students were excited to have discovered a method for uncovering some of their own participatory memories of infancy (some of these memories were reported in the "Author's View" section in Chapter 6), and many expressed a desire to continue with their somatic awareness explorations.

Most of the students also agreed that this qualitative study was scientifically valid for the study of infancy in general. Some typical statements were, "It is important to state that an adult cannot experience exactly what an infant can experience but through these lessons he/she may gain insight into how that infant may move between developmental stages," and "One of the greatest benefits the lessons provide for adults is that the lessons help adults sympathize with infants."

Although almost all the students reported having participatory memories, expressed surprise at the intensity of the memories, and commented on their inability to explain them in logical ways, virtually all remained skeptical about whether this method was a scientifically valid way of contacting their own infant experience. Some wondered whether it was possible to decide whether the participatory memories they experienced were from real events during infancy or from their own adult imagination. "Although I am not sure if the lessons made me in contact with my *own* infant experience, I do think I contacted *an* infant experience by becoming more in touch with my body." These methods are "tools to help us empathize with other infant's experiences rather than a way of remembering our own." They argued that no one could know the experiences of an infant because the infant's emotions are simpler than ours and because there is no way for the infant to communicate. So how could the adult participatory memories be verified? Thus, while they all had surprising and valuable experiences and agreed that the lessons helped them become aware of something inside themselves about which they had been unaware, few were willing to say conclusively that this "something" came from their infancy.

My students were aware, in the end, that qualitative research cannot prove anything. Qualitative research is personal, the story of an individual's life and experience. It reads more like a novel than like a traditional scientific report. Students were also aware of the indeterminism that enters into the creation of their lives: the route from infancy to adulthood is not clear and logical, and it would be impossible to trace all the developmental pathways that led from past to present and back to the past.

Yet the students all agreed that even under these constraints, qualitative research on themselves is still a valuable tool for understanding who we are as human beings and the contribution of the infancy period to human life. One student said, "I feel that people who are concerned with the 'scientific merit' of these lessons should experience them for themselves." This is a way of saying that the validity of the method itself cannot be proven by traditional scientific means. Its validity derives from direct experience with the method, just as the validity of the lessons for understanding infancy derives only from direct engagement with the movements.

As we have seen from research on the observed infant, events that occurred during infancy do in fact have some impact on later life, even if we cannot trace that impact to a specific event for specific people. Whether or not we can consciously remember our infancy, patterns of movement, thought, and feeling from infancy persist in our minds and bodies and contribute to the person we are today. It is not necessary to consciously or conceptually remember something, from any age period in your life, for it to have an influence over you. Conversely, just because you remember something does not mean that it had a major influence on who you are today. The point is that we are historical beings: who we are is partly the result of who we were. The specific links between our past and present, however, are unlikely to ever be fully sorted out. We are always transforming the past as we make it into the present, and there are indeterministic factors that enter into this transformation.

Does indeterminism actually occur in human development? Only a qualitative case study can answer that question, which is another way of saying that you should trust yourself and your own life experiences to provide an answer. As you encounter infants and young children in personal and professional roles, and as you enter into the infant's world through the lessons and exercises in this book, you will have to piece together the general principles from current research with your own personal experiences. It will be up to you to bridge the gap between the abstract and the specific. In doing so, you will be rewarded with a deepening understanding of human life and human development, with all its richness and surprises.

SUMMARY

Development as a Complex Dynamic Process

■ Research should focus on the process by which desirable and undesirable developmental outcomes are formed.

■ Developmental outcomes are determined by multiple factors.

■ Human development in complex family and social systems is regulated by both deterministic and nondeterministic factors. Research has fewer ways to capture the nondeterministic effects.

■ Variability is inherent in developmental processes so that the same experience affects each person differently.

Research on Continuity between Early and Later Development

■ Continuity is the extent to which aspects of the individual are preserved from one age to another.

■ There are many forms of continuity, as shown in Table 12.1.

Perinatal Factors

■ Outcomes for perinatal factors depend on the quality of the environment and on the severity of the initial disorder.

Motor Development

■ In early infancy, motor skills can be enhanced in the short term, but there seems to be little long-term benefit.

■ Motor skill enrichment programs show more lasting effects when they begin after the age of 2 years.

Parental Contributions

■ Little is known about the long-term effects of maternal employment; however, few short-term effects have been found.

■ Different considerations must be applied to the effects of child care for children under 6 months of age than for older children.

■ Attachment shows strong continuity with early mother-infant relationships and with later social and emotional competence.

■ The concept of the internal working model may best explain this continuity.

■ Guided participation and authoritative and proactive caregiving styles are associated with long-term patterns of child cognitive, social, and emotional competence.

- Problems in the research make it difficult to determine whether the continuity is due to the parent, the child, or external mediating factors.

Risk and Disadvantage

- Economic disadvantage has long-term effects on development, usually due to the increased stress on the family. Other stress-producing factors also create the opportunity for negative outcomes.

- Intervention is typically helpful in alleviating the effects of risk and disadvantage if it includes both a child and a parent education component and, where necessary, nutrition and health care.

Culture

- Cultures differ according to whether they focus on individual achievement or on the family and group, and this affects the development of empathy, sharing, and cooperation.

- It is important to take account of variability within cultures, which may sometimes be as great as that between cultures.

Gender

- Few long-term influences on sex-role behavior can be found during infancy.

- Gender may mediate a child's response to the environment and the caregiver's response to the child, creating the possibility of differential outcomes.

Intellectual Development

- Specific aspects of the physical and social environment are linked to specific long-term cognitive developmental outcomes and only for specific groups of children.

- Some information-processing factors, including habituation and attention, may show unmediated long-term consistency.

Temperament

- There are many different definitions of temperament.

- Temperament is difficult to measure and shows consistency for some but not all infants.

Developmental Systems of Multiple Interacting Factors

- Development is composed of multiple interacting factors in a dynamic system.

- Each person is a unique individual and will have their own pathway of change through time.

 ON THE WEB

www.isisweb.org   The International Society on Infant Studies web site gives information on research in infancy. It provides links to membership, conferences, journals, employment, governance, the society's newsletter, members' e-mail, infant facts, training grants, and related topics. Papers and journals are also available through this site.

www.childtrends.org   Child Trends is a non-profit organization that studies children, youth, and families through research, data collection, and data analysis. It provides links to current research projects, press releases, current news items, a list-serv, and "The Child Indicator," a newsletter intended "to communicate the major developments within each sector of the child and youth indicators field to the larger community of interested users." This site is updated regularly.

www.infant-parent.com   The Infant-Parent Institute provides information on the history and courses that they teach along with training films for infant mental health. The site also includes links to the institute's most frequently requested lecture and workshop topics and registration and order forms.

www.injoyvideos.com   This is a promotional web site that provides educational videos on pregnancy, childbirth, postpartum care, breast-feeding, baby care, teen issues, and parenting.

www.childdevmedia.com   Child Development Media is a promotional site selling educational videos to parents, professionals, and students. These videos and training materials contain information on early intervention, early education, child and adolescent development, and parent education.

GLOSSARY

Buffering   The ability of the environment to maintain infant development on a typical course in spite of deviations caused by early infant risk factors.

Compensation   The provision of additional environmental support for infants who suffer from early deficits.

Continuity   The preservation of individual characteristics across ages.

Determinism   The view that all natural phenomena are the result of some specifiable set of causes.

Environmental specificity   Continuities between the environment and the individual's development are found only for specific facets of the individual with specific features of the environment. Specific individuals are better able to profit from some environments than from others.

Historical processes   Developmental processes that are not simple accumulations of past events but are uniquely emergent creations that can never be exactly repeated.

Indeterminism   The idea that not all natural phenomena can be predicted from known laws or principles.

Self-righting   The ability of the infant organism to assimilate those aspects of the environment that serve to return development to a more typical pathway.

Stability   Continuity with respect to group ranking, when individuals preserve their ranking with respect to the same reference group over age.

Temperament   Lasting individual differences in emotional expressiveness and general responsiveness to the environment.

Appendix 1-A
Infant Development Growth Charts

Girls' Physical Growth NCHS Percentiles: Birth to 36 Months—Part 1

Adapted from P. V. V. Hamill, T. A. Drizd, C. L. Johnson, R. B. Reed, A. F. Roche, & W. M. Moore, Physical growth: National Center for Health Statistics percentiles, 1979. *American Journal of Clinical Nutrition, 32,* 607–629. Data from the Fels Longitudinal Study, Wright State University School of Medicine, Yellow Springs, OH. Copyright © Ross Laboratories. Reprinted with permission of Ross Laboratories.

Appendix 1-B
Infant Development Growth Charts
Girls' Physical Growth NCHS Percentiles: Birth to 36 Months—Part 1

Adapted from P. V. V. Hamill, T. A. Drizd, C. L. Johnson, R. B. Reed, A. F. Roche, & W. M. Moore, Physical growth: National Center for Health Statistics percentiles, 1979. *American Journal of Clinical Nutrition, 32,* 607–629. Data from the Fels Longitudinal Study, Wright State University School of Medicine, Yellow Springs, OH. Copyright © Ross Laboratories. Reprinted with permission of Ross Laboratories.

Appendix 1-C
Infant Development Growth Charts
Boys' Physical Growth NCHS Percentiles: Birth to 36 Months—Part 2

Adapted from P. V. V. Hamill, T. A. Drizd, C. L. Johnson, R. B. Reed, A. F. Roche, & W. M. Moore, Physical growth: National Center for Health Statistics percentiles, 1979. *American Journal of Clinical Nutrition, 32,* 607– 629. Data from the Fels Longitudinal Study, Wright State University School of Medicine, Yellow Springs, OH. Copyright © Ross Laboratories. Reprinted with permission of Ross Laboratories.

Appendix 1-D
Infant Development Growth Charts
Boys' Physical Growth NCHS Percentiles: Birth to 36 Months—Part 2

DATE	AGE	LENGTH	WEIGHT	HEAD CIRC	COMMENT

Appendix 2
Careers in the Field of Infancy

Health-Related Careers

Pediatrics
Pediatrician
Neonatologist
Infant intensive care worker

Nursing and Women's Health
Women's health nursing
Pediatric nursing
Intensive care unit nursing
Neonatal nursing
Obstetrician/gynecologist
Midwife
Doula

Technical
Biomedical engineer
Intensive care technician
Designer/marketer of health
and safety equipment

Nutritional
Nutritionist

Dietitian
Baby food salesperson

Early Intervention Programs
Infant stimulation specialist
Rehabilitation/special education worker
Early intervention specialist, and program designer and assessor
Placement and adoption/foster care worker
Social worker/child protection worker
Audiologist/speech therapist
Child life specialist
Physical therapist
Massage therapist for infants and mothers
Feldenkrais, Rosen method, or Watsu practitioner

Pediatric Psychology
Developmental tester
Follow-up assessor and researcher
Psychosomatic disorders specialist
Infant mental health specialist

Education-Related Careers

Infant Care
Day-care teacher, supervisor,
or administrator
Infant/toddler nursery program teacher,
supervisor, or administrator

Parent Education
Parent educator
Family life educator
Parent-child programmer

Counselor for teenage parents
Psychotherapist or psychiatrist
Marriage and family counselor

College Teaching and Research
Researcher
College teacher
Administrator of college programs in early childhood and child
development

Other Careers with Infants

Baby product salesperson, designer,
or manufacturer
Toy salesperson, designer, or manufacturer
Baby clothing salesperson, designer,
or manufacturer
Environmental and furniture designer
for nurseries and day care centers
Journalist

Writer/producer of books and other media for young children
Legislative aide
Policy analyst
Child advocate
Web site designer
Media specialist

References

Abel, E. L., Randall, C. L., & Riley, E. P. (1983). Alcohol consumption and prenatal development. In B. Tabakoff, P. B. Sutker, & C. L. Randall (Eds.), *Medical and social aspects of alcohol abuse*. New York: Plenum Press.

Aber, J. L., Belsky, J., Slade, A., & Crnic, K. (1999). Stability and change in mothers' representations of their relationship with their toddlers. *Developmental Psychology, 35*(4), 1038–1047.

Abramovitch, R., Corter, C., & Landau, B. (1979). Sibling interaction in the home. *Child Development, 50,* 997–1003.

Abramovitch, R., Corter, C., Pepler, D. J., & Stanhope, L. (1986). Sibling and peer interaction: A final follow-up and a comparison. *Child Development, 57,* 217–229.

Achenbach, T. M., Phares, V., Howell, C. T., Rauh, V. A., & Nurcombe, B. (1990). Seven-year outcome of the Vermont intervention program for low-birthweight infants. *Child Development, 61,* 1672–1681.

Achermann, J., Dinneen, E., & Stevenson-Hinde, J. (1991). Clearing up at 2.5 years. *British Journal of Developmental Psychology, 9,* 365–376.

Acredolo, L., & Goodwyn, S. (1985). Symbolic gesturing in language development. *Human Development, 28,* 40–49.

Acredolo, L., & Goodwyn, S. (1988). Symbolic gesturing in normal infants. *Child Development, 59,* 450–466.

Adams, R. J., & Passman, R. H. (1981). The effects of preparing two-year-olds for brief separations from their mothers. *Child Development, 52,* 1068–1070.

Adamson, L. B. (1995). *Communication development during infancy.* Dubuque, IA: WCB Brown & Benchmark.

Adamson, L. B., & Bakeman, R. (1985). Affect and attention: Infants observed with mothers and peers. *Child Development, 56,* 582–593.

Adamson, L. B., Bakeman, R., Smith, C. B., & Walters, A. S. (1987). Adults' interpretation of infants' acts. *Developmental Psychology, 23,* 383–387.

Adinolfi, A. M. (1971). The postnatal development of synaptic contacts in the cerebral cortex. In M. B. Sterman, D. J. McGinty, & A. M. Adinolfi (Eds.), *Brain development and behavior* (pp. 182–196). New York: Academic Press.

Adler, S. A. (1997). Selective integration of temporally distinct perceptual information in infant memory. *Infant Behavior and Development, 20,* 3–28.

Adolph, K. E. (1997). Learning in the development of infant locomotion. *Monographs of the Society for Research in Child Development, 62*(3), 1–140.

Adolph, K. E., Gibson, E. J., & Eppler, M. A. (1990). *Perceiving affordances of slopes: The ups and downs of toddler's locomotion.* Report of Emory Cognition Project. Atlanta, GA: Emory University.

Adolph, K. E., Vereijken, B., & Denny, M. A. (1998). Learning to crawl. *Child Development, 69*(5), 1299–1312.

Adolph, K. E., Vereijken, B., Denny, M. A., Gill, V. S., & Lucero, A. (1995, June). *Increased balance requirements constrain variability in infant crawling.* Poster presented at the American Psychological Society, New York.

Adrien, J. L., Lenoir, P., Martineau, J., Perrot, A., Hameury, L., Larmande, C., & Sauvage, D. (1993). Blind ratings of early symptoms of autism based upon family home movies. *Journal of the American Academy of Child Adolescent Psychiatry, 32,* 617–626.

Affonso, D. (1977). "Missing pieces": A study of postpartum feelings. *Birth and the Family Journal, 4,* 159–164.

Agiobu-Kemmer, I. (1986). Cognitive and affective aspects of infant development. In H. V. Curran (Ed.), *Nigerian children: Developmental perspectives* (pp. 42–67). London: Routledge & Kegan Paul.

Aguiar, A., & Baillargeon, R. (1998). Eight-and-a-half-month-old infants' reasoning about containment events. *Child Development, 69*(3), 636–653.

Ainsworth, M. (1979). Attachment as related to mother-infant interaction. In R. Hinde & J. Rosenblatt (Eds.), *Advances in the study of behavior* (pp. 115–148). New York: Academic Press.

Ainsworth, M., & Bell, S. (1970). Attachment, exploration, and separation: Illustrated by the behavior of one-year-olds in a strange situation. *Child Development, 41,* 49–67.

Ainsworth, M., Bell, S., & Stayton, D. (1971). Individual differences in strange situation behavior of one-year-olds. In H. R. Schaffer (Ed.), *The origins of human and social relations* (pp. 240–262). London: Academic Press.

Ainsworth, M., Blehar, M. C., Waters, E., & Wall, S. (1978). *Patterns of attachment.* Hillsdale, NJ: Erlbaum.

Alan Guttmacher Institute. (1994). *Sex and America's teenagers.* New York, New York: Author.

Alessandri, S. M., & Lewis, M. (1996). Differences in pride and shame in maltreated and nonmaltreated preschoolers. *Child Development, 67*(4), 1857–1869.

Alessandri, S. M., Sullivan, M. W., Imaizumi, S., & Lewis, M. (1993). Learning and emotional responsivity in cocaine-exposed infants. *Developmental Psychology, 29,* 989–997.

Alexander, G. R., & Korenbrot, C. C. (1995). The role of prenatal care in preventing low birth weight. *The Future of Children, 5,* 103–120.

Allen, D. A., Affleck, G., McGrade, B. J., & McQueeney, M. (1984). Effects of single-parent status on mothers and their high-risk infants. *Infant Behavior and Development, 7,* 347–359.

Allen, S. (1998). A qualitative analysis of the process, mediating variables and impact of traumatic childbirth. *Reproductive and Infant Psychology, 16,* 107–131.

Allman, J., Rosin, A., Kumar, R., & Hasenstaub, A. (1998). Parenting and survival in anthropoid primates: Caretakers live longer. *Proceedings of the National Academy of Sciences of the United States of America, 95,* 6866–6869.

Als, H., Duffy, F. H., & McAnulty, G. B. (1988). Behavioral differences between preterm and full-term newborns as measured with the APIB system scores: I. *Infant Behavior and Development, 11,* 305–318.

Alvarez, W. F. (1985). The meaning of maternal employment for mothers and their perceptions of their three-year-old children. *Child Development, 56,* 350–360.

Amabile, T. A., & Rovee-Collier, C. (1991). Contextual variation and memory retrieval at six months. *Child Development, 62,* 1155–1166.

American Academy of Pediatrics. (1997). Breastfeeding and the use of human milk: Policy statement. *Pediatrics, 100*(6), 1035–1039.

American Academy of Pediatrics, Committee on Nutrition. (1981). On the feeding of solid food to infants. *Pediatrics, 68,* 435–443.

Ammerman, S. D., Perelli, E., Adler, N., & Irwin, C. E. (1992). Do adolescents understand what physicians say about sexuality and health? *Clinical Pediatrics, 31,* 590–595.

Anders, T. F., Goodlin-Jones, B. L., & Zelenko, M. (1998). Infant regulation and sleep-wake state development. *Zero to Three 19*(2), 5–8.

Anderson, A. S., Purvis, G. A., & Chopra, J. G. (1979). The introduction of mixed feeding in infancy. In *Pediatric nutrition handbook* (pp. 83–99). Evanston, IL: American Academy of Pediatrics.

Anderson, D. R., & Levin, S. R. (1976). Young children's attention to "Sesame Street." *Child Development, 47,* 806–811.

Anderson, D. R., & Lorch, E. P. (1983). Looking at television: Action or reaction? In J. Bryant & D. R. Anderson (Eds.), *Children's understanding of television: Research on attention and comprehension* (pp. 1–33). New York: Academic Press.

Anderson, G. C. (1999). Kangaroo care of the premature infant. In E. Goldstein & A. Sostek (Eds.), *Nurturing the premature infant: Developmental intervention in the neonatal intensive care nursery* (pp. 351–366). Oxford, England: Oxford University Press.

Anderson, G. C., Burroughs, A. K., & Measel, C. P. (1983). Nonnutritive sucking opportunities: A safe and effective treatment for preterm neonates. In T. Field & A. Sostek (Eds.), *Infants born at risk* (pp. 215–245). New York: Grune & Stratton.

Andersson, B. E. (1992). Effects of day-care on cognitive and socioemotional competence of thirteen-year-old Swedish schoolchildren. *Child Development, 63,* 20–36.

Anisfeld, M. (1979). Interpreting "imitative" responses in early infancy. *Science, 205,* 214–215.

Antonelli, P. L. (1985). *Mathematical essays on growth and the emergence of form.* Edmonton, Canada: University of Alberta Press.

Apgar, V. (1953). A proposal for a new method of evaluation in the newborn infant. *Current Research in Anesthesia and Analgesia, 32,* 260.

Arehart-Treichel, J. (1979, December 1). Down's syndrome: The father's role. *Science News,* 381–382.

Areias, M. E., Kumar, R., Barros, H., & Figueiredo, E. (1996). Correlates of postnatal depression in mothers and fathers. *British Journal of Psychiatry, 169*(1), 36–41.

Arend, R., Gove, F. L., & Sroufe, L. A. (1979). Continuity of individual adaptation from infancy to kindergarten: A predictive study of ego-resiliency and curiosity in preschoolers. *Child Development, 50,* 950–959.

Arendt, R., Singer, L., Angelopoulos, J., Bass-Busdiecker, O., & Mascia, J. (1998). Sensorimotor development in cocaine-exposed infants. *Infant Behavior and Development, 21*(4), 627–640.

Arterberry, M., Yonas, A., & Bensen, A. S. (1989). Self-produced locomotion and the development of responsiveness to linear perspective and texture gradients. *Developmental Psychology, 25*(6), 976–982.

Asendorpf, J. B., & Baudonniere, P. M. (1993). Self-awareness and other-awareness: Mirror self-recognition and synchronic imitation among unfamiliar peers. *Developmental Psychology, 29,* 88–95.

Asendorpf, J. B., Warkentin, V., & Baudonniere, P. (1996). Self-awareness and other-awareness II: Mirror self-recognition, social contingency awareness, and synchronic imitation. *Developmental Psychology, 32*(2), 313–321.

Aslin, R. N. (1981). Development of smooth pursuit in human infants. In D. F. Fisher, R. A. Monty, & J. W. Sanders (Eds.), *Eye movements: Cognition and visual perception* (pp. 540–557). Hillsdale, NJ: Erlbaum.

Aslin, R. N. (1987). Visual and auditory development in infancy. In J. D. Osofsky (Ed.), *Handbook of infant development* (2nd ed., pp. 146–169). New York: Wiley.

Atkinson, L., Chisholm, V. C., Scott, B., Goldberg, S., Vaughn, B. E., Blackwell, J., Dickens, S., & Tam, F. (1999). Maternal sensitivity, child functional level, and attachment in Down syndrome. *Monographs of the Society for Research in Child Development, 64*(3), 46–66.

Aureli, T. (1994). Shared focus in mother-child joint activity in the second year of life. *Early Development & Parenting, 3,* 145–152.

Aureli, T. (1997). *L'osservazione del comportamento del bambino.* Bologna, Italy: Società editrice il Mulino.

Aviezer, O., Sagi, A., Joels, T., & Ziv, Y. (1999). Emotional availability and attachment representations in Kibbutz infants and their mothers. *Developmental Psychology, 35*(3), 811–821.

Axia, G., Bonichini, S., & Benini, F. (1999). Attention and reaction to distress in infancy: A longitudinal study. *Developmental Psychology, 35*(2), 500–504.

Baddeley, A. (1994). The remembered self and the enacted self. In U. Neisser & R. Fivush (Eds.), *The remembering self: Construction and accuracy in the self-narrative* (pp. 236–242). Cambridge, England: Cambridge University Press.

Bahrick, L. E. (1987). Infants' intermodal perception of two levels of temporal structure in natural events. *Infant Behavior and Development, 10,* 387–416.

Bahrick, L. E. (1988). Intermodal learning in infancy: Learning on the basis of two kinds of invariant relations in audible and visible events. *Child Development, 59,* 197–209.

Bahrick, L. E., Netto, D., & Hernandez-Reif, M. (1998). Intermodal perception of adult and child faces and voices by infants. *Child Development, 69*(5), 1263–1275.

Bahrick, L. E., & Pickens, J. N. (1988). Classification of bimodal English and Spanish language passages by infants. *Infant Behavior and Development, 11,* 277–296.

Bai, D. L., & Bertenthal, B. I. (1992). Locomotor status and the development of spatial search skills. *Child Development, 63,* 215–226.

Baillargeon, R. (1987). Object permanence in 3½- and 4½-month-old infants. *Developmental Psychology, 23,* 655–664.

Baillargeon, R., & DeVos, J. (1991). Object permanence in young infants: Further evidence. *Child Development, 62,* 1227–1246.

Baillargeon, R., & Graber, M. (1988). Evidence of location memory in 8-month-old infants in a nonsearch AB task. *Developmental Psychology, 24,* 502–511.

Baillargeon, R., Needham, A., & DeVos, J. (1992). The development of young infants' intuitions about support. *Early Development & Parenting, 1,* 69–78.

Baird, P. A., & Sadovnick, A. D. (1987). Life expectancy in Down's syndrome. *Journal of Pediatrics, 110,* 849–854.

Baird, P. A., Yee, I. M., & Sadovnick, A. D. (1994). Population-based study of long-term outcomes after amniocentesis. *Lancet, 344* (8930), 1134–1136.

Bakeman, R., & Adamson, L. B. (1984). Coordinating attention to people and objects in mother-infant and peer-infant interaction. *Child Development, 55,* 1278–1289.

Bakeman, R., & Brown, J. (1980). Analyzing behavioral sequences: Differences between preterm and full-term infant-mother dyads during the first months of life. In D. Sawin (Ed.), *Psychosocial risks in infant-environment transactions* (pp. 390–415). New York: Brunner-Mazel.

Bakeman, R., & Brownlee, J. (1980). The strategic use of parallel play: A sequential analysis. *Child Development, 51,* 873–878.

Baker, R. L., & Mednick, B. R. (1984). *Influence on human development: A longitudinal perspective.* The Hague: Kluwer-Nijhoff.

Balamore, U., & Wozniak, R. H. (1984). Speech-action coordination in young children. *Developmental Psychology, 20,* 850–858.

Baldwin, D. A. (1993). Early referential understanding: Infants' ability to recognize referential acts for what they are. *Developmental Psychology, 29,* 832–843.

Baldwin, D. A. (1995). Understanding the link between joint attention and language. In C. Moore & P. J. Dunham (Eds.), *Joint attention: Its origins and role in development* (pp. 131–158). Hillsdale, NJ: Erlbaum.

Baldwin, D. A., & Markman, E. M. (1989). Establishing word-object relations: A first step. *Child Development, 60,* 381–398.

Baldwin, D. A., Markman, E. M., Bill, B., Desjardins, R. N., Irwin, J. M., & Tidball, G. (1996). Infants' reliance on a social criterion for establishing word-object relations. *Child Development, 67,* 3135–3153.

Baldwin, D. A., Markman, E. M., & Melartin, R. L. (1993). Infants' ability to draw inferences about nonobvious object properties: Evidence from exploratory play. *Child Development, 64,* 711–728.

Ball, R. M., & Pianta, R. C. (1993). Relations between maternal network size and maternal behaviour with five-year-olds across levels of maternal background and child ability. *Early Development & Parenting, 2,* 209–216.

Balog, J. (1976). A new look at our infant mortality. *Birth and the Family Journal, 3,* 15–23.

Bandura, A. (1977). *Social learning theory.* Englewood Cliffs, NJ: Prentice-Hall.

Bandura, A. (1989). Human agency in social cognitive theory. *American Psychologist, 44*(9), 1175–1184.

Bandura, A. (1996). *Social foundations of thought and action: A social cognitive theory.* Englewood Cliffs, NJ: Prentice-Hall.

Bane, M. J., & Ellwood, D. T. (1989). One fifth of the nation's children: Why are they poor? *Science, 245,* 1047–1053.

Bard, K. A. (1994). Evolutionary roots of intuitive parenting: Maternal competence in chimpanzees. *Early Development and Parenting, 3,* 19–28.

Bard, K. A., Platzman, K. A., Lester, B. M., & Suomi, S. J. (1992). Orientation to social and nonsocial stimuli in neonatal chimpanzees and humans. *Infant Behavior and Development, 15,* 43–56.

Barden, R. C., Ford, M. E., Jensen, A. G., Rogers-Salyer, M., & Salyer, K. E. (1989). Effects of craniofacial deformity in infancy on the quality of mother-infant interactions. *Child Development, 60,* 819–824.

Barglow, P. (1987a). Effect of maternal absence due to employment on the quality of infant-mother attachment in a low-risk sample. *Child Development, 58,* 945–954.

Barglow, P. (1987b). Some further comments about infant day-care research. *Zero to Three, 8,* 26–28.

Barnard, K. E., Bee, H. L., & Hammond, M. A. (1984). Developmental changes in maternal interactions with term and preterm infants. *Infant Behavior and Development, 7,* 101–113.

Barness, L. A. (1981). [Letter to the editor.] *Pediatrics, 67,* 166.

Barnett, D., Ganiban, J., & Ciccheti, D. (1999). Maltreatment, negative expressivity, and the development of type D attachments from 12 to 24 months of age. *Monographs of the Society for Research in Child Development, 64*(3), 97–118.

Barnett, R. C., & Baruch, G. K. (1987). Determinants of fathers' participation in family work. *Journal of Marriage and the Family,* 29–40.

Baron-Cohen, S., Allen, J., & Gillberg, C. (1992). Can autism be detected at 18 months? *British Journal of Psychiatry, 161,* 839–843.

Baron-Cohen, S., Cox, A., Baird, G., Sweettenham, J., & Nightingale, N. (1996). Psychological markers in the detection of autism in infancy in a large population. *British Journal of Psychiatry, 168*(2), 158–163.

Barr, R. G. (1990). The early crying paradox: A modest proposal. *Human Nature, 1,* 355–389.

Barr, R. G., & Hayne, H. (1999). Developmental changes in imitation from television during infancy. *Child Development, 70*(5), 1067–1081.

Barr, R. G., Quek, V. S. H., Cousineau, D., Oberlander, T. F., Brian, J. A., & Young, S. N. (1994). Effects of intraoral sucrose on crying, mouthing, and hand-mouth contact in newborn and six-week-old infants. *Developmental Medicine Child Neurology, 36,* 608–618.

Barr, R. G., Rotman, A., Yaremko, J., Leduc, D., & Francoeur, T. E. (1992). The crying of infants with colic: A controlled empirical description. *Pediatrics, 90,* 14–21.

Barratt, M. S., & Roach, M. A. (1995). Early interactive processes: Parenting by adolescent and adult single mothers. *Infant Behavior and Development, 18,* 97–109.

Barratt, M. S., Roach, M. A., & Leavitt, L. A. (1996). The impact of low-risk prematurity on maternal behavior and toddler outcomes. *International Journal of Behavioral Development, 19*(3), 581–602.

Barrera, M. E., & Maurer, D. (1981). Discrimination of strangers by the three-month-old. *Child Development, 52,* 558–563.

Barrera, M. E., Rosenbaum, P. L., & Cunningham, C. E. (1987). Corrected and uncorrected Bayley scores: Longitudinal developmental patterns in low and high birth weight preterm infants. *Infant Behavior and Development, 10,* 337–346.

Barrett, D. E., Radke-Yarrow, M., & Klein, R. E. (1982). Chronic malnutrition and child behavior: Effects of early caloric supplementation on social and emotional functioning at school age. *Developmental Psychology, 18,* 541–556.

Barrett, K. C. (1995). A functionalist approach to shame and guilt. In J. P. Tangney & K. W. Fischer (Eds.), *Self-conscious emotions: The psychology of shame, guilt, embarrassment, and pride* (pp. 25–63). New York: Guilford Press.

Barrett, K. C., & Campos, J. J. (1987). Perspectives on emotional development II: A functionalist approach to emotions. In J. D. Osofsky (Ed.), *Handbook of infant development* (2nd ed., pp. 555–578). New York: Wiley.

Barrett, K. C., & Nelson-Goens, G. C. (1997). Emotion communication and the development of the social emotions. In K. C. Barrett (Ed.), *New directions in child development: The communication of emotion: Current research from diverse perspectives, 77* (pp. 69–88). San Francisco: Jossey-Bass.

Barrile, M., Armstrong, E. S., & Bower, T. G. R. (1999). Novelty and frequency as determinants of newborn preference. *Developmental Science, 2*(1), 47–52.

Barss, V. A., Benacerraf, B. R., & Frigoletto, F. D. (1985). Ultrasonographic determination of chorion type in twin gestation. *Obstetrics and Gynecology, 66,* 779–783.

Barth, R. P., Fetro, J. V., Leland, N., & Volkan, K. (1992). Preventing adolescent pregnancy with social and cognitive skills. *Journal of Adolescent Research, 7,* 208–232.

Barton, M. E., & Tomasello, M. (1991). Joint attention and conversation in mother-infant-sibling triads. *Child Development, 62,* 517–529.

Bass, M., Kravath, R. E., & Glass, L. (1986). Death scene investigation in sudden infant death. *New England Journal of Medicine, 315,* 100–105.

Bates, E., Camaioni, L., & Volterra, V. (1975). The acquisition of performatives prior to speech. *Merrill-Palmer Quarterly, 21,* 205–226.

Bates, E., O'Connell, B., & Shore, C. (1987). Language and communication in infancy. In J. D. Osofsky (Ed.), *Handbook of infant development* (2nd ed., pp. 149–203). New York: Wiley.

Bates, E., Thal, D., Whitesell, K., Fenson, L., & Oakes, L. (1989). Integrating language and gesture in infancy. *Developmental Psychology, 25,* 1104–1119.

Bates, J. E. (1980). The concept of difficult temperament. *Merrill-Palmer Quarterly, 26,* 299–319.

Bates, J. E. (1987). Temperament in infancy. In J. D. Osofsky (Ed.), *Handbook of infant development* (2nd ed., pp. 35–69). New York: Wiley.

Bates, J. E., & Bayles, K. (1984). Objective and subjective components in mothers' perceptions of their children from age 6 months to 3 years. *Merrill-Palmer Quarterly, 30,* 111–130.

Bates, E., Carlson-Luden, V., & Bretherton, I. (1980). Perceptual aspects of tool using in infancy. *Infant Behavior and Development, 3,* 127–140.

Bates, J. E., Freeland, C. A., & Lounsbury, M. L. (1979). Measurement of infant difficultness. *Child Development, 50,* 794–803.

Bates, J. E., Maslin, C. A., & Frankel, K. A. (1985). Attachment security, mother-child interaction, and temperament as predictors of behavior-problem ratings at age three years. *Monographs of the Society for Research in Child Development, 50* (Serial No. 209), 167–193.

Bates, E., O'Connell, B., & Shore, C. (1987). Language and communication in infancy. In J. D. Osofsky (Ed.), *Handbook of infant development* (2nd ed., pp. 149–203). New York: Wiley.

Bates, J. E., Olson, S. L., Pettit, G. S., & Bayles, K. (1982). Dimensions of individuality in the mother-infant relationship at 6 months of age. *Child Development, 53,* 446–461.

Bates, J. E., Wachs, T. D., & Emde, R. N. (1994). Toward practical uses for biological concepts of temperament. In J. E. Bates & T. D. Wachs (Eds.), *Temperament: Individual differences at the interface of biology and behavior* (pp. 275–306). Washington, DC: American Psychological Association.

Bateson, M. C. (1975). Mother-infant exchanges: The epigenesis of conversation interaction. *Annals of the New York Academy of Science, 263,* 101–113.

Bateson, P. P. G. (1966). The characteristics and context of imprinting. *Biological Review, 41,* 177–220.

Battin, M., Ling, E. W., Whitfield, M. F., Mackinnon, M., & Effer, S. B. (1998). Has the outcome for extremely low gestational age (ELGA) infants improved following recent advances in neonatal intensive care? *American Journal of Perinatology, 15*(8), 469–477.

Bauer, P. J. (1993). Memory for gender-consistent and gender-inconsistent event sequences by twenty-five-month-old children. *Child Development, 64,* 285–297.

Bauer, P. J. (1996). What do infants recall of their lives? Memory for specific events by one- to two-year-olds. *American Psychologist, 51*(1), 29–41.

Bauer, P. J., & Dow, G. A. (1994). Episodic memory in 16- and 20-month-old children: Specifics are generalized but not forgotten. *Developmental Psychology, 30,* 403–417.

Bauer, P. J., Schwade, J. A., Wewerka, S. S., & Delaney, D. (1999). Planning ahead: Goal-directed problem solving by 2-year-olds. *Developmental Psychology, 35*(8), 1321–1337.

Baumrind, D. (1973). The development of instrumental competence through socialization. In A. Pick (Ed.), *Minnesota symposium on child development, 11,* 1112–1132. Minneapolis: University of Minnesota Press.

Baumrind, D. (1993). The average expectable environment is not good enough: A response to Scarr. *Child Development, 64,* 1299–1317.

Bayley, N. (1969). *The Bayley scale of infant development.* (Manual). Stanford, CA: Psychological Corporation.

Beck, R. A., Kambiss, S., & Bass, J. W. (1993). The retreat of Hemophilus influenzae type B invasive disease: Analysis of and immunization program and implications for OTO-HNS. *Otolaryngological Head and Neck Surgery, 109,* 712–721.

Becker, J. (1977). A learning analysis of the development of peer oriented behavior in nine-month-old infants. *Developmental psychology, 13,* 481–491.

Becker, P. T., Houser, B. J., Engelhardt, K. F., & Steinmann, M. J. (1993). Father and mother contributions to family functioning when the child has a mental delay. *Early Development and Parenting, 2,* 145–155.

Beckwith, L., & Cohen, S. E. (1978). Preterm birth: Hazardous obstetrical and postnatal events as related to caregiver-infant behavior. *Infant Behavior and Development, 1,* 403–412.

Beckwith, L., Cohen, S. E., & Hamilton, C. E. (1999). Maternal sensitivity during infancy and subsequent life events relate to attachment representation at early adulthood. *Developmental Psychology, 35*(3), 693–700.

Beckwith, L., Rodning, C., & Cohen, S. (1992). Preterm children at early adolescence and continuity and discontinuity in maternal responsiveness from infancy. *Child Development, 63,* 1198–1208.

Bell, R., Weller, G., & Waldrop, M. (1971). Newborn and preschooler: Organization of behavior and relations between periods. *Monographs of the Society for Research in Child Development, 36* (Serial No. 142), 1–130.

Bell, R. Q., & Costello, N. S. (1964). Three tests for sex differences in tactile sensitivity in the newborn. *Biologia Neonatorum, 7,* 335–347.

Bellagamba, F., & Tomasello, M. (1999). Re-enacting intended acts: Comparing 12- and 18-month-olds. *Infant Behavior and Development, 22*(2), 277–282.

Belsky, J. (1980). Child maltreatment: An ecological integration. *American Psychologist, 35,* 320–335.

Belsky, J. (1981). Early human experience: A family perspective. *Developmental Psychology, 17,* 3–23.

Belsky, J. (1984). The determinants of parenting: A process model. *Child Development, 55,* 83–96.

Belsky, J. (1995). Expanding the ecology of human development: An evolutionary perspective. In P. Moen & G. H. Elder (Eds.), *Examining lives in context: Perspectives on the ecology of human development* (pp. 545–561). Washington, DC: American Psychological Association.

Belsky, J. (1996). Parent, infant, and social-contextual antecedents of father-son attachment security. *Developmental Psychology, 32*(5), 905–913.

Belsky, J., & Braungart, J. M. (1991). Are insecure-avoidant infants with extensive day-care experience less stressed by and more independent in the strange situation? *Child Development, 62,* 567–671.

Belsky, J., Goode, M. K., & Most, R. K. (1980). Maternal simulation and infant exploratory competence; Cross-sectional, correlational, and experimental analyses. *Child Development, 51,* 1168–1178.

Belsky, J., & Isabella, R. A. (1985). Marital and parent-child relationships in family of origin and marital change following the birth of a baby: A retrospective analysis. *Child Development, 56,* 342–349.

Belsky, J., & Most, R. K. (1981). From exploration to play: A cross-sectional study of infant free play behavior. *Developmental Psychology, 17,* 630–639.

Belsky, J., & Rovine, M. J. (1988). Nonmaternal care in the first year of life and the security of infant-parent attachment. *Child Development, 59,* 157–167.

Belsky, J., Rovine, M. J., & Taylor, D. G. (1984). The Pennsylvania infant and family development project III: The origins of individual differences in infant-mother attachment: Maternal and infant contributions. *Child Development, 55,* 718–728.

Belsky, J., Ward, M. J., & Rovine, M. (1986). Prenatal expectations, postnatal experiences, and the transition to parenthood. In R. D. Ashmore & D. M. Brodzinsky (Eds.), *Thinking about the family: Views of parents and children* (pp. 15–38). Hillsdale, NJ: Erlbaum.

Belsky, J., Woodworth, S., & Crnic, K. (1996). Trouble in the second year: Three questions about family interaction. *Child Development, 67,* 556–578.

Bendersky, M., & Lewis, M. (1998). Arousal modulation in cocaine-exposed infants. *Developmental Psychology, 34*(3), 555–564.

Benn, R. K. (1986). Factors promoting secure attachment relationships between employed mothers and their sons. *Child Development, 57,* 1224–1231.

Bennett, W. J. (1987). The role of the family in the nurture and protection of the young. *American Psychologist, 42,* 246–250.

Benson, J. B. (1993). Season of birth and onset of locomotion: Theoretical and methodological implications. *Infant Behavior and Development, 16,* 69–81.

Berg, W. K. (1975). Cardiac components of defense responses in infants. *Psychophysiology, 12,* 224.

Berg, W. K., & Berg, K. M. (1979). Psychophysiological development in infancy: State, sensory function, and attention. In J. D. Osofsky (Ed.), *Handbook of infant development* (pp. 283–343). New York: Wiley.

Berg, W. K., & Berg, K. M. (1987). Psychophysiological development in infancy: State, startle, and attention. In J. D. Osofsky (Ed.), *Handbook of infant development* (2nd ed., pp. 121–145). New York: Wiley.

Berger, J., & Cunningham, C. C. (1983). Development of early vocal behaviors & interactions in Down's syndrome and non-handicapped infant-mother pairs. *Developmental Psychology, 19,* 322–331.

Berk, L. E. (1986). Development of private speech among preschool children. *Early Child Development and Care, 24,* 113–136.

Berko, J. (1958). The child's learning of English morphology. *Word, 14,* 150–177.

Berlin, L. J., Cassidy, J., & Belsky, J. (1995). Loneliness in young children and infant-mother attachment: A longitudinal study. *Merrill-Palmer Quarterly, 41,* 91–103.

Berlin, L. J., O'Neal, C., & Brooks-Gunn, J. (1998). What makes early intervention programs work? The program, its participants, and their interactions. *Zero to Three, 18*(4), 4–15.

Berman, P. W., Goodman, V., Sloan, V. L., & Fernandez, L. (1978). Preference for infants among black and white children: Sex and age differences. *Child Development, 49,* 917–919.

Berman, P. W., Monda, C. C., & Merscough, R. P. (1977). Sex differences in young children's responses to an infant: An observation within a day-care setting. *Child Development, 48,* 711–715.

Berrueta-Clement, J. R., Schweinhart, L. J., Barnett, W. S., Epstein, A. S., & Weikart, D. P. (1984). *Changed lives: The effects of the Perry Preschool Program on youths through age 19 (Monograph No. 8).* Ypsilanti, MI: High Scope/Educational Research Foundation.

Bertenthal, B. I., & Bai, D. L. (1989). Infants' sensitivity to optical flow for controlling posture. *Developmental Psychology, 25,* 936–945.

Bertenthal, B. I., Campos, J. J., & Barrett, K. C. (1984). Self-produced locomotion: An organizer of emotional, cognitive, and social development in infancy. In R. N. Emde & R. J. Harmon (Eds.), *Continuities and discontinuities in development* (pp. 175–210). New York: Plenum Press.

Bertenthal, B. I., & Pinto, J. (1993). Complementary processes in the perception and production of human movements. In L. B. Smith & E. Thelen (Eds.), *A dynamic systems approach to development: Applications* (pp. 209–239). Cambridge, MA: MIT Press.

Bertenthal, B. I., Proffitt, D. R., & Cutting, J. E. (1984). Infant sensitivity to figural coherence in biomechanical motions. *Journal of Experimental Child Psychology, 37,* 213–230.

Bertenthal, B. I., Proffitt, D. R., Kramer, S. J., & Spetner, N. B. (1987). Infants' encoding of kinetic displays varying in relative coherence. *Developmental Psychology, 23*(2), 171–178.

Berthiaume, M., David, J., Saucier, J. F., & Borgeat, F. (1998). Correlates of pre-partum depressive symptomatology: A multivariate analysis. *Reproductive and Infant Psychology, 16,* 45–56.

Bettes, B. A. (1988). Maternal depression and motherese: Temporal and intonational features. *Child Development, 59,* 1089–1096.

Bever, T. G. (1970). The cognitive basis for linguistic structures. In J. R. Haynes (Ed.), *Cognition and the development of language* (pp. 40–72). New York: Wiley.

Bhatt, R. S., Rovee-Collier, C., & Weiner, S. (1994). Developmental changes in the interface between perception and memory retrieval. *Developmental Psychology, 30,* 151–162.

Bigelow, A. E. (1992). Locomotion and search behavior in blind infants. *Infant Behavior and Development, 15,* 179–189.

Bigelow, A. E. (1998). Infants' sensitivity to familiar imperfect contingencies in social interaction. *Infant Behavior and Development, 21*(1), 149–162.

Bigelow, A. E., MacDonald, D., & MacDonald, L. (1995). The development of infants' search for their mothers, unfamiliar people, and objects. *Merrill-Palmer Quarterly, 41,* 191–205.

Bigelow, A., MacLean, J., Wood, C., & Smith, J. (1990). Infants' responses to child and adult strangers: An investigation of height and facial configuration variables. *Infant Behavior and Development, 13,* 21–32.

Bijeljac-Babic, R., Bertoncini, J., & Mehler, J. (1993). How do 4-day-old infants categorize multisyllabic utterances? *Developmental Psychology, 29,* 711–721.

Bijou, S. W., & Baer, D. M. (1965). *Child development: Vol. 2. Universal stage of infancy.* New York: Appleton-Century-Crofts.

Bingol, N., Fuchs, M., Diaz, V., Stone, R. K., & Gromisch, D. S. (1987). Teratogenicity of cocaine in humans. *Journal of Pediatrics, 110*(1), 93–96.

Biringen, Z., Emde, R. N., Campos, J. J., & Appelbaum, M. I. (1995). Affective reorganization in the infant, the mother, and the dyad: The role of upright locomotion and its timing. *Child Development, 66,* 499–514.

Birth (June 1988). Report for American College of Obstetricians and Gynecologists. *Birth, 15,* 113.

Black, L., Steinschneider, A., & Sheehe, P. R. (1979). Neonatal respiratory instability and infant development. *Child Development, 50,* 561–564.

Black, M. M., & Krishnakumar, A. (1998). Children in low-income, urban settings: Interventions to promote mental health and well-being. *American Psychologist, 53*(6), 635–646.

Blackford, J. U., & Walden, T. A. (1998). Individual differences in social referencing. *Infant Behavior and Development, 21*(1), 89–102.

Blackman, J. A., Lindgren, S. D., Hein, H. A., & Harper, D. C. (1987). Long-term surveillance of high-risk children. *American Journal of Diseases of Children, 141,* 1293–1299.

Blackwell, C. C., Weir, D. M., Busuttil, A., Saadi, A. T., Essery, S. D., Raza, M. W., James, V. S., & MacKenzie, D. A. (1994). The role of infectious agents in sudden infant death syndrome. *FEMS Immunological Medicine and Microbiology, 9,* 91–100.

Blake, A., Stewart, A., & Turcan, D. (1975). Parents of babies of very low birth weight: Long-term follow-up. In Ciba Foundation Symposium (Ed.), *Parent-infant interaction* (pp. 150–177). New York: Elsevier.

Blake, J., McConnell, S., Horton, G., & Benson, N. (1992). The gestural repertoire and its evolution over the second year. *Early Development and Parenting, 1,* 127–136.

Blank, A., Mofenson, L. M., Willoughby, A., & Yaffe, S. J. (1994). Maternal and pediatric AIDS in the United States: The current situation and future research directions. *Acta-Paediatrica-Supplement, 400,* 106–110.

Blank, M., & Klig, S. (1982). The child and the school experience. In C. B. Kopp & J. B. Krakow (Eds.), *The child: Development in social context* (pp. 456–513). Reading, MA: Addison-Wesley.

Blass, E. M. (1997). Changing influences of sucrose and visual engagement in 2- to 12-week-old human infants: Implications for maternal face recognition. *Infant Behavior and Development, 20*(4), 423–434.

Blass, E. M., & Ciaramitaro, V. (1994). A new look at some old mechanisms in human newborns: Taste and tactile determinants of state, affect, and action. *Monographs of the Society for Research in Child Development, 59,* 1–102.

Blass, E. M., Fillion, T. J., Rochat, P., Hoffmeyer, L. B., & Metzger, M. A. (1989). Sensorimotor and motivational determinants of hand-mouth coordination in 1- to 3-day-old human infants. *Developmental Psychology, 25,* 963–975.

Blass, E. M., Ganchrow, J. R., & Steiner, J. E. (1984). Classical conditioning in newborn humans 2 to 48 hours of age. *Infant Behavior and Development, 7,* 223–235.

Blehar, M. C., Lieberman, A., & Ainsworth, M. (1977). Early face-to-face interaction and its relation to later mother-infant attachment. *Child Development, 48,* 182–194.

Bloch, H. (1990). Status and function of early sensory-motor coordination. In H. Bloch & B. I. Bertenthal (Eds.), *Sensory-motor organiza-*

tions and development in infancy and early childhood (pp. 163–178). The Netherlands: Kluwer Academic.

Block, J. A., & Block, J. (1980). The role of ego-control and ego-resiliency in the organization of behavior. In W. A. Collins (Ed.), *Minnesota symposia on child psychology* (Vol. 13, pp. 1550–1574). Hillsdale, NJ: Erlbaum.

Bloom, K., D'Odorico, L., & Beaumont, S. (1993). Adult preferences for syllabic vocalizations: Generalizations to parity and native language. *Infant Behavior and Development, 16,* 109–120.

Bloom, K., & Lo, E. (1990). Adult perceptions of vocalizing infants. *Infant Behavior and Development, 13,* 209–219.

Bloom, L., & Beckwith, R. (1989). Talking with feeling: Integrating affective and linguistic expression in early language development. *Cognition and Emotion, 3*(4), 313–342.

Bloom, L., Margulis, C., Tinker, E., & Fujita, N. (1996). Early conversations and word learning: Contributions from child and adult. *Child Development, 67,* 3154–3175.

Bloom, L., Merkin, S., & Wootten, J. (1982). Wh-questions: Linquistic factors that contribute to the sequence of acquisition. *Child Development, 53,* 1084–1092.

Bloom, L., Rocissano, L., & Hood, L. (1976). Adult-child discourse: Developmental interaction between information processing and linguistic knowledge. *Cognitive Psychology, 8,* 521–552.

Bluglass, K., & Hassall, C. (1979). Alternative forms of community support after sudden infant death. *Medicine, Science and the Law, 19,* 240–245.

Blurton-Jones, N., Ferreira, C., Brown, M., & MacDonald, L. (1978). The association between perinatal factors and later night waking. *Developmental Medicine and Child Neurology, 20,* 427–434.

Bocci, V., von Brenmen, K., Corradeschi, F., Franchi, F., Luzzi, E., & Paulesu, L. (1993). Presence of interferon-gamma and interleukin-6 in colostrum of normal women. *Lymphokine-Cytokine Research, 12,* 21–24.

Boddy, J. M., & Skuse, D. H. (1994). The process of parenting in failure to thrive. *Journal of Child Psychology and Psychiatry and Allied Disciplines, 35,* 401–424.

Bodle, J. H., Zhou, L. Y., Shore, C. M., & Dixon, W. E. (1996). Transfer by responsibility in parent-child play during the second year. *Early Development and Parenting, 5*(4), 185–194.

Boehm, L. (1977). The development of independence: A comparative study. *Child Development, 28,* 85–92.

Bohannon, J. N., III, & Stanowicz, L. (1988). The issue of negative evidence: Adult responses to children's language errors. *Developmental Psychology, 24,* 684–689.

Bohlin, G., & Hagekull, B. (1993). Stranger wariness and sociability in the early years. *Infant Behavior and Development, 16,* 53–67.

Bohlin, G., Hagekull, B., Germer, M., Anderson, K., & Lindberg, L. (1989). Avoidant and resistant reunion behaviors as predicted by maternal interactive behavior and infant temperament. *Infant Behavior and Development, 12,* 105–117.

Bohlin, G., Hagekull, B., & Lindberg, L. (1994). Infantile colic and parental experiences. *Early Development and Parenting, 3,* 63–69.

Bonin, M., Pomerleau, A., & Malcuit, G. (1998). A longitudinal study of visual attention and psychomotor development in preterm and full-term infants during the first six months of life. *Infant Behavior and Development, 21*(1), 103–118.

Bookstein, F. L., Sampson, P. D., Streissguth, A. P., & Barr, H. M. (1996). Exploiting redundant measurement of dose and developmental outcome: New methods from the behavioral teratology of alcohol. *Developmental Psychology, 32*(3), 404–415.

Boom, D. C. van den (1994). The influence of temperament and mothering on attachment and exploration: An experimental manipulation of sensitive responsiveness among lower-class mothers with irritable infants. *Child Development, 65,* 1457–1477.

Boom, D. C. van den, & Gravenhorst, J. B. (1995). Prenatal and perinatal correlates of neonatal irritability. *Infant Behavior and Development, 18,* 117–121.

Boom, D. C. van den, & Hoeksma, J. B. (1994a). The effect of infant irritability on mother-infant interaction: A growth-curve analysis. *Developmental Psychology, 30*(4), 581–590.

Boom, D. C. van den, & Hoeksma, J. B. (1994b). How is development conceptualized in mother-child interaction? In W. Koops, J. Hoeksma, & D. C. van den Boom (Eds.), *Early mother-child interaction and attachment: Old and new approaches.* Amsterdam: Elsevier.

Bornstein, M. H. (1985). Habituation of attention as a measure of visual information processing in human infants: Summary, systematization, and synthesis. In G. Gottlieb & N. A. Krasnegor (Eds.), *Measurement of audition and vision in the first year of postnatal life: A methodological overview* (pp. 260–281). Norwood, NJ: Ablex.

Bornstein, M. H., & Benasich, A. A. (1986). Infant habituation: Assessments of short-term reliability and individual differences at five months. *Child Development, 57,* 87–99.

Bornstein, M. H., Haynes, O. M., Pascual, L., Painter, K., & Galperin, C. (1999). Play in two societies: Pervasiveness of process, specificity of structure. *Child Development, 70*(2), 317–331.

Bornstein, M. H., & Krinsky, S. J. (1985). Perception of symmetry in infancy: The salience of vertical symmetry and the perception of pattern wholes. *Journal of Experimental Child Psychology, 39,* 1–19.

Bornstein, M. H., Krinsky, S. J., & Benasich, A. A. (1986). Fine orientation discrimination and shape constancy in infants. *Journal of Experimental Child Psychology, 41,* 49–60.

Bornstein, M. H., & Sigman, M. D. (1986). Continuity in mental development from infancy. *Child Development, 57,* 251–274.

Bornstein, M. H., Tal, J., Rahn, C., Galperin, C. Z., Pecheux, M., Lamour, M., Toda, S., Azuma, H., Ogino, M., & Tamis-LeMonda, C. S. (1992). Functional analysis of the contents of maternal speech to infants of 5 and 13 months in four cultures: Argentina, France, Japan, and the United States. *Developmental Psychology, 28,* 593–603.

Bornstein, M. H., & Tamis-LeMonda, C. S. (1995). Parent-child symbolic play: Three theories in search of an effect. *Developmental Review, 15,* 382–400.

Bornstein, M. H., Tamis-LeMonda, C. S., Tal, J., Ludemann, P., Toda, S., Rahn, C. W., Pecheux, M. G., Azuma, H., & Vardi, D. (1992). Maternal responsiveness to infants in three societies: The United States, France, and Japan. *Child Development, 63,* 808–821.

Boss, J. A. (1994). First trimester prenatal diagnosis: Earlier is not necessarily better. *Journal of Medical Ethics, 20,* 146–151.

Botting, N., Powls, A., Cooke, R. W., & Marlow, N. (1998). Cognitive and educational outcome of very-low-birthweight children in early adolescence. *Developmental Medicine and Child Neurology, 40*(10), 652–660.

Bowerman, M. (1978). Systematizing semantic knowledge: Changes over time in the child's organization of word meaning. *Child Development, 49,* 977–987.

Bowlby, J. (1969). *Attachment and loss: Vol. 1. Attachment.* New York: Basic Books.

Bowlby, J. (1980). *Attachment and loss: Vol. 3. Loss, sadness and depression.* New York: Basic Books.

Bowman, M. C., & Saunders, D. M. (1994). Community attitudes to maternal age and pregnancy after assisted reproductive technology: Too old at 50 years? *Human Reproduction, 9,* 167–171.

Boyce, W. T., Schaefer, C., & Uitti, C. (1985). Permanence and change: Psychosocial factors in the outcome of adolescent pregnancy. *Social Science Medicine, 21*(11), 1279–1287.

Brackbill, Y. (1971). Cumulative effects of continuous stimulation on arousal level in infants. *Child Development, 42,* 17–26.

Brackbill, Y. (1979). Obstetrical medication and infant behavior. In J. Osofsky (Ed.), *Handbook of infant development* (pp. 380–402). New York: Wiley.

Bradley, R. H., & Caldwell, B. M. (1976). The relation of infants' home environment to mental test performance at fifty-four months: A follow-up study. *Child Development, 47,* 1172–1173.

Bradley, R. H., & Caldwell, B. M. (1995). Caregiving and the regulation of childgrowth and development: Describing proximal aspects of caregiving systems. *Developmental Review, 15,* 38–85.

Bradley, R. H., Whiteside, L., Mundfrom, D. J., Casey, P. H., Kelleher, K. J., & Pope, S. K. (1994). Early indications of resilience and their relation to experiences in the home environments of low birthweight, premature children living in poverty. *Child Development, 65,* 346–360.

Braine, M. D. S. (1976). Children's first word combinations. *Monographs of the Society for Research in Child Development, 164* (Serial No. 164), pp. 1–104.

Brake, S. C., Fifer, W. P., Alfasi, G., & Fleischman, A. (1988). The first nutritive sucking response of premature newborns. *Infant Behavior and Development, 11,* 1–19.

Branchfeld, S., Goldberg, S., & Sloman, J. (1980). Parent-infant interaction in free play at 8 and 12 months: Effects of prematurity and immaturity. *Infant Behavior and Development, 3,* 289–306.

Bråten, S. (1998). Infant learning by altercentric participation: The reverse of egocentric observation in autism. In S. Bråten (Ed.), *Intersubjective communication and emotion in early ontogeny. Studies in emotion and social interaction, 2nd series* (pp. 105–124). New York: Cambridge University Press.

Braungart-Rieker, J., Garwood, M. M., Powers, B. P., & Notaro, P. C. (1998). Infant affect and affect regulation during the still-face paradigm with mothers and fathers: The role of infant characteristics and parental sensitivity. *Developmental Psychology, 34*(6), 1428–1437.

Brauth, S. E., Hall, W. S., & Dooling, R. J. (Eds.) (1991). *Plasticity of development.* Cambridge, MA: MIT Press.

Brazelton, T. B. (1977). Implications of infant development among the Mayan Indians of Mexico. In P. H. Liederman, S. R. Tulkin, & A. Rosenfeld (Eds.), *Culture and infancy* (pp. 336–352). New York: Academic Press.

Brazelton, T. B., Koslowski, B., & Main, M. (1974). The origins of reciprocity. In M. Lewis & L. Rosenblum (Eds.), *The effect of the infant on its caregiver* (pp. 150–185). New York: Wiley.

Brazelton, T. B., Nugent, J. K., & Lester, B. M. (1987). Neonatal behavioral assessment scale. In J. D. Osofsky (Ed.), *Handbook of infant development* (2nd ed., pp. 92–120). New York: Wiley.

Breitmayer, B. J., & Ramey, C. T. (1986). Biological nonoptimality and quality of postnatal environment as codeterminants of intellectual development. *Child Development, 57,* 1151–1165.

Bremmer, J. (1978). Egocentric vs. allocentric spatial coding in nine-month-old infants: Factors influencing choice of code. *Developmental Psychology, 14,* 346–355.

Brennan, P. A., Grekin, E. R., & Mednick, S. A. (1999). Maternal smoking during pregnancy and adult male criminal outcomes. *Archives of General Psychiatry, 56,* 215–219.

Bretherton, I. (1985). Attachment theory: Retrospect and prospect. *Monographs of the Society for Research in Child Development, 50* (Serial No. 209), 3–35.

Bretherton, I. (1987). New perspectives on attachment relations: Security, communication, and internal working models. In J. D. Osofsky (Ed.), *Handbook of infant development* (2nd ed., pp. 1061–1100). New York: Wiley.

Bretherton, I., Fritz, J., Zahn-Waxler, C., & Ridgeway, D. (1986). Learning to talk about emotions: A functionalist perspective. *Child Development, 57,* 529–548.

Bridges, L. J., & Connell, J. P. (1991). Consistency and inconsistency in infant emotional and social interactive behavior across contexts and caregivers. *Infant Behavior and Development, 14,* 471–487.

Bridges, L. J., Connell, J. P., & Belsky, J. (1988). Similarities and differences in infant-mother and infant-father interaction in the strange situation: A component process analysis. *Developmental Psychology, 24,* 92–100.

Bridges, L. J., Grolnick, W. S., & Connell, J. P. (1997). Infant emotion regulation with mothers and fathers. *Infant Behavior and Development, 20,* 47–57.

Brighi, A. (1997). Patterns of mother-infant interaction and contingency learning in full-term infants. *Early Development and Parenting, 6*(1), 37–45.

Bril, B., & Breniere, Y. (1993). Posture and independent locomotion in early childhood: Learning to walk or learning dynamic postural control? In G. J. P. Savelsbergh (Ed.), *The development of coordination in infancy* (pp. 337–358). Amsterdam: Elsevier.

Bril, B., & Sabatier, C. (1986). The cultural context of motor development: Postural manipulations in the daily life of Bambara babies (Mali). *International Journal of Behavioral Development, 9,* 439–453.

Brody, G. H., Stoneman, Z., & MacKinnon, C. (1982). Role asymmetries among school-age children, their younger siblings, and their friends. *Child Development, 53,* 1364–1370.

Broerse, J., & Elias, G. (1994). Changes in the content and timing of mothers' talk to infants. *British Journal of Developmental Psychology, 12,* 131–145.

Bromwich, R., & Parmalee, A. (1979). An intervention program for preterm infants. In T. Field, A. Sostek, S. Goldberg, & H. Shuman (Eds.), *Infants born at risk: Behavior and development* (pp. 66–79). New York: Springer Medical and Scientific Books.

Bronfenbrenner, U. (1979). *The ecology of human development: Experiments by nature and design.* Cambridge, MA: Harvard University Press.

Bronfenbrenner, U. (1986). Ecology of the family as a context for human development: Research perspectives. *Developmental Psychology, 22*(6), 723–742.

Bronfenbrenner, U., & Evans, G. W. (2000). Developmental science in the 21st century: Emerging questions, theoretical models, research designs and empirical findings. *Social Development, 9*(1), 115–125.

Bronson, G. W. (1972). Infants' reactions to unfamiliar persons and novel objects. *Monographs of the Society for Research in Child Development, 47* (Serial No. 148), 1–46.

Brookhart, J., & Hock, E. (1976). The effects of experimental context and experiential background on infants' behavior toward their mothers and a stranger. *Child Development, 47,* 333–340.

Brooks, J., & Lewis, M. (1976). Infants' responses to strangers: Midget, adult, and child. *Child Development, 47,* 323–332.

Brooks-Gunn, J., & Furstenberg, F. (1986). Antecedents and consequences of parenting: The case of adolescent motherhood. In A. Fogel & G. F. Melson (Eds.), *Origins of nurturance: Developmental, biological, and cultural perspectives on caregiving* (pp. 166–185). Hillsdale, NJ: Erlbaum.

Brooks-Gunn, J., Klebanov, P. K., Liaw, F., & Spiker, D. (1993). Enhancing the development of low-birthweight, premature infants: Changes in cognition and behavior over the first three years. *Child Development, 64,* 736–753.

Brooks-Gunn, J., & Lewis, M. (1982). Affective exchanges between normal and handicapped infants and their mothers. In T. Field & A. Fogel (Eds.), *Emotion and early interaction* (pp. 17–41). Hillsdale, NJ: Erlbaum.

Brown, J., Bakeman, R., Snyder, P., Frederickson, W., Morgan, S., & Helper, R. (1975). Interactions of black inner-city mothers with their newborn infants. *Child Development, 46,* 677–686.

Brown, J. R., & Dunn, J. (1992). Talk with your mother or your sibling? Developmental changes in early family conversations about feelings. *Child Development, 63,* 336–349.

Brown, R. (1973). *A first language: The early stages.* Cambridge, MA: Harvard University Press.

Brown, R., Cazden, C., & Bellugi-Klima, V. (1969). The child's grammar from I to III. In J. P. Hill (Ed.), *Minnesota Symposium of Child Psychology* (Vol. 2). St. Paul: University of Minnesota Press.

Brownell, C. A. (1986). Convergent developments: Cognitive-developmental correlates of growth in infant/toddler peer skills. *Child Development, 57,* 275–286.

Brownell, C. A. (1988). Combinatorial skills: Converging developments over the second year. *Child Development, 59,* 675–685.

Bruer, J. (1999). *The myth of the first three years.* New York: Free Press.

Bruner, J. (1983). *Child's talk: Learning to use language.* New York: Norton.

Brunner, D. P., Munch, M., Biedermann, K., Huch, R., Huch, A., & Borbely, A. A. (1994). Changes in sleep and sleep electroencephalogram during pregnancy. *Sleep, 17,* 576–582.

Bryant, P. E., & Trabasso, T. (1971). Transitive inferences and memory in young children. *Nature, 232,* 456–458.

Bryne, J. M., & Horowitz, F. D. (1979). Rocking as a soothing intervention: The influence of direction and type of movement. *Infant Behavior and Development, 2,* 209–214.

Buehler, B. A., Rao, V., & Finnell, R. H. (1994). Biochemical and molecular teratology of fetal hydantoin syndrome. *Neurological Clinics, 12,* 741–748.

Buka, S. L., & Lipsitt, L. P. (1991). Newborn sucking behavior and its relation to grasping. *Infant Behavior and Development, 14,* 59–67.

Bukatko, D., & Daehler, M. W. (1995). *Child development: A thematic approach* (2nd ed.). Boston: Houghton Mifflin.

Bullock, M., & Lutkenhaus, P. (1988). The development of volitional behavior in the toddler years. *Child Development, 59,* 664–674.

Burack, J. A., Shulman, C., Katzir, E., Schaap, T., Brennan, J. M., Iarocci, G., Wilansky, P., & Amir, N. (1999). Cognitive and behavioral development of Israeli males with fragile X and Down syndrome. *International Journal of Behavioral Development, 23*(2), 519–531.

Burchinal, M. R., Bryant, D. M., Lee, M. W., & Ramey, C. T. (1992). Early day care, infant-mother attachment, and maternal responsivenss in the infant's first year. *Early Childhood Research Quarterly, 7,* 383–396.

Burchinal, M. R., Campbell, F. A., Bryant, D. M., Wasik, B. H., & Ramey, C. T. (1997). Early intervention and mediating processes in cognitive performance children of low-income African American families. *Child Development, 68*(5), 935–954.

Burchinal, M. R., Lee, M., & Ramey, C. (1989). Type of day-care and preschool intellectual development in disadvantaged children. *Child Development, 60,* 128–137.

Burchinal, M. R., Roberts, J. E., Nabors, L. A., & Bryant, D. M. (1996). Quality of center child care and infant cognitive language development. *Child Development, 67,* 606–620.

Burgess, R. L. (1979). Child abuse: A social interactional analysis. In B. B. Lakey & A. E. Kazdin (Eds.), *Advances in clinical child psychology* (pp. 405–430). New York: Plenum Press.

Burgess, R. L., & Conger, R. D. (1978). Family interaction in abusive, neglectful and normal families. *Child Development, 49,* 1163–1173.

Bushnell, E. W. (1982). Visual-tactual knowledge in 8- and 9½- and 11-month old infants. *Infant Behavior and Development, 5,* 63–75.

Bushnell, E. W., & Boudreau, J. P. (1993). Motor development and the mind: The potential role of motor abilities as a determinant of aspects of perceptual development. *Child Development, 64,* 1005–1021.

Buss, A. H., & Plomin, R. (1984). *Temperament: Early developing personality traits.* Hillsdale, NJ: Erlbaum.

Buss, K. A., & Goldsmith, H. H. (1998). Fear and anger regulation in infancy: Effects on the temporal dynamics of affective expression. *Child Development, 69*(2), 359–374.

Butler, J., & Rovee-Collier, C. (1989). Contextual gating of memory retrieval. *Developmental Psychobiology, 22,* 533–552.

Butterworth, G. (1977). Object disappearance and error in Piaget's stage IV task. *Journal of Experimental Child Psychology, 23,* 391–401.

Butterworth, G. (1990). Self-perception in infancy. In D. Cicchetti & M. Beeghly (Eds.), *The self in transition: Infancy to childhood* (pp. 119–137). Chicago: University of Chicago Press.

Butterworth, G. (1993). Dynamic approaches to infant perception and action: Old and new theories about the origins of knowledge. In L. B. Smith & E. Thelen (Eds.), *A dynamic systems approach to development: Applications. MIT Press/Bradford Books series in cognitive psychology* (pp. 171–187). Cambridge, MA: MIT Press.

Butterworth, G. (2000). Joint visual attention in infancy. In J. G. Bremner & A. Fogel (Eds.), *Handbook of infancy research* (pp. 221–239). Oxford, England: Blackwell.

Butterworth, G., & Cochran, E. (1980). Towards a mechanism of joint visual attention in human infancy. *International Journal of Behavioral Development, 3,* 253–272.

Byers, T., Grahm, S., & Rzepka, T. (1985). Lactation and breast cancer: Evidence for a negative association in premenopausal women. *American Journal of Epidemiology, 121,* 664–674.

Cain, L. P., Kelly, D. H., & Shannon, D. C. (1980). Parents' perceptions of the psychological and social impact of home monitoring. *Pediatrics, 66,* 37–41.

Cairns, R. (1979). *Social development: The origins and plasticity of interchanges.* San Francisco: W. H. Freeman.

Caldera, Y. M., Huston, A. C., & O'Brien, M. (1989). Social interactions and play patterns of parents and toddlers with feminine, masculine, and neutral toys. *Child Development, 60,* 70–76.

Caldwell, B. M. (1986). Day care and early environmental adequacy. In W. Fowler (Ed.), Early experience and the development of competence. *New Directions for Child Development, 32,* 11–30.

Calhoun, M. L., Rose, T. L., Hanft, B., & Sturkey, C. (1991). Social reciprocity interventions: Implications for developmental therapists. Physical and Occupational Therapy in *Pediatrics, 11,* 45–56.

Calkins, S., & Fox, N. A. (1994). Individual differences in the biological aspects of temperament. In J. E. Bates & T. D. Wachs (Eds.), *Temperament: Individual differences at the interface of biology and behavior* (pp. 199–217). Washington, DC: American Psychological Association.

Calkins, S. D., & Johnson, M. C. (1998). Toddler regulation of distress to frustrating events: Temperamental and maternal correlates. *Infant Behavior and Development, 21*(3), 379–395.

Calkins, S. D., Fox, N. A., & Marshall, T. R. (1996). Behavioral and physiological antecedents of inhibited and uninhibited behavior. *Child Development, 67,* 523–540.

Calkins, S. D., Gill, K. L., Johnson, M. C., & Smith, C. L. (1999). Emotional reactivity and emotional regulation strategies as predictors of social behavior with peers during toddlerhood. *Social Development, 8*(3), 310–334.

Calkins, S. D., Smith, C. L., Gill, K. L., & Johnson, M. C. (1998). Maternal interactive style across contexts: Relations to emotional, behavioral, and physiological regulation during toddlerhood. *Social Development, 7*(3), 350–369.

Callaghan, J. W. (1981). A comparison of Anglo, Hopi, and Navajo mothers and infants. In T. M. Field, A. M. Sostek, P. Vietze, & P. H. Leiderman (Eds.), *Culture and early interactions* (pp. 503–536). Hillsdale, NJ: Erlbaum.

Callaghan, T. C. (1999). Early understanding and production of graphic symbols. *Child Development, 70*(6), 1314–1324.

Camaioni, L. (2000). Early language. In J. G. Bremner & A. Fogel (Eds.), *Handbook of infancy research* (pp. 605–635). Oxford, England: Blackwell.

Camaioni, L., Aureli, T., Bellagamba, F., & Fogel, A. (1999). *The transition from conventional to symbolic shared reference in mother-infant communication.* Paper presented at the 9th European Conference on Developmental Psychology.

Camaioni, L., Baumgartner, E., & Perucchini, P. (1991). Content and structure in toddlers' social competence with peers from 12 to 36 months of age. *Early Child Development and Care, 67,* 17–27.

Camaioni, L., Perucchini, P., Muratori, F. & Milone, A. (1997). A longitudinal examination of the communicative gestures deficit in young children with autism. *Journal of Autism and Developmental Disorders, 27,* 715–725.

Campbell, D. W., & Eaton, W. O. (1999). Sex differences in the activity level of infants. *Infant and Child Development, 8*(1), 1–17.

Campbell, S. B., Cohn, J. F., & Meyers, T. (1995). Depression in first-time mothers: Mother-infant interaction and depression chronicity. *Developmental Psychology, 31,* 349–357.

Campos, J. J. (1976). Heart rate: A sensitive tool for the study of emotional development in the infant. In L. P. Lipsitt (Ed.), *Developmental psychobiology: The significance of infancy* (pp. 405–426). Hillsdale, NJ: Erlbaum.

Campos, J. J., & Barrett, K. C. (1984). Toward a new understanding of emotions and their development. In C. E. Izard, J. Kagan, & R. B. Zajonc (Eds.), *Emotions, cognition, and behavior* (pp. 229–263). New York: Cambridge University Press.

Campos, J. J., Campos, R., & Barrett, K. (1989). Emergent themes in the study of emotional development and emotion regulation. *Developmental Psychology, 25*(3), 394–402.

Campos, J. J., Emde, R. N., Gaensbauer, T., & Henderson, C. (1975). Cardiac and behavioral interrelations in the reactions of infants to strangers. *Developmental Psychology, 11,* 589–601.

Campos, J. J., Langer, A., & Krowitz, A. (1970). Cardiac responses on the visual cliff in prelocomotor human infants. *Science, 170,* 196–197.

Campos, R. G. (1989). Soothing pain-elicited distress in infants with swaddling and pacifiers. *Child Development, 60,* 781–792.

Camras, L. A. (1993). A dynamic systems perspective on expressive development. In K. Strongman (Ed.), *International review of studies on emotion* (pp. 210–224). New York: Wiley.

Canfield, R. L., & Haith, M. M. (1991). Young infants' visual expectations for symmetric and asymmetric stimulus sequences. *Developmental Psychology, 27,* 198–208.

Caplan, M., Vespo, J., Pedersen, J., & Hay, D. F. (1991). Conflict and its resolution in small groups of one- and two-year-olds. *Child Development, 62,* 1513–1524.

Capra, F. (1996). *The web of life.* New York: Anchor Books.

Carew, J. V. (1980). Experience and the development of intelligence in young children at home and in day care. *Monographs of the Society for Research in Child Development, 45* (6-sup-7), 1–115.

Carlile, K. S., & Holstrum, W. J. (1989). Parental involvement behaviors: A comparison of Chamorro and Caucasian parents. *Infant Behavior and Development, 12,* 479–494.

Carlson, E. A. (1998). A prospective longitudinal study of attachment disorganization/disorientation. *Child Development, 69*(4), 1107–1128.

Carlson, V., Cicchetti, D., Barnett, D., & Braunwald, K. (1989). Disorganized/disoriented attachment relationships in maltreated infants. *Developmental Psychology, 25,* 525–531.

Carlsson, S. G., Fagerberg, H., Horneman, G., Hwang, C., Larsson, K., Rodholm, M., Schaller, J., Danielsson, B., & Gundewall, C. (1979). Effects of various amounts of contact between mother and child on the mother's nursing behavior: A follow-up study. *Infant Behavior and Development, 2,* 209–214.

Carmen, R. del, Pedersen, F. A., Huffman, L. C., & Bryan, Y. E. (1993). Dyadic distress management predicts subsequent security of attachment. *Infant Behavior and Development, 16,* 131–147.

Caron, A. J., Caron, R. F., & Antell, S. E. (1988). Infant understanding of containment: An affordance perceived or a relationship conceived? *Developmental Psychology, 24,* 620–627.

Caron, A. J., Caron, R. F., & Carlson, V. R. (1979). Infant perception of the invariant shape of objects varying in slant. *Child Development, 50,* 716–721.

Caron, A. J., Caron, R. F., & MacLean, D. J. (1988). Infant discrimination of naturalistic emotional expressions: The role of face and voice. *Child Development, 59,* 604–616.

Caron, R. F., Caron, A. J., & Myers, R. S. (1982). Abstraction of invariant face expressions in infancy. *Child Development, 53,* 1008–1015.

Carpenter, M., Akhtar, N., & Tomasello, M. (1998). Fourteen- through 18-month-old infants differentially imitate intentional and accidental actions. *Infant Behavior and Development, 21*(2), 315–330.

Carpenter, M., Nagell, K., & Tomasello, M. (1998). Social cognition, joint attention, and communicative competence from 9 to 15 months of age. *Monographs of the Society for Research in Child Development, 63*(4), 1–176.

Caruso, D. A. (1993). Dimensions of quality in infants' exploratory behavior: Relationships to problem-solving ability. *Infant Behavior and Development, 16,* 441–454.

Caspi, A., & Silva, P. A. (1995). Temperamental qualities at age three predict personality traits in young adulthood: Longitudinal evidence from birth cohort. *Child Development, 66,* 486–498.

Cassidy, J. (1994). Emotion regulation: Influences of attachment relationships. *Monographs of the Society for Research in Child Development, 59,* 228–249.

Cassidy, J., & Berlin, L. J. (1994). The insecure/ambivalent pattern of attachment: Theory and research. *Child Development, 65,* 971–991.

Cassidy, J. W., & Standley, J. M. (1995). The effect of music listening on physiological responses of premature infants in the NICU. *Journal of Music Therapy, 32*(4), 208–227.

Catherwood, D. (1993). The robustness of infant haptic memory: Testing its capacity to withstand delay and haptic interference. *Child Development, 64,* 702–710.

Caudill, W., & Weinstein, H. (1969). Maternal care and infant behavior in Japan and America. *Psychiatry, 32,* 12–43.

Caughy, M. O., DiPietro, J. A., & Strobino, D. M. (1994). Day-care participation as a protective factor in the cognitive development of low-income children. *Child Development, 65,* 457–471.

Centers for Disease Control (1995, June). Recommended childhood immunization schedule—United States, 1995. *Morbidity and Mortality Weekly Report, 44,* no. RR-5, 1–8.

Cernoch, J. M., & Porter, R. H. (1985). Recognition of maternal axillary odors by infants. *Child Development, 56,* 1593–1598.

Cervantes, C. A., & Callanan, M. A. (1998). Labels and explanations in mother-child emotion talk: Age and gender differentiation. *Developmental Psychology, 34*(1), 88–98.

Chandler, M., Fritz, A. S., & Hala, S. (1989). Small-scale deceit: Deception as a marker of two-, three-, and four-year-olds' early theories of mind. *Child Development, 60,* 1263–1277.

Charman, T., Swettenham, J., Baron-Cohen, S., Cox, A., Baird, G., & Drew, A. (1997). Infants with autism: An investigation of empathy, pretend play, joint attention, and imitation. *Developmental Psychology, 33*(5), 781–789.

Chase-Lansdale, P. L., & Owen, M. T. (1987). Maternal employment in a family context: Effects on infant-mother and infant-father attachments. *Child Development, 58,* 1505–1512.

Chen, Z., & Sanchez, R. P., & Campbell, T. (1997). From beyond to within their grasp: The rudiments of analogical problem solving in 10- to 13-month-olds. *Developmental Psychology, 33*(5), 790–801.

Cherlin, A. J., & Furstenberg, F. F., Jr. (1986). *The new American grandparent.* New York: Basic Books.

Chin-Quee, D. S., & Scarr, S. (1994). Lack of early child care effects on school-age children's social competence and academic achievement. *Early Development and Parenting, 3,* 103–112.

Chisholm, J. S. (1983). *Navajo infancy: An ethological study of child development.* New York: Aldine.

Chisholm, K. (1998). A three year follow-up of attachment and indiscriminate friendliness in children adopted from Romanian orphanages. *Child Development, 69*(4), 1092–1106.

Chomitz, V. R., Cheung, L. W. Y., & Liebermann, E. (1995). The role of lifestyle in preventing low birth weight. *The Future of Children, 5,* 121–138.

Chomsky, N. (1975). *Reflections on language.* New York: Pantheon.

Christensen, H., Poyser, C., Pollitt, P., & Cubis, J. (1999). Pregnancy may confer a selective cognitive advantage. *Journal of Reproductive and Infant Psychology, 17*(1), 7–25.

Chubet, C. T. (1988). *Feeding your baby: Breast, bottle, and baby foods.* Stamford, CT: Longmeadow Press.

Cicchetti, D., & Mans, L. (1976, September). *Down's syndrome and normal infants' responses to impending collision.* Paper presented at the meeting of the American Psychological Association, Washington, DC.

Cielinski, K. L., Vaughn, B. E., Seifer, R., & Contreras, J. (1995). Relations among sustained engagement during play, quality of play, and mother-child interaction in samples of children with Down syndrome and normally developing toddlers. *Infant Behavior and Development, 18*(2), 163–176.

Clark, E. V. (1978). Strategies for communicating. *Child Development, 49,* 953–959.

Clark, H. H., & Clark, E. V. (1977). *Psychology and language: An introduction to psycholinguistics.* New York: Harcourt Brace Jovanovich.

Clark, J. E., Truly, T. L., & Phillips, S. J. (1993). On the development of walking as a limit-cycle system. In L. B. Smith & E. Thelen (Eds.), *A dynamic systems approach to development: Applications* (pp. 71–93). Cambridge, MA: MIT Press.

Clark, J. E., Whitall, J., & Phillips, S. J. (1988). Human interlimb coordination: The first 6 months of independent walking. *Developmental Psychobiology, 21,* 445–456.

Clark, R., Hyde, J. S., Essex, M. J., & Klein, M. H. (1997). Length of maternity leave and quality of mother-infant interactions. *Child Development, 68*(2), 364–383.

Clarke-Stewart, A. (1978). And daddy makes three: The father's impact on mother and young child. *Child Development, 44,* 466–478.

Clarke-Stewart, A. (1984). Day care: A new context for research and development. In M. Perlmutter (Ed.), *Minnesota symposia on child psychology* (Vol. 17, pp. 1015–1034). Hillsdale, NJ: Erlbaum.

Clarke-Stewart, K. A. (1998). Historical shifts and underlying themes in ideas about rearing young children in the United States: Where have we been? Where are we going? *Early Development and Parenting, 7,* 101–117.

Clifton, R. K., Perris, E., & Bullinger, A. (1991). Infants' perception of auditory space. *Developmental Psychology, 27,* 187–197.

Clifton, R. K., Rochat, P., Litovsky, R. Y., & Perris, E. E. (1991). Object representation guides infants' reaching in the dark. *Journal of Experimental Psychology: Human Perception and Performance, 17,* 323–329.

Clifton, R. K., Rochat, P., Robin, D. J., & Berthier, N. E. (1994). Multimodal perception in the control of infant reaching. *Journal of Experimental Psychology: Human Perception and Performance, 20,* 876–886.

Coale, A. J., & Banister, J. (1994). Five decades of missing females in China. *Demography, 31,* 459–479.

Cofer, L. F., Grice, J. W., Sethre-Hofstad, L., Radi, C. J., Zimmerman, L. K., Palmer-Seal, D., & Santa-Maria, G. (1999). Developmental perspectives on morningness-eveningness and social interactions. *Human Development, 42,* 169–198.

Cogswell, M. E., Serdula, M. K., Hungerford, D. W., & Yip, R. (1995). Gestational weight gain among average-weight and overweight women: What is excessive? *American Journal of Obstetrics and Gynecology, 172,* 705–712.

Cohen, D. L. (1993). Stress Head Start quality, but spotlight 0–3. *Education Week, 12,* 10–20.

Cohen, L., Zilkha, S., Middleton, J., & O'Donnohue, N. (1978). Perinatal mortality: Assisting parental affirmation. *American Journal of Orthopsychiatry, 48,* 727–731.

Cohen, L. B., DeLoache, J. S., & Strauss, M. S. (1979). Infant visual perception. In J. Osofsky (Ed.), *Handbook of infant development* (pp. 419–435). New York: Wiley.

Cohen, L. B., & Oakes, L. M. (1993). How infants perceive a simple causal event. *Developmental Psychology, 29,* 421–433.

Cohen, L. B., & Strauss, M. S. (1979). Concept acquisition in the human infant. *Child Development, 50,* 419–424.

Cohen, L. J., & Campos, J. J. (1974). Father, mother and stranger as elicitors of attachment behaviors in infancy. *Developmental Psychology, 10,* 146–154.

Cohen, N. L., & Tomlinson-Keasey, C. (1980). The effects of peers and mothers on toddlers' play. *Child Development, 51,* 921–924.

Cohen, P., Kasen, S., Brook, J. S., & Hartmark, C. (1998). Behavior patterns of young children and their offspring: A two-generation study. *Developmental Psychology, 34*(6), 1202–1208.

Cohen, R. (1981). Factors influencing maternal choice of childbirth alternatives. *Journal of the American Academy of Child Psychiatry, 20,* 1–15.

Cohen, S. E., & Beckwith, L. (1979). Preterm infant intervention with the caregiver in the first year of life and competence at age two. *Child Development, 50,* 767–776.

Cohler, B. J., & Grunebaum, H. V. (1981). *Mothers, grandmothers, and daughters: Personality and childcare in three-generation families.* New York: Wiley.

Cohn, J. F., Campbell, S. B., Matias, R., & Hopkins, J. (1990). Face-to-face interactions of postpartum depressed and nondepressed mother-infant pairs at 2 months. *Developmental Psychology, 26*(1), 15–23.

Cohn, J. F., & Elmore, M. (1988). Effect of contingent changes in mothers' affective expression on the organization of behavior in 3-month-old infants. *Infant Behavior and Development, 11,* 493–505.

Cohn, J. F., Matias, R., Tronick, E. Z., Lyons-Ruth, K., & Connell, D. (1986). Face-to-face interactions, spontaneous and structured, of mothers with depressive symptoms. In T. Field & E. Z. Tronick (Eds.), *Maternal depression and child development, New directions for child development* (pp. 31–46). San Francisco: Jossey-Bass.

Cohn, J. F., & Tronick, E. Z. (1983). Three-month-old infants' reaction to simulated maternal depression. *Child Development, 54,* 185–193.

Cohn, J. F., & Tronick, E. Z. (1988). Mother-infant face-to-face interaction: Influence in bidirectional and unrelated to periodic cycles in either partner's behavior. *Developmental Psychology, 24*(3), 386–392.

Coldren, J. T., & Colombo, J. (1994). The nature and processes of preverbal learning: Implications from nine-month-old infants' discrimination problem solving. *Monographs of the Society for Research in Child Development, 59,* 1–94.

Cole, P. M., Barrett, K. C., & Zahn-Waxler, C. (1992). Emotion displays in two-year-olds during mishaps. *Child Development, 63,* 314–324.

Coleman, J. M., Pratt, R. R., Stoddard, R. A., Gerstmann, D. R., & Abel, H. H. (1997). The effects of the male and female singing and speaking voices on selected physiological and behavioral measures of premature infants in the intensive care unit. *International Journal of Arts Medicine, 5*(2), 4–11.

Coles, R. (1971). *The South goes north.* Boston: Little, Brown.

Coley, R. L., & Chase-Lansdale, P. L. (1998). Adolescent pregnancy and parenthood: Recent evidence and future directions. *American Psychologist, 53*(2), 152–166.

Coll, C. T. G., Halpern, L. F., Vohr, B. R., Seifer, R., & Oh, W. (1992). Stability and correlates of change of early temperament in preterm and full-term infants. *Infant Behavior and Development, 15,* 137–153.

Colletta, N. D. (1981). Social support and the risk of maternal rejection by adolescent mothers. *Journal of Psychology, 109,* 191–197.

Colletta, N. D., & Lee, D. (1983). The impact of support for black adolescent mothers. *Journal of Family Issues, 4,* 127–143.

Collins, J. E. (1994). Fetal surgery: Changing the outcome before birth. *Journal of Obstetrics, Gynecology & Neonatal Nursing, 23,* 166–169.

Collis, G. M., & Schaffer, H. R. (1975). Synchronization of visual attention in mother-infant pairs. *Journal of Child Psychology and Psychiatry, 16,* 315–320.

Colombo, J., Frick, J. E., Ryther, J. S., Coldren, J. T., & Mitchell, D. W. (1995). *Merrill-Palmer Quarterly, 41,* 104–113.

Colombo, J., Mitchell, D. W., Coldren, J. T., & Freeseman, L. J. (1991). Individual differences in infant visual attention: Are short lookers faster processors or feature processors? *Child Development, 62,* 1247–1257.

Colombo, J., Mitchell, D. W., O'Brien, M., & Horowitz, F. D. (1987). The stability of visual habituation during the first year of life. *Child Development, 58,* 474–487.

Colombo, J., Moss, M., & Horowitz, F. D. (1989). Neonatal state profiles: Reliability and short-term prediction of neurobehavioral status. *Child Development, 60,* 1102–1110.

Connell, J. P. (1985). A component process approach to the study of individual differences and developmental change in attachment system functioning. In M. E. Lamb, R. A. Thompson, W. Gardner, & E. L. Charnov, (Eds.), *Infant-mother attachment* (pp. 223–247). Hillsdale, NJ: Erlbaum.

Conner, J. M., & Nelson, E. C. (1999). Neonatal intensive care: Satisfaction measured from a parent's perspective. *Pediatrics, 103,* 336–349.

Connolly, K., & Dalgleish, M. (1989). The emergence of a tool-using skill in infancy. *Developmental Psychology, 25,* 894–912.

Conrad, R. (1998). Darwin's baby and baby's Darwin: Mutual recognition in observational research. *Human Development, 41*(1), 47–64.

Cooper, R. P., Abraham, J., Berman, S., & Staska, M. (1997). The development of infants' preference for motherese. *Infant Behavior and Development, 20*(4), 477–488.

Cooper, R. P., & Aslin, R. N. (1989). The language environment of the young infant: Implications for early perceptual development. *Canadian Journal of Psychology, 43,* 247–265.

Cooper, R. P., & Aslin, R. N. (1994). Developmental differences in infant attention to the spectral properties of infant-directed speech. *Child Development, 65,* 1663–1677.

Copstick, S., Taylor, K., Hayes, R., & Morris, N. (1986). The relation of time of day to childbirth. *Journal of Reproductive and Infant Psychology, 4*(1–2), 13–22.

Corkum, V., & Moore, C. (1995). Development of joint visual attention in infants. In C. Moore & P. J. Dunham (Eds.), *Joint attention: Its origins and role in development* (pp. 61–83). Hillsdale, NJ: Erlbaum.

Corter, C. (1977). Brief separation and communication between infant and mother. In T. Alloway, P. Pliner, & L. Krames (Eds.), *Attachment behavior* (pp. 143–168). New York: Plenum Press.

Corter, C., Abramovitch, R., & Pepler, D. J. (1983). The role of the mother in sibling interaction. *Child Development, 54,* 1599–1605.

Cossette, L., Malcuit, G., & Pomerleau, A. (1991). Sex differences in motor activity during early infancy. *Infant Behavior and Development, 14,* 175–186.

Coster, W. J., Gersten, M. S., Beeghly, M., & Cicchetti, D. (1989). Communicative functioning in maltreated toddlers. *Developmental Psychology, 25*(6), 1020–1029.

Cotterell, J. L. (1986). Work and community influences on the quality of child rearing. *Child Development, 57,* 362–374.

Cottrell, B. H., & Shannahan, M. K. (1987). A comparison of fetal outcome in birth chair and delivery table births. *Research in Nursing and Health, 10,* 239–243.

Cowan, C. P., & Cowan, P. A. (1981). *Couple role arrangements and satisfaction during family formation.* Boston: Society for Research in Child Development.

Cox, M. C., Owen, M. T., Henderson, V. K., & Margand, N. A. (1992). Prediction of infant-father and infant-mother attachment. *Developmental Psychology, 28,* 474–483.

Cox, M. C., Owen, M. T., Lewis, J. M., & Henderson, V. K. (1989). Marriage, adult adjustment, and early parenting. *Child Development, 60,* 1015–1024.

Crain-Thoreson, C., & Dale, P. (1992). Do early talkers become early readers? Linguistic precocity, preschool language, and emergent literacy. *Developmental Psychology, 28,* 421–429.

Craton, L. G. (1996). The development of perceptual completion abilities: Infants' perception of stationary, partially occluded objects. *Child Development, 67*(3), 890–904.

Cravioto, J., & Arrieta, R. (1983). Malnutrition in childhood. In M. Rutter (Ed.), *Developmental neuropsychiatry* (pp. 515–538). New York: Guilford Press.

Crawford, J. W. (1982). Mother-infant interaction in premature and full-term infants. *Child Development, 53,* 957–962.

Crittenden, P. M. (1985). Social networks, quality of child rearing, and child development. *Child Development, 56,* 1299–1313.

Crnic, K., & Greenberg, M. (1987). Maternal stress, social support, and coping: Influences on the early mother-child relationship. In C. Boukydis (Ed.), *Research on support for parents and infants in the postnatal period* (pp. 25–40). Norwood, NJ: Ablex.

Crockenberg, S. B. (1981). Infant irritability, mother responsiveness, and social support influences on the security of infant-mother attachment. *Child Development, 52,* 857–865.

Crockenberg, S. B. (1987). Support for adolescent mothers during the postnatal period: Theory and research. In C. Boukydis (Ed.), *Research on support for parents and infants in the postnatal period* (pp. 3–24). Norwood, NJ: Ablex.

Crockenberg, S. B., & Acredolo, C. (1983). Infant temperament ratings: A function of infants, of mothers, or both? *Infant Behavior and Development, 6,* 61–72.

Crockenberg, S. B., & McCluskey, K. (1986). Change in maternal behavior during the baby's first year of life. *Child Development, 57,* 746–753.

Crockenberg, S. B., & Smith, P. (1982). Antecedents of mother-infant interaction and infant irritability in the first three months of life. *Infant Behavior and Development, 6,* 61–72.

Cronin, C. M. G., Shapiro, C. R., Casiro, O. G., & Cheang, M. S. (1995). The impact of very low-birth-weight infants on the family is long lasting. *Archives of the Pediatric and Adolescent Medicine, 149,* 151–158.

Crook, C. K. (1978). Taste perception in the newborn infant. *Infant Behavior and Development, 1,* 52–69.

Crouter, A. C., Perry-Jenkins, M., Huston, T. L., & McHale, S. M. (1987). Processes underlying father involvement in dual-earner and single-earner families. *Developmental Psychology, 23,* 431–440.

Crowley, P. H., Gulati, D. K., Hayden, T. L., Lopez, P., & Dyer, R. A. (1979). A chiasma-hormonal hypothesis relating Down's syndrome and maternal age. *Nature, 280,* 417–419.

Cruz-Sanchez, F. F., Lucena, J., Ascaso, C., Tolosa, E., Quinto, L., & Rossi, M. L. (1997). Cerebellar cortex delayed maturation in sudden infant death syndrome. *Journal of Neuropathology and Experimental Neurology, 56*(4), 340–346.

Cuisinier, M., Janssen, H., de Graauw, D., & Hoogduin, K. (1998). Predictors of maternal reactions to excessive crying of newborns. Findings from a prospective study in a naturalistic situation. *Early Development and Parenting, 7,* 41–49.

Cummings, J. S., Pellegrini, D. S., Notarius, C. I., & Cummings, E. M. (1989). Children's responses to angry adult behavior as a function of marital distress and history of interparent hostility. *Child Development, 60,* 1035–1043.

Curry, M. (1979). Contact during the first hour with the wrapped or naked newborn: Effect on maternal attachment at 36 hours and three months. *Birth and the Family Journal, 6,* 227–235.

Cutillo, D. M., Hammond, E. A., Reeser, S. L., Kershner, M. A., Lukin, B., Godmilow, L., & Donnenfeld, A. E. (1994). Chorionic villus sampling utilization following reports of a possible association with fetal limb defects. *Prenatal Diagnosis, 14,* 327–332.

Dahl, R. E., Scher, M. S., Williamson, D. E., Robles, N., & Day, N. (1995). A longitudinal study of prenatal marijuana use: Effects of sleep and arousal at age 3 years. *Archives of Pediatric and Adolescent Medicine, 149,* 145–150.

Dale, P. S. (1976). *Language development: Structure and function* (2nd ed.). New York: Holt, Rinehart and Winston.

Damast, A. M., Tamis-LeMonda, C. S., & Bornstein, M. H. (1996). Mother-child play: Sequential interactions and the relation between maternal beliefs and behaviors. *Child Development, 67*(4), 1752–1766.

Danforth, D. N. (Ed.) (1977). *Obstetrics and gynecology* (3rd ed.). New York: Harper & Row.

Daniels, D., Plomin, R., & Greenhalgh, J. (1984). Correlates of difficult temperament in infancy. *Child Development, 55,* 1184–1194.

Dannemiller, J. L., & Stephens, B. R. (1988). A critical test of infant pattern preference models. *Child Development, 59,* 210–216.

Darj, E., & Nordstrom, M. L. (1999). The Misgav Ladach method for ceasarean section compared to the Pfanenstiel method. *Acta Obstetrica et Gynecologica Scandinavica, 78,* 37–41.

Darwin, C. R. (1859). *The origin of species.* New York: Modern Library.

Davenport-Slack, B., & Boylan, C. H. (1974). Psychological correlates of childbirth pain. *Psychosomatic Medicine, 36,* 215–223.

Davis, D. (1967). Family process in mental retardation. *American Journal of Psychiatry, 124,* 340–350.

Davis, D. (1985). Infant car safety: The role of perinatal caregivers. *Birth, 12*(Supplement), 21–27.

Davis, H. (1978). A description of aspects of mother-infant vocal interaction. *Journal of Child Psychology and Psychiatry, 19,* 379–386.

Dawson, G., Frey, K., Panagiotides, H., Yamada, E., Hessl, D., & Osterling, J. (1999). Infants of depressed mothers exhibit atypical frontal electrical brain activity during interactions with mother and with a familiar, nondepressed adult. *Child Development, 70*(5), 1058–1066.

DeBoysson-Bardies, B. (1990). Some reflexions on sensory-motor organization of speech during the first year of life. In H. Bloch & B. I. Bertenthal (Eds.), *Sensory-motor organizations and development in infancy and early childhood* (pp. 457–466). The Netherlands: Kluwer Academic.

DeBoysson-Bardies, B., Sagant, L., & Durand, C. (1984). Discernible differences in the babbling of infants according to target language. *Journal of Child Language, 11,* 1–15.

DeCasper, A. J., & Fifer, W. P. (1980). Of human bonding: Newborns prefer their mothers' voices. *Science, 208,* 1174–1176.

DeCasper, A. J., & Sigafoos, A. D. (1983). The intrauterine heartbeat: A potent reinforcer for newborns. *Infant Behavior and Development, 6,* 19–26.

DeCasper, A. J., & Spence, M. J. (1986). Prenatal maternal speech influences newborns' perception of speech sounds. *Infant Behavior and Development, 9,* 133–150.

DeChateau, P. (1980). Early post-partum contact and later attitudes. *International Journal of Behavioral Development, 3,* 273–286.

DeChateau, P. (1987). Parent-infant socialization in several western European countries. In J. D. Osofsky (Ed.), *Handbook of infant development* (2nd ed., pp. 642–668). New York: Wiley.

Delevati, N. M., & Bergamasco, N. H. P. (1999). Pain in the neonate: An analysis of facial movements and crying in response to nociceptive stimuli. *Infant Behavior and Development, 22*(1), 137–143.

DeLoache, J. S., & Plaetzer, B. (1985, April). *Tea for two: Joint mother-child symbolic play.* Presented at the meeting of the Society for Research in Child Development, Toronto, Canada.

DeLoache, J. S., Sugarman, S., & Brown, A. L. (1985). The development of error correction strategies in young children's manipulative play. *Child Development, 56,* 928–939.

DeMeis, D. K., Hock, E., & McBride, S. L. (1986). The balance of employment and motherhood: Longitudinal study of mothers' feelings about separation from their first-born infants. *Developmental Psychology, 22,* 627–632.

Demos, V. E. (1982). Facial expressions of infants and toddlers: A descriptive analysis. In T. Field & A. Fogel (Eds.), *Emotion and early interaction* (pp. 188–209). Hillsdale, NJ: Erlbaum.

den Bak, I. M., & Ross, H. S. (1996). I'm telling: The content, context, and consequences of children's tattling on their siblings. *Social Development, 5*(3), 292–309.

Denham, S. (1986). Social cognition, prosocial behavior and emotion in preschoolers: Contextual validation. *Child Development, 57,* 194–201.

Denzin, N. K. & Lincoln, Y. S. (1994). *Handbook of qualitative research.* Thousand Oaks, CA: Sage Publications.

Desor, J. A., Miller, O., & Turner, R. (1973). Taste in acceptance of sugars by human infants. *Journal of Comparative and Physiological Psychology, 85,* 496–501.

Desrochers, S., Morissette, P., & Ricard, M. (1995). Two perspectives on pointing in infancy. In C. Moore & P. J. Dunham (Eds.), *Joint attention: Its origins and role in development* (pp. 85–101). Hillsdale, NJ: Erlbaum.

DeStefano, C. T., & Mueller, E. (1982). Environmental determinants of peer social activity in 18-month-old males. *Infant Behavior and Development, 5,* 175–183.

deVilliers, J. C., & deVilliers, P. A. (1973). A cross-sectional study of the acquisition of grammatical morphemes in child speech. *Journal of Pyscholinguistic Research, 2,* 267–278.

De Wolff, M. S., & van Ijzendoorn, M. H. (1997). Sensitivity and attachment: A meta-analysis on parental antecedents of infant attachment. *Child Development, 68*(4), 571–591.

Diamond, A. (1988). Abilities and neural mechanisms underlying AB performance. *Child Development, 59,* 523–527.

Diamond, A., & Doar, B. (1989). The performance of human infants on a measure of frontal cortex function, the delayed response task. *Developmental Psychobiology, 22*(3), 271–294.

Diamond, A., Prevor, M. B., Callender, G., & Druin, D. P. (1997). Prefrontal cortex cognitive deficits in children treated early and continuously for PKU. *Monographs of the Society for Research in Child Development, 62*(4), 1–205.

Dick-Read, G. (1972). *Childbirth without fear: The original approach to natural childbirth* (Rev. ed.). H. Wessel & H. Ellis (Eds.). New York: Harper & Row. (Original work published 1933)

Dickson, K. L., Fogel, A., & Messinger, D. (1997). The social context of smiling and laughter in infants. In M. Mascolo & S. Griffen (Eds.), *The development of emotion* (pp. 253–273). New York: Plenum Press.

Dickson, K. L., Walker, H., & Fogel, A. (1997). The relationship between smile-type and play-type during parent-infant play. *Developmental Psychology, 33,* 925–933.

Dickstein, S., & Parke, R. D. (1988). Social referencing in infancy: A glance at fathers and marriage. *Child Development, 59,* 506–511.

DiLalla, L. F., & Watson, M. W. (1988). Differentiation of fantasy and reality: Preschoolers' reactions to interruptions in their play. *Developmental Psychology, 24,* 286–291.

DiPietro, J. A., Hodgson, D. M., Costigan, K. A., & Johnson, T. R. B. (1996). Fetal neurobehavioral development. *Child Development, 67*(5), 2553–2567.

DiPietro, J. A., Larson, S. K., & Porges, S. W. (1987). Behavioral and heart rate pattern differences between breast-fed and bottle-fed neonates. *Developmental Psychology, 23*(4), 467–474.

Dittrichová, J., Brichacek, V., Mandys, F., Paul, K., Sobotkova, D., Tautermannova, M., Vondracek, J., & Zezulakova, J. (1996). Relationship of early behavior to later developmental outcome for preterm children. *International Journal of Behavioral Development, 19*(3), 517–532.

Dixon, S. D., LeVine, R. A., Richman, A., & Brazelton, T. B. (1984). Mother-child interaction around a teaching task: An African-American comparison. *Child Development, 55,* 1252–1264.

Dondi, M. (1999). Maturità e specificità del comportamento facciale nelle più precoci fasi dello sviluppo. *Giornale Italiano di Psicologia, 26*(1), 23–53.

Dondi, M., Simion, F., & Caltran, G. (1999). Can newborns discriminate between their own cry and the cry of another newborn infant? *Developmental Psychology, 35*(2), 418–426.

Donovan, W. L., & Leavitt, L. A. (1989). Maternal self-efficacy and infant attachment: Integrating physiology, perceptions, and behavior. *Child Development, 60,* 460–472.

Donovan, W. L., Leavitt, L. A., & Walsh, R. O. (1998). Conflict and depression predict maternal sensitivity to infant cries. *Infant Behavior and Development, 21*(3), 505–517.

Dougherty, T. M., & Haith, M. M. (1997). Infant expectations and reaction time as predictors of childhood speed of processing and IQ. *Developmental Psychology, 33*(1), 146–155.

Dow, K. E., & Reopelli, R. J. (1985). Ethanol neurotoxicity: Effects on neurite formation and neutrotrophic factor production in vitro. *Science, 228,* 591–593.

Drachman, D. B., & Coulombre, A. J. (1962). Experimental clubfoot and arthorogryposis multiplex congenita. *Lancet, 2,* 523–536.

Dragonas, R., Petrogiannis, K., & Adam, H. (1997). Working women, their emotional well-being and pregnancy in Greece. *Journal of Reproductive and Infant Psychology, 15,* 239–256.

Dressler, W. (1985). Extended family relationships, social support, and mental health in a southern black community. *Journal of Health and Social Behavior, 26,* 39–48.

Drotar, D., & Irvin, N. (1979). Disturbed maternal bereavement following infant death. *Child Care, Health and Development, 5,* 239–247.

Dubowitz, L. M. S., Dubowitz, V., & Goldberg, C. (1970). Clinical assessment of gestational age in the newborn infant. *Journal of Pediatrics, 77,* 1–10.

Dull, H. (1997). *Watsu: Freeing the body in water* (2nd ed.). Harbin, CA: Harbin Springs.

Dunham, P. J., & Dunham, F. (1995). Developmental antecedents of taxonomic and thematic strategies. *Developmental Psychology, 31,* 483–493.

Dunham, P. J., & Dunham, F. (1996). The semantically reciprocating robot: Adult influences on children's early conversational skills. *Social Development, 5*(3), 261–274.

Dunham, P. J., Dunham, F., & Curwin, A. (1993). Joint-attentional states and lexical acquisition at 18 months. *Developmental Psychology, 29,* 827–831.

Dunham, P. J., Dunham, F., Hurshman, A., & Alexander, T. (1989). Social contingency effects on subsequent perceptual-cognitive tasks in young infants. *Child Development, 60,* 1486–1496.

Dunham, P. J., Dunham, F., Tran, S., & Akhtar, N. (1991). The nonreciprocating robot: Effects on verbal discourse, social play, and social referencing at two years of age. *Child Development, 62,* 1489–1502.

Dunn, D. T., Newell, M. L., Ades, A. E., & Peckham, C. S. (1992). Risk of human immunodeficiency virus type 1 transmission through breastfeeding. *Lancet, 340,* 585–588.

Dunn, J. (1975). Consistency and change in styles of mothering. In Ciba Foundation Symposium (Ed.), *Parent-infant interaction* (pp. 108–135). New York: Elsevier.

Dunn, J. (1998). Siblings, emotion, and the development of understanding. In S. Bråten (Ed.), *Intersubjective communication and emotion in early ontogeny. Studies in emotion and social interaction, 2nd series* (pp. 158–168). Cambridge, England: Cambridge University Press.

Dunn, J., Bretherton, I., & Munn, P. (1987). Conversations about feeling states between mothers and their young children. *Developmental Psychology, 23,* 132–139.

Dunn, J., & Kendrick, C. (1980). Interactions between young siblings in the context of family relationships. In M. Lewis & L. Rosenblum

(Eds.), *The child and its family* (pp. 334–369). New York: Plenum Press.

Dunn, J., & Kendrick, C. (1981). Social behavior of young siblings in the family context: Differences between same-sex and different-sex dyads. *Child Development, 52,* 1265–1273.

Dunn, J., & Kendrick, C. (1982). *Siblings: love, envy, and understanding.* Cambridge, MA: Harvard University Press.

Dunn, J., Kreps, C., & Brown, J. (1996). Children's family relationships between two and five: Developmental changes and individual differences. *Social Development, 5*(3), 230–250.

Dunn, J., & Munn, P. (1985). Becoming a family member: Family conflict and the development of social understanding in the second year. *Child Development, 56,* 480–492.

Dunn, J., & Munn, P. (1987). Development of justification in disputes with mother and sibling. *Developmental Psychology, 23,* 791–798.

Dunn, J., Plomin, R., & Daniels, D. (1986). Consistency and change in mothers' behavior toward young siblings. *Child Development, 57,* 348–356.

Dunn, J., & Shatz, M. (1989). Becoming a conversationalist despite (or because of) having an older sibling. *Child Development, 60,* 399–410.

Dunsmore, J. C., & Halberstadt, A. G. (1997). How does family emotional expressiveness affect children's schemas? In K. C. Barrett (Ed.), *New directions in child development: The communication of emotion: Current research from diverse perspectives, 77* (pp. 45–68). San Francisco: Jossey-Bass.

Dupont, F. (1989). *Daily life in ancient Rome* (C. Woodall, Trans.). Oxford, England: Blackwell.

Dworetzky, J. P., & Davis, N. J. (1989). *Human development: A life span approach.* St. Paul, MN: West.

Dyer, A. B., Lickliter, R., & Gottlieb, G. (1989). Maternal and peer imprinting in mallard ducklings under experimentally simulated natural social conditions. *Developmental Psychobiology, 22,* 463–475.

Dyregrov, A., & Matthiesen, S. B. (1987). Stillbirth, neonatal death, and sudden infant death (SIDS): Parental reactions. *Scandinavian Journal of Psychology, 28,* 104–114.

Eakins, P. S. (Ed.). (1986). *The American way of birth.* Philadelphia: Temple University Press.

Easterbrooks, M. A. (1989). Quality of attachment to mother and to father: Effects of perinatal risk status. *Child Development, 60,* 825–830.

Easterbrooks, M. A., & Goldberg, W. (1984). Toddler development in the family: Impact of father involvement and parenting characteristics. *Child Development, 55,* 740–752.

Easterbrooks, M. A., & Goldberg, W. (1985). Effects of early maternal employment on toddlers, mothers, and fathers. *Developmental Psychology, 21,* 774–783.

Ebert, J. D., & Sussex, I. M. (1970). *Interacting systems in development* (2nd ed.). New York: Holt, Rinehart and Winston.

Eckerman, C. O. (1993). Toddler's achievement of coordinated action with conspecifics: A dynamic systems perspective. In L. B. Smith & E. Thelen (Eds.), *A dynamic systems approach to development: Applications* (pp. 333–357). Cambridge, MA: MIT Press.

Eckerman, C. O., & Whatley, J. L. (1977). Toys and social interaction between infant peers. *Child Development, 48,* 1645–1656.

Eckerman, C. O., Davis, C. C., & Didow, S. M. (1989). Toddlers' emerging ways of achieving social coordinations with a peer. *Child Development, 60,* 440–453.

Eckerman, C. O., & Didow, S. M. (1989). Toddlers' social coordinations: Changing responses to another's invitation to play. *Developmental Psychology, 25,* 794–804.

Eckerman, C. O., Hsu, H., Molitor, A., Leung, E. H. L., & Goldstein, R. F. (1999). Infant arousal in an en-face exchange with a new partner: Effects of prematurity and perinatal biological risk. *Developmental Psychology, 35*(1), 282–293.

Eckerman, C. O., Oehler, J. M., Medvin, M. B., & Hannan, T. E. (1994). Premature newborns as social partners before term age. *Infant Behavior and Development, 17,* 55–70.

Eckerman, C. O., & Stein, M. R. (1990). How imitation begets imitation and toddlers' generation of games. *Developmental Psychology, 26,* 370–378.

Eckerman, C. O., & Whatley, J. L. (1975). Infants' reactions to unfamiliar adults varying in novelty. *Developmental Psychology, 11,* 562–566.

Eckerman, C. O., Whatley, J. L., & Kutz, S. (1975). Growth of social play with peers during the second year of life. *Developmental Psychology, 11,* 42–49.

Eckerman, C. O., Whatley, J. L., & McGehee, L. J. (1979). Approaching and contacting the object another manipulates: A social skill of the one-year-old. *Developmental Psychology, 15,* 585–593.

Edwards, C. P. (1984). The age group labels and categories of preschool children. *Child Development, 55,* 440–452.

Egeland, B., & Hiester, M. (1995). The long-term consequences of infant day-care and mother-infant attachment. *Child Development, 66,* 474–485.

Egeland, B., & Sroufe, L. A. (1981). Developmental sequelae of maltreatment in infancy. *New Directions for Child Development, 11,* 77–92.

Eilers, R. E., & Gavin, W. J. (1981). The evaluation of infant speech perception skills: Statistical techniques and theory development. In R. Stark (Ed.), *Language behavior in infancy and early childhood* (pp. 219–243). New York: Elsevier.

Eilers, R. E., Oller, D. K., Levine, S., Basinger, D., Lynch, M. P., & Urbano, R. (1993). The role of prematurity and socioeconomic status in the onset of canonical babbling in infants. *Infant Behavior and Development, 16,* 297–315.

Eimas, P. D., & Quinn, P. C. (1994). Studies on the formation of perceptually based basic-level categories in young infants. *Child Development, 65,* 903–917.

Eimas, P. D., Siqueland, E. R., Jusczyk, P., & Vigorito, J. (1971). Speech perception in infants. *Science, 171,* 303–306.

Einspieler, C., Widder, J., Holzer, A., & Kenner, T. (1988). The predictive value of behavioral risk factors for sudden infant death. *Early Human Development, 18,* 101–109.

Eisenberg, R. B. (1976). *Auditory competence in early life.* Baltimore: University Park Press.

Eizirik, L. S., Bohlin, G., & Hagekull, B. (1994). Interaction between mother and pre-term infant at 34 weeks post-conceptional age. *Early Development and Parenting, 3,* 171–180.

Elder, G., Nguyen, T., & Caspi, A. (1985). Linking family hardship to children's lives. *Child Development, 56,* 361–375.

Ellis, S., & Rogoff, B. (1982). The strategies and efficacy of child versus adult teachers. *Child Development, 53,* 730–735.

Ellsworth, C. P., Muir, D. W., & Hains, S. M. J. (1993). Social competence and person-object differentiation: An analysis of the still-face effect. *Developmental Psychology, 29*(1), 63–73.

Emde, R. N., Gaensbauer, T. J., & Harmon, R. J. (1976). Emotional expression in infancy. *Psychological Issues, 10*(1).

Emde, R. N., Plomin, R., Robinson, J., Corley, R., DeFries, J., Fulker, D. W., Reznick, J. S., Campos, J., Kagan, J., & Zahn-Waxler, C. (1992). Temperament, emotion, and cognition at fourteen months: The MacArthur longitudinal twin study. *Child Development, 63,* 1437–1455.

Entwisle, D. R., & Alexander, K. L. (1987). Long-term effects of cesarean delivery on parents' beliefs and children's schooling. *Developmental Psychology, 23,* 676–682.

Entwisle, D. R., & Doering, S. (1981). *The first birth: A turning point.* Baltimore: John Hopkins University Press.

Erickson, M. F., Sroufe, L. A., & Egeland, B. (1985). Relationship between quality of attachment and behavior problems in preschool in a high-risk sample. In I. Bretherton & E. Waters (Eds.), *Growing points of attachment theory and research. Monographs of the Society for Research in Child Development, 50* (Serial No. 209), 147–166.

Erikson, E. (1950). *Childhood and society.* New York: Norton.

Escalona, S. K., & Corman, H. H. (1968). *Albert Einstein scales of sensorimotor development.* Unpublished manuscript.

Escobar, G. J., Yanover, M., Gardner, M. N., Goembeski, D., Armstrong, M. A., Shum, F., & Kipnis P. (1998). Structured review of neonatal deaths in a managed care organization. *Pediatric Perinatal Epidemiology, 12*(4), 422–436.

Espy, K. A., Riese, M. L., & Francis, D. J. (1997). Neurobehavior in preterm neonates exposed to cocaine, alcohol, and tobacco. *Infant Behavior and Development, 20*(3), 297–309.

Eyer, D. (1996). *Motherguilt: How our culture blames mothers for what's wrong with society.* New York: Random House.

Fabrena, H., Jr., & Nutini, H. (1994). Sudden infant and child death as a cultural phenomenon: A Tlaxcalan case study. *Psychiatry, 57,* 225–243.

Fagan, J. F. (1979). The origins of facial pattern recognition. In M. H. Bornstein and W. Kessen (Eds.), *Psychological development from infancy: Image to intention* (pp. 616–649). Hillsdale, NJ: Erlbaum.

Fagard, J., & Jacquet, A. (1989). Onset of bimanual coordination and symmetry versus asymmetry of movement. *Infant Behavior and Development, 12,* 229–235.

Fagen, J. W., Ohr, P. S., Singer, J. M., & Klein, S. J. (1989). Crying and retrograde amnesia in young infants. *Infant Behavior and Development, 12,* 13–24.

Fagen, J. W., Prigot, J., Carroll, M., Pioli, L., Stein, A., & Franco, A. (1997). Auditory context and memory retrieval in young infants. *Child Development, 68*(6), 1057–1066.

Fagot, B. I. (1997). Attachment, parenting, and peer interactions of toddler children. *Developmental Psychology, 33*(3), 489–499.

Fagot, B. I., & Hagan, R. (1991). Observations of parent reactions to sex-stereotyped behaviors: Age and sex effects. *Child Development, 62,* 617–628.

Fagot, B. I., & Kavanagh, K. (1993). Parenting during the second year: Effects of children's age, sex, and attachment classification. *Child Development, 64,* 258–271.

Fagot, B. I., & Leinbach, M. D. (1989). The young child's gender schema: Environmental input, internal organization, *Child Development, 60,* 663–672.

Fagot, B. I., & Leinbach, M. D., & Hagan, R. (1990). Gender labeling and the adoption of sex-typed behaviors. *Developmental Psychology, 22,* 440–443.

Fagot, B. I., Leinbach, M. D., & O'Boyle, C. (1992). Gender labeling, gender stereotyping, and parenting behaviors. *Developmental Psychology, 28,* 225–230.

Falkner, F. (Ed.) (1985). *Prevention of infant mortality and morbidity.* Basel, Switzerland: Karger.

Fantz, R. L. (1961). The origin of form perception. *Scientific American, 204,* 66–72.

Fantz, R. L., Fagan, J. F., & Miranda, S. B. (1975). Early visual selection. In L. B. Cohen & P. Salapatek (Eds.), *Infant perception: From sensation to cognition* (Vol. 1, pp. 130–155). New York: Academic Press.

Fares, S. L., & Adler, N. E. (1998). "Top-of-the-head" descriptions of baby and self: Links to reported health behaviors and social context in early pregnancy. *Journal of Social and Personal Relationships, 15*(4), 555–564.

Farran, D. C., & Haskins, R. (1980). Reciprocal influence in the social interactions of mothers and three-month-old children from different socioeconomic backgrounds. *Child Development, 51,* 780–791.

Farver, J. M., & Howes, C. (1993). Cultural differences in American and Mexican mother-child pretend play. *Merrill-Palmer Quarterly, 39,* 344–358.

Farver, J. M., & Wimbarti, S. (1995). Paternal participation in toddlers' pretend play. *Social Development, 4,* 17–29.

Feeney, G. (1994). Fertility decline in East Asia. *Science, 266,* 1518–1523.

Fein, R. (1976). The first weeks of fathering: The importance of choices and supports for new parents. *Birth and the Family Journal, 3,* 53–58.

Feiring, C., Fox, N. A., Jaskir, J., & Lewis, M. (1987). The relation between social support, infant risk status and mother-infant interaction. *Developmental Psychology, 23,* 400–405.

Feiring, C., & Lewis, M. (1981). Middle class differences in cognitive development. In T. M. Field, A. M., Sostek, P. Vietze, & P. H. Leiderman (Eds.), *Culture and early interactions* (pp. 73–97). Hillsdale, NJ: Erlbaum.

Feiring, C. Lewis, M., & Starr, M. D. (1984). Indirect effects and infants' reactions to strangers. *Developmental Psychology, 20,* 485–491.

Feldenkrais, M. (1981). *The elusive obvious.* Cupertino, CA: Meta Publications.

Feldman, R., Greenbaum, C. W., & Yirmiya, N. (1999). Mother-infant affect synchrony as an antecedent of the emergence of self-control. *Developmental Psychology, 35*(1), 223–231.

Feldman, S. S., & Nash, S. C. (1978). Interest in babies during young adulthood. *Child Development, 49,* 617–622.

Feldman, S. S., & Nash, S. C. (1979a). Changes in responsiveness to babies during adolescence. *Child Development, 50,* 942–949.

Feldman, S. S., & Nash, S. C. (1979b). Sex differences in responsiveness to babies among mature adults. *Developmental Psychology, 15,* 430–436.

Feldman, S. S., & Nash, S. C. (1986). Antecedents of early parenting. In A. Fogel & G. F. Melson (Eds.), *Origins of nurturance: Developmental, biological, and cultural perspectives on caregiving* (pp. 128–136). Hillsdale, NJ: Erlbaum.

Fenson, C., Kagan, J., Kearsley, R. B., & Zelazo, P. R. (1976). The developmental progression of manipulative play in the first two years. *Child Development, 47,* 232–236.

Fenson, L., Sapper, V., & Minner, D. G. (1974). Attention and manipulative play in the one-year-old child. *Child Development, 45,* 757–764.

Ferland, M. B., & Mendelson, M. J. (1989). Infants' categorization of melodic contour. *Infant Behavior and Development, 12,* 341–355.

Fernald, A. (1985). Four-month-old infants prefer to listen to motherese. *Infant Behavior and Development, 8,* 181–195.

Fernald, A. (1989). Intonation and communicative intent in mothers' speech to infants: Is the melody the message? *Child Development, 60,* 1497–1510.

Fernald, A. (1993). Approval and disapproval: Infant responsiveness to vocal affect in familiar and unfamiliar languages. *Child Development, 64,* 657–674.

Fernald, A., & Kuhl, P. (1987). Acoustic determinants of infant preference for motherese speech. *Infant Behavior and Development, 10,* 279–293.

Fernald, A., & Morikawa, H. (1993). Common themes and cultural variations in Japanese and American mothers' speech to infants. *Child Development, 64,* 637–656.

Fernald, A., & Simon, T. (1984). Expanded intonation contours in mothers' speech to newborns. *Developmental Psychology, 20,* 104–113.

Fernald, A., Taeschner, T., Dunn, J., Papousek, M., DeBoysson-Bardies, B., & Fukui, I. (1989). A cross-language study of prosodic modifications in mothers' and fathers' speech to preverbal infants, *Journal of Child Language, 16,* 477–501.

Field, T. (1979). Differential behavioral and cardiac responses of 3-month-old infants to mirror and peer. *Infant Behavior and Development, 2,* 179–84.

Field, T. (1981a). Interaction coaching for high-risk infants and their parents. In H. Moss (Ed.), *Prevention and human sciences* (pp. 316–333). New York: Haworth Press.

Field, T. (1981b). Infant arousal, attention and affect during early interactions. In L. P. Lipsitt & C. Rovee-Collier (Eds.), *Advances in infancy research* (Vol. 1, pp. 121–144). Norwood, NJ: Ablex.

Field, T. (1982). Affective and physiological changes during manipulated interactions of high-risk infants. In T. Field & A. Fogel (Eds.), *Emotion and early interaction* (pp. 480–501). Hillsdale, NJ: Erlbaum.

Field, T. (1987). Affective and interactive disturbances in infants. In J. D. Osofsky (Ed.), *Handbook of infant development* (2nd ed., pp. 70–91). New York: Wiley.

Field, T. (1991). Young children's adaptations to repeated separations from their mothers. *Child Development, 61,* 539–547.

Field, T. (1994). The effects of mother's physical and emotional unavailability on emotion regulation. *Monographs of the Society for Research in Child Development, 59,* 208–227.

Field, T. (1998). Maternal depression effects on infants and early interventions. *Preventive Medicine, 27,* 200–203.

Field, T. (1998). Touch therapy effects on development. *International Journal of Behavioral Development, 22*(4), 779–797.

Field, T., Dempsey, J. R., Hatch, J., Ting, G., & Clifton, R. K. (1979). Cardiac and behavioral responses to repeated tactile and auditory stimulation by preterm and term neonates. *Developmental Psychology, 15,* 406–416.

Field, T., Gewirtz, J. L., Cohen, D., Garcia, R., Greenberg, R., & Collins, K. (1984). Leave-takings and reunions of infants, toddlers, preschoolers, and their parents. *Child Development, 55,* 628–635.

Field, T., Greenberg, R., Woodson, R., Cohen, D., & Garcia, R. (1984). A descriptive study on the facial expressions of infants during Brazelton neonatal assessments. *Infant Mental Health Journal, 5,* 61–71.

Field, T., Grizzle, N., Scafidi, F., Abrams, S., Richardson, S., Kuhn, C., & Schanberg, S. (1996). Massage therapy for infants of depressed mothers. *Infant Behavior and Development, 19,* 107–112.

Field, T., Grizzle, N., Scafidi, F., & Schanberg, S. (1996). Massage and relaxation therapies' effects on depressed adolescent mothers. *Adolescence, 31,* 903–911.

Field, T., Healy, B., Goldstein, S., Perry, S., Bendell, D., Schanberg, S., Zimmerman, E. A., & Kuhn, C. (1988). Infants of depressed mothers show "depressed" behavior even with nondepressed adults. *Child Development, 59,* 1569–1579.

Field, T., Healy, B., & LeBlanc, W. G. (1989). Sharing and synchrony of behavior states and heart rate in nondepressed versus depressed mother-infant interactions. *Infant Behavior and Development, 12,* 357–376.

Field, T., Ignatoff, E., Stringer, S., Brennan. J., Greenberg, R., Widmayer, S., & Anderson, G. (1982). Non-nutritive sucking during tube feedings: Effects on preterm neonates in an intensive care unit. *Pediatrics, 70,* 381–384.

Field, T., Morrow, C., & Adlestein, D. (1993). Depressed mothers' perceptions of infant behavior. *Infant Behavior and Development, 16,* 99–108.

Field, T., Sandberg, D., Garcia, R., Vega-Lahr, N., Goldstein, S., & Guy, L. (1985). Pregnancy problems, postpartum depression, and early mother-infant interactions. *Developmental Psychology, 21,* 1152–1156.

Field, T. & Sostek, A. (1983). *Infants born at risk: Physiological, perceptual and cognitive processes.* New York: Grune & Stratton.

Field, T., Vega-Lahr, N., & Jagadish, S. (1984). Separation stress of nursery school infants and toddlers graduating to new classes. *Infant Behavior and Development, 7,* 277–284.

Field, T., Vega-Lahr, N., Scafidi, F., & Goldstein, S. (1986). Effects of maternal unavailability on mother-infant interactions. *Infant Behavior and Development, 9,* 473–478.

Field, T., & Widmayer, S. M. (1980). Developmental follow-up on infants delivered by caesarean section and general anesthesia. *Infant Behavior and Development, 3,* 253–264.

Field, T., Widmayer, S. M., Stringer, S., & Ignatoff, E. (1980). Teenage, lower class, black mothers and their preterm infants: An intervention and developmental follow-up. *Child Development, 51,* 426–436.

Field, T., Woodson, R., Greenberg, R., & Cohen, D. (1982). *Discrimination and imitation of facial expressions by neonates.* Paper presented at the International Conference on Infant Studies, Austin, TX.

Fifth Special Report to the U.S. Congress on Alcohol and Health (1984). *Alcohol Health and Research World, 9,* 1–72.

Finkelstein, N., Dent, C., Gallacher, K., & Ramey, C. (1978). Social behavior of infants and toddlers in a day-care environment. *Developmental Psychology, 14,* 257–262.

Fiorentino, M. R. (1981). *A basis for sensorimotor development—normal and abnormal: The influence of primitive, postural reflexes on the development and distribution of tone.* Springfield, IL: Charles C. Thomas.

Fischer, J., & Rozenberg, C. (1999). The maternity care coalition: Strategy for survival in the context of managed care and welfare reform. *Zero to Three, 19*(4), 14–19.

Fischer, K. W. (1987). Relations between brain and cognitive development. *Child Development, 58,* 623–632.

Fish, M., Stifter, C. A., & Belsky, J. (1991). Conditions of continuity and discontinuity in infant negative emotionality: Newborn to five months. *Child Development, 62,* 1525–1537.

Fisher, C. B., Ferdinandsen K., & Bornstein, M. H. (1981). The role of symmetry in infant form perception. *Child Development, 52,* 457–462.

Fivaz-Depeursinge, E., & Corboz-Warnery, A. (1999). *The primary triangle: A developmental systems view of mother, fathers, and infants.* New York: Basic Books.

Fivush, R. (1994). Constructing narrative, emotion, and self in parent-child conversations about the past. In U. Neisser & R. Fivush (Eds.), *The remembering self: Construction and accuracy in the self-narrative* (pp. 205–232). Cambridge, England: Cambridge University Press.

Fleming, A. S., & Orpen, G. (1986). Psychobiology of maternal behavior in rats, selected other species and humans. In A. Fogel & G. F. Melson (Eds.), *Origins of nurturance: Developmental, biological, and cultural perspectives on caregiving* (pp. 184–208). Hillsdale, NJ: Erlbaum.

Fleming, A. S., Ruble, D. N., Flett, G. L., & Shaul, D. L. (1988). Postpartum adjustment in first-time mothers: Relations between mood, maternal attitudes, and mother-infant interactions. *Developmental Psychology, 24,* 71–81.

Fleming, A. S., Ruble, D. N., Flett, G. L., & Van Wagner, V. (1990). Adjustment in first-time mothers: Changes in mood and mood content during the early postpartum months. *Developmental Psychology, 26,* 137–143.

Fogel, A. (1977). Temporal organization in mother-infant face-to-face interaction. In H. R. Schaffer (Ed.), *Studies in mother-infant interaction* (pp. 119–152). New York: Academic Press.

Fogel, A. (1979). Peer vs. mother directed behavior in 1- to 3-month-old infants. *Infant Behavior and Development, 2,* 215–226.

Fogel, A. (1981). The ontogeny of gestural communication: The first six months. In R. Stark (Ed.), *Language behavior in infancy and early childhood* (pp. 17–44). New York: Elsevier.

Fogel, A. (1982a). Affect dynamics in early infancy: Affective tolerance. In T. Field & A. Fogel (Eds.), *Emotion and early interaction* (pp. 15–56). Hillsdale, NJ: Erlbaum.

Fogel, A. (1982b). Early adult-infant face-to-face interaction: Expectable sequences of behavior. *Journal of Pediatric Psychology, 7,* 1–22.

Fogel, A. (1982c). Emotional development. In H. Mitzel (Ed.), *Encyclopedia of educational research* (pp. 455–489). New York: Macmillan.

Fogel, A. (1985). Coordinative structures in the development of expressive behavior in early infancy. In G. Zivin (Ed.), *The development of expressive behavior: Biology-environment interactions* (pp. 249–267). New York: Academic Press.

Fogel, A. (1990a). The process of developmental change in infant communicative action: Using dynamic systems theory to study individual ontogenies. In J. Colombo & J. Fagen (Eds.), *Individual differences in infancy: Reliability, stability, and prediction* (pp. 177–201). Hillsdale, NJ: Erlbaum.

Fogel, A. (1990b). Sensorimotor factors in communicative development. In H. Bloch & B. Bertenthal (Eds.), *Sensorimotor organization and development in infancy and early childhood. NATO ASI Series* (pp. 54–80). The Netherlands: Kluwer Academic.

Fogel, A. (1993). *Developing through relationships.* Chicago: University of Chicago Press.

Fogel, A. (2000). A relational perspective on the development of self and emotion. In J. A. Bosma & E. S. Kunnen (Eds.), *Identity and emotions: A self-organizational perspective.* Cambridge, England: Cambridge University Press.

Fogel, A., & Branco, A. U. (1997). Meta-communication as a source of indeterminism in relationship development. In A. Fogel, M. Lyra, & J. Valsiner (Eds.), *Dynamics and indeterminism in developmental and social processes* (pp. 138–155). Hillsdale, NJ: Erlbaum.

Fogel, A., Dedo, J. Y., & McEwen, I. (1992). Effect of postural position and reaching on gaze during mother-infant face-to-face interaction. *Infant Behavior and Development, 15,* 231–244.

Fogel, A., Dickson, K. L., Hsu, H., Messinger, D., Nelson-Goens, G. C., & Nwokah, E. (1997). Communicative dynamics of emotion. In K. C. Barrett (Ed.), *New directions in child development: The communication of emotion: Current research from diverse perspectives, 77* (pp. 5–24). San Francisco: Jossey-Bass.

Fogel, A., & Hannan, T. E. (1985). Manual actions of 2- to 3-month-old human infants during social interaction. *Child Development, 56,* 1271–1279.

Fogel, A., Karns, J., & Kawai, M. (1990). Lateral asymmetry in attention for 3-month-old human infants during face-to-face interaction with mother. *Developmental Psychology 23,* 1–14.

Fogel, A., & Lyra, M. (1997). Dynamics of development in relationships. In F. Masterpasqua & P. Perna (Eds.), *The psychological meaning of chaos: Self-organization in human development and psychotherapy* (pp. 75–94). Washington, DC: American Psychological Association.

Fogel, A., Lyra, M. C., & Valsiner, J. (Eds.). (1997). *Dynamics and indeterminism in developmental and social processes.* Hillsdale, NJ: Erlbaum.

Fogel, A., Melson, G. F., Toda, S., & Mistry, J. (1987). Young children's responses to unfamiliar infants: The effects of adult involvement. *International Journal of Behavioral Development, 10,* 37–50.

Fogel, A., & Melson, G. F. (1988). *Child development.* St. Paul, MN: West.

Fogel, A., Nelson-Goens, G. C., Hsu, H., & Shapiro, A. F. (in press). Mother-infant peekaboo and tickle games at 6 and 12 months: The dynamics of positive emotion, attention, and communication. *Child Development.*

Fogel, A., Nwokah, E., Dedo, J., Messinger, D., Dickson, K. L., Matusov, E., & Holt, S. A. (1992). Social process theory of emotion: A dynamic systems perspective. *Social Development, 1,* 122–142.

Fogel, A., Nwokah, E., Hsu, H. C., Dedo, J. Y., & Walker, H. (1993). Posture and communication in mother-infant interaction. In G. J. P. Savelsbergh (Ed.), *The development of coordination in infancy* (pp. 395–422). Amsterdam: Elsevier.

Fogel, A., Nwokah, E., & Karns, J. (1993). Parent-infant games as dynamic social systems. In K. B. MacDonald (Ed.), *Parents and children playing* (pp. 391–417). Albany, NY: SUNY Press.

Fogel, A., Stevenson, M. B., & Messinger, D. (1992). A comparison of the parent-child relationship in Japan and the United States. In J. L. Roopnarine & D. B. Carter (Eds.), *Parent-child relations in diverse cultural settings* (pp. 205–230). Norwood, NJ: Ablex.

Fogel, A., & Thelen, E. (1987). Development of early expressive and communicative action: Reinterpreting the evidence from a dynamic systems perspective. *Developmental Psychology, 23,* 747–761.

Fogel, A., Toda, S., & Kawai, M. (1988). Mother-infant face-to-face interaction in Japan and the United States: A laboratory comparison using 3-month-old infants. *Developmental Psychology, 24,* 398–406.

Ford, J. H., MacCormac, L., & Hiller, J. (1994). Pregnancy and lifestyle study: Association between occupational and environmental exposure to chemicals and reproductive outcome. *Mutation Research, 313,* 153–164.

Forestier, D. F., Kaplan, C., & Cox, W. (1988). Prenatal diagnosis and management of bleeding disorders with fetal blood sampling. *American Journal of Obstetrics and Gynecology, 158,* 939–946.

Forrest, J. D., & Fordyce, R. R. (1993). Women's contraceptive attitudes and use in 1992. *Family Planning Perspectives, 25,* 175–179.

Forrest, J. D., & Fordyce, R. R. (1993b). Locomotor coordination in infancy: The transition from walking to running. In G. J. P. Savelsbergh (Ed.), *The development of coordination in infancy* (pp. 359–393). Amsterdam: Elsevier.

Forrester, L. W., Phillips, S. J., & Clark, J. E. (1993). Locomotor coordination in infancy: The transition from walking to running. In G. J. P. Savelsbergh (Ed.), *The development of coordination in infancy* (pp. 359–393). Amsterdam: Elsevier.

Fox, C. R., & Gelfand, D. M. (1994). Maternal depressed mood and stress as related to vigilance, self-efficacy, and mother-child interactions. *Early Development and Parenting, 3,* 233–243.

Fox, N. A. (1977). Attachment of kibbutz infants to mother and metapelet. *Child Development, 48,* 1228–1239.

Fox, N. A. (1985). Sweet/sour—interest/disgust: The role of approach-withdrawal in the development of emotions. In T. Field & N. Fox (Eds.), *Social perception in infancy* (pp. 165–181). Norwood, NJ: Ablex.

Fox, N. A. (1989). Psychophysiological correlates of emotional reactivity during the first year of life. *Developmental Psychology, 25,* 364–372.

Fox, N. A., & Davidson, R. J. (1988). Patterns of brain electrical activity during the expression of discrete emotions in ten-month-old infants. *Developmental Psychology, 24,* 230–236.

Fox, N. A., Kimmerly, N. L., & Schafer, W. D. (1991). Attachment to mother/attachment to father: A meta-analysis. *Child Development, 62,* 210–225.

Fox, R., & McDaniels, C. (1982). The perception of biological motion by human infants. *Science, 218,* 486–487.

Fraiberg, S. (1974). Gross motor development in infants blind from birth. *Child Development, 45,* 114–126.

Francis, P. L., Self, P. A., & Horowitz, F. D. (1987). The behavioral assessment of the neonate: An overview. In J. D. Osofsky (Ed.), *Handbook of infant development* (2nd ed., pp. 170–208). New York: Wiley.

Franco, F., Fogel, A., Messinger, D., & Frazier, C. (1996). Cultural differences in physical contact between Hispanic and Anglo mother-infant dyads living in the United States. *Early Development and Parenting, 5,* 119–127.

Frankenburg, W. K., Dodd, J. B., Fandal, A. W., Kuzuk, E., & Cohrs, M. (1975). *DDST: Reference manual* (Rev. ed.). Denver: Ladoka Project and Publication Foundation.

Frazier, P. A., Byer, A. L., Fischer, A. R., Wright, D. M., & DeBord, K. A. (1996). Adult attachment style and partner choice: Correlational and experimental findings. *Personal Relationships, 3*(2), 117–136.

Freeman, N. H. (1980). *Strategies of representation in young children: Analysis of spatial skill and drawing processes.* London: Academic Press.

Freeman, R. (1990). Intrapartum fetal monitoring—A disappointing story (editorial; comment). *New England Journal of Medicine, 322*(9), 624–626.

Freud, A. (1965). *Normality and pathology in childhood.* New York: International Universities Press.

Freud, S. (1900/1953). [*The interpretation of dreams.*] In J. Strachey (Ed. and Trans.), *The standard edition of the complete works of Sigmund Freud* (Vol. 3, pp. 485–699). London: Hogarth Press. (Original work published 1900)

Freud, S. (1903/1953). [*Three essays on the theory of sexuality.*] In J. Strachey (Ed. and Trans.), *The standard edition of the complete works of Sigmund Freud* (Vol. 7, pp. 1550–1669). London: Hogarth Press. (Original work published 1903)

Frick, J. E., Colombo, J., & Saxon, T. F. (1999). Individual and developmental differences in disengagement of fixation in early infancy. *Child Development, 70*(3), 537–548.

Friedman, S. L., & Jacobs, B. S. (1981). Sex differences in neonates' behavioral responsiveness to repeated auditory stimulation. *Infant Behavior and Development, 4,* 175–183.

Friedman, S. L., Randolph, S., & Kochanoff, A. (2000). Child care research at the dawn of a new millennium: Taking stock of what we know. In J. G. Bremner & A. Fogel (Eds.), *Handbook of infancy research* (pp. 415–437). Oxford, England: Blackwell.

Friedrich-Cofer, L. K. (1986). Body, mind, and morals in the framing of social policy. In L. K. Friedrich-Cofer (Ed.), *Human nature of public policy: Scientific views of women, children and families* (pp. 97–173). New York: Praeger.

Frigoletto, F. D., Greene, M. F., Benacerraf, B. R., Barss, V. A., & Saltzman, D. H. (1986). Ultrasonographic fetal surveillance in the management of the isoimmunized pregnancy. *New England Journal of Medicine, 315,* 430–432.

Frodi, A. M., & Lamb, M. E. (1978). Sex differences in responsiveness to infants: A developmental study of psychophysiological and behavioral responses. *Child Development, 49,* 1182–1188.

Frodi, A. M., & Lamb, M. E. (1980). Child abuser's response to infant smiles and cries. *Child Development, 51,* 238–241.

Frodi, A. M., Lamb, M. E., Leavitt, L. A., & Donovan, W. L. (1978). Father's and mother's responses to infant smiles and cries. *Infant Behavior and Development, 1,* 187–198.

Frosch, C. A., Mangelsdorf, S. C., & McHale, J. L. (1998). Correlates of marital behavior at 6 months postpartum. *Developmental Psychology, 34*(6), 1438–1449.

Furdon, S. A., Pfeil, V. C., & Snow, K. (1998). Operationalizing Donna Wong's principle of atraumatic care: Pain management in the NICU. *Pediatric Nursing, 24*(4), 336–342.

Furman, W., Rahe, D. F., & Hartup, W. W. (1979). Rehabilitation of socially withdrawn preschool children through mixed-age and same-age socialization. *Child Development, 50,* 915–922.

Furrow, D. (1984). Social and private speech at two years. *Child Development, 55,* 355–362.

Furstenberg, F. F., Jr., Brooks-Gunn, J., & Morgan, P. (1987). *Adolescent mothers in later life.* New York: Cambridge University Press.

Gaddini, R. (1970). Transitional objects and the process of individuation. *Journal of the American Academy of Child Psychiatry, 9,* 347–365.

Galvin, E. S. (1989). Children and child care in China: Some observations. *Children Today, 19–23.*

Gandelman, R. (1992). *The psychobiology of behavioral development.* New York: Oxford University Press.

Gandour, M. J. (1989). Activity level as a dimension of temperament in toddlers: Its relevance for the organismic specificity hypothesis. *Child Development, 60,* 1092–1098.

Garbarino, J. A. (1976). A preliminary study of some ecological correlates of child abuse: The impact of socioeconomic stress on mothers. *Child Development, 47,* 178–185.

Garbarino, J. A. (1982). Sociocultural risk: Dangers to competence. In C. Kopp & J. B. Krakow (Eds.), *The child: Development in a social context* (pp. 246–268). Reading, MA: Addison-Wesley.

Garbarino, J. A. (1992). The meaning of poverty in the world of children. *American Behavioral Scientist, 35,* 220–237.

Garbarino, J. A. (1993). Children's response to community violence: What do we know? *Infant Mental Health Journal, 14,* 103–115.

Garbarino, J. A., & Crouter, A. (1978). Defining the community context for parent-child relations: The correlates of child maltreatment. *Child Development, 49,* 604–616.

Garcia-Coll, C., Kagan, J., & Reznick, J. S. (1984). Behavioral inhibition in young children. *Child Development, 55,* 1005–1019.

Gardner, C. A. (1989). Is an embryo a person? *Nation,* 557–559.

Gardosi, J., Hutson, N., & Lynch, C. (1989). Randomized, controlled trial of squatting in the second stage of labor. *Lancet, 2,* 74–77.

Garner, P. W., Jones, D. C., & Palmer, D. J. (1994). Social cognitive correlates of preschool children's sibling caregiving behavior. *Developmental Psychology, 30,* 905–911.

Garvey, C. (1974). Some properties of social play. *Merrill-Palmer Quarterly, 20,* 163–180.

Gatts, J. D., Wallace, D. H., Glasscock, G. F., McKee, E., & Cohen, R. S. (1994). A modified newborn intensive care unit environment may shorten hospital stay. *Journal of Perinatology, 14,* 422–427.

Gavidia-Payne, S., & Stoneman, Z. (1997). Family predictors of maternal and paternal involvement in programs for young children with disabilities. *Child Development, 68*(4), 701–717.

Gelfand, D. M. (2000). Infant mental health in a changing society. In J. G. Bremner & A. Fogel (Eds.), *Handbook of infancy research* (pp. 362–385). Oxford, England: Blackwell.

Gelfand, D. M., & Teti, D. M. (1990). The effects of maternal depression on children. *Clinical Psychology Review, 10,* 329–353.

Gelfand, D. M., Teti, D. M., & Fox, C. E. R. (1992). Sources of parenting stress for depressed and nondepressed mothers of infants. *Journal of Clinical Child Psychology, 21,* 262–272.

Geller, G., Tambor, E. S., Chase, G. A., Hofman, K. J., Faden, R. R., & Holtzman, N. A. (1993). Incorporation of genetic counselling in primary care practice. *Archives of Family Medicine, 2,* 1119–1125.

Gelles, R. (1978). Violence toward children in the United States. *American Journal of Orthopsychiatry, 48,* 580–592.

Gelman, S. A., Collman, P., & Maccoby, E. E. (1986). Inferring properties from categories vs. inferring categories from properties: The case of gender. *Child Development, 57,* 396–404.

Gentner, D. (1978). On relational meaning: The acquisition of verb meaning. *Child Development, 49,* 988–998.

George, C., & Main, M. (1979). Social interactions in young abused children: Approach, avoidance, and aggression. *Child Development, 50,* 306–318.

Gerken, L., Landau, B., & Remez, R. E. (1990). Function morphemes in young children's speech perception and production. *Developmental Psychology, 26,* 204–216.

Gerner, E. M. (1999). Emotional interaction in a group of preterm infants at 3 and 6 months of corrected age. *Infant and Child Development, 8,* 117–128.

Gesell, A. (1925). *The mental growth of the preschool child.* New York: Macmillan.

Gesell, A. (1928). *Infancy and human growth.* New York: Macmillan.

Gewirtz, J. L. (1972). *Attachment and dependency.* New York: Halsted Press.

Gianino, A., & Tronick, E. Z. (1988). The mutual regulation model: The infant's self and interactive regulation and coping and defensive capacities. In T. M. Field, P. M. McCabe, & N. Schneiderman (Eds.), *Stress and coping across development* (pp. 300–323). Hillsdale, NJ: Erlbaum.

Gibson, E. J., Owsley, C. J., Walker, A., & Megaw-Nyce, J. (1979). Development of the perception of invariants: Substance and shape. *Perception, 8*(6), 609–619.

Gibson, E. J., Riccio, G., Schmuckler, M. A., Stoffregen, T. A., Rosenberg, D., & Taormina, J. (1987). Detection of the traversability of surfaces by crawling and walking infants. *Journal of Experimental Psychology: Human Perception and Performance, 13,* 533–544.

Gibson, E. J., & Walk, R. D. (1960). The "visual cliff." *Scientific American, 202,* 64–71.

Gibson, J. J. (1966). *The senses considered as perceptual systems.* Boston, MA: Houghton Mifflin.

Gielen, A. C., O'Campo, P. J., Faden, R. R., Kass, N. E., & Xue, X. (1994). Interpersonal conflict and physical violence during the childbearing years. *Social Science and Medicine, 39,* 781–787.

Gies, F., & Gies, J. (1987). *Marriage and the family in the Middle Ages.* New York: Harper & Row.

Gil, D. G. (1970). *Violence against children: Physical child abuse in the United States.* Cambridge, MA: Harvard University Press.

Ginsburg, C. (1999). Body-image, movement, and consciousness: Examples from a somatic practice in the Feldenkrais method. *Journal of Consciousness Studies, 6*(2–3), 79–91.

Ginsburg, G. P., & Kilbourne, B. K. (1988). Emergence of vocal alternation in mother-infant interchanges. *Journal of Child Language, 15,* 221–235.

Glazer, S. (1993a). Outlook, testing theories. *C. Q. Researcher, 3,* 304–306.

Glazer, S. (1993b). Preventing teen pregnancy. *C. Q. Researcher, 3,* 409–431.

Glink, P. (1998). A collaborative effort in perinatal support for birthing teens. *Zero to Three, 18*(5), 44–50.

Gloger-Tippelt, G. S., & Huerkamp, M. (1998). Relationship change at the transition to parenthood and security of infant-mother attachment. *International Journal of Behavioral Development, 22*(3), 633–655.

Godfrey, A. B., & Kilgore, A. (1998). An approach to help very young infants sleep through the night. *Zero to Three, 19*(2), 15–21.

Goldberg, S. (1983). Parent-to-infant bonding: Another look. *Child Development, 54,* 1355–1382.

Goldfarb, J. (1993). Breastfeeding, AIDS, and other infectious diseases. *Clinical Perinatology, 20,* 225–243.

Goldfield, E. C. (1989). Transition from rocking to crawling: Postural constraints on infant movement. *Developmental Psychology, 25,* 913–919.

Goldfield, E. C. (1993). Dynamic systems in development: Action systems. In L. B. Smith & E. Thelen (Eds.), *A dynamic systems approach to development: Applications* (pp. 51–70). Cambridge, MA: MIT Press.

Golding, J., & Peters, T. J. (1985). What else do SIDS risk prediction scores predict? *Early Human Development, 12,* 247–260.

Goldman, M. B. (1994). Sudden infant death syndrome: Back to sleep campaign. *Caring, 13,* 52–55.

Goldman-Rakic, P. S. (1987). Development of cortical circuitry and cognitive function. *Child Development, 58,* 601–622.

Goldsmith, D. F., & Rogoff, B. (1997). Mothers' and toddlers' coordinated joint focus of attention: Variations with maternal dysphoric symptoms. *Developmental Psychology, 33*(1), 113–119.

Goldsmith, H. H., & Alansky, J. (1987). Maternal and infant temperamental predictors of attachment: A meta-analytic review. *Journal of Consulting and Clinical Psychology, 55,* 805–816.

Goldsmith, H. H., Buss, K. A., & Lemery, K. S. (1997). Toddler and childhood temperament: Expanded content, stronger genetic evidence, new evidence for the importance of environment. *Developmental Psychology, 33*(6), 891–905.

Goldsmith, H. H., Buss, A. H., Plomin, R., Rothbart, M. K., Thoman, A., Chess, S., Hinde, R. A., & McCall, R. B. (1987). Roundtable: What is temperament? Four approaches. *Child Development, 58,* 505–529.

Goldsmith, H. H., & Campos, J. J. (1990). The structure of temperamental fear and pleasure in infants: A psychometric perspective. *Child Development, 61,* 1944–1964.

Goldsmith, H. H., & Gottesman, I. I. (1981). Origins of variation in behavioral style: A longitudinal study of temperament in young twins. *Child Development, 52,* 91–103.

Goldsmith, H. H., Lemery, K. S., Buss, K. A., & Campos, J. J. (1999). Genetic analyses of focal aspects of infant temperament. *Developmental Psychology, 35*(4), 972–985.

Golinkoff, R. M., & Ames, G. J. (1979). A comparison of fathers' and mothers' speech with their young children. *Child Development, 50,* 28–32.

Golomb, C. (1974). *Young children's sculpture and drawing: A study in representation development.* Cambridge, MA: Harvard University Press.

Golub, M. S. (1996). Labor analgesia and infant brain development. *Pharmacology of Biochemical Behavior, 55*(4), 619–628.

Golub, M. S., Macintosh, M. S., & Baumrind, N. (1998). Developmental and reproductive toxicity of inorganic arsenic: Animal studies and human concerns. *Journal of Toxicology and Environmental Health, 1*(3), 199–241.

Goodman, J. C., McDonough, L., & Brown, N. B. (1998). The role of semantic context and memory in the acquisition of novel nouns. *Child Development, 69*(5), 1330–1344.

Goodnow, J. (1977). *Children drawing.* Cambridge, MA: Harvard University Press.

Goodwyn, S. W., & Acredolo, L. P. (1993). Symbolic gesture versus word: Is there a modality advantage for onset of symbol use? *Child Development, 64,* 688–701.

Goossens, F. A., & van Ijzendoorn, M. H. (1990). Quality of infants' attachments to professional caregivers: Relation to infant-parent attachment and day-care characteristics. *Child Development, 61,* 832–837.

Gordon, S. (1982). Teenage sexuality. In M. Schwarz (Ed.), *TV and teens* (pp. 136–138). Reading, MA: Addison-Wesley.

Gordon, T. (1988). The case against disciplining children at home or in school. *Person-Centered Review, 3,* 59–85.

Gorman, K. S., & Pollitt, E. (1992). Relationship between weight and body proportionality at birth, growth during the first year of life, and cognitive development at 36, 48, and 60 months. *Infant Behavior and Development, 15,* 279–296.

Gottfried, A. W., Rose, S. A., & Bridger, W. H. (1977). Cross-modal transfer in human infants. *Child Development, 48,* 118–123.

Gottlieb, G. (1991a). Experiential canalization of behavioral development: Theory. *Developmental Psychology, 27,* 4–13.

Gottlieb, G. (1991b). Experiential canalization of behavioral development: Results. *Developmental Psychology, 27,* 35–39.

Gottlieb, G. (1995). Some conceptual deficiencies in "developmental" behavior genetics. *Human Development, 38*(3), 131–141.

Goubet, N., & Clifton, R. K. (1998). Object and event representation in 6½-month-old infants. *Developmental Psychology, 34*(1), 63–76.

Gould, S. J. (1994). The evolution of life on earth. *Scientific American,* 85–91.

Graham, F. K., Anthony, B. J., & Zeigler, B. L. (1984). The orienting response and developmental processes. In D. Siddle (Ed.), *Orienting and habituation: Perspectives in human research* (pp. 166–183). New York: Wiley.

Graham, F. K., Leavitt, L., Strock, B., & Brown, H. (1978). Precocious cardiac orienting in a human anencephalic infant. *Science, 199,* 322–324.

Grandin, T., & Scariano, M. (1986). *Emergence: Labeled autistic.* Novato, CA: Arena Press.

Granrud, C. E., & Yonas, A. (1984). Infants' perception of pictorially specified interposition. *Journal of Experimental Child Psychology, 37,* 500–511.

Granrud, C. E., Yonas, A., & Opland, E. A. (1985). Infants' sensitivity to the depth cue of shading. *Perception and Psychophysics, 37,* 415–419.

Grant, V. J. (1994). Sex of infant differences in mother-infant interaction: A reinterpretation of past findings. *Developmental Review, 14,* 1–26.

Green, J. A., Gustafson, G. E., Irwin, J. R., Kalinowski, L. L., & Wood, R. M. (1995). Infant crying: Acoustics, perception, and communication. *Early Development and Parenting, 4*(4), 161–175.

Green, J. A., Gustafson, G. E., & McGhie, A. C. (1998). Changes in infants' cries as a function of time in a cry bout. *Child Development, 69*(2), 271–279.

Green, J. E., Dorfman, A., Jones, S. L., Bender, S., Patton, L., & Schulman, J. D. (1988). Chorionic villus sampling: Experience with an initial 940 cases. *Obstetrics and Gynecology, 71,* 208–212.

Green, J. M. (1998). Postnatal depression or perinatal dysphoria? Findings from a longitudinal community-based study using the Edinburgh Postnatal Depression Scale. *Journal of Reproductive and Infant Psychology, 16*(2–3), 143–155.

Greenberger, E., O'Neil, R., & Nagel, S. K. (1994). Linking workplace and homeplace: Relations between the nature of adults' work and their parenting behaviors. *Developmental Psychology, 30,* 990–1002.

Greenfield, P., & Smith, J. H. (1976). *The structure of communication in early language development.* New York: Academic Press.

Greenleaf, P. (1978). *Children throughout the ages: A history of childhood.* New York: Barnes & Noble.

Greenough, W. T., Black, J. E., & Wallace, C. S. (1987). Experience and brain development. *Child Development, 58,* 539–559.

Greenspan, S., & Wieder, S. (1997). An integrated approach to interventions for young children with severe difficulties in relating and communicating. *Zero to Three, 17*(5), 5–17.

Grieser, D. L., & Kuhl, P. K. (1988). Maternal speech to infants in a tonal language: Support for universal prosodic features in motherese. *Developmental Psychology, 24*(1), 14–20.

Grieser, D. L., & Kuhl, P. K. (1989). Categorization of speech by infants: Support for speech-sound prototypes. *Developmental Psychology, 25,* 577–588.

Grigoroiu-Serbanescu, M. (1981). Intellectual and emotional development in premature children from 1 to 5 years. *International Journal of Behavioral Development, 4,* 183–200.

Grimes, D. A. (1994). The morbidity and mortality of pregnancy: Still risky business. *American Journal of Obstetrics and Gynecology, 170,* 1489–1494.

Grimm, E. (1967). Psychological and social factors in pregnancy, delivery and outcome. In S. Richardson & A. Guttmacher (Eds.), *Childbearing: Its social and psychological aspects* (pp. 305–348). Baltimore: Williams & Wilkins.

Grobstein, C. (1988). *Science and the unborn.* New York: Basic Books.

Grodstein, F., Goldman, M. B., & Cramer, D. W. (1994). Infertility in women and moderate alcohol use. *American Journal of Public Health, 84,* 1429–1432.

Grolnick, W. S., Bridges, L. J., & Connel, J. P. (1996). Emotion regulation in two-year-olds: Strategies and emotional expression in four contexts. *Child Development, 67,* 928–941.

Grolnick, W. S., Cosgrove, T. J., & Bridges, L. J. (1996). Age-graded change in the initiation of positive affect. *Infant Behavior and Development, 19,* 153–157.

Grossman, K., Grossman, K. E., Spangler, G., Suess, G., & Unzner, L. (1985). Maternal sensitivity and newborns' orientation responses as related to quality of attachment in northern Germany. *Monographs of the Society for Research in Child Development, 50* (Serial No. 209), 233–256.

Grover, S., & Permezel, M. (1994). What's new?: Gynaecology. *Medical Journal of Australia, 161,* 330–331.

Gruen, A. (1987). The relationship of sudden infant death and parental unconscious conflicts. *Pre- and Perinatal Psychology Journal, 2,* 50–56.

Gruendel, J. M. (1977). Referential extension in early language development. *Child Development, 48,* 1567–1576.

Grunwaldt, E., Bates, T., & Guthrie, D. (1960). The onset of sleeping through the night in infancy. *Pediatrics, 26,* 667–668.

Grych, J. H., & Clark, R. (1999). Maternal employment and development of the father-infant relationship in the first year. *Developmental Psychology, 35*(4), 893–903.

Guerin, D. W., Gottfried, A. W., & Thomas, C. W. (1997). Difficult temperament and behaviour problems: A longitudinal study from 1.5 to 12 years. *International Journal of Behavioral Development, 21*(1), 71–90.

Guillain, A., Foxonet, C., Petersen, A., & Ramos, M. (1997). Socialization and cognition in children between the age of 18 and 24 months. *Early Development and Parenting, 6*(2), 59–71.

Gunnar, M. (1994). Psychoendocrine studies of temperament and stress in early childhood: Expanding current models. In J. E. Bates & T. D. Wachs (Eds.), *Temperament: Individual differences at the interface of biology and behavior* (pp. 175–198). Washington, DC: American Psychological Association.

Gunnar, M., Leighton, K., & Peleaux, R. (1984). Effects of temporal predictability on the reactions of 1-year-olds to potentially frightening toys. *Developmental Psychology, 20,* 449–458.

Gunnar, M., Mangelsdorf, S., Larson, M., & Hertsgaard, L. (1989). Attachment, temperament, and adrenocortical activity in infancy: A study of psychoendocrine regulation. *Developmental Psychology, 25,* 355–363.

Gunnar, M., Senior, K., & Hartup, W. W. (1984). Peer presence and the exploratory behavior of eighteen- and thirty-month-old children. *Child Development, 55,* 1103–1109.

Gunnar, M. R., & Stone, C. (1984). The effects of positive maternal affect on infant responses to pleasant, ambiguous, and fear-provoking toys. *Child Development, 55,* 1231–1236.

Gunter, N., & LaBarbera, R. (1980). The consequences of adolescent childbearing on postnatal development. *International Journal of Behavioral Development, 3,* 191–214.

Gusella, J. L., Muir, D., & Tronick, E. Z. (1988). The effect of manipulating maternal behavior during an interaction on three- and six-month-olds' affect and attention. *Child Development, 59,* 1111–1124.

Gustafson, G. E. (1984). The effects of the ability to locomote on infants' social and exploratory behaviors: An experimental study. *Developmental Psychology, 20,* 397–405.

Gustafson, G. E., & Green, J. A. (1989). On the importance of fundamental frequency and other acoustic features in cry perception and infant development. *Child Development, 60,* 772–780.

Gustafson, G. E., & Green, J. A. (1991). Developmental coordination of cry sounds with visual regard and gestures. *Infant Behavior and Development, 14,* 51–57.

Gustafson, G. E., Green, J. A., & Kalinowski, L. L. (1995, March). *Crying and vocalizing: A nascent system for communicating different meanings?* Poster presented at the meeting of the Society for Research in Child Development, Indianapolis, IN.

Gustafson, G. E., Green, J. A., & West, M. J. (1979). The infant's changing role in mother-infant games: The growth of social skills. *Infant Behavior and Development, 2,* 301–308.

Gustafson, G. E., & Harris, K. L. (1990). Women's responses to young infants' cries. *Developmental Psychology, 26,* 144–152.

Guthrie, H. A. (1979). *Introduction to nutrition.* St. Louis: Mosby.

Gutman, A., & Turnure, J. (1979). Mothers' production of hand gestures while communicating with their pre-school children under various task conditions. *Developmental Psychology, 15,* 197–203.

Guttmacher, A. (1973). *Pregnancy, birth and family planning: A guide for expectant parents in the 1970s.* New York: Viking Press.

Guyer, B., MacDorman, M. F., Martin, J. A., Peters, K. D., & Strobino, D. M. (1998). Annual summary of vital statistics: 1997. *Pediatrics, 102*(6), 1333–1349.

Hack, M., Klein, N. K., & Taylor, H. G. (1995). Long-term developmental outcomes of low birth weight infants. *The Future of Children, 5,* 176–196.

Hagekull, B., Stenberg, G., & Bohlin, G. (1993). Infant-mother social referencing interactions: Description and antecedents in maternal sensitivity and infant irritability. *Early Development and Parenting, 2,* 183–191.

Hagerman, R. J. (1996). Biomedical advances in developmental psychology: The case of fragile X syndrome. *Developmental Psychology, 32*(3), 416–424.

Haight, W., Masiello, T., Dickson, K. L., Huckeby, E., & Black, J. E. (1994). The everyday contexts and social functions of spontaneous mother-child pretend play in the home. *Merrill-Palmer Quarterly, 40,* 509–522.

Haight, W., & Miller, P. J. (1992). The development of everyday pretend play: A longitudinal study of mothers' participation. *Merrill-Palmer Quarterly, 38,* 331–349.

Haight, W. L., Wang, X., Fung, H. H., Williams, K., & Mintz, J. (1999). Universal, developmental, and variable aspects of young children's play: A cross-cultural comparison of pretending at home. *Child Development, 70*(6), 1477–1488.

Hains, S. M. J., & Muir, D. W. (1996). Effects of stimulus contingency in infant-adult interactions. *Infant Behavior and Development, 19,* 49–61.

Haith, M. M. (1980). *Rules that babies look by: The organization of newborn visual activity.* Hillsdale, NJ: Erlbaum.

Haith, M. M., Bergman, T., & Moore, M. (1977). Eye contact and face scanning in early infancy. *Science, 198,* 853–855.

Hala, S., Chandler, M., & Fritz, A. S. (1991). Fledgling theories of mind: Deception as a marker of three-year-olds' understanding of false belief. *Child Development, 62,* 83–97.

Hallock, M. B., Worobey, J., & Self, P. A. (1989). Behavioral development in chimpanzee *(Pan troglodytes)* and human newborns across the first month of life. *International Journal of Behavioral Development, 12,* 527–540.

Halonen, J. S., & Passman, R. (1978). Pacifier's effects upon play and separations from the mother for the one-year-old in a novel environment. *Infant Behavior and Development, 1,* 70–78.

Hamilton, L. R. (1989). Variables associated with child maltreatment and implications for prevention and treatment. *Early Child Development, 42,* 31–56.

Hanawalt, B. A. (1993). *Growing up in medieval London: The experience of childhood in history.* New York: Oxford University Press.

Hanna, E., & Meltzoff, A. N. (1993). Peer imitation by toddlers in laboratory, home and day-care contexts: Implications for social learning and memory. *Developmental Psychology, 29,* 701–710.

Hannan, T. E. (1987). A cross-sequential assessment of the occurrences of pointing in three- to twelve-month-old infants. *Infant Behavior and Development, 10,* 11–22.

Hansen, M. (1993). Surrogacy contract upheld; California Supreme Courts says such agreements don't violate public policy. *American Psychological Association, 79,* 34.

Harding, C. G., & Golinkoff, R. M. (1979). The origins of intentional vocalizations in prelinguistic infants. *Child Development, 50,* 33–40.

Hardy, J. B., Aston, N. M., Brooks-Gunn, J., Shapiro, S., & Miller, T. L. (1998). Like mother, like child: Intergenerational patterns of age at first birth and associations with childhood and adolescent characteristics and adult outcomes in the second generation. *Developmental Psychology, 34*(6), 1220–1232.

Hardyck, C., & Petrinovich, L. F. (1977). Left-handedness. *Psychological Bulletin, 84,* 385–404.

Hareven, T. K. (1982). *Family time and industrial time.* New York: Cambridge University Press.

Hareven, T. K. (1985). Historical changes in the family and the life course: Implications for child development. *Monographs of the Society for Research in Child Development, 50* (Serial No. 211), 8–23.

Harkins, D. A., & Michel, G. F. (1988). Evidence for a maternal effect on infant hand-use preferences. *Developmental Psychology, 21,* 535–541.

Harley, K., & Reese, E. (1999). Origins of autobiographical memory. *Developmental Psychology, 35*(8), 1338–1348.

Harlow, H., & Harlow, M. (1965). The affectional systems. In A. Schrier, H. Harlow, & F. Stollnitz (Eds.), *Behavior of non-human primates* (Vol. 2). New York: Academic Press.

Harris, M., Jones, D., & Grant, J. (1985). The social-interactional context of maternal speech to infants: An explanation for the event-bound nature of early word use? *First Language, 5,* 89–100.

Harris, P. L. (1989). *Children and emotion: The development of psychological understanding.* New York: Basil Blackwell.

Harris, P. L. (1998). Fictional absorption: Emotional responses to make-believe. In S. Bråten (Ed.), *Intersubjective communication and emotion in early ontogeny. Studies in emotion and social interaction, 2nd series* (pp. 336–353). Cambridge, England: Cambridge University Press.

Harris, P. L., & Kavanaugh, R. D. (1993). Young children's understanding of pretense. *Monographs of the Society for Research in Child Development, 58,* 1–92.

Hart, B., & Risley, T. R. (1992). American parenting of language-learning children: Persisting differences in family-child interactions observed in natural home environments. *Developmental Psychology, 28,* 1096–1105.

Hart, S., Field, T., Del Valle, C., & Letourneau, M. (1998). Infants protest their mothers' attending to an infant-size doll. *Social Development, 7*(1), 54–61.

Hart, S., Field, T., Letourneau, M., & Del Valle, C. (1998). Jealousy protests in infants of depressed mothers. *Infant Behavior and Development, 21*(1), 137–148.

Harter, S. (1983). Developmental perspectives on the self-system. In P. H. Mussen (Series Ed.) & E. M. Hetherington (Vol. Ed.), *Handbook of child psychology: Vol. 4. Socialization, personality, and social development* (pp. 176–194). New York: Wiley.

Hartley, L. (1995). *Wisdom of the body moving.* Berkeley, CA: North Atlantic Books.

Hartmann, A. F., Radin, M. B., & McConnell, B. (1992). Parent-to-parent support: A critical component of health care services for families. *Issues in Comprehensive Pediatric Nursing, 15,* 55–67.

Hartmann, H., & Molz, G. (1979). Unexpected death in infancy. In J. Howells (Ed.), *Modern perspectives in the psychiatry of infancy* (pp. 360–395). New York: Brunner-Mazel.

Harty, J. R. (1990). Pharmacotherapy in infantile autism. *Focus on Autistic Behavior, 5,* 1–15.

Harwood, R. L., Schölmerich, A., Schulze, P. A., & Gonzalez, Z. (1999). Cultural differences in maternal beliefs and behaviors: A study of middle-class Anglo and Puerto Rican mother-infant pairs in four everyday situations. *Child Development, 70*(4), 1005–1016.

Hatton, D. D., Bailey, D. B., Burchinal, M. R., & Ferrell, K. A. (1997). Developmental growth curves of preschool children with vision impairments. *Child Development, 68*(5), 788–806.

Hauser-Cram, P. (1996). Mastery motivation in toddlers with developmental disabilities. *Child Development, 67,* 236–248.

Hauser-Cram, P., Warfield, M. E., Shonkoff, J. P., Krauss, M. W., Upshur, C. C., & Sayer, A. (1999). Family influences on adaptive development in young children with Down syndrome. *Child Development, 70*(4), 979–989.

Hawley, T. L., & Disney, E. R. (1992). Crack's children: The consequences of maternal cocaine abuse. *Social Policy Report: Society for Research in Child Development, 6,* 1–22.

Hawley, P. H., & Little, T. D. (1999). On winning some and losing some: A social relations approach to social dominance in toddlers. *Merrill-Palmer Quarterly, 45*(2), 185–214.

Hay, D. F., Caplan, M., Castle, J., & Stimson, C. A. (1991). Does sharing become increasingly "rational" in the second year of life? *Developmental Psychology, 27,* 987–993.

Hay, D. F., Murray, P., Cecire, S., & Nash, A. (1985). Social learning of social behavior in early life. *Child Development, 56,* 43–57.

Hayne, H., & Findlay, N. (1995). Contextual control of memory retrieval in infancy: Evidence for associative priming. *Infant Behavior and Development, 18*(2), 195–207.

Hayne, H., & Rovee-Collier, C. (1995). The organization of reactivated memory in infancy. *Child Development, 66,* 893–906.

Hazell, L. (1975). A study of 300 elective home births. *Birth and the Family Journal, 2,* 11–18.

Hazen, N. (1982). Spatial exploration and spatial knowledge: Individual and developmental differences in very young children. *Child Development, 53,* 826–833.

Hazlewood, V. (1977). The role of auditory stimuli in crying inhibition in the neonate. *Journal of Audiology Research, 17,* 225–240.

Healy, B. T. (1989). Autonomic nervous system correlates of temperament. *Infant Behavior and Development, 12,* 289–304.

Hebb, D. O. (1949). *The organization of behavior.* New York: Oxford University Press.

Heckhausen, J. (1988). Becoming aware of one's competence in the second year: Developmental progression within the mother-child dyad. *International Journal of Behavioral Development, 11,* 305–326.

Heimann, M. (1989). Neonatal imitation, gaze aversion, and mother-infant interaction. *Infant Behavior and Development, 12,* 495–505.

Heimann, M., Ullstadius, E., Dahlgren, S. O., & Gillberg, C. (1992). Imitation in autism: A preliminary research note. *Behavioral Neurology, 5,* 219–227.

Heinicke, C. M. (1984). Impact of pre-birth parent personality and marital functioning on family development: A framework and suggestions for further study. *Developmental Psychology, 20,* 1044–1053.

Heinicke, C. M., Diskin, S. D., Ramsey-Klee, D. M., & Oates, D. S. (1986). Pre- and post-birth antecedents of 2-year-old attention, capacity for relationships, and verbal expressiveness. *Developmental Psychology, 22,* 777–787.

Heinicke, C. M., & Guthrie, D. (1992). Stability and change in husband-wife adaptation and the development of the positive parent-child relationship. *Infant Behavior and Development, 15,* 109–127.

Heinicke, C. M., & Lampl, E. (1988). Pre- and post-birth antecedents of 3- and 4-year-old attention, IQ, verbal expressiveness, task orientation, and capacity for relationships. *Infant Behavior and Development, 11,* 381–410.

Heinicke, C. M., & Westheimer, I. (1966). *Brief separations.* New York: Academic Press.

Heinonen, O., Sloane, D., & Shapiro, S. (1976). *Birth defects and drugs in pregnancy.* Littleton, MA: Publishing Sciences Group.

Helmrath, T., & Steinitz, E. (1978). Death of an infant: Parental grieving and the failure of social support. *Journal of Family Practice, 6,* 785–790.

Helweg, L. A., Lundemose, J. B., & Bille, H. (1994). Overheating and sudden infant death: Temperature regulation in relation to the prone position, the possible pathogenesis of sudden infant death. *Ugeskrift For Laeger, 156,* 7193–7196.

Henshaw, S. K. (1994). Recent trends in the legal status of induced abortion. *Journal of Public Health Policy, 15,* 165–172.

Herault, J., Matineau, J., Petit, E., & Perrot, A. (1994). Genetic markers in autism: Association study on short arm of chromosome 11. *Journal of Autism and Developmental Disorders, 24,* 233–236.

Hernandez, D. J. (1997). Child development and the social demography of childhood. *Child Development, 68*(1), 149–169.

Heshusius, L. (1994). Freeing ourselves from objectivity: Managing subjectivity or turning toward a participatory mode of consciousness? *Educational Researcher, 23*(3), 15–22.

Hespos, S. J., & Rochat, P. (1997). Dynamic mental representation in infancy. *Cognition, 64,* 153–188.

Hess, E. H. (1959). Imprinting. *Science, 130,* 133–141.

Hesse, E., & van Ijzendoorn, M. H. (1998). Parental loss of close family members and propensities towards absorption in offspring. *Developmental Science, 1*(2), 299–305.

Hetherington, E. M., & Parke, R. D. (1993). *Child psychology: A contemporary viewpoint* (4th ed.). New York: McGraw-Hill.

Hewlett, B. S., Lamb, M. E., Shannon, D., Leyendecker, B., & Schölmerich, A. (1998). Culture and early infancy among central African foragers and farmers. *Developmental Psychology, 34*(4), 653–661.

Higgins, C. I., Campos, J. J., & Kermoian, R. (1996). Effect of self-produced locomotion on infant postural compensation to optic flow. *Developmental Psychology, 32*(5), 836–841.

Hildebrandt, K. H., Lake, M. A., & Parry, T. B. (1994). Infant coping with everyday stressful events. *Merrill-Palmer Quarterly, 40* (2), 171–189.

Hilder, A. S. (1994). Ethnic differences in the sudden infant death syndrome: What we can learn from immigrants to the UK. *Early Human Development, 38,* 143–149.

Hill, W. L., Borovsky, D., & Rovee-Collier, C. (1988). Continuities in infant memory development. *Developmental Psychobiology, 21,* 43–62.

Hirst, W. (1994). The remembered self in amnesics. In U. Neisser & R. Fivush (Eds.), *The remembering self: Construction and accuracy in the self-narrative* (pp. 253–276). Cambridge, England: Cambridge University Press.

Hobson, R. P. (1990). On the origins of self and the case of autism. *Development and Psychopathology, 2,* 163–181.

Hobson, R. P. (1991). Against the theory of "theory of mind." *British Journal of Developmental Psychology, 9*(1), 33–51.

Hobson, R. P. (1993). The emotional origins of social understanding. *Philosophical Psychology, 6,* 227–249.

Hock, E., & DeMeis, D. K. (1990). Depression in mothers of infants: The role of maternal employment. *Developmental Psychology, 26,* 285–291.

Hodapp, R. M., Goldfield, E. C., & Boyatzis, C. J. (1984). The use and effectiveness of maternal scaffolding in mother-infant games. *Child Development, 55,* 772–781.

Hodnett, E. D., & Osborn, R. W. (1989). Effects of continuous intrapartum professional support on childbirth outcomes. *Research in Nursing and Health, 12*(5), 289–297.

Hofer, M. A. (1981). *The roots of human behavior: An introduction to the psychobiology of early development.* New York: Freeman.

Hoff-Ginsberg, E. (1986). Function and structure in maternal speech: Their relation to the child's development of syntax. *Developmental Psychology, 22,* 155–163.

Hoff-Ginsberg, E., & Shatz, M. (1982). Linguistic input and the child's acquisition of language. *Psychological Bulletin, 92,* 3–26.

Hoffman, M. (1975). Developmental synthesis of affect and cognition and its implications for altruistic motivation. *Developmental Psychology, 11,* 607–622.

Holden, C. (1988). Family planning: A growing gap. *Science, 242,* 370–371.

Holden, G. W. (1983). Avoiding conflict: Mothers as tacticians in the supermarket. *Child Development, 54,* 233–240.

Holden, G. W. (1985). How parents create a social environment via proactive behavior. In T. Garling & J. Valsiner (Eds.), *Children within environments: Towards a psychology of accident prevention* (pp. 160–186). New York: Plenum Press.

Holden, G. W., Thompson, E. E., Zambarano, R. J., & Marshall, L. A. (1997). Child effects as a source of change in maternal attitudes toward corporal punishment. *Journal of Social and Personal Relationships, 14*(4), 481–490.

Holland, R. L., & Smith, D. A. (1989). Management of the second stage of labor. A review (Part II). *South Dakota Journal of Medicine, 42,* 5–8.

Hollenbeck, A. R., Gewirtz, J. L., Seloris, S. L., & Scanlon, J. W. (1984). Labor and delivery medication influences parent-infant interaction in the first post-partum month. *Infant Behavior and Development, 7,* 201–210.

Holt, S. A., Fogel, A., & Wood, R. W. (1998). Innovation in social games. In M. D. P. de Lyra & J. Valsiner (Eds.), *Construction of psychological processes in interpersonal communication: Vol. 4. Child development in culturally structured environments* (pp. 787–823). Norwood, NJ: Ablex.

Hong, K., & Townes, B. (1976). Infant's attachment to inanimate objects: A cross-cultural study. *Journal of the American Academy of Child Psychiatry, 15,* 49–61.

Honig, A. S., & Deters, K. (1996). Grandmothers and mothers: An intergenerational comparison of child-rearing practices with pre-schoolers. *Early Development and Parenting, 5*(1), 47–55.

Hooker, D. (1952). *The prenatal origin of behavior.* Lawrence: University of Kansas Press.

Hopkins, B., & Butterworth, G. (1997). Dynamical systems approaches to the development of action. In J. G. Bremner & A. Slater (Eds.), *Infant development: Recent advances* (pp. 75–100). Hove, England: Psychology Press/Erlbaum.

Hopkins, B., Janssen, B., Kardaun, O., & van der Schoot, T. (1988). Quieting during early infancy: Evidence for a developmental change? *Early Human Development, 18,* 111–124.

Hopkins, B., & von Wulfften Palthe, T. (1987). The development of state during early infancy. *Developmental Psychobiology, 20*(2), 165–175.

Hormann, E. (1977). Breast feeding the adopted baby. *Birth and the Family Journal, 4,* 165–173.

Hornik, R., & Gunnar, M. R. (1988). A descriptive analysis of infant social referencing. *Child Development, 59,* 626–634.

Hornik, R., Risenhoover, N., & Gunnar, M. R. (1987). The effects of maternal positive, neutral and negative affective communications on infant responses to new toys. *Child Development, 58,* 937–944.

Hoshi, N., & Chen, S. J. (1998). Emotion communication of Japanese mothers and their infants. *Research and clinical center for child development: Annual report 1997–1998, 21,* 27–34.

Hossain, Z., Field, T., Gonzalez, J., Malphurs, J., Del Valle, C., & Pickens, J. (1994). Infants of "depressed" mothers interact better with their nondepressed fathers. *Infant Mental Health Journal, 15,* 348–357.

Hossain, Z., Field, T., Pickens, J., Malphurs, J., & Del Valle, C. (1997). Fathers' caregiving in low-income African-American and Hispanic-American families. *Early Development and Parenting, 6*(2), 73–82.

Howard, J. (1978). The influence of children's developmental dysfunctions on marital quality and family interaction. In R. M. Lerner & G. B. Spanier (Eds.), *Child influences on marital and family interaction* (pp. 501–532). New York: Academic Press.

Howard, S. S. (1995). Treatment of male infertility. *New England Journal of Medicine, 332,* 312–317.

Howe, N. (1991). Sibling-directed internal state language, perspective taking, and affective behavior. *Child Development, 62,* 1503–1512.

Howes, C. (1988). Relations between early child care and schooling. *Developmental Psychology, 24,* 53–57.

Howes, C. (1997). Children's experiences in center-based child care as a function of teacher background and adult:child ratio. *Merrill-Palmer Quarterly, 43*(3), 404–425.

Howes, C., Galinsky, E., & Kontos, S. (1998). Child care caregiver sensitivity and attachment. *Social Development, 7*(1), 23–36.

Howes, C., & Matheson, C. C. (1992). Sequences in the development of competent play with peers: Social and social pretend play. *Developmental Psychology, 28,* 961–974.

Howes, C., Phillips, D. A., & Whitebook, M. (1992). Thresholds of quality: Implications for the social development of children in center-based child care. *Child Development, 63,* 449–460.

Howes, C., & Smith, E. W. (1995). Children and their child care caregivers: Profiles of relationships. *Social Development, 4,* 45–59.

Howes, C., & Stewart, P. (1987). Child's play with adults, toys, and peers: An examination of family and child-care influences. *Developmental Psychology, 23,* 423–430.

Hrdy, S. B. (1999). *Mother nature: A history of mothers, infants, and natural selection.* Pantheon.

Hsieh, F. J., Shyu, M. K., Sheu, B. C., Lin, S. P., Chen, C. P., & Huang, F. Y. (1995). Limb defects after chorionic villus sampling. *Obstetrics and Gynecology, 85,* 84–88.

Hsu, H. C., Fogel, A., & Cooper, R. B. (in press). Infant vocal development during the first six months: Speech quality and melodic complexity. *Infant and Child Development.*

Hubert, N. C., Wachs, T. D., Peters-Martin, P., & Gandour, M. J. (1982). The study of early temperament: Measurement and conceptual issues. *Child Development, 53,* 571–600.

Hudson, J. A., & Sheffield, E. G. (1998). Déjà vu all over again: Effects of reenactment on toddlers' event memory. *Child Development, 69*(1), 51–67.

Huffman, L. C., Bryan, Y. E., Carmen, R. del, Pedersen, F. A., Doussard-Roosevelt, J. A., & Porges, S. W. (1998). Infant temperament and cardiac vagal tone: Assessments at twelve weeks of age. *Child Development, 69*(3), 624–635.

Huffman, L. C., Bryan, Y. E., Pedersen, F. A., Lester, B. M., Newman, J. D., & Carmen, R. del. (1994). Infant cry acoustics and maternal ratings of temperament. *Infant Behavior and Development, 17,* 45–53.

Hughes, M. A., McCollum, J., Sheftel, D., & Sanchez, G. (1994). How parents cope with the experience of neonatal intensive care. *Children's Health Care, 23*(1), 1–14.

Hughes, P. F., & Morrison, J. (1994). Grandmultiparity: Not to be feared? An analysis of grandmultiparous women receiving modern antenatal care. *International Journal of Gynecological Obstetrics, 44,* 211–217.

Humphrey, M., & Kirkwood, R. (1982). Marital relationship among adopters. *Adoption and Fostering, 6,* 44–48.

Hunt, H. T. (1995). *On the nature of consciousness: Cognitive, phenomenological, and transpersonal perspectives.* New Haven, CT: Yale University Press.

Hunter, F. T., McCarthy, M. E., MacTurk, R. H., & Vietze, P. M. (1987). Infants' social-constructive interactions with mothers and fathers. *Developmental Psychology, 23,* 249–254.

Hunter, R. S., Kilstrom, N., Kraybill, E. N., & Loda, F. (1978). Antecedents of child abuse and neglect in premature infants: A prospective study in a newborn intensive care unit. *Pediatrics, 61,* 629–635.

Hunziker, U. A., & Barr, R. G. (1986). Increased carrying reduces infant crying: A randomized controlled trial. *Pediatrics, 77,* 641–648.

Huston, A. C. (1994). Children in poverty: Designing research to affect policy. *Social Policy Report: Society for Research in Child Development, 8,* 1–11.

Hutcheson, J. J., Black, M. M., & Starr, R. H. (1993). Developmental differences in interactional characteristics of mothers and their children with failure to thrive. *Journal of Pediatric Psychology, 18,* 453–466.

Huttenlocher, P., & Dabholkar, A. (1997). Regional differences in synaptogenesis in human cerebral cortex. *Journal of Comparative Neurology* (4), 387.

Huttenlocher, J., Haight, W., Bryk, A., Seltzer, M., & Lyons, T. (1991). Early vocabulary growth: Relation to language input and gender. *Developmental Psychology, 27,* 236–248.

Hyde, J. S., Essex, M. J., & Horton, F. (1993). Fathers and parental leave: Attitudes and experiences. *Journal of Family Issues, 14,* 616–623.

Hyman, C. A., & Mitchell, R. (1977). A psychological study of child battering. *Health Visitor, 48,* 294–296.

Hyssala, L., Hyttinen, M., Tautava, P., & Sillanpaa, M. (1993). The Finnish family competence study: The transition to fatherhood. *Journal of Genetic Psychology, 154,* 199–208.

Illingworth, R. S. (1966). *The development of the infant and young child: Normal and abnormal* (3rd ed.). London: E. & S. Livingstone.

Imbens-Bailey, A., & Pan, B. A. (1998). The pragmatics of self- and other-reference in young children. *Social Development, 7*(2), 217–233.

Ingersoll, E. W., & Thoman, E. B. (1994). The breathing bear: Effects on respiration in premature infants. *Physiology and Behavior, 56,* 855–895.

Isabella, R. A. (1993). Origins of attachment: Maternal interactive behavior across the first year. *Child Development, 64,* 605–621.

Isabella, R. A. (1998). Origins of attachment: The role of context, duration, frequency of observation, and infant age in measuring maternal behavior. *Journal of Social and Personal Relationships, 15*(4), 538–554.

Isabella, R. A., & Belsky, J. (1991). Interactional synchrony and the origins of infant-mother attachment: A replication study. *Child Development, 62,* 373–384.

Isabella, R. A., Belsky, J., & von Eye, A. (1989). Origins of infant-mother attachment: An examination of interactional synchrony during the infant's first year. *Developmental Psychology, 25*(1), 12–21.

Ispa, J. (1981). Peer support among Soviet day care toddlers. *International Journal of Behavioral Development, 4,* 255–270.

Izard, C. E. (1981, April). *The primacy of emotion in human development.* Paper presented at the meeting of the Society for Research in Child Development, Boston, MA.

Izard, C. E., Haynes, M. O., Chisholm, G., & Baak, K. (1991). Emotional determinants of infant-mother attachment. *Child Development, 62,* 906–917.

Izard, C. E., Hembree, E. A., & Huebner, R. R. (1987). Infants' emotion expressions to acute pain: Developmental change and stability of individual differences. *Developmental Psychology, 23,* 105–113.

Izard, C. E., & Malatesta, C. Z. (1987). Perspectives on emotional development I: Differential emotions theory of early emotional development. In J. D. Osofsky (Ed.), *Handbook of infant development* (2nd ed., pp. 494–554). New York: Wiley.

Jack, K. E., & Chao, C. R. (1992). Female voluntary surgical contraception via minilaparotomy under local anesthesia. *International Journal of Gynecological Obstetrics, 39,* 111–116.

Jacklin, C. N., Wilcox, K. T., & Maccoby, E. E. (1988). Neonatal sex-steroid hormones and cognitive abilities at six years. *Developmental Psychobiology, 21,* 567–574.

Jackson, J. F. (1993). Human behavioral genetics, Scarr's theory, and her views on interventions: A critical review and commentary on their implications for African American children. *Child Development, 64,* 1318–1332.

Jacobson, J. L. (1981). The role of inanimate objects in early peer interaction. *Child Development, 52,* 618–626.

Jacobson, J. L., Boersma, D. C., Fields, R. B., & Olson, K. L. (1983). Paralinguistic features of adult speech to infants and small children. *Child Development, 54,* 436–442.

Jacobson, S. W. (1979). Matching behavior in the young infant. *Child Development, 50,* 425–430.

Jacobson, S. W., Fein, G. G., Jacobson, J. L., Schwartz, P. M., & Dowler, J. K. (1985). The effect of intrauterine PCB exposure on visual recognition memory. *Child Development, 56,* 853–860.

Jacobson, S. W., & Frye, K. F. (1991). Effect of maternal social support on attachment: Experimental evidence. *Child Development, 62,* 572–582.

Jacobson, S. W., Jacobson, J. L., O'Neill, J. M., Padgett, R. J., Frankowski, J. J., & Bihun, J. T. (1992). *Child Development, 63,* 711–724.

Jaroszewicz, A. M., & Boyd, I. H. (1973). Clinical assessment of gestational age in the newborn. *South African Medical Journal, 47,* 2123–2124.

Jarvis, P. A., & Creasey, G. L. (1991). Parental stress, coping, and attachment in families with an 18-month-old infant. *Infant Behavior and Development, 14,* 383–395.

Jarvis, P. A., Myers, B. J., & Creasey, G. L. (1989). The effects of infants' illness on mothers' interactions with prematures at 4 and 8 months. *Infant Behavior and Development, 12,* 25–35.

Jelliffe, D. B., & Jelliffe, E. F. P. (1988). Breastfeeding: General review. In D. B. Jelliffe & E. F. P. Jelliffe (Eds.), *Programmes to promote breast-feeding* (pp. 3–11). Oxford, England: Oxford University Press.

Johnson, H., Glassman, M. B., Fiks, K. B., & Rosen, T. S. (1987). Path analysis of variables affecting 36-month outcome in a population of multi-risk children. *Infant Behavior and Development, 10,* 451–465.

Johnson, J. L., McAndrew, F. T., & Harris, P. B. (1991). Sociobiology and the naming of adopted and natural children. *Ethology and Sociobiology, 12,* 365–375.

Johnson, L. G. (1983). Giftedness in preschool: A better time for development than identification. *Roeper Review, 5,* 13–15.

Johnson, M. H. (2000). Functional brain development during infancy. In J. G. Bremner & A. Fogel (Eds.), *Handbook of infancy research* (pp. 130–154). Oxford, England: Blackwell.

Johnson, M. H., Dziurawiec, S., Ellis, H., & Morton, J. (1991). Newborns' preferential tracking of face-like stimuli and its subsequent decline. *Cognition, 40,* 1–19.

Johnson, S., Slaughter, V., & Carey, S. (1998). Whose gaze will infants follow? The elicitation of gaze-following in 12-month-olds. *Developmental Science, 1*(2), 233–238.

Johnson, T. R. B., Besinger, R. E., & Thomas, R. L. (1989). The latest clues to fetal behavior and well-being. *Contemporary Pediatrics,* 66–84.

Jones, C. (1987). *Mind over labor.* New York: Viking.

Jones, C. P., & Adamson, L. B. (1987). Language use in mother-child and mother-child-sibling interactions. *Child Development, 58,* 356–366.

Jones, L. C., & Hermann, J. A. (1992). Parental division of infant care: Contextual influences and infant characteristics. *Nursing Research, 41,* 228–234.

Jones, L. C., & Thomas, S. A. (1989). New fathers' blood pressure and heart rate: Relationships to interaction with their newborn infants. *Nursing Research, 38,* 237–241.

Jones, N. A., Field, T., Fox, N. A., Davalos, M., Malphurs, J., Carraway, K., Schanberg, S., & Kuhn, C. (1997). Infants of intrusive and withdrawn mothers. *Infant Behavior and Development, 20,* 175–186.

Jones, O. (1977). Mother-child communication with pre-linguistic Down's syndrome and normal infants. In H. R. Schaffer (Ed.), *Studies in mother-infant interaction* (pp. 76–109). London: Academic Press.

Jones, S. S. (1996). Imitation or exploration? Young infants' matching of adults' oral gestures. *Child Development, 67*(5), 1952–1969.

Jones, S. S., Collins, K., & Hong, H. W. (1991). An audience effect on smile production in 10-month-old infants. *Psychological Science, 2,* 45–49.

Jones, S. S., Raag, T., & Collins, K. L. (1990). Smiling in older infants: Form and maternal response. *Infant Behavior and Development, 13,* 147–165.

Jones, S. S., Smith, L. B., & Landau, B. (1991). Object properties and knowledge in early lexical learning. *Child Development, 62,* 499–516.

Judd, J. M. (1985). Assessing the newborn from head to toe. *Nursing '85, 15,* 34–41.

Juffer, F., & Rosenboom, L. G. (1997). Infant-mother attachment of internationally adopted children in the Netherlands. *International Journal of Behavioral Development, 20*(1), 93–107.

Juffer, F., Rosenboom, L. G., Hoksbergen, R. A. C., Riksen-Walraven, J. M. A., & Kohnstamm, G. A. (1997). Attachment and intervention in adoptive families with and without biological children. In W. Koops, J. B. Hoeksma, & D. C. van den Boom (Eds.), *Development of interaction and attachment: Traditional and non-traditional approaches* (pp. 93–108). Amsterdam: Royal Netherlands Academy of Arts and Sciences.

Jusczyk, P. W. (1985). The high-amplitude sucking technique as a methodological tool in speech perception research. In G. Gottlieb & N. A. Krasnegor (Eds.), *Measurement of audition and vision during the first year of postnatal life: A methodological overview* (pp. 414–438). Norwood, NJ: Ablex.

Jusczyk, P. W., Cutler, A., & Redanz, N. J. (1993). Infants' preference for the predominant stress patterns of English words. *Child Development, 64,* 675–687.

Jusczyk, P. W., Kennedy, L. J., & Jusczyk, A. (1995). Young infants' retention of information about syllables. *Infant Behavior and Development, 18*(1), 27–41.

Kagan, J. (1987). Perspectives on infancy. In J. D. Osofsky (Ed.), *Handbook of infant development* (2nd ed., pp. 1150–1198). New York: Wiley.

Kagan, J. (1989). *Unstable ideas.* Cambridge, MA: Harvard University Press.

Kagan, J., Arcus, D., Snidman, N., Feng, W. Y., Hendler, J., & Greene, S. (1994). *Reactivity in infants: A cross-national comparison.* Developmental Psychology, 30, 342–345.

Kagan, J., Kearsley, R., & Zelazo, P. (1978). *Infancy: Its place in human development.* Cambridge, MA: Harvard University Press.

Kagan, J., & Reznick, J. S. (1984). Cardiac reaction as an index of task involvement. *Australian Journal of Psychology, 36,* 135–147.

Kagan, J., Reznick, J. S., & Snidman, N. (1987). The physiology and psychology of behavioral inhibition in children. *Child Development, 58,* 1459–1473.

Kagan, J., Reznick, J. S., Snidman, N., Gibbons, J., & Johnson, M. O. (1988). Childhood derivatives of inhibition and lack of inhibition to the unfamiliar. *Child Development, 59,* 1580–1589.

Kagan, J., Snidman, N., & Arcus, D. (1998). Childhood derivatives of high and low reactivity in infancy. *Child Development, 69*(6), 1483–1493.

Kaitz, M., Meirov, H., & Landman, I. (1993). Infant recognition by tactile cues. *Infant Behavior and Development, 16,* 333–341.

Kaler, S. R., & Kopp, C. B. (1990). Compliance and comprehension in very young toddlers. *Child Development, 61,* 1997–2003.

Kalmar, M. (1996). The course of intellectual development in preterm and fullterm children: An 8-year longitudinal study. *International Journal of Behavioral Development, 19*(3), 491–516.

Kaltenbach, K., Weinraub, M., & Fullard, W. (1980). Infant wariness toward strangers reconsidered: Infant's and mother's reactions to unfamiliar persons. *Child Development, 51,* 1197–1202.

Kanazawa, T., Shimizu, S., Kamada, J., Tanabe, H., & Itoigawa, N. (1997). Intelligence and learning disabilities in 6- to 8-year-old children weighing under 1,000 grams at birth. *International Journal of Behavioral Development, 20*(1), 179–188.

Kaplan, P. S., Bachorowski, J., & Zarlengo-Strouse, P. (1999). Child-directed speech produced by mothers with symptoms of depression fails to promote associative learning in 4-month-old infants. *Child Development, 70*(3), 560–570.

Kapoor, S. K., Amand, K., & Kumar, G. (1994). Risk factors for stillbirths in a secondary level hospital at Ballabgarh, Haryana: A case control study. *Indian Journal of Pediatrics, 61,* 161–166.

Karcew, S. (1994). Fetal consequences and risks attributed to the use of prescribed and over-the-counter (OTC) preparations during pregnancy. *International Journal of Clinical Pharmacological Therapy, 32,* 335–343.

Karmel, M. (1959). *Thank you, Doctor Lamaze: A mother's experiences in painless childbirth.* Philadelphia: Lippincott.

Karns, J. T. (2000). Health, nutrition, and safety. In J. G. Bremner & A. Fogel (Eds.), *Handbook of infancy research* (pp. 438–460). Oxford, England: Blackwell.

Karr-Morse, R., & Wiley, M. S. (1997). *Ghosts from the nursery: Tracing the roots of violence.* New York: Atlantic Monthly Press.

Karrer, R., Monti, L., & Ackles, P. K. (1989, October). *Late ERP's of one-month-old infants in a visual oddball task.* Presented at the Society for Psychophysiological Research, New Orleans.

Karzon, R. G. (1985). Discrimination of polysyllabic sequences by one-to four-month-old infants. *Journal of Experimental Child Psychology, 39,* 326–342.

Kataria, S., Frutiger, A. D., Lanford, B., & Swanson, M. S. (1988). Anterior fontanel closure in healthy term infants. *Infant Behavior and Development, 11,* 229–233.

Katz, V. L., & Kuller, J. A. (1994). Recurrent miscarriage. *American Journal of Perinatology, 11,* 386–387.

Kaufmann, R., & Kaufmann, F. (1980). The face schema in 3- and 4-month-old infants: The role of dynamic properties of the face. *Infant Behavior and Development, 3*, 331–339.

Kawakami, K., Takai-Kawakami, K., Kurihara, H., Shimizu, Y., & Yanaihara, T. (1996). The effect of sounds on newborn infants under stress. *Infant Behavior and Development, 19*, 375–379.

Kaye, K. (1977). Toward the origin of dialogue. In H. R. Schaffer (Ed.), *Studies in mother-infant interaction* (pp. 75–120). New York: Academic Press.

Kaye, K. (1982). *The mental and social life of babies.* Chicago: University of Chicago Press.

Kaye, K., & Fogel, A. (1980). The temporal structure of face-to-face communication between mothers and infants. *Developmental Psychology, 16*, 454–464.

Kaye, K., & Marcus, J. (1978). Imitation over a series of trials without feedback. *Infant Behavior and Development, 1*, 141–155.

Kaye, K., & Wells, A. J. (1980). Mother's jiggling and the burst-pause pattern of neonatal feeding. *Infant Behavior and Development, 3*, 29–46.

Keith-Speigel, P. (1983). *Children and consent to participate in research.* In G. B. Melton & M. J. Saks (Eds.), *Children's competence to consent* (pp. 179–211). New York: Plenum Press.

Keller, A., Ford, L. H., & Meacham, J. A. (1978). Dimensions of self-concept in preschool children. *Developmental Psychology, 14*, 483–489.

Keller, H., Chasiotis, A., Risau-Peters, J., Volker, S., Zach, U., & Restemeier, R. (1996). Psychobiological aspects of infant crying. *Early Development and Parenting, 5*(1), 1–13.

Kelley, M. L., Smith, T. S., Green, A. P., Berndt, A. E., & Rogers, M. C. (1998). Importance of fathers' parenting to African-American toddler's social and cognitive development. *Infant Behavior and Development, 21*(4), 733–744.

Kemper, T. L., & Bauman, M. L. (1993). The contribution of neuropathologic studies to the understanding of autism. *Neurological Clinics, 11*, 175–187.

Kendrick, C., & Dunn, J. (1980). Caring for a second baby: Effects on interaction between mother and firstborn. *Developmental Psychology, 16*, 303–311.

Kennedy, D., & Koren, G. (1998). Valproic acid use in psychiatry: Issues in treating women of reproductive age. *Journal of Psychiatry and Neuroscience, 23*(4), 223–228.

Kennedy, K. I., Fortney, J. A., Bonhomme, M. G., Potts, M., Lamptey, P., & Carswell, W. (1990). Do the benefits of breastfeeding outweigh the risk of postnatal transmission of HIV via breastmilk? *Tropical Doctor, 20*, 25–29.

Kent, R. D. (1981). Articulatory-acoustic perspectives on speech development. In R. Stark (Ed.), *Language development in infancy and early childhood* (pp. 105–106). New York: Elsevier.

Kermoian, R., & Campos, J. J. (1988). Locomotor experience: A facilitator of spatial cognitive development. *Child Development, 59*, 908–917.

Kessen, W., Haith, M., & Salapatek, P. (1970). Human infancy: A bibliography and guide. In P. H. Mussen (Ed.), *Carmichael's manual of child psychology* (3rd ed., pp. 808–856). New York: Wiley.

Ketting, E., & Visser, A. P. (1994). Contraception in the Netherlands: The low abortion rate explained. *Patient and Educational Counseling, 23*, 161–171.

Kiely, M., Drum, M. A., & Kessel, W. (1998). Early discharge: Risks, benefits, and who decides. *Clinical Perinatology, 25*, 539–553.

Kier, C. A., & Lewis, C. N. (1993). Sibling attachment: The development of a new infant-based measure (SPPIR). *Early Development and Parenting, 2*, 243–246.

Kilbride, H. W., Johnson, D. L., & Streissguth, A. P. (1977). Social class, birth order, and newborn experience. *Child Development, 48*, 1686–1688.

Killen, M., & Wainryb, C. (2000). Independence and interdependence in diverse cultural contexts. In S. Harkness & C. Raeff (Eds.), *Variability in the social construction of the child. New directions for child and adolescent development* (No. 87, pp. 5–21). San Francisco: Jossey-Bass, Inc.

Kisilevsky, B. S., Hains, S. M. J., Lee, K., Muir, D. W., Xu, F., Fu, G., Zhao, Z. Y., & Yang, R. L. (1998). The still-face effect in Chinese and Canadian 3- to 6-month-old infants. *Developmental Psychology, 34*(4), 629–639.

Kisilevsky, B. S., & Muir, D. W. (1984). Neonatal habituation and dishabituation to tactile stimulation during sleep. *Developmental Psychology, 20*, 367–373.

Kitchen, W., & Murton, L. J. (1985). Survival rates of infants with birth weight between 501 and 1,000 g. *American Journal of Diseases of Children, 139*, 470–471.

Klaus, M. H., Jerauld, R., Kreger, N. C., McAlpine, W., Steffa, M., & Kennell, J. H. (1972). Maternal attachment importance of the first post-partum days. *New England Journal of Medicine, 46*, 187–192.

Klaus, M. H., Kennell, J. H., Plumb, N., & Zeuhlke, S. (1970). Human maternal behavior at the first contact with her young. *Pediatrics, 46*, 187–192.

Klein, B. P. (1985). Caregiving arrangements by employed women with children under a year of age. *Developmental Psychology, 21*(3), 403–406.

Klein, R. P., & Durfee, J. T. (1976). Effects of stress on attachment behavior in infants. *Journal of Genetic Psychology, 132*, 321–322.

Kleitman, N. (1963). *Sleep and wakefulness.* Chicago: University of Chicago Press.

Klerman, L. V., & Goldenberg, R. L. (1999). Prenatal care: A new perspective. *Zero to Three, 19*(4), 3–8.

Klimes-Dougan, B., & Kopp, C. B. (1999). Children conflict tactics with mothers: A longitudinal investigation of the toddler and preschool years. *Merrill-Palmer Quarterly, 45*(2), 226–241.

Klinnert, M. D. (1984). The regulation of infant behavior by maternal facial expression. *Infant Behavior and Development, 7*, 447–465.

Klinnert, M. D., Emde, R. N., Butterfield, P., & Campos, J. J. (1986). Social referencing: The infant's use of emotional signals from a friendly adult with mother present. *Developmental Psychology, 22*, 427–432.

Klinnert, M. D., Gavin, L. A., Wamboldt, F. S., & Mrazek, D. A. (1992). Marriages with children at medical risk: The transition to parenthood. *Journal of the American Academy of Child and Adolescent Psychiatry, 31*(2), 334–342.

Klopfer, P. (1988). Metaphors for development: How important are experiences early in life? *Developmental Psychobiology, 21*, 671–678.

Kochanska, G., Coy, K. C., Tjebkes, T. L., & Husarek, S. J. (1998). Individual differences in emotionality in infancy. *Child Development, 69*(2), 375–390.

Kochanska, G., Forman, D. R., & Coy, K. C. (1999). Implications of the mother-child relationship in infancy for socialization in the second year of life. *Infant Behavior and Development, 22*(2), 249–265.

Kochanska, G., Tjebkes, T. L., & Forman, D. R. (1998). Children's emerging regulation of conduct: Restraint, compliance, and internalization from infancy to the second year. *Child Development, 69*(5), 1378–1389.

Koepke, J. E., & Bigelow, A. E. (1997). Observations of newborn suckling behavior. *Infant Behavior and Development, 20*(1), 93–98.

Koepke, J. E., Hamm, M., Legerstee, J., & Russell, M. (1983). Neonatal imitation: Two failures to replicate. *Infant Behavior and Development, 6*, 97–102.

Koester, L. S. (1994). Early interactions and the socioemotional development of deaf infants. *Early Development and Parenting, 3*, 51–60.

Kogan, N., & Carter, A. S. (1996). Mother-infant reengagement following the still-face: The role of maternal emotion availability in infant affect regulation. *Infant Behavior and Development, 19*, 359–370.

Kojima, H. (1986). Becoming nurturant in Japan: Past and present. In A. Fogel & G. F. Melson (Eds.), *Origins of nurturance: Developmen-*

tal, biological, and cultural perspectives on caregiving (pp. 359–376). Hillsdale, NJ: Erlbaum.

Kolbert, K., & Miller, A. (1994). Government in the examining room: Restrictions on the provision of abortion. Journal of Medical Women's Association, 49, 153–155.

Konner, M. (1975). Relations among infants and juveniles in comparative perspective. In M. Lewis & L. A. Rosenblum (Eds.), Friendship and peer relations (pp. 108–140). New York: Wiley.

Konner, M. (1977). Infancy among the Kalahari Desert San. In P. H. Leiderman, S. R. Tulkin, & A. Rosenfeld (Eds.), Culture and infancy (pp. 680–699). New York: Academic Press.

Kontos, D. (1978). A study of the effects of extended mother-infant contact on maternal behavior at one and three months. Birth and the Family Journal, 5, 133–140.

Kontos, S., Howes, C., Shinn, M., & Galinsky, E. (1997). Children's experience in family child care and relative care as a function of family income and ethnicity. Merrill-Palmer Quarterly, 43(3), 386–403.

Koomen, H. M. Y., & Hoeksma, J. B. (1992). Maternal interactive behavior towards children with and children without cleft lip and palate. Early Development and Parenting, 1, 169–181.

Koops, W. (1996). Historical developmental psychology: The sample case of paintings. International Journal of Behavioral Development, 19(2), 393–413.

Kopp, C. B. (1982). Antecedents of self-regulation: A developmental perspective. Developmental Psychology, 18, 199–214.

Kopp, C. B. (1989). Regulation of distress and negative emotions: A developmental view. Developmental Psychology, 25, 343–354.

Kopp, C. B., & Parmelee, A. (1979). Prenatal and perinatal influences on infant behavior. In J. Osofsky (Ed.), Handbook of infant development (pp. 215–247). New York: Wiley.

Kopp, C. B., & Vaughn, B. E. (1982). Sustained attention during exploratory manipulation as a predictor of cognitive competence in preterm infants. Child Development, 53, 174–182.

Korn, S. J., Chess, S., & Fernandez, P. (1978). The impact of children's physical handicaps on marital quality and family interaction. In R. M. Lerner & G. B. Spanier (Eds.), Child influences on marital and family interaction (pp. 285–308). New York: Academic Press.

Korner, A. (1987). Preventive intervention with high-risk newborns: Theoretical, conceptual, and methodological perspectives. In J. D. Osofsky (Ed.), Handbook of infant development (2nd ed. pp. 503–534). New York: Wiley.

Korner, A., Brown, B. W., Reade, E. P., Stevenson, D. K., Fernbach, S. A., & Thom, V. A. (1988). State behavior of preterm infants as a function of development, individual and sex differences. Infant Behavior and Development, 11, 111–124.

Kornfeld, J. R. (1971). Theoretical issues in child phonology. Proceedings of the Seventh Annual Meeting of the Chicago Linguistics Society (pp. 454–468). Chicago: University of Chicago Press.

Kornhaber, A., & Woodward, K. L. (1981). Grandparent/grandchild: The vital connection. Garden City, NY: Anchor Press.

Korte, D., & Scaer, R. (1990). A good birth, a safe birth. New York: Bantam.

Kotch, J. B., & Cohen, S. R. (1986). SIDS counselors' reports of own and parents' reactions to reviewing the autopsy report. Omega Journal of Death and Dying, 16, 129–139.

Krafchuk, E. E., Tronick, E., & Clifton, R. K. (1983). Behavioral and cardiac responsiveness to sound in preterm neonates varying in risk status: A hypothesis of their paradoxical reactivity. In T. Field & A. Sostek (Eds.), Infants born at risk (pp. 144–164). New York: Grune & Stratton.

Kramer, L., & Gottman, J. M. (1992). Becoming a sibling: "With a little help from my friends." Developmental Psychology, 28, 685–699.

Kramer, L., Perozynski, L. A., & Chung, T. Y. (1999). Parental responses to sibling conflict: The effects of development and parent gender. Child Development, 70(6), 1401–1414.

Kravitz, H., Goldenberg, D., & Neyhus, A. (1978). Tactual exploration by normal infants. Developmental Medicine and Child-Neurology, 20(6), 720–726.

Kremenitzer, J. P., Vaughan, H. G., Jr., Kurtzberg, D., & Dowling, K. (1979). Smooth-pursuit eye movements in the newborn infant. Child Development, 50, 442–448.

Kropp, J. P., & Haynes, O. M. (1987). To identify general and specific emotion signals of infants. Child Development, 58, 187–190.

Kuchuk, A., Vibbert, M., & Bornstein, M. H. (1986). The perception of smiling and its experiential correlates in three-month-old infants. Child Development, 57, 1054–1061.

Kuczaj, S. A. (1978). Children's judgements of grammatical and ungrammatical irregular past-tense verbs. Child Development, 49, 319–326.

Kuczaj, S. A., & Maratsos, M. P. (1983). Initial verbs of yes-no questions: A different kind of general grammatical category. Developmental Psychology, 19, 440–444.

Kuczynski, L., & Kochanska, G. (1995). Function and content of maternal demands: Developmental significance of early demands for competent action. Child Development, 66, 616–628.

Kuczynski, L., Zahn-Waxler, C., & Radke-Yarrow, M. (1987). Development and content of imitation in the second and third years of life: A socialization perspective. Developmental Psychology, 23, 276–282.

Kuhl, P. K. (1981). Auditory category formation and developmental speech perception. In R. Stark (Ed.), Language behavior in infancy and early childhood (pp. 155–170). New York: Elsevier.

Kuhl, P. K. (1998). Language, culture, and intersubjectivity: The creation of shared perception. In S. Bråten (Ed.), Intersubjective communication and emotion in early ontogeny. Studies in emotion and social interaction, 2nd series (pp. 297–315). Cambridge, England: Cambridge University Press.

Kulin, N. A., Pastuszk, A., Sage, S. R., Schick-Boschetto, B., Spivey, G., Feldkamp, M., Ormond, K., Matsui, D., Stein-Schechman, A. K., Cook, L., Brochu, J., Rieder, M., & Koren, G. (1998). Pregnancy outcome following maternal use of the new selective serotonin reuptake inhibitors. Journal of the American Medical Association, 279, 609–610.

Kuller, J. A., & Katz, V. L. (1994). Miscarriage: A historical perspective. Birth, 21, 227–228.

Kumar, T. C. (1994). The value and use of different contraceptive methods. Human Reproduction, 9, 578–585.

Kurzweil, S. R. (1988). Recognition of mother from multisensory interactions in early infancy. Infant Behavior and Development, 11, 235–243.

Laakso, M. L., Poikkeus, A. M., & Lyytinen, P. (1999). Shared reading interaction in families with and without genetic risk for dyslexia: Implications for toddlers' language development. Infant and Child Development, 8, 179–195.

Labrell, F. (1994). A typical interaction behavior between fathers and toddlers: Teasing. Early Development and Parenting, 3, 125–130.

Lamb, M. E. (1977). The development of mother-infant and father-infant attachments in the second year of life. Developmental Psychology, 13, 637–648.

Lamb, M. E. (1978a). Influences of the child on marital quality and family interaction during the prenatal, perinatal and infancy periods. In R. M. Lerner & G. B. Spanier (Eds.), Child influences on marital and family interaction (pp. 259–289). New York: Academic Press.

Lamb, M. E. (1978b). Interactions between eighteen-month-olds and their preschool-aged siblings. Child Development, 49, 51–59.

Lamb, M. E. (1978c). Qualitative aspects of mother- and father-infant attachments. Infant Behavior and Development, 1, 265–277.

Lamb, M. E. (1982). The bonding phenomenon: Misinterpretations and their implications. Journal of Pediatrics, 101, 555–557.

Lamb, M. E., & Bornstein, M. H. (1987). Development in infancy (2nd ed.). New York: Random House.

Lamb, M. E., Frodi, A. M., Frodj, M., & Hwang, C. P. (1982). Characteristics of maternal and paternal behavior in traditional and nontraditional Swedish families. *International Journal of Behavior and Development, 5,* 131–141.

Lamb, M. E., Gaensbauer, T. J., Malkin, C. M., & Schultz, L. A. (1985). The effects of child maltreatment on security of infant-adult attachment. *Infant Behavior and Development, 8,* 35–45.

Lamb, M. E., Pleck, J. H., Charnov, E. L., & Levine, J. A. (1987). A biosocial perspective on paternal behavior and involvement. In J. B. Lancaster, A. Rossi, J. Altmann, & L. R. Sherrod (Eds.), *Parenting across the lifespan: Biosocial perspectives* (pp. 66–87). Chicago: Aldine.

Lamb, M. E., Sternberg, K. J., & Prodromidis, M. (1992). Nonmaternal care and the security of infant-mother attachment: A reanalysis of the data. *Infant Behavior and Development, 15,* 71–83.

Lamb, M. E., Thompson, R., Gardner, W., Charnov, E., & Estes, D. (1984). Security of infantile attachment as assessed in the strange situation: Its study and biological interpretation. *Behavioral and Brain Sciences, 7,* 127–147.

Lampert, R. W., & Schochet, S. S. (1968). Demyelination and remyelination in lead neuropathy. *Journal of Neuropathology and Experimental Neurology, 27,* 527–545.

Landau, B., & Spelke, E. (1988). Geometric complexity and object search in infancy. *Developmental Psychology, 24,* 512–521.

Landau, R. (1976). Extent that the mother represents the social stimulation to which the infant is exposed: Findings from a cross-cultural study. *Developmental Psychology, 12,* 399–405.

Landesman-Dwyer, S. (1981). Maternal drinking and pregnancy outcome. *Applied Research in Mental Retardation, 3,* 241–263.

Landry, S. H. (1995). The development of joint attention in premature low birth weight infants: Effects of early medical complications and maternal attention-directing behaviors. In C. Moore & P. J. Dunham (Eds.), *Joint attention: Its origins and role in development* (pp. 223–250). Hillsdale, NJ: Erlbaum.

Landry, S. H., & Chapieski, M. L. (1989). Joint attention and infant toy exploration: Effects of Down's syndrome and prematurity. *Child Development, 60,* 103–118.

Landry, S. H., Chapieski, M. L., & Schmidt, M. (1986). Effects of maternal attention-directing strategies on preterms' response to toys. *Infant Behavior and Development, 9,* 257–269.

Landry, S. H., Garner, P. W., Swank, P. R., & Baldwin, C. D. (1996). Effects of maternal scaffolding during joint toy play with preterm and full-term infants. *Merrill-Palmer Quarterly, 42*(2), 177–199.

Landry, S. H., Smith, K. E., Miller-Loncar, C. L., & Swank, P. R. (1997). Predicting cognitive-language and social growth curves from early maternal behaviors in children at varying degrees of biological risk. *Developmental Psychology, 33*(6), 1040–1053.

Landry, S. H., Smith, K. E., Miller-Loncar, C. L., & Swank, P. R. (1998). The relation of change in maternal interactive styles to the developing social competence of full-term and preterm children. *Child Development, 69*(1), 105–123.

Langkamp, D. L., & Harris, S. (1992). Predicting preschool motor and cognitive performance in appropriate-for-gestational-age children born at 32 weeks gestation. *Early Development and Parenting, 1,* 89–96.

Langlois, J. H., Ritter, J. M., Casey, R. J., & Sawin, D. B. (1995). Infant attractiveness predicts maternal behaviors and attitudes. *Developmental Psychology, 31,* 464–472.

Langlois, J. H., Ritter, J. M., Roggman, L. A., & Vaughn, L. S. (1991). Facial diversity and infant preferences for attractive faces. *Developmental Psychology, 27,* 79–84.

Langlois, J. H., Roggman, L. A., Casey, R. J., Ritter, J. M., Rieser-Danner, L. S., & Jenkins, V. Y. (1987). Infant preferences for attractive faces: Rudiments of a stereotype? *Developmental Psychology, 23,* 363–369.

Langlois, J. H., Roggman, L. A., & Rieser-Danner, L. A. (1990). Infants' differential social responses to attractive and unattractive faces. *Developmental Psychology, 26,* 153–159.

Largo, R. H. (1993). Early motor development in preterm children. In G. J. P. Savelsbergh (Ed.), *The development of coordination in infancy* (pp. 425–444). Amsterdam: Elsevier.

Laughlin, C. D. (1991). Pre- and perinatal brain development and enculturation: A biogenetic structural approach. *Human Nature, 2,* 171–213.

Lavelli, M. (1999). Attenzione visiva e relative pattern espressivi nel contesto della comunicazione precoce con la madre: La transizione del secondo mese. Unpublished doctoral dissertation. Università degli studi di Milano.

Lavelli, M., & Fogel, A. (1998). *Developmental changes in early mother-infant face-to-face communication.* Presented at the International Conference on Infant Studies, Atlanta, GA.

Lavelli, M., & Poli, M. (1998). Early mother-infant interaction during breast- and bottle-feeding. *Infant Behavior and Development, 21*(4), 667–684.

Lawson, K. R., Parrinello, R., & Ruff, H. A. (1992). Maternal behavior and infant attention. *Infant Behavior and Development, 15,* 209–229.

Lawson, K. R., & Ruff, H. A. (1984). Infants' visual following: The effects of size and sound. *Developmental Psychology, 20,* 427–434.

Lazar, I., & Darlington, R. (1982). Lasting effects of early education: A report from the Consortium for Longitudinal Studies. *Monographs of the Society for Research in Child Development, 47* (Serial No. 195), 1–151.

Leach, P. (1997). Infant care from infants' viewpoint: The views of some professionals. *Early Development and Parenting, 6*(2), 47–58.

Leadbeater, B. J., Bishop, S. J., & Raver, C. C. (1996). Quality of mother-toddler interactions, maternal depressive symptoms, and behavior problems in preschoolers of adolescent mothers. *Developmental Psychology, 32*(2), 280–288.

Leboyer, F. (1975). *Birth without violence.* New York: Knopf.

Lecanuet, J.-P., Granier-Deferre, C., Jacquet, A.-Y., Capponi, I., & Ledru, L. (1993). Prenatal discrimination of a male and a female voice uttering the same sentence. *Early Development and Parenting, 2,* 217–228.

Lee, C., & Bates, J. (1985). Mother-child interaction at age two years and perceived difficult temperament. *Child Development, 56,* 1314–1325.

Lee, V. E., Brooks-Gunn, J., & Schnur, E. (1988). Does Head Start work? A 1-year follow-up comparison of disadvantaged children attending Head Start, no preschool, and other preschool programs. *Developmental Psychology, 24,* 210–222.

Lee, V. E., Brooks-Gunn, J., Schnur, E., & Liaw, F. R. (1990). Are Head Start effects sustained? A longitudinal follow-up comparison of disadvantaged children attending Head Start, no preschool, and other preschool programs. *Child Development, 61,* 495–507.

Lefebvre, F., Bard, H., Veilleux, A., & Martel, C. (1988). Outcome at school age of children with birth weights of 1,000 grams or less. *Developmental Medicine and Child Neurology, 30*(2), 170–180.

Leftwich, M., & Collins, F. (1994). Parental smoking, depression, and child development. *Journal of Pediatric Psychology, 19,* 557–569.

Leger, D. W., Thompson, R. A., Merritt, J. A., & Benz, J. J. (1996). Adult perception of emotion intensity in human infant cries: Effects of infant age and cry acoustics. *Child Development, 67,* 3238–3249.

Legerstee, M. (1991). Changes in the quality of infant sounds as a function of social and nonsocial stimulation. *First Language, 11,* 327–343.

Legerstee, M. (1992). A review of the animate-inanimate distinction in infancy: Implications for models of social and cognitive knowing. *Early Development and Parenting, 1,* 59–67.

Legerstee, M. (1997). Contingency effects of people and objects on subsequent cognitive functioning in three-month-old infants. *Social Development, 6*(3), 307–321.

Legerstee, M., & Bowman, T. G. (1989). The development of responses to people and a toy in infants with Down's syndrome. *Infant Behavior and Development, 12,* 465–477.

Legerstee, M., Pomerleau, A., Malcuit, G., & Feider, H. (1987). The development of infants' responses to people and a doll: Implications for research in communication. *Infant Behavior and Development, 10,* 81–95.

Legerstee, M., & Weintraub, J. (1997). The integration of person and object attention in infants with and without Down syndrome. *Infant Behavior and Development, 20*(1), 71–82.

Le Goff, J. (1987). *The medieval world.* (L. G. Cochrane, Trans.). London, England: Collins and Brown.

Leiberman, A. F. (1977). Preschoolers' competence with a peer: Relations with attachment and peer experience. *Child Development, 48,* 1277–1287.

Leifer, J. S., & Lewis, M. (1983). Maternal speech to normal and handicapped children: A look at question-asking behavior. *Infant Behavior and Development, 6,* 175–187.

Leifer, M. (1980). *Psychological effects of motherhood: A study of first pregnancy.* New York: Praeger.

Leitch, D. B. (1999). Mother-infant interaction: Achieving synchrony. *Nursing Research, 48*(1), 55–58.

Lelorde, G., Barthelemy, C., Martineau, J., & Bruneau, N. (1991). Free acquisition, free imitation, physiological curiosity and exchange and development therapies in autistic children. *Brain Dysfunction, 4,* 335–347.

Lemery, K. S., & Goldsmith, H. H. (1999). Genetically informative designs for the study of behavioral development. *International Journal of Behavioral Development, 23*(2), 293–317.

Lemery, K. S., Goldsmith, H. H., Klinnert, M. D., & Mrazek, D. A. (1999). Developmental models of infant and childhood temperament. *Developmental Psychology, 35*(1), 189–204.

Lemmer, C. M. (1987). Early discharge: Outcomes in primiparas and their infants. *Journal of Obstetric and Gynecological Nursing,* 230–236.

Lempers, J. D., Flavell, E. R., & Flavell, J. H. (1977). The development in very young children of tacit knowledge concerning visual perception. *Genetic Psychology Monographs, 95,* 3–53.

Lenneberg, E. H. (1969). On explaining language. *Science, 164,* 635–643.

Leonard, R. (1993). Mother-child disputes as arenas for fostering negotiation skills. *Early Development and Parenting, 2,* 157–167.

Lesko, W., & Leski, M. (1984). *The maternity sourcebook.* New York: Warner Books.

Leslie, G. I., Gibson, F. L., McMahon, C., Tennant, C., & Saunders, D. M. (1998). Infants conceived using in-vitro fertilization do not over-utilize health care resources after the neonatal period. *Human Reproduction, 13*(8), 2055–2059.

Lester, B. M. (1976). Spectrum analysis of the sounds of well-nourished and malnourished infants. *Child Development, 47,* 237–241.

Lester, B. M., Boukydis, Z. C. F., Garcia-Coll, C. T., Hole, W., & Peucker, M. (1992). Infantile colic: Acoustic cry characteristics, maternal perception of cry, and temperament. *Infant Behavior and Development, 15,* 15–26.

Lester, B. M., & Dreher, M. (1989). Effects of marijuana use during pregnancy on newborn cry. *Child Development, 60,* 765–771.

Lester, B. M., & Zeskind, P. S. (1978). Brazelton scale physical size correlates of neonatal cry features. *Infant Behavior and Development, 1,* 393–402.

Leung, E., & Rheingold, H. L. (1981). Development of pointing as a social gesture. *Developmental Psychology, 17,* 215–220.

Levitt, M. J., Weber, R. A., & Clark, M. C. (1986). Social network relationships as sources of maternal support and well-being. *Developmental Psychology, 22,* 310–316.

Levitt, P., Reinoso, B., & Jones, L. (1998). The critical impact of early cellular environment on neuronal development. *Preventive Medicine, 27*(2), 180–183.

Levy, G. (in press). Detection of race-related categories by 10-month-old infants. *Infant Behavior and Development.*

Levy, G., & Haaf, R. A. (1994). Detection of gender-related categories by 10-month-old infants. *Infant Behavior and Development, 17,* 457–459.

Levy, H. L., Karolkewicz, V., Houghton, S. A., & MacCready, R. A. (1970). Screening the "normal" population in Massachusetts for phenylketonuria. *New England Journal of Medicine, 282,* 1455–1458.

Levy, T. M. (Ed.) (2000). *Handbook of attachment interventions.* San Diego, CA: Academic Press.

Levy, Y. (1999). Early metalinguistic competence: Speech monitoring and repair behavior. *Developmental Psychology, 35*(3), 822–834.

Levy-Shiff, R. (1994). Individual and contextual correlates of marital change across the transition to parenthood. *Developmental Psychology, 30,* 591–601.

Levy-Shiff, R., Dimitrovsky, L., Shulman, S., & Har-Even, D. (1998). Cognitive appraisals, coping strategies, and support resources as correlates of parenting and infant development. *Developmental Psychology, 34*(6), 1417–1427.

Levy-Shiff, R., Goldschmidt, I., & Har-Even, D. (1991). Transition to parenthood in adoptive families. *Developmental Psychology, 27,* 131–140.

Levy-Shiff, R., Sharir, H., & Mogilner, M. B. (1989). Mother– and father–preterm infant relationship in the hospital preterm nursery. *Child Development, 60,* 93–102.

Lew, A. R., & Butterworth, G. (1995). The effects of hunger on hand-mouth coordination in newborn infants. *Developmental Psychology, 31,* 456–463.

Lewis, C., Kier, C., Hyder, C., Prenderville, N., Pullen, J., & Stephens, A. (1996). Observer influences on fathers and mothers: An experimental manipulation of the structure and function of parent-infant conversation. *Early Development and Parenting, 5*(1), 57–68.

Lewis, M. (1995). Embarrassment: The emotion of self-exposure and evaluation. In J. P. Tangney & K. W. Fischer (Eds.) *Self-conscious emotions: The psychology of shame, guilt, embarrassment, and pride* (pp. 198–218). New York: Guilford Press.

Lewis, M., & Brooks-Gunn, J. (1979). *Social cognition and the acquisition of self.* New York: Plenum Press.

Lewis, M., & Feiring, C. (1978). The child's social world. In R. M. Lerner & G. B. Spanier (Eds.), *Child influences on marital and family interaction* (pp. 119–150). New York: Academic Press.

Lewis, M., & Feiring, C. (1989). Infant, mother, and mother-infant interaction behavior and subsequent attachment. *Child Development, 60,* 831–837.

Lewis, M., & Michalson, L. (1983). *Children's emotions and moods.* New York: Plenum Press.

Lewis, M., & Ramsay, D. S. (1995). Developmental change in infants' responses to stress. *Child Development, 66,* 657–670.

Lewis, M., Alessandri, S. M., & Sullivan, M. W. (1992). Differences in shame and pride as a function of children's gender and task difficulty. *Child Development, 63,* 630–638.

Lewis, M., Stanger, C., & Sullivan, M. W. (1989). Deception in 3-year-olds. *Developmental Psychology, 25,* 439–443.

Lewis, M., Sullivan, M. W., Ramsay, D. S., & Alessandri, S. M. (1992). Individual differences in anger and sad expressions during extinction: Antecedents and consequences. *Infant Behavior and Development, 15,* 443–452.

Lewis, M., Sullivan, M. W., Stanger, C., & Weiss, M. (1989). Self development and self-conscious emotions. *Child Development, 60,* 146–156.

Lewis, M., Young, G., Brooks, J., & Michalson, L. (1975). The beginning of friendship. In M. Lewis & L. Rosenblum (Eds.), *Friendship and peer relations* (pp. 305–341). New York: Wiley.

Lewis, M. D. (1993). Emotion-cognition interactions in early infant development. *Cognition and Emotion, 7,* 145–170.

Lewis, M. D. (1995). Cognition-emotion feedback and the self-organization of developmental paths. *Human Development, 38* (2), 71–102.

Lewis, M. D. (1993). Early socioemotional predictors of cognitive competency at 4 years. *Developmental Psychology, 29,* 1036–1045.

Lewis, M. D., Koroshegyi, C., Douglas, L., & Kampe, K. (1997). Age-specific associations between emotional responses to separation and cognitive performance in infancy. *Developmental Psychology, 33*(1), 32–42.

Lewis, M. D., Lamey, A. V., & Douglas, L. (1999). A new dynamic systems method for the analysis of early socioemotional development. *Developmental Science, 2*(4), 457–475.

Lewis, M. D., & Ramsay, D. S. (1997). Stress reactivity and self-recognition. *Child Development, 68*(4), 621–629.

Lewis, S. E., & Nicolson, P. (1998). Talking about early motherhood: Recognizing loss and reconstructing depression. *Reproductive and Infant Psychology, 16,* 177–197.

Lewit, E. M., & Baker, L. S. (1995). Unintentional injuries. *Future of Children, 5,* 214–231.

Lewit, E. M., Baker, L. S., Corman, H., & Shiono, P. H. (1995). The direct cost of low birth weight. *Future of Children, 5,* 35–56.

Lewkowicz, D. J. (1988). Sensory dominance in infants: 1. Six-month-old infants' response to auditory-visual compounds. *Developmental Psychology, 24,* 155–171.

Lewkowicz, D. J. (1994). Limitations on infants' response to rate-based auditory-visual relations. *Development Psychology, 30,* 880–892.

Lewkowicz, D. J. (1996). Infants' response to the audible and visible properties of the human face: 1. Role of the lexical-syntactic content, temporal synchrony, gender, and manner of speech. *Developmental Psychology, 32*(2), 347–366.

Ley, R. G., & Koepke, J. E. (1982). Attachment behavior out of doors: Naturalistic observations of sex and age differences in the separation behavior of young children. *Infant Behavior and Development, 5,* 195–201.

L'Hoir, M., Westers, P., Konig, P., Visser, A., Guedeke, M., & Wolters, W. (1994). Parental management of infants born following a cot-death victim who were monitored compared to infants who, despite similar histories, were not monitored: A controlled study. *European Journal of Pediatrics, 153,* 694–699.

Liaw, F., & Brooks-Gunn, J. (1993). Patterns of low-birth-weight children's cognitive development. *Developmental Psychology, 29,* 1024–1035.

Lickliter, R., & Hellewell, T. B. (1992). Contextual determinants of auditory learning in Bobwhite quail embryos and hatchlings. *Developmental Psychobiology, 25,* 017–031.

Lieberman, E., Lang, J. M., Frigoletto, F., Richardson, D. K., Ringer, S. A., & Cohen, A. (1997). Epidural analgesia, intrapartum fever, and neonatal sepsis evaluation. *Pediatrics, 99*(3), 415–419.

Lieberman, A. F., Weston, D. R., & Pawl, J. H. (1991). Preventive intervention and outcome with anxiously attached dyads. *Child Development, 62,* 199–209.

Lindahl, L. B., & Heimann, M. (1997). Research report: Social proximity in early mother-infant interactions: Implications for gender differences? *Early Development and Parenting, 6*(2), 83–88.

Lindsay, J. A., Johnson, H. M., Wallace, F. M., & Soos, J. M. (1994). Can superantigens trigger sudden infant death? *Medical Hypotheses, 43,* 81–85.

Lipsitt, L. P. (1979a). Infants at risk: Perinatal and neonatal factors. *International Journal of Behavioral Development, 2,* 23–42.

Lipsitt, L. P. (1979b). The pleasures and annoyances of infants: Approach and avoidance behavior. In E. Thoman (Ed.), *The origins of the infant's social responsiveness* (pp. 105–119). Hillsdale, NJ: Erlbaum.

Lipsitt, L. P. (1981). Infant learning. In T. Field, A. Huston, H. Quay, L. Troll, & G. Finley (Eds.), *Review of human development* (pp. 256–279). New York: Wiley.

Lipsitt, L. P., Engen, T., & Kaye, H. (1963). Developmental changes in the olfactory threshold of the neonate. *Child Development, 34,* 371–376.

Lipsitt, L. P., Sturges, W. Q., & Burke, P. (1979). Perinatal indicators and subsequent crib death. *Infant Behavior and Development, 2,* 325–328.

Liptak, G. S., Keller, B. B., Feldman, A. W., & Chamberlain, R. W. (1983). Enhancing infant development and parent practitioner interaction with the Brazelton Neonatal Behavioral Assessment Scale. *Pediatrics, 72,* 71–78.

Little, A. B. (1988). There's many a slip 'twixt implantation and the crib (editorial). *New England Journal of Medicine, 319*(4), 241–242.

Little, J., & Vainio, H. (1994). Mutagenic lifestyles? A review of evidence of associations between germ-cell mutations in humans and smoking, alcohol consumption and use of "recreational" drugs. *Mutation Research, 313,* 131–151.

Lock, A. (1980). *The guided reinvention of language.* New York: Academic Press.

Lock, A. (2000). Preverbal communication. In J. G. Bremner & A. Fogel (Eds.), *Handbook of infancy research* (pp. 504–521). Oxford, England: Blackwell.

Locke, J. L. (1979). The child's processing of phonology. In W. A. Collins (Ed.), *Minnesota symposia on child psychology: Vol. 12. Children's language and communication* (pp. 1261–1289). Hillsdale, NJ: Erlbaum.

Locke, J. L. (1993). *The child's path to spoken language.* Cambridge, MA: Harvard University Press.

Lodish, H. F. (1995). Through the glass lightly. *Science, 267,* 1609–1611.

Loehlin, J. C. (1989). Partitioning environmental and genetic contributions to behavioral development. *American Psychologist, 44*(10), 1285–1292.

Lollis, S. P. (1990). Effects of maternal behavior on toddler behavior during separation. *Child Development, 61,* 99–103.

Lorenz, K. Z. (1952). The comparative method in studying innate behavior. *Symposium of the Society for Experimental Biology, 41,* 221–268.

Lorenz, K. Z. (1965). *Evolution and modification of behavior.* Chicago: University of Chicago Press.

Losoya, S. H., Callor, S., Rowe, D. C., & Goldsmith, H. H. (1997). Origins of familial similarity in parenting: A study of twins and adoptive siblings. *Developmental Psychology, 33*(6), 1012–1023.

Lounsbury, M. L., & Bates, J. E. (1982). The cries of infants of differing levels of temperamental difficultness: Acoustic properties and effects on listeners. *Child Development, 53,* 677–686.

Lowinger, S. (1999). Infant irritability and early mother-infant reciprocity patterns. *Infant and Child Development, 8*(2), 71–84.

Lozoff, B. (1998). Explanatory mechanisms for poorer development in iron deficient anemic infants. In *Nutrition, health, and child development* (Pan-American Health Organization Scientific Monograph No. 566) (pp. 1–89). Washington, DC: Pan-American Health Organization.

Lozoff, B., Klein, N. K., Nelson, E. C., McClish, D. K., Manual, M., & Chacon, M. E. (1998). Behavior of infants with iron-deficiency anemia. *Child Development, 69*(1), 24–36.

Lubic, R. W. (1999). Giving birth is powerful! *Zero to Three, 19*(4), 20–24.

Ludemann, P. M. (1991). Generalized discrimination of positive facial expressions by seven- and ten-month-old infants. *Child Development, 62,* 55–67.

Ludemann, P. M., & Nelson, C. A. (1988). Categorical representation of facial expressions by 7-month-old infants. *Developmental Psychology, 24,* 492–501.

Ludington-Hoe, S. M., & Swinth, J. (1996). Developmental aspects of kangaroo care. *Journal of Obstetric, Gynecologic, and Neonatal Nursing, 25*(8), 691–703.

Lundy, B. L., Jones, N. A., Field, T., Nearing, G., Davalos, M., Pietro, P. A., Schanberg, S., & Kuhn, C. (1999). Prenatal depression effects on neonates. *Infant Behavior and Development, 22*(1), 119–129.

Lunt, R., & Law, D. (1974). A review of the chronology of eruption of deciduous teeth. *Journal of the American Dental Association, 89,* 872–879.

Lupe, P. J., & Gross, T. L. (1986). Maternal upright posture and mobility in labor: A review. *Obstetrics and Gynecology, 67* (5), 727–734.

Lyons, S. (1998). A prospective study of post traumatic stress symptoms 1 month following childbirth in a group of 42 first-time mothers. *Reproductive and Infant Psychology, 16,* 91–105.

Lyons-Ruth, K., Alpern, L., & Repacholi, B. (1993). Disorganized infant attachment classification and maternal psychosocial problems as predictors of hostile-aggressive behavior in the preschool classroom. *Child Development, 64,* 572–585.

Lyons-Ruth, K., Bronfman, E., & Parsons, E. (1999). Maternal frightened, frightening, or atypical behavior and disorganized infant attachment patterns. *Monographs of the Society for Research in Child Development, 64*(3), 67–96.

Lyons-Ruth, K., Connell, D. B., Grunebaum, H. U., & Botein, S. (1990). Infants at social risk: Maternal depression and family support services as mediators of infant development and security of attachment. *Child Development, 61,* 85–98.

Lyons-Ruth, K., Easterbrooks, M. A., & Cibelli, C. D. (1997). Infant attachment strategies, infant mental lag, and maternal depressive symptoms: Predictors of internalizing and externalizing problems at age 7. *Developmental Psychology, 33*(4), 681–692.

Lyra, M., & Ferreira, M. (1987, August). *Dialogue and the construction of the mother-infant dyad.* Paper presented at the International Society for Behavioral Development Conference, Tokyo, Japan.

Lyra, M. C., & Rossetti-Ferreira, M. C. (1995). Transformation and construction in social interaction: A new perspective on analysis of the mother-infant dyad. In J. Valsiner (Ed.), *Child development within culturally structured environments (Vol. 3). Comparative-cultural and coconstructionist perspectives* (pp. 316–351). Norwood, NJ: Ablex.

MacFarlane, A. (1975). Olfaction in the development of social preferences in the human neonate. In Ciba Foundation Symposium (Ed.), *Parent-infant interaction* (pp. 605–617). New York: Elsevier.

Madden, M. E. (1994). The variety of emotional reactions to miscarriage. *Journal of Women's Health, 21,* 85–104.

Madsen, M. C., & Shapira, A. (1970). Cooperative and competitive behavior of urban Afro-American, Anglo-American, Mexican-American, and Mexican village children. *Developmental Psychology, 3,* 16–20.

Magid, K., & McKelvey, C. A. (1987). *High risk: Children without a conscience.* New York: Bantam.

Mahler, M., Pine, F., & Bergman, A. (1975). *The psychological birth of the human infant.* New York: Basic Books.

Main, M., & Cassidy, J. (1988). Categories of response to reunion with the parent at age 6: Predictable from infant attachment classifications and stable over a 1-month period. *Developmental Psychology, 24,* 415–426.

Main, M., & George, C. (1985). Responses of abused and disadvantaged toddlers to distress in agemates: A study in the day care setting. *Developmental Psychology, 21,* 407–412.

Main, M., Kaplan, N., & Cassidy, J. (1985). Security in infancy, childhood, and adulthood: A move to the level of representation. In I. Bretherton & E. Waters (Eds.), Growing points of attachment theory and research. *Monographs of the Society for Research in Child Development, 50* (Serial No. 209), 66–104.

Main, M., & Solomon, J. (1986). Discovery of an insecure disorganized/disoriented attachment pattern: Procedures, findings, and implications for the classification of behavior. In M. Yogman & T. B. Brazelton (Eds.), *Affective development in infancy* (pp. 95–124). Norwood, NJ: Ablex.

Main, M., & Weston, D. R. (1981). The quality of the toddler's relationship to mother and father: Related to conflict behavior and the readiness to establish new relationships. *Child Development, 52,* 932–940.

Malatesta, C. Z., Culver, C., Tesman, J. R., & Shepard, B. (1989). The development of emotion expression during the first two years of life. *Monographs of the Society for Research in Child Development, 54* (Serial No. 219), 1–104.

Malatesta, C. Z., Grigoryev, P., Lamb, C., Albin, M., & Culver, C. (1986). Emotion socialization and expressive development in preterm and full-term infants. *Child Development, 57,* 316–330.

Malatesta, C. Z., & Haviland, J. M. (1982). Learning display rules: The socialization of emotion expression in infancy. *Child Development, 53,* 991–1003.

Malatesta-Magai, C., Leak, S., Tesman, J., Shepard, B., Culver, C., & Smaggia, B. (1994). Profiles of emotional development: Individual differences in facial and vocal expression of emotion during the second and third years of life. *International Journal of Behavioral Development, 17,* 239–269.

Malphurs, J. E., Raag, T., Field, T., Pickens, J., & Nogueras-Pelaez, M. (1996). Touch by intrusive and withdrawn mothers with depressive symptoms. *Early Development and Parenting, 5*(2), 111–115.

Mandell, F., McAnulty, E., & Reece, R. M. (1980). Observations of paternal response to sudden unanticipated infant death. *Pediatrics, 65,* 221–225.

Mandler, J. M., & McDonough, L. (1998). On developing a knowledge base in infancy. *Developmental Psychology, 34*(6), 1274–1288.

Mandy, A., Gard, P. R., Ross, K., & Valentine, B. H. (1998). Psychological sequelae in women following either parturition or nongynecological surgery. *Reproductive and Infant Psychology, 16,* 133–141.

Mangelsdorf, S. C. (1992). Developmental changes in infant-stranger interaction. *Infant Behavior and Development, 15,* 191–208.

Mangelsdorf, S. C., Plunkett, J. W., Dedrick, C. F., Berlin, M., Meisels, S. J., McHale, J. L., & Dichtellmiller, M. (1996). Attachment security in very low birth weight infants. *Developmental Psychology, 32*(5), 914–920.

Maratsos, M., Kuczaj, S., Fox, D., & Chalkley, M. (1979). Some empirical studies in the acquisition of transformational relations: Passives, negatives, and the past tense. In W. A. Collins (Ed.), *Minnesota symposia on child psychology: Vol. 12. Children's language and communication* (pp. 1242–1260). Hillsdale, NJ: Erlbaum.

Marcos, H. (1995). Mother-child and father-child communication in the second year: A functional approach. *Early Development and Parenting, 4,* 49–61.

Marcos, H., & Chanu, M. K. (1992). Learning how to insist and clarify in the second year: Reformulation of requests in different contexts. *International Journal of Behavioral Development, 15,* 359–376.

Marcos, H., & Verba, M. (1990, April). *Referential communication with adults and infants in the second year.* Paper presented at the International Conference on Infant Studies, Montreal, Canada.

Marcovitch, S., Goldberg, S., Gold, A., & Washington, J. (1997). Determinants of behavioural problems in Romanian children adopted in Ontario. *International Journal of Behavioral Development, 20*(1), 17–31.

Marcovitch, S., & Zelazo, P. D. (1999). The a-not-b error: Results from a logistic meta-analysis. *Child Development, 70*(6), 1297–1313.

Marcus, G. F., Pinker, S., Ullman, M., & Hollander, M. (1992). Overregularization in language acquisition. *Monographs of the Society for Research in Child Development, 57*(4), 1–182.

Marecek, J. (1987). Counseling adolescents with problem pregnancies. *American Psychologist, 42,* 89–93.

Markman, H. J., & Kadushin, F. S. (1986). Preventive effects of Lamaze training for first-time parents: A short-term longitudinal study. *Journal of Consulting Clinical Psychology, 54*(6), 872–874.

Marlier, L., Schaal, B., & Soussignan, R. (1998a). Bottle-fed neonates prefer an odor experienced in utero to an odor experienced postnatally in the feeding context. *Developmental Psychobiology, 33*(2), 133–145.

Marlier, L., Schaal, B., & Soussignan, R. (1998b). Neonatal responsiveness to the odor of amniotic and lacteal fluids: A test of perinatal chemosensory continuity. *Child Development, 69*(3), 611–623.

Martin, R. P., Noyes, J., Wisenbaker, J., & Huttunen, M. O. (1999). Prediction of early childhood negative emotionality and inhibition from maternal distress during pregnancy. *Merrill-Palmer Quarterly, 45*(3), 370–391.

Martinez-Frias, M. L., Rodriguez-Pinilla, E., Bermejo, E., & Prieto, L. (1998). Prenatal exposure to sex hormones: A case-control study. *Teratology, 57*(1), 8–12.

Martini, M., & Kirkpatrick, J. (1981). Early interactions in Marquesas islands. In T. M. Field, A. M. Sostek, P. Vietze, & P. H. Leiderman (Eds.), *Culture and early interactions.* Hillsdale, NJ: Erlbaum.

Masataka, N. (1992). Motherese in a signed language. *Infant Behavior and Development, 15,* 453–460.

Masataka, N. (1999). Preference for infant-directed singing in 2-day-old hearing infants of deaf parents. *Developmental Psychology, 35*(4), 1001–1005.

Mascolo, M. F., & Fischer, K. W. (1995). Development transformations in appraisals for pride, shame, and guilt. In J. P. Tangney & K. W. Fischer (Eds.), *Self-conscious emotions: The psychology of shame, guilt, embarrassment, and pride* (pp. 64–113). New York: Guilford Press.

Masur, E. F. (1993). Transitions in representational ability: Infants' verbal, vocal, and action imitation during the second year. *Merrill-Palmer Quarterly, 39,* 437–456.

Masur, E. F., & Rodemaker, J. E. (1999). Mothers' and infants' spontaneous vocal, verbal, and action imitation during the second year. *Merrill-Palmer Quarterly, 45*(3), 392–412.

Matas, L., Arend, R. A., & Sroufe, L. A. (1978). Continuity of adaptation in the second year: The relationship between quality of attachment and later competence. *Child Development, 49,* 547–556.

Matheny, A. P., Jr., Wilson, R. S., & Thoben, A. S. (1987). Home and mother: Relations with infant temperament. *Developmental Psychology, 23,* 323–331.

Matias, R., & Cohn, J. E. (1993). Are max-specified infant facial expressions during face-to-face interaction consistent with differential emotions theory? *Developmental Psychology, 29,* 524–531.

Maun, A. R., Williams, R. S., Graber, B., & Myers, W. G. (1994). The passage of Florida's statute on assisted reproductive technology. *Obstetrics and Gynecology, 84,* 889–893.

Maurer, D. (1985). Infants' perception of facedness. In T. M. Field & N. A. Fox (Eds.), *Social perception in infants* (pp. 73–100). Norwood, NJ: Ablex.

Maurer, D., & Salapatek, P. (1976). Developmental changes in the scanning of faces by young infants. *Child Development, 47,* 523–527.

Mauthner, N. S. (1998). Re-assessing the importance and role of the marital relationship in postnatal depression: Methodological and theoretical implications. *Reproductive and Infant Psychology, 16,* 157–175.

Mayer, S., & Musatti, T. (1992). Towards the use of symbol: Play with objects and communication with adults and peers in the second year. *Infant Behavior and Development, 15,* 1–13.

Mayes, L. C., Carter, A. S., & Stubbe, D. (1993). Individual differences in exploratory behavior in the second year of life. *Infant Behavior and Development, 16,* 269–284.

Mayes, L. C., Feldman, R., Granger, R. H., Haynes, O. M., Bornstein, M. H., & Schottenfeld, R. (1997). The effects of polydrug use with and without cocaine on mother-infant interaction at 3 and 6 months. *Infant Behavior and Development, 20*(4), 489–502.

Mayes, L. C., Granger, R. H., Bornstein, M. H., & Zuckerman, B. (1992). The problem of prenatal cocaine exposure. *Journal of the American Medical Association, 267,* 406–408.

Mayes, L. C., Granger, R. H., Frank, M. A., Schottenfeld, R., & Bornstein, M. H. (1993). Neurobehavioral profiles of neonates exposed to cocaine prenatally. *Pediatrics, 91,* 778–783.

Mayes, L. C., & Kessen, M. (1989). Maturational changes in measures of habituation. *Infant Behavior and Development, 12,* 437–450.

McCalin, M., & Mandell, F. (1994). Sudden infant death syndrome: The nurse counselor's response to bereavement counseling. *Journal of Community Health Nursing, 11,* 177–186.

McCall, R. B., & Carriger, M. S. (1993). A meta-analysis of infant habituation and recognition memory performance as predictors of later IQ. *Child Development, 64,* 57–79.

McCarty, M. E., Clifton, R. K., & Collard, R. R. (1999). Problem solving in infancy: The emergence of an action plan. *Developmental Psychology, 35*(4), 1091–1101.

McClearn, G. E. (1970). Genetic influences on behavior and development. In P. H. Mussen (Ed.), *Child psychology* (3rd ed., Vol. 1). New York: Wiley.

McClure, V. S. (1989). *Infant massage: A handbook for loving parents.* New York: Bantam Books.

McConkie, R. A., & Iafolla, A. K. (1993). Medium-chain acyl CoA dehydrogenase deficiency: Its relationship to SIDS and the impact on genetic counseling. *Journal of Genetic Counseling, 2,* 17–27.

McCormick, C. M., & Maurer, D. M. (1988). Unimanual hand preferences in 6-month-olds: Consistency and relation familial-handedness. *Infant Behavior and Development, 11,* 21–29.

McCune, L. (1989, April). *Toward an integrative theory of early language acquisition: Evidence from longitudinal trends in vocal behavior.* Paper presented at the biennial meeting of the Society for Research in Child Development, Kansas City, MO.

McCune, L. (1995). A normative study of representational play at the transition to language. *Developmental Psychology, 31,* 198–206.

McCune-Nicholich, L. (1981). Toward symbolic functioning: Structure of early pretend games and potential parallels with language. *Child Development, 52,* 785–797.

McDonald, D. (1978). Paternal behavior at first contact with the newborn in a birth environment without intrusions. *Birth and the Family Journal, 5,* 123–132.

McDonald, M. A., Sigman, M., Espinosa, M. P., & Neumann, C. G. (1994). Impact of temporary food shortage on children and their mothers. *Child Development, 65*(2), 404–415.

McDonald, R., & Avery, D. (1983). *Dentistry for the child and adolescent* (4th ed.). St. Louis, MO: Mosby.

McDonnell, P. M., Anderson, V. E. S., & Abraham, W. C. (1983). Asymmetry and orientation of arm movements in three- to eight-week-old infants. *Infant Behavior and Development, 6,* 287–298.

McDonough, L., & Mandler, J. M. (1998). Inductive generalization in 9- and 11-month-olds. *Developmental Science, 1*(2), 227–232.

McGlaughlin, A., & Grayson, A. (1999). A prospective study of crying during the first year of infancy. *Journal of Reproductive and Infant Psychology, 17*(1), 41–52.

McGraw, M. B. (1935). *Growth: A study of Johnny and Jimmy.* New York: Appleton.

McGuire, J. (1988). Gender stereotypes of parents with two-year-olds and beliefs about gender differences in behavior. *Sex Roles, 19,* 233–240.

McIntosh, J. R., & Koonce, M. P. (1989). Mitosis. *Science, 246,* 622–628.

McKee, J. (1974). Selections from "Two legs to stand on." In J. Milgram & D. Sciarra (Eds.), *Childhood revisited* (pp. 41–55). New York: Macmillan. (Original work published 1955)

McKenna, J. J. (1987). An anthropological perspective on the sudden infant death syndrome: A testable hypothesis of the possible role of parental breathing cues in promoting infant breathing stability: I. *Pre- and Perinatal Psychology Journal, 2,* 93–135.

McKenna, J. J. (1988). An anthropological perspective on the sudden infant death syndrome: The neurological and structural bases of speech breathing and why SIDS appears to be a species-specific malady: II. *Pre- and Perinatal Psychology Journal, 2,* 149–178.

McKenna, J. J., & Mosko, S. (1994). Sleep and arousal, synchrony and independence, among mothers and infants sleeping apart and together (same bed): An experiment in evolutionary medicine. *Acta Paediatricia Supplement, 397*, 94–102.

McKenna, J. J., Mosko, S., Richard, C., Drummond, S., Hunt, L., Cetel, M. B., & Arpaia, J. (1994). Experimental studies of infant-parent co-sleeping: Mutual physiological and behavioral influences and their relevance to SIDS (sudden infant death syndrome). *Early Human Development, 38*, 187–201.

McKenzie, B., & Over, R. (1983). Young infants fail to imitate facial and manual gestures. *Infant Behavior and Development, 6*, 85–95.

McKenzie, B. E., Skouteris, H., Day, R. H., Hartman, B., & Yonas, A. (1993). Effective action by infants to contact objects by reaching and leaning. *Child Development, 64*, 415–429.

McKenzie, B. E., Tootell, H. E., & Day, R. H. (1980). Development of visual size constancy during the first year of human infancy. *Developmental Psychology, 16*, 163–174.

McKim, M. K. (1987). Transition to what? New parents' problems in the first year. *Family Relations Journal of Applied Family and Child Studies, 36*, 22–25.

McLaughlin, B. (1983). Child compliance to parental control techniques. *Developmental Psychology, 19*, 667–673.

McLoyd, V. C. (1990). The impact of economic hardship on black families and children: Psychological distress, parenting, and socioemotional development. *Child Development, 61*, 311–346.

McLoyd, V. C. (1998). Socioeconomic disadvantage and child development. *American Psychologist, 53*(2), 185–204.

McLoyd, V. C., & Wilson, L. (1991). The strain of living poor: Parenting, social support, and child mental health. In A. C. Huston (Ed.), *Children in poverty: Child development and public policy* (pp. 105–135). New York: Cambridge University Press.

McMahon, C. A., Tennant, C., Ungerer, J., & Saunders, D. (1999). Don't count your chickens: A comparative study of the experience of pregnancy after IVF conception. *Journal of Reproductive and Infant Psychology, 17*(4), 345–356.

McNeill, D. (1970). *The acquisition of language.* New York: Harper & Row.

McPherson, M. G. (1983). Improving services to infants and young children with handicapping conditions and their families: The Division of Maternal and Child Health as collaborator. *Zero to Three, 4*, 1–6.

McShane, J. (1980). *Learning to talk.* Cambridge, England: Cambridge University Press.

McTurk, R. H., McCarthy, M. E., Vietze, P. M., & Yarrow, L. J. (1987). Sequential analysis of mastery behavior in 6- to 12-month-old infants. *Developmental Psychology, 23*, 199–203.

Mead, M., & Newton, N. (1967). Cultural patterning of perinatal behavior. In S. Richardson & A. Guttmacher (Eds.), *Childbearing: Its social and psychological aspects* (pp. 76–104). Baltimore: Williams & Wilkins.

Mead, R. (1999, August 9). Annals of reproduction: Eggs for sale. *The New Yorker, 75*, 56–65.

Meadow-Orlans, K. P., & Spencer, P. E. (1996). Maternal sensitivity and the visual attentiveness of children who are deaf. *Early Development and Parenting, 5*(4), 213–223.

Meares, R., Grimwalde, J., & Wood, C. (1976). A possible relationship between anxiety in pregnancy and puerperal depression. *Journal of Psychosomatic Research, 20*, 605–610.

Meder, A. (1989). Effects of hand-rearing on the behavioral development of infant and juvenile gorillas. *Developmental Psychobiology, 22*, 357–376.

Meer, A. L. H. van der, Weel, F. R. van der, & Lee, D. N. (1995). The functional significance of arm movements in neonates. *Science, 267*, 693–696.

Mehl, L., Peterson, G., Sokolsky, W., & Whitt, M. (1976). Outcomes of early discharge after normal birth. *Birth and the Family Journal, 3*, 101–107.

Meins, E., Fernyhough, C., Russell, J., & Clark-Carter, D. (1998). Security of attachment as a predictor of symbolic and mentalising abilities: A longitudinal study. *Social Development, 7*(1), 1–24.

Melchor, J. C., Rodriguez-Alarcon, J., Fernandez-Liebrez, L., Benito, J. A., Linares, A., & Aranguren, G. (1994). Delayed childbearing and pregnancy outcome. *Zentralblatt für Gynäkologie, 116*, 566–570.

Melson, G. (1980). *The family as an ecosystem.* New York: Burgess.

Melson, G., & Cohen, A. (1981). Contextual influences on children's activity: Sex differences in effects of peer presence and interpersonal attraction. *Genetic Psychology Monographs, 103*, 243–260.

Melson, G., & Fogel, A. (1982). Young children's interest in unfamiliar infants. *Child Development, 53*, 693–700.

Melson, G., & Fogel, A. (1988, March). The development of nurturance in young children. *Young Children*, 57–65.

Melson, G., Fogel, A., & Toda, S. (1986). Children's ideas about infants and their care. *Child Development, 57*, 1519–1527.

Melson, G., Hsu, H. C., & Ladd, G. W. (1993). The parental support networks of mothers and fathers: A multidimensional approach. *Early Development and Parenting, 2*, 169–182.

Meltzoff, A. (1988). Infant imitation and memory: Nine-month-olds in immediate and deferred tests. *Child Development, 59*, 217–225.

Meltzoff, A., & Moore, M. K. (1989). Imitation in newborn infants: Exploring the range of gestures imitated and the underlying mechanisms. *Developmental Psychology, 25*, 954–962.

Meltzoff, A., & Moore, M. K. (1994). Imitation, memory, and the representation of persons. *Infant Behavior and Development, 17*, 83–99.

Meltzoff, A., & Moore, M. K. (1997). Explaining facial imitation: A theoretical model. *Early Development and Parenting, 6*(1), 179–192.

Meltzoff, A., & Moore, W. (1977). Imitation of facial and manual gestures by human neonates. *Science, 198*, 75–78.

Mennella, J. A. (1997). A cross-cultural perspective. *Nutrition Today, 32*(4), 144–151.

Mercer, R. T., Ferketich, S., May, K., DeJoseph, J., & Sollid, D. (1988). Further exploration of maternal and paternal fetal attachment. *Research in Nursing and Health, 11*, 83–95.

Meredith, H. (1975). Somatic changes during human pre-natal life. *Child Development, 46*, 603–610.

Messer, D. J., Rachford, D., McCarthy, M. E., & Yarrow, L. J. (1987). Assessment of mastery behavior at 30 months: Analysis of task-directed activities. *Developmental Psychology, 23*(6), 771–781.

Messinger, D. S., Dolcourt, J., King, J., Bodnar, A., & Beck, D. (1996). The survival and developmental outcome of extremely low birthweight infants. *Infant Mental Health Journal, 17*(4), 375–385.

Messinger, D. S., & Fogel, A. (1998). Give and take: The development of conventional infant gestures. *Merrill-Palmer Quarterly, 44*(4), 566–590.

Messinger, D., Fogel, A., & Dickson, K. L. (1998). What's in a smile? *Developmental Psychology, 35*(3), 701–708.

Messmer, P. R., Rodriguez, S., Adams, J., Wells-Gentry, J., Washburn, K., Zabaleta, I., & Abreu, S. (1999). Effect of kangaroo care on sleep time for neonates. *Pediatric Nursing, 23*(4), 408–414.

Metosky, P., & Vondra, J. (1995). Prenatal drug exposure and play and coping in toddlers: A comparison study. *Infant Behavior and Development, 18*, 15–25.

Meyer, L., Mailloux, J., Marcoux, S., Blanchett, P., & Meyer, F. (1987). Maternal and neonatal morbidity in instrumental deliveries with the Kobayashi vacuum extractor and low forceps. *Acta Obstetrica et Gynecologica Scandinavica, 66*(7), 643–647.

Meyers, B. J., & Kaltenbach, K. (1992). Cocaine-exposed infants: Myths and misunderstandings. *Zero to Three, 12*, 1–5. Arlington, VA: National Center for Clinical Infant Programs.

Michaelson, K. L., et al. (1988). *Childbirth in America: Anthropological perspectives.* South Hadley, MA: Bergin & Garvey.

Michel, G. F., & Harkins, D. A. (1986). Postural and lateral asymmetries in the ontogeny of handedness during infancy. *Developmental Psychobiology, 19*, 247–258.

Miebert, C. J. (1991). Dimensions of subjectivity in parents' ratings of infant temperament. *Child Development, 62,* 352–361.

Milewski, A. E. (1976). Infant's discrimination of internal and external pattern elements. Journal of Experimental *Child Psychology, 22,* 229–246.

Miller, P. J., Mintz, J., Hoogstra, L., Fung, H., & Potts, R. (1992). The narrated self: Young children's construction of self in relation to others in conversational stories of personal experience. *Merrill-Palmer Quarterly, 38,* 45–67.

Miller, W. R. (1964). The acquisition of formal features of language. *American Journal of Orthopsychiatry, 34,* 862–867.

Mintzer, D., Als, H., Tronick, E. A., & Brazelton, T. B. (1985). Parenting an infant with a birth defect: The regulation of self-esteem. *Zero to Three, 5,* 1–7.

Mitra, S. C., Ganesh, V., & Apuzzio, J. J. (1994). Effect of maternal cocaine abuse on renal arterial flow and urine output of the fetus. *American Journal of Obstetrics and Gynecology, 171,* 1556–1559.

Mix, K. S., Levine, S. C., & Huttenlocher, J. (1997). Numerical abstraction in infants: Another look. *Developmental Psychology, 33*(3), 423–428.

Miyake, K., Chen, S., & Campos, J. J. (1985). Infant temperament, mother's mode of interaction, and attachment in Japan: An interim report. In I. Bretherton & E. Waters (Eds.). *Growing points of attachment theory and research. Monographs of the Society for Research in Child Development, 50* (Serial No. 209), 276–297.

Molfese, V. J., DiLalla, L. F., & Bunce, D. (1997). Prediction of the intelligence test scores of 3- to 8-year-old children by home environment, socioeconomic status, and biomedical risks. *Merrill-Palmer Quarterly, 43*(2), 219–234.

Molina, M., & Jouen, F. (1998). Modulation of the palmar grasp behavior in neonates according to texture property. *Infant Behavior and Development, 21*(4), 659–667.

Molnar, G. E. (1978). Analysis of motor disorder in retarded infants and young children. *American Journal of Mental Deficiency, 83,* 213–222.

Moon, C., Cooper, R. P., & Fifer, W. P. (1993). Two-day-olds prefer their native language. *Infant Behavior and Development, 16,* 495–500.

Moore, C., Angelopoulos, M., & Bennett, P. (1997). The role of movement in the development of joint visual attention. *Infant Behavior and Development, 20,* 83–92.

Moore, T. R., Sorg, J., Miller, L., Key, T. C., & Resnik, R. (1986). Hemodynamic effects of intravenous cocaine on the pregnant ewe and fetus. *American Journal of Obstetrics and Gynecology, 155,* 883–888.

Morales, M., Mundy, P., & Rojas, J. (1998). Following the direction of gaze and language development in 6-month-olds. *Infant Behavior and Development, 21*(2), 373–377.

Moran, G., Krupka, A., Tutton, A., & Symons, D. (1987). Patterns of maternal and infant imitation during play. *Infant Behavior and Development, 10,* 477–491.

Morange-Majoux, F., Cougnot, P., & Bloch, H. (1997). Hand tactual exploration of textures in infants from 4 to 6 months. *Early Development and Parenting, 6,* 127–135.

Moreno, C., Ardanaz, E., Olivera, J. E., Castilla, J., & de Pedro, C. J. (1994). A temporal-spatial cluster of sudden infant death syndrome in Navarre, Spain. *European Journal of Epidemiology, 10,* 129–134.

Morrongiello, B. A., Fenwick, K. D., & Chance, G. (1990). Sound localization acuity in very young infants: An observer-based testing procedure. *Developmental Psychology, 26,* 75–84.

Morrongiello, B. A., & Rocca, P. T. (1987). Infants' localization of sounds on the horizontal plane: Effects of auditory and visual cues. *Child Development, 58,* 918–927.

Mosier, C. E., & Rogoff, B. (1994). Infants' instrumental use of their mothers to achieve their goals. *Child Development, 65,* 70–79.

Moss, M., Colombo, J., Mitchell, D. W., & Horowitz, F. D. (1988). Neonatal behavioral organization and visual processing at three months. *Child Development, 59,* 1211–1220.

Moustakas, C. (1994). *Phenomenological research methods.* Thousand Oaks, CA: Sage Publications.

Mueller, E., Bleier, M., Krakow, J., Hegedus, K., & Cournoyer, P. (1977). The development of peer verbal interaction among two-year-old boys. *Child Development, 48,* 284–287.

Mueller, E., & Brenner, J. (1977). The growth of social interaction in a toddler play group: The role of peer experience. *Child Development, 48,* 854–861.

Mueller, E., & Lucas, T. (1975). A developmental analysis of peer interaction among toddlers. In M. Lewis & L. Rosenblum (Eds.), *Friendship and peer relations* (pp. 65–90). New York: Wiley.

Mullen, M., Snidman, N., & Kagan, J. (1993). Free-play behavior in inhibited and uninhibited children. *Infant Behavior and Development, 16,* 383–389.

Mumme, D. L., Fernald, A., & Herrera, C. (1996). Infants' responses to facial and vocal emotional signals in a social referencing paradigm. *Child Development, 67,* 3219–3237.

Munakata, Y. (1997). Perseverative reaching in infancy: The roles of hidden toys and motor history in the *AB* task. *Infant Behavior and Development, 20*(3), 405–416.

Mundy, P., & Gomes, A. (1998). Individual differences in joint attention skill development in the second year. *Infant Behavior and Development, 21*(3), 469–482.

Mundy, P., Kasari, C., & Sigman, M. (1992). Nonverbal communication, affective sharing, and intersubjectivity. *Infant Behavior and Development, 15,* 377–381.

Munn, P., & Dunn, J. (1989). Temperament and the developing relationship between siblings. *International Journal of Behavioral Development, 12,* 433–451.

Murai, N., Murai, N., & Takahashi, I. (1978). A study of moods in postpartum women. *Tohoku Psychologica Ioliak, 37,* 32–40.

Murphy, C. M. (1978). Pointing in the context of a shared activity. *Child Development, 49,* 371–380.

Murray, A. D. (1988). Newborn auditory brainstem evoked responses (ABRs): Longitudinal correlates in the first year. *Child Development, 59,* 1542–1554.

Murray, L., Fiori-Cowley, A., Hooper, R., & Cooper, P. (1996). The impact of postnatal depression and associated adversity on early mother-infant interactions and later infant outcomes. *Child Development, 67*(5), 2512–2526.

Murray, L., & Trevarthen, C. (1985). Emotional regulation of interactions between two-month-olds and their mothers. In T. Field & N. Fox (Eds.), *Social perception in infants.* Norwood, NJ: Ablex.

Myers, B. J. (1982). Early intervention using Brazelton training with middle-class mothers and fathers of newborns. *Child Development, 53,* 462–471.

Myers, B. J. (1987). Mother-infant bonding: The status of this critical-period hypothesis. In M. H. Bornstein (Ed.), *Sensitive periods in development: Interdisciplinary perspectives* (pp. 108–137). Hillsdale, NJ: Erlbaum.

Myers, B. J., Jarvis, P. A., & Creasey, G. L. (1987). Infants' behavior and their mothers and grandmothers. *Infant Behavior and Development, 10,* 245–259.

Nachmias, M., Gunnar, M., Mangelsdorf, S., Parritz, R. H., & Buss, K. (1996). Behavioral inhibition and stress reactivity: The moderating role of attachment security. *Child Development, 67,* 508–522.

Nadel, J., Carchon, I., Kervella, C., Marcelli, D., & Plantey-Reserbat, D. (1999). Expectancies for social contingency in 2-month-olds. *Developmental Science, 2*(2), 164–173.

Nadel, J., & Fontaine, A. (1989). Communication by imitation: A developmental and comparative approach to transitory social competence. In B. H. Schneider & G. Attili (Eds.), *Social competence in developmental perspective* (pp. 131–144). The Netherlands: Kluwer Academic.

Nadel, J., & Tremblay-Leveau, H. (1999). Early perception of social contingencies and interpersonal intentionality: Dyadic and triadic paradigms. In P. Rochat (Ed.), *Early social cognition* (pp. 391–415). Mahwah, NJ: Lawrence Erlbaum Associates.

Naeye, R. (1980). Sudden infant death. *Scientific American, 242,* 56–62.

Nagan, H. Y., Miu, P., Ko, L., & Ma, H. K. (1990). Long-term neurological sequelae following vacuum extractor delivery. *Australia and New Zealand Journal of Obstetrical Gynaecology, 30*(2), 111–114.

Naigles, L. G., & Kako, E. T. (1993). First contact in verb acquisition: Defining a role for syntax. *Child Development, 64,* 1665–1687.

Nakano, S. (1995). Let your toddler journey to separation: Child separation and reconstruction of playful interactions in the Japanese mother and child. *Research and Clinical Center for Child Development, 17,* 23–44.

Nakazima, S. (1972). Phonemicization and symbolization in language development. In E. H. Lenneberg & E. Lenneberg (Eds.), *Foundations of language development: A multidisciplinary approach* (Vol. 1, pp. 306–332). New York: Academic Press.

National Safety Council. (1987). *Accident facts.* Chicago: Author.

Nazzi, T., Floccia, C., & Bertoncini, J. (1998). Discrimination of pitch contours by neonates. *Infant Behavior and Development, 21*(4), 779–784.

Needham, A., & Baillargeon, R. (1998). Effects of prior experience on 4.5-month-old infants' object segregation. *Infant Behavior and Development, 21*(1), 1–24.

Nehlig, A., & Debry, G. (1994). Potential teratogenic and neurodevelopmental consequences of coffee and caffeine exposure: A review of human and animal data. *Neurotoxicology and Teratology, 16,* 531–543.

Neisser, U. (1991). Two perceptually given aspects of the self and their development. Special Issue: The development of self: The first three years. *Developmental Review, 11* (3), 197–209.

Nelson, C. A. (1985). The perception and recognition of facial expressions in infancy. In T. M. Field & N. A. Fox (Eds.), *Social perception in infants* (pp. 101–125). Norwood, NJ: Ablex.

Nelson, C. A. (1987). The recognition of facial expressions in the first two years of life: Mechanisms of development. *Child Development, 58,* 889–909.

Nelson, C. A. (1994). Neural bases of infant temperament. In J. E. Bates & T. D. Wachs (Eds.), *Temperament: Individual differences at the interface of biology and behavior* (pp. 47–82). Washington, DC: American Psychological Association.

Nelson, J. R., Jr. (1982). The politics of federal day care regulations. In E. Zigler & E. Gordon (Eds.), *Day care: Scientific and social policy issues* (pp. 277–305). Boston: Auburn House.

Nelson, K. (1973). Structure and strategy in learning to talk. *Monographs of the Society for Research in Child Development, 38* (Serial No. 149), 1–136.

Nelson, K. (1978). How children represent knowledge of their world in and out of language: A preliminary report. In R. S. Siegler (Ed.), *Children's thinking: What develops?* (pp. 213–240). Hillsdale, NJ: Erlbaum.

Nelson, K. (1981). Individual differences in language development: Implications for development and language. *Developmental Psychology, 17,* 170–187.

Nelson, K., Rescorla, L., Gruendel, J., & Benedict, H. (1978). Early lexicons: What do they mean? *Child Development, 49,* 960–968.

Nelson, N. M., Enkin, M. W., Saigel, S., Bennett, K. J., Milner, R., & Sackett, D. L. (1980). A randomized clinical trial of the Leboyer approach to childbirth. *New England Journal of Medicine, 299,* 655–660.

Nettlebladt, P., Fagerstrom, C., & Udderberg, N. (1976). The significance of reported childbirth pain. *Journal of Psychosomatic Research, 20,* 215–221.

Neumann, P. J., Gharib, S. D., & Weinstein, M. C. (1994). The cost of a successful delivery with in vitro fertilization. *New England Journal of Medicine, 331,* 239–243.

Newman, D. L., Caspi, A., Moffitt, T. E., & Silva, P. A. (1997). Antecedents of adult interpersonal functioning: Effects of individual differences in age 3 temperament. *Developmental Psychology, 33*(2), 206–217.

NICHD Early Child Care Research Network (1996). Characteristics of infant child care: Factors contributing to positive caregiving. *Early Childhood Research Quarterly, 11,* 269–306.

NICHD Early Child Care Research Network (1997a). Child care in the first year of life. *Merrill-Palmer Quarterly, 43*(3), 340–360.

NICHD Early Child Care Research Network (1997b). Familial factors associated with characteristics of nonmaternal care for infants. *Journal of Marriage and the Family, 59,* 389–408.

NICHD Early Child Care Research Network (1997c). Poverty and patterns of child care. In G. J. Duncan & J. Brooks-Gunn (Eds.), *Consequences of growing up poor* (pp. 100–130). New York: Russell Sage.

NICHD Early Child Care Research Network (1998a). Early child care and self-control, compliance, and problem behavior in 24 and 36 months. *Child Development, 69*(4), 1145–1170.

NICHD Early Child Care Research Network (1998b). Relations between family predictors and child outcomes: Are they weaker for children in child care? *Developmental Psychology, 34*(5), 1119–1128.

NICHD Early Child Care Research Network (1999). Chronicity of maternal depressive symptoms, maternal sensitivity, and child functioning at 36 months. *Developmental Psychology, 35*(8), 1297–1310.

Nicolich, L. M. (1977). Beyond sensorimotor intelligence: Assessment of symbolic maturity through analysis of pretend play. *Merrill-Palmer Quarterly, 23,* 89–100.

Nichols, F. H., & Humenick, S. S. (1988). *Childbirth education: Practice, research, and theory.* Philadelphia: W. B. Saunders.

Ninio, A. (1979). The naive theory of the infant and other maternal attitudes in two subgroups in Israel. *Child Development, 50,* 976–980.

Ninio, A. (1980). Picture-book reading in mother-infant dyads belonging to two subgroups in Israel. *Child Development, 51,* 587–590.

Ninio, A. (1983). Joint book reading as a multiple vocabulary acquisition device. *Developmental Psychology, 19,* 445–451.

Nwokah, E., Davies, P., Islam, A., Hsu, H., & Fogel, A. (1993). Vocal affect in three-year-olds: A quantitative acoustic analysis of child laughter. *Acoustical Society of America, 94,* 3076–3090.

Nwokah, E., & Fogel, A. (1993). Laughter in mother-infant emotional communication. *Humor, 6–2,* 137–161.

Nwokah, E., Hsu, H., Dobrowolska, O., & Fogel, A. (1994). The development of laughter in mother-infant communication: Timing parameters and temporal sequences. *Infant Behavior and Development, 16,* 23–25.

Oakes, L. M., Coppage, D. J., & Dingel, A. (1997). By land or by sea: The role of perceptual similarity in infants' categorization of animals. *Developmental Psychology, 33*(3), 396–407.

Oakes, L. M., Plumert, J. M., Lansink, J. M., & Merryman, J. D. (1996). Evidence for task-dependent categorization in infancy. *Infant Behavior and Development, 19,* 425–440.

Oakes, L. M., & Tellinghuisen, D. J. (1994). Examining in infancy: Does it reflect active processing? *Developmental Psychology, 30,* 748–756.

O'Brien, M., Asay, J. H., & McCluskey-Fawcett, K. (1999). Family functioning and maternal depression following premature birth. *Reproductive and Infant Psychology, 17*(2), 175–188.

O'Brien, M., & Huston, A. C. (1985). Development of sex-typed play behavior in toddlers. *Developmental Psychology, 21,* 866–871.

O'Connell, B., & Bretherton, I. (1984). Toddler's play, alone and with mother: The role of maternal guidance. In I. Bretherton (Ed.), *Symbolic play* (pp. 337–366). Orlando, FL: Academic Press.

O'Conner, M. J., Sigman, M., & Brill, N. (1987). Disorganization of attachment in relation to maternal alcohol consumption. *Journal of Consulting and Clinical Psychology, 55,* 831–836.

Oehler, J. M., & Eckerman, C. O. (1988, April). *Regulatory effects of human speech and touch in premature infants prior to term age.*

Presentation at the International Conference on Infant Studies, Washington, DC.

Ogunyemi, D., Hullett, S., Leeper, J., & Risk, A. (1998). Prepregnancy body mass index, weight gain during pregnancy, and perinatal outcome in a rural black population. *Journal of Maternal and Fetal Medicine, 7*(4), 190–193.

O'Hara, M. W. (1997). The nature of postpartum depressive disorders. In L. Murray & P. J. Cooper (Eds.), *Postpartum depression and child development* (pp. 3–31). New York: Guilford Press.

O'Hara, M. W., Schlechte, J. A., Lewis, D. A., & Varner, M. W. (1991). Controlled prospective study of postpartum mood disorders: Psychological, environmental, and hormonal variables. *Journal of Abnormal Psychology, 100*(1), 63–73.

Olds, S. B., London, M. L., & Ladewig, P. A. (1984). Nursing assessment of the newborn. *Maternal-newborn nursing: A family-centered approach* (pp. 660–707). Menlo Park, CA: Addison-Wesley.

Oller, D. K. & Eilers, R. E. (1988). The role of audition in infant babbling. *Child Development, 59,* 441–449.

Olson, S. L., Bates, J. E., & Bayles, K. (1984). Mother-infant interaction and the development of individual differences in children's cognitive competence. *Developmental Psychology, 20,* 166–179.

Olson, S. L., Bates, J. E., & Kaskie, B. (1992). Caregiver-infant interaction antecedents of children's school-age cognitive ability. *Merrill-Palmer Quarterly, 38,* 309–330.

O'Neill, D. K. (1996). Seven-year-old children's sensitivity to a parent's knowledge state when making requests. *Child Development, 67,* 659–677.

Oppenheim, D., Sagi, A., & Lamb, M. E. (1988). Infant-adult attachments on the kibbutz and their relation to socioemotional development 4 years later. *Developmental Psychology, 24,* 427–433.

O'Reilly-Green, C., & Cohen, W. R. (1993). Pregnancy in women aged 40 and older. *Obstetrics and Gynecology, 20,* 313–331.

Osofsky, H., Rosenthal, M., & Butterbaugh, G. (1999). Addressing infertility: Opportunities for the mental health professional to support families. *Zero to Three, 19*(4), 25–31.

Oster, H. (1978). Facial expression and affect development. In M. Lewis & L. A. Rosenblum (Eds.), *The development of affect* (pp. 43–75). New York: Plenum Press.

Oster, H., Hegley, D., & Nagel, L. (1992). Adult judgments and fine-grained analysis of infant facial expressions: Testing the validity of a priori coding formulas. *Developmental Psychology, 28,* 1115–1131.

Osterling, J., & Dawson, G. (1994). Early recognition of children and autism: A study of first birthday home videotapes. *Journal of Autism and Developmental Disorders, 24,* 247–257.

Otaki, M., Durrett, M., Richards, P., Nyquist, L., & Pennebaker, J. (1986). Maternal and infant behavior in Japan and America: A partial replication. *Journal of Cross-Cultural Psychology, 17,* 251–268.

Oviatt, S. L. (1978, April). *Qualitative change in the language comprehension of 9- to 17-month-old infants: An experimental approach.* Paper presented at the International Conference on Infant Studies, Providence, RI.

Ozonoff, S., & South, M. (2000). Early social development in young children with autism: Theoretical and clinical implications. In J. G. Bremner & A. Fogel (Eds.), *Handbook of infancy research* (pp. 72–96). Oxford, England: Blackwell.

Paiva, J. V., Hutto, C., Antunes, C., & Scott, G. (1994). Correlation between timing of rupture of amniotic membranes and risk of HIV-1 perinatal transmission. *International Conference on AIDS, 10,* 307–308.

Palkovitz, R. (1984). Parental attitude and fathers' interactions with their 5-month-old infants. *Developmental Psychology, 20,* 1054–1060.

Palkovitz, R. (1985). Fathers' birth attendance, early contact, and extended contact with their newborns: A critical review. *Child Development, 56,* 392–408.

Palmer, C. F. (1989). The discriminating nature of infants' exploratory actions. *Developmental Psychology, 25,* 885–893.

Palo, P., Piiroinen, O., Honkonen, E., Lakkala, T., & Aula, P. (1994). Transabdominal chorionic villus sampling and amniocentesis for prenatal diagnosis: 5 years' experience at a university centre. *Prenatal Diagnosis, 14,* 157–162.

Panneton, R. K., & DeCasper, A. J. (1986, April). *Newborns' postnatal preference for a prenatally experienced melody.* Paper presented at the International Conference on Infant Studies, Los Angeles, CA.

Papousek, H. (1967). Conditioning during early postnatal development. In Y. Brackbill & G. G. Thompson (Eds.), *Behavior in infancy and early childhood* (pp. 268–284). New York: Free Press.

Papousek, H., & Papousek, M. (1977). Mothering and the cognitive headstart: Psychobiological considerations. In H. R. Schaffer (Ed.), *Studies in mother-infant interaction* (pp. 63–88). London: Academic Press.

Papousek, H., & Papousek, M. (1987). Intuitive parenting: A dialectic counterpart of the infant's integrative competence. In J. D. Osofsky (Ed.), *Handbook of infant development* (2nd ed., pp. 302–331). New York: Wiley.

Papousek, M. (1989). Determinants of responsiveness to infant vocal expression of emotional state. *Infant Behavior and Development, 12,* 507–524.

Papousek, M. (1994). Melodies in caregivers' speech: A species-specific guidance towards language. *Early Development and Parenting, 3,* 5–17.

Papousek, M., Bornstein, M. H., Nuzzo, C., Papousek, H., & Symmes, D. (1990). Infant responses to prototypical melodic contours in parental speech. *Infant Behavior and Development, 13,* 539–545.

Papousek, M., & Papousek, H. (1981). Musical elements in the infant's vocalization: Their significance for communication, cognition, and creativity. In L. P. Lipsitt & C. K. Rovee-Collier (Eds.), *Advances in infancy research* (Vol. 1, pp. 64–86). Norwood, NJ: Ablex.

Papousek, M., Papousek, H., & Bornstein, M. H. (1985). The naturalistic vocal environment of young infants: On the significance of homogeneity and variability in parental speech. In T. M. Field & N. A. Fox (Eds.), *Social perception in infants* (pp. 171–186). Norwood, NJ: Ablex.

Papousek, M., Papousek, H., & Symmes, D. (1991). The meanings of melodies in motherese in tone and stress languages. *Infant Behavior and Development, 14,* 415–440.

Papousek, M., & von Hofacker, N. (1995). Persistent crying and parenting: Search for a butterfly in a dynamic system. *Early Development and Parenting, 4*(4), 209–224.

Parfitt, R. R. (1977). *The birth primer.* Philadelphia: Running Press.

Park, K. A., & Waters, E. (1989). Security of attachment and preschool friendship. *Child Development, 60,* 1076–1081.

Park, S., Belsky, J., Putnam, S., & Crnic, K. (1997). Infant emotionality, parenting, and 3-year inhibition: Exploring stability and lawful discontinuity in a male sample. *Developmental Psychology, 33*(2), 218–227.

Parke, R., & Collmer, C. W. (1975). Child abuse: An interdisciplinary analysis. In E. Hetherington (Ed.), *Review of the child development research* (Vol. 5, pp. 87–102). Chicago: University of Chicago Press.

Parke, R. D., & Sawin, D. B. (1980). The family in early infancy: Social interactional and attitudinal analyses. In F. A. Pedersen (Ed.), *The father-infant relationship: Observational studies in the family setting* (pp. 244–268). New York: Praeger Special Studies.

Parke, R. D., & Tinsley, B. R. (1981). The father's role in infancy: Determinants of involvement in caregiving and play. In M. E. Lamb (Ed.), *The role of the father in child development* (2nd ed., pp. 310–329). New York: Wiley.

Parke, R. D., & Tinsley, B. R. (1987). Family interaction in infancy. In J. D. Osofsky (Ed.), *Handbook of infant development* (2nd ed., pp. 332–353). New York: Wiley.

Parker, B., McFarlane, J., & Soeken, K. (1994). Abuse during pregnancy: Effects on maternal complications and birth weight in adult and teenage women. *Obstetrics and Gynecology, 84,* 323–328.

Parmelee, A. H., Jr., Schulz, H. R., & Disbrow, M. W. (1961). Sleep patterns of the newborn. *Journal of Pediatrics, 58,* 241–250.

Parrinello, R. M., & Ruff, H. A. (1988). The influence of adult intervention on infants' level of attention. *Child Development, 59,* 1125–1135.

Parritz, R. H. (1996). A descriptive analysis of toddler coping in challenging circumstances. *Infant Behavior and Development, 19,* 171–180.

Parten, M. B. (1932). Social participation among preschool children. *Journal of Abnormal and Social Psychology, 27,* 243–269.

Pascalis, O., de Schonen, S., Morton, J., Deruelle, C., & Fabre-Grenet, M. (1995). Mother's face recognition by neonates: A replication and extension. *Infant Behavior and Development, 18,* 79–85.

Passman, R. H. (1977). Providing attachment objects to facilitate learning and reduce distress: Effects of mothers and security blankets. *Developmental Psychology, 13,* 25–28.

Passman, R. H., & Weisberg, P. (1975). Mothers and blankets as agents for promoting play and exploration by young children in a novel environment: The effects of social and non-social attachment objects. *Developmental Psychology, 11,* 170–177.

Patterson, C. J., Kupersmidt, J. B., & Vaden, N. A. (1990). Income level, gender, ethnicity, and household composition as predictors of children's school-based competence. *Child Development, 61,* 485–494.

Patterson, M. L., & Werker, J. F. (1999). Matching phonetic information in lips and voice is robust in 4.5-month-old infants. *Infant Behavior and Development, 22*(2), 237–247.

Patton, M. Q. (1990). *Qualitative evaluation and research methods* (2nd ed.). London: Sage.

Paulson, G., & Gottlieb, G. (1968). Developmental reflexes: The reappearance of foetal and neonatal reflexes in aged patients. *Brain, 91,* 37–52.

Pawl, J. H. (1992). Interventions to strengthen relationships between infants and drug-abusing or recovering parents. *Zero to Three, 13,* 6–10.

Pearson, J. L., Hunter, A. G., Ensminger, M. E., & Kellam, S. G. (1990). Black grandmothers in multigenerational households: Diversity in family structure and parenting involvement in Woodlawn community. *Child Development, 61,* 434–442.

Pecheux, M. G., Labrell, F., & Pistorio, M. (1993). What do parents talk about to infants? *Early Development and Parenting, 2,* 89–97.

Peckham, C. S. (1993). Mother-to-child transmission of HIV: Risk factors and timing. *International Conference on AIDS, 9,* abstract no. PS-04-2.

Pedersen, D. R., & Moran, G. (1996). Expressions of the attachment relationship outside of the strange situation. *Child Development, 67*(3), 915–927.

Pedersen, F., Suwalsky, J. T., Cain, R. L., & Zaslow, M. J. (1987). Paternal care of infants during maternal separations: Associations with father-infant interaction at one year. *Psychiatry, 50,* 193–205.

Pedlow, R., Sanson, A., Prior, M., & Oberklaid, F. (1993). Stability of maternally reported temperament from infancy to 8 years. *Developmental Psychology, 29,* 998–1007.

Peduto, V. A., Musu, M., Gatto, G., & Ghilli, L. (1994). Sudden infant death syndrome (SIDS): Risk conditions and intervention strategies. *Minerva-Anesthesiology, 60,* 393–402.

Peiper, A. (1963). *Cerebral function in infancy and childhood.* New York: Consultants Bureau.

Pelaez-Nogueras, M., Field, T., Cigales, M., Gonzalez, A., & Clasky, S. (1994). Infants of depressed mothers show less "depressed" behavior with their nursery teachers. *Infant Mental Health Journal, 15,* 358–367.

Pelaez-Nogueras, M., Field, T. M., Hossain, Z., & Pickens, J. (1996). Depressed mothers' touching increases infants' positive affect and attention in still-face interactions. *Child Development, 67*(4), 1780–1792.

Pellegrini, A. D., & Smith, P. K. (1998). Physical activity play: The nature and function of a neglected aspect of play. *Child Development, 69*(3), 577–598.

Peña, I. C., Teberg, A. J., & Hoppenbrouwers, T. (1987). The Gesell developmental schedule in Hispanic low-birth weight infants during the first year of life. *Infant Behavior and Development, 10,* 199–216.

Perlman, M., & Ross, H. S. (1997). The benefits of parent intervention in children's disputes: An examination of concurrent changes in children's fighting styles. *Child Development, 68*(4), 690–700.

Perris, E. E., & Clifton, R. K. (1988). Reaching in the dark toward sound as a measure of auditory localization in infants. *Infant Behavior and Development, 11,* 473–491.

Perris, E. E., Myers, N. A., & Clifton, R. K. (1990). Long-term memory for a single infancy experience. *Child Development, 61,* 1796–1807.

Perrucci, C., & Targ, D. (1988). Effect of plant closing on marriage and family life. In P. Voydanoff & L. Majka (Eds.), *Families and economic distress* (pp. 135–153). Newbury Park, CA: Sage.

Peterson, C. (1999). Children's memory for medical emergencies: 2 years later. *Developmental Psychology, 35*(6), 1493–1506.

Peterson, C., & Bell, M. (1996). Children's memory for traumatic injury. *Child Development, 67,* 3045–3070.

Peterson, C., & Rideout, R. (1998). Memory for medical emergencies experienced by 1- and 2-year-olds. *Developmental Psychology, 34*(5), 1059–1072.

Peterson, G., & Peters, D. (1985). The socialization values of low-income Appalachian white and rural black mothers: A comparative study. *Journal of Comparative Family Studies, 16,* 75–91.

Petitto, L. (1985, October). *On the use of prelinguistic gestures in hearing and deaf children: Implications for theories of language acquisition.* Paper presented at the Tenth Annual Boston University Conference on Language Acquisition, Boston, MA.

Pettit, G. S., & Bates, J. E. (1984). Continuity of individual differences in the mother-infant relationship from 6 to 13 months. *Child Development, 55,* 729–739.

Phillips, D., McCartney, K., & Scarr, S. (1987). Child-care quality and children's social development. *Developmental Psychology, 23,* 537–543.

Phillips, R. D., Wagner, S. H., Fells, C. A., & Lynch, M. (1990). Do infants recognize emotion in facial expressions?: Categorical and "metaphorical" evidence. *Infant Behavior and Development, 13,* 71–84.

Phipps-Yonas, S. (1980). Teenage pregnancy and motherhood: A review of the literature. *American Journal of Orthopsychiatry, 50,* 403–431.

Piaget, J. (1952). *The origins of intelligence in children.* New York: International Universities Press.

Piaget, J. (1954). *The construction of reality in the child.* New York: Ballantine Books.

Piaget, J. (1962). *Play, dreams and imitation in childhood.* New York: Norton.

Piaget, J., & Inhelder, B. (1969). *The psychology of the child.* New York: Basic Books.

Pickens, J. N., & Field, T. (1995). Facial expressions and vagal tone of infants of depressed and non-depressed mothers. *Early Development and parenting, 4,* 83–89.

Pieraut-Lebonniec, G. (1990). Reaching and hand adjusting to the target properties. In H. Bloch & B. I. Bertenthal (Eds.), *Sensory-motor organizations and development in infancy and early childhood* (pp. 301–314). Boston, MA: Kluwer Academic.

Pine, J. M., Lieven, E. V. M., & Rowland, C. F. (1997). Stylistic variation at the "single-word" stage: Relations between maternal speech characteristics and children's vocabulary composition and usage. *Child Development, 68*(5), 807–819.

Pipes, P. L. (1985). *Nutrition in infancy and early childhood* (2nd ed.). St. Louis: Mosby.

Pipp, S., Easterbrooks, M. A., & Brown, S. R. (1993). Attachment status and complexity of infants' self- and other-knowledge when tested with mother and father. *Social Development, 2,* 4–12.

Pipp, S., Easterbrooks, M. A., & Harmon, R. J. (1992). The relation between attachment and knowledge of self and mother in one- to three-year-old infants. *Child Development, 63* (3), 738–750.

Pipp, S., Fischer, K. W., & Jennings, S. (1987). Acquisition of self- and mother knowledge in infancy. *Developmental Psychology, 23*, 86–96.

Pipp-Siegel, S., Siegel, C. H., & Dean, J. (1999). Neurological aspects of the disorganized/disoriented attachment classification system: Differentiating quality of the attachment relationship from neurological impairment. *Monographs of the Society for Research in Child Development, 64*(3), 25–44.

Pistrang, N. (1984). Women's work involvement and experience of new motherhood. *Journal of Marriage and Family*, 433–446.

Placek, P. J. (1986). Commentary: Cesarean rates still rising. *Statistical Bulletin, 67*, 9.

Pleck, J. H. (1983). Husbands' paid work and family roles: Current research issues. In H. Lopata & J. H. Pleck (Eds.), *Research in the interweave of social roles: Vol. 3. Families and jobs* (pp. 575–605). Greenwich, CT: JAI Press.

Pleck, J. H., & Rustad, M. (1980). *Husbands' and wives' time in family work and paid work in 1975–1976 study of time use.* Unpublished paper. Wellesley College Center for Research on Women.

Plomin, R. (1990). The role of inheritance in behavior. *Science, 248*, 183–188.

Plomin, R. (1994). Nature, nurture, and social development. *Social Development, 3*, 37–53.

Plomin, R., & Rutter, M. (1998). Child development, molecular genetics, and what to do with genes once they are found. *Child Development, 69*(4), 1223–1242.

Plomin, R., & Saudino, K. J. (1994). Quantitative genetics and molecular genetics. In J. E. Bates & T. D. Wachs (Eds.) *Temperament: Individual differences at the interface of biology and behavior* (pp. 143–171). Washington, DC: American Psychological Association.

Plunkett, J. W., Klein, T., & Meisels, S. J. (1988). The relationship of preterm infant-mother attachment to stranger sociability at 3 years. *Infant Behavior and Development, 11*, 83–96.

Polansky, N. (1976). Analysis of research on child neglect: The social work viewpoint. In Herner and Co. (Eds.), *Four perspectives on the status of child abuse and neglect research* (pp. 602–638). Washington, DC: National Center on Child Abuse and Neglect.

Pollitt, E., Garza, C., & Leibel, R. L. (1984). Nutrition and public policy. In H. W. Stevenson & A. E. Siegel (Eds.), *Child development research and social policy* (pp. 421–470). Chicago: University of Chicago Press.

Pollitt, E., Golub, M., Gorman, K., Grantham-McGregor, S., Levitsky, D., Schurch, B., Strupp, B., & Wachs, T. (1996). A reconceptualization of the effects of undernutrition on children's biological, psychosocial, and behavioral development. *Social Policy Report: Society for Research in Child Development, 10*(5).

Porcher, F. K. (1992). HIV infected pregnant women and their infants: Primary health care implications. *Nurse Practitioner, 17*, 46–54.

Porter, R. H., Cernoch, J. M., & Perry, S. (1983). The importance of odors in mother-infant interactions. *Maternal Child Nursing Journal, 12*(3), 147–154.

Porter, R. H., Makin, J. W., Davis, L. B., & Christensen, K. M. (1992). Breast-fed infants respond to olfactory cues from their own mother and unfamiliar lactating females. *Infant Behavior and Development, 15*, 85–93.

Portes, P., Dunham, R., & Williams, S. (1986). Assessing child-rearing style in ecological settings: Its relation to culture, social class, early age intervention and scholastic achievement. *Adolescence, 21*, 723–735.

Posada, G., Gao, Y., Wu, F., Posada, R., Tascon, M., Schölmerich, A., Sagi, A., Kondo-Ikemura, K., Haaland, W., & Synnevaag, B. (1995). The secure-base phenomenon across cultures: Children's behavior, mothers' preferences, and experts' concepts. *Monographs of the Society for Research in Child Development, 244*(60), 27–48.

Poulin-Dubois, D., Serbin, L. A., & Derbyshire, A. (1998). Toddlers' intermodal and verbal knowledge about gender. *Merrill-Palmer Quarterly, 44*(3), 338–354.

Poulin-Dubois, D., Serbin, L. A., Kenyon, B., & Derbyshire, A. (1994). Infants' intermodal knowledge about gender. *Developmental Psychology, 30*, 436–442.

Powell, D. R. (2000). Early intervention and risk. In J. G. Bremner & A. Fogel (Eds.), *Handbook of infancy research.* Oxford, England: Blackwell.

Powell, M. (1991). The psychosocial impact of Sudden Infant Death Syndrome on siblings. Committee of the Health Psychology Interest Group of the Psychological Society of Ireland: Having babies: Issues in reproductive and infant psychology. *Irish Journal of Psychology, 12*, 235–247.

Power, T. G., Chapieski, M. L., & McGrath, M. P. (1985). Assessment of individual differences in infant exploration and play. *Developmental Psychology, 21*, 974–981.

Power, T. G., & Parke, R. D. (1986). Patterns of early socialization: Mother- and father-infant interaction in the home. *International Journal of Behavioral Development, 9*, 331–341.

Prechtl, H. F. R. (1977). *The neurological examination of the full term newborn infant* (2nd ed.). London: Heinemann.

Preisler, G. (1997). Social and emotional development of blind children: A longitudinal study. In V. Lewis & G. M. Collis (Eds.), *Blindness and psychological development in young children* (pp. 69–85). Leicester, England: BPS Books.

Pressman, E. K., DiPietro, J. A., Costigan, K. A., Shupe, A. K., & Johnson, T. R. B. (1998). Fetal neurobehavioral development: Associations with socioeconomic class and fetal sex. *Developmental Psychobiology, 33*(1), 79–91.

Pridham, K. F. (1998). Guided participation and development of caregiving competencies for families of low birth-weight infants. *Journal of Advanced Nursing, 28*(5), 948–958.

Prigogine, I., & Stengers, I. (Eds.) (1984). *Order out of chaos: Man's new dialogue with nature.* New York: Bantam Books.

Provence, S. (1982). Infant day care: Relationships between theory and practice. In E. F. Zigler & E. W. Gordon (Eds.), *Day care: Scientific and social policy issues* (pp. 33–35). Boston: Auburn House.

Provence, S., & Naylor, A. (1983). *Working with disadvantaged parents and children: Scientific issues and practice.* New Haven, CT: Yale University Press.

Prysak, M., Lorenz, R. P., & Kisly, A. (1995). Pregnancy outcome in nulliparous women 35 years and older. *Obstetrics and Gynecology, 85*, 65–70.

Puddifoot, J. E., & Johnson, M. P. (1999). Active grief, despair, and difficulty coping: Some measured characteristics of male response following their partner's miscarriage. *Journal of Reproductive and Infant Psychology, 17*(1), 89–93.

Puffer, R. R., & Serrano, C. V. (1973). *Patterns of mortality in childhood (PAHO Scientific Publication No. 262).* Washington, DC: Pan American Health Organization.

Pye, C. (1986). Quiche Mayan speech to children. *Journal of Child Language, 13*(1), 85–100.

Quinn, P. C., Cummins, M., Kase, J., Martin, E., & Weissman, S. (1996). Development of categorical representations for *above* and *below* spatial relations in 3- to 7-month-old infants. *Developmental Psychology, 32*(5), 942–950.

Quinn, T. C. (1995). The epidemiology of the acquired immunodeficiency syndrome in the 1990s. *Emergency Medical Clinics of North America, 13*, 1–25.

Rabain-Jamin, J., & Wornham, W. L. (1993). Practices and representations of child care and motor development among West Africans in Paris. *Early Development and Parenting, 2*, 107–119.

Radke-Yarrow, M., & Zahn-Waxler, C. (1984). Roots, motives, and patterns in children's pro-social behavior. In E. Staub, D. Bartal, J. Karylowski, & J. Reykowski (Eds.), *The development and maintenance of pro-social behaviors* (pp. 68–89). New York: Plenum Press.

Radke-Yarrow, M., Zahn-Waxler, C., Richardson, D. T., Susman, A., & Martinez, P. (1994). Caring behavior in children of clinically depressed and well mothers. *Child Development, 65,* 1405–1414.

Ragozin, A. S., Bashan, R. B., Crnic, K. A., Greenberg, M. T., & Robinson, N. M. (1982). Effects of maternal age on parenting role. *Developmental Psychology, 18,* 627–634.

Ramey, C. T., & Campbell, F. A. (1991). Poverty, early childhood education, and academic competence: The Abecedarian experience. In A. C. Huston (Ed.), *Children in poverty: Child development and public policy* (pp. 190–221). New York: Cambridge University Press.

Ramey, C. T., & Ramey, S. L. (1998). Early intervention and early experience. *American Psychologist, 53*(2), 109–120.

Ramey, S. L. (1999). Head Start and preschool education: Toward continued improvement. *American Psychologist, 54*(5), 344–346.

Ramig, P. R. (1993). High reported spontaneous stuttering recovery rates: Fact or fiction? *Language, Speech, and Hearing Services in Schools, 24,* 156–160.

Ramsay, D. S. (1980). Onset of unimanual handedness in infants. *Infant Behavior and Development, 3,* 377–386.

Ramsey, C. N., Abell, T. N., & Baker, L. C. (1986). The relationship between family functioning, life events, family structure, and the outcome of pregnancy. *Journal of Family Practice, 22,* 521–527.

Rapoport, R., Rapoport, R. N., & Strelitz, A. (1977). *Fathers, mothers and society: Toward new alliances.* New York: Basic Books.

Rappoport, D. (1976). Pour une naissance sans violence: Résultats d'une première enquête. *Bulletin de Psychologie, 29,* 552–560.

Rauh, V. A., Achenbach, T. M., Nurcombe, B., Howell, C. T., & Teti, D. M. (1988). Minimizing adverse effects of low birthweight: Four-year results of an early intervention program. *Child Development, 59,* 544–553.

Rautava, P., Koski, M. L., Sillanpaa, M., & Tuominen, J. (1992). The Finnish family competence study: Childbearing attitudes in pregnant nulliparae. *Acta Paedopsychiatrica, 55,* 3–8.

Raver, C. C. (1996). Relations between social contingency in mother-child interaction and 2-year-olds' social competence. *Developmental Psychology, 32*(5), 850–859.

Raver, C. C. (1996). Success at catching and keeping toddler's attention: An examination of joint attention among low-income mothers and their 2-year-olds. *Early Development and Parenting, 5*(4), 225–236.

Reardon, P., & Bushnell, E. W. (1988). Infants' sensitivity to arbitrary pairings of color and taste. *Infant Behavior and Development, 11,* 245–250.

Rebuffat, E., Groswasser, J., Kelmanson, I., Sottiaux, M., & Kahn, A. (1994). Polygraphic evaluation of night-to-night variability in sleep characteristics and apneas in infants. *Sleep, 17,* 329–332.

Recchia, S. L. (1997). Social communication and response to ambiguous stimuli in toddlers with visual impairments. *Journal of Applied Developmental Psychology, 18*(3), 297–316.

Reddy, V. (1991). Playing with others' expectations: Teasing and mucking about in the first year. In A. Whiten (Ed.), *Natural theories of mind: Evolution, development, and simulation of everyday mindreading* (pp. 143–158). Cambridge, MA: Basil Blackwell.

Reddy, V. (2000). Mind knowledge in the first year: Understanding attention and intention. In J. G. Bremner & A. Fogel (Eds.), *Handbook of infancy research* (pp. 155–181). Oxford, England: Blackwell.

Reeb, K. G., Graham, A. V., Zyzanski, S. J., & Kitson, G. C. (1987). Predicting low birthweight and complicated labor in urban black women: A biopsychosocial perspective. *Social Science and Medicine, 25,* 1321–1327.

Reed, G., & Leiderman, P. H. (1981). Age-related changes in attachment behavior in polymatrically reared infants: The Kenyan Gusii. In T. Field, T. M. Sostek, P. Vietze, & P. Leiderman, (Eds.), *Culture and early interactions* (pp. 85–101). Hillsdale, NJ: Erlbaum.

Reese, M. (1985). Moshe Feldenkrais's work with movement: A parallel approach to Milton Erickson's hypnotherapy. In J. K. Zeig (Ed.), *Ericksonian psychotherapy: Vol. 1: Structures* (pp. 213–229). New York: Brunner-Mazel.

Reilly, J., McIntire, M., & Bellugi, U. (1985, October). *Faces: The relationship between language and affect.* Paper presented at the 10th Annual Boston University Conference on Language Development, Boston, MA.

Reimers, M., & Fogel, A. (1992). The evolution of joint attention to objects between infants and their mothers: Diversity and convergence. *Analise Psicologica, 1,* 81–89.

Reinecke, M. A., & Fogel, A. (1994). The development of referential offering in the first year. *Early Development and Parenting, 3,* 181–186.

Reissland, N. (1988). Neonatal imitation in the first hour of life: Observations in rural Nepal. *Developmental Psychology, 24,* 464–469.

Reissland, N., & Harris, P. (1991). Children's use of display rules in pride-eliciting situations. *British Journal of Developmental Psychology, 9,* 431–435.

Reite, M., Kaemingk, K., & Boccia, M. L. (1989). Maternal separation in bonnet monkey infants: Altered attachment and social support. *Child Development, 60,* 473–480.

Remez, L. (1996). Few married women use a method in Côte d'Ivoire, but fertility is decreasing. *International Family Planning Perspectives, 22*(3), 130–132.

Repacholi, B. M., & Gopnik, A. (1997). Early reasoning about desires: Evidence from 14- and 18-month olds. *Developmental Psychology, 33*(1), 12–21.

Reynolds, A. J. (1998). Developing early childhood programs for children and families at risk: Research-based principles to promote long-term effectiveness. *Children and Youth Services Review, 20*(6), 503–523.

Reznick, J. S., Kagan, J., Snidman, N., Gersten, M., Baak, K., & Rosenberg, A. (1986). Inhibited and uninhibited children: A follow-up study. *Child Development, 57,* 660–680.

Rheingold, H. L. (1982). Little children's participation in the work of adults: A nascent prosocial behavior. *Child Development, 53,* 114–125.

Rheingold, H. L., Cook, K. V., & Kolowitz, V. (1987). Commands activate the behavior and pleasure of 2-year-old children. *Developmental Psychology, 23,* 146–151.

Rheingold, H. L., Hay, D. F., & West, M. J. (1976). Sharing in the second year of life. *Child Development, 47,* 1148–1158.

Rhodes, J. E. (1993). Easing postpartum school transitions through parent mentoring programs. *Prevention in Human Services, 10,* 169–178.

Ricard, M., & Decarie, T. G. (1993). Distance-maintaining in infants' reaction to an adult stranger. *Social Development, 2,* 154–161.

Ricciuti, H. N. (1974). Fear and the development of social attachments in the first year of life. In M. Lewis & L. Rosenblum (Eds.), *The origins of fear* (pp. 39–58). New York: Wiley.

Ricciuti, H. N., & Poresky, R. H. (1972). Emotional behavior and development in the first year of life: An analysis of arousal, approach-withdrawal, and affective responses. In A. Pick (Ed.), *Minnesota symposia on child psychology* (Vol. 6, pp. 200–221). Minneapolis: University of Minnesota Press.

Richards, M. P. M. (1977). An ecological study of infant development in an urban setting in Britain. In P. Leiderman, S. Tulkin, & A. Rosenfeld (Eds.), *Culture and infancy: Variations in the human experience* (pp. 504–525). New York: Academic Press.

Richardson, D. K., Gray, J. E., Gortmaker, S. L., Goldman, D. A., Pursley, D. M., & McCormick, M. C. (1998). Declining severity adjusted mortality: Evidence of improving neonatal intensive care. *Pediatrics, 102*(4), 893–899.

Richardson, G. A., Day, N. L., & Taylor, P. M. (1989). The effect of pre-natal alcohol, marijuana, and tobacco exposure on neonatal behavior. *Infant Behavior and Development, 12,* 199–209.

Rickman, M. D., & Davidson, R. J. (1994). Personality and behavior in parents of temperamentally inhibited and uninhibited children. *Developmental Psychology, 30,* 346–354.

Ricks, S. S. (1985). Father-infant interactions: a review of empirical research. *Family Relations, 34,* 505–511.

Ridgeway, D., Waters, E., & Kuczaj, S. A., II. (1985). Acquisition of emotion-descriptive language: Receptive and productive vocabulary norms for ages 18 months to 6 years. *Developmental Psychology, 21,* 901–908.

Rieck, M., Arad, I., & Netzer, D. (1996). Developmental evaluation of very-low-birthweight infants: Longitudinal and cross-sectional studies. *International Journal of Behavioral Development, 19*(3), 549–562.

Riese, M. L. (1987). Longitudinal assessment of temperament from birth to 2 years: A comparison of full-term and preterm infants. *Infant Behavior and Development, 10,* 347–363.

Riley, C. A., & Trabasso, T. (1974). Comparatives, logical structures, and encoding in a transitive inference task. *Journal of Experimental Psychology, 17,* 187–203.

Ritter, J. M., Casey, R. J., & Langlois, J. H. (1991). Adults' responses to infants varying in appearance of age and attractiveness. *Child Development, 62,* 68–82.

Rizzo, T. A., Metzger, B. E., Dooley, S. L., & Cho, N. H. (1997). Early malnutrition and child neurobehavioral development: Insights from the study of children of diabetic mothers. *Child Development, 68*(1), 26–38.

Roberts, C., & Lowe, C. (1975). Where have all the conceptions gone? *Lancet, 1,* 498–499.

Roberts, K., & Cuff, M. D. (1989). Categorization studies of 9- to 15-month-old infants: Evidence for superordinate categorization? *Infant Behavior and Development, 12,* 265–288.

Robertson, J., & Robertson, J. (1971). Young children in brief separation: A fresh look. *Psychoanalytic Study of the Child, 26,* 264–315.

Robertson, S. S. (1987). Human cyclic motility: Fetal-newborn continuities and newborn state differences. *Developmental Psychobiology, 20,* 425–442.

Robertson, S. S. (1990). Temporal organization in fetal and newborn movement. In H. Bloch & B. I. Bertenthal (Eds.), *Sensory-motor organizations and development in infancy and early childhood* (pp. 105–122). The Netherlands: Kluwer Academic.

Robinson, C. H. (1978). *Fundamentals of normal nutrition* (3rd ed.). New York: Macmillian.

Robinson, J., Little, C., & Biringen, Z. (1993). Emotional communication in mother-toddler relationship: Evidence for early gender differentiation. *Merrill-Palmer Quarterly, 39,* 496–515.

Robinson, J. L., Kagan, J., Reznick, J. S., & Corley, R. (1992). The heritability of inhibited and uninhibited behavior: A twin study. *Developmental Psychology, 28* (6), 1030–1037.

Robson, A., & Cline, B. (1998). Developmental consequences of intrauterine growth retardation. *Infant Behavior and Development, 21*(2), 331344.

Rochat, P. (1987). Mouthing and grasping in neonates: Evidence for early detection of what hard or soft substances afford for action. *Infant Behavior and Development, 10,* 435–449.

Rochat, P. (1989). Object manipulation and exploration in 2- to 5-month-old infants. *Developmental Psychology, 25,* 871–884.

Rochat, P. (1992). Self-sitting and reaching in 5- to 8-month-old infants: The impact of posture and its development on early eye-hand coordination. *Journal of Motor Behavior, 24,* 210–220.

Rochat, P., Blass, E. M., & Hoffmeyer, L. B. (1988). Oropharyngeal control of hand-mouth coordination in newborn infants. *Developmental Psychology, 24,* 459–463.

Rochat, P., & Goubet, N. (1995). Development of sitting and reaching in 5- to 6-month-old infants. *Infant Behavior and Development, 18,* 53–68.

Rochat, P., Goubet, N., & Senders, S. J. (1999). To reach or not to reach? Perception of body effectivities by young infants. *Infant and Child Development, 8,* 129–148.

Rochat, P., & Hespos, S. J. (1997). Differential rooting response by neonates: Evidence for an early sense of self. *Early Development and Parenting, 6*(3–4), 105–112.

Rochat, P., & Morgan, R. (1995). Spatial determinants in the perception of self-produced leg movements by 3- to 5-month-old infants. *Developmental Psychology, 31,* 626–636.

Rochat, P., Querido, J. G., & Striano, T. (1999). Emerging sensitivity to the timing and structure of protoconversation in early infancy. *Developmental Psychology, 35*(4), 950–957.

Rochat, P., & Senders, S. J. (1990, April). *Sitting and reaching in infancy.* Paper presented at the Seventh International Conference on Infant Studies, Montreal, Canada.

Rocissano, L., Slade, A., & Lynch, V. (1987). Dyadic synchrony and toddler compliance. *Developmental Psychology, 23,* 698–704.

Rock, A. M. L., Trainor, L. J., & Addison, T. L. (1999). Distinctive messages in infant-directed lullabies and play songs. *Developmental Psychology, 35*(2), 527–534.

Rodholm, M., & Larsson, K. (1979). Father-infant interaction at the first contact after delivery. *Early Human Development, 3,* 21–27.

Rogers, S. J., & DiLalla, D. L. (1990). Age of symptom onset in young children with pervasive developmental disorders. *Journal of American Academy of Child and Adolescent Psychiatry, 29,* 863–872.

Roggman, L. A., Langlois, J. H., Hubbs-Tait, L., & Rieser-Danner, L. A. (1994). Infant day-care, attachment, and the "file drawer problem." *Child Development, 65,* 1429–1443.

Rogoff, B. (1990). *Apprenticeship in thinking: Cognitive development in social context.* New York: Oxford University Press.

Rogoff, B., Mistry, J., Goncu, A., & Mosier, C. (1993). Guided participation in cultural activity by toddlers and caregivers. *Monographs of the Society for Research in Child Development, 58* (8 Serial No. 236), 1–179.

Rogoff, B., Mosier, C., Mistry, J., & Goncu, A. (1989). Toddlers' guided participation in cultural activity. *Cultural Dynamics, 2,* 209–237.

Rogowski, J. (1998). Cost-effectiveness of care for very low birth weight infants. *Pediatrics, 102*(1), 35–43.

Rogowski, J. (1999). Measuring the cost of neonatal and perinatal care. *Pediatrics, 103*(5), 329–335.

Ronnqvist, L., & Hofsten, C. von. (1994). Neonatal finger and arm movements as determined by a social and an object context. *Early Development and Parenting, 3,* 81–94.

Rooks, J. P., Weatherby, N. L., Ernst, E. K. M., Stapleton, S., Rosen, D., & Rosenfeld, A. (1989). Outcome of care in birth centers. *New England Journal of Medicine, 321,* 1804–1811.

Rose, S. A., & Feldman, J. F. (1997). Memory and speed: Their role in the relation of infant information processing to later IQ. *Child Development, 68*(4), 630–641.

Rose, S. A., Feldman, J. F., & Wallace, I. F. (1988). Individual differences in infants' information processing: Reliability, stability, and prediction. *Child Development, 59,* 1177–1197.

Rose, S. A., Feldman, J. F., Wallace, I. F., & McCarton, C. (1989). Infant visual attention: Relation to birth status and developmental outcome during the first 5 years. *Developmental Psychology, 25,* 560–576.

Rose, S. A., Futterweit, L. R., & Jankowski, J. J. (1999). The relation of affect to attention and learning in infancy. *Child Development, 70*(3), 549–559.

Rose, S. A., & Ruff, H. A. (1987). Cross-modal abilities in human infants. In J. D. Osofsky (Ed.), *Handbook of infant development* (2nd ed., pp. 318–362). New York: Wiley.

Rose, S. A., Schmidt, K., & Bridget, W. H. (1976). Cardiac and behavioral responsivity to tactile stimulation in premature and full-term infants. *Developmental Psychology, 12,* 311–320.

Rosen, K. S., & Burke, P. B. (1999). Multiple attachment relationships within families: Mothers and fathers with two young children. *Developmental Psychology, 35*(2), 436–444.

Rosen, K. S., & Rothbaum, F. (1993). Quality of parental caregiving and security of attachment. *Developmental Psychology, 29,* 358–367.

Rosen, W. D., Adamson, L. B., & Bakeman, R. (1992). An experimental investigation of infant social referencing: Mothers' messages and gender differences. *Developmental Psychology, 28,* 1172–1178.

Rosenblatt, J. S. (1972). Learning in newborn kittens. *Scientific American, 277,* 18–25.

Rosenblith, J. F., & Sims-Knight, J. E. (1985). *In the beginning: Development in the first two years.* Belmont, CA: Brooks/Cole.

Rosenfield, J. A., Zahorik, P. M., Saint, W., & Murphy, G. (1993). Women's satisfaction with birth control. *Journal of Family Practice, 36,* 169–173.

Rosenstein, D., & Oster, H. (1988). Differential facial responses to four basic tastes in newborns. *Child Development, 59,* 1555–1568.

Rosenthal, N. K. (1991). The relation of peer interaction among infants and toddlers in family day care to characteristics of the child care environment. *Journal of Reproductive and Infant Psychology, Special Issues: International Perspective on Day Care for Young Children, 9,* 151–167.

Rosenthal, N. K. (1999). Out-of-home child care research: A cultural perspective. *International Journal of Behavioral Development, 23*(2), 477–518.

Rosett, H. L. (1980). The effects of alcohol on the fetus and offspring. In O. J. Kalant (Ed.), *Alcohol and drug problems in women. Neurobehavioral Toxicology and Teratology, 6,* 379–385.

Ross, H. S. (1996). Negotiating principles of entitlement in sibling property disputes. *Developmental Psychology, 32*(1), 90–101.

Ross, H. S., Conant, C. L., Cheyne, J. A., & Alevizos, E. (1992). Relationships and alliances in the social interaction of kibbutz toddlers. *Social Development, 1,* 1–17.

Ross, H. S., & Goldman, B. D. (1977a). Establishing new social relations in infancy. In T. Alloway, P. Pliner, & L. Krames (Eds.), *Attachment behavior* (pp. 225–239). New York: Plenum Press.

Ross, H. S., & Goldman, B. D. (1977b). Infant's sociability toward strangers. *Child Development, 48,* 638–642.

Ross, H. S., & Lollis, S. P. (1987). Communication within infant social games. *Developmental Psychology, 23,* 241–248.

Rossi, A. (1968). Transition to parenthood. *Journal of Marriage and the Family, 30,* 26–39.

Rothbart, M. K. (1986). Longitudinal observation of infant temperament. *Developmental Psychology, 22,* 356–365.

Rothbart, M. K., & Derryberry, D. (1981). Development of individual differences in temperament. In M. E. Lamb (Ed.), *Advances in developmental psychology* (Vol. 1, pp. 191–230). Hillsdale, NJ: Erlbaum.

Rothbart, M. K., Derryberry, D., & Posner, M. I. (1994). A psychobiological approach to the development of temperament. In J. E. Bates & T. D. Wachs (Eds.), *Temperament: Individual differences at the interface of biology and behavior* (pp. 83–116). Washington, DC: American Psychological Association.

Rothbart, M. K., & Posner, M. I. (1985). Temperament and the development of self-regulation. In L. C. Hartlage & C. F. Telzrow (Eds.), *The neuropsychology of individual differences: A developmental perspective* (pp. 93–123). New York: Plenum Press.

Rounds, K. A. (1991). Early intervention services for very young children and their families under P.L. 99-457. *Special issues: Learning disabilities. Child and Adolescent Social Work Journal, 8,* 489–499.

Rovee-Collier, C., & Barr, R. (2000). Infant learning and memory. In J. G. Bremner & A. Fogel (Eds.), *Handbook of infancy research.* Oxford, England: Blackwell.

Rovee-Collier, C. K., Enright, M., Lucas, D., Fagan, J., & Gekoski, M. J. (1981). The forgetting of newly acquired and reactivated memories of 3-month-old infants. *Infant Behavior and Development, 4,* 317–331.

Rovee-Collier, C. K., Evancio, S., & Earley, L. A. (1995). The time window hypothesis: Spacing effects. *Infant Behavior and Development, 18,* 69–78.

Roy, T. S., Andrews, J. E., Seidler, F. J., & Slotkin, T. A. (1998). Nicotine evokes cell death in embryonic rat brain during neurulation. *Journal of Pharmacology and Experimental Therapy, 287*(3), 1136–1144.

Rubenstein, J., & Howes, C. (1976). The effects of peers on toddler interaction with mother and toys. *Child Development, 47,* 597–605.

Rubenstein, J., Howes, C., & Pedersen, F. A. (1982). Second order effects of peers on mother-toddler interaction. *Infant Behavior and Development, 5,* 185–194.

Rubin, D. H., Krasilnikoff, B., Leventhal, J. M., Weile, B., & Berget, A. (1986). Effect of passive smoking on birth-weight. *Lancet, 2,* 415–417.

Rubin, G. B., Fagen, J. W., & Carroll, M. H. (1998). Olfactory context and memory retrieval in 3-month-old infants. *Infant Behavior and Development, 21*(4), 641–658.

Rubin, K. H., Hastings, P., Chen, X., Stewart, S., & McNichol, K. (1998). Intrapersonal and maternal correlates of aggression, conflict, and externalizing problems in toddlers. *Child Development, 69*(6), 1614–1629.

Rubinstein, A. J., Kalakanis, L., & Langlois, J. H. (1999). Infant preferences for attractive faces: A cognitive explanation. *Developmental Psychology, 35*(3), 848–855.

Ruda, M. A., Ling, Q.-D., Hohmann, R. G., Peng, Y. B., & Tachibana, T. (2000). Altered nocireceptive neuronal circuits after neonatal peripheral inflammation. *Science, 289*(5479), 628–630.

Ruff, H. A. (1978). Infant recognition of invariant forms of objects. *Child Development, 49,* 293–306.

Ruff, H. A. (1984). Infant's manipulative exploration of objects: Effects of age and object characteristics. *Developmental Psychology, 20,* 9–20.

Ruff, H. A. (1985). Detection of information specifying the motion of objects by 3- and 5-month-old infants. *Developmental Psychology, 21,* 295–305.

Ruff, H. A. (1986). Components of attention during infants' manipulative exploration. *Child Development, 57,* 105–114.

Ruff, H. A., & Kohler, C. J. (1978). Tactual-visual transfer in six-month-old infants. *Infant Behavior and Development, 1,* 259–264.

Ruff, H. A., & Lawson, K. R. (1990). Development of sustained, focused attention in young children during free play. *Developmental Psychology, 26,* 85–93.

Ruff, H. A., Lawson, K. R., Parrinello, R., & Weissberg, R. (1990). Long-term stability of individual differences in sustained attention in the early years. *Child Development, 61,* 60–75.

Ruff, H. A., Saltarelli, L. M., Capozzoli, M., & Dubiner, K. (1992). The differentiation of activity in infants' exploration of objects. *Developmental Psychology, 28* (5), 851–861.

Ruffwarg, H. P., Muzio, J. N., & Dement, W. C. (1966). Ontogenetic development of the human sleep-dream cycle. *Science, 153,* 604–619.

Ruopp, R. R., & Travers, J. (1982). Janus faces of day care: Perspectives on quality and cost. In E. Zigler & E. Gordon (Eds.), *Day care: Scientific and social policy issues* (pp. 165–190). Boston: Auburn House.

Russell, M. J., Mendelson, T., & Peeke, H. V. (1983). Mothers' identification of their infant's odors. *Ethology and Sociobiology, 4*(1), 29–31.

Rutter, M. (1979). Maternal deprivation, 1972–1978: New findings, new concepts, new approaches. *Child Development, 50,* 283–305.

Rutter, M. (1987). Continuities and discontinuities from infancy. In J. D. Osofsky (Ed.), *Handbook of infant development* (2nd ed.). New York: Wiley.

Ryan, V., & Wilson, K. (1995). Non-directive play therapy as a means of recreating optimal infant socialization patterns. *Early Development and Parenting, 4*(1) 29–38.

Sachs, J., & Devin, J. (1976). Young children's use of age-appropriate speech styles in social interaction and role-playing. *Journal of Child Language, 3,* 81–98.

Sagi, A. (1981). Mothers' and non-mothers' identification of infant cries. *Infant Behavior and Development, 4,* 37–40.

Sagi, A., Donnell, F., van Ijzendoorn, M. H., Mayseless, O. & Aviezer, O. (1994). Sleeping out of home in a kibbutz communal arrangement: It makes a difference for infant-mother attachment. *Child Development, 65,* 992–1004.

Sagi, A., van Ijzendoorn, M. H., Scharf, M., Joels, T., Koren-Karie, N., Mayseless, O., & Aviezer, O. (1997). Ecological constraints for inter-generational transmission of attachment. *International Journal of Behavioral Development, 20*(2), 287–299.

Sagi, A., Lamb, M. E., Lewkowicz, K. S., Shoham, R., Dvir, R., & Estes, D. (1985). Security of infant-mother, -father, and -metapelet attachments among kibbutz-reared Israeli children. In I. Bretherton & E. Waters (Eds.), *Growing points of attachment theory and research. Monographs of the Society for Research in Child Development, 50* (Serial No. 209), 257–275.

Salapatek, P., & Banks, M. S. (1978). Infant sensory assessment: Vision. In F. D. Minifie & L. L. Lloyd (Eds.), *Communicative and cognitive abilities: Early behavioral assessment* (pp. 86–107). Baltimore: University Park Press.

Salk, L. (1973). The role of the heartbeat in relations between mother and infant. *Scientific American, 228,* 24–29.

Sameroff, A. J. (1984). Developmental systems: Contexts and evolution. In P. H. Mussen (Ed.), *Handbook of child psychology: Vol. I. History, theory, and methods* (4th ed., pp. 237–294). New York: Wiley.

Sameroff, A. J., & Chandler, M. (1975). Reproductive risk and the continuum of caretaking casualty. In F. Horowitz (Ed.), *Review of child development research* (pp. 303–331). Chicago: University of Chicago Press.

Sameroff, A. J., & Emde, R. N. (1989). *Relationship disturbances in early childhood: A developmental approach.* New York: Basic Books.

Sameroff, A. J., & Seifer, R. (1983). Familial risk and child competence. *Child Development, 54,* 1254–1268.

Sameroff, A. J., Seifer, R., & Elias, P. K. (1982). Sociocultural variability in infant temperament ratings. *Child Development, 53,* 164–173.

Samuels, C. A. (1985). Attention to eye contact opportunity and facial motion by three-month-old infants. *Journal of Experimental Child Psychology, 40,* 105–114.

Samuels, C. A., Scholz, K., & Edmundson, S. (1992). The effects of baby bath and massage by fathers on the family system: The Sunraysia Australia intervention project. *Early Development and Parenting, 1,* 39–49.

Samuels, H. R. (1980). The effect of an older sibling on infant locomotor exploration of a new environment. *Child Development, 51,* 606–609.

Sancier, B., & Mapp, P. (1992). Who helps working women care for the young and old? *Affiliate Journal of Women and Social Work, 7,* 61–62.

Sander, L. W. (1962). Issues in early mother-child interaction. *Journal of the American Academy of Child Psychiatry, 1,* 141–166.

Sander, L. W., Stechler, G., Burns, P., & Lee, A. (1979). Change in infant and caregiver variables over the first two months of life: Integration of action in early development. In E. B. Thoman (Ed.), *Origins of the infant's social responsiveness* (pp. 349–407). Hillsdale, NJ: Lawrence Erlbaum Associates.

Sandman, C. A., Wadhwa, P., Hetrick, W. H., Porto, M., & Peeke, H. V. S. (1997). Human fetal heart rate dishabituation between thirty and thirty-two weeks' gestation. *Child Development, 68*(6), 1031–1040.

Sansavini, A. (1997). Neonatal perception of the rhythmical structure of speech: The role of stress patterns. *Early Development and Parenting, 6*(1), 3–13.

Sansavini, A., Bertoncini, J., & Giovanelli, G. (1997). Newborns discriminate the rhythm of multisyllabic stressed words. *Developmental Psychology, 33*(1), 3–11.

Sansavini, A., Rizzardi, M., Alessandroni, R., & Giovanelli, G. (1996). The development of Italian low- and very-low-birthweight infants from birth to 5 years: The role of biological and social risks. *International Journal of Behavioral Development, 19*(3), 533–547.

Sardana, R. (1985). Examining for defects. *Nursing Mirror, 160,* 38–42.

Savage-Rumbaugh, S., Murphy, J., Sevcik, R. A., Brakke, K. E., Williams, S. L., & Rumbaugh, D. M. (1993). Language comprehension in ape and child. *Monographs of the Society for Research in Child Development, 58* (3–4, Serial No. 233), 1–221.

Savelsbergh, G. J. P., & van der Kamp, J. (1993). The coordination of infant's reaching, grasping, catching and posture: A natural physical approach. In G. J. P. Savelsbergh (Ed.), *The development of coordination in infancy* (pp. 289–317). Amsterdam: Elsevier.

Sawin, D., & Parke, R. (1979). Fathers' affectionate stimulation and care-giving behaviors with newborn infants. *Family Coordinator, 28,* 509–513.

Scaife, M., & Bruner, J. S. (1975). The capacity for joint visual attention in the infant. *Nature, 253,* 265–266.

Scaramella, L. V., Conger, R. D., Simons, R. L., & Whitbeck, L. B. (1998). Predicting risk for pregnancy by late adolescence: A social contextual perspective. *Developmental Psychology, 34*(6), 1233–1245.

Scarr, S. (1984). *Mother care/other care.* New York: Basic Books.

Scarr, S. (1992). Developmental theories for the 1990s: Development and individual differences. *Child Development, 63*(1), 1–19.

Scarr, S. (1993). Biological and cultural diversity: The legacy of Darwin for development. *Child Development, 64,* 1333–1353.

Scarr, S., & Eisenberg, M. (1993). Child care research: Issues, perspectives, and results. *Annual Review of Psychology, 44,* 613–632.

Scarr, S., & McCartney, K. (1983). How people make their own environments: A theory of genotype-environment effects. *Child Development, 21,* 391–402.

Scarr, S., & McCartney, K. (1988). Far from home: An experimental evaluation of the mother-child home program in Bermuda. *Child Development, 59,* 531–543.

Schachter, F. F. (1979). *Everyday mother talk to toddlers: Early intervention.* New York: Academic Press.

Schachter, F. S., & Stone, R. K. (1985). Difficult sibling, easy sibling: Temperament and the within-family environment. *Child Development, 56,* 1335–1344.

Schafer, G., Plunkett, K., & Harris, P. L. (1999). What's in a name? Lexical knowledge drives infant preferences in the absence of referential input. *Developmental Science, 2*(2), 187–194.

Schaffer, H. R., & Crook, C. K. (1979). Maternal control techniques in a directed play situation. *Child Development, 50,* 989–996.

Schaffer, H. R., & Crook, C. K. (1980). Child compliance and maternal control techniques. *Developmental Psychology, 16,* 54–56.

Schaffer, H. R., & Emerson, P. (1964). Patterns of response to physical contact in early human development. *Journal of Child Psychiatry and Psychology, 5,* 1–13.

Schaller, J., Carlsson, S. G., & Larsson, K. (1979). Effects of extended post-partum mother-child contact on the mother's behavior during nursing. *Infant Behavior and Development, 2,* 319–324.

Schanberg, S., Bartolome, J., & Kuhn, C. (1987, January). *Touching and the brain.* Paper presented at the American College of Neuropsychopharmacology, San Juan, Puerto Rico.

Schiffman, P. C., Westlake, R. E., Santiago, T. V., & Edelman, N. H. (1980). Ventilatory control in parents of victims of sudden-infant-death syndrome. *New England Journal of Medicine, 302,* 486–491.

Schindler, P. J., Moely, B. E., & Frank, A. L. (1987). Time in day care and social participation of young children. *Developmental Psychology, 23,* 255–261.

Schleidt, M., & Genzel, C. (1990). The significance of mother's perfume for infants in the first weeks of their life. *Ethology and Sociobiology, 11,* 145–155.

Schlesinger, M., & Langer, J. (1999). Infants' developing expectations of possible and impossible tool-use events between ages 8 and 12 months. *Developmental Science, 2*(2), 195–205.

Schmitz, S., Fulker, D. W., Plomin, R., Zahn-Waxler, C., Emde, R. N., & DeFries, J. C. (1999). Temperament and problem behavior during early childhood. *International Journal of Behavioral Development, 23*(2), 333–355.

Schmuckler, M. A. (1996). Visual-proprioceptive intermodal perception in infancy. *Infant Behavior and Development, 19,* 221–232.

Schneider, K. J. (1998). Toward a science of the heart: Romanticism and the revival of psychology. *American Psychologist, 53*(3), 277–289.

Schneider, M. L., Roughton, E. C., Koehler, A. J., & Lubach, G. R. (1999). Growth and development following prenatal stress exposure in primates: An examination of ontogenetic vulnerability. *Child Development, 70*(2), 263–274.

Schneider-Rosen, K., & Wenz-Gross, M. (1990). Patterns of compliance from eighteen to thirty months of age. *Child Development, 61,* 104–112.

Schölmerich, A., Fracasso, M. P., Lamb, M. E., & Broberg, A. G. (1995). Interactional harmony at 7 and 10 months of age predicts security of attachment as measured by Q-sort ratings. *Social Development, 4,* 64–68.

Schölmerich, A., Lamb, M. E., Leyendecker, B., & Fracasso, M. P. (1997). Mother-infant teaching interactions and attachment security in Euro-American and Central-American immigrant families. *Infant Behavior and Development, 20,* 165–174.

Scholz, K., & Samuels, C. A. (1992). Neonatal bathing and massage intervention with fathers, behavioral effects 12 weeks after birth of the first baby: The Sunraysia Australia Intervention Project. *International Journal of Behavioral Development, 15,* 67–81.

Schreiber, J. (1977). Birth, the family and the community: A southern Italian example. *Birth and the Family Journal, 4,* 153–157.

Schuetze, P., Lewis, A., & DiMartino, D. (1999). Relation between time spent in daycare and exploratory behaviors in 9-month-old infants. *Infant Behavior and Development, 22*(2), 267–276.

Schuetze, P., & Zeskind, P. S. (1997). Relation between reported maternal caffeine consumption during pregnancy and neonatal state and heart rate. *Infant Behavior and Development, 20*(4), 559–562.

Schulman-Galambos, C., & Galambos, R. (1979). Brain stem evoked response audiometry in newborn hearing screening. *Archives of Otolaryngology, 105,* 86–90.

Schwartz, A., Campos, J., & Baisel, E. (1973). The visual cliff: Cardiac and behavioral correlates on the deep and shallow sides at 5 and 9 months of age. *Journal of Experimental Child Psychology, 15,* 85–99.

Schwartz, P. (1983). Length of daycare attendance and attachment behavior in eighteen-month-old infants. *Child Development, 54,* 1073–1078.

Schweinhart, L. J., & Weikart, D. P. (1979, April). *Perry preschool effects in adolescence.* Paper presented to the biennial meeting of the Society for Research in Child Development, San Francisco, CA.

Seifer, R., Sameroff, A. J., Anagnostopolou, R., & Elias, P. K. (1992). Mother-infant interaction during the first year: Effects of situation, maternal mental illness, and demographic factors. *Infant Behavior and Development, 15,* 405–426.

Seifer, R., Sameroff, A. J., Barrett, L. C., & Krafchuk, E. (1994). Infant temperament measured by multiple observations and mother report. *Child Development, 65,* 1478–1490.

Seifer, R., & Schiller, M., Sameroff, A. J., Resnick, S., & Riordan, K. (1996). Attachment, maternal sensitivity, and infant temperament during the first year of life. *Developmental Psychology, 32*(1), 12–25.

Seitz, V., Rosenbaum, L. K., & Apfel, N. H. (1985). Effects of family support intervention: A ten-year follow-up. *Child Development, 56,* 376–391.

Self, P., & Horowitz, F. D. (1979). The assessment of the newborn infant. In J. Osofsky (Ed.), *Handbook of infant development* (pp. 240–268). New York: Wiley.

Seligman, M. E. P., & Maier, S. (1967). Failure to escape traumatic shock. *Journal of Experimental Psychology, 74,* 1–9.

Sell, E. J., Hill-Mangan, S., & Holberg, C. J. (1992). Natural course of behavioral organization in premature infants. *Infant Behavior and Development, 15*(4), 461–478.

Selman, R. L. (1980). *The growth of interpersonal understanding: Developmental and clinical analyses.* New York: Academic Press.

Serifica, F. C. (1978). The development of attachment behaviors: An organismic-developmental perspective. *Human Development, 21,* 119–140.

Service, R. F. (1994). Barriers hold back new contraception strategies. *Science, 266,* 1489.

Service V., Lock, A., & Chandler, P. (1989). Individual differences in early communicative development: A social constructivist perspective. In S. Tetzchner, L. Siegel & L. Smith (Eds.), *The social cognitive aspects of normal atypical language development* (pp. 23–49). New York: Springer-Verlag.

Seto, A., Einarson, T., & Koren, G. (1997). Pregnancy outcome following first trimester exposure to antihistamines: Meta-analysis. *American Journal of Perinatology, 14*(3), 199–124.

Sewall, M. (1930). Some causes of jealousy in young children. *Smith College Studies in Social Work, 1,* 6–22.

Shahmoon-Shanok, R. (1999). Adopting parenthood: An enduring transformation marking identity and intimacy capacities. *Zero to Three, 19*(4), 32–36.

Shand, N., & Kosawa, Y. (1985). Japanese and American behavior types at three months: Infants and infant-mother dyads. *Infant Behavior and Development, 8,* 225–240.

Shapira, A., & Madsen, M. C. (1969). Cooperative and competitive behavior of kibbutz and urban children in Israel. *Child Development, 40,* 609–617.

Sharan, P. (1988). One view of the cultural context for the study of child-rearing in India. *Newsletter of the International Society for the Study of Behavioral Development, 13,* 1–3.

Shatz, M. (1978). The relationship between cognitive processes and the development of communication skills. In C. B. Keasey (Ed.), *Nebraska symposium on motivation.* Lincoln: University of Nebraska Press.

Shatz, M., & Gelman, R. (1973). The development of communication skills: Modifications in the speech of young children as a function of listener. *Monographs of the Society for Research in Child Development, 38* (Serial No. 152), 1–37.

Sheppard, J. J., & Mysak, E. D. (1984). Ontogeny of infantile oral reflexes and emerging chewing. *Child Development, 55,* 831–843.

Sherrod, K. B., Crawley, S., Petersen, G., & Bennett, P. (1978). Maternal language to prelinguistic infants: Semantic aspects. *Infant Behavior and Development, 1,* 335–346.

Sherrod, K. B., Friedman, S., Crawley, S., Drake, D., & Devrieux, J. (1977). Maternal language to prelinguistic infants: Syntactic aspects. *Child Development, 48,* 1662–1665.

Sherrod, K. B., O'Conner, S., Vietze, P. M., & Altemeier, W. A. (1984). Child health and maltreatment. *Child Development, 55,* 1174–1183.

Shirley, M. M. (1931). *The first two years: A study of twenty-five babies: Vol. 1. Postural and locomotor development.* Minneapolis: University of Minnesota Press.

Shirley, M. M. (1933). *The first two years: A study of twenty-five babies (Vol. 3)*. Minneapolis: University of Minnesota Press.

Shnider, S. (1981). Choice of anesthesia for labor and delivery. *Journal of Obstetrics and Gynecology, 58* (5 Suppl.), 24S-34S.

Shonkoff, J. P., Hauser-Cram, P., Krauss, M. W., & Upshur, C. C. (1992). Development of infants with disabilities and their families. *Monographs of the Society for Research in Child Development, 57,* 1–163.

Shore, C. (1986). Combinatorial play: Conceptual development, and early multiword speech. *Developmental Psychology, 22*(2), 184–190.

Shulman, S., Becker, A., & Sroufe, L. A. (1999). Adult-child interactions as related to adult's family history and child's attachment. *International Journal of Behavioral Development, 23*(4), 959–976.

Shwalb, B. J., Shwalb, D., & Shoji, J. (1994). Structure and dimensions of maternal perceptions of Japanese infant temperament. *Developmental Psychology, 30,* 131–141.

Shy, K. K., Luthy, D. A., Bennett, F. C., Whitfield, M., Larson, E. B., Belle, G. van, Hughes, J. P., Wilson, J. A., & Stenchever, M. A. (1990). Effects of electronic fetal-heart-rate monitoring, as compared with periodic ausculation, on the neurological development of premature infants. *New England Journal of Medicine, 322*(9), 588–593.

Siegal, L. S. (1981). Infant tests as predictors of cognitive and language development at two years. *Child Development, 52,* 545–557.

Siegal, M., & Storey, R. M. (1985). Day care and children's conceptions of moral and social rules. *Child Development, 56,* 1001–1008.

Sigman, M., Cohen, S. E., Beckwith, L., & Parmelee, A. H. (1981). Social and familial influences on the development of preterm infants. *Journal of Pediatric Psychology, 6,* 1–13.

Sigman, M., Cohen, S. E., Beckwith, L., & Parmelee, A. H. (1986). Infant attention in relation to intellectual abilities in childhood. *Developmental Psychology, 22,* 788–792.

Sigman, M., & Kasari, C. (1995). Joint attention across contexts in normal and autistic children. In C. Moore & P. J. Dunham (Eds.), *Joint attention: Its origins and role in development* (pp. 189–203). Hillsdale, NJ: Erlbaum.

Sigman, M., Neumann, C., Carter, E., Cattle, D. J., D'Souza, S., & Bwibo, N. (1988). Home interactions and the development of Embu toddlers in Kenya. *Child Development, 59,* 1251–1261.

Sigman, M., & Ruskin, E. (1999). Continuity and change in the social competence of children with autism, Down syndrome, and developmental delays. *Monographs of the Society for Research in Child Development, 64*(1), 1–139.

Silberner, J. (1986). Survival of the fetus. *Science News, 130,* 234–235.

Silver, M. (1985). Life after Tay-Sachs. *Jewish Monthly, 99,* 14–23.

Silverman, I., Dickens, S. E., Eals, M., & Fine, J. (1993). Perceptions of maternal and paternal solicitude by birth children and adoptees: Relevance for maternal bonding theory. *Early Development and Parenting, 2,* 135–144.

Simons, R. L., Lorenz, F. O., Wu, C. I., & Conger, R. D. (1993). Social network and marital support as mediators and moderators of the impact of stress and depression on parental behavior. *Developmental Psychology, 29,* 368–381.

Singer, L. M., Brodzinsky, D. M., Ramsay, D., Steir, M., & Waters, E. (1985). Mother-infant attachment in adoptive families. *Child Development, 56,* 1543–1551.

Singer, L. M., Salvator, A., Guo, S., Collin, M., Lilien, L., & Baley, J. (1999). Maternal psychological distress and parenting stress after the birth of a very low-birth-weight infant. *Journal of the American Medical Association, 281*(9), 799–805.

Singh, V. K., Warren, R. P., Odell, J. D., Warren, W. L., & Cole, P. (1993). Antibodies to myelin basic protein in children with autistic behavior. *Brain Behavior and Immunization, 7,* 97–103.

Siskind, V., Schofield, F., Rice, D., & Bain, C. (1989). Breast cancer and breastfeeding: Results from an Australian case-control study. *American Journal of Epidemiology, 130,* 229–236.

Sitskoorn, M. M., & Smitsman, A. W. (1995). Infants' perception of dynamic relations between objects: Passing through or support? *Developmental Psychology, 31,* 437–447.

Sitskoorn, M. M., & Smitsman, A. W. (1997). Perception of dynamic object relations in infancy. *Infant Behavior and Development, 20,* 141–150.

Skarin, K. (1977). Cognitive and contextual determinants of stranger fear in six- and eleven-month-old infants. *Child Development, 48,* 537–544.

Skeoch, C., Rosenberg, K., Turner, T., Skeoch, H., & McIlwaine, G. (1987). Very low birthweight survivors: Illness and readmission to hospital in the first 15 months of life. *British Medical Journal, 295,* 579–580.

Skinner, B. F. (1938). *The behavior of organisms.* Englewood Cliffs, NJ: Prentice-Hall.

Slaby, R. G., & Frey, K. S. (1975). Development of gender constancy and selective attention to same-sex models. *Child Development, 46,* 849–856.

Slade, A. (1986). Symbolic play and separation-individuation: A naturalistic study. *Bulletin of the Menninger Clinic, 50,* 541–563.

Slade, A. (1987a). A longitudinal study of maternal involvement and symbolic play during the toddler period. *Child Development, 58,* 367–375.

Slade, A. (1987b). Quality of attachment and early symbolic play. *Developmental Psychology, 23,* 78–85.

Slater, A., Morison, V., & Rose, D. (1984). Habituation in the newborn. *Infant Behavior and Development, 7,* 183–200.

Slater, A., von der Schulenbur, C., Brown, E., Badenoch, M., Butterworth, G., Parsons, S., & Samuels, C. (1998). Newborn infants prefer attractive faces. *Infant Behavior and Development, 21*(2), 345–354.

Slaughter, D. T. (1980). Social policy issues affecting infants. In B. Weissbourd & J. Musick (Eds.), *Infants: Their social environments* (pp. 150–178). Chicago: National Association for the Education of Young Children.

Slobin, D. (1970). Universals of grammatical development in children. In G. B. Flores d'Arcais & W. J. M. Levelt (Eds.), *Advances in psycholinguistics* (pp. 12–38). Amsterdam: North-Holland.

Smeeding, T. M., & Torrey, B. B. (1988). Poor children in rich countries. *Science, 242,* 873–877.

Smialek, A. (1978). Observations on immediate reactions of families to sudden infant death. *Pediatrics, 62,* 160–165.

Smidt-Jensen, S., & Hahnemann, N. (1988). Transabdominal chorionic villus sampling for fetal diagnosis: Technical and obstetrical evaluation of 100 cases. *Prenatal Diagnosis, 8,* 7–17.

Smigel, K. L. (1988). Breast-feeding linked to decreased cancer risk for mother, child. *Journal of the National Cancer Institute, 80,* 1362–1363.

Smith, P. B., & Pederson, D. R. (1988). Maternal sensitivity and patterns of infant-mother attachment. *Child Development, 59,* 1097–1101.

Smith, R. (1999, March). The timing of birth. *Scientific American, 280*(3), 68–75.

Smotherman, W. P., & Robinson, S. R. (1987). Prenatal expression of species-typical action patterns in the rat fetus. *Journal of Comparative Psychology, 101*(2), 190–196.

Smyth, J. M., & Pennebaker, J. W. (1999). Sharing one's story. In C. R. Snyder (Ed.), *Coping: The psychology of what works* (pp. 70–89). Oxford, England: Oxford University Press.

Snow, C. E. (1977). The development of conversation between mothers and babies. *Journal of Child Language, 4,* 1–22.

Snow, C. E. (1984). Parent-child interaction and the development of communicative ability. In R. Schiefelbusch & J. Pickar (Eds.), *The acquisition of communicative competence* (pp. 377–403). Baltimore: University Park Press.

Snow, M. E., Jacklin, C. N., & Maccoby, E. E. (1981). Birth-order differences in peer sociability at thirty-three months. *Child Development, 52,* 589–595.

Sogaard, A. J., Kritz-Silverstein, D., & Wingard, D. L. (1994). Finnmark heart study: Employment status and parenthood as predictors of psychological health in women, 20–49 years. *International Journal of Epidemiology, 23*, 82–90.

Soken, N. H., & Pick, A. D. (1992). Intermodal perception of happy and angry expressive behaviors by seven-month-old infants. *Child Development, 63*, 787–795.

Soken, N. H., & Pick, A. D. (1999). Infants' perception of dynamic affective expressions: Do infants distinguish specific expressions? *Child Development, 70*(6), 1275–1282.

Sokolov, J. L. (1993). A local contingency analysis of the fine-tuning hypothesis. *Developmental Psychology, 29*, 1008–1023.

Sollie, D., & Miller, B. (1980). The transition to parenthood as a critical time for building family strengths. In N. Stinnet & P. Knaub (Eds.), *Family strengths: Positive models of family life* (pp. 19–36). Lincoln: University of Nebraska Press.

Sorce, J., Emde, R., Campos, J., & Klinnert, M. (1985). Maternal emotional signaling: Its effect on the visual cliff behavior of 1-year-olds. *Developmental Psychology, 21*, 195–200.

Sorenson, E. R. (1979). Early tactile communication and the patterning of human organization: A New Guinea case study. In M. Bullowa (Ed.), *Before speech* (pp. 217–229). New York: Cambridge University Press.

Sostek, A. M., & Anders, T. F. (1977). Relationships among the Brazelton neonatal scale, Bayley infant scales and early temperament. *Child Development, 48*, 320–323.

Sostek, A. M., Smith, Y. F., Katz, K. S., & Grant, E. G. (1987). Developmental outcome of preterm infants with intraventricular hemorrhage at one and two years of age. *Child Development, 58*, 779–786.

Spangler, G., & Grossmann, K. E. (1993). Biobehavioral organization in securely and insecurely attached infants. *Child Development, 64*, 1439–1450.

Speltz, M. L., Endriga, M. C., Fisher, P. A., & Mason, C. A. (1997). Early predictors of attachment in infants with cleft lip and/or palate. *Child Development, 68*(1), 12–25.

Spemann, H. (1938). *Embryonic development and induction.* New Haven, CT: Yale University Press.

Spence, M. J., & Freeman, M. S. (1996). Newborn infants prefer the maternal low-pass filtered voice, but not the maternal whispered voice. *Infant Behavior and Development, 19*, 199–212.

Speraw, S. R. (1994). The experience of miscarriage: How couples define quality in health care delivery. *Journal of Perinatology, 14*, 208–215.

Spieker, S. J., & Bensley L. (1994). Roles of living arrangements and grandmother social support in adolescent mothering and infant attachment. *Developmental Psychology, 30*, 102–111.

Spiker, D., Ferguson, J., & Brooks-Gunn, J. (1993). Enhancing maternal interactive behavior and child social competence in low birth weight, premature infants. *Child Development, 64*, 754–768.

Spinillo, A., Iasci, A., Dal-Maso, J., Di-Lenardo, L., Grella, P., & Guaschino, S. (1994). The effect of fetal infection with human immunodeficiency virus type 1 on birthweight and length of gestation. *European Journal of Obstetrics and Gynecology, 57*, 13–17.

Spitz, H. H. (1992). Does the Carolina Abecedarian early intervention project prevent sociocultural mental retardation? *Intelligence, 16*, 225.

Spitz, R. (1965). *The first year of life.* New York: International Universities Press.

Spock, B. (1957). *Baby and child care.* New York: Pocket Books.

Sprafkin, J., & Silverman, T. (1982). Sex on prime time. In M. Schwarz (Ed.), *TV and teens* (pp. 130–135). Reading, MA: Addison-Wesley.

Sroufe, L. A. (1979). Socioemotional development. In J. Osofsky (Ed.), *Handbook of infant development* (pp. 462–516). New York: Wiley.

Sroufe, L. A. (1983). Individual patterns of adaptation from infancy to preschool. In M. Perlmutter (Ed.), *Minnesota symposia on child psychology* (Vol. 16, pp. 165–182). Hillsdale, NJ: Lawrence Erlbaum.

Sroufe, L. A. (1989). Relationships, self, and individual adaptation. In A. J. Sameroff and R. N. Emde (Eds.), *Relationships disturbances in early childhood: A developmental approach* (pp. 70–94). New York: Basic Books.

Sroufe, L. A. (1995). *Emotional development: The organization of emotional life in the early years.* Cambridge, England: Cambridge University Press.

Sroufe, L. A., & Waters, E. (1976). The ontogenesis of smiling and laughter: A perspective on the organization of development in infancy. *Psychological Review, 83*, 173–186.

Sroufe, L. A., & Wunsch, J. P. (1977). The development of laughter in the first year of life. *Child Development, 43*, 1326–1344.

Stack, D. M. (2000). The salience of touch and physical contact during infancy: Unravelling some of the mysteries of the somaesthetic sense. In J. G. Bremner & A. Fogel (Eds.), *Handbook of infancy research* (pp. 268–292). Oxford, England: Blackwell.

Stack, D. M., & Arnold, S. L. (1998). Changes in mothers' touch and hand gestures influence infant behavior during face-to-face interchanges. *Infant Behavior and Development, 21*(3), 451–468.

Stack, D. M., & LePage, D. E. (1996). Infants' sensitivity to manipulations of maternal touch during face-to-face interactions. *Social Development, 5*(1), 41–55.

Stack, D. M., & Muir, D. W. (1992). Adult tactile stimulation during face-to-face interactions modulates five-month-olds' affect and attention. *Child Development, 63*, 1509–1525.

Stanton, A. N., Scott, D. J., & Downhan, M. A. (1980). Is overheating a factor in some unexpected infant deaths? *Lancet, 78*(5), 1054–1057.

Stark, R. E. (1978). Features of infant sounds: The emergence of cooing. *Journal of Child Language, 3*, 379–390.

Stark, R. E., Rose, S. N., & McLagen, M. (1975). Features of infant sounds: The first eight weeks of life. *Journal of Child Language, 2*, 205–222.

Starkey, D. (1981). The origins of concept formation: Object sorting and object preference in early infancy. *Child Development, 52*, 489–497.

Stattin, H., & Klackenberg-Larsson, I. (1991). The short- and long-term implications for parent-child relations of parents' prenatal preferences for their child's gender. *Developmental Psychology, 27*(1), 141–147.

Stayton, D. J., Ainsworth, M. D. S., & Main, M. B. (1973). The development of separation behavior in the first year of life: Protest, following, greeting. *Developmental Psychology, 9*, 213–225.

Steele, H., Steele, M., Croft, C., & Fonagy, P. (1999). Infant-mother attachment at one year predicts children's understanding of mixed emotions at six years. *Social Development, 8*(2), 161–178.

Steele, H., Steele, M., & Fonagy, P. (1996). Associations among attachment classifications of mothers, fathers, and their infants. *Child Development, 67*, 523–540.

Stein, A., Cambell, E. A., Day, A., McPherson, K., & Cooper, P. J. (1987). Social adversity, low birth weight, and preterm delivery. *British Medical Journal, 295*, 291–293.

Stein, Z., & Susser, M. (1985). Effects of early nutrition on neurological and mental competence in human beings. *Psychological Medicine, 15*, 717–726.

Steiner, J. E. (1973). The gustofacial response: Observation on normal and anencephalic newborn infants. In J. F. Bosma (Ed.), *Fourth symposium on oral sensation and perception.* (DHEW Publication No. NIH 73–546) (pp. 15–28). Bethesda, MD: Department of Health, Education, and Welfare.

Steiner, J. E. (1977). Facial expressions of the neonate infant indicating the hedonics of food-related chemical stimuli. In J. M. Weiffenbach (Ed.), *Taste and development* (pp. 204–219). Bethesda, MD: Department of Health, Education, and Welfare.

Stella-Prorok, E. M. (1983). Mother-child language in the natural environment. In K. E. Nelson (Ed.), *Children's language* (pp. 389–407). Hillsdale, NJ: Erlbaum.

Stenberg, C., Campos, J. J., & Emde, R. N. (1983). The facial expression of anger in seven-month-old infants. *Child Development, 54,* 178–184.

Stenberg, G., & Hagekull, B. (1997). Social referencing and mood modification in 1-year-olds. *Infant Behavior and Development, 20,* 209–217.

Sterman, M. B., & Hoppenbrouwers, T. (1971). The development of sleep-waking and rest-activity patterns from fetus to adult in man. In M. B. Sterman, D. J. McGinty, & A. M. Adinolfi (Eds.), *Brain development and behavior* (pp. 203–228). New York: Academic Press.

Stern, D. N. (1977). *The first relationship.* Cambridge, MA: Harvard University Press.

Stern, D. N. (1985). *The interpersonal world of the infant: A view from psychoanalysis and developmental psychology.* New York: Basic Books.

Stern, D. N. (1995). *The motherhood constellation.* New York: Basic Books.

Stern, D. N., Jaffe, J., Beebe, B., & Bennett, S. J. (1975). Vocalizing in unison and in alternation: Two modes of communication within the mother-infant dyad. *Annals of the New York Academy of Science, 263,* 89–100.

Stern, D. N., Spieker, S., Barnett, R. K., & MacKain, K. (1983). The prosody of maternal speech: Infant age and context related changes. *Journal of Child Language, 10,* 1–15.

Sternberg, R. J., & Davidson, J. E. (1985). Cognitive development in the gifted and talented. In F. D. Horowitz & M. O'Brien (Eds.), *The gifted and talented: Developmental perspectives* (pp. 37–74). Washington, DC: American Psychological Association.

Stevens, B., Johnston, C., Franck, L., Petryshen, P., Jack, A., & Foster, G. (1999). The efficacy of developmentally sensitive interventions and sucrose for relieving procedural pain in very low birth weight neonates. *Nursing Research, 48,* 35–43.

Stevens, J. H. (1984). Black grandmothers' & black adolescent mothers' knowledge about parenting. *Developmental Psychology, 20,* 1017–1025.

Stevens, J. H. (1988). Social support, locus of control, and parenting in three low-income groups of mothers: Black teenagers, black adults, and white adults. *Child Development, 59,* 635–642.

Stevenson, M. R., & Black, K. N. (1988). Paternal absence and sex-role development: A meta-analysis. *Child Development, 59,* 793–814.

Stewart, A. (1983). Severe perinatal hazards. In M. Rutter (Ed.), *Developmental neuropsychiatry* (pp. 117–132). New York: Churchill Livingstone.

Stewart, D. E. (1994). Incidence of postpartum abuse in women with a history of abuse during pregnancy. *Canadian Medical Association Journal, 151,* 1601–1604.

Stewart, D. E., & Cecutti, A. (1993). Physical abuse in pregnancy. *Canadian Medical Association Journal, 149,* 1257–1263.

Stewart, R. A. (1981). Supplementary foods: Their nutritional role in infant feedings. In J. Bond, L. Filer, G. LeVeille, A. Thomson, & W. Weil (Eds.), *Infant and child feeding* (pp. 101–128). New York: Academic Press.

Stewart, R. A. (1983). Sibling interaction: The role of the older child as teacher for the younger. *Merrill-Palmer Quarterly, 29,* 47–68.

Stewart, R. A., Mobley, L. A., Van Tuyl, S. S., & Salvador, M. A. (1987). The firstborn's adjustment to the birth of a sibling: A longitudinal assessment. *Child Development, 58,* 341–355.

Stiefel, G. S., Plunkett, J. W., & Meisels, S. J. (1987). Affective expression among preterm infants of varying levels of biological risk. *Infant Behavior and Development, 10,* 151–164.

Stifter, C. A., Coulehan, C. M., & Fish, M. (1993). Linking employment to attachment: The mediating effects of maternal separation anxiety and interactive behavior. *Child Development, 64,* 1451–1460.

Stifter, C. A., Fox, N. A., & Porges, S. W. (1989). Facial expressivity and vagal tone in 5- and 10-month-old infants. *Infant Behavior and Development, 12,* 127–137.

Stifter, C. A., & Moyer, D. (1991). The regulation of positive affect: Gaze aversion activity during mother-infant interaction. *Infant Behavior and Development, 14,* 111–123.

Stiles, J. (1995). The early use and development of graphic formulas: Two case study reports of graphic formula production by 2-to-3-year-old children. *International Journal of Behavioral Development, 18*(1), 127–149.

Stipek, D. (1995). The development of pride and shame in toddlers. In J. P. Tangney & K. W. Fischer (Eds.), *Self-conscious emotions: The psychology of shame, guilt, embarrassment, and pride* (pp. 237–252). New York: Guilford Press.

St. James-Roberts, I., Conroy, S., & Wilsher, K. (1998). Links between maternal care and persistent infant crying in the early months. *Child Care, Health, and Development, 24*(5), 353–376.

St. James-Roberts, I., & Plewis, I. (1996). Individual differences, daily fluctuations, and developmental changes in amounts of infant waking, fussing, crying, feeding, and sleeping. Child Development, 67(5), 2527–2540.

Stockman, I. J., & Vaughn-Cooke, F. (1992). Lexical elaboration in children's locative action expressions. *Child Development, 63,* 1104–1125.

Stone, L. J., Smith, H., & Murphy, L. (1973). *The competent infant.* New York: Basic Books.

Stone, W. L., Lemanek, K. L., Fishel, P. T., Fernandez, M. C., & Altemeier, W. A. (1990). Play and imitation skills in the diagnosis of autism in young children. *Pediatrics, 86,* 267–272.

Stoneman, Z., Brody, G. H., & MacKinnon, C. (1984). Naturalistic observations of children's activities and roles while playing with their siblings and friends. *Child Development, 55,* 617–627.

Strassberg, Z., & Treboux, D. (2000). Interpretations of child emotion expressions and coercive parenting practices among adolescent mothers. *Social Development, 9*(1), 80–95.

Straus, M. A. (1995). *Beating the devil out of them: Corporal punishment in American families.* New York: Lexington Books.

Straus, M. A., & Stewart, J. H. (1999). Corporal punishment by American parents: National data on prevalence, chronicity, severity, and duration, in relation to child and family characteristics. *Clinical Child and Family Psychology Review, 2*(2), 55–70.

Strauss, A., & Corbin, J. (1990). *Basics of qualitative research: Grounded theory procedures and techniques.* Newbury Park, CA: Sage.

Strauss, M. S., & Curtis, L. E. (1981). Infant's perception of numerosity. *Child Development, 52,* 1146–1152.

Streissguth, A. P., Barr, H. M., Sampson, P. D., & Bookstein, F. L. (1994). Prenatal alcohol and offspring development: The first fourteen years. *Drug and Alcohol Dependency, 36,* 89–99.

Streissguth, A. P., Martin, D. C., Barr, H. M., Sandman, B. M., Kirchner, G. L., & Darby, B. L. (1984). Intrauterine alcohol and nicotine exposure: Attention and reaction time in 4-year-old children. *Developmental Psychology, 20,* 533–541.

Streri, A., & Spelke, E. S. (1989). Effects of motion and figural goodness on haptic object perception in infancy. *Child Development, 60,* 1111–1125.

Striano, T., & Rochat, P. (1999). Developmental link between dyadic and triadic social competence in infancy. *British Journal of Developmental Psychology, 17,* 1–12.

Striano, T., & Rochat, P. (in press). Emergence of selective social referencing in infancy. *Infancy.*

Strobino, B. A., & Pantel-Silverman, J. (1987). First-trimester vaginal bleeding and the loss of chromosomally normal and abnormal conceptions. *American Journal of Obstetrics and Gynecology, 157,* 1150–1154.

Stuchbery, M., Matthey, S., & Barnett, B. (1998). Postnatal depression and social supports in Vietnamese, Arabic, and Anglo-Celtic mothers. *Social Psychiatry and Psychiatric Epidemiology, 33*(10), 483–490.

Sugarman, S. (1982). The development of preverbal communication: Its contribution and limits in promoting the development of language. In R. Schiefelbusch & L. Pickar (Eds.), *Communicative competence: Acquisition and intervention* (pp. 410–449). Baltimore: University Park Press.

Sullivan, M. W., Rovee-Collier, C. K., & Tynes, D. M. (1979). A conditioning analysis of infant longterm memory. *Child Development, 50,* 152–162.

Sun, L. C., & Roopnarine, J. L. (1996). Mother-infant, father-infant and involvement in childcare and household labor among Taiwanese families. *Infant Behavior and Development, 19,* 121–129.

Suomi, S. J. (1987). Genetic and maternal contributions to individual differences in rhesus monkey biobehavioral development. In N. A. Krasnegor, E. M. Blass, M. A. Hofer, & W. P. Smotherman (Eds.), *Perinatal development: A psychobiological perspective* (pp. 397–420). New York: Academic Press.

Suomi, S. J., & Harlow, H. F. (1972). Social rehabilitation of isolate reared monkeys. *Developmental Psychology, 6,* 487–496.

Super, C. (1976). Environmental effects on motor development: The case of "African infant precocity." *Developmental Medicine and Child Neurology, 18,* 561–567.

Super, C. (1981). Behavioral development in infancy. In R. Munroe & B. Whiting (Eds.), *Handbook of cross-cultural human development* (pp. 95–128). New York: Garland.

Super, C., Herrera, M. G., & Mora, J. O. (1990). Long-term effects of food supplementation and psychosocial intervention on the physical growth of Colombian infants at risk of malnutrition. *Child Development, 61,* 29–49.

Susman-Stillman, A., Kalkoske, M., Egeland, B., & Waldman, I. (1996). Infant temperament and maternal sensitivity as predictors of attachment security. *Infant Behavior and Development, 19,* 33–47.

Suwalsky, J. T., & Klein, R. P. (1980). Effects of naturally occurring nontraumatic separations from mother. *Infant Mental Health Journal, 1,* 196–201.

Swain, I. U., Zelazo, P. R., & Clifton, R. K. (1993). Newborn infants' memory for speech sounds retained over 24 hours. *Developmental Psychology, 29,* 312–323.

Swan, A. M. (1993). Helping children who stutter: What teachers need to know. *Childhood Education, 69,* 138–141.

Swets-Gronert, F. (1984, August). *Temperament in young children.* Paper presented at the European Conference on Development Psychology, Groningen, the Netherlands.

Swoboda, P. J., Kass, J., Morse, P. A., & Leavitt, L. A. (1978). Memory factors in vowel discrimination of normal and at-risk infants. *Child Development, 49,* 332–339.

Symons, D. K., & McLeod, P. J. (1994). Maternal, infant, and occupational characteristics that predict postpartum employment patterns. *Infant Behavior and Development, 17,* 71–82.

Symons, D. K., & Moran, G. (1987). The behavioral dynamics of mutual responsiveness in early face-to-face mother-infant interaction. *Child Development, 58,* 1488–1495.

Takahashi, K. (1986). Examining the strange-situation procedure with Japanese mothers and 12-month-old infants. *Developmental Psychology, 22,* 265–270.

Tamis-LeMonda, C. S., & Bornstein, M. H. (1989). Habituation and maternal encouragement of attention in infancy as predictors of toddler language, play, and representational competence. *Child Development, 60,* 738–751.

Tamis-LeMonda, C. S., & Bornstein, M. H. (1990). Language, play, and attention at one year. *Infant Behavior and Development, 13,* 85–98.

Tamis-LeMonda, C. S., Bornstein, M. H., Baumwell, L., & Damast, A. M. (1996). Responsive parenting in the second year: Specific influences on children's language and play. *Early Development and Parenting, 5*(4), 173–183.

Tamis-LeMonda, C. S., Bornstein, M. H., Cyphers, L., Toda, S., & Ogino, M. (1992). Language and play at one year: A comparison of toddlers and mothers in the United States and Japan. *International Journal of Behavioral Development, 15,* 19–42.

Tan, L. E. (1985). Laterality and motor-skills in four-year-olds. *Child Development, 56,* 119–124.

Tanner, J. M. (1970). Physical growth. In P. H. Mussen (Ed.), *Manual of child psychology* (3rd ed., pp. 77–156). New York: Wiley.

Tanguay, P. E. (1990). Early infantile autism: What have we learned in the past 50 years? *Brain Dysfunction, 3,* 197–207.

Tardif, T. (1996). Nouns are not always learned before verbs: Evidence from Mandarin speakers' early vocabularies. *Developmental Psychology, 32*(3), 492–504.

Tardif, T., Gelman, S. A., & Xu, F. (1999). Putting the "noun bias" in context: A comparison of English and Mandarin. *Child Development, 70*(3), 620–635.

Tardif, T., & Wellman, H. M. (2000). Acquisition of mental state language in Mandarin- and Cantonese-speaking children. *Developmental Psychology, 36*(1), 25–43.

Taub, H. B., Goldstein, K. M., & Caputo, D. V. (1977). Indices of neonatal prematurity as discriminators of development in middle childhood. *Child Development, 48,* 797–805.

Taylor, H., Baker, D., ALSPAC and the Study Team. (1997). Employment, parity, and single parenthood: Their impact on health in pregnancy. *Journal of Reproductive and Infant Psychology, 15,* 221–237.

Taylor, R. (1989). Cracking cocaine's legacy in babies of drug abusers. *Journal of NIH Research, 1,* 29–32.

Taylor, S. D. (1994). Demand for predictive genetic testing for Huntington's disease in Australia, 1987 to 1993. *Medical Journal of Australia, 161,* 351–355.

Technical Bulletin Number 189 (1994). Exercise during pregnancy and the postpartum period. *International Journal Gynecology and Obstetrics, 45,* 65–70.

Teitelbaum, P., Teitelbaum, O., Nye, J., Fryman, J., & Maurer, R. G. (1998). Movement analysis in infancy may be useful for early diagnosis of autism. *Proceedings of the National Academy of Sciences of the United States of America, 95,* 13982–13987.

Templeton, A., & Morris, J. K. (1998). Reducing the risk of multiple births by transfer of two embryos after in vitro fertilization. *New England Journal of Medicine, 339*(9), 573–577.

Terjesen, N. C., & Wilkins, L. P. (1979). A proposal for a model of a sudden infant death syndrome act: Help for the "other" victims of SIDS. *Family Law Quarterly, 12,* 285–308.

Termine, N. T., & Izard, C. E. (1988). Infants' responses to their mothers' expressions of joy and sadness. *Developmental Psychology, 24,* 223–229.

Terr, L. (1994). *Unchained memories.* New York: Basic Books.

Tessier, R., Nadeau, L., Boivin, M., & Tremblay, R. E. (1997). The social behavior of 11- to 12-year-old children born as low birthweight and/or premature infants. *International Journal of Behavioral Development, 21*(4), 795–811.

Teti, D. M., & Ablard, K. E. (1989). Security of attachment and infant-sibling relationships: A laboratory study. *Child Development, 60,* 1519–1528.

Teti, D. M., Bond, L. A., & Gibbs, E. D. (1988). Mothers, fathers, and siblings: A comparison of play styles and influence upon infant cognitive level. *International Journal of Behavioral Development, 11,* 415–432.

Teti, D. M., & Gelfand, D. M. (1991). Behavioral competence among mothers of infants in the first year: The mediational role of maternal self-efficacy. *Child Development, 62,* 918–929.

Teti, D. M., Gelfand, D. M., Messinger, D. S., & Isabella, R. (1995). Maternal depression and the quality of early attachment: An examination of infants, preschoolers, and their mothers. *Developmental Psychology, 31,* 364–376.

Teti, D. M., & Lamb, M. E. (1989). Socioeconomic and marital outcomes of adolescent marriage, adolescent childbirth, and their co-occurrence. *Journal of Marriage and the Family, 51*, 203–212.

Teti, D. M., Lamb, M. E., & Elster, A. B. (1987). Long-range socioeconomic and marital consequences of adolescent marriage in three cohorts of adult males. *Journal of Marriage and the Family, 49*, 499–506.

Teti, D. M., Nakagawa, R. D., & Wirth, O. (1991). Security of attachment between preschoolers and their mothers: Relations among social interaction, parenting stress, and mothers' sorts of the attachment Q-set. *Developmental Psychology, 27*, 440–447.

Teti, D. M., O'Connell, M. A., & Reiner, C. D. (1996). Parenting sensitivity, parental depression and child health: The mediational role of parental self-efficacy. *Early Development and Parenting, 5*(4), 237–250.

Tharapel, A. T., Tharapel, S. A., & Bannerman, R. M. (1985). Recurrent pregnancy losses and parental chromosome abnormalities: A review. *British Journal of Obstetrics and Gynecology, 92*, 899–914.

Thelen, E. (1989). The (re)discovery of motor development: Learning new things from an old field. *Developmental Psychology, 25*, 946–949.

Thelen, E. (1990). Dynamical systems and the generation of individual differences. In J. Colombo & J. Fagen (Eds.), *Individual differences in infancy: Reliability, stability, prediction* (pp. 19–43). Hillsdale, NJ: Erlbaum.

Thelen, E., Bradshaw, G., & Ward, J. A. (1981). Spontaneous kicking in month-old infants: Manifestation of a human central locomotor program. *Behavioral and Neural Biology, 32*, 45–53.

Thelen, E., & Fogel, A. (1989). Toward an action-based theory of infant development. In J. Lockman & N. Hazen (Eds.), *Action in social context: Perspectives on early development* (pp. 23–64). New York: Plenum Press.

Thelen, E., Skala, K. D., & Kelso, J. A. (1987). The dynamic nature of early coordination: Evidence from bilateral leg movements in young infants. *Developmental Psychology, 23*, 179–186.

Thelen, E., & Smith, L. B. (Eds.) (1994). *A dynamic systems approach to the development of cognition and action.* Cambridge, MA: MIT Press.

Thelen, E., & Ulrich, B. D. (1991). Hidden skills. *Monographs of the Society for Research in Child Development, 56*, 1–106.

Thike, K. B., Wai, K. T., Oo, N., & Yi, K. H. (1993). Contraceptive practice before female sterilization. *Asia Oceania Journal of Obstetrics and Gynecology, 19*, 241–248.

Thoman, E. B. (1993). Obligation and option in the premature nursery. *Developmental Review, 13*, 1–30.

Thoman, E. B., Acebo, C., Dreyer, C. A., Becker, P. T., & Freese, M. P. (1979). Individuality in the interactive process. In E. B. Thomas (Ed.), *Origins of the infant's social responsiveness* (pp. 305–338). Hillsdale, NJ: Erlbaum.

Thoman, E. B., Barnett, C., & Leiderman, P. H. (1971). Feeding behaviors of newborn infants as a function of parity of the mother. *Child Development, 42*, 1471–1483.

Thoman, E. B., Leiderman, P. H., & Olson, J. P. (1972). Neonate-mother interactions during breast feeding. *Developmental Psychology, 6*, 110–118.

Thomas, A., & Chess, S. (1977). *Temperament and development.* New York: Brunner/Mazel.

Thompson, C. (1995). Umbilical cords: Turning garbage into clinical gold. *Science, 268*, 805–806.

Thompson, L. A., Fagan, J. F., & Fulker, D. W. (1991). Longitudinal prediction of specific cognitive abilities from infant novelty preference. *Child Development, 62*, 530–538.

Thompson, L. M., Murphy, P., O'Hara, J., & Wallymahmed, A. (1997). Levels of daily hassles and uplifts in employed and non-employed pregnant women. *Journal of Reproductive and Infant Psychology, 15*, 271–280.

Thompson, R. A. (1998). Empathy and its origins in early development. In S. Bråten (Ed.), *Intersubjective communication and emotion in early ontogeny. Studies in emotion and social interaction, 2nd series* (pp. 144–157). Cambridge, England: Cambridge University Press.

Thompson, R. A., Connell, J. P., & Bridges, L. J. (1988). Temperament, emotion, and social interactive behavior in the strange situation: A component process analysis of attachment system functioning. *Child Development, 59*, 1102–1110.

Thompson, R. A., & Lamb, M. E. (1982). Stranger sociability and its relationships to temperament and social experiences during the second year. *Infant Behavior and Development, 5*, 277–287.

Thorpe, K. J., Dragonas, T., & Golding, J. (1992). The effects of psychosocial factors on the mother's emotional well-being during early parenthood: A cross-cultural study of Britain and Greece. *Journal of Reproductive and Infant Psychology, 10*, 205–217.

Thorpe, L. A. & Trehub, S. E. (1989). Duration illusion and auditory grouping in infancy. *Developmental Psychology, 25*, 122–127.

Tiedemann, D. (1927). Tiedemann's observations on the development of the mental faculties of children (S. Langer, Trans.). *Pedagogical Seminary and Journal of Genetic Psychology, 34*, 205–230.

Tinsley, B. R., & Parke, R. D. (1984). Grandparents as support and socialization agents. In M. Lewis (Ed.), *Beyond the dyad* (pp. 89–102). New York: Plenum Press.

Titus, S. L. (1976). Family photographs and transition to parenthood. *Journal of Marriage and the Family, 38*, 525–530.

Tizard, B., & Rees, J. (1974). A comparison of the effects of adoption, restoration to the natural mother, and continued institutionalization on the cognitive development of four-year-old children. *Child Development, 45*, 92–99.

Tizard, J., & Tizard, B. (1971). The social development of 2-year-old children in a residential nursery. In H. R. Schaffer (Ed.), *The origin of human social relations* (pp. 337–358). London: Academic Press.

Toda, S., & Fogel, A. (1989, April). *Infant behavior in the still-face situation at 3 and 6 months.* Paper presented at the Society for Research in Child Development, Kansas City, MO.

Toda, S., & Fogel, A. (1993). Infant response to the still-face situation at 3 and 6 months. *Developmental Psychology, 29*, 532–538.

Toda, S., Fogel, A., & Kawai, M. (1990). Maternal speech to three-month-old infants in the United States and Japan. *Journal of Child Language, 17*, 279–294.

Tomasello, M. (1995). Joint attention as social cognition. In C. Moore & P. J. Dunham (Eds.), *Joint attention: Its origins and role in development* (pp. 103–130). Hillsdale, NJ: Erlbaum.

Tomasello, M., Call, J., & Gluckman, A. (1997). Comprehension of novel communicative signs by apes and human children. *Child Development, 68*(6), 1067–1080.

Tomasello, M., & Farrar, M. J. (1986). Joint attention and early language. *Child Development, 57*, 1454–1463.

Tomasello, M., Mannle, S., & Kruger, A. C. (1986). Linguistic environment of 1- to 2-year-old twins. *Developmental Psychology, 22*, 169–176.

Tomasello, M., Savage-Rumbaugh, S., & Kruger, A. C. (1993). Imitative learning of actions on objects by children, chimpanzees, and enculturated chimpanzees. *Child Development, 64*, 1688–1705.

Toselli, M., Farneti, P., & Salzarulo, P. (1998). Maternal representation and care of infant sleep. *Early Development and Parenting, 7*, 73–78.

Touraine, J. L., Sanhadji, K., & Firouzi, R. (1994). Susceptibility of human fetal cells to HIV infection, in vitro and in viol in the SICD-HU Model. *International Conference on AIDS, 10*, 307 (abstract no. PC0157).

Towers, C. V., Deveikis, A., Asrat, T., Nageotte, M. P., & Freeman, R. K. (1993). Role of "bloodless C section" to decrease maternal child HIV transmission: A pilot study. *International Conference on AIDS, 9*, 712 (abstract no. P0–C16–2978).

Trainor, L. J. (1996). Infant preferences for infant-directed versus noninfant-directed playsongs and lullabies. *Infant Behavior and Development, 19,* 83–92.

Trainor, L. J., Clark, E. D., Huntley, A., & Adams, B. A. (1997). The acoustic basis of preferences for infant-directed singing. *Infant Behavior and Development, 20*(3), 383–396.

Trainor, L. J., & Zacharias, C. A. (1998). Infants prefer higher-pitched singing. *Infant Behavior and Development, 21*(4), 799–806.

Trause, M. A. (1977). Stranger responses: Effects of familiarity, stranger's approach and sex of infant. *Child Development, 48,* 1657–1661.

Trause, M. A., Boslett, M., Voos, D., Rudd, C., Klaus, M., & Kennell, J. (1978). A birth in the hospital: The effect on the sibling. *Birth and the Family Journal, 5,* 207–210.

Trehub, S. E., Bull, D., & Thorpe, L. A. (1984). Infants' perception of melodies: The role of melodic contour. *Child Development, 55,* 821–830.

Trehub, S. E., Thorpe, L. A., & Morrongiello, B. A. (1987). Organizational processes in infants' perception of auditory patterns. *Child Development, 58,* 741–749.

Trehub, S. E., Unyk, A. M., & Trainor, L. J. (1993). Adults identify infant-directed music across cultures. *Infant Behavior and Development, 16,* 193–211.

Trevarthen, C. (1973). Behavioral embryology. In E. C. Carterette & M. P. Friedman (Eds.), *Handbook of perception: Vol. 3. Biology of perceptual systems* (pp. 61–78). New York: Academic Press.

Trevarthen, C. (1977). Descriptive analysis of infant communicative behavior. In H. R. Schaffer (Ed.), *Studies of mother-infant interaction* (pp. 227–270). London: Academic Press.

Trevarthen, C. (1980). Neurological development and the growth of psychological functions. In J. Sants (Ed.), *Developmental psychology and society* (pp. 46–95). New York: St. Martin's Press.

Trevarthen, C. (1998). The concept and foundations of infant intersubjectivity. In S. Bråten (Ed.), *Intersubjective communication and emotion in early ontogeny. Studies in emotion and social interaction, 2nd series* (pp. 15–46). New York: Cambridge University Press.

Trevarthen, C., Aitken, K., Papoudi, D., & Robarts, J. (1998). *Children with autism: Diagnosis and interventions to meet their needs* (2nd ed.). Philadelphia: Jessica Kingsley.

Trevarthen, C., & Hubley, P. (1978). Secondary intersubjectivity: Confidence, confiding and acts of meaning in the first year. In A. Lock (Ed.) *Action, gesture, and symbol: The emergence of language* (pp. 183–227). New York: Academic Press.

Trickett, P. K., & Susman, E. J. (1988). Parental perceptions of child-rearing practices in physically abusive and nonabusive families. *Developmental Psychology, 24,* 270–276.

Tronick, E., Als, H., Adamson, L., Weise, S., & Brazelton, T. B. (1978). The infant's response to entrapment between contradictory messages in face-to-face interaction. *Journal of Child Psychiatry, 17,* 1–13.

Tronick, E. Z., Thomas, R. B., & Daltabuit, M. (1994). The Quechua Manta pouch: A caretaking practice for buffering the Peruvian infant against the multiple stressors of high altitude. *Child Development, 65,* 1005–1013.

Turkheimer, M., Bakeman, R., & Adamson, L. B. (1989). Do mothers support and peers inhibit skilled object play in infancy? *Infant Behavior and Development, 12,* 37–44.

Ungerer, J., Brody, L., & Zelazo, P. (1978). Long-term memory for speech in 2- to 4-week-old infants. *Infant Behavior and Development, 1,* 177–186.

Ungerer, J., & Sigman, M. (1984). The relation of play and sensorimotor behavior to language in the second year. *Child Development, 55,* 1448–1455.

Ungerer, J., Zelazo, P. R., Kearsley, R. D., & O'Leary, K. (1981). Developmental changes in the representation of objects in symbolic play from 18 to 34 months of age. *Child Development, 52,* 186–195.

United Nations Department of Economic and Social Affairs (1986). *Demographic yearbook.* New York: United Nations.

United States Bureau of the Census. (1988). *Current Population Reports,* Series P-70, No. 20. Washington, DC: U.S. Government Printing Office.

Uzgiris, I. C. (1983). Imitation in infancy: Its interpersonal aspects. In M. Perlmutter (Ed.), *Minnesota symposia on child psychology* (Vol. 17, pp. 1–32). Hillsdale, NJ: Erlbaum.

Uzgiris, I. C., & Hunt, J. M. (1975). *Toward ordinal scales of psychological development in infancy.* Champaign: University of Illinois Press.

Valdez-Menchaca, M. C., & Whitehurst, G. J. (1992). Accelerating language development through picture book reading: A systematic extension to Mexican day care. *Developmental Psychology, 28,* 1106–1114.

Valenzuela, M. (1997). Maternal sensitivity in a developing society: The context of urban poverty and infant chronic undernutrition. *Developmental Psychology, 33*(5), 845–855.

van Beek, Y., & Samson, J. F. (1994). Communication in preterm infants: Why is it different? *Early Development and Parenting, 3,* 37–50.

Vandell, D. L. (1979). Effects of a playgroup experience on mother-son and father-son interaction. *Developmental Psychology, 15,* 379–385.

Vandell, D. L. (1980). Sociability with peer and mother during the first year. *Developmental Psychology, 16,* 335–361.

Vandell, D. L., Hyde, J. S., Plant, E. A., & Essex, M. J. (1997). Fathers and "others" as infant-care providers: Predictors of parents' emotional well-being and marital satisfaction. *Merrill-Palmer Quarterly, 43*(3), 361–385.

Vandell, D. L., Owen, M. T., Wilson, K. S., & Henderson, V. K. (1988). Social development in infant twins: Peer and mother-child relationships. *Child Development, 59,* 168–177.

Vandell, D. L., & Ramanan, J. (1992). Effects of early and recent maternal employment on children from low-income families. *Child Development, 63,* 938–949.

Vandell, D. L., & Wilson, K. S. (1987). Infants' interactions with mother, sibling, and peer: Contrasts and relations between interaction systems. *Child Development, 58,* 176–186.

Vandell, D. L., Wilson, K. S., & Buchanan, N. R. (1980). Peer interaction in the first year of life: An examination of its structure, content, and sensitivity to toys. *Child Development, 51,* 481–488.

Van de Perre, P., Simonon, A., Hitimana, D. G., Dabis, F., Msellati, P., Mukamabano, B., Butera, J. B., Van-Goethem, C., Karita, E., & Lepage, P. (1993). Infective and anti-infective properties of breastmilk from HIV-1–infected women. *Lancet, 341,* 914–918.

Van de Walle, G. A., & Spelke, E. (1996). Spatiotemporal integration and object perception in infancy: Perceiving unity versus form. *Child Development, 67,* 2621–2640.

VanDoorninck, W. J., Caldwell, B. M., Wright, C., & Frankenburg, W. K. (1981). The relationship between twelve-month home stimulation and school achievement. *Child Development, 52,* 1080–1083.

van Geert, P. (1991). A dynamic systems model of cognitive and language growth. *Journal of Psychological Review, 98* (1), 3–53.

van Geert, P. (1993). A dynamic systems model of cognitive growth: Competition and support under limited resource conditions. In L. B. Smith & E. Thelen (Eds.), *A dynamic systems approach to development: Applications. MIT Press/Bradford Books series in cognitive psychology* (pp. 265–331). Cambridge, MA: MIT Press.

van Geert, P. (1998). We almost had a great future behind us: The contribution of non-linear dynamics to developmental-science-in-the-making. *Developmental Science, 1*(1), 143–159.

Van Giffen, K., & Haith, M. H. (1984). Infant visual response to Gestalt geometric forms. *Infant Behavior and Development, 7,* 335–346.

van Ijzendoorn, M. H., Goldberg, S., Kroonenberg, P. M., & Frenkel, O. J. (1992). The relative effects of maternal and child problems on the quality of attachment: A meta-analysis of attachment in clinical samples. *Child Development, 63,* 840–858.

van Ijzendoorn, M. H., & Kroonenberg, P. M. (1988). Cross-cultural patterns of attachment: A meta-analysis of the strange situation. *Child Development, 59,* 147–156.

Varela, F. J., Thompson, E., Rosch, E. (1991). *The embodied mind: Cognitive science and human experiences.* Cambridge, MA: MIT Press.

Vaughn, B. E., Bradley, C. F., Joffe, L. S., Seifer, R., & Barglow, P. (1987). Maternal characteristics measured prenatally are predictive of ratings of temperamental "difficulty" on the Carey Infant Temperament Questionnaire. *Developmental Psychology, 23,* 152–161.

Vaughn, B. E., Deane, K. E., & Waters, E. (1985). The impact of out-of-home care on child-mother attachment quality: Another look at some enduring questions. In I. Bretherton & E. Waters (Eds.), *Growing points of attachment theory and research. Monographs of the Society for Research in Child Development, 50* (1–2, Whole No. 209), 110–135.

Vaughn, B. E., Egeland, B., Sroufe, L. A., & Waters, E. (1979). Individual differences in infant-mother attachment at twelve and eighteen months: Stability and change in families under stress. *Child Development, 50,* 971–975.

Vaughn, B. E., Grove, F. L., & Egeland, B. (1980). The relationship between out-of-home care and the quality of infant-mother attachment in an economically disadvantaged population. *Child Development, 51,* 1203–1214.

Vaughn, B. E., Kopp, C. B., & Krakow, J. B. (1984). The emergence and consolidation of self-control from 18 to 30 months of age: Normative trends and individual differences. *Child Development, 55,* 990–1004.

Vaughn, B. E., Kopp, C. B., Krakow, J. B., Johnson, K., & Schwartz, S. S. (1986). Process analyses of the behavior of very young children in delay tasks. *Developmental Psychology, 22,* 752–759.

Vaughn, B. E., Stevenson-Hinde, J., Waters, E., Kotsaftis, A., Lefever, G. B., Shouldice, A., Trudel, M., & Belsky, J. (1992). Attachment security and temperament in infancy and early childhood: Some conceptual clarifications. *Developmental Psychology, 28,* 463–473.

Vaughn, B. E., Taraldson, B. J., Crichton, L., & Egeland, B. (1981). The assessment of infant temperament: A critique of the Carey Infant Temperament Questionnaire. *Infant Behavior and Development, 4,* 1–18.

Velde, E. R., & Cohlen, B. J. (1999). The management of infertility. *New England Journal of Medicine, 340*(3), 224–226.

Ventura, S. J., Mathews, T. J., & Curtin, S. C. (1998). Declines in teenage birth rates, 1991–97: National and state patterns. *National Vital Statistics Report, 47*(12), 1–17.

Vereijken, C. M. J. L., Riksen-Walraven, J. M., & Kondo-Ikemura, K. (1997). Maternal sensitivity and infant attachment security in Japan: A longitudinal study. *International Journal of Behavioral Development, 21*(1), 35–49.

Verlinsky, Y., & Kuliev, A. (1994). Human preimplantation diagnosis: Needs, efficiency and efficacy of genetic and chromosomal analysis. *Baillieres Clinical Obstetrics and Gynacology, 8,* 177–196.

Vertes, R. P. (1986). A life-sustaining function for REM sleep: A theory. *Neuroscience and Behavioral Reviews, 10*(4), 371–376.

Vibbert, M., & Bornstein, M. H. (1989). Specific associations between domains of mother-child interaction and toddler referential language and pretense play. *Infant Behavior and Development, 12,* 163–184.

Vohr, B. R., & Coll, C. T. G. (1985). Neurodevelopmental and school performance of very-low-birth-weight infants: A seven-year longitudinal study. *Pediatrics, 76,* 345–350.

Volling, B. L., & Belsky, J. (1992). Infant, father, and marital antecedents of infant-father attachment security in dual-earner and single-earner families. *International Journal of Behavioral Development, 15,* 83–100.

Volling, B. L., & Elins, J. L. (1998). Family relationships and children's emotional adjustment as correlates of maternal and paternal differential treatment: A replication with toddler and preschool siblings. *Child Development, 69*(6), 1640–1656.

Volling, B. L., & Feagans, L. V. (1995). Infant day care and children's social competence. *Infant Behavior and Development, 18*(2), 177–188.

Von Hemel, J. O., Majoor-Krakauer, D. F., Jahoda, M. G. J., & Sachs, E. S. (1986). First trimester diagnosis from chorionic villi of a der(15), t(9;15), (q33;Q14)mat identified by DA/DAPI staining. *Journal of Medical Genetics, 23,* 89–90.

Von Hofsten, C., & Spelke, E. S. (1985). Object perception and object-directed reaching in infancy. *Journal of Experimental Psychology: General, 114,* 198–212.

Vorhees, C. V., & Mollnow, E. (1987). Behavioral teratogenesis: Long-term influences on behavior from early exposure to environmental agents. In J. D. Osofsky (Ed.), *Handbook of infant development* (pp. 599–616). New York: Wiley.

Vygotsky, L. S. (1978). *Mind in society.* Cambridge, MA: Harvard University Press.

Vyt, A. (1993). Infant and parental pathways to pre-school cognitive competence. *Early Development and Parenting, 2,* 197–207.

Wachs, T. D. (1982). Early experience and early cognitive development: The search for specificity. In I. Uzgiris & J. Hunt (Eds.), *Research with scales of psychological development in infancy* (pp. 371–400). Champaign: University of Illinois Press.

Wachs, T. D. (1987). Specificity of environmental action as manifest in environmental correlates of infant's mastery motivation. *Developmental Psychology, 23,* 782–790.

Wachs, T. D. (1988). Relevance of physical environment influences for toddler temperament. *Infant Behavior and Development, 11,* 431–445.

Wachs, T. D. (1993). Nature of relations between the physical and social microenvironment of the two-year-old child. *Early Development and Parenting, 2,* 81–87.

Wachs, T. D. (2000). *Necessary but not sufficient: The respective roles of single and multiple influences on individual development.* Washington, DC: American Psychological Association.

Wachs, T. D., & Bates, J. E. (2000). Temperament. In J. G. Bremner & A. Fogel (Eds.), *Handbook of infancy research* (pp. 28–45). Oxford, England: Blackwell.

Wachs, T. D., Bishry, Z., Sobhy, A., McCabe, G., Galal, O., & Shaheen, F. (1993). Relation of rearing environment to adaptive behavior of Egyptian toddlers. *Child Development, 64,* 586–604.

Wachs, T. D., & Gandour, M. J. (1983). Temperament, environment, and six-month cognitive-intellectual development: A test of the organismic specificity hypothesis. *International Journal of Behavioral Development, 6,* 135–152.

Wachs, T. D., & Gruen, G. E. (1982). *Early experience and human development.* New York: Plenum Press.

Waddington, C. H. (1966). *Principles of development and differentiation.* New York: Macmillan.

Wade, J. (1996). *Changes of mind: A holonomic theory of the evolution of consciousness.* New York: State University of New York Press.

Wakschlag, L. S., Chase-Lansdale, P. L., & Brooks-Gunn, J. (1996). Not just "Ghosts from the nursery": Contemporary intergenerational relationships and parenting in young African-American families. *Child Development, 67*(5), 2131–2147

Wakschlag, L. S., & Hans, S. L. (1999). Relation of maternal responsiveness during infancy to the development of behavior problems in high-risk youths. *Developmental Psychology, 35*(2), 569–579.

Walden, T. A., & Ogan, T. A. (1988). The development of social referencing. *Child Development, 59,* 1230–1240.

Waldenstrom, U. (1999). Effects of birth center care on fathers' satisfaction with care, experience of the birth and adaption to fatherhood. *Journal of Reproductive and Infant Psychology, 17*(4), 357–368.

Waletzky, L. (1979). Husbands' problems with breast-feeding. *American Journal of Orthopsychiatry, 49,* 349–353.

Walker, B. E., & Quarles, J. (1976). Palate development in mouse foetuses after tongue removal. *Archives of Oral Biology, 21,* 405–412.

Walker-Andrews, A. S., & Lennon, E. (1991). Infants' discrimination of vocal expressions: Contributions of auditory and visual information. *Infant Behavior and Development, 14,* 131–142.

Wallach, M. A. (1985). Creativity testing and giftedness. In F. D. Horowitz & M. O'Brien (Eds.), *The gifted and talented: Developmental perspectives* (pp. 99–123). Washington, DC: American Psychological Association.

Walton, G. E., Bower, N. J. A., & Bower, T. G. R. (1992). Recognition of familiar faces by newborns. *Infant Behavior and Development, 15,* 265–269.

Ward, M. J., Vaughn, B. E., & Robb, M. D. (1988). Social-emotional adaptation and infant-mother attachment in siblings: Role of the mother in cross-sibling consistency. *Child Development, 59,* 643–651.

Wartner, U. G., Grossmann, K., Fremmer-Bombik, E., & Suess, G. (1994). Attachment patterns at age six in south Germany: Predictability from infancy and implications for preschool behavior. *Child Development, 65*(4), 1014–1027.

Wasik, B. H., Ramey, C. T., Bryant, D. M., & Sparling, J. J. (1990). A longitudinal study of two early intervention strategies: Project CARE. *Child Development, 61,* 1682–1696.

Wasserman, G. A., Allen, R., & Solomon, C. R. (1985). At-risk toddlers and their mothers: The special case of physical handicap. *Child Development, 56,* 73–83.

Waters, E. (1983). The stability of individual differences in infant attachment: Comments on the Thompson, Lamb, and Estes contributions. *Child Development, 54,* 516–520.

Waters, E., Vaughn, B., & Egeland, B. (1980). Individual differences in infant-mother attachment relationships at age one: Antecedents in neonatal behavior in an urban, economically disadvantaged sample. *Child Development, 51,* 208–216.

Watson, J. S. (1973). Smiling, cooing, and "the game." *Merrill-Palmer Quarterly, 18,* 323–339.

Waxman, S. R., & Senghas, A. (1992). Relations among word meanings in early lexical development. *Developmental Psychology, 28,* 862–873.

Webster, J., Sweett, S., & Stolz, T. A. (1994). Domestic violence in pregnancy: A prevalence study. *Medical Journal of Australia, 161,* 466–470.

Wedenberg, E. (1956). Auditory tests on newborn infants. *Acta Otolaryngologica, 46,* 446–461.

Weed, S., & Jensen, L. (1993). A second year evaluation of three abstinence sex education programs. *Journal of Research and Development in Education, 26,* 92–96.

Weinberg, M. K., & Tronick, E. Z. (1994). Beyond the face: An empirical study of infant affective configurations of facial, vocal, gestural, and regulatory behaviors. *Child Development, 65,* 1503–1515.

Weinberg, M. K., Tronick, E. Z., Cohn, J. F., & Olson, K. L. (1999). Gender differences in emotional expressivity and self-regulation during early infancy. *Developmental Psychology, 35*(1), 175–188.

Weinraub, M., Clements, L. P., Sockloff, A., Ethridge, T., Gracely, E., & Myers, B. (1984). The development of sex role stereotypes in the third year: Relations to gender labeling, sex-typed toy preference and family characteristics. *Child Development, 55,* 1493–1503.

Weinraub, M., & Lewis, M. (1977). The determinants of children's responses to separation. *Monographs of the Society for Research in Child Development, 42* (Serial No. 172), 1–127.

Weinraub, M., & Putney, E. (1978). The effects of heights on infant's social responses to unfamiliar persons. *Child Development, 49,* 598–603.

Weinraub, M., & Wolf, B. M. (1983). Effects of stress and social supports on mother-child interactions on single- and two-parent families. *Child Development, 54,* 1297–1311.

Weintraub, K. S., & Furman, L. N. (1987). Child care: Quality, regulation, and research. *Social Policy Report: Society for Research in Child Development, 2,* 27–68.

Weir, R., & Feldman, W. (1975). A study of infant feeding practices. *Birth and the Family Journal, 2,* 63–64.

Weir, R. H. (1966). Questions on the learning of phonology. In F. Smith & G. A. Miller (Eds.), *The genesis of language: A psycholinguistic approach* (pp. 112–140). Cambridge, MA: MIT Press.

Wellman, H. M., Cross, D., & Bartsch, K. (1986). Infant search and object permanence: A meta-analysis of the A-not-B error. *Monographs of the Society for Research in Child Development, 51* (3, Serial No. 214), 1–51.

Wellman, H. M., & Lempers, J. D. (1977). The naturalistic communicative abilities of two-year-olds. *Child Development, 48,* 1052–1057.

Welsh, M. C., Pennington, B. F., Ozonoff, S., Rouse, B., & McCabe, E. R. B. (1990). Neuropsychology of early-treated phenylketonuria: Specific executive function deficits. *Child Development, 61,* 1697–1713.

Wenckstern, S., Weizmann, F., & Leenaars, A. A. (1984). Temperament and tempos of play in eight-month-old infants. *Child Development, 55,* 1195–1199.

Wendland-Carro, J., Piccinini, C. A., & Millar, W. S. (1999). The role of an early intervention on enhancing the quality of mother-infant interaction. *Child Development, 70*(3), 713–721.

Wente, A., & Crockenberg, S. (1976). Transition to fatherhood: Prenatal Lamaze preparation, adjustment difficulty and the adult husband-wife relationship. *Family Coordinator, 25,* 351–357.

Wentworth, N., & Haith, M. M. (1992). Event-specific expectations of 2- and 3-month-old infants. *Developmental Psychology, 28,* 842–850.

Were, E. O., & Karanja, J. K. (1994). Attitudes of males to contraception in a Kenyan rural population. *East African Medical Journal, 71,* 106–109.

Werker, J. F., & Lalonde, C. E. (1988). Cross-language speech perception: Initial capabilities and developmental change. *Developmental Psychology, 24,* 674–683.

Werker, J. F., & Tees, R. C. (1984). Cross-language speech perception: Evidence for perceptual reorganization during the first year of life. *Infant Behavior and Development, 7,* 49–63.

Werner, E. (1979). *Cross-cultural child development.* Monterey, CA: Brooks-Cole.

Werner, E. (1986, April). *The infant's view of planet Earth.* Paper presented at the International Conference on Infant Studies, Los Angeles, CA.

Werner, E., Bierman, J., & French, F. (1971). *The children of Kauai.* Honolulu: University of Hawaii Press.

Wertsch, J. V., & Tulviste, P. (1992). L. S. Vygotsky and contemporary development psychology. *Developmental Psychology, 28,* 548–557.

West, L., & Fogel, A. (April, 1990). *Maternal guidance of object interaction.* Paper presented at the International Conference on Infant Studies, Montreal, Canada.

West, M. J., & Rheingold, H. L. (1978). Infant stimulation of maternal instruction. *Infant Behavior and Development, 1,* 205–215.

Westbrook, M. (1978). Analyzing affective responses to past events: Women's reactions to a childbearing year. *Journal of Clinical Psychology, 34,* 967–971.

Weston, J. A., Coolton, M., Halsey, S., & Covington, S. (1993). A legacy of violence in nonorganic failure to thrive. *Child Abuse and Neglect, 17,* 709–714.

Wheeler, S. R. (1994). Psychosocial needs of women during miscarriage or ectopic pregnancy. *American Obstetrical and Gynecological Nursing Journal, 68,* 221–231.

Whiffen, V. E. (1988). Vulnerability to postpartum depression: A prospective multivariate study. *Journal of Abnormal Psychology, 97*(4), 467–474.

White, E. (1992). Foster parenting the drug affected baby. *Zero to Three, 13,* 13–16.

Whitehurst, G. J., & Vasta, R. (1975). Is language acquired through imitation? *Journal of Psycholinguistic Research, 4,* 37–59.

Whitehurst, G. J., Falco, F. L., Lonigan, C. J., Fischel, J. E., DeBaryshe, B. D., Valdez-Menchaca, M. C., & Caulfield, M. (1988). Accelerating language development through picture book reading. *Developmental Psychology, 24,* 552–559.

Whiten, A., & Milner, P. (1986). The educational experiences of Nigerian infants. In H. V. Curran (Ed.), *Nigerian children: Developmental perspectives* (pp. 260–280). London: Routledge & Kegan Paul.

Whiting, B. (1974). Folk wisdom and child-rearing. *Merrill-Palmer Quarterly, 20,* 9–19.

Whiting, B., & Whiting, J. W. (1975). *Children of six cultures: A psychocultural analysis.* Cambridge, MA: Harvard University Press.

Whiting, J. (1981). Environmental constraints on infant care practices. In R. Monroe, R. Monroe, & B. Whiting (Eds.), *Handbook of cross-cultural development* (pp. 67–89). New York: Garland Publishing.

Wicki, W. (1999). The impact of family resources and satisfaction with division of labor on coping and worries after the birth of the first child. *International Journal of Behavioral Development, 23*(2), 431–456.

Wideman, M. V., & Singer, J. E. (1984). The role of psychological mechanisms in preparation for childbirth. *American Psychologist, 39,* 1357–1371.

Widmayer, S. M., Peterson, L. M., Lerner, M., Carnahan, S., Calderon, A., Wingerd, J., & Marshall, R. (1990). Predictors of Haitian-American infant development at twelve months. *Child Development, 61,* 410–415.

Wiehe, V. R. (1989). Child abuse: An ecological perspective. *Early Child Development and Care, 42,* 141–149.

Wiesenfeld, A. R., Malatesta, C. Z., & DeLoache, L. (1981). Differential parental response to familiar and unfamiliar infant distress signals. *Infant Behavior and Development, 4,* 281–295.

Wigfield, R., Gilbert, R., & Fleming, P. J. (1994). SIDS: Risk reduction measures. *Early Human Development, 38,* 161–164.

Wijnroks, L. (1998). Early maternal stimulation and the development of cognitive competence and attention of preterm infants. *Early Development and Parenting, 7,* 19–30.

Wilcox, A. J., Weinberg, C. R., & Baird, D. D. (1995). Timing of sexual intercourse in relation to ovulation. Effects on the probability of conception, survival of the pregnancy, and sex of the baby. *New England Journal of Medicine, 333*(7), 1517–1521.

Wilcox, T., & Baillargeon, R. (1998). Object individuation in young infants: Further evidence with an event-monitoring paradigm. *Developmental Science, 1*(1), 127–142.

Wilkie, C. F., & Ames, E. W. (1986). The relationship of infant crying to parental stress in the transition to parenthood. *Journal of Marriage and the Family, 48,* 545–550.

Williams, D. (1999). *Like colour to the blind: Soul searching and soul finding.* London: Jessica Kingsley.

Wilson, M. N. (1986). The black extended family: An analytical consideration. *Developmental Psychology, 22,* 246–258.

WIN News (1992). Safe motherhood: New estimates show uneven progress. *Women's International Network News, 18,* 35–36.

Winick, M., Knarig, K., & Harris, R. (1975). Malnutrition and environmental enrichment by early adoption. *Science, 190,* 1173–1175.

Winnicott, D. (1971). *Playing and reality.* New York: Basic Books.

Winslow, M., & Guitar, B. (1994). The effects of structured turn-taking on disfluencies: A case study. *Language, Speech, and Hearing Services in Schools, 25,* 251–257.

Winston, R. M. L., & Handyside, A. H. (1993). New challenges in human in vitro fertilization. *Science, 260,* 932–936.

Wolf, D., & Gardner, H. (1979). Style and sequence in early symbolic play. In N. Smith & M. Franklin (Eds.), *Symbolic function in childhood* (pp. 64–92). Hillsdale, NJ: Erlbaum.

Wolff, P. H. (1966). The causes, controls, and organization of behavior in the neonate. *Psychological Issues, 5,* (Monograph No. 17).

Wolff, P. H. (1987). *The development of behavioral states and the expression of emotions in early infancy: New proposals for investigation.* Chicago: University of Chicago Press.

Wolff, P. H. (1993). Behavioral and emotional states in infancy: A dynamic perspective. In L. B. Smith & E. Thelen (Eds.), *A dynamic systems approach to development: Applications* (pp. 189–208). Cambridge, MA: MIT Press.

Wong, V., & Wong, S. N. (1991). Brainstem suditory evoked potential study in children with autistic disorder. *Journal of Autism and Developmental Disorders, 21,* 329–340.

Woods, N. S., Eyler, F. D., Behnke, M., & Conlon, M. (1993). Cocaine use during pregnancy: Maternal depressive symptoms and infant neurobehavior over the first month. *Infant Behavior and Development, 16,* 83–98.

Woodson, R., Drinkwin, J., & Hamilton, C. (1985). Effects of nonnutritive sucking on state and activity: Term-preterm comparisons. *Infant Behavior and Development, 8,* 435–441.

Woodson, R., & Hamilton, C. (1988). The effect of nonnutritive sucking on heart rate in preterm infants. *Developmental Psychobiology, 21* (3), 207–213.

Woodward, A. L. (1999). Infants' ability to distinguish between purposeful and non-purposeful behaviors. *Infant Behavior and Development, 22*(2), 145–160.

Woodward, A. L., & Hoyne, K. L. (1999). Infants' learning about words and sounds in relation to objects. *Child Development, 70*(1), 65–77.

Woodward, A. L., & Sommerville, J. A. (2000). Twelve-month-old infants interpret action in context. *Psychological Sciences, 11*(1), 73–77.

Woodward, A. L., Markman, E. M., & Fitzsimmons, C. M. (1994). Rapid word learning in 13- and 18-month-olds. *Developmental Psychology, 30*(4), 553–556.

Wooten, S. (1995). *Touching the body, reaching the soul: How touch influences the nature of human beings.* Santa Fe, NM: Rosen Method Center Southwest.

World Health Organization (1976). *New trends and approaches in the delivery of maternal and child care in health services.* (Tech. Rep. Series No. 600). Geneva: Author.

World Health Organization (1985). *The quantity and quality of breast milk.* Geneva: Author.

Worobey, J., & Belsky, J. (1982). Employing the Brazelton scale to influence mothering: An experimental comparison of three strategies. *Developmental Psychology, 18,* 736–743.

Worobey, J., & Blajda, V. M. (1989). Temperament ratings at 2 weeks, 2 months, and 1 year: Differential stability of activity and emotionality. *Developmental Psychology, 25,* 257–262.

Worobey, J., & Lewis, M. (1989). Individual differences in the reactivity of young infants. *Developmental Psychology, 25,* 663–667.

Wright, L. (1994). Prenatal diagnosis in the 1990s. *Journal of Obstetrical and Gynecological Neonatal Nursing, 23,* 506–515.

Wynn, K. (1998). Numerical competence in infants. In C. Donlan (Ed.), *The development of mathematical skills. Studies in developmental psychology* (pp. 3–25). Hove, England: Psychology Press/Taylor & Francis.

Yale Bush Center Infant Care Leave Project (1985). *Facts on parents in the workforce and infant care.* New Haven, CT: Author.

Yale, M. E., Messinger, D. S., Cobo-Lewis, A. B., Oller, D. K., & Eilers, R. E. (1999). An event-based analysis of the coordination of early infant vocalization and facial actions. *Developmental Psychology, 35*(2), 505–513.

Yalom, I. D. (1968). Postpartum blues syndrome. *Archives of General Psychiatry, 28,* 16–27.

Yarrow, L. J., Rubenstein, J. L., & Pedersen, F. A. (1975). *Infant and environment: Early cognitive and motivational development.* Washington, DC: Hemisphere Publishing.

Yates, D. J., & Bremner, J. G. (1988). Conditions for Piagetian stage IV search errors in a task using transparent occluders. *Infant Behavior and Development, 11,* 411–417.

Yoder, P. J. (1989). Maternal question use predicts later language development in specific-language-disordered children. *Journal of Speech and Hearing Disorders, 54,* 347–355.

Yonas, A., Pettersen, L., & Granrud, C. E. (1982). Infants' sensitivity to familiar size as information for distance. *Child Development, 53,* 1285–1290.

Yoshikawa, H. (1999). Welfare dynamics, support services, mothers' earnings, and child cognitive development: Implications for contemporary welfare reform. *Child Development, 70*(3), 779–801.

Young, G., & Lewis, M. (1979). Effects of familiarity and maternal attention on infant peer relations. *Merrill-Palmer Quarterly, 25,* 105–120.

Young, G., Segalowitz, S. J., Misek, P., Alp, I. E., & Boulet, R. (1983). Is early reaching left handed? Review of manual specialization research. In G. Young, S. J. Segalowitz, C. M. Corter, & S. Trehub (Eds.), *Manual specialization and the developing brain* (pp. 337–353). New York: Academic Press.

Young, I. D., Rickett, A. B., & Clarke, M. (1986). Genetic analysis of malformations causing perinatal mortality. *Journal of Medical Genetics, 23,* 58–63.

Young, S. K., Fox, N. A., & Zahn-Waxler, C. (1999). The relations between temperament and empathy in 2-year-olds. *Developmental Psychology, 35*(8), 1189–1197.

Youngblut, J. M., Loveland-Cherry, C. J., & Horan, M. (1993). Maternal employment, family functioning, and preterm infant development at 9 and 12 months. *Research in Nursing and Health, 16,* 33–43.

Younger, B., & Gotlieb, S. (1988). Development of categorization skills: Changes in the nature or structure of infant form categories? *Developmental Psychology, 24,* 611–619.

Younger, B. A., & Fearing, D. D. (1999). Parsing items into separate categories: Developmental changes in infant categorization. *Child Development, 70*(2), 291–303.

Zachry, W. (1978). Ordinality and interdependence of representation and language development in infancy. *Child Development, 49,* 681–687.

Zahn-Waxler, C., Radke-Yarrow, M., Wagner, E., & Chapman, M. (1992). Development of concern for others. *Developmental Psychology, 28,* 126–136.

Zahn-Waxler, C., & Robinson, J. (1995). Empathy and guilt: Early origins of feelings of responsibility. In J. P. Tangney & K. W. Fischer (Eds.) *Self-conscious emotions: The psychology of shame, guilt, embarrassment, and pride* (pp. 143–173). New York: Guilford Press.

Zahn-Waxler, C., Robinson, J. L., & Emde, R. N. (1992). The development of empathy in twins. *Developmental Psychology, 28,* 1038–1047.

Zarbatany, L., & Lamb, M. E. (1985). Social referencing as a function of information source: Mothers versus strangers. *Infant Behavior and Development, 8,* 25–33.

Zarling, C. L., Hirsch, B. J., & Landry, S. (1988). Maternal social networks and mother-infant interactions in full-term and very low birthweight preterm infants. *Child Development, 59,* 178–185.

Zaslow, M. J., & Eldred, C. A. (Eds.) (1997). The promise and limitations of parenting education for teen mothers on welfare: Lessons from the New Chance Observational Study. *Parenting behavior in a sample of young mothers in poverty: Results of the New Chance Observational Study.* Washington, D.C.: Child Trends.

Zebrowitz, L. A., & Montepare, J. M. (1992). Impressions of babyfaced individuals across the life span. *Developmental Psychology, 28,* 1143–1152.

Zeitz, D. (1969). *Child welfare: Services and perspectives.* New York: Wiley.

Zelazo, N. A., Zelazo, P. R., Cohen, K. M., & Zelazo, P. D. (1993). Specificity of practice effects on elementary neuromotor patterns. *Developmental Psychology, 29,* 686–691.

Zelazo, P. R. (1976). From reflexive to instrumental behavior. In L. P. Lipsitt (Ed.), *Developmental psychobiology: The significance of infancy* (pp. 232–267). Hillsdale, NJ: Erlbaum.

Zelazo, P. R., Brody, L. R., & Chaikan, H. (1984). Neonatal habituation and dishabituation of head turning to rattle sounds. *Infant Behavior and Development, 7,* 311–321.

Zentner, M. R., & Kagan, J. (1998). Infants' perception of consonance and dissonance in music. *Infant Behavior and Development, 21*(3), 483–492.

Zeskind, P. S. (1980). Adult responses to cries of low and high risk infants. *Infant Behavior and Development, 3,* 167–178.

Zeskind, P. S., & Barr, R. G. (1997). Acoustic characteristics of naturally occurring cries of infants with "colic." *Child Development, 68*(3), 394–403.

Zeskind, P. S., & Iacino, R. (1984). Effects of maternal visitation to preterm infants in the neonatal intensive care unit. *Child Development, 55,* 1887–1893.

Zeskind, P. S., & Iacino, R. (1987). The relation between length of hospitalization and the mental and physical development of preterm infants. *Infant Behavior and Development, 10,* 217–221.

Zeskind, P. S., Klein, L., & Marshall, T. R. (1992). Adults' perceptions of experimental modifications of durations of pauses and expiratory sounds in infant crying. *Developmental Psychology, 28,* 1153–1162.

Zeskind, P. S., & Lester, B. M. (1978). Acoustic features of auditory perceptions of the cries of newborns with prenatal complications. *Child Development, 49,* 580–589.

Zeskind, P. S., & Lester, B. M. (1981). Analysis of cry features in newborns with differential fetal growth. *Child Development, 52,* 207–212.

Zeskind, P. S., & Marshall, T. R. (1988). The relation between variations in pitch and maternal perceptions of infant crying. *Child Development, 59,* 193–196.

Zeskind, P. S., & Marshall, T. R. (1991). Temporal organization in neonatal arousal: Systems, oscillations, and development. In M. Weiss & P. Zelazo (Eds.), *Newborn attention: Biological constraints and the influence of experiences* (pp. 22–62). Norwood, NJ: Ablex.

Zeskind, P. S., Marshall, T. R., & Goff, D. M. (1992). Rhythmic organization of heart rate in breast-fed and bottle-fed newborn infants. *Early Development and Parenting, 1,* 79–87.

Zeskind, P. S., Wilhite, A., & Marshall, T. R. (1993). Infant cry as a graded signal: Expiratory sounds alter mothers' perceptions. *Early Development and Parenting, 2,* 99–105.

Zevalkink, J., Riksen-Walraven, J. M., & Van Lieshout, C. F. M. (1999). Attachment in the Indonesian caregiving context. *Social Development, 8*(1), 21–40.

Zimmermann, P., Fremmer-Bombik, E., Spangler, G., & Grossmann, K. E. (1995, March). *Attachment in adolescence: A longitudinal perspective.* Poster presented at the Biennial Meeting of the Society for Research in Child Development, Indianapolis, IN.

Zimmerman, R. K., & Grebink, G. S. (1992). Childhood immunizations: A practical approach for clinicians. *American Family Physician, 45,* 1759–1772.

Zlatin, M. A. (1973). *Explorative mapping of the vocal tract and primitive syllabification in infancy: The first six months.* Purdue University Contributed Papers, Fall.

Zlochower, A. J., & Cohn, J. F. (1996). Vocal timing in face-to-face interaction of clinically depressed and nondepressed mothers and their 4-month-old infants. *Infant Behavior and Development, 19,* 371–374.

Zukow, P. G. (1980). A microanalytic study of the role of the caregiver in the relationship between and language acquisition during the one word period (Doctoral dissertation, University of California, 1980). *Dissertation Abstracts International, 42,* 18.

Zukow, P. G. (1986). The relationship between interaction with the caregiver and the emergence of play activities during the one-word period. *British Journal of Developmental Psychology, 4,* 223–234.

Zukow, P. G. (1990). Socio-perceptual bases for the emergence of language: An alternative to innatist approaches. *Developmental Psychobiology, 23,* 705–726.

Zukow-Goldring, P. (1996). Sensitive caregiving fosters the comprehension of speech: When gestures speak louder than words. *Early Development and Parenting, 5*(4), 195–211.

Zukow-Goldring, P. (1997). A social ecological realist approach to the emergence of the lexicon: Educating attention to amodal invariants in gesture and speech. In C. Dent-Read & P. Zukow-Goldring (Eds.), *Evolving explanations of development: Ecological approaches to organism-environment systems* (pp. 199–250). Washington, DC: American Psychological Association.

Name Index

523

Subject Index

Photo Credits